THE CANADIAN YEARBOOK OF INTERNATIONAL LAW

2008

ANNUAIRE CANADIEN DE DROIT INTERNATIONAL

The Canadian Yearbook of International Law

VOLUME XLVI   2008   TOME XLVI

Annuaire canadien de Droit international

Published under the auspices of
THE CANADIAN BRANCH, INTERNATIONAL LAW ASSOCIATION
AND
THE CANADIAN COUNCIL ON INTERNATIONAL LAW

Publié sous les auspices de
LA SECTION CANADIENNE DE L'ASSOCIATION DE DROIT INTERNATIONAL
ET
LE CONSEIL CANADIEN DE DROIT INTERNATIONAL

UBCPress·Vancouver·Toronto

Printed in Canada on acid-free paper

ISBN 978-0-7748-1780-6
ISSN 0069-0058

Canadian Cataloguing in Publication Data

The National Library of Canada has catalogued this publication as follows:

The Canadian yearbook of international law — Annuaire canadien de droit international

Annual.
Text in English and French.
"Published under the auspices of the Canadian Branch, International Law Association and the Canadian Council on International Law."
ISSN 0069-0058

1. International Law — Periodicals.
I. International Law Association. Canadian Branch.
II. Title: Annuaire canadien de droit international.
JC 21.C3   341'.05   C75-34558-6E

Données de catalogage avant publication (Canada)

Annuaire canadien de droit international — The Canadian yearbook of international law

Annuel.
Textes en anglais et en français.
"Publié sous les auspices de la Branche canadienne de l'Association de droit international et le Conseil canadien de droit international."
ISSN 0069-0058

1. Droit international — Périodiques.
I. Association de droit international. Section canadienne.
II. Conseil canadien de droit international.
III. Titre: The Canadian yearbook of international law.
JC 21.C3   341'.05   C75-34558-6E

www.ubcpress.ca

The Board of Editors, the Canadian Branch of the International Law Association, the Canadian Council on International Law, and the University of British Columbia are not in any way responsible for the views expressed by contributors, whether the contributions are signed or unsigned.

Les opinions émises dans le présent *Annuaire* par nos collaborateurs, qu'il s'agisse d'articles signés, ne sauraient en aucune façon engager la responsabilité du Comité de rédaction, de la Section canadienne du Conseil canadien de droit international ou de l'Université de la Colombie-Britannique.

Communications to the Yearbook should be addressed to:

Les communications destinées à l'Annuaire doivent être adressées à:

THE EDITOR, THE CANADIAN YEARBOOK OF INTERNATIONAL LAW
FACULTY OF LAW, COMMON LAW SECTION
UNIVERSITY OF OTTAWA
57 LOUIS PASTEUR
OTTAWA, ONTARIO K1N 6N5 CANADA

Contents / Matière

Book Reviews / Recensions de livres

THE CANADIAN YEARBOOK OF INTERNATIONAL LAW

2008

ANNUAIRE CANADIEN DE DROIT INTERNATIONAL

Objectivity and Statutory Interpretation: End Use in the Canadian Customs Tariff

MAUREEN IRISH

INTRODUCTION

On 1 January 1988, Canada replaced its previous customs tariff with the Harmonized Commodity Description and Coding System.[1] The Harmonized System (HS) is contained in an international convention negotiated under the auspices of the World Customs Organization in Brussels.[2] One of the distinctive features of the Canadian tariff prior to implementation of the HS was the presence of many end use items, with reduced or zero rates of duty that reflected policies favouring particular domestic economic sectors or activities. The items depended on actual use of the imported goods, not on evidence of chief or principal use in the general market. Such end use items are not part of the six-digit nomenclature of the HS.

The objective approach to interpretation has a central place in tariff administration around the world. The European Union applies the HS and has a long history of previous application of the

---

Maureen Irish is a professor in the Faculty of Law at the University of Windsor. I am grateful to Windsor students who have provided assistance on customs tariff law over a number of years: Cindy Dickinson, Robert Shapiro, Shannon Derrick, and Rachel Manno. Their research was supported by funding from the Law Foundation of Ontario. Part of this article draws from my doctoral thesis at McGill University, supported by the Foundation for Legal Research. As in the past, I express my appreciation to A.L.C. de Mestral for his kind supervision of both my LL.M. and D.C.L. theses.

[1] *Customs Tariff*, R.S.C. 1985 (3d Supp.), c. 41, rep. and sub. *Customs Tariff*, S.C. 1997, c. 36. For the pre-Harmonized System (HS) legislation and tariff schedule, see *Customs Tariff*, R.S.C. 1985, c. C-54.

[2] International Convention on the Harmonized Commodity Description and Coding System, Brussels, 14 June 1983, Can. T.S. 1988 No. 38 (in force 1 January 1988).

Brussels Tariff Nomenclature, which is the basis for the development of the HS. Cases decided by the European Court of Justice (ECJ) are influential for discussions within the World Customs Organization. Many decisions of the court have established that "in accordance with settled case-law, in the interests of legal certainty and ease of verification, the decisive criterion for the classification of goods for customs purposes is in general to be sought in their objective characteristics and properties, as defined in the wording" of the tariff.[3] According to the decisions, the intended use of a product

3   *Staatssecretaris van Financiën v. Kamino International Logistics BV,* Case C-376/07, 19 February 2009, at para. 31. See *Kip Europe SA, Hewlett Packard International SARL v. Administration des douanes, Direction générale des douanes et droits indirects,* Cases C-362/07 and C-363/07, 11 December 2008; *JVC France SAS v. Administration des douanes — Direction nationale du renseignement et des enquêtes douanières,* Case C-312/07, [2008] E.C.R. I-4165; *Codirex Expeditie BV v. Staatssecretaris van Financiën,* Case C-400/06, [2007] E.C.R. I-7399; *F.T.S. International BV v. Belastingdienst — Douane West,* Case C-310/06, [2007] E.C.R. I-6749; *Turbon International GmbH v. Oberfinanzdirektion Koblenz,* Case C-250/05 , [2006] E.C.R. I-10531; *Sachsenmilch AG v. Oberfinanzdirektion Nürnberg,* Case C-196/05, [2006] E.C.R. I-5161; *Possehl Erzkontor GmbH v. Hauptzollamt Duisberg,* Case C-445/04, [2005] E.C.R. I-10721; *Ikegami Electronics (Europe) GmbH v. Oberfinanzdirektion Nürnberg,* Case C-467/03, [2005] E.C.R. I-2389; *Skatteministeriet v. Imexpo Trading A/S,* Case C-379/02, [2004] E.C.R. I-9273; *Lohmann GmbH & Co. KG v. Oberfinanzdirektion Koblenz,* Cases C-260 to C-263/00, [2002] E.C.R. I-10045; *Biochem Zusatzstoffe Handels- und Produktions GmbH v. Oberfinanzdirektion Nürnberg,* Case C-259/00, [2002] E.C.R. I-2461; *Turbon International GmbH v. Oberfinanzdirektion Koblenz,* Case C-276/00, [2002] E.C.R. I-1389; *CBA Computer Handels- und Beteiligungs GmbH v. Hauptzollamt Aachen,* Case C-479/99, [2001] E.C.R. I-4391; *Vau De Sport GmbH & Co. KG v. Oberfinanzdirektion Koblenz,* Case C-288/99, [2001] E.C.R. I-3683; *Peacock AG v. Hauptzollamt Paderborn,* Case C-339/98, [2000] E.C.R. I-8947; *Fábrica de Queijo Eru Portuguesa Ld. v. Tribunal Técnico Aduaneiro de Segunda Instância,* Case C-42/99, [2000] E.C.R. I-7691; *Mövenpick Deutschland GmbH für das Gastgewerbe v. Hauptzollamt Bremen,* Case C-405/97, [1999] E.C.R. I-2397; *ROSE Elektrotechnic GmbH & Co. KG v. Oberfinanzdirektion Köln,* Case C-280/97, [1999] E.C.R. I-689; *Glob-Sped AG v. Hauptzollamt Lörrach,* Case C-328/97, [1998] E.C.R. I-8357; *Laboratoires Sarget SA v. Fonds d'Intervention et de Régularisation du Marché du Sucre (FIRS),* Case C-270/96, [1998] E.C.R. I-1121; *Techex Computer + Grafik Vertriebs GmbH v. Hauptzollamt München,* Case C-382/95, [1997] E.C.R. I-7363; *Leonhard Knubben Speditions GmbH v. Hauptzollamt Mannheim,* Case C-143/96, [1997] E.C.R. I-7039; *Laboratoires de Thérapeutique Moderne (LTM) v. Fonds d'Intervention et de Régularisation du Marché du Sucre (FIRS),* Case C-201/96, [1997] E.C.R. I-6147; *Rank Xerox Manufacturing (Nederland) BV v. Inspecteur der Invoerrechten en Accijnzen,* Case C-67/95, [1997] E.C.R. I-5401; *Codiesel — Sociedade de Apoio Técnico à Indústria Ld v. Conselho Técnico Aduaneiro,* Case C-105/96, [1997] E.C.R. I-3465; *Fábrica de Queijo Eru Portuguesa Ld v. Alfândega de Lisboa (Tribunal Técnico Aduaneiro de Segunda Instância),* Case C-164/95, [1997] E.C.R. I-3441; *Ludwig Wünsche & Co. v. Hauptzollamt Hamburg-Jonas,* Cases C-274/95, C275/95, and C276/95, [1997] E.C.R.

"may constitute an objective criterion for classification if it is inherent to the product, and that inherent character must be capable of being assessed on the basis of the product's objective characteristics and properties."[4] According to this approach, if the intended use is not inherent in the physical characteristics of the goods, it should not be a factor in determining classification.[5]

After the adoption of the HS, end use items in the Canadian tariff were preserved through codes for a transition period. The current legislation has a new definition of "for use in," which is the

---

I-2091; *VOBIS Microcomputer AG v. Oberfinanzdirektion München*, Case C-121/95, [1996] E.C.R. I-3047; *Patrick Colin and Daniel Dupré*, Cases C-106/94 and C-139/94, [1995] E.C.R. I-4759; *Ministre des Finances v. Société Pardo & Fils and Camicas SARL*, Cases C-59/94 and C-64/94, [1995] E.C.R. I-3159; *Gausepohl-Fleisch GmbH v. Oberfinanzdirektion Hamburg*, Case C-33/92, [1993] Rec. I-3047; *Hauptzollamt Mannheim v. Boehringer Mannheim GmbH*, Case C-381/90, [1992] Rec. I-3495; *Ludwig Post v. Oberfinanzdirektion München*, Case C-120/90, [1991] E.C.R. I-2391 at I-2405–06; *Ministère public v. Fauque*, Cases C-153/88 to C-157/88, [1990] E.C.R. I-649. For earlier cases, see *Günther Henck v. Hauptzollamt Emden*, Case 36/71, [1972] Rec. 187, and other decisions discussed in Maureen Irish, "Interpretation and Naming: The Harmonized System in Canadian Customs Tariff Law" (1993) 31 Can. Y.B. Int'l L. 89 at 142–44. Jurisprudence of the European Court of Justice is available online at <http://curia.europa.eu>.

4 *Siebrand BV v. Staatssecretaris van Financiën*, Case C-150/08, 7 May 2009, at para. 38 [*Siebrand BV*]. See *Metherma GmbH & Co. KG v. Hauptzollamt Düsseldorf*, Case C-403/07, 27 November 2008; *BVBA Van Landeghem v. Belgische Staat*, Case C-486/06, [2007] E.C.R. I-10661; *Medion AG v. Hauptzollamt Duisberg, Canon Deutschland GmbH v. Hauptzollamt Krefeld*, Cases C-208/06 and C-209/06, [2007] E.C.R. I-7963; *Olicom A/S v. Skatteministeriet*, Case C-142/06, [2007] E.C.R. I-6675; *Sunshine Deutschland Handelsgesellschaft mbH v. Kauptzollamt Kiel*, Case C-229/06, [2007] E.C.R. I-3251; *RUMA GmbH v. Oberfinanzdirektion Nürnberg*, Case C-183/06, [2007] E.C.R. I-1559; *B.A.S. Trucks BV v. Staatssecretaris van Financiën*, Case C-400/05, [2007] E.C.R. I-311; *Anagram International Inc. v. Inspecteur van de Belastingdienst — Douanedistrict Rotterdam*, Case C-14/05, [2006] E.C.R. I-6763; *Uroplasty BV v. Inspecteur van de Belastingdienst — Douanedistrict Rotterdam*, Case C-514/04, [2006] E.C.R. I-6721; *Kawasaki Motors Europe NV v. Inspecteur van de Belastingdienst — Douanedistrict Rotterdam*, Case C-15/05, [2006] E.C.R. I-3657; *Proxxon GmbH v. Oberfinanzdirektion Köln*, Case C-500/04, [2006] E.C.R. I-1545; *Intermodal Transports BV v. Staatssecretaris van Financiën*, Case C-495/03, [2005] E.C.R. I-8151; *DFDS BV v. Inspecteur van de Belastingdienst — Douanedistrict Rotterdam*, Case C-396/02, [2004] E.C.R. I-8439; *Krings GmbH v. Oberfinanzdirektion Nürnberg*, Case C-130/02, [2004] E.C.R. I-2121; *Holz Geenen GmbH v. Oberfinanzdirektion München*, Case C-309/98, [2000] E.C.R. I-1975; *Hauptzollamt Hamburg-St. Annen v. Thyssen Haniel Logistic GbmH*, Case C-459/93, [1995] E.C.R. I-1381.

5 *Hauptzollamt Osnabrück v. Kleiderwerke Hela Lampe GmbH & Co. KG*, Case 222/85, [1986] E.C.R. 2449. See *Handelsonderneming J.Mikx BV v. Minister van Enonomische Zaken*, Case 90/85, [1986] E.C.R. 1695.

key phrase that previously identified end use items. In this article, I outline what happened during the transition and examine Canadian cases on types of "use" items under the HS nomenclature over the twenty years of experience since implementation. I also discuss the previous end use items briefly.

The review of "use" items provides the background for a discussion of the suitable interpretive approach for the HS. In the pre-HS Canadian tariff, judicial interpretation of end use items had become quite purposive, following Parliament's presumed intention to offer encouragement to particular economic activities. In order to ensure favourable tariff treatment for the named activities, end use items were given wide coverage and accorded increasingly high priority over other items. I argue that, while strong purposive interpretation such as this is inappropriate for the current system, it is also incorrect to assume that objects announce their identity in their observable, physical characteristics alone. As explained later in this article, the path suggested is instead a middle ground, referred to as participatory interpretation, which takes into account the use of the goods. Although the current EC approach is long established, I argue that it is too objective and that recent Canadian cases point the way to a more suitable interpretive approach. The following sections address the theories of interpretation, then the experience of Canadian cases having to do with use that have occurred since implementation, and, finally, the decisions under the previous system that involve end use items, including coverage and priorities.

OBJECTIVITY, PARTICIPATION, AND PURPOSE

Along with the growth of legislation since the middle part of the last century, the common law world has turned increasingly to the study of theories of statutory interpretation. An approach that follows the presumed intent of legislators has wide support in the literature.[6] In the famous exchange in 1958 between H.L.A. Hart and

---

6 Pierre-André Côté, *The Interpretation of Legislation in Canada,* 3rd edition (Scarborough: Carswell, 2000); Ruth L. Sullivan, *Sullivan on the Construction of Statutes,* 5th edition (Markham: LexisNexis, 2008); Randal N. Graham, *Statutory Interpretation: Theory and Practice* (Toronto: Emond Montgomery, 2001); Stéphane Beaulac, *Handbook on Statutory Interpretation: General Methodology, Canadian Charter and International Law* (Markham: LexisNexis, 2008); John Willis, "Statute Interpretation in a Nutshell" (1938) 16 Can. Bar Rev. 1; William N. Eskridge Jr., "The Case of the Speluncean Explorers: Twentieth-Century Statutory Interpretation in a Nutshell" (1993) 61 Geo. Wash. L. Rev. 1731.

Lon Fuller, both scholars accepted purposive interpretation. While arguing that rules have a core of settled meaning, Hart thought that judges could consider legislators' purposes and aims to deal with questions in the penumbra of uncertainty surrounding words. Purposive interpretation could be used, for example, to decide whether a rule prohibiting vehicles in the park applied to bicycles, roller skates, toy automobiles, and airplanes.[7] Fuller, on the other hand, denied that interpretation could ever be anything other than purposive. Since rules are not expressed as individual nouns but, rather, as full sentences or paragraphs, he argued that it is impossible to read them without forming some notion of the goals intended. In this view, the purpose is easier to apply in some situations than in others, but interpretation should always look towards the intended policy. Fuller characterized Hart's theory of the settled core as formalist, as presuming that the existence of law requires that at least some meanings be reached through categorization and deductive logic alone without reference to legislative purpose. According to Fuller, rules never have a determined core of meaning that is independent of context.[8]

Hart's distinction between the core of settled meaning and the surrounding penumbra of uncertainty has been much debated. In his theory, the settled core provides the predictability that allows law to guide behaviour.[9] Current criticism of the divide, even in

[7] H.L.A. Hart, "Positivism and the Separation of Law and Morals" (1958) 71 Harv. L. Rev. 593 at 607 and 613.

[8] Lon L. Fuller, "Positivism and Fidelity to Law: A Reply to Professor Hart" (1958) 71 Harv. L. Rev. 630 at 637–38 and 661–69. Hart also criticized formalism and the description of legal reasoning as merely the application of deductive logic to facts that presented themselves already neatly classified (at 602 and 607–12).

[9] Gerald Postema, "Positivism and the Separation of Realists from Their Skepticism: Normative Guidance, the Rule of Law and Legal Reasoning," in Peter Cane, ed., *The Hart-Fuller Debate: Fifty Years On* (Oxford: Hart Publishing, forthcoming 2009), see conference papers available online at <http://law.anu.edu.au/JFCALR/hart_fuller.asp>. Postema notes that Hart also discussed the operation of practical reasoning in the penumbra. Decision making in the penumbra was apparently the usual situation for Hart: "[A]fter all is said and done we must remember ... how exceptional is this feeling that one way of deciding a case is imposed upon us as the only natural or rational elaboration of some rule. Surely it cannot be doubted that, for most cases of interpretation, the language of choice between alternatives ... better conveys the realities of the situation ... [H]ere if anywhere we live among uncertainties between which we have to choose, and ... the existing law imposes only limits on our choice and not the choice itself." Hart, *supra* note 7 at 629.

analytical jurisprudence, might now question whether the source of ambiguity is in the words alone, rather than in the understanding of context.[10] There is probably general agreement now that the vehicles in the park example supposes a legal rule applying at a particular time in a particular culture.[11] It is, indeed, difficult to imagine what would be left of the settled core if, in the future, people were transported in "bubble-like devices that ride on a cushion of air and are essentially invisible, emit no sounds or pollutants, and cause no injury or pain if they hit someone."[12] As Brian Bix notes, legal interpretation is more complex than "a sharp division between unreflective application (in the core) and arbitrary choice (in the penumbra)."[13]

At the same time, attention to context and culture does not lead to the conclusion that anything goes. Timothy Endicott argues that no legal theorist supports a thesis of radical indeterminacy of language. "Please pass the pickles" has meaning, in this view, even though the context will determine which pickles are meant and where they are to be passed.[14] Attention to context, particularly in critical theory, leads to emphasis on voice and the perspectives of the recipients of communication. For those affected by marginalization, Hart's skepticism over the moral value of any given legal system is likely more reassuring than Fuller's view that procedural rule of law will guarantee a minimum level of morality.[15] Ngaire

---

10 Frederick Schauer, "(Re)taking Hart," book review of Nicola Lacey, *A Life of H.L.A. Hart: The Nightmare and the Noble Dream* (Oxford: Oxford University Press, 2004), (2006) 119 Harv. L. Rev. 852 at 865–67. See Thomas Morawetz, "Law as Experience: Theory and the Internal Aspect of Law" (1999) 52 S. M. U. L. Rev. 28 at 39: "[Hart's] account was limited by the assumption, inherent in the philosophical strategies of his time, that the openness and indeterminacies of law as a social practice were to be explained through the indeterminacies of language."

11 See Pierre Schlag, "No Vehicles in the Park" (1999–2000) 23 Seattle U.L. Rev. 381 at 387.

12 Larry Alexander, "All or Nothing at All? The Intentions of Authorities and the Authority of Intentions," in Andrei Marmor, ed., *Law and Interpretation: Essays in Legal Philosophy* (Oxford: Clarendon Press, 1995) 357 at 358.

13 Brian Bix, "Legal Reasoning, the Rule of Law and Legal Theory: Comments on Gerald Postema, 'Positivism and the Separation of the Realists from their Skepticism,'" in Peter Cane, *supra* note 9 at 9 (conference paper).

14 Timothy A.O. Endicott, "Linguistic Indeterminacy" (1996) 16 Oxford J. Legal Stud. 667 at 688.

15 Fuller, *supra* note 8 at 636. While questioning Hart's separation of law and morality, Leslie Green agrees that law can be consistent with overwhelming iniquity

Naffine comments on the legal systems of the 1958 debaters: the United Kingdom (Hart) and the United States (Fuller). The two systems might not have been considered particularly worthy by those marginalized at the time, including a married woman in England with no legal defence against marital rape and an African-American in the United States when segregation was legally accepted.[16] The perspectives of those subject to the rule must be part of the context for communication to be effective. Words have meaning in context, but you will not wind up with the pickles if there is no one who understands what they are and that the appropriate response is to pick up the dish and hand it along.

For tariff classification, the choice of interpretive approaches is wider than the alternatives examined in the Hart-Fuller debate. Rejecting purposive interpretation for the HS does not lead to a formalist approach as the only alternative. It is not necessary to argue that concepts or objects generate their own pre-attached labels in order to maintain that words mean something. As well, the social context is not a matter to be addressed only after the words themselves have been found wanting. Current discussions of legal theory pay increased attention to the ways in which language has meaning for recipients of communication, whether that language comprises full sentences or the isolated nouns of a heading or sub-heading of the HS.[17] Even if the legislative purpose involves an intent to classify goods by objective physical characteristics alone, it is argued here that naming will and should include an awareness of experience that is an integral part of language. The theory advanced in this article adopts Fuller's observation of the importance of context, which is applied here to individual nouns as well as to sentences. It also agrees generally with Hart's observation of settled meanings.

The field of cognitive science has produced important insights into the process of classification in language. In his study of cognition, George Lakoff elaborated a theory of categorization that depends

---

and observes that mere rule of law is "not an unqualified human good." Leslie Green, "Positivism and the Inseparability of Law and Morals" (2008) N.Y.U. L. Rev. 1035 at 1058. See also Brian Bix, "H.L.A. Hart and the Hermeneutic Turn in Legal Theory" (1999) 52 S.M.U. L. Rev. 167 at 195–98.

16 Ngaire Naffine, "The Common Discourse of Hart and Fuller," in Peter Cane, *supra* note 9.

17 See, for example, Bernard J. Hibbitts, "Making Sense of Metaphors: Visuality, Aurality and the Reconfiguration of American Legal Discourse" (1994) 16 Cardozo L. Rev. 229.

on idealized cognitive models. According to this theory, categories of things are determined not by the physical properties of objects themselves but, rather, by the ways in which human beings experience them. Basic level categories, for example, are neither the most general nor the most specific labels but, rather, the ones most convenient for human use. At the basic level, category members are perceived as having common overall shape, which is reflected in a common image. Humans usually interact with them through a common physical motion. These categories are the ones most easily learned by children and most easily remembered. Knowledge is commonly organized at this level. The words chosen as labels tend to be short. Basic level categories can be used in neutral contexts. "There is a dog on the porch," for example, is neutral, while a particular circumstance is required to replace the word "dog" with either "mammal" or "wire-haired terrier." The word "chair" conjures up an image with a shape, while the word "furniture" is more general, more abstract. The naming of "chair back," "chair seat," and "table leg" indicate the importance of human interaction and imagination. The labels, thus, come not from the objects observed but, rather, from the experience of observers.[18]

Steven Winter has applied these insights to legal interpretation.[19] He maintains that language is embodied and imaginative, but is neither arbitrary nor unpredictable. We use experience and cultural knowledge to form complex categories that are not necessarily limited to objects or matters sharing common properties. The category for "hand," for example, includes some extensions based on metaphor ("hour hand," "the upper hand") and metonymy ("all hands on deck," "a hand of cards," "lend a hand," "give a hand," "hand that to me") and not just a core group with shared characteristics.[20] Human interaction forms the categories. It is use, for example, that puts a shoe brush and hairbrush together, even though

---

[18] George Lakoff, *Women, Fire and Dangerous Things: What Categories Reveal about the Mind* (Chicago: University of Chicago Press, 1987) esp. at 43–52. The title of the book comes from a category in Dyirbal, an Aboriginal language of Australia, which contains linkages quite different from those in European languages (at 92ff.).

[19] Steven L. Winter, *A Clearing in the Forest: Law, Life and Mind* (Chicago: University of Chicago Press, 2001); Steven L. Winter, "Transcendental Nonsense, Metaphoric Reasoning, and the Cognitive Stakes for Law" (1988) 137 U. Penn. L. Rev. 1105; Steven L. Winter, "The Cognitive Dimension of the *Agon* between Legal Power and Narrative Meaning" (1989) 87 Mich. L. Rev. 2225.

[20] Winter, *Clearing in the Forest, supra* note 19 at 73.

their physical properties may differ.[21] Idealized cognitive models (ICMs) that are widely understood produce clear, settled meanings. Prototype effects also appear so that some things will be considered stronger or better examples of the category. These prototypes can have an influence on reasoning. Robins and sparrows, for example, are seen as better "birds" than penguins or ducks. Winter reports that, in one experiment, people who were told that robins on an isolated island had a serious disease thought it likely to spread to ducks but did not think that a similar disease of ducks was as likely to affect robins when the fact pattern was reversed.[22] According to Winter, Hart's core of settled meaning simply describes prototypes that are widely accepted.[23]

Winter addresses the vehicle in the park question by discussing the ICMs of parks and vehicles. The following is his description of the ICM of "vehicle":

[T]he concept "vehicle" is structured relative to human purpose and use. Vehicles carry us and our goods, and they do so with greater speed and efficiency than walking. The concept "vehicle" entails mobility, transportability, and an energy source. Vehicles have varied greatly over the course of human experience, from rickshaws, chariots, Conestoga wagons, and cars to jet airplanes; their energy sources range from other humans to animals to the internal combustion engine and beyond. But, in a given culture at a given moment, there are only a few conventional modes of transportation that are common and recurrent. These will inevitably share the conditions of the vehicle ICM.[24]

Human intervention and experience, thus, come with the labels as part of the ordinary operation of language, as the tacit knowledge that frames the categories and determines how language will be understood by the recipients of the communication.[25] A vehicle consists not just of its observable physical components but also of its intended use.[26] Certainty and predictability derive from culture and social practices:

---

[21] *Ibid.* at 22.

[22] *Ibid.* at 76, citing Lance J. Rips, "Inductive Judgments about Natural Categories" (1975) 14 J. Verbal Learning & Verbal Behaviour 665.

[23] Winter, *Clearing in the Forest, supra* note 19 at 304, 316–17.

[24] *Ibid.* at 203–4.

[25] *Ibid.* at 203.

[26] Frederick Bowers, *Linguistic Aspects of Legislative Expression* (Vancouver: UBC Press, 1989) at 141. For further discussion of classification, see 139–64.

The "purpose" of the rule need not be abstracted as a reified entity because our common experience with vehicles and their respective hazards informs us immediately of what the concern is likely to be. Of course, the target will be different in Victorian England than in 1958, but no person of those respective eras would miss the reference.[27]

Analysis of such ICMs may assist with many aspects of legal theory. Attention to categorization and prototypes could provide insight into how we determine similarities and differences[28] and might encourage us to examine ever more closely the assumptions of decision makers to see which voices speak for the interpretive community.[29]

This study of categories and ICMs in language differs from the explicit analysis of socio-economic goals or legislative policy that is usually associated with purposive statutory interpretation. Context tells us what the words mean within a culture, a trade, or an interpretive community. The sense of experience that is part of language will be an automatic part of any inquiry into the meaning of words. This inquiry may not necessarily involve a deliberate analysis of legislative "purpose" as something outside and distinct from language. Just as it is possible to have a conversation without distancing oneself and wondering specifically what one's interlocutor is trying to accomplish, so statutory interpretation can proceed by considering the meanings of words in social practice without a separate inquiry as to intended legislative policy. For tariff classification and the HS, interpretation should not be guided by the specific socio-economic goals of any particular government. An awareness of the use of goods and the commercial understandings of trade participants must, however, be part of the interpretation if the system is to work effectively.

To return to the vehicles in the park example, there are several Canadian tariff decisions that deal with the classification of vehicles. The decisions demonstrate the importance of the international

---

27 Winter, "Transcendental Nonsense," *supra* note 19 at 1178. As Winter points out, we would probably now consider that a child's tricycle was permitted in the park and, indeed, was one of the uses protected by the rule, although some nineteenth-century views would have resisted allowing such recreational activities to disturb the pastoral calm of a park (Winter, *Clearing in the Forest, supra* note 19 at 204–5).

28 Winter, *Clearing in the Forest, supra* note 19 at 238–39.

29 Jay M. Feinman, "Jurisprudence of Classification" (1989) 41 Stanford L. Rev. 661 at 709–10.

context and also appear to reflect the idealized cognitive model described by Winter. In 2004, the Federal Court of Appeal decided that all-terrain vehicles (ATVs) were not "motorcycles" but were instead "motor cars and other vehicles principally designed for the transport of persons." ATVs are four-wheeled, motorized, off-road vehicles. The Canadian International Trade Tribunal (CITT) had accepted the importer's argument that the goods were motorcycles, but the Federal Court of Appeal allowed the Attorney General's appeal.[30] The heading for motor vehicles lists use for the transport of persons as part of the description. In this instance, the HS explanatory note that confirmed the classification as motor vehicles added extra detail beyond Winter's ICM for vehicles as entailing mobility, transportability, and an energy source.

In *Canadian Tire Corporation Ltd. v. Deputy Minister of National Revenue for Customs and Excise,* the Deputy Minister argued that imported goods were vehicles even though they did not have an energy source. The goods were plastic carts with a manually operated reel for the storage of garden hoses. Since the carts had wheels,

---

[30] According to the Federal Court of Appeal, the Canadian International Trade Tribunal (CITT) was clearly wrong, since the tribunal had used its own interpretation of what constituted a "motor-car type steering system" and had decided that the elaboration of that term in an HS Explanatory Note was not adequate to distinguish motorcycles from other motor vehicles. *Suzuki Canada Inc. v. Commissioner of the Canada Customs and Revenue Agency,* [2003] C.I.T.T. No. 35 (Apps. AP-99–114, AP-99–115, AP-2000–08), rev'd [2004] F.C.J. No. 615 (C.A.), leave to appeal dismissed [2004] S.C.C.A. No. 243, foll'd *Arctic Cat Sales Inc. v. Commissioner of the Canada Border Services Agency,* [2006] C.I.T.T. No. 8 (Apps. AP-2005–005, AP-2005–010, AP-2005–011, AP-2005–020). In *Suzuki,* the Federal Court of Appeal reached the same result as it had in an earlier dispute where the importer argued unsuccessfully that all-terrain vehicles (ATVs) were tractors rather than motor vehicles: *Yamaha Motor Canada Ltd. v. Commissioner of the Canada Customs and Revenue Agency,* [2000] C.I.T.T. No. 106 (App. AP-99–105), aff'd, [2002] F.C.J. No. 101 (C.A.). In an HS Explanatory Note, tractors are defined by their use as "vehicles constructed essentially for hauling or pushing another vehicle, appliance or load" and this did not cover ATVs. On the application of the tractor heading to lawnmowers, see *Marubeni Canada Ltd. v. Deputy Minister of National Revenue for Customs and Excise (DMNRCE),* [1994] C.I.T.T. No. 154 (App. AP-93–311) (finding the imported goods to be tractors); *Ford New Holland Canada Ltd. v. DMNRCE,* [1995] C.I.T.T. No. 7 (App. AP-93–388) (also tractors); *Steen Hansen Motorcycles Ltd. v. DMNRCE,* [1997] C.I.T.T. No. 48 (App. AP-95–065) (finding the imported goods to be powered mowers); *Honda Canada Inc. v. DMNRCE,* [1999] C.I.T.T. No. 3 (App. AP-97–111) (also powered mowers); *AYP (Canada) Inc. v. DMNRCE,* [1999] C.I.T.T. No. 85 (Apps. AP-97–063, AP-97–067, AP-97–077, AP-97–079, AP-97–084, AP-97–085, AP-97–096, AP-97–103, AP-97–115, AP-97–136), aff'd [2001] F.C.J. No. 736 (also powered mowers).

the argument was that they were "vehicles ... not mechanically propelled ... for the transport of goods." The CITT decided, however, that the goods were more specifically described as mechanical appliances, a decision in accordance with Winter's ICM.[31] In its reasoning, the CITT referred to two dictionary definitions that emphasized that vehicles were for carriage, conveyance, or transport, reflecting the importance of purpose and use.

The importance of use for carriage or transport in the ICM also had an effect on interpretation despite a definition contained in the legislation. Prior to 1986, Canadian customs legislation contained a provision defining the word "vehicle." The definition stated:

In this Act, or in any other law relating to the customs ... "vehicle" means any cart, car, wagon, carriage, barrow, sleigh, aircraft or other conveyance of any kind whatever, whether drawn or propelled by steam, by animals, or by hand or other power, and includes the harness or tackle of the animals, and the fittings, furnishings and appurtenances of the vehicle.[32]

Prairie Equipment & Radiators Limited v. Deputy Minister of National Revenue for Customs and Excise was an early appeal decided by the Tariff Board, which was the predecessor to the CITT. In this decision, the board reluctantly found excavating equipment to be a vehicle within the definition and recommended that the government restrict its wide application.[33] When no amendment was forthcoming, the board ruled in *General Supply Co. of Canada v. Deputy Minister of National Revenue for Customs and Excise* that a power shovel was machinery rather than a motor vehicle, and the Exchequer Court confirmed that the "vehicle" definition did not apply.[34] The court said that the motor vehicle item did not cover

---

31 *Canadian Tire Corporation Ltd. v. DMNRCE*, [1995] C.I.T.T. No. 68 (App. AP-94-157).

32 *Customs Act*, R.S.C. 1970, c. C-40, s. 2(1), rep. S.C. 1986, c. 1. At the time, the *Customs Tariff* contained a provision confirming that "[t]he expressions mentioned in section 2 of the *Customs Act*, whenever they occur herein or in any Act relating to the customs, have the meaning assigned to them respectively by that section." *Customs Tariff*, R.S.C. 1970, c. C-41, s. 2(3).

33 *Prairie Equipment & Radiators Limited v. DMNRCE* (1952), 1 T.B.R. 56 (T.B., App. 247).

34 *General Supply Co. of Canada v. DMNRCE* (1952), 1 T.B.R. 76 (T.B., App. 269), aff'd [1954] Ex.C.R. 340, 1 T.B.R. 81 (Ex.Ct.). The decision was foreshadowed by an excise tax decision: *J.H. Ryder Machinery Company Ltd. v. DMNRCE* (1952), 1 T.B.R. 75 (T.B., App. 262)

everything capable of moving from one location to another but only "conveyances" designed for the purpose of carrying goods or passengers. The decision demonstrates the importance of the experiential understanding of what a "vehicle" is, since the excavating equipment and the power shovel did actually carry material from one spot to another and thus would be within a formalist application of the definition, as the Tariff Board had found initially.

The definition was still causing problems in 1975, in the appeal *J.H. Ryder Machinery Limited v. Deputy Minister of National Revenue for Customs and Excise*, which concerned large cranes used for handling bulky machinery, pipes, and pre-fabricated housing. The board in this decision allowed the appeal and determined that the cranes were machinery rather than motor vehicles as the department had maintained. The board commented on the wide definition of "vehicle," which could be traced back in the *Customs Act* at least as far as 1883. The definition was wide apparently to cover any possible means of smuggling goods across the border, and it was not intended as a definition of what the tariff item for motor vehicles would include.[35] There were thus sufficient indications in the context to confirm that the very limited mobility of the cranes meant that they were not conveyances within the definition. On this purposive interpretation of the definition, the cranes were not covered. Excavating equipment and large cranes might not be within the usual meaning of "vehicles" and probably not within the ICM as described by Winter. One can wonder whether they would be permitted in the park, but that would never have been a likely spot for application of the *Customs Act* definition.

This article examines Canadian cases dealing with intended use under the HS and also end use items in the previous Canadian tariff. The theory advanced criticizes the idea that predictability requires emphasizing objective, physical characteristics of goods. With the adoption of the HS, it would be a mistake to abandon all consideration of use and attempt to classify goods solely according

---

[35] *J.H. Ryder Machinery Limited v. DMNRCE* (1975), 6 T.B.R. 278 (T.B., App. 1095). See also *Burrard Amusements Limited v. DMNRCE* (1960), 2 T.B.R. 210 (T.B., App. 524); *Canadian Reynolds v. DMNRCE* (1972) C.Gaz.1972.I.1067 (T.B., App. 967); *Mont Sutton v. DMNRCE* (1972) C.Gaz.1972.I.1927 (T.B., App. 983); *J.R. Macdonald v. DMNRCE* (1980), 7 T.B.R. 156, 2 C.E.R. 228 (T.B., App. 1493); *Universal Go-Tract Limited v. DMNRCE* (1981), 7 T.B.R. 392, 3 C.E.R. 239 (T.B., App. 1683), aff'd (1982) 4 C.E.R. 381 (F.C.A.); *AG Marketing v. DMNRCE* (1985), 10 T.B.R. 228, 10 C.E.R. 105 (T.B., App. 2309); *Magnatrim v. DMNRCE* (1988), 18 C.E.R. 13 (T.B., App. 2841).

to physical properties. The approach that is advocated, which is called participatory interpretation, looks to the use of goods, including both function and purpose, and the perspectives of those dealing with them in the full commercial context. Meaning entails a sense of the understanding of language in human experience, such as the notion that a vehicle involves the conveyance of people and goods. Participatory interpretation considers physical characteristics of imports along with other indications of their intended purpose, including price, advertising, and distribution.

The approach to use is more narrow in European Community (EC) case law. The intended use of goods may be considered but only if it is inherent in the product's objective characteristics and properties.[36] In the *Staatssecretaris van Financiën v. Kamino International Logistics BV* decision, for example, the ECJ dealt with the classification of computer screens. The Amsterdam Court of Appeal had classified them as of a kind used principally for automatic data processing since the resolution and brightness of the screens meant that they were suitable for designers and graphic artists who would be viewing the screen at close range. As well, the Amsterdam Court of Appeal noted that the monitors were marketed by the manufacturer exclusively for professional users and were too expensive for other possible applications such as displaying video for DVD players, camcorders, and computer games. The ECJ supported the result but on the basis of the technical characteristics of the screens alone, with no mention of the price or of the manufacturer's marketing system.[37] The opinion of the Advocate General in the case expressly rejects any consideration of packaging indications and advertising to assist with classification, for fear of potential abuse, since products could be advertised for one use when the public knows that there

---

36 *Siebrand BV, supra* note 4 at para. 38. The Tariff Board of Canada had some minor experience with a requirement that use be reflected in physical characteristics of goods. In a decision in 1954, the board over-ruled a practice that the department had followed for "many years" to accept end use certificates for entry under an item covering "articles of glass ... designed to be cut" (*Reference re Administration of Tariff Item 326e* (1954), 1 T.B.R. 192 (T.B., App. 322)). In interpreting this wording, the board decided that the crucial factor was not whether the glass was actually to be embellished later by cutting but, rather, whether it was of a particular quality indicating that the manufacturer had *designed* it for this purpose. For similar items, see *Terochem Laboratories Limited v. DMNRCE* (1986), 11 T.B.R. 223, 11 C.E.R. 319 (T.B., App. 2401); *Western Medi-Aid Products Ltd. v. DMNRCE* (1986), 11 T.B.R. 229, 11 C.E.R. 326 (T.B., Apps. 2357).

37 *Staatssecretaris van Financiën v. Kamino International Logistics BV,* Case C-376/07, 19 February 2009 *[Kamino]*.

is another surreptitious use.[38] This seems an odd approach, unless it could be shown that the marketing of the screens to professional users was in some way deceptive. Without some indication of the intended use, it is difficult to see how courts are to assess the various physical characteristics. Looking at the complete commercial context, the Amsterdam Court of Appeal had found that the only "sensible and useful use" of the goods was for designers, graphic artists, and similar professional users.[39] The full participatory approach of the Amsterdam Court of Appeal is to be preferred, since it is most likely to reflect the understandings of commercial participants. The ECJ in *Kamino* adopts a somewhat participatory approach since use is considered, but the court applies an artificial filter and does not conduct a complete participatory interpretation.

The ECJ has paid some attention to marketing. In *Ikegami Electronics (Europe) GmbH v. Oberfinanzdirektion Nürnberg*, the court considered the manner in which video surveillance machines were marketed as part of its determination that they had a specific function other than automatic data processing.[40] In *Siebrand BV v. Staatssecretaris van Financiën*, the court stated that the name under which goods were marketed was an objective characteristic.[41]

A focus directed solely to physical characteristics does not, in fact, provide a secure guarantee against circumvention. In *BVBA Van Landeghem v. Belgische Staat*, the court was deciding whether pickup trucks were principally for the transport of persons (10 percent duty) or for the transport of goods (22 percent duty). It determined that the trucks were for personal transport because they had luxurious interiors with adjustable leather seats, a stereo and compact disc player, electric windows and mirrors, extra seats with safety belts behind the driver's seat, and deluxe sports rims. The sports rims, in particular, were an "obvious characteristic" demonstrating the intended use since the rims had no practical value.[42] Given the

---

[38] Opinion of Advocate General Mengozzi, 10 September 2008, *Staatssecretaris van Financiën v. Kamino International Logistics BV*, Case C-376/07, at para. 74.

[39] *Kamino, supra* note 37 at para. 26.

[40] *Ikegami Electronics (Europe) GmbH v. Oberfinanzdirektion Nürnberg*, Case C-467/03, [2005] E.C.R. I-2389.

[41] *Siebrand BV, supra* note 4 at para. 38. In *Hauptzollamt Hamburg-St. Annen v. Thyssen Haniel Logistic GbmH*, Case C-459/93, [1995] E.C.R. I-1381, price was a factor indicating that the amino acid mixture in question was intended for medical use, since it was too expensive for use as a food additive (at para. 16).

[42] *BVBA Van Landeghem v. Belgische Staat*, Case C-486/06, [2007] E.C.R. I-10661 at para. 40.

significant difference in duty levels, I suggest it would have made more sense to consider how much the sports rims cost before putting significant emphasis on this one feature. It would also have been helpful to have information on how the trucks were being advertised and distributed.

HARMONIZED SYSTEM: PARTICIPATORY INTERPRETATION

The following sections examine end use and other use items since the HS was implemented in 1988. The first section deals with end use items and a definition that emphasizes physical characteristics, as applied in the cases. The next section examines descriptions that mention use explicitly but do not contain the statutory phrase "for use in." The final section looks at decisions that adopt a participatory approach to interpretation, including "best use" cases that consider the full commercial context.

Prior to implementation of the HS, as many as 40 percent of the items in the Canadian tariff had a specific end use or end user provisions, in which classification depended on the use to which the goods were put after they were imported.[43] These items provided concessions to a particular industry or activity, allowing importation either free of duty or at a reduced rate. Instead of drafting very detailed descriptions of relevant goods so that only a given industry or activity could benefit, the legislator provided for the end use directly and stipulated that the use had to be met in order for the goods to qualify. The following are two examples of end use items in the pre-1988 Canadian tariff before the adoption of the HS:

Self-propelled trucks ... parts of the foregoing; all the foregoing for use exclusively in the operation of logging.

Articles and materials which enter into the cost of manufacture of the goods enumerated in Tariff Items 40900–1, 40902–1 ... when imported for use in the manufacture of the goods enumerated in the aforesaid tariff items.[44]

---

43 Tariff Board, *Reference No. 163, Canada's Customs Tariff According to the Harmonized System,* Vol. I (1985) at 5.

44 Previous tariff items 41105–1 and 44200–1, quoted from Thomas Lindsay and Bruce Lindsay, *Outline of Customs in Canada,* 6th edition (Vancouver: Erin Publishers, 1985) at 13. The French version of end use items usually referred to goods "devant servir à/dans" the particular use.

The logging item contained a naming element that had to be met along with the end use — that is, "self-propelled trucks" or "parts." The second item, on the other hand, was wider and all embracing, with no real naming element except "articles and materials." The crucial factor was that imports were for use in the manufacture of goods in the listed items, which had to do with milking machines, cream separators, and other agricultural machinery.

Classification under end use items depended on the actual use of the goods imported, not on their primary, normal, or ordinary use.[45] Customs treatment therefore was not completely finalized at the time of entry. If goods were diverted from the qualifying use, they had to be reclassified at the initiative of the importer or customs officials.[46] In consequence, the status of goods could not depend solely on observable physical characteristics. The tariff items themselves demanded that interpretation look beyond the goods to an examination of the commercial context.[47]

END USE IN THE HS TARIFF

The transition to the HS required a careful examination of previous end use items to move goods into the new system without affecting rates more than necessary. In Reference 163, the Tariff Board was asked to study the idea of transferring as many of these concessionary items as possible to the HS tariff. Of the 738 items included in the reference, the board recommended moving about one-third into the six-digit tariff without end use qualifications and retaining about another one-third of the items at the seven- and eight-digit level of the Canadian tariff, which contains some detailed descriptions applying only in national legislation and not as part of the

---

[45] *Superior Brake & Hydraulic Specialists Ltd. v. DMNRCE* (1986), 11 T.B.R. 13, 10 C.E.R. 271 (T.B., Apps. 2245, 2254).

[46] *R. v. Confection Alapo Inc.* (1980), 2 C.E.R. 249 (F.C.T.D.); *R. v. Paragon Computer* (1985), 12 C.E.R. 185 (B.C.C.A.).

[47] The items seemed to carry with them an automatic sense of the tariff in application. Cost factors could have an influence, as in *Alex L. Clark Limited v. DMNRCE* (1967), 4 T.B.R. 53 (T.B., App. 860). In this appeal, the board decided that imported tape was not "for use in the recording and reproduction of sound" even though it could function quite well for this purpose. The imported goods were actually computer tape, which was more expensive than ordinary audio tape, and the price differential may have helped the board to determine that the end use would not be met.

common six-digit HS nomenclature.[48] To preserve existing rates for the remaining items, a list of statutory concessions identified by four-digit code numbers was included in a schedule of the tariff during a ten-year period. The codes were repealed at the beginning of 1998 when Parliament adopted a revised customs tariff.[49]

The new legislation included a definition of "for use in," the key phrase that traditionally identified an end use item. In the current Canadian tariff, the phrase is defined to mean that goods are "wrought or incorporated into, or attached to, other goods referred to in that tariff item."[50] Goods with a less direct physical connection are defined as "to be employed in" the listed activity or sector.[51]

Disputes arose over the transition to the HS and the codes. In *Asea Brown Boveri Inc. v. Deputy Minister of National Revenue for Customs and Excise*, the appellant was unsuccessful in arguing for classification in a code that covered "parts ... for use in the manufacture of capacitors." Although the appellant argued that it had imported such goods duty-free prior to the implementation of the HS, the CITT ruled that the imported goods were themselves capacitors, rather than just parts, and that the code was inapplicable.[52] In *Diamant Boart Truco Ltd. v. Deputy Minister of National Revenue for Customs and Excise*, the appellant succeeded in retaining duty-free status for imported circular saw blades that were held to be "for use in stone-cutting machines" within the wording of a tariff amendment that the appellant argued had been adopted by Parliament specifically for the imported goods, at the appellant's request.[53]

---

48 Tariff Board, *Reference No. 163, Canada's Customs Tariff According to the Harmonized System*, Vol. V, Part 3 (1988) (Consolidation of Concessionary Provisions — Statutory Concessionary Tariff Items) at 4–5.

49 *Customs Tariff*, S.C. 1997, c. 36. Chapter 99 of the revised tariff contains some end use items and is not subject to the rule of specificity in General Interpretative Rule 3(a).

50 See *Customs Tariff*, R.S.C. 1985 (3d Supp.), c. 41, s. 4, rep. and sub. *Customs Tariff*, S.C. 1997, c. 36, s. 2(1). The French version of the new definition applies the same requirement to the phrases "devant servir à" and "devant servir dans." A similar definition was actually added to the earlier *Customs Tariff* in February 1987, prior to implementation of the HS: *An Act to Amend the Customs Tariff and the Duties Relief Act*, S.C. 1987, c. 29, s. 1.

51 In the French version, this definition refers to goods *"devant être utilisé pour"* or *"devant être utilisé dans"* the particular sector.

52 *Asea Brown Boveri Inc. v. DMNRCE*, [1991] C.I.T.T. No. 48 (App. AP-89–180).

53 *Diamant Boart Truco Ltd. v. DMNRCE*, [1992] C.I.T.T. No. 89 (App. AP-90–166). The item did not cover the imported drill bits at issue in a subsequent appeal,

Disputes over interpretation of the code items could involve general questions of scope of the descriptions.[54] In *Computalog Ltd. v. Deputy Minister of National Revenue for Customs and Excise,* the CITT dealt with the classification of electric cable that was used to lower logging instruments below the surface in oil and gas wells. In part of its reasons for rejecting classification under a code item, the tribunal decided that fitting the cable with the required connectors at either end was not manufacturing, and thus the cable was not "for use in the manufacture" of certain goods, as required by the code.[55] In *Northern Alberta Processing Co. v. Deputy Minister of National Revenue for Customs and Excise,* the CITT rejected the application of a code item for goods that enter into the cost of the manufacture of fertilizer in part because the appellant made only a component for fertilizer, not the fertilizer itself, and was therefore

---

however: *Universal Grinding Wheel Division of Unicorn Abrasive of Canada Ltd. (now Diamant Boart Craelius Inc.) v. DMNRCE,* [1994] C.I.T.T. No. 10 (Apps. AP-90-213, AP-90-214). Continuity was also at issue when the codes were terminated in 1998. In *Formica Canada,* the appellant argued that goods previously covered by a code should be classified in the tariff item that was indicated for that code in the concordance table provided along with the amendment. The tribunal rejected this argument and held that the revised wording of an exclusion in the item was now wide enough to exclude the goods, which were polymers or copolymers of phenol-formaldehyde: *Formica Canada Inc. v. Commissioner of the Canada Customs and Revenue Agency,* [2002] C.I.T.T. No. 18 (App. AP-2000–041) at para. 24. The classification under the previous code had been confirmed in *Formica Canada Inc. v. DMNRCE,* [1998] C.I.T.T. No. 5 (App. AP-96–205), aff'd. [1999] F.C.J. No. 580 (C.A.). In the 1998 decision, the exclusionary language in the code at the time was held insufficient to cover polymers.

54 For cases interpreting various code descriptions, see *Jolly Jumper Inc. v. DMNRCE,* [1992] C.I.T.T. No. 109 (App. AP-91–235); *Kimberly-Clark Canada Inc. v. DMNRCE,* [1994] C.I.T.T. No. 28 (App. AP-92–303); *Hibernia Management and Development Company Ltd. v. DMNRCE,* [1998] C.I.T.T. No. 35 (App. AP-96–228); *Boehringer Mannheim Canada Ltd. v. Commissioner of the Canada Customs and Revenue Agency,* [2001] C.I.T.T. No. 17 (App. AP-99–104). See also *Clariant (Canada) Inc. v. Commissioner of the Canada Customs and Revenue Agency,* [2002] C.I.T.T. No. 8 (App. AP-2000–022).

55 *Computalog Ltd. v. DMNRCE,* [1994] C.I.T.T. No. 82 (App. AP-92–265). To the same effect, see *Flextube Inc. v. DMNRCE,* [1999] C.I.T.T. No. 16 (App. AP-95–097) [*Flextube Inc.*]; *Nowsco Well Services Ltd. v. DMNRCE,* [1999] C.I.T.T. No. 39 (App. AP-95–128). For a review of definitions of manufacturing commonly used in customs and sales tax law, see *Movado Group of Canada, Inc. v. Minister of National Revenue,* [1998] C.I.T.T. No. 60 (App. AP-97–027) (attaching a strap to a watch head did not constitute manufacturing or production).

too remote from the listed use.[56] In *Sandvik Tamrock Canada Ltd. v. Deputy Minister of National Revenue for Customs and Excise,* the Federal Court of Appeal determined that rods for rock-drilling jumbo drills were articles "for use in extracting machinery for extracting minerals directly from the working face of a mine" and thus within a description in chapter 99 of the tariff. The tribunal had said that the drills did not actually extract material since they were used to create holes for explosives, but the Federal Court of Appeal took a wider view of "extracting machinery" and reversed the tribunal's decision. A narrow view would have made the tariff description inapplicable to any machinery used in hard-rock mining, which is the main form of mining in Canada.[57]

One difficulty over interpretation of the "for use in" codes and other concessionary provisions had to do with the effect of the statutory definition requiring goods to be "wrought into, attached to or incorporated into other goods" in order to qualify. The pre-HS customs tariff took a much wider approach to the interpretation of end use items, not dependent on this physical connection. Since the codes were intended to preserve the benefits of the previous system during the transition, it could have been argued that the previous approach should continue when they were interpreted. The legislation appeared to rule out this possibility. The definition in the legislation adopting the HS at the beginning of 1988 allowed some room for discussion, since it applied "unless the context otherwise requires." The language, however, stated quite specifically that the definition of the expression "for use in" applied "wherever it occurs in a tariff item in Schedule I or a code in Schedule II."[58] The appellant in *Atlas Alloys, a Division of Rio Algom Ltd. v. Deputy*

---

56 *Northern Alberta Processing Co. v. DMNRCE,* [1996] C.I.T.T. No. 79 (App. AP-94–307). As well, on the facts, it was not clear that any of the appellant's output was actually used for the commercial production of fertilizer.

57 *Sandvik Tamrock Canada Ltd. v. DMNRCE,* [2000] C.I.T.T. No. 45 (App. AP-99–083), rev'd [2001] F.C.J. No. 1692 (C.A.). If the view of the CITT had prevailed, the tariff description would have covered only a mechanical device used in soft-rock mining such as coal mining, which directs the rock or ore along a conveyor system to the back of the machine. The Federal Court of Appeal used purposive interpretation, the approach that applied to the pre-HS end use items in the decisions of the Tariff Board. As discussed later in the section on coverage of those end use items, the case law of the European Court of Justice takes a narrower view of explicit use descriptions and likely would have agreed with the CITT result.

58 *Customs Tariff,* R.S.C. 1985 (3d Supp.), c. 41, s. 4.

Minister of National Revenue for Customs and Excise tried to avoid the statutory definition for a code in a duty reduction order that was neither Schedule I nor Schedule II, but the CITT ruled that the order and Schedule II were closely related enactments and the definition would apply.[59] The definition also applied in *Flextube Inc. v. Deputy Minister of National Revenue for Customs and Excise,* involving codes in Schedule II, where it seemed to entail the idea that the physical connection had to be permanent.[60] While this assumption may have some support in the language requiring goods to be "wrought into" or "incorporated into" other goods, it should be noted that the definition in English also refers to goods that are merely "attached to" other goods. As well, *Flextube* involved a special end use item for goods that were "for use in the manufacture of" other goods, rather than an ordinary end use item. Other cases have rejected a requirement that the physical link be permanent.[61]

There are some differences between the English and French versions of the statutory definition. The definition was originally placed in section 4 of the *Customs Tariff* when the HS was adopted:

4. The expression "for use in," wherever it occurs in a tariff item in Schedule I or a code in Schedule II in relation to goods, means, unless the context otherwise requires, that the goods must be wrought into, attached to or incorporated into other goods as provided for in that tariff item or code.

In French, section 4 read as follows:

59　*Atlas Alloys, a Division of Rio Algom Ltd. v. DMNRCE,* [1996] C.I.T.T. No. 96 (App. AP-95-194).

60　*Flextube Inc., supra* note 55 at para. 35. The tribunal has also used definitions from Schedule I in Schedule II, citing s. 68(3) of the *Customs Tariff,* R.S.C. 1985 (3d Supp.), c. 41: "The words and expressions used in Schedule II, wherever those words and expressions are used in Schedule I, have the same meanings as in Schedule I." *Simmons Canada Inc. and Les Entreprises Sommex Ltée v. DMNRCE,* [1997] C.I.T.T. No. 92 (Apps. AP-96-063, AP-96-085, AP-96-089); *Richards Packaging Inc. and Duopac Packaging Inc. v. DMNRCE,* [1999] C.I.T.T. No. 12 (Apps. AP-98-007, AP-98-010), aff'd [2000] F.C.J. No. 2027 (C.A.). In *Richards,* a definition that was stated to apply only for classification within a subheading in a particular HS chapter was nevertheless applied to a code in a duty reduction order.

61　See, for example, *Sony of Canada Ltd. v. DMNRCE,* [1996] C.I.T.T. No. 87 (App. AP-95-262) [*Sony of Canada*], discussed later in this article, in which a tape cartridge was held to be "for use in" a magnetic tape drive, despite the fact that it was not permanently attached to the drive.

4. Les expressions "devant servir dans" et "devant servir à," mentionnées en regard d'un numéro tarifaire de l'annexe I ou d'un code de l'annexe II, signifient que, sauf indication contraire du contexte, les marchandises en cause entrent dans la composition d'autres marchandises par voie d'ouvraison, de fixation ou d'incorporation, selon ce qui est indiqué en regard de ce numéro ou code.[62]

The definition was moved to section 2(1) when the legislation was replaced with a new customs tariff at the beginning of 1998, with some amendments in both versions:

2(1). The definitions in this subsection apply in this Act ... "for use in," whenever it appears in a tariff item, in respect of goods classified in the tariff item, means that the goods must be wrought or incorporated into, or attached to, other goods referred to in that tariff item.

In French, the relevant part of section 2(1) reads as follows:

2(1). Les définitions qui suivent s'appliquent á la présente loi ... "devant servir dans" ou "devant servir à" Mention dans un numéro tarifaire, applicable aux marchandises qui y sont classées et qui doivent entrer dans la composition d'autres marchandises mentionées dans ce numéro tarifaire par voie d'ouvraison, de fixation ou d'incorporation.[63]

In both sets of definitions, it will be noted that the English and French do not quite match. In French, goods are to enter into the composition of other goods by the various means listed, while in English, goods could meet the definition by being merely "attached to" other goods. In the appeal *Sony of Canada Ltd. v. Deputy Minister of National Revenue for Customs and Excise*, the Deputy Minister was unsuccessful in arguing that the French version was clearer and that one good must be a component of another in order to qualify. The tribunal disagreed and held that a tape cartridge was "for use in" a tape drive, as it was physically connected and functionally joined. The physical connection did not have to be permanent. When in operation, the cartridge was locked into the drive and was necessary for the tape drive to function.[64]

---

62 *Customs Tariff*, R.S.C. 1985 (3d Supp.), c. 41.

63 *Customs Tariff*, S.C. 1997, c. 36.

64 *Sony of Canada, supra* note 61. The tribunal mentioned that the code language at issue was not "for use in the manufacture of" but simply "for use in." The

The requirement that goods be functionally linked added an abstract element to what could be a definition looking to physical characteristics alone. In *Sony*, the tape was not only physically attached but was also needed for the tape deck to function. This issue was raised in the *Asea Brown Boveri* series of appeals involving equipment for electrical transmission stations. The question was whether the equipment qualified for code classification as "for use in ... process control apparatus." The tribunal held that certain equipment qualified if it was involved in the control function and was for use in a station or substation with a control centre.[65] Despite being physically connected, equipment failed to qualify if it did not react or respond in some way to direction from the process control apparatus.[66] In *Prins Greenhouses Ltd. v. Deputy Minister of National Revenue for Customs and Excise*, various components were held to be for use in an integrated greenhouse system, as they were involved in its function of controlling climate and environment for plant growth.[67]

---

tribunal rejected an argument that the French version required goods to be attached directly to each other in *Asea Brown Boveri Inc. v. DMNRCE*, [1996] C.I.T.T. No. 76 (App. AP-95–189). In that appeal, equipment was held to be for use in process control apparatus since it was attached to the electrical transmission system for a station that had a control centre. In *Jam Industries*, the wording "entrer dans la composition" had some influence on the tribunal's decision, in which synthesizers, digital pianos, and digital organs were held not be "articles for use in ... automatic data processing machines" (that is, computers), since the synthesizers, pianos, and organs did not complement the function of the computers. Rather, the musical instruments could be played on their own and the computer, when attached, would only complement the functions of the instruments. *Jam Industries Ltd. v. President of the Canada Border Services Agency*, [2006] C.I.T.T. No. 32 (App. AP-2005–006), aff'd. [2007] F.C.J. No. 768 (C.A.).

65 *Asea Brown Boveri Inc. v. DMNRCE*, [1998] C.I.T.T. No. 36 (Apps. AP-93–392, AP-93–393, AP-94–001, AP-94–002, AP-94–007, AP-94–019, AP-94–020, AP-94–026, AP-94–028, AP-94–030, AP-94–033, AP-94–043, AP-94–055, AP-94–060, AP-94–064, AP-94–068, AP-94–077, AP-94–079, AP-94–097, AP-96–118); *Asea Brown Boveri Inc. v. DMNRCE*, [1999] C.I.T.T. No. 99 (App. AP-97–123); *Asea Brown Boveri Inc. v. DMNRCE*, [2000] C.I.T.T. No. 17 (App. AP-98–001). See further *Asea Brown Boveri Inc. v. Commissioner of the Canada Customs and Revenue Agency*, [2005] C.I.T.T. No. 75 (Apps. AP-2002–027, AP-2002–029 to AP-2002–033, AP-2002–108).

66 *Asea Brown Boveri Inc. v. DMNRCE*, [1999] C.I.T.T. No. 100 (App. AP-97–137), rev'd on other grounds [2001] F.C.J. No. 658 (T.D); *Asea Brown Boveri Inc. v. DMNRCE*, [2000] C.I.T.T. No. 16 (Apps. AP-97–124, AP-97–125). See further *Asea Brown Boveri Inc. v. Commissioner of the Canada Customs and Revenue Agency*, [2003] C.I.T.T. No. 39 (App. AP-2002–004).

67 *Prins Greenhouses Ltd. v. DMNRCE*, [2001] C.I.T.T. No. 28 (App. AP-99–045).

Another requirement was that there be some actual use of the goods in the application chosen. Sometimes the destination of the goods is clear from their nature, but, in other situations, it may be more difficult for an importer to prove what the end use will be. The importer in the series of appeals in *Entrelec Inc. v. Deputy Minister of National Revenue for Customs and Excise* was a wholesaler that sold only about 30 percent of the imports in question directly to final end users. It produced evidence by way of end use certificates and testimony, but the CITT found that the end use was demonstrated for only 14 percent of the goods imported.[68] The qualifying use did not have to be the sole use of the goods[69] so long as the requirements of physical connection and functional link were met. In the appeal *PHD Canada Distributing Ltd. v. Commissioner of the Canada Customs and Revenue Agency*, compact discs containing music were held to be for use in automatic data-processing machines (the CD drives), even though the drives could function with more complicated CDs containing other data. The CITT found that since data from the music CD was processed in the drive and the computer, the CDs were functionally joined to the active operation of the drive. It was not necessary for the playing of music CDs to be the primary function of the CD drive.[70] It was also not necessary for the qualify-

---

68 *Entrelec Inc. v. DMNRCE*, [1998] C.I.T.T. No. 76 (App. AP-97–029), rev'd [2000] F.C.J. No. 1499 (C.A.); *Entrelec v. Commissioner of the Canada Customs and Revenue Agency*, [2003] C.I.T.T. No. 20 (App. AP-2000–051), aff'd [2004] F.C.J. 717 (C.A.). In the previous system for end use items, the burden of proof was normally on the importer, since the circumstances concerning use would be within the knowledge of the importer and subsequent purchasers. The burden could sometimes be difficult for importers to meet, especially if the end use involved sales at the retail level. In the *Keymar* appeal, for example, the imported kerosene heaters were suitable for use on boats, but the distribution and marketing of the goods were not sufficiently limited to prove that they were "for use exclusively in the ... equipment of ships or vessels." *Keymar Equipment Ltd. v. DMNRCE* (1983), 9 T.B.R. 1, 6 C.E.R. 104 (T.B., Apps. 1898 etc.), aff'd. (1985), 10 C.E.R. 87 (F.C.A.).

69 *Kappler Canada Ltd. v. DMNRCE*, [1995] C.I.T.T. No. 69 (App. AP-94–232) (protective suits were for use in a noxious atmosphere since they were used for asbestos removal, even though there were other possible uses).

70 *PHD Canada Distributing Ltd. v. Commissioner of the Canada Customs and Revenue Agency*, [2002] C.I.T.T. No. 100 (App. AP-99–116). See also *Imation Canada Inc. v. Commissioner of the Canada Customs and Revenue Agency*, [2001] C.I.T.T. No. 84 (App. AP-2000–047) (film was for use in a laser imager); *Sony of Canada Ltd. v. Commissioner of the Canada Customs and Revenue Agency*, [2004] C.I.T.T. No. 11 (App. AP-2001-097) (magnetic tape recorders were for use in computers if they

ing use to last a long time. In *Agri-Pack v. Commissioner of the Canada Customs and Revenue Agency,* onion bags were for use in machinery for bagging, filling, or packing fresh vegetables even though each bag would be attached to a machine and filled only once and thereafter would serve for storage.[71]

These decisions show how participatory interpretation crept into a statutory definition that appears to refer only to observable, physical characteristics. To qualify, goods must be involved in the functional unit in a certain way. Circumstances are judged through a focus on the function and purpose of goods. This is not a question of interpreting in accordance with legislative purposes but, rather, in accordance with the operation of the assumptions behind ordinary communication by way of language.

CLASSIFICATION BY EXPLICIT USE

Some tariff descriptions refer to the use of goods without being end use classifications. The goods are not "for use in" a particular sector. Use is mentioned explicitly, however, as part of the description. Standard formulations are that the goods are "of a kind used with" some other goods or "of a kind used in" a certain application.[72]

In *Ballarat Corporation Ltd. v. Deputy Minister of National Revenue for Customs and Excise,* time switches were found to be "of a kind used with" certain listed goods, including table fans, household dehumidifiers, and window air conditioners. The Deputy Minister submitted that there was nothing inherent in the design, construction, or composition of the switches to make them suitable solely or principally for that use, but the tribunal declined to read in such a condition. According to the tribunal, if Parliament intended to require

---

were imported with linking cables and software). Even if it were met, the description "articles for use in ... automatic data processing machines" might give way to a more specific description, as occurred in *Pelco Worldwide Headquarters v. President of the Canada Border Services Agency,* [2007] C.I.T.T. No. 63 (Apps. AP-2006–016, AP-2006–018), where digital video recorders were held to be video recording apparatuses.

[71] *Agri-Pack v. Commissioner of the Canada Customs and Revenue Agency,* [2004] C.I.T.T. No. 129 (App. AP-2003–010), aff'd but ref'd back on other grounds [2005] F.C.J. No. 2059 (C.A.).

[72] *Winners Only (Canada) Ltd. v. DMNRCE,* [1996] C.I.T.T. No. 35 (App. AP-94–142): "wooden furniture of a kind used in offices and parts thereof"; *Bio Agri Mix Ltd. v. Commissioner of the Canada Customs and Revenue Agency,* [2000] C.I.T.T. No. 104 (App. AP-99–085): "preparations of a kind used in animal feeding."

that the imports be designed to be used primarily in a certain way, the description would have said so specifically. To be classified in the tariff item, imports had to be capable of, or suitable for, use with the listed goods, but there was no need to demonstrate primary use or any actual use at all. The imported switches in *Ballarat* had physical features making them suitable for use with listed goods. They were therefore "of a kind used with" those goods.[73] This fairly wide approach to the phrase "of a kind used with" was at issue in *Black & Decker Canada Inc. v. Deputy Minister of National Revenue for Customs and Excise*, in which thermostats for frying pans did not qualify, even though they operated on the same principle as other thermostats that were actually used or capable of being used with the listed goods. The imported thermostats were specifically designed for particular frying pans and were not suitable for use with listed goods. The tribunal ruled that the "kind" was not so wide as to include imports that were, in fact, incapable of the mentioned use.[74]

Classification by explicit use also covers descriptions that refer to goods being "for" a particular purpose. In *Costco Canada Inc. v. Commissioner of the Canada Customs and Revenue Agency*, the tribunal said that the phrase "of a kind used for domestic purposes" had the same meaning as "for domestic purposes." The tariff item in question had originally contained the first phrase, which was replaced by the second phrase partway through the series of importations in dispute. Since the item was not an end-use provision, the tribunal stated that the imported benches did not have to be used exclusively around domiciles in order to be primarily for use in a domestic setting. The tribunal examined the physical characteristics, design, and price of the benches and decided that they met the domestic purpose requirement, since they were "clearly made to be used in a domestic setting, such as a private garden, a backyard lawn or a patio."[75] The

---

73 *Ballarat Corporation Ltd. v. DMNRCE,* [1995] C.I.T.T. No. 85 (App. AP-93–359) [*Ballarat*]. To the same effect, see *Noma Industries Limited v. DMNRCE,* [1997] C.I.T.T. No. 22 (App. AP-96–061).

74 *Black & Decker Canada Inc. v. DMNRCE,* [1997] C.I.T.T. No. 12 (Apps. AP-95–020, AP-95–046, AP-96–069). Evidence of actual use helped to persuade the tribunal that imported coiled steel tubing was "of a kind used in drilling for oil or gas" in *Flextube Inc., supra* note 55.

75 *Costco Canada Inc. v. Commissioner of the Canada Customs and Revenue Agency,* [2001] C.I.T.T. No. 7 (App. AP-2000–05) at para. 18. Goods were found to be "electro-thermic appliances of a kind used for domestic purposes" in *Sunbeam Corp. (Canada) v. DMNRCE,* [1997] C.I.T.T. No. 21 (App. AP-96–054), a dispute that did not involve the interpretation of the domestic purposes condition. See also

tribunal looked at the same factors, along with marketing, in *Alliance Rona Home Inc. v. Commissioner of the Canada Customs and Revenue Agency*, to decide that the imported folding chairs were not "for domestic purposes" since they were not primarily made to be used in a domestic setting.[76] This emphasis on primary purpose goes beyond the requirement of suitability or capability that was applied to the phrase "of a kind used with." It may be natural to expect that when goods are to be "for" a certain purpose, that purpose should be their primary purpose. In *Canadian Tire Group Ltd. v. President of the Canada Border Services Agency*, the tribunal held that a heat gun was not "of a kind used for domestic purposes" since there was evidence of business use by a contractor, even though the product manual stated that the goods were not warranted for industrial or commercial use.[77]

In 2006 and 2007, the Federal Court of Appeal dealt with two appeals on the question of whether goods were "articles for Christmas festivities." In *Decolin Inc. v. President of the Canada Border Services Agency*, the CITT held that tablecloths and other table linen decorated with Christmas motifs met the description, due to evidence of their short marketing season. The dispute had to do with an amendment to the Explanatory Notes effective after importation of the goods that would have excluded table linen from the heading. The Court of Appeal upheld the tribunal's decision that the amendment did not apply to the imported linens.[78] In *3319067 Canada Inc. (Universal Lites) v. President of the Canada Border Services Agency*, the

---

Johnson & Johnson Inc. v. Commissioner of the Canada Customs and Revenue Agency, [2004] C.I.T.T. No. 53 (App. AP-2003–030) ("of a kind used for household or sanitary purposes").

[76] *Alliance Rona Home Inc. v. Commissioner of the Canada Customs and Revenue Agency*, [2002] C.I.T.T. No. 78 (App. AP-2001–065). In *Euro-Line Appliances v. DMNRCE*, [1997] C.I.T.T. No. 9 (App. AP-95–230), the tribunal looked to marketing, use, and physical features to decide that the goods in issue were "household-type" washing machines. See further *Black & Decker Canada Inc. v. DMNRCE*, [1992] C.I.T.T. No. 143 (App. AP-90–192), in which the tribunal decided that goods could be domestic appliances even if they were for domestic chores outside the four walls of a house.

[77] *Canadian Tire Group Ltd. v. President of the Canada Border Services Agency*, [2007] C.I.T.T. No. 93 (App. AP-2006–038) at para. 38.

[78] *Decolin Inc. v. President of the Canada Border Services Agency*, [2005] C.I.T.T. No. 58 (App. AP-2004–011), aff'd [2006] F.C.J. No. 1963 (C.A.). The tribunal was of the view that it would be unfair to give retroactive effect to the amendment. The Court of Appeal nevertheless noted with apparent approval the tribunal's practice

imported net lights also had a short marketing season, but the tribunal held that they were covered by a more specific heading for lamps and lighting fittings. Within that heading, the tribunal majority ruled that the goods were "other electric lamps and lighting fittings." One member of the tribunal dissented and, applying the *Ballarat* decision,[79] would have found that the goods were "lighting sets of a kind used for Christmas trees." According to the dissent, the net lights did not have to be solely or even principally used to decorate indoor Christmas trees to meet this description; use on outdoor trees and shrubbery would have been sufficient for classification in the tariff item, which would also have reflected the seasonal nature of the goods. The decision of the majority was affirmed on appeal.[80] In *Universal Lites,* consideration of use operated at several levels. Although the goods might have met the requirement of principal use "for Christmas festivities," this description was rejected for a more specific one. Within the heading chosen, there was disagreement among tribunal members over whether the goods met a less onerous use requirement to be "of a kind used for Christmas trees." The majority, upheld on appeal, decided that the phrase did not cover the use of the imported goods.

Other descriptions mentioning an express use have required interpretation by the CITT and the judicial system, with varying approaches to the connection to use. The Federal Court of Appeal decided that vitamins and iron supplements were "medicaments ... for therapeutic ... uses" even though they were not used to treat a specific disease. It was sufficient that they were taken in order to

---

of considering any amendment to the Explanatory Notes, even an amendment effective after the importation of the goods in question. The Canada Border Services Agency argued unsuccessfully that the amendment, which Canada had proposed at the World Customs Organization (WCO), simply clarified the heading without changing its scope. In *Franklin Mint Inc. v. President of the Canada Border Services Agency,* [2006] C.I.T.T. No. 63 (App. AP-2004–061), Christmas plates were articles for Christmas festivities even though they could be purchased year round, since they were for display use during the holiday season (para. 52). Christmas calendars containing chocolates did not qualify as articles for Christmas festivities, however, in *Morris National Inc. v. President of the Canada Border Services Agency,* [2007] C.I.T.T. No. 20 (App. AP-2005–039), since the packaging did not change the fact that the goods were predominantly chocolates (para. 20).

79 *Ballarat, supra* note 73.

80 *3319067 Canada Inc. (Universal Lites) v. President of the Canada Border Services Agency,* [2006] C.I.T.T. No. 34 (App. AP-2004–017), aff'd. [2007] F.C.J. No. 925 (C.A.).

prevent disease or ailment.[81] This fairly wide interpretation of the use also appears in the Court of Appeal's decision issued on the same day that goods could be for therapeutic uses without proof of medical efficacy so long as they were actually used to prevent or treat a disease or ailment.[82] Other disputes have involved a range of descriptions: "instruments ... used in ... surgical ... sciences,"[83] "articles of apparel and clothing accessories ... specially designed for use in sports,"[84] hand rails, corner guards, and wall guards "prepared for use in structures,"[85] "butter substitutes and preparations suitable for use as butter substitutes."[86]

Descriptions that explicitly mention use without including the phrase "for use in" are not bound by the statutory definition of that

---

[81] *Flora Manufacturing & Distributing Ltd. v. DMNRCE*, [2000] F.C.J. No. 1196 (C.A.), rev'g [1998] C.I.T.T. No. 68 (App. AP-97–052). See *DSM Nutritional Products Canada Inc. v. President of the Canada Border Services Agency*, [2008] C.I.T.T. No. 83 (App. AP-2007–012), in which the CITT explicitly refused to follow a WCO Classification Opinion and found the goods there in question to be medicaments. On the interpretation of "medicaments," see further *Upjohn Inter-American Corporation v. DMNRCE*, [1992] C.I.T. .T. No. 8 (Apps. AP-90–197, AP-90–146); *Pfizer Canada Inc. v. Commissioner of the Canada Customs and Revenue Agency*, [2003] C.I.T.T. No. 86 (Apps. AP-2002–038 to AP-2002–090); *Roche Vitamins Canada Inc. v. Commissioner of the Canada Customs and Revenue Agency*, [2006] C.I.T.T. No. 10 (App. AP-2003–036).

[82] *Yves Ponroy Canada v. DMNRCE*, [2000] F.C.J. No. 1202 (C.A.), affirming the following four decisions: *Yves Ponroy Canada v. DMNRCE*, [1997] C.I.T.T. No. 126 (App. AP-96–117); *Flora Manufacturing & Distributing Ltd. v. DMNRCE*, [1998] C.I.T.T. No. 47 (App. AP-97–002); *Flora Manufacturing & Distributing Ltd. v. DMNRCE*, [1998] C.I.T.T .No. 69 (App. AP-97–058); *Hilary's Distribution Ltd. v. DMNRCE*, [1998] C.I.T.T. No. 72 (App. AP-97–010). In these four decisions, the CITT had evidence showing that the goods were used for the treatment of disease and had some curative powers.

[83] *Heco Medical Group Inc. v. DMNRCE*, [1996] C.I.T.T. No. 44 (App. AP-95–089).

[84] *International Imports for Competitive Shooting Equipment Inc. v. DMNRCE*, [1999] C.I.T.T. No. 69 (App. AP-98–076). The phrase covered gloves used and designed for the sport of target shooting. See *Sigvaris Corporation v. President of the Canada Border Services Agency*, [2009] C.I.T.T. No. 3 (App. AP-2007–009).

[85] *ERV Parent Co. Ltd. v. DMNRCE*, [1997] C.I.T.T. No. 115 (Apps. AP-95–127, AP-95–191). The phrase covered components that had no other uses. They were "prepared" in the sense of having been treated, as they had been bent and drilled for installation and the remaining work could be done onsite.

[86] *Reference Regarding the Tariff Classification of Certain Butteroil Blends*, [1999] CITT No. 25. The tribunal majority decided that the butter oil blend at issue did not qualify, because it could not "take the place of butter in substantially all respects and in substantially all conditions" (at para. 79). The blend was used primarily for making ice cream. It did not have the taste or texture of butter. One tribunal

phrase requiring goods to be "wrought into, attached to or incorporated into other goods."[87] In *Record Tools Inc. v. Deputy Minister of National Revenue for Customs and Excise,* the CITT decided that woodturning tools were "interchangeable tools for machine-tools" even though the tools only lean against the machine tool (a wood lathe) when they are used. They are not fitted into the lathe or attached or incorporated in any other way. They are nevertheless "for machine tools" since they are necessary for a wood lathe to function and neither the lathe nor the tools are intended to perform independently of the other.[88] Had the description referred instead to "interchangeable tools for use in machine-tools," the statutory definition might have led to the conclusion that a more concrete physical link was needed. All of the parties agreed that a wood lathe was a "machine-tool." This was the only way in which tools were used with wood lathes. The item for "interchangeable tools" could easily have covered nothing in relation to wood lathes if physical incorporation had been required. *Record Tools,* thus, is an example of wider, participatory interpretation involving classification by commercial application of the goods rather than simply by physical characteristics.

---

member dissented, citing *Ballarat, supra* note 73, to the effect that the phrase "suitable for use as a butter substitute" imposed a lesser requirement than meeting substantially all the purposes of butter. Since the blend could replace butter in the making of ice cream, it acted as a butter substitute, in the view of the dissenting member. The dissenting member also stated that the blend would meet a commercial reality or commercial fitness test for interpretation of the phrase "suitable for use" in some pre-HS US jurisprudence cited to the tribunal (para. 102, citing *United States v. F. W. Myers & Co., Inc.* 60 C.C.P.A. 134, 476 F. 2d 1377, (1973) C.C.P.A. LEXIS 370, C.A.D. 1097; *Keer, Maurer and Company v. United States,* 46 C.C.P.A. 110, 1959 CCPA LEXIS 191, C.A.D. 710; *Kahlen v. United States (No. 448),* United States Court of Customs Appeals, 12 October 1911 at 208). According to the dissenting member, if a product is commercially used as a substitute for butter, then it would meet a commercial fitness test of being suitable for use as a substitute.

87 *Customs Tariff,* S.C. 1997, c. 36, s. 2.

88 *Record Tools Inc. v. DMNRCE,* [1997] C.I.T.T. No. 95 (App. AP-96–225). In *Gladu Tools Inc. v. President of the Canada Border Services Agency,* [2005] C.I.T.T. No. 55 (App. AP-2004–018), the tribunal decided that knives fitted into tools that were in turn installed on woodworking machines should be classified as "knives ... for machines ... for woodworking," rejecting an argument by the Canada Border Services Agency (CBSA) that the knives had to be mounted directly onto the machines to qualify (at para. 35). The decision was reversed on appeal on other grounds. *Gladu Tools Inc. v. President of the Canada Border Services Agency,* [2007] F.C.J. No. 781 (C.A.).

PARTICIPATORY INTERPRETATION AND "BEST USE"

Many Canadian decisions since 1988 demonstrate participatory interpretation, which takes account of the commercial context and trade understandings. Participatory interpretation goes beyond physical characteristics of goods and classifies according to human factors, including function and intended use of the goods, as shown through price, marketing, and distribution. As interpretation theory, participatory interpretation emphasizes the viewpoint of the recipient of the communication and reflects the influence of ICMs, as described by Steven Winter.

Interpretation by intended use and purpose may help to determine the essential character of goods. This could be a focus on what products actually accomplish, such as the goalie pads in *Bauer Nike Hockey Inc. v. President of the Canada Border Services Agency*[89] or the bearings that determined the classification of roller glides for drawers in *Groupe Cabico Inc. v. President of the Canada Border Services Agency.*[90] The essential character might be the function that gives the article its name.[91] It will be the principal function of the goods, reflecting their fundamental purpose.[92] In *Brooks Wetsuits Ltd. v. Minister of National Revenue,* there was no dispute that the spray skirt worn by kayakers kept water out of the kayak. The issue was whether it was a safety device or insulation for the kayaker in cold waters. Finding that the purpose was protection of the kayaker, the Federal Court (Trial Division) determined that the spray skirt was an accessory to wetsuits.[93] When a function is explicitly mentioned, goods must be involved in the function to qualify.[94] As well, the

---

[89] *Bauer Nike Hockey Inc. v. President of the Canada Border Services Agency,* [2006] C.I.T.T. No. 58 (App. AP-2005–019). See also *Power Twins Performance Parts Ltd. v. Commissioner of the Canada Customs and Revenue Agency,* [2003] C.I.T.T. No. 59 (App. AP-2002–022) (face shields).

[90] *Groupe Cabico Inc. v. President of the Canada Border Services Agency,* [2007] C.I.T.T. No. 92 (App. AP-2006–004).

[91] *Asea Brown Boveri Inc. v. DMNRCE ,* AP-89–180, [1991] C.I.T.T. No. 48 (App. AP-89–180).

[92] *Pelco Worldwide Headquarters v. President of the Canada Border Services Agency,* [2007] C.I.T.T. No. 63 (Apps. AP-2006–016, AP-2006–018); *Carlon Canada Limited v. DMNRCE,* [1995] C.I.T.T. No. 46 (App. AP-94–168).

[93] *Brooks Wetsuits Ltd. v. Minister of National Revenue,* [1999] F.C.J. No. 1547 (T.D.).

[94] *Spectra/Premium Industries Inc. v. President of the Canada Border Services Agency,* [2008] C.I.T.T. No. 16 (App. AP-2006–053), paras. 32–34, aff'd [2009] F.C.J. No. 313 (C.A.). As discussed later in the section on the coverage of the previous

involvement needs to be discernible at the time of importation and not dependent on events occurring after that time.[95]

The role of ICMs is strong. In *Rona Corporation Inc. v. President of the Canada Border Services Agency*, gazebos with steel frames, fabric roofs, and fabric bug-screen sides were classified as steel structures rather than tents. Although the gazebos provided shelter, the tribunal determined that since they required complex assembly and were intended to be semi-permanent, they were not within the meaning of tents "in common parlance."[96] In *N.C. Cameron & Sons Ltd. v. President of the Canada Border Services Agency*, the ICM may have even overtaken the tariff wording in the decision of the majority. The appeal involved imported figurines that the majority decided could not be classified as dolls because they were too fragile to be played with as toys. The dissenting member disagreed, however, noting that the Explanatory Note also referred to "dolls intended for decorative purposes," in addition to "dolls designed for the amusement of children."[97] The disagreement between majority and dissent illustrates the influence of interpretation by the intended purpose of the goods.

Purpose can determine the essential character of goods. In the appeal *Mon-Tex Mills Ltd. v. Commissioner of the Canada Customs and Revenue Agency*, the CITT held that decorative shower curtains with liners were curtains since the main weight and value of the goods were in the curtain. The Federal Court of Appeal reversed, however, saying that the tribunal's decision was unreasonable. According to the Court of Appeal, essential character refers to the fundamental nature of goods, their reason for existence, which in this case was to prevent the leakage of water from showers. It was the vinyl liner, therefore, that provided the essential character and the goods were

---

end use items, the Tariff Board took a wider approach to interpretation of those items. The decision in *Spectra/Premium* is similar to the case law of the European Court of Justice, noted in that section. See further *Interprovincial Corrosion Control Company Limited v. DMNRCE*, [1997] C.I.T.T. No. 59 (App. AP-96–041); *Hibernia Management and Development Company Ltd. v. DMNRCE*, [1998] C.I.T.T. No. 35 (App. AP-96–228).

95 *Opal Optical Ltd. v. DMNRCE*, [1994] C.I.T.T. No. 65 (App. AP-92–385).

96 *Rona Corporation Inc. v. President of the Canada Border Services Agency*, [2008] C.I.T.T. No. 13 (App. AP-2006–033) at para. 30.

97 *N.C. Cameron & Sons Ltd. v. President of the Canada Border Services Agency*, [2007] C.I.T.T. No. 50 (App. AP-2006–022) at para. 21.

articles of plastic.⁹⁸ Similarly, in *Mammoet Canada Eastern Ltd. v. President of the Canada Border Services Agency*, the tribunal determined that the hydraulic equipment for lifting on certain heavy-duty transporters constituted "the entire purpose" of the transporters,⁹⁹ which were therefore trucks with lifting equipment rather than trailers.¹⁰⁰ In *816392 Ontario Ltd. (c.o.b. Freedom Motors) v. Deputy Minister of National Revenue for Customs and Excise*, the tribunal held that minivans did not change their essential character when they were exported to the United States to be made wheelchair accessible and then re-imported into Canada. They were still designed for the transportation of persons and had not become new or commercially different products. The minivans were therefore classified in heading 98.22 as goods returned to Canada after repair or alteration in the United States and were dutiable only on the value of the alteration.¹⁰¹ Note that it is not the intent of the particular importer that determines, even if there is no dispute as to that intent.¹⁰² Marketing, advertising, and prices will be important factors to indicate the purpose. In *Norsk Fitness Products Inc. v. President of the Canada Border Services Agency*, ankle, knee, elbow, and back supports that contained magnets derived their essential character from the magnets, as the pricing and marketing showed that the goods were purchased for the intended effect of magnetic therapy

---

98 *Mon-Tex Mills Ltd. v. Commissioner of the Canada Customs and Revenue Agency*, [2004] F.C.J. No. 1712 (C.A.), rev'g [2003] C.I.T.T. No. 81 (App. AP-2002–103).

99 *Mammoet Canada Eastern Ltd. v. President of the Canada Border Services Agency*, [2006] C.I.T.T. No. 26 (Apps. AP-2004–024 to AP-2004–046) at para. 25.

100 An Explanatory Note helped to identify the purpose of goods in *Supertek*, which dealt with the classification of small battery-operated push-on lights. Although the lights could be carried, the tribunal decided they were not "portable lamps" since, according to the Explanatory Note, this description was for lamps "designed for use when carried in the hand or on the person." The lights at issue would normally be fastened to a wall in a closet or cupboard. *Supertek Canada Inc. v. Commissioner of the Canada Customs and Revenue Agency*, [2003] C.I.T.T. No. 41 (App. AP-2001–095).

101 *816392 Ontario Ltd. (c.o.b. Freedom Motors) v. DMNRCE*, [1996] C.I.T.T. No. 86 (Apps. AP-95–299, AP-96–053). See further *Dominion Sample Ltd. v. Commissioner of the Canada Customs and Revenue Agency*, [2003] F.C.J. No. 1567, at paras. 44–47.

102 Pepper spray was still an offensive weapon, even though the importer intended to use it to defend against dogs, bears, and other animals. *Roozen v. DMNRCE*, [1999] C.I.T.T. No. 17 (App. AP-96–057).

to reduce pain, even though medical evidence did not support such a claim.[103]

One line of Canadian cases seems almost directly linked to the notion of ICMs, with special emphasis on purpose. This line of cases mentioned the intended design and "best use." The "best use" approach was argued by counsel in the appeal *Zellers Inc. v. Deputy Minister of National Revenue for Customs and Excise*, which dealt with whether pillows in the shape of animals qualified as toys. The tribunal decided that they did and allowed the appeal, noting that the goods were more like toys than pillows.[104] The appellant had argued that the description as toys was a better one, suggesting three tests for interpretation: (1) appearance; (2) design and best use; and (3) marketing and distribution.[105] The tribunal allowed the appeal but only under General Interpretative Rule 3(c), as the last in numerical order rather than as the more accurate description.[106] The best use test became part of the tribunal's reasoning in *Regal Confections Inc. v. Deputy Minister of National Revenue for Customs and Excise*, an appeal over whether various small containers holding candies were toys or confectionery. The tribunal mentioned with approval counsel's arguments in favour of appearance, design, best use, marketing, and distribution, while noting that these were individual factors that might be helpful to consider and that their importance would vary according to the particular product.[107] In the decision, the tribunal held that a motorized dispenser sold with two packages of candy qualified as a toy due to the use of the dispenser as an independent collectible article of play.[108] In a later case, the *Regal* factors were considered indicative but not determinative in

---

103 *Norsk Fitness Products Inc. v. President of the Canada Border Services Agency*, [2006] C.I.T.T. No. 44 (App. AP-2003–045).

104 *Zellers Inc. v. DMNRCE*, [1998] C.I.T.T. No. 53 (App. AP-97–057) at para. 57.

105 *Ibid.* at para. 48.

106 For an earlier case using participatory interpretation to decide that small play tents were toys rather than tents, see *World Famous Sales of Canada Inc. v. DMNRCE*, [1994] C.I.T.T. No. 124 (App. AP-93–263).

107 *Regal Confections Inc. v. DMNRCE*, [1999] C.I.T.T. No. 51 (Apps. AP-98–043, AP-98–044, AP-98–051) at para. 22. See further *Havi Global Solutions (Canada) Limited Partnership v. President of the Canada Border Services Agency*, [2008] C.I.T.T. No. 67 (App. AP-2007–014); *Korhani Canada Inc. v. President of the Canada Border Services Agency*, [2008] C.I.T.T. No. 79 (App. AP-2007–008).

108 *Ibid.* at para. 30. On the interpretation of toys, see further *Franklin Mint Inc. v. President of the Canada Border Services Agency*, [2006] C.I.T.T. No. 63 (App.

Partylite Gifts Ltd. v. Commissioner of the Canada Customs and Revenue Agency, an appeal in which glass candleholders were held to be non-electrical candlesticks rather than glassware. The tribunal considered their design, best usage, and marketing, noting that glassware would not usually be in a package with instructions on how to prevent a fire.[109]

Some decisions of the ECJ provide hints of similar participatory interpretation that explores the intended use. An example is the decision in *Neckermann Versand AG v. Hauptzollamt Frankfurt am Main-Ost* that knitted pyjamas can be classified as pyjamas even if they are not wholly and exclusively suitable for wearing in bed. It is sufficient if their general appearance and fabric demonstrate that this function is the main use intended.[110] This seems a sensible way of giving effect to the ordinary meaning of pyjamas — of how the language would be understood in general speech — even though the court's reasoning is still tied to objective characteristics inherent in the goods. There is no need to take the view that consideration of use threatens certainty and predictability, so that imported jeans fastening left over right in *Hauptzollamt Osnabrück v. Kleiderwerke Hela Lampe GmbH & Co. KG* had to be classified as men's garments rather than women's garments, despite evidence that jeans worn by women also fastened in the same way.[111] In his opinion in *Neckermann Versand,* Advocate General Jacobs raised the question of uniformity. He suggested that it would not be sufficient to look to the intended use in just one member state since local customs and conditions could vary. The habits of the EC as a whole had to be considered in this view in order to ensure uniform application of the common customs tariff. The question of differing usage had to be addressed,

---

AP-2004–061); *N.C. Cameron & Sons Ltd. v. President of the Canada Border Services Agency,* [2007] C.I.T.T. No. 50 (App. AP-2006–022).

[109] *Partylite Gifts Ltd. v. Commissioner of the Canada Customs and Revenue Agency,* [2004] C.I.T.T. No. 18 (App. AP-2003–008) at paras. 41, 44, aff'd. [2005] F.C.J. No. 753 (C.A.).

[110] *Neckermann Versand AG v. Hauptzollamt Frankfurt am Main-Ost,* Case C-395/93, [1994] E.C.R. I-4027. Goods were also classified by their main use in *Wiener S.I. GmbH v. Hauptzollamt Emmerich,* Case C-338/95, [1997] E.C.R. 6495; *Anagram International Inc. v. Inspecteur van de Belastingdienst — Douanedistrict Rotterdam,* Case C-14/05, [2006] E.C.R. I-6763

[111] *Hauptzollamt Osnabrück v. Kleiderwerke Hela Lampe GmbH & Co. KG,* Case 222/85, [1986] E.C.R. 2449. See also *Handelsonderneming J.Mikx BV v. Minister van Enonomische Zaken,* Case 90/85, [1986] E.C.R. 1695.

but it would normally be part of the choice of context. It is un-likely, for example, that there would be a global perspective on the function of snow boots. In addition, usage can change over time, which may have been part of the problem in *Hela Lampe*.

Certainty is not in the physical features of goods alone. The per-spectives of trade participants must be considered in order to avoid having a tariff isolated from commercial reality. The Canadian cases on "best use" do this well in that they look to the full commercial context without requiring a link to inherent physical characteristics.

END USE PRIOR TO THE HS

The following sections examine decisions of the Tariff Board, which was the predecessor of the CITT, in its interpretation of pre-HS end use items. Relying on presumed legislative purpose, the Tariff Board gave the end use items wide coverage and granted them priority over other items.

COVERAGE

The Tariff Board decisions adopted a purposive approach to inter-pretation of end use items. The board was not just classifying im-ported goods against a commercial background but also deciding whether Parliament intended a tariff concession for these goods given their involvement in a particular economic activity or sector. When the end use was for manufacturing, the board would con-sider whether the activity in Canada was sufficient to justify beneficial tariff treatment. Coverage could be fairly wide, especially for "all-embracing" end use items that included any articles and materials meeting a given end use.

In a number of appeals, the question to resolve was whether the specific activity in which the imported goods would be involved was part of the general activity covered by the end use. Interpretation was fairly generous in favour of wide coverage. In three early deci-sions on an end use item for logging operations, the board ruled that the following were covered: trucks that transported logs to the log dump,[112] railway cars owned by a logging company but used by a common carrier to transport logs to the log dump,[113] machinery

---

[112] *Reference re Logging Motor Trucks* (1951), 1 T.B.R. 51 (T.B., App. 243).

[113] *Fleetwood Logging Company v. DMNRCE* (1954), 1 T.B.R. 161 (T.B., App. 308), aff'd [1954] Ex.C.R. 695, 1 T.B.R. 162.

used by a logging company or one of its contractors for the construction and maintenance of roads, camps, log dumps, wharves, and docks as well as machinery used by a logging company for fire prevention.[114] In *Fleetwood Logging Company v. Deputy Minister of National Revenue for Customs and Excise,* concerning railway cars, the Exchequer Court on appeal specifically mentioned the legislative purpose of assisting the logging industry and remarked that a contrary result would create a disadvantage for logging companies that did not have log dumps on their own property and thus had to use common carriers.

A generous view of what processes were included in a metallurgical operation for chemical conversion, extraction, reduction, and recovery appears in a later series of appeals involving the Sherritt Gordon plant in Fort Saskatchewan.[115] The board also took a wide approach in *Ersco Canada Ltd. v. Deputy Minister of National Revenue for Customs and Excise,*[116] in which the phrase "fire brick ... for use exclusively in the construction or repair of a furnace, kiln, or other equipment of a manufacturing establishment" was held to cover

---

[114] *Reference ... on Logging Camp Machinery* (1956), 1 T.B.R. 258 (T.B., App. 380). See also *Port Arthur Shipbuilding Company v. DMNRCE* (1955), 1 T.B.R. 236 (T.B., App. 340).

[115] *Industrial and Road Equipment Ltd. v. DMNRCE, Canadian Chromalox Co. v. DMNRCE, Sherritt Gordon Mines Limited v. DMNRCE, Clark Compressor Co. v. DMNRCE* (1958), 2 T.B.R 110 (T.B. Apps. 441, 449, 451, 461), aff'd (*sub nom Dorr-Oliver Long Ltd. v. Sherritt Gordon Mines Ltd.*) (1959) 2 T.B.R. 113 (Ex. Ct.); *Sherritt Gordon Mines Ltd. v. DMNRCE* (1961), 2 T.B.R. 231 (T.B., App. 548). The pipe fittings in *Sherritt Gordon Mines Ltd. v. DMNRCE* (1961), 2 T.B.R. 234 (T.B., App. 549) would have been covered by the same end use item as well, except that they were not sufficiently complex to be described as "apparatus," as the item required. See further *Ocelot Chemicals v. DMNRCE* (1985), 10 T.B.R. 286, 10 C.E.R. 208 (T.B., App. 2019), in which the board confirmed a settlement between the parties to the effect that catalyst carriers and reformer tube assemblies were included in a tariff item for "machinery and apparatus for use in the distillation or recovery of products from natural gas ... parts thereof," under a rather wide interpretation of the word "recovery" in trade usage to mean "production."

[116] *Ersco Canada Ltd. v. DMNRCE* (1981), 7 T.B.R. 432, 3 C.E.R. 263 (T.B., App. 1571). See also *Canadian Pacific Limited v. DMNRCE* (1985), 10 T.B.R. 252, 10 C.E.R. 121 (T.B., App. 2331). A similarly wide view was taken in an *Excise Tax Act* appeal, *Underwater Gas Developers Ltd. v. DMNRCE* (1960), 2 T.B.R. 203 (T.B., App. 516), in which work boats and a hydraulic lift used in their repair and maintenance were covered by an end use item for the development of natural gas wells since they were part of a drilling operation in Lake Erie.

brick used for abrasion resistance in various areas of a factory and was not limited to equipment incidental to kilns or furnaces.[117]

The interpretation of end use items could be quite specifically purposive, following Parliament's presumed intention to give a tariff concession to a particular activity. In the appeal *Malden Mills of Canada Ltd. v. Deputy Minister of National Revenue for Customs and Excise*, for example, the board was willing to read a qualification into an item for "fabrics ... sent abroad for electrostatic flocking ... for use in Canadian manufactures" in order to exclude fabrics that had received additional processing abroad before being re-imported. The goods still met the literal wording of the item but were excluded presumably because of legislative intent to encourage manufacturing in Canada.[118] The purposive approach was most common in the interpretation of very wide end use items — those covering imports "for use in the manufacture of" listed goods and especially all-embracing items covering "articles and materials for use in the manufacture of" goods. Here, the intention to encourage the domestic activity was central and obvious. When the item covered just about any imports that were to be used in the manufacturing process, there was not even a named category for which border inspection could take place. "Articles and materials" is, after all, a very wide phrase.[119] For such items, the legislative intent was obvious and paramount.

---

[117] A more narrow view of the physical scope of an end use item was taken in the *Major Irrigation* appeal concerning equipment used for handling potatoes. The board held that the equipment was not agricultural machinery since it was used for highway shipment as well as on the farm and the qualification "for use on the farm for farm purposes only," which appeared several times in the tariff item, was taken to apply to the whole item: *Major Irrigation (1974) Limited v. DMNRCE* (1982), 8 T.B.R. 446, 5 C.E.R. 93 (T.B., App. 1830). See also *Heavy Duty Products v. DMNRCE* (1962), 2 T.B.R. 282 (T.B., App. 590), in which stainless steel sinks for washing milking apparatus did not qualify as "equipment for milking parlours" since for sanitary reasons they could not be used in the milking parlours themselves where the cows were kept; *Martin & Stewart Ltd. v. DMNRCE* (1983), 8 T.B.R. 502, 5 C.E.R. 126 (T.B., App. 1659), in which hides and skins were not farm produce within the phrase "wire and twine for baling farm produce" because they had been too far processed from the point at which the animal passed the farm gate. See further *Caristrap Corporation v. DMNRCE* (1967), 4 T.B.R. 61 (T.B., App. 863).

[118] *Malden Mills of Canada Ltd. v. DMNRCE* (1982), 8 T.B.R. 126, 4 C.E.R. 89 (T.B., App. 1772).

[119] However, see, *contra*, dissent of Tariff Board member Bertrand in *Universal Grinding Wheel v. DMNRCE* (1984), 9 T.B.R. 194, 6 C.E.R. 236 (T.B., App.2057), aff'd (1986), 11 C.E.R. 157 (F.C.A.).

The main question in most of the "for use in the manufacture of" appeals was whether or not a given activity could be characterized as manufacturing. In classification decisions in this area, interpretation was usually generous in favour of finding that the activity qualified as manufacturing, with the exception of one Supreme Court of Canada decision involving a claim for a drawback, not a tariff duty on importation. In the Supreme Court of Canada decision, the appellant Research-Cottrell was claiming under a drawback item for "materials ... when used in the manufacture of" certain machinery and apparatus — in this case, eight electrostatic precipitators installed at the Inco plant in Copper Cliff.[120] The drawback claimed was for imported components of the precipitators, which Research-Cottrell said it had manufactured in Canada. Only the Exchequer Court agreed that this activity was manufacturing, on the theory that the precipitators did not exist until they were assembled from domestic and imported parts in Canada and, thus, that they had to have been manufactured in Canada. This analysis was rejected by the majority in the Supreme Court of Canada since it would have resulted in any assembly activity being considered manufacturing and this was not a necessary conclusion as a matter of law. The dissent of Justice Louis-Philippe Pigeon in the Supreme Court of Canada (Chief Justice John Cartwright concurring) would have accepted the Exchequer Court's reasoning and rejected the Tariff Board's analysis, which had examined "whether assembly and erection were of sufficient importance to justify the benefit of the drawback ... a factor which ought not to enter into consideration on the construction of the tariff item," according to Pigeon J.'s dissent.[121] In the result, while the Supreme Court of Canada decision involves a narrow interpretation of manufacturing, it seems to vindicate the strong purposive approach taken by the Tariff Board in first instance. In its declaration, the board had stated that

[t]he intent of the drawback items ... is clearly the encouragement of the manufacture in Canada of the goods or articles described ... as opposed to their acquisition abroad. In such a context it hardly seems a reasonable construction of the word manufacture to extend the benefits of the drawback items to imported goods which are simply assembled and erected on site.[122]

---

120 *DMNRCE v. Research-Cottrell (Canada) Ltd.,* [1968] S.C.R. 684, 68 D.L.R. (2d) 194, rev'g [1967] 2 Ex.C.R. 3, 3 T.B.R. 251, rev'g (1965), 3 T.B.R. 248 (T.B., App. 790) [*Research-Cottrell*].

121 *Research-Cottrell* S.C.R., *supra* note 120 at 688.

122 *Research-Cottrell* T.B.R., *supra* note 120 at 250.

When the issue arose in ordinary tariff classification decisions not involving drawback claims, the Tariff Board tended to be more generous on the question of whether assembly could qualify as manufacturing. In the appeal *RCA Victor Company v. Deputy Minister of National Revenue for Customs and Excise*, the board distinguished the situation from that in *Research-Cottrell*, where the components had been simply shipped to the site and assembled there.[123] In *RCA Victor*, the appellant put together radio-relaying equipment at its plant in Montreal and then further assembled and installed it in various relaying stations in the Canadian Pacific/Canadian National telecommunications system. The board rejected the department's submission that only the activity in Montreal was manufacturing and held that the work at the relay stations was also part of the full process. All of the imported equipment, therefore, qualified as "for use in the manufacture of" radio apparatus.[124]

In the appeals *Harry D. Shields Limited v. Deputy Minister of National Revenue for Customs and Excise* and *Kipp Kelly Limited v. Deputy Minister of National Revenue for Customs and Excise*, the board again dealt with the question of assembly and manufacturing. In *Harry D. Shields*, the board decided that the assembly of bicycles qualified as manufacturing since it was a complex process involving investment of capital and labour and was also an essential link in production that added new qualities and properties.[125] The department's practice of deciding according to percentages of Canadian material content was rejected since it was not authorized in the tariff item. In the *Kipp Kelly* appeals,[126] involving diesel engines of a class or kind not made in Canada imported for assembly in electric generating sets, the board similarly rejected the Canadian content factor and found the operations to be manufacturing, despite evidence

---

123 *RCA Victor Company v. DMNRCE* (1966), 3 T.B.R. 311 (T.B., App. 834).

124 See also *J. & P. Coats (Canada) Limited v. DMNRCE* (1965), 3 T.B.R. 236 (T.B., App. 781) (goods can be for use in the manufacture of products "without entering into every part of the whole process of manufacture" so long as they are for use in some part of that process — at 238); *Geigy Chemical Corporation v. DMNRCE* (1966), 3 T.B.R. 285 (T.B., App. 806).

125 *Harry D. Shields Limited v. DMNRCE* (1980), 7 T.B.R. 1, 2 C.E.R. 1 (T.B., App. 1489). The board was using tests drawn from excise tax decisions. See discussion in Maureen Irish, "Machinery Remission: Transparency and the Rule of Law" (1994) 23(2) Can. Bus. L. J. 161 at 183–86.

126 *Kipp Kelly Limited v. DMNRCE* (1977), 6 T.B.R. 493 (T.B., App. 1182); *Kipp Kelly Limited v. DMNRCE* (1980), 7 T.B.R. 102, 2 C.E.R. 129 (T.B., App. 1479), aff'd (1981), [1982] 1 F.C. 571, 3 C.E.R. 196 (F.C.A.).

in the first *Kipp Kelly* appeal to the effect that the value added in Canada was less than 15 percent of the value of the finished product. The board emphasized that it was deciding in the context of the particular tariff item. It may be that the decision was influenced by the fact that the engines had to be of a class or kind not made in Canada in order to qualify. The item, in other words, was intended for components that could not be sourced locally, and it may have been contemplated that Canadian content in the finished goods would not be high.[127]

In most cases, the approach was generous in favour of finding an activity to be manufacturing.[128] Even when the analysis was not directly purposive, there was still a strong sense of the system in context, and interpretation was generally participatory. In the appeal *Calko Mills Ltd. v. Deputy Minister of National Revenue for Customs and Excise*, for example, the board had to determine whether imported yarn was for use in the manufacture of cotton sewing thread. To decide whether the end product was sewing thread, the board looked to the actual use made of it by the appellant and found that it did not qualify because it was used for weaving rather than conventional sewing.[129]

---

[127] The board did not go so far as to say that everything required to prepare the finished product was manufacturing. In the *City of Sherbrooke* appeal, automatic scales used in the purification of municipal water were not "for use in Canadian manufactures," since this was simply treatment of the water, not manufacturing of goods: *Sherbrooke (City of) v. DMNRCE* (1981), 7 T.B.R. 386, 3 C.E.R. 214 (T.B., App. 1495). See also *North-West Bindery Limited v. DMNRCE* (1971), 5 T.B.R. 133 (T.B., App. 950). And, at the beginning of the process, it cannot be said that everything done to collect and prepare the necessary raw materials qualifies as manufacturing: *Ayerst, McKenna & Harrison Limited v. DMNRCE* (1969), 4 T.B.R. 398 (T.B., App. 920), aff'd (1970), 4 T.B.R. 404 (Ex.Ct.) — containers used to collect urine from pregnant mares and transport it to premises where estrogen was produced were not "apparatus, equipment ... for the manufacture of ... hormones." The *Ayerst* decision may be constrasted with *3M Canada Inc. v. DMNRCE* (1984), 9 T.B.R. 262, 7 C.E.R. 299 (T.B., App. 2069), in which coated papers used to transfer photographs by laser fax for newspapers were found to be used in "production" of the newspapers even though they did not become a physical part of the final paper.

[128] In *Unident Limited v. DMNRCE* (1979), 6 T.B.R. 771, 1 C.E.R. 64 (T.B., App. 1377), the reconstruction of damaged teeth was the manufacturing of dental surgical prostheses. See also *Novocol Chemical Manufacturing Company v. DMNRCE* (1988), 13 T.B.R. 183, 16 C.E.R. 132 (T.B., App. 2731).

[129] *Calko Mills Ltd. v. DMNRCE* (1975), 6 T.B.R. 199 (T.B., App. 1064). See also *Promo-Wear Ltd. v. DMNRCE* (1981), 7 T.B.R. 267, 3 C.E.R. 32 (T.B., App. 1568), in which actual use was relevant in the board's decision that the imported urethane foam rolls were used in the manufacture of tips and sides of caps.

In the purely objective approach to classification, the importer's intentions concerning use of the goods was irrelevant. In the appeal *Allied Toys & Enterprises Limited v. Deputy Minister of National Revenue for Customs and Excise*, for example, the imported goods were classified as cigarette holders even though the importer planned to use them in the manufacture of toys.[130] The intentions of the particular importer and subsequent purchasers were crucial, however, for the interpretation of end use items. In the appeal *Joy Manufacturing Co. (Canada) Ltd. v. Deputy Minister of National Revenue for Customs and Excise*, the Tariff Board, choosing between two end use items, decided that transporter belts were parts of filters rather than parts of conveyors because the importer purchased them specifically for filters and the conveying of material was only a minor part of their intended function.[131] The importer's intentions also meant that an imported scow was not a vessel "destined for use or service in Canadian waters" in the appeal *Autoport Limited v. Deputy Minister of National Revenue for Customs and Excise*, since by the time of importation it had been determined that repairs to upgrade the scow for transportation use were too expensive and that it would have to be left simply as a permanent part of the wharf.[132]

In some decisions of the Tariff Board, explicit use tariff descriptions were treated as end use items and given wide coverage. In the appeal *Industrial and Road Equipment Ltd. v. Deputy Minister of National Revenue for Customs and Excise*, the board decided that "apparatus for chemical conversion, extraction, reduction or recovery" meant apparatus *for use in* the various processes and covered equipment that did not itself perform any of the listed functions.[133]

---

130 *Allied Toys & Enterprises Limited v. DMNRCE* (1959), 2 T.B.R. 188 (T.B., App. 499).

131 *Joy Manufacturing Co. (Canada) Ltd. v. DMNRCE* (1984), 9 T.B.R. 155, 6 C.E.R. 208 (T.B., App. 2083). See also *Ingenuity Incorporated v. DMNRCE* (1987), 12 T.B.R. 416, 15 C.E.R. 52 (T.B., App. 2602).

132 *Autoport Limited v. DMNRCE* (1984), 9 T.B.R. 316, 7 C.E.R. 45 (T.B., App. 2058), referring specifically to *Great Canadian Oil Sands Supply Ltd. v. DMNRCE*, [1976] 2 F.C. 281 (C.A.).

133 The overall tariff item involved was end use, since it covered "sundry articles of metal ... for use in metallurgical operations." *Industrial and Road Equipment Ltd. v. DMNRCE, Canadian Chromalox Co. v. DMNRCE, Sherritt Gordon Mines Limited v DMNRCE, Clark Compressor Co. v. DMNRCE* (1958), 2 T.B.R 110 (T.B. Apps. 441, 449, 451, 461), aff'd (*sub nom Dorr-Oliver Long Ltd. v. Sherritt Gordon Mines Ltd.*) (1959) 2 T.B.R. 113 (Ex. Ct.). See further *Naramata Co-operative Growers Exchange v. DMNRCE* (1964), 3 T.B.R. 144 (T.B., App. 726); *Cascade Co-operative Union v. DMNRCE, Vernon Fruit Union v. DMNRCE* (1966), 3 T.B.R. 281 (T.B., Apps. 804, 823).

Similarly, in the *Landis and Gyr Inc. v. Deputy Minister of National Revenue for Customs and Excise* appeal, the board decided that "meters for indicating and/or recording" meant meters *for the purpose of indicating and/or recording* and that the measurements did not have to be in a form to be read by humans.[134] This interpretation is significantly wider than the decision in *Astro-Med GmbH* v. *Oberfinanzdirektion Berlin* in the case law of the ECJ, which held that a converter was not machinery for measuring since it simply displayed measurements taken by other apparatus and did not itself perform a measuring function.[135]

For explicit use descriptions, participatory interpretation involving trade experience and the commercial context was common, even if these were not treated as end use items.[136] In appeals involving one such tariff description for

> books and pamphlets, and replacement pages therefore, for the promotion of religion, medicine and surgery, the fine arts, law, science, technical training, and the study of languages, not including dictionaries,

evidence on the specialized distribution chains for certain books helped to prove that they were "for the promotion of religion."[137]

---

134 *Landis and Gyr Inc. v. DMNRCE* (1963), 3 T.B.R. 122 (T.B., App. 708). The item was subsequently held applicable to a whole host of machine-readable indicators: *Aritech Inc. (Canada) v. DMNRCE* (1985), 10 T.B.R. 81, 9 C.E.R. 29 (T.B., App. 2156); *United Industrial Products Ltd. v. DMNRCE* (1986), 13 C.E.R. 111 (T.B. . App. 2528); *Akhurst Machinery Ltd. v. DMNRCE* (1987), 12 T.B.R. 181, 14 C.E.R. 98 (T.B., App. 2630); *MTI Canada Ltd. v. DMNRCE* (1988), 13 T.B.R. 154, 16 C.E.R. 109 (T.B., App. 2776); *Ripley's Farm v. DMNRCE* (1988), 13 T.B.R. 280, 16 C.E.R. 153 (T.B., App. 2681); *Stewart Warner Corp. of Canada v. DMNRCE* (1988), 17 C.E.R. 188 (T.B., App. 2838). See also *Nord Photo Engineering Inc. v. DMNRCE*, C.Gaz.1978.I.3951 (T.B., Apps. 1273,1276).

135 *Astro-Med GmbH v. Oberfinanzdirektion Berlin*, Case C-108/92, [1993] Rec. I-3797. To the same effect, see also *Siemens Nixdorf Informationssysteme AG v. Hauptzollamt Augsburg*, Case C-11/93, [1994] E.C.R. I-1945; *Techmeda Internationale Medizinisch-Technische Marketing- und Handels-GmbH & Co. KG v. Oberfinanzdirektion Köln*, Case C-356/93, [1994] E.C.R. I-2371; *GoldStar Europe GmbH v. Hauptzollamt Ludwigshafen*, Case C-401/93, [1994] Rec. I-5587.

136 *Simark Controls Ltd. v. DMNRCE* (1985), 10 T.B.R. 221, 9 C.E.R. 270 (T.B., App. 2278), esp. at 225. See *Foxboro Canada Inc. v. DMNRCE* (1986), 11 T.B.R. 384, 12 C.E.R. 118 (T.B., App. 2418), aff'd (1988), 17 C.E.R. 1 (F.C.A.).

137 *Home Evangel Books Limited v. DMNRCE*, C.Gaz.1977.I.2629 (T.B., App. 1185); *Dawn Distributors v. DMNRCE* (1982), 8 T.B.R. 338, 4 C.E.R. 409 (T.B., App. 1781).

In an earlier appeal, when the appellant did not present such evidence concerning similar manuals for Sunday School teachers, the goods did not qualify.[138] In the appeal *Oppenheimer Bros. & Company v. Deputy Minister of National Revenue for Customs and Excise*, the Tariff Board considered company advertising to decide that Clorox bleach could qualify under a tariff item covering "non-alcoholic preparations or chemicals for disinfecting" even though disinfecting was only secondary to the product's main function of bleaching. The decision was affirmed by the Supreme Court of Canada.[139]

In the pre-HS tariff, decisions on the scope of end use items were made within a system in which it was presumed that customs officials had power to follow the goods after importation to make sure that the end use was met. This sort of monitoring may not have occurred too often, but the acknowledgement that it could happen added a sense of the provisions in application to the entire interpretive process. For these items, interpretation was often participatory, reflecting the commercial context and understandings, including the use of goods. In addition, especially when the item covered imports "for use in the manufacture of" certain goods, a purposive approach favouring the presumed economic policy of the legislator had a strong influence on interpretation.

PRIORITIES

Prior to the adoption of the HS, certain types of end use items were given very wide coverage, in accordance with presumed legislative

---

138 *Scripture Press v. DMNRCE* (1958), 2 T.B.R. 172 (T.B., App. 490). For other appeals interpreting parts of this tariff item, see *Thonger Agencies Limited v. DMNRCE* (1950), 1 T.B.R. 34 (T.B., App. 213) — technical business manual not covered; *Leland Publishing Co. Ltd. v. DMNRCE* (1957), 2 T.B.R. 16 (T.B., App. 397), aff'd (1958) 2 T.B.R. 17 (Ex.Ct.) — encyclopedias not covered; *McClelland & Stewart Limited v. DMNRCE*, C.Gaz.1977.I.3286 (T.B., App. 1180) — history book not covered; *A la Tricoteuse Inc. v. DMNRCE*, C.Gaz.1979.I.679, (T.B., App. 1332) — macramé instruction book not covered; *RCA Limited v. DMNRCE* (1979), 6 T.B.R. 824, 1 C.E.R. 154 (T.B., App. 1307) — technical servicing manual not covered. See also *PTL Television Network of Canada v. DMNRCE* (1982), 8 T.B.R. 389, 5 C.E.R. 25 (T.B., App. 1814), for an appeal concerning a comparable end user item: "[F]or the use of any society or institution incorporated or established solely for religious, educational, scientific or literary purposes."

139 *Oppenheimer Bros. & Company v. DMNRCE* (1957), 2. T.B.R. 21 (T.B., App.398), aff'd (*sub nom Javex Co. v. Oppenheimer Bros. & Co.*) (1959), 2 T.B.R. 28 (Ex.Ct.), aff'd [1961] S.C.R. 170, (1961) 2 T.B.R. 35, 26 D.L.R. (2d) 523. The company advertising was presented to show what the product was supposed to do in ordinary household use.

intention to benefit the named industry or activity. Particularly after a 1976 decision of the Federal Court of Appeal, a purposive approach was also used to determine priorities between items. End use items increasingly received top priority over other tariff items, even specific naming (*"eo nomine"*) items.

In order to administer the customs tariff, Revenue Canada had to establish a certain hierarchy among types of tariff items to deal with situations in which goods could qualify under more than one item. The hierarchy was not expressed in the legislation but had developed through several years of practice.[140] The hierarchy was as follows:

1. All-embracing items
2. *Eo nomine* items
3. End use items
4. *Eo nomine* items n.o.p.
5. End use items n.o.p.
6. Other items:
   a. basket items
   b. according-to-material items
   c. residual item 71100–1

The "n.o.p." meant "not otherwise provided," indicating that the item included only those goods not covered elsewhere in the tariff. Basket items were simply very general naming (*eo nomine*) items such as "electrical apparatus" or "machines" that would be expected to give way to more specific items. According-to-material items were those that referred to the constituent material, such as "manufactures, articles or wares of iron or steel." The really difficult problem in characterization of tariff items under this hierarchy was the question of all-embracing items that had priority over everything else. End use items of the type "materials and articles for use in the manufacture of" were usually listed in the all-embracing category, along with another tariff item covering scientific apparatus for use by public hospitals, museums, libraries, and educational institutions. In effect, the hierarchy attempted to take these very generalized end use items and give them a special priority, distinguishing them from ordinary end use items such as "self-propelled trucks ... for use exclusively in the operation of logging," which had a certain

---

140 Thomas Lindsay and Bruce Lindsay, *Outline of Customs in Canada,* 6th edition (Vancouver: Erin Publishers, 1985) at 13.

naming element as well as the required end use. It seemed that the very general, "super end use" items were to have priority in order to make sure that the concession granted by the legislators was actually effective. When the legislative intent to favour a particular end use was so clear, then anything that could qualify under that item was to be classified there even if it might also be covered by another item.

The case that disrupted this hierarchy and seemed to say that all end use items had over-riding priority was the appeal *Great Canadian Oil Sands Supply Limited v. Deputy Minister of National Revenue for Customs and Excise* involving dump trucks for use in the Alberta tar sands.[141] The trucks had been classified as "machinery and apparatus ... for operating oil-sands by mining operations." The appellant maintained that because of their special suitability for use in the wet silt conditions of the tar sands, they were of a separate class or kind not made in Canada and thus eligible for duty-free entry under a concessionary subcategory. The Federal Court of Appeal in 1976 adopted the dissenting opinion from the Tariff Board level and agreed that this was a separate class or kind since the determination had to be made in light of the required end use. Quoting the dissent from Tariff Board member Dauphinée, the Court of Appeal stated that,

> where end use is enacted as part of an item, the item becomes only in part a description of goods as such. Classification must then be based both upon the goods as described, and the use as designated ... Where a use provision is enacted use becomes more than a facet of the evidence as to the nature of the goods, it becomes the basis for classification under the item. This will exclude for purposes of findings of class or kind, all goods that do not meet this end use requirement, inasmuch as they will not be the goods described in the item.[142]

In this part of its decision, the court thus indicated a strong tendency to favour the stated end use in order to give effect to the legislative

---

[141] *Great Canadian Oil Sands Supply Limited v. DMNRCE* (1975), 6 T.B.R. 116 (T.B., App. 1051), rev'd [1976] 2 F.C. 281, 6 T.B.R. 160 (F.C.A.). See further *Great Canadian Oil Sands Supply Ltd. v. DMNRCE* (1979), 6 T.B.R. 915, 1 C.E.R. 239 (T.B., App. 1386), rev'd. *DMNRCE v. Suncor Inc. (formerly Great Canadian Oil Sands)* (1981), 3 C.E.R. 340 (F.C.A.), reheard (1982), 8 T.B.R. 116, 4 C.E.R. 83 (T.B., App. 1386).

[142] *Great Canadian Oil Sands Supply* T.B.R., *supra* note 141 at 165–66, quoting Tariff Board dissent at 151.

concession granted to the industry in question. Concerning priorities for end use items, the Court of Appeal and all members of the Tariff Board agreed on certain other comments favouring end use items that were elicited because of arguments put forward by the intervenant at the Tariff Board level, who did not participate in the appeal. The intervenant had argued that instead of being "machinery and apparatus ... for operating oil-sands by mining operations," the trucks should be classified as "diesel-powered self-propelled dump trucks ... for off-highway use in carrying minerals or other excavated materials at mines." Since the trucks were used to carry excavated material at the tar sands site, they qualified under both items, and the Tariff Board majority even stated that the off-highway dump truck item was more precise and specific.[143] The board nevertheless decided in favour of the oil sands item because of the strong legislative intent to encourage tar sands development. In support of its decision on the conflict between these two end use items, the board majority stated:

[W]hen it is clear that the legislator has enacted a tariff classification of goods specifically for use by a particular industry, then that classification should have precedence where it applies, even if such goods are more precisely described in another tariff item.[144]

This statement was supported by the dissenting member of the board[145] and by the Court of Appeal.[146] In the context of the decision, the board majority was actually only deciding as between two end use items and choosing the one that referred more directly to a particular industry. Since the oil sands item was for "machinery and apparatus" that met the declared use, the item could have been seen as a general, all-embracing, super end use item at the top of the hierarchy without calling the whole system into question. The statement, however, seemed to have a much wider meaning and seemed to give the priority position to all end use items, moving them all up to the top of the list above naming items. Almost any end use item could be interpreted as being enacted "for use by a particular industry." The statement implied that they should all be given priority over naming items even when those items described the goods very precisely.

[143] *Ibid.* at 138.
[144] *Ibid.* at 140.
[145] *Ibid.* at 147–48.
[146] *Ibid.* at 164.

There had never been any doubt in previous decisions that end use items would have priority over *eo nomine* "not otherwise provided" items, which covered only those goods "not otherwise provided" for elsewhere in the tariff.[147] The question posed by the comments in *Great Canadian Oil Sands* was really about the conflict between end use items and ordinary unconditional *eo nomine* items. After *Great Canadian Oil Sands,* decisions of the board gave top priority to end use items without distinguishing among the types of end use. In some appeals, the board would cite the comments of the majority decision in the case, approved by the Court of Appeal, and state that end use had precedence because the legislator had demonstrated an intention to favour a particular industry.[148] In others, the board would cite the dissent, which was also approved by the Court of Appeal, and emphasize that in an end use item, use was the basis for classification and not just a facet of the evidence. End use items regularly had priority over *eo nomine* items — both *eo nomine* "not otherwise provided" and ordinary, unconditional *eo nominee* — and the scope of the end use would be interpreted widely in the actual commercial context.[149] In *Universal Grinding Wheel v. Deputy Minister of National Revenue for Customs and Excise,* the imported goods were classified as "materials and articles for use exclusively in the manufacture of" dental instruments rather than under a specific *eo nomine* item for grinding wheels.[150] The end use item had priority according to the authority of *Great Canadian Oil*

---

147 See *General Supply Co. of Canada v. DMNRCE,* [1954] Ex.C.R. 340 at 347, 1 T.B.R. 81 at 85 (Ex.Ct.); *Super Electric Supply Co. v. DMNRCE* (1970), C.Gaz.1970.I.2850 (T.B., App. 947); *Canadian Reynolds Metals Co. v. DMNRCE* (1972), C.Gaz.1972.I.1067 (T.B., App. 851); *DMNRCE v. Ferguson Industries Ltd.* (1972), 4 T.B.R. 368 (S.C.C.), rev'g (1970), 4 T.B.R. 357 (Ex.Ct.), aff'g (1969), 4 T.B.R. 344 (T.B., App. 911) — reheard (1973), 4 T.B.R. 379 (T.B., App. 911); *Applied Electronics Ltd. v. DMNRCE* (1988), 13 T.B.R. 98, 16 C.E.R. 60 (T.B., App. 2661).

148 *Pharmacia (Canada) Limited v. DMNRCE* (1976), 6 T.B.R. 403 (T.B., Apps. 1164, 1165); *Amoco Canada Petroleum Co. v. DMNRCE* (1977), C.Gaz.1978.I.829 (T.B., App. 1193); *Centrilift Hughes v. DMNRCE* (1987), 12 T.B.R. 191, 14 C.E.R. 130 (T.B., App. 2539).

149 *Johnson & Johnson Limited v. DMNRCE* (1982), 8 T.B.R. 147, 4 C.E.R. 146 (T.B., App. 1653); *Redi Garlic Distributors Inc. v. DMNRCE* (1984), 9 T.B.R. 385, 8 C.E.R. 126 (T.B., App. 2141); *Kulka Distributors Ltd. v. DMNRCE* (1985), 10 T.B.R. 48, 8 C.E.R. 258 (T.B., App. 2128); *Indel-Davis Ltd. v. DMNRCE* (1987), 12 T.B.R. 589, 15 C.E.R. 223 (T.B., App. 2775); *Applied Electronics Ltd. v. DMNRCE* (1988), 13 T.B.R. 98, 16 C.E.R. 60 (T.B., App. 2661).

150 *Universal Grinding Wheel v. DMNRCE* (1984), 9 T.B.R. 194, 6 C.E.R. 236 (T.B., App. 2057), aff'd (1986), 11 C.E.R. 157 (F.C.A.).

Sands and also because such priority was necessary to give the item useful effect to benefit manufacturers of dental instruments. In the appeal *Coopérative Fédérée de Québec à Montréal v. Deputy Minister of National Revenue for Customs and Excise*, potato waste products that were re-processed for compounding in animal and poultry feed were classified under an end use item covering "feeds, n.o.p., for animals and poultry, and ingredients for use therein, n.o.p.," rather than under an *eo nomine* item for "potato products ... n.o.p."[151] The end use item had priority according to the authority of *Great Canadian Oil Sands*. In the Federal Court of Appeal, the concurring judgement of Justice James Hugessen took the purposive argument further and looked to detailed economic policy. Since the end use item prescribed duty-free entry, it was for the benefit of producers of animals and poultry, and since the potato products item carried a duty of 10 percent it was for the benefit of the Canadian potato industry. Granting free entry to these goods made from potato waste gave effect to the policy behind both items.[152]

In summary, it was clear that in *Great Canadian Oil Sands* and subsequent decisions, the Tariff Board was developing a position that differed quite substantially from the hierarchy that the department had established. Not only was the board not distinguishing among varieties of end use items, but it was also giving all end use items top priority in classification, even over very specific *eo nomine* items, in order to give effect to the presumed intentions of Parliament. Even if the customs tariff had not been revised to adopt the HS, the question of priorities among various tariff items was in need of examination and revision.

CONCLUSION

The HS has been widely adopted as a customs and statistical nomenclature. In this global context, a purposive approach to statutory interpretation emphasizing the socio-economic goals behind implementation of the legislation is not suitable. There is no reason to believe that the purposes of the legislators of any particular country are those of the entire HS. It could not be expected that the

---

[151] *Coopérative Fédérée de Québec à Montréal v. DMNRCE* (1984), 9 T.B.R. 381, 8 C.E.R. 121 (T.B., App. 2134), aff'd (1987), 13 C.E.R. 338, 76 N.R. 218 (F.C.A.). See *Cargill Ltd. v. DMNRCE* (1990), 3 T.C.T. 2409 (C.I.T.T., AP-2802).

[152] The other two judges in the Federal Court of Appeal, Pratte J. and Marceau J., filed separate concurring judgments that did not adopt the economic analysis.

classification of goods in the HS should depend on the wishes of domestic legislators to encourage specific sectors through the imposition or reduction of a customs duty. Pre-HS Canadian end use cases gave special weight to legislative intent in favour of particular domestic economic sectors. This sort of direct inquiry into domestic policy is out of place in the interpretation of the HS. The general policy behind the HS favours developing consensus views on reliable tariff classification. This goal will not be met if interpretation looks to the domestic economic policy of each state that adopts the HS.

Canadian decisions on the previous end use items applied a strongly purposive approach to interpretation that is not appropriate for the HS. The decisions also illustrate, however, a classification system that looks beyond observable, physical characteristics of the goods to review their use in commercial context. It is the thesis of this article that such use considerations must be taken into account for successful interpretation of the HS. The case law of the ECJ goes too far in assuming that classification must always be based on the physical features of goods. Meaning comes not just from the observed physical characteristics of goods but also from their intended use and the understandings of those who use them. An attempt to isolate language from interpretation and human intervention is not likely to succeed. Recent Canadian cases provide examples of the preferable approach, which not only considers physical features of goods but also takes account of use as indicated through commercial factors such as price, marketing, and distribution.

Empirical observation of physical characteristics of goods will not guarantee certainty or uniformity, since naming that ignores use is artificial. There is a greater chance of attracting a consensus if interpretation is participatory and looks to all factors involved, including use. The use criterion refers to goods in their condition as imported, but there is no reason to require special physical features in order to trigger participatory interpretation. In the HS, authorities will not vary classification with each importer and monitor use separately, but this does not mean that interpretation must depend only on objective, physical characteristics. The participatory approach is not limited to instances in which customs authorities are willing to monitor use of particular imports.

Formalism is not the only alternative to purposive interpretation. The choices are wider than those explored in the debate between H.L.A Hart and Lon Fuller in 1958. Steven Winter has applied insights from the cognitive sciences to legal interpretation, highlighting the importance of human imagination and contextual understanding. Even for the naming of tangible goods, objectivity in interpretation is not the answer. Communication requires participants on both sides of the activity. For language to operate effectively, there must be readers as well as writers, listeners as well as speakers. To be successful, tariff classification must take account of market factors and the use of goods.

Sommaire

L'objectivité et l'interprétation des lois: l'utilisation finale et le Tarif des douanes canadien

Le Système harmonisé de désignation et de codification des marchandises (Système harmonisé) est adopté par les plus importants pays commerçants du monde, y inclus le Canada. Les décisions de la Cour européenne de justice sont influentes pour l'interprétation du Système harmonisé. Selon ces décisions, les marchandises doivent être classées pour fins du Système harmonisé sur la base de leurs caractéristiques physiques, tandis que les caractéristiques qui se rapportent à leur utilisation suite à leur importation ne doivent être considérées que dans la mesure où celles-ci sont reflétées dans les caractéristiques physiques. L'auteur rejette cette approche étroite et affirme que l'interprétation ne sera utile que si elle est faite à la lumière du contexte commercial complet, y compris l'utilisation après l'importation, la publicité, la distribution et les indicateurs du marché tels que les prix. L'article passe en revue la jurisprudence canadienne depuis la mise en œuvre du Système harmonisé en 1988, ainsi que certains arrêts interprétant la nomenclature canadienne avant 1988, qui comprenait de nombreux éléments tarifaires qui dépendaient de l'utilisation finale des marchandises après leur importation.

Summary

Objectivity and Statutory Interpretation: End Use in the Canadian
Customs Tariff

*The Harmonized Commodity Description and Coding System (Harmonized
System) has been adopted by the major trading nations of the world, including Canada. Decisions of the European Court of Justice are influential for
interpretation of the Harmonized System. According to these decisions, goods
should be classified under the Harmonized System on the basis of their
physical characteristics, while factors that relate to use after importation
should be considered only if they are reflected in the physical characteristics.
The author rejects this narrow approach and argues that interpretation will
be successful only if it is done in light of the full commercial context, including use after importation, advertising, distribution, and market indicators
such as price. The article reviews Canadian case law since implementation
of the Harmonized System in 1988 as well as some decisions interpreting
the pre-1988 Canadian nomenclature, which contained many tariff items
that depended on the end use of goods after importation.*

La notion de conditionnalité reconsidérée dans les relations Nord-Sud: une approche favorisant le plein exercice des droits économiques dans les pays en développement

PIERRE-FRANÇOIS MERCURE

INTRODUCTION

L'État, par ses structures parlementaire et judiciaire, impose un arbitrage à ses justiciables sur l'importance relative de droits dont ils sont titulaires, dans l'éventualité où ces derniers entrent en conflit. Lorsqu'une telle situation se présente entre sujets de droit au niveau international, il n'existe aucun mode institutionnalisé de conciliation obligatoire de ceux-ci.[1] Ainsi en est-il, lorsque le principe de la liberté commerciale[2] est confronté, dans certaines circonstances, au droit au travail.[3] Cette problématique se pose avec une grande acuité dans le contexte des relations Nord-Sud, dans l'hypothèse où les droits en opposition sont, d'une part, un droit de l'État à caractère économique et d'autre part, un droit de l'homme à caractère économique tel, le droit à la nourriture, le droit à la santé ou le droit à l'éducation.[4]

Pierre-François Mercure, Vice-doyen à l'enseignement et professeur, Faculté de droit, Université de Sherbrooke.

[1] W.A. Schabas, *Précis du droit international des droits de la personne*, Cowansville, Éditions Yvon Blais, 1997, aux pp. 49–132.

[2] Qui constitue notamment un droit fondamental des États, Q.D. Nguyen, P. Daillier et A. Pellet, 7e éd., *Droit international public*, Paris, L.G.D.J., 2002, à la p. 1195.

[3] R. Howse et M. Mutua, *Protection des droits humains et mondialisation de l'économie: un défi pour l'OMC*, Montréal, Centre international des droits de la personne et du développement démocratique. 2000.

[4] Nous référons aux droits économiques et sociaux prévus dans le *Pacte international relatif aux droits économiques, sociaux et culturels* ou les mêmes droits prévus dans d'autres conventions. Nous excluons le droit de participer à la vie culturelle, prévu au paragraphe 15(1) du *Pacte* ou le même droit prévu dans d'autres conventions, pour les raisons qui seront évoquées plus tard dans cette communication. *Pacte international relatif aux droits économiques, sociaux et culturels*, 1966,

Lorsqu'un pays en développement est confronté au dilemme de devoir rembourser une dette qu'il a contractée auprès d'un pays développé conformément aux modalités convenues avec ce dernier ou de suspendre son remboursement afin de fournir des services sociaux de base à sa population, ce sont les droits dont les deux États sont investis qui s'opposent. Le droit de l'État créancier au remboursement de la dette contractée par l'État débiteur entre en contradiction avec le droit de l'État débiteur de ne pas respecter intégralement l'entente convenue ou de suspendre son application afin qu'il soit en mesure d'assurer le plein exercice des droits de l'homme (modifier dans tout le texte) à caractère économique.

Les prémices de ce conflit de droits entre les États résident, comme il sera exposé, dans les fondements du transfert financier du pays développé au pays en développement, principalement de la réalisation, par le pays en développement, des conditions qui lui sont imposées par le pays développé dans l'entente. Lorsque le transfert financier résulte d'un prêt consenti par une institution financière multilatérale à un pays en développement, la condition-nalité imposée par la première au deuxième prend sa source, soit dans l'entente, soit dans les statuts ou les actes de l'institution fi-nancière multilatérale. Que le créancier soit un État ou une orga-nisation internationale, c'est, par conséquent, le droit positif des transferts de flux financiers du Nord vers le Sud qui est la source de la conditionnalité que subissent les pays en développement. Dans ces deux situations, ce sont les droits des pays développés qui sont favorisés au détriment de ceux du pays en développement. Lorsque le créancier est une institution financière multilatérale, cette situa-tion est en grande partie attribuable au contrôle qu'exercent les pays développés sur le processus décisionnel de ce type d'organisa-tion internationale, puisqu'ils en sont les principaux bailleurs de fonds.

L'arbitrage entre les droits du débiteur et ceux du créancier est-il réalisable et si oui comment peut-il se matérialiser? Un État débiteur jouirait-il d'un droit d'échanger sa collaboration dans la résolution de problématiques mondiales, par exemple la protection de l'envi-ronnement, contre des concessions financières de la part d'un État créancier, afin de favoriser l'application de modalités pour rendre

---

943 R.T.N.U. 13; R.T.C. 1976, no 46. Afin de faciliter la lecture du texte, nous utiliserons l'expression *droits économiques* afin de référer aux droits de l'homme à caractère économique et social.

effectif des droits économiques dans l'État débiteur? La collaboration des pays en développement dépendrait alors de la réalisation d'une condition: la renégociation des dispositions de l'entente économique qui entravent la réalisation des droits économiques.

L'État débiteur serait-il investi d'un droit qui lui permettrait de rééquilibrer la situation financière dans laquelle il se trouve et qui origine du droit international positif, pour une large part favorable aux intérêts des pays développés? Aucune source de droit international public, ne fait expressément référence à un tel droit. Son existence sera néanmoins démontrée. Ce droit, que nous appelons "droit à la conditionnalité universelle" pour les raisons qui seront exposées,[5] existerait dans les faits au profit d'un pays en développement, lorsque le contexte économique prévalant de l'ordre promu par les pays développés ou une organisation internationale contrôlée par ces derniers, aurait des effets négatifs ou inhibiteurs sur l'application de droits économiques dans le pays en développement.[6]

C'est en situant notre analyse dans le contexte des relations Nord-Sud, qu'un regard critique sera porté sur la question de savoir si les pays en développement sont investis d'un droit qui leur permettrait de rendre effectif les droits économiques. Afin que notre étude soit la plus complète possible, il est logique de rechercher, dans une première partie, la source de la notion de conditionnalité dans le droit propre aux relations internationales entre pays développés et pays en développement et d'expliquer, dans une deuxième partie, que la notion de conditionnalité peut-être le fondement d'un droit dont le rôle serait de stimuler le recentrage du rapport de force entre le Nord et le Sud.

Le droit à la conditionnalité universelle s'articule autour de la notion de conditionnalité dans le contexte de la pratique de l'échange entre pays en développement et pays développés. Il est donc requis, en introduction, de circonscrire la notion sous cet angle. Il sera donc procédé à l'analyse de la conditionnalité de premier niveau dans la pratique de l'échange Nord-Sud, puis à

---

[5] Ce type de conditionnalité sera caractérisé de conditionnalité de troisième niveau. *Cf., infra* note 9.

[6] Nous avons présenté la notion de conditionnalité universelle dans le contexte de la sécurité alimentaire des pays en développement dans un article paru en 2003. *Cf.* Pierre-François Mercure, "La sécurité alimentaire du tiers-monde: cadre conceptuel de l'action des pays en développement dans le contexte de la mondialisation," *Les Cahiers de Droit* 44 (2003), à la p. 779.

celle de la conditionnalité de deuxième niveau dans le même contexte. Nous étudierons, finalement, l'émergence de la conditionnalité de troisième niveau, appelé "conditionnalité universelle," au profit des pays en développement.

LA NOTION DE CONDITIONNALITÉ DE PREMIER NIVEAU DANS LA PRATIQUE DE L'ÉCHANGE NORD-SUD

Les grandes découvertes des 15e et 16e siècles, l'industrialisation et finalement la libéralisation progressive des marchés commerciaux depuis la création de l'Accord général sur les tarifs douaniers et le commerce (GATT) constituent trois périodes charnières dans l'augmentation du volume des échanges commerciaux entre les États. Le troc, devenu l'accord de compensation,[7] constitua la première forme d'échange entre les États. Cette pratique qui ne concernait à l'origine que le transfert réciproque des marchandises évolua graduellement vers des comportements multiformes des relations interétatiques. Les États vinrent, ainsi, à échanger entre eux des biens contre des devises, des services contre des devises, des biens contre des services et des services contre des services. L'expression "monnaie d'échange" est fréquemment utilisée lors de l'étude de telles situations. La pratique des États se fonde sur une notion que l'on pourrait qualifier de conditionnalité de premier niveau: la contrepartie de chacun des États est assurée par le versement de celle de l'autre État. La réalisation de l'échange n'est motivée que par la volonté de chacune des parties de se procurer un bien (ou une devise) détenu par l'autre partie ou celle de recevoir un service de celle-ci.

L'échange entre les parties se fait entre partenaires égaux et pleinement consentants. La volonté d'aucune de celles-ci n'est altérée par des considérations autres que celle de participer à une transaction équitable, c'est-à-dire une transaction dans laquelle les deux parties trouvent un avantage. L'échange s'effectue dans le contexte d'un rapport de force équilibré entre les États.

La source de la conditionnalité réside dans le contrat intervenu entre les parties, c'est-à-dire dans la transaction qui s'établit entre deux protagonistes dont le pouvoir de négociation est équivalent: la conditionnalité origine, par conséquent, du consentement libre qui s'établit entre les parties. Si tel n'est pas le cas: mentionnons,

---

7 Cette dernière expression est couramment utilisée dans le commerce international contemporain. *Le Petit Robert,* Paris, 2000.

par exemple, une situation où un État économiquement puissant oblige son contractant, un État pauvre, à accepter un échange iné- quitable, en brandissant le spectre de mettre un terme à un avan- tage financier qu'il lui accorde, l'échange serait alors accompli dans le contexte de l'application de la notion qui peut-être qualifiée de conditionnalité de deuxième niveau.

C'est surtout dans le contexte des relations Nord-Sud que la pra- tique de la conditionnalité de deuxième niveau s'est développée, en raison précisément de l'état d'infériorité d'une des deux parties à la transaction, par rapport à l'autre partie. La période de décolo- nisation des années 1950–60 fut déterminante dans l'élargissement de ce type de comportement aux États; les pays développés ayant joué le rôle d'États puissants et les pays en développement ayant joué celui d'États faibles.

LA NOTION DE CONDITIONNALITÉ DE DEUXIÈME NIVEAU DANS LA PRATIQUE DE L'ÉCHANGE NORD-SUD

La distinction fondamentale qui existe entre la notion de condition- nalité de premier niveau et la notion de conditionnalité de deux- ième niveau réside dans la capacité pour le pays en développement de négocier librement avec son partenaire — pays développé ou organisation internationale contrôlée par des pays développés — les modalités de l'entente. La liberté du pays en développement est complète dans le premier cas et cette dernière est occultée dans le deuxième cas.

La notion de conditionnalité de deuxième niveau se calque sur un schéma de ce type: un pays développé ou une organisation in- ternationale contrôlée par des pays développés, effectue une tran- saction avec un pays en développement et impose des conditions à ce dernier afin de réaliser la transaction. Les deux cas de figure les plus fréquents sont les suivants: (1) les conditions peuvent être mentionnées expressément par écrit dans la convention conclue entre les parties. Cette dernière peut être qualifiée de convention principale; (2) elles peuvent aussi ne pas être indiquées dans celle- ci, mais être incluses dans une autre entente, qui pourrait être qualifiée de convention parallèle. Cette dernière a comme objectif de motiver, pour ne pas dire obliger, le pays en développement à signer l'entente principale.

La conditionnalité incluse dans la convention principale pourrait être qualifiée de conditionnalité interne, tandis que la condition- nalité incluse dans l'entente parallèle pourrait être qualifiée de conditionnalité externe. Les deux types de conditionnalités prennent leur source dans la convention principale. La conditionnalité interne peut aussi prendre sa source dans les statuts d'une organisation internationale, dans l'hypothèse où une telle entité est l'un des contractants et qu'elle est contrôlée par des pays développés. Le fondement des conditionnalités interne et externe est néanmoins, toujours, le droit qui s'applique aux parties, c'est-à-dire, la convention principale ou les statuts de l'organisation internationale.

Les programmes de politiques économiques[8] imposés aux pays en développement par le Fonds monétaire international (FMI) et la Banque mondiale (BM), se fondent sur la notion de conditionnalité interne de deuxième niveau, puisque les décaissements des organismes dépendent de la mise en œuvre des prescriptions qu'ils imposent aux pays en développement dans des accords approuvés par leurs conseils d'administration. La conditionnalité externe de deuxième niveau peut être illustrée par la situation suivante. Un pays développé accorde un prêt à un pays en développement aux conditions du marché, sans qu'aucune clause de sauvegarde ne soit prévue au contrat. La situation économique du pays en développement se détériore et ce dernier indique au pays développé qu'il veut renégocier les conditions du prêt. Le pays développé refuse la demande du pays en développement et l'informe qu'il sera mis fin à une entente commerciale qui lie les deux États dans l'hypothèse où le pays en développement imposerait un moratoire sur le remboursement du prêt.

La conditionnalité de deuxième niveau se situe hors du contexte d'une entente s'appuyant sur un rapport de force équilibré entre les partenaires. Le pays en développement n'a aucun pouvoir sur une conditionnalité de ce type à l'intérieur du cadre des négociations portant sur la convention principale ou sur la convention parallèle. Des conditions non négociables lui sont imposées. Les pays en développement considèrent qu'une pratique de cette nature constitue

---

8 Auparavant appelés les programmes d'ajustement structurel (PAS). Les institutions financières multilatérales accordent des prêts aux États à la condition qu'ils adoptent des programmes de politiques économiques, c'est-à-dire des programmes de stabilisation économique ainsi que des réformes structurelles en profondeur. M. Chossudovsky, *La Mondialisation de la pauvreté*, Montréal, Écosociété, 1998, à la p. 47. L'auteur indique: "L'ajustement structurel est souvent considéré comme étant subdivisé en deux phases distinctes: (1) la stabilisation macroéconomique 'à court terme', comprenant la dévaluation, la libéralisation des prix et l'austérité fiscale; (2) la mise en œuvre d'un certain nombre de réformes structurelles fondamentales imposant une certaine politique à suivre." *Ibid.* à la p. 48.

une atteinte à leur souveraineté. Cette conditionnalité pose un problème lorsqu'elle menace la réalisation de droits économiques. Le pays en développement, en se fondant sur les attributs découlant de la souveraineté, devrait pouvoir exercer librement le choix des options qui s'offrent à lui. Il pourrait alors décider de respecter intégralement les modalités de la conditionnalité de deuxième niveau qui lui est imposée et il ne pourrait plus alors assurer la réalisation des droits économiques au profit de sa population. Il aurait aussi le choix d'imposer à son cocontractant une renégociation de l'entente, incluant celle des modalités de la conditionnalité de deuxième niveau, afin de se placer dans une situation qui lui permettrait de rencontrer ses obligations au titre des droits économiques.

Dans l'éventualité où les pays en développement opteraient pour la deuxième hypothèse, il devrait démontrer qu'il est titulaire d'un droit qui lui permettrait de demander l'assouplissement de la conditionnalité de deuxième niveau pour être en mesure de respecter ses obligations relativement aux droits économiques.

L'ÉMERGENCE D'UN DROIT À UNE CONDITIONNALITÉ DE TROISIÈME NIVEAU AU PROFIT DES PAYS EN DÉVELOPPEMENT[9]

La conditionnalité de troisième niveau se situe à l'extérieur du cadre des négociations des ententes principale et parallèle entre les États. Elle est invoquée par le pays en développement afin que le rapport de force qui s'est établi entre les parties à l'entente principale ou parallèle devienne plus équilibré. Elle vise l'aménagement ou la modification de conditions économiques qui empêchent ou ralentissent la mise en application des droits économiques dans le pays en développement.

Le droit à la conditionnalité de troisième niveau, que nous appelons le droit à la conditionnalité universelle, se définit comme le droit d'un État, de rendre conditionnelle, c'est-à-dire de soumettre à un processus d'échange, sa participation à la résolution de problématiques mondiales, en contrepartie du réaménagement ou, à tout le moins, de l'assouplissement des conditions économiques qui empêchent la réalisation d'un droit économique.[10] Le droit

---

[9] Les caractéristiques de la notion de conditionnalité universelle exposées dans le texte qui suit sont tirées d'un article que nous avons écrit en 2003. *Supra* note 6.

[10] Il pourrait s'agir, mais non obligatoirement, de l'application de certains éléments du Nouvel ordre économique international (NOEI).

pourrait donc être invoqué, lorsqu'un contexte économique rigoureux imposé à un État paralyse ou nuit à une intervention de sa
part, afin de rendre effectif un droit économique. L'exercice du
droit permettrait aux pays en développement d'obtenir des concessions des pays développés. Les concessions obtenues stimuleraient
l'application des droits économiques dans les pays en développement, en échange de leur collaboration dans la résolution de problématiques mondiales.

Le qualificatif "universelle" a été attribué à la notion de conditionnalité de troisième niveau pour les raisons qui suivent. Premièrement, tous les secteurs d'activités pourraient faire l'objet
d'échanges entre les parties. Les pays en développement utilise-
raient la conditionnalité de troisième niveau dans des domaines où
ils détiennent un pouvoir de négociation équivalent à celui dont
disposent les pays développés. Il s'agit de secteurs qui intéressent
la communauté internationale dans son ensemble puisqu'ils touchent des problématiques universelles. Leur résolution requiert le
concours de tous les États. Les secteurs suivants, où l'implication
des pays en développement est essentielle pour le bien-être collectif, peuvent être mentionnés à titre d'exemple: la lutte antiterro-
riste; la protection de l'environnement global; le contrôle de la
croissance démographique; la migration internationale et la réduction des vagues de réfugiés; la réglementation de l'utilisation de
l'énergie nucléaire; l'adoption de mesures destinées à contrôler la
production et le trafic de stupéfiants; la libéralisation du commerce; le contrôle des maladies transmissibles telles que le palu-
disme et le VIH/sida; la stabilité financière; la paix mondiale.[11]

Deuxièmement, tous les États sont théoriquement investis du droit
à la conditionnalité de troisième niveau. Elle ne s'appliquerait, dans
les faits, qu'aux pays en développement et plus particulièrement à
ceux de ces derniers inclus dans la catégorie des pays les moins
avancés (PMA) ou dans les autres sous-catégories de pays en développement.[12] Un seul État ou un groupe de ceux-ci pourrait l'invoquer à l'encontre d'États pris individuellement ou collectivement,

---

[11] Ces exemples sont tirés du résumé par le Programme des Nations Unies pour
le développement (PNUD), *Les biens publics à l'échelle mondiale, La coopération
internationale au XXIe siècle*, 1999, à la p. 10, disponible en ligne à: <http://www.
undp.org/globalpublicgoods/TheBook/thebook.html>. I. Kaul, I. Grunberg,
M. A. Stern, *Global Public Goods, International Cooperation in the 21st Century*, New
York, Oxford University Press, 1999.

[12] Pays en développement sans littoral, petits États insulaires en développement
(PEID) et pays pauvres très endettés (PPTE).

mais aussi à l'encontre d'organisations régionales ou universelles à caractère commercial ou économique, lorsque le mécanisme décisionnel de l'organisation est contrôlé par des pays développés, en droit ou dans les faits.[13]

Troisièmement, les entités juridiques entre lesquelles pourrait s'exercer le droit à la conditionnalité universelle, d'une part un pays en développement ou un groupe de ceux-ci et, d'autre part, un pays développé, un groupe de ceux-ci ou une organisation internationale, seraient liées à deux niveaux. Elles seraient liées à un premier niveau en ce qui concerne des questions économiques au sens large, c'est-à-dire qu'un pays développé, un groupe de ceux-ci ou une organisation internationale pourrait avoir, par exemple, consenti un prêt à un pays en développement ou un groupe de ceux-ci. Les entités parties à la convention de prêt seraient aussi liées à un deuxième niveau: la promotion des droits de l'homme à caractère économique. Si le prêt est consenti par un pays développé à un pays en développement, les deux États seraient alors signataires de conventions relatives à la protection de droits de l'homme à caractère économique. Dans l'hypothèse où le prêteur serait une organisation internationale, les pays développés détenant un poids déterminant dans la décision d'accorder ou non le prêt, devraient être signataires de conventions relatives à la protection de droits de l'homme à caractère économique avec le pays en développement. Les entités juridiques seraient liées aux deux niveaux, soit par des traités au sens de la Convention de Vienne sur le droit des traités,[14] soit par toute autre entente contractuelle, ce qui inclut les ententes verbales et les actes concertés non conventionnels (*gentlemen's agreements*). Les deux volets ou les deux *negotii*, pourraient être inclus dans le même *instrumentum*.[15]

[13] Il s'agit donc d'un droit qui s'exerce sans qu'il y ait application des notions de responsabilité du droit international. En ce qui concerne les organisations internationales, consulter, Pierre Klein, *La responsabilité des organisations internationales*, Bruxelles, Éditions Bruylant, 1998.

[14] P.-M. Dupuy, 2e éd., *Les grands textes de droit international public*, Paris, Dalloz, 2000, à la p. 201.

[15] Il pourrait s'agir, par exemple, des statuts d'organisations internationales ou régionales à vocation économique, qui prévoiraient le respect des droits de l'homme, lorsque les organisations internationales concernées exerceraient leurs activités. Ce n'est toutefois pas le cas de la BIRD et du FMI dont les chartes constitutives ne font aucune mention du respect des droits fondamentaux de la personne dans leurs activités courantes avec les États débiteurs, qu'il s'agisse de droits civils, politiques ou économiques. En ce qui concerne les décisions prises par les dirigeants de la BIRD, il est indiqué à l'article IV section 10 des Statuts

Le droit à la conditionnalité universelle constituerait un droit à
l'échange qui pourrait être exercé à tout moment lors des négociations précédant la conclusion d'une entente à caractère économique
au sens large. L'État, titulaire du droit, serait celui qui échangerait
sa collaboration à la résolution de problématiques mondiales. Le
droit consisterait, pour l'État, à troquer son concours avec un État
ou une organisation internationale avec lequel il est lié, en contrepartie d'une modification des modalités d'un traité ou d'une entente, de nature ou à incidence économique. Le droit à la
conditionnalité universelle constituerait une réponse à la rigueur
excessive de la conditionnalité de deuxième niveau imposée à l'État
débiteur, soit par l'entente économique qui le lie à l'État ou l'organisation internationale créancier, soit par les statuts de l'organisation internationale. Dans les deux situations, le droit positif
constitue la source de la notion de conditionnalité dans les relations
entre le pays développé et le pays en développement.

LE DROIT POSITIF COMME SOURCE DE LA NOTION DE CONDITIONNALITÉ DANS LES RELATIONS ENTRE PAYS DÉVELOPPÉS ET PAYS EN DÉVELOPPEMENT

Les relations Nord-Sud ont une place importante à la notion de
conditionnalité. Cette dernière est intimement liée au développement économique et social des pays en développement. Lorsqu'elle
agit au deuxième niveau, elle a comme conséquence de porter atteinte au libre consentement des États dans leurs transactions. Nous
étudierons l'application de la conditionnalité dans le contexte du
développement et nous expliquerons que la pratique de la conditionnalité de deuxième niveau engendre une iniquité dans
l'échange pour les pays en développement.

L'APPLICATION DE LA CONDITIONNALITÉ DANS LE CONTEXTE DU DÉVELOPPEMENT

La pratique de la conditionnalité origine de différents secteurs du
droit international public. Ce constat explique les différentes formes

---

de la BIRD: *Leurs décisions seront fondées exclusivement sur des considérations économiques* ..., adoptés à Bretton Woods le 22 juillet 1944. R.T.N.U., vol. 2, à la p. 135.
Sur cette question consulter: I.F.I. Shihata, "La Banque mondiale et les droits
de l'homme," *RBDI* 1 (1999), aux pp. 86–96; P. Klein, "Les institutions financières
internationales et les droits de la personne," *RBDI* 1 (1999), aux pp. 97–114; G.
Niyungeko, "L'impact du programme d'ajustement structurel sur le respect des
droits économiques et sociaux au Burundi," *RBDI* 1 (1999), aux pp. 8–18.

qu'elle revêt. Il permet aussi de comprendre la variabilité des éléments de l'échange.

Les différentes formes de la conditionnalité[16]

La conditionnalité se fonde sur une pratique ancienne des États. Elle balise leur comportement et assure, conséquemment, une stabilité dans les relations internationales. La conditionnalité vise la survenance de facteurs dont l'effet est de modifier un statut juridique ou d'en créer un nouveau. En ce qui concerne, par exemple, les règles d'acquisition territoriale, la reconnaissance juridique de l'acquisition du territoire par un État repose sur la présence de certains éléments. L'un de ceux-ci a été établi par la jurisprudence internationale: l'occupation effective. La réalisation de cette dernière, qui constitue la condition, confère un statut juridique particulier au territoire. Le droit, dans ce cas, qui émane de décisions de la Cour internationale de justice (CIJ) est la source de la conditionnalité. La coutume ou une convention peut aussi être à l'origine de la conditionnalité. Cette dernière pourrait, de la même façon, découler d'une sentence arbitrale.

Dans son sens traditionnel, la notion de conditionnalité vise le déclenchement d'un processus qui crée une situation de droit. Elle a cependant évolué et elle s'est introduite progressivement dans les secteurs économique et financier, notamment dans certains de ceux-ci qui sont propres aux relations Nord-Sud, créant un domaine du droit particulier à ce contexte. Elle peut alors être de type "contrepartie" ou de type "substitution" et elle s'exerce sur une base bilatérale ou multilatérale.

La conditionnalité de type "contrepartie" exprime l'accomplissement préalable ou simultané d'un engagement dont l'objectif est d'assurer le versement d'une prestation à caractère financier. Les concours du FMI et l'aide liée permettent d'illustrer cette situation. Dans le premier cas, les États emprunteurs, membres de l'organisme, doivent rencontrer un certain nombre de conditions afin d'obtenir une prestation financière de celui-ci. Ces conditions jettent

---

[16] Le contenu de cette section est tiré d'une communication présentée par le professeur Alain Piquemal, le 13 avril 1995 à l'Institut du droit de la Paix et du Développement de l'Université de Nice–Sophia Antipolis, non rapporté. Voir aussi: A. Piquemal, "La notion de conditionnalité et les organisations internationales économiques et financières" dans *Mélanges en l'honneur du Doyen Paul Isoart*, Paris, Pedone, 1996, aux pp. 306–18; Alain Vandervorst, *La conditionnalité écologique dans les organisations financières internationales*, Thèse de doctorat, Rouen, 1999.

les bases des programmes de politiques économiques qui seront mis en force dans l'État emprunteur. Les acteurs de la pratique sont, d'une part, une organisation internationale contrôlée par des pays développés et d'autre part, un pays en développement. La conditionnalité s'exerce alors dans un contexte multilatéral.

Dans le cas de l'aide liée, la conditionnalité réside dans l'utilisation de la prestation financière accordée au pays en développement afin qu'il achète des biens et des services à une entreprise de la même nationalité que celle de l'État qui consent l'aide, par définition un pays développé. La réalisation de la condition confère, en bout de ligne, le statut juridique de donataire au pays en développement. La conditionnalité, qui découle d'une convention entre les parties, impose, indéniablement, des contraintes économiques au pays en développement. Les acteurs de la pratique sont deux États dans ce cas: un pays en développement et un pays développé. La condition-nalité agit alors dans un contexte bilatéral.[17]

La conditionnalité de type "substitution" entraîne un changement de la situation juridico-économique des États. Les mécanismes conditionnels pour la mise en place des organisations d'intégration économiques régionales, les unions douanières et les zones de libre-échange (ZLE), sont inclus dans cette catégorie. L'accomplissement d'un certain nombre d'actions est requis pour aboutir au statut de l'union douanière ou de la ZLE, notamment l'abaissement, voire la suppression des barrières tarifaires. Dans le cas de l'union-doua-nière, l'établissement d'un tarif extérieur commun (TEC) est, de plus, requis. La situation juridico-économique modifiée aboutit à la mise en œuvre effective de l'union douanière ou de la ZLE. La conditionnalité agit, dans ce cas, dans un contexte multilatéral, puisque l'État qui désire joindre la ZLE ou l'union douanière doit respecter les conditions imposées par les États signataires du traité instituant le nouvel espace économique et promouvant l'intégration économique.

La conditionnalité de type "substitution" doit être distinguée d'un autre type de conditionnalité exprimée, elle aussi, dans des rapports multilatéraux. Cette dernière ne concerne pas un changement de

---

[17] La conditionnalité de type politique pourrait aussi s'établir dans des relations bilatérales, par exemple une conditionnalité politique d'alignement pour obtenir de l'aide financière. Au temps de la guerre froide, l'ex-URSS accordait essen-tiellement son assistance financière aux États qui se déclaraient socialistes. Il est intéressant de consulter sur cette question Z. Laïdi, dir., *L'URSS vue du Tiers Monde*, Paris, Éditions Karthala, 1984.

la situation juridico-économique d'un État, mais permet l'attribution d'avantages liés au statut d'État. Elle est imposée aux États en contrepartie de leur participation à une organisation internationale. Cette conditionnalité peut être soit économique, soit géographique et politique. La première situation peut être illustrée par la participation des États à l'Organisation de coopération et de développement économiques (OCDE). Afin de devenir membre de cet organisme, l'État doit, notamment, pratiquer l'économie de marché. La deuxième situation peut être illustrée par le Conseil de l'Europe. L'État doit être localisé dans l'espace géographique européen et pratiquer une politique démocratique afin de pouvoir devenir membre de l'organisme. D'autres exemples sont fournis par les prestations versées par des institutions financières multilatérales. Les concours financiers de l'Agence internationale pour le développement (AID) sont conditionnés par l'appartenance de l'État bénéficiaire au groupe des PMA. Tel est aussi le cas de la Banque islamique de développement qui n'accorde de prêts qu'à des États islamiques ou des communautés islamiques.

La variabilité des éléments de l'échange

Toute tentative de systématisation des pratiques d'échange Nord-Sud s'appuyant sur la notion de conditionnalité se heurte à la problématique d'identifier le niveau de cette dernière. Le fait que les pays en développement et les pays développés trouvent leur compte dans les ententes qu'ils concluent, ne permet pas de faire abstraction de l'avantage que représente, en soi, pour les pays développés, leur poids économique, lors du processus de négociation avec les pays en développement. De plus, s'il est difficile d'imaginer qu'un pays en développement utilise la conditionnalité de deuxième niveau pour mieux équilibrer la transaction entre les parties, lors d'un échange avec un pays développé, la situation inverse est fréquente. Dans le premier cas, il faudrait parler de conditionnalité de troisième niveau, plutôt que de conditionnalité de deuxième niveau. La pratique des États est, en effet, bien établie quant à l'échange entre des pays en développement et des pays développés faisant intervenir une conditionnalité de deuxième niveau imposée par les pays développés. La frontière entre, d'une part, la conditionnalité de premier niveau et celle de deuxième niveau et, d'autre part, entre cette dernière et la conditionnalité de troisième niveau est, par conséquent, difficile à tracer avec précision.

Nous présenterons donc une typologie des pratiques d'échange entre les pays en développement et les pays développés basée, non pas sur le niveau de la conditionnalité, puisque le classement est difficilement réalisable pour la raison énoncée au paragraphe précédent, mais sur la nature de la prestation accordée par le pays en développement. Cette dernière est essentiellement de deux types: un bien localisé sur son territoire et un comportement relativement à des problématiques universelles.

La prestation du pays en développement constituée par un bien localisé sur son territoire

La pratique Nord-Sud en matière de développement économique et social s'articule autour du concept de l'échange. Ce dernier est reconnu par le système normatif international lorsqu'il y a nationalisation. L'État est autorisé, au nom de la réalisation du droit à la nationalisation, à se réapproprier des ressources et donc, à demander à un autre État ou à une entreprise privée étrangère, que la propriété de ces dernières soit transférée à son profit, moyennant une compensation de sa part.[18] Par l'exercice de ce droit, un pays en développement devient maître des ressources minérales et énergétiques situées sur son territoire, mais jusque-là exploitées par des étrangers. Il récupère, ainsi, des ressources qui lui procureront les revenus essentiels pour son développement.[19]

Les nationalisations d'entreprises étrangères, moins fréquentes depuis la fin des années 1960,[20] visent donc un contrôle économique afin de promouvoir le droit au développement des États. Une indemnisation sert de contrepartie à l'échange.[21] Les pays en développement invoquent le principe de la souveraineté permanente sur les ressources naturelles au soutien des nationalisations qu'ils réalisent. Ce fut notamment le cas pour le pétrole, l'une des ressources les plus fréquemment nationalisées par les pays en

---

18 Sur cette question consulter: G. Feuer et H. Cassan, *Droit international du développement*, 2e éd., Paris, Dalloz, 1991, aux pp. 209–31.

19 C'est en vertu du principe de la souveraineté territoriale qu'un État peut nationaliser, exerçant ainsi un élément de la souveraineté permanente sur les ressources naturelles dont il est investi. Nguyen *et al.*, *supra*, note 2 à la p. 1089.

20 Il s'agit comme l'indiquent Feuer et Cassan d'une pratique en déclin. *Supra* note 18 à la p. 210.

21 La nationalisation doit respecter trois conditions: (1) l'opération doit se faire pour des motifs d'intérêt public; (2) le propriétaire doit recevoir une indemnisation adéquate; (3) il doit épuiser les voies de recours dans l'État qui nationalise. Il s'agit des principes formulés au paragraphe 4 de la résolution 1803 (XVII) que l'on retrouve dans *ibid.*, à la p. 213.

développement, puisque les gisements exploités sont surtout localisés sur leur territoire.[22]

Le Nord et le Sud trouvent un *modus vivendi* sur le partage d'une ressource, lorsque l'économie du Nord dépend, dans une large mesure, de la ressource naturelle localisée dans un pays du Sud. Tel fut le cas pour le pétrole, où il a été convenu que les pays en développement étaient et resteraient propriétaires de la ressource, mais accepteraient de la vendre aux pays développés à un coût raisonnable, en contrepartie de l'engagement, de la part des pays développés, du respect de la souveraineté des pays exportateurs.[23] Tel fut le cas, aussi, pour d'autres ressources localisées principalement sur le territoire de pays en développement par exemple, les ressources génétiques. La protection de ces dernières est assurée par la Convention sur la diversité biologique[24] qui repose "sur la réalisation de l'hypothétique équilibre entre l'accès par les P.D. aux ressources génétiques et celui par les P.E.D. aux technologies du génie génétique."[25] L'échange, dans ce cas, se fait entre le pays en développement qui permet le prélèvement d'espèces floristiques sur son territoire, en contrepartie d'un transfert de technologie d'un pays développé à un pays en développement. Une ressource est alors échangée contre un service. Bien que le contexte soit différent, notamment parce qu'il concerne les relations entre deux pays en développement, le même esprit anime le programme pétrole contre médecins, intervenu entre Cuba et le Venezuela.

La pratique Nord-Sud de l'échange peut aussi se réaliser sous la forme de troc, par le transfert à un pays développé, d'un bien appartenant à un pays en développement, en contrepartie du transfert

---

[22] Les pays développés ont invoqué, quant à eux, lors du premier choc pétrolier de 1973, le concept de patrimoine commun de l'humanité (PCH) afin de requérir le partage équitable de la ressource. L'intérêt économique des groupes de protagonistes, pays en développement ou pays développé, dicte le choix qu'ils font des concepts juridiques qu'ils jugent pertinents à leur cause. Comme le rapporte M. Bedjaoui, le représentant de la Grande-Bretagne soutenait que l'État producteur ne possède sur ses richesses qu'une simple garde ne conférant au gardien qu'un droit relatif de gestion. M. Bedjaoui, "Non-alignement et droit international," *R.C.A.D.I.*, vol. III, nᵒ 151 (1976), à la p. 445.

[23] Le compromis fut la conciliation de la souveraineté des États sur les ressources avec l'intérêt international.

[24] Texte dans Dupuy, *supra* note 14 à la p. 692.

[25] P.-F. Mercure, "Le rejet du concept de patrimoine commun de l'humanité afin d'assurer la gestion de la diversité biologique," *A.C.D.I.*, vol. XXXIII, nᵒ 281 (1995), à la p. 300.

à ce dernier, d'un bien d'une autre nature appartenant au pays développé. La plupart du temps, le pays développé transfère au pays en développement un bien localisé sur son territoire et inversement le pays en développement transfère au pays développé un bien d'une autre nature localisé sur son territoire. Cette pratique est illustrée par les échanges pétrole contre nourriture qui se sont déroulés entre l'Irak et les pays développés, par l'intermédiaire du Conseil de sécurité de l'Organisation des Nations Unies (ONU), au cours des années 1990. Dans ce cas, une ressource énergétique indispensable pour l'occident est échangée contre d'autres ressources, cette fois-ci vitales pour les pays en développement: des médicaments et des denrées alimentaires de base.[26]

La pratique de l'échange entre des pays en développement et des pays développés concerne, traditionnellement, des biens ou des services. Les relations Nord-Sud sont cependant de plus en plus marquées par des échanges entre des biens du Nord, sous forme matérielle ou de nature pécuniaire, et un comportement des pays en développement relativement à des enjeux universels. Ce dernier se situe dans le cadre de l'entente convenue entre les États et constitue, conséquemment, une conditionnalité de premier niveau. La collaboration des pays en développement à la résolution de problématiques universelles dans le contexte de la conditionnalité de troisième niveau, sera étudiée à la prochaine section.

La prestation du pays en développement constituée par un comportement relativement à des problématiques universelles

Certains pays en développement ont profité du contexte de la guerre froide afin d'obtenir des concessions de nature économique des États-Unis ou de l'ex-URSS, en contrepartie de leur adhésion à l'idéologie politique de l'un ou l'autre des pays.[27] La prestation du pays en développement est alors constituée par le comportement qu'il adopte conformément au système politique qu'il choisit. La menace que représentait l'expansion du communisme en Asie a amené les États-Unis à procéder à des transferts financiers publics importants dans certains pays de ce continent, notamment en Corée du sud. Les flux financiers seraient à l'origine du développement

---

[26] A. Bencheneb, "Pétrole contre nourriture: l'ONU et les contrats internationaux d'assouplissement de l'embargo consécutif à la guerre du Golfe," *J.D.I.*, vol. 4 (1997), à la p. 945.

[27] Laïdi, *supra* note 17.

économique fulgurant de ce pays.[28] Le comportement de certains pays en développement afin de soutenir le capitalisme ou le communisme, s'inscrivait dans la problématique universelle que représentait la guerre froide.

La prestation des pays en développement est aussi constituée par le comportement qu'ils adoptent dans les échanges dette-environnement. Ces derniers ont comme objectif la réduction de la dette extérieure d'un pays en développement et la protection de l'environnement global, deux enjeux qui constituent, à l'évidence, des problématiques universelles. Le pays en développement qui en bénéficie s'engage, à l'égard du pays développé créancier, à adopter des mesures de réhabilitation de l'environnement, en contrepartie du réaménagement ou de l'annulation partielle de sa dette extérieure. La conditionnalité, dans ce cas, peut avoir un fondement bilatéral ou multilatéral; la pratique de ces échanges se réalisant, dans cette dernière situation, par l'entremise du Club de Paris.

Ce type d'échange qui s'articule autour de la gestion de la dette extérieure d'un pays en développement rappelle ceux intervenus à la fin du 19e et au début du 20e siècle, lors des crises de la dette extérieure de pays d'Amérique latine où les États européens avaient accepté de ne pas intervenir militairement afin de recouvrer leurs créances, en échange de l'adoption d'un comportement déterminé de la part des pays débiteurs: leur collaboration au remboursement de la dette.[29] La conditionnalité se situait, dans ce cas, à l'extérieur de la convention principale et avait pour objectif l'accomplissement par les États d'Amérique latine de leur obligation de rembourser la dette contractée avec les États créanciers européens. La conditionnalité s'exerçait alors dans un contexte multilatéral, puisque les États créanciers agissaient de façon concertée et entendaient mettre collectivement en œuvre leurs menaces afin d'inciter, voire d'obliger, les pays débiteurs à trouver une solution à une problématique que l'Europe considérait comme universelle à l'époque: la stabilité des engagements financiers interétatiques.

---

[28] Comme le rapporte H. Ben Hammouda: "la menace communiste en Asie, a amené les États-Unis à avoir une attitude bienveillante à l'égard des pays asiatiques et à favoriser une forte croissance économique pour éloigner la pauvreté et diminuer par conséquent les risques de contagion révolutionnaire." H. Ben Hammouda, "Mondialisation, marginalisation de l'Afrique et perspectives d'avenir," dans Centre Tricontinental, dir., *À la recherche d'alternatives — Un autre monde est-il possible?*, Paris, L'Harmattan, 2001, aux pp. 103–22.

[29] Ces affaires ont donné naissance à la doctrine de Monroe. Nguyen *et al.*, *supra* note 2 aux pp. 75–76 et 936.

L'atteinte de l'universalité des règles du droit international public constitue un objectif primordial dans un monde globalisé. Il est ainsi important que le plus grand nombre possible d'États adhèrent à la coutume en tant que source normative. Un rapport de force s'est établi entre les pays en développement et les pays développés sur cette question, qui constituait un enjeu universel pendant la grande période de décolonisation dans les années 1950 et 1960. La majorité des pays en développement manifestait une réticence à être soumis aux coutumes internationales préexistantes, élaborées, notamment, par les anciens États colonisateurs.

Le différend fut résolu par l'application d'une conditionnalité de premier niveau. La reconnaissance des États nouvellement indépendants — essentiellement des pays en développement — par les États souverains à l'époque — essentiellement des pays développés — était conditionnelle à l'acceptation par les États du premier groupe, des coutumes élaborées sans leur participation. Ainsi, comme le rapporte le professeur Claude Emanuelli: "Cependant, les États nouveaux sont ... présumés avoir tacitement accepté d'être liés par les règles coutumières préexistantes. Cette acceptation tacite serait la contrepartie de leur reconnaissance par les États en place ou de leur admission à l'ONU."[30] Puisque la question de l'admission d'un nouvel État à l'ONU relève de l'Assemblée générale des Nations Unies (AGNU) et que cette dernière était contrôlée, au moment de sa création, par les pays développés, la conditionnalité se réalisait dans un contexte multilatéral entre, d'une part, l'AGNU et d'autre part, le pays en développement. Un vote positif de l'AGNU, quant à l'admission d'un État à cet organisme, revêtait une signification qui n'échappait pas aux pays en développement: celle de leur reconnaissance comme État nouvellement indépendant.[31]

Le contrôle des flux migratoires du Sud vers le Nord, notamment ceux de migrants économiques, constitue une autre problématique universelle dont l'issue est directement liée au comportement des pays en développement. La position de l'Union européenne (UE) sur cette question doit être mentionnée, car elle illustre bien la façon dont s'articule la conditionnalité dans un tel contexte. Le Conseil de l'Union européenne, soucieux de réduire le nombre

---

30 C. Emanuelli, *Droit international public*, Montréal, Wilson et Lafleur, 2004, à la p. 63. Il s'agit de la position de la majorité des auteurs volontaristes.

31 J. Touscoz, *Le principe d'effectivité dans l'ordre international*, Paris, L.G.D.J., 1964, à la p. 36.

d'immigrants qui entrent illégalement sur le territoire de ses États membres adopte la position suivante en 2002:

Le Conseil européen estime qu'il est nécessaire de procéder à une évaluation systématique des relations avec les pays tiers qui ne coopèrent pas dans la lutte contre l'immigration illégale. Cette évaluation sera prise en compte dans les relations entre l'Union européenne et ses États membres et les pays concernés, *dans tous les domaines pertinents.* Une coopération insuffisante de la part d'un pays pourrait rendre plus difficile *l'approfondissement des relations* entre le pays en question et l'Union."[32]

Le Conseil européen laisse entendre, notamment, que les États bénéficiaires de l'aide publique au développement (APD) accordée par l'UE, doivent collaborer à réduire le flot des migrants en provenance de leur territoire et à destination de l'UE, à défaut de quoi cette dernière pourrait mettre un terme aux transferts financiers au chapitre de l'APD en faveur de ces États. Les États visés sont évidemment les pays en développement qui connaissent une forte émigration vers le continent européen. La conditionnalité imposée multilatéralement par l'UE vise à obtenir la collaboration de ces derniers dans la résolution d'une problématique universelle.

Il peut être affirmé, dans toutes ces situations, que le pouvoir de négociation des pays en développement est équivalent à celui des pays développés, puisque la monnaie d'échange dont disposent les pays en développement revêt une très grande importance pour les pays développés. Cette dernière est, en effet, liée à des problématiques universelles qui concernent tous les États et donc les pays développés. Ces échanges Nord-Sud s'effectuent dans le contexte de l'application de la notion de conditionnalité de premier niveau. Le pouvoir de négociation des pays en développement est affaibli lorsqu'il y a application de la notion de conditionnalité de deuxiè-

---

[32] Conclusions de la présidence du Conseil européen de Séville (21 et 22 juin 2002), 2002, à la p. 11, disponible en ligne à: <http://www.consilium.europa. eu/ueDocs/cms_Data/docs/pressdata/fr/ec/72640.pdf>. Consulter aussi (2002, à la p. 9): <http://register.consilium.europa.eu/pdf/fr/02/st09/09796-r1f2.pdf>; (2002, à la 12): <http://www.consilium.europa.eu/ueDocs/cms_ Data/docs/pressdata/fr/jha/71020.pdf>; (2002): <http://www.consilium. europa.eu/ueDocs/cms_Data/docs/pressdata/fr/gena/71148.pdf>; Union européenne, "Conclusions de la présidence du conseil européen de Séville 21 et 22 juin 2002 (extraits)," *Cultures & Conflits* 45 (printemps 2002), disponible en ligne à: <http://www.conflits.org/index791.html.>; (2002): <http://www.rfi. fr/actufr/articles/030/article_15314.asp>.

me niveau. Dans cette situation, les pays développés créent le droit et ils sont donc responsables de la norme de laquelle la pratique de la conditionnalité découle.

LA PRATIQUE DE LA CONDITIONNALITÉ DE DEUXIÈME NIVEAU: UN SYSTÈME INÉQUITABLE POUR LES PAYS EN DÉVELOPPEMENT

L'iniquité dont sont victimes les pays en développement dans la pratique de la conditionnalité de deuxième niveau, découle de la divergence des intérêts économiques du groupe par rapport à ceux des pays développés sur la question du développement. Elle est aussi tributaire de la conception traditionnellement différente du Nord et du Sud quant à l'importance relative des droits de l'homme.

Les intérêts économiques divergents des pays en développement et des pays développés sur la question du développement

Deux visions économiques s'opposent dans la résolution de la problématique du développement: celle des pays en développement, qui demeure théorique et celle des pays développés qui s'applique dans les faits. La suprématie économique des pays développés permet à ces derniers d'imposer leur philosophie dans l'élaboration des règles commerciales et dans la gouvernance macroéconomique exercée par les institutions financières multilatérales. Cette situation est liée à un processus décisionnel biaisé des organisations à caractère économique qui servent de relais à la promotion des intérêts des États développés.

La philosophie économique de la triade: Organisation mondiale du commerce (OMC), Fonds monétaire international (FMI) et Banque mondiale (BM)

Il est paradoxal de constater que malgré l'accroissement significatif, depuis des décennies, de la richesse globale de l'humanité, les pays en développement, qui constituent la majorité des États, ne disposent toujours pas suffisamment de ressources financières afin de mettre en œuvre les droits économiques et sociaux prioritaires. Cette constatation oblige à se questionner sur les causes qui empêchent les pays en développement de s'acquitter des obligations qu'ils ont à l'égard de leur population à ce chapitre.

L'analyse de la question requiert de mesurer les conséquences sur les pays en développement de la philosophie économique de l'Organisation mondiale du commerce (OMC), de la BM et du FMI, puisque ces organismes agissent comme les principaux leviers de la répartition de la richesse entre les États.

Le Consensus de Washington[33] constitue la pierre angulaire de la philosophie économique de la BIRD et du FMI. Il comporte quatre préceptes: déréglementation, privatisation, stabilité macro-économique et compression budgétaire.[34] Il vise à donner une forme ultra libérale à la mondialisation et à obtenir, à terme, la libéralisation des marchés financiers. Il est le fruit d'ententes informelles conclues dans les années 1980 et 1990 entre les principales sociétés transnationales et banques privées américaines, la BM, le FMI et la Réserve fédérale américaine.

Le libre-échange et la mondialisation ont irrévocablement modifié les relations économiques internationales depuis la fin du second conflit mondial. *L'Accord général sur le les tarifs douaniers et le commerce* est l'instrument privilégié de ce changement qui répudie les pratiques protectionnistes de l'entre-guerres. Il est le fruit d'une démarche anglo-américaine et se fonde sur le libre jeu des forces du marché. Seules les considérations commerciales animaient ses fondateurs, lors de sa création en 1947. Elles visaient l'augmentation des revenus réels, le relèvement des niveaux de vie et le plein emploi. Les objectifs de l'Organisation mondiale du commerce (OMC) sont identiques, puisque *l'Accord de Marrakech* les reprend, en ajoutant, néanmoins, qu'ils doivent être atteints conformément au concept de développement durable, qui vise à préserver l'environnement d'une manière compatible avec les besoins des États signataires dont les niveaux de développement économique sont inégaux.

Le système OMC-GATT et le Consensus de Washington s'accordent parfaitement, d'un point de vue idéologique, puisque la réalisation de l'objectif du premier — la libéralisation des marchés — ne peut qu'être stimulée par la mise en œuvre des préceptes du Consensus de Washington.

C'est par l'imposition de mesures visant des programmes de politiques économiques que le FMI et la BM conditionnent leurs prêts

---

[33] Sur le Consensus de Washington, consulter, GEMDEV, *Mondialisation, les mots et les choses,* Paris, Karthala, 1999; R. Reich, *L'Économie mondialisée,* Paris, Dunod, 1993; Centre Tricontinental, *supra* note 28. Ce terme fut inventé par John Williamson, économiste à la BM.

[34] Commission des droits de l'homme, 59e session, *Exposé oral de M. Jean Ziegler, rapporteur spécial sur le droit à l'alimentation* (5 avril 2002, à la p. 3), disponible en ligne à: <http://www.unhchr.ch/huricane/huricane.nsf/424e6fc8b8e55fa680 2566b0004083d9/dod65fa45948132ac1256b92004dab37?OpenDocument>.

aux pays en développement. En effet, la modification des structures macroéconomiques des pays en développement est presque toujours requise afin de mettre en force les décisions de la triade. Ceci s'explique par le fait que la conditionnalité de deuxième niveau imposée aux pays en développement par ces organismes,[35] s'inspire des préceptes du Consensus de Washington. Or, selon les décideurs de la triade qui, comme il sera exposé dans la partie qui suit, défendent les intérêts des pays développés, les pays en développement n'en font jamais assez pour donner l'orientation ultra libérale à leur économie afin de concrétiser les préceptes du Consensus de Washington.

C'est aussi par la mise en œuvre de programmes de politiques économiques, imposés par la BM et le FMI, lors de l'octroi de concours financiers, que les pays en développement participent au fonctionnement du système commercial international administré par l'OMC qui leur est en grande partie défavorable. L'application des programmes de politiques économiques heurte, bien souvent de plein fouet, la réalisation des droits économiques des citoyens des pays en développement.

Les programmes de politiques économiques sont mis en vigueur dans des pays en développement qui connaissent des difficultés économiques en amont de toute intervention des institutions financières multilatérales; il est, par conséquent, malaisé d'évaluer leurs effets sur la réalisation des droits économiques. Les problèmes économiques des pays en développement résultent, soit d'une gouvernance déficiente de l'État, soit d'influences économiques extérieures négatives ou d'autres types d'influences extérieures négatives ou encore d'une combinaison des deux.[36] Il peut tout de même être affirmé, sans risque d'erreur, que la philosophie économique véhiculée par les institutions financières multilatérales, favorise les pays développés au détriment des pays en développement.

---

35 Un nombre grandissant d'économistes affirment néanmoins qu'un "consensus post-Washington qui sans remettre en question les préceptes fondamentaux du consensus antérieur" doit tenir compte de la protection de l'environnement, de la répartition de la richesse et de la promotion de la démocratie. *Intégration hémisphérique et démocratique dans les Amériques: Symposium de Windsor,* 3-5 juin 2000 (2002, à la p. 3), disponible en ligne à: <http://www.ichrdd.ca/francais/commdoc/publications/devDemo/windsor2000/rappSymposiumFraGlossaire.html>.

36 Consulter à ce sujet, T. Mkandawire et C. C. Soludo, *Notre continent notre avenir: Perspectives africaines sur l'ajustement structurel,* Ottawa, Éditions du CRDI, 1999, aux pp. 83–90.

Cette dernière prive, en effet, les pays en développement des ressources financières qui seraient nécessaires à la réduction de la pauvreté et par voie de conséquence à la mise en œuvre des droits économiques.

Un processus décisionnel favorable aux intérêts des pays développés

Les décisions de la triade traduisent invariablement la philosophie économique du Consensus de Washington. Ceci relève de l'évidence pour le FMI et la BM, puisque ce sont les États qui disposent d'un droit de veto dans les décisions prises par ces organismes qui promeuvent le plus activement le Consensus de Washington. Les États-Unis sont titulaires, ainsi, d'un droit de veto sur toute modification des chartes constitutives de ces organisations, car ils possèdent 17,35 p. 100 des voix de celles-ci et que 85 p. 100 des voix sont requises afin de les modifier.[37] Les pays en développement considèrent que la règle du *un dollar une voix* qui préside aux décisions de la BM et du FMI doit être repensée, car elle met en exergue un déficit démocratique. Ils considèrent que ces organismes doivent revenir à leur fonction originelle qui consiste à assurer la régulation du système économique mondial et ne pas envisager la seule rentabilité du capital. Cet objectif, ne peut être atteint, selon les pays en développement, sans que l'État puisse jouer son rôle de garant des objectifs sociaux.[38]

Le processus décisionnel de l'OMC semble, de prime abord, plus démocratique que celui de la BM et du FMI, les décisions s'y prenant par consensus. Sous le couvert de ce dernier, le consentement des pays en développement à des concessions commerciales leur est, cependant, extirpé de force dans la plupart des cas. La dynamique des négociations défavorise, en effet, les pays en développement. Les négociations multilatérales portant sur un domaine convenu entre les parties consultatives se font en effet à armes inégales, les pays en développement, notamment les PMA, ne disposant pas des ressources techniques nécessaires afin de défendre leurs positions.

Les représentants des pays développés déterminent les règles du jeu avant et pendant les rencontres portant sur les négociations lors

---

[37] Vingt-deux pays d'Afrique se partagent 1,17 p. 100 des voix. A. Zacharie et É. Toussaint, *Sortir du consensus de Washington* (2002), disponible en ligne à: <http://risal.collectifs.net/article.php3?id_article=370>.

[38] Centre tricontinental, *supra* note 28 à la p. 25.

des cycles commerciaux et les enfreignent si leurs intérêts sont menacés.[39] L'écart est important entre, d'une part, les promesses de mieux-être et de croissance économique faites par l'OMC aux pays en développement et les règles du jeu qui leurs sont présentées et d'autre part, la manière dont se comportent les pays développés et les concessions qu'ils obtiennent en bout de ligne des pays en développement.

Le traité de l'OMC fut, par ailleurs, imposé aux États du Tiers-Monde lors des négociations de l'Uruguay Round. Les pays en développement subissaient une récession économique accentuée par la crise de l'endettement et devaient affronter les problèmes politiques qui découlaient de cette situation.[40] De plus, les pays en développement n'étaient pas adéquatement préparés à se mesurer aux États développés dans des négociations hautement techniques.[41]

Le discours des défenseurs de l'OMC sur les bienfaits du libre-échange pour l'ensemble de la communauté internationale a été interrompu lors de la 5e Conférence ministérielle de l'OMC à Cancun le 14 septembre 2003, durant le cycle de négociation de Doha.[42] Plus de vingt-deux pays en développement se sont retirés de la table de négociations manifestant ainsi leur opposition aux politiques agricoles protectionnistes des pays développés et démontrant que

---

[39] Propos rapportés par R.-P. Paringaux, "L'agriculture indienne à l'épreuve de l'OMC," *Le Monde diplomatique* (septembre 2002), à la p.7. Sur le comportement des pays développés lors des négociations, consulter A. Bertrand et L. Kalafatides, *OMC, le pouvoir invisible*, Paris, Fayard, 2002, aux pp.15–24 et 41–61.

[40] La fin de la bipolarité augmentait aussi la pression politique et économique sur les pays en développement. B. Founou-Tchuigoua, "La dimension panafricaine du défi à la mondialisation néo-libérale," dans Centre tricontinental, *Et si l'Afrique refusait le marché?*, Paris, L'Harmattan, 2001, à la p. 120.

[41] "La plupart subissaient même des pressions relevant du chantage." *Ibid.* Sur le déroulement des négociations lors de l'Uruguay Round, consulter Bertrand et Kalafatides, *supra* note 39 aux pp. 41–61.

[42] Le cycle de Doha devait faire en sorte, tel que mentionné dans la Déclaration ministérielle adoptée le 14 novembre 2001, que le commerce international puisse jouer "un rôle majeur dans la promotion du développement économique et la réduction de la pauvreté." Art. 2, *Déclaration ministérielle*, adoptée le 14 novembre 2001, OMC Quatrième session Doha, 9–14 novembre 2001 WT/MIN(01)DEC/1. Voir aussi l'article 3 consacré aux pays les moins avancés. Sur ces négociations, consulter: I. Bensidoun, A. Chevallier et G. Gaulier, "Pour le Sud, y a-t-il eu gain à l'ouverture?," *Problèmes économiques* n° 2.743 (2002), à la p. 3. C'est tout le débat d'une protection temporaire des industries naissantes dont il est question.

les pays pauvres n'entendaient pas jouer le jeu du libre-échange inconditionnel.[43]

Cet événement s'inscrit parfaitement bien dans le cours de l'histoire des négociations commerciales internationales où les pays en développement ne sont que de simples spectateurs ne jouissant d'aucun véritable pouvoir de négociation face aux pays développés. Il manifeste fondamentalement le souci des pays en développement de donner une primauté aux droits de l'homme sur le libre commerce comme le rapporteur à la Commission des droits de l'homme des Nations Unies l'a déjà demandé.[44]

L'application du credo du Consensus de Washington menace donc directement la réalisation des droits économiques et sociaux dans les pays en développement.[45] La difficulté de concilier les droits dont le Nord et le Sud font la promotion constitue un autre obstacle majeur à la réalisation du droit au développement dans les pays en développement.

La conception traditionnellement différente du Nord et du Sud quant à l'importance relative des droits de l'homme

Les relations Nord-Sud ont toujours été caractérisées par une conception différente des droits de l'homme. Elle concerne la distinction entre, d'une part, les droits civils et politiques et, d'autre part, les droits économiques, sociaux et culturels. Les droits civils et politiques sont prioritairement promus par les pays développés et les droits économiques, sociaux et culturels sont, à l'inverse, prioritairement promus par les pays en développement. Les conceptions du Nord et du Sud en matière de droits de l'homme varient aussi sous l'angle de l'individualité et de la collectivité des droits de

---

[43] É. Desrosiers, "Échec fracassant de la conférence de Cancun," *Le Devoir* (15 septembre 2003), à la p. A1. Voir à ce sujet B. Cassen, "La guerre commerciale, seul horizon du libre-échange," *Le Monde diplomatique* (septembre 2003), à la p. 22; J. Berthelot, "Le trois aberrations des politiques agricoles," *Le Monde diplomatique* (septembre 2003), à la p. 22, disponible en ligne (2003) à: <http://www.monde-diplomatique.fr.>.

[44] Commission des droits de l'homme, *supra* note 34 à la p. 5. Les participants à la conférence tenue à Doha, en novembre 2001, ont cependant décidé de ne pas considérer le droit à l'alimentation dans les pourparlers, malgré les nombreuses propositions à cet effet. *Ibid.*

[45] Voir notamment, en ce qui concerne le droit à la nourriture, Commission des droits de l'homme, *Au droit à la nourriture s'oppose le consensus de Washington*, *supra* note 34 à la p. 3.

l'homme: les pays en développement donnent préséance au volet collectif des droits de l'homme, tandis que les pays développés donnent préséance au volet individuel des droits de l'homme. La tension Nord-Sud sur le sujet, qui remonte aux années 1960 et 1970, a connu un répit dans les années 1980, avant de connaître un regain dans les années 1990, du à l'essor de la conditionnalité politique imposée aux pays en développement. Par cette dernière, les pays développés ont fait du respect des droits civils et politiques, un pré-requis aux transferts publics de flux financiers du Nord vers le Sud, que ce soit sous forme de prêt ou d'aide publique au développement.[46]

L'importance plus grande que les pays développés accordent aux droits civils et politiques par rapport aux droits économiques, sociaux et culturels tient au fait que, selon eux, les droits de l'homme doivent se limiter à protéger l'individu contre l'État. Cela ne vise pour ainsi dire, selon leur conception, que les droits devant assurer une démocratie participative dans un État de droit.[47] Il est impératif que l'État, dans son optique, conserve toute la latitude possible dans le secteur économique et le fait de consentir des droits à caractère économique aux individus est traditionnellement perçu comme une menace pour le capitalisme.[48]

Selon les pays en développement, les droits économiques, sociaux et culturels conditionnent l'exercice de tous les droits de l'homme, c'est-à-dire que les droits et libertés accordés à l'individu dépendent de la disponibilité de ressources financières suffisantes dans les coffres de l'État.[49] La déclaration de Téhéran adoptée en 1968 confirme cette position: "La jouissance complète des droits civils et politiques est impossible sans celle des droits économiques, sociaux et culturels."[50] La position défendue par les pays en développement

---

46 Catherine Schneider, "Au cœur de la coopération internationale de l'Union européenne: quelle stratégie à venir pour la conditionnalité politique?" dans Hubert Thierry, dir., *Droit international et coopération internationale, Hommage à Jean-André Touscoz*, France Europe Éditions, Nice, 2007, aux pp. 750–78.

47 K. Mbaye, "Introduction," dans *Droit international, bilan et perspectives*, t. 2, Paris, Pedone, 1991, à la p. 1121.

48 Il ne faut cependant pas négliger, comme le rapporte Schabas, "l'idéologie social-démocrate qui animait les puissances occidentales pendant et après la crise économique des années 1930." Schabas, *supra* note 1 à la p. 39.

49 V. Kartashkin, "Les pays socialistes et les droits de l'homme," dans K. Vasak, *Les dimensions internationales des droits de l'homme*, Paris, UNESCO, 1978, à la p. 680.

50 *Proclamation de Téhéran*, Acte final de la Conférence internationale des droits de l'homme, Doc. NU A/CONF 32/41 (1968) 3.

résulte de leur conception de la place qu'occupe le développement économique dans la réalisation des droits de l'homme. Le premier doit nécessairement précéder les deuxièmes. C'est d'ailleurs ce que la résolution 1161 du 26 novembre 1957 indique: "un développement économique et social ... contribuerait à favoriser et à maintenir ... le progrès social et l'élévation du niveau de vie ainsi que la reconnaissance et le respect des droits de l'homme et des libertés fondamentales."[51] Les pays en développement érigent le développement économique en droit au développement et ce dernier constitue la matrice de tous les droits économiques et sociaux.

La préoccupation des pays en développement à l'égard du développement économique fournit la raison pour laquelle ils considèrent avant tout le droit au développement comme un droit collectif, sans exclure sa dimension individuelle, puisque la personne en est le bénéficiaire ultime.[52] Les pays en développement considèrent que le degré d'autonomie de l'État, notamment dans le secteur économique, est une garantie préalable pour l'exercice des autres droits de l'homme. L'État exercerait ses attributs dans le domaine économique en se fondant sur le droit au développement dont il est titulaire au nom de la collectivité qu'il représente. Ces considérations amenèrent les pays en développement et les États socialistes à demander l'inclusion du droit à l'autodétermination dans les deux Pactes et de son corollaire, la souveraineté permanente sur les ressources naturelles, afin de leur conférer des droits essentiels à leur développement économique. Les pays en développement affirmèrent, par la suite, le lien indissociable entre le droit au développement et les droits de l'homme, le premier devant précéder les deuxièmes. La primauté va donc pour les pays en développement aux droits collectifs ou droits de la troisième génération.

L'attachement des pays en développement au volet collectif du droit au développement est tellement important que c'est ce droit qu'ils opposent aux pays développés lorsque ces derniers demandent leur collaboration dans le secteur de l'environnement[53] ou

---

51 *Progrès économique et social équilibré et intégré*, Rés. AG 1161 (XII), Doc. Off. AG NU, 12e sess., supp. no 18, Doc. NU A/3805 (1957) 17.

52 Sur cette question consulter, A. Kerdoun, "Le droit au développement en tant que droit de l'homme: portée et limites," *R.Q.D.I.*, vol. 17.1 (2004), à la p. 80.

53 Les pays en développement soutiennent, qu'en ce qui les concerne, leur développement économique doit recevoir la priorité sur la protection de l'environnement global pour laquelle leur collaboration est demandée.

dans la lutte contre le terrorisme.[54] C'est aussi en se fondant sur ce droit qu'ils exercent la conditionnalité de troisième niveau.

Les pays développés considèrent, quant à eux, que les droits et libertés individuels constituent le fondement des droits de l'homme que les peuples n'ont que des droits limités.

Les droits économiques s'opposeraient directement, selon les pays développés, au droit à la liberté du commerce qui, selon eux, constitue la pierre angulaire du droit international moderne. Bien que prioritairement centré sur l'individu, il constitue aussi, le seul droit collectif véritablement promu par les pays développés. Il s'appliquerait donc aux groupes et aux États, en plus des individus.

Le droit à la liberté de commerce heurterait de plein fouet le droit au développement puisqu'il restreindrait les options politiques et économiques des pays en développement, qui n'auraient d'autre choix que qu'adhérer à un ordre international élaboré par ses promoteurs: organisations internationales contrôlées par les pays développés, entreprises transnationales et États développés.[55] Le droit à la liberté de commerce appliqué rigidement par ces derniers, au cours des années 1960 et 1970, a ainsi écarté les droits économiques de la philosophie néolibérale de l'après-guerre qui, jusqu'à un certain point, tendait à les intégrer.

La philosophie à la base de la création de la triade complique la conciliation des principes de l'économie de marché avec les droits économiques et sociaux. La problématique est amplifiée par la mondialisation et l'un de ses principaux effets sur la gouvernance: la difficulté pour l'État d'assumer ses responsabilités au niveau de la distribution équitable de la richesse.[56]

Dans ce contexte, ce qui est vrai pour les droits dont sont investis les individus s'applique aussi pour ceux dont peuvent se prévaloir les groupes: collectivités et États. Compte tenu de l'esprit qui anime les décideurs de la mondialisation, la conditionnalité de troisième niveau, comme il sera vu à la deuxième partie, permet, au niveau international, la reconnaissance de droits économiques pour le

---

54 J. Lesourne, "Essai de prospective mondiale après le 11 septembre," *Futuribles*, n° 269 (2001), aux pp. 35–42.

55 D. Carreau et P. Juillard, *Droit international économique,* 4e éd., Paris, LGDJ, 1998, à la p. 41.

56 "Les néo-libéraux ont donc limité la perception que les gens ont du travail, réduisant toujours plus l'économique à la logique exclusive du marché, et marginalisant le rôle redistributif de l'État." W. Dierckxsens, "Vers une alternative citoyenne," dans Centre tricontinental, *supra* note 28 à la p. 135.

bénéfice de la population des pays en développement. Elle constitue, lorsque les droits des pays en développement et ceux des pays développés entrent en conflit, un mécanisme assurant une conciliation de ceux-ci. Les États vulnérables seraient même les titulaires d'un droit visant l'équité dans les relations internationales, dont elle constituerait le pivot.

Le droit des pays développés s'impose aux pays en développement, comme le droit du plus fort devient la loi du plus faible. Ainsi, la vision économique du Nord et sa conception des droits de l'homme s'appliquent naturellement aux pays en développement. Cette suprématie du droit des pays développés dans ces domaines sert d'assise au déclenchement de la pratique de la conditionnalité de troisième niveau qui permet l'aménagement d'un rapport de force plus équilibré entre les deux groupes.

LA NOTION DE CONDITIONNALITÉ COMME FONDEMENT À UN DROIT POUR LES ÉTATS EN DÉVELOPPEMENT: LE RECENTRAGE DU RAPPORT DE FORCE ENTRE LES ÉTATS

L'état de nécessité[57] existe en droit international afin qu'un État se libère d'une obligation qu'il a contractée sans que sa responsabilité internationale puisse être engagée sur la base de la non-exécution de celle-ci. Tel que l'a conçu la CDI dans son projet intitulé *Responsabilité de l'État pour fait internationalement illicite*,[58] l'État qui serait à l'origine d'un "fait non conforme à l'une de ses obligations internationales" ne pourrait voir sa responsabilité engagée lorsque la défense de l'état de nécessité serait retenue, puisque cette dernière constituerait une cause d'exclusion de l'illicéité du fait en question. La nécessité se fonderait sur un événement "accompli

---

[57] Sur le concept consulter Nguyen *et al., supra* note 2 aux pp. 223–24 et 786–87. Le droit à la conditionnalité universelle prend aussi sa source dans les mesures de rétorsion et les contre-mesures; ces dernières sont prévues aux articles 47 à 50 du *Projet de codification du droit de la responsabilité internationale des États.* Voir *supra* note 14 à la p. 719. Elles pourraient être appliquées contre un État; à la fois, créancier d'un autre État qui voit sa marge de manœuvre réduite quant au respect des droits humains fondamentaux, mais aussi, signataire avec l'État débiteur d'un traité international portant sur les droits de l'homme. L'État créancier ne respecterait pas l'obligation de collaborer à l'application des droits humains fondamentaux qu'il a contractée avec l'État débiteur. Ce qui ouvrirait la porte aux mesures. L'échange proposé par l'État débiteur constituerait une mesure de rétorsion ou une contre-mesure. Sur ces notions, consulter Nguyen *et al., supra* note 2 aux pp. 957–62.

[58] *Projet de codification du droit, ibid,* art. 25–27.

dans la sphère de la liberté que le droit laisse aux sujets pour pourvoir à leur propre conservation."[59] Les États jouiraient ainsi d'une liberté d'action qui ferait partie de leur domaine réservé.[60] La pratique du recours au droit à la conditionnalité universelle trouve sa source dans le concept de l'état de nécessité.

L'objectif de la mise en œuvre du droit à la conditionnalité universelle ne serait pas que l'État débiteur puisse se libérer d'une obligation internationale qu'il aurait contractée. Il serait toujours lié par cette dernière, mais il pourrait et il jouirait du droit de renégocier les termes de l'obligation contractée. Si le créancier et le débiteur ne parvenaient pas à s'entendre, ce dernier aurait le droit de mettre fin à l'entente sur la base de l'état de nécessité. Le droit à la conditionnalité universelle permettrait, jusqu'à un certain point, une réversibilité de la pratique de la conditionnalité de deuxième niveau. L'objectif de la conditionnalité universelle serait un rééquilibrage des rapports contractuels entre les parties. L'État A qui imposerait une conditionnalité de deuxième niveau à l'État B afin d'assurer l'exécution d'une obligation conventionnelle, pourrait se voir imposer une conditionnalité de troisième niveau par l'État B afin qu'il assouplisse les modalités de l'entente conventionnelle qui menace la réalisation des droits économiques dans l'État B. Ce dernier jouirait d'un droit à l'utilisation de la conditionnalité de troisième niveau afin de créer un contexte propice à la mise en application des droits économiques. La conditionnalité de troisième niveau permettrait, ainsi, le rééquilibrage des droits des parties. Le droit à la conditionnalité universelle constituerait ainsi, en quelque sorte, le droit du plus faible à la révision de la conditionnalité de deuxième niveau.

L'ÉTAT DE NÉCESSITÉ: SOURCE DE LA PRATIQUE DU RECOURS
AU DROIT À LA CONDITIONNALITÉ UNIVERSELLE

La notion de l'état de nécessité peut servir de fondement au respect des obligations d'un État envers sa population en vertu de son droit

---

59 D. Anzilotti, *Cours de droit international* (trad. de G. Gidel), réédition, Paris, Éditions Panthéon-Assas, 1999, à la p. 513. La position à l'effet que l'état de nécessité est une circonstance excluant ou atténuant la responsabilité doit être distinguée de celle de l'exclusion de l'illicéité. T. Christakis, "Nécessité n'a pas de loi?" dans *La nécessité en droit international*, Colloque de la SFDI, Paris, Pedone, 2007, à la p. 11.

60 Consacré par l'article 2 paragraphe 7 de la Charte des Nations Unies. Consulter à ce sujet, G. Arangio-Ruiz, "Le domaine réservé, l'organisation internationale et le rapport entre le droit international et le droit interne," *R.C.A.D.I.*, vol. 225 (1990), aux pp. 9–484.

constitutionnel ou de conventions internationales qui le lient.[61] Certains auteurs ont avancé qu'un pays débiteur pourrait ainsi, "refuser un programme d'ajustement structurel rendant impossible le financement public des services sociaux de base."[62]

Si le droit pour un État de ne pas honorer une obligation internationale à caractère économique qu'il aurait contractée par traité ou convenu par toute autre forme d'entente, peut se justifier par la nécessité qu'il a de fournir des services sociaux de base à sa population, il aurait aussi, sur la même base, le droit de demander à son cocontractant de renégocier avec lui les termes des ententes à caractère économique qui entravent l'application d'un droit économique. Qui peut le plus, peut le moins. La notion de l'état de nécessité peut être invoquée dans les deux situations. Ces dernières renvoient à deux visions de l'état de nécessité: la circonstance excluant l'illicéité et la circonstance atténuant la responsabilité. Dans les deux situations, cependant, les conditions d'application de l'état de nécessité dans les domaines économique et financier sont les mêmes.

Les deux visions de l'état de nécessité: la circonstance excluant l'illicéité et la circonstance atténuant la responsabilité

L'état de nécessité est associé au droit international de la responsabilité de l'État à cause des travaux de la CDI dans ce domaine.[63]

La réticence de plusieurs commissaires à l'introduction de ce concept en responsabilité internationale comme une circonstance excluant l'illicéité d'un acte, n'a pu être levée que par l'adoption de conditions rigoureuses afin qu'il puisse être invoqué.[64] Il est

---

[61] H. Ruiz Diaz, *L'État de nécessité la dette extérieure: Mécanisme juridiques de non-paiement, moratoire ou suspension de paiement*, document préparé pour le Comité pour l'annulation de la dette du Tiers-Monde (CADTM), 2000, à la p. 7, disponible en ligne à: <http://users.skynet.be/cadtm/>. Selon l'auteur qui s'appuie sur la décision du Barrage de Gabcikovo-Nagymaros, "le concept s'applique à tout type de convention ou accord international, quel que soit la nature de ladite convention ou son contenu." *Ibid.* à la p. 5. "Affaire relative au projet Gabcikovo–Nagymaros (Hongrie/Slovaquie) (1997) C.I.J. 92, 25 septembre," *I.L.M.* 37 (1998), à la p. 162, disponible en ligne à: <http://www.icj-cij.org/cij /cdocket/chs/chsjudgment/chs_cjudgment_970925.htm>.

[62] Zacharie et Toussaint, *supra* note 37 à la p. 3.

[63] Le concept a été débattu au sein de la Commission du droit international qui l'a codifié à l'article 25 du *Projet de codification du droit de la responsabilité internationale des États*, *supra* note 14 [*Projet de la CDI*].

[64] Voir à ce sujet J. Salmon, *Faut-il codifier l'état de nécessité en droit international?*, dans J. Makarczyk, dir., *Études de droit international en l'honneur du Juge M. Lachs*, The Hague/Boston, M. Nijhoff, 1984, aux pp. 244 et suiv.

nécessaire, afin de comprendre ces dernières, de distinguer les règles primaires des règles secondaires en matière de responsabilité internationale. Les premières concernent la violation par un État d'obligations conventionnelles relatives, par exemple, au droit des traités; les deuxièmes concernent les obligations qui découlent de cette violation et qui déclenchent les conséquences associées au droit de la responsabilité des États, notamment, la réparation du préjudice subi.[65] Les obligations primaires et secondaires des États sont donc respectivement associées aux règles primaires et secondaires en matière de responsabilité internationale.

Il existe des barrières extrinsèques relatives à la nature de l'obligation primaire et des obstacles intrinsèques à la nature de l'obligation secondaire.[66] Les premières sont de deux types. Le premier résulte de l'article 25 (2) a) du Projet de la CDI en vertu duquel l'état de nécessité ne peut-être invoqué si l'obligation internationale en question exclut la possibilité d'invoquer l'état de nécessité. Le deuxième résulte de l'article 26 à l'effet que l'état de nécessité ne peut jamais justifier la violation d'une "obligation découlant d'une norme impérative du droit international général."

En ce qui concerne les obstacles intrinsèques, ils sont codifiés par l'article 25 (1) et (2) b) du Projet de la CDI. Ils permettent de délimiter précisément les contours de l'état de nécessité afin d'éviter que les États invoquent trop fréquemment ce motif pour se libérer de certaines de leurs obligations internationales. Ils sont au nombre de cinq: (1) l'existence d'un péril grave et imminent; (2) le péril doit porter atteinte à un intérêt essentiel; (3) le fait incriminé doit constituer le seul moyen de protéger un intérêt essentiel contre un péril grave et imminent; (4) l'intérêt sacrifié, qui se fonde sur un droit, doit être inférieur à l'intérêt sauvegardé; (5) l'État auteur du fait illicite "ne doit pas avoir contribué à la survenance de l'état de nécessité."[67]

C'est sur le terrain de l'illicéité que s'est développé l'état de nécessité. La CIJ a confirmé la position de la CDI dans l'arrêt *Gabčíkovo-Nagymaros*.[68] La cour y affirme le caractère coutumier de l'état de nécessité, en écartant son application dans le litige qu'elle doit trancher: "L'état de nécessité constitue une cause, reconnue par le

---

65 Emanuelli, *supra* note 30 à la p. 569 (voir la note 557).

66 Christakis, *supra* note 59 aux pp. 19 et suiv.

67 *Ibid.* aux pp. 23 et suiv.

68 Projet *Gabcikovo-Nagymaros*, *supra* note 61 aux paras. 47–48.

droit international coutumier, d'exclusion de l'illicéité d'un fait non conforme à une obligation internationale."[69] La sentence *LG&E v. The Argentine Republic,*[70] qui sera commentée ultérieurement, constitue, néanmoins, la seule décision ayant retenu l'état de nécessité comme une circonstance excluant l'illicéité d'un fait non conforme à une obligation internationale. Dans celle-ci, le tribunal impose aux parties les conséquences de l'état de nécessité. Il a ainsi décidé que l'état de nécessité libérait entièrement l'État emprunteur de son obligation de rembourser une dette.

Si la jurisprudence reconnaît la faculté pour un État d'invoquer l'état de nécessité en matière économique et financière, elle est cependant muette sur les conséquences de la nécessité économique et financière, une fois qu'elle est admise. Comme l'a écrit la juriste Orianne Osuna, qui a consacré une étude sur la question:

Les conséquences de l'admission de la nécessité économique ne sont donc pas établies de façon précise ... il est difficile de dire si la nécessité en matière économique ou financière est considérée comme une circonstance excluant l'illicéité ou si elle a un autre effet, comme la suspension provisoire de l'obligation internationale ou l'atténuation de la responsabilité de l'État qui l'invoque.[71]

Les tribunaux ont, en effet, évité d'aborder de front cette question; toutefois les jugements démontrent sans conteste qu'ils ont emprunté tout autant l'avenue de l'état de nécessité comme une circonstance atténuant la responsabilité, que celle de l'état de nécessité comme une circonstance excluant l'illicéité, afin de fonder leurs conclusions.

Cet énoncé est confirmé par les décisions rendues en matière de remboursement de la dette extérieure de pays en difficulté de paiement. Les tribunaux devaient décider si la responsabilité internationale d'un État devait être engagée dans la situation de non-exécution d'une obligation internationale par celui-ci, afin de lutter contre une crise économique et financière. Les décisions

---

[69] Notons la réserve de Christakis, *supra* note 59 à la p. 41. *Rec.* CIJ, 1997, § 51 de l'arrêt.

[70] CIRDI Case No. ARB/02/01 (United States/Argentina BIT), 2001, disponible en ligne à: <http://ita.law.uvic.ca/index.htm> (ci-après *LG&E c. Argentine*).

[71] O. Osuna, "L'apport de la jurisprudence internationale en matière de nécessité économique et financière avant 1945," dans *La nécessité en droit international, supra* note 59, à la p. 361.

rapportées reconnaissent la répudiation pure et simple de la dette ou elles prévoient sa suspension.[72] Les décisions rendues dans ce domaine ont d'ailleurs servi d'arguments à des juristes qui défendent l'idée que l'état de nécessité peut être invoqué afin de répudier ou de suspendre le remboursement de la dette extérieure des pays en développement, dans le cadre de relations interétatiques, mais aussi à l'égard d'organisations internationales.[73]

Le professeur Théodore Christakis écrit, quant à lui:

> il semble que, dans un certain nombre de cas, des organes, juridictionnels et autres, ont tenu compte de l'état de nécessité en tant que circonstance atténuant la responsabilité, en tant que correctif pour des cas exceptionnels où l'application stricte du droit aurait amené à des résultats manifestement injustes.[74]

La plupart des décisions auxquelles l'auteur fait référence concernent le domaine économique et financier. Ce dernier y voit les indices d'une pratique des États qui pourrait être à la base d'une coutume, à l'effet que l'état de nécessité constituerait une circonstance atténuant leur responsabilité.[75]

L'état de nécessité ferait donc partie du droit coutumier dans deux situations. Premièrement, dans le cas de l'exclusion de l'illicéité d'un fait non conforme à une obligation internationale et deuxièmement dans le cas de l'atténuation de la responsabilité d'un fait non conforme à une obligation internationale. En consacrant le caractère coutumier de l'état de nécessité dans ces deux situations, les tribunaux consacrent, par la même occasion, les conséquences juridiques qui découlent de l'état de nécessité. L'état de nécessité peut alors libérer entièrement ou partiellement l'État débiteur de l'obligation internationale.

---

[72] Consulter à ce sujet les commentaires du rapporteur spécial Roberto Ago, A/ CN.4/318 Add. 5-7, "Additif au 8ème rapport sur la responsabilité des États par M. Roberto Ago," *A.C.D.I.*, vol. II, no 1 (1980), à la p. 22, para. 21.

[73] *Cf. supra* note 61. Voir aussi H.R. Diaz, *La force majeure: la situation en Argentine—La dette extérieure: mécanismes juridiques de non-paiement, moratoire ou suspension de paiement,* document préparé pour Attac-Québec, 2002, disponible en ligne à: <http://www.quebec.attac.org/article.php3?id_article=116>; H.R. Diaz, *La force majeure. La dette extérieure: mécanismes juridiques de non-paiement, moratoire ou suspension de paiement,* document préparé pour Attac-France, 2002, disponible en ligne à: <http://www.france.attac.org/spip.php?article304>.

[74] Christakis, *supra* note 59 à la p. 56.

[75] *Ibid.* aux pp. 56 et suiv.

La mise en œuvre de la conditionnalité universelle permettrait alors à l'État qui l'invoque d'atténuer les conséquences rigides de l'entente financière qu'il a contracté avec un autre État ou une organisation internationale. Elle permettrait aussi à l'État débiteur de se libérer de son l'obligation, s'il ne parvient pas à s'entendre avec son créancier.

Les conditions d'application de l'état de nécessité dans les domaines économique et financier

L'état de nécessité peut être soulevé lorsque existe une situation de "danger pour l'existence de l'État, pour sa survie politique ou même économique."[76] La survie économique réfère "aux ressources dont un État peut disposer pour continuer à satisfaire les besoins de la population, particulièrement en matière de santé, d'éducation, culturelle et sociale."[77] Cette situation présente un intérêt évident quant à la réalisation des droits économiques, puisqu'elle est le plus fréquemment tributaire des ressources financières dont dispose l'État.

La sentence *C.M.S. Gaz Transmission Company c. The Argentine Republic,* rendue par le Centre international pour le règlement des différends internationaux (CIRDI) en 2005,[78] est intéressante à ce niveau, puisque le tribunal expose les conditions requises afin que l'état de nécessité puisse être invoqué dans le contexte du remboursement de la dette d'un pays en développement, avant de retenir le principe comme une circonstance atténuant la responsabilité d'un État. Mentionnons, avant d'analyser la sentence, que la jurisprudence de la CIJ et des tribunaux arbitraux impose des conditions plus contraignantes dans les domaines économique et financier, ce qui comprend le remboursement de la dette extérieure d'un pays, que dans d'autres domaines, afin que puisse être retenu l'état de nécessité.

La première condition est qu'il appartient à l'État qui invoque l'état de nécessité de démontrer l'existence de la crise qui l'empêche d'honorer ses obligations internationales. C'est cependant au tribunal d'apprécier la gravité de cette dernière relativement aux

---

[76] La survie politique réfère à une situation "d'impossibilité politique de gouverner ou d'instabilité sociale." Ph. Cahier, "Cours de droit international public," *R.C.A.D.I.* (1985), à la p. 290. Diaz, *supra* note 61.

[77] *Ibid.*

[78] CIRDI Case No. ARB/01/08 (United States/Argentina BIT), 2002, disponible en ligne à: <http://ita.law.uvic.ca/index.htm> (ci-après *CMS c. Argentine*).

conséquences sur ces mêmes obligations. La deuxième condition est que la crise financière doit menacer l'existence même de l'État.[79] Le critère semble plus exigeant que le "péril grave et imminent pour un intérêt essentiel de l'État" prévu à l'article 25 du Projet de la CDI. La troisième condition est que le non-respect de l'obligation internationale constitue l'unique moyen de protéger l'intérêt de l'État, c'est-à-dire que seul le non-respect de cette obligation doit pouvoir permettre à l'État de survivre.[80]

La sentence *CMS c. Argentine*, assouplit la deuxième condition. Le tribunal considère que la situation dans laquelle se trouvait l'Argentine afin de ne pas honorer ses obligations constituait une "crise sévère," qui ne menaçait pas l'existence de l'État, et refuse d'exclure l'illicéité de l'acte sur la base du droit coutumier. Le tribunal endosse alors, en quelque sorte, le critère de l'article 25 du Projet de la CDI. C'est du moins le constat que font certains juristes à la suite de leur analyse de la décision.[81] Ils soulignent cependant l'étrangeté du raisonnement du tribunal. Ce dernier interprète, en effet, le péril grave et imminent dont parle l'article 25, comme signifiant une situation de "*total collapse*" dans laquelle devrait se trouver un État.[82] L'Argentine ne s'étant pas retrouvée dans une telle situation afin de ne pas honorer son obligation de remboursement et pour éviter qu'elle ne puisse invoquer l'état de nécessité, le tribunal fait reposer son raisonnement en définissant l'état de nécessité en fonction de l'obligation primaire, c'est-à-dire de la clause de sauvegarde incluse dans le traité conclu entre les États-Unis et l'Argentine.[83]

Cette décision est très critiquée et avec raison, car son fondement, quant au critère de l'acuité de la crise économique, aurait dû reposer sur l'obligation secondaire. Elle est cependant conforme aux autres décisions en matière de crises financière et économique quant aux conséquences de l'admission de la nécessité économique qui permet un assouplissement des conditions de remboursement du prêt, plutôt qu'une répudiation pure et simple de l'obligation. Le raisonnement ondoyant du tribunal amène finalement à une atténuation de la responsabilité de l'Argentine.

---

79 Osuna, *supra* note 71 à la p. 363.

80 *Ibid.* aux pp. 363–64.

81 Christakis, *supra* note 59 à la p. 62.

82 *Ibid.*, note 221.

83 *Ibid.*

Dans la sentence *LG&E c. Argentine,* le tribunal juge cependant que l'état de nécessité constitue une circonstance excluant l'illicéité. Il fonde sa décision sur la clause de sauvegarde contenue à l'article XI du traité bilatéral Argentine/États-Unis afin de reconnaître l'état de nécessité. Le Tribunal décide "d'exclure l'illicéité de l'acte d'un État sur la base de l'état de nécessité en allant d'ailleurs jusqu'au bout de cette logique et en refusant toute obligation d'indemnisation pour la période en question."[84] Le tribunal ne réfère qu'accessoirement à la règle secondaire en matière d'État de nécessité.[85] Il considère que la crise argentine revêtait le caractère de gravité de l'article XI du traité bilatéral Argentine/États-Unis et qu'alors, le non-remboursement de la dette était autorisé. Le tribunal indique que la coutume basée sur l'article 25 du Projet de la CDI supporte cette conclusion. Le CIRDI, dans cette décision, fait équivaloir l'article XI du traité bilatéral à l'article 25 du Projet de la CDI quant à l'acuité de la crise économique permettant d'invoquer l'état de nécessité. Il doit s'agir d'une crise sévère, tandis que dans la sentence *CMS c. Argentine,* le CIRDI indique que l'article 25 du Projet de la CDI équivaut à une situation de "*total collapse.*"

Nous pouvons tirer deux conclusions de ces sentences. La première porte sur les conditions pour invoquer l'état de nécessité; l'autre concerne les conséquences de l'application du principe, lorsqu'il est retenu. La première conclusion est que pour que l'état de nécessité soit reconnu, l'une des conditions à respecter réside dans la survenance d'une crise sévère, cette expression signifiant que des troubles économiques importants se produisent dans l'État, mais que ceux-ci ne mettent pas en jeu son existence. Le seuil de déclenchement afin que soit retenu l'état de nécessité est la survenance d'une crise sévère et, par conséquent, celle d'une situation de "*total collapse,*" puisque cette notion signifie que le contexte économique s'est dégradé depuis l'atteinte du seuil de la crise sévère. Selon le CIRDI, le péril grave et imminent mentionné à l'article 25 du Projet de la CDI signifie donc la survenance d'une crise sévère. La deuxième conclusion qui peut être tirée de ces décisions et qui est conforme à ce qui a été présenté plus haut est que: la conséquence de la reconnaissance de l'état de nécessité, peut être soit l'exclusion de l'illicéité du non-remboursement de la dette par

---

[84] *Ibid.* à la p. 63. Le tribunal se réfère à l'article 25 du projet de la Commission du droit international (CDI) afin de confirmer ses conclusions sur l'applicabilité de la règle primaire. *Ibid.* à la p. 43.

[85] *Ibid.,* aux pp. 63 et 43, voir la note 155.

l'état débiteur, soit une atténuation de l'obligation de remboursement de l'État débiteur. Dans le premier cas, l'État débiteur est
déchargé de l'obligation de remboursement, tandis que dans le
deuxième cas, il est tenu à un remboursement partiel. Ces arbitra-
ges seront cependant suivis par d'autres.[86]

Lorsque le remboursement d'une dette qu'un État a contracté
par traité lui impose des contraintes économiques qui menacent la
mise en œuvre de droits économiques prioritaires, il peut être soutenu qu'un tel contexte constitue une crise sévère pour cet État.
L'état de nécessité constitue alors le fondement de l'exercice de la
conditionnalité universelle par l'État débiteur, afin de négocier le
réaménagement de la dette avec l'État ou l'organisation internationale créancier. Dans l'hypothèse où l'État créancier et l'État débiteur
ne pourraient s'entendre sur des modalités à cet effet, l'État débiteur
serait en droit de refuser le remboursement de la dette.

LE DROIT À LA CONDITIONNALITÉ UNIVERSELLE: LE DROIT DU PLUS
FAIBLE À LA RÉVISION DE LA PRATIQUE DE LA CONDITIONNALITÉ DE
DEUXIÈME NIVEAU

Les droits de l'homme à caractère économique sont liés au droit à
la conditionnalité universelle comme il sera démontré en étudiant
le contexte de ce dernier. Nous exposerons, par la suite, les balises
de la pratique du droit à la conditionnalité universelle.

Le contexte du droit à la conditionnalité universelle

La mise en œuvre des droits économiques est en grande partie
tributaire des politiques adoptées par l'État sur la base de son domaine réservé. Le droit à la conditionnalité universelle concourt
directement à la mise en œuvre des droits économiques en assurant
la préservation du domaine réservé de l'État. Il stimule l'ajustement
des droits du créancier par rapport à ceux du débiteur. Son fondement réside dans l'obligation de réaliser les droits de l'homme à
caractère économique.

Un droit voué à la préservation du domaine réservé de l'État

Le concept de souveraineté permet à l'État d'adopter le comportement international qu'il désire avec la seule limitation de l'im-
médiateté normative qui l'oblige à se soumettre "directement,

---

[86] *Ibid.*, à la p. 63.

immédiatement, au droit international,"[87] notamment à respecter les droits de l'homme et plus particulièrement les droits de l'homme à caractère économique. Ces derniers font partie, en effet, des "préoccupations légitimes de la communauté internationale,"[88] mais ne sont pas pour autant exclus du domaine réservé de l'État. Leur mise en œuvre dépend de l'organisation du système économique et social de l'État et ce dernier est tout à fait justifié, et serait même obligé, d'intervenir dans l'hypothèse où l'action des institutions financières multilatérales contrecarre la réalisation des droits de l'homme à caractère économique.[89]

L'État doit, afin de préserver l'autonomie qui lui est nécessaire pour la mise en œuvre des droits économiques dans les limites de son domaine réservé, utiliser la conditionnalité universelle. Cette dernière est requise afin d'obliger les États et les institutions financières multilatérales créancières à rendre compatibles leurs exigences économiques avec les politiques de l'État débiteur visant l'application des droits économiques. L'État débiteur impose ainsi à l'État ou à l'institution financière multilatérale créancière, les conséquences de l'appariement ou de l'association qu'il opère entre le respect de droits économiques prévus dans les conventions auxquelles il est signataire, et sa collaboration avec eux afin de résoudre les défis contemporains de la société internationale.

Le comportement de l'État débiteur est autorisé par la liberté d'action[90] dont il jouit et fait partie de son domaine réservé.[91] L'État définit ainsi les contours de son comportement socio-économique dans le contexte de la mondialisation en précisant, du même coup, le contenu de son domaine réservé qui "dépend des nécessités de la vie internationale, telles qu'elles s'expriment par le développement du droit international positif."[92] Les programmes de politiques

---

87 Nguyen *et al.*, supra note 2 à la p. 425 (tel que de respecter les règles du *jus cogens* et les ententes internationales qu'il a conclues avec d'autres États).

88 D. Carreau, *Droit international*, 7e éd., no 1, Paris, Pedone, 2001, à la p. 374.

89 *Ibid.* L'organisation économique et sociale de l'État échapperait à son domaine réservé, compte tenu de l'"ingérence" des institutions financières multilatérales dans ce domaine.

90 Nguyen *et al.*, *supra* note 2 aux pp. 430 et suiv.

91 Consacré par l'art. 2, para. 7 de la Charte des Nations Unies. Consulter à ce sujet Arangio-Ruiz, *supra* note 60.

92 *Ibid.* à la p. 372. L'auteur appuie son commentaire sur la décision *Affaire des décrets de nationalité en Tunisie et au Maroc (Tunisie/Maroc)* (1923) C.P.J.I., no. 4, 7 février.

économiques, imposés par les institutions financières multilatérales et qui nuisent à l'application des droits économiques, portent atteinte au domaine réservé de l'État puisqu'ils lui imposent un comportement qui contrecarre bien souvent sa stratégie de mise en application des droits de l'homme ou limite les choix de politiques qu'il voudrait adopter à ce niveau.[93]

Un droit favorisant l'ajustement des droits du créancier par rapport à ceux du débiteur

Lors des négociations de toute entente économique qui lie un pays développé à un pays en développement, il peut être soutenu que le droit du créancier reçoit un traitement plus avantageux que celui du débiteur. Le droit du créancier est mieux protégé que celui du débiteur, puisqu'il est défendu par la partie dont le poids dans la négociation est le plus important. La mise en œuvre de la conditionnalité universelle permet à l'État débiteur de bonifier son pouvoir de négociation et, par conséquent, de préserver l'intégrité de ses droits.

La conditionnalité universelle doit être distinguée de la situation où l'État débiteur brandit le spectre de ne pas respecter l'intégralité d'une entente à caractère économique puisque, à son avis, cette dernière menace la mise en application de droits économiques. Une telle situation constitue une conditionnalité de deuxième niveau. Bien que l'objectif de cette dernière soit toutefois le même que celui de la conditionnalité universelle, c'est-à-dire de favoriser la réalisation des droits économiques, le résultat de la mise en œuvre de la conditionnalité de deuxième niveau, dans une situation de ce type, diffère de celui de la conditionnalité universelle. La mise en œuvre de la conditionnalité de deuxième niveau est, en effet, l'annihilation totale ou partielle du droit du créancier sur la base de l'intérêt du débiteur, tandis que la conditionnalité universelle vise le rééquilibrage de droits: le droit du créancier à être remboursé de la dette qu'il détient à l'égard du débiteur et le droit du débiteur de pourvoir à la réalisation de droits économiques. La conditionnalité universelle permet de mieux situer les droits des parties créancières et débitrices l'une par rapport à l'autre, tandis que la conditionnalité de deuxième niveau est susceptible de créer une confusion quant à la portée des droits.

La conditionnalité universelle autorise les parties à procéder à l'évaluation des droits qu'ils défendent dans un esprit de conciliation

---

[93] *Cf.*, *supra* note 12.

de ceux-ci. La conditionnalité de deuxième niveau, bien qu'elle autorise la conciliation des droits défendus par les parties, s'exerce, bien souvent, dans un esprit de confrontation. Le droit à conditionnalité universelle promeut, en bout de ligne, la réalisation des droits économiques et la réalisation de l'entente économique. La conditionnalité de deuxième niveau favorise, avant tout, la réalisation des droits économiques au détriment de la réalisation de l'entente économique.

La conditionnalité de troisième niveau ne modifie donc pas le droit du créancier au remboursement de la dette; elle ne fait que changer des modalités. La conditionnalité de deuxième niveau définit, jusqu'à un certain point, un nouveau droit au remboursement. Le résultat de la négociation peut amener la caducité du remboursement de la totalité ou d'une partie de la dette. La conditionnalité universelle a comme objectif de permettre une nouvelle négociation de l'entente où les droits des parties seront pris en considération d'une manière plus équitable. La conditionnalité de deuxième niveau revêt un caractère d'unilatéralité en faveur du débiteur, car le créancier n'a pas vraiment de pouvoir de négociation.

La conditionnalité de deuxième niveau et la conditionnalité universelle sont autonomes, en ce sens qu'elles peuvent être utilisées séparément. Néanmoins, elles peuvent être utilisées conjointement et dans ce cas, elles accroissent le pouvoir de négociation de l'État débiteur en faveur de la réalisation des droits économiques.

Un droit fondé sur l'obligation de réalisation des droits économiques

Les droits à un environnement sain, à la paix ou au développement constituent des droits de la troisième génération ou des droits de solidarité. Ils ont comme objectif la création d'un contexte universel propice au mieux être de la collectivité. Leur mise en œuvre repose sur la coopération internationale. Le droit à la conditionnalité universelle serait un droit inclus dans cette catégorie. Il constituerait, en quelque sorte, un droit de nature procédurale dont l'application permettrait la réalisation des droits prioritaires de la personne à caractère économique.

Le droit à la conditionnalité universelle permettrait d'atteindre l'ordre sur le plan social et sur le plan international auquel l'article 28 (Déclaration universelle des droits de l'homme) réfère pour la mise en œuvre des droits et libertés énoncés dans la Déclaration. Le droit à la conditionnalité universelle constituerait, ainsi, un droit tout autant individuel que collectif, tout comme le droit au

développement. Le droit à la conditionnalité universelle a une filiation morale qui ne soulève aucun doute.

Puisque la composante essentielle du droit à la conditionnalité
universelle est le développement social des États — car il vise l'application de droits prioritaires de la personne à caractère économique — il prendrait ancrage dans les mêmes concepts que ceux dont
est issu le droit au développement, c'est-à-dire, le *jus cogens* et la
solidarité internationale.[94] Il aurait aussi comme fondement les
sources du droit dont il ferait la promotion. Ainsi, il serait en filiation avec le droit à la vie,[95] dans un processus visant à rendre les
droits économiques effectifs.[96]

La conditionnalité universelle constitue tout autant un droit
qu'une obligation pour les pays en développement. Ils auraient le
devoir de mettre en œuvre ce droit de nature procédurale afin
d'assurer la réalisation des droits économiques. L'obligation des
États prendrait sa source dans les moyens de faire la promotion des
droits de l'homme. Les obligations de coopération et de solidarité
qui incombent à tous les États à ce niveau agissent comme le pivot
de l'intervention des États.[97] Elles découlent des articles suivants:
55 et 56 de la Charte des Nations-Unies; 28 de la Déclaration universelle des droits de l'homme et 2 du Pacte international relatif
aux droits économiques, sociaux et culturels.

Selon le paragraphe 55(c) et l'article 56 de la Charte, les membres
"s'engagent à agir, tant conjointement que séparément ... en vue
d'assurer le respect universel et effectif des droits de l'homme."
L'article 28 de la *Déclaration*, proclame qu'un ordre international
doit être promu afin que les droits et libertés énoncés dans la présente Déclaration puissent y trouver plein effet. L'article 2 du *Pacte*

94 Sur les sources du droit au développement, consulter Bedjaoui, *supra* note 22
   aux pp. 1255 et suiv.

95 Explicitement consacré par la Déclaration universelle des droits de l'homme,
   supra note 14, art. 3 et le Pacte international relatif aux droits civils et politiques,
   supra note 14 à la p. 71, para. 6(1) et implicitement par la Charte des Nations-
   Unies, *supra* note 14. Pour certains, tous les droits de la troisième génération
   découleraient du droit à la vie. Comme le rapporte K. Baslar: "*all the so-called
   third generation of human rights should take their cue from imperative norm of the right
   to life.*" K. Baslar, *The Concept of the Common Heritage of Mankind in International
   Law*, La Haye, Martinus Nijhoff, 1998, à la p. 322.

96 Il est admis que le droit à la nourriture a comme fondement le droit à la vie,
   tout comme le droit au développement.

97 Consulter P.-F. Mercure, "L'obligation alimentaire des pays en développement
   à l'égard de leur population: la normativité du mécanisme de développement
   durable," *A.C.D.I.* (2002), aux pp. 107–12.

est particulièrement important. Il dispose, que par la coopération internationale, les États doivent "assurer progressivement le plein exercice des droits reconnus dans le présent Pacte *par tous les moyens appropriés.*" La conditionnalité universelle constitue sans contredit l'un de ces moyens. Les États auraient ainsi l'obligation de l'utiliser afin d'assurer la réalisation des droits économiques.

Le même exercice d'interprétation de la Déclaration sur le droit au développement indique aussi clairement, l'obligation d'agir des États en ce domaine: "Les États doivent prendre des mesures pour éliminer les obstacles au développement résultant du non respect ... des droits économiques, sociaux et culturels."[98] La Charte africaine des droits de l'homme et des peuples crée un devoir de solidarité entre les membres en édictant que "le principe de solidarité et de relations amicales ... est applicable aux rapports entre les États."[99] Les manquements aux devoirs de coopération et de solidarité imposés aux États par les conventions internationales mentionnées sont susceptibles d'engager leur responsabilité internationale.[100]

Il est nécessaire, à ce point, d'envisager l'encadrement de l'exercice du droit à la conditionnalité universelle afin que ce dernier soit conforme au droit international positif.

Les balises de l'exercice du droit à la conditionnalité universelle[101]

L'exercice du droit à la conditionnalité universelle répond à des conditions objectives et subjectives. Les premières concernent les ententes liant les États, tandis que les deuxièmes sont relatives au comportement de l'État qui invoque le droit.

Les conditions objectives: les ententes liant les États

Les acteurs de la mise en œuvre de la conditionnalité universelle, l'État débiteur et l'État créancier, doivent être liés conventionnellement par deux ententes. Il s'agit de la condition de l'existence de

---

[98] Déclaration sur le droit au développement, adoptée le 4 décembre 1986, AGNU Rés. 41/128, au para. 6 (3).

[99] Charte africaine des droits de l'homme et des peuples, adoptée à Nairobi le 27 juin 1981, entrée en vigueur le 21 octobre 1986. Texte dans *International Legal Materials*, vol. XXI, n° 1 (janvier 1982), aux pp. 58–68.

[100] L. André et J. Dutry, "La responsabilité internationale des États pour les situations d'extrême pauvreté," *R.B.D.I.* 58 (1999), aux pp. 62 et suiv.

[101] Nous approfondissons dans cette section les conditions de la mise en œuvre du droit à la conditionnalité universelle telles que présentées dans Mercure, *supra* note 6 aux pp. 808–12.

deux conventions. Deux autres conditions sont requises. La condition de l'attribution des conséquences de la conditionnalité à une entente économique et celle à l'effet que le droit économique protégé doit être fondamental.

(a) L'existence de deux conventions

Le droit à la conditionnalité universelle peut-être invoqué par un État lorsque ce dernier considère que la mise en œuvre d'une entente à caractère économique à laquelle il participe aura des conséquences telles sur ses finances publiques qu'elle empêchera l'application de dispositions relatives à un droit de la personne à caractère économique prévu dans une autre entente à laquelle il participe. L'État est donc lié par deux ententes: l'une qui possède un caractère économique dans laquelle il est débiteur à l'égard d'un sujet de droit extérieur à l'entente, et l'autre qui est relative à des droits économiques dans laquelle il est débiteur à l'égard de l'un de ses sujets de droit. Les mesures de mise en œuvre de celles-ci s'avèrent être incompatibles ou, à tout le moins, difficilement réconciliables.

(b) L'attribution des conséquences de la conditionnalité à une entente économique

Les difficultés économiques auxquelles est confronté l'État débiteur doivent résulter de la mise en œuvre de la conditionnalité de deuxième niveau qui lui est imposée par une organisation internationale régionale ou universelle, par un ou des États ou par des regroupements de ces entités. On peut penser à des programmes de politiques économiques de la BM et du FMI qui contrecarraient ou simplement diminueraient la capacité de l'État de rendre effectif des droits prioritaires à caractère économique. Ces conditions de deuxième niveau doivent découler de mesures économiques prises afin de donner effet aux dispositions d'une entente à laquelle participe l'État. Ce dernier doit pouvoir attribuer à une entente de nature économique au moins, le contexte économique à l'origine des difficultés qu'il rencontre afin de rendre effectif le droit prioritaire de la personne à caractère économique.

(c) Un droit économique fondamental

Le droit atteint doit être prévu dans le Pacte international relatif aux droits économiques, sociaux et culturels ou dans toute autre entente universelle ou régionale prévoyant des dispositions analogues à celles prévues dans le Pacte. Il doit, en effet, s'agir d'un droit à caractère économique protégé par la communauté internationale et l'État qui entend exercer son droit à la conditionnalité universelle et doit être lié par le Pacte ou l'entente universelle ou régionale.

Puisque l'application de la conditionnalité universelle constitue une mesure exceptionnelle pour une situation extrême, les droits protégés doivent être des droits économiques prioritaires; c'est-à-dire les droits assimilables, en quelque sorte, à ceux du noyau dur des droits économiques. Le droit protégé doit donc être un droit fondamental ou prioritaire à caractère économique. Ainsi, l'atteinte au droit de toute personne de former avec d'autres des syndicats et de s'affilier au syndicat de son choix[102] et celle de jouir de conditions de travail justes et favorables[103] ne justifieraient pas, à notre avis, la mise en application du droit à la conditionnalité universelle. Les droits prévus à l'article 15 du Pacte (participer à la vie culturelle; bénéficier du progrès scientifique et de ses applications; bénéficier de la protection des intérêts moraux et matériels qui découlent de toute production scientifique, littéraire ou artistique), seraient dans la même situation.

Les conditions subjectives: le comportement de l'État qui invoque le droit

L'État qui invoque le droit à la conditionnalité universelle doit avoir agi de bonne foi, c'est-à-dire que son comportement ne doit pas avoir été à l'origine du contexte économique précaire dans lequel il se trouve. Il s'agit de l'application de la théorie des mains propres. Il ne doit pas non plus chercher à se libérer entièrement de l'obligation contractée si cela n'est pas essentiel à la réalisation des droits économiques. Il s'agit de la condition de l'obligation de réalisation de l'entente économique par l'État débiteur.

(a) La théorie des mains propres

Le fait que l'État ait mis en œuvre les dispositions qui intègrent les conditions économiques prévues dans la conditionnalité de deuxième niveau dans son ordre juridique interne, ne constitue évidemment pas une cause rédhibitoire à l'exercice du droit à la conditionnalité

---

[102] Art. 8(1) a) du Pacte, *supra* note 4.

[103] *Ibid.* art. 7.

universelle. La conditionnalité universelle constitue précisément une réponse à l'exercice de la conditionnalité de deuxième niveau par la partie créancière. Il est présumé, dans cette dernière situation, que les conditions économiques de l'entente sont imposées à l'État débiteur. Le pouvoir de négociation de ce dernier est lié, c'est-à-dire n'est pas libre et ses décisions économiques sont sujettes à un questionnement quant à leur acceptation véritable par ses dirigeants. Cette présomption pourrait être renversée par une démonstration de la partie adverse que les conditions de l'entente ont été librement consenties par l'État débiteur, c'est-à-dire que ce dernier a considéré que les conditions de deuxième niveau n'auraient raisonnablement aucune conséquence sur le niveau de développement économique de l'État et conséquemment sur les droits économiques.

La démonstration par l'État créancier du consentement libre de l'État débiteur aux conditions de deuxième niveau est évidemment difficile à faire, car le premier doit prouver que le deuxième a été en mesure d'anticiper que les conditions économiques imposées par la conditionnalité de deuxième niveau nuiraient à l'application de dispositions requises pour donner effet à un droit économique. Si l'État créancier démontre que l'État débiteur était raisonnablement en mesure d'anticiper de telles conséquences, cela revient à dire, à toutes fins utiles, qu'il a contribué à créer la situation problématique dans laquelle il se trouve. L'État a pris de mauvaises décisions ou s'est abstenu de prendre les décisions requises afin d'empêcher qu'il se retrouve dans une situation problématique. Dans les deux cas, il est fautif; dans un de ceux-ci par action et dans l'autre par omission. Il a contribué à son propre malheur.

En droit de la responsabilité, tant dans le droit interne des États, qu'en droit international, un tel comportement du sujet de droit, constitue un facteur qui l'empêche d'invoquer l'état de nécessité. Cette condition, qui est souvent traduite par la doctrine des mains propres, constitue un principe général de droit en matière de responsabilité, qui a d'ailleurs été codifié à l'article 25 du Projet de la CDI. Cette dernière indique, dans son rapport de 2001, que l'État ne peut invoquer l'État de nécessité si "sa contribution à la survenance de la situation de nécessité est substantielle et non pas simplement accessoire ou secondaire."[104]

---

[104] *Cf., Rapport de la CDI*, A/56/10, 2001, à la p. 208. Sur cet aspect, consulter Christakis, *supra* note 59 à la p. 29.

(b) L'obligation de réalisation de l'entente économique par l'État débiteur

L'État débiteur ne doit pas demander l'annulation de l'obligation économique et financière, ce qui équivaudrait à du chantage. Il doit demander, de bonne foi, l'assouplissement ou le réaménagement de l'obligation. Un parallèle peut être fait entre cette obligation de l'État débiteur et celle qui existe lorsque l'état de nécessité est invoqué par un État en matière de responsabilité. L'état de nécessité constituerait une circonstance atténuant l'obligation de réparer et non une circonstance excluant l'illicéité.[105] Il peut être cité afin d'illustrer cette affirmation l'affaire *Booker c. Guyana*[106] dans laquelle, suite à une nationalisation d'entreprise, la Guyane demandait une renégociation de l'indemnité qu'elle avait versé à l'entreprise, c'est-à-dire une atténuation des conséquences des mesures prises et non pas d'être considéré comme non responsable du non paiement de l'indemnité.

CONCLUSION

Le travail que nous avons accompli devrait faire l'objet d'études plus approfondies relativement à trois aspects. Le premier, qui est fondamental, consiste à déterminer dans quels domaines une pratique d'échange s'est développée entre les États et à identifier si cette dernière peut éventuellement être la base d'une règle coutumière. Il serait aussi important, indépendamment de toute pratique des États, de déterminer le plus exhaustivement possible, quelles sont les problématiques mondiales qui requièrent une collaboration Nord-Sud et qui sont susceptibles, par conséquent, d'ouvrir la porte à la mise en branle de la notion de conditionnalité universelle. La liste est bien plus longue que les quelques situations qui ont été mentionnées dans notre étude.

Le deuxième aspect concerne la détermination plus précise, d'une part, des conditions juridiques afin de pouvoir invoquer la notion de conditionnalité universelle et d'autre part, des conséquences qui découlent du déclenchement d'un processus d'échange qui intègre la notion. Le premier volet consiste à faire une réflexion approfondie sur les balises de la pratique du droit à la conditionnalité universelle, en portant une attention particulière à la question

---

[105] *Ibid.* aux pp. 45–63.

[106] L'arbitrage a été réglé hors cours le 11 octobre 2003; voir la décision n⁰ 85, disponible en ligne à: <http://icsid.worldbank.org/ICSID/FrontServlet? requestType=GenCaseDtlsRH&actionVal=ListConcluded>.

de l'application de la théorie des mains propres et à celle du seuil requis pour que le processus d'échange intégrant la notion de conditionnalité universelle puisse être déclenché. Dans ce dernier cas, il importe de développer des critères afin que l'État puisse justifier le non-respect de l'entente économique sur la base des obligations qu'il a envers sa population. La question de l'identification précise du type de droits économiques visés se pose alors: le spectre des droits économiques susceptibles de déclencher le processus de mise en application du droit à la conditionnalité universelle est-il aussi large que celui des droits économiques du Pacte international sur les droits économiques, sociaux et culturels ou est-il restreint à une catégorie de ceux-ci; par exemple, les droits économiques fondamentaux ou prioritaires tel qu'expliqué précédemment? Le deuxième volet concerne, notamment, la question des types d'assouplissements ou de réaménagements que l'État débiteur peut demander à son partenaire, compte tenu, que le droit à la conditionnalité universelle ne peut avoir comme conséquence de libérer totalement l'État de l'obligation à caractère économique.

Le troisième aspect concerne les modalités de la mise en œuvre effective de la notion de conditionnalité universelle selon la nature des protagonistes concernés, selon qu'ils agissent comme débiteurs ou créanciers; c'est-à-dire, les États, les regroupements de ceux-ci ou les organisations internationales. Pour ce qui est du regroupement d'États, il serait intéressant qu'une analyse ultérieure porte sur l'interaction entre un État et un groupe d'États dans les hypothèses où l'État agit comme débiteur et créancier, mais aussi sur l'interaction entre deux groupes d'États lorsque ces derniers sont les acteurs de l'échange. En ce qui concerne l'organisation internationale, il serait important d'identifier des critères juridiques afin de déterminer quel groupe d'intérêts représente les organisations internationales les plus susceptibles d'être concernées par l'exercice du droit à la conditionnalité universelle: les pays en développement ou les pays développés.

Le processus de la mondialisation doit s'accomplir d'une manière qui soit compatible avec la mise en œuvre effective des droits économiques dans les pays en développement. Cela constitue une condition péremptoire afin que les États puissent gérer sans heurts les défis contemporains auxquels ils sont confrontés, notamment la protection de l'environnement global. Les pays en développement, par exemple, n'accepteront pas de participer à la gestion de la crise des changements climatiques à moins que les pays développés et les organisations internationales contrôlées par eux acceptent de faire des concessions au niveau économique. La monnaie d'échange des pays en développement sera ainsi constituée de leur acceptation de collaborer à la réduction des gaz à effet de serre. Une telle situation rappelle le débat Nord-Sud de la Conférence de Stockholm en 1972, mais aussi le rapport *Notre avenir à tous* de la Commission mondiale sur l'environnement et le développement dans lequel fut formellement présenté pour la première fois le concept de développement durable.

La conciliation environnement–développement n'est pas achevée et la problématique des changements climatiques mettra à l'épreuve l'aptitude des États à intégrer la question des droits économiques dans son action globale. La notion de conditionnalité universelle peut jouer un rôle déterminant à cet égard. L'adaptation des institutions intra et interétatiques afin d'encadrer sa mise en œuvre ne devrait pas constituer une tâche trop ardue pour les États, puisque ces derniers interagissent déjà dans l'esprit de l'échange qui constitue la *realpolitik* depuis la naissance de l'État nation.

Summary

Rethinking the Notion of Conditionality in North-South Relations: Towards an Approach That Favours the Full Exercise of Developing Countries' Economic Rights

International conventions regulating economic matters are often shaped by the concerns of the stronger party to the agreement at the expense of the weaker party. This situation, which is one of the consequences of factual inequalities between states, results in a rigorous conditionality that is dictated to developing countries when they enter into debtor-creditor relationships with developed countries or international organizations. Such developing countries are then confronted with a dilemma: reimburse the incurred debt in accordance with the terms of the conditionality, thereby hindering the implementation of economic human rights, such as the rights to education, health, shelter, and food, among others, or give precedence to those rights over debt repayment obligations. Developing countries have invoked the "state of necessity" argument since the beginning of the twentieth century, but international decisions pertaining to these concerns show that this argumentation has met with only limited success.

The right to universal conditionality is rooted in the positive law of North-South financial transfers, which is one-sided, since it carries a conditionality that is prejudicial towards developing countries. However, the notion of

conditionality can also be a source of rights for developing countries, the implementation of which would have as its main objective the enactment of economic human rights, which have been hindered by the strict observance of the notion of conditionality in economic agreements. In this study of the notion of conditionality within the context of North-South relations, an attempt is made to demonstrate the existence of the right to universal conditionality, of which the prevailing doctrine has never taken account. Thus, the notion of conditionality is examined within a dual perspective. On the one hand, conditionality is a product of the economic conventions that bind debtors, yet, on the other, it also serves as the foundation for the rights of debtors relative to their creditors. In both cases, the debtors are developing countries, while the creditors are either developed countries or international organizations.

Sommaire

La notion de conditionnalité reconsidérée dans les relations Nord-Sud: une approche favorisant le plein exercice des droits économiques dans les pays en développement

Les conventions internationales à caractère économique sont souvent modelées sur les préoccupations de la partie la plus puissante à l'entente au détriment de la partie la plus faible. Cette situation, qui est l'une des conséquences de l'inégalité de faits entre les États, s'exprime par une conditionnalité rigoureuse imposée aux pays en développement lorsqu'ils s'engagent avec un pays développé ou une organisation internationale créanciers. Le pays en développement est alors confronté au dilemme de devoir rembourser la dette contractée conformément aux modalités de la conditionnalité, mettant en péril la mise en application de droits de la personne à caractère économique : droit à l'éducation, à la santé, au logement, à la nourriture, etc., ou de donner préséance à ces droits sur son obligation de remboursement de la créance. Les pays en développement ont avancé l'argument de l'état de nécessité, avec un succès limité, comme en témoignent les décisions internationales relatives à cette préoccupation des états qui remonte au début du 20e siècle.

Le droit à la conditionnalité universelle aurait comme fondement le droit positif des transferts financiers Nord-Sud, qui est inéquitable car il intègre une conditionnalité préjudiciable aux pays en développement. La notion de conditionnalité constituerait ainsi, la source d'un droit pour les pays en développement, dont l'application aurait comme objectif le rétablissement des droits de la personne à caractère économique qui ont été restreints par l'application stricte de la notion de conditionnalité dans l'entente écono-mique. C'est à travers l'étude de la notion de conditionnalité dans le contexte des relations Nord-Sud que cet article tente de démontrer l'exis-tence du droit à la conditionnalité universelle dont la doctrine n'a jamais fait état. La notion de conditionnalité est ainsi envisagée sous une double perspective: celle où elle origine de la convention économique qui lie le dé-biteur et le créancier et celle où elle sert de fondement à un droit du débiteur à l'égard du créancier. Dans les deux situations, le débiteur est un pays en développement et le créancier est un pays développé ou une organisation internationale.

The Future of the Law of Occupation

KRISTEN E. BOON

Introduction

The law of occupation has become the subject of great contemporary interest because of two prominent, although *sui generis*, situations: the long-term Israeli occupation of the Gaza Strip, the West Bank, and the Golan Heights, and the "transformative" occupation of Iraq. In both situations, the occupying powers have resisted the label of belligerent occupier and selectively applied the 1907 Hague Regulations and the 1949 Geneva Conventions to the territories in question.[1] In Iraq, a further level of complexity arose when the Security Council used its Chapter VII powers to finesse certain aspects of the law of occupation to address circumstances

Kristen E. Boon is an Associate Professor of Law at Seton Hall University School of Law. This piece was inspired by the author's forthcoming article "Obligations of the New Occupier: The Contours of a Jus Post Bellum" (2008) 31 Loy. L.A. Int'l & Comp. L. Rev. 101, which addresses the normative framework for a *jus post bellum*. The present article addresses specific legal challenges that confront the law of occupation and the evolving *jus post bellum*. Thanks to Cathy Adams, Lieutenant Colonel Al Goshi, Tristan Ferrero, Keith Morrill, Sylvain Vite, and David Wippman for their very helpful ideas and insights. I would also like to express my gratitude to Maja Basioli in the Seton Hall Law Library for her resourcefulness and support and to Jeremy Watson for his excellent research assistance.

1 Regulations Respecting the Laws and Customs of War on Land, annexed to Hague Convention Respecting the Laws and Customs of War on Land, 18 October 1907, 36 Stat. 2277, 187 C.T.S. 227 [Hague Regulations]; Geneva Convention I for the Amelioration of the Condition of the Wounded and Sick in Armed Forces in the Field, 12 August 1949, 75 U.N.T.S. 31; Geneva Convention II for the Amelioration of the Condition of Wounded, Sick and Shipwrecked Members of Armed Forces at Sea, 12 August 1949, 75 U.N.T.S. 85; Geneva Convention III Relative to the Treatment of Prisoners of War, 12 August 1949, 75 U.N.T.S. 135; Geneva Convention IV Relative to the Protection of Civilian Persons in Time of War, 12 August 1949, 75 U.N.T.S. 287 [Geneva Convention IV].

107

particular to that intervention, prompting a volley of inquiries into the future role of the Security Council in updating, amending, and administering the law of occupation. The unique circumstances of these occupations have sparked vigorous debate over the future of the law of occupation. Specifically, is the widely accepted, but largely unenforced, law of occupation capable of regulating transitions between conflict and peace in the twenty-first century? Changing military and technological capacities, the growing involvement of the United Nations in peace building, and the shifting motivations and security considerations informing decisions to intervene and withdraw from foreign territories are factors that were not foreseen when the law of occupation was codified.

Although judicial decisions interpreting the Hague Regulations and the fourth Geneva Convention Relative to the Protection of Civilian Persons in Time of War (Geneva Convention IV) are rare, some recent cases have advanced doctrinal issues behind the scenes of this larger debate about the relevance of occupation law. In 2005, for example, the International Court of Justice (ICJ) found in the *Case Concerning Armed Activities on the Territory of the Congo (Dem. Rep. Congo v. Uganda)* that Uganda was an occupying power in the Ituri region of the Congo, while raising the legal threshold for the application of the law of occupation ever so slightly.[2] In a highly contested advisory opinion issued in 2004 on the *Legal Consequences of the Construction of a Wall in the Occupied Palestinian Territory,* the ICJ reiterated that international human rights must be respected in times of occupation.[3] The Eritrea-Ethiopia Claims Commission determined that there had been a belligerent occupation along parts of the front between the two countries, and it found Eritrea liable for acts of physical abuse of civilians and destruction of property.[4]

---

2 *Case Concerning Armed Activities on the Territory of the Congo (Dem. Rep. Congo v. Uganda),* [2005] I.C.J. Rep. 1 [*Armed Activities*] (see discussion in text accompanying notes 44 and 45 later in this article).

3 *Legal Consequences of the Construction of a Wall in the Occupied Palestinian Territory,* [2004] I.C.J. Rep. 104 [*Construction of a Wall*] (acknowledging that the International Covenant on Civil and Political Rights (ICCPR), *infra* note 90, is applicable outside of a state's territory to acts of an occupying state committed in the exercise of its jurisdiction). See also *Legality of the Threat or Use of Nuclear Weapons, Advisory Opinion,* [1996] I.C.J. Rep. 226 [*Nuclear Weapons*] (announcing the court's opinion that the ICCPR's protections do not cease during wartime).

4 Eritrea-Ethiopia Claims Commission, *Partial Award (Central Front), Ethiopia's Claim 2,* [2004] 43 I.L.M 1275 at 128, <http://www.pca-cpa.org/upload/files/ET%20Partial%20Award(1).pdf> [*Ethiopia's Partial Award*].

The Commission for Reception, Truth and Reconciliation in Timor-Leste similarly documented the effects of the Indonesian occupation of East Timor, noting the extensive militarization of the East Timorese society and the implementation of governmental bodies by Indonesia.[5] Moreover, discrete questions of occupation law have arisen before the International Criminal Tribunal for the Former Yugoslavia (ICTY). In the *P. v. Naletilic & Martinovic* case, for example, the trial chamber considered the factual circumstances required to trigger occupation law at length and determined that some instances of belligerent occupation had occurred in the Former Yugoslavia.[6] Russia's 2008 intervention in South Ossetia is widely considered to constitute an occupation of Georgia, although a case filed before the ICJ in Georgia only alleges breach of the International Convention on the Elimination of All Forms of Racial Discrimination.[7] Reaching further back into history, the practical import of this body of law is illustrated by numerous examples of occupation in the last century alone, including, but not limited to, the occupations of northern Cyprus, Namibia, the Dodecanese Islands, and the Axis occupations of territories in Europe, Asia, and North Africa generally.[8]

This article examines recent developments in the notoriously open-textured law of occupation that have arisen as it has been variously ignored, invoked, challenged, examined, and ultimately reformed through practice. In particular, I discuss the triggers for beginning and ending an occupation, including recent jurisprudence on the "effective control" test. I examine who can be an occupier,

---

[5] Commission for Reception, Truth, and Reconciliation in East Timor, *Chega! The Report of the Commission for Reception, Truth, and Reconciliation in Timor-Leste* (2005), East Timor and Indonesia Action Network, <http://www.etan.org/news/2006/cavr.htm> at pt. 4, paras. 159–72.

[6] *P. v. Naletilic & Martinovic*, IT-98–34-T (2003) at paras. 210–33 and 587) (WL) [*Naletilic*].

[7] International Convention on the Elimination of All Forms of Racial Discrimination, 21 December 1965, 660 U.N.T.S. 197. *Russian Federation: Legal Aspects of War in Georgia*, Law Library of Congress (2008–01474), <http://www.loc.gov/law/help/russian-georgia-war.php> at 14: "Russia's military deployed in the regions may be recognized as an occupational force and Russia may be forced to withdraw its armed forces from the territory of Georgia." See also *Application of the International Convention on the Elimination of All Forms of Racial Discrimination (Georgia v. Russian Federation)*, International Court of Justice, <http://www.icj-cij.org/docket/index.php?p1=3&p2=3&code=GR&case=140&k=4d>.

[8] Yoram Dinstein, *The International Law of Belligerent Occupation* (Cambridge: Cambridge University Press, 2009) at paras. 18–25; Eyal Benvenisti, *The International Law of Occupation* (The Hague: T.M.C. Asser Press, 2004) at 32–98.

the question of "multiple occupiers" under unified command, and the obligations of occupiers in the areas of legislation and institutional reform. I also consider the challenges of UN involvement in transitional situations, including the applicability of the law of occupation to UN forces and the role of the Security Council in adapting the law of occupation to new contingencies. I conclude with a discussion of the principle of "conservationism" and the relationship between the law of occupation and *jus post bellum* in order to provide an assessment of possible "futures" for the law of occupation. I argue that *jus post bellum* is needed to create a normative framework for all actors exercising governmental powers in transitional situations, eliminating accountability gaps that currently permeate occupation situations. A *jus post bellum* will raise questions of scope, application, and enforceability. Nonetheless, it is a critical frontier as the law of occupation confronts new situations with multilateral actors in weak institutional environments.

Sources of Dissatisfaction with the Law of Occupation

The law of occupation is codified in two principal instruments: the 1907 Hague Regulations and the 1949 Geneva Convention IV. It is uncontested that the Hague Regulations have entered into customary international law and that the Geneva Conventions complement, rather than abrogate, the Hague Regulations.[9] Acceptance of the Geneva Conventions (although not the Optional Protocols) is, at the time of writing, universal, with 194 state parties. It is thus a great tragedy that this wide support for the law of occupation is not reflected in practice — instead, the principles of occupation law are notoriously poorly enforced, which has led many to question their viability as a workable set of legal standards.[10] The reasons for their insufficient implementation are worth discussing as an initial matter since they contextualize the debate over the future of the law of occupation.

The majority of scholars and states today consider the law of occupation to be inadequate for the realities of modern occupation as well as with the demands of peace building and post-conflict

---

9 *Construction of a Wall, supra* note 3 at para. 89; *Ethiopia's Partial Award, supra* note 4 at para. 16; *Nuclear Weapons, supra* note 3 at para. 75.

10 Tristan Ferrero, "Enforcement of Occupation Law in Domestic Courts: Issues and Opportunities" (2008) 41 Israel L. Rev. 331 at 332, where he states that "[o]ne can only be struck by the gap existing between the high degree of elaboration of IHL norms and the high degree of their formal acceptance by the community of states on the one hand and their actual disrespect in the field on the other."

reconstruction by analogy.[11] The reasons for this dissatisfaction are manifold. First, the Hague Regulations and the Geneva Conventions do not contain any internal review, reporting, or accountability mechanisms. Article 1 of Geneva Convention IV requires that all "High Contracting Parties undertake to respect and to ensure respect for the present Convention in all circumstances."[12] Commentaries from the International Committee of the Red Cross (ICRC) indicate the special importance of a state's obligations *vis-à-vis* itself and, at the same time, *vis-à-vis* others:

[B]]y undertaking at the very outset to respect the clauses of the Convention, the Contracting Parties drew attention to the special character of that instrument. It is not an engagement concluded on a basis of reciprocity, binding each party to the contract only in so far as the other party observes its obligations. It is rather a series of unilateral engagements solemnly contracted before the world as represented by the other Contracting Parties.[13]

The Geneva Conventions are limited, however, by the absence of institutional enforcement mechanisms.[14] Breaches of the law of belligerent occupation are largely questions of state responsibility that are difficult to enforce due to the limited jurisdiction of international courts and tribunals.[15] Moreover, the convention does not create an individual right of action for persons claiming breach of the

---

[11] See, e.g., Grant T. Harris, "The Era of Multilateral Occupation" (2006) 24 Berkeley J. Int'l L. 1 at 9, where he states that "[t]he international law of occupation has become essentially irrelevant as a force that compels action by occupying powers. Occupants rarely comply with the letter or spirit of that body of law. As a result, the law of occupation's legal authority and status are uncertain." Carsten Stahn, "Jus Ad Bellum, Jus In Bello ... Jus Post Bellum? — Rethinking the Conception of the Law of Armed Forces" (2006) 17 E.J.I.L. 921 at 928: "The norms of international humanitarian law are therefore only to a limited extent relevant to the broader process of building peace after conflict." Brett H. McGurk, "Revisiting the Law of National-Building: Iraq in Transition" (2004–5) 45 Va. J. Int'l L. 451 at 453.

[12] Geneva Convention IV, *supra* note 1; Benvenisti, *supra* note 8 at 4.

[13] International Committee of the Red Cross, Respect for the Convention Commentary to Article 1 of the Convention (IV) relative to the Protection of Civilian Persons in Time of War International Humanitarian Law Treaties and Documents, <http://www.icrc.org/ihl.nsf/COM/380–600004?OpenDocument>.

[14] The lack of enforcement mechanisms is a general problem in international law, although it is particularly pronounced with regard to the use of force and the law of occupation.

[15] Ferrero, *supra* note 10 at 335.

provisions on belligerent occupation. Article 9 of Geneva Convention IV references a "protecting power" institution, which was inherited from the 1929 Convention Relative to the Treatment of Prisoners of War.[16] In theory, this power involves the appointment of a neutral third state that will "safeguard the interests of the Parties to the conflict."[17] In practice, however, it is the ICRC who notifies states of their obligations under the law of occupation. Occupiers have thus engaged in what Eyal Benvenisti calls a "pattern of denial" about the applicability of occupation law.[18] Most occupiers do not acknowledge that they are bound, whether because they are interested in permanent control of the territory, because the status of the territory is disputed, or because they wish to avoid the considerable burdens and liabilities created by Geneva Convention IV. Enforcement of international humanitarian law has, in the main, been limited to individual criminal liability through domestic criminal proceedings or international criminal courts such as the International Criminal Court, International Criminal Tribunal for Rwanda, and the ICTY.[19]

A second reason why the law of occupation is criticized is that it creates somewhat unrealistic burdens on occupying powers. Under Article 55 of Geneva Convention IV, the occupying power is required "[t]o the fullest extent of the means available to it ... of ensuring the food and medical supplies of the population; it should, in particular, bring in the necessary foodstuffs, medical stores and other articles if the resources of the occupied territory are inadequate." Article 56 similarly provides that the occupying power has "the duty of ensuring and maintaining, with the cooperation of national and

---

16 Convention Relative to the Treatment of Prisoners of War, 27 July 1929, 75 U.N.T.S. 135, 6 U.S.T. 3316. This term is defined in Article 2(2) of Protocol Additional to the Geneva Conventions of 12 August 1949, and Relating to the Protection of Victims of International Armed Conflicts, 8 June 1977, 1125 U.N.T.S. 3, 16 I.L.M. 1391 [Additional Protocol I], as "a neutral or other State not a Party to the conflict which has been designated by a Party to the conflict and accepted by the adverse Party and has agreed to carry out the functions assigned to a Protecting Power under the Convention and this Protocol." For the history of the provision, see *Commentary on the Geneva Conventions,* International Humanitarian Law – Treaties and Documents, <http://www.icrc.org/ihl.nsf/COM/380–600012?OpenDocument>.

17 Geneva Convention IV, *supra* note 1, Article 9; see also Ferrero, *supra* note 10 at 335 (who calls this institution "a dead letter").

18 Benvenisti, *supra* note 8 at 149.

19 Note however, that Ferraro considers regional courts to be a growing locus of enforcement. Ferraro, *supra* note 10.

local authorities, the medical and hospital establishments and services, public health and hygiene in the occupied territory ... and measures necessary to combat the spread of contagious diseases and epidemics." Articles 59 through 63 create further requirements with regard to relief consignments and oblige the occupying power, "if the whole or part of the population of an occupied territory is inadequately supplied ... to agree to relief schemes on behalf of the said population, and ... facilitate them by all the means at its disposal." The combined effect of these provisions is to place onerous obligations on an occupying power for ensuring the welfare of the occupied population. These obligations go above and beyond the legal duties owed to a state's own population. The result has been that *de facto* occupiers have repeatedly denied their status as occupiers to avoid being saddled with the burdens of full compliance.[20]

A third limitation of the law of occupation is that it applies to only a subset of contemporary war-to-peace transitions. In order for the full protections of Geneva Convention IV to apply, the conflict must be of an international character, the invader must be actually exercising authority, and the actors in question must be contracting parties to the Geneva Conventions.[21] The provisions on belligerent occupation in Geneva Convention IV, therefore, do not clearly apply to internal conflicts, to multilateral peacekeeping missions, or to the period after a formal occupation but before a stable peace.[22] Moreover, the Geneva Conventions are based on the assumption that occupations must follow the defeat of a functioning national government, whereas, in reality, occupations are increasingly taking

---

[20] K.A. Cavanaugh, "Rewriting Law: The Case of Israel and the Occupied Territory," in David Wippman and Matthew Evangelista, eds., *New Wars, New Laws? Applying the Laws of War in Twenty-First Century Conflicts* (Dobb's Ferry, NY: Transnational Publishers, 2005) at 227 and 239 (discussing Israel's objections to the applicability of the law of occupation in Gaza).

[21] The obligations in conflicts that are considered "not of an international character" are significantly less burdensome, as per common Article 3 of the Geneva Conventions. See, e.g., Geneva Convention IV, *supra* note 1, Article 3.

[22] As the UK *Manual on the Law of Armed Conflict* states: "[T]he application of the law of armed conflict to internal hostilities thus depends on a number of factors. In the first place, it does not apply at all unless an armed conflict exists. If an armed conflict exists, the provisions of Common Article 3 apply. Should the dissidents achieve a degree of success and exercise the necessary control over a part of the territory, the provisions of Additional Protocol II come into force. Finally, if the conflict is recognized as conflict falling within Additional Protocol I, Article 1 (4), it becomes subject to the Geneva Conventions and Protocol I." UK Ministry of Defence, *The Manual on the Law of Armed Conflict* (Oxford and New York: Oxford University Press, 2004) at para. 3.9.

place in territories that have weak domestic institutions to begin with. Occupiers, and, where the occupation has become multilateralized through UN involvement, the international community, have thus advocated and implemented transformative programs. As Steven Ratner writes, "this sort of cognitive dissonance — the disconnect between the ways international law and organizations have conceptualized occupations and territorial administrations and the ways these missions are actually carried out — is no longer tenable."[23]

When the Geneva Conventions were negotiated in 1949, the law of occupation was a forward-looking body of law. The conventions did not presume that war was being fought by sovereigns that had no interest in the domestic circumstances of an occupied territory.[24] Instead, they foresaw the deep involvement of civilian populations in contemporary conflicts and, as a result, were called a sort of bill of rights for occupied populations.[25] Nonetheless, there is little question today that the law of occupation is at a crossroads. Has the law of occupation been rendered irrelevant? Or should it be reinvigorated for its central purpose of short-term military occupations and joined by a new set of principles, a *jus post bellum*, which are applicable to war-to-peace transitions?[26] The issues examined in the following sections represent some of the ways this debate has unfolded.

EFFECTIVE CONTROL AS A TRIGGER FOR THE LAW OF OCCUPATION

When does an occupation begin? An occupation begins when "effective control" of a territory is established by a foreign entity. The test is derived from Hague Regulation 42, which provides: "[T]erritory is considered occupied when it is actually placed under the authority of the hostile army. The occupation extends only to the territory where such authority has been established and can be exercised."[27] In the 2004 case, *Construction of a Wall*, the ICJ confirmed

---

23 Steven R. Ratner, "Foreign Occupation and International Territorial Administration: The Challenges of Convergence" (2005) 16 E.J.I. L. 695 at 697.

24 Martti Koskenniemi, "Occupied Zone: A Zone of Reasonableness" (2008) 41 Isr. L. Rev. 13 at 31.

25 Benvenisti, *supra* note 8 at 105.

26 Adam Roberts, "Transformative Military Occupation" (2006) 100 A.J.I.L. 580 (arguing that the law of occupation can accommodate modern circumstances of occupation); see generally Carsten Stahn and Jann K. Kleffner, eds., *Jus Post Bellum: Towards a Law of Transition from Conflict to Peace* (The Hague: T.M.C. Asser Press, 2008); Kristen Boon, "Obligations of the New Occupier: The Contours of a *Jus Post Bellum*" (2008) 31 Loy. L.A. Int'l & Comp. L. Rev. 101.

27 Hague Regulations, *supra* note 1, Article 42.

the ongoing relevance of this provision, holding that "territory is considered occupied when it is actually placed under the authority of the hostile army, and the occupation extends only to the territory where such authority has been established and can be exercised."[28] A state of occupation is consequentially determined on the facts. It makes no difference whether an occupation has received Security Council approval or whether it is labelled an "invasion," "liberation," or "occupation," or whether it follows a formal declaration as such.[29]

Several observations follow this fact-based approach in the law of occupation. First, belligerent occupation is predicated upon a lack of consent — it requires a non-consensual and coercive presence by a hostile army.[30] A state of occupation will not exist where a foreign presence has been invited in or where a previously hostile force is later made welcome by consent of the occupied territory in question. For example, although Security Council Resolution 1546 proclaimed that the occupation of Iraq ended on 30 June 2004 upon the dissolution of the Coalition Provisional Authority (CPA), in the view of the ICRC it was the consent of the interim Iraqi government to the presence of multinational forces that ended the occupation.[31] By the same logic, a belligerent occupation will exist when a state withdraws its consent to the existence of foreign troops within its territory.[32] Second, occupation requires neither a showing of prior armed conflict nor a formal declaration of war.[33] Article 2(2) of the Geneva Convention IV provides that the convention "shall also apply to all cases of partial or total occupation of the territory *even if the said occupation meets with no armed resistance.*"[34] The presumption that occupation is part of a war to peace transition is therefore incorrect — although occupation often does follow

---

[28] *Construction of a Wall, supra* note 3 at 78 ("territory is considered occupied when it is actually placed under the authority of the hostile army, and the occupation extends only to the territory where such authority has been established and can be exercised.") See also Dinstein, *supra* note 8 at para. 96.

[29] Daniel Thurer, *Current Challenges to the Law of Occupation* (Official Statement, November 2005, at 2), International Committee of the Red Cross (ICRC), <http://www.icrc.org/web/eng/siteengo.nsf/html/occupation-statement-211105>.

[30] Dinstein, *supra* note 8 at para. 78.

[31] Security Counsel Resolution 1546, U.N.S.C. 4987 Mtg, UN Doc. S/RES/1546 (2004). See also Thurer, *supra* note 29 at 8–9.

[32] Dinstein, *supra* note 8 at para. 70.

[33] *Ibid.* at paras. 70–71.

[34] Geneva Convention IV, *supra* note 1, Article 2(2).

conflict, it need not as a matter of law. Third, the actual territory under effective control may advance and recede during fighting. There is no requirement that an entire territory be continuously occupied during a belligerent occupation or that the area occupied remain fixed. Instead, Article 2(2) of the convention clearly applies to situations of partial occupation.[35] In sum, the law of occupation places far greater weight on the factual context of an occupation than on the legal declarations of states. As the UK's *Manual on the Law of Armed Conflict* states, "the law will apply even if none of the parties recognize the existence of a state of war provided that an armed conflict is in fact in existence."[36]

The effective control test set out earlier has two elements. First, for a state of occupation to exist, the ousted government must be incapable of exercising its authority.[37] As Article 41 of the *Manuel des lois de la guerre sur terre*, which was adopted in 1880 by the Institut de Droit International, states:

Territory is regarded as occupied when, as the consequence of invasions by hostile forces, the State to which it belongs *has ceased, in fact, to exercise its authority therein,* and the invading State is alone in a position to maintain order there. The limits within which this state of affairs exists determine the extent and duration of the occupation.[38]

This first element clarifies the distinction between the mere invasion or passage of troops through an area and the displacement of indigenous authorities, which creates the situation for foreign troops to implement measures of stabilization.[39] Only the latter is sufficient to meet the effective control test. Moreover, in cases where the prior government was weak or has collapsed, this branch of the test will be easily met.

---

[35] See Geneva Convention IV, *supra* note 1, Article 2(2).

[36] UK Ministry of Defence, *supra* note 22 at para. 3.2.3.

[37] Eyal Benvenisti, *The Law on the Unilateral Termination of Occupation,* in Andreas Zimmermann and Thomas Giegerich, eds., *Veröffentlichungen des Walther-Schücking-Instituts für Internationales Recht an der Universität Kiel* (2009) at 2 [forthcoming].

[38] Institut de droit international, M. Gustave Moynier, rapporteur, *Manuel des lois de la guerre sur terre* (*Oxford Manual on Land Warfare*) (1880), <http://www.idi-iil. org/idiF/resolutionsF/1880_oxf_02_fr.pdf>, Article 41 [emphasis added].

[39] Compare Gerhard von Glahn, *The Occupation of Enemy Territory: A Commentary on the Law and Practice of Belligerent Occupation* (Minneapolis: University of Minnesota Press, 1957) at 28. See also Adam Roberts, *What Is a Military Occupation?* (1984) 55 Br. Y.B. Int'l L. 249 at 256.

The second element of the effective control test is not universally accepted. Must the occupying force actually exercise authority or does it simply need to have the potential to exercise its authority?[40] There are different schools of thought over whether effective control requires actual control or, simply, potential control by the occupying power. The *Manuel des lois de la guerre sur terre*, as can be seen earlier, requires that the state simply have the potential for effective control. This position has been advocated by the trial chamber of the ICTY in the *Nateltilic* case, which stated that "the occupying power must *be in position to substitute its own authority* for that of the occupied authorities, which must have been rendered incapable of functioning publicly."[41] Some national military manuals also adopt this approach,[42] as did Judge Pieter Kooijmans in his separate opinion in the *Armed Activities* case.[43]

[40] See generally Benvenisti, *supra* note 37; Marten Zwanenburg, "The Law of Occupation Revisited: The Beginning of an Occupation" (2007) 10 Y.B. Int'l Human. L. 99 at 110 (arguing that it is only necessary that the occupying power be in a position to substitute its own authority for that of the former government).

[41] *Naletilic, supra* note 6 at para. 217 [emphasis added] (the tribunal set out four additional guidelines in applying the effective control test, which also point towards the importance of prospective ability to control: "(ii) the enemy's forces have surrendered, been defeated or withdrawn. In this respect, battle areas may not be considered as occupied territory. However, sporadic local resistance, even successful, does not affect the reality of occupation. (iii) the occupying power has a sufficient force present, or the capacity to send troops within a reasonable time to make the authority of the occupying power felt. (iv) a temporary administration has been established over the territory. (v) The occupying power has issued and enforced directions to the civilian population").

[42] UK Ministry of Defence, *supra* note 22 at para. 11.3 ("the occupying power is in a position to substitute its own authority for that of the former government." Note however, that paragraph 11.3.2 states that "occupation does not take effect merely because the main forces of the country have been defeated but depends on whether authority is actually being exercised over the civilian population"). See also National Defense Canada, *Law of Armed Conflict at the Operational and Tactical Levels* Canada, 2001 (Ottawa: Office of the Judge Advocate General, 2001) at para. 1203(4) ("the invader should be in a position to substitute his own authority for that of the legitimate government"). However, see German military manual entitled *Humanitarian Law in Armed Conflicts — Manual* (Bonn: Federal Ministry of Defence of the Federal Republic of Germany, 1992) at VR II 3, stating that "the occupying power must be able to actually exercise its authority" and the United States, *The Law of Land Warfare*, Field Manual 27–10 (Washington, DC: Department of the Army, 1940) para. 356, requiring that "the invader has successfully substituted its own authority for that of the legitimate government in the territory invaded."

[43] *Armed Activities, supra* note 2 at paras. 45–50 (concluding that "[a]s long as Uganda maintained its hold on these locations, it remained the effective authority and thus the Occupying Power, until a new state of affairs developed").

The majority decision in the *Armed Activities* case adopts the stricter "actual control" test. In determining whether Ugandan forces were occupying the Ituri region of the Democratic Republic of the Congo (DRC), the court stated:

[T]he Court will need to satisfy itself that the Ugandan armed forces in the DRC were not only stationed in particular locations but also that they had substituted their own authority for that of the Congolese Government. In that event, any justification given by Uganda for its occupation would be of no relevance; nor would it be relevant whether or not Uganda had established a structured military administration of the territory occupied.[44]

The court was careful to note that the mere presence of Ugandan troops in the DRC did not create a situation of occupation: "[T]he territorial limits of any zone of occupation by Uganda in the DRC cannot be determined by simply drawing a line connecting the geographical locations where Ugandan troops were present."[45] If it had, the court stated that it would not matter whether or not the substituted authority rose to the level of a structured military administration, indicating that actual control does not require an elaborate administrative presence.[46] In his separate opinion, however, Kooijmans J. noted that the creation of a power vacuum in the region should be sufficient because the requirement for substitution of the occupant's authority for that of the territorial power had led to an unwarranted narrowing of the criteria of the law of belligerent occupation as these had been interpreted in customary law since 1907.[47]

As is evident, the apparent simplicity of the effective control test has been difficult to apply in practice. Effective control is a *conditio sine qua non* of occupation, yet it is extremely difficult to objectively determine how much control is "effective control."[48] The degree of effective control that is required is fact specific — it may depend on the terrain, the density of the population, and other considerations.[49] In addition, effective control of land is usually seen to be central to the doctrine, meaning that supremacy in air

---

[44] *Ibid.* at para. 173.

[45] *Ibid.* at para. 174.

[46] *Ibid.*

[47] *Ibid.* at para. 44.

[48] Dinstein, *supra* note 8 at para. 98; see also Benvenisti, *supra* note 37 at 4.

[49] Dinstein, *supra* note 8 at para. 98.

and on water will not be sufficient.[50] This issue has had very concrete implications since the decision by the Israeli government on 12 September 2005 to "disengage" from the Gaza Strip. Yuval Shany documents the raging debate over whether Israel should be considered an occupying power because it retains control over the Gaza airspace, maritime zones, and over peripheral borders and because it may send troops back into Gaza at any time.[51] Some posit that although Israel continues to exercise influence over Gaza, it falls short of the "effective control" required for belligerent occupation.[52] The Palestinian Negotiations Affairs Department has argued, in response, that Israel continues to occupy Gaza, substituting, in effect, its former direct means of control with a new and indirect means of control.[53]

The debate over potential versus effective control involves more than clarity of criteria — it also reflects the reality that occupying powers may avoid the final steps of establishing an administration in order to skirt the duties of occupation. Conversely, an occupier may withdraw from an occupation before the local administration has been established, leaving a situation of great instability in its wake. In either case, application of the more onerous "actual control" test may undermine the protections of individuals that lie at the heart of the Geneva Conventions.[54] The broader "potential" control test is supported by the theory of indirect control in belligerent occupation. An occupying power is not required to exercise its powers directly. Occupation can take place by proxy or by indirect control, where an occupying power operates through local rebel groups[55] or local officials to carry out its mandate.[56] This may include the creation of new administrative structures or the adoption of existing bureaucracies, as long as the occupying power exercises paramount authority.[57] The key inquiry is whether the occupying

---

[50] *Ibid.* at para. 100.

[51] Yuval Shany, "Binary Law Meets Complex Reality" (2008) 41 Isr. L. Rev. 68 at 71.

[52] *Ibid.* at 72.

[53] *Ibid.*

[54] See discussion later in this article on the protections of individuals after the cessation of an occupation.

[55] Zwanenburg, *supra* note 40 at 121 (discussing the implications in *Armed Activities, supra* note 2).

[56] See *Loizidou v. Turkey,* (1995) 310 E.C.H.R. (Ser. A) 453.

[57] Dinstein, *supra* note 8 at paras. 135–37.

power has exclusive governmental or administrative authority in the occupied territory, independently of the displaced sovereign.[58] Given the Geneva Convention's primary focus on the protection of civilian populations, and the poor enforcement record of the law of occupation as a general matter, any further weakening of the triggers for invoking the law of occupation will limit the relevance of the law of occupation going forward.

SINGLE VERSUS MULTIPLE OCCUPIERS

Typically, an occupying power is identified as the central government of the state that has carried out the invasion and subsequent occupation.[59] However, occupation is not a lone endeavour by definition. Territory may be partitioned with each occupier exercising effective control over a separate area.[60] Alternatively, territory may be occupied by more than one occupier if the effective control test set out earlier is met. For example, a multi-member coalition jointly occupied Iraq in 2003–4, where members of the Coalition of the Willing, including the United Kingdom, the United States, Romania, Poland, Spain, and Australia acted under unified command.[61] Although Security Council Resolution 1483 identified only the United States and the United Kingdom as occupiers, and not other members of the Coalition of the Willing, the ICRC took the position that the Security Council's resolution was not conclusive because the effective control test requires an assessment of the facts on the ground. As such, in determining which countries to remind of their obligations under the Geneva Conventions, the ICRC examined whether countries sent combat personnel and whether the national contingents in question had been assigned responsibility for exercising

58 Daphna Shraga, "Military Occupation and UN Transitional Administrations: The Analogy and Its Limitations," in Marcelo G. Kohen, ed., *Promoting Justice, Human Rights and Conflict Resolution through International Law* (Leiden: Brill, 2007) 479 at 481.

59 Roberts, *supra* note 26 at 585; although as Roberts notes in an earlier work, there have been examples of occupation by non-state entities. Roberts, *supra* note 39 at 292.

60 Dinstein, *supra* note 8 at para. 111 (discussing the joint occupation of Poland during the Second World War).

61 The application of this test would exclude Japan, however, who only sent non-governmental organizations. See discussion later in this article on the effect of the Security Council resolution that only referred to the United Kingdom and United States as occupying powers.

effective control over a portion of Iraqi territory.[62] If they had, the ICRC considered them occupiers, filling in the gaps in the Security Council's resolution.

In cases where internationally wrongful acts occur, multiple occupiers might be held liable under principles of joint and several liability for any "common adventures."[63] In Iraq, for example, questions have arisen as to whether the United Kingdom and the United States were liable for violations of international law, even if they were not directly involved in the acts.[64] According to this theory, victims would be able to recover their losses against either of the occupiers, on the grounds that particular elements of the damage were attributable to each.[65] Although judicial determination of such theories is unlikely to be tested before the ICJ, the potential for joint occupier responsibility in Iraq may well affect the willingness of states to participate in joint occupations in the future.[66]

Since responsibility for wrongful acts, whether for single or multiple occupiers, should give rise to reparations, at least in theory, some *de minimus* forms of accountability are implied in the law of occupation.[67] Governance in occupied territories is increasingly

---

[62] Thurer, *supra* note 29 at 5 (in total, the ICRC sent interventions to nine states in addition to the United States and the United Kingdom, which included states that the ICRC considered were exercising control over protected persons).

[63] Christine Chinkin, "The Continuing Occupation? Issues of Joint and Several Liability and Effective Control," in Phil Shiner and Andrew Williams, eds., *The Iraq War and International Law* (Portland: Hart Publishing, 2008) 161 at 176.

[64] Davd Scheffer, "Beyond Occupation Law" (2003) 97 A.J.I.L. 842 at 855 (listing actions that would be internationally wrongful if proven).

[65] *Ibid.* at 172.

[66] The UK *Manual on the Law of Armed Conflict, supra* note 22 at para. 11.3.3, simply encourages occupying powers to address such a situation by separate agreement: "in cases where two or more states jointly occupy territory (following a coalition military campaign, for example), it is desirable that there be an agreement between them setting out the relationship between the occupying powers."

[67] Richard Stewart, *Accountability, Participation, and the Problem of Disregard in Global Regulatory Governance* (2008) at 17 [draft on file with author] (describing legal accountability generally as "involve[ing] a legal proceeding initiated by a plaintiff account holder for the tribunal to determine whether a defendant accountee violated legal standards applicable to his conduct and thereby violated the account holder's rights. The tribunal may impose liability or other sanctions for unlawful or wrongful conduct by the accountee. Such actions may be brought against private actors, including trustees and other fiduciaries, or against public authorities and officials. There are specified procedures for rendering account, and the court uses established standards and gives reasons for its evaluation").

subject to international scrutiny, and, despite the difficult local conditions that often occur after conflict, authorities that do not respect the basic principles of transparency and accountability have been widely criticized and forced to reform their practices.[68] Thus, international administrations, even though unelected, are increasingly challenged in public fora to account for wrongful acts, as the outcry over the treatment of detainees in Abu Ghraib demonstrates. Indeed, one of the reasons why the concept of occupation has become increasingly complex is the demand for the respect of basic principles of self-rule and self-determination in all situations.[69] Enforcement and accountability go hand in hand, making the search for effective judicial remedies critical to the future of the law of occupation.[70] As a matter of legitimacy, if not legality, the accountability deficit in the law of occupation must be addressed in order for this body of law to retain its currency.[71]

THE OCCUPIER'S POWER TO LEGISLATE

A key presumption behind international humanitarian law is that belligerent occupation is temporary. During an occupation, the sovereignty of the occupied state becomes dormant, while the occupier exercises *de facto* ruling authority in recognition of the ongoing, but displaced, sovereignty of the state.[72] As Gerhard von Glahn explains, "the occupant does not in any way acquire sovereign rights in the occupied territory but exercises a temporary right of

---

[68] Simon Chesterman, *You the People: The United Nations, Transitional Administrations, and State Building* (Oxford: Oxford University Press, 2004) at 143.

[69] Benvenisti, *supra* note 8 at 189.

[70] Ferrero, *supra* note 10 at 355 (advocating the use of third state courts to enforce the law of occupation).

[71] The ILC's draft Articles on State Responsibility and the Responsibility of International Organizations demonstrate the developing legal bases for holding power holders to account in transitional situations where a breach of an international obligation has occured. See, e.g., *Report of the United Nations Secretary General*, UN Doc. A/51/389 (1996) 4, para. 6: "[T]he principle of State responsibily — widely accepted to be applicable to international organizations — that damage caused in breach of an international obligation and which is attributable to the State (or to the Organization) entails the international responsibility of the State (or of the Organization)."

[72] Dinstein, *supra* note 8 at para. 113; Shraga, *supra* note 58 at 481. See also UK Ministry of Defence, *supra* note 22 at 11.9 ("during the occupation, the sovereignty of the occupied state does not pass to the occupying power. It is suspended").

administration on a trustee basis until such time as the final disposition of the occupied territory is determined."[73] As such, it is generally accepted that occupants may not make fundamental or irreversible changes to the fabric of society.[74] Moreover, an occupying power may not apply their domestic laws to the area in question.[75]

One of the most hotly debated provisions of the law of occupation in recent times is the scope of an occupier's legislative powers, given the transformative occupation of Iraq. Although the United States and the United Kingdom reluctantly recognized their status as occupying powers in Iraq, they embarked on an aggressive campaign to reform domestic laws and institutions.[76] During the CPA's fourteen months in existence, it enacted twelve regulations, one hundred orders, and issued seventeen explanatory memoranda on subjects ranging from domestic criminal law to tax reform.[77] Economic development was a clear priority for the CPA, as evidenced by the multitude of reforms targeting the economy, which included legal changes, the direct involvement of the World Bank and the International Monetary Fund (IMF) in the reconstruction effort, and the improvement of infrastructure and the management of natural resources in Iraq.[78] Institutional changes were vast as well. The process of "de-Ba'athification" of Iraqi society involved the elimination of party structures and government ministries that were

---

[73] von Glahn, *supra* note 39 at 31.

[74] See also National Defense Canada, *supra* note 42 at para. 1205 ("[g]enerally speaking, the occupant is not entitled to alter the existing form of government, to upset the constitution and domestic laws of the occupied territory, or to set aside the rights of the inhabitants").

[75] von Glahn, *supra* note 39 at 94 ("the occupant cannot apply his own domestic laws to the occupied territory until proper title has been secured to the area in question").

[76] Letter dated 8 May 2003 from the Permanent Representatives of the United Kingdom of Great Britain and Northern Ireland and the United States of America to the United Nations addressed to the President of the Security Council, 2003, UN Doc. S/2003/538 at paras. 90–93 [Letter to Security Council]. See also Kristen Boon, "Legislative Reform in Post-Conflict Zones" (2005) 50 McGill L.J. 285 at 314–15 (discussing the implications of the letter, and legislative reform in Iraq under the Coalition Provisional Authority (CPA)).

[77] See generally Greg Fox, *The Occupation of Iraq* (2005) 36 Geo. J. Int'l L. 195.

[78] Kristen E. Boon, "Open for Business: International Financial Institutions, Post-Conflict Economic Reform, and the Rule of Law" (2007) 39 N.Y.U. J. Int'l & Pol. 513.

used to "oppress the Iraqi people and as institutions of torture, repression and corruption."[79]

As Article 43 of the Hague Regulations sets out, the power to legislate in an occupied territory involves taking "all measures ... to restore, and ensure, as far as possible, public order and safety, while respecting, unless absolutely prevented, the laws in force in the country."[80] It should be noted that the French text of this article, which is the original and authoritative text, uses the terms "public order and life" rather than "public order and safety." In English, the promotion of "safety" has been a focal point for justifying change to domestic laws, whereas, in French, the very different word "life" implies the "entire social and commercial life of the community."[81] In either case, the occupying power is not given carte blanche to suspend or modify the existing laws or introduce its own laws. Instead, it must meet the threshold of "empechement absolu" or "absolutely prevented" in order to act. Marco Sassoli writes that while changes may be made to restore and maintain public order and civil life, occupying powers should stay as close as possible to similar local standards and the local cultural, legal, and economic traditions.[82]

Article 64 of the Geneva Conventions provides guidance as to when domestic laws can legitimately be suspended:

Art. 64. The penal laws of the occupied territory shall remain in force, with the exception that they may be repealed or suspended by the Occupying Power in cases where they constitute a threat to its security or an obstacle to the application of the present Convention.[83]

...

The Occupying Power may, however, subject the population of the occupied territory to provisions which are essential to enable the Occupying Power to fulfill its obligations under the present Convention, to maintain the orderly government of the territory, and to ensure the security of the Occupying Power, of the members and property of the occupying forces or

---

[79] *Ibid.*

[80] Hague Regulations, *supra* note 1, Article 43.

[81] Dinstein, *supra* note 8 at para. 203

[82] Marco Sassoli, "Article 43 of the Hague Regulations and Peace Operations in the Twenty-First Century" (2004) at 1 [paper on file with author].

[83] As Dinstein notes, Article 64 is considered to clarify and amplify Article 43. Dinstein, *supra* note 8 at para. 258(b).

administration, and likewise of the establishments and lines of communication used by them.[84]

Although Article 64 refers to penal law, it is typically accepted that it should be construed as being applicable to every type of law, therefore affecting the competence of the occupying power to suspend and modify both civil and penal laws.[85] The occupying power is consequently permitted to legislate, according to the ICRC commentaries, in three situations:

(a) It may promulgate provisions required for the application of the Convention in accordance with the obligations imposed on it by the latter in a number of spheres: child welfare, labour, food, hygiene and public health etc.
(b) It will have the right to enact provisions necessary to maintain the "orderly government of the territory" in its capacity as the Power responsible for public law and order.
(c) It is, lastly, authorized to promulgate penal provisions for its own protection.[86]

In sum, it is uncontroverted that the Geneva Conventions will prevail if there are conflicts with domestic legislation. Any laws that prevent the occupying power from carrying out its duties under the convention, or that contain discriminatory or inhumane provisions, may similarly be abrogated. Moreover, the law of occupation recognizes that an occupying power may be required to act to guarantee its own security, such as repealing laws urging the population to resist the enemy and suspending laws on the right to bear arms, suffrage laws, and sometimes free speech.[87]

---

[84] Geneva Convention IV, *supra* note 1, Article 64.

[85] As the ICRC commentary states, "the idea of the continuity of the legal system applies to the whole of the law (civil law and penal law) in the occupied territory. The reason for the Diplomatic Conference making express reference only to respect for penal law was that it had not been sufficiently observed during past conflicts; there is no reason to infer a contrario that the occupation authorities are not also bound to respect the civil law of the country, or even its constitution." International Humanitarian Law – Treaties and Documents, <http://www.icrc. org/ihl.nsf/COM/380–600071?OpenDocument> [ICRC commentary]. See also Dinstein, *supra* note 8 at para. 258(c).

[86] ICRC commentary, *supra* note 85.

[87] Dinstein, *supra* note 8 at para. 260; von Glahn, *supra* note 39 at 98.

The central debate in interpreting the Hague Regulations and the Geneva Conventions has been over what legislative acts are necessary to promote public order and government. Since public order and legislative action are closely linked and sometimes required as a matter of human rights law, a permissive interpretation of "orderly government" would grant an occupier great scope to reform the laws.[88] The UK's *Manual on the Law of Armed Conflict* goes even further by acknowledging that an occupying power may "repeal or amend laws that are contrary to international law and is also entitled to make changes mandated or encouraged by the UN Security Council."[89] There is consequently a great spectrum of attitudes over what approach to legislative reform is permitted by the law of occupation.

What is clear is that an increasing number of international and national courts are weighing in on the relationship between human rights and international humanitarian law, and specifically on whether human rights should apply during times of war. Since the Geneva Conventions are somewhat dated — they were concluded before the International Covenant on Civil and Political Rights and the Additional Protocols to the Geneva Conventions came into existence — there is an increasing disconnect between human rights and international humanitarian law.[90] The ICJ,[91] the Inter-American Commission on Human Rights,[92] the European Commission of Human Rights, the European Court of Human Rights,[93] and the

---

[88] Sassoli, *supra* note 82 at 3.

[89] UK Ministry of Defence, *supra* note 22 at para. 11.11.

[90] International Covenant on Civil and Political Rights, G.A. Res. 2200A (XXI), 21 U.N. GAOR Supp. (No. 16) at 52, UN Doc. A/6316 (1966), 999 U.N.T.S. 171 [ICCPR]; Additional Protocol 1, *supra* note 16.

[91] See *Nuclear Weapons, supra* note 3 at para. 25 (announcing the court's opinion that the ICCPR's protections do not cease during wartime); *Construction of a Wall, supra* note 2 at paras. 104–13 (acknowledging that the ICCPR is applicable outside of a state's territory to acts of an occupying state committed in the exercise of its jurisdiction); *Armed Activities, supra* note 2 (holding the ICCPR and other human rights treaties applicable to Uganda's armed occupation of the Democratic Republic of Congo).

[92] See, e.g., *Coard v. U.S.* (1999), Inter-Am Comm. H.R., No. 109/99, Doc. OEA/ser.L./V/II.85,doc.9rev. (holding that human rights laws were violated by US armed forces operating in Grenada).

[93] See *Loizidou v. Turkey* (1995), 310 E.C.H.R. (Ser. A) (holding that the application of the European Convention on Human Rights is not limited to the national territory of the high contracting parties); *Bankovic v. Belgium* (2001) E.C.H.R.

Human Rights Committee,[94] have all acknowledged the application of international human rights law in wartime. These decisions illustrate the limits on the exercise of governmental authority during occupations and reinforce that some human rights are non-derogable even in times of emergency.[95] While these decisions do not go so far as to require "positive" content for new laws and, thus, do not resolve the hard cases of whether an occupant has a duty to repeal laws that contravene human rights standards (for example, domestic laws that limit women's rights to work or to own property), they do provide some possible directions for clarifying an occupant's legislative powers.

At present, Article 43 of the Hague Regulations and Article 64 of Geneva Convention IV, provide little more than a convenient tool for occupants to invoke as they see fit. As Benvenisti writes, if an occupant wished, it could intervene in practically all aspects of life, and, if it was in an occupant's interest to refrain from action, it could invoke the "limits" imposed on its powers.[96] It goes almost without saying that the legacy of laws enacted during an occupation is of practical consequence — many sovereigns will decide to keep the laws in place for the good of the population and often are pressured to do so as a matter of public order.[97] The rise of the welfare state, and the greater involvement of governments in economic and social rights, has meant that the simple and open-ended principles of Article 43 of the Hague Regulations and Article 64 of the Geneva Conventions are subject to expansive and changing interpretations. The occupation of Iraq has made it clear that more specific guidelines on an occupant's legislative powers and duties will be necessary in order to ease the inherent conflict of interest between the security

---

335 at para. 71 (holding that European Convention applies where the occupier, "though use of effective control of the relevant territory ... as a consequence of military occupation ... exercise[s] all or some of the public powers normally to be exercised by th[e occupied territory's] government").

94 General Comment no. 31, UN Doc. CCPR/C/21/Rev.1/Add. 13 (29 March 2004).

95 ICCPR, *supra* note 90, Articles 6–8; see also Roberts, *supra* note 39 at 250.

96 Benvenisti, *supra* note 8 at 11.

97 von Glahn, *supra* note 39 at 258 (von Glahn makes the point, however, that if the occupant takes an act in violation of international law, subsequent acts stemming from the initial violation would not bind the returned sovereign because of their illegal foundation); Boon, *supra* note 78 at 548 (discussing the pressure on Iraq to maintain laws enacted during the occupation).

of the occupying power and the self-determination and welfare of the citizens of an occupied territory as well as provide some concrete guidance on legal reform.[98]

CESSATION OF AN OCCUPATION AND ONGOING OBLIGATIONS

The end of an occupation is normally triggered by the loss of effective control or by the general close of military operations.[99] In theory, although rarely in reality, the ousted sovereign may also return and regain possession of the territory. Nonetheless, when the occupying power is expelled from, or loses its grip over, an occupied territory by a successful rebellion, it may also cede effective control, signalling the end of an occupation.[100] Benvenisti notes that the end of an occupation will depend on which effective control test is used: "[U]nder the test of actual control, occupation ends when the occupant no longer exercises its authority in the occupied territory. Under the test of potential control, occupation ends when the occupant is no longer capable of exercising its authority."[101]

Occupations may also end by the transfer of authority to an indigenous local government.[102] Such was the theory behind the Security Council's Resolution 1546, which proclaimed that "by 30 June 2004, the occupation will end and the Coalition Provisional Authority will cease to exist, and that Iraq will reassert its full sovereignty."[103] When authority was transferred from the CPA to the newly established Iraqi interim government, however, this conclusion was cast into doubt as a matter of law because foreign troops remained in the territory with effective control. It is thus significant that the ICRC relied on the Iraqi government's consent to the presence of multinational forces as an indication that the coalition forces were no longer hostile and that the occupation had terminated.[104]

---

[98] Benvenisti, *supra* note 8 at 210.

[99] Geneva Convention IV, *supra* note 1, Article 6(2) and (3). In theory, occupations can also end under the doctrine of deballatio, but this is now largely considered to be defunct. See Benvenisti, *supra* note 8 at 94–96.

[100] Dinstein, *supra* note 8 at para. 102.

[101] Benvenisti, *supra* note 8 at 9.

[102] Benvenisti, *supra* note 35 at n. 3.

[103] Security Council Resolution 1546, *supra* note 31 at para. 2. For a critical assessment of this theory, see Sir Adam Roberts, *The End of Occupation in Iraq*, Policy Brief, 28 June 2004, <http://www.ihresearch.org/iraq/feature>.

[104] Thurer, *supra* note 29 at 8–9.

Recent occupations have created occasion to reflect on what obligations follow the cessation of "effective control."[105] Article 4 of the Geneva Convention IV provides that "persons protected by the Convention are those who, at a given moment and in any manner whatsoever, find themselves, in case of a conflict or occupation, in the hands of a Party to the conflict or Occupying Power of which they are not nationals."[106] The ICRC commentaries make clear that when a party to the conflict or an occupying power has individuals "in their hands," the Geneva Conventions create obligations that continue beyond the official end of an occupation.[107] In other words, some provisions of the conventions, and particularly those that focus on individual rights and humane treatment, extend past the temporal framework of effective control. For example, numerous provisions of the laws of war apply even before an occupation begins, including many set out in the 1899 and 1907 Hague Regulations and in Geneva Convention IV. As Adam Roberts writes, "there is general evidence of a tendency to think of the laws of war as a set of minimum rules to be observed in the widest possible range of situations."[108] Similarly, Article 6 of the Geneva Conventions provides that certain obligations will survive the end of an occupation. In the case of occupied territories, "the application of the present

---

105 See *Int'l Comm. of the Red Cross, Iraq Post Transfer,* 2004, <http://www.icrc.org/web/eng/siteengo.nsf/html/63KKj8>.

106 Geneva Convention IV, *supra* note 1, Article 4. The International Criminal Tribunal for the Former Yugoslavia has also taken this position, noting that "the application of the law of occupation as it affects 'individuals' as civilians protected under Geneva Convention IV does not require that the occupying power have actual authority." For the purposes of individuals rights, therefore, a state of occupation exists upon their falling into "the hands of the occupying power," otherwise civilians would be left, during an intermediate period, with less protection than that attached to them once occupation is established. *Naletilic, supra* note 5 at paras. 219–22.

107 The ICRC commentaries state that "the expression 'in the hands of' need not necessarily be understood in the physical sense; it simply means that the person is in territory which is under the control of the Power in question." International Humanitarian Law – Treaties and Documents, <http://www.icrc.org/ihl.nsf/COM/380–600007?OpenDocument>. See also UK Ministry of Defence, *supra* note 22 at para. 3.10 (providing that the application of the law of armed conflict continues until the termination of the occupation, even if military operations ceased at a later date, and noting that persons in the power of the adversary continue to benefit from the relevant provisions of the conventions and protocol until their final release, and repatriation or re-establishment).

108 Roberts, *supra* note 39 at 256.

Convention shall cease one year after the general close of military operations; however the Occupying Power shall be bound, for the duration of the occupation, to the extent that such Power exercises the functions of government in such territory, by the provisions of the following Articles of the present Convention, Protected persons whose release, repatriation or re-establishment may take place after such dates shall meanwhile continue to benefit by the present Convention."[109] The provisions cited in Article 6 include the humane treatment of protected persons and fundamental rules for the treatment of individuals who are in the hands of a power of which they are not a national.

These ongoing obligations became the subject of great debate in Iraq on the issue of the treatment of detainees post-occupation. Where the multinational forces exercised authority over persons or property in Iraq, and carried out functions in lieu of the interim government in specific fields, the ICRC continued to apply the rules on occupation relevant to these activities in order to ensure that the protected persons received the protection of the convention despite the CPA's decision to withdraw.[110] Nonetheless, an investigation by the American military into the situation at Abu Ghraib revealed the pervasive confusion over the laws applicable to detainees both during and after the occupation.[111] Although the letters annexed to Security Council Resolution 1546 were interpreted as permitting the multinational forces to continue to detain individuals after the transfer of sovereignty to Iraq, they gave little practical guidance to the occupying powers for those detainees still under their control.[112] Since this time, the US military has developed a new internal policy applying Geneva Convention IV to post-occupation detention situations. A lacuna still exists in the international legal framework, however, which will be necessary to clarify the legal obligations in numerous non-occupation security detentions that are taking place globally.

---

[109] Geneva Convention IV, *supra* note 1, Article 6.

[110] Thurer, *supra* note 29 at 9.

[111] Lieutenant General Anthony R. Jones, *AR 15–6 Investigation of the Abu Ghraib Detention Facility and 205th MI Brigade* <http://www.wshein.com/media/Catalog/3/331980.pdf> (2004) at 14–15 and 27.

[112] See Lisa Ashenaz Croke, Washington Refuses to Relinquish Legal Authority to 'Sovereign' Iraq, 6 July 2004, <http://www.newstandardnews.net>; see generally Ashley S. Deeks, *Administrative Detention in Armed Conflicts* 40 Case Western Reserve J. Int'l L. (2009) 403 at 420.

THE APPLICATION OF THE LAW OF OCCUPATION TO THE UNITED NATIONS

There has been vigorous debate over whether the law of occupation applies to UN peacekeeping missions and international administrations. As a result of the commonalities between belligerent occupation and territorial control by a state or group of states over territory that they do not have title to,[113] some have argued that international humanitarian law should apply to international territorial administrations under UN auspices.[114] At a practical level, many of the legal reforms advocated by the UN transitional administrations in Kosovo and East Timor were similar to those later adopted by the CPA in Iraq. For example, in both cases, the temporary administrations passed laws on the establishment of basic governmental structures and security, repealed discriminatory laws, set up the judicial system, promulgated economic and financial reform, and created institutions and structures for eventual self-government.[115] Many recent interventions have had some multilateral component as well, making them indistinguishable from the traditional belligerent occupying power in the eyes of those living the territory in question.[116] The parallels in approach, governance structure, international involvement, and sometimes in goals, between regimes of belligerent occupation and the activities of international organizations in transitional activities reveal the current legal framework to be unsatisfactory and incomplete.

The limits of the analogy between international territorial administrations and belligerent occupations have nonetheless been made apparent. The conditions for entry, exit, and the modes of governance are distinguishable.[117] Daphna Shraga, a senior humanitarian lawyer at the United Nations argues that "the laws of occupation

---

113 Ralphe Wilde, *International Territorial Administration: How the Civilizing Mission Never Went Away* (Oxford: Oxford University Press, 2008) at 312 (discussing the parallels, and the fact that the administration is not composed of representatives of the territory itself, but instead has the identity of the "other").

114 Benvenisti, *supra* note 8 at XVI ("the law of occupation should apply to any case of 'effective control' of a power (be it one or more states or an international organization, such as the United Nations"); Laurie Blank, *The Role of International Financial Institutions in International Humanitarian Law Working Group* (January 2002) 42 Peaceworks, <http://www.usip.org/pubs/peaceworks/pwks42.pdf>.

115 Boon, *supra* note 76 at 314–15.

116 Ratner, *supra* note 23 at 696.

117 *Ibid.* at 699–700.

have never been applicable to any [UN operation] *de jure* or by analogy." She notes that traditional UN peacebuilding operations in the Congo, Lebanon, Cyprus, and Somalia were mandated to "assist" the government or national authorities in place and did not displace the legitimate sovereign or replace it with its own system of governance.[118] Later UN missions in west Irian, Cambodia, and eastern Slavonia were given the authority to administer and legislate and, in the exceptional cases of East Timor and Kosovo, granted full executive and legislative authority on a consensual basis.[119] Moreover, because international organizations do not have standing to become parties to international treaties such as the Geneva Conventions (they are not high contracting parties), they will only be legally bound if they voluntarily accept the obligations of the law of occupation.[120]

While the United Nations has acknowledged that it is bound by some principles of humanitarian law applicable to peacekeepers, it has not adopted the governance provisions of the law of belligerent occupation.[121] The hesitation often comes from the very different circumstances under which the United Nations intervenes in countries. Several provisions of humanitarian law are difficult to apply outside of the state-to-state structure because they reference regulations, laws, and orders that are applicable to the detaining power or they presume the occupying power has its own population.[122] Nonetheless, the area of biggest debate has involved the *status quo ante* principle that is central to the law of occupation. Whereas the law of occupation presumes that there is an order to restore and creates obligations on the occupying power that are consonant with this goal, UN-sponsored interventions have usually taken place in order to protect a citizenry from its government or because there was no effective government in the first place. In other words, most international administrations have been established for

118 Shraga, *supra* note 58 at 481.

119 *Ibid.*

120 See Scheffer, *supra* note 64 at 852; Fox, *supra* note 77 at 222–30.

121 In 1999, the United Nations accepted the application of some humanitarian principles for forces under UN command. UN Secretariat, *UN Secretary General's Bulletin: Observance by United Nations Forces of International Humanitarian Law*, UN Doc. ST/SGB/1999/13 (1999).

122 Garbriele Porreto and Sylvain Vite, *The Application of International Humanitarian Law and Human Rights Law to International Organizations*, Research Paper Series no. 1/2006, (Geneva: University Center for International Humanitarian Law, 2006) at 25–26.

the very purpose of effectuating, facilitating, or overseeing political and constitutional changes.[123] Thus, despite the occasional decision by international transitional administrations to selectively adopt principles from the law of occupation (the UN mission in Kosovo, for example, decided that the existing laws would remain in force until, and unless displaced by, the introduction of UN regulations), many have subscribed to the position that the intention of the Security Council was never, and will never, be to recognize or guarantee that the territory placed under UN administration would revert back to the ousted sovereign at the end of the UN mandate. One of the key questions in regard to the future of the law of occupation is thus whether the *status quo ante* should be upheld in situations of multilateral occupation.

Occupiers are obliged to protect the civilian population by acting as trustees and reserving fundamental political and legal changes to future governments representing the occupied population.[124] This principle has been described as one of "conservationism," which involves three presumptions: occupations are temporary, non-transformative, and limited in scope.[125] Roberts describes the law of occupation as being inherently conservative in nature: "[T]he idea of military intervention with a transformative purpose stands in tension with the existing system of international law as it applies to states."[126] The fundamental premise that occupiers will conserve the laws and institutions of an occupied territory has, however, been

---

[123] *Ibid.* at 28.

[124] Rudiger Wolfrum, *The Adequacy of International Humanitarian Law Rules on Belligerent Occupation: To What Extent May Security Council Resolution 1483 Be Considered a Model for Adjustment?*, in Michael N. Schmitt, ed., *International Law and Armed Conflict: Exploring the Faultlines: Essays in Honour of Yoram Dinstein* (Leiden, The Netherlands: Martinus Nijhoff Publishers, 2007) 497 at 498. Compare Gregory Fox, *Humanitarian Occupation* (Cambridge: Cambridge University Press, 2008) at 29–33 (arguing that the mandate system did not require the promotion of political rights or self-government and that there was very little international oversight).

[125] Nehal Bhuta, *The Antinomies of Transformative Occupation* (2005) 16 Eur. J. Int'l L. 721 at 726 (describing occupation as a temporary state of fact); Christopher Greenwood, *The Administration of Occupied Territory in International Law*, in Emma Playfair, ed., *International Law and the Administration of Occupied Territories: Two Decades of Israeli Occupation of the West Bank and Gaza Strip* (Oxford: Clarendon Press, 1992) 241 at 265–66 (describing the temporary authority of occupiers); Fox, *supra* note 124 at 235.

[126] Roberts, *supra* note 26 at 619.

challenged at its roots.[127] The transformative occupation of Iraq, and the sweeping social and institutional reforms that took place in both Japan and Germany after the Second World War, revealed concerted efforts to eradicate existing national institutions.[128] Indeed, the Allies' main goal during the post-war occupation of Japan and Germany was to replace existing national institutions with democratic ones in their stead.[129]

CONSERVATIONISM VERSUS *JUS POST BELLUM*

The absence of a generally applicable international legal framework regulating transitions from conflict to peace, has sparked proposals for a new category of law: a *jus post bellum. Jus post bellum* derives its name from two existing bodies of law: *jus ad bellum* and *jus in bello,* which are applicable, respectively, to the initiation of war and to conduct in war, including the law of occupation. While the scope and content of *jus post bellum* are only developing, a significant contribution of a *jus post bellum* would be to fill existing gaps and establish a uniform legal regime that is applicable to the exercise of public authority during transitions. A *jus post bellum* would apply to all actors exercising governance functions, including the United Nations and belligerent occupants, and it would provide parameters for intervention in recognition of the right of self-determination. One of the principal differences between the law of occupation and *jus post bellum* involves the approach to the *status quo ante,* with the latter abandoning the strictures of conservationism.[130] Nonetheless, the *in bello* law of belligerent occupation would have obvious areas of overlap with a *jus post bellum* in the overarching connections

---

127 It should be noted, however, that rapid and wholesale transformation has not been the objective of all occupations. Some occupations have had limited purposes. Benvenisti, *supra* note 8 at 181–82, discussing the coalition's occupation of southern and northern Iraq, and the Israeli occupation of southern Lebanon). For a discussion of the principle of conservationism in prolonged occupation, see Adam Roberts, *Prolonged Military Occupation: The Israeli-Occupied Territories since 1967* (1990) 84 A.J.I.L. 44 at 44–105 (stating that even in a prolonged occupation, occupying powers must avoid making drastic changes).

128 The occupations of Germany and Japan took place before the Geneva Conventions were codified. Article 43 of the Hague Regulations of 1907, *supra* note 1, provided the principal source of regulation. See Fox, *supra* note 124 at 259 (illustrating why some argued the Hague Regulations did not apply to these occupations).

129 Benvenisti, *supra* note 8 at 91.

130 See the discussion later in this article.

between the temporary administration of territories and international peace and security. Moreover, the law of occupation provides helpful content to the provision of assistance to civilian populations in war time situations — obligations that are not reflected in other bodies of law such as human rights. In my view, *jus post bellum* is based on four emerging norms in international law: accountability, good economic governance, stewardship, and proportionality in intervention and result.[131]

ACCOUNTABILITY

Occupation governments are by their very nature unelected and thus not subject to the typical constraints of a democratic system. Still, whether constituted by states alone or in combination with international organizations, they must meet basic criteria of accountability in order to be perceived as legitimate. Whereas, historically, accountability of international organizations was conceived of as flowing solely from international organizations to the entities that delegated their power to the organization, a *jus post bellum* expands these duties in recognition of the public functions that international organizations can and often do play. In the last decade, international organizations have enlarged the scope of their activities dramatically, rendering limited accountability models outmoded. For example, the transitional administrations in Kosovo and East Timor expanded the United Nations's traditional peace-building presence dramatically because the administrations exercised broad public powers with a direct impact on individual interests.

The draft Articles on State Responsibility and the Responsibility of International Organizations, and certain national decisions limiting the scope of privileges and immunities of international organizations involved in governance activities demonstrate the developing legal bases for holding power holders to account where breaches of international obligations have occurred. *Jus post bellum* would build on these secondary rules by identifying primary rules of accountability that would be implemented during the exercise of power, not only *ex ante*. The source of the obligations would arise from applicable rules of international law (including international humanitarian and human rights law), state responsibility, the internal rules of the international organization and, in some cases, national law.

---

[131] See generally Boon, *supra* note 26.

Accountability requires monitoring by independent agencies and the opportunity for judicial contestation. Such principles could be put into practice by national courts or by the Security Council itself, through the creation of independent expert review mechanisms, modeled on the World Bank's Inspection Panel, or through new ad hoc judicial bodies.

GOOD ECONOMIC GOVERNANCE

Good economic governance is a second pillar of *jus post bellum*. Economic reconstruction is now a standard component of peace-building operations and occupations because poverty, the mis-management of natural resources, and food or currency crises can create conflict. The connection between economic stability and durable peace is well established, and the Security Council is now regularly including principles of good governance in its Chapter VII resolutions.[132] The Security Council has thus urged the lawful and transparent exploitation of natural resources, encouraged "certificate of origin" schemes such as the Kimberley process for diamond certification, and now includes substantive economic objectives in its peacekeeping mandates.[133] In the peace-building context, the Security Council has underscored the importance of economic rehabilitation and good economic governance in many regions, including Eastern Slavonia, Kosovo, East Timor, the Congo, Liberia, Afghanistan, and Iraq.[134] The economic dimensions of conflict (including the causes of war, the effects of spoilers such as

132 See Paul Collier, Post-Conflict Economic Recovery (April 2006) [unpub-lished], <http://users.ox.ac.uk/~econpco/research/pdfs/IPA-PostConflict EconomicRecovery.pdf> (noting that typically there is a 39 percent risk that peace will collapse within the first five years, and a 32 percent risk that it will collapse in the next five years); Paul Collier, *Policy for Post-Conflict Societies: Re-ducing the Risks of Renewed Conflict,* Working Paper no. 28135 (New York: World Bank, 2000) at 3–4 (stating that the three highest risks for post-conflict societies are a high dependency on natural resource rents, a downturn in economic opportunities, and ethnic dominance).

133 "The Kimberley Process Certification Scheme (KPCS) imposes extensive require-ments on its members to enable them to certify shipments of rough diamonds as 'conflict-free.' As of November 2008, the KP has 49 members, representing 75 countries, with the European Community and its member states counting as an individual participant." See <http://www.kimberleyprocess.com>.

134 See discussion in Kristen Boon, "Coining a New Jurisdiction: The Security Council as Economic Peacekeeper" (2008) 41 Vand. J. Transnat'l L. 991 at 1032–33.

warlords and militias, and economic measures to combat corruption) are becoming central to contemporary concepts of collective security.[135] Although there are no treaties that comprehensively address or define good economic governance, principles of transparency, anti-corruption, and, in some situations, public ownership of national resources, illustrate this emerging norm.

STEWARDSHIP

A third principle of *jus post bellum* is stewardship. This concept derives from the mandate system of the League of Nations as well as the special obligations of occupiers to the occupied recognized in the Hague Regulations and the Geneva Conventions. In the context of occupation, this obligation has been understood as one of trusteeship, requiring that administrators respect the rights and safeguard the interests of inhabitants under their purview. While there have been vociferous objections to the colonial overtones of the trusteeship model, and great criticism of the fanciful nature of this obligation in the occupation context, the occupation of Iraq shows the continuing relevance of stewardship duties, or *modified* trusteeship duties, to *jus post bellum*. In Iraq, the Security Council and the CPA deliberately expanded the trusteeship duties, recognizing the dependence of the people of Iraq on the international community. The Security Council, for example, required the CPA to "promote the welfare of the Iraqi people through the effective administration of the territory."[136] CPA Order no. 2 stated that all assets of the Iraqi Ba'ath Party that had been transferred or acquired were subject to seizure by the CPA "on behalf and for the benefit of the Iraqi people."[137] As such, international protection of certain rights and goods, including the right to sovereignty over natural resources in the period preceding self-determination, continues to have purchase in *post bellum* interventions by states and international organizations. Nonetheless, these obligations are limited. They must be of finite

---

[135] See Boon, *supra* note 78. See also Laurence Boisson De Chazournes, *Collective Security and Economic Interventionism of the UN: The Need for a Coherent and Integrated Approach* (2007) 10 J. Int'l Econ. L. 51 at 52 (discussing emerging practice of integrating economic elements into collective security arrangements).

[136] Security Council Resolution 1483, UN Doc. S/RES/1483 (22 May 2003) at para. 4.

[137] Coalition Provisional Authority, *Dissolution of Entities with Annex A*, Order no. 2 (23 August 2003) at para. 2, <http://www.cpa-iraq.org/regulations/index.html# Regulations>.

duration, be carefully delineated, and there must be opportunities to hold the power holder to account, through private rights of action or accountability mechanisms as defined earlier.

PROPORTIONALITY

A final principle of *jus post bellum* is proportionality. The scope of reforms taken in pursuit of establishment of a durable peace must be proportionate to the legal end goals of the occupations or peace-building missions in question. Moreover, *jus post bellum* must not infringe on the right to self-determination. It is also relevant to the *post bellum* assessment because proportionality derives from the "just war" doctrine, whereby the recourse of the resort to force is assessed against the wrongs committed, and the deployed countermeasures must be proportionate in turn. Factors that weigh in favour of deeper intervention include the collapse of central institutions, the absence of a functioning legal system, and laws that are contrary to major international human rights treaties. Elements that auger for a "lighter footprint" by foreign states or entities will include a modern legal system, a functioning civil society, a history of a democratic, elected governance, and respect for human rights and universal norms.

THE ROLE OF THE SECURITY COUNCIL

The Security Council's extensive involvement in Iraq has been held up as an alternative approach to updating the law of occupation. Since the Council has shown its willingness to adapt and vary the law of occupation in Iraq, some have contended that the future of the law of occupation lies with the Security Council.[138] For example, the Security Council overrode certain conservationist principles by authorizing economic reconstruction, legal reform, and the creation of a new representative government.[139] The Security Council also promoted the welfare of the Iraqi people through the establishment of a development fund for Iraq, and it has encouraged the entry of the World Bank and the IMF into Iraq, enlisting their support and

---

138 Scheffer, *supra* note 64 at 847–51.

139 Security Council Resolution 1483, *supra* note 135 at para. 8 (appointing a special representative to undertake these tasks in coordination with the CPA). See also Fox, *supra* note 76 at 273 (noting that the CPA in Iraq relied on Security Council Resolution 1483, as well as other substantive international standards, as a basis for its regulations).

assistance in economic strategies.[140] The key inquiry, however, in whether the Security Council's involvement is preferable to an independent body of principles, such as a *jus post bellum*, is whether the Council's involvement in Iraq is good precedent.

Overall, the Security Council's intervention in the occupation of Iraq has been met with mixed reviews. On the positive side, the Security Council broadened the CPA's presence to include international interests while reaffirming that the sovereignty of Iraq lay in the Iraqi people themselves. Furthermore, the Security Council's recommendations were tailored to the situation in Iraq and took into account the dominant role of oil in the national economy. On the other hand, the Security Council was criticized for not requiring that the new government in Iraq be created on the basis of democratic elections. In addition, the Council's resolutions were not explicit enough to give good guidance on how to interpret changes to the law of occupation. Indeed, because the Security Council is not an expert legal body, many provisions in the resolutions were too vague to apply to the situations that arose. For example, the Security Council recognized the United Kingdom and the United States as occupying powers but did not acknowledge or define the role of other coalition members such as Romania and Poland.

Despite the Council's critical role in multilateral interventions as a general matter, therefore, its attempts to rewrite the law of occupation should not be viewed as a source of neutral *renouvellement*. It is unrealistic to expect it to consistently and impartially intervene where the interests of its permanent members are involved. Ultimately, occupiers may be given the upper hand under Security Council regimes, and this structural drawback is an important reason why a new legal instrument outlining *post bellum* principles of governance in transitional situations is needed.

CONCLUSION

The lack of an overarching legal framework in international occupations and war-to-peace transitions more generally is problematic. It creates gaps in international responsibility and raises problems of inter-operability among institutions and actors on the ground.[141] The occupation of Iraq vividly illustrates this problem. The CPA and the coalition forces were bound by the Geneva

[140] Boon, *supra* note 77 at 539.
[141] *Ibid.* at 542–43.

Conventions and the Hague Regulations. The United Nations, the World Bank, the IMF, and other international institutions had not declared adherence to the conventions and were instead bound by their own charters. Even the World Bank and the IMF, who were invited into Iraq by the Security Council, were only required to give "due regard" to Chapter VII resolutions as per their relationship agreements with the United Nations.[142] The absence of standardized principles has created great disorder on the ground, undercutting the legitimacy and coherence of the occupation and transition.

A primary goal of *jus post bellum* is durable peace. Conflict prevention, peacekeeping, peace building, and post-conflict reconstruction have this central goal in common. Although there is little present momentum for codifying new instruments in this field, several developments indicate emerging norms relevant to a *jus post bellum*. First, the report on the "Responsibility to Protect," which was written by the International Commission on Intervention and State Sovereignty, emphasizes that modern interventions cannot end after military conflict and should instead contain a "responsibility to rebuild."[143] This obligation includes the responsibility to implement sustainable reconstruction and rehabilitation and to prevent the conditions that might lead the conflicts to repeat themselves.[144] A second development of note is the creation of the Peacebuilding Commission in 2005. This UN organ has a mandate to integrate peace-building strategies from the outset of UN interventions and is emerging as a co-ordinating power dedicated to peace building.[145] Third, efforts are underway to clarify the crime of aggression, and, given the interrelated concepts of war and peace, exploration of its content will add substance to the obligations for building a durable peace.

The debate over the law of occupation has largely taken place through the lens of two very unique and highly contested occupations of the last thirty years. The task now is to step back from the

---

142 *Ibid.* at 560.

143 See International Commission on Intervention and State Sovereignty, *Report: The Responsibility to Protect* (December 2001) at XI, <http://www.iciss.ca/pdf/Commission- Report.pdf>. See also Stahn, *supra* note 11 at 931.

144 UN Secretary-General, *Report of the Secretary-General on Implementing the Responsibility to Protect*, UN Doc. A/63/677 (12 January 2009).

145 Peacebuilding Commission, Working Group on Lessons Learned, *Meeting on Peacebuilding Strategic Frameworks, Indicators, and Monitoring Mechanisms* (19 September 2007), <http://www.un.org/peace/peacebuilding/pbc-lessons.shtml> at "Summary Notes of the Chair."

immediate circumstances and assess how the law of occupation can be reformed to provide better guidance going forward. I have highlighted three concrete steps for action: (1) improve enforcement on the ground as well as the accountability mechanisms; (2) delineate the legislative powers of an occupant; and (3) create a legal instrument setting out general principles of a *jus post bellum* applicable to the governance activities of occupants and international organizations alike.

Sommaire

L'avenir de la loi de l'occupation

Le droit de l'occupation suscite actuellement beaucoup d'intérêt en raison de deux situations importantes, quoique distinctes: l'occupation de longue durée par l'Israël de la bande de Gaza, de la Cisjordanie et du plateau du Golan; et l'occupation "transformatrice" de l'Irak. Dans ces deux cas, les puissances occupantes ont résisté cette appellation et ont appliqué de manière sélective, aux territoires en question, le Règlement de La Haye de 1907 et les Conventions de Genève de 1949. Les circonstances particulières de ces occupations ont suscité un débat animé sur l'avenir du droit de l'occupation. À savoir: Le droit de l'occupation, largement accepté mais souvent inappliqué, est-il capable de gérer la transition entre les situations de conflit armé et de paix au XXIe siècle? Cet article passe en revue l'évolution récente du droit de l'occupation, bien connu pour son ambiguïté, à la lumière du fait qu'il est variablement écarté, contesté, invoqué, examiné et, ultimement, transformé par la pratique. En particulier, l'article discute des éléments déclencheurs qui marquent le début et la fin d'une occupation, ainsi que la jurisprudence récente sur le test du "contrôle effectif." Il analyse également la question de qui peut être un occupant, la question des "occupants multiples" sous commandement unifié, et les obligations des occupants dans les domaines de la législation et de la réforme institutionnelle. L'auteure considère, de plus, les défis posés par la participation des Nations Unies (ONU) dans les situations transitionnelles, notamment l'applicabilité de la loi de l'occupation aux forces de l'ONU et le rôle du Conseil de sécurité dans l'adaptation de la loi de l'occupation. L'auteure termine en discutant du principe du "conservatisme," et de la relation entre le droit de l'occupation et du jus post bellum, *afin de fournir une évaluation "d'avenirs possibles" de la loi de l'occupation.*

Summary

The Future of the Law of Occupation

The law of occupation has become the subject of great contemporary interest because of two prominent, although sui generis, *situations: the long-term Israeli occupation of the Gaza Strip, the West Bank, and the Golan Heights and the "transformative" occupation of Iraq. In both situations, the occupying powers resisted the label of belligerent occupier and selectively applied the 1907 Hague Regulations and the 1949 Geneva Conventions to the territories in question. The unique circumstances of these occupations have sparked vigorous debate over the future of the law of occupation. To wit, is the widely accepted, but largely unenforced, law of occupation capable of regulating transitions between armed conflict and peace in the twenty-first century? This article examines recent developments in the notoriously open-textured law of occupation that have arisen as this law has been variously ignored, invoked, challenged, examined, and ultimately reformed through practice. In particular, it discusses the triggers for beginning and ending an occupation, including recent jurisprudence on the "effective control" test. The article examines who can be an occupier, the question of "multiple occupiers" under unified command, and the obligations of occupiers in the areas of legislation and institutional reform. The author also considers the challenges of UN involvement in transitional situations, including the applicability of the law of occupation to UN forces and the role of the Security Council in adapting the law of occupation. The author concludes with a discussion of the principle of "conservationism" and the relationship between the law of occupation and jus post* bellum, *in order to provide an assessment of possible "futures" of the law of occupation.*

Civil Disobedience and International Law: Sketch for a Theoretical Argument

FRÉDÉRIC MÉGRET

The recent demonstrations in Iran and the widely heard calls to passive resistance have again put the issue of systematic disobedience in the international limelight. The claims of the protesters of Teheran and beyond are anchored in domestic politics and traditions, but invocations of international human rights have also featured prominently, if implicitly. Indeed, in the last few years, an increasing number of actions of civil disobedience have been framed in relation to international law or values. Thomas Franck already noted in the early 1990s that "[w]hat is rarely noted ... is that obedience to national authority is currently most often challenged in connection with the dissenting citizen's sense of an international or supranational obligation and in connection with some sense of an 'ought' which has its roots in a perceived international order."[1] What was true then is even more true now, and international law has enjoyed a quite unique popularity among activists of various stripes. Groups are either seizing international law's authority to justify acts of disobedience, claiming that the goals they promote through disobedience are supported by international law, and arguing that a domestic law or practice is in violation of international

Frédéric Mégret is in the Faculty of Law at McGill University and is Canada Research Chair in the Law of Human Rights and Legal Pluralism. I am grateful to the Social Science and Humanities Research Council for the award of a grant for my "Rethinking 'Resistance to Oppression': Civil Disobedience, Armed Rebellion and International Law" project. This article is an early and exploratory outcome of that project. Thanks are also due to comments from participants in the 2007 Oslo New International Law Conference and the Ljubljana International Studies Association/ World International Studies Committee 2008 meeting. Invaluable research assistance was provided by Amar Khoday, Sara Phillips, and Allison Rhoades.

[1] T.M. Franck, *The Power of Legitimacy among Nations* (Oxford: Oxford University Press, 1990).

law or even that international law implicitly confers upon them a residual power to implement its norms.

Although this is not an entirely new phenomenon,[2] it has gained an amplitude that testifies to profound mutations of the international sphere. Domestically felt injustices are increasingly analyzed as violations of international law that are seen most prominently, but not only, as violations of international human rights law. In many cases, individuals and social groups are taking seriously the fact that international law exists and that it is, under some form or other, binding on the states under whose jurisdiction they fall. The fact that states are not complying with their international obligations is then considered to legitimize actions taken in violation of domestic laws in the spirit of non-violent resistance generally, conscientious objection, and, at times, civil disobedience. At the same time, invocations of international law have become more sophisticated. They rely less on a sort of blanket, top-down authority to disobey *à la Nuremberg* (which international law probably does not provide in any unambiguous way) and more on a claim of being at the vanguard of efforts to not only implement, but also to create and re-imagine, international law.

However, what does it mean for international law that it has increasingly served as a rallying cry for domestic and transnational civil society in such ways? Apart from the fact that others draw on its authority, what should international law's position be *vis-à-vis* domestic civil disobeyers? Can international law countenance civil disobedience without undermining order and sovereignty to the point where its historical project becomes unrecognizable? Conversely, what does it mean for civil disobedience that it is increasingly anchoring itself in the perceived incontrovertibility of international norms? Does international law really provide authority for disobedience and, if so, what sort of disobedience? Can international law make disobedience legal or at least legitimate?

International lawyers and scholars have until recently reflected little on these issues.[3] Although the discipline has been quite active in understanding the increasing contribution that transnational

---

2 Already, Henry Thoreau's tax boycott following the annexation of California was based on the Mexican war being contrary to international law.

3 With a few notable exceptions. See, for example, Balakrishnan Rajagopal, *International Law from Below: Development, Social Movements, and Third World Resistance* (Cambridge: Cambridge University Press, 2003). Rajagopal, however, is not interested in civil disobedience specifically.

civil society can make to the development and ordinary implementation of international law, for example, it seems to have had more difficulty in understanding the space for more radical direct action. If anything, the analysis is still dominated by formalist debates on the municipal status of international law or by jurisdictional debates on the sensitivity of domestic courts to international norms. International lawyers seem at times almost agnostic about the issue, torn between sympathy for the goals on the one hand and a perhaps lingering unease with projects of activist challenges to the legitimacy of the state from within, on the other. As a result, Richard Falk's now relatively old call to "conceive of a doctrine of civil disobedience on an international level" has been largely unheard in the realm of academic international lawyers.[4]

Most theorizing on civil disobedience, moreover, has tended to be the province of moral and political theorists, who typically discount the existence and relevance of positive law.[5] There has also been a tendency to frame the debate of disobedience in ways that emphasize purely domestic debates,[6] which seem out of touch with civil disobedience's increasingly cosmopolitan horizon. If anything, it is attorneys, who, in occasionally defending individuals who have committed acts of civil disobedience, have spearheaded new developments, but they have generally done so from the point of view of criminal or constitutional law rather than international law.

---

[4] R.A. Falk, "The Adequacy of Contemporary Theories of International Law: Gaps in Legal Thinking" (1964) 50 Va. L. Rev. 231 at 255.

[5] For example, the classical moral theory dilemma is whether there is a moral obligation to obey/disobey the law. The question is often raised as if the law itself had little interesting to say on the issue, except presumably the stubborn assertion that it is binding.

[6] For example, many books on civil disobedience do not mention international law once. H.A. Bedau, *Civil Disobedience in Focus* (New York: Routledge, 1991). The vast majority of writings on civil disobedience come from the United States where, for all the occasional references to international law, the debate remains dominated either by domestic political theory or domestic constitutional concerns. In particular, the treatment of civil disobedience in political theory typically emphasizes the nature of the problem in, to use Rawls's expression, "the special case of a nearly just society." J. Rawls, *A Theory of Justice* (Cambridge, MA: Belknap Press, 1999) at 319; see also, R.M. Dworkin, *A Matter of Principle* (Oxford: Oxford University Press, 1986) at 105. Dworkin defines civil disobedience as not "challenging the legitimacy of the government or of the dimensions of the political community." However, that is arguably what many civil disobeyers have done, and it does not seem crucial to a proper understanding of civil disobedience that they do not.

Moreover, although civil disobeyers themselves have been more prone to rely on the authority of international law, they generally do so in instrumental ways that do not do justice to the role that international law might properly be expected to play.

As a result, there has been remarkably little theoretical work to join the dots conceptually between civil disobedience as a particular method of political protest, and international law as a historical and ideological project that is increasingly weighing on domestic normative outcomes. In fact, there might even be said to exist a cultural and social gap between grassroots activists invoking international law and the more rarefied culture of an international legal profession that is simultaneously progressive in its project and characteristically conservative in its assumptions. This lack of interest is misguided, not only because of the factual circumstance that international law is increasingly invoked by civil disobeyers but also because of the impact that civil disobedience can have on the theory and practice of international law and vice versa. There is a risk that international law may become disconnected from some of the actual ways in which it is promoted and upheld and that its theory may become out of touch with its practice. And, conversely, there is a risk that civil disobeyers will imperfectly understand what constraints come with invoking international law.

This article seeks to examine the genesis, meaning, and potential of such developments both for international law and for the concept of civil disobedience. It will operate at a relatively high degree of generality, and its ambition is to merely sketch out what might be a cogent theoretical argument linking the two. In the process, it will seek to tease out the prolegomenon of what might be a normative theory of civil disobedience in relation to international law. In this respect, I will not be directly interested in what positive international law says on the topic of civil disobedience — as I will endeavour to show, it has said remarkably little — but what it arguably *should* or *might* say that is consistent with its premises and its broad historical circumstances. The article will, in other words, solicit legal imagination beyond the usual inventory of authority and precedents.[7]

7 This article is part of a larger project funded by the Social Sciences and Humanities Research Council to critically re-examine a neglected tradition of "resistance" in international law, in order to recapture some of international law's subversive potential, whose emphasis is, to use the expression of Balakrishna Rajagopal, on the construction of "international law from below."

I want to take this initial tension — between a global civil society avid to draw on the authority of international law to engage in alternative forms of protest and an international law apparently reluctant to get drawn into the confrontational waters of disobedience — as my starting point. I begin by broadly outlining the historical and normative record of civil disobedience and international law as two interconnected themes. I then show how the lack of a well-conceived analytical framework to think about the two in more dynamic ways has been problematic for both and how a greater *rapprochement* would make sense in a variety of ways. Finally, I try to evaluate ways in which international law might legitimize civil disobedience and in which civil disobedience might cogently rely on international law.

Civil Disobedience and International Law: The Record

I define civil disobedience as the tradition, forged by the likes of Thoreau, Gandhi, Luther King, and Luthuli, of violating domestic law to protest the unjustness of specific laws or of an entire legal and political regime.[8] I have chosen civil disobedience as the focus of this article because civil disobedience is a specifically legal form of challenge to the state, one that relies on the dramatization of the confrontation between state and individual before the courts and that is therefore particularly appropriate to examine conflicts of authority between legal orders. However, civil disobedience is itself only a small part of a broader tradition of non-violent resistance, itself the heir to pluri-secular thought on the conditions of legitimate resistance to power, particularly that of the sovereign.

At the heart of the concept of resistance is the idea that there are circumstances in which the law must be opposed because it is deemed fundamentally and decisively unjust. It is this very public motivation, therefore, that distinguishes civil disobeyers from ordinary criminals. Non-violent resistance and civil disobedience are distinct from mere political protest in that they involve a violation of the law rather than simply a legal opposition to the policies of the state.[9] Disobeyers, moreover, are not simply stating their "disagreement" with a policy or their refusal to be part of it, such as with

---

[8] See H.D. Thoreau, *On the Duty of Civil Disobedience* (N.p.: Forgotten Books, 2008). M.L. King and J. Jackson, *Why We Can't Wait* (New York: Signet Classics, 2000).

[9] International law, particularly international human rights law, has had considerable things to say on the latter, protecting as it does such key civil and political

conscientious objectors.[10] The latter do not particularly seek to convince, as much as to live "according to their conscience."[11] Like the version adhered to by Henry David Thoreau, their version of disobedience is an intimate and relatively narrow one that involves a retreat from the world rather than an engagement with it.[12] Instead, civil disobeyers want to effect change, by signalling the degree to which a particular policy offends their sense of justice and raising its costs. Some disobeyers may "seek" or at least "accept" their punishment, particularly in regimes that are otherwise considered legitimate, but this will not be considered a necessary condition of all civil disobedience in this article.[13] A sophisticated understanding of civil disobedience suggests an attempt to "turn the legal machinery against itself" and force it to show its "true nature" (political "jujitsu") in a way that will be politically damaging.[14] Although civil disobedience relies on the courage and steadfastness of its actors, it is not sacrificial in the sense of seeking punishment for the sake of it. Rather, in forcing the state to punish them, disobeyers hope to challenge it either through numbers (creating an impossibility of repression) or through a sort of counter-exemplarity (in being forced to punish, the state exposes its unjustness).

PRACTICES OF DISOBEDIENCE

I want to begin this section by giving a few examples of civil disobedience that have drawn substantial inspiration from international law.

---

rights as freedom of expression or freedom of assembly as well as various provisions protecting the integrity and freedom of individuals. In other words, the state is not at liberty to prohibit or frustrate a number of manifestations of political dissent.

10　The debates on conscientious objection, and "conscience-inspired" civil disobedience are sometimes unhelpfully confused. The former is not really a transformative, as much as a privacy-based, claim; the latter considers that it is not enough to be part of something, she also wants that something changed for her conscience to be assuaged.

11　A. Sagi and R. Shapira, "Civil Disobedience and Conscientious Objection" (2002) 36 Isr. L.R. 181.

12　W.A. Herr, "Thoreau: A Civil Disobedient?" (1974) 85 Ethics 87.

13　The willingness to accept one's punishment is characteristic of civil disobedience launched in broadly democratic and rule of law-based societies, not fundamentally oppressive ones. In this respect, my understanding of civil disobedience is closer to that of Howard Zinn. See H. Zinn, *Disobedience and Democracy: Nine Fallacies of Law and Order* (N.p.: South End Press, 2002).

14　D. Hess and B. Martin, "Repression, Backfire, and the Theory of Transformative Events" (2006) 11(2) Mobilization: An International Quarterly 249.

Example 1: Civil disobedience against war and occupation

The first great wave of civil disobedience against war occurred in the 1960s in the wake of the Vietnam War. Although this disobedience was no doubt partly inspired by discontentment with the draft system, it also capitalized fully on arguments taken from international law, denouncing the war as one of aggression and imperialism.[15] Threats of massive civil disobedience were also agitated in the United States in response to the possibility of an invasion of Nicaragua.[16] Most recently, civil disobedience initiatives against the invasions of Afghanistan and Iraq, as well as against the so-called "war on terror," have been extensively justified by reference to international law. For example, in 2006, four Dominican nuns in Ithaca faced trial in the United States for pouring their own blood on recruitment materials and the American flag in protest against the Iraq war. The defence of the "Saint Patrick's Four" — as they became know — was that they were legally justified by virtue of trying to stop a war that was illegal under international law.[17]

Although terror attacks launched by Palestinian groups get the lion's share of media coverage, it is also undeniable that a sustained effort of civil disobedience has been launched against the Israeli occupation of territories beyond the Green line.[18] This campaign draws significantly on international law, including a long litany of Security Council resolutions demanding Israeli withdrawal. The civil disobedience movement in East Timor has also drawn largely on the register of international law.[19]

---

[15] Interestingly, one of the great figures of civil disobedience, Martin Luther King, often emphasized the fact that the Vietnam War was, above all, in violation of international law. See Martin Luther King, "The Casualties of the War in Vietnam," National Institute, Los Angeles, 25 February 1967 (emphasizing violations of the Charter of the United Nations and the principle of self-determination).

[16] Christian Smith, *Resisting Reagan: The US Central America Peace Movement* (Chicago: University of Chicago Press, 1996).

[17] B. Quigley, "The St. Patrick's Four: Jury Votes 9–3 to Acquit Peace Activists Despite Admission They Poured Blood in Military Recruiting Center" (2004) 61 Guild Practitioner 110.

[18] Mubarak E. Awad, "Non-Violent Resistance: A Strategy for the Occupied Territories" (1984) 13(4) J. Palestine Stud. 22; Gene Sharp, "The Intifadah and Nonviolent Struggle" (1989) 19(1) J. Palestine Stud. 22.

[19] M.J. Stephan, "Nonviolent Insurgency: The Role of Civilian-Based Resistance in the East Timorese, Palestinian, and Kosovo Albanian Self-Determination Movements" (Ph.D. thesis, Fletcher School of Law and Diplomacy, 2005) [unpublished].

Example 2: Civil disobedience against armament

Civil disobedience has been used particularly extensively to mount campaigns against major armament initiatives that were seen as contravening or having the potential to contravene international law. Some of the original actions in this genre were taken by German pacifists during the interwar who denounced through their newspapers Germany's rearmament, which was in violation of the Versailles treaty, and were tried for high treason as a result. The emergence of nuclear weapons, because of their potentially worldwide impact, had a unique catalyzing influence on the development of ideas about resistance based on international principles.[20] The Ploughshares movement in the United States focused, among other things, on the perceived illegality under international law of weapons of mass destruction, particularly inter-continental missiles. The original "call to action" that emerged in 1981 in Madison, Wisconsin, emphasized that these constituted a "threat to global society." Many related acts of civil disobedience were subsequently framed as being in defence of international law. In the early 1980s, for example, the German peace movement successfully challenged the installation of Pershing missiles on German soil, thanks to a sustained action of civil disobedience that constantly invoked not only the German constitution but also the role it ascribed to international law and the prohibition on the use of force contained in the Charter of the United Nations. The "Trident" movement in the United Kingdom has drawn extensively on the International Court of Justice's advisory opinion on nuclear weapons to justify its actions.[21]

Example 3: Civil disobedience against colonization and racism

Civil disobedience was originally conceived by Henry Thoreau as a way of protesting the institution of slavery. Some of the earliest cases of known civil disobedience campaigns against colonizers involve the movement led by Kimbangu in the Congo in the 1920s. Mahatma Gandhi used civil disobedience — specifically the doctrine of Satyagraha — to challenge first the Apartheid government, then British colonization. Civil disobedience was used throughout colonial Africa (for example, in Zambia and Congo) and beyond to

---

[20] R. Falk, "Citizenship and the Modern State: The Spirit of Thoreau in the Age of Trident" (1985) 9 Aus. J. Leg. Phil. 254.

[21] C. Hilson, "Framing the Local and the Global in the Anti-Nuclear Movement: Law and the Politics of Place" (2009) 36 J.L. & Soc'y 94.

achieve self-determination in contexts where it was denied.[22] A systematic policy of civil disobedience was resorted to in the American South to counter segregation. Although religiously inspired, the boycotts and sit-ins of the civil rights movement made a forceful connection with the ideal of the Universal Declaration of Human Rights and its premise of racial equality.[23] In the 1980s, civil disobeyers the world over engaged in various forms of protest against the interests of the Apartheid state, typically to undermine its diplomatic credentials and commercial interests.[24] The South African and Namibian resistance both legitimized their campaigns of civil disobedience (for example, the Defiance Campaign) by reference to the UN General Assembly resolutions condemning the regime.

In recent years, civil disobedience has been used particularly to defend migrants and refugees. The acts in question are often the work of asylum seekers themselves, who have been known to storm out of the camps within which they are confined as a form of protest. On other occasions, it is external well-wishers who have invaded camps,[25] provided asylum seekers with fake passports to escape to "safe" destinations,[26] destroyed camp installations,[27] provided sanctuary,[28] or left food and water to assist in perilous journeys.[29] The

---

[22] M.J. Stephan, "Strategic Nonviolence: Fighting for Statehood: The Role of Civilian-Based Resistance in the East Timorese, Palestinian, and Kosovo Albanian Self-Determination Movements" (2006) 30 Fletcher F. World Aff. 57.

[23] Universal Declaration of Human Rights, 10 December 1948, UNGA Resolution 217A III at art. 25(1).

[24] I.J. Gassama, "Reaffirming Faith in the Dignity of Each Human Being: The United Nations, NGOs, and Apartheid" (1995) 19 Fordham Int'l L.J. 1464.

[25] Liz Fekete, "Civil Disobedience Campaign against Detention Centres Launched," *Independent Race and Refugee News Network* (19 May 2002), <https://www.irr.org.uk/cgi-bin/news/open.pl?id=5257>.

[26] Patricia Karvela and Elizabeth Colman, "Raids Hit 'Passport Racket,'" *The Australian* (2 December 2004).

[27] On the "Shut Down the Camp" initiative in Denmark, see Luk Lejren, "Shut Down the Camp," Luk Lejren, <http://luklejren.dk/spip.php?article14>.

[28] C. Patsias and L. Vaillancourt, *Les églises comme dernier refuge face à la loi: les dilemmes de la désobéissance civile au sein des sociétés démocratiques* (Colloque international du Sodrus, L'asile religieux entre désobéissance et obligation légale, Université de Sherbrooke, 7–8 February 2007, <http://www.usherbrooke.ca/politique_appliquee/2e_cycle/cahiers/cahier-6.pdf> [unpublished].

[29] On the "No More Deaths" movement and its role in the US-Mexico border, see M. Caminero-Santangelo, "Responding to the Human Costs of US Immigration Policy: No More Deaths and the New Sanctuary Movement" (2009) 7(1) Latino

1951 Convention Relating to the Status of Refugees is typically invoked, and states are faulted for failing to honour their existing commitments.[30]

Example 4: Civil disobedience in defence of democracy and human rights

Solidarnosc effectively used a civil disobedience campaign to precipitate the end of communism in Poland, in the name of an ideal of democracy and human rights.[31] In the last decades, the populations of Kosovo, the Ukraine, the Baltic states, Myanmar, Sudan, Tibet, Chile, South Korea, Indonesia, Taiwan, China, Ethiopia, the Philippines, Bangladesh, El Salvador, Guatemala, Bolivia, Lebanon, Western Sahara, Cameroon, and Iran have all engaged in various forms of civil disobedience as a way to remedy what they have considered to be a denial of democracy.[32] Civil disobeyers have targeted specific policies that undermined democracy and human rights transnationally, such as those led by the Central Intelligence Agency in Central America in the 1980s and 1990s.

Civil disobedience has also been at the forefront of action in favour of human rights.[33] From the demonstrations of the "mothers of the disappeared" in Buenos Aires to Tien An Men, civil disobedience is one of the preferred tactics of grass root human rights movements. An interesting example of civil disobedience in defence of human rights relates to women's struggles since at least the time of the suffragettes. Wajeha al-Huwaider, a Saudi women's rights activist, for example, has challenged the Saudi "guardianship" system frontally by, for example, engaging in illegal acts of driving (broadcast on Youtube). At about the same time, Lubna Hussein, a Sudanese

---

Studies 112; M.A. Failinger, "No More Deaths: On Conscience, Civil Disobedience, and a New Role for Truth Commissions" (2006) 75 U.M.K.C. L. Rev. 401. See also the earlier, S.B. Coutin, "Smugglers or Samaritans in Tucson, Arizona: Producing and Contesting Legal Truth" (1995) American Ethnologist 549.

30 Convention Relating to the Status of Refugees, 28 July 1951, 189 U.N.T.S. 150.

31 Erik Neveu, *Sociologie des mouvements sociaux* (Paris: La découverte, 2000) at 3. See also A. Roberts, *Civil Resistance in the East European and Soviet Revolutions* (Boston: Albert Einstein Institution, 1991).

32 S. Zunes, "Unarmed Insurrections against Authoritarian Governments in the Third World: A New Kind of Revolution" (1994) 15(3) Third World Q. 403.

33 Kumi Naidoo, "Time for Global Civil Disobedience?: Five Things to Advance the Universal Declaration of Human Rights," *Huffington Post* (10 December 2008), <http://www.huffingtonpost.com>.

journalist, decided to forsake her UN immunity and challenge the law under which she was threatened with sixty lashes for wearing "indecent clothing in public" (trousers). Civil disobedience has also been used by sex workers[34] and by the Dalit in India.[35]

Example 5: Civil disobedience and international economic justice

Perhaps one of the most notable cases of transnational non-violent resistance is the sort that has challenged global economic govern-ance in the last decade, as incarnated by various international sum-mits (G-8, World Trade Organization (WTO), Davos, and so on).[36] The 2001 "summer of resistance" in Genoa marked in many ways the peak of a movement that emerged in Seattle, which is sometimes described as anti-globalization but is better understood as a move-ment vying for global economic rules that would be more equitable and favourable to the least well-off as well as more sustainable. Civil disobedience has often been orchestrated with a view to securing, and in reference to, the international regime of labour rights.[37] Social groups have pressured states or sub-state entities to adopt selective purchasing laws, in violation of WTO rules, in order to push certain normative agendas (for example, the Massachusetts ban on purchases from companies that invest in Burma).[38]

Example 6: Civil disobedience in defence of the environment

One of the most recent developments in the field of internation-ally oriented civil disobedience is the trend towards disobedience aimed at protecting the environment. Al Gore recently urged young Americans to engage in civil disobedience actions to fight the con-struction of new coal-powered power plants, a call that was followed

---

[34] P. Kotiswaran, "Preparing for Civil Disobedience: Indian Sex Workers and the Law" (2001) 21 B.C. Third World L.J. 161.

[35] C. Bob, "'Dalit Rights Are Human Rights': Caste Discrimination, International Activism, and the Construction of a New Human Rights Issue" (2007) 29(1) Hum. Rts. Q. 167.

[36] D. Rucht, "Social Movements Challenging Neo-Liberal Globalization" (2006) Civil Society: Berlin Perspectives 189.

[37] S.F. Diamond, "Bridging the Divide: An Alternative Approach to International Labor Rights after the Battle of Seattle" (2001) 29 Pepp. L. Rev. 115.

[38] M.D. Barker, "Flying over the Judicial Hump: A Human Rights Drama Featuring Burma, the Commonwealth of Massachusetts, the WTO, and the Federal Courts" (2000) 32 Geo. J. Int'l L. 51.

in March 2009 by mass civil disobedience to shut down the Capital Power Plant.[39] A new breed of radical environmentalism has emerged that invokes the register of resistance and disobedience with a view to "saving the planet."[40] Greenpeace has long been willing to spectacularly violate the law to bring attention to certain environmental depredations. Villagers protesting the construction of a dam in Bangladesh have invoked the recommendations of the World Commission on Dams.[41] Captain Paul Watson, an Australian environmental activist accused of piracy by Japan after obstructing Japanese whaling ships, regularly refers to the fact that the international whale regime was being violated. Anti-biotech crop movements have invoked the Convention on Biological Diversity or the Cartagena Protocol on Biosafety.[42]

In all of these cases, therefore, one is confronted with a newly energized civil society (domestic or transnational) that claims international authority to, essentially, violate domestic law. To be precise, international law may not always be invoked as such (for example, because civil disobeyers do not get their day in court), but it is clearly the basis for a logic of confrontation with the state. Moreover, appeals to international law routinely mesh with appeals to global justice, where the specificity of the system of inter-state regulation traditionally known as international law is challenged and claims are made directly to a mix of positive norms and global values. The regularity with which international law is invoked points to a new and dramatic trend, even in cases where civil disobeyers take issue, implicitly or explicitly, with some of the limitations of international law.

At a certain level, transnational relations and globalization have been at the origin of the diffusion of models of political action that may at one point have been quite peculiar to certain political traditions. For example, Hannah Arendt once described civil

---

[39] "Largest Civil Disobedience on Global Warming in U.S. History Turns up the Heat on Congress," *Greenpeace USA* (3 March 2009), <http://www.greenpeace.org/usa/news/largest-civil-disobedience-on>.

[40] C.C.G. Hernandez, "Radical Environmentalism: New Civil Disobedience" (2007) 6 Seattle J. Social Justice 289.

[41] Rezwan, "Bangladesh, India: No to Tipaimukh Dam," *Global Voices* (27 May 2009), <http://globalvoicesonline.org/2009/05/27/bangladesh-india-no-to-tipaimukh-dam>.

[42] Convention on Biological Diversity, 5 June 1992, 31 I.L.M. 818 (1992); Cartagena Protocol on Biosafety, 29 January 2000, <http://sedac.ciesin.org/pidb/texts-menu.html>.

disobedience as a distinctly American phenomenon, critically shaped by US political culture.[43] However, ideas about civil disobedience have become globally diffused.[44] One could even argue that civil disobedience has absorbed over the years a number of neighbouring and indigenous political practices, which have become dominated by its particular language. In some ways, civil disobedience used international law as a vehicle, one ideally suited to rally support transnationally and supranationally. The fact that civil disobedience has become a global practice, nonetheless, is not the same thing as explaining the normative role that international law might play within it. This role needs to be first understood by an examination of the record of international law arguments in actual civil disobedience cases.

CIVIL DISOBEDIENCE BEFORE THE COURTS

The record of international law in civil disobedience cases is decidedly a mixed one, although it should be said that civil disobedience has, for understandable reasons, generally fared poorly judicially. Civil disobedience is always marked by an appeal to something higher than a particular legal order. At times, a "better understanding of what domestic law actually says" is all that will be invoked. This will be particularly true of countries such as the United States with a vigorous constitutional rights tradition, from which competing understandings of the law can be inferred. At times, especially in federal states, there will be room to invoke federal provisions against those of various constituent entities. However, quite often an alternative understanding of positive domestic law will not be readily available or will be insufficient. It is in those cases that international law has assumed a more prominent role, either as a principal or supplementary argument. It is not the goal of this article to delve in any detail into those cases. However, it is important to note the symptomatic fact that in most cases where disobeyers invoked

---

43 H. Arendt, *Crises of the Republic* (New York: Harcourt, Brace and Jovanovich, 1972) at 49–102.

44 J. Smith and H. Johnston, *Globalization and Resistance: Transnational Dimensions of Social Movements* (Lanham, MD: Rowman and Littlefield, 2002); S. Chabot, "Transnational Diffusion and the African American Reinvention of Gandhian Repertoire" (2000) 5(2) Mobilization: An International Quarterly 201; G. Hayes, "Vulnerability and Disobedience: New Repertoires in French Environmental Protests" (2006) 15(5) Environmental Politics 821; and S. Scalmer, "The Labor of Diffusion: The Peace Pledge Union and the Adaptation of the Gandhian Repertoire" (2002) 7(3) Mobilization: An International Quarterly 269.

international law courts have either eluded the question altogether or dealt only with the peripheral aspects of it from the point of view of international law.

There are, first, a number of cases where civil disobedience arguments have simply not been heard because the legal system is not characterized by the rule of law or respect for the rights of the accused. In other words, the system is already so heavily rigged against protestors of any sort that civil disobedience is "lost on the system," as it were. Civil disobedience is at its most effective in "intermediate" conditions — ones where the system may not be irreproachable but where it is at least open enough to give the defendants a fair hearing. Civil disobeyers are, paradoxically, dependent on the very system they challenge. In addition, even if the rights of the defence are not grossly violated, several procedural obstacles may be put in the defendants' way. For example, judges have often ruled evidence of political motive as inadmissible, thus preventing juries from making their own minds up about the worthiness of such motives.[45] This ruling has happened in contexts where one might expect juries to be more sensitive to extreme dilemmas of justice and the law.[46] Individuals who have persisted in emphasizing their political and internationally inclined motives have occasionally been held in contempt.

A second obstacle relates to the broader issue of the applicability of international law domestically. Many cases of civil disobedience invoking international law have been lost because, particularly in dualist countries, the system rejects the idea that international law can be applicable directly or is part of the law of the land. Further, even if international law is applicable, this remains a far cry from accepting that it confers rights upon individuals to essentially act upon international law's authority. Quite often, civil disobeyers have been denied standing to claim arguments directly drawn from traditional international law.

A third more general obstacle lies in the general antipathy of courts towards justifying any form of disobedience. It goes without saying that respect for the law is seen as being central by courts and

---

[45] M.C. Loesch, "Motive Testimony and a Civil Disobedience Justification" (1990) 5 N.D. J. L. Ethics & Public Pol'y 1070.

[46] A great many comments on civil disobedience in the US context emphasize this aspect and insist that, at the very least, juries should be able to hear arguments drawn from civil disobedience. This is a procedural rather than a substantive position and, as such, rather incomplete (not to mention that the jury issue will not be relevant in all jurisdictions).

lawyers.[47] This is evident in such doctrinal constructs as the exclusion of motive, which is a central tenet of the criminal law that is very resistant to invocations of even the highest order,[48] except as part of a limited set of recognized defences (necessity and self-defence). Strong principled reasons reinforce this idea, including the equality between defendants (that is, a crime should not be defensible simply because it was committed for the "right" reasons). There is no reason to think that appeals to international law would radically or immediately challenge this stance.

This is not to deny that there have been a few cases where civil disobedience has been recognized by the courts on the basis of international norms.[49] These are typically decisions from lower courts, based on fairly ad hoc reasoning that encountered sympathetic judges or juries. They are nonetheless testimony to the power of arguments taken both from civil disobedience and international law. For example, in the Scottish Trident case,[50] a number of individuals were acquitted of having damaged nuclear submarines because a judge found that the very threat of nuclear Armageddon was arguably contrary to international law principles.[51] These cases nonetheless remain episodic and are not necessarily the most interesting from the point of view of civil disobedience.

However, it is important to note that not every acquittal in a civil disobedience case is a victory for international law. In fact, most cases where international law arguments have been heard (successfully or not) have tended to be dominated by reasoning that was much more characteristic of criminal law, rather than international law. The risk is that the radicality and the specificity of the acts involved will be minimized or even trivialized. For example, in *United*

---

[47] J.A. McMorrow, "Civil Disobedience and the Lawyer's Obligation to the Law" (1991) 48 Wash. & Lee L. Rev. 139.

[48] For a contrary argument, see C.P. Colby, "Civil Disobedience: A Case for Separate Treatment" (1967) 14 Wayne L. Rev. 1165.

[49] For reference to a few US cases, see M. Lippman, "Civil Resistance: Revitalizing International Law in the Nuclear Age" (1992) 13 Whittier L. Rev. 17 at 47.

[50] *Lord (Trident) v. Angela Zelter, Bodil Ulla Roder, Ellen Moxley,* Advocate's Reference no. 1 of 2000 by Her Majesty's advocate referring for the opinion of the High Court on points of law, 30 March 2001.

[51] C.J. Moxley, "The Unlawfulness of the United Kingdom's Policy of Nuclear Deterrence: The Invalidity of the Scots High Court's Decision in Zelter" (2001) Jurid. Rev. 319. See also R.E. Schwartz, "Chaos, Oppression, and Rebellion: The Use of Self-Help to Secure Individual Rights under International Law" (1994) 12 B.U. Int'l L.J. 255.

States v. Murdock, the disobedient was held to have engaged in a mistake of law about whether the 5th Amendment actually had been violated by an obligation to divulge tax information to the government.[52] The disobeyer, in other words, was "confused" about his legal duties. This sort of case (which was not specifically about international law) hardly upholds a strong and principled vision of civil disobedience, preferring to see the protester as someone who is fundamentally misguided. Civil disobedience is made into an excuse rather than a justification, and the focus is thus on indulgence *vis-à-vis* the particular characteristics of the accused, rather than on any endorsement of his cause. Another way of having a relatively benign attitude to civil disobedience, but which has the risk of marginalizing it, is to sentence individuals to substantial probation terms and require them, for example, to undergo psychological counselling or to pledge to refrain from other actions.

Even in cases based on a defence of necessity (the majority in the United States), internationally motivated civil disobedience is mixed up, often for understandably tactical reasons, with concepts that may be quite alien to it and that may distort what is at stake.[53] For example, the central idea behind necessity — that the action was causally required and the only one available to avoid a greater harm in a situation of urgency — is ill-suited to understanding the specificity of civil disobedience as a form of political protest rather than the sort of last-ditch effort to avert a greater danger traditionally envisaged by the criminal law (for example, burning a red light to bring someone to the Emergency). Most acts of civil disobedience are not "necessary" in the way that is envisaged by the necessity defence. They will not necessarily lead to the result they intend to bring about, do not respond to an absolutely imminent danger, and are not necessarily the only means available. They belong to the register of political action rather than to the register of the criminal law.

The judgment of civil disobeyers is merely that a state is too steeped in its ways, after a variety of other tactics have been tried, to listen to anything other than the (relatively) drastic action. Civil disobedience is a desperate measure, and I will argue later that it should be a last resort, but this is not the same as saying it is

---

[52] *United States v. Murdock*, 290 U.S. 389 (1933). Also *Keegan v. United States*, 325 U.S. 478 (1945).

[53] The reverse is of course also true — although less interesting for the purposes of this article — in that civil disobedience distorts, or at least purports to distort, the common law defence of necessity. See *United States v. Schoon*, 971 F.2d at 199 (1992).

unmistakably the only means to avoid a disaster. The necessity defence also manages to minimize and misconstrue the international law element in civil disobedience cases, by essentially relying on international law as a form of *fact*, entered as evidence of the greater harm that the accused intended to avert rather than as normative authority for the disobedience *per se*. International law should be more than a yardstick to measure the potency of dangers. It can act, as will be seen, as a specific vector of the legality/illegality of certain international or domestic conduct and thus operates on an axiological scale rather than purely on an evidentiary axis.

The problem seems to be that most cases where civil disobedience arguments based on international law have been heard were not above all *international law cases hearing truly international law defences*. Even if they interpret international law, domestic cases almost always do so from a vantage point that is imperfectly international and thus offer a rather weak vision of how civil disobedience and international law might relate to each other. There have been no cases heard by international tribunals that would truly raise the issue of the legality/legitimacy of civil disobedience under international law.[54] What is needed is a "purer" international legal argument than that which can be obtained from a few domestic decisions, one that focuses on civil disobedience as an "international law defence."

INTERNATIONAL LAW AND CIVIL DISOBEDIENCE: PROSPECTS FOR *RAPPROCHEMENT*

In this section, I consider both the obstacles to, and the potential for, international law and civil disobedience to operate a rapprochement. Although both problems are linked, they remain analytically independent.

INTERNATIONAL LAW AND THE POTENTIAL CONTRIBUTION OF CIVIL DISOBEDIENCE

Apart from the lack of cases, the normative project of international law is one that is certainly not naturally inclined to make any

---

[54] The exception are a few European Court of Human Rights cases related to civil disobedience, in which the court re-qualified the purported disobedience as being, in fact, an exercise in a legitimate freedom of expression. Since it was not for the state to punish the conduct in question in the first place, the issue of civil disobedience did not truly arise in any strong sense. See case of *Irfan Temel and others v. Turkey* (2009), Application no. 36458/02, Judgment, 3 March 2009, European Court of Human Rights <http://www.echr.coe.int>.

strong connection with civil disobedience. To begin with, civil disobedience is something that occurs in the domestic sphere and is (or was), as such, not immediately cognizable by international law. International law, moreover, is historically committed to sovereignty, order, and the maintenance of the supremacy of institutions of international regulation. It has thus been broadly unsympathetic to what is often perceived as agitation by individuals.

Three notable obstacles stand in the way of a greater recognition of civil disobedience. First, there is a focus on the *international* means of implementing international law, where civil disobedience largely occurs sub- or transnationally. The solution to international problems is typically presented as coming from above rather than from below, in ways that are often quite unquestioned and have to do with the biases of the discipline. Second, there is a focus on the formal means of implementing international law. International law is ill at ease with notions of resistance and struggle, preferring the pacifying and managerial language of conflict prevention and resolution, diplomacy, and the settlement of disputes. International law is to be developed and implemented through conferences, committees, and experts. The third notable obstacle is a focus on the state as the principal subject of international law. Historically, at least, this focus has made it problematic to conceive of a role for individuals or civil society that is more than residual or marginal.

Moreover, and perhaps most problematically, international law has a notable legitimist bend, traditionally preferring order over justice, to use the language of Hedley Bull.[55] International law is attracted to "real and actual power" (something manifested, for instance, in its doctrine of statehood) regardless of its legitimacy, which it sees as the best basis for stability and predictability. For all of its evolutions in the last decades, international law remains a system of norms wedded to the protection of a certain vision of sovereignty. By contrast, civil disobedience is the apotheosis of a certain legal insolence directed at state authority. States are obviously generally very skeptical and wary of it, but international lawyers will often oblige, resisting any move that would expose them to accusations of interference in domestic affairs.

Notwithstanding, there is no doubt that international law could benefit from a better understanding of the role of civil disobedience, precisely when that disobedience is broadly based upon its

---

55 H. Bull, A. Hurrell, and S. Hoffmann, *The Anarchical Society: A Study of Order in World Politics* (New York: Columbia University Press, 2002).

claimed authority. To begin with, it is worth stressing that most civil disobedience that is justified by invocations of international law is also often, paradoxically, a challenge to international law or at least to a certain vision of international law. Civil disobeyers gladly invoke the authority of international law, but they sometimes have a very personal — some might say unorthodox or utopian — view of what international law stands for. Civil disobedience based on an international ideal, in this context, has often foreshadowed and helped bring about major shifts in international norms. In a sense, many acts of civil disobedience have been foundational acts of norm setting. For example, Gandhian civil disobedience largely anticipated the international norm of decolonization, even as it occasionally sought to assert that its project was fully compatible with an international legal order in the making, one which it intended to bring about through its very acts. Indigenous peoples' so-called "tribal disobedience" has powerfully shaped the normative agenda that eventually led to a much greater international recognition of their specific rights.[56] One could also argue that issues of international economic justice, which had been defended unsuccessfully by Third World states during the era of the new international economic order, were put back on the international agenda by the actions of civil resisters. The tension between international law as it is and international law as it should be has always been one of the most productive tensions of the international normative edifice, and it is one on which civil disobedience draws heavily.

As such, civil disobedience has been a way not only of contesting domestic law but also of re-imagining the role of international law in relation to it as well as the role of international law *tout court*. For example, among the most notable forms of disobedience is the sort that arises to challenge both the state and global governance structures that are seen as being insufficiently democratic or as promoting policies that are incompatible with international principles. Of course, in some cases, civil disobeyers will more than anticipate the course of international law's evolution. For example, the Ploughshare's movement seemed to assume that the very possession of nuclear weapons was illegal and sought to justify acts of depredation by the need to avoid nuclear Armageddon. As it turned out, when the International Court of Justice eventually dealt with the issue of nuclear weapons, it was more circumspect about when and why the

[56] R.O. Porter, "Tribal Disobedience" (2005) 11 Tex. J. on Cl. & Cr. 137.

use of nuclear weapons would be illegal. Nonetheless, the Plough-share challenge did capture early on something crucial, namely that legal or illegal, weapons of mass destruction pose a tremendous threat to the very possibility of international life. It also helped stigmatize the excesses of a particular military-strategic discourse that seemed as if it could do entirely without the restraint of norms. In other words, the movement "overshot," but not by a long way, and captured the essence of an international normative regime in the making before international law had had a chance to express itself on the matter. Trident campaigners were prompt, at any rate, to see the advisory opinion as "having given great potential to the legal arguments for non-violent direct action."[57] Similarly, environmental activists involved in uprooting biotech crops such as José Bové, have taken "direct action ... without waiting for international law" in an attempt to "reclaim the commons" that has since influenced the declaration on indigenous rights.[58]

Second, it is trite to say that international law is immersed in a perpetual compliance and implementation crisis, which at times threatens its very ambition. This crisis is particularly pronounced with norms that articulate societal and human-oriented interests (whose constituency is often shut out by the system) rather than those based on state interest (which has obvious defenders). It is a crisis, moreover, that is a by-product of the endless difficulty of imposing law in a society of equals. Typically, international law seeks to transcend the crisis "from above" through more international institutions and jurisdictions. Although this route has accomplished much in the last century, it remains very dependent on some form of voluntary submission that is rarely forthcoming, not to mention that the existence of international mechanisms is certainly no guarantee that they will be respected. The system is particularly inappropriate, moreover, to deal with "persistent offenders" — that is, states that are not minimally committed to respecting their international obligations. A number of obvious pathologies of international order (for example, the recurring emphasis on the use of international force as the ultimate guarantee of the regime) clearly flow from this enforcement deficit. In addition to this crisis of compliance, and

---

[57] Janet Bloomfield, "Resisting the British Bomb: Recent Times," in D. Holdstock and F. Barnaby, eds., *The British Nuclear Weapons Programme, 1952–2002* (N.p.: Routledge, 2003).

[58] A. Starr, *Global Revolt: A Guide to the Movements against Globalization* (New York: Zed Books, 2005) at 63.

indeed partly as a result of it, international law is undergoing a chronic crisis of legitimacy. The gap between international law's promise and its reality, as well as the dubious paradox of its authority (international law relies on the very states that it seeks to constrain) severely weakens its claim to speak on behalf of the system's supposed ultimate beneficiaries. There is a looming sense that the international discourse's infatuation with the idea of an "international community" is in severe need of updating.[59]

These crises that international law is experiencing make it all the more striking that it has seemed largely oblivious to the tradition of civil disobedience. Bottom-up action by social movements in defence of international norms through disobedience carries considerable potential, precisely where top-down international law is at its weakest, namely when confronted with persistent violators. In fact, the record of disobedience in terms of upholding the international principles that inspired it has already been considerable, particularly when efforts were deployed systematically and with considerable popular support.[60] For example, Gandhian civil disobedience was an extremely significant development in bringing about the end of British colonial domination in India. It can be seen as having ushered in the era of decolonization based on the international ideal of collective self-determination. The US civil rights movement's success in bringing about the demise of segregation was also largely based on very strong campaigns of civil disobedience. Perhaps an even clearer example is that of the fight against Apartheid and the South African occupation of Namibia.

It is this hidden debt that should be acknowledged to renew thinking about international law's modes of enforcement. International law is in fact already deeply indebted to popular resistance and has been since at least the eighteenth- and nineteenth-century liberal revolutions. Civil disobedience that is consonant with international goals can also, in the process, substantially recast international law's own claim to authority — not so much as the *fait brut* of state power but, rather, as a bedrock of popular struggles.[61] Civil

---

[59] Arjun Appadurai, "Broken Promises" (2002) 132 Foreign Policy 42.

[60] On the theme of the effectiveness of civil disobedience, see M.J. Stephan and E. Chenoweth, "Why Civil Resistance Works: The Strategic Logic of Nonviolent Conflict" (2008) 33(1) International Security 7.

[61] Frédéric Mégret, "Le droit international peut-il être un droit de résistance? Dix conditions pour un renouveau de l'ambition normative internationale" (2008) 39 Études internationales 39.

disobedience is largely a device of popular empowerment against the dictates of the state. It possesses in itself a profoundly emancipatory and liberating potential. It highlights the role of international law as a key arbiter of normative disputes between citizens and the state. In this context, arguments to the effect that the encouragement of civil disobedience risks undermining the traditional pillars of international law tend to be a *petitio principi* and in danger of reifying sovereignty as absolute and immutable. Sovereignty is today as much the product of popular struggles as it is a grant from international authority.

There are also more principled reasons why a high degree of compatibility between civil disobedience and international law is evident, regardless of the actual international law cause that is pursued. First, civil disobedience is not only used to promote human rights, but it is also arguably consonant *in itself* with the ethos of human rights. Civil disobedience is the manifestation of a fundamental human aspiration to live according to the highest principles of justice and ultimately to one's conscience. It exalts, as does the tradition of human rights by and large, the idea of the self-determining, rational, and free individual as an end in itself and a guarantee against oppression. It relies on key liberties such as the freedom of thought and the freedom of expression (even though it may go further than what would routinely be tolerated by states as falling under these rights). Civil disobedience is thus "profoundly human" and can be understood as a value that is worth protecting in itself because of the way it underscores the importance of being able to take a stand against policies that one deems fundamentally unjust. This stance, in turn, militates in favour of at least a tolerance of "civil disobedience" regardless of whether it is ultimately justified as well as the idea that there should be a reasonable accommodation of individuals' conscience in a liberal state.[62]

Second, civil disobedience, from the point of view of international law, appears as a fundamental political virtue. Civil disobedience is in many ways a manifestation of what is best in human beings as *homo politicus:* a willingness to sacrifice well-being for the sake of the greater good, often in conjunction with others and as a manifestation of solidarity. Moreover, civil disobedience, which is sometimes opposed to the democratic ethos and presented as elitist, can also be deeply democratic in certain cases — "a constituent part of the

---

62 There are many defenses of civil disobedience of this sort. See V. Haksar, "The Right to Civil Disobedience" (2003) 41 Osgoode Hall L.J. 407.

political culture of a developed democratic community."[63] It is "good" that people are willing to sacrifice for the common interest, and some scholars have advanced models of civil disobedience as a serious counter-weight within traditional separation of power theory.[64] This sort of traditional democratic defence of civil disobedience can be reframed along more cosmopolitan lines. Civil disobedience in the name of international law manifests an aspiration by individuals to behave as citizens of the world and to take international law seriously. Even though their vision of international law may occasionally be unorthodox, their commitment is certainly something that reinforces cosmopolitan bonds and is part of the making of the international community. At a time when the idea of global democracy is the object of keen interest,[65] it would be regrettable if some of the ways in which this ethos is already expressing itself were not taken into account. Internationally motivated civil disobedience could be seen as a rare political virtue, the willingness to defend certain supranational ideals even against one's own state or community.

In times of crisis, it is worth remembering that international law does put a big onus on individuals in positions of responsibility to be able to distinguish right from wrong by relying on the authority of international law to disobey manifestly unlawful orders. A culture sympathetic to civil disobedience is one that would pave the road to these more radical forms of disobedience, which arguably constitute a formidable hope for peace. The justification for civil disobedience, then, would lie not in the Nuremberg defence per se (at least not always) but, rather, in the need to keep the Nuremberg social type (the alert, morally responsible, and not blindly obedient citizen) alive as a democratic ideal. The fact that civil disobeyers are willing to accept the law's sanction at least in democratic contexts also evidences a deep willingness to take the system for what it is, accept its overall authority, and seek to have it reform itself rather than be overthrown. From a democratic point of view, this

[63] J. Habermas and M. Calhoun, "Right and Violence: A German Trauma" (1985) 1 Cultural Critique 125 at 136.

[64] Benjamin Beauverger, *La désobéissance civique, de nouvelles perspectives pour la séparation des pouvoirs* (Congrès de Paris: VIIe Congrès français de droit constitutionnel, Paris 2008), <http://www.droitconstitutionnel.org/>.

[65] See, for example, J. Marks and S. Crawford, "The Global Democracy Deficit: An Essay in International Law and its Limits," in D. Archibugi and D. Held, eds., *Reimagining Political Community: Studies in Cosmopolitan Democracy* (Stanford, CA: Stanford University Press, 1998).

willingness to help change the system from within is embedded in a deeply communal ethos (my opponent is not an "other" but the one I need to learn to live with).

Third, civil disobedience and more generally passive resistance seem compatible with international law's bias in favour of the non-violent resolution of conflicts.[66] Although international lawyers may be uneasy with transgression, they are even more uneasy with violence. This bias against violence is expressed above all in the relations between states (the prohibition on the use of force), but it probably applies with equal, if not greater, force in the relations of non-state actors to states. In a context where terrorism (essentially, non-state violence) and domestic conflicts are increasingly presented as the greatest threats to international order, there would seem to be a strong vested interest for the international community to help create spaces of resistance somewhere between opposition and rebellion, which do not make resort to force an appealing result or even the only recourse.[67] Indeed, the rise of civil disobedience movements often coincides with the decline in resort to armed struggle[68] and is frequently framed in direct opposition to the latter.[69] Moreover, civil disobedience will in many (although not all) cases involve a certain willingness to "work with the system" rather than to overthrow it (as in the typical revolutionary framework), something that can only mesh well with international law's emphasis on gradualist domestic change. Finally, large-scale civil disobedience, because of its inclusive nature (in contrast to armed action, which is typically "elitist") and its reliance on "counter-institutions" (as in Kosovo or Palestine), typically paves the way to much smoother transitions. The "civil courage" that is at the root of civil disobedience has also been held to represent an essential basis of a "tolerant

---

[66] L. Kutner, "Due Process of Rebellion" (1972) 7 Val. U.L. Rev. 1 at 50.

[67] Indeed, civil disobeyers themselves have often pointed out that their approach is often the only alternative to violent confrontation, since the status quo is intolerable. For example, Luther King emphasized civil disobedience as the only "alternative to riots."

[68] Zunes, *supra* note 32 at 406. M.J. Stephan and J. Mundy, "A Battlefield Transformed: From Guerilla Resistance to Mass Nonviolent Struggle in the Western Sahara" (2006) 8(3) J. Military and Strategic Stud. 2.

[69] See, for example, the discussion of the petition, first printed in al-Quds on 19 June 2002 and signed by prominent Palestinian public figures condemning resort to suicide bombings against Israeli civilians in L.A. Allen, "Palestinians Debate 'Polite' Resistance to Occupation" (2002) Middle East Report 38.

post-colonial socio-political system which allows for dissenting views."[70]

CIVIL DISOBEDIENCE AND THE POTENTIAL CONTRIBUTION OF INTERNATIONAL LAW

Civil disobedience has a significant historical and philosophical pedigree, is booming in practice, and yet is paradoxically in an apparent constant state of crisis. Although it can be credited with great accomplishments in twentieth-century politics, for example, civil disobedience is an intrinsically perilous venture that pits civil society against the forces of the powers that be. Since it asks much of individuals and groups (including the risk of repression, criminal sanction, and imprisonment or worse, it is also rare. Civil disobedience remains a relatively marginal, exceptional, and precarious means of political struggle dependent on very peculiar conditions. Indeed, one might say that civil disobedience suffers from its own crisis of potency and efficiency. On the "legitimist" side, civil disobedience is attacked as being too willing to break the law, to keen to shun the normal routes of democratic participation or judicial redress, and too presumptuous in claiming to enforce some "higher law." On the "radical" side, civil disobedience is criticized by those who would resort to violence as being too "civil" and possibly complicit at a certain level with the very injustices it is trying to correct (witness, for example, the criticism by part of the new Tibetan generation of the Dalai Lama's leadership).

At least one reason for these limitations is what one might call civil disobedience's own enduring crisis of legitimacy or authority. The question "what is an 'unjust' law and when should it be disobeyed" might equally be framed as "what is Law and why should it be obeyed in the first place?"[71] Clearly, few political practices have

---

[70] H. Melber, "The Virtues of Civil Courage and Civil Disobedience in the Historical Context of Namibia and South Africa" (2001) 28(2) Politikon 236 at 236.

[71] Indeed, one of the criticisms of civil disobedience theorizing is too great a readiness to accept certain basic assumptions about what makes law constraining. M.S Howenstein, "Procrustes and His Bed: Limits of the Modern Theory of Civil Disobedience" (1997) 21 Legal Stud. F. 541. On the relationship between obedience and disobedience, law and non-law, and a critique of the idea that law morally (always) requires obedience, see H. Zinn, "Law, Justice and Disobedience" (1990) 5 N.D. J. L., Ethics & Public Pol'y 899. See also D. Lyons, "Moral Judgment, Historical Reality, and Civil Disobedience" (1998) Philosophy and Public Affairs 31.

been as enmeshed in jurisprudential dilemmas about authority, power, and legitimacy as civil disobedience. To the extent that the issue of the justification of legal obedience does not receive a clear answer, it is hardly surprising that the issue of disobedience remains fraught with ambiguity.[72] Stated in simple terms, the foundational problem of civil disobedience is that, as a claim to political or legal action, it cannot rest on any authority granted by the state, since it is precisely the state that it seeks to challenge. Any purported "legality" of civil disobedience, therefore, can almost by definition not be rooted in positive legality.[73]

This has always raised considerable jurisprudential problems and confined civil disobedience to a relatively precarious philosophical foothold based on appeals to conscience and a mix of supra-legal values. Non-statist principles of justification are typically either higher religious principles (a notable Christian tradition that arguably runs from Saint Augustine to Martin Luther King) or a secularized version of the latter (for example, the tradition of natural law) or morality (for example, the Fuller tradition). These have historically provided strong motivation to spur individuals into action and will undeniably continue to do so, but they have also put civil disobedience at odds with much of the modern legal project by placing civil disobedience "outside the law," not only in the sense that it is in opposition to law but also in the sense that it is in some ways "extra-legal." Civil disobedience has been based on an anti-positivist, naturalist ethos, and the problem has been framed typically as being, for example, one of morality versus law or legitimacy versus legality.

Although this may be precisely "the point" for some civil disobeyers, it undeniably comes at a cost. Appeals to "higher law" have trouble hiding the fact that such "law" is altogether of a different kind than the one with which the courts are accustomed to dealing. Civil disobedience runs into major difficulties, notably in a modern or post-modern world that is skeptical of transcendance or even a common world view or claims about justice. The difficulty of grounding civil disobedience in something less subjective than appeals to one's conscience has also occasionally hindered civil disobedience's ability to act as a rallying platform for broad concerted political action. It increases the solipsism of the disobeyer, even as appeals

---

72 See A.J. Simmons, "Civil Disobedience and the Duty to Obey the Law," in R. Frey and C. Wellman, eds., *A Companion to Applied Ethics* (Cornwall, UK: Wiley-Blackwell, 2003) at 50.

73 C. Cohen, "Civil Disobedience and the Law" (1966) 21 Rutgers L. Rev. 1.

to conscience can make it very difficult to distinguish between legitimate and illegitimate civil disobedience (and there has certainly been some of the latter). This has sometimes threatened to push civil disobedience towards conscientious objection, in the sense that disobeyers merely invoke their more or less idiosyncratic preferences without a very strong basis to challenge legal orders.

In this context, greater recourse to international legal arguments arguably has the potential to renew the promise of civil disobedience. By powerfully reframing the state's acts as the source of illegality, they cast themselves as advanced defenders of true, super-legality, not so much disobeyers as "law enforcement agents in relation to the government."[74] Some theorists of civil disobedience, for instance, have argued that to be successful, and even legitimate, it should proceed from within the law — that is, offer a better view of what the law should be (on the basis, presumably, of a theory about the law) — rather than argue its case entirely from outside. Sophie Turenne, for example, has argued that such "intra-legal" defence of civil disobedience should be based on "human rights," pointing at principles that "over-ride the law as currently applied."[75] Aside from the issue of whether human rights law only, or international law generally, provide the appropriate normative vantage point, there is certainly a case that invoking international law can be a way of at least partly escaping Ronald Dworkin's criticism of "policy disobedience" as being a form of "civil blackmail"[76] (where a minority simply seeks to impose its views on society through civil disobedience).[77] The civil disobeyer who invokes international law (regardless of whether she is right about what international law actually says) is in a posture where she is not simply conducting politics by other means but, fundamentally challenging the state's behaviour from the point of view of its own international obligations.[78]

---

[74] Falk, *supra* note 20 at 263.

[75] S. Turenne, "Judicial Responses to Civil Disobedience: A Comparative Approach" (2004) 10(4) Res Publica 379. It is interesting that Turenne mixes invocations of human rights with references to the European Convention on Human Rights as a "federating element of European societies," which makes "consideration of the civil disobedient's claims imperative."

[76] Dworkin, *supra* note 6 at 112.

[77] S.M. Bauer and P.J. Eckerstrom, "The State Made Me Do It: The Applicability of the Necessity Defense to Civil Disobedience" (1986) 39 Stan. L. Rev. 1173 at 1176, n. 1117.

[78] This is reflected by the increasing tendency of civil disobedience to be framed in terms of "civil resistance," where violation of the law is not acknowledged.

The argument here is not that international law might provide some incontrovertible and unproblematic basis for civil disobedience in a way that natural law does not. International law is in some ways as fraught with complexity and uncertainty as the naturalist tradition it sought to displace, and its position on issues such as disobedience is anything but clear. Indeed, one should caution some enthusiastic grassroots international lawyers that international law does not stand for all the emancipatory and lofty goals they ascribe to it. Short of justifying disobedience per se, however, international law does routinely point to the invalidity of certain domestic norms and practices, particularly as they affect human rights. Independently of its precise status domestically, there is no doubt that it operates from within the same broad realist and positivist paradigm as domestic law. Conflicts between disobeyers and the state can thus be solved within a fairly conventional axiological conflict of norms framework, based on the superiority of international law, which is generally affirmed and recognized by all. By contrast, the relationship between natural and domestic law was always more problematic, in that it involved a conflict of concepts of law rather than a mere conflict of legal order and norms.

Moreover, and perhaps more importantly, international law provides a reference point that is potentially profoundly communal and that can thus anchor practices of civil disobedience in a more concrete cosmopolitan reality than the cosmopolitan utopia of naturalist thinking. International law can help rescue civil disobedience from its occasional solipsism and parochialism, to make it more rooted in certain common bonds of humanity. According to one participant in the Save Darfur campaign, for example, framing civil disobedience in terms of what it can do for international law "will strengthen the movement's spiritual and moral foundation by transforming conscience and compassion into civil initiative to uphold international laws on genocide, war crimes and crimes against humanity."[79] Aside from the instrumental logic displayed in this statement, there is no doubt that international law provides a platform for sustained transnational dialogue that is in many ways the antithesis of Thoreau's withdrawing into pained solitude or even the civil rights movement's sacrificial logic. Given that a classic

---

M. Lippman, "Civil Resistance: The Dictates of Conscience and International Law versus the American Judiciary" (1990) 6 Fla. J. Int'l L. 5 at 7.

[79] Tim Nonn, "Charting a New Course for the Darfur Movement," The Promise of Engagement, <http://bechamilton.com/?p=1050>.

critique of civil disobedience is that, especially in democracies, it is a manifestation of elite arrogance, resort to international law can help recharacterize disobedience not as an assertion of "knowing better" but, rather, as essentially an act of selflessness backed by international authority.

Reinforcing the normative status of civil disobedience might significantly reinforce the practice of civil disobedience. It is a fact sometimes neglected that disobedience involves considerable personal courage in a context where one may be condemned by the community as well as the state apparatus. More than simply a "moral" support, international law might provide limited but real safeguards against the state. International law can help to make the state liable for repressing acts of disobedience beyond the call of the criminal law. International law also represents the promise of rehabilitation for those who have been condemned unjustly by a prior regime as a result of acts of disobedience.[80] Finally, the recognition of a certain international privilege of disobedience has consequences for certain cases of extradition, and it may be easier to recharacterize a "crime" as a legitimate act of disobedience "from outside" than from within the society where the act occurred.

Of course, there is always a danger that, in contributing to "normalize" and even in some cases "legalize" civil disobedience, international law might "take the sting out" of the practice. To be what it is, or at least to be effective, civil disobedience arguably needs to, at the very least, violate the law to provoke it. "Legalizing" civil disobedience from the vantage point of international law might be doing disobedience a fundamental disservice (or so the argument goes). Indeed, it might unduly extend the domain of the law to areas that should remain purely political, a defining moment and act of defiance not robbed of its unique courage by merely being made into an instance of "decentralized implementation." A further, more jurisprudential, argument is that the law cannot define the conditions of its own violation without ceasing to be law. An argument specifically against the *international* legalization of civil disobedience is that international law may unduly restrict the conditions of disobedience. The international agenda may at times be benign and emancipatory, but it has also often itself been oppressive, hegemonic, and partial. There is an aspect of self-determination inherent in civil disobedience that cautions against trying to set up a uniform

---

[80] W.M. Reisman, "The Tormented Conscience: Applying and Appraising Unauthorized Coercion" (1983) 32 Emory L.J. 499.

formula for it (in a context where international law would presumably have to come up with some sort of broad formula if it were not to risk legitimizing all forms of disobedience).

It is difficult not to have sympathy for the argument that one should not, under the guise of promoting civil disobedience, end up destroying it. However, the argument is surely flawed. For one thing, the fact that civil disobedience is legitimate or legal under international law will probably hardly by itself suffice in practice to convince judges domestically to acquit defendants. More importantly, civil disobeyers are not legally masochistic and would probably not forfeit an opportunity to win a case if one emerged (as Dworkin put it, "if an act of civil disobedience can achieve its point without punishment, then this is generally better for all concerned").[81] If, against all odds, a case is to be won in court against the state, vindicating the disobeyer's argument, this would be a first step towards changing the law that most disobeyers would welcome. Civil disobeyers who invoke international law to allege the unjustness of the domestic laws they violate are, in a sense, "upholders" rather than "violators" of international law and have no reason to want to accept their punishment.[82] Indeed, as rightly emphasized by Francis Anthony Boyle in a recent book, "old style" civil disobedience that gladly embraced its punishment as part of a sort of Socratic recognition of the fundamental legitimacy of the norms of the state is a little *passé*.[83] Perhaps precisely because modern day civil disobeyers are aware of the deep connection they have established with international norms — and it is the disobeyers themselves who seek out international law's authority — they are less willing than their predecessors to pay the price of their transgression. The ability to speak, fundamentally, the same legal language as the state means that civil disobeyers do not need to make amends for putting their conscience first, since their conscience, precisely, demands of them that they put law (including international law) above obedience.

81 Dworkin, *supra* note 6 at 115. This is validated by history. For example, "freedom riders" in the American South were eventually vindicated by the Supreme Court of the United States, which found that their interpretation of the law, not the South's police, was the right one. Needless to say, they did not complain that they were not ultimately punished for their acts. In other words, being punished for having violated an unjust law is not ultimately the goal of disobeyers, although it may certainly be a tactical goal.

82 C. Dworkin, "Civil Disobedience: The Case against Prosecution" (1968) 10(6) N.Y. Rev. Books 6.

83 F.A. Boyle, *Protesting Power: War, Resistance, and Law* (Lanham, MD: Rowman and Littlefield Publishers, 2007) at 41.

Towards Internationally Legitimate Civil Disobedience?

If civil disobedience were to be considered legitimate from the point of view of international law, how would it be, and to what effect? In an effort to open, rather than foreclose, the debate, I suggest what might be a few key parameters that should be taken into account, both from the point of view of civil disobedience itself and international law. The main point here is that international law should lean in favour of recognizing civil disobedience only in very limited cases but that it should very much recognize it in those few cases. Although I am not concerned in this article with whether civil disobedience has been legitimized under positive international law (since the initial argument is that it has had little to say on the matter), I do note that there is an "air of reality," or at least a certain plausibility, to the idea. For example, the Universal Declaration on Human Rights indicates in its preamble that it is "essential that human rights should be protected by the rule of law," lest man "be compelled to have recourse, as a last resort, to rebellion against tyranny and oppression."[84] The international community, through the UN General Assembly, has on countless occasions insisted that people have a right to resistance in certain circumstances that goes as far as armed resistance (and therefore surely encompasses, *a fortiori*, less internationally anomalous forms of resistance such as civil disobedience). There are strong elements of international practice that point to advantageous treatment of disobeyers for the purposes of asylum and non-extradition. Quite a significant number of countries have constitutionalized a right to resist oppression, and there is a significant practice of "amnestying" civil disobeyers once the moment of confrontation is passed.[85] There are therefore at least scattered traces of civil disobedience being made legal and legitimate in some cases.

The greatest fear raised by an increased legitimization of civil disobedience is that it becomes a recipe for chaos. It is one thing to think that sovereignty can be abused in some cases but that does not mean that civil disobedience will, in all or even most cases, be legitimate. Three major questions arise, traditionally, that can be reframed from the perspective of international law: justificatory (on what grounds might civil disobedience be defended internationally?), substantive (civil disobedience for or because of what?), and

---

84 Universal Declaration of Human Rights, *supra* note 23.
85 This was the case for example after the Vietnam War.

procedural (civil disobedience by whom, when, and how?). These are obviously not watertight analytical categories, and they interact to a considerable extent.

JUSTIFYING CIVIL DISOBEDIENCE UNDER INTERNATIONAL LAW

Perhaps the best-known suggestion to justify civil disobedience internationally is the "Nuremberg precedent," which is the idea that obeying orders is not a defence to an accusation of having committed an international crime.[86] This principle theoretically opens the way for an obligation to disobey certain orders, even though the conditions for such disobedience are rarely spelled out in the law because of understandable state reluctance. As Francis Boyle has argued, "the Nuremberg judgment privileges all citizens of nations engaged in war crimes to act in a measured but effective way to prevent the continuing commissions of those crimes."[87] The argument, then, is that "orders" can be analogized with "laws," so that there is a duty to disobey certain domestic laws that are in flagrant contradiction with international law, at the risk of being found complicit otherwise.[88] The European Court of Human Rights' confirmation of the condemnation of German Democratic Republic border guards on the grounds that they should have known that laws allowing them to fire on would-be escapees were in violation of the International Covenant on Civil and Political Rights is an interesting example of precisely this sort of consequence.[89] The retroactive condemnation of individuals for their failure to understand that their acts were in violation of international law surely has, as its flip side, an *ex ante* validation of the acts of would-be disobeyers confronted with fundamentally criminal laws.

However, the scope of the Nuremberg defence is narrow in several ways. It only really applies to the worst international crimes. As we will see, international crimes are certainly a likely international motive to justify disobedience, but they are probably not the only motive. Second, the Nuremberg defence only, or at least primarily, deals with individuals who would be directly in a position to commit

---

86　Falk, *supra* note 20 at 261–63.

87　Boyle, *supra* note 83 at 10.

88　B.D. Lambek, "Necessity and International Law: Arguments for the Legality of Civil Disobedience" (1986) 5 Yale L. & Pol'y Rev. 472 at 489–91.

89　*Streletz, Kessler and Krenz v. Germany* (2001), 33 E.H.R.R. 31. However, it is important to note that the case involved officials and not ordinary citizens. International Covenant on Civil and Political Rights, 999 U.N.T.S. 171.

such crimes[90] rather than members of the general population who may think of disobeying. In other words, it is more of an incentive for those in power to abandon ship, than it is one for ordinary citizens to stop the ship from pursuing its course. Of course, the Nuremberg precedent has been extended to more and more categories of individuals, from the military to the highest political authorities and from those in formal hierarchies to those in informal ones. Yet a key difference remains, which is that individuals will be liable only if they are in a position where they are the recipients of orders directly and if, in obeying these orders, they will actively participate, or be complicit, in crimes. Ordinary individuals, in failing to disobey, may well fail to stand up to their highest moral duties as citizens, but they will not actually commit crimes. This defence has been accordingly quite easily rejected, especially in US courts.[91] Moreover, in seeking to extend the Nuremberg defence to all civil disobeyers, civil disobeyers have tended to aggrandize themselves (in equating their responsibility with that of those who are directly executing policies) even as they diminish their motives (guilt avoidance rather than political courage).[92]

Although the Nuremberg precedent provides some of the inspiration for the idea of an obligation to disobey in certain select circumstances, therefore, it is hardly a blueprint for the more broad political form of disobedience envisaged in this article. What is needed is to base a right of civil disobedience (rather than a duty) under a broader concept of international law. I propose what is, in essence, a largely conceptual, even aesthetic, justification of civil disobedience from an international perspective. The idea is to imagine what might emerge as an exceptional "defence of international law" defence, which is based not on the fundamental invalidity of certain domestic laws or policies from the viewpoint of international law. In order to develop such a theory, I suggest that international law needs to develop a better theory of agency and of transgression.

---

[90] This is consonant, at least in the common law, with the quite central idea that one cannot commit crimes by omission except in cases where a prior duty to act exists. This duty to act is typically a function of a higher degree of responsibility imposed in certain cases, in the case of the military a higher capacity to provoke harm.

[91] See, for example, *United States v. Montgomery*, 772 F.2d 733 (11th Cir. 1985).

[92] In *State v. Marley*, 54 Haw. 450, 509 P.2d (1973), the court dismissed as "frivolous any contention that (the defendants) were legally obligated to act to avoid criminal liability" under Nuremberg principles.

First, perhaps one of the biggest difficulties in forging an international theory of civil disobedience is developing an adequate theory of international human *agency*. The Nuremberg defence, as has been suggested, is not an authority for the fact that individuals should generally be decentralized actors of international law. Rather, it merely tells individuals that they should not, in executing certain orders (or, at best, following certain laws), become criminals under international law. In other words, it asks individuals to, in a sense, shun and escape international subjecthood by not committing international crimes and to remain in the relative anonymity of passivity rather than know the spectacular infamy of mankind's enemies. Individuals are asked only to refrain from acting in a certain way in very specific situations rather than doing something generally for international law. This in some ways the exact opposite of what civil disobedience in the name of international law seeks to uphold, which is potentially a much more positive role for all defending international norms.

Significant strides have no doubt been accomplished in the direction of greater recognition of a more positive role of individuals as actors (beyond simply authors of international crimes). The role of individuals and non-state actors in fostering compliance is increasingly appreciated. The existence of a right of petition before several regional human rights courts and even before certain universal human rights bodies is evidence of the growing stature of individuals. This role, however, is only partial and formal. There are many situations where the international system offers not even the appearance of a remedy to individuals or groups locked in a confrontation with their state. Typically, moreover, the vision of civil society promoted by international law is one where non-governmental organizations and social movements are "gentle helpers" and promoters of international law rather than at the vanguard of its simultaneous reinvention and defence. International law, in other words, has hardly kept up with the many ways in which it is in fact constituted by the restless and unruly forces of activism ("less civil society and more civil disobedience," to use the words of Naomi Klein, seems to be the broad orientation).

A better understanding of the contribution of civil disobedience to international law might draw on legal anthropology and a better grasp of how international law is in fact constituted by all those who claim to act in its name — however unauthorized they may be by the system itself.[93] It might, drawing on legal pluralism, try to understand this emerging sense of agency in the language of its actors themselves. Indeed, while some non-state actors are keen to shun the international limelight, many social groups involved in civil disobedience claim and seek a plenitude of subjecthood commensurate with their de facto role. For example, an increasingly frequent claim made by civil disobeyers is that they must rise to the occasion (of international law's coming into being) even when and *because* states or the international community will not.[94] Hence, the argument was made early on in the context of action against nuclear weapons that "individuals have a right to insist that international law is upheld by their governments."[95] Trident Ploughshares activists argue that the United Kingdom is not actively negotiating nuclear disarmament according to the 1968 Treaty on the Non-Proliferation of Nuclear Weapons,[96] and, if individuals resort to civil disobedience to enforce human rights, it is because they are "vindicating the inalienable international human rights of all individuals in those instances in which the international community has been unwilling or unable to institute democratic reforms."[97]

---

[93] See, in particular, S.B. Coutin, "Enacting Law through Social Practice: Sanctuary as a Form of Resistance," in Sally F. Falk, ed., *Law and Anthropology: A Reader* (Hoboken: Wiley-Blackwell, 2005) 278.

[94] In this respect, an argument for decentralized enforcement through civil resistance might emphasize that, for all of its drive to centralization and institutionalization, the international community remains in an embryonic state and is often incapable of honouring some of its most cherished international commitments. See Frédéric Mégret, "Beyond the 'Salvation Paradigm': Responsibility to Protect (Others) v. the Power of Protecting Oneself" (2009) 40 Security Dialogue [forthcoming in 2009]. Also M.J. Stephan and J. Mundy, "A Battlefield Transformed: From Guerilla Resistance to Mass Nonviolent Struggle in the Western Sahara" (2006) 8(3) J. Military and Strategic Stud. 2 at 10–12; R. Falk, "The East Timor Ordeal: International Law and Its Limits" (2000) 32(1–2) Bulletin of Concerned Asian Scholars 49; and R. Wedgwood, "Gallant Delusions" (2002) 132 Foreign Policy 44.

[95] G. Delf, *Humanizing Hell!: The Law v. Nuclear Weapons* (N.p.: Hamish Hamilton, 1985) at 53.

[96] *Lord Advocate's Reference No. 1 of 2000*, (2002) 122 I.L.R. at 651, [2000] H.C.J.T. 1. (defendants arguing that they "acted in the knowledge that the only effective remedy open to us to prevent a nuclear holocaust was to join with other 'global citizens' in an effort to enforce the law ourselves as the Government, judiciary, police and other institutions were not willing to do it themselves").

[97] M. Lippman, "The Right of Civil Resistance under International Law and the Domestic Necessity Defense" (1989) 8 Penn State Int'l L. Rev. 349 at 350. See

As a result of this failure by states to honour their commitments or generally stand in defence of international law, certain civil disobeyers are claiming a radical new form of direct agency under international law. Those working for "Sanctuary," an organization providing assistance to refugees from Central America in the United States that it judges to have been unlawfully denied asylum, effectively and symbolically sought to "substitute" the state by directly granting sanctuary. Nuclear protesters who damaged missiles argued that they were engaged, literally, in "disarmament." Captain Paul Watson, the Australian activist involved in actions against Japanese whaling ships argues that his actions are justified by the UN World Charter for Nature.[98] Implicit in these claims is an increasing sense of disintermediation — that international law's injunctions apply to all and that it is everybody's business to ensure that they are respected. International law, in other words, whatever the arcane debates about its formal status domestically, has already largely been received and accepted by public opinion as a framework of reference that is profoundly legitimizing political action by a sort of "international law" *avant garde*. This sense of radical international agency is based on the idea, as described by Boyle, that "civil resisters are the sheriffs enforcing international law" in circumstances where states violate it.[99]

The basis for such a position could plausibly be held to lie in the idea that international law is increasingly, de facto, a cosmopolitan, rather than simply an interstate, law, one whose subjects are

---

also Valérie Le Héno, *La désobéissance: un Moteur d'évolution* (2009), Scribd, <http://www.scribd.com/doc/10054900/La-desobeissance-Un-Moteur-devolution>: (*"parce que les autorités et pouvoirs politiques désobéissent, eux, à leur promesse de tout faire pour que les Droits de l'Homme sortent de leur idéalité"*).

98 See "Captain Paul Watson Responds to the Director-General of the Japanese Institute of Cetacean Research," *Sea Sheppard News* (27 December 2005), <http://www.seashepherd.org/news-and-media/news-051227-1.html>. As it happens, the argument is sketchy at best from a legal positive point of view. The provision invoked — section 21 — of the Charter is merely a standard reference to the fact that non-state entities "to the extent that they are able ... shall" implement relevant provisions. In addition, the Charter is really only a soft law argument. However, merely pointing out the unorthodoxy of Captain Watson's sort of reasoning would miss the point, in that this agency is claimed even if it is not actually conferred by international law. UN General Assembly, World Charter for Nature, Doc. A/Res/37/7 (28 October 1982),

99 Boyle, *supra* note 83 at 41.

significantly (even principally) individuals.[100] Old constructs, such as the idea that treaties are exclusively agreements between states, increasingly appear formalistic when their existence is clearly meant to create objective situations of enjoyment by individuals. This is something that human rights bodies at least have extensively recognized through the idea of the "special character" of human rights treaties. [101] However, even with international norms that may seem to retain a more explicit interstate dimension — the prohibition of aggression or the protection of the environment — it will become increasingly difficult to claim a primacy of state interest when populations are just as likely to be affected as sovereigns. The idea that certain norms are *erga omnes* — literally, owed to all and therefore the responsibility of all — might also be understood to be legitimizing, at a deeper level, direct action by non-state actors.[102]

Second, international law is still very much in need of a concept of what might be termed "legitimate transgression." This is perhaps one of the hardest steps for international lawyers to take, as it involves potentially undermining the state's authority in certain cases but also, more generally, the idea of law itself. "What do international lawyers make of disobedience?" Tom Franck once asked, a question that to this day remains unanswered.[103] Of course, the state's authority may be undermined only for the sake of upholding international law, but it is hard not to see how it is simultaneously one of the pillars of international order that is shaken. As much as the question of disobedience, it is perhaps the question of *obedience* that must be asked in the first place. Does international law *actually* require individuals to obey domestic law and, if so, to what extent?[104]

---

[100] There is obviously an old tradition in international law that has defended this point of view, most notably in France with the likes of Duguit and Scelle. Interestingly, Duguit also considered that there were significant limits to obedience to unjust laws. See D. Hiez, *La désobéissance civile: Approches politiques et juridiques* (Villeneuve-d'Ascq: Presses universitaires du Septentrion, 2008) at 59.

[101] Frédéric Mégret, "The Nature of Human Rights Obligations," in Daniel Moeckli et al., eds., *International Human Rights Law* (Oxford: Oxford University Press) [forthcoming in 2010].

[102] It is interesting in this respect to reflect on the fact that the idea of *erga omnes* norms is often framed as being that the violation of certain norms "shocks the conscience of humanity." The fact that the expression "humanity" is used suggests that something more is at stake than states being "shocked."

[103] Franck, *supra* note 1 at 11.

[104] The issue of the moral authority of the state to govern is, probably much more than in international law, a central concern in political and moral theory. See

This is a more complex question than it seems. Traditionally, one might argue that international law is indifferent to the domestic organization of states (their laws, famously, cannot be invoked as a defence for failure to execute an international obligation) and is therefore at least agnostic about whether citizens are required to, or actually, respect domestic law. As Brad Roth has underlined, "[t]hat I accept the legitimacy of a foreign government's authority over a foreign land may imply that I am bound not to seek its overthrow, but does not imply that I believe its subjects are bound not to rebel."[105] In theory, one can imagine that international law would have no problem with a state that was largely unregulated or anarchic (as long as this anarchy did not overspill) or with one that put great emphasis on individual conscience to uphold certain values even in defiance of domestic positive law. And, in some cases at least, as has been seen, international law specifically legitimizes disobedience to domestic law (that is, through a Nuremberg-type defence).

On the other hand, the very criteria of statehood traditionally emphasize that a state is only a state to the extent that it has a government, in addition to a territory and a population, which is capable of exerting authority over both.[106] Indeed, the ability to exert obedience from one's subjects specifically features as one of the criteria of de facto statehood.[107] Although this authority might be exercised by brute force, it is more likely that most of the time it will be ensured at least partly through law. Since law (and obedience to it) are natural ingredients of governmentality and statehood, therefore, it is doubtful that international law would side easily with civil disobeyers. In fact, international law at least protects each state's law from external interference, by prescribing in detail the limits of each state's jurisdiction, particularly in cases of domestic strife.[108]

D. Copp, "The Idea of a Legitimate State" (1999) Philosophy and Public Affairs 3; C.H. Wellman and A.J. Simmons, *Is There a Duty to Obey the Law?* (Cambridge: Cambridge University Press, 2005).

[105] B.R. Roth, *Governmental Illegitimacy in International Law* (Oxford: Oxford University Press, 2001).

[106] *Island of Palmas case* (1928) 1 R.I.A.A. 829, 839 (Arbitrator Huber), 4 I.L.R. 3.

[107] Agenda Item 61, UN GAOR, 5th Sess., UN Doc. A/AC.38/L.21 (1950) at 6 (Annexes): "[A] government ... should be recognized if that government ... has the obedience of the bulk of the population of that territory in such a way that this control, authority, and obedience appear to be of a permanent character").

[108] See, for example, the Convention on Duties and Rights of States in the Event of Civil Strive, 10 February 1928, 134 L.N.T.S. 45 (entered into force 21 May 1928).

This suggests that, in international legal eyes, domestic systems of law are at least something worth protecting from the outside.

Domestically, international law also often encourages a sort of law-abiding bias, if only to better secure its own legitimacy. For example, jurisdictionally, the rule of exhaustion of domestic remedies, which applies in contexts as diverse as diplomatic protection, commercial arbitration, or human rights petitions suggests that at the very least individuals should resort to domestic remedies before they engage in anything more rash (it is this initial deferral to sovereignty that then makes supranational remedies appear legitimate). The fact that the international community has been involved in so much peace and state building (at the core of which is often legal reform), moreover, is testimony to a certain ingrained international interest in working institutions of the state.

How can this tension be reconciled under the prism of civil disobedience? Several arguments can be hinted at here. The tension described earlier is one that does not take into account the fact that, for all of its commitment to domestic order, international law is in fact increasingly not indifferent to the *tenor* of domestic law. States are constantly required to implement international law, and international bodies routinely criticize aspects of domestic law that are incompatible with international obligations — in some cases, very harshly and in a way that leaves no doubt about the fundamental unjustness of the entire legal system involved. In cases where a system is judged to be so corrupt as to be incapable of providing a remedy, the rule of exhaustion of local remedies will be lifted.[109]

Indeed, in exploring the validity of disobedience, international law might re-explore its own complex debt to transgression and the complex dialectics of conformity and breach.[110] For example, one might point out the already fundamentally decentralized nature of international enforcement, whether it be through counter-measures, self-defence, and various other unilateral acts relying on a degree of self-help. This decentralized nature is the inevitable result of an international system whose "ability to self-correct and self-enforce is much more limited (than the domestic system's) creating gaps

---

[109] It should be noted in passing, though, that international law's increasing proclivity to reflect on the legitimacy of domestic systems may also provide arguments against civil disobedience — for example, when it considers that a state is legitimate domestically and finds little cause to resort to extreme tactics.

[110] R.E. Goodin, "Toward an International Rule of Law: Distinguishing International Law-Breakers from Would-be Law-Makers" (2005) 9(1) Journal of Ethics 225.

between aspiration and authority, procedures and policy."[111] The justification for decentralized enforcement via civil disobedience would be essentially the same that is used for certain unilateral measures in the inter-state system, a topic that has witnessed a revival of interest of late.[112] Decentralized responses to breaches of international norms are justified because of the anarchic character of the system and a fundamental recognition of the fact that the actors whose interests are directly threatened are in many cases the most suited to offer at least a first line of response to illegality.[113] Indeed, even in highly centralized domestic systems with significant adjudicatory capability, civil disobedience has been presented as being key to updating the law in the face of significant majority obstruction.

THE SUBSTANTIVE THRESHOLD OF CIVIL DISOBEDIENCE

In terms of the sort of situation that might justify civil disobedience, it is easy to conceive that there would be extreme cases where international law should have no qualms about supporting state defiance. If genocide is underway, for example, surely international law is not so sovereignty oriented that it could remain indifferent to those who seek to oppose genocide by peaceful means. By the same token, simply because international law says something is illegal does not mean it requires or even allows individuals to do something rash and incongruous by international law's quietist standards. Civil disobedience is a radical tactic, which should be reserved for radical violations of essential norms. To claim otherwise would be deeply destructive of sovereign and the inter-state system, in ways that are

---

[111] J.K. Cogan, "Noncompliance and the International Rule of Law" (2006) 31 Yale J. Int'l L. 189 at 190.

[112] Cogan's theorization of "operational noncompliance" is very relevant here, even though it only seems to apply to states and not civil society. *Ibid.* Also N.J. Wheeler, "Humanitarian Vigilantes or Legal Entrepreneurs: Enforcing Human Rights in International Society" (2000) 3(1) Critical Review of International Social and Political Philosophy 139.

[113] Of course, the domestic system defined by the state is in a sense exactly the contrary of a decentralized system, and, under normal conditions, its constituent parts (individuals, citizens) are characteristically not supposed to "take the law in their own hands." However, if this system is fundamentally unjust and in contravention of fundamental international norms, one can argue that the domestic legal order either dissolves or is sidelined by international law, so that the individual finds herself as a sort of newfound depository of international personhood. The civil disobeyer thus operates in a decentralized system, left vacant by the waning of a fundamentally "unjust" domestic order.

not justified by the gravity of the violations. There are certainly strong international legal arguments in favour of the recognition of "some value to adherence to law ... for its own sake."[114]

Three general criteria can help us map the conceptual terrain of what might be internationally legitimate civil disobedience.[115] In line with this article's overall aim, a first criterion would be the degree to which the civil disobedience is a response to major violations of international law. One situation might be where an entire regime (rather than just a specific law) is deemed, under some sort of Radbruch formula, to lack entirely in legitimacy because its laws do not exhibit the minimum conditions of lawfulness.[116] In other cases, the justification of disobedience may be tied to particular policies or laws that, although they do not evidence a breakdown of the very idea of law, at least indicate a violation of international law. In this respect, the international norms in question should probably be connected to the protection of some fundamental human value. Civil disobedience is not an appropriate strategy to protect values of which individuals are not the significant beneficiaries, and state interest *per se* is better guaranteed by states, at least when the state is in a position to protect its interests.[117]

---

114 Richard A. Falk and Saul H. Mendlovitz, *The Strategy of World Order* (New York: World Law Fund, 1966) at 310.

115 In addition, one should probably add a non-criterion, which is the issue of whether the state laws/policy involved are either domestic or international. I think that should be largely irrelevant if the laws/policies involved actually intersect with any of the listed criteria. Although civil disobedience will often be primarily geared towards domestic decisions, it may very well target the state's foreign policy or, more likely, a mix of domestic and foreign policies (draft dodging in the context of the Vietnam War, for example, was based both on anti-imperialist "international" grounds and on a "domestic" resistance against the draft, which, at least in the circumstances, was seen as an abuse of its power by the state).

116 In the *East German Border Guards* case before various German courts after re-unification, the ideas of legal philosopher Gustav Radbruch (that a legal system loses this quality if it excessively departs from certain standards of justice, a line of argument also associated with Fuller in the Anglo-American tradition) were largely accepted. See P.E. Quint, "The Border Guard Trials and the East German Past-Seven Arguments" (2000) 48 Am. J. Comp. L. 541.

117 One can imagine certain situations of state deliquescence — for example, an occupation — where it would be legitimate for civil disobeyers to stand up for the interests of an absent sovereign. On this subject more generally, see F. Mégret, "*Grandeur et déclin de l'idée de résistance à l'occupation: à propos des 'insurgés'*" (2010) Revue belge de droit international [forthcoming in 2010].

Furthermore, a criterion of sheer gravity of the violations at stake would be required before civil disobedience was considered legitimate from the point of view of international law. This gravity could be evaluated both from the angle of the type of value involved (life, physical integrity, discrimination, political participation, and so on) and the generalized, systematic, repeated, or perverse character of the violations. Without going into too much detail, one obvious candidate for civil disobedience is the avoidance, minimization, or interruption of the commission of *international crimes,* at the very least the International Criminal Court's so-called core crimes (genocide, crimes against humanity, and war crimes). It would be fundamentally contradictory if the international community were to, on the one hand, promote these norms as essential to its very survival and constitutive of its normative aspirations and, on the other hand, demand of individuals that they be led by their state "like lambs to the slaughter," out of an anachronistic reification of sovereignty, and entirely defer to international law's traditional means of dealing with atrocities, even when those have been found wanting.

In line with international law's supposed normative move towards a legal order more concerned with the dignity of the individual, I would also argue that certain generalized or systematic violations of human rights, even though they may not fit the definition of international crimes, might also internationally justify actions of civil disobedience. The violations should be of the sort that evidence not isolated and accidental instances by some state agents but, rather, a deliberate policy of denying certain basic rights. In addition, the severe undermining of democracy, and instances of tyranny, dictatorship, or totalitarianism, would all correspond to the sort of situation where civil disobedience is internationally legitimate both on account of the rights dimension and human values involved and of international law's own increasing support of forms of democratic entitlement.

THE PROCEDURAL THRESHOLD OF CIVIL DISOBEDIENCE

The substantive threshold for justifying civil disobedience may in many cases be less important in the absolute than a variety of contextual circumstances surrounding it. In other words, the commission of some international crimes might not warrant civil disobedience, and some crimes or violations of international law that are much less grave than international crimes might occasionally warrant civil disobedience. In this respect, the important question seems to be less which violations of international law would entitle the populace to civil disobedience and more a question of what the actual conditions are in which this disobedience might be actualized.

Perhaps most crucially, international law would be most sympathetic to acts of civil disobedience that respected certain temporal conditions. International law should not seek to legitimize civil disobedience too early (at the risk of unnecessarily undermining the authority of the state) or too late (at the risk of failing to stand by the values that it and civil disobedience jointly seek to uphold). Something like *subsidiarity*, therefore, should be the key legal criterion of determining whether civil disobedience is chronologically opportune. International support for civil disobedience should be reserved for those cases where all means that do not involve violating the law have been exhausted. It would, in other terms, clearly have to be a last resort. However, what defines a last resort will in turn depend on the degree of unjustness of the policies and the type of regime confronted.

Specifically, one can see two sorts of alternative avenues whose impossibility would have to be established before civil disobedience was engaged in. First, political action not involving a violation of the law would have to be the preferred option. International law could not want to encourage frivolous manifestations of civil disobedience when changes to laws or policies could be obtained through democratic means. Whether such action is possible will of course depend on the availability and openness of democratic institutions.[118] Civil disobeyers regularly allege (whether the claims are true is another issue) that their actions are rendered legitimate by the dysfunction of the normal institutions of democracy or, of course, the total absence of it.[119] One would have to be able to invoke a very substantial absence or dysfunction of democratic

---

[118] Allowance may be made for the more or less functional character of the democracy in relation to the problem at hand. For example, one of the key theoretical justifications of civil disobedience in defence of the environment even in democracies is that democracies have been very bad at taking the sort of massive action that would be required by a threat such as catastrophic global warming.

[119] See, for example, "Declaration of Francis A. Boyle," in *USA v. Carol Gilbert, Jackie Marie Hudson and Ardeth Platte*, Criminal Case no. 02-CR-509 R B (N.D. Col. 2002) (United States District Court for the District of ColoradoChapters, <http://chapters.scarecrowpress.com/07/425/0742538923ch1.pdf> (alleging a "breakdown in the Constitutional principle of checks and balances which implements the separation of powers").

institutions to avail oneself of international law's authority in disobeying domestic law.

In particular, international law would not legitimize the civil disobedience of a democratic minority that simply finds itself on the "losing side" of any number of democratic decisions. It is in the nature of democracy that it will make discontents, and to allow these to resist the law is something that would clearly undermine democratic arrangements and popular sovereignty. On the other hand, if those on the "losing side" of democratic decision making are so on the basis of some discriminatory ground (race, ethnicity, religion, disability, sexual orientation) and if there seems no prospect of their obtaining fundamental political change through the normal routes and within a reasonable time, then civil disobedience may be the only means available. This would seem to be the case in most situations where civil disobedience would be substantively justified. For example, a state engaged in Apartheid or genocide is unlikely to simultaneously be receptive to political forces engaged in stopping these practices. However, the overlap may not be complete, and one can see how democratic action could in some cases effectively obtain changes in policies involving even relatively grave human rights violations.

A second type of avenue that would need to be explored prior to any action in civil disobedience being launched is the availability of legal and judicial remedies. Particularly (although not only) in cases where democracy is dysfunctional, the court system can continue to provide, if it is itself functional, a measure of remedy for violations of rights and policies that infringe the constitution or even international law. At the very least, therefore, in the same way that receivability of a case before international mechanisms (particularly the human rights type) is conditional upon the exhaustion of domestic remedies, individuals contemplating civil disobedience should have exhausted both domestic and international jurisdictional or quasi-jurisdictional remedies. However, in the same way that the rule of exhaustion of domestic remedies knows of exceptions when it is very unlikely that such a remedy could be obtained, civil disobedience should be contemplated if the domestic and international remedies are unavailable or illusory.

Another significant issue relates to the more or less representative character of the groups involved in civil disobedience. Civil disobedience raises a classic dilemma of jurisprudence when it comes to the authority of particular groups to engage in such acts. Since civil disobedience arises to challenge unjust/illegal state policies to which the state is likely to be strongly wedded, the state's structures of deliberation and representation are likely to be part of the problem. In other words, the normal mechanisms for identifying authority and responsibility are precisely what will be found wanting. This means that civil disobedience can, and has only ever emerged, in "ground-up" fashion as it were from an effort at self-organization by civil society, which must per hypothesis proceed bereft of any prior legitimacy or procedures to establish it. Civil disobedience's only legitimacy is, and has been historically, an appeal to certain higher principles, the ability to coalesce individuals under a common banner and ultimately to convince society (and, arguably, the world at large) of the justness of its cause. The history of civil disobedience, therefore, belongs more to the history of grass root political movements than it does to the reality of formal and organized democratic political representation.

This is unavoidable to an extent, but it can also create intractable dilemmas of legitimacy. The international system could have a role to play in helping define the contours of what sort of groups speak for a constituency broad enough to justify disobedience. One criterion might be related to a number of organic characteristics. For example, civil disobeyers should be minimally representative of the population or groups they claim to represent or in whose name at least they claim to act. Another criterion might be that civil disobedient groups be at least proto-democratic so that, for example, a civil disobedience movement that was based on the cult status of some charismatic figure would not be considered to be as legitimate as one that was born from an open deliberative process. The idea would not be for international law to require that groups that were perpetrating civil disobedience exhibit all of the characteristics of formal political organizations, but that at least their internal functioning should not be too far apart from the values that they profess, on the one hand, and international law's own slant in favour of representative and democratic governance, on the other.

Finally, the very manner in which civil disobedience action is undertaken has a bearing on how it should be received internationally. Here, I leave aside issues of "style" of civil disobedience of which there are many, and on which international law has little to say, as long as the broad parameters of the practice are adhered to. The important idea is that civil disobedience campaigns should be proportional and even tailored to the evil that they seek to redress.[120]

---

[120] See *Williams v. Wallace*, 240 F. Supp. 100 (M.D. Ala. 1965).

Given that this is the rule in inter-state relations (that is, a lawful countermeasure is one that is proportionate), the same should apply to non-state actors. Civil disobedience is, and should remain in any event, an exorbitant exception to international law's otherwise legitimist stance in favour of state sovereignty (and its ability to sanction its citizens for violations of the law) and the normal functioning of institutions. It should only be legitimate to the extent that it is strictly necessary to obtain the repeal of a particular law or policy. In other words, it should not become a blank cheque for any manner of disobedience. Typically, the violation of criminal law would not be contemplated by internationally legitimate civil disobedience, except, and to the extent, that the criminal law is itself manifestly unjust (for example, a criminal law that punishes individuals belonging to certain racial groups from sitting in certain buses). The use of violence would in itself, and by definition, be incompatible with civil disobedience. The extent, gravity, and timing of civil disobedience should be orchestrated to maximize its political impact while minimizing its disruption potential to innocent third parties, if need be through symbolic action rather than simply on the basis of individuals' sense of personal outrage at a certain law or policy. Civil disobedience that would exceed these (admittedly hard to define precisely) boundaries might well lose the legal backing that it might otherwise get from international law. All of these limitations on the "freedom" to disobey are consonant with an international approach that is broadly sympathetic when the stakes warrant it but wary of the slippery slope that all confrontation with the organs of the state can entail.

CONCLUSION

This article has sought to argue that although international law and civil disobedience operate on two apparently irreducible dimensions, there are in fact more links between them than catches the eye. It has argued, in fact, that both could gain from greater conceptual interaction with each other. International law in its current predicament certainly needs all of the resources that it can attract to reinvent itself and reinforce its promise. It is dubious that it can do so by relying exclusively on the inter-state world or through such theoretical constructs as the "international community." Civil disobedience, on the other hand, as a manifestation of civil society's resistance to certain fundamentally unjust practices, is a formidable idea but one that has often been caught in inextricable dilemmas of authority. It is a project that can gain considerably from its inscription in a cosmopolitan horizon of confrontation and questioning. On this path, one thing that is needed is a rediscovery of the extent to which international law is already profoundly indebted to a certain "esprit de résistance," despite its occasional self-presentation as a fully sufficient system, disconnected from popular politics and fundamental issues of state legitimacy.

In this context and to recapitulate, one possible argument in favour of greater recognition of the complementarity of civil disobedience and international law might be an argument about the potential disjunction between international law's substantive norms and its preferred method to develop and enforce them. The relative neglect in which civil disobedience stood was sustainable as long as international law was primarily conceived as a law between states. If this was the case, then what might be individuals' legitimacy in trying to uphold international principles of which they were not even the beneficiaries, let alone the subjects? However, international law has gradually set up a potential situation of crisis for itself by increasingly portraying itself as a law focused on the promotion of basic human rights for all or, at least, as a law that is ultimately destined to benefit individuals. It is respect for these very human rights (civil, political, economic, social, and cultural) that the new generation of civil disobeyers, trained and socialized in the ways of "international civil society," is invoking in increasingly sophisticated ways.

There thus emerges a situation of at least *objective collusion* between international law's aims and civil disobedience's actions undertaken to pursue these aims (directly or indirectly, explicitly or implicitly). To the extent that international law does not entirely keep abreast of this development, there arises a strange chiasm between the legal system's substantive goals and the reality of how that law is actually brought into being and enforced — on the one hand, an almost metaphysical idealization of the individual and, on the other hand, a compulsive reliance on the state. This puts international law in the not altogether untenable, but complex, situation where it may disapprove of action (civil disobedience) taken in defence of its own substantive norms, presumably on the basis that the action violates some higher order norm (of order, obedience, or sovereignty). Of course, this is in a sense only superficially a paradoxical situation. The international system may aspire to some end, but not so much so that it is willing to fundamentally change its preferred means of attaining this end (which, in the case of human rights, still sees deference to sovereignty as being unavoidable).

The promotion of international human rights law, for example, is itself embedded in compromises between rights and sovereignty.[121]

By the same token, ends and means are hardly rigidly separable. The end itself (for example, a world oriented towards the protection of some concept of human dignity) may condition a certain vision of the means needed to implement it (that is, civil disobedience in at least some cases). Inversely, the means themselves (say, sovereignty's toolbox) project, and are predated by, a certain vision of ends (an international legal system geared towards the maintenance of sovereignty as its ordering concept). There is a danger that in treating ends and means as belonging to irreducible analytical categories, international law's "method" may become more important than its "goals" and that the system may end up "losing its soul" by not recognizing the tension between the ends and means for what it is — that is, ultimately a debate *between ends*. Put slightly differently, international law's ontology and its epistemology cannot remain forever apart without producing considerable normative strain. Once the system becomes aware of this strain, it opens itself up to some fundamental possibilities for reordering. It may be therefore that, in the long run, a legal system's compliance mechanisms are likely to emulate its substantive aspirations. To the extent that international law is increasingly governed by concerns for the human being at the level of its substantive norms, one can conjecture that it may also increasingly see fit to rely on human beings to promote compliance with those norms.

The argument put forward here is not necessarily one that may be directly used in cases of civil disobedience before domestic courts, where more familiar routes may continue to be favoured. However, it does recognize that international law has its own stake in how civil disobedience is treated domestically, when some of its central norms are involved. It does not necessarily militate in favour of straightforward acquittals that will likely not be forthcoming and that civil disobeyers may not specifically seek. Rather, the reference to international law can safeguard the overall legitimacy of civil disobedience and, if nothing else, reinforce its status domestically, even as it inscribes in it something broader than individual conscience. As such, it does argue in favour of a certain indulgence, lest vocations be entirely discouraged, in that civil disobedience is an expression of admirable political courage, and in some cases at least, profoundly

---

[121] For example, individuals often have to exhaust domestic remedies before they can bring a case to an international body.

conducive to the values that international law stands for. It may seem meaningless to speak of a right to, or a privilege of, civil disobedience,[122] but there is probably a right to have even one's misguided civil disobedience recognized as something different than ordinary criminality, when exactly the opposite has often been true.

It may be that the alliance between certain forms of political protest and the substantive goals of international law will often only be contingent and even accidental. Civil disobeyers who objectively defend international values will often not be spurred to do so by some formal aspiration to have international law "obeyed" for the sake of it. Indeed, they may find that their aspirations clash with those of the established international legal order. International law, on the other hand, may have qualms about "letting the genie out of the box" and be particularly wary of undermining some of the statist foundations of its authority by engaging in strategies that coerce the state from below. Nonetheless, if it is the case that the international legal order is "serious" about focusing on the fate of human beings, as has certainly long been its promise, then individuals, and more generally the *forces vives* of society (both domestic and global), should feel increasingly internationally empowered to stand up to unjust orders. I foresee much prospect for not only challenging and reordering hierarchies in this process but also for freeing untold energies that have the potential to reshape international law and the way we think of it.

Of course, an international law that is willing to encourage civil disobedience is one that should be ready to see these tools periodically turned against it. It would be an international law at once ready to buttress authority and to undermine it — a law of constraint and of emancipation and one that is likely to emerge from a maelstrom of encounters. As Christian Bay put it, retracing the thought of Camus, "[a] commitment to civil disobedience is as necessary for the full growth of the individual as a human being as the steady supply of individuals prepared to commit civil disobedience is necessary for the protection and development of a human rights-oriented society."[123] The same could be said of international society and the recognition of the foundational character of transgression

---

[122] Although proposals of the sort have no doubt been made. See, for example, Marcus G. Raskin, *The Common Good: Its Politics, Policies, and Philosophy* (New York: Routledge, 1986) at 298; Lippman, *supra* note 97.

[123] Christian Bay, "Civil Disobedience," in T. Parsons and D. Sills, eds., *International Encyclopedia of the Social Sciences* (New York: Macmillan-Free Press, 1968) at 478.

by global citizens, which would be an apt recognition of the debt that all legal systems, paradoxically, owe to the resistance occasionally expressed against them.[124]

Sommaire

Désobéissance civile et droit international: esquisse d'un argument théorique

Cet article soutient qu'il y a une tendance croissante de la société civile de recourir à la désobéissance civile par rapport aux valeurs juridiques internationaux. Mais le droit international ne s'est pas adapté à cette tendance. En fait, tant le droit international que la désobéissance civile bénéficierait d'une meilleure compréhension de leur interaction. L'article retrace brièvement des arguments tirés du droit international dans les cas de désobéissance civile, met en évidence les contraintes théoriques du débat, et cherche à établir quelques fondements de base pour une théorie juridique internationale de la désobéissance civile légitime.

Summary

Civil Disobedience and International Law: Sketch for a Theoretical Argument

This article argues that there is an increasing trend of civil society resorting to civil disobedience in relation to international legal values. International law, however, has not caught up with this trend. In fact, both international law and civil disobedience can gain much from a better understanding of their interaction. The article briefly traces the record of arguments drawn from international law in civil disobedience cases, highlights the theoretical constraints of the debate, and seeks to establish some basic foundations for an international legal theory of legitimate civil disobedience.

---

[124] Etienne Balibar has developed this idea of "foundational transgression." See E. Balibar, "L'État d'urgence démocratique," *Le Monde* (19 February 1997).

Canadian International Human Rights Obligations in the Context of Assisted Human Reproduction

VERÓNICA B. PIÑERO

If we want to see our visions of children's rights prevail across communities, some of which currently lack our judgment, we must engage in dialogue. Our aim must be the enlargement of a shared common sense. Children's rights discourse must not be seen, as it frequently is, as a foreign imposition, rather as an element of shared common sense.

— *Michael Freeman, "Article 3: The Best Interest of the Child"*

INTRODUCTION

In 1986, an Argentinean movie won an Academy Award for best foreign film. This film, *The Official Story,* is about an Argentinean middle-class married woman (Alicia) who discovers that her adopted daughter (Gaby) is the child of a murdered political prisoner. Of course, her husband was aware of the scam: it was through his political contacts that he obtained Gaby. Alicia refused to see what was going on during that period (1976–83) and never questioned the child's origins. However, one day she awakens to the horrors being perpetrated by the Argentinean military government and decides to inquire about Gaby's biological origins. She finally meets Gaby's grandmother, who wants Gaby to be returned to her biological family. During an argument that Alicia has with her husband about this request, he states that ultimately they are Gaby's family and "who cares" about the biological family. Alicia does not agree

Verónica B. Piñero, LL.L., M.C.A., LL.M., LL.D. candidate, University of Ottawa. I am grateful to Danilo D'Addio Chammas and Mariana De Lorenzi for their insightful comments on some parts of this article. John Cecchetti kindly assisted me in editing this article, for which I am very thankful. The Social Sciences and Humanities Research Council of Canada generously funded the writing of this article.

with this statement and professes: "I do care, I do not want to do this to Gaby."[1] Alicia's cry reflects not only a mother's unconditional love for her child, but also the recognition of Gaby's need to know who she is — in other words, Gaby's identity.

The discussion in this article addresses Alicia's cry about Gaby's need to know her identity. However, its context does not involve the Argentinean "dirty war" but, rather, the Canadian regulation of assisted human reproduction.[2] The *Assisted Human Reproduction Act*, when regulating the disclosure of the donor's identity to the recipients of reproductive materials, notes that "the identity of the donor — or information that can reasonably be expected to be used in the identification of the donor — shall not be disclosed without the donor's written consent."[3] This article argues that Canada, by not allowing the donor's offspring access to the donor's identity, ignores — and consequently is in violation of — international human rights law on health, identity, and family relations. The first part of the article explores the international human rights treaties on identity, health, and family relations that Canada has signed, ratified, or acceded to as well as the international scholarship developed on the subject. The second part discusses whether Canada's legal system is in line with the relevant international human rights obligations identified earlier and whether there is scope for judicially interpreting it in such a way that would conform to these obligations.

INTERNATIONAL HUMAN RIGHTS LAW ON IDENTITY, HEALTH, AND FAMILY RELATIONS[4]

What is the international human rights framework that creates obligations for states with respect to persons within their territory

---

1   *La Historia Oficial* [*The Official Story*], directed by Luis Puenzo (1985).

2   Sara Wilson's research compared the disclosure of the biological parents' identity in the case of the children of the disappeared (Argentina), with adoption and donor insemination regulation (United Kingdom). She justifies her methodology from a child's rights standpoint: "[F]rom the perspective of the children, on which I concentrate in this paper, there are marked similarities between the situation of the children in all three cases: many of them have had very little or no contact with their biological 'genitors,' and have very little or no information about them, or even that they exist." "Identity, Genealogy and the Social Family: The Case of Donor Insemination" (1997) 11 Int'l J. L., Pol'y & Family 270 at 279.

3   *An Act Respecting Assisted Human Reproduction and Related Research*, S.C. 2004, c. 2 at s. 18(3) [*Assisted Human Reproduction Act*].

4   This section explores the universal and the American human rights systems. Concerning the American regional human rights system, Canada is not a party

(or subject to their jurisdiction) in the field of health, identity, and family relations? What is the "content" of these obligations? Can we argue that the interests of artificially procreated individuals in health, identity, and family relations matters are considered "rights" under international human rights law? In the event of a positive answer, how is this protection accorded? This section first explores international obligations on health rights and then focuses on identity rights. As a corollary to this discussion, this section comments on the right to family relations as regulated in international human rights law.

INTERNATIONAL OBLIGATIONS ON HEALTH RIGHTS

From an international perspective, the right to health is a core human right indispensable for the exercise of other human rights. This right was first regulated in a multilateral convention in the 1965 International Convention on the Elimination of All Forms of Racial Discrimination, whose Article 5(e)(iv) guarantees to everybody, "without distinction as to race, colour, or national or ethnic origin ... the right to public health, medical care, social security and social services."[5] The most comprehensive regulation came one

---

to either the American Convention on Human Rights, *infra* note 89, or the Additional Protocol to the American Convention on Human Rights in the Area of Economic, Social and Cultural Rights, *infra* note 90. The study of the European and the African regional human rights systems is beyond the scope of this article.

5 International Convention on the Elimination of All Forms of Racial Discrimination, 21 December 1965, UNGA Resolution 2106 (XX), Can. T. S. 1970/28 at art. 5(e)(iv) (entered into force on 4 January 1969; entered into force for Canada 14 October 1970) [ICERD].

Early attempts to regulate this right can be found in the Geneva Declaration of the Rights of the Child, 26 September 1924, G.A. Res. 1386 (XIV), 14 U.N. GAOR Supp. (No. 16) at 19, UN Doc. A/4354 (1959) at art. 2 (adopted and proclaimed by the League of Nations): "[T]he child that is sick must be nursed"; in the Universal Declaration of Human Rights, 10 December 1948, UNGA Resolution 217 A III at art. 25(1) [UDHR]: "Everyone has the right to a standard of living adequate for the health and well-being of himself and of his family, including food, clothing, housing and medical care and necessary social services"; in the American Declaration on the Rights and Duties of Man, 1948, O.A.S. Res. XXX, adopted by the Ninth International Conference of American States (1948), reprinted in *Basic Documents Pertaining to Human Rights in the Inter-American System*, OEA/Ser.L.V/II.82 doc.6 rev.1 at 17 (1992) at Article XI [ADRDM]: "Every person has the right to the preservation of his health through sanitary and social measures relating to food, clothing, housing and medical care, to the extent

year later with the adoption of the International Covenant on Economic, Social and Cultural Rights (ICESCR) in 1966: "The States Parties to the present Covenant recognize the right of everyone to the enjoyment of the highest attainable standard of physical and mental health."[6] In 1979, the Convention on the Elimination of All Forms of Discrimination against Women brought a new dimension to this right: "States Parties shall take all appropriate measures to eliminate discrimination against women in the field of health care in order to ensure, on a basis of equality of men and women, access to health care services, including those related to family planning."[7] A child-oriented perspective on the right to health was introduced in 1989 with the adoption of the Convention on the Rights of the Child (CRC):

> States Parties recognize the right of the child to the enjoyment of the highest attainable standards of health and to facilities for the treatment of illness and rehabilitation of health. States Parties shall strive to ensure that no child is deprived of his or her right of access to such health care services.[8]

None of these conventions make explicit reference to health rights in the context of assisted human reproduction, nor do they plainly refer to any health-related context.[9] All of these instruments, which

---

permitted by public and community resources"; and in the Declaration of the Rights of the Child, 20 November 1959 UNGA Resolution 1386(XIV) at principle 4: "The child shall enjoy the benefits of social security. He shall be entitled to grow and develop in health; to this end, special care and protection shall be provided both to him and to his mother, including adequate pre-natal and post-natal care."

6   International Covenant on Economic, Social, and Cultural Rights, 16 December 1966 UNGA Resolution 2200A (XXI) Can. T.S. 1976/46 at art. 12(1) (entered into force on 3 January 1976; entered into force for Canada 19 August 1976) [ICESCR].

7   Convention on the Elimination of All Forms of Discrimination against Women, 18 December 1979, Can. T.S. 1982/31 at art. 12(1) (entered into force on 3 September 1981; entered into force for Canada 9 January 1982) [CEDAW]. With regard to health rights in the work environment, see Article 11(1)(f).

8   Convention on the Rights of the Child, 20 November 1989, UNGA Resolution 44/25, Can. T.S. 1992/3 at art. 24(1) (entered into force on 2 September 1990; entered into force for Canada 12 January 1992) [CRC].

9   During the negotiations of the text of the CRC, there were two unsuccessful attempts to regulate genetic engineering. One was brought by the government of Colombia, as a comment to the first Polish draft to the convention (1978). The

were ratified or acceded to by Canada, regulate states parties' obligations to recognize the right for the persons under their jurisdiction to the highest attainable standards of health without any sort of distinction. Under this legal framework, it is necessary to evaluate how international law regulates states parties' obligations in the domain of health rights. For instance, under the ICESCR, states parties are required to take steps "to achieve the full realization" of the right to health.[10] In regard to this right, and following an analysis of the nature of the general legal obligations undertaken by states parties to the ICESCR (Article 2(1)), the Committee on Economic, Social and Cultural Rights (CESCR)[11] recognized the adoption of domestic legislation as an "indispensable element" for granting the right to health.[12] However, how much time is necessary in order for states to pass legislation that observes and implements the ICESCR? Article 2(1) of the ICESCR regulates the general legal obligations of states parties and the pace at which these obligations have to be implemented:

Each State Party to the present Covenant undertakes to take steps, individually and through international assistance and co-operation, especially economic and technical, to the maximum of its available resources, *with a view to achieving progressively the full realization of the rights recognized in the present Covenant* by all appropriate means, including particularly the adoption of legislation measures.[13]

---

second attempt was a proposal submitted to the Commission on Human Rights by the World Association of Children's Friends (a non-governmental organization) following the second reading of the convention (1989). Office of the United Nations High Commissioner for Human Rights, *Legislative History of the Convention on the Rights of the Child*, volume II (New York and Geneva: United Nations, 2007) 898–99, <http://www.ohchr.org/EN/PublicationsResources/Pages/ReferenceMaterial.asp>.

10 ICESCR, *supra* note 6 at art. 12(2).

11 The Committee on Economic, Social and Cultural Rights (CESCR) is the monitoring body of the ICESCR, *supra* note 6 at Part IV. See also United Nations Economic and Social Council, Resolution 1985/17 Establishing the Committee on Economic, Social and Cultural Rights, 28 May 1985.

12 CESCR, *General Comment 3 on the Nature of States Parties Obligations* (Article 2, part 1), 14 December 1990, at para. 3, Office of the High Commissioner for Human Rights <http://www.unhchr.ch/tbs/doc.nsf/(Symbol)/94bdbaf59b43a424c12563edoo52b664?Opendocument> [*General Comment 3*].

13 ICESCR, *supra* note 6 at art. 2(1) [emphasis added].

According to Article 2(1) of the ICESCR on the interpretation of a time frame, the CESCR clarifies the meaning of the term "progressive realization" to mean that it

imposes an obligation to move as expeditiously and effectively as possible towards that goal. Moreover, any deliberately retrogressive measures in that regard would require the most careful consideration and would need to be fully justified by reference to the totality of the rights provided for in the Covenant and in the context of the full use of the maximum available resources.[14]

According to *General Comment 3 on the Nature of States Parties Obligations*, states parties to the ICESCR have to implement the rights regulated therein, among them the right to health, as promptly as possible. Indeed, the "right to the highest attainable standard of health" is an important obligation for states parties to the ICESCR and requires legislation that leads to its full implementation. The enacted domestic legislation, as stated in the ICESCR, should not discriminate against any sort of group:

The States Parties to the present Covenant undertake to guarantee that the rights enunciated in the present Covenant will be exercised without discrimination of any kind as to race, colour, sex, language, religion, political or other opinion, national or social origin, property, *birth or other status*.[15]

This statement raises a compelling question. If Canadian legislation does not allow offspring to access donors' identifying information unless the latter consents to it, is the legislation being contrary to the international human rights framework on health rights identified earlier? This idea can be illustrated through an example. Suppose that Marie decides to anonymously donate her eggs for artificial insemination. She successfully completes the physical check requirements for so doing, and her eggs are extracted. Some time

---

14 *General Comment 3, supra* note 12 at para. 9. Audrey Chapman is against the notion of "progressive realization" for assessing states parties' compliance with economic, social, and cultural rights since, as she argues, this "is inexact and renders these rights difficult to monitor." Audrey Chapman, "A 'Violation Approach' for Monitoring the International Covenant on Economic, Social and Cultural Rights" (1996) 18 Hum. Rights Q. 23 at 23.

15 ICESCR, *supra* note 6 at art. 2(2) [emphasis added].

later, a woman is artificially inseminated with Marie's eggs and a baby girl (Camille) is born as a result of the procedure. By this time, Marie is diagnosed with a severe case of breast cancer that fortunately responds well to treatment. Marie is advised to tell her daughters about this possible genetic condition. Sadly, this health-related information does not appear in Marie's donor file since the diagnosis was rendered after her eggs were extracted. As a result, Camille will never have access to information on the latent risks of her developing breast cancer. Is it possible to claim that Camille has been granted the "right to the highest attainable standard of health"?[16]

In a subsequent general comment, the CESCR explicitly refers to the content of the "right to the highest attainable standard of health" as regulated in the ICESCR: "The right to health is not to be understood as a right to be *healthy*. The right to health contains both freedoms and entitlements. *The freedoms include the right to control one's health and body.*"[17] And it continues: "The Committee interprets the right to health, as defined in article 12.1, *as an inclusive right extending not only to timely and appropriate health care but also to the underlying determinants of health, such as ... access to health-related education and information.*"[18] Moreover, when highlighting the "interrelated and essential elements" that belong to the full implementation of the right to health, the committee identifies "information accessibility" as a core requirement and defines it as including "the right to seek, receive and impart information and ideas concerning

16 Comité Consultatif National d'Éthique pour les sciences de la vie et de la santé, *Avis no. 90. Accès aux origines, anonymat et secret de la filiation* (2005) at 4, Comité Consultatif National d'Éthique pour les sciences de la vie et de la santé, <http://www.ccne-ethique.fr/docs/fr/aviso90.pdf>. Eric Blyth reports how donor-conceived people have identified the lack of updated information about donors as a health issue: "With increasing awareness of the importance of genetics and of personal genetic biographies, donor-conceived people have begun to itemize the information they want about their genetic and social heritage and to emphasize the need for this information to be updated and *not to cease at the point of donation.*" "Information on Genetic Origins in Donor-Assisted Conception: Is Knowing Who You Are a Human Rights Issue?" (2002) 5 Human Fertility 185 at 187 [emphasis added]. See also Joanna Rose's and E.M.'s personal accounts on the relevance of the subject in *Rose & Anor v. Secretary of State for Health Human Fertilisation and Embryology Authority*, [2002] E.W.H.C. 1593 (Admin) (26 July 2002) at paras. 7 and 12, respectively.

17 CESCR, *General Comment 14 on the Right to the Highest Attainable Standard of Health* (Article 12 of the ICESCR), 11 May 2000, at para. 8, Office of the High Commissioner for Human Rights <http://www2.ohchr.org/english/bodies/cescr/comments.htm> [emphasis added] [*General Comment 14*].

18 *Ibid.* at para. 11 [emphasis added].

health issues."[19] Is Camille, the baby girl in our earlier example, being granted access to health-related education and information? Unfortunately, under current Canadian legislation on assisted human reproduction, Camille does not have access to health-related information that can lead her to "timely and appropriate health care." Camille's health rights — as regulated by the ICESCR — are being neglected by the Canadian domestic legislation on assisted human reproduction.

Another principle of the right to health is the observance of confidentiality. However, this right does not limit access to health-related information to people who have a valid interest, such as Camille in the earlier example. The CESCR's *General Comment 14 on the Right to the Highest Attainable Standard of Health* states that "information accessibility" is not absolute: "[A]ccessibility of information should not impair the right to have personal health data treated with confidentiality."[20] What does the word "confidentiality" mean in this phrase? From the literal context of both this paragraph and the entire commentary, it seems that the committee did not want to equate "accessibility" to "openness" but, rather, to limit the latter. This interpretation is clearly stated in the Committee on the Rights of the Child's[21] *General Comment 4 on Adolescent Health and Development in the Context of the Convention on the Rights of the Child,* which requires states parties to implement the principle of accessibility: "Health facilities, goods and services should be known and easily accessible (economically, physically and socially) to all adolescents, without discrimination."[22] Moreover, in regard to "confidentiality," the committee notes: "Confidentiality should be guaranteed, when necessary."[23] It seems that the intention of both committees when regulating the notion of "confidentiality" was to

---

19 *Ibid.* at para. 12(b)(iv).

20 *Ibid.*

21 The Committee on the Rights of the Child is the monitoring body of the CRC, *supra* note 8 at Part II.

22 Committee on the Rights of the Child, *General Comment 4 on Adolescent Health and Development in the Context of the Convention on the Rights of the Child,* 1 July 2003, at para. 41(b) and para. 24, Office of the High Commissioner for Human Rights <http://www.unhchr.ch/tbs/doc.nsf/898586b1dc7b4043c1256a450044f331/309e8c3807aa8cb7c1256d2doo38caaa/$FILE/G0340816.pdf>: "Adolescents have the right to access adequate information essential for their health and development and for their ability to participate meaningfully in society."

23 *Ibid.*

protect the privacy of the persons accessing health-related information and to prevent private health-related information from being openly available. However, there was no intention to limit access to such private health-related information. Article 9 of the Universal Declaration on the Human Genome and Human Rights clearly supports this interpretation:

In order to protect human rights and fundamental freedoms, limitations to the principles of consent and confidentiality may only be prescribed by law, *for compelling reasons within the bounds of public international law and the international law of human rights*.24

In other words, the information "sought," "received," or "imparted" may not necessarily be public information. However, this does not mean that people cannot have access to this information. There are compelling reasons under international human rights law, such as the full observance of the right to health, that limit the principle of confidentiality.25

The Committee on the Rights of the Child considers the child's best interest a core principle that should guide the enactment of legislation implementing the right to health. Referring to the CRC, the CESCR notes that "[i]n all policies and programmes aimed at guaranteeing the right to health of children and adolescent their best interest shall be a primary consideration."26 Moreover, according to Article 4, when explaining the nature of the obligations regulated therein, states parties are required to enact legislation that observes the convention's rights: "States Parties shall undertake

---

24 Universal Declaration on the Human Genome and Human Rights, 11 November 1997, General Conference of the United Nations Educational, Scientific and Cultural Organisation, 29th Sess. UNGA Resolution 53/152, 9 December 1998 [emphasis added].

25 For a similar perspective, see Asbjørn Eide and Wenche Barth Eide, "Article 24 The Right to Health," in André Alen et al., eds., *A Commentary on the United Nations Conventions on the Rights of the Child* (Leiden: Martinus Nijhoff Publishers, 2006) at 22. Michael Freeman, also writing for this series of volumes that intended to discuss the "scope" of different articles of the CRC, has critically commented about the authors' lack of discussion of children's health rights in the assisted reproduction domain: "What obligations are there [Article 24 of the CRC] to the children of reproductive technology?" Michael Freeman, "Book Review: A. Eide and W.B. Eide 'Article 24: The Right to Health'" (2007) 15 Int'l J. Children's Rights 315 at 317.

26 *General Comment 14, supra* note 17 at para. 24. See also Eide and Eide, *supra* note 25 at 5.

all appropriate legislative, administrative, and other measures for the implementation of the rights recognized in the present Convention."[27] With regard to the extent of these obligations, Mervat Rishmawi notes that "the formula used in the CRC is meant to be inclusive of any measures that should be taken to implement the Convention."[28] This means that when a state ratifies the CRC, it assumes the obligation to make the rights regulated therein effective in its jurisdiction. A. Eide and W.B. Eide, when analyzing the states parties' obligations under the CRC, refer to the methodological analysis employed by the CESCR in *General Comment 14*.[29] According to these authors, the duties of a state when becoming a party to the CRC with respect to the implementation of the right to health can be classified as obligations to respect, protect, and fulfil. The enactment of legislation that implements the right to health as internationally regulated is considered within the obligation to fulfil and, consequently, is an important step towards the effective implementation and observance of the CRC:

As with all other human rights, the obligations of the State concerning the right of the child to enjoy the highest attainable standard of health falls into three broad categories: the obligations to *respect, protect* and *fulfill*. In turn, the obligation to fulfill contains obligations to facilitate, provide and promote. The obligation to *respect* requires States to refrain from interfering directly or indirectly, with the enjoyment by the child of its right to health or with the rights of parents or guardians to take the necessary steps for the health of the child. The obligation to *protect* requires States to take measures that prevent third parties from causing harm to the child's health, or from interfering with the access of the child to health care. The State is also obliged to take measures, when necessary, to protect the child against abuse or neglect by the child's parents. *Finally, the obligation to fulfill requires States to adopt appropriate legislative, administrative, budgetary, judicial, promotional and other measures towards the full realization of the right of the child to health.*[30]

With respect to the obligation to fulfil, the CESCR recognizes this sort of duty as a "positive measure": "The obligation to *fulfill* requires

27 CRC, *supra* note 8 at art. 4(1).

28 Mervat Rishmawi, "Article 4: The Nature of States Parties' Obligations," in Alen et al., *supra* note 25 at 4.

29 *General Comment 14, supra* note 17 at para. 33.

30 Eide and Eide, *supra* note 25 at 6–7 [emphasis added].

States Parties, *inter alia,* to give sufficient recognition to the right to health in the national, political and legal system."[31] Similar views have been expressed by the Committee on the Rights of the Child in regard to states parties' legal obligations in relation to the health and development of adolescents under the CRC:

> States Parties must take all appropriate legislative, administrative and other measures for the realization and monitoring of the rights of adolescents to health and development as recognized in the Convention. *To this end, States Parties must notably fulfill the following obligations ...* (b) *To ensure that adolescents have access to the information that is essential for their health and development.*[32]

When Camille is denied "access to the information that is essential for her health and development," her health rights embodied in the CRC are not being reflected in Canadian domestic legislation.

In sum, the right to health as regulated in international human rights law is a comprehensive right including many different aspects, among them the right to access to health-related information. States parties to the enumerated conventions, among them Canada, have a positive obligation to facilitate, provide, and promote in their territories the highest attainable standards of health, mostly through the enactment of domestic legislation that implements and observes the international requirements. "Access to health information" is considered a core element for evaluating whether international obligations on health rights have been successfully and effectively implemented domestically.

INTERNATIONAL OBLIGATIONS ON IDENTITY RIGHTS

According to Michael Freeman, most of the literature on artificially procreated individuals has focused its attention on the notion of identity. It is a subject of "interest which is of greatest concern to

---

[31] *General Comment 14, supra* note 17 at para. 36.

[32] Committee on the Rights of the Child, *supra* note 22 at para. 39 [emphasis added]. See as well Eide and Eide, *supra* note 25 at 1: "[The CRC] does not provide a right of the child to be healthy — no legal instrument can do that — but it spells out obligations of States Parties to adopt measures which, if implemented, will ensure the highest attainable standard of health taking into account the genetic and other biological predispositions of the individual child and the risks that children are exposed to."

those who have been artificially-procreated."[33] For Douglas Hodgson, the importance of the right to identity "is reflected by the position of Articles 7 and 8 at the beginning of the Convention [CRC] directly after the child's inherent right to life."[34] The Waller Committee in Australia has also recognized the importance of identity rights to human beings: "Whether or not a person pursues her or his origins, it should be possible for everyone to discover them. In this sense, everyone has a strong interest in being able to discover some information about her or his origin."[35] Surprisingly, the only international regulation on the right to identity is in the CRC:

Article 8. (1) States Parties undertake to respect the right of the child to preserve his or her identity, including nationality, name and family relations as recognized by law without unlawful interference.

(2) Where a child is illegally deprived of some or all of the elements of his or her identity, States Parties shall provide appropriate assistance and protection, with a view to reestablishing speedily his or her identity.[36]

This article did not exist in the first Polish draft to the CRC in 1978, and it was not until 1985 that it was presented to the working group

---

[33] Michael Freeman, "The New Birth Right? Identity and the Child of the Reproduction Revolution" (1996) 4 Int'l J. Children's Rights 273 at 277. See also Katherine O'Donovan, "A Right to Know One's Parentage?" (1988) 2 Int'l J. L. & Family 27; Wilson, *supra* note 2.

[34] Douglas Hodgson, "The International Legal Protection of the Child's Right to a Legal Identity and the Problem of Statelessness" (1993) 7 Int'l J. L. & Family 255 at 256.

[35] The Committee to Consider the Social, Ethical and Legal Issues Arising from In Vitro Fertilization (Louis Waller, Chair), *Report on the Disposition of Embryos Produced by In Vitro Fertilization* (Melbourne: F.D. Atkinson Government Printer, 1984), para. 3.30, 26; cited in Louis Waller and Debbie Mortimer, "The Gifts of Life-Donating Gametes and the Consequences," in Michael Freeman and Andrew D.E. Lewis, eds., *Law and Medicine: Current Legal Issues 2000*, vol. 3 (New York: Oxford University Press, 2000) 303 at 304.

[36] CRC, *supra* note 8 at art. 8. A different attempt to regulate identity rights can be found in the Convention on the Prevention and Punishment of the Crime of Genocide, 9 December 1948, Can. T.S. 1949/27 at art. II (e) (entered into force on 12 January 1951): "In the present Convention, genocide means any of the following acts committed with intent to destroy, in whole or in part, a national, ethnical, racial or religious group, as such ... Forcibly transferring children of the group to another group."

by the Argentinean government.[37] As noted in the introduction to this article, Argentina had just elected a democratic government in 1983, and this article reflected the problems that Argentina was dealing with locally. Political prisoners' children, abducted along with their parents or having been born to female political prisoners while in illegal detention, had been given to individuals connected to the militia or the police for adoption, and their biological families were looking for them.[38] The representative of Argentina wanted to address this particular problem and consequently introduced the following article:

The child has the inalienable right to retain his true and genuine personal, legal and family identity ... In the event that a child has been fraudulently deprived of some or all of the elements of his identity, the State must give him special protection and assistance with a view to re-establishing his true and genuine identity as soon as possible. In particular, this obligation of the State includes restoring the child to his blood relation to be brought up.[39]

The notion of "family identity" brought much discussion since the concept was unknown in many states. As a result of this inquiry, the delegation of the Netherlands wanted to introduce the phrase "as recognized by law" after the words "family identity."[40] As well, the delegation of Norway sought to replace the phrase "family identity" with the words "family relations."[41] In the end, the draft article was

---

[37] Office of the United Nations High Commissioner for Human Rights, *Legislative History of the Convention on the Rights of the Child*, volume I (New York and Geneva: United Nations, 2007) at 383, Office of the High Commissioner for Human Rights <http://www.ohchr.org/EN/PublicationsResources/Pages/ReferenceMaterial.asp>.

[38] The partial relocation of these children has been an extremely difficult task since many of them had been registered as having been born in the families who had really adopted them. During the Argentinean military government, individuals associated with the militia or the police forces had access to the official registries and were able to falsify the information related to the kidnapped child. Up to the present, many children (adults) do not know their biological origins. See Informe de la Comisión Nacional sobre la Desaparición de Personas, *Nunca Más* (Buenos Aires: EUDEBA, 1984), Proyecto Desaparecidos, <http://www.desaparecidos.org/arg/conadep/nuncamas/nuncamas.html >.

[39] Office of the United Nations High Commissioner for Human Rights, *supra* note 37 at 383.

[40] *Ibid.* at 385.

[41] *Ibid.*

modified accordingly. During the second reading of this article in 1988–89, the representative of Mexico unsuccessfully attempted to modify the wording to make the commitments of the states parties more explicit and as well to include in the formulation of the article the biological elements of identity.[42]

As Jaap Doek notes, the origin of the article is not related to cases of medically assisted procreation. Nevertheless, he notes that, "in the light of the present day developments and a dynamic interpretation of the CRC, it can be considered to include in the right to preserve your identity, the right to be informed about your (biological) origins."[43] Considering that Doek was the chairperson of the Committee on the Rights of the Child for the period between 2001 and 2007 (and a member from 1999 to 2007), his understanding about the legal implications of Article 8 of the CRC should be taken seriously. In addition, many authors note that the list of elements fundamental to the preservation of identity enumerated in Article 8.1 (nationality, name, and family relations) is nonexhaustive.[44] Therefore, the biological origins of a child are also included within the notion of identity. Indeed, Doek argues that it is not clear whether the limiting qualification "as recognized by law" in the first paragraph of the article should be linked to "identity" or "to family relations." As noted earlier, the original version referred to the notion of "family identity," and since this was an unknown concept for many domestic juridical systems the representative from the Netherlands suggested that the phrase "as recognized by law" be added. The limitation of "as recognized by law" was not meant to restrict the notion of identity but the notion of "family identity," which now reads "family relations."

[42] *Ibid.* at 387.

[43] Jaap E. Doek, "Article 8: The Right to Preservation of Identity, and Article 9: The Right Not to Be Separated from His or Her Parents," in Alen et al., *supra* note 25 at 12. Freeman understands the right to identity in a negative — and maybe broader — fashion. He argues "that the right to identity is a right not to be deceived about one's true origins." Freeman, *supra* note 33 at 291.

[44] Geraldine Van Bueren, *The International Law on the Rights of the Child* (The Hague: Martinus Nijhoff Publishers, 1998) at 119; Doek, *supra* note 43 at 8; Jaime Sergio Cerda, "The Draft Convention on the Rights of the Child: New Rights" (1990) 12(1) Hum. Rights Q. 115 at 116 (Cerda was the Argentinean sponsor of Article 8 of the CRC); George Stewart, "Interpreting the Child's Right to Identity in the U.N. Convention on the Rights of the Child" (1992) 26(3) Family L. Q. 221 at 224.

The second paragraph of Article 8 also protects the interests on identity of assisted human reproduction offspring. In response, Doek notes that

paragraph 2 of Article 8 of the CRC has not been written with artificial procreation in mind. But the obligation to respect the right of the child to preserve her or his identity, requires the State Party to undertake all legislative, administrative or other measures (Article 4 of the CRC) to implement that right, interpreting it in a dynamic manner and with the present day conditions in mind.[45]

In addition, the notion of "illegally" in the second paragraph of Article 8, as Geraldine Van Bueren highlights, "applies both when the deprivation is illegal under domestic law and when the deprivation of identity is contrary to international law. To interpret article 8 only to include the former would open up a dangerous loophole."[46] According to Van Bueren, the elements of identity are regulated both by domestic law and international law. And as noted earlier, Doek states that even though Article 8 of the CRC was intended to address a specific situation, a dynamic interpretation of its wording would allow us to include in it the situation of children who were artificially conceived through the genetic material of anonymous donors and are interested in being informed about the donor's identity. Therefore, under international law, information relating to a child's biological origins is considered to be part of his/her identity and consequently protected by Article 8 of the CRC. Any sort of interference with this mandate will be contrary to international law and, as a result, "illegal" according to Article 8 (second paragraph) of the CRC.

INTERNATIONAL OBLIGATIONS ON THE RIGHTS OF FAMILY RELATIONS

International law recognizes the importance of the family as the basic unit upon which society is organized and, for this reason, requires states to protect it. However, neither the notion of "family" nor who the "family members" are considered to be has been defined under international law. In 1948, the American Declaration on the Rights and Duties of Man (ADRDM) recognized that "[e]very person has the right to the protection of the law against abusive

---

[45] Doek, *supra* note 43 at 13.
[46] Van Bueren, *supra* note 44 at 119.

attacks upon his honor, reputation, and his private and family life,"[47] and it provided protection accordingly: "Every person has the right to establish a family, the basic element of society, and to receive protection therefore."[48] That same year, the Universal Declaration of Human Rights (UDHR) was adopted, recognizing an analogous protection: "No one shall be subjected to arbitrary interference with his privacy, family, home or correspondence, nor to attacks upon his honour and reputation. Everyone has the right to the protection of the law against such interference or attacks."[49] As well, the declaration states that "[t]he family is the natural and fundamental group unit of society and is entitled to protection by society and the State."[50] Similar protection was provided by the two international covenants adopted in 1966. The ICESCR states that "[t]he widest possible protection and assistance should be accorded to the family, which is the natural and fundamental group unit of society, particularly for its establishment and while it is responsible for the care and education of dependent children."[51] The International Covenant on Civil and Political Rights (ICCPR) brought a civil rights perspective to the right to family relations and provided for proper protection as well. First, Article 17(1) notes that "[n]o one shall be subjected to arbitrary or unlawful interference with his privacy, family, or correspondence, nor to unlawful attacks on his honour and reputation."[52] Second, Article 23(1) states that "[t]he family is the natural and fundamental group unit of society and is entitled to protection by society and the State."[53]

The protection of the right to family relations received a child-oriented perspective with the enactment of the CRC. This convention introduced three new articles on the subject. Article 16(1), with an almost identical formulation to the ICCPR, states that "[n]o child shall be subjected to arbitrary or unlawful interference with his or her privacy, family, or correspondence, not to unlawful attacks

---

[47] ADRDM, *supra* note 5 at art. V.

[48] *Ibid.* at art. VI.

[49] UDHR, *supra* note 5 at art. 12.

[50] *Ibid.* at art. 16(3).

[51] ICESCR, *supra* note 6 at art. 10(1).

[52] International Covenant on Civil and Political Rights, 16 December 1966, UNGA Resolution 2200A (XXI), Can. T. S. 1976/47 at art. 17(1) (entered into force on 23 March 1976; entered into force for Canada 19 August 1976) [ICCPR].

[53] *Ibid.* at art. 23(1).

on his or her honour and reputation."[54] Article 20(1) regulates the child's right to a family environment: "A child temporarily or permanently deprived of his or her family environment, or in whose own best interests cannot be allowed to remain in that environment, shall be entitled to special protection and assistance provided by the State."[55] Finally, Article 7(1) regulates the child's right to know his or her parents: "The child shall be registered immediately after birth and shall have the right from birth to a name, the right to acquire a nationality and, as far as possible, the right to know and be cared for by his or her parents."[56]

The purpose of this part of the article is to analyze, under international law, which family relations rights offspring have with regard to anonymous donors. The underlying question is whether the earlier provisions apply to such offspring. In this regard, it is worth highlighting that a right to a family *per se* does not exist under international law. What international law recognizes is the importance of the family as the basic unit of society and the necessity to protect it. In the context of assisted human reproduction, we need to draw a distinction between two separate — albeit related — inquiries: first, the family relations that offspring have with their half-siblings; and, second, the family relations that offspring have with the anonymous donor.

With respect to the first question, Eric Blyth has reported that offspring are interested in, and willing to know about, the existence of half-siblings: how many half-siblings they have, their age, gender, and whereabouts.[57] This fact is no surprise. James Dwyer argues that siblings' relationships "are the most important relationships in the lives of some children and central to the life of most, typically entailing emotional ties stronger than those with any other nonparent relatives, such as grandparents, aunts, uncles, and cousins."[58] Astonishingly, under international law, there is no express provision that regulates children's right to access and contact with their siblings. Nevertheless, Van Bueren argues that a child's right "to access

---

[54] CRC, *supra* note 8 at art. 16(1). See also the para. 5 of the preamble to the CRC.

[55] *Ibid.* at art. 20(1).

[56] *Ibid.* at art. 7(1).

[57] Eric Blyth, "Donor Assisted Conception and Donor Offspring Rights to Genetic Origins Information" (1998) 6 Int'l J. Children's Rights 237 at 244–45; Blyth, *supra* note 16 at 188.

[58] James G. Dwyer, *The Relationship Rights of Children* (Cambridge: Cambridge University Press, 2006) at 59–60.

and contact with siblings falls within article 16 of the UN Convention as amounting to unlawful interference with the family."[59] Paraphrasing this author, any obstruction (either material or legal) of siblings' relationship could be considered as being contrary to the CRC. Moreover, both the UDHR and the ICCPR recognize the right to protection against "arbitrary interference" and "arbitrary or unlawful interference" (respectively) with the family, and, as a result, they expand the legal protection to adults as well.[60] With respect to "siblings' relationships," any sort of distinction between offspring and children born without the use of artificial technologies could be construed as being contrary to Article 2(1) of the CRC. According to this article, the rights stated in the CRC should be implemented by states parties "without discrimination of any kind,"[61] including "birth or other status."[62] In addition, protection against discrimination is accorded by both the UDHR and the ICCPR "without distinction of any kind, such as ... birth or other status."[63] Therefore, it can be argued that not allowing offspring access to their (possible) siblings amounts to "arbitrary or unlawful interference with his or her privacy [and] family."[64]

To date, the interest in establishing and preserving one's relationship with siblings has been addressed only by Van Bueren and not in the context of assisted human reproduction. Our understanding, which favours a dynamic interpretation of the CRC as Doek offers,[65] is that the protection offered to children against arbitrary or illegal intrusions under Article 16(1) of the CRC, which, according to Van Bueren, protects siblings' relationships, should include artificially procreated individuals. Similar conclusions arise from Article 12 of the UDHR (protection against arbitrary interference) and Article 17(1) of the ICCPR (protection against arbitrary or illegal interference). Moreover, as noted in the previous subsection, the notion of "illegal intrusion" should not be limited to domestic law but should be inclusive of international human rights law. In other

---

59 Van Bueren, *supra* note 44 at 83.

60 UDHR, *supra* note 5 at art. 12; ICCPR, *supra* note 52 at art. 17(1) (respectively).

61 CRC, *supra* note 8 at art. 2(1).

62 *Ibid.*

63 UDHR, *supra* note 5 at art. 2(1); ICCPR, *supra* note 52 at art. 2(1).

64 CRC, *supra* note 8 at art. 16(1); UDHR, *supra* note 5 at art. 12; and ICCPR, *supra* note 52 at art. 17(1).

65 Doek, *supra* note 43 at 12.

words, the notion of "illegal intrusion" refers to any sort of conduct that can be considered to be contrary to domestic law and/or international human rights law.[66] Referring to Article 17 of the ICCPR, the Human Rights Committee holds that

[t]he term "unlawful" means that no interference can take place except in cases envisaged by the law. Interference authorized by States can only take place on the basis of law, *which itself must comply with the provisions, aims and objectives of the Covenant* [ICCPR].[67]

With regard to the term "arbitrary interference," which is also stated in Article 17 of the ICCPR, the Human Rights Committee understands that this expression

can also extend to interference provided for under the law. The introduction of the concept of arbitrariness is intended to guarantee that even interference provided for by law should be in accordance with the provisions, aims and objectives of the Covenant and should be, in any event, reasonable in the particular circumstances.[68]

With respect to the relationship between the anonymous donor and the offspring, it would be difficult to argue that there is a right to family relations. The child that is conceived through the donor's genetic material will be born in a family, and the donor will not be considered to be a member of that family. However, under international law, every child is granted "as far as possible, the right to know and be cared for by his or her parents."[69] Ineta Ziemele notes that

---

[66] For example, the enactment of legislation by a state party to the CRC that does not observe the international human rights law recognized to individuals therein.

[67] Human Rights Committee, *General Comment 16 on the Right to Respect of Privacy, Family, and Home and Correspondence, and Protection of Honour and Reputation* (Art. 17), 8 April 1988, at para. 3, Office of the High Commissioner for Human Rights, <http://www2.ohchr.org/english/bodies/hrc/comments.htm>. The Human Rights Committee is the monitoring body of the ICCPR, *supra* note 52 at Part IV [emphasis added].

[68] *Ibid.* at para. 4.

[69] CRC, *supra* note 8 at art. 7(1). Nigel Cantwell and Anna Holzscheiter understand that Articles 7(1) and 20 of the CRC are closely related. Nigel Cantwell and Anna Holzscheiter, "Article 20: Children Deprived of Their Family Environment," in Alen et al., *supra* note 25 at 5.

[s]ome exchanges between the CRC Committee and States in the framework of the State reports suggest that the CRC Committee takes the view that the term "parents" in the context of Article 7 and the aims of the CRC *includes biological parents* and that the child has the right to know, as far as possible, who they are. This right is both part of Article 7 and Article 3 of the CRC since *it is considered to be in the best interest of the child to know, as far as possible, the child's birth parents.*[70]

What does the phrase "as far as possible" mean? It is important to be clear about its meaning since, as Freeman notes, this qualification could limit the application of this article.[71] To decipher its full meaning, it is helpful to explore the legislative history of the CRC one more time. Article 7, as regulated in the CRC's first Polish draft in 1978, only stated that "[t]he child shall be entitled from his birth to a name and a nationality."[72] During the period of 1979–88, most of the discussion surrounding this article only focused on how to implement the child's right to a nationality, which was a conflicted topic among negotiating states back then. It was not until the 1988 technical review that the UN Educational, Social, and Cultural Organization proposed adding a new paragraph to this article, which read: "The child shall have the right from birth to respect for his/her human, racial, national and cultural identity and dignity, as well as have the duty to respect the human, racial, national and cultural identity and dignity of others."[73] This text was adopted by the working group, but during the second reading in 1989 the delegation of Egypt, on behalf of nine Arab countries, proposed an amendment to it: "The child shall have the right from his birth to know and belong to his parents, as well as the right to a name and to acquire a nationality."[74] As the delegation of Egypt explained,

---

[70] Ineta Ziemele, "Article 7: The Right to Birth Registration, Name and Nationality, and the Right to Know and Be Cared for by Parents," in Alen et al., *supra* note 25 at 26 [emphasis added].

[71] Michael Freeman, "The Rights of the Artificially Procreated Child," in *The Moral Status of Children: Essays on the Rights of the Child* (The Hague: Kluwer Law International, 1997) at 196.

[72] Office of the United Nations High Commissioner for Human Rights, *supra* note 37 at 370.

[73] *Ibid.* at 376.

[74] *Ibid.* at 378.

the purpose of the first amendment was that of ensuring the psychological stability of the child, which was of equal importance to his physical and mental growth and helped to form his personality. *In most cases the right to know his parents was quite essential to the child* and equal to his right to a name or a nationality, which were only important to him at a certain age.[75]

The delegations of West Germany, the Soviet Union, and the United States expressed some concern about this proposal since their legislations regulated the right to "secret adoptions," and, consequently, the right to know one's parents could not be applied.[76] As a result, the representative of the United States introduced a new proposal: "The child shall have the right from birth to a name and registration and to acquire a nationality, and, as far as possible, to know and be cared for by his or her parents."[77] This last amendment created some concern since some participants viewed the words "as far as possible" "as giving rise to an arbitrary interpretation of this article."[78] Therefore, a new discussion arose in which the observers for New Zealand and Sweden proposed that the phrase "as far as possible" should be replaced by the phrases "subject to the provisions of this Convention" or "as far as possible and subject to the provisions of the Convention," respectively.[79] In addition, the representative of the United States suggested adding the wording "in the best interests of the child."[80] Once the final text was adopted, the representative of Sweden stated that "his delegation was able to join in the consensus on article 2 [current Article 7] on the understanding that the provisions of this article should be interpreted in the best interests of the child."[81]

According to the legislative history of the CRC, the phrase "as far as possible" should be interpreted to take into consideration the best interest of the child. Moreover, as the legislative history documents, the only reason why this phrase was added was to take into consideration the "secret" adoption procedures regulated in some Western countries. In response, Ziemele notes that

---

[75] *Ibid.* [emphasis added].

[76] *Ibid.*

[77] *Ibid.* at 379.

[78] *Ibid.*

[79] *Ibid.*

[80] *Ibid.*

[81] *Ibid.* at 380.

[t]he limitation "as far as" possible presupposes that there might be circumstances which may limit the right of the child to know the biological parents. In any event, often there will be a need to weigh all the circumstances, *but an absolute prohibition on the right to know biological parents is contrary to the CRC.*[82]

Both Ziemele and the legislative history of the CRC lead us to conclude that a complete prohibition on the right to know biological parents would be contrary to the CRC. Moreover, any sort of distinction for exercising this right — for instance, this right only being recognized in the context of adoption procedures and not in the context of assisted human reproduction — could be considered to be contrary to Article 2(1) of the CRC (prohibition against discrimination).[83] As a final note, Eric Blyth and Abigail Farrand report that the Austrian government has interpreted Article 7 of the CRC as giving offspring the right to know about their genetic father on reaching the age of fourteen years old (egg and embryo donation are illegal in Austria).[84]

CANADA AND INTERNATIONAL HUMAN RIGHTS LAW

As noted in the previous section, international human rights law on health, identity, and family relations recognizes the interests of artificially conceived individuals as human rights to observe and protect. Having analyzed its content previously, the article now discusses whether the Canadian legal system is in line with the relevant international human rights obligations identified earlier and whether there is scope for judicially interpreting it in such a way that would conform to these obligations. This subsection first explores whether the international human rights law has been explicitly or implicitly implemented in Canadian law and even if it can be deemed to be part of customary international law (and, therefore, directly applicable in Canada through common law). The second subsection focuses on whether the existing Canadian law can be interpreted consistently with the relevant international human rights obligations.

---

82 Ziemele, *supra* note 70 at 27 [emphasis added].

83 CRC, *supra* note 8 at art. 2(1).

84 Eric Blyth and Abigail Farrand, "Anonymity in Donor-Assisted Conception and the UN Convention on the Rights of the Child" (2004) 12 Int'l J' on Children's Right 89 at 94–95.

It is beyond the scope of this article to discuss whether the regulation of assisted human reproduction is a power that belongs to Parliament or to the provincial legislatures. It is worth noting that on 19 June 2008, the Quebec Court of Appeal held that many sections of the *Assisted Human Reproduction Act* (sections 8–19, 40–53, 60, 61, and 68) were unconstitutional because they were not within the jurisdiction of the federal government. By the time of writing, the Attorney General of Canada had appealed this decision, and the governments of British Columbia, Alberta, Saskatchewan, and New Brunswick had been granted leave to intervene in the litigation. To date, the Supreme Court of Canada has not rendered a decision on the subject.[85] In other words, despite the fact that the *Assisted Human Reproduction Act* has been constitutionally challenged, Parliament's legislative power has not been overruled.[86] Hence, it is assumed that the regulation of assisted human reproduction is a subject matter for which the Parliament of Canada has competence in regulating.[87]

DOES INTERNATIONAL HUMAN RIGHTS LAW HAVE DIRECT EFFECT IN THE CANADIAN LEGAL SYSTEM?

From the outset, it is necessary to identify the status of international human rights law in Canada for assessing the Canadian observance. Concerning the universal human rights system, Canada has acceded to the ICCPR (1976) and the ICESCR (1976) and has

---

[85] *Renvoi fait par le gouvernement du Québec en vertu de la Loi sur les renvois à la Cour d'appel, L.R.Q. ch. R-23, relativement à la constitutionnalité des articles 8 à 19, 40 à 53, 60, 61 et 68 de la Loi sur la procréation assistée, L.C. 2004, ch. 2 (Dans l'affaire du),* 2008 Q.C.C.A. 1167, leave to appeal to S.C.C. requested (Docket 32750). On 11 March 2009, the Attorney General of British Columbia gave notice of withdrawal.

[86] *Assisted Human Reproduction Act, supra* note 3. For a discussion supporting Parliament's legislative power for regulating assisted human reproduction, see Martha Jackman, "The Constitution and the Regulation of New Reproductive Technologies," in *Overview of Legal Issues in New Reproductive Technologies,* volume 3 of the Research Studies of the Royal Commission on New Reproductive Technologies (Ottawa: Supply and Services Canada, 1994) at 1.

[87] As a result, an analysis of Article 27 of the Vienna Convention on the Laws of Treaties is beyond the scope of this article ("[a] Party may not invoke the provisions of its internal law as justification for its failure to perform a treaty. This rule is without prejudice to article 46"). Vienna Convention on the Law of Treaties, 23 May 1969, Can. T.S. 1980/37 (entered into force on 27 January 1980; entered into force for Canada 27 January 1980 [Vienna Convention].

ratified the CRC (1991). As well, Canada has subscribed to the UDHR (1948). However, we need to draw a distinction between the obligations under the ICCPR, the ICESCR, and the CRC as well as the obligations under the UDHR. With regard to the former, once a state becomes a party to either treaty, it assumes at the international level the obligation to observe its regulation and to perform it in good faith.[88] On the other hand, the status of the UDHR is contentious. While some scholars argue that its provisions (or part of them) have become customary international law, others argue that the UDHR is a non-binding legal instrument (soft law). States are asked to implement it in their legal systems, but its non-observance cannot be considered to be a breach of international law. The ICESCR and the ICCPR have codified the wording of this declaration, and Canada is party to both covenants.

Canada is also a member of a multinational organization that operates within a regional geographic area — the Organization of American States (OAS). With respect to the American human rights system, Canada has neither signed nor acceded to the American Convention on Human Rights[89] or the Additional Protocol to the American Convention on Human Rights in the Area of Economic, Social, and Cultural Rights.[90] The only OAS human rights document relevant to this discussion that applies to Canada is the ADRDM.[91] Even though it was originally adopted as a non-binding declaration, the ADRDM has been held to be a source of international obligations for the states members to the OAS by both the Inter-American Court on Human Rights and the Inter-American Commission on Human Rights.[92] Indeed, with regard to Canada, the Inter-American Commission on Human Rights held that

---

88 Vienna Convention, *supra* note 87 at art. 26.

89 American Convention on Human Rights, 22 November 1969, OAS Treaty Series No. 36; 1144 UNTS 123; 9 ILM 99 (1969) (entered into force on 18 July 1978).

90 Additional Protocol to the American Convention on Human Rights in the Area of Economic, Social, and Cultural Rights, 17 November 1988, O.A.S. Treaty Series No. 69 (1988), Basic Documents Pertaining to Human Rights in the Inter-American System, Doc. OEA/Ser.L.V/II.82 doc.6 rev.1 at 67 (1992) (entered into force on 16 November 1999).

91 ADRDM, *supra* note 5.

92 Inter-American Court on Human Rights, *Interpretation of the American Declaration of the Rights and Duties of Man Within the Framework of Article 64 of the American Convention on Human Rights,* Advisory Opinion OC-10/89 (14 July 1989) at paras. 35–45; Inter-American Commission on Human Rights, *James Terry Roach and Jay Pinkerton (United States),* Resolution no. 3/87, Case 9647 (22 September 1987)

[t]he State is a member State of the Organization of American States but is not a Party to the American Convention on Human Rights. Consequently, the State is subject to the Commission's jurisdiction as regards to the American Declaration of the Rights and Duties of Man, as provided for in Article 49 of the Commission's Rules of Procedure. Canada deposited its instrument of ratification of the OAS Charter on January 8, 1990.[93]

Accordingly, the Inter-American Commission of Human Rights is competent to examine petitioners' claims that have "occurred subsequent to the State's ratification of the OAS Charter"[94] (competence *ratione temporis*), which comprise violations of human rights protected under the ADRDM (competence *ratione materiae*) alleged to have taken place within Canada (competence *ratione loci*).[95]

Once the status of international human rights law has been identified, the next question is how international law applies to Canada (reception system).[96] As Gibran van Ert notes, Canada is a hybrid jurisdiction. While conventional international law has to be implemented by legislation before taking direct effect in Canadian law (dualist system), customary international law is incorporated directly by the common law (monist system).[97] The Canadian

---

at paras. 46–49; Inter-American Commission on Human Rights, *Rafael Ferrer-Mazorra et al. (United States)*, Report 51/01, Case 9903 (4 April 2001) at para. 171; Statute of the Inter-American Commission on Human Rights (approved by Resolution no. 447 of the General Assembly of the Organization of American States, October 1979) at art. 20.

93 Inter-American Commission on Human Rights, *Grand Chief Michael Mitchell (Canada)*, Report no. 74/03, Petition 790/01 (22 October 2003) at para. 30.

94 *Ibid.*

95 *Ibid.* at para. 31.

96 Actually, a necessary "in-between" step is to determine whether Canada introduced a unilateral statement (reservation or statement of understanding) to any of the human rights instruments identified in section 1 that would limit Canadian international obligations. See Vienna Convention, *supra* note 87 at arts. 19–23. When becoming a state party to the CRC, Canada only entered two reservations (detention of young offenders along with adult offenders and Aboriginal customary adoption) and one statement of understanding (Aboriginal rights). Canada did not enter any reservation or statement of understanding when accessing the ICESCR. With respect to the ICCPR, Canada objected a reservation made by the government of Maldives and made a declaration recognizing the competence of the Human Rights Committee. See Office of the United Nations High Commissioner for Human Rights, United Nations Treaty Collection, <http://treaties.un.org/Pages/Treaties.aspx?id=4&subid=A&lang=en>.

97 Gibran van Ert, *Using International Law in Canadian Courts*, 2nd edition (Toronto: Irwin Law, 2008) at 3.

conventional international law reception system requires that in order to be considered part of Canadian law, treaty-based obligations must be implemented domestically through legislation (either through statute or regulation). However, international human rights conventions bind Canada as a matter of international law. Once Canada ratifies or accedes to a treaty and the treaty is in force, Canada is bound to observe it.[98] If Canada violates the treaty, international responsibility may arise. Nonetheless, Canadian courts do not recognize the applicable treaty within Canada unless it has been implemented domestically or its provisions have become customary international law and therefore directly applicable in Canada through the common law. The reason for this limitation is the "democratic deficit" concerning the negotiation and ratification of international conventions. In Canada, the power to sign and ratify international conventions is an executive act derived from the Royal prerogative. Parliament, which represents the legislative branch, is not involved in this process. In an attempt to address the "democratic deficit," international treaties are not directly incorporated in the Canadian legal system and require an act of Parliament through legislation to be enforceable domestically.[99] It is worth noting that since Canada is a federal system the power of Parliament to implement an international treaty is limited by the exclusive powers of the provincial legislatures.[100]

---

98 *Ibid.* at 150 and 163.

99 Canada, Standing Senate Committee on Human Rights, *Who's in Charge Here? Effective Implementation of Canada's International Obligations with Respect to the Rights of Children* (November 2005) at 35, Parliament of Canada <http://www.parl. gc.ca/38/1/parlbus/commbus/senate/com-e/huma-e/rep-e/rep19nov05-e. htm>; Elizabeth Eid, "Interaction between International and Domestic Human Rights Law: A Canadian Perspective," paper presented at the Sino-Canadian International Conference on the Ratification and Implementation of Human Rights Covenants: Beijing, China, October 2001, at 2–3, International Centre for Criminal Law Reform and Criminal Justice Policy <http://www.icclr.law.ubc. ca/Publications/Reports/E-Eid.PDF>.

100 *Constitution Act, 1867* (U.K.) 30 & 31 Vict., c. 3, reprinted in R.S.C. 1985, App. II, No. 5 at ss. 91–92. Donald Fleming and John McEvoy contend that the principle of *pacta sunt servanda* also applies to the provinces: "[I]t is wrong, in our view, to consider that only federal Canada is obliged to international human rights obligations to which the provinces have agreed to bind themselves. In such cases, the provinces (and territories) are also subject to the *pacta sunt servanda* principle." Donald J. Fleming and John P. McEvoy, "Domestic Implementation of Canada's International Human Rights Obligations," in Oonagh E. Fitzgerald, eds., *The Globalized Rule of Law: Relationships between International and Domestic Law* (Toronto: Irwin Law, 2006) at 542.

Scholars argue that conventional international law can be implemented explicitly or implicitly. According to Elizabeth Eid and Hoori Hamboyan,

[t]he term *explicit implementation* means that there has been a definite legislative act that has transformed the international treaty provisions into a domestic statute or regulation. The phrase "implicit implementation" refers to legislation, programs, and policies that have been relied upon by the government to confirm pre-existing compliance with a human rights treaty upon ratification.[101]

"Explicit implementation" requires Parliament to enact a statute or a regulation that expressly refers to the convention as being part of the Canadian law. Authors differ about how this enactment can be done. "[T]extual incorporation of the whole or part of the treaty" and "scheduling the text and referring to all or part" are examples of how it might be done.[102] Many scholars claim that "explicit implementation" is not achieved when an international convention is only identified in the preamble to a statute. Consider, for example, the preamble to the *Youth Criminal Justice Act:*

Whereas Canada is a Party to the United Nations Convention on the Rights of the Child and recognizes that young persons have rights and freedoms, including those stated in the Canadian Charter of Rights and Freedoms and the Canadian Bill of Rights, and have special guarantees of their rights and freedoms.[103]

Most scholars do not accept that this preamble constitutes explicit implementation of the CRC into the Canadian youth criminal justice system.[104]

On the other hand, "implicit implementation" relies upon existing domestic law, policies, or programs that already observe the treaties.

---

101 Elizabeth Eid and Hoori Hamboyan "Implementation by Canada of Its International Human Rights Treaty Obligations: Making Sense Out of the Nonsensical," in Fitzgerald, *supra* note 100 at 451.

102 For a more comprehensive list, see Armand De Mestral and Evan Fox-Decent, "Implementation and Reception: The Congeniality of Canada's Legal Order to International Law," in Fitzgerald, *supra* note 100 at 42–56.

103 *An Act in Respect of Criminal Justice for Young Persons and to Amend and Repeal Other Acts,* S.C. 2002, c. 1.

104 Eid and Hamboyan, *supra* note 101 at 455.

Eid and Hamboyan, along with van Ert, refer to this method as the common Canadian practice for implementing international human rights law. Consequently, no additional legislation for implementing the treaties needs to be passed.[105] Donald Fleming and John McEvoy, for example, report that it took almost ten years for Canada to accede to the ICCPR and the ICESCR because the federal government undertook a federal-provincial consultation to ensure that both provincial and federal legislation were in compliance with the human rights law declared in those covenants.[106] As a result, when Canada became party to the covenants it was deemed that they had been implicitly implemented and, therefore, were part of the Canadian legal system.[107]

In *Baker v. Canada (Minister of Citizenship and Immigration)*, Justice Claire L'Heureux-Dubé, speaking for the majority of the Supreme Court of Canada, held that the CRC was an unimplemented convention and, therefore, not part of Canadian law.[108] Despite this finding, she acknowledged the relevance of this law in Canada: "[T]he values reflected in international human rights law may help inform the contextual approach to statutory interpretation and judicial review."[109] Indeed, she held that the best interests of the child — one of the leading principles of the CRC — was an important factor to consider when exercising discretion: "[W]here the interests of children are minimized, in a manner inconsistent with Canada's humanitarian and compassionate tradition and the Minister's guidelines, the decision will be unreasonable."[110] Conversely, the minority took the view that the majority brought into the Canadian system a principle that existed in a non-implemented treaty (unincorporated convention). According to the minority, the appellant indirectly achieved what she could not have achieved directly,

---

[105] *Ibid.* at 451–52; van Ert, *supra* note 97 at 234, 246, and 249.

[106] Fleming and McEvoy, *supra* note 100 at 527.

[107] "Prior to accession [to the ICCPR and the ICESCR] the federal government obtained the agreement of the provinces, all of whom undertook to take measures for implementation of the Covenants in their respective jurisdiction," *Re Public Service Employee Relations Act (Alberta)* [1987] 1 S.C.R. 313 at para. 61.

[108] *Baker v. Canada (Minister of Citizenship and Immigration)*, [1999] 2 S.C.R. 817 at para. 69 [*Baker*].

[109] *Ibid.* at para. 70. See Jutta Brunnée and Stephen J. Toope, "A Hesitant Embrace: The Application of International Law by Canadian Courts" (2002) 49 C.Y.I.L. 3 at 5.

[110] *Baker, supra* note 108 at para. 75

"namely, to give force and effect within the domestic legal system to international obligations undertaken by the executive alone that have yet to be subject to the democratic will of Parliament."[111] Freeman and van Ert point out convincingly that the Court treated the CRC as a "supposedly unimplemented" convention "though in fact the CRC has prompted abundant federal and provincial legislative activity."[112] However, as we will argue later in this article, it seems that the majority in *Baker* treated the "best interests of the child" as customary international law — even though this was never explicitly stated.

While the argument that the CRC is an unimplemented treaty is shared by most Canadian courts, [113] the Standing Senate Committee on Human Rights took a different position. According to this committee, the CRC has been implicitly implemented by means of the *Canadian Charter of Rights and Freedoms*[114] and pre-existing federal and provincial legislation:

The *Convention on the Rights of the Child* is currently deemed to be implemented by means of the *Canadian Charter of Rights and Freedoms*, federal and provincial human rights legislation, and other federal and provincial legislation pertaining to matters addressed in the Convention. In essence, this is a policy-based approach to Canada's international obligations. The government relies on pre-existing laws, using existing mechanisms and applying the Convention through them, rather than relying on specific

111 *Ibid.* at para. 80.

112 Mark Freeman and Gibran van Ert, *International Human Rights Law* (Toronto: Irwin Law, 2004) at 165.

113 *Idahosa v. Canada (Public Safety and Emergency Preparedness)*, 2007 FC 1200 (T.D.) at para. 25; *Okoloubu v. Canada (Minister of Citizenship and Immigration)*, 2007 FC 1069 (T.D.) at para. 9; *Lennox and Addington Famiy and Children's Services v. T.S.*, (2000) 6 R.F.L. (5th) 331 at para. 23; *Paterson v. Canada (Minister of Citizenship and Immigration)*, [2000] F.C.J. 139 (T.D.) at para. 17; *Holder v. Canada (Minister of Citizenship and Immigration)*, [1999] F.C.J. 956 (T.D.) at para. 5; *Suresh v. Canada (Minister of Citizenship and Immigration)*, [1999] F.C.J 865 (T.D.) at para. 44; *Strachan v. Canada (Minister of Citizenship and Immigration)*, [1998] F.C.J. No. 1715 (T.D.) at para. 9; *R. v. James*, [1998] O.J. No. 1438 at para. 10; *Baker v. Canada (Minister of Citizenship and Immigration)*, [1996] F.C.J. 1570 (C.A.) at paras. 18 and 40; *Baker v. Canada (Minister of Citizenship and Immigration)*, [1995] F.C.J. 1441 (T.D.) at para. 39; *Langner v. Canada (Minister of Employment and Immigration)*, [1995] F.C.J. 469 (C.A.) at para. 11. In comparison, see *R. v. Sharpe*, [1999] B.C.J. 1555 (C.A.) at para. 236 (J. McEachern dissenting); *R. v. B.M.*, [1998] O.J. No. 3398 at paras. 8 and 21.

114 *Canadian Charter of Rights and Freedoms*, Part I of the *Constitution Act, 1982*, being Schedule B to the *Canada Act 1982* (U.K.), 1982, c. 11 [*Charter*].

legislation to ensure that children's rights recognized under the Convention are respected across the board.[115]

...

The argument is that because the federal government worked to ensure that Canada fulfills its obligations indirectly through the conformity of pre-existing legislation with the Convention, it does not have to directly incorporate the Convention by means of enabling or any other more explicit form of legislation.[116]

The complexity of the status of the CRC in Canadian domestic law is even more evident if we take into consideration how the federal and provincial governments report to the Committee on the Rights of the Child on the implementation of the CRC within Canada. Canada's first report in 1994 highlighted the difficulties arising from its federal system and how it overcame them:

In Canada, responsibility for implementing the rights set forth in the *Convention on the Rights of the Child* is shared by the Government of Canada, the provincial governments, and, following a delegation of authority by the Parliament of Canada, the territorial governments. Therefore, consultations were conducted with all jurisdictions before ratification took place.[117]

According to the second report submitted by Canada in 2001, there is no doubt that the CRC has had a direct effect on the Canadian domestic system:

The *Convention on the Rights of the Child* plays an important role in the development and implementation of children's rights in Canada. From 1993 to 1997, the Government of Canada introduced numerous measures to enhance the well-being of children. During this time, the Convention influenced Government of Canada policy strategies, action plans, and initiatives. It affected judicial decisions concerning the *Canadian Charter of Rights and Freedoms*, relevant legislation and the common law.[118]

---

[115] Canada, Standing Senate Committee on Human Rights, *supra* note 99 at 4, see also 43–44 and 62–63.

[116] *Ibid.* at 63. See also Eid, *supra* note 99 at 4–5.

[117] Canada, *Initial Reports of States Parties Due in 1994: Canada,* 28 July 1994, Doc. CRC/C/11/Add.3 at para. 1, Office of the United Nations High Commissioner for Human Rights, <http://www2.ohchr.org/english/bodies/crc/past02.htm#9>.

[118] Canada, *Second Periodic Reports of States Parties Due in 1999: Canada,* 12 March 2003, Doc. CRC/C/83/Add.6 at para. 7, Committee on the Rights of the Child

In light of these arguments, it is our understanding that the CRC has been implicitly implemented in Canada and, therefore, that it is part of the Canadian domestic law. It is evident that the main problem of the "implicit implementation" procedure is that the implementing legislation sometimes can be difficult to identify. Eid and Hamboyan suggest that this could be solved "if upon ratification, a statement was prepared listing the domestic statutes, regulations, and policies that were relied upon as assenting conformity with the treaty. Such a statement could be tabled in Parliament along with the treaty."[119]

The status of the ADRDM within Canada possesses its own challenges as well. Originally adopted as a human rights declaration, the ADRDM is nowadays considered a legally binding human rights instrument by the Inter-American Court on Human Rights and the Inter-American Commission on Human Rights. Nonetheless, such a status has been quite controversial: the United States, for instance, has objected to the ADRDM being considered a legally binding human rights document ever since it was adopted.[120] The controversy arose again in 1989 when the Inter-American Court of Human Rights held that the ADRDM had legally binding effects.[121] When Canada joined the OAS in 1990, the advisory opinion on the legal status of the ADRDM had already been rendered. As a result, as the Standing Senate Committee on Human Rights stated in 2003, it would be difficult for Canada to adhere to the US position since Canada became a member of the OAS after the Inter-American Court of Human Right's 1989 advisory opinion.[122] On the other hand, Canadian courts have been reluctant to identify the status of the ADRDM within Canada. Some recent decisions seem to hesitate

---

<http://www2.ohchr.org/english/bodies/crc/past.htm#34>. The third and four reports were due on 11 January 2009, Canadian Heritage <http://www.unhchr. ch/tbs/doc.nsf/898586b1dc7b4043c1256a450044f331/995a15056ca61d16 c1256df000310995/$FILE/G0344648.pdf>.

119 Eid and Hamboyan, *supra* note 101 at 461.

120 David Forsythe, "Human Rights, The United States and The Organization of American States" (1991) 13 Hum. Rights Q. 66 at 76–77.

121 Inter-American Court on Human Rights, *supra* note 92.

122 Canada, Standing Senate Committee on Human Rights, *Enhancing Canada's Role in the OAS: Canadian Adherence to the American Convention on Human Rights* (May 2003) at 134, Parliament of Canada <http://www.parl.gc.ca/37/2/parlbus/ commbus/senate/com-e/huma-e/rep-e/rep04may03-e.htm>.

whether this human rights declaration has legally binding effects in Canada,[123] and, if so, what its effects for Canadian courts are.[124]

To summarize, there are two possibilities for arguing that a treaty-based international norm is effective in Canada and, as a result, directly applicable: (1) either Parliament has implemented the conventional international human rights law explicitly; or (2) the conventional international human rights law can be considered already implemented domestically by the time of ratification or accession ("implicit implementation"). As noted earlier, the ICCPR, the ICESCR, and the CRC can be considered "implicitly implemented" and, as a consequence, directly applicable in Canada.[125] On the other hand, the status of the ADRDM within Canada is not clear — being identified primarily as a "regional declaration," the ADRDM is not generally referred to in Canadian case law as a source of human rights law.

Canadian courts have an obligation to draw a distinction between norms that are binding on Canada under international law (ratified or acceded to treaties) and norms that do not bind Canada internationally (such as soft law and international treaties to which Canada is not a party).[126] As a result, Canadian courts have had to

---

123 *Ikejiani Ebele Okoloubu v. The Minister of Citizenship and Immigration*, 2007 FC 1069 (T.D.) at para. 6: "The *American Declaration on the Rights and Duties of Men*, which actually precedes the Covenant [ICCPR], is not in fact a treaty."

124 *Oumou Diakité v. The Minister of Citizenship and Immigration and of Public Safety and Emergency Preparedness*, 2009 FC 165 (T.D.) at para. 1: Shore J. found that the ADRDM imposed a persuasive interpretation on the court to take into account the best interests of the child and that "[t]he principles and obligations should be considered while making a decision in this case." See, *e.g.*, *Jeanne Mauricette v. the Minister of Public Safety and Emergency Preparedness*, 2008 FC 420 at para. 27

125 *Contra Ahani v. Canada (A.G.)* (2002), 58 O.R. (3d) 107 (C.A.) at paras. 16 and 31: "Although Canada is a Party to the Covenant [ICCPR] and to the Protocol [Optional Protocol to the ICCPR], it has not incorporated either into its domestic law": "Canada has never incorporated either the Covenant or the Protocol into Canadian law by implementing legislation. Absent implementing legislation, neither has any legal effect in Canada" (respectively). However, Rosenberg J. was in dissent in this decision, relying on Articles 26 and 27 of the Vienna Convention (instead of on the convention being implicitly implemented), and he noted that "[t]he federal government has undertaken to perform this Covenant in good faith. It has also undertaken not to invoke the provision of its internal law as justification for failure to perform." *Ibid.* at para. 70. He was referring here to the requisite of domestic implementation of international treaties for them having legal effect within Canada.

126 Brunnée and Toope, *supra* note 109 at 6–7. Regarding non-ratified treaties, signatories states still have the obligation not to defeat the object and purpose of the treaty. Vienna Convention, *supra* note 87 at art. 18(1).

interpret domestic law in conformity with the norms that bind Canada under international law (former group) as far as possible, while the norms that do not bind Canada under international law can help inform the interpretation of domestic law (latter group). Indeed, the norms that bind Canada internationally could be divided into implemented and unimplemented international law norms. The consequence of such a division is that the implemented norms are directly applicable in Canada according to the Canadian reception system of conventional international law. However, as previously highlighted, a treaty commitment is no less binding on Canada internationally for being unimplemented in Canadian law — both implemented and unimplemented norms bind Canada under international law. Indeed, if these norms are not observed by Canada, international responsibility may arise.

As a final note on treaty-based international law, some authors have criticized the requirement of implementation for international law to have effect within Canada as being overly restrictive. According to Jutta Brunnée and Stephen Toope, who have analyzed *Attorney General for Canada v. Attorney General for Ontario*, "traditionally, Canadian law did not categorically require statutory implementation."[127] This statement refers to the distinction between self-executing treaties versus treaties that do not have such an effect. While the former take immediate effect in the domestic legislation, the latter require some degree of implementing legislation for the international norms to be enforceable within the state party. The argument favouring self-executing treaties has been clearly identified by the CESCR when it refers to the status of the ICESCR in domestic law:

In general, legally binding international human rights standards should operate directly and immediately within the domestic legal system of each State Party, thereby enabling individuals to seek enforcement of their rights before national courts and tribunals.[128]

A question may arise whether the international human rights law identified in the first section of this article, in addition to being

---

[127] Brunnée and Toope, *supra* note 109 at 27; *Attorney General for Canada v. Attorney General for Ontario*, [1937] A.C. 326 (P.C.) at 347.

[128] CESCR, *General Comment 9 on the Domestic Application of the Covenant*, 3 December 1998, at para. 4, Office of the High Commissioner for Human Rights, <http://www.unhchr.ch/tbs/doc.nsf/(Symbol)/4ceb75c5492497d9802566d5005160 36?Opendocument> [*General Comment 9*].

regulated in international human rights treaties, can also be considered to be customary international law and, therefore, directly applicable in Canada through the common law. Article 38(1) of the Statute of the International Court of Justice identifies international custom as a source of international law, along with international treaties and general principles of law.[129] This is a controversial idea. Even though the human rights law discussed in the first section is widely recognized to be rights under customary international law, there is no agreement whether the rights to health, identity, and family relations are customary international law.[130] One argument could be that, if the UDHR is considered to have attained customary status, both the rights to health and family relations would be deemed to have achieved such a condition. Nevertheless, as noted earlier, the status of the UDHR as customary international law is still contentious.[131]

The difficulty regarding the recognition of the right to identity as part of customary international law rests on the requirement of "state practice." As Brunnée and Toope note, "[t]he existence of a binding rule of custom is proven with reference to two distinct, but inter-related, elements: state practice and *opinio juris.*"[132] When

---

[129] *Statute of the International Court of Justice,* annexed to the Charter of the United Nations, 26 June 1945, Can. T. S. 1945/7 at art. 38(1). Brunnée and Toope, *supra* note 109 at 12, note that general principles of law are rarely argued before Canadian courts.

[130] The Human Rights Committee, when regulating the matters that could be entered as reservations by states parties to the ICCPR and its protocols, identified some provisions in the covenant that represent customary international law. Human Rights Committee, *General Comment 24 on Issues Relating to Reservations Made Upon Ratification or Accession to the Covenant or the Optional Protocols Thereto, or in Relation to Declarations under Article 41 of the Covenant,* 4 November 1994, at paras. 8–9, Office of the High Commissioner for Human Rights, <http://www2.ohchr.org/english/bodies/hrc/comments.htm>.

[131] In *Francis (Litigation guardian of) v. Canada (Minister of Citizenship and Immigration,* [1998] O.J. No. 1791 at para. 10, McNeely J. seems to suggest that the CRC could be considered part of international customary law: "Since fundamental justice like natural justice is not the creation of any particular national judicial system, the United Nations Convention on the Rights of the Child may be looked at. This convention does not purport to create rights but to declare them. Its ratification by so many countries including Canada suggests that the rights declared therein are consistent with the views of justice in the adopting countries."

[132] Brunnée and Toope, *supra* note 109 at 15.

regulating human donor-assisted reproduction, for instance, European countries have addressed donor anonymity in very different ways. While some countries have expressly banned the use of donors (Italy), others have not regulated this domain (Luxemburg). Indeed, some countries protect donor anonymity (France), others forbid anonymity and allow access to identifiable information regarding donors (Sweden), and others have double-track systems that allow both anonymous and identity-registered donors (Belgium).[133] In this context, it is very difficult to identify a consistent and unambiguous state practice that allows a customary right to identity to emerge.

On the other hand, it can be argued that "the best interests of the child," a guiding principle of the CRC, has become customary international law and, as a result, has direct effect in the Canadian legal system through the common law. In *Baker*, the majority of the Supreme Court of Canada held that the "best interests of the child" was an important factor to consider when exercising discretion, even though the CRC was an unimplemented convention.[134] In fact, such a position was not unexpected. We argue that the Supreme Court of Canada's approach to the "best interests of the child" as a Canadian value had already been advanced by L'Heureux-Dubé J. in her dissenting vote in *Young v. Young*, where she traced the origin and application of this principle in family law:

[T]he best interest test is universally recognized as the foundation of modern family law around the world and is legislatively entrenched in both common law and civil jurisdictions in the United States, Australia and Europe. Moreover, the need to make the best interests of the child the primary consideration in all actions concerning children, including legal proceedings, is specifically recognized in international human rights law documents such as the United Nations Convention on the Rights of the Child.[135]

---

133 See Mariana De Lorenzi and Verónica Pinero, "Assisted Human Reproduction Offspring and the Fundamental Right to Identity: the Recognition of the Right to Know One's Origins under the European Convention on Human Rights" (2009) 6(1) Personalized Medicine 79.

134 *Baker, supra* note 108 at para. 75

135 *Young v. Young,* [1993] 4 S.C.R. 3 at para. 91 [*Young*]. L'Heureux-Dubé J. held a similar position in *P.(D.) v. S.(C).,* [1993] 4 S.C.R. 141 at para. 101 (this time for the majority).

According to L'Heureux-Dubé J., the "best interests of the child" had been applied by courts for decades "and the case law provides a large body of jurisprudence to which courts may resort when considering factors relevant to the best interest test."[136] An opportunity to discuss the "best interest test" arose again in 1996 in *V.W. v. D.S.*, a decision dealing with the international abduction of a child by her father. L'Heureux-Dubé J. (for the minority) held that "the interests of children are of paramount importance in matters relating to their custody."[137] For her, "[t]his objective is in keeping with the universal recognition that the interests of the child must prevail, as stated in a number of international documents in addition to the Convention [on the Civil Aspects of International Child Abduction], such as the Convention on the Rights of the Child."[138] In *Gordon v. Goertz*, which is the companion case to *V.W. v. D.S.*, L'Heureux-Dubé J. (for the minority) traced the "best interest test" in treaty-based international law:

International awareness of children's right is illustrated by various international documents such as the League of Nations Declaration of the Rights of the Child (1924), the United Nations Declaration of the Rights of the Child (1959) and the 1989 United Nations Convention on the Rights of the Child, Can. T.S. 1992 No. 3, art. 3(1) of which recognizes the need to make the best interests of the child the primary consideration in all actions concerning children, including legal proceedings.[139]

When *Baker* was decided in 1999, L'Heureux-Dubé J. held that the "best interests of the child" was an important factor, albeit not the prevailing factor, which the decision maker had to take into account when assessing an administrative application that could affect the interests of children. Otherwise, the decision would be unreasonable.[140] Some years later, in *Canadian Foundation for Children, Youth and the Law v. Canada (Attorney General)*, a decision dealing with the constitutionality of section 43 of the *Criminal Code*, Chief Justice Beverley McLachlin (for the majority) identified the best interests of the child as "an established legal principle in international and

---

136 *Young, supra* note 135 at para. 95.

137 *V.W. v. D.S.*, [1996] 2 S.C.R. 108 at para. 76.

138 *Ibid.*

139 *Gordon v. Goertz*, [1996] 2 S.C.R. 26 at 87.

140 *Baker, supra* note 108 at para. 75.

domestic law."[141] Indeed, according to her, the "best interests of the child" is a legal principle, even though it is not a principle of fundamental justice since it "fails to meet the second criterion for a principle of fundamental justice: consensus that the principle is vital or fundamental to our societal notion of justice."[142] She argued that Article 3(1) of the CRC regulates this principle as being "a primary consideration" instead of "the primary consideration" for decision makers to evaluate when dealing with a situation that could affect children.[143]

In sum, the "best interests of the child" has solidified as a norm of customary international law, besides having been explicitly included as a legal consideration by many Canadian statutes.[144] However, as noted in *Canadian Foundation*, the "best interests of the child" is a legal principle, albeit not a principle of fundamental justice.[145] On the other hand, the status of the rights to health, family relations, and identity as customary international law is controversial. The rights to health and family relations are regulated in many international human rights documents, among them the UDHR. If this declaration was considered customary international law, those rights would have direct effect in Canadian law through the common law. With respect to the right to identity, it lacks the requirement of "state practice" for being considered as a customary international norm.

CAN CANADIAN LAW BE INTERPRETED CONSISTENTLY WITH INTERNATIONAL HUMAN RIGHTS OBLIGATIONS?

The regulation of assisted human reproduction in Canada has never been a simple matter. After a Royal Commission of Inquiry on

---

[141] *Canadian Foundation for Children, Youth and the Law v. Canada (Attorney General)*, 2004 SCC 4 at para. 9 [*Canadian Foundation*]. *Criminal Code*, R.S.C. 1985, c. C-46, s. 264.

[142] *Canadian Foundation, supra* note 141 at para. 10.

[143] *Ibid.* Actually, the latter formulation belongs to the Declaration of the Rights of the Child: "[T]he best interests of the child shall be the paramount consideration." Declaration of the Rights of the Child, 20 November 1959, UNGA Resolution 1386(XIV) at principle 2.

[144] *Canadian Foundation, supra* note 141 at para. 9. See *Khadr v. Canada (Prime Minister)*, 2009 FC 405 (T.D.) at para. 73. In the *R. v. D.B.*, 2008 SCC 25 at paras. 59–60, the Supreme Court of Canada found that the "presumption of diminished moral culpability for young persons is a long-standing legal principle. It is also a legal principle that finds expression in Canada's international commitment [CRC]."

[145] *Canadian Foundation, supra* note 141 at para. 10.

Reproductive Technology,[146] a House of Commons' report,[147] and a bill reintroduced many times in Parliament,[148] the *Assisted Human Reproduction Act* finally received royal assent on 29 March 2004.[149] During this process, academics, politicians, policy makers, and individuals discussed many diverse and controversial issues, among them, the protection of donors' privacy and the welfare of children born through these technologies. As we discuss later in this article, both areas have always been in conflict because this controversy has a binary dimension — while some donors do not want to make their identifiable information available to offspring (lack of knowledge), their offspring may want to have access to such information (access to knowledge). Although Parliament has left this conflict unsolved, Canadian courts — we argue — could make use of the presumption of observance of international law as a judicial policy and favour an interpretation of the statute that is in accordance with international human rights law.[150]

The regulation of assisted human reproduction in Canada was passed after many years of debates. In 1993, after four years of consultation, the Royal Commission on New Reproductive Technologies submitted its report. The government introduced a bill regulating the matter in 1996, which died on the order paper because of the 1997 election.[151] Health Canada submitted draft legislation to the House of Commons Standing Committee on

---

146 Royal Commission on New Reproductive Technologies, *Proceed with Care: Final Report* (Ottawa: Minister of Government Services Canada, 1993).

147 House of Commons, Standing Committee on Health, *Assisted Human Reproduction: Building Families* (December 2001), Parliament of Canada <http://www2.parl.gc.ca/content/hoc/Committee/371/HEAL/Reports/RP1032041/healrpo2/healrpo2-e.pdf>.

148 Bill C-47, *Human Reproductive and Genetic Technologies Act*, 2nd Sess., 35th Parl., 1996; Bill C-56, *Act Respecting Human Assisted Reproduction*, 1st Sess., 37th Parl., 2002; Bill C-13, *Act Respecting Assisted Human Reproduction*, 2nd Sess., 37th Parl., 2002; Bill C-6, *Act Respecting Assisted Human Reproductive Technologies and Related Research*. 3rd Sess., 37th Parl., 2004.

149 *Assisted Human Reproduction Act*, *supra* note 3.

150 Van Ert discusses the Canadian leading cases on the presumption of observance of international law as a judicial policy chronologically. Van Ert, *supra* note 97 at 139–59.

151 Bill C-47, *Human Reproductive and Genetic Technologies Act*, 2nd Sess., 35th Parl., 1996.

Health for consideration in 2001, and the committee presented its report entitled "Building Families" in December of that year.[152] The committee opposed the protection of donors' identifiable information — as recommended by Health Canada — and called for an open-track system through which offspring could have access to donors' identifiable information. In the committee's own words, "where there is a conflict between the privacy rights of a donor and the rights of a resulting child to know its heritage, the rights of the child should prevail."[153] As a result, the majority of the committee recommended that "[c]onsent to the release of identifying information be mandatory before accepting an individual as a sperm, egg, or embryo donor."[154] On the other hand, the Canadian Alliance's minority report severely criticized this recommendation on the grounds that it did not afford enough protection to an offspring's right to identity. Health Canada's bill attached a higher weight to donors' privacy rights than to an offspring's right to access to information regarding their origins. Thus, as the Canadian Alliance argued, regulation protecting an offspring's access to information had to be explicitly stated:

That the final legislation contain clear statement to the effect that where the privacy rights of the donors of human reproductive materials conflict with the rights of children to know their genetic and social heritage, that the rights of the children shall prevail.[155]

In regard to the relationship between donors and offspring, the committee clearly recommended that "[n]o legal responsibilities respecting offspring, financial or otherwise, should arise out of a donation."[156]

Health Canada redrafted the bill in 2002 — allegedly taking into consideration the House of Commons Standing Committee on Health's report — and tabled it in the House of Commons. However, many of the recommendations of the committee — such as

---

[152] House of Commons, *supra* note 147.

[153] *Ibid.* at 21.

[154] *Ibid.* at 38 (Recommendation 19.a). This report had four dissenting minority reports.

[155] *Ibid.* at 81.

[156] *Ibid.* at 22.

the recognition of an offspring's right to identity — had not been included, and this brought diverse reactions from parliamentarians.[157] During the second reading of the bill, most parliamentarians opposed the bill as it did not allow an offspring access to a donor's identifiable information.[158] On the other hand, only one parliamentarian was in favour of protecting donors' privacy rights.[159] Members of the House of Commons Standing Committee on Health, where the bill was sent after receiving second reading, along with expert witnesses, were quite concerned about an offspring not having access to donors' identifying information. According to them, this was contrary to the committee's original recommendations and to the stated principle of the bill (children's interests being the primary concern).[160] Yet, other members agreed with how donors' privacy protection had been regulated.[161]

When Parliament prorogued, the bill was reinstated at the same point in the legislative process the following session (House of

---

[157] Bill C-56, *Act Respecting Human Assisted Reproduction*, 1st Sess., 37th Parl., 2002.

[158] *House of Commons Debates* (21 May 2002) at 11528, 11572 (Hon. Rob Merrifield); *House of Commons Debates* (21 May 2002) at 11530, 11534 (Hon. Réal Ménard); *House of Commons Debates* (21 May 2002) at 11540 (Hon. André Bachand); *House of Commons Debates* (21 May 2002) at 11545 (Hon. Paul Szabo); *House of Commons Debates* (21 May 2002) at 11547–11548 (Hon. Diane Ablonczy); *House of Commons Debates* (21 May 2002) at 11548 [Hon. Betty Hinton]; *House of Commons Debates* (21 May 2002) at 11570 [Hon. Reg Alcock]; *House of Commons Debates* (21 May 2002) at 11572 [Hon. Bev Desjarlais]; *House of Commons Debates* (21 May 2002) at 11572 [Hon. Reg Alcock]; *House of Commons Debates* (21 May 2002) at 11575, 11579 [Hon. James Lunney]; *House of Commons Debates* (21 May 2002) at 11579 [Hon. Joe Comartin]; *House of Commons Debates* (22 May 2002) at 11607 [Hon. Gary Lunn]; *House of Commons Debates* (22 May 2002) at 11610 [Hon. Larry Spencer]; *House of Commons Debates* (22 May 2002) at 11616 [Hon. Gurmant Grewal]; *House of Commons Debates* (24 May 2002) at 11727 [Hon. Ken Epp]; *House of Commons Debates* (27 May 2002) at 11739, 11749 [Hon. Reed Elley]; *House of Commons Debates* (27 May 2002) at 11743 [Hon. Jim Gouk].

[159] *House of Commons Debates* (27 May 2002) at 11771 [Hon. Rahim Jaffer].

[160] Canada, House of Commons Standing Committee on Health, *Evidence* (30 May 2002); Canada, House of Commons Standing Committee on Health, *Evidence* (12 June 2002); Canada, House of Commons Standing Committee on Health, *Evidence* (13 June 2002).

[161] Canada, House of Commons Standing Committee on Health, *Evidence* (30 May 2002); Canada, House of Commons Standing Committee on Health, *Evidence* (12 June 2002).

Commons Standing Committee on Health).[162] Again, the binary controversy between an offspring's right to know the identity of their genetic donors and a donor's right to keep their information private arose. What is worth noting is that when the Privacy Commissioner of Canada was invited to the committee to discuss the matter his opinion was that this discussion did not deal with privacy rights versus identity rights but, rather, with donors' attitudes if their identifiable information was made available. After consulting with Health Canada, the Privacy Commissioner of Canada was advised that an open-track system would "much discourage people from becoming donors and open up a whole host of legal issues and concerns," such as child support — a matter that falls under civil rights and property and thus is beyond the jurisdiction of Parliament. Indeed, as Privacy Commissioner of Canada, he believed that an offspring's right to identity was paramount: "[P]hilosophically, my view would be closer to the view of this committee — namely, that the rights of offspring should take precedence over the rights of the donor."[163] On the other hand, health professionals working or supervising clinics specialized in reproductive medicine presented most of the arguments against an open-track system that would allow access to donors' identifiable information.[164] When

---

[162] Bill C-13, *Act Respecting Assisted Human Reproduction*, 2nd Sess., 37th Parl., 2002. On 12 December 2002, when the bill was reprinted as amended by the Standing Committee on Health, the title of the bill was changed into the *Act Respecting Assisted Human Reproductive Technologies and Related Research*.

[163] Canada, House of Commons Standing Committee on Health, *Evidence* (21 November 2002) (George Radwanski). Jennifer Stoddart, current Privacy Commissioner of Canada, reversed this position and held that "donors should have the right to control access to their identities, except in specific circumstances that raise health or safety concerns." Standing Senate Committee on Social Affairs, Science and Technology, *Bill C-6, Act Respecting Assisted Human Reproduction and Related Research* (3 March 2004) at 3:17.
   Suzi Leather, chair of the Human Fertilisation and Embryology Authority of the United Kingdom, presented an argument similar to Radwanski's. According to her, "there should be a move toward the removal of donor anonymity." However, this should not applied retroactively. Canada, House of Commons Standing Committee on Health, *Evidence* (2 December 2002, morning meeting) (Suzi Leather). See also Olivia Pratten's and Barry Stevens' testimonies (assisted human reproduction offspring): Canada, House of Commons Standing Committee on Health, *Evidence* (2 December 2002, afternoon meeting).

[164] Canada, House of Commons Standing Committee on Health, *Evidence* (20 November 2002).

the committee began the clause-by-clause study of the bill, one of the voted amendments was to make the interest of children born through the application of reproduction technologies a paramount principle:

(a) the health and well-being of children born through the application of assisted human reproductive technologies must be given priority in all decisions respecting their use.[165]

As a result, this principle — which was placed second in Health Canada's draft legislation — was placed first.[166]

The next clause-by-clause vote that is relevant for our discussion was the protection of donors' identifiable information. As noted in clause 18(3), which became Article 18(3) when the bill received Royal assent, an offspring could not have access to a donor's identity:

The Agency shall, on request, disclose health reporting information relating to a donor of human reproductive material or of an *in vitro* embryo to a person undergoing an assisted reproduction procedure using that human reproductive material or embryo, to a person conceived by means of such a procedure and to descendants of a person so conceived, but the identity of the donors — or information that can reasonably be expected to be used in the identification of the donor — shall not be disclosed without the donor's written consent.[167]

During the discussion of this clause in the committee, there was an attempt to bring an exception that would allow an offspring access to a donor's identity. However, this exception would only apply to offspring conceived after the bill came into force (non-retroactive).[168] Yet, legal counsel from the Department of Justice

---

[165] Bill C-13, *An Act Respecting Assisted Human Reproductive Technologies and Related Research*, 2nd Sess., 37th Parl., 2002 (reprinted on 12 December 2002) at clause 2.

[166] Canada, House of Commons Standing Committee on Health, *Evidence* (3 December 2002, afternoon meeting) (Hon. Yolande Thibeault).

[167] Bill C-13, *supra* note 165 at clause 18(3).

[168] The proposed amendment read: "Despite subsection (3), the identity of a donor referred to in that subsection shall be disclosed to any person conceived by means of an assisted reproduction procedure and to any descendant of a person so conceived upon application by the person or descendant at any time after

advised the committee that such an amendment could entitle offspring to claim child support and/or make a claim against the donor's state.[169] As these matters were under the exclusive provincial legislative power, Parliament did not have jurisdiction to address them. The amendment was not supported by the committee (six nays and five yeas).[170] The committee reported to the House of Commons, and after several debates the bill received its third reading and was passed to the Senate.[171] The bill was read for the second time in the Senate and referred to the Standing Senate Committee on Social Affairs, Science and Technology before Parliament prorogued (12 November 2003).

The following session, the bill was reinstated at the same point in the legislative process.[172] The committee presented its report on 9 March 2004 and passed the bill without amendments.[173] However, it noted that there were several matters, among them an offspring's right to identity, that needed to be addressed when regulations were drafted and during the three-year review.[174] According to the committee, before allowing the release of donors' identifiable information, family law needed to be amended in all jurisdictions so sperm donors were not deemed to be the fathers of the offspring:

---

they have attained the age of 18 years. Canada, House of Commons Standing Committee on Health, *Evidence* (9 December 2002, morning meeting) (Hon. Rob Merrifield).

[169] Canada, House of Commons Standing Committee on Health, *Evidence* (9 December 2002, morning meeting) (Hon. Glenn Rivard).

[170] Canada, House of Commons Standing Committee on Health, *Evidence* (9 December 2002, afternoon meeting). There was an attempt to re-examine the vote on that amendment the following day since its text was available only in English; yet this was unsuccessful. Canada, House of Commons Standing Committee on Health, *Evidence* (10 December 2002, morning and afternoon meetings) (Hon. Réal Ménard).

[171] *House of Commons Debates* (28 October 2003) at 8882.

[172] Pursuant to the order made on 10 February 2004, Bill C-6 (previously Bill C-13, 2nd Session, 37th Parliament) was deemed to have been read the second time in the House of Commons and referred to a committee, reported with amendments, concurred in at the report stage, and read the third time and passed to the Senate; *House of Commons Debates* (10 February 2004). In the Senate, the bill received its first and second reading and was referred to the committee. *Senate Debates* (11 February 2004) at 130; and *Senate Debates* (13 February 2004) at 187.

[173] *Bill C-6, An Act respecting assisted human reproduction and related research* (3 March 2004), 3rd Sess., 37th Parl., at 3:5.

[174] *Ibid.* at 3:6.

These witnesses testified that currently under family law in all but two provinces and one territory, a non-anonymous sperm donor is deemed to be the father of any child(ren) born as the consequence of his sperm. The Committee was told that the anonymity provision cannot change until family law is changed in all jurisdictions. Additionally, family law does not assign maternity to egg donors currently in any Canadian jurisdiction. The position was clearly expressed that Canada should not make donor identification mandatory before family law has been appropriately addressed to protect donors.

The Committee understands the difficulty in requiring donor identification at this time. However, we would observe that this issue should be carefully examined when this legislation is reviewed within three years.[175]

The bill received royal assent on 29 March 2004. As noted earlier, the domestic regulation of donors' privacy rights in the context of assisted human reproduction is ambiguous. While Article 18.3 prohibits access to donors' identifiable information unless they so consent, Article 2.a states that the interests of the children born through the application of these technologies are paramount. Is it feasible to reconcile both norms? Unfortunately, reconciliation is almost impossible since some donors want their personal information to be kept secret unless decided otherwise, while offspring assert that having access to donors' identifiable information is in their "best interest." What was the intention of the Canadian legislature when enacting the *Assisted Human Reproduction Act?* As noted, parliamentarians were very much in favour of protecting an offspring's right to identity; however, they had concerns regarding the impact of offspring's access to donors' identifiable information on family law.

In sum, taking into consideration the legal history of the regulation of assisted human reproduction in Canada, there are two possible interpretations, one favouring the donor's right to privacy and the other supporting an offspring's access to this information as part of their best interests. And here lies the role of the presumption of conformity with international law. While the controversy that lies under the current regulation of assisted human reproduction will always exist, one solution favours international human rights law that Canada has signed and ratified, and the other rejects it. In *R. v. Hape,* Justice Louis LeBel (for the majority of the Supreme

175 *Ibid.* at 3:9.

Court of Canada) commented on the role of the judiciary in relation to international law:

[T]he presumption of conformity is based on the rule of judicial policy that, as a matter of law, courts will strive to avoid constructions of domestic law pursuant to which the state would be in violation of its international obligations, unless the wording of the statute clearly compels that result.[176]

Whereas a judicial interpretation favouring donors' rights to keep their information private would reject major international human rights law that binds Canada, an interpretation providing offspring with access to donors' identifiable information would observe international human rights treaties to which Canada is a party — some of them already implicitly implemented in Canada (the ICCPR, the ICESCR, and the CRC). The use of the presumption of conformity as a judicial policy has also been favoured by the CESCR with respect to the treatment of the ICESCR in domestic courts:

It is generally accepted that domestic law should be interpreted as far as possible in a way which conforms to a State's international legal obligations. Thus, when a domestic decision maker is faced with a choice between an interpretation of domestic law that would place the state in breach of the Covenant and one that would enable the State to comply with the Covenant, international law requires the choice of the latter.[177]

The Human Rights Committee took a similar position with respect to the ICCPR:

[U]nless Covenant rights are already protected by their domestic laws or practices, States Parties are required on ratification to make such changes to domestic laws and practices as are necessary to ensure their conformity with the Covenant. Where there are inconsistencies between domestic law and the Covenant, article 2 requires that the domestic law or practice be changed to meet the standards imposed by the Covenant's substantive guarantees.[178]

---

[176] *R. v. Hape*, 2007 SCC 26 at para. 53.

[177] *Ibid.*, at para. 15. On the notion of states parties' violations to the right to health and determining which actions or omissions amount to a violation of this right, see *General Comment 14, supra* note 17 at part III.

[178] Human Rights Committee, *General Comment 31 on the Nature of the General Legal Obligations Imposed on States Parties to the Covenant,* 26 May 2004, at para. 13,

In sum, if Canadian courts were to favour offspring's right to identity over donors' privacy rights through the application of the principle of conformity to international law when interpreting the *Assisted Human Reproduction Act,* such an approach would be consistent with major international human rights law binding on Canada.[179]

Finally, the Standing Senate Committee on Human Rights, while examining the Canadian implementation of international obligations with respect to children's rights, found that "Canada does not take its international human rights obligations seriously enough."[180] Indeed, some years later, this same committee found that

the best interests of the child are not being served by current adoption and donor insemination policies across the country. *Children have a right to their own identity — to know who they are —* and this right is not always being effectively protected in Canada. *A large part of this right entails the child's need to know the identity of his or her biological parents.*[181]

CONCLUSION

In Canada, the fundamental question is "whose rights should prevail?" Should Canada give priority to the donor's right to privacy or

---

Office of the High Commissioner for Human Rights, <http://www.unhchr.ch/tbs/doc.nsf/(Symbol)/CCPR.C.21.Rev.1.Add.13.En?Opendocument>.

179 *Assisted Human Reproduction Act, supra* note 3.

180 Canada, Standing Senate Committee on Human Rights, *supra* note 99 at 68. Rishmawi, *supra* note 28 at 24, notes that "the CRC Committee if of the view that, in the event of a conflict between the CRC and national legislation or practice, the Convention should prevail. This is based on Article 27 of the Vienna Convention on the Law of Treaties."

181 Canada, Standing Senate Committee on Human Rights, *Children: The Silenced Citizens. Effective Implementation of Canada's International Obligations with Respect to the Rights of Children,* Final Report of the Standing Senate Committee on Human Rights (April 2007) at 113, Parliament of Canada <http://www.parl.gc.ca/39/1/parlbus/commbus/senate/Com-e/huma-e/rep-e/rep10apr07-e.htm> [emphasis added]. Accordingly, the committee recommended that "federal-provincial-territorial negotiations on adoption proposed in Recommendation 10 should include consideration of access to a biological parent's identity and of the benefits of identity disclosure vetos. The Committee also recommends that Assisted Human Reproduction Canada review the legal and regulatory regime surrounding sperm donor identity and access to a donor's medical history to determine how the best interests of the child can better be served" (at 115).

to the offspring's rights to health, identity, and family relations?[182] As discussed in this article, Canada is a party to numerous international human rights instruments and, consequently, must observe international law on health, identity, and family relations. To date, Canada gives priority to the donor's right to privacy, despite the compelling — and compulsory — international legal framework on offspring's rights to identity, health, and family relations. We do accept that donors have rights, but these rights have to be prioritized when they conflict. As Freeman and Van Ert note, human rights are not absolute rights and their scope of application is limited by other rights that are limited between themselves.[183] Accordingly, the donor's right to privacy should be limited by an offspring's rights to health, identity, and family relations. In Canada, the donor's right to privacy has not been adequately interpreted in a manner that also observes and protects the offspring's rights to health, identity, and family relations. Finally, and ironically, the *Assisted Human Reproduction Act* fails to observe its own first principle, which states: "[T]he health and well-being of children born through the application of the assisted human reproductive technology *must be given priority in all decisions respecting their use.*"[184]

Summary

Canadian International Human Rights Obligations in the Context of Assisted Human Reproduction

In Canada, as in most countries, assisted human reproduction has become accessible treatment for individuals who wish to conceive. Scientific advancements in the area of human reproduction have led to the enactment of

---

182 Michelle Giroux, "Le droit fondamental de connaître ses origines biologiques," in Tara Collins et al, eds., *Droits de l'enfant. Actes de la Conférence internationale / Ottawa 2007. Rights of the Child.* Proceedings of the International Conference / Ottawa 2007 (Montreal: Wilson and Lafleur, 2008) at 371.

183 Freeman and van Ert, *supra* note 112 at 35. See also Vienna Declaration and Programme of Action, UN Doc. A/CONF.157/23 (12 July 1993) at para. 5 (adopted at the World Conference on Human Rights): "All human rights are universal, indivisible and interdependent and interrelated. The international community must treat human rights globally in a fair and equal manner, on the same footing, and with the same emphasis."

184 *Assisted Human Reproduction Act, supra* note 3 at s. 2 (a) [emphasis added].

legislation that attempts to regulate this novel field. The Canadian Assisted Human Reproduction Act *(2004) identifies the health and well-being of children born through reproductive technologies as a paramount principle in all decisions respecting their use. On the other hand, and surprisingly, the statute restricts access by offspring to information that can lead to identification of their genitors. The disclosure of donors' identity to the recipients of reproductive materials is quite limited. According to this article, this legislation is in violation of international human rights law on health, identity, and family relations to which Canada is a party. The first part of the article explores international human rights law on identity, health, and family relations rights that Canada has signed, ratified, or acceded to. The second part discusses whether the Canadian legal system is in line with the relevant international human rights obligations identified earlier and asserts that there is scope for judicially interpreting Canadian law in such a way that would conform to those obligations.*

Sommaire

Les obligations du Canada en vertu du droit international des droits de la personne

Au Canada, comme dans la plupart des pays, la procréation assistée est devenue un traitement accessible aux personnes qui souhaitent concevoir. Les progrès scientifiques dans le domaine de la procréation ont mené à la promulgation de la législation qui tente de réglementer ce nouveau domaine. La Loi sur la procréation assistée *(2004) du Canada identifie la santé et le bien-être des enfants nés grâce à des technologies de reproduction comme principe primordial dans toutes les décisions concernant leur utilisation. D'autre part, et chose surprenante, la loi restreint l'accès par ces enfants à l'information qui pourrait les amener à identifier leurs géniteurs. La divulgation de l'identité du donneur au receveur(s) du matériel de reproduction est très limitée. Selon l'auteure, cette réglementation est en violation du droit international des droits de la personne se rapportant à la santé, l'identité et les relations familiales auquel le Canada est sujet. La première partie de l'article passe en revue le droit international des droits de la personne sur l'identité, la santé et les relations familiales auquel le Canada a adhéré. La deuxième partie examine si le système juridique canadien est en conformité avec les obligations internationales relatives aux droits de la personne identifiés ci-dessus et affirme qu'il existe une marge d'interprétation judiciaire du droit canadien qui permettrait le respect de ces obligations.*

Protecting Civilians during the Fight against Transnational Terrorism: Applying International Humanitarian Law to Transnational Armed Conflicts

KARINNE COOMBES

INTRODUCTION: COMBATING TERRORISM AND PROTECTING CIVILIANS

In July 2006, Israeli Prime Minister Ehud Olmert promised "a very painful and far-reaching response" when Hezbollah militants entered Israel from Lebanon, killed eight and captured two Israeli soldiers.[1] The result was a thirty-three-day conflict between Israel and Hezbollah, which had major effects on both Lebanon and Israel.[2] The widespread destruction and the civilian deaths arising from this conflict led Derek Gregory to query if, "in the dust of the shattered village of Qana [in Lebanon], in the rubble of Beirut's suburbs, and above all in the broken bodies filling the mortuaries, are we witnessing not only the deaths of hundreds of civilians but also the death of the idea of the civilian?"[3] Since the terrorist attacks

Karinne Coombes, B.A., B.Sc., M.A., LL.B. This article is drawn largely from a research essay submitted as a requirement of the joint M.A./LL.B. program between the Norman Paterson School of International Affairs (NPSIA) at Carleton University and the Faculty of Law at the University of Ottawa. I would like to thank Chris Penny from NPSIA and John Currie from the Faculty of Law for supervising my research. This article benefited greatly from their insightful comments and suggestions.

[1] See Commission of Inquiry on Lebanon, *Report of the Commission of Inquiry on Lebanon*, UN HRC, 3d Sess., UN Doc. A/HRC/RES/3/3 (2006) at para. 40.

[2] *Ibid.* ("large parts of Lebanese civilian infrastructure, including roads, bridges ... [the] Beirut Airport, ports, water and sewage treatment plants, electrical facilities, fuel stations, commercial structures, schools and hospitals, as well as private homes" were targets of attack by Israel. As a result, over 900,000 people in Lebanon were displaced, while an estimated 1,191 were killed and 4,409 injured, with children accounting for one-third of the casualties. In Israel, the toll was "43 civilian deaths, 997 injuries, 6,000 homes affected, and 300,000 persons ... displaced by Hezbollah's attacks" at paras. 76–78).

[3] Derek Gregory, "Death of the Civilian?" Editorial (2006) 24 Environment and Planning D 633 at 633.

in the United States on 11 September 2001, there has arguably been an increased recognition of the threat posed by transnational terrorism,[4] which has spurred action at national and international levels. Civilians enjoy a protected status under international law. However, the incident described earlier — and others like it[5] — illustrates recent challenges that transnational terrorism and the fight against it pose to international law and its ability to protect civilians from harm. When a state uses force in order to protect its population from the threat of terrorist attacks, such action can itself threaten the rights and lives of innocent civilians. The International Commission of Jurists has voiced such concern about counter-terrorist activity:

> The world faces a grave challenge to the rule of law and human rights. Previously well-established and accepted legal principles are being called into question in all regions of the world through ill-conceived responses to terrorism. Many of the achievements in the legal protection of human rights are under attack.[6]

United Nations Security Council (UNSC) resolutions also illustrate the growing recognition that counter-terrorist action can violate international law. While Resolution 1618 of 2005 reaffirms "the need to combat by all means, *in accordance with the Charter of the United Nations,* threats to international peace and security caused by terrorist acts," Resolution 1822 of 2008 reaffirms

> the need to combat by all means, in accordance with the Charter of the United Nations *and international law, including applicable international human*

---

4   The qualifier "transnational" is used to distinguish non-state from "international" or state-sponsored terrorism. Non-state actors committing terrorist attacks in the territory of other states will be considered transnational terrorism for the purposes of this article. Such groups can be located in one state or many.

5   Consider, for example, the Israel-Hamas conflict in Gaza from 27 December 2008 to 18 January 2009. The United States has claimed — and acted upon — the right to strike terrorist organizations located in Pakistan near the border with Afghanistan should Pakistan prove unwilling or unable to eliminate the threat of attacks in Afghanistan. Turkey has used military force against Kurds in northern Iraq; and Columbia attacked members of the Revolutionary Armed Forces of Colombia located in Ecuador in March 2008.

6   International Commission of Jurists, *Berlin Declaration,* 28 August 2004, <http://icj.org/IMG/pdf/Berlin_Declaration.pdf>.

rights, refugee, and humanitarian law, threats to international peace and security caused by terrorist acts.[7]

This difference in language arguably illustrates the international community's growing concern for breaches of international law arising from counter-terrorist activities. John Bolton, former US permanent ambassador to the United Nations stated during the 2006 Israel-Hezbollah conflict that there is "certainly no moral equivalence between an act of terrorism directed at [a] civilian population and the tragic loss [of civilian life that results]" and "the tragic loss of civilian life as a consequence of military action."[8] Although this statement may be normatively compelling and is legally correct when counter-terrorist military action conforms to the requirements of the law, it will be argued that it risks undermining the protection international law provides to innocent civilians[9] if it is used to justify acts that breach international law.

This article will explore the ability of international law — particularly international humanitarian law (IHL) — to protect innocent civilians from harm in the context of the fight against transnational terrorism. To achieve the goal of allowing states to protect their populations from the threat of terrorism, while at the same time respecting the rule of law and the rights of innocent civilians, it is argued that, while IHL must remain applicable only to armed conflicts, it must also evolve so that it clearly applies to "transnational" armed conflicts (that is, armed conflicts between State A and a non-state actor based in State B, where State A uses force in the territory of State B without State B's consent).[10] Currently, it is not

---

[7] Security Council (SC) Resolution 1618, UN SCOR, UN Doc. S/RES/1618 (2005), preamble [emphasis added]; SC Resolution 1822, UN SCOR, UN Doc. S/RES/1822 (2008), preamble [emphasis added].

[8] John R. Bolton, *Remarks on the Draft Resolution on the Middle East,* New York City, 13 July 2006, <http://www.state.gov/p/io/rls/rm/68972.htm>.

[9] The term "innocent civilian" will be used in contrast to individuals who engage in terrorist attacks or armed conflicts, as they arguably retain the status of "civilian" despite their potential participation in an armed conflict with a state. See *Public Committee against Torture in Israel v. Government of Israel,* HCJ 769/02 (11 December 2006) at paras. 31–40 and the authorities referred to therein [*Targeted Killings*].

[10] "Transnational" highlights the aspects distinguishing these conflicts from "international" or "non-international" armed conflicts — although the conflict transcends national boundaries, the opposing parties are not states. See Geoffrey S. Corn, "Hamdan, Lebanon, and the Regulation of Hostilities: The Need

clear that such conflicts fall within either of the traditional understandings of the recognized forms of armed conflict. Unlike "international" armed conflicts, the parties to the conflict are not states
(or their agents), while unlike "non-international" armed conflicts,
the conflict is not an internal civil one. Some states have used this
potential gap in the law to argue that their use of force is not regulated by IHL in such circumstances or that certain aspects of IHL
do not apply.[11] It is argued that this gap must be closed in order to
ensure an appropriate balance that allows states to respond to the
threat of terrorism while safeguarding the rights and lives of innocent civilians. Outside of the context of an armed conflict, other
rules of international and domestic law properly regulate the state's
use of counter-terrorist force.

The discussion is divided into four sections. The first section explores terrorism, its relation to international law, and how the law
constrains state action. The second section examines the legal regulation of the use of force by states and the laws that apply during
armed conflicts. The third section canvasses the protection that IHL
provides to civilians, while the fourth section considers the argument
that IHL must evolve in order to apply to transnational armed conflicts. It will be argued that while recognizing a third category of
armed conflict could permit the development of rules specific to
these conflicts, the application of IHL to transnational armed conflicts should be achieved by recognizing non-international armed
conflicts as a residual category that regulates all armed conflicts to
which a non-state actor is a party (without being an agent of a state).

TERRORISM AND INTERNATIONAL LAW

THE THREAT OF TRANSNATIONAL TERRORISM

With rapid technological advances and a "shrinking world" fuelled
by globalization, the ability of non-state actors to attack populations

---

to Recognize a Hybrid Category of Armed Conflict" (2007) 40 Vand. J. Transnat'l
L. 295 (uses the term "transnational"); Roy Schondorf, "Extra-State Armed
Conflicts: Is There a Need for a New Legal Regime?" (2004) 37 N.Y.U.J. Int'l L.
& Pol. 1 (uses the term "extra-state"); Gabor Rona, "Interesting Times for Inter-
national Humanitarian Law: Challenges from the 'War on Terror'" (2003) 27
Fletcher Forum of World Affairs 55 at 58 ("to avoid confusion with ['international
armed conflict'] a term whose use connotes state action, it would be better to
speak of this type of armed conflict as 'interstate' or 'transnational'").

11 See the discussion in note 216.

worldwide has arguably increased in recent years. The attacks in the United States on 11 September 2001 may be considered a striking illustration of the emergence of an arguably new phenomenon[12] that the UNSC has recognized as a threat to international peace and security:non-state actors able to launch deadly attacks outside of the state(s) in which they are based.[13] As the international community attempts to address the threat posed by these activities, the first question that arises is: what is "terrorism"? Despite many attempts, the international community has been largely unsuccessful at defining "terrorism."[14] In 2004, the UN secretary-general's High Level Panel on Threats, Challenges and Change recommended that terrorism be defined as

---

[12] Consider, e.g., Georges Abi-Saab, "The Proper Role of International Law in Combating Terrorism" (2002) 1 Chinese J. Int'l L. 305 at 306 (Georges Abi-Saab, a former judge of the Appeals Chamber of the International Criminal Tribunal for the former Yugoslavia [ICTY], believes that the events of 11 September 2001 triggered a "shock of recognition" regarding the risk of terrorism that previously had been contemplated but not truly understood); Christopher Greenwood, *Essays on War in International Law* (London: Cameron May, 2006) at 409 ("while international terrorism did not begin on that day, the scale of the attacks, the loss of life which they caused, and the means with which they were carried out set them apart from all prior terrorist atrocities no matter how awful"); International Committee of the Red Cross (ICRC), *International Humanitarian Law and the Challenges of Contemporary Armed Conflict* (Geneva: ICRC, 2003) at 17 [ICRC Report 2003] (recognizing the rise of "transnational networks capable of inflicting deadly violence on targets in geographically distant states").

[13] See, e.g., SC Resolution 1373, UN SCOR, UN Doc. S/RES/1373 (2001).

[14] In 1934, member states of the League of Nations discussed drafting a convention outlawing terrorism. This led to the adoption of the Convention on the Prevention and Punishment of Terrorism in 1937, which defined terrorism as: "[a]ll criminal acts directed at a State and intended or calculated to create a state of terror in the minds of particular persons or groups of persons or the general public," but it never entered into force due to an inability to approve this definition. See United Nations Counter-Terrorism Committee, *The Role of the Counter-Terrorism Committee and its Executive Directorate in the International Counter-Terrorism Effort*, <http://www.un.org/terrorism/pdfs/fact_sheet_1.pdf> [*Counter-Terrorism Fact Sheet*]. In 1994, a UN General Assembly (UNGA) Resolution defined terrorism as "criminal acts intended or calculated to provoke a state of terror in the general public, a group of persons or particular persons for political purposes" and provided that such acts were "in any circumstances unjustifiable whatever the considerations of a political, philosophical, ideological, racial, ethnic, religious, or other nature." See *Measures to Eliminate International Terrorism*, GA Res. 49/60, UN GAOR 49th Sess., UN Doc. A/RES/49/60 (1994).

any action ... intended to cause death or serious bodily harm to civilians or non-combatants, when the purpose of such attack, by its nature or context, is to intimidate a population, or to compel a Government or an international organization to do or to abstain from doing any act.[15]

United Nations Secretary-General Kofi Annan endorsed this definition in 2005.[16] In the same year, the UN member states agreed on the need for a "clear and unqualified condemnation of terrorism" addressing the issue "in all its forms and manifestations, committed by whomever, wherever and for whatever purposes" and to work towards a common definition of, and a comprehensive convention against, terrorism.[17] Despite this expressed commitment, efforts have stalled. Concern with the proposed definitions has been repeatedly expressed, in many instances due to the potential identification as terrorists of groups of peoples seeking self-determination[18] and the requirement of proving the intent to induce fear that has been central to some definitions. Some commentators have questioned the ability to criminalize "terrorism," arguing that it would not be just to hold someone accountable for "terrorism" if it remains undefined.[19] The lack of a precise definition, however, has not prevented the criminalization of many aspects of terrorism under national law and international treaties.[20]

In light of the definitional difficulties, Rosalyn Higgins has claimed that "[t]errorism is a term without legal significance. It is merely a

15 United Nations High-Level Panel on Threats, Challenges and Change, *A More Secure World: Our Shared Responsibility*, UN Doc. A/59/565 (2004) at para. 164.

16 Kofi Annan, *In Larger Freedom: Towards Development, Security and Human Rights for All*, UN Doc. A/59/2005 (2005) at para. 91.

17 *Counter-Terrorism Fact Sheet, supra* note 14.

18 Such concern is illustrated by the saying: "One man's terrorist is another man's freedom fighter."

19 Helen Duffy, *The "War on Terror" and the Framework of International Law* (New York: Cambridge University Press, 2005) at 40.

20 Thirteen international agreements address specific acts of terrorism, including the International Convention for the Suppression of Terrorist Bombings; the International Convention for the Suppression of the Financing of Terrorism; and the International Convention for the Suppression of Acts of Nuclear Terrorism: see UN, International Instruments to Counter Terrorism. To view all of these conventions, see United Nations, <http://www.un.org/terrorism/instruments. shtml>; Robert P. Barnridge, Jr., *Non-State Actors and Terrorism: Applying the Law of State Responsibility and the Due Diligence Principle* (The Hague: T.M.C. Asser Press, 2008) at 121–22.

convenient way of alluding to activities, whether of states or individuals, widely disapproved of and in which the methods used are either unlawful, or the targets protected or both."[21] Despite the lack of a consensus on the definition, Pierre-Marie Dupuy notes common elements: "Terror exercised on a civilian population as a political weapon is evidently at the core of any definition of terrorism, the international element being provided by the physical origin of the act and/or nationality of the wrongdoers."[22] Since at least 109 possible definitions of terrorism have been proposed,[23] this article will not endorse one, but it will consider the core elements to be: (1) the use of armed violence; (2) directed against a civilian population; (3) as a political weapon. It should also be noted that, under any legal regime, acts of terrorism are unlawful and are therefore legally significant — they violate IHL during times of armed conflict and international and domestic criminal law outside of an armed conflict.[24]

INTERNATIONAL LEGAL OBLIGATIONS AND STATE ACTIONS

International law is historically state-centric since states are its traditional subjects and its underlying principle is state sovereignty. Despite this foundation, a state's freedom of action remains constrained by its international legal obligations, as a second principle of international law is that a state incurs responsibility when it or its agents, including its military forces, violate its international legal obligations.[25] It will be argued that the ability for international law to afford protection to civilians may be challenged during the fight against transnational terrorism when states use force

---

21 Higgins, cited in Duffy, *supra* note 19 at 18.

22 Pierre-Marie Dupuy, "State Sponsors of Terrorism: Issues of Responsibility," in Andrea Bianchi, ed., *Enforcing International Law Norms against Terrorism* (Portland: Hart, 2004) at 5.

23 *Ibid.*

24 ICRC Report 2003, *supra* note 12 at 7 ("whatever the motives, intentional and direct attacks against civilians in armed conflict ... are strictly prohibited under IHL. So are acts or threats of violence the primary purpose of which is to spread terror among the civilian population. Outside of armed conflict, acts of violence aimed against civilians are crimes under international and domestic criminal laws").

25 *State Responsibility for Internationally Wrongful Acts*, UN GAOR, 56th Sess., Annex, Agenda Item 162, UN Doc. A/RES/56/83 (2001), art. 1 [*Articles on State Responsibility*].

against non-state actors outside of their territory. Such situations highlight the underlying tension between state sovereignty and the binding nature of international law. Through sovereignty, states enjoy freedom from interference in their internal affairs as a matter of custom and treaty.[26] However, sovereignty is not without limits, as international law places legal constraints on state activity. As such, a state will be bound by its international legal obligations when responding to the threat of transnational terrorism. It will be argued that transnational terrorism poses particular difficulties for states because the participation of non-state actors at an international level can make applying international law difficult due to its state-centric nature. Furthermore, while states will endeavour to protect their populations from harm threatened by transnational terrorism, international law limits the lawful scope of their responses to this threat.

IHL is a specialized body of international law that applies to armed conflicts. By regulating the conduct of hostilities and limiting the scope of lawful actions of the parties to armed conflicts, IHL has the potential to provide significant protection to individuals during armed conflicts. However, difficulty in assessing the lawfulness of a state's reaction to the threat of transnational terrorism may arise because an armed conflict between a state and a non-state actor based in another state's territory (without the territorial state's consent) may not fit within the traditional understandings of armed conflicts to which IHL applies.[27] In light of the pressure on states to respond to transnational terrorism in a manner that conforms with international law, the International Committee of the Red Cross (ICRC) has recognized that "the overriding legal and moral challenge presently facing the international community" is to combat the threat of terrorism "while preserving existing standards of protection provided by international law, including international humanitarian law."[28]

---

[26] Regarding customary status, see *Case Concerning Military and Paramilitary Activities In and Against Nicaragua (Nicaragua v. United States of America)*, [1986] I.C.J. Rep. 14 at para. 205 [*Nicaragua*]; as a matter of treaty, Charter of the United Nations, at art. 2(1).

[27] As will be explored later in this article, international humanitarian law (IHL) traditionally applies during armed conflicts that arise between states (as international armed conflicts) or between a state and non-state actor contained within the territory of the state (a non-international armed conflict).

[28] ICRC Report 2003, *supra* note 12 at 8.

THE USE OF ARMED FORCE AGAINST TRANSNATIONAL TERRORISM

A fundamental feature of "transnational" terrorism is that a non-state actor commits terrorist attacks outside of the state(s) in which it is based. To combat this threat, some states have proved willing to use armed force against suspected terrorists despite the fact that they are located in another state.[29] This situation may challenge the law regulating the extra-territorial use of force, which developed in response to inter-state conflicts. Although it is well settled that IHL applies to armed conflicts between two or more states, or those that remain contained within a state, its application to conflicts between a state and a non-state actor based in another state can be unclear. Before examining some of the legal protections individuals enjoy under IHL, the law regulating the state's extra-territorial use of force will be briefly explored.

THE USE OF FORCE BY STATES: *JUS AD BELLUM* AND *JUS IN BELLO*

The law regulating the recourse to the use of force by a state, *jus ad bellum*, is a separate branch of law from IHL, or *jus in bello*, which regulates the conduct of hostilities during an armed conflict. It is well accepted at international law that there is a binding prohibition on the state's extra-territorial use of force. Although using force was once an accepted means of statecraft, states are now obliged to settle disputes peacefully.[30] The only widely recognized exceptions to this prohibition are individual or collective acts of self-defence and force authorized by the UNSC to maintain international peace and security.[31] Although *jus ad bellum* will not be a focus of this

---

29 See, e.g., note 5 in this article.

30 This prohibition is recognized as a matter of treaty and customary law. See, e.g., *Kellogg-Briand Pact*, 27 August 1928, 46 U.S. Stat. 2343, art. 1 (the parties agree to "renounce [war] as an instrument of national policy in their relations with one another"); Charter of the United Nations, art. 2(4) ("[a]ll members shall refrain in their international relations from the threat or use of force against the territorial integrity or political independence of any state, or in any manner inconsistent with the Purposes of the United Nations"). The customary status of this prohibition was confirmed by the International Court of Justice (ICJ) and may be considered *jus cogens*. See *Nicaragua, supra* note 26 at para. 190. See also Marco Sassoli and Antoine A. Bouvier, eds. *How Does Law Protect in War?* 2nd edition (Geneva: ICRC, 2006) vol. 1 at 104 ("Today the use of force between States is prohibited by a peremptory rule of international law").

31 *Ibid.* UN Charter, arts. 51 and 42. The right to use force in self-defence has been recognized as a principle of customary international law, see *Nicaragua, supra* note 26 at para. 181.

article, it is important to recognize the destabilizing effects that the use of force in counter-terrorist activities may have on the strength and stability of international law — if states routinely use armed force contrary to international law, this could weaken the long-standing prohibition on the inter-state use of force. Pertinent to this discussion, a weakened prohibition on the use of force may result in less protection for innocent civilians, as an increased incidence of the use of force could correspond to an increased potential for persons to suffer harm. A possible counter-argument is that the prohibition on the use of force may interfere with a state's ability to protect itself and its population from terrorism, to the extent that violations could increase the protection of civilians. While this reasoning may hold true for populations threatened by transnational terrorism, it will be argued that a weakened prohibition on the use of force by states would pose a greater threat to international peace and security as well as to the rights and lives of innocent civilians at large. It is recognized, however, that for international law to remain relevant — and respected — it must allow states (or an international organization acting on their behalf) to effectively respond to the threat of transnational terrorism. Therefore, a balance must be attained that allows states to protect their populations while ensuring adequate protection of the rights and lives of innocent civilians when states use force to combat this threat.

As noted earlier, IHL regulates the means and methods of how states may lawfully use force. However, as is evident from its alternative name, the law of armed conflict, IHL only applies during armed conflicts. As such, it is important to understand what constitutes an "armed conflict" at international law and how the use of force in the context of transnational terrorism can challenge the legal protections that civilians might enjoy under IHL. It should be noted that predicating the application of IHL on the existence of an armed conflict does not result in a lack of legal protection when a state uses force outside of an armed conflict. In these circumstances, international human rights law (IHRL) may apply. Indeed, IHL is considered to have a *lex specialis* character such that, despite its application during an armed conflict, it does not completely displace IHRL, which is considered *lex generalis*.[32]

---

[32] The ICJ recognized the *lex specialis* character of IHL in *Legality of the Threat or Use of Nuclear Weapons*, Advisory Opinion, [1996] I.C.J. Rep. 226 at para. 25 [*Nuclear Weapons*].

INTERNATIONAL HUMANITARIAN LAW, ARMED CONFLICTS,
AND TERRORISM

There is a long history of international agreements purporting to regulate the conduct of armed hostilities between states.[33] Many treaties address the law of armed conflicts, while customary international law and general principles of law also play significant roles in defining the content of IHL.[34] Two principal series of treaties known as the "Hague Law" and the "Geneva Law" provide the substance of modern IHL. In the past, these sets of treaties were conceptualized as distinct branches of the law of armed conflict, with the Hague Law providing rules regarding the conduct of hostilities and the Geneva Law the protection of civilians and others *hors de combat*.[35] As the International Court of Justice (ICJ) has found, these two branches "have gradually formed one single complex system, known today as international humanitarian law."[36] Despite the title "international *humanitarian* law," the law regulating armed conflicts remains a fundamental compromise between military necessity[37] and the protection of humanity from undue suffering.

---

[33] See, e.g., Yoram Dinstein, *The Conduct of Hostilities under the Law of International Armed Conflict* (New York: Cambridge University Press, 2004) at 9 (The earliest such instrument is the 1856 Paris Declaration Respecting Maritime Law).

[34] See Jean-Marie Henckaerts and Louise Doswald-Beck, eds., *Customary International Humanitarian Law* (Cambridge: Cambridge University Press, 2005). The importance of customary law was highlighted in 1899 through "Martens Clause" in the preamble of the Convention with Respect to the Laws and Customs of War on Land, 29 July 1899, Avalon Project, Yale Law School, <http://avalon.law.yale.edu/19th_century/hague02.asp> [Hague Convention]. The Protocol Additional to the Geneva Conventions of 12 August 1949, and Relating to the Protection of Victims of Non-International Armed Conflicts, 8 June 1977, 1125 U.N.T.S. 609 [Additional Protocol II] contains a modern version ("In cases not covered by this Protocol or by other international agreements, civilians and combatants remain under the protection and authority of the principles of international law derived from custom, from the principles of humanity and from the dictates of public conscience," at art. 1(2)); see also *ibid.* at 7.

[35] See Dinstein, *supra* note 33 at 13 (this approach "was never really justified").

[36] *Nuclear Weapons, supra* note 32 at para. 75.

[37] Regarding "military necessity," see, e.g., *Instructions for the Government of Armies of the United States in the Field (Lieber Code)*, 24 April 1863, <http://www.icrc.org/ihl.nsf/FULL/110?OpenDocument> ("[m]ilitary necessity admits of all direct destruction of life or limb of 'armed' enemies, and of other persons whose destruction is incidentally 'unavoidable' in the armed contests of the war; it allows of the capturing of every armed enemy, and every enemy of importance to the

Modern legal protection for individuals who do not, or can no longer, take part in fighting is found in the four 1949 Geneva Conventions, which enjoy universal acceptance.[38] In 1977, two Additional Protocols (Additional Protocol I and Additional Protocol II) were added to the Geneva Conventions, which address issues arising under international and non-international armed conflicts respectively.[39] The protocols complement rather than supercede the Geneva Conventions, and their adoption led to the merger of the Hague and Geneva Laws.[40] Although the protocols do not enjoy universal ratification, some of their content reflects customary international law.[41]

---

hostile government, or of peculiar danger to the captor; it allows of all destruction of property, and obstruction of the ways and channels of traffic, travel, or communication, and of all withholding of sustenance or means of life from the enemy ... Men who take up arms against one another in public war do not cease on this account to be moral beings, responsible to one another and to God ... Military necessity does not admit of cruelty — that is, the infliction of suffering for the sake of suffering or for revenge, nor of maiming or wounding except in fight, nor of torture to extort confessions. It does not admit of the use of poison in any way, nor of the wanton devastation of a district. It admits of deception, but disclaims acts of perfidy; and, in general, military necessity does not include any act of hostility which makes the return to peace unnecessarily difficult," arts. 15–16).

38 The four 1949 Geneva Conventions superseded the previous 1929 Geneva Conventions: Geneva Convention for the Amelioration of the Condition of the Wounded and Sick in Armies in the Field (first drafted in 1864 and revised and replaced in 1906 and 1929) and the Geneva Convention Relative to the Treatment of Prisoners of War. Geneva Convention I for the Amelioration of the Condition of the Wounded and Sick in Armed Forces in the Field, 12 August 1949, 75 U.N.T.S. 31; Geneva Convention II for the Amelioration of the Condition of Wounded, Sick and Shipwrecked Members of Armed Forces at Sea, 12 August 1949, 75 U.N.T.S. 85; Geneva Convention III Relative to the Treatment of Prisoners of War, 12 August 1949, 75 U.N.T.S. 135; Geneva Convention IV Relative to the Protection of Civilian Persons in Time of War, 12 August 1949, 75 U.N.T.S. 287 [Geneva Convention IV]. Of particular importance to this study is Geneva Convention IV. Regarding ratification status, see ICRC, *The Geneva Conventions: The Core of International Humanitarian Law*, <http://www.icrc.org/Web/Eng/siteengo.nsf/htmlall/genevaconventions>.

39 Protocol Additional to the Geneva Conventions of 12 August 1949, and Relating to the Protection of Victims of International Armed Conflicts, 8 June 1977, 1125 U.N.T.S. 3 [Additional Protocol I]; Additional Protocol II, *supra* note 34.

40 Sassoli and Bouvier, *supra* note 30, vol. 1 at 123.

41 ICRC, *supra* note 38 (168 states have ratified the Additional Protocol I and 164 states have ratified Additional Protocol II). Regarding customary status, see Henckaerts and Doswald-Beck, *supra* note 34. A third additional protocol exists:

An important aspect of IHL is its binding nature on all parties to a conflict, irrespective of the cause and regardless of whether war has been declared or recognized by any of the parties.[42] IHL also applies equally to all parties to a conflict, independent of the legality of the recourse to the use of force,[43] and remains effective even if a party denounces its application.[44] Furthermore, non-adherence to IHL cannot justify in-kind reprisals.[45] As such, if IHL applied to an armed conflict between a state and a non-state actor in the context of transnational terrorism, its provisions would bind both the state and non-state actor, and the state would be unable to deny the application of IHL simply by arguing that unlawful terrorist attacks instigated the conflict.

Armed conflicts have been divided into two distinct categories — international and non-international — to which different rules apply. Traditionally, IHL has regulated hostilities during international (state-to-state) armed conflicts, while non-international (internal) armed conflicts have been shielded from the law through the state's freedom from interference in its internal affairs granted by state sovereignty.[46] However, in 1949, minimal protection was

---

Protocol Additional to the Geneva Conventions of 12 August 1949, and Relating to the Adoption of an Additional Distinctive Emblem, 8 December 2005.

[42] Leslie C. Green, *The Contemporary Law of Armed Conflict*, 3rd edition (Manchester: Manchester University Press, 2008) at 53.

[43] See, e.g., Dinstein, *supra* note 33 at 5 ("[b]reaches of [IHL] cannot be justified on the ground that the enemy is responsible for commencing the hostilities in flagrant breach of the *jus ad bellum*"); Gerald L. Neuman, "Humanitarian Law and Counterterrorist Force" (2003) E.J.I.L. 283 at 284. See especially Additional Protocol I, *supra* note 39 at preamble ("[t]he provisions of the Geneva Conventions of 12 August 1949 and of this Protocol must be fully applied in all circumstances to all persons who are protected by those instruments, without any adverse distinction based on the nature or origin of the armed conflict or the causes espoused by or attributed to the Parties to the conflict"). Although IHL applies to all parties in a conflict, this is not to say that the obligations will always be identical. In certain circumstances, IHL obligations may vary to a degree between parties to the same conflict (for example, when a state has ratified the Convention on the Prohibition of the Use, Stockpiling, Production and Transfer of Anti-Personnel Mines and on Their Destruction banning the use of land mines but another state has not and it continues to use them without violating IHL).

[44] See Green, *supra* note 42 at 23.

[45] See, e.g., Sassoli and Bouvier, *supra* note 30 at 297 (when a state takes countermeasures against another state for a breach of an international obligation, "[t]hose measures must themselves conform to IHL," while reprisals against protected persons and the civilian population by parties to a conflict are prohibited).

[46] See Green, *supra* note 42 at 66.

afforded to persons taking no part in hostilities during non-international armed conflicts through Common Article 3 to the Geneva Conventions. Although brief, Common Article 3 was significant because it provided the first legal regulation for non-international armed conflicts.[47] With Additional Protocol II, non-international armed conflicts became subject to further regulation. Despite this codification, the precise requirements for international and non-international armed conflicts remain subject to debate because they were not clearly defined in a treaty. Illustrating the difficulty that may arise by leaving the characterization of an armed conflict to states, Additional Protocol II contains rather restrictive requirements for its application in comparison to Common Article 3, which was intended to stop the practice of states denying the application of IHL to armed conflicts contained within their territory.[48] It is argued that this experience underscores the importance of clarifying whether a transnational armed conflict fits within the recognized categories of armed conflict.

International Armed Conflicts

International armed conflict is, by far, the most regulated form of conflict. Applicable treaties include the 1899 and 1907 Hague Regulations, the Geneva Conventions, and Additional Protocol I.[49] Reflecting the state-centric nature of international law, international armed conflict is traditionally understood as occurring between two or more states.[50] This understanding is evident from Common

47 See Corn, *supra* note 10 at 307 (Common Article 3 was "a major step forward in humanitarian regulation of conflict"). The significance of Common Article 3 will be explored in more detail later in this article.

48 See Yves Sandoz et al., eds., *Commentary on the Additional Protocols of 8 June 1977 to the Geneva Conventions of 12 August 1949* (ICRC: Geneva, 1987) at para. 1348; Liesbeth Zegveld, *Accountability of Armed Opposition Groups in International Law* (Cambridge: Cambridge University Press, 2002) at 143 ("the absence of a definition of an internal armed conflict in Common Article 3 proved to leave states too much freedom in their determination of the applicability of the law"). As will be discussed later in this article, a result is that there may be non-international armed conflicts to which only Common Article 3 applies and those to which both Common Article 3 and Additional Protocol II apply.

49 Regulations Respecting the Laws and Customs of War on Land, annexed to Hague Convention Respecting the Laws and Customs of War on Land, 18 October 1907, 36 Stat. 2277, 187 C.T.S. 227 [Hague Regulations]; ICRC Report 2003, *supra* note 12 at 8–9.

50 The only widely accepted exceptions are wars of national liberation and cases of complete or total occupation of the territory of one state by another. See, e.g.,

Article 2 of the Geneva Conventions, which provides that the treaties apply to armed conflicts that occur between "two or more High Contracting Parties." The Geneva Conventions do not further define "international armed conflict." However, the ICRC commentary provides some guidance, which suggests that international armed conflicts arise when a dispute between states results in the use of armed force by a state: "Any difference arising between two States and leading to the intervention of armed forces is an armed conflict within the meaning of Article 2."[51] The commentary further indicates that there is no threshold of violence to be exceeded for such circumstances to be considered an international armed conflict.[52] Relying on this understanding, it may be difficult to classify the use of force by State A against a non-state actor based in State B as an international armed conflict, when State B is not responsible for the actions of the non-state actor and does not participate as a party to the conflict.[53] When, however, an agency relationship exists between State B and the non-state actor, such that the non-state actor's actions may be attributable to State B, an international armed conflict can arise between the states.[54] Without this agency relationship, it may be argued that the situation is not an international

---

Sassoli and Bouvier, *supra* note 30 at 109 ("[d]uring the Diplomatic Conference that lead to the adoption of the two Additional Protocols of 1977, this conception [limiting international armed conflict to States] was challenged and it was finally recognized that 'wars of national liberation' should also be considered international armed conflicts"); Geneva Convention IV, *supra* note 38, art. 2 (the Geneva Conventions apply "to all cases of partial or total occupation of the territory of a High Contracting Party, even if the said occupation meets with no armed resistance").

51 Oscar Uhler et al., *Commentary on the Geneva Conventions of 12 August 1949*, vol. 4 (ICRC: Geneva, 1958) at 19.

52 See *ibid.* ("[i]t makes no difference how long the conflict lasts, or how much slaughter takes place"). However, see ICRC, *Summary Report of 27th Round Table: International Humanitarian Law and Other Legal Regimes: Interplay in Situations of Violence* (The Hague: ICRC, 2003) at 3 (an argument may be made that a *de minimis* exception exists regarding the scale and intensity for an armed conflict so that minor border incursions and skirmishes between states would not amount to an armed conflict).

53 See, e.g., Michael N. Schmitt, "'Direct Participation in Hostilities' and 21st Century Hostilities," in Horst Fisher et al., eds., *Crisis Management and Humanitarian Protection* (Berlin: BWV, 2004) 505 at 523, <http://www.michaelschmitt.org/images/Directparticipationpageproofs.pdf>.

54 See, e.g., *Articles on State Responsibility*, *supra* note 25, ch. 2 (a state is responsible for conduct that is attributable to it); Schondorf, *supra* note 10 at 37.

armed conflict because: (1) State B is not a party to the conflict; (2) there is no underlying dispute between the states; and (3) the force is not "directed" at State B.[55] (In making this argument, it should be stressed that there is no requirement under IHL for both states to use force for an international armed conflict to exist.) A counter-argument, however, is that the non-consensual use of force by State A in the territory of State B — whether or not it is opposed by force — is sufficient for finding that an international armed conflict exists, despite the fact that the force is directed against the non-state actor and not State B.

There is a lack of consensus among scholars whether such situations would be considered an international armed conflict. Marco Sassoli recognizes the potential difficulty of classifying transnational conflicts, noting that, "*controversially,* the law of international armed conflict applies when a state is directing hostilities against a transnational armed group on the territory of another state without the agreement of the latter state (e.g., Israel in Lebanon in 2006, if we consider the acts of Hezbollah to not be attributable to Lebanon)."[56] In contrast, Gabor Rona appears to require the parties to an international armed conflict to be states:

An international armed conflict is one in which two or more states are parties to the conflict. Armed conflicts that fall outside of this category are those in which a state is engaged in conflict with a transnational armed group whose actions cannot be attributed to a state.[57]

A recent opinion paper by the ICRC regarding the definition of armed conflicts provides that opposing parties to an international armed conflict must be states, and it also notes that they "occur[]

---

[55] See Corn, *supra* note 10 at 304.

[56] Marco Sassoli, *Transnational Armed Groups and International Humanitarian Law,* Occasional Paper Series no. 6 (Harvard University: Program on Humanitarian Policy and Conflict Research, 2006) at 5 [emphasis added]; see also Jonathan Somer, "Acts of Non-State Armed Groups and the Law Governing Armed Conflict" *ASIL Insights* (24 August 2006), <http://www.asil.org/insights060824.cfm> ("[i]f the acts of Hezbollah are deemed attributable to a state, the conflict is considered to be international and the Geneva Conventions will apply in their entirety").

[57] Rona, *supra,* note 10 at 58; see also Derek Jinks, "September 11 and the Laws of War" (2003) Y.J. Int'l L. 1 at 12 ("[a]bsent proof that al Qaeda acted on behalf of a state or that a state has recognized al Qaeda as a 'belligerent,' the only potentially applicable body of law [to the acts of 11 September] is the law of war governing internal armed conflicts").

when *one or more States* have recourse to armed force *against another State,* regardless of the reasons or the intensity of this confrontation."[58] As such, it may be argued that a transnational armed conflict is not international because the parties are not states (or non-state actors whose actions are attributable to a state), and the force used by State A is directed at the non-state actor and not State B. Clearly, a terrorist group whose actions cannot be attributable to a state cannot be a party for the purposes of finding that an international armed conflict exists because it is not a state. As noted earlier, however, it may be more difficult to maintain that State A is not directing armed force at State B. This difficulty will increase when State A controls some of State B's territory. Since transnational armed conflicts are rare, there is limited state practice and *opinio juris* to resolve this issue. However, the 2006 Israel-Hezbollah conflict may provide limited guidance. There are divergent views on the nature of this conflict, which underscores the difficulty in classifying these situations.[59] Kenneth Anderson notes that the general (albeit not universal) view is that when there are mixed parties (that is, a non-state group as a separate party to an armed conflict to which the territorial state is a party), the nature of the conflict is characterized with respect to each party.[60] The result could be concurrent conflicts

---

[58] ICRC, *Opinion Paper: How Is the Term "Armed Conflict" Defined in International Humanitarian Law?* (March 2008), <http://www.icrc.org/web/eng/siteeng0. nsf/htmlall/armed-conflict-article-170308/$file/Opinion-paper-armed-conflict. pdf> at 1 [emphasis added].

[59] See, e.g., Commission of Inquiry, *supra* note 1 at paras. 8–9 ("[t]he hostilities that took place from 12 July to 14 August constitute an international armed conflict to which conventional and customary international humanitarian law and international human rights law are applicable ... the Commission highlights its *sui generis* nature in that active hostilities took place only between Israel and Hezbollah fighters"). Compare Corn, *supra* note 10 at 305 ("neither Israel nor Lebanon took the position that the hostilities fell into the category of international armed conflict"). It is not apparent, however, that they took the opposite position. See Government of Israel, *Preserving Humanitarian Principles While Combating Terrorism,* April 2007, <http://www.mfa.gov.il/MFA/Terrorism-+ Obstacle+to+Peace/Terrorism+from+Lebanon-+Hizbullah/Preserving+ Humanitarian+Principles+While+Combating+Terrorism+-+April+2007.htm> (Israel did not classify the conflict, but "held itself bound to apply the principles of humanitarian law").

[60] Kenneth Anderson, *Is the Israel-Hezbollah Conflict an International Armed Conflict?* <http://kennethandersonlawofwar.blogspot.com/2006/07/is-israel-hezbollah-conflict.html> (he concludes that if Lebanon's armed forces were involved in the fighting, the armed conflict between Israel and Lebanon would have been international, while the conflict between Israel and Hezbollah would not).

of different natures: the conflict between the states would be international, while the conflict between the non-state actor and State A would not. Jonathan Somer concludes that an international armed conflict would have existed where Israel exercised control over Lebanese territory on the basis that the Geneva Conventions apply to situations of partial or total occupation even where there is no armed resistance.[61] Highlighting the difficulty in characterizing the nature of such conflicts, Somer notes that "[a]n argument also exists ... that the conflict is international in nature, not as a result of any issue of attribution or occupation, but simply because Common Article 2 applies as soon as Israel attacked Lebanese territory."[62]

This article is principally concerned with the nature of the armed conflict between State A and the non-state actor. Although the question of how the law protects civilians may be moot with respect to the actions of State A if there were concurrent armed conflicts of different natures (because State A would likely be bound by the rules applicable to international armed conflicts when it acts in State B's territory regardless of its target), the nature of the conflict between State A and the non-state actor would remain relevant because the law applicable to the non-state actor would be determined by the nature of the conflict. The nature of the conflict is also important because of the uncertainty regarding whether an international armed conflict would even exist. State A, for example, could arguably not trigger the application of the Geneva Conventions if it did not control any of State B's territory. Finally, an armed conflict could arise where there is no identifiable government in State B to support the existence of an international armed conflict. Should a state engage in an armed conflict with a non-state actor in a failed state, the nature of the conflict may be relevant for both parties.[63]

Human Rights Watch endorses this position and that of Somer, *supra* note 56, see Human Rights Watch, "Civilians under Assault: Hezbollah's Rocket Attacks on Israel in the 2006 War" (2007) 19(3) Human Rights Watch Reports at 21 ("[a]t least to the extent of armed hostilities between the states of Israel and Lebanon and Israeli control over Lebanese territory, the 2006 conflict was an international armed conflict").

61 Somer, *ibid.*

62 *Ibid.*

63 Regarding the application of IHL in failed states, see Sassoli and Bouvier, *supra* note 30, vol. 2 at 770–75.

Non-International Armed Conflicts

Historically, non-international armed conflicts have been subject to less regulation than international. The principal treaties and treaty provisions applicable to non-international armed conflicts are Common Article 3 and Additional Protocol II. Common Article 3 provides limited humanitarian protection during armed conflicts "not of an international character occurring in the territory of one of the High Contracting Parties," while Additional Protocol II "develops and supplements [Common Article 3] ... without modifying its existing conditions of application."[64] Additional Protocol II largely applies to situations of civil war[65] and requires a threshold level of violence to be reached since the protocol provides that it "shall not apply to situations of internal disturbances and tensions, such as riots, isolated and sporadic acts of violence and other acts of a similar nature, as not being armed conflicts."[66]

There is significant debate regarding the potential classification of an armed conflict between a state and a non-state actor based in another state as non-international. In some instances, this characterization may be straightforward, such as when State B invites State A to use force in its territory. In such cases, State A would be an agent of State B, and a non-international armed conflict would exist when the requirements of an armed conflict are met.[67] The characterization of the conflict is more difficult, however, when State A uses force without State B's consent. As noted earlier, the traditional conception of a non-international armed conflict is an internal civil war. When a state uses force against a non-state actor

---

[64] Geneva Convention IV, *supra* note 38, art. 3; Additional Protocol II, *supra* note 34, art. 1.

[65] Additional Protocol II, *supra* note 34, art. 1(1) ("[t]his Protocol ... shall apply to all armed conflicts which are not covered by Article 1 of [Additional Protocol I] ... *and* which take place *in the territory* of a High Contracting Party *between its armed forces and dissident armed forces or other organized armed groups* which, under responsible command, exercise such control over a part of its territory as to enable them to carry out sustained and concerted military operations and to implement this Protocol" [emphasis added]).

[66] *Ibid.*, art. 1(2).

[67] The current conflict in Afghanistan may be considered a non-international armed conflict, as international forces are engaged in a conflict against insurgents with the consent of the current Afghanistan government. Although beyond the scope of this article, such situations may raise difficult questions regarding the IHL obligations that apply, as State B may be party to Additional Protocol II when State A is not.

based in another state, this force does not easily fit within this definition. Since conflicts that fall outside of the categories of "international" or "non-international" are relatively uncommon, there are few historical examples from which state practice can be drawn. Therefore, most arguments regarding the appropriate classification revolve around the interpretation of treaties.[68] At least three different interpretations of the requirements for non-international armed conflicts are possible: (1) they must be contained within the territory of a single state; (2) they must be situations of internal civil war between the territorial state and an armed opposition group or between such groups; or (3) they are any armed conflict that is not international.[69]

As noted earlier, Common Article 3 and Additional Protocol II respectively provide that they apply when the conflict occurs "in the territory" of "one" or "a" "High Contracting Party."[70] Some authors believe that this wording effectively limits non-international armed conflicts to those contained within the territory of a single state.[71] The drafting history and a plain reading of Common Article 3 support this interpretation.[72] The ICRC commentary notes, for example, that it was initially recommended that Common Article 3 begin with: "In the case of armed conflict *within the borders of a State*, the Convention shall be applied."[73] The *Manual on the Law of*

---

[68] Schondorf, *supra* note 10 at 52–53; Sassoli, *supra* note 56 at 2 ("the fact remains that most armed conflicts are either clearly international or clearly non-international").

[69] Jinks, *supra* note 57 at 38–41. Since a later section of this article will explore the argument that a new category of armed conflict is necessary, this part will largely canvass rather than critically evaluate these positions.

[70] See Geneva Convention IV, *supra* note 38, art. 3; Additional Protocol II, *supra* note 34, art. 1(1).

[71] See, e.g., Natasha Balendra, "Defining Armed Conflict" (2008) 29 Cardozo L. Rev. 2461 at 2469; Schmitt, *supra* note 53 at 523 ("[n]either the Common Article [3] nor the additional Protocol [II] applies ... to a conflict in which a shadowy group of terrorists from multiple countries targets a government or its citizens globally"); Schondorf, *supra* note 10 at 50 ("[l]egislative history ... support[s] the view that the provision's purpose was to deal only with armed conflicts within the territorial boundaries of a high contracting party"); Rona, *supra* note 10. Due to its universality, Common Article 3 would apply when a non-international armed conflict arises in any state, but Additional Protocol II would be limited to states parties to the treaty.

[72] Jinks, *supra* note 57 at 40.

[73] Uhler et al., *supra* note 51 at 41–42 [emphasis added].

Non-International Armed Conflict, which is used to teach IHL at the International Institute of Humanitarian Law in San Remo, provides that non-international armed conflicts must remain contained within a single state.[74] The Rome Statute of the International Criminal Court (Rome Statute) may also support this interpretation since its provision criminalizing war crimes committed during non-international armed conflicts "applies to armed conflicts that take place *in the territory of a State* when there is protracted armed conflict between governmental authorities and organized armed groups or between such groups."[75] Since all armed conflicts must occur within a state (unless it is on the high seas), it is difficult to see why this phrase would be included if there were no intention to indicate a territorial restriction. Roy Schondorf argues that it may be difficult to characterize a transnational armed conflict as non-international because the drafting history and "the treaty's language does not seem to cover [such] armed conflicts because [these] armed conflicts do not take place within the territory of the state."[76] Despite this claim, competing interpretations are possible due to Common Article 3's language.[77]

A second possible interpretation of these treaties is that, as the drafting history of Common Article 3 and the detailed provisions of Additional Protocol II arguably show, they were intended to regulate internal civil wars.[78] The ICRC commentary notes, for

---

[74] Michael N. Schmitt et al., *The Manual on the Law of Non-International Armed Conflict with Commentary* (San Remo, Italy: International Institute of Humanitarian Law, 2006) at 2 (non-international armed conflicts do not "encompass conflicts extending to the territory of two or more States").

[75] Rome Statute of the International Criminal Court, 17 July 1998, 2187 U.N.T.S. 3, art. 8(2)(f) [emphasis added] [Rome Statute].

[76] Schondorf, *supra* note 10 at 50. This argument may be less persuasive because, on its face, Common Article 3 does not require the territorial state to be the one that is using force during an armed conflict.

[77] See note 65, in contrast to Common Article 3. Additional Protocol II provides that it applies only when the territorial state is engaged in an armed conflict with a non-state actor that has reached a threshold level of organization and exerts control over a portion of the state's territory.

[78] See, e.g., Schondorf, *supra* note 10; Uhler et al., *supra* note 51; Green, *supra* note 42 at 343 ("[a] non-international armed conflict has traditionally been one in which the governmental authorities are opposed by groups within that state seeking to overthrow those authorities by force of arms"); John P. Cerone, "Status of Detainees in Non-International Armed Conflict, and Their Protection in the Course of Criminal Proceedings: The Case of *Hamdan v. Rumsfeld*" *ASIL Insight,* 14 July 2006, <http://www.asil.org/insights060714.cfm> ("the

example, "useful" criteria for determining the existence of a non-international armed conflict that suggest that Common Article 3 applies to internal civil wars.[79] Some support for this interpretation may be drawn from state practice, as the UK *Manual of the Law of Armed Conflict* provides:

> If the situation *in a country* amounts to an armed conflict, the law of armed conflict applies … If it is an armed conflict *between the forces of a state and dissident or anti-government armed forces*, or if it is an armed conflict between factions *within a state*, Common Article 3 to the Geneva Conventions applies.[80]

Although not produced by a state, the *Manual on the Law of Non-International Armed Conflict* may support understanding non-international armed conflicts as internal civil wars, as it defines them as "armed confrontations occurring *within the territory of a single State* and in which the armed forces of no other State are *engaged against the central government.*"[81] The Rome Statute may also support the requirement for the territorial State to be involved —

---

paradigm case of non-international armed conflict is internal conflict, e.g., a civil war"); Gabor Rona, "When Is a War Not a War? The Proper Role of the Law of Armed Conflict in the 'Global War on Terror'" (presentation at the International Action to Prevent and Combat Terrorism in Copenhagen, 15 March 2004), <http://www.icrc.org/web/eng/siteengo.nsf/html/5XCMNJ> ("[w]hen the 'war on terror' amounts to the use of armed force within a State, between a State and a rebel group or between rebel groups within the State, the situation *may* amount to a non-international armed conflict" [emphasis in original]); Institute of International Law, *Resolution on the Application of IHL and Fundamental Human Rights in Armed Conflicts in which Non-State Entities are Parties* (Berlin, 1999), online: <http://www.idi-iil.org/idiE/resolutionsE/1999_ber_03_en.PDF> ("the expression 'armed conflicts in which non-State entities are parties' means *internal* armed conflicts between *a government's armed forces and those of one or several non-State entities*, or between several non-State entities" [emphasis added]).

79 Uhler et al., *supra* note 51 at 41–42. The criteria are discussed later in note 106.

80 *Manual of the Law of Armed Conflict*, at para. 3.5, cited in Green, *supra* note 42 at 73 [emphasis added].

81 Schmitt et al., *supra* note 74 at 2 [emphasis added] (it is noted that this wording is not conclusive as requiring non-international armed conflicts to be civil wars. The manual's commentary does not directly address the nature of a transnational armed conflict: "Non-international armed conflicts do not include conflicts in which two or more States are engaged against each other … When a foreign State extends its military support to the government of a State within which a

either directly or indirectly by another state acting as an agent — by providing that non-international armed conflicts occur "between governmental authorities and organized armed groups or between such groups." Potentially supporting this interpretation, the ICRC has noted that

[n]on-international armed conflicts are *protracted armed confrontations* occurring between governmental armed forces and the forces of one or more armed groups, or between such groups arising on the territory of a State.[82]

Although the above may not necessarily exclude an armed conflict in State B in which the forces of State A are engaged against non-state actors but not against the central government, it may support the understanding of non-international armed conflicts as internal civil conflicts because the references to government and governmental authorities would presumably refer to the government of the territorial state.[83] Further, transnational armed conflicts may not fit within this framework because a non-state terrorist organization may not be a dissident group with respect to the territorial state. It should be noted that, despite the traditional or paradigmatic understanding of non-international armed conflicts as an internal civil war, the concept could be capable of evolution through state practice.

A third understanding of non-international armed conflict is based upon reading Common Article 3 so that it applies to *all* armed conflicts that are "not of an international character." As Sassoli has noted, the use of the phrase "in the territory of [a/one] High Contracting Party" could merely indicate that Common Article 3 and Additional Protocol II purport to bind only the states that have ratified the treaties rather than indicate a territorial restriction to

---

non-international armed conflict is taking place, the conflict remains non-international in character. Conversely, should a foreign State extend military support to an armed group acting against the government, the conflict will become international in character").

[82] ICRC, *Opinion Paper, supra* note 58 at 5 [emphasis in original].

[83] An alternative interpretation may be that these provisions simply show that another state cannot be engaged against the state government for the conflict to remain non-international and not necessarily require the state government to be involved. For other ambiguous statements, see note 78 in this article; see also *ibid.*

the application of the treaties' provisions.[84] The argument against imposing territorial restrictions on non-international armed conflicts is strengthened because it may be desirable for internal conflicts that spill over into neighbouring states without involving the neighbouring state's armed forces to remain "non-international." The Statute for the International Criminal Tribunal for Rwanda may support this position since it authorized the tribunal to enforce the rules of non-international armed conflicts when the Rwandan conflict had spill-over effects.[85] In light of this situation, Liesbeth Zegveld concludes that "internal armed conflicts are distinguished from international conflicts by the parties involved rather than by the territorial scope of the conflict."[86]

Sassoli argues that non-international armed conflicts should be considered a residual category, stating that "every armed conflict not classified as international is perforce a non-international armed conflict," and he notes that, "[f]rom the perspective and purpose of IHL, [such an] interpretation must be correct, as there would otherwise be a gap in protection, which could not be explained by States' concerns about their sovereignty."[87] Jurisprudence may support this broad interpretation.[88] The ICJ arguably adopted this position in *Case Concerning Military and Paramilitary Activities In and Against Nicaragua (Nicaragua v. United States of America)*, when it recognized that the protections in Common Article 3 applied to international armed conflicts as a matter of customary law:

---

84 See Sassoli, *supra* note 56 at 9.

85 Statute of the International Tribunal for Rwanda, Annex to SC Resolution 955, UN SCOR, UN Doc. S/Res/955 (1994), arts. 1, 7; see Sassoli, *supra* note 56 (the ICTR Statute "confirms that even a conflict spreading across borders remains a non-international armed conflict"). However, see Rome Statute, *supra* note 75, as the Rome Statute appears to maintain the traditional territorial limitation for non-international armed conflicts.

86 Zegveld, *supra* note 48 at 136. Although Zegveld's characterization may resolve the territorial issue, it is unclear whether she would consider that an outside state could be a party to an armed conflict with a non-state armed group and maintain the internal/non-international classification.

87 Marco Sassoli, "Use and Abuse of the Laws of War in 'The War on Terrorism'" (2004) 22 Law & Inequality 195 at 201; see also ICRC, *supra* note 58 at 1.

88 Cerone, *supra* note 78 ("international authorities including the [ICJ] and the [ICTY] ... interpret the phrase 'conflict not of an international character' as being residual, covering any armed conflict that is not inter-state"); compare notes 98 and 99 (the ICTY has arguably recognized the territorial requirement of a non-international armed conflict).

[Common] Article 3 ... *defines certain rules to be applied in the armed conflicts of a non-international character.* There is no doubt that, *in the event of international armed conflicts, these rules also constitute a minimum yardstick,* in addition to the more elaborate rules which also apply to international conflicts; and *they are rules which, in the Court's opinion, reflect what the Court in 1949 called "elementary considerations of humanity"* [and were held to form part of customary law applicable to international armed conflicts in *Corfu Channel*].[89]

This holding is widely considered to extend Common Article 3 as a "minimum yardstick" to *all* armed conflicts — presumably, international, non-international, or otherwise. One could argue that an extension of these principles to armed conflicts regardless of the characterization as international or non-international supports understanding non-international armed conflicts as a residual category. It should be recalled, however, that the court in *Nicaragua* was *not* applying Common Article 3 but was, rather, using it to identify general principles of IHL applicable to "international" and "non-international" armed conflicts.[90] Although these principles may apply to international and non-international armed conflicts, one may question the ability of using *Nicaragua* to identify the legal requirements of a non-international armed conflict. The Supreme Court of the United States, however, arguably endorsed the residual category interpretation of non-international armed conflicts in *Hamdan v. Rumsfeld,* when the majority held that "[t]he term 'conflict not of an international character' is used here [in Common Article 3] in contradistinction to a conflict between nations."[91] Like

---

[89] *Nicaragua, supra* note 26 at para. 218; see *Corfu Channel (United Kingdom of Great Britain and Northern Ireland v. Albania),* [1949] I.C.J. Rep. 4 at 22 [emphasis added]. The court further stated in *Nicaragua* that, "general principles of humanitarian law include a particular prohibition [on encouraging violations the principles in Common Article 3], accepted by States and extending to activities *which occur in the context of armed conflicts, whether international in character or not*" at para. 255 [emphasis added].

[90] See *Nicaragua, supra* note 26 at paras. 217–18.

[91] *Hamdan v. Rumsfeld,* 548 U.S. 557 (2006) at 67 [*Hamdan*] (Justice Stevens further noted that "[Common Article 3] ... affords some minimal protection ... to individuals ... who are involved in a conflict 'in the territory' of a signatory"). Since every armed conflict must occur within the territory of a signatory due to the universality of the Geneva Conventions, Stevens J. may arguably have been noting the potential territorial limitation of Common Article 3. *Hamdan* may be of limited support for resolving the classification of transnational armed conflicts because the Court did not discuss the requirements of an "armed conflict" and

Sassoli, Derek Jinks advocates a broad interpretation in order to avoid an "inexplicable regulatory gap in the Geneva Conventions" when armed conflicts fall outside of the traditional conceptions of "international" and "non-international."[92] Rejecting this approach, Roy Schondorf argues that "[t]his interpretation ... is not particularly convincing," and he maintains that "[t]here is also neither historical nor academic support for reading Common Article 3 as suggesting anything other than that the conflict must occur within the territory of the state that is a party to the conflict."[93] Although Common Article 3 does not contain this requirement on its face, Schondorf considers the view of Sassoli and Jinks "flawed" because it "bends reality to conform to outdated classifications," and he asserts that,

[r]ather than argue that a situation that is essentially different from [a non-international] armed conflict should be governed by the laws pertaining to [non-international] armed conflicts, it is preferable to recognize that a gap exists ... and to focus academic discussions on what should be done about this gap.[94]

In light of this debate, the need to clarify the application of IHL to armed conflicts is readily apparent. Even Sassoli notes that "[i]t may be that a law specific to such transnational armed conflicts could be elaborated."[95]

Armed Conflicts and the Fight against Transnational Terrorism

In addition to the potential difficulty in characterizing the nature of an armed conflict between a state and a non-state actor based in another state, there may be other hurdles to cross in order to recognize the existence of an armed conflict when states use force against extra-territorial transnational terrorist groups. Determining when IHL applies is complicated by the fact that IHL treaties do not define "armed conflict." Theodor Meron recognizes this difficulty:

---

did not rule on the argument raised by the US government that its conflict with al Qaeda in Afghanistan was distinct from its conflict with the Taliban and was unique because of its extra-territorial character, see *Hamdan* at 65–66.

[92] Jinks, *supra* note 56 at 40.

[93] Schondorf, *supra* note 10 at 50–51.

[94] *Ibid.* at note 131.

[95] Sassoli, *supra* note 87 at 220.

"The thresholds of applicability of [IHL] and the characterization of conflicts [as international or non-international] are among the most controversial issues in international humanitarian law."[96] Although IHL may apply when counter-terrorism action "amounts to, or involves, armed conflict," a fundamental question is: what is an armed conflict?[97]

In *Prosecutor v. Tadic* (Jurisdiction), the Appeals Chamber of the International Criminal Tribunal for the Former Yugoslavia (ICTY) considered this issue and held that "an armed conflict exists whenever there is *a resort to armed force between States* or *protracted armed violence* between *governmental authorities* and *organised armed groups* or between such groups *within a State.*"[98] This definition was adopted in all cases before the ICTY.[99] Indicating a measure of acceptance of this definition, the Rome Statute reflects this definition for non-international armed conflicts, although it does not define international armed conflict.[100] It is clear that this definition recognizes that a threshold of armed violence must be exceeded to trigger the application of IHL to non-international armed conflicts (and arguably recognizes a territorial and/or party limitation). Whether violence exceeds this threshold must be determined on a case-by-case basis. The jurisprudence of the ICTY suggests that this threshold "should be interpreted in a flexible manner" and does not require "military operations be carried out in a sustained or continuous manner."[101] It is unclear if intensity of violence, rather than duration, can render armed violence "protracted."[102]

---

[96] Theodor Meron, *Humanization of International Law* (Boston: Martinus Nijhoff, 2006) at 29.

[97] ICRC Report 2003, *supra* note 12 at 18.

[98] *Prosecutor v. Tadic*, IT-94-1, Decision on the Defence Motion for Interlocutory Appeal on Jurisdiction (2 October 1995) (ICTY, Appeals Chamber) [*Tadic* case] at paras. 67 and 70 [emphasis added]. This definition appears on its face to support the traditional classification of international and non-international armed conflicts, see the discussion earlier in this article.

[99] Sonja Boelaert-Suominen, "The Yugoslavia Tribunal and the Common Core of Humanitarian Law Applicable to All Armed Conflicts" (2000) 13 Leiden J. Int'l L. 619 at 632.

[100] See Rome Statute, *supra* note 75, art. 8(2)(f).

[101] Boelaert-Suominen, *supra* note 99 at 635.

[102] Rona, *supra* note 10 at 62–63. See Sassoli, *supra* note 56 at 7 (protracted armed violence cannot be the appropriate threshold because "it is not foreseeable at the outset of a given conflict" and "[i]t is difficult to imagine that the obligation to respect IHL does not arise readily at the inception of a conflict but only from

As noted earlier, a non-state actor must be sufficiently organized to be identifiable as a party to a conflict. The ICRC underscores the importance of this requirement:

The very logic underlying IHL requires identifiable parties in the above sense because this body of law — while not affecting the parties' legal status — establishes equality of rights and obligations among them under IHL (not domestic law) when they are at war. The parties' IHL rights and obligations are provided for so that both sides know the rules within which they are allowed to operate and so that they are able to rely on similar conduct by the other side.[103]

In contrast to the *Tadic* case, Additional Protocol II requires a non-state armed group to be under "responsible" command and exert a certain level of control over the state's territory.[104] This restrictive definition, however, only applies to the application of Additional Protocol II, as Common Article 3 does not contain a similar definition.[105] Although Common Article 3 does not define non-international armed conflicts, the ICRC commentary provides criteria that it considered "useful as a means of distinguishing a genuine armed conflict from a mere act of banditry or an unorganized and short-lived insurrection."[106] These criteria would severely

---

that time when hostilities become protracted"). Supporting the argument that intensity may suffice, the Inter-American Commission on Human Rights held that IHL applied to a conflict lasting only two days, see *Abella (Argentina)*, 18 November 1997, Doc. OEA/Ser.L/V/II.98 doc. 6 rev. (1998). See ICRC, *supra* note 58 at 5 ("[t]he armed confrontation must reach a *minimum level of intensity* and the parties involved in the conflict must show *a minimum of organisation*") [emphasis in original].

103 ICRC Report 2003, *supra* note 12 at 19.

104 Additional Protocol II, *supra* note 34, art. 1(1).

105 See Sandoz et al., *supra* note 48 at para. 4454 (since Common Article 3 applies simultaneously, it will continue to apply even if a non-international armed conflict fails to meet the criteria of Additional Protocol II); Sassoli and Bouvier, *supra* note 30 at 90 ("[i]t should be noted that this fairly restrictive definition [found in Additional Protocol II] applies only to Protocol II. The definition does not apply to Article 3 common to the Geneva Conventions. Practically, there are thus situations of non-international armed conflict to which only Article 3 will apply, the level of organization of the dissidents groups being insufficient for Protocol II to apply").

106 Uhler et al., *supra* note 51 at 35-36 ("(1) That the Party in revolt against the de jure Government possesses an organized military force, an authority responsible for its acts, acting within a determinate territory and having the means of

limit the application of Common Article 3; however, Sonja Boelaert-Suominen argues that, in light of the ICTY jurisprudence, "it can be safely concluded that the threshold suggested by the ICRC commentary has failed to crystallise into customary international law."[107] Of significance, there is no requirement in a non-international armed conflict for non-state actors to exercise control over the territory or have a responsible command: "All that is required is ... *protracted* [or intense] armed violence between *organised* armed groups."[108]

Rona rejects calls for a new category of armed conflict but believes that IHL can regulate armed conflicts arising during the fight against transnational terrorism when the general criteria of an armed conflict are satisfied.[109] First, the parties to the conflict must be identifiable. Consistent with the position of the ICRC, Rona considers that the concept of a "party" suggests a minimum level of organization because "[t]here can be no assessment of rights and responsibilities under humanitarian law in war without identifiable parties."[110] Second, the territory in which the conflict is occurring must be identifiable. Third, the requisite threshold of armed violence must be exceeded. And, fourth, the beginning and end of

---

respecting and ensuring respect for the Convention; (2) That the legal Government is obliged to have recourse to the regular military forces against insurgents organized as military and in possession of a part of the national territory; (3) (a) That the de jure Government has recognized the insurgents as belligerents; or (b) that it has claimed for itself the rights of a belligerent; or (c) that it has accorded the insurgents recognition as belligerents for the purposes only of the present Convention; or (d) that the dispute has been admitted to the agenda of the Security Council or the General Assembly of the United Nations as being a threat to international peace, a breach of the peace, or an act of aggression; (4)(a) That the insurgents have an organisation purporting to have the characteristics of a State, (b) That the insurgent civil authority exercises de facto authority over persons within a determinate territory, (c) That the armed forces act under the direction of the organized civil authority and are prepared to observe the ordinary laws of war, (d) That the insurgent civil authority agrees to be bound by the provisions of the Convention").

107 Boelaert-Suominen, *supra* note 99 at 634.

108 *Ibid.* [emphasis in original].

109 Rona, *supra* note 10 at 55–74.

110 *Ibid.* at 60. Such consistency is to be expected in light of the fact that Rona was serving as a legal advisor in the Legal Division of the ICRC at the time of his writing; see also Duffy, *supra* note 19 at 219 (an essential factor for the existence of any armed conflict is the "resort to force between two or more *identifiable* parties") [emphasis added].

the conflict must be identifiable in order to determine when IHL begins and ceases to apply.[111] Applying IHL to the use of force against non-state terrorist groups may be difficult because these requirements may not be easily met. Regarding the US "War on Terror," the ICRC notes that

it is difficult to see how a loosely connected, clandestine network of [terrorist] cells ... could qualify as a "party" to the conflict. Many questions remain without answer, such as what discrete networks are at issue? What acts of terrorism perpetrated at geographically distinct points in the world can be linked to those networks? What would be the characterization of purely individual acts?[112]

Although some groups such as Al-Qaeda may lack the structure to be identifiable as a party to a conflict, it is conceivable that non-state actors could reach this level of organization. Groups such as Hezbollah in Lebanon, for example, may be sufficiently organized — and territorially concentrated — to be capable of being parties. Further difficulty in applying IHL to the War on Terror arises due to the territorial and temporal scope of such a "war," as a worldwide campaign "against terrorism" cannot occur in an identifiable territory and its beginning and end may not be capable of identification (when is terrorism vanquished?). Although the War on Terror *itself* does not fit the requirements of an armed conflict to which IHL would apply, it is conceivable that an armed conflict may arise *within* the context of a rhetorical War on Terror, such as the US-led conflict against the Taliban and Al-Qaeda in Afghanistan. Leaving aside the conflict's classification as international or non-international, it does demonstrate some of the criteria: a protracted level of armed violence was exceeded; the parties are sufficiently organized;[113] it occurs within an identifiable territory; and its beginning and end are (or presumably will be) identifiable.

The ICRC has also recognized that an armed conflict may exist between a state and a non-state terrorist organization and that this

---

111 *Ibid.* at 62. That is not to say that the end must be identified for IHL to be triggered, although it should be eventually identifiable as certain obligations cease and arise at the end of an armed conflict.

112 ICRC Report 2003, *supra* note 12 at 19.

113 Regarding Al-Qaeda, its operations in Afghanistan may be sufficiently organized for it to be considered a party to the conflict notwithstanding the fact that its "cells" worldwide may not be so organized.

determination must be made on a case-by-case basis.[114] Like Rona, however, the ICRC does not address the potential difficulty that may arise in classifying the nature of such an armed conflict. Concern for the appropriate classification is not purely academic, as different rules apply to international and non-international armed conflicts.[115] It is not suggested that IHL should apply automatically to the use of armed force between a state and a non-state actor based in another state, as there are important reasons for maintaining the restrictions on the application of IHL, including the fact that IHL may provide less protection to individuals than other applicable bodies of law.[116] Rather, it is argued that, when the general requirements of an armed conflict are met, the application of IHL should not be barred due to the potential uncertainty in identifying the armed conflict as international or non-international in character. The difficulty in characterizing armed conflicts that arguably fall outside of the traditional categories has fuelled considerable debate and sparked calls for recognizing a new category to deal with these "new" situations.[117] The final section will explore the merits and shortcomings of such an approach.

IHL AND THE PROTECTION OF CIVILIANS DURING COUNTER-TERRORISM ACTIVITIES

MORAL BASIS FOR THE PROTECTION OF INNOCENT CIVILIANS

Concern for humanity during armed conflict has been an integral part of IHL, such that one may argue that "[t]he concern to limit

[114] ICRC Report 2003, *supra* note 12 at 20 ("[i]n some instances the violence involved will amount to a situation covered by IHL ... while in others, it will not").

[115] The fact that there are two sets of rules that apply to international and non-international armed conflict has been subject to significant criticism, and arguments have been made that there should be a single definition of armed conflict in order for the distinction between international and non-international armed conflicts to be discarded. See, e.g., James G. Stewart, "Towards a Single Definition of Armed Conflict in International Humanitarian Law: A Critique of Internationalized Armed Conflict" (2003) 85 Int'l Rev. Red Cross 313. Despite this concern, many of the protections provided to victims of war in international armed conflicts also apply during non-international armed conflicts as part of customary IHL. See Henckaerts and Doswald-Beck, *supra* note 34.

[116] Under IHRL, a state may be required to show that it was absolutely necessary for it to use lethal force against suspected terrorists based in another state, which is not required under IHL; see David Kretzmer, "Targeted Killing of Suspected Terrorists: Extra-Judicial Executions or Legitimate Means of Defence?" (2005) 16 E.J.I.L. 171.

[117] See, Corn, *supra* note 10; Schondorf, *supra* note 10; but see Rona, *supra* note 10.

the effects of war to the fighters themselves may be as old as war itself."[118] There are at least seven possible reasons why non-combatants should be spared from harm: (1) they are innocent; (2) they are not fighting; (3) they are defenceless; (4) killing them is unnecessary; (5) it reduces the casualties of war; (6) sparing women and children allows the species to survive; and (7) killing them is against "the rules of the game."[119] Colm McKeogh concludes that none of these reasons alone supports the "principle of non-combatant immunity," and it is "justice that requires that innocent civilians should not be killed in war."[120] He notes as support that,

[a]s innocents, the justification of punitive killing does not apply to them. As non-combatants, the justification of preventative killing does not apply to them. As civilians, the justification of consensual killing does not apply to them. They have not agreed to occupy the role of instrument; they have not consented to be treated as a means to a military or political end; they have done, and are doing, nothing that warrants attack on them. It is then the most fundamental principles of justice which require that civilians be immune from targeting in war.[121]

In light of the compelling normative reasons to protect innocent civilians from harm and the increased concern that has been shown for the rights of individuals through the progressive development of human rights, it is argued that it is appropriate to use the protection of innocent civilians — those threatened by transnational terrorism and a state's fight against it — as a basis for exploring the ability of IHL to regulate armed conflicts in the context of transnational terrorism. It is recognized that there may be a danger in over-stating individual rights to the point that states could lose the ability to effectively protect their populations from the threat of transnational terrorism. Faced with a legal regime leading to such a result, it is likely that states would not comply with its requirements.[122] As such, a balance should be sought between the state's

---

118 Colm McKeogh, *Innocent Civilians: The Morality of Killing in War* (Chippenham, UK: Palgrave, 2002) at 2.

119 *Ibid.* at 5.

120 *Ibid.* at 155.

121 *Ibid.* at 165.

122 See, e.g., Bertil Duner, "Disregard for Security: The Human Rights Movement and 9/11," in Magnus Ranstorp and Paul Wilkinson, eds., *Terrorism and Human Rights* (New York: Routledge, 2008) 78 at 79 ("[t]here is a certain tendency

desire to protect itself and its citizens and its duty to respect the rights and lives of individuals beyond its borders when it exercises power affecting such persons. Although innocent civilians will suffer death and injury when states use force against the threat of transnational terrorism, it remains to be determined if such harm is in accordance with the applicable rules of law.

IHL AND THE PROTECTION OF CIVILIANS DURING ARMED CONFLICTS

One of the underlying humanitarian features of IHL is the concern with the protection of individuals who take no part in the conduct of hostilities (that is, innocent civilians and persons *hors de combat*), which has progressively developed to such an extent that the UN Human Rights Council has found that "the protection of civilians is a fundamental precept of IHL."[123] As noted earlier, the substance of IHL will depend upon the armed conflict's classification as international or non-international. Therefore, the characterization of an armed conflict between a state and a non-state actor may be important because it could determine the protections that civilians enjoy and provide a means of determining the lawfulness of state and non-state action.

As previously discussed, international armed conflict is more highly regulated by treaties than non-international armed conflict. Despite this disproportionate treatment, customary international law has developed such that non-international armed conflicts are becoming increasingly regulated. Meron argues that the ICTY has played an integral role in blurring the distinction between international and non-international armed conflict when it relates to the protection of innocents.[124] In *Tadic* (Merits), the Appeals Chamber of the ICTY questioned the rationality of predicating the rules protecting civilians on the legal classification of the conflict:

---

among leading human rights [nongovernmental organizations] to take the other side of the relationship — security against terrorism — rather lightly").

123 Commission of Inquiry, *supra* note 1 at para. 82.

124 Theodor Meron, "Cassese's *Tadic* and the Law of Non-International Armed Conflicts," in Lal Chand Vorah et al., eds., *Man's Inhumanity to Man: Essays in Honour of Antonio Cassese* (The Hague: Kluwer Law International, 2003) at 536 (as a result of the jurisprudence of the ICTY, "there has been a broadening of international law applicable to non-international armed conflicts, often through elimination of the distinctions between international and non-international armed conflicts").

Why protect civilians from belligerent violence, or ban rape, torture or the wanton destruction of hospitals, churches, museums or private property, as well as proscribe weapons causing unnecessary suffering when two sovereign States are engaged in war and yet refrain from enacting the same bans or providing the same protection when armed violence has erupted "only" within the territory of a sovereign State? If international law, while of course duly safeguarding the legitimate interests of States, must gradually turn to the protection of human beings, it is only natural that the ... dichotomy [between international and non-international armed conflicts] should gradually lose its weight.[125]

Similarly, the ICTY Appeals Chamber held in *Prosecutor v. Delalic et al. (Celebici Camp)* that maintaining unequal protection for innocent civilians during non-international armed conflicts would be against the underlying purpose of the Geneva Conventions.[126] Given this trend of convergence, the ICRC undertook a comprehensive study of customary IHL, producing an authoritative treatise on the subject.[127] Its findings are extremely relevant to identifying the protections that IHL affords to civilians, as many of these rules have been recognized as customary law applicable to both international and non-international armed conflicts.[128]

Recognition of the Protected Status of the "Civilian" under IHL

At its core, IHL is a compromise that seeks to balance military necessity with the desire to protect humanity from the devastation of conflict. As Yoram Dinstein notes,

---

125 *Prosecutor v. Tadic*, IT-94-1, Judgment (15 July 1999) (ICTY, Appeals Chamber) at para. 97 [*Tadic* (Merits)].

126 *Prosecutor v. Delalic et al. (Celebici Camp)*, IT-96-21-T (20 February 2001) (ICTY, Appeals Chamber) at para. 172 [*Delalic*] ("[i]n light of the fact that the majority of the conflicts in the contemporary world are internal, to maintain a distinction between the two legal regimes and their criminal consequences in respect of similarly egregious acts *because of the difference in nature of the conflicts would ignore the very purpose of the Geneva Conventions, which is to protect the dignity of the human person*") [emphasis added]; see Meron, *supra* note 96 at 33.

127 Henckaerts and Doswald-Beck, *supra* note 34.

128 ICRC Report 2003, *supra* note 12 at 16 ("[t]he Study confirms that the principle of distinction, the definition of military objectives, the prohibition of indiscriminate attacks, the principle of proportionality and the duty to take precautions in attack are all part of customary international law, regardless of the type of armed conflict involved").

[IHL] in its entirety is predicated on a subtle equilibrium between two diametrically opposed impulses: military necessity and humanitarian considerations. If military necessity were to prevail completely, no limitation of any kind would have been imposed on the freedom of action between belligerent States ... Conversely, if benevolent humanitarianism were the only beacon to guide the path of armed forces, war would have entailed no bloodshed, no destruction and no human suffering; in short, war would not be war.[129]

The result is a legal regime that seeks to define a "middle road" such that states involved in armed conflicts are given leeway to inflict destruction when it is necessary, while their freedom of action is circumscribed in the name of humanitarianism.[130]

Restrictions on the methods and means of warfare have existed for much of human history.[131] However, during medieval times, the notion of a "just war" meant that "once the cause was just, any means to achieve the end [were] permissible."[132] Eventually, the concept of "chivalrous warriors fighting just wars ... under official authority" resulted in laws protecting the "privileged class of belligerents."[133] The progressive codification of IHL gave rise to a relatively high level of legal protection for civilians. The Hague Convention of 1899 is an early manifestation of such protection, as it prohibited the bombardment of undefended settlements.[134] Of significance, the "Martens Clause" was incorporated into its preamble, which provides that "in cases not included in the Regulations ... populations and belligerents remain under the protection and empire of the principles of international law, as they result from the usages established between civilized nations, from the laws of humanity and the requirements of the public conscience."[135]

---

[129] Dinstein, *supra* note 33 at 16.

[130] *Ibid.* at 9, 17 (such concern was first codified in the 1868 St Petersburg Declaration: "[T]he progress of civilization should have the effect of alleviating as much as possible the calamities of war").

[131] See, e.g., Green, *supra* note 42.

[132] Judith Gail Gardam, "Proportionality and Force in International Law" (1993) 87 A.J.I.L. 395.

[133] Kenneth Watkin, *Combatants, Unprivileged Belligerents and Conflicts in the 21st Century* Background Paper (Cambridge, MA: Program on Humanitarian Policy and Conflict Research, Harvard University, 2003) at 6.

[134] Hague Convention, *supra* note 34, art. 25.

[135] *Ibid.*, preamble. See Rupert Ticehurst, "The Martens Clause and the Laws of Armed Conflict" (1997) 317 Int'l Rev. Red Cross 125.

Although the substance of this clause is subject to interpretation, its effect may be characterized as a reminder to states that sources outside of treaties can limit lawful state action, and it may also arguably reverse the general permissive nature of international law (that is, that which is not prohibited is permitted).[136] As Justice Mohammed Shahbuddeen of the ICJ has noted,

[the Martens] Clause provided its own self-sufficient and conclusive authority for the proposition that there were already in existence principles of international law under which considerations of humanity could themselves exert legal force to govern military conduct in cases in which no relevant rule was provided by conventional law.[137]

The changing nature of warfare and its heightened destructive capacity have been an impetus for enhancing the legal protection of civilians. The First and Second World Wars were particularly important in this respect, as the involvement of entire societies in the war effort gave rise to the concept of the "total war," which was used to justify making non-combatants objects of attack. Under the total war theory, it was argued that "enemy non-combatants could only be preserved from harm at great peril to any country that hoped to prevail."[138] A result was "the strategic bombardment of cities not only to disrupt the production of armaments but also to terrorize civilian populations in the hopes of breaking their resolve to support the war effort."[139] Although not formally adopted, the 1923 Rules of Aerial Warfare reflected concern for the effects of hostilities on civilians, as it sought to outlaw "aerial bombardment for the purpose of terrorizing the civilian population, of destroying or damaging private property not of military character, or of injuring the non-combatant."[140] In 1938, the League of Nations declared that international law forbade bombing civilian populations.[141] The increasing concern for civilians during armed conflict lead to Geneva Convention IV, which is explicitly designed for the "[p]rotection of civilian persons in the time of war."

[136] Ticehurst, *supra* note 135.

[137] *Nuclear Weapons, supra* note 32 (Shahbuddeen J. (dissent)).

[138] J. Marshall Beier, "Discriminating Tastes: 'Smart' Bombs, Non-Combatants, and Notions of Legitimacy in Warfare" (2003) 34 Security Dialogue 418.

[139] *Ibid.*

[140] Gregory, *supra* note 3 at 634.

[141] *Ibid.*

Despite this recognition of the protected status of civilians, a formal definition of a civilian was not established until 1977 through Additional Protocol I.[142] The definition has been widely accepted by states such that customary IHL recognizes as civilians "all persons who are not members of the armed forces," while the "civilian population comprises all persons who are civilians."[143] This definition applies to both international and non-international armed conflicts, although the ICRC has noted that state practice "is ambiguous as to whether members of armed opposition groups are considered members of armed forces or civilians" during non-international conflicts.[144]

Civilians and the Principle of Distinction

The principle of distinction requires states to, as much as is feasible, limit the effects of war to combatants (that is, those taking an active part in hostilities) and military objectives. This principle was first set out in the 1868 Declaration of St Petersburg, which asserted that "the only legitimate object which States should endeavour to accomplish during war is to weaken the military forces of the enemy."[145] The modern principle provides that "[t]he parties to the conflict must at all times distinguish between civilians and combatants," while "[a]ttacks may only be directed against combatants" and "must not be directed against civilians."[146] The principle exists as customary law applicable to both international and non-international armed conflicts.[147]

---

142 See Additional Protocol I, *supra* note 39, art. 50(1) ("[a] civilian is any person who does not belong to one of the categories of persons referred to in Article 4A(1), (2), (3) and (6) of the Third Convention [certain prisoners of war] and Article 43 of this Protocol [armed forces]"). See also Uhler et al., *supra* note 51 at 21 (although "civilian" remained undefined in the Geneva Conventions, this should not be understood as a lack of concern for humanity: "it must not be forgotten that the Conventions [were] drawn up first and foremost to protect individuals, and not to serve State interests"). Gregory, *supra* note 3 at 634.

143 Henckaerts and Doswald-Beck, *supra* note 34 at 17, "rule 5."

144 *Ibid.*

145 Declaration of St Petersburg, 29 November 1868 (Avalon Project, Yale Law School), <http://avalon.law.yale.edu/19th_century/decpeter.asp>, preamble.

146 Henckaerts and Doswald-Beck, *supra* note 34 "rule 1" at 3 (although the authors do not clearly state this in Rule 1, it is qualified by the fact that civilians who are directly participating in hostilities may be lawful targets of attack).

147 See *ibid.* This customary status has been recognized by the ICJ and other international tribunals. *Nuclear Weapons, supra* note 32 at paras. 61 and 434.

The principle of distinction also protects civilians from the adverse effects of hostilities by requiring states to distinguish between civilian "objects" and military objectives. The requirement to restrict attacks to military objectives, which is customary law applicable to international and non-international armed conflicts, was codified in Additional Protocol I.[148] A lawful military objective must: (1) be tangible; (2) contribute effectively to the military action of the enemy by its "nature, location, purpose or use"; and (3) offer a definite military advantage if destroyed, captured or neutralized.[149] This understanding of military objectives also reflects customary international law applicable to international and non-international armed conflicts.[150] Since these criteria must be fulfilled "in the circumstances ruling at the time,"[151] Sassoli argues that the drafters "avoid[ed] too large an interpretation" of the lawful objects of attack and "exclud[ed] *indirect* contributions and *possible* advantages."[152] Without these restrictions, he argues that "the limitation to 'military' objectives [and thereby the protection afforded to civilians by the principle of distinction] could be too easily undermined."[153] In addition to being considered unlawful targets of attack, civilians also enjoy protection from the effects of indiscriminate

---

148 Additional Protocol I, *supra* note 39 (Art. 48 identifies the "basic rule": "In order to ensure respect for and protection of the civilian population and civilian objects, the Parties to the conflict shall at all times distinguish between the civilian population and combatants and between civilian objects and military objectives and accordingly shall direct their operations only against military objectives"). Regarding customary status, see Henckaerts and Doswald-Beck, *supra* note 34, "rule 7" at 25, 27–28 (although a similar codification of this rule was dropped from the draft of Additional Protocol II prior to its acceptance, "it has been argued that the concept of general protection [of civilians] in Article 13(1) of [Additional Protocol II] is broad enough to cover it" in non-international armed conflicts. They support the conclusion that the principle of distinction applies in non-international armed conflicts with treaties dealing with the conduct of hostilities during non-international armed conflicts concluded after Additional Protocol II, numerous military manuals, national legislation, state practice, and the *Nuclear Weapons* case).

149 Additional Protocol I, *supra* note 39, art. 52(2).

150 Henckaerts and Doswald-Beck, *supra* note 34, "rule 8" at 29–32.

151 Additional Protocol I, *supra* note 39, art. 52(2).

152 Marco Sassoli, *Legitimate Targets of Attack under IHL*, Background Paper (Cambridge, MA: Program on Humanitarian Policy and Conflict Research, Harvard University, 2004) at 3 [emphasis in original].

153 *Ibid.*

attacks.[154] Like most of the protections that IHL affords to civilians, the prohibition on indiscriminate attacks applies as customary law to international and non-international armed conflicts.[155] As such, states would be obliged to abide by the principle of distinction during an armed conflict in the context of counter-terrorism if it were classified as either international or non-international.

Principle of Proportionality

Complementing the principle of distinction is the principle of proportionality. This principle highlights the fine balance that IHL seeks between protecting the interests of humanity and taking into account the realities of war, since it requires parties to a conflict to consider foreseeable collateral damage (that is, injury to civilians and civilian objects) in relation to the military advantage expected to arise from the attack. As a matter of customary law applicable to international and non-international armed conflicts,[156] the principle operates so that the

[154] Additional Protocol I, *supra* note 39, art. 51 (4) (the protocol expressly prohibits indiscriminate attacks and identifies, but does not limit, such attacks as: "(a) those which are not directed at a specific military objective; (b) those which employ a method or means of combat which cannot be directed at a specific military objective; or (c) those which employ a method or means of combat the effects of which cannot be limited as required by [the] Protocol; and consequently, in each such case, are of a nature to strike military objectives and civilians or civilian objects without distinction"); see Henckaerts and Doswald-Beck, *supra* note 34 at 41 ([t]he Mexico delegation stated that art. 51 "cannot be the subject of any reservations whatsoever since these would be inconsistent with the aim and purpose of Protocol I and undermine its basis").

[155] Henckaerts and Doswald-Beck, *supra* note 34, "rule 12" at 40.

[156] See Additional Protocol I, *supra* note 39 (the requirement for proportionality in attack is codified with respect to international armed conflicts in arts. 51(5) (b) and 57); see also Henckaerts and Doswald-Beck, *supra* note 34 at 48–49 (although not specifically mentioned in Additional Protocol II with respect to non-international armed conflicts, "it has been argued that [the principle of proportionality] is inherent to the principle of humanity which was explicitly made applicable to the Protocol in its preamble and that, as a result, the principle of proportionality cannot be ignored in the application of the Protocol" to non-international armed conflicts. The conclusion that the principle of proportionality applies during non-international armed conflict as customary IHL is supported by its codification in treaties subsequent to the adoption of Additional Protocol II, its widespread inclusion in military manuals, pleadings of states before the ICJ in *Nuclear Weapons*, the jurisprudence of international judicial organs, and the fact that, "[n]o official contrary practice was found [in the ICRC study] with respect to either international or non-international armed conflicts").

[l]aunching of an attack which may be expected to cause incidental loss of civilian life, injury to civilians, damage to civilian objects, or a combination thereof, which would be excessive in relation to the concrete and direct military advantage anticipated, is prohibited.[157]

Rona succinctly summarizes the principle of proportionality and its effect:

[T]he principle of proportionality concedes ... that it is not always feasible to limit damage to military objectives. Even if civilians are not the targets of attack, they may be affected. Otherwise legitimate military objectives are not rendered out-of-bounds simply because of a risk of "collateral damage." Thus, the principle of proportionality, like that of distinction, requires that combatants take precautionary measures to minimize civilian harms and to refrain from attacks that are likely to result in incidental civilian damage or casualties that are excessive in relation to the concrete and direct military advantage anticipated.[158]

Although the principle of proportionality and its effect on the conduct of hostilities may be easily summarized, its practical application poses a significant challenge due to the fact that it is often not clear what would be considered disproportionate. Proportionality remains to be determined on a case-by-case basis, and difficulty arises due to the subjective nature of the assessment, as the law "requires balancing [by a party about to use force during an armed conflict] between two opposing goals: the swift achievement of the military goal with the minimum losses of one's own combatants and the protection of the other party's civilian population."[159] Questions also arise regarding how "military advantage" should be interpreted. Judith Gail Gardam finds that the term "concrete and direct military advantage" in Article 51(5)(b) of Additional Protocol I "requires that proportionality be assessed in relation to each individual attack, rather than on a cumulative basis."[160] The ICRC has noted that this position is not universally accepted, as some states "have stated that the expression 'military advantage' refers to the advantage anticipated from the military attack considered as a whole and not only

---

[157] Henckaerts and Doswald-Beck, *supra* note 34 at 46, "rule 14."

[158] *Ibid.* at 66–67.

[159] Gardam, *supra* note 132 at 409.

[160] *Ibid.* at 407.

from isolated or particular parts of that attack."[161] The ICRC commentary notes that the intent was "to show that the advantage concerned should be substantial and relatively close, and that advantages which are hardly perceptible and those which would only occur in the long term should be disregarded."[162] Whether military advantage must relate to the specific act in question or the overall conduct of hostilities, determinations of proportionality will remain subjective and difficult. Gardam believes that the rule "allows a considerable degree of latitude for interpretation before a particular attack will be considered indiscriminate," which "operates in the interest of the military rather than that of civilians."[163]

Despite its subjective nature, proportionality must be continually assessed.[164] The ICRC commentary identifies various factors that must be taken into account when a party to an armed conflict assesses the danger an attack poses to the civilians and civilian objects, including: the location of the object of attack; the terrain; the accuracy of the weapons to be used; weather conditions that could affect the conduct of the attack; the nature of the military objectives concerned; and the skill of the combatants undertaking the attack.[165] The commentary further notes that "[a]ll these factors together must be taken into consideration whenever an attack could hit incidentally civilian persons and objects," and it presents a "clearcut" example of when the conclusion is simple, as "the presence of a soldier on leave obviously cannot justify the destruction of a village."[166] Much more difficult situations are conceivable in the context of counter-terrorist activity. Would it be proportionate to attack the home of a suspected terrorist at night when it is known that his large family lives within the home and would likely perish

---

[161] Henckaerts and Doswald-Beck, *supra* note 34 at 49.

[162] Sandoz et al., *supra* note 48 at para. 2209. This temporal element is contested, as "concrete and direct" does not necessarily equate to immediate or soon.

[163] Gardam, *supra* note 132 at 407.

[164] See *ibid* ("[f]irst, proportionality is a factor in the selection of the target. If civilian losses are inevitable, because of either the intermingling of civilian and military targets or the dual character of the target itself, these must be balanced against the military advantage. Second, the means and methods of attack must be assessed. Some weapons are more likely to involve indiscriminate damage than others ... Finally, even if these requirements are met, the conduct of the attack itself must not be negligent and involve unnecessary civilian casualties").

[165] Sandoz et al., *supra* note 48 at para. 2212.

[166] *Ibid.* at para. 2213.

in the attack?[167] Despite any uncertainty in making a determination of proportionality, it "must above all be a question of common sense and good faith for military commanders ... In every attack they must carefully weigh up the humanitarian and military interests at stake."[168]

Positive Obligations under the Precautionary Principle

A third obligation that complements the principles of distinction and proportionality is the "precautionary principle," whereby the parties to an armed conflict are under a "duty to take precautionary measures to implement the principle of distinction"[169] and attempt to ensure the proportionality of an attack. The duty to take precautions applies as customary international law applicable to international and non-international armed conflicts:

In the conduct of military operations, constant care must be taken to spare the civilian population, civilians and civilian objects. All feasible precautions must be taken to avoid, and in any event minimise, incidental loss of civilian life, injury to civilians and damage to civilian objects.[170]

In order to meet this obligation, the parties to an armed conflict are required to: (1) do everything feasible to verify that targets of attack are lawful military objectives and not civilians or civilian objects; (2) take precautions to avoid and minimize incidental effects on civilians and civilian objects; (3) refrain from launching a disproportionate attack; (4) cancel attacks if the state subsequently becomes aware that the target is not a lawful military objective

---

[167] Consider, e.g., the attack by Israel against the home of a Hamas leader, Nizar Rayyan, during the 2008–9 Israel-Hamas conflict, in which Rayyan, his four wives, and nine of his children were killed. Isabel Kershner, "In Broadening Offensive, Israel Steps Up Diplomacy," *New York Times* (2 January 2009) at A6; see also *Targeted Killings, supra* note 9 at para. 8 (On 22 July 2002, Israel destroyed the house of wanted terrorist Salah Shehade, killing him, his wife and family, and twelve neighbours). Further difficulty may also arise during counter-terrorist activity because non-state terrorists may not be considered "combatants" under IHL but, rather, civilians who lose their immunity from attack when they directly participate in hostilities. See, e.g., *Targeted Killings, supra* note 9; and Schmitt, *supra* note 53.

[168] Sandoz et al., *supra* note 48 at paras. 2208–9.

[169] Rona, *supra* note 10 at 66.

[170] Henckaerts and Doswald-Beck, *supra* note 34 at 51, "rule 15."

and if the effects on civilians and civilian objects "would be excessive in relation to the concrete and direct military advantage anticipated"; and (5) give "effective advance warning ... of attacks which may affect the civilian population" when circumstances permit.[171] In light of the requirement to take precautions to ensure the protection of civilians in both international and non-international armed conflicts, should a state's use of force against a non-state terrorist organization occur during an armed conflict to which IHL applies it would likely be bound to employ such precautions.[172]

THE CHALLENGE OF ASYMMETRICAL CONFLICTS

A conflict between a state and a non-state actor is almost always asymmetrical in nature, with the state enjoying a significant military advantage. In such situations, it is common for the disadvantaged party to employ tactics in an effort to overcome its disadvantage. Terrorist attacks are often characterized as such a tactic. Since the group cannot prevail over the state militarily, it seeks to gain an advantage by targeting the vulnerable civilian population. Although the disadvantaged party will likely breach IHL, it does not — and should not — excuse the other party from respecting its obligations under IHL.[173]

Aside from directing attacks at civilians, non-state actors may use other tactics that breach IHL. Common tactics include "[t]he asymmetrically disadvantaged party either feign[ing] protected status or us[ing] proximity to protected individuals and objects to deter attacks."[174] By concealing themselves within the civilian population, this tactic arguably "turns the IHL principle of distinction on its head by incentivising its violation."[175] The danger these tactics pose to

---

[171] Additional Protocol I, *supra* note 39, art. 57.

[172] State practice in such circumstances is evident from the 2006 Israel-Hezbollah conflict and the 2008–9 conflict between Israel and Hamas, as Israel used leaflets and telephone calls to warn civilians of attacks.

[173] See, e.g., Additional Protocol I, *supra* note 39 at art. 51(8) ("[a]ny violation of these prohibitions shall not release the Parties to the conflict from their legal obligations with respect to the civilian population and civilians").

[174] Michael N. Schmitt, "Asymmetrical Warfare and International Humanitarian Law," in Wolff Heintschel von Heinegg and Volker Epping, eds., *International Humanitarian Law Facing New Challenges: Symposium in Honour of Knut Ipsen* (New York: Springer, 2007) 11 at 23.

[175] *Ibid.* at 22.

civilians and the challenge they present to states responding to them is illustrated by the tactic of "human shielding," which occurs when a party attempts to protect its position from attack by deliberately placing civilians in the line of fire. It is prohibited in international and non-international armed conflicts under customary IHL.[176] Although a party may benefit from its breach of IHL, civilians being used as involuntary shields are not lawful targets of direct attack and must be included in the proportionality considerations by a party planning to attack.[177] As Michael N. Schmitt notes, "[t]here have been suggestions that involuntary shields should not be included in the calculation of incidental injury, lest the lawbreakers benefit from their misconduct."[178] This argument should not be accepted because it clearly contradicts the principle that violations of IHL do not release the other party of its legal obligations and could severely undermine the protections the law provides to innocent civilians.

It is readily apparent that the tactics employed by a non-state terrorist group can challenge the ability for states to effectively respond to the threat they pose. It is argued that this difficulty does not, and should not, legitimize breaches of the law in the name of counterterrorism, because accepting the contrary may threaten the rights of innocent civilians and the rule of law itself.[179] It is evident that IHL may provide significant protection to innocent civilians when a state uses force during an armed conflict. It is argued that IHL should apply when a state's use of force against a non-state terrorist group based in another state occurs during a situation that meets

---

[176] Henckaerts and Doswald-Beck, *supra* note 34 at 337–40, "rule 97."

[177] This does not mean that a state will be automatically barred from attacking the object being shielded. Involuntary human shields must be factored into the proportionality consideration. If the target is a valid military objective, it may be possible for the state to attack it and not violate IHL as long as the resulting civilian casualties are not disproportionate to the valid military objective sought.

[178] Schmitt, *supra* note 174 at 27; voluntary human shields would be lawful targets of attack because their activities constitute direct participation in hostilities.

[179] *Ibid.* at 47–48 ("when asymmetry disrupts the presumption [that the parties to an armed conflict will abide by the rules of IHL] and one side violates the agreed rules, the practical incentive for compliance by the other fades. Instead, IHL begins appearing as if it operates to the benefit of one's foes. When that happens, the dictates of the law appear out of step with reality, perhaps even 'quaint' ... [T]he real danger is not so much that the various forms of asymmetry will result in violations of IHL. Rather, it is that asymmetries may unleash a dynamic that undercuts the very foundations of this body of law").

the general requirements of an armed conflict. In other words, the application of IHL should not be barred due to potential uncertainty regarding the nature of the armed conflict between the state and the non-state actor. This approach may strike a balance that allows states to protect their populations from serious threats of terrorism while maintaining concern for the rights of innocent civilians. This is not to say, however, that the rigours of the law should be relaxed due to the difficulty of combating an asymmetrically disadvantaged party. To accept otherwise could lead down a slippery slope towards eroding the protection that innocent civilians have progressively attained during and outside of armed conflicts. If a state's actions against suspected terrorists are contrary to international law — IHRL, IHL, or any other applicable law — it should be held responsible for these violations.

Should a New Category of Armed Conflict Be Recognized?

Even when a level of protracted or intense violence is reached between a state and an organized non-state actor based in another state, it may be unclear if IHL applies because the situation may not easily fit the traditional understanding of an international or non-international armed conflict.[180] Some commentators have argued that IHL must evolve so that it clearly applies to conflicts between states and non-state terrorist organizations based in other states.[181] Others contend that this evolution is unnecessary and that other legal regimes — such as IHRL, and domestic and international criminal law — can and should apply to these situations.[182] This section will advance an argument that is somewhat in between these positions, arguing that, in light of the goals of allowing states to protect their populations from the threat of transnational terrorism and protecting innocent civilians during counter-terrorism activities, IHL should apply when the use of force between a state and a non-state actor based in another state constitutes an armed conflict.

---

[180] See the discussion earlier in this article; see also Thomas M. Franck, "Criminals, Combatants, or What? An Examination of the Role of Law in Responding to the Threat of Terrorism" (2004) 98 A.J.I.L. 686 ("Al Qaeda — to take the most prominent example [of a terrorist group] — does not readily fit the mold of either a crime family or an enemy state. Yet it is in response to these models that national criminal laws and international laws of war have been developed" at 686).

[181] See, e.g., Corn, *supra* note 10; and Schondorf, *supra* note 10.

[182] See, e.g., Rona, *supra* note 10.

When this threshold is not reached, other legal regimes would protect civilian populations, while *jus ad bellum* — and potentially IHRL[183] — would define the permissible extent of the use of force by states against suspected terrorists. This section will consider the arguments in favour and against recognizing a third category of armed conflict when a state engages in protracted or intense armed violence with an organized non-state actor based in another state. It will be argued that, while a limited evolution of IHL may be useful to dispel ambiguity regarding its application to the fight against transnational terrorism, recognizing a third category is not the best approach for achieving its application. Rather, non-international armed conflicts should be interpreted expansively to achieve the application of IHL.

MEETING CONFLICTING GOALS THROUGH THE CAREFUL
EXPANSION OF IHL

Rona rejects calls for an evolution in IHL to encompass the use of force by states against non-state terrorist groups based in another state in large part due to the belief that IHL should not apply to situations such as the "War on Terror."[184] The author agrees that, for IHL to apply to counter-terrorist actions, the situation must constitute an armed conflict. A declaration of "war" against terrorism does not, and should not, trigger IHL. When, however, the situation amounts to an armed conflict, IHL should apply despite the fact that the situation may not clearly fit within the traditional categories of armed conflict. It is recognized that the application of IHL should be made with care because its over-application could undermine the rights that individuals may otherwise enjoy. Rona notes this danger and argues that, by invoking the concept of war,

---

[183] It may be argued that states would be bound to abide by their obligation under IHRL to not deprive individuals arbitrarily of the right to life when using extraterritorial force against suspected or known terrorists, as the right arguably ranks as a peremptory norm of international law. See, e.g., Kretzmer, *supra* note 116 at 184–85; Rene Provost, *International Humanitarian Law and Human Rights* (New York: Cambridge University Press, 2002) at 19–21; Noëlle Quénivet, "The Right to Life in International Humanitarian Law and Human Rights Law," in Roberta Arnold and Noëlle Quénivet, eds., *International Humanitarian Law and Human Rights Law: Towards a New Merger in International Law* (Boston: Martinus Nijhoff, 2008) 331 at 331; Alex P. Schmid, "Terrorism and Human Rights: A Perspective from the United Nations," in Ranstorp and Wilkinson, *supra* note 122, 19 at 19–20.

[184] See, e.g., Rona, *supra* note 10.

the United States may be seeking to justify actions that may otherwise be unlawful:

> The error of the United States' choice of nomenclature is neither insignificant nor innocent. The U.S. view, if accepted as a statement of law, would serve as a global waiver of domestic and international criminal and human rights laws that regulate, if not prohibit, killing. Turning the whole world into a rhetorical battlefield cannot legally justify, though it may in practice set the stage for, a claimed license to kill people or detain them without recourse to judicial review anytime, anywhere. This is a privilege that ... exists under limited conditions and may only be exercised by lawful combatants and parties to armed conflict.[185]

Rona does not accept claims that IHL is inadequate or outdated in the context of transnational terrorism and asserts that other legal regimes provide adequate means of addressing the threat posed. Although Rona notes that IHL properly applies during an armed conflict in the context of transnational terrorism, he does not address the fact that the conflict may defy the common understandings of international and non-international armed conflicts and thereby render the application of IHL unclear.[186] In light of this potential gap, it is argued that a careful expansion of the application of IHL can be supported because it allows states to respond to a credible and serious terrorist threat while maintaining the stringent requirements for the lawful denial of the right to life outside of armed conflicts. This approach could ensure protection for innocent civilians, while permitting the use of force against suspected terrorists to protect a state's population from a terrorist attack for which there is credible evidence and the absolute necessity of taking that action can be proven. It is argued that this approach strikes a proper balance because it allows states to protect their populations while protecting the rights and lives of innocent civilians.

Avoiding Derogations from IHRL

In light of the desire to protect innocent civilians from harm due to transnational terrorism and the fight against it, there is a strong argument that IHL should not apply because it may provide less

---

[185] *Ibid.* at 64.

[186] *Ibid.* at 58–59 ("[a]n international armed conflict is one in which two or state are parties to the conflict" while non-international "historically ... involv[e] rebels within a state against the state or other rebels").

protection for individuals than IHRL. This is unsurprising given IHL's inherent compromise between military necessity and humanitarian concerns.[187] As Rona has cautioned, "fiddling with the boundaries or, more accurately, with the overlap between humanitarian law and other legal regimes can have profound, long-term, and decidedly 'un-humanitarian' consequences on the delicate balance between state and personal security, human rights, and civil liberties."[188] Although IHL may be more protective of individual rights in some respects,[189] overall, it provides less protection than IHRL because killing combatants and civilians who directly participate in hostilities without making prior efforts to detain them is not generally an arbitrary deprivation of the right to life during an armed conflict.[190] Further, innocent civilians "are at a greater risk under IHL due to the fact that they can be killed or injured so long as it is not disproportionate to the military objective being sought"[191] and if incidental and feasible precautions are taken by the attacking state. Although innocent civilians are protected by the principle of proportionality under IHL, it may be argued that IHRL imposes greater restrictions on the use of lethal force because it would be proportionate under IHRL "only if it is absolutely necessary to achieve a legitimate aim such as protecting another individual's life."[192] When no armed conflict exists, the high threshold of absolute necessity under IHRL — and thereby the evidentiary burden to show that the force was used in response to a credible threat — must be satisfied. In contrast, under IHL, the state would only have to ensure that the "collateral damage" inflicted on civilians and

---

187 *Ibid.* at 57 ("[i]n return for these protections [that IHL provides], humanitarian law elevates the essence of war — killing and detaining people without trial — into a right, if only for persons designated as 'privileged combatants'").

188 *Ibid.* at 58.

189 See Balendra, *supra* note 71 at 2494 (IHL may be considered more protective than IHRL, because it: (1) imposes binding obligations on a non-state actor who is party to a conflict, whereas IHRL is only binding upon states; (2) provides for individual criminal responsibility for the commission of war crimes, whereas IHRL is enforceable only against state entities; and (3) imposes obligations from which states and non-state actors cannot lawfully derogate, whereas IHRL may be derogated from in certain circumstances).

190 *Ibid.* at 2497.

191 *Ibid.* at 2498.

192 *Ibid.* It may be argued, however, that IHL could provide increased protection for innocent civilians because it explicitly requires the consideration of collateral damage when a state uses force, unlike IHRL.

civilian objects is not excessive in relation to the military objective sought and that it took precautions to limit such harm. Since there is an increased risk of harm to innocent civilians if IHL applies to such activity outside of an armed conflict, it is argued that IHL should remain applicable only to armed conflicts.[193] The increased risk to civilians under IHL and the adequacy of other legal regimes to allow a state to respond to the threat of terrorism bolsters the argument that a "War on Terror" should not, in itself, constitute an armed conflict.[194]

A NECESSARY STEP IN THE CONTINUED EVOLUTION OF IHL

Multiple factors support the application of IHL to transnational armed conflicts. First, IHL has historically evolved in response to the changing nature of conflict. As David Wippman notes, "[i]n the past, important developments in international humanitarian law have commonly followed major conflicts" in which new methods and concepts of warfare — such as mustard gas, tanks, aerial bombardment, and machine guns in the First World War and the total war theory being used to justify indiscriminate attacks on civilians during the Second World War — illustrated that IHL was inadequate for meeting its goals.[195] And, when the protections provided by the Geneva Conventions were shown to have "failed to address adequately many important issues," a major international conference led to the adoption of the two Additional Protocols.[196] These events clearly illustrate that IHL is capable of adapting in order to address

---

[193] *Ibid.* at 2498 (given the increased potential for violations of the right to life, some commentators maintain that targeted strikes "presumptively violate the principle of proportionality under IHL because of the potential risk to civilians"); see, e.g., Vincent-Joel Proulx, "If the Hat Fits, Wear It, If the Turban Fits, Run for your Life: Reflections on Indefinite Detention and Targeted Killing of Suspected Terrorists" (2005) Hastings L. J. 801. An argument in favour of apply IHL, however, is that it would provide a means of finding non-state actors liable under international criminal law, which is not possible under IHRL.

[194] See Rona, *supra* note 10 at 69 ("[t]here is little evidence that domestic and international laws and institutions of crime and punishment are not up to the task when terrorism and the War on Terror do not rise to the level of armed conflict. But there are powerful reasons to conclude that the application of humanitarian law in those circumstances would do more harm than good").

[195] David Wippman, "Do New Wars Call for New Laws?" in David Wippman and Matthew Evangelista, eds., *New Wars, New Laws? Applying the Laws of War in the 21st Century* (Ardsley, NY: Transnational, 2005) 1 at 1–2.

[196] *Ibid.* at 2.

the changing nature of conflict. It is argued that transnational terrorism may represent a further change in the nature of armed conflict that requires a limited reconsideration or clarification of IHL and its application.[197]

Second, this evolution may be justified because it would bring the legal regime into conformity with the current practices of some states. Given the uncertainty in defining non-international armed conflict, many states already apply the principles of IHL to armed conflicts regardless of their classification as international or non-international. Such policies are evident in the military manuals of both the United States and the United Kingdom.[198] In light of this practice, recognizing a new category of armed conflict may not be a major evolution, and could be accepted by states. Further, some states have already proved willing to recognize that IHL would apply when a state engages in an armed conflict with a non-state actor based in another state.[199] There is no consensus, however, that IHL applies in these circumstances. As Geoffrey Corn argues, an "evolution [in IHL] is necessary to effectively reconcile the expectations of both professional military forces and the international community with the applicability of the law regulating combat operations."[200] Although some states may, as a matter of policy, abide by IHL regardless of the legal classification of an armed conflict, it would be preferable to recognize the application of IHL to these circumstances as a matter of law because it would dispel uncertainty and allow for a clarification of the rules applicable to this new form of armed conflict. Customary international law requires the belief of the state that the law requires the practice in which it is engaged. If states apply the principles of IHL as a matter of policy, it could be argued that such belief is not present. As such, states accepting the proposed application of IHL should indicate their belief that the law requires this approach.

A third factor that supports ensuring the application of IHL to these "new" armed conflicts may be found in the Martens Clause. As discussed earlier, the Martens Clause illustrates that there are

<hr>

[197] *Ibid.* at 3.

[198] Corn, *supra* note 10.

[199] See *ibid.* at 321 and 329 ("operations such as those launched by Israel against Hezbollah defy categorization as either international or internal armed conflicts," however, "[t]he prospect of an unregulated battlefield is simply unacceptable in the international community — a fact that is demonstrated by the response to [this] conflict in Lebanon").

[200] *Ibid.* at 299.

fundamental principles that should regulate the conduct of hostilities even when the codified law does not provide for their application. The ICJ has confirmed the ability of the Martens Clause to support developments in IHL, since it recognized that the clause "has proved to be an effective means of addressing the rapid evolution of military technology."[201] Corn argues that the Martens Clause has an important role to play in the context of transnational terrorism:

The clause provides additional support for the proposition that no conflict can be permitted to fall outside the regulation of the foundational principles of the laws of war. Accordingly, the Martens Clause bolsters the rationale for adopting a new conflict classification category, because it suggests that the requirement to ensure humanitarian regulation of de facto conflict was historically considered preeminent to the technical interpretation of treaty obligations.[202]

Meron notes that "[i]t is generally agreed that the Clause means, at the very least, that adoption of a treaty regulating particular aspects of the law of war does not deprive the affected persons of the protection of those norms of customary humanitarian law that were not included in the codification,"[203] and he concludes that, "[i]n appropriate circumstances, it provides an additional argument against a finding of *non liquet*."[204] Since the fundamental principles of IHL form part of customary international law applicable to international and non-international armed conflicts, a gap in the law that would result in IHL not regulating a form of armed conflict should not be tolerated. Given that it is unclear whether transnational armed conflicts fit within the recognized categories of armed conflict, IHL must either evolve or be clarified so that states cannot deny its application to this type of conflict. As the preceding analysis shows, such evolution or clarification would build upon a strong existing foundation. Attempts by states to argue that these situations fall within a gap in the law should be resisted by other states in order to clearly show that this interpretation of the law is not widely accepted.

---

[201] *Nuclear Weapons, supra* note 32 at para. 78.

[202] Corn, *supra* note 10 at 338–39.

[203] Meron, *supra* note 96 at 27.

[204] *Ibid.* at 27–28.

THE APPLICATION OF INTERNATIONAL HUMANITARIAN LAW TO
TRANSNATIONAL ARMED CONFLICTS

There are three potential means of achieving regulation by IHL of armed conflicts between a state and a non-state actor based in another state. They could be considered as a distinct new category or recognized as a sub-category of either international or non-international armed conflicts. This section will set forth the proposed scope and law applicable to a new category of transnational armed conflict before evaluating if this category would be a necessary or practical means of ensuring the application of IHL in these situations. While recognizing that a third category could be superior to expanding one of the existing categories of armed conflict because it would permit the development of rules tailored to the unique characteristics of such conflicts, it will be argued that the more practical approach may be for non-international armed conflicts to be understood as a residual category encompassing transnational armed conflicts. Such an approach would avoid confusion regarding the applicable rules of IHL and could forestall potential efforts by states to develop rules that could result in less protection to innocent civilians.

Proposed Characteristics of a New Category of IHL

The threshold of protracted or intense armed violence as described in the *Tadic* case and as it applies to non-international armed conflicts would be an appropriate trigger for the application of IHL to transnational armed conflicts. A major argument against endorsing a threshold approach for determining the application of IHL is that it could act as an incentive for the state to escalate violence and thereby be subject to less restrictive rules than under IHRL. Despite the fact that a state may have more latitude in using lethal force under the armed conflict model, the risk that a state would escalate violence to trigger IHL may be overstated. When a state uses force in self-defence against a terrorist group in another state, it would likely remain bound by the requirements of *jus ad bellum*, including the requirement that the force used be proportionate to the threat and the armed attack to which the state is responding.[205]

---

[205] Proportionality has been recognized by the ICJ as a principle of customary international law applicable when a state uses force in self-defence. See *Nuclear Weapons, supra* note 32 at para. 41; *Nicaragua, supra* note 26 at para. 176; and *Case Concerning Oil Platforms (Islamic Republic of Iran v. United States of America)*, [2003] I.C.J. Rep. 161 at paras. 73–77.

Where protracted or intense armed force would be disproportionate and a state uses such force, this action would be contrary to *jus ad bellum* and the state would breach its international legal obligations.[206]

Advocating a new category of armed conflict, Corn proposes that the existence of an armed conflict be based on the satisfaction of two criteria: (1) the use of a state's armed forces in response to a threat; and (2) the authorization by a state for these forces to "engage an enemy not exclusively in response to hostile act or intent, but based on status identification."[207] Although Corn asserts that these criteria "provide an effective means of determining the existence of any armed conflict," they suffer from a major flaw. Predicating the existence of an armed conflict — and thereby the application of IHL — on the *content* of a state's directive to its armed forces as indicative that the state *considers itself* bound by IHL is not acceptable because it would leave the application of IHL subject to the discretion of the state. From a practical perspective, Corn's approach could prove unworkable because states do not routinely publicize their directives to their military forces. Furthermore, targeted strikes that would otherwise constitute extra-judicial killings because they do not meet the requirements of IHRL outside of an armed conflict could trigger the application of IHL because the strike: (1) was carried out by the state's armed forces; and (2) the orders to kill were made upon the target's *status* as a suspected terrorist.[208] By

---

206 Treating *jus ad bellum* separately from *jus in bello*, the recourse to the use of force against a terrorist group based in another state would fall under the scope of Article 2(4) of the UN Charter as "international relations" because it involves the use of cross-border force, despite the fact that the force is not directed at the territorial state's armed forces and the territorial state is not a party to any resultant armed conflict.

207 Corn, *supra* note 10 at 346 (the authorization to employ force based on the "status" of an enemy reflects the fact that a State's armed forces are not limited under IHL to using force only in self-defence and is a means Corn proposes to distinguish the deployment of armed forces by a state during an armed conflict from deployments for other international purposes (such as peace-keeping operations), where the armed forces are only entitled to use force in self-defence).

208 See, e.g, Kretzmer, *supra* note 116 at 178–79 (the use of lethal force is arguably not "arbitrary" and therefore not contrary to the right to life guaranteed under IHRL provided that the use of lethal forces is absolutely necessary to protect the state's civilians from unlawful violence by the target); Balendra, *supra* note 71 at 2505.

predicating the application of IHL, to some extent, upon the discretion of the state, it is argued that this would undermine the fundamental principle that IHL binds all parties to an armed conflict equally, whether or not they recognize the existence of an armed conflict. Although the threshold approach adopted by the ICTY is subject to competing interpretations, this approach is arguably appropriate because it currently provides a means of determining the existence of an armed conflict that may be familiar to states and the international community.

If a new category of armed conflict were recognized, its rules would remain to be determined. At a minimum, it is likely that the principles contained within Common Article 3 would apply, which is supported by the ICJ's characterization in *Nicaragua* that such protections are a minimum yardstick that is applicable to all armed conflicts.[209] It is further argued that the aspects of IHL that apply as a matter of customary law to non-international armed conflicts should also apply.[210] This position is supported by the fact that these rules are consistent with the fundamental features of IHL, which Marco Sassoli and Antoine Bouvier have identified as: the principles of humanity, necessity, proportionality, and distinction; the prohibition against causing unnecessary suffering; and the maintenance of *jus in bello* independent from *jus ad bellum*.[211] As will be discussed later in this section, the rules of IHL that only apply to international armed conflicts should not apply to transnational armed conflicts. This would likely be crucial to gaining acceptance by states of a new category of armed conflict because — unlike some of the rules of international armed conflict — none of these principles of IHL would provide legitimacy to a non-state actor that is party to the conflict.[212]

Schondorf argues that there are important advantages to recognizing a third category, since a legal void is avoided while maintaining flexibility to permit the future development of specific norms applicable to transnational armed conflicts.[213] Allowing for the future development of rules tailored to the unique challenges posed

---

[209] See the discussion earlier in this article.

[210] See the discussion earlier in this article.

[211] Sassoli and Bouvier, *supra* note 30 at 141–42; see Schondorf, *supra* note 10 at 56.

[212] See Corn, *supra* note 10 at 348 (he notes that vesting "undeserved status or legitimacy" remains "a critical concern for national security decision-makers").

[213] Schondorf, *supra* note 10 at 55.

by such conflicts may be the strongest argument in favour of recognizing a third category. As an example of a specialized rule, Schondorf notes that, since a state exercises force in another state's territory without consent during a transnational armed conflict, it could be beneficial to impose greater restrictions on the permissible scope of the state's action, such that every use of armed force during such a conflict would have to meet the requirements of self-defence.[214] In light of the *lex specialis* nature of IHL, it could also be appropriate to draw upon IHRL when identifying the applicable rules, which could result in more protection for innocent civilians.

If a third category were recognized, the precise content of the law would remain to be determined by state practice and would likely require future codification. As will be discussed, states would ultimately determine the applicable rules, which may be a central weakness of this approach. Further, although one may argue that the fundamental principles of IHL should apply as a matter of customary law, this argument may be difficult to support when characterizing transnational armed conflicts as a "new" phenomenon because state practice to this effect would be limited. Despite arguing in favour of a new category, Schondorf concedes that, while "there ... may be room to consider convening a conference in order to clarify the issues in the law of [transnational] armed conflict," there are risks associated with premature attempts. Due to the delicate political situation surrounding transnational armed conflicts, such attempts could be unsuccessful and undermine IHL.[215]

It is evident that there is considerable debate regarding the ability for international or non-international armed conflicts to encompass situations that do not easily fit within their traditional scope. One benefit of recognizing a new category of transnational armed conflict is that it may silence such debate. As such, confusion regarding the application of IHL to the conflict could be avoided, and it could forestall claims by states that such situations fall into a gap in the law to which even the settled rules of IHL do not apply.[216]

---

[214] *Ibid.* at 64. Although such an approach would result in increasing the protection of civilians because it would limit the ability of the state to use force, it may run the controversial risk of conflating *jus ad bellum* and *jus in bello*.

[215] *Ibid.* at 77–78. In light of the fact that some states would desire to "roll back" the restrictions on their actions during armed conflicts, even a "successful" attempt could be a cause for concern.

[216] See, e.g., the US position in *Hamdan, supra* note 91 (arguing that Common Article 3 would not apply to its armed conflict with Al-Qaeda) and Israel's

However, a strong argument against recognizing a third category is that it could increase, rather than decrease, uncertainty regarding the applicable rules.[217] Since state consent would be a key feature of distinguishing a transnational, from a non-international, armed conflict, it may be difficult to determine which law applies should the territorial state not openly declare if it has consented to the outside state's activities — or that such activity is even occurring.[218] Although this article has focused on armed conflicts arising between a state and a non-state actor in the context of transnational terrorism, it should be noted that recognizing a third category of armed conflict would have implications in other contexts. Although terrorist organizations may have little desire to comply with the requirements of the law, the same cannot be said for all non-state actors that could be party to an armed conflict with an outside state. If the nature of the conflict is dependent upon the consent of the territorial state, it may be difficult for non-state actors to determine what its legal obligations are under IHL. This could lend support to the argument, discussed later, that clarity regarding the applicable law could be achieved if non-international armed conflicts were considered a residual category that applies absent a direct conflict between states (or their agents) rather than recognize a new category.

Should International Armed Conflicts Encompass Transnational Armed Conflicts?

An argument may be made that transnational armed conflicts should be considered a sub-category of international armed conflicts. Al-

---

argument in *Targeted Killings*, *supra* note 9 at para. 11 (that there is a category of persons under IHL known as "unlawful combatants" to which the protections of IHL do not apply: "These are people who take active and continuous part in an armed conflict, and therefore should be treated as combatants, in the sense that they are legitimate targets of attack, and they do not enjoy the protections granted to civilians. However, they are not entitled to the rights and privileges of combatants, since they do not differentiate themselves from the civilian population and since they do not obey the laws of war").

217 See Sassoli, *supra* note 87 at 220–21 ("[a] new law [applicable to transnational armed conflicts] would inevitably create a third category ... adding to the existing difficulties in classifying situations under the laws of war").

218 Consider, e.g., Pakistan's position regarding the ongoing US strikes in its territory: Mark M. Azzetti and David E. Sanger, "Obama Expands Missile Strikes Inside Pakistan," *New York Times* (20 February 2009), <http://www.nytimes.com/2009/02/21/washington/21policy.html>.

though similar to international armed conflicts in some respects,[219] it is argued that the classification of transnational should be avoided because international armed conflicts should remain restricted to those to which states (or their agents) are parties. Schondorf identifies a potentially problematic result of classifying transnational armed conflicts as international, which would arguably pose a greater threat to the rights and lives of innocent civilians — it would "extend[] the scope of the conflict instead of containing it, rendering the military installations of [the territorial state] legitimate military targets."[220] The validity of this claim may be questioned, however, because it would be unlikely that such objects could be considered lawful targets of attack if the territorial state were not a true party to the conflict because their value as a military objective would be absent, while it would be imprudent — militarily and politically — for State A to unnecessarily escalate hostilities by targeting State B's military installations. This may, however, illustrate the difficulty of adapting the rules of international armed conflict to the *sui generis* armed conflict where the territorial state is not a party to the conflict despite the fact that another state uses force in its territory without its consent.[221]

There are further arguments against expanding the scope of international armed conflicts. First, it may be unlikely that states would accept this approach due to concerns that it would grant a measure of legitimacy to non-state armed groups. This argument is supported by the fact that states have historically resisted applying certain rules of IHL applicable to international armed conflicts to non-international armed conflict for this reason.[222] As such, it is likely that states would resist applying rules of IHL that could provide an air of legitimacy to the terrorist group's cause and would reject

---

[219] They are similar, for example, because a state uses force in another state's territory, and the logistics of hostilities are the same because the targets are located abroad, see Schondorf, *supra* note 10 at 35–36.

[220] *Ibid.* at 27.

[221] Commission of Inquiry, *supra* note 1 at para. 9 (the commission noted the "*sui generis*" character of the conflict because Lebanon did not engage in the hostilities occurring in its territory).

[222] The argument states raise in denying the application of such things as combatant status and prisoner of war rights to non-state actors engaged in a non-international armed conflict with a state is that it would grant legitimacy to such actors and their cause. Potential legitimacy may arise because non-state actors enjoying combatancy status could be entitled to lawfully engage in armed conflict.

the notion that members of a non-state terrorist group could be entitled to prisoner-of-war status and avoid prosecution for participating in the armed conflict.[223] In contrast, it could be argued that the rules of international armed conflict should apply because offering combatancy status to non-state actors who meet the obligations of such status could act as an incentive for them to abide by the rules of IHL.[224] Although denying combatancy status may provide little incentive for non-state actors to comply with IHL, it is argued that this position may be of limited persuasion for terrorist organizations,[225] while states have historically proven to be reluctant to provide this status in other contexts.

[223] See Additional Protocol I, *supra* note 39, art. 43(2) ("combatants" are members of the armed forces of a party to a conflict (other than medical personnel and chaplains), who "have the right to directly participate in hostilities"); Henckaerts and Doswald-Beck, *supra* note 34 at 395 (prisoner of war (POW) status does not exist in non-international armed conflicts). Without combatancy status, non-state actors cannot claim POW status if apprehended (even during an international armed conflict where this status exists), cannot lawfully engage in combat, and may be liable for prosecution as a result of their participation. Although not benefiting from combatancy status, such persons are not without protection under IHL. If in the power of the opposing party, such individuals would retain rights as persons *hors de combat*, which are protected as "fundamental guarantees" under customary IHL including the rights to humane treatment, not to be subject to torture, and so on. See Henckaerts and Doswald-Beck, *supra* note 34 at 299 and on. Although the ability for states to lawfully engage in targeting of suspected and known terrorists based in other states and the status of non-state actors who engage in hostilities with a state in the context of transnational terrorism are important issues, they will not be examined in this article in detail. For discussions of these issues, see *Targeted Killings*, *supra* note 9 and Schmitt, *supra* note 53.

[224] See, e.g., Charles H.B. Garraway, "25 Years of the Two Additional Protocols: Their Impact on the Waging of War; Challenges from New Types of Armed Conflicts," in Guido Ravasi and Gian Luca Berto, eds., *Proceedings of the 26th San Remo Round Table, 2002* (Milan: Edizioni Nagard, 2004) 145 at 152 and 154 ("there is little incentive to comply with international law if all it is saying is that '*You remain a criminal. However, if you insist on being a criminal, this is how to be a good criminal*' ... By labeling those who engage in asymmetric warfare as criminals and international outlaws, we actually remove any incentive for them to conform [to IHL]") [emphasis in original].

[225] Given that non-state terrorist groups use tactics that are, by their nature, contrary to IHL, it may be unlikely that extending combatancy status to such actors would result in their compliance with IHL. This position is arguably more persuasive in other armed conflicts involving non-state armed groups — particularly for groups seeking independence — whereby IHL compliance can be a mechanism to strengthen the group's claim to legitimacy despite their concurrent characterization as criminal by the state against which they are fighting. Such conflicts,

A second reason why international armed conflicts should not be expanded to encompass transnational armed conflicts is because there is arguably a low threshold required to trigger the application of IHL to an international armed conflict.[226] If such situations were considered a form of international armed conflicts, one could argue that IHL would apply the moment a state uses force against a non-state actor based in another state, regardless of the level of violence. Applying IHL in such circumstances (for example, a targeted strike against a suspected terrorist) may provide less protection to individuals than they would otherwise enjoy. There may also be a strong argument that internal armed conflicts that spill over into neighbouring states without involving that state's armed forces should remain classified as non-international. In light of these reasons, it is argued that ensuring the application of IHL to transnational armed conflicts should not be achieved by the expansion of international armed conflicts.

Should Non-International Armed Conflicts Encompass Transnational Armed Conflicts?

Transnational armed conflicts may share more similarities with the traditional conception of non-international armed conflicts than international conflicts due to the fact that a non-state actor is a party to the conflict. Given these similarities, they are likely to be asymmetrical, with the non-state actor usually lacking legitimacy (at least in the view of the state engaged in the conflict) and may be more likely to be marked by breaches of IHL.[227] As such, the argument that transnational armed conflicts should be classified as non-international may be compelling. As Corn argues, "[t]he ultimate question ... is whether it is best to continue to try and fit the proverbial square 'armed conflict' peg into the round Common Article 3 hole, or whether the time has come to endorse a new category."[228]

---

however, may already qualify as "international." See Additional Protocol I, *supra* note 39, art. 1 (4) (Additional Protocol I applies to, and may provide combatant status for, non-state actors engaged in "armed conflicts in which peoples are fighting against colonial domination and alien occupation and against racist régimes in the exercise of their right of self-determination").

[226] See the discussion earlier in this article. See *Delalic, supra* note 126 at para. 184 ("the existence of armed force between States is sufficient of itself to trigger the application of [IHL]").

[227] Schondorf, *supra* note 10 at 38–40.

[228] Corn, *supra* note 10 at 329.

Authors advocating the recognition of a third category of armed conflict often support their position with the argument that non-international armed conflicts provide insufficient protection to non-combatants (that is, civilians). Schondorf, for example, states that transnational armed conflicts "raise important issues surrounding civilian protections that ... would justify the application of the rules concerning the protection of non-combatants in [international] armed conflicts to the situation," and he argues that classifying them as non-international would "offer non-combatants less protection than that afforded to non-combatants in [international] armed conflicts even though nothing, as a theoretical or practical matter, justifies adopting a theory that affords non-combatants inferior protection in [transnational] armed conflicts."[229] In making such assertions, however, these authors do not consider the convergence between the rules of IHL that protect innocent civilians during international and non-international armed conflicts that has occurred. As noted earlier, despite the fact that international armed conflicts remain more highly regulated and once provided significantly more protection to innocent civilians than non-international armed conflict, many of these rules now apply to non-international armed conflict as part of customary international law.[230] In light of this convergence, recognizing a third category of armed conflict in the name protecting innocent civilians may not be as pressing as some authors contend.

As discussed earlier, there also may be textual support in Common Article 3 for considering non-international armed conflicts to be a residual category that would encompass transnational armed conflicts, as the universally accepted treaty provision may be interpreted as applying to any armed conflict that is "not of an international character."[231] If non-international armed conflicts were so interpreted, this would ensure that a relatively well-developed body of law would apply to such conflicts. It may also prevent states from using a new category of armed conflict to advance arguments that could decrease the legal impediments for their use of force against suspected terrorists that could result in an increased risk of harm to innocent civilians.[232] As noted, a potential benefit of recognizing a

---

229 Schondorf, *supra* note 10 at 40.

230 See the discussion earlier in this article.

231 See the discussion earlier in this article.

232 See the discussion at note 218.

new category of armed conflict may be the development of rules specific to the context of such situations. The opportunity to develop new rules, however, could leave innocent civilians at a greater risk of harm, as an inherent risk may be that states would use this opportunity to their tactical advantage.[233] In the name of securing their populations from the threat of attacks by non-state actors, states could seek to ease the restrictions on the lawful conduct of hostilities in a manner that could endanger the rights and lives of innocent civilians. While supporting his argument that a third category of transnational armed conflict should be recognized because it could permit the development of rules specific to these "unique" situations, Schondorf provides an example of such a rule that could have a destabilizing effect on the rights of innocent civilians because it could undermine the principle of distinction: "[I]t is possible that the use of civilian clothing [by a state's armed forces], which is prohibited in other types of armed conflict but allowed in law enforcement operations, should be allowed in certain types of operations in [transnational] armed conflicts."[234]

There may also be practical difficulty in creating a third category of armed conflict with rules specific to its context, as it would likely require the creation of an international treaty. Since treaties only bind the ratifying states, an attempt to formalize a third category of armed conflict and its applicable rules that does not meet with widespread state acceptance could result in greater uncertainty regarding the rules governing the conduct of hostilities during these conflicts. States that are party to such conflicts but have not ratified the treaty could claim that they are not bound by its rules. Sassoli notes, for example, that "[i]t is doubtful whether a new law for transnational conflicts ... would be acceptable to the United States and whether such a law would be accepted and respected in the future by other States involved in such conflicts" because such law would "necessarily also give some rights to the non-State actors involved."[235] In light of the protection that innocent civilians currently enjoy during non-international armed conflicts and the universality of Common Article 3 and the fundamental protections

---

[233] See, e.g, Sassoli, *supra* note 87 at 220 ("any revision [of IHL] introduces the risk that States will take advantage of it to weaken rather than strengthen their obligations and the corresponding rights of war victims").

[234] Schondorf, *supra* note 10 at 59.

[235] Sassoli, *supra* note 87 at 220

of IHL, a risk of recognizing a third category is that it may ultimately prove less protective than applying the law of non-international armed conflicts to transnational armed conflicts.

It is clear that there is a great deal of uncertainty regarding the legal effect of an armed conflict between a state and a non-state actor based in another state. Although it may be ultimately preferable to recognize a third category of armed conflict because specific rules could be developed for these situations, this may not be the most practical approach in light of the fact that states — not academics — would determine the law applicable to a new category. In order to ensure the ability for states to protect their populations from the threat of transnational terrorism in a manner that respects the rights and lives of innocent civilians, it is argued that IHL should apply when an armed conflict arises between a state and a non-state actor based in another state. The simplest means of ensuring this application may be to adopt the understanding of non-international armed conflicts as a residual category encompassing *all* armed conflicts that do not arise between states.[236] Considering non-international armed conflicts as a residual category may, to some extent, avoid uncertainty regarding when IHL is triggered and

---

[236] Just as recognizing a new category of transnational armed conflict would require state acceptance, so too would achieving the proposed clarification/expansion of non-international armed conflicts. Although the traditional or paradigmatic non-international armed conflict is an internal civil war, state practice coupled with *opinio juris* could support applying the rules of non-international armed conflict as the plain words of Common Article 3 arguably provide: to armed conflicts that are not international (that is, state-to-state) in character. States could indicate through formal statements that the rules of non-international armed conflicts apply — as a matter of law — to these situations. Such statements could build upon the decisions in *Nicaragua* and *Hamdan* as support for applying the fundamental principles of IHL to all armed conflicts even if they fall outside of the common understandings of the traditional categories. An important step could be for states to revise their military manuals to ensure that their armed forces are clearly bound to apply the rules of non-international armed conflicts to such situations. As the ICRC study has shown, these manuals provide a useful means of identifying customary IHL. Although doing so may be difficult due to the political nature of the issue, states could also pass a resolution in the UN General Assembly indicating their understanding of non-international armed conflicts as a residual category. Since states have proven to be concerned that the fight against transnational terrorism can threaten the rights of innocent civilians, there may be sufficient support for such a resolution so that it could be passed with a significant majority so that — although non-binding — it could arguably reflect widespread state *opinio juris* despite the fact that state practice may be nascent because these types of armed conflicts remain relatively rare.

decrease the ability for states engaged in armed conflicts with non-state actors that transcend national boundaries to claim that their activities are not regulated by IHL. It is argued that such an approach arguably represents a modest evolution in IHL by bringing under its umbrella a form of conflict that was not considered when the major IHL treaties were ratified and that it would ensure that states are bound — at a minimum — by the elementary considerations of humanity in their fight against transnational terrorism.

Conclusion: Respecting International Law in the Fight against Terrorism

The binding nature of international law in the context of the fight against transnational terrorism is underscored by a compelling purpose — the protection of innocent civilians. It is apparent that international law provides substantial protection for the rights and lives of innocent civilians. This protection, however, is only as strong as the adherence of states — and non-state actors — to their legal obligations. In light of the fact that customary international law is developed by state practice, it is argued that violations of the law should attract international condemnation. States should not tolerate breaches of the law simply because it is difficult to "fight" terrorism. If states endorse or acquiesce to tactics that do not respect the rule of law and the rights of individuals, the risk of harm to innocent civilians may be grave.

It has been argued that IHL should apply when an armed conflict arises between a state and a non-state actor based in another state. In light of the potential uncertainty regarding the application of IHL to circumstances that fall outside of the traditional conceptions of international and non-international armed conflicts, non-international armed conflicts should be understood as a residual category that encompasses all armed conflicts to which the parties are not states. It must be recognized, however, that there may be a danger in the over-application of IHL because it can provide less protection for individuals than IHRL. As such, IHL should not apply when a non-state actor cannot be identified as a party to the conflict or when the other requirements of an armed conflict are not present. This approach may balance the desire of states to protect their populations from the threat of transnational terrorism, while attempting to ensure respect for the rights of innocent civilians. Such an approach is necessary because a legal regime that benefits individual rights to the detriment of a state's security could lead to disrespect for the law and an erosion of its binding character through continued violations.

Whether or not a situation amounts to an armed conflict, states remain bound to their legal obligations — including IHRL or IHL — when responding to the threat of terrorism. There is no question that abiding by the law regarding the use of lethal force — on both a domestic and international level — will pose challenges to combating terrorism, as legal obligations will restrict the actions that states can take against suspected terrorists. It is argued that states should attempt to comply with the law despite these challenges. Maintaining stringent restraints on the use of lethal force by states against suspected terrorists could also increase the incentive for states to explore other means than using armed force to combat the threat of terrorism, while they may retain the right to use force when it is necessary. The consequence of an approach that disregards the rule of law must be avoided: "[I]t is precisely by declaring an all-out war that one falls into the terrorists' trap, since one simply follows them in their scorched-earth policy of burning bridges between civilizations and driving civilian populations with them over the precipice."[237]

Given their customary nature, there is a risk that many international legal obligations could be weakened if breaches are met with acquiescence from other states. At a minimum, states should protest breaches of international law that occur during the fight against transnational terrorism. Ideally, states would be held accountable for serious breaches of IHL and gross breaches of IHRL.[238] If states prevent and react to the threat of transnational terrorism in ways that respect international law and the rights of individuals, it is hoped that the destabilizing effects of terrorism may be minimized. The words of Sergio Vieira de Mello, the late UN High Commissioner for Human Rights who died in a terrorist attack, underscore the importance of ensuring the protection of innocent civilians and respect for the rule of law: "I am convinced that the best — the only — strategy to isolate and defeat terrorism is by respecting human rights, fostering social justice, enhancing democracy and upholding the primacy of the rule of law."[239]

237 Frederic Megret, "'War'? Legal Semantics and the Move to Violence" (2002) 13 E.J.I.L. 361 at 391.

238 See *Basic Principles and Guidelines on the Right to a Remedy and Reparation for Victims of Gross Violations of International Human Rights Law and Serious Violations of International Humanitarian Law*, General Assembly Resolution 60/147, UN GAOR 60th Sess. UN Doc. A/Res/60/147 (2006).

239 Quoted in Schmid, *supra* note 183.

Sommaire

Les protection des civils durant la lutte contre le terrorisme trans-national: l'application du droit international humanitaire aux conflits armés transnationaux

Cet article examine comment le droit international humanitaire peut proté-ger les civils innocents dans le contexte de la lutte contre le terrorisme trans-national. Afin de permettre aux États de protéger leurs populations contre la menace du terrorisme tout en respectant la primauté du droit et les droits des individus, l'auteure fait valoir que, bien que le droit international hu-manitaire ne doit s'appliquer qu'aux conflits armés, il doit évoluer de sorte à ce qu'il s'applique clairement aux conflits armés "transnationaux" (à savoir, les conflits armés entre un État A et un acteur non-étatique située dans le territoire d'un État B, où l'État A a recours à la force armée sans le consentement de l'État B). Plutôt que de reconnaître une troisième, nou-velle catégorie de conflits armés à ces fins, l'auteure affirme que la catégorie des conflits armés non-internationaux doit être interprétée comme une caté-gorie résiduelle qui comprend tous les conflits armés où les parties ne sont pas exclusivement des États et / ou leurs représentants.

Summary

Protecting Civilians during the Fight against Transnational Terror-ism: Applying International Humanitarian Law to Transnational Armed Conflicts

This article explores how international humanitarian law (IHL) may apply to protect innocent civilians during the fight against transnational terror-ism. To achieve the goal of allowing states to protect their populations from the threat of terrorism while respecting the rule of law and the rights of in-dividuals, it is argued that, while IHL should remain applicable only to armed conflicts it must evolve so that it clearly applies to "transnational" armed conflicts (that is, armed conflicts between State A and a non-state actor based in State B, where State A uses force in the territory of State B without State B's consent). Rather than recognizing a new third category of armed conflict to cover these situations, it is argued that non-international armed conflicts should be understood as a residual category that regulates all armed conflicts to which the parties are states and/or their agents.

Notes and Comments /
Notes et commentaires

Khadr's Twist on *Hape:*
Tortured Determinations of
the Extraterritorial Reach of the
Canadian *Charter*

INTRODUCTION

On 23 May 2008, the Supreme Court of Canada released a judgment in one of the many legal proceedings spawned by Canadian citizen Omar Khadr's detention and prosecution by US military authorities in Guantánamo Bay.[1] In this particular case, the issue raised was the applicability of the *Canadian Charter of Rights and Freedoms* to the actions of Canadian officials, including officers of the Canadian Security and Intelligence Service (CSIS), in interrogating Khadr at Guantánamo Bay and passing the fruits of such interrogations to US authorities.[2] As a result, the Court was required to address, for the second time in less than a year, the applicability of the *Charter* to the actions of Canadian government officials abroad.[3] Also for the second time in less than a year, the Court determined that resolution of this issue was governed by the content of Canada's international legal obligations.

The Court's unanimous and unsigned judgment in *Canada (Justice) v. Khadr* is remarkable in a number of respects. Perhaps most notable is its startling brevity,[4] particularly given the complexity and

---

[1] *Canada (Justice) v. Khadr,* 2008 SCC 28 [*Khadr*].

[2] *Canadian Charter of Rights and Freedoms,* Part I of the *Constitution Act, 1982,* being Schedule B of the *Canada Act 1982* (U.K.) 1982, c. 11 [*Charter*].

[3] The Court had previously addressed this issue in *R. v. Hape,* [2007] 2 S.C.R. 292, 2007 SCC 26 (released 7 June 2007) [*Hape*].

[4] The judgment comprises a total of forty-two paragraphs. Excluding prefatory and concluding statements, factual recitations, descriptions of lower court decisions, and analysis devoted to procedural matters, the Court devoted a mere

importance of its central issue and the critical commentary[5] generated by the judgment upon which it is premised — the Court's June
2007 majority opinion in *R. v. Hape*.[6] *Hape* essentially held, on dubious international legal grounds, that "extraterritorial application
of the *Charter* is impossible."[7] *Khadr* confirms that rule but holds
that it is subject to an exception "if Canada was participating in a
process that was violative of Canada's binding obligations under
international law."[8] *Khadr*'s brevity of analysis in asserting, justifying,
and applying this exception raises, yet leaves unexamined and unanswered, a number of uncertainties and questions that will be
commented on in the following discussion.

Moreover, while *Khadr* evades application of *Hape*'s principle of
the non-applicability of the *Charter* abroad (the *Hape* principle) on
the basis of an exception to that principle ostensibly propounded
in *Hape* itself,[9] the exception to the *Hape* principle that is applied
by the Court in *Khadr* (the *Khadr* exception) is in fact wholly novel.
Certainly, insofar as it limits the damage generated by *Hape*'s ill-
considered amputation of the *Charter*'s extraterritorial reach, the
Khadr exception is to be welcomed. However, in purporting to apply
an exception to the *Hape* principle already recognized in *Hape* itself,
the Court in *Khadr* implicitly and unanimously confirms the *Hape*

---

twelve paragraphs to discussion and resolution of the case's central substantive
issue, the applicability of the *Charter* to the actions of Canadian government actors abroad. *Khadr, supra* note 1 at paras. 16–27. Of these, four paragraphs are
devoted to establishing the legal principles governing this issue (*ibid.* at paras.
16–19), whereas the remaining eight paragraphs relate to their application to
the facts of the case (*ibid.* at paras. 20–27).

5 See, for example, K. Roach, "*R. v. Hape* Creates Charter-Free Zones for Canadian
   Officials Abroad" (2007) 53 Criminal L.Q. 1; J.H. Currie, "Weaving a Tangled
   Web: *Hape* and the Obfuscation of Canadian Reception Law" (2007) 45 Can.
   Y.B. Int'l L. 55; F. Larocque et al., "L'incorporation de la coutume internationale
   en common law canadienne" (2007) 45 Can. Y.B. Int'l L. 173.; N. Gal-Or, "*R. v.
   Hape*: International Law before the Supreme Court of Canada" (2008) 66 Ad-
   vocate 885; H.S. Fairley, "International Law Comes of Age: *Hape v. The Queen*"
   (2008) 87 Can. B. Rev. 229; A. Attaran, "Have Charter, Will Travel? Extraterritoriality in Constitutional Law and Canadian Exceptionalism" (2009) 87 Can.
   B. Rev. 515.

6 *Hape, supra* note 3.

7 *Ibid.* at para. 85.

8 *Khadr, supra* note 1 at para. 19.

9 *Ibid.* at para. 18.

principle. This further entrenchment of the geographically limited reach of the *Charter*'s protections, at least as a starting point, is a development to be regretted. Just as importantly, this approach also deprives the Court of the opportunity to weigh the merits and examine the many implications of the new exception that it in fact announces in *Khadr*. The missed opportunity to correct *Hape*'s erroneous starting point, and the conceptual confusion generated by the Court's logically strained efforts to sidestep it in *Khadr*, will also be the subject of comment.

Khadr also raises important constitutional questions of a procedural, substantive, and remedial order. For example, its full-faith reliance on legal findings by a foreign court in deciding a matter of domestic constitutional importance;[10] its cursory examination of the content of relevant protections under section 7 of the *Charter*;[11] and its perfunctory curtailment of the *Charter*'s remedial scope in extraterritorial cases — even where the *Charter* is found to apply in principle — are all matters deserving of critical scrutiny.[12] Given that the international legal dimensions of the case are largely confined to issues of the *Charter*'s extraterritorial applicability, however, this will be the focus of this comment.

FACTUAL BACKGROUND

Omar Ahmed Khadr, a Canadian national, was detained by US military authorities in Afghanistan on 27 July 2002, when he was fifteen years of age. US authorities alleged that Khadr, in addition to participating unlawfully in combat operations against US and coalition forces in Afghanistan and murdering an American soldier during those operations, had conspired with members of the Al-Qaeda terrorist organization to commit terrorist acts against the US and coalition forces in Afghanistan. Accordingly, following his initial detention in Afghanistan, Khadr was transferred by US authorities to a US detention centre in Guantánamo Bay, Cuba. This detention centre had been established in 2001 by order of the US president for purposes of detaining and prosecuting individuals suspected of having links with the Al-Qaeda terrorist network or otherwise being involved in terrorist activities.[13]

10 *Ibid.* at paras. 21–24.

11 *Ibid.* at paras. 29, 31–32.

12 *Ibid.* at paras. 33–35.

13 *Ibid.* at paras. 5–6.

Pursuant to the presidential order establishing the Guantánamo Bay detention centre, detainees were to have no recourse to American, foreign, or international courts or tribunals for any remedy whatsoever. Rather, detainees were to be subject to the exclusive jurisdiction of military commissions established at Guantánamo Bay by the US secretary of defence for purposes of their prosecution. Having determined that the application of normal rules of criminal procedure was "not practicable" in the circumstances of such prosecutions, the US president issued subsequent orders establishing special rules for the military commissions that significantly departed from normal criminal procedure protections relating to the admissibility of evidence as well as the rights to counsel, disclosure, and trial by an independent tribunal.[14]

Khadr was not formally charged with any offence until November 2005. At that time, he was charged with having committed the offences of conspiracy, murder by an unprivileged belligerent, attempted murder by an unprivileged belligerent, and aiding the enemy. Prior to being charged, he was repeatedly interrogated by US authorities. In addition, he was interviewed on a number of occasions, including in February and September 2003, by Canadian officials, including members of CSIS. These interviews, summaries of which were shared with US authorities, touched upon issues related to the charges subsequently laid by the United States against Khadr.[15] At the time of writing, Khadr's prosecution by a US military commission continues.

Upon being charged by US authorities, Khadr sought disclosure from the Minister of Justice and the Attorney General of Canada, the Canadian Minister of Foreign Affairs, the Director of CSIS, and the Commissioner of the Royal Canadian Mounted Police, of any documents in Canada's possession, including records of the interviews conducted by Canadian officials in Guantánamo Bay, which were relevant to the charges he was facing in the US military commission proceedings. He relied in this regard on the disclosure rules set out by the Supreme Court of Canada in *R. v. Stinchcombe*.[16] His request for disclosure was formally denied in January 2006.[17]

---

14 *Ibid.* at para. 6.

15 *Ibid.* at paras. 7–8.

16 *R. v. Stinchcombe*, [1991] 3 S.C.R. 326 [*Stinchcombe*].

17 *Khadr, supra* note 1 at para. 8.

LOWER COURT DECISIONS

In light of Canada's failure to disclose the records requested, Khadr applied on 3 January 2006 for an order of *mandamus* in the Federal Court. Khadr's position was that, *per Stinchcombe*,[18] section 7 of the *Charter* gave him a constitutional right to disclosure of any materials in the possession of the federal Crown relevant to the charges against him. He also relied on the British Columbia Court of Appeal's 2003 decision in *Purdy v. Canada (Attorney General)* for the proposition that this right extended to situations where the charges against him were being prosecuted by foreign authorities in a foreign jurisdiction.[19]

On 25 April 2006, Justice Konrad von Finckenstein dismissed the application.[20] Framing the question in terms of whether section 7 of the *Charter* applies "in the circumstances in which [Khadr] finds himself,"[21] von Finckenstein J. accepted, on the basis of the Supreme Court of Canada's then-prevailing ruling in *R. v. Cook*,[22] that "the [*Charter*] rights of Canadians when interrogated abroad by Canadian law enforcement agents are protected in certain circumstances."[23] Whether this was so in any given case, however, depended on whether there was "a reasonable foreseeable connection between Canada's actions and the violation of the Charter."[24] *Purdy* was distinguishable in its application of this test,[25] von Finckenstein J. found, in that it addressed a joint Canada-US investigation that had been carried out primarily in Canada.[26] As there had been no investigation of, and no charges against, Khadr in Canada, von Finckenstein J. concluded that the necessary causal connection between the actions of Canadian officials and the threat to Khadr's

---

[18] *Stinchcombe, supra* note 16.

[19] *Purdy v. Canada (Attorney General)* (2003), 226 D.L.R. (4th) 761 (B.C.S.C.), aff'd (2003), 230 D.L.R. (4th) 361 (B.C.C.A.) [*Purdy*].

[20] *Khadr v. Canada (Minister of Justice)* (2006), 290 F.T.R. 313, 2006 FC 509 [*Khadr* (FC)].

[21] *Ibid.* at para. 10.

[22] *R. v. Cook,* [1998] 2 S.C.R. 597 [*Cook*].

[23] *Khadr* (FC), *supra* note 20 at para. 12.

[24] *Ibid.* at para. 13, citing *Suresh v. Canada (Minister of Citizenship and Immigration),* [2002] 1 S.C.R. 3, 2002 SCC 1 at para. 54 [*Suresh*].

[25] *Purdy, supra* note 19.

[26] *Khadr* (FC), *supra* note 20 at paras. 17–20.

rights to life, liberty, and security of the person had not been established, and section 7 of the *Charter* accordingly had no application.[27]

On appeal, the Federal Court of Appeal essentially agreed with von Finckenstein J.'s analysis of the relevant law but differed in its appreciation of the facts.[28] In particular, the Federal Court of Appeal noted that the interviews by Canadian officials had been carried out in part for law enforcement purposes, that they covered matters that were the subject of the charges subsequently laid against Khadr by US authorities, and that summaries of those interviews had been provided to US authorities prior to those charges being laid. As a result, Canadian officials had assisted US authorities in conducting their investigation of Khadr and in preparing a case against him. The Federal Court of Appeal found that this may have made it more likely that charges would be laid against Khadr and, thus, may have increased the likelihood that he would be deprived of his right to life, liberty, and security of the person. This established a sufficient causal connection between the actions of Canadian officials and the potential deprivation of Khadr's section 7 rights to warrant application of section 7 of the *Charter* in his case, contrary to von Finckenstein J.'s finding.[29]

The Federal Court of Appeal accordingly proceeded to evaluate Khadr's argument on the substantive application of section 7 to his case. It determined that Khadr had made a *prima facie* case that he was at substantial risk of not being able to make full answer and defence to the charges pending against him before the US military commission if he were denied access to relevant information in the possession of the federal Crown.[30] The Federal Court of Appeal accordingly concluded that Khadr had a right to disclosure of such information, subject to privilege and public interest immunity claims that might be raised by the Crown and reviewed by a court of law.[31] The Court therefore ordered that the Crown produce all relevant documents within its possession to a judge of the Federal Court, who would in turn determine to which particular documents Khadr was entitled pursuant to section 7 of the *Charter, Stinchcombe,* and

---

[27] *Ibid.* at paras. 20, 22.
[28] *Khadr v. Canada (Minister of Justice),* [2008] 1 F.C.R. 270, 2007 FCA 182 at paras. 29–32, 34 [*Khadr* (FCA)]. Note that this decision was released approximately one month prior to the release of the Supreme Court of Canada's judgment in *Hape, supra* note 3.
[29] *Khadr* (FCA), *supra* note 28 at para. 34.
[30] *Ibid.* at para. 37.
[31] *Ibid.*

the relevant rules governing claims to privilege and public interest immunity,[32] including those pursuant to sections 38 and following of the *Canada Evidence Act*.[33]

THE SUPREME COURT OF CANADA'S DECISION

Both the Federal Court's and the Federal Court of Appeal's decisions were rendered prior to the Supreme Court of Canada's ruling in *Hape*,[34] which effectively overturned *Cook*[35] and rewrote the rules governing extraterritorial applicability of the *Charter*. Thus, while it dismissed the appeal against the order of the Federal Court of Appeal, the Supreme Court of Canada based its decision on different legal grounds than the courts below and, ultimately, varied the terms of the Federal Court of Appeal's order.

The Supreme Court of Canada's starting point was that, if the interviews and process to which Khadr was subject had occurred in Canada, he "would have been entitled to full disclosure under the principles in *Stinchcombe*."[36] Yet Canada argued that, pursuant to *Hape*, the *Charter* had no application to the actions of Canadian officials at Guantánamo Bay and that there was, therefore, no basis for such a disclosure order. The Supreme Court of Canada noted, however, that its ruling in *Hape* had been premised on "international law principles against extraterritorial enforcement of domestic laws and the principle of comity"[37] and that *Hape* "stated an important exception to the principle of comity" in cases of "clear violations of international law and fundamental human rights."[38] Thus, reasoned the Court, the issue was whether "Canada was participating in a process that was violative of Canada's binding obligations under international law."[39] If so, the *Charter* applied; if not, it did not.[40]

Sidestepping the need to determine for itself "the legality of the process at Guantánamo Bay under which Khadr was held at the time that Canadian officials participated in that process," the Court noted that the Supreme Court of the United States (USSC) had

---

[32] *Ibid.* at paras. 42, 44.

[33] *Canada Evidence Act*, R.S.C. 1985, c. C-5.

[34] *Hape, supra* note 3.

[35] *Cook, supra* note 22; *Hape, supra* note 3 at para. 182 (per Binnie J., concurring).

[36] *Khadr, supra* note 1 at para. 16.

[37] *Ibid.* at para. 17.

[38] *Ibid.* at para. 18; *Hape, supra* note 3 at paras. 51, 52, 101.

[39] *Khadr, supra* note 1 at paras. 19–20.

[40] *Ibid.*

already done so. In particular, the Court observed that the USSC had previously found "that the detainees had illegally been denied access to *habeas corpus* and that the procedures under which they were to be prosecuted violated the Geneva Conventions."[41] This, the Court held, was sufficient to permit it to conclude that "the regime providing for the detention and trial of Khadr at the time of the CSIS interviews constituted a clear violation of fundamental human rights protected by international law."[42] Since sharing summaries of its interviews of Khadr with US authorities had made Canada a participant in that regime — although merely conducting these interviews "may not" have — the *Charter* applied, and Canada was subject to a section 7 duty of disclosure.[43]

However, that duty of disclosure was not necessarily coterminous with, but only "analogous to," that which would apply in the case of government conduct occurring in Canada.[44] In particular, because applicability of the *Charter* to the actions of Canadian officials abroad hinged on their participation in a foreign process that violated Canada's international legal obligations, "[t]he scope of the disclosure obligation in this context is defined by the nature of Canada's participation in the foreign process."[45] Accordingly, rather than ordering disclosure of all materials in Canada's possession that might be relevant to the US charges against Khadr, as ordered by the Federal Court of Appeal in accordance with *Stinchcombe*, the Supreme Court of Canada ordered disclosure of all records of the interviews conducted by Canadian officials and of any information given to US authorities as a direct consequence of those interviews.[46]

---

41 *Ibid.* at paras. 21–23, relying upon *Rasul v. Bush*, 542 U.S. 466 (2004) and *Hamdan v. Rumsfeld*, 126 S. Ct. 2749 (2006) [*Hamdan*]. Geneva Convention I for the Amelioration of the Condition of the Wounded and Sick in Armed Forces in the Field, 12 August 1949, 75 U.N.T.S. 31; Geneva Convention II for the Amelioration of the Condition of Wounded, Sick and Shipwrecked Members of Armed Forces at Sea, 12 August 1949, 75 U.N.T.S. 85; Geneva Convention III Relative to the Treatment of Prisoners of War, 12 August 1949, 75 U.N.T.S. 135; Geneva Convention IV Relative to the Protection of Civilian Persons in Time of War, 12 August 1949, 75 U.N.T.S. 287 [Geneva Conventions].

42 *Khadr, supra* note 1 at para. 24.

43 *Ibid.* at paras 26–27, 31.

44 *Ibid.* at paras. 30–31.

45 *Ibid.* at para. 32.

46 *Ibid.* at para. 37. This order was made subject to consideration, by a Federal Court judge, of any privilege or public interest immunity claims by the government, including any under sections 38 ff. of the *Canada Evidence Act, supra* note 33.

DISCUSSION

In order to appreciate the significance of, and difficulties posed by, the Court's judgment in *Khadr*, it is first necessary to recall the majority ruling in *Hape*, upon which *Khadr* is premised, and to touch briefly on its principal shortcomings. It will be remembered that in *Hape*, a bare majority of the Court, unbidden by the Crown and unassisted by any submissions on Canada's international legal obligations, overturned the Court's own relatively recent ruling on the extraterritorial reach of the *Charter*[47] and held that "extraterritorial application of the *Charter* is impossible."[48] The *Hape* majority's sole legal basis for doing so were Canada's international legal obligations flowing from the principles of the sovereign equality of states and non-intervention, as well as the prohibition of state exercises of extraterritorial enforcement jurisdiction.[49] According to the majority, the conclusion that the *Charter* could have no application to the actions of Canadian officials abroad followed from these international legal principles and obligations in one of two ways. First, the majority articulated a novel rule of *Charter* interpretation to the effect that "courts should seek to ensure compliance with Canada's binding obligations under international law where the express words are capable of supporting such a conclusion."[50] Given (1) the *Charter*'s silence as to its territorial reach; (2) principles of international law that generally forbid states from exercising enforcement

---

[47] *Cook, supra* note 22. While the majority in *Hape, supra* note 3, did not expressly overrule *Cook*, and the official report of the former indicates that *Cook* was "distinguished," it is difficult to see how the majority's conclusion concerning the impossibility of the extraterritorial application of the *Charter* can be reconciled with *Cook*'s earlier finding that such application, while rarely justified, is nevertheless permissible in limited circumstances. See also the concurring judgment of Binnie J. in *Hape, supra* note 3 at para. 182, commenting that the majority judgment "effectively overrules *Cook*." It is also notable that the circumstances contemplated in *Cook* appear to bear no direct relation to the circumstances identified by the Court in *Khadr, supra* note 1, as justifying such exceptional extraterritorial application.

[48] *Hape, supra* note 3 at para. 85.

[49] *Ibid.* at paras. 40–46, 57–65. While the majority in *Hape* does also refer in the course of its reasons to the principle of comity, it makes clear that it does not consider comity to be legally binding. Rather, "comity is more a principle of interpretation than a rule of law, because it does not arise from formal obligations" (*ibid.* at para. 47); and "[i]nternational law is a positive legal order, whereas comity, which is of the nature of a principle of interpretation, is based on a desire for states to act courteously towards one another" (*ibid.* at para. 50).

[50] *Ibid.* at para. 56.

jurisdiction abroad;[51] and (3) the majority's assumption that the application of the *Charter* to the actions of Canadian officials abroad would amount to an exercise of extraterritorial enforcement jurisdiction,[52] the majority in *Hape* thus concluded that the *Charter*'s reach must be territorially limited to Canada. In the alternative, the majority reasoned that, in light of international law's constraints on the exercise of extraterritorial enforcement jurisdiction, Parliament "has no jurisdiction to authorize enforcement abroad."[53] As a result, enforcement abroad fell outside the "authority of Parliament," as that expression is used in section 32(1) of the *Charter,* and, hence, the reach of the *Charter*'s application provision.[54]

The majority judgment in *Hape* is deeply problematic on many levels. At the level of mere principle and public policy, *Hape* appears aberrant on its face in writing a blank cheque to Canadian governments to violate the *Charter* with impunity as long as they do so abroad. If "extraterritorial application of the *Charter* is impossible,"[55] it seems to follow that all the world beyond Canada's borders is a *Charter*-free zone in which Canadian government actors are free to (and apparently do, judging from the facts of *Hape* itself) act in ways that would otherwise be constitutionally impermissible.[56] The implications of such an approach are particularly breathtaking given the very many ways in which Canadian officials *are* active abroad. The profound asymmetry between the *fact* of extensive extraterritorial governmental activity and *Hape*'s principle of non-applicability of the *Charter* to such activity is both confounding and troubling. That Canadian officials should in fact be competent to act abroad and yet not be subject to any *Charter* constraints in doing so seems at best counter-intuitive and at worst unwise.

It might nevertheless be defensible to sacrifice the common sense public interest in constitutionally constraining all exercises of governmental authority on the altar of some higher principle — for example, the need to ensure respect for Canada's international legal obligations. Yet here too the case for the *Hape* principle falters.

---

[51] *Ibid.* at paras. 40–46, 57–65, and 96–101.

[52] *Ibid.* at para. 85.

[53] *Ibid.* at para. 94.

[54] *Ibid.* at paras. 69, 94, and 103–6. Section 32(1) of the *Charter, supra* note 2, provides that it applies to "the Parliament and government of Canada in respect of *all matters within the authority of Parliament*" [emphasis added].

[55] *Hape, supra* note 3 at para. 85.

[56] Roach, *supra* note 5.

Even accepting the *Hape* majority's overly simplistic characterization of international law's general prohibition of state exercises of extraterritorial enforcement jurisdiction,[57] no such exercise of jurisdiction would in fact occur if a Canadian court were to apply the *Charter*, in a Canadian court proceeding, to the extraterritorial actions of Canadian officials. The only exercise of enforcement jurisdiction in such a situation occurs in Canada — the location where the court proceeding occurs. A court proceeding in Canada — even one in which the Court applies Canadian rules of law to events that have occurred abroad — involves no exercise of "power"[58] or coercive jurisdiction in any other state's territory. The only extraterritorial exercise of jurisdiction in such a case is *prescriptive* rather than enforcement in nature. That is, a court sitting only in Canada (and thus exercising enforcement jurisdiction only in Canada) and applying a Canadian rule of law to events occurring abroad is simply defining the *prescriptive* reach of that rule, not *enforcing* it abroad. This fundamental distinction between extraterritorial exercises of *prescriptive* and *enforcement* jurisdiction — the former broadly permissible in international law on a number of bases,[59] the latter more tightly circumscribed[60] — is fatally confused by the majority in *Hape*.

57 *Hape, supra* note 3 at para. 69: "In the absence of consent Canada cannot exercise its enforcement jurisdiction over a matter situated outside Canadian territory." In fact, the core of the international legal prohibition on extraterritorial exercises of enforcement jurisdiction is limited in its application to enforcement *in another's state's territory*, not outside one's own. See, e.g., *The Case of the SS "Lotus" (France v. Turkey)* (1927), P.C.I.J. (Ser. A) No. 10 at 18–19 [*Lotus*]: "Now the first and foremost restriction imposed by international law upon a State is that — failing the existence of a permissive rule to the contrary — it may not exercise its power in any form *in the territory of another State* [emphasis added]." Furthermore, international law is rife with rules, not based on consent, that permit states to exercise enforcement jurisdiction outside their own territory. To cite but two examples by way of illustration: the right of states to arrest ships flying their flag, or engaged in piracy, on the high seas (see United Nations Convention on the Law of the Sea, 10 December 1982, 1833 U.N.T.S. 3 (entered into force 16 November 1994), arts. 94, 97, 99, 101–109, 113–14); and the right of states to use armed force against other states in self-defence (see Charter of the United Nations, 26 June 1945, Can. T.S. 1945 No. 7 (in force 24 October 1945), art. 51).

58 *Lotus, supra* note 57 at 19.

59 See I. Brownlie, *Principles of Public International Law*, 7th edition (Oxford: Oxford University Press, 2008) at 300–8; J.H. Currie, *Public International Law*, 2nd edition (Toronto: Irwin Law, 2008) at 339–54; M.N. Shaw, *International Law*, 5th edition (Cambridge: Cambridge University Press, 2003) at 578–93.

60 Brownlie, *supra* note 59 at 309–11; Currie, *supra* note 59 at 335–39; Shaw, *supra* note 59 at 577.

Indeed, while alluding in a number of places to these different conceptions of extraterritorial jurisdiction, the majority repeatedly conflates them,[61] culminating in its flawed conclusion that defining the prescriptive reach of the *Charter* to encompass Canadian governmental action abroad would be tantamount to enforcing it abroad.[62] Once this error in reasoning is exposed, a critical premise for the majority's conclusion that the *Charter* cannot be applied in domestic judicial proceedings to official Canadian activity abroad evaporates.

Nor does the *Hape* majority's alternative argument for limiting the *Charter*'s extraterritorial reach fare any better. The only source for that secondary argument's critical premise, that extraterritorial enforcement falls outside the "authority of Parliament" and thus the scope of section 32(1) of the *Charter*,[63] is a purported rule of customary international law.[64] However, the majority offers no basis for treating such a rule as determinative, in a domestic legal setting, of a domestic constitutional matter — the scope of parliamentary legislative authority.[65] Indeed, that the authority of Parliament is plenary within the classes of subjects enumerated in section 91 of the *Constitution Act, 1867*,[66] that it extends to extraterritorial

---

61 See, for example, *Hape, supra* note 3: "While extraterritorial jurisdiction —prescriptive, enforcement, or adjudicative — exists under international law, *it* is subject to strict limits under international law that are based on ... the territoriality principle" (at para. 65) [emphasis added]. See also para. 69 (making the logical leap between the premise that Canada has no *enforcement jurisdiction over a matter* situated outside Canada's territory, and the conclusion that the *matter itself* therefore falls outside the authority of Parliament); and para. 85 (reasoning that the *Charter* cannot *apply* to extraterritorial conduct — a question of its prescriptive reach — if it cannot be *enforced* extraterritorially, thus collapsing the distinction between prescriptive and enforcement jurisdiction entirely).

62 *Ibid.* at para. 85. Note particularly the assertion that "enforcement is necessary for the *Charter* to apply." This is a clear negation of the international legal distinction between enforcement and prescriptive jurisdiction.

63 *Ibid.* at paras. 69, 94, and 103–6.

64 See analysis on this point in Currie, *supra* note 5 at 88–89.

65 See *ibid.* at 89–93.

66 See, for example, Statute of Westminster 1931 (U.K.), 22 Geo. 5, c. 4, s. 3, which confers on Parliament "*full power* to make laws having extra-territorial *operation*" [emphasis added]. See also *Interpretation Act*, R.S.C. 1985, c. I-21, s. 8(3); *Croft v. Dunphy*, [1933] A.C. 156 (J.C.P.C.) [*Croft*]; *Society of Composers, Authors and Music Publishers of Canada v. Canadian Assn. of Internet Providers*, [2004] 2 S.C.R. 427 at para. 141 (per LeBel J.); P.W. Hogg, *Constitutional Law of Canada*, 5th edition Supp. (looseleaf) (Scarborough, ON: Thomson Carswell, 2007) at paras.

enforcement action,[67] and that it even includes the power to violate international law itself[68] are all well-settled axioms of Canadian constitutional law. It therefore seems plain that the *Hape* majority's secondary basis for denying the extraterritorial reach of the *Charter* is equally devoid of merit.[69]

In sum, the *Hape* principle appears flawed both on its merits and in the construction of the legal arguments deployed to justify it. In this context, *Khadr*'s retrenchment of that principle, even if only partial, is at first blush a welcome development. In particular, *Khadr* appears, on its surface, satisfactorily to address many of the public policy concerns raised by the *Hape* principle. According to *Khadr*, at least in cases where official conduct abroad amounts to participation in breaches of Canada's international legal obligations, the *Charter* will apply notwithstanding *Hape*'s "impossibility" dictum.[70] Given that *Charter* protections have generally — although not necessarily or consistently[71] — been interpreted by the courts to provide protection at least as great as that provided in Canada's corresponding international human rights obligations[72] and that international law generally "informs" *Charter* interpretation,[73] *Khadr*'s international

---

12.2, 13.2; and R. Sullivan, *Statutory Interpretation* (Concord, ON: Irwin Law, 1997) at 34.

67 *Croft, supra* note 66 at 167 (affirming the *vires* of anti-smuggling legislation that authorized the seizure of vessels outside Canadian territory, and holding that the *British North America Act, 1867* "imposed no territorial restriction in terms and their Lordships see no justification for inferring it").

68 See R. St. J. Macdonald, "The Relationship between International Law and Domestic Law in Canada," in R. St. J. Macdonald, G.L. Morris, and D.M. Johnston, eds., *Canadian Perspectives on International Law and Organization* (Toronto: University of Toronto Press, 1974), 88 at 119; *Hape, supra* note 3 at paras. 39, 53 and 68.

69 See Currie, *supra* note 5 at 93–94.

70 *Khadr, supra* note 1 at paras. 18–19.

71 See analysis in Currie, *supra* note 5 at 71–85.

72 See *Slaight Communications Inc. v. Davidson*, [1989] 1 S.C.R. 1038 at 1056–57 [*Slaight Communications*] (per Dickson C.J.) (quoting his earlier comment in *Reference re Public Service Employee Relations Act (Alta.)*, [1987] 1 S.C.R. 313 at 349, dissenting on another point); *Health Services and Support — Facilities Subsector Bargaining Assn. v. British Columbia*, [2007] 2 S.C.R. 391, 2007 SCC 27 at para. 70 [*Health Services*]: "[T]he *Charter* should be presumed to provide at least as great a level of protection as is found in the international human rights documents that Canada has ratified."

73 See, for example, *United States v. Burns*, [2001] 1 S.C.R. 283 at paras. 79–81 [*Burns*] (endorsing the views that international law is "of use" in interpreting

law *caveat* should effectively mean that the *Charter* will henceforth apply in a wide array of situations in which its provisions are in fact violated by Canadian officials abroad. As a result, much of the "asymmetry" introduced by *Hape* between factual exercises of government authority abroad on the one hand, and *Charter* control of such authority on the other, is erased.

However, the correspondence between Canada's international legal obligations (including its international human rights obligations) and the *Charter*'s protections is not necessarily complete. As suggested earlier, *Hape*'s interpretive presumption of *Charter* conformity with Canada's international legal obligations is an innovation in the Court's *Charter* jurisprudence[74] and has not even been consistently applied by the Court since *Hape*.[75] Nor have the various other approaches taken by the Court to the relationship between *Charter* guarantees and Canada's international legal obligations

---

the *Charter* and that international human rights law "should inform" and "must be relevant and persuasive" to such interpretation); *Suresh, supra* note 24 at paras. 46 (*Charter* interpretation "*is informed* ... by international law, including *jus cogens*" [emphasis added]); and at para. 60 ("in seeking the meaning of the Canadian Constitution, the courts *may be informed* by international law" [emphasis added]); *Health Services, supra* note 72 at para. 20 ("international law ... *may inform* the interpretation of *Charter* guarantees"); and para. 69 ("Canada's international obligations *can assist* courts charged with interpreting the *Charter*'s guarantees" [emphasis added]). See also *Canadian Foundation for Children, Youth and the Law v. Canada (Attorney General)*, [2004] 1 S.C.R. 76 at paras. 9–10; *Charkaoui v. Canada (Minister of Citizenship and Immigration)*, [2007] 1 S.C.R. 350 at para. 90; discussion in J. Brunnée and S.J. Toope, "A Hesitant Embrace: The Application of International Law by Canadian Courts" (2002) 40 Can. Y.B. Int'l L. 3 at 33–35; and S. Beaulac, "Le droit international et l'interprétation législative: oui au contexte, non à la présomption," in O. Fitzgerald, ed., *Règle de droit et mondialisation: Rapports entre le droit international et le droit interne* (Toronto: Irwin Law, 2007) 413.

74 See Currie, *supra* note 5 at 75–76.

75 *Health Services, supra* note 72, released the day after *Hape*, makes no mention of the *Hape* presumption of *Charter* conformity at all but, instead, relies on a variation of the "minimum content" rule articulated in *Slaight Communications, supra* note 72, and of the more flexible "may inform" approach articulated in *Burns, supra* note 73, and *Suresh, supra* note 24: see *Health Services, supra* note 72 at paras. 20, 69–70. *Khadr* itself merely refers to, without clearly endorsing, *Hape*'s presumption of *Charter* conformity (see *Khadr, supra* note 1 at para. 18), and subsequently refers to the more discretionary "may inform" approach espoused in *Burns, supra* note 73, and *Suresh, supra* note 24 (see *Khadr, supra* note 1 at para. 29).

always or even generally called for close reconciliation of the two.[76] In some instances, therefore, the substantive content of *Charter* protections may well exceed those provided by international law, and, as a result, government acts abroad may in some cases be inconsistent with the former but not the latter.[77] In such cases, the *Charter* will continue not to apply to the extent of this "gap," *per Hape* and *Khadr*. The curious result would appear to be to transform Canada's international legal obligations from a "floor," below which the *Charter*'s protections should not drop,[78] into a "ceiling" above which they effectively cannot rise whenever government officials act outside Canadian territory. No rational basis for thus denying Canadians (and potentially others) the "full benefit of the *Charter*'s protection" beyond Canadian territory is articulated by the Court.[79]

Indeed, the latter observation underscores a curious feature of the *Khadr* judgment. In fact, no basis *at all* is articulated by the Court for the *Khadr* exception. The reason for this is that the Court does not purport to formulate the exception in *Khadr*. Rather, the Court intimates that the exception was in fact established as part of the majority's reasoning in *Hape* itself:

> 17. The government argues that ... the *Charter* does not apply to the conduct of Canadian agents operating outside Canada. It relies on *R. v. Hape* ... where a majority of this Court held that Canadian agents participating in an investigation into money laundering in the Carribean were not bound by *Charter* constraints in the manner in which the investigation was conducted. This conclusion was *based on international law principles* against extraterritorial enforcement of domestic laws *and the principle of comity* which implies acceptance of foreign laws and procedures when Canadian officials are operating abroad.

---

[76] See, in particular, the highly discretionary approach to such reconciliation called for in the authorities collected in note 73.

[77] Also notable in this regard is the Court's finding in *Khadr, supra* note 1 at paras. 30–32, that *Charter* breaches occurring abroad do not necessarily attract the same level of remedial protection as they would if committed in Canada, notwithstanding a prior finding that the *Charter* applies to such breaches in principle. This would seem to suggest even greater potential for divergence between the substance of *Charter* protections, normally interpreted in light of Canada's international legal obligations in the domestic context, and their content in the extraterritorial context.

[78] *Per Slaight Communications* and *Health Services*, both *supra* note 72.

[79] *R. v. Big M Drug Mart Ltd.*, [1985] 1 S.C.R. 295 at 344 [*Big M Drug Mart*].

18. In *Hape*, however, the Court stated an important exception *to the principle of comity*. While not unanimous on all the principles governing extraterritorial application of the *Charter*, the Court was united on the principle that comity cannot be used to justify Canadian participation in activities of a foreign state or its agents that are contrary to Canada's international obligations. It was held that the deference required by the principle of comity "ends where clear violations of international law and fundamental human rights begin" ... The Court further held that in interpreting the scope and application of the *Charter*, the courts should seek to ensure compliance with Canada's binding obligations under international law ...

19. If the Guantanamo Bay process under which Mr. Khadr was being held was in conformity with Canada's international obligations, the *Charter* has no application and Mr. Khadr's application for disclosure cannot succeed: *Hape*. However, if Canada was participating in a process that was violative of Canada's binding obligations under international law, the *Charter* applies to the extent of that participation.[80]

This passage does not, however, tell the whole story. It certainly is true that, in speaking of the principle of comity, Justice Louis LeBel, for the majority in *Hape*, alluded to Canada's international legal obligations and human rights commitments as establishing the operative limits of that principle.[81] What is missing from *Khadr's* account of the majority's opinion in *Hape*, however, is the sharp distinction drawn between the "non-binding" principle of comity and the "binding" principles of international law.[82] For the *Hape* majority, *binding* international legal principles prohibiting the

---

80 *Khadr, supra* note 1 at paras. 17–19 [emphasis added]. It is unclear whether the substitution of "and" for "of" in the restatement of *Hape's* presumption of conformity appearing in the final sentence of para. 19 is intentional, although it may confirm the intended applicability of the presumption to interpretation of the *Charter* generally and not merely s. 32(1), as argued in Currie, *supra* note 5 at note 89.

81 *Hape, supra* note 3 at paras. 51–52.

82 The Court also takes a certain liberty when it asserts that "[w]hile not unanimous on all the principles governing extraterritorial application of the *Charter*, the Court was united on the principle that comity cannot be used to justify Canadian participation in activities of a foreign state or its agents that are contrary to Canada's international obligations." *Khadr, supra* note 1 at para. 18. In fact, Binnie J., in concurring reasons, explicitly declined to endorse such a proposition on the basis of the record and submissions before the Court in *Hape*. *Hape, supra* note 3 at paras. 186–88 (per Binnie J., concurring).

extraterritorial exercise of enforcement jurisdiction, coupled with the presumption of *Charter* conformity with Canada's international legal *obligations, required* a territorially limited interpretation of the *Charter*'s reach.[83] By contrast, the *non-binding* principle of comity merely provided additional support for the conclusion reached on the basis of Canada's binding international legal obligations.[84] And, being non-binding, it is not surprising (or controversial) that the majority in *Hape* should have concluded that the principle of comity must ultimately yield to respect for Canada's international legal obligations, including those of a human rights character.[85]

So while, as stated by the Court in *Khadr, Hape* recognized an exception to the non-binding principle of *comity*, it did not recognize an exception to the binding principles of *international law*, which, according to the majority, made extraterritorial application of the *Charter* legally impossible. It certainly did not hold that these international legal principles cease to be applicable, as with the principle of comity, whenever Canadian officials participate abroad in a process "violative of Canada's binding obligations under international law" — thus clearing the way for extraterritorial application of the *Charter*.[86] Yet that is precisely the effect of the rule asserted, without supporting argument, in the first sentence of paragraph 19 quoted earlier — and attributed by the Court simply to "*Hape*."[87]

Thus, it is submitted that the real exception to the *Hape* principle was not established in *Hape*, as intimated in the passage quoted earlier, but, rather, is an innovation of *Khadr* itself. The importance of the Court's finding in *Khadr* that Canadian officials participated in a US process that violated Canada's international legal obligations lies not in that finding's ouster of comity considerations (which are non-binding in any event). Its real significance is that it is apparently used by the Court to override binding international legal obligations that, according to *Hape*, forbid extraterritorial application of the *Charter*. The former is consistent with some *dicta* from *Hape;* the latter is not.

Why does this matter? What difference does it make whether the exception applied in *Khadr* was established in *Hape* (as intimated

---

[83] *Hape, supra* note 3 at paras. 40–46, 57–69.

[84] *Ibid.* at paras. 47–52, 96–101.

[85] *Ibid.* at paras. 50, 52, 101.

[86] *Khadr, supra* note 1 at para. 19.

[87] *Ibid.*

by the Court) or rather in *Khadr* itself, as long as the effect of the exception on the *Hape* principle is clear?

There are in fact several reasons for which the Court's approach to this issue is significant. First, and perhaps somewhat formally, it is submitted that the Court, as the ultimate authority on the legal meaning of the Canadian Constitution, has an obligation to explain its interpretations of the Constitution in general, and of the *Charter* in particular, in clear and transparent terms. In a constitutional democracy in which government and legislative action is subject to the review jurisdiction of the courts, the rule of law demands nothing less. Had the Court openly acknowledged in *Khadr* that it was modifying the *Hape* principle by articulating a new exception to it, it would naturally have been incumbent on the Court to provide some reasoned, intelligible, and persuasive basis for doing so. However, by purporting not to introduce, but merely to *apply*, an exception to the *Hape* principle already propounded in *Hape* itself, the Court effectively sidesteps the need to explain itself. Of course, this would not be problematic if the Court had indeed pioneered and justified the exception in *Hape*. Yet as seen earlier, this was not the case. The majority in *Hape* provided a plausible (albeit brief) explanation for why the non-binding principle of comity must yield to binding principles of international law.[88] It did not provide any explanation at all for, or even allude to, the proposition that binding principles of international law forbidding extraterritorial application of the *Charter* must yield to other binding principles of international law that may or may not be related to permissible extraterritorial exercises of enforcement jurisdiction. The result of this failure to explain the legal basis for such a proposition, in either *Hape* or *Khadr*, is to give the *Khadr* exception, whether desirable or justifiable or not, an air of arbitrariness that undermines its authority.[89]

The implications of such a failure are not merely formal, however; they are also substantive and practical. Substantively, the issue that naturally arises is *how* or *why* Canada's participation abroad, in a process that is inconsistent with its international legal obligations, leads to applicability of the *Charter* to that participation? It is submitted that among the many questions that would necessarily have to be answered in order to provide a satisfactory basis for such a rule are the following.

---

88 *Ibid.* at paras. 50, 52, 101.

89 For discussion of similar concerns arising from the majority judgment in *Hape*, *supra* note 3, see Currie, *supra* note 5 at 94–96.

First, given that the issue is the extraterritorial applicability of the *Charter,* and assuming that this issue should be resolved in a manner consistent with Canada's international legal obligations, why would any such obligations that do not address the extraterritorial scope of Canada's human rights commitments or its jurisdictional competence be relevant? The *Hape* principle, at least, rests on the Court's understanding of Canada's international legal obligations that have a bearing on its extraterritorial jurisdiction. These are sensible considerations in interpreting the *Charter's* geographic reach, in that the former might be breached by too broad an approach to the latter. In contrast, the *Khadr* exception apparently rests on Canada's international legal obligations *whether or not* they relate to Canada's extraterritorial competence. For example, in *Khadr,*[90] the Court relies on US breaches of the international human right of *habeas corpus*[91] as well as the right to be tried by a "regularly constituted court" under Common Article 3 of the 1949 Geneva Conventions.[92] While these international legal rights may be relevant in interpreting the substantive content of certain *Charter* guarantees,[93] how are they relevant in determining whether the *Charter* reaches their occurrence abroad?[94] Would they be further breached by a mere judicial determination that the *Charter* does not apply to their violation abroad? If not, why do they compel the conclusion that the *Charter* must in fact apply to such violations?

90 *Khadr, supra* note 1 at paras. 21–23.

91 See, *e.g.,* International Covenant on Civil and Political Rights, 16 December 1966, 999 U.N.T.S. 171, art. 9(4) (in force 23 March 1976; Article 41 entered into force 28 March 1979) [ICCPR].

92 Geneva Conventions, *supra* note 41.

93 Per the authorities collected in notes 72 and 73.

94 A distinction must be drawn between these rights and any correlative rules that may speak to states' obligations to respect them extraterritorially. These particular rights may indeed be attended by correlative state obligations to respect them beyond national territory. See, e.g., *Legal Consequences of the Construction of a Wall in the Occupied Palestinian Authority (Advisory Opinion),* [2004] I.C.J. Rep. 136 at paras. 108–11 (concluding at para. 111 that "the Court considers that the *International Covenant on Civil and Political Rights* is applicable in respect of acts done by a State in the exercise of its jurisdiction outside its own territory"); UN Human Rights Committee, *General Comment 31,* UN GAOR, 59th Sess., Supp. no. 40, vol. 1, UN Doc. A/59/40 (2004) at para. 12; UN Human Rights Committee, *Lopez v. Uruguay,* Communication no. 52/1979, UN Doc. CCPR/C/13//D//52/1979 (1981); C. Forcese, *National Security Law: Canadian Practice in International Perspective* (Toronto: Irwin Law, 2007) at 29–30. However, the Court's proposition is not limited to international legal obligations having such extraterritorial scope.

Second, in a confrontation between Canada's international legal obligations that purportedly compel it not to apply the *Charter* extraterritorially, on the one hand, and its international legal obligations that (for reasons not made clear by the Court) compel just such an extraterritorial application, on the other, why should the latter prevail? This is one of the central questions avoided by the Court in *Khadr* in characterizing the issue as a confrontation between the (non-binding) principle of comity and Canada's binding international legal obligations. And yet, as seen earlier, the Court's basis for the *Hape* principle rests primarily on respect for Canada's *binding* international legal obligations and not on mere comity considerations. So why does one set of binding international legal obligations yield to another, as necessarily implied by the *Khadr* exception?

Third, even assuming that violations of some of Canada's international legal obligations oust the constraining effects of other obligations that would otherwise exclude the *Charter*'s application abroad, why does it necessarily follow that the *Charter* in fact applies abroad? Presumably, such ouster would liberate the *Charter* from the constraints of the *Hape* principle, but it is unclear why the result should not therefore be a return to first principles. That is, in the absence of any textual guidance in the *Charter* itself and, *ex hypothesi*, of any international legal constraints on the *Charter*'s extraterritorial application, the question whether the *Charter should* apply to official acts abroad would remain to be addressed. The Court in *Khadr* seems to leap to the conclusion that it should, but it does not explain why. Should the starting position not rather be that, since neither the text of the *Charter* nor international law determines its extraterritorial applicability, some other basis or interpretive tool must be identified in order to resolve the issue one way or the other?

Fourth, why is the issue whether Canada has *participated in a process* that violates its international legal obligations, rather than, simply, whether it has violated such obligations? This way of structuring the test appears to move the crucial inquiry away from the actions of Canadian officials themselves and to focus it, instead, on foreign conduct. In *Khadr*, this shift leads the Court to devote virtually its entire analysis to an examination of whether "the process at

---

Rather, the *Khadr* exception refers to Canadian participation in foreign violations of "Canada's binding obligations under international law" without qualification, which must necessarily include those clearly limited to its own territory. See *Khadr, supra* note 1 at paras. 18–19.

Guantanamo Bay" rather than the conduct of Canadian officials — whether by way of their participation in that process or otherwise — "was a process that violated Canada's binding obligations under international law."[95] Two aspects of this "process" are deemed by the Court to be violations of "fundamental human rights protected by international law":[96] detention without access to the right of *habeas corpus*[97] and the procedural rules for US military commissions.[98] Yet at no point does the Court's inquiry lead it to ask whether Canada or Canadian officials are responsible for these violations, nor is it evident how they could possibly be. How could Canada be responsible for US executive orders denying access to the right of *habeas corpus* or adequate procedural protections in the US military commissions process? Is it meaningful to ask whether *foreign* conduct violates *Canada's* binding obligations under international law? What if the process, contrary to the facts in *Khadr,* is inconsistent with Canada's international legal obligations but does not violate the international legal obligations of the foreign state in question?[99] Is the purpose to determine whether it would have violated Canada's international legal obligations *had* the process been a Canadian one? If so, does there not have to be some examination

[95] *Khadr, supra* note 1 at para. 21.

[96] *Ibid.* at para. 24.

[97] *Ibid.* at para. 22.

[98] *Ibid.* at para. 23. Note that this mischaracterizes somewhat the USSC's finding in *Hamdan, supra* note 41. The USSC judgment ultimately turned on whether the military commission established by the US president to prosecute Hamdan had been authorized by Congress. The majority found that it had not because the relevant congressional enabling legislation required that such a commission be consistent with the "law of war." Part of the "law of war," Common Article 3 of the Geneva Conventions, *supra* note 41, requires that tribunals be "regularly constituted" pursuant to domestic law, and American law requires that some practical need to deviate from standard court-martial practice be demonstrated before a military commission is established. As no such demonstration had been made, the establishment of the commission did not comply with American law, which meant that the "regularly constituted" requirement of Common Article 3 was not met, the commission was thus not consistent with the "law of war" and, in turn, not authorized by the congressional enabling legislation (per Stevens J., for the Court, at 69–70, 72; per Kennedy J., concurring, at pp. 8–10). While a plurality went further and found that a number of the commission's procedural aspects departed from the procedural requirements of Common Article 3, the majority judgment limited itself to finding inconsistency with the *constitution,* rather than the *procedures,* of the commission.

[99] Might this not require some deference to the foreign process, assuming that process was consistent with the foreign state's international legal obligations?

of the meaning of "participation" and of the extent to which such participation by Canada in the process (rather than the process itself) violates Canada's international legal obligations? No such analysis is conducted by the Court. Rather, the Court simply asserts that making available the product of the CSIS interviews to US authorities, though possibly not the interviews themselves, amounts to Canadian participation in the process[100] and that "that participation … would be contrary to Canada's binding international obligations."[101] No reasons for this leap of logic are provided, nor is it self-evident why such sharing of information would be contrary to Canada's international obligations to grant access to the right of *habeas corpus* and adequate due process guarantees to persons detained or prosecuted by it.[102]

None of these questions are unanswerable, of course. While attempting to formulate and defend adequate answers to them all would exceed the scope and purpose of this comment, some preliminary suggestions may be made by way of illustration. For example, a possible answer to the first question might be that only those of Canada's obligations that require it to extend relevant international human rights protections beyond its borders will be relevant to the application of the *Khadr* exception. This approach would be most readily reconciled with the Court's jurisprudence calling for (varying degrees of) consistency between Canada's international legal obligations and interpretation of the *Charter*.[103] Another, more controversial, answer might be that, as the *Charter* is premised on the supremacy of the rule of law,[104] its application abroad is justifiable whenever necessary and useful in curtailing violations of Canada's international legal obligations, of whatever character.

The second question could conceivably be answered by resorting to some "hierarchy of norms" theory in international or even domestic constitutional law. For example, if the obligations in whose

---

100 *Khadr, supra* note 1 at para. 27.

101 *Ibid.* at para. 25.

102 This is particularly so given that, at the time of the sharing of information (to the end of 2004), Khadr was not subject to any military commission process, charges against him having only been laid in November 2005. At best, therefore, the process's violation of the "regularly constituted court" requirement of Common Article 3 of the Geneva Conventions, *supra* note 41, was purely prospective in Khadr's case at the time of Canadian "participation" therein.

103 See the authorities collected in notes 72 and 73.

104 *Charter, supra* note 2, preamble: "Whereas Canada is founded upon principles that recognize the *supremacy of … the rule of law*" [emphasis added].

violation Canada was found to be participating were of a *jus cogens* character, this might be argued to provide a basis for superseding the obligations underpinning the *Hape* principle, which arguably are not of a *jus cogens* character.[105] Or, less elaborately, it might be argued that more specific international legal obligations — for example, those relating to the protection of human rights — supersede those of a more general nature — for example, those respecting the sovereign equality of states or the territorial limits of enforcement jurisdiction.[106] In the alternative, a domestic rule of *Charter* interpretation might be deployed to resolve the conflict of norms. For example, there is arguable authority for the proposition that Canada's international human rights obligations are "relevant and persuasive" in interpreting the *Charter* but that Canada's international legal obligations of a non-human rights character may merely "inform" such interpretation.[107] If this difference of approach signals a hierarchy of the relevance of different classes of international legal obligations to *Charter* interpretation, it might resolve the clash of obligations apparently engendered by founding both the *Hape* principle and the *Khadr* exception to it on the same obligation to ensure respect for Canada's international legal obligations.

---

[105] See generally C. Tomuschat and J.M. Thouvenin, *The Fundamental Rules of the International Legal Order: Jus Cogens and Obligations Erga Omnes* (Leiden: Martinus Nijhoff, 2006).

[106] See, e.g., the International Law Commission's discussion of the *lex specialis* doctrine in its report on the fragmentation of international law. International Law Commission, "Conclusions of the Work of the Study Group on the Fragmentation of International Law: Difficulties Arising from the Diversification and Expansion of International Law," in *Report of the International Law Commission on the Work of its Fifty-Eighth Session*, U.N.G.A.O.R., 61st Sess., Supp. No. 10, UN Doc. A/61/10 (2006), II Yearbook of the International Law Commission (Part Two) at paras. 5–10. Such an analysis would remedy one of the principal failings of the majority opinion in *Hape, supra* note 3, which considered general principles of international law constraining the exercise of extraterritorial jurisdiction but failed to consider whether any of Canada's international legal obligations — for example, of a human rights character — might modify the applicability of those general principles in Canada's relations with the United Kingdom (which exercises sovereignty over the Turks and Caicos Islands, the location of the extraterritorial acts at issue). See further Currie, *supra* note 5 at 82–84.

[107] See *Burns, supra* note 73 at paras. 79–81 (international law is "of use" in interpreting the *Charter*, but international human rights law "*should* inform" and "*must be* relevant and *persuasive*" to such interpretation [emphasis added]); *Health Services, supra* note 72 at para. 70 ("the *Charter should be presumed* to provide at least as great a level of protection as is found in the *international human rights*

A possible answer to the third question might flow from the first answer to the first question suggested earlier. If application of the *Khadr* exception were limited to Canada's international legal obligations that require it to extend relevant international human rights protections beyond its borders, this, in itself, would be sufficient to justify interpreting the silence of section 32(1) of the *Charter* as being permissive. Another possible approach to resolving the question might simply be to resort to the general rule that, given its very nature, "large and liberal" interpretations of the *Charter*'s protections are called for.[108] In other words, in the absence of any textual or international legal constraints on applying the *Charter* to official acts abroad, why should it not reach such acts? Still another answer might be that in a constitutional democracy no exercise of public power should escape the reach of the constitution that authorizes it, such that to the extent government actors are competent to act abroad such actions should be consistent with the *Charter*.[109]

On the fourth question raised earlier, an obvious answer would seem to be that what is in fact relevant is whether *Canada*'s conduct, rather than a foreign process, is or was consistent with Canada's international legal obligations. Alternatively, if for some reason it is felt necessary to focus primarily on the international legality of the foreign process and only secondarily on that of Canada's participation in it, many of the concerns identified earlier could be addressed by defining "participation" in terms derived from the rules of attributability in the law of state responsibility.[110] For example, if

---

documents that Canada has ratified" [emphasis added]) and para. 20 (*"international law ... may inform* the interpretation of *Charter* guarantees" [emphasis added]).

108 *Hunter v. Southam*, [1984] 2 S.C.R. 145 at 156. See also *Big M Drug Mart, supra* note 79 at 344; *Reference Re British Columbia Motor Vehicle Act*, [1985] 2 S.C.R. 486 at 499; *Eldridge v. British Columbia*, [1997] 3 S.C.R. 624 at para. 53.

109 *Operation Dismantle v. The Queen*, [1985] 1 S.C.R. 441 at paras. 28, 38 (per Dickson C.J.) and paras. 50–67 (per Wilson J.).

110 See the International Law Commission's "Draft Articles on State Responsibility," in *Report of the International Law Commission on the Work of its Fifty-Third Session*, U.N.G.A.O.R., 56th Sess., Supplement No. 10 (A/56/10), c. IV.E.1, UN Doc. A/CN.4/L. 602/Rev. 1 (2001) [*Draft Articles*]. See also the *Commentaries to the Draft Articles on Responsibility of States for Internationally Wrongful Acts* in *ibid.*, c. IV.E.2 [*Commentaries*]. The *Draft Articles* and the ILC *Commentaries* accompanying them are also conveniently reproduced in J. Crawford, *The International Law Commission's Articles on State Responsibility: Introduction, Text and Commentaries* (Cambridge: Cambridge University Press, 2002).

Canada were to "acknowledge and adopt" the foreign process as its own,[111] or if this process were "placed at the disposal of" Canada by the foreign state,[112] this would establish an international legal connection between the international legal shortcomings of the foreign process and Canada's participation therein. It would also ground the key conclusion that Canada had thereby violated its international legal obligations and thereby exposed itself to *Charter* scrutiny.

The point here is not to promote any particular answer to the substantive questions raised by the *Khadr* exception but, rather, to underscore that such questions *are* raised by this exception and yet are *not* addressed in any way by the Court. In other words, very significant — though not insurmountable — legal and logical questions are raised by the *Khadr* exception as formulated by the Court. These questions require answers. Moreover, the foregoing exercise illustrates that answering these questions, whether in one of the ways suggested earlier or entirely differently, may have an impact on the nature and scope of the *Khadr* exception itself. For example, addressing the first question raised earlier in the manner first suggested may significantly narrow the scope of the *Khadr* exception. Yet this is precisely the substantive importance and benefit of requiring reasoned justification of such a judge-made rule of law. The need to defend a rule rationally rather than assert it arbitrarily may lead to a better understanding of its implications and, hence, beneficial modifications to its scope and application. In lieu of a seemingly arbitrary or axiomatic rule to be accepted in blind faith, a rule that is shown to mesh with the prevailing legal context and sound policy considerations may in fact respond more appropriately to the circumstances that call for its articulation in the first place.

Finally, the *practical* relevance of the Court's approach of purportedly applying an exception propounded in *Hape* is that it thereby implicitly affirms the *Hape* principle itself as the general rule. Indeed, it is a classic case of the exception proving the rule — giving the rule, moreover, the implicit stamp of approval of the whole Court rather than the bare majority it commanded in *Hape*. This is very much to be regretted in light of the serious shortcomings of the *Hape* principle and its underlying rationales, as outlined earlier.

Moreover, by failing squarely to acknowledge its creation of an exception to the *Hape* principle in *Khadr*, the Court is not compelled to address the underlying reasons for which such an exception

---

[111] *Draft Articles, supra* note 110, art. 11.

[112] *Ibid.*, art. 6.

might be needed in the first place. Had the Court done so, it is possible that it would also have had to face some of the more unsustainable implications of the *Hape* principle, as starkly illustrated on the facts of *Khadr.* It may seem of no great moment to deny the benefit of detailed protections against unreasonable search and seizure to a corrupt Canadian businessman carrying out money laundering activities abroad,[113] especially in the name of the noble principle of upholding international law. It is altogether another matter to realize that a rule justifying such a denial will also in principle deny *Charter* protections to a Canadian child detained, interrogated, and prosecuted by a foreign state, with Canadian government participation, in violation of some of the most fundamental international legal obligations to which Canada is a party as well as some of the *Charter*'s most basic guarantees. In short, the facts of *Khadr* expose the untenability in principle of the *Hape* ruling. Rather than face this untenability, the Court in *Khadr* effectively evades it by reading down *Hape* in a manner that superficially makes it appear less untenable. In doing so, the Court not only misses its chance to disavow the bare majority judgment in *Hape;* it also deepens the legal and logical morass currently governing, in the name of respect for Canada's international legal obligations, the extraterritorial applicability of the *Charter.*

Conclusions

On 21 May 2009, the Supreme Court of Canada dismissed an application for leave to appeal from a judgment of the Federal Court of Appeal in *Amnesty International Canada v. Chief of the Defence Staff for the Canadian Forces.*[114] In this case, Amnesty International Canada and the British Columbia Civil Liberties Association had sought a declaration from the Federal Court that sections 7, 10, and 12 of the *Charter* apply to detainees held by the Canadian Forces in Afghanistan as well as to transfers of those detainees to Afghan authorities. In this context, the applicants moved for a determination of the following questions:

1. Does the *Charter* apply during the armed conflict in Afghanistan to the detention of non-Canadians by the Canadian Forces or

---

[113] That is, the fact situation faced by the Court in *Hape, supra* note 3.

[114] *Amnesty International Canada v. Canada (Chief of the Defence Staff),* application for leave to appeal dismissed, 21 May 2009 (S.C.C.).

their transfer to Afghan authorities to be dealt with by those authorities?

2. If the answer to the above question is "no" then would the *Charter* nonetheless apply if the applicants were ultimately able to establish that the transfer of the detainees in question would expose them to a substantial risk of torture?

In the Federal Court, Justice Anne MacTavish answered both of these questions in the negative on the basis of *Hape* (*Khadr* having not yet been released by the Supreme Court of Canada).[115] The Federal Court of Appeal, rejecting the applicant's appeal after the Supreme Court of Canada's decision in *Khadr,* held that "*Khadr* has not changed the principles applicable to the concepts of territoriality and of comity set out by the Supreme Court of Canada in *Hape.*"[116] According to the Federal Court of Appeal, *Khadr* stood only for the proposition that "deference and comity end where clear violations of international law and fundamental human rights begin" but not "that the Charter then applies as a consequence of these violations."[117] Rather, "all the circumstances in a given situation must be examined before it can be said that the *Charter* applies."[118] Finding that the circumstances raised in *Amnesty International* differed from those in *Khadr* and *Hape,* the Court of Appeal accordingly affirmed MacTavish J.'s conclusion that the *Charter* had and could have no application to the actions of the Canadian Forces in Afghanistan.

Whatever else might be said about the reasoning of the Federal Court and Federal Court of Appeal in *Amnesty International,* it is at least of concern that the latter should interpret *Khadr* as neither amending the *Hape* principle nor providing for application of the *Charter* abroad in cases of "clear violations of international law and fundamental human rights."[119] How this can be so is difficult to understand. Still more difficult to understand is why the Supreme Court of Canada should have felt no need to clarify the law on this crucial point. As discussed earlier and, it is submitted, illustrated

[115] *Amnesty International v. Canada (Chief of the Defence Staff),* 2008 FC 336 (12 March 2008).

[116] *Amnesty International v. Canada (Chief of the Defence Staff),* 2008 FCA 401 (17 December 2008) at para. 9.

[117] *Ibid.* at para. 20.

[118] *Ibid.*

[119] *Khadr, supra* note 1 at para. 18.

by the judgments in *Amnesty International,* the *Hape/Khadr* regime for the determination of the applicability of the *Charter* to the acts of Canadian officials abroad is mired in legal and logical incoherence and uncertainty that cries out for rectification, or at least clarification, by the Court. In denying leave to appeal from the judgment of the Federal Court of Appeal in *Amnesty International,* the Supreme Court of Canada has foregone yet another opportunity to provide intelligibility and predictability to this critical intersection between Canada's constitutional and international legal obligations.

John H. Currie
Faculty of Law, University of Ottawa

Sommaire

Le virage *Khadr / Hape:* déterminations tourmentées de la portée extraterritoriale de la *Charte* canadienne

Ce commentaire discute de la décision de la Cour suprême du Canada dans l'affaire Khadr (mai 2008), dans laquelle la Cour énonce une exception au principe formulé dans l'arrêt Hape (juin 2007). Selon Hape, l'application de la Charte canadienne des droits et libertés (la Charte) à la conduite des fonctionnaires canadiens à l'étranger est "impossible." Selon Khadr, par contre, ce principe ne tient pas si cette conduite constitue une participation à un processus qui viole les obligations juridiques internationales du Canada. L'auteur applaudit ce rejet partiel du principe Hape qui, soutient-on, est mal fondé en droit international. Toutefois, l'auteur remet en question le refus de la Cour de s'adresser aux nombreux défauts de Hape ou de justifier de quelque façon l'exception qu'il affirme, de façon apparemment arbitraire, dans Khadr. Ces refus, on fait valoir, ne servent qu'à approfondir les incohérences juridiques et logiques qui caractérisent actuellement, au nom du respect des obligations juridiques internationales du Canada, les règles régissant l'applicabilité extraterritoriale de la Charte.

Summary

Khadr's Twist on *Hape*: Tortured Determinations of the Extraterritorial Reach of the Canadian *Charter*

This comment reviews the Supreme Court of Canada's May 2008 decision in Canada (Justice) v. Khadr, *in which the Court announced an exception to its June 2007 holding in* R. v. Hape. *Hape* held, *on international legal grounds, that application of the* Canadian Charter of Rights and Freedoms *to the acts of Canadian officials abroad is "impossible."* Khadr *held that this was not so if the acts of Canadian officials abroad amount to participation in a process that violates Canada's international legal obligations. The author welcomes this partial retrenchment of the* Hape *principle, which, it is argued, is ill-founded in international law. However, the author is also critical of the Court's failure to engage directly with* Hape*'s many flaws or to justify in any way the seemingly arbitrary exception to it propounded in* Khadr. *These failures, it is argued, serve only to deepen the legal and logical incoherencies that currently characterize, in the name of respect for Canada's international legal obligations, the rules governing the extraterritorial applicability of the* Charter.

Un nouveau chantier transatlantique: l'entente France-Québec sur la reconnaissance des qualifications professionnelles

E n marge du XIIᵉ Sommet de la Francophonie, le premier ministre du Québec et le président de la République française signaient dans la Vieille Capitale l'*Entente entre le Québec et la France en matière de reconnaissance mutuelle des qualifications professionnelles*[1] (ci-après *Entente France-Québec de 2008*). Le chef du gouvernement du Québec et le chef de l'État français sont convenus de mettre en place un système facilitant la libre circulation des personnes exerçant une profession ou un métier réglementé sur leur territoire respectif. Le ton solennel donné à la conclusion de cette entente internationale se voulait une réflexion du caractère ambitieux et innovateur de son objet, soit un renforcement significatif de la mobilité professionnelle entre le Québec et la France, la création d'un nouvel espace économique et l'approfondissement du dialogue transatlantique francophone.

Cette nouvelle entente internationale entre la France et le Québec s'ajoute à près d'une centaine d'ententes conclues au fil d'une longue tradition de coopération entre les deux parties, amorcée en 1964.[2] Les ententes aussi structurantes que l'*Entente France-Québec*

---

[1] Entente entre le Québec et la France en matière de reconnaissance mutuelle des qualifications professionnelles, 17 octobre 2008, No. référence 2008–12 (application: 17 octobre 2008) [ci-après Entente France-Québec de 2008], disponible en ligne à: <http://www.mri.gouv.qc.ca/fr/informer/ententes/pdf/2008–12.pdf>.

[2] Sur les relations France-Québec, voir généralement Serge Joyal et Paul-André Linteau, dir., *France, Canada, Québec: 400 ans de relations d'exception*, Montréal, Presses de l'Université de Montréal, 2008; Frédéric Bastien, *Le poids de la coopération: le rapport France-Québec*, Montréal, Québec-Amérique, 2006; Québec, Ministère des Relations internationales, *France-Québec. Portrait d'une relation en mouvement* par Sophie Niquette, Québec, Gouvernement du Québec, 2002; Frédéric Bastien, *Relations particulières: la France face au Québec après de Gaulle*, Montréal, Boréal, 1999.

de 2008 sont cependant moins fréquentes dans les relations internationales du Québec. Il faut probablement remonter à l'entente en matière de sécurité sociale conclue en 1979[3] pour retrouver un accord aussi dense et étendu entre Paris et Québec, car c'est un véritable système de reconnaissance mutuelle des qualifications professionnelles qui est institué par l'entente de 2008.

Le système franco-québécois de reconnaissance mutuelle des qualifications professionnelles mis en place sera d'abord situé dans le contexte général du régime de reconnaissance mutuelle des qualifications professionnelles de la Communauté européenne (CE), dont l'influence est significative, puis, plus spécialement, dans celui de la nouvelle politique internationale du Québec. Les grandes lignes du système seront ensuite esquissées, ce qui permettra de brosser un premier tableau de l'avancement de la mise en œuvre de l'Entente. Des observations sur quelques questions qui présentent un intérêt particulier seront finalement formulées, en ce qui concerne l'impact du nouveau système sur la protection du public, ainsi que sa licéité au regard du droit international économique.

LE CONTEXTE DE L'ENTENTE FRANCE-QUÉBEC DE 2008

L'INFLUENCE SIGNIFICATIVE DE L'APPROCHE DE LA COMMUNAUTÉ EUROPÉENNE

Le discours gouvernemental ne manque pas d'inspiration pour qualifier l'Entente France-Québec de 2008: "une entente sans précédent en matière de reconnaissance des qualifications professionnelles";[4] "une avancée concrète et sans précédent";[5] "[l'Entente]

---

3   Entente entre le gouvernement de la République française et le gouvernement du Québec en matière de sécurité sociale, 12 février 1979, No. référence 1979-02 (abrogée), disponible en ligne à: <http://www.mri.gouv.qc.ca/fr/informer/ententes/pdf/1979-02.pdf>. Cette entente a été remplacée par l'*Entente en matière de sécurité sociale entre le gouvernement du Québec et le gouvernement de la République française*, 17 février 2003, No. référence 2003-20 (entrée en vigueur: 1er novembre 2006), disponible en ligne à: <http://www.mri.gouv.qc.ca/fr/informer/ententes/pdf/2003-20.pdf>. Voir généralement Gérald Goldstein, "L'Entente France-Québec en matière de sécurité sociale," *Revue québécoise de droit international*, vol. 4 (1987), à la p. 203.

4   Québec, ministère des Relations internationales, Communiqué, "Mobilité des travailleurs. Signature d'une entente historique entre la France et le Québec" (17 octobre 2008), disponible en ligne à: <http://www.mri.gouv.qc.ca/fr/informer/salle_de_presse/communiques/textes/2008/2008_10_17.asp>.

5   *Ibid.*

ne représente rien de moins qu'une nouvelle liberté: la liberté de travailler, d'être reconnu, de créer et de pouvoir construire sans contraintes dans le pays ami";[6] "nous, Québécois et Français, sommes les premiers au monde à créer un nouvel espace de mobilité pour nos citoyens respectifs";[7] "nous savons déjà que cette ouverture fera date, constituant en effet une initiative unique."[8] Cette surenchère de qualificatifs ne doit pas voiler le modèle antérieur que constitue le régime communautaire de reconnaissance mutuelle des qualifications professionnelles.[9] Extrêmement sophistiqué au plan juridique et fort de longues années d'application dans les relations entre les États membres de la CE, ce dernier a influencé de manière significative l'entente Sarkozy-Charest. Sans rien enlever au nouveau système franco-québécois de reconnaissance mutuelle des qualifications professionnelles, le modèle antérieur de la CE permet d'aborder l'analyse du nouveau système d'une manière plus nuancée et plus éclairante.

Le raffinement du régime communautaire de reconnaissance mutuelle des qualifications professionnelles tient au fait que celui-ci s'inscrit dans un cadre juridique et institutionnel supranational, qui est défini par le Traité instituant la Communauté européenne[10] (ci-après Traité CE). Ce régime s'applique aux vingt-sept États membres de la CE, ainsi qu'aux trois autres États membres de l'Espace économique européen.[11] Les obligations internationales qui en

---

6 *Ibid.*

7 Québec, Assemblée nationale, *Journal des débats*, vol. 41, n° 4 (10 mars 2009), à la p. 139 (M. Jean Charest).

8 *Ibid.*, vol. 41, n° 16 (7 avril 2009), aux pp. 1537–47 (M. Pierre Arcand).

9 En toute justice, les documents gouvernementaux qui ne sont pas rédigés dans le feu de l'action emploient un ton nettement plus mesuré, contrairement aux communiqués de presse ou aux débats parlementaires. Par exemple, une brochure gouvernementale présente l'Entente France-Québec de 2008 comme "une première entre l'Europe et l'Amérique," ce qui est beaucoup plus juste et met en lumière son réel intérêt. Québec, ministère des Relations internationales, *La reconnaissance des qualifications professionnelles. Entente France-Québec. Une nouvelle passerelle entre la France et le Québec*, Québec, Gouvernement du Québec, 2008, disponible en ligne à: <http://www.mri.gouv.qc.ca/fr/pdf/Depliant_entente_qualif_prof_FrQc.pdf>.

10 Traité instituant la Communauté européenne, 25 mars 1957, 294 R.T.N.U. 16 (version consolidée publiée dans [2002] J.O.C.E. C 325/1) [ci-après Traité CE].

11 Accord sur l'espace économique européen, 2 mai 1992, 1803 R.T.N.U. 1, art. 31, 97–104 et annexe VIII (entrée en vigueur: 1er janvier 1994). Il s'agit de l'Islande, du Liechtenstein et de la Norvège. Un régime particulier de liberté de circulation des personnes s'applique en outre entre la Suisse et les États

découlent s'appliquent directement dans le droit national des États membres, en raison du principe de "l'effet direct"; ceux-ci sont par ailleurs obligés de transposer les directives communautaires pertinentes dans leur droit interne.[12] En outre, tout manquement à ses obligations par un État membre peut faire l'objet d'un recours par la Commission européenne ou un autre État membre auprès de la Cour de justice des Communautés européennes ou encore d'un recours privé devant les tribunaux internes de l'État fautif. Le régime communautaire a été mis en place en deux étapes: la première dite de "l'harmonisation négative" procède directement de l'application des dispositions du Traité CE; la seconde dite de "l'harmonisation positive" procède de l'adoption de directives par le législateur communautaire.

Harmonisation négative de la reconnaissance des qualifications professionnelles

Le droit communautaire primaire, qui est posé par le Traité CE, interdit toute discrimination fondée sur la nationalité d'un ressortissant d'un État membre. C'est en raison de cette interdiction que l'on parle d'harmonisation "négative." La règle du traitement national est posée concernant le droit d'établissement de tout ressortissant d'un État membre dans un autre État membre.[13] Cela signifie que la nationalité d'un ressortissant européen ne peut l'empêcher de s'installer dans un État membre, pour y exercer une activité professionnelle sur une base permanente. Mais cela signifie aussi que celui-ci reste tenu de remplir les autres conditions exigées

---

membres de la CE. Celui-ci étend de manière graduelle le régime communautaire de reconnaissance mutuelle des qualifications professionnelles aux relations Suisse-CE. Accord entre la Confédération suisse, d'une part, et la Communauté européenne et ses États membres, d'autre part, sur la libre circulation des personnes, 21 juin 1999 [2002], J.O.C.E. L 114/6, R.O. 2002 1529 (entrée en vigueur : 1er juin 2002).

12 Traité CE, *supra* note 12, art. 249; *Reyners c. Belgique*, 2–74, [1974] C.J.C.E. rec. 631, para. 32.

13 Traité CE, *ibid.*, art. 43. En droit communautaire, le droit d'établissement s'oppose à la libre prestation des services: le premier renvoie à l'établissement d'un prestataire de service dans un autre État que son État d'origine, pour y exercer son activité professionnelle sur une base permanente; la libre prestation des services renvoie au professionnel qui demeure établi dans son État d'origine, mais qui se rend dans un autre État pour y exercer son activité professionnelle sur une base temporaire, ou qui offre ses services à des destinataires situés dans un autre État sans se déplacer physiquement (*ibid.*, art. 49).

dans l'État d'accueil pour exercer la profession. Par exemple, si l'appartenance à un ordre professionnel national est exigée pour l'exercice d'une profession donnée, les ressortissants européens doivent en faire partie, tout comme les ressortissants de l'État d'accueil. Dans une cause célèbre, le refus par l'Ordre national des avocats de Belgique d'admettre un ressortissant néerlandais, qui avait reçu toute sa formation universitaire en Belgique, a été jugé contraire au droit d'établissement garanti par le Traité CE.[14]

Cette interdiction de principe de toute discrimination fondée sur la nationalité reste cependant soumise à une exception importante. Un État membre peut fermer l'accès à une profession aux ressortissants européens, si cette profession consiste en des activités participant, même à titre occasionnel, à "l'exercice de l'autorité publique."[15] La Cour de Luxembourg a déjà jugé que la profession d'avocat ne tombe pas sous la coupe de cette exception.[16] Jusqu'à tout récemment, l'on prenait pour acquis que la profession de notaire relevait, elle, de l'exception; toutefois la France et plusieurs autres États membres font actuellement l'objet d'un recours en manquement initié par la Commission européenne, qui conteste la fermeture de la profession de notaire dans ces États pour les ressortissants européens.[17]

Pour le reste, seules les mesures non-discriminatoires "excessives" ont été jugées interdites, au cas par cas, au regard du droit d'établissement garanti par le Traité CE. Les mesures non-discriminatoires interdites sont des mesures qui gênent ou rendent moins attrayant le droit d'établissement, d'une manière non nécessaire et disproportionnée.[18] L'exemple classique d'une mesure non-discriminatoire excessive est celui de l'interdiction d'avoir plus d'un centre d'activité dans la CE;[19] le droit d'établissement

---

[14] *Reyners, supra* note 12.

[15] Traité CE, *supra* note 10, art. 45.

[16] *Reyners, supra* note 12 aux paras. 54–55.

[17] *Commission c. France,* "Recours en manquement introduit par la Commission" (12 février 2008), C-50/08 [2008], J.O.U.E. C 128/18. Un recours semblable a aussi été initié par la Commission contre l'Allemagne (C-54/08), l'Autriche (C-53/08), la Belgique (C-47/08), la Grèce (C-61/08), le Luxembourg (C-51/08) et les Pays-Bas (C-157/09).

[18] *Gebhard c. Consiglio dell'Ordine degli Avvocati e Procuratori di Milano,* C-55/94 [1995], C.J.C.E. Rec. I-4165 aux paras. 33–37.

[19] Voir *Ordre des avocats au barreau de Paris c. Klopp,* 107/83 [1984], C.J.C.E. rec. 2971.

comporte donc le droit au "double établissement," c'est-à-dire le droit de s'établir dans plus d'un État membre. Il signifie aussi que les États membres ont l'obligation de prendre en considération l'équivalence des diplômes des ressortissants européens qui souhaitent s'établir sur leur territoire, pour y exercer une profession réglementée.[20] Du reste, les obstacles non-discriminatoires "non excessifs" ou "raisonnables" ne sont pas du tout levés par le Traité CE. Ce dernier ne prévoit pas la manière dont les États membres doivent procéder à l'examen de l'équivalence des qualifications professionnelles, ce qui signifie que cette prise en considération pourrait diverger d'un État à l'autre. Ceci explique pourquoi une action positive du législateur communautaire a été nécessaire, pour compléter l'harmonisation du droit d'établissement dans la CE.

Harmonisation positive de la reconnaissance des qualifications professionnelles

L'harmonisation positive de la reconnaissance des qualifications professionnelles s'est faite au moyen d'une panoplie de directives éparses, adoptées et modifiées sur plus d'une trentaine d'années. Cette constellation d'instruments communautaires, visant à faciliter le droit d'établissement prévu par le Traité CE, a fait l'objet d'une importante refonte en 2005, avec l'adoption de la directive 2005/36/CE.[21] Cette nouvelle directive unique, qui a remplacé l'ensemble des instruments antérieurs concernant la reconnaissance des qualifications professionnelles, n'apporte pas de modification fondamentale. Elle codifie plutôt l'acquis communautaire concernant toutes les professions et les métiers, en plus d'y greffer un nouveau régime général de libre prestation des services,[22] et d'y ajouter un processus facultatif d'harmonisation des formations.[23]

Dans ses premières directives d'harmonisation, le législateur communautaire a suivi une approche sectorielle assez fastidieuse dans les domaines de la santé et de l'architecture. Ces directives procédaient d'abord à *l'harmonisation* du contenu des formations nationales, pour ensuite instaurer un régime de reconnaissance

---

20 *Gebhard, supra* note 18, aux para. 38.

21 CE, *Directive 2005/36/CE du Parlement européen et du Conseil du 7 septembre 2005 relative à la reconnaissance des qualifications professionnelles* [2005], J.O. L 255/22, art. 53(3).

22 *Ibid.*, art. 5–9.

23 *Ibid.*, art. 15.

automatique des qualifications professionnelles.[24] En 1989, une nouvelle approche générale était introduite, avec l'adoption d'une directive unique pour l'ensemble des professions qui n'avaient pas encore fait l'objet d'une directive sectorielle.[25] Cette nouvelle approche se caractérise principalement par l'abandon du travail fastidieux d'harmonisation du contenu des formations nationales, ainsi que de l'automaticité de la reconnaissance mutuelle des qualifications

[24] CE, *Directive 77/452/CEE du Conseil, du 27 juin 1977, visant à la reconnaissance mutuelle des diplômes, certificats et autres titres d'infirmier responsable des soins généraux et comportant des mesures destinées à faciliter l'exercice effectif du droit d'établissement et de libre prestation de services* [1977], J.O.C.E. L 176/1; CE, *Directive 77/453/CEE du Conseil, du 27 juin 1977, visant à la coordination des dispositions législatives, réglementaires et administratives concernant les activités de l'infirmier responsable des soins généraux* [1977], J.O.C.E. L 176/8; CE, *Directive 78/686/CEE du Conseil, du 25 juillet 1978, visant à la reconnaissance mutuelle des diplômes, certificats et autres titres du praticien de l'art dentaire et comportant des mesures destinées à faciliter l'exercice effectif du droit d'établissement et de libre prestation de services* [1978], J.O.C.E. L 233/1; CE, *Directive 78/687/CEE du Conseil, du 25 juillet 1978, visant à la coordination des dispositions législatives, réglementaires et administratives concernant les activités du praticien de l'art dentaire* [1978], J.O.C.E. L 233/10; CE, *Directive 78/1026/CEE du Conseil, du 18 décembre 1978, visant à la reconnaissance mutuelle des diplômes, certificats et autres titres de vétérinaire et comportant des mesures destinées à faciliter l'exercice effectif du droit d'établissement et de libre prestation de services* [1978], J.O.C.E. L 362/1; CE, *Directive 78/1027/CEE du Conseil, du 18 décembre 1978, visant à la coordination des dispositions législatives, réglementaires et administratives concernant les activités du vétérinaire* [1978], J.O.C.E. L 362/7; CE, *Directive 80/154/CEE du Conseil, du 21 janvier 1980, visant à la reconnaissance mutuelle des diplômes, certificats et autres titres de sage-femme et comportant des mesures destinées à faciliter l'exercice effectif du droit d'établissement et de libre prestation de services* [1980], J.O.C.E. L 33/1; CE, *Directive 80/155/CEE du Conseil, du 21 janvier 1980, visant à la coordination des dispositions législatives, réglementaires et administratives concernant l'accès aux activités de la sage-femme et l'exercice de celles-ci* [1980], J.O.C.E. L 33/8; CE, *Directive 85/384/CEE du Conseil du 10 juin 1985 visant à la reconnaissance mutuelle des diplômes, certificats et autres titres du domaine de l'architecture et comportant des mesures destinées à faciliter l'exercice effectif du droit d'établissement et de libre prestation de services* [1985], J.O.C.E. L 223/15; CE, *Directive 85/432/CEE du Conseil du 16 septembre 1985 visant à la coordination des dispositions législatives, réglementaires et administratives concernant certaines activités du domaine de la pharmacie* [1985], J.O.C.E. L 253/34; CE, *Directive 85/433/CEE du Conseil du 16 septembre 1985 visant à la reconnaissance mutuelle des diplômes, certificats et autres titres en pharmacie, et comportant des mesures destinées à faciliter l'exercice effectif du droit d'établissement pour certaines activités du domaine de la pharmacie* [1985], J.O.C.E. L 253/37; CE, *Directive 93/16/CEE du Conseil, du 5 avril 1993, visant à faciliter la libre circulation des médecins et la reconnaissance mutuelle de leurs diplômes, certificats et autres titres* [1993], J.O.C.E. L 164/1.

[25] CE, *Directive 89/48/CEE du Conseil du 21 décembre 1988 relative à un système général de reconnaissance des diplômes d'enseignement supérieur qui sanctionnent des formations professionnelles d'une durée minimale de trois ans* [1989], J.O.C.E. L 19/16.

professionnelles. Le système général de reconnaissance instauré par la directive 89/48/CEE a été complété en 1992, par un système complémentaire de reconnaissance mutuelle des qualifications professionnelles, qui visait les métiers, c'est-à-dire les formations de courte durée ne nécessitant pas d'études universitaires.[26]

Malgré la refonte importante apportée par la directive 2005/36/CE, les lignes de force du régime communautaire de reconnaissance mutuelle des qualifications professionnelle demeurent les mêmes, qu'il s'agisse des systèmes régis par l'ancienne ou la nouvelle approche.[27] Les systèmes sectoriels dans les domaines de la santé et de l'architecture sont maintenus et sont toujours fondés sur l'harmonisation des formations nationales et la reconnaissance automatique des qualifications professionnelles.[28] Le système général de reconnaissance mutuelle des qualifications professionnelles est également reconduit, tout comme le système complémentaire pour les métiers.[29] C'est l'influence du système général qui est la plus apparente dans l'Entente France-Québec de 2008.

Plutôt que d'harmoniser les formations nationales, comme le font les systèmes sectoriels, le système général favorise le maintien de la diversité des formations à travers la CE, en s'appuyant sur le principe de la confiance mutuelle entre les États membres quant à *l'équivalence* des formations professionnelles offertes sur leur territoire respectif. Plutôt que de prévoir la reconnaissance automatique de l'équivalence des formations, comme le font aussi les systèmes

---

[26] CE, *Directive 92/51/CEE du Conseil, du 18 juin 1992, relative à un deuxième système général de reconnaissance des formations professionnelles, qui complète la directive 89/48/ CEE* [1992], J.O.C.E. L 209/24; CE, *Directive 1999/42/CE du Parlement européen et du Conseil du 7 juin 1999 instituant un mécanisme de reconnaissance des diplômes pour les activités professionnelles couvertes par les directives de libéralisation et portant mesures transitoires, et complétant le système général de reconnaissance des diplômes* [1999], J.O.C.E. L 201/77.

[27] Voir généralement Jacques Pertek, *Diplômes et professions en Europe*, Bruxelles, Bruylant, 2008; Christophe Fouassier, "Le système général de reconnaissance des diplômes: la confiance mutuelle et ses limites," *Revue des affaires européennes*, no. 1 (2005), à la p. 31; Jacques Pertek, dir., *La reconnaissance des qualifications dans un espace européen des formations et des professions*, Bruxelles, Bruylant, 1998; Jean-Marc Favret, "Le système général de reconnaissance des diplômes et des formations professionnelles en droit communautaire : l'esprit et la méthode," *Revue trimestrielle de droit européen*, nº 2 (1996), à la p. 259; Jacques Pertek, "La reconnaissance mutuelle des diplômes d'enseignement supérieur," *Revue trimestrielle de droit européen* (1989), à la p. 623.

[28] *Directive 2005/36/CE, supra* note 21, art. 21–49.

[29] *Ibid.*, art. 16–20.

sectoriels, le système général prévoit une *présomption juridique de comparabilité* des qualifications professionnelles.[30] Cette présomption n'est pas irréfragable et elle peut être renversée par l'État d'accueil, qui peut décider d'imposer des "mesures de compensation." Trois motifs peuvent justifier le renversement de la présomption de comparabilité des formations nationales. Il s'agit premièrement d'une différence d'au moins un an dans la durée de la formation entre l'État d'origine et l'État d'accueil; deuxièmement, de différences substantielles dans le contenu des formations respectives; troisièmement, de différences dans le domaine d'activités couvert par la profession dans chacun des États.[31]

Les mesures de compensation que l'État d'accueil peut imposer pour permettre au demandeur d'obtenir la reconnaissance de ses qualifications professionnelles peuvent consister soit en l'imposition d'un stage d'adaptation (d'une durée maximum de trois ans), soit d'épreuves d'aptitudes.[32] L'imposition des mesures de compensation doit être modulée selon le cas individuel de chaque demandeur, en application du principe de proportionnalité, en ce qui concerne particulièrement la prise en considération de l'expérience qu'il a acquise après avoir obtenu ses qualifications professionnelles. Le choix entre un stage ou une épreuve appartient en principe au demandeur, mais les professions juridiques font ici l'objet d'un traitement particulier, en raison du caractère sensible de la formation en droit national pour celles-ci. Le choix entre le stage d'adaptation ou l'épreuve d'aptitudes appartient dans ce cas à l'État d'accueil, et la mise en œuvre du système général indique que la majorité des États membres a opté pour l'imposition d'une épreuve d'aptitudes, en raison des différences substantielles dans la formation nationale, et ce, de manière systématique pour tous les avocats migrants.[33]

L'application systématique des épreuves d'aptitudes pour les avocats migrants a eu pour effet de détourner complètement l'esprit

---

[30] *Ibid.*, art. 13.

[31] *Ibid.*, art. 14.

[32] *Ibid.*

[33] Jacques Pertek, "Les professions juridiques et judiciaires dans l'Union européenne: libre circulation dans l'espace européen, reconnaissance mutuelle des qualifications, équivalence des autorisations nationales d'exercice," *Revue française de droit administratif,* no 3 (1999) à la p. 633; Katarzyna Gromek-Broc, "Le barreau européen franchit les frontières: vicissitudes de la directive d'établissement pour les avocats," *Recueil Dalloz,* no 8 (2001), à la p. 641.

du système général de reconnaissance des qualifications professionnelles. En vertu du principe de proportionnalité, l'imposition d'une telle épreuve devait être faite sur une base individuelle et modulée selon les lacunes dans la formation de chaque demandeur. En pratique, les États membres imposent systématiquement des épreuves d'aptitudes générales à tous les demandeurs étrangers, ce qui a eu pour résultat de créer un effet dissuasif chez les demandeurs potentiels, entravant sérieusement la mise en œuvre du système général à l'égard des avocats migrants.[34] Cette paralysie du système général a amené le législateur communautaire à créer un nouveau système de reconnaissance mutuelle pour le titre d'avocat, s'ajoutant au système général de reconnaissance des diplômes, destiné à faciliter la libéralisation de l'exercice de cette profession dans la CE.[35]

Dans l'hypothèse ou les qualifications professionnelles du demandeur sont reconnues, que ce soit en application de la présomption de comparabilité ou après qu'il ait subi avec succès les mesures correctrices, l'effet juridique de la reconnaissance est que ce dernier peut alors intégrer totalement la profession dans l'État d'accueil.[36] Le demandeur devra cependant remplir les autres exigences requises pour exercer la profession, comme le versement d'une cotisation, le maintien d'une moralité irréprochable, etc. Tout refus de la part d'un État d'accueil de reconnaître les qualifications professionnelles d'un demandeur doit pouvoir faire l'objet d'un recours juridictionnel de droit interne.[37]

Une nouvelle directive a été adoptée en 2006 afin de poursuivre la libéralisation de la prestation des services et du droit d'établissement.[38] La directive 2006/123/CE vise à éliminer les obstacles au

[34] Pertek, *ibid.* à la p. 634.

[35] CE, *Directive 98/5/CE du Parlement européen et du Conseil du 16 février 1998 visant à faciliter l'exercice permanent de la profession d'avocat dans un État membre autre que celui où la qualification a été acquise* [1998], J.O.C.E. L 77/36. Voir généralement Jacques Pertek, "L'Europe des professions d'avocat après la directive 98/5 sur l'exercice permanent dans un autre État membre," *Revue du Marché commun et de l'Union européenne,* n⁰ 445 (2001), à la p. 106; Matthew S. Podell, "When Zeal for European Unity Overcomes Common Sense: The Lawyers' Directive," *Boston College International & Comparative Law Review,* vol. 23 (1999), à la p. 57.

[36] *Directive 2005/36/CE, supra* note 21, art. 4 et 53. Les professionnels migrants doivent cependant avoir le droit additionnel de faire usage de leur titre d'origine, en plus du titre de l'État d'accueil (*ibid.,* art. 54).

[37] *Ibid.,* art. 51.

[38] CE, *Directive 2006/123/CE du Parlement européen et du Conseil du 12 décembre 2006 relative aux services dans le marché intérieur* [2006], J.O.U.E. L 376/36. Voir généralement Kerstin Peglow, "La libre prestation de services dans la directive

commerce des services qui ne sont levés ni par le Traité CE et l'interdiction des mesures non-discriminatoires excessives, ni par le régime communautaire de reconnaissance mutuelle des qualifications professionnelles. L'articulation juridique de cette nouvelle directive avec l'acquis communautaire est complexe, mais son objectif fondamental est clair: elle traduit la volonté de la CE de libéraliser davantage l'exercice des professions. La directive 2006/123/CE oblige les États membres à passer en revue et à justifier toutes les restrictions à l'exercice d'une profession qui subsistent sur leur territoire. Les obstacles qui sont visés sont par exemple la forme juridique sous laquelle un prestataire de service peut opérer, le nombre de salariés qu'il peut employer, la fixation de tarifs obligatoires pour des services professionnels, le maintien de catégories au sein d'une profession, etc. La directive "services" donnera donc l'impulsion à un vaste processus d'analyse de la réglementation de l'ensemble des professions à travers l'Europe.

En plus de transparaître de manière évidente du système franco-québécois de reconnaissance mutuelle des qualifications professionnelles mis en place par l'Entente France-Québec de 2008, l'influence significative du régime communautaire — du système général de reconnaissance en particulier — est aussi visible dans certaines dispositions de l'Entente, qui se réfèrent explicitement à la directive 2005/36/CE.[39] La terminologie employée par l'Entente, ainsi que son approche qui consiste à prévoir la reconnaissance mutuelle des qualifications, sans pour autant procéder à l'harmonisation des formations nationales, sont autant de manifestations de cette influence. Cette dernière est aussi reconnue de manière explicite dans certains documents gouvernementaux ou dans les débats parlementaires qui ont portés sur l'Entente.[40] Pour

---

n° 2006/123/CE: réflexions sur l'insertion de la directive dans le droit communautaire existant," *Revue trimestrielle de droit européen*, n° 1 (2008), à la p. 67; Stéphanie Francq et Olivier De Schutter, "La proposition de directive relative aux services dans le marché intérieur: reconnaissance mutuelle, harmonisation et conflit de lois dans l'Europe élargie," *Cahiers de droit européen*, (2005), à la p. 604.

39 Entente France-Québec de 2008, *supra* note 1, Annexe II, section I.

40 France, ministère des Affaires étrangères et Européennes, "Informations pratiques sur l'Entente France-Québec en matière de reconnaissance mutuelle des qualifications professionnelles," disponible en ligne à: <http://www.anaem.ca/entente.php>; Québec, ministère des Relations internationales, *La politique internationale du Québec: plan d'action 2006–2009. Rapport d'étape 2007–2008*, Québec, Gouvernement du Québec, 2009, à la p. 71, disponible en ligne à:

se réaliser, la transposition du régime communautaire dans les relations France-Québec a toutefois elle-même été catalysée par la
nouvelle politique internationale du Québec.

LA NOUVELLE POLITIQUE INTERNATIONALE DU QUÉBEC

L'entente Sarkozy-Charest s'inscrit pleinement dans la nouvelle
politique internationale du Québec,[41] qui a redéployé son action à
l'étranger autour de cinq axes prioritaires.[42] Cet *aggiornamento* suc-
cède à trois énoncés québécois de politique internationale antérieurs
à celui de 2006, qui datent respectivement de 1985, 1991 et 2001.[43]
L'amélioration de la libre circulation des professionnels et des gens
de métier cadre parfaitement dans l'un des axes de la nouvelle
politique, qui vise à favoriser la croissance et la prospérité du Québec. L'un des moyens envisagés pour atteindre cet objectif est de
développer le capital humain du Québec, en attirant notamment

---

<http://www.mri.gouv.qc.ca/fr/pdf/rapport_etape.pdf> [ci-après Québec,
Rapport d'étape 2007–2008]; Québec, Assemblée nationale, *Journal des débats*, vol.
41, n° 16 (7 avril 2009), aux pp. 1537–47 (Mme Louise Beaudoin).

41 Québec, ministère des Relations internationales, *La politique internationale du
Québec: la force de l'action concertée*, Québec, Gouvernement du Québec, 2006,
[ci-après *Politique internationale du Québec*], disponible en ligne à: <http://www.
mri.gouv.qc.ca/fr/pdf/Politique.pdf>.

42 Les cinq axes de la politique internationale du Québec sont: le renforcement
de la capacité d'action et d'influence de l'État; l'action en faveur de la croissance
et de la prospérité du Québec; la contribution à la sécurité du Québec et du
continent nord-américain; la promotion de l'identité et de la culture du Québec;
la contribution à l'effort de solidarité internationale. *Politique internationale du
Québec, ibid.* à la p. 23.

43 Voir Québec, ministère des Relations internationales, *Le Québec dans le monde: le
défi de l'interdépendance. Énoncé de politique de relations internationales*, Québec,
Gouvernement du Québec, 1985; Québec, ministère des Affaires internationales,
*Le Québec et l'interdépendance: le monde pour horizon. Éléments d'une politique d'affaires
internationales*, Québec, Gouvernement du Québec, 1991; Québec, ministère des
Relations internationales, *Le Québec dans un ensemble international en mutation:
plan stratégique 2001–2004*, Québec, Gouvernement du Québec, 2001. Voir généralement Jean-Roch Côté, "Une analyse discursive de trois énoncés québécois
de politique internationale," *Études internationales*, vol. 37 (2006), à la p. 121;
Luc Bernier, *De Paris à Washington: la politique internationale du Québec*, Sainte-Foy,
Presses de l'Université du Québec, 1996; Louis Bélanger, *Deux analyses sur l'évolution de la politique internationale du Québec, 1989–1992*, Sainte-Foy, Université
Laval, Institut québécois des hautes études internationales, 1996. Louis Balthazar
et al., *Trente ans de politique extérieure du Québec: 1960-1990*, Sillery, Septentrion,
1993; Paul Painchaud, dir., *Le Canada et le Québec sur la scène internationale*, Montréal, Presses de l'Université du Québec, 1977.

davantage d'immigrants qualifiés et en facilitant leur intégration à la vie économique québécoise. La reconnaissance des compétences et des diplômes est désignée comme l'instrument privilégié de cette intégration.[44] L'Entente France-Québec de 2008 concrétise donc les ambitions du Québec à cet égard et entend contribuer à la réalisation d'un objectif fondamental de sa politique internationale.

L'importance pour le Québec de faciliter la mobilité de la main d'œuvre s'explique entre autres par la nécessité de maintenir son équilibre démographique avec des immigrants qualifiés, qui pourront répondre aux besoins du marché du travail. De plus, dans une économie du savoir fondée sur la formation de la main d'œuvre, le Québec a tout intérêt à tirer profit des individus formés à l'étranger qui vivent sur son territoire. Un système attractif de reconnaissance des qualifications professionnelles pourrait également être un vecteur de recrutement de chercheurs et de spécialistes étrangers. Cette ouverture des professions et métiers réglementés aux étrangers doit bien sûr se conjuguer avec la protection du public. C'est d'abord à l'aulne de cet impératif que doivent se mesurer les initiatives de libéralisation de leur exercice. Elles doivent également être compatibles avec les obligations internationales qui s'appliquent aux parties dans le domaine économique.

Des initiatives visant à faciliter l'intégration des immigrants à la vie économique québécoise avaient déjà été prises en 2005, pour préparer le terrain à la reconnaissance de leurs diplômes et de leurs compétences.[45] Par exemple, les conditions de délivrance des permis d'exercice d'une profession ont été assouplies par une modification législative, pour permettre aux ordres professionnels de créer de nouvelles catégories de permis mieux adaptées à la situation des candidats formés à l'étranger.[46] Les ordres professionnels ont également été invités par le gouvernement du Québec à passer en revue leurs pratiques afin d'identifier les éventuels obstacles à l'accès aux professions réglementées. Enfin, le gouvernement a aussi entrepris d'élargir l'accès des immigrants aux formations d'appoint prescrites par les ordres professionnels. L'Entente France-Québec de 2008 constitue donc une nouvelle étape dans un processus déjà entamé, qui profite du cadre et de l'élan donné par la nouvelle politique internationale du Québec.

[44] *Politique internationale du Québec, supra* note 41 à la p. 56.

[45] *Ibid.*

[46] *Loi modifiant le Code des professions concernant la délivrance de permis*, L.Q. 2006, c. 20.

La conclusion d'ententes internationales avec des organismes réglementaires ou des établissements d'enseignement à l'étranger, est l'une des mesures envisagées explicitement par le gouvernement du Québec dans le plan d'action qui accompagne sa politique internationale.[47] Ces ententes sont destinées à permettre la réalisation des objectifs fixés par la politique internationale, en créant des passerelles entre ordres professionnels québécois et étrangers pour accélérer le processus de reconnaissance des compétences des immigrants. Le plan d'action ne prévoit pas de manière générale la conclusion d'ententes directement avec un État étranger, ni de manière spécifique la conclusion d'une entente avec la France. L'approche horizontale et intégrée de l'entente Sarkozy-Charest semble avoir dépassé les ambitions originales du Québec à cet égard, en proposant un cadre global pour le règlement de la question de la reconnaissance mutuelle des qualifications des personnes exerçant des professions ou des métiers réglementés au Québec ou en France.

Même s'il n'est pas prévu explicitement par le plan d'action du Québec, le choix de la France comme premier partenaire pour la conclusion d'une telle entente internationale n'est guère étonnant. Partenaire privilégié de l'action internationale du Québec depuis ses origines, la France occupe une place unique dans la politique internationale du Québec.[48] Leur relation a atteint une maturité telle qu'ils cultivent maintenant des liens étroits dans pratiquement tous les secteurs d'activité. Aire d'action prioritaire du Québec,[49] la France lui permet par ailleurs de puiser dans un bassin important d'immigrants qualifiés francophones. La préservation de l'identité québécoise étant l'une des missions premières du gouvernement du Québec, la facilitation de l'intégration d'immigrants provenant de la France contribue en outre à renforcer la pérennité de la langue française, caractéristique au cœur de la spécificité québécoise.

Dans son préambule, l'Entente rappelle justement qu'elle se fonde sur la confiance réciproque existant entre la France et le Québec, confiance qui s'incarne notamment par la tradition de

---

[47] Québec, ministère des Relations internationales, *La politique internationale du Québec: plan d'action 2006–2009*, Québec, Gouvernement du Québec, 2006, à la p. 55, disponible en ligne à: <http://www.mri.gouv.qc.ca/fr/pdf/plan_action.pdf>.

[48] *Politique internationale du Québec*, *supra* note 41 à la p. 33.

[49] *Ibid.* à la p. 107.

coopération universitaire et de mobilité étudiante qui les unit.[50]
C'est sur la base de cette confiance qu'est mis en place le système
franco-québécois de reconnaissance mutuelle des qualifications
professionnelles.

LA MISE EN PLACE D'UN SYSTÈME FRANCO-QUÉBÉCOIS DE
RECONNAISSANCE MUTUELLE DES QUALIFICATIONS PROFESSIONNELLES

UNE APPROCHE GLOBALE ET INTÉGRÉE

L'Entente France-Québec de 2008 vise à faciliter l'établissement
permanent sur le territoire d'une partie de professionnels ou gens
de métier qualifiés sur le territoire de l'autre partie. Cet établissement est facilité par la simplification du processus de reconnaissance des qualifications professionnelles entre les parties, et signifie
que le candidat pourra intégrer totalement la profession ou le
métier sur le territoire où il veut s'installer.[51] Si elle participe de la
même idée, l'Entente ne fait cependant pas naître un véritable
"droit d'établissement" juridiquement contraignant à charge des
parties, comme il en existe un dans la CE.[52] Elle ne vise pas non
plus la question de la libre prestation des services, entendue au sens
de l'exercice temporaire de sa profession ou de son métier sur un
autre territoire que celui sur lequel une personne est établie, question faisant également l'objet de garanties juridiques dans la CE.[53]
Enfin le système franco-québécois mis en place ne touche pas du
tout aux questions relatives à l'immigration, au droit de séjour et
au permis de travail.[54] Pour reprendre les mots du professeur Jacques Pertek, l'Entente vise à fournir les clés de deux des trois verrous
qui bloquent le libre exercice d'une profession ou d'un métier au

---

[50] Entente France-Québec de 2008, *supra* note 1, préambule, 3e para.

[51] *Ibid.*, art. 6.

[52] Voir *supra* note 13 et le texte correspondant.

[53] *Ibid.*

[54] Entente France-Québec de 2008, *supra* note 1, art. 10. Il faut rappeler que plusieurs de ces questions relèvent de la compétence fédérale au Canada et échap-
peraient de toute façon aux compétences du Québec, à l'exception notable de
la sélection des immigrants, qui est une compétence mixte et fait l'objet d'arrangements intergouvernementaux. *Loi constitutionnelle de 1867* (R.-U.) 30 & 31
Vict., c. 3, reproduite dans L.R.C. 1985, app. II, n° 5, art. 92(25) et 95; Henri
Brun, Guy Tremblay et Eugénie Brouillet, *Droit constitutionnel*, 5e éd., Cowansville,
Yvon Blais, 2008, aux pp. 521–24; Peter W. Hogg, *Constitutional Law of Canada*,
feuilles mobiles, Thomson, Toronto, 2007, aux paras. 26.1, 26.2 et 46.1(b).

Québec ou en France: elle interdit les exigences de nationalité et elle facilite la satisfaction des conditions nationales de qualifications professionnelles applicables.[55]

Les professions et métiers visés sont tous ceux dont l'exercice est réglementé au Québec ou en France, ce qui couvre à la fois ceux dont les actes sont réservés exclusivement à leurs membres et ceux dont seulement le port d'un titre leur est réservé.[56] Il faut exclure de cette intégration de principe les "Officiers publics et ministériels" que les parties ont explicitement choisi de soustraire du système franco-québécois. La profession notariale est exclue de part et d'autres, tandis que la France exclut en outre les professions d'administrateur et mandataire judiciaires, d'avocat au Conseil d'État et à la Cour de cassation, d'avoué, de commissaire-priseur judiciaire, de greffier des tribunaux de commerce et d'huissier de justice.[57] L'éventail des professions soumises au système est donc légèrement plus large au Québec, mais les conséquences pratiques de ce déséquilibre semblent négligeables. La profession d'huissier de justice ne sera vraisemblablement pas libéralisée par le Québec sans réciprocité — faute d'homologue avec qui négocier — alors que les autres professions françaises exclues ne sont pas réglementées spécifiquement au Québec, comme les commissaires-priseurs judiciaires ou n'y ont pas d'équivalent direct, comme les avocats au Conseil d'État ou à la Cour de cassation et les autres professions juridiques françaises exclues.

La libéralisation de l'exercice des professions et métiers visés n'est pas opérée directement par l'Entente; cette dernière pose plutôt un cadre global et intégré devant orchestrer ce processus. L'opération est en réalité déléguée aux "autorités compétentes" respectives des parties, c'est-à-dire à leurs organismes de réglementation professionnelle, qui sont enjoints de déterminer si la conclusion d'un "arrangement de reconnaissance mutuelle" (ARM) est possible.[58] Cet exercice auquel sont conviés les organismes québécois et français est étroitement encadré par une "procédure commune" qui

---

[55] Pertek, *supra* note 33 aux pp. 625–26. Le troisième verrou auquel l'Entente ne touche pas est celui, déjà mentionné, des conditions générales d'entrée et de séjour sur le territoire national qui sont fixées par les États.

[56] *Entente France-Québec de 2008*, *supra* note 1, art. 4 et Annexe I, section I, para. 1.

[57] *Ibid.*, Annexe II, section II.

[58] *Ibid.*, art. 1. La liste exhaustive des autorités compétentes visées est dressée à l'annexe II de l'*Entente*. Pour la partie québécoise, il s'agit entre autres des 44 ordres professionnels régis par le *Code des professions*, à l'exception de la

doit être appliquée selon un échéancier strict.[59] L'exercice consiste essentiellement à examiner les équivalences entre les qualifications professionnelles et à prévoir à l'avance les étapes à franchir pour obtenir la reconnaissance de ses qualifications par une autre partie, l'idée étant de réduire les embûches au strict minimum. Si les organismes estiment que la conclusion d'un ARM est possible au terme de l'exercice, ils ont l'obligation de convenir d'un tel texte avec leur homologue, alors qu'il leur est au contraire interdit de le faire si leur conclusion à cet égard est négative.[60] Les autorités compétentes conservent ainsi une marge de manœuvre importante dans le processus de libéralisation, et l'obligation qui leur est imposée est celle de se prêter à l'exercice de déterminer si la conclusion d'un ARM est opportune et de conclure un ARM dans l'affirmative, en suivant la procédure commune, alors que l'obligation qui pèse sur le Québec et la France est celle de prendre tous les moyens à leur disposition pour que les autorités compétentes remplissent leur propre obligation de moyen.[61]

Puisque les organismes de réglementation compétents sont enjoints de mettre en œuvre l'Entente, celle-ci ne semble contenir aucune disposition qui puisse être directement invocable par les particuliers d'une partie qui voudraient bénéficier — à supposer que le droit constitutionnel d'une partie le permette — immédiatement de la reconnaissance de leurs qualifications professionnelles

---

Chambre des notaires du Québec. *Code des professions*, L.R.Q., c. C-26, Annexe I. Pour la partie française, il s'agit d'un emprunt à la liste des autorités compétentes dressées en vertu du régime communautaire de reconnaissance mutuelle des qualifications professionnelles. Voir *Directive 2005/36/CE, supra* note 21, art. 53(3).

59 Entente France-Québec de 2008, *supra* note 1, art. 5, Annexe III. L'échéancier de la libéralisation de l'exercice des professions et métiers réglementés est réparti en deux listes, dont la première comprend les professions et métiers prioritaires pour lesquels des ARM doivent être négociés avant le 31 décembre 2009, et la seconde comprend les autres dont la libéralisation est moins urgente, puisque les ARM doivent être négociés avant le 31 mars 2010 ou toute autre date déterminée par le Comité bilatéral. Il faut souligner que le langage employé par l'Entente semble préjuger de la conclusion des autorités compétentes quant à l'opportunité de conclure un ARM, alors qu'elle leur laisse pourtant la liberté de juger de cette opportunité au moyen de la procédure commune (*Ibid.*, art. 5). Parmi les professions prioritaires, il faut mentionner celles d'architecte, d'arpenteur-géomètre, d'avocat, de comptable, de dentiste, d'ingénieur, de médecin, de pharmacien et de travailleur social.

60 *Ibid.*, art. 5, Annexe I, art. 6, 12–13.

61 *Ibid.*, art. 1.

dans l'autre partie.[62] L'Entente ne semble faire naître aucun droit individuel puisqu'elle est explicitement destinée à être mise en œuvre au moyen d'ARM et de modifications à être apportées aux législations française et québécoise et de mesures réglementaires et administratives.[63]

L'approche globale et intégrée de l'Entente France-Québec de 2008 se matérialise non seulement sur le plan matériel, mais aussi sur le plan institutionnel. Un Comité bilatéral est institué avec la mission de veiller à la bonne marche du système franco-québécois de reconnaissance mutuelle des qualifications professionnelles.[64] Il est spécialement chargé de fournir des avis consultatifs sur les projets d'ARM soumis par les autorités compétentes et de documenter les flux de professionnels et de gens de métiers induits par l'Entente.[65] Le Comité bilatéral doit aussi faire annuellement rapport aux gouvernements du Québec et de la France sur la mise en œuvre de l'Entente, rapport dont copie doit être déposée pour information à la Commission permanente de coopération franco-québécoise, ce qui parachève le caractère global et intégré du système mis en place. Pour avoir une vue complète de ce système, il est cependant indispensable de se pencher sur la procédure commune que les autorités compétentes doivent suivre en vue de conclure des arrangements sectoriels et de mettre véritablement le système en application.

---

62 Il s'agit d'une différence importante avec le régime de reconnaissance des qualifications professionnelles de la Communauté européenne, où les dispositions pertinentes du traité de Rome jouissent de l'effet direct et où le défaut de la France d'avoir transposé la directive sur le droit d'établissement des avocats dans les délais prescrits a, par exemple, permis aux particuliers de l'invoquer directement devant les tribunaux français pour bénéficier de ses dispositions, malgré l'inexistence d'une loi de transposition. Voir *supra* note 12 et le texte correspondant; *Van Binsbergen c. Bestuur van de Bedrijfsvereninging Metaalnijverheid*, C-33/74 [1974], Rec. C.J.C.E. 1299; C.A. Pau, 21 mai 2001, D. 2002.Jur.121 (note de Bernard Blanchard).

63 Entente France-Québec de 2008, *supra* note 1, préambule, 6e para., art. 1–2.

64 *Ibid.*, art. 8, Annexe IV. Le Comité bilatéral doit se réunir au moins une fois par année et il est composé d'un coprésident de rang ministériel de chaque partie, accompagné chacun de cinq autres représentants. Un secrétariat composé de deux sections et dirigé par deux secrétaires généraux fournit un soutien administratif au Comité bilatéral.

65 La procédure commune prévue par l'Entente pour encadrer sa mise en œuvre par les autorités compétentes leur impose l'obligation de soumettre au Comité bilatéral tout projet d'ARM pour avis consultatif. Le Comité doit également être informé de tout ARM conclus par les autorités compétentes. Entente France-Québec de 2008, *ibid.*, Annexe I, section II, art. 17 et 18. Voir *infra* note 77 et le texte correspondant pour une discussion sur la procédure commune.

LE CHAMP D'APPLICATION DE LA PROCÉDURE COMMUNE
ET DU SYSTÈME FRANCO-QUÉBÉCOIS

Les organismes de réglementation professionnelle ont l'obligation de suivre la procédure commune prévue par l'Entente pour déterminer l'opportunité de conclure un ARM avec leur homologue de l'autre partie, ainsi que pour orienter le contenu de cet arrangement sectoriel. Trois conditions sont fixées pour déterminer si la procédure commune peut être appliquée par les autorités compétentes, mais l'Entente manque de clarté à cet égard.

Double réglementation du métier ou de la profession

Premièrement, il est indispensable qu'une profession ou un métier fasse l'objet d'une réglementation dans les deux parties pour que les autorités compétentes soient obligées d'appliquer la procédure commune et puissent conclure un ARM.[66] Ce principe de la double réglementation signifie que lorsqu'une profession ou un métier fait l'objet d'une réglementation dans une seule partie, l'autorité compétente pertinente n'est soumise à aucune obligation par l'Entente. Toutefois, le Québec et la France sont alors soumis à une obligation moindre de coopérer afin de faciliter la reconnaissance des qualifications professionnelles sur le territoire qui réglemente la profession ou le métier, en s'inspirant de la procédure commune.[67] L'Entente n'oblige donc nullement une partie à déréglementer l'exercice d'une profession parce que celle-ci ne serait pas réglementée par l'autre partie, au nom d'un principe du plus petit dénominateur commun. Le Comité bilatéral aura sans doute un rôle important à jouer dans un tel cas et il sera certainement l'instrument de mise en œuvre de cette obligation de coopération.

Problème de la territorialité des qualifications professionnelles

Les deuxièmes et troisièmes conditions posées par l'Entente, pour déterminer si une autorité compétente doit appliquer la procédure

---

66 Entente France-Québec de 2008, *ibid.*, art. 5a). À la lumière de cette première condition d'application de la procédure commune, il semble que l'exclusion par la France des professions juridiques non réglementées spécifiquement au Québec n'aurait pas été nécessaire, puisque la conclusion d'un ARM serait de toute façon interdite à leur égard. Voir *supra* note 57 et le texte correspondant.

67 *Ibid.*, art. 9. Par l'exclusion des professions juridiques non réglementées spécifiquement au Québec, mentionnée ci-dessus, la France aura voulu les soustraire complètement au système franco-québécois et surtout à cette obligation de coopération.

commune pour éventuellement conclure un ARM, sont sibyllines à deux égards. Il est prévu que le titre de formation visé par la reconnaissance mutuelle doit avoir été obtenu d'une "autorité reconnue de la France ou du Québec *sur leurs territoires* respectifs," et que l'aptitude légale d'exercer une profession ou un métier "est en vigueur et a été obtenue *sur le territoire* de la France ou du Québec."[68] La somme du titre de formation et de l'aptitude légale à exercer une profession ou un métier réglementé constitue les qualifications professionnelles d'un individu au sens de l'Entente.

Le premier aspect équivoque de ces dispositions est la question de savoir si ces conditions sont cumulatives ou non: le diplôme *et* le permis d'exercice doivent-ils avoir été tous deux obtenus au Québec ou en France? Dans l'affirmative, l'individu qui aurait obtenu son diplôme à l'extérieur du Québec ou de la France, mais qui aurait néanmoins réussi à y intégrer une profession ou un métier réglementé serait-il exclu du champ d'application de l'Entente? La question n'est pas que théorique, puisque la réalité de la mobilité étudiante et professionnelle en Europe veut qu'il soit possible pour un individu d'obtenir son diplôme à l'extérieur de la France, pour ensuite y intégrer une profession ou un métier réglementé, à l'aide du régime communautaire de libre circulation des diplômes et des professions par exemple. L'adéquation avec la réalité de la mobilité étudiante au Québec se pose aussi, puisqu'il est possible qu'un individu ait acquis son diplôme ailleurs qu'au Québec et y ait ensuite intégré une profession: si les deux conditions précitées sont cumulatives, un tel cas est-il exclu du système franco-québécois de reconnaissance mutuelle des qualifications professionnelles?

Pour ne prendre qu'un exemple, les individus détenant un diplôme de premier cycle en droit délivré — à l'extérieur du Québec — par l'Université d'Ottawa sont automatiquement admissibles pour devenir membre du Barreau du Québec et y intégrer la profession d'avocat, au même titre que les individus détenant un tel diplôme délivré par une université québécoise.[69] Si les conditions de détenir un diplôme et un permis d'exercice provenant du Québec ou de la France sont cumulatives, cela semble devoir signifier que les avocats québécois diplômés de l'Université d'Ottawa sont exclus du système franco-québécois de reconnaissance mutuelle des diplômes.

---

[68] *Ibid.*, art. 5(b) et (c) [soulignés de l'auteur].

[69] *Loi sur le Barreau*, L.R.Q., c. B-1, art. 44; *Règlement sur la formation professionnelle des avocats*, R.Q., c. B-1, r.7.3, art. 5(2); *Règlement sur les diplômes délivrés par les établissements d'enseignement désignés qui donnent droit aux permis et aux certificats de spécialistes des ordres professionnels*, R.Q., c. C-26, r.1.1, art. 1.03.

Puisque la satisfaction de la première condition concernant le principe de la double réglementation semble devoir être impérative, et en l'absence des conjonctions "et" ou "ou," qui préciseraient la coordination entre ces conditions, il semble qu'il faille conclure que ces conditions sont cumulatives. Si c'est le cas, la raison de l'obligation que le diplôme ait été obtenu d'une autorité reconnue de la France ou du Québec sur leurs territoires respectifs demeure obscure. Pourquoi ne pas s'être contenté d'exiger que le permis d'exercice ait été obtenu au Québec ou en France? Les parties ont-elles voulu exclure les individus y ayant intégré une profession sans y avoir obtenu leur diplôme? Le seul cas qui semble échapper à cette exclusion serait celui de l'individu ayant obtenu son diplôme au Québec et ayant intégré la profession en France ou vice-versa. La mise en œuvre de l'Entente devrait apporter des réponses à ces questions, mais il est probable que des clarifications, voire des modifications, seront nécessaires.

La portée du caractère probablement cumulatif des deuxièmes et troisièmes conditions d'application de la procédure commune pourrait, cependant, être atténuée par une interprétation plus libérale du territoire d'obtention du titre de formation. D'une part, la disposition générale de l'Entente qui prévoit les trois conditions d'application de la procédure commune parle clairement du titre de formation "obtenu d'une autorité reconnue de la France ou du Québec sur leurs territoires respectifs"[70] elle insiste sur le fait que le diplôme doit avoir été obtenu d'une institution d'enseignement située sur le territoire québécois ou français. D'autre part, la définition du terme "titre de formation" prévue dans l'annexe de l'Entente dispose qu'il s'agit de tout diplôme "délivré par une autorité reconnue *ou désignée* par la France ou le Québec"[71]; cette disposition particulière ne comporte aucune référence au territoire sur lequel a été obtenu le diplôme, mais insiste plutôt sur le fait qu'il doit avoir été obtenu d'une institution d'enseignement reconnue ou désignée par la France ou le Québec, ce qui pourrait être suffisamment large pour inclure les diplômes étrangers reconnus par la France ou le Québec. Dans un tel cas, le caractère cumulatif des deuxièmes et troisièmes conditions serait moins problématique, puisque les diplômes étrangers reconnus par la France ou le Québec, et ayant permis à leur titulaire d'y intégrer une profession ou un métier réglementé, seraient couverts par le système franco-québécois.

[70] Entente France-Québec de 2008, *supra* note 1, art. 5.
[71] *Ibid.*, Annexe I, section I, para. 2 [soulignés de l'auteur].

Comment réconcilier ces définitions, qui semblent contradictoi-
res? La disposition particulière peut-elle l'emporter sur la disposition
générale, au point de gommer la référence expresse au territoire
sur lequel a été obtenu le diplôme? Il est permis d'en douter.[72] Si
cette référence au territoire où a été obtenu le diplôme devait être
gommée, cela signifierait-il que le système franco-québécois serait
aussi ouvert aux diplômes étrangers reconnus à l'avance dans la
réglementation — comme c'est le cas des diplômes en droit de
l'Université d'Ottawa — ainsi qu'aux diplômes étrangers reconnus
a posteriori de manière *ad hoc*? Cela signifierait-il plutôt qu'il est
seulement ouvert aux diplômes étrangers reconnus à l'avance?
Cette confusion se répercute dans la mise en œuvre de l'Entente
jusqu'à maintenant, puisque la pratique des organismes de réglementation professionnelle est divergente. Alors que certains ARM
comportent une exigence de territorialité québécoise ou française
du diplôme, comme la disposition générale, d'autres ARM n'en
comportent pas, comme la disposition particulière. Il est donc à
prévoir que le Comité bilatéral sera appelé à se pencher sur cette
question assez rapidement.

Le deuxième aspect équivoque des deuxièmes et troisièmes
conditions d'application de la procédure commune — détenir un
diplôme et un permis d'exercice provenant du Québec ou de la
France — est celui de leur fonction exacte. S'agit-il réellement de
conditions visant à circonscrire l'obligation des autorités compétentes d'appliquer la procédure commune en vue de la conclusion
éventuelle d'un ARM, comme le titre de la disposition qui prévoit
les trois conditions et son premier alinéa le laissent entendre?[73]
Pourtant, si cela se conçoit bien pour la première condition (concernant la double réglementation), la manière dont sont rédigées les
deux autres conditions semble surtout servir à déterminer les cas

---

[72] La déclaration d'ouverture du ministre des Relations internationales, prononcée
lors du débat sur l'adoption de la motion d'approbation parlementaire de l'Entente France-Québec de 2008, va dans le sens de l'interprétation fondée sur la
disposition générale prévoyant l'exigence de territorialité québécoise ou française
du diplôme: "Est donc visée par cette entente toute personne, sans égard à sa
nationalité, qui a obtenu son titre de formation sur le territoire de la France ou
du Québec ainsi que son aptitude légale d'exercer une profession ou un métier
réglementé sur ledit territoire." Québec, Assemblée nationale, *Journal des débats*,
vol. 41, n° 16 (7 avril 2009), aux pp. 1537–47 (M. Pierre Arcand). Voir aussi
dans le même sens les commentaires de la porte-parole de l'opposition officielle
en matière de relations internationales et de francophonie. *Ibid.* aux pp. 1537–47
(Mme Louise Beaudoin).

[73] Entente France-Québec de 2008, *supra* note 1, art. 5.

individuels (détenir un diplôme ou un permis provenant du Québec ou de la France) qui pourraient bénéficier du système franco-québécois de reconnaissance mutuelle des qualifications professionnelles, sans viser pour autant de manière générale, l'application de la procédure commune par les autorités compétentes. Si tel est le cas — et cette interprétation semble devoir l'emporter en toute logique, au risque de paralyser l'application de la procédure commune — la rédaction de l'Entente manque aussi de cohérence et de clarté à cet égard. Ces conditions viseraient en somme à circonscrire le champ d'application non pas de l'obligation d'appliquer la procédure commune, mais plutôt celui des ARM que les autorités compétentes devront éventuellement conclure.

Interdiction de la discrimination fondée sur la nationalité

Une dernière condition est prévue par l'Entente France-Québec de 2008, non pas pour conditionner le déclenchement de l'application de la procédure commune, mais plutôt pour encadrer le contenu des ARM à être conclus. La nationalité de l'individu qui demande la reconnaissance de ses qualifications professionnelles doit être indifférente à l'octroi de cette reconnaissance.[74] Le système franco-québécois mis en place n'est donc pas réservé exclusivement aux ressortissants français et aux ressortissants canadiens qui résident au Québec. Le point focal de l'Entente est le caractère français ou québécois des qualifications professionnelles obtenues, sans égard à la nationalité du bénéficiaire, ce qui est en phase avec les flux d'immigration qui caractérisent les sociétés française et québécoise. Le contraste avec l'exigence que le diplôme ait été obtenu au Québec ou en France, si cette interprétation de l'Entente est juste, ne manque pas d'étonner.

LE FONCTIONNEMENT DE LA PROCÉDURE COMMUNE EN VUE
DE LA CONCLUSION D'UN ARM

De manière assez trompeuse, la procédure commune que doivent suivre les organismes de réglementation professionnelle, qui constitue pourtant le cœur du système franco-québécois de reconnaissance mutuelle des qualifications professionnelles, n'est pas prévue dans le corps du texte de l'Entente, mais figure plutôt en annexe de celle-ci. Pour présider à son application, lorsque celle-ci peut s'appliquer selon les conditions exposées ci-dessus, l'Entente

---

[74] *Ibid.*, art. 6.

France-Québec de 2008 prévoit cinq grands principes directeurs.[75] En ce qui concerne l'intérêt du public, sa protection doit être assurée, la qualité des services professionnels maintenue et les normes relatives à la langue française respectées. En ce qui concerne l'intérêt des bénéficiaires du système, la procédure doit être appliquée de manière équitable, transparente et réciproque, tandis que la reconnaissance mutuelle des qualifications professionnelles qui est octroyée au terme du processus doit être effective. Les bénéficiaires doivent intégrer la profession ou le métier sur le territoire d'accueil, et tout refus individuel à cet égard doit pouvoir faire l'objet d'un recours effectif, devant une autorité dont la composition est différente de celle qui a rendu la décision.[76]

Vérification de l'équivalence globale des qualifications professionnelles

La première étape de la procédure commune consiste à vérifier l'équivalence globale entre le domaine d'activité couvert par la profession ou le métier réglementé, et celle entre les qualifications professionnelles exigées pour l'exercer.[77] Contrairement au régime de la CE, le système franco-québécois ne pose pas le principe de l'équivalence des qualifications professionnelles comme une présomption juridique devant être renversée pour ne pas s'appliquer.[78] Les organismes de réglementation professionnelle sont chargés d'établir positivement l'existence factuelle de cette équivalence globale. Si au terme de cette vérification, ils en viennent à la conclusion que le domaine de la profession ou du métier qu'ils régissent et les qualifications pour l'exercer sont effectivement globalement équivalents, les organismes ont alors l'obligation de conclure un ARM qui prévoit la reconnaissance mutuelle *automatique* des qualifications professionnelles.[79]

Quel doit être l'effet juridique concret de cette reconnaissance des qualifications professionnelles? Tant l'Entente que la procédure commune sont équivoques quant à la latitude des organismes de réglementation professionnelle à cet égard. L'Entente dispose que la reconnaissance "permet aux bénéficiaires de remplir les exigences de qualification professionnelle requises pour l'obtention" du permis d'exercice de la profession ou du métier sur le territoire d'accueil, ce qui permet alors aux bénéficiaires de déposer une

---

75 *Ibid.*, art. 3.
76 *Ibid.*, art. 6–7.
77 *Ibid.*, Annexe I, section II, art. 1.
78 Voir *supra* note 30 et le texte correspondant.
79 *Ibid.*, Annexe I, section II, art. 6–7.

demande d'autorisation d'exercice de la profession ou du métier.[80] La procédure commune ne fournit pas davantage de détails sur la marge de manœuvre réglementaire dont jouissent les organismes professionnels à ce stade, puisqu'elle prescrit simplement les conditions dans lesquelles les organismes doivent reconnaître les qualifications professionnelles du demandeur.[81] L'organisme professionnel doit-il intégrer totalement les demandeurs bénéficiant du système franco-québécois dans la profession ou le métier réglementé, au même titre que les individus ayant obtenu leurs qualifications professionnelles localement? Leur statut doit-il être absolument identique? À l'inverse, l'organisme professionnel conserve-t-il à ce stade une certaine latitude, qui lui permettrait d'émettre un permis d'exercice distinct pour ces demandeurs, comportant certaines obligations différentes, comme l'utilisation conjointe de la mention du titre professionnel d'origine ou des restrictions particulières, comme l'interdiction de poser certains actes? Selon un document d'information publié par le gouvernement du Québec, la première interprétation, celle voulant que l'intégration du demandeur soit *totale* et *identique* à celle des individus qualifiés localement, semble devoir l'emporter.[82]

Si un différend devait survenir à ce sujet entre des organismes de réglementation professionnelle et les gouvernements des parties, il reviendrait vraisemblablement au Comité bilatéral de le régler, et celui-ci penchera certainement du côté de l'interprétation gouvernementale puisqu'il est composé exclusivement de représentants des gouvernements. Cette interprétation semble au demeurant plus en phase avec l'économie générale de l'Entente et du principe directeur de l'effectivité de la reconnaissance mutuelle des qualifications professionnelles. L'intégration totale des bénéficiaires du système aux mêmes conditions que les candidats qualifiés localement signifie qu'ils doivent alors remplir les autres conditions normales d'entrée dans la profession ou le métier réglementé, comme présenter une demande de permis d'exercice, acquitter la cotisation professionnelle, satisfaire aux exigences de moralité s'il

---

[80] *Ibid.*, art. 6.
[81] *Ibid.*, Annexe I, section II, art. 7 *in fine*. Voir aussi Annexe I, section II, art. 8–11 *in fine*.
[82] Québec, ministère des Relations internationales, *Entente France-Québec sur la reconnaissance mutuelle des qualifications professionnelles. Procédure commune de reconnaissance des qualifications professionnelles (schéma)*, disponible en ligne à: <http://www.mri.gouv.qc.ca/fr/pdf/procedure_commune_entente_qualif_prof_FrQc_fr.pdf>. Ce document indique qu'une fois les qualifications professionnelles reconnues: "[1]es autorités compétentes délivrent l'autorisation d'exercer *aux mêmes conditions* que celles auxquelles sont soumises les personnes exerçant une profession réglementée de la Partie d'accueil" [soulignés de l'auteur].

y a lieu, remplir les exigences déontologiques, remplir les exigences en matière d'assurance responsabilité professionnelle et remplir les exigences de connaissances linguistiques.

Désignation des mesures de compensation imposées en cas de différences substantielles des qualifications professionnelles

Les cas de reconnaissance automatique des qualifications entre des professions ou des métiers réglementés risquent d'être relativement peu fréquents, compte tenu de la diversité dans l'organisation des professions et des métiers entre le Québec et la France. La procédure commune prévoit néanmoins l'obligation de conclure un ARM lorsque le domaine d'activité couvert par la profession ou le métier ou les qualifications professionnelles exigées pour l'exercer ne sont globalement pas équivalents et comportent des différences substantielles, mais en autant qu'il ne s'agit pas de différences insurmontables.[83]

Une première différence substantielle peut porter sur le domaine d'activité respectif de la profession ou du métier réglementé au Québec et en France, qui survient lorsqu'une activité couverte dans une partie ne l'est pas dans l'autre et que cette activité fait l'objet d'une formation spécifique portant sur des matières substantiellement différentes de celles couvertes par la formation dans la partie où l'activité n'est pas couverte par la profession ou le métier.[84] Une deuxième différence substantielle peut porter sur le diplôme exigé pour intégrer la profession ou le métier, qui survient lorsque les matières couvertes par la formation exigée au Québec ou en France diffèrent de manière importante en termes de durée ou de contenu, et que la connaissance de ces matières est essentielle.[85] Une troisième différence substantielle peut porter sur le "programme d'apprentissage," ce qui semble comprendre par exemple les exigences de stage, exigé au Québec ou en France pour intégrer la profession ou le métier, qui survient lorsque ceux-ci diffèrent de manière importante en termes de durée ou de contenu, et que l'acquisition de ces compétences appliquées est essentielle.[86]

Lorsque de telles différences substantielles sont constatées, les organismes professionnels doivent fixer à l'avance les mesures de compensation permettant aux demandeurs québécois ou français

---

[83] Entente France-Québec de 2008, *supra* note 1, Annexe I, section II, art. 2, 6, 8–11.

[84] *Ibid.*, Annexe I, section II, art. 3(1). L'Entente emploie le terme "champ de pratique."

[85] *Ibid.*, art. 3(2).

[86] *Ibid.*, art. 3(3).

de les combler, afin de leur permettre d'obtenir la reconnaissance de leurs qualifications professionnelles par l'autre partie. Dans ce cas de figure, la reconnaissance n'est donc plus automatique, mais *conditionnelle* à la satisfaction par le demandeur de ces mesures de compensation, qui seront prévues par l'ARM qu'ils ont l'obligation de conclure. La libre circulation des professionnels et des gens de métiers entre le Québec et la France est donc facilitée par la fixation à l'avance et de manière générale des étapes à franchir pour pouvoir y intégrer totalement une profession ou un métier réglementé, ce qui élimine désormais le caractère aléatoire et individualisé que ce parcours peut souvent revêtir pour les demandeurs étrangers.

Les organismes de réglementation professionnelle conservent à nouveau une certaine marge de manœuvre dans l'établissement des mesures de compensation qu'ils souhaitent prescrire dans l'ARM. La procédure commune pose le principe de la sévérité graduelle des mesures de compensation pour combler les différences substantielles identifiées par les organismes, lors de leur vérification de l'équivalence globale du domaine d'activité couvert par la profession ou le métier réglementé et des qualifications professionnelles exigées pour l'exercer.[87] Les organismes doivent imposer la mesure de compensation la moins restrictive possible et une préférence est clairement exprimée pour la reconnaissance de l'expérience professionnelle à ce titre, quoique les différences portant sur le domaine d'activité couvert par la profession ou le métier ne puissent jamais être compensées par l'expérience acquise par le demandeur.[88] Autrement, la mesure de compensation prescrite peut consister en l'imposition d'un stage d'adaptation, ou si cela s'avère insuffisant pour combler les différences substantielles, l'imposition d'une épreuve d'aptitude ou encore, dans le pire des cas, l'imposition d'une formation complémentaire.[89] Lorsque le demandeur satisfait aux mesures de compensation qui lui sont imposées par l'organisme professionnel d'accueil aux termes de l'ARM, celui-ci obtient donc la reconnaissance de ses qualifications professionnelles, ce qui lui permet alors de demander formellement son intégration totale à la profession ou au métier visé dans le territoire d'accueil.[90]

---

[87] *Ibid.*, art. 5(3).

[88] *Ibid.*, art. 4 et 8.

[89] *Ibid.*, art. 5(1) et 5(2).

[90] *Ibid.*, art. 8–11. Voir *supra* note 78 et le texte correspondant, pour une discussion sur l'effet juridique concret de la reconnaissance des qualifications professionnelles aux termes de l'Entente France-Québec de 2008.

Différences insurmontables dans les qualifications professionnelles

Il est finalement possible que lors de la vérification de l'équivalence globale du domaine couvert par la profession ou le métier et des qualifications professionnelles exigées pour l'exercer, les organismes professionnels en viennent à la conclusion que les différences qui existent sont telles qu'il est impossible de les surmonter par l'imposition de mesures de compensation. Lorsqu'une incompatibilité semblable est établie, l'Entente interdit purement et simplement la conclusion d'un ARM.[91] Le système franco-québécois empêche donc la reconnaissance mutuelle des qualifications professionnelles entre ces professions ou métiers réglementés.

En somme, l'entente Charest-Sarkozy ne détermine nullement à l'avance les professions ou les métiers qui bénéficient du système franco-québécois de reconnaissance mutuelle des qualifications professionnelles. Ce sont les organismes de réglementation professionnelle québécois et français qui se voient confier la responsabilité de mettre en œuvre le système, et ils conservent à ce titre une importante marge de manœuvre. D'une part, ce sont ces organismes qui procèdent à l'évaluation factuelle de l'équivalence globale du domaine d'activité couvert par la profession ou le métier qu'ils régissent respectivement au Québec et en France et les qualifications professionnelles exigées pour l'y exercer. D'autre part, ce sont également eux qui doivent fixer les mesures de compensation prescrites si des différences substantielles existent entre le Québec et la France à l'égard du domaine couvert par la profession ou le métier ou des qualifications professionnelles exigées pour l'exercer. Cette marge de manœuvre s'exprimera dans la décision sur l'opportunité de conclure un ARM ou non, ainsi que dans le choix et dans la modulation des mesures de compensation éventuellement prescrites par l'ARM, ce qui rend indispensable une analyse des ARM conclus jusqu'à maintenant pour compléter cette première étude de l'Entente France-Québec de 2008.

L'ÉTAT D'AVANCEMENT DES ARM ET L'ACQUIS DU SYSTÈME FRANCO-QUÉBÉCOIS

L'approche globale et intégrée du système franco-québécois de reconnaissance mutuelle des qualifications professionnelles se caractérise notamment par l'établissement d'un échéancier strict et détaillé pour la conclusion des ARM par les organismes de

---

[91] *Ibid.*, Annexe I, section II, art. 12–13.

réglementation professionnelle. Au 1er juillet 2009, cet échéancier est déjà largement respecté, puisque dix-huit ARM ont été conclus, dont sept visent une profession prioritaire et onze un métier prioritaire.[92] Cela signifie que les ARM ont déjà été conclus pour tous les métiers prioritaires, tandis que plus de la moitié des professions prioritaires ont déjà fait l'objet d'un ARM. En ce qui concerne les cinq autres professions prioritaires, les autorités compétentes se sont déjà engagées à finaliser la conclusion d'un ARM dans les délais prescrits,[93] bientôt imitées par trois autres professions non prioritaires.[94]

[92] Les professions prioritaires qui ont fait l'objet d'un ARM sont celles d'architecte, d'arpenteur-géomètre, d'avocat, de comptable-agréé, de comptable général licencié, d'ingénieur et de travailleur social. Québec, ministère des Relations internationales, *Bilan de la signature des arrangements de reconnaissance mutuelle (ARM) des qualifications professionnelles pour les métiers et professions réglementés au Québec et en France*, disponible en ligne à: <http://www.mri.gouv.qc.ca/fr/grands_dossiers/qualifications_professionnelles/bilan_ARM.asp> (dernière modification: 6 juillet 2009). Au 1er juillet 2009, les ARM visant les onze métiers prioritaires n'avaient encore été signés que par la partie française. À cette date, la signature de la partie québécoise n'avait toujours pas été apposée, mais elle est censée n'être qu'une formalité. Cela signifie cependant que la date formelle de conclusion de ces ARM reste alors à déterminer.

[93] *Engagement à conclure un arrangement en vue de la reconnaissance mutuelle des qualifications professionnelles entre le Conseil national de l'Ordre des chirurgiens-dentistes de la France et l'Ordre des dentistes du Québec*, 17 octobre 2008, disponible en ligne à: <http://www.ofiicanada.ca/pdf/earm_dentistes.pdf>; *Engagement à conclure un arrangement en vue de la reconnaissance mutuelle des qualifications professionnelles entre le Conseil national de l'Ordre des médecins de France et le Collège des médecins du Québec*, 17 octobre 2008, disponible en ligne à: <http://www.ofiicanada.ca/pdf/earm_medecins.pdf>; *Engagement à conclure un arrangement en vue de la reconnaissance mutuelle des qualifications professionnelles des médecins vétérinaires entre le Conseil supérieur de l'Ordre des vétérinaires de France et l'Ordre des médecins vétérinaires du Québec*, 17 octobre 2008, disponible en ligne à: <http://www.ofiicanada.ca/pdf/earm_veterinaires.pdf>; *Engagement à conclure un arrangement en vue de la reconnaissance mutuelle des qualifications professionnelles entre le Conseil national de l'Ordre des pharmaciens de France et l'Ordre des pharmaciens du Québec*, 17 octobre 2008, disponible en ligne à: <http://www.ofiicanada.ca/pdf/earm_pharmaciens.pdf>; *Engagement à conclure un arrangement en vue de la reconnaissance mutuelle des qualifications professionnelles des sages-femmes entre l'Ordre national des sages-femmes de France et l'Ordre des sages-femmes du Québec*, 17 octobre 2008, disponible en ligne à: <http://www.ofiicanada.ca/pdf/earm_sages-femmes.pdf>.

[94] Les professions non prioritaires qui se sont engagées à conclure un ARM sont celles d'opticien d'ordonnance, de physiothérapeute et de technologue en radiologie. Des discussions sont aussi déjà envisagées par les autorités compétentes en vue de s'engager à conclure un ARM en ce qui concerne les professions d'infirmière et d'orthophoniste. Québec, ministère des Relations internationales,

Mis en regard de la procédure commune, ces engagements anticipés à conclure un ARM semblent signifier que les autorités compétentes ont déjà effectué une partie de la première étape de vérification de l'équivalence globale des professions et métiers qu'elles réglementent et qu'elles excluent d'emblée toute incompatibilité insurmontable. Il s'agit de la seule conclusion logique au vu de leur engagement à conclure un ARM, puisque la procédure commune en interdirait autrement la conclusion dans un tel cas. Incidemment, aucune incompatibilité insurmontable n'a été identifiée jusqu'à maintenant entre des professions ou des métiers réglementés. L'approche globale et intégrée de l'Entente France-Québec de 2008 porte fruit puisque les autorités chargées de l'appliquer au moyen d'arrangements sectoriels sont activement engagées dans sa mise en œuvre.

Patron commun des ARM et difficultés particulières

Un patron commun se dégage déjà des ARM conclus jusqu'à maintenant, à l'exception des deux premiers, concernant les professions d'architecte et d'ingénieur, qui diffèrent légèrement des autres. Dans un premier temps, un préambule offre un sommaire de l'Entente France-Québec de 2008, puis il mentionne l'examen comparé de la formation et des qualifications professionnelles requis par la procédure commune et auquel les autorités compétentes se sont livrées, ainsi que les résultats de cette analyse comparée. L'objet de l'ARM est toujours précisé, soit d'établir les conditions de la reconnaissance des qualifications professionnelles dans le secteur visé, ainsi que la portée de l'ARM, qui est calquée sur celle de l'Entente, sous réserve des commentaires ci-dessous, en ce qui concerne les individus qui pourront en bénéficier et l'épineuse question du territoire sur lequel a été obtenu le titre de formation. Les définitions et les principes directeurs de l'Entente sont également repris par les ARM. Des dispositions administratives prévoient l'endroit et la procédure de traitement des demandes individuelles de reconnaissance des qualifications professionnelles. Le cœur des ARM est toujours constitué par les dispositions posant les conditions de reconnaissance de la formation et des qualifications professionnelles.

"Entente France-Québec sur la reconnaissance des qualifications professionnelles — Le ministre Arcand se réjouit de la signature de 14 nouveaux arrangements de reconnaissance mutuelle," Communiqué (27 avril 2009), disponible en ligne à: <http://www.mri.gouv.qc.ca/fr/informer/salle_de_presse/communiques/textes/2009/2009_04_27.asp>.

Ces dispositions diffèrent évidemment d'un ARM à l'autre, mais certaines tendances générales peuvent être observées.[95]

La jouissance d'une expérience professionnelle préalable sur le territoire d'origine peut-elle être un critère d'admissibilité au système franco-québécois de reconnaissance mutuelle des qualifications professionnelles? Certains ARM qui portent sur des métiers prioritaires prévoient que seuls les candidats français qui détiennent déjà une telle expérience sur leur territoire d'origine peuvent demander la reconnaissance de leurs qualifications professionnelles au Québec.[96] Puisqu'il s'agit d'une condition d'admissibilité, cela signifie que ces candidats sont écartés d'emblée du système et que les autorités compétentes ont jugé qu'il était impossible de combler ce manque d'expérience par des mesures de compensation. Une telle approche est-elle conforme à l'esprit ou à la lettre de l'Entente? Il est permis d'en douter? L'Entente ne vise-t-elle pas précisément à permettre à des individus ayant complété leur formation professionnelle sur leur territoire d'origine de voir leurs qualifications être reconnue plus facilement. L'imposition d'un stage d'adaptation au Québec n'aurait-il pas permis aux techniciens constructeurs de bois, aux techniciens en métallerie ou aux mécaniciens de transport par câbles et de remontées mécaniques français de gagner l'expérience requise pour combler la différence substantielle entre les programmes de formation des deux parties? Jusqu'à présent, cette approche n'a heureusement pas été suivie dans les ARM qui portent sur des professions.

Qu'en est-il du traitement réservé par les ARM à la question du champ d'application du système franco-québécois? Le diplôme du candidat doit-il obligatoirement avoir été obtenu d'une institution d'enseignement située au Québec ou en France pour qu'il soit admissible au système de reconnaissance mutuelle des qualifications professionnelles? L'ambiguïté de l'Entente France-Québec de 2008 à cet égard a été soulignée précédemment et sa mise en œuvre

---

[95] Voir le tableau qui figure en annexe, pour un panorama complet du contenu des ARM conclus en ce qui concerne les professions réglementées prioritaires.

[96] *Arrangement en vue de la reconnaissance mutuelle des qualifications professionnelles pour le métier de charpentier-menuisier au Québec et le métier de technicien constructeur de bois en France*, art. 5.3, disponible en ligne à: <http://www.ofiicanada.ca/pdf/ARM_charpentier_menuisier.pdf> [ci-après *ARM des charpentiers-menuisiers*]; *Arrangement en vue de la reconnaissance mutuelle des qualifications professionnelles pour le métier de serrurier de bâtiment au Québec et le métier de technicien en métallerie en France*, art. 5.3, disponible en ligne à: <http://www.ofiicanada.ca/pdf/ARM%20serruriers.pdf> [ci-après *ARM des serruriers de bâtiment*]; *Arrangement en vue de la*

indique que celle-ci subsiste.[97] Si quelques ARM calquent les dispositions de l'Entente qui en fixent la portée, important du coup la même ambiguïté,[98] la majorité des ARM reformule légèrement ses dispositions, en éliminant la mention "sur leur territoire respectif."[99] Ces derniers ARM conservent toutefois la formule introductive "sur le territoire de la France ou du Québec," ce qui semble neutraliser l'effet de l'élimination de ladite mention, et laisse subsister un doute sur l'obligation ou non d'avoir obtenu son diplôme au Québec

---

reconnaissance mutuelle des qualifications professionnelles pour le métier de mécanicien ou mécanicienne de remontées mécaniques au Québec et le métier de mécanicien ou mécanicienne de transport par câbles et de remontées mécaniques en France, art. 5.3, disponible en ligne à: <http://www.ofiicanada.ca/pdf/ARM%20mecaniciens.pdf>.

97 Voir *supra* note 68 et le texte correspondant.

98 *Arrangement en vue de la reconnaissance mutuelle des qualifications professionnelles des architectes entre l'Ordre des architectes du Québec et l'Ordre des architectes de France,* 9 avril 2009, art. 2, disponible en ligne à: <http://www.mri.gouv.qc.ca/fr/pdf/Bilan_ARM_entente_qualif/ARM_architectes.pdf> [ci-après *ARM des architectes*]; *Arrangement en vue de la reconnaissance mutuelle des qualifications professionnelles entre l'Ordre des comptables agréés du Québec et l'Ordre des experts-comptables de France,* 27 avril 2009, art. 2, disponible en ligne à: <http://www.mri.gouv.qc.ca/fr/pdf/Bilan_ARM_entente_qualif/ARM_Comptables_agréés.pdf> [ci-après *ARM des CA*].

99 *Arrangement en vue de la reconnaissance mutuelle des qualifications professionnelles entre l'Ordre des arpenteurs-géomètres du Québec et le ministre d'État, ministre de l'Écologie, de l'Énergie, du Développement durable et de l'Aménagement du territoire et l'Ordre des géomètres-experts de France,* 9 juin 2009, art. 2, disponible en ligne à: <http://www.mri.gouv.qc.ca/fr/pdf/Bilan_ARM_entente_qualif/ARM_arpenteurs.pdf> [ci-après *ARM des arpenteurs-géomètres*]; *Arrangement en vue de la reconnaissance mutuelle des qualifications professionnelles entre le Barreau du Québec et le Conseil national des barreaux,* 30 mai 2009, art. 2, disponible en ligne à: <http://www.mri.gouv.qc.ca/fr/pdf/Bilan_ARM_entente_qualif/ARM_avocats.pdf> [ci-après *ARM des avocats*]; *Arrangement en vue de la reconnaissance mutuelle des qualifications professionnelles entre l'Ordre professionnel des comptables généraux licenciés du Québec et l'Ordre des experts-comptables de France,* 27 avril 2009, art. 2, disponible en ligne à: <http://www.mri.gouv.qc.ca/fr/pdf/Bilan_ARM_entente_qualif/ARM_Comptables_généraux.pdf> [ci-après *ARM des CGA*]; *Arrangement en vue de la reconnaissance mutuelle des qualifications professionnelles entre l'Ordre des ingénieurs du Québec et la Commission des titres d'ingénieurs de France et le Conseil national des ingénieurs et scientifiques de France,* 17 octobre 2008, art. 2, disponible en ligne à: <http://www.mri.gouv.qc.ca/fr/pdf/Bilan_ARM_entente_qualif/ARM_ingenieurs.pdf> [ci-après *ARM des ingénieurs*]; *Arrangement en vue de la reconnaissance mutuelle des qualifications professionnelles entre l'Ordre professionnel des travailleurs sociaux du Québec et le ministre du Travail, des Relations sociales, de la Famille, de la Solidarité et de la Ville français [sic],* 27 avril 2009, art. 2, disponible en ligne à: <http://www.mri.gouv.qc.ca/fr/pdf/Bilan_ARM_entente_qualif/ARM_Travailleurs_sociaux.pdf> [ci-après *ARM des travailleurs sociaux*].

ou en France. Cette épineuse question demeure donc entière malgré l'adoption de plusieurs ARM.

Un effet pervers de l'approche globale et intégrée du système franco-québécois, avec son échéancier strict et la pression politique réelle qu'il fait subir aux autorités compétentes pour qu'elles livrent des résultats, pourrait-il être de faire en sorte que les ARM conclus ne soient qu'une fuite en avant? Cette hypothèse semble se vérifier dans le cas de certains ARM qui portent sur des métiers prioritaires, puisqu'ils prévoient que les mesures de compensation requises pour combler les différences substantielles identifiées sont encore indéterminées et feront l'objet d'un addenda.[100]

Typologie des formes de reconnaissance mutuelle prévues par les ARM

Deux ARM seulement — ceux qui portent sur la profession d'ingénieur et de travailleur social — prévoitent la *reconnaissance automatique* des qualifications professionnelles. Cette automaticité ne joue que pour les ingénieurs québécois, ce qui signifie que les autorités compétentes françaises ont estimé qu'il n'y a pas de différences substantielles entre la formation reçue en France ou au Québec, et que l'ingénieur québécois peut devenir ingénieur français sans mesure de compensation.[101] En revanche, l'automaticité de la reconnaissance ne joue pour le moment que pour les travailleurs sociaux français qui désirent s'établir au Québec.[102] Il s'agit de la forme la plus avancée — et la plus rare, ce qui n'étonne guère — de reconnaissance mutuelle des qualifications professionnelles dans le système franco-québécois.

Une forme un peu plus fréquente de reconnaissance mutuelle des qualifications professionnelle dans le système franco-québécois

---

[100] *Arrangement en vue de la reconnaissance mutuelle des qualifications professionnelles pour le métier de mécanicien ou mécanicienne de machines fixes (classe 4) au Québec et le métier de technicien ou technicienne de maintenance de systèmes énergétiques et climatiques en France*, art. 5.1, disponible en ligne à: <http://www.ofiicanada.ca/pdf/ARM%20syst%20energet%20et%20climatiques.pdf>; *Arrangement en vue de la reconnaissance mutuelle des qualifications professionnelles pour le métier de couvreur au Québec et le métier d'étancheur du bâtiment et des travaux publics en France*, art. 5.4, disponible en ligne à: <http://www.ofiicanada.ca/pdf/ARM%20couvreurs.pdf>; *Arrangement en vue de la reconnaissance mutuelle des qualifications professionnelles pour le métier de poseur de revêtement souples au Québec et le métier de solier moquettiste en France*, art. 5.4, disponible en ligne à: <http://www.ofiicanada.ca/pdf/ARM%20solier_moquettistes.pdf>.

[101] *ARM des ingénieurs, supra* note 99, art. 5.

[102] *ARM des travailleurs sociaux, supra* note 99, art. 5.2.

est celle que nous proposons d'appeler la *reconnaissance quasi-automatique.* Celle-ci consiste à n'imposer comme mesure de compensation que l'acquisition de connaissances dans le domaine déontologique et de la réglementation professionnelle pour les professions ou dans le domaine de la santé et de la sécurité au travail pour les métiers.[103] Les professions d'architecte et d'avocat appartiennent à cette catégorie, ce qui ne manque pas d'étonner en ce qui concerne cette dernière, compte tenu du caractère éminemment local du droit positif et particulièrement des règles de procédure. La libéralisation de l'exercice de la profession d'avocat dans la CE, pour prendre un exemple bien étudié dans la littérature, a été semée de beaucoup plus d'embûches.[104]

De manière prévisible, la forme de reconnaissance mutuelle des qualifications professionnelles la plus fréquente dans les ARM est la *reconnaissance conditionnelle.* Celle-ci consiste à prescrire l'imposition de mesures de compensation significatives pour combler les différences substantielles dans la formation professionnelle reçue dans le territoire d'origine. La majorité des professions et des métiers prioritaires appartiennent à cette catégorie et toute la palette des mesures de compensation possible est exploitée: stage d'adaptation, épreuve d'aptitude et formation complémentaire. Cependant, tel que mentionné précédemment, aucune différence insurmontable n'a encore été observée entre des professions ou des métiers prioritaires, ce qui signifie que la forme la moins avancée de reconnaissance mutuelle — le refus pur et simple — n'existe pas dans le système franco-québécois, à l'exception bien entendu des professions juridiques ou judiciaires qui en ont été exclues d'entrée de jeu.

Effets de la reconnaissance des qualifications professionnelles dans les ARM

Quels enseignements peut-on tirer des ARM conclus à ce jour quant aux effets de la reconnaissance des qualifications professionnelles? Conformément à l'Entente, le candidat qui voit ses qualifications être reconnues dans le territoire d'accueil acquiert le droit d'y demander son admission dans la profession ou le métier réglementé aux mêmes conditions que celui y ayant acquis sa formation professionnelle. Le candidat pourra exercer la profession ou le

---

[103] *ARM des architectes, supra* note 98, art. 6.2 et 6.4; *ARM des avocats, supra* note 97, art. 5.1 et 5.2. Pour les métiers prioritaires, voir par exemple *ARM des charpentiers-menuisiers, supra* note 96, art. 5.3; *ARM des serruriers de bâtiment, supra* note 96, art. 5.3.

[104] Voir *supra* note 35 et le texte correspondant.

métier sur le territoire d'accueil aux mêmes conditions que les autres membres, c'est-à-dire qu'il pourra porter le titre et poser les actes réservés, moyennant le versement de la cotisation profession-nelle, le respect des règles déontologiques, la souscription d'une assurance responsabilité professionnelle, la démonstration de bonnes mœurs, etc.

Deux questions demeurent quant à l'effet de la reconnaissance mutuelle des qualifications professionnelles. D'une part, le statut du candidat qui intègre une profession ou un métier réglementé grâce au système franco-québécois doit-il être identique aux autres membres? L'ARM qui porte sur la profession d'ingénieur soulève cette question puisqu'il prévoit que l'ingénieur québécois admis en France doit porter avec son titre professionnel une mention précisant qu'il a obtenu ses qualifications professionnelles à l'étran-ger.[105] Une telle différenciation des professionnels ou des gens de métier selon l'origine de leurs qualifications est-elle permise par l'Entente? L'ambiguïté du texte de l'Entente que nous avons sou-lignée ci-dessus sur l'effet de la reconnaissance mutuelle pourrait peut-être supporter une telle différenciation, mais sa très grande rareté indique selon nous qu'elle serait plutôt contraire à l'esprit de l'Entente. Il est instructif de noter que la seule profession qui a introduit cette différenciation des titres professionnels pouvant être employés est aussi la seule à avoir adopté la reconnaissance auto-matique des qualifications professionnelles.

D'autre part, une fois que le candidat a été admis dans la profes-sion ou le métier réglementé sur le territoire d'accueil grâce au système franco-québécois, doit-il maintenir son statut professionnel d'origine? L'Entente ne comporte aucune disposition explicite sur cette question. Selon nous, le statut professionnel d'origine du demandeur n'est pertinent qu'au stade de la demande de recon-naissance des qualifications professionnelles, comme condition donnant accès au système franco-québécois de reconnaissance mutuelle. Puisque l'esprit de l'*Entente France-Québec de 2008* est de faciliter l'*établissement permanent* des candidats dans le territoire d'accueil, plutôt que la prestation temporaire de services, cela im-plique une intégration complète et définitive dans la profession ou le métier réglementé sur le territoire d'accueil. Dès que le candidat est admis dans la profession ou le métier sur le territoire d'accueil, il est à notre avis tout à fait libre de renoncer à son adhésion à la profession ou au métier sur son territoire d'origine.

---

[105] *ARM des ingénieurs, supra* note 99, art. 5.

Effet politique dynamisant de l'Entente au-delà de ses objectifs

Deux développements originaux doivent finalement être mentionnés concernant l'acquis du système franco-québécois de reconnaissance mutuelle des qualifications professionnelles. L'effet dynamisant de l'entente Sarkozy-Charest sur les organismes de réglementation professionnelle est d'abord illustré par la signature d'une entente additionnelle concernant la profession d'architecte, qui opère en amont du système franco-québécois.[106] Celle-ci vise les candidats qui ne sont pas encore membre de l'ordre professionnel sur leur territoire d'origine, mais qui y sont admissibles. Ces candidats échappent au système franco-québécois puisqu'ils n'ont pas de permis d'exercice de la profession d'architecte dans leur territoire d'origine.

Cet effet dynamisant de l'Entente est aussi illustré avec la profession de travailleur social par l'intégration de la formation complémentaire, requise pour jouir de la reconnaissance des qualifications professionnelles, directement dans le cursus universitaire sur le territoire d'origine.[107] Cet effet original de l'entente Sarkozy-Charest sur la formation universitaire, au-delà des autorités compétentes, intègre donc à l'avance les mesures de compensation au cœur de la formation dans le territoire d'origine. Les travailleurs sociaux québécois qui auront suivis ces cours, lors de leurs études universitaires au Québec, pourront à terme bénéficier de la reconnaissance automatique de leurs qualifications professionnelles en France. Pour être opérationnel, cet aménagement suppose la collaboration active des universités québécoises, elles qui ne sont pas *a priori* visées par l'Entente France-Québec de 2008. Il s'agit en définitive d'une forme — légère — d'harmonisation des formations nationales qui n'est pas exigée par l'Entente.

Mesures de mise en œuvre prises par le gouvernement du Québec

Si les ARM conclus jusqu'à présent permettent de faire une première évaluation de l'acquis du système franco-québécois de reconnaissance mutuelle des qualifications professionnelles, pour que l'Entente France-Québec de 2008 soit pleinement mise en œuvre,

---

106 *Entente afin de faciliter la reconnaissance mutuelle des qualifications professionnelles des diplômés en architecture entre l'Ordre des architectes du Québec et l'Ordre des architectes de France*, 9 avril 2009, disponible en ligne à: <http://www.oaq.com/wmfichier/ENTENTE.pdf>.

107 *ARM des travailleurs sociaux, supra* note 99, art. 5.1.

il faudra attendre que la législation et la réglementation professionnelle soient modifiées.[108] Au Québec, le projet de loi 3 a été
adopté au printemps 2009, afin d'outiller les ordres professionnels
sur le plan réglementaire, pour leur permettre d'exécuter leur
ARM.[109] Ces modifications donneront force de loi en droit interne
aux engagements des gouvernements et des autorités compétentes,
ce qui permettra alors au système de déployer ses effets à destination
des professionnels et des gens de métier migrants qui en sont les
bénéficiaires. À l'instar de ce qui s'est produit en droit communautaire, il est à prévoir que cette panoplie de normes de nature différente — entente internationale, ARM, loi, règlement, décision
administrative — fera l'objet de contestations judiciaires, puisque
le système franco-québécois vise à faciliter la mobilité professionnelle des individus et leur donne ainsi un intérêt juridique réel dans
son fonctionnement. Cette jurisprudence pourrait contribuer à
faire avancer le "droit québécois des relations internationales,"[110]
notamment au chapitre de l'invocabilité et du statut juridique des
ententes internationales.

La création du poste de Commissaire aux plaintes concernant les
mécanismes de reconnaissance des compétences professionnelles,
au sein de l'Office des professions du Québec, a également été
proposée avec le projet de loi 53.[111] Cette initiative récente vise à
prévoir une voie de recours originale pour les individus qui s'esti-
meront lésés par la décision d'un ordre professionnel, portant sur
leur demande de reconnaissance de qualifications professionnelles

---

[108] Entente France-Québec de 2008, *supra* note 1, art. 2.

[109] P.L. 3, *Loi permettant la mise en œuvre de l'Entente entre le Québec et la France en matière de reconnaissance mutuelle des qualifications professionnelles ainsi que d'autres ententes du même type*, 1ère sess., 39e lég., Québec, 2009 (sanctionné le 10 juin 2009), L.Q. 2009, c. 16.

[110] Voir Daniel Turp, "La doctrine Gérin-Lajoie et l'émergence d'un droit québécois des relations internationales," dans Stéphane Paquin avec la collaboration de Louise Beaudoin, Robert Comeau et Guy Lachapelle, dir., *Les relations interna- tionales du Québec depuis la Doctrine Gérin-Lajoie (1965–2005). Le prolongement externe des compétences internes*, Québec, Presses de l'Université Laval, 2006, à la p. 49; Daniel Turp, "Le consentement de l'État du Québec aux engagements interna- tionaux et sa participation aux forums internationaux," dans Sienho Yee et Jacques-Yvan Morin, dir., *Multiculturalism and International Law: Essays in Honour of Edward McWhinney*, Leyde, Martinus Nijhoff, 2009, à la p. 719.

[111] P.L. 53, *Loi instituant le poste de Commissaire aux plaintes concernant les mécanismes de reconnaissance des compétences professionnelles*, 1ère sess., 39e lég., Québec, 2009 (présenté le 10 juin 2009).

acquises à l'étranger.[112] Le Commissaire n'aura pas compétence uniquement sur les demandes présentées suivant le système franco-québécois, puisque sa compétence sera générale et ouverte à toutes les demandes de cette nature, ce qui traduit l'engagement sérieux du gouvernement du Québec pour la mobilité professionnelle. Le sérieux de la politique du gouvernement se traduit aussi par la mise sur pied du "Fonds d'appui à la mobilité de la main d'œuvre," doté de 5 000 000 $, pour soutenir les efforts des ordres professionnels et des autres autorités compétentes dans la mise en œuvre de l'Entente France-Québec de 2008.[113]

OBSERVATIONS SUR DES QUESTIONS CHOISIES

LE SYSTÈME FRANCO-QUÉBÉCOIS ET LA PROTECTION DU PUBLIC

Il convient de s'interroger sur la question de savoir si le système franco-québécois de reconnaissance mutuelle des qualifications professionnelles est conforme à son objectif — et au principe directeur — voulant qu'il assure la protection du public. À l'instar du système professionnel québécois, le système franco-québécois confie la responsabilité de veiller à la protection du public aux ordres professionnels et aux autres autorités compétentes. En visant uniquement à faciliter l'établissement des demandeurs, c'est-à-dire leur intégration permanente et définitive à la profession ou au métier réglementé dans l'État d'accueil, la protection du public est effectivement confiée aux autorités compétentes. À ce titre, il faut toutefois rappeler que l'Entente France-Québec de 2008 elle-même ne semble pas permettre aux autorités compétentes d'exiger que le professionnel migrant mentionne son titre ou ses qualifications professionnelles d'origine. Le consommateur ne sera pas obligatoirement informé de l'origine étrangère des qualifications professionnelles de son fournisseur de services, ce qui signifie que le système franco-québécois est entièrement fondé sur la confiance envers le jugement des autorités compétentes pour assurer la protection du public. Cette confiance s'exprime dans la compétence confiée aux autorités de négocier des ARM en évaluant l'équivalence

---

112 Après examen des plaintes individuelles, le commissaire ne pourrait que présenter ses conclusions et ses recommandations à l'ordre professionnel concerné, ce qui signifie que ce processus sera purement consultatif ne saurait constituer le recours effectif contre les décisions des autorités compétentes qui est requis par l'Entente France-Québec de 2008. Voir *supra* note 1, art. 7.

113 Québec, *Rapport d'étape 2007–2008*, *supra* note 40 à la p. 72.

des qualifications professionnelles et en prescrivant si nécessaire des mesures de compensation.

Pour déterminer si le public est suffisamment protégé, il est indispensable d'examiner la manière dont les autorités compétentes se sont acquittées de leur tâche. Par exemple, en ce qui concerne la profession d'avocat, l'approche choisie par le Barreau du Québec et le Conseil national des barreaux de France est celle de la reconnaissance quasi-automatique des qualifications professionnelles. Il n'y a pratiquement aucune mesure de compensation qui est imposée aux demandeurs; seule la réussite d'une épreuve d'aptitude sur la réglementation professionnelle et la déontologie est exigée. Aucun stage d'adaptation n'est exigé, ni aucune formation complémentaire en droit national de l'État d'accueil. Cette situation pourrait conduire à des résultats paradoxaux, comme celui de l'avocat français qui n'a absolument jamais touché au droit fédéral canadien ou au droit québécois, mais qui pourrait voir son établissement complet au Québec être beaucoup plus facile que l'avocat qui provient du Canada anglais et qui a consacré toute sa carrière au droit fiscal fédéral, au droit criminel ou au droit constitutionnel. L'avocat canadien-anglais pourrait ne se voir octroyer qu'un permis spécial de conseiller juridique canadien, plutôt qu'un permis général comme l'avocat migrant français.[114]

Il est permis de s'interroger sur le niveau d'équivalence du droit substantif et du droit procédural entre le Québec et la France, particulièrement dans les domaines du droit relevant au Québec des compétences fédérales, comme le droit criminel, ou encore dans le domaine du droit constitutionnel, qui ont peu à voir avec la tradition juridique civiliste. La facilitation du droit d'établissement des avocats entre le Québec et la France est allée très loin, trop peut-être, au détriment de la protection du public. Il faut rappeler que ce dernier n'est pas informé de la manière dont un avocat est devenu membre du Barreau, ce qui signifie qu'il n'a aucun moyen de savoir que les connaissances de l'avocat migrant en droit national n'ont pas été contrôlées. La confiance des autorités compétentes envers la capacité d'autorégulation du marché des services juridiques peut étonner.

Le *Code de déontologie des avocats* exige en effet que l'avocat québécois n'accepte que les mandats qu'il estime avoir la compétence

---

[114] *Règlement sur la délivrance des permis spéciaux du Barreau du Québec*, R.Q., c. C-26, r. 19.1.1.1, art. 7–9.

d'accomplir.[115] Cette obligation déontologique lui impose de recourir à l'aide nécessaire s'il n'est pas suffisamment préparé pour
fournir un service professionnel, ce qui pourrait remplir le rôle
d'une sorte d'obligation d'agir de concert avec un avocat expéri-
menté. Par ailleurs, l'avocat québécois ne doit pas faire de la fausse
représentation quant à son niveau de competence.[116] Cela signifie
que le Barreau du Québec n'interviendra qu'après qu'une faute
déontologique ait été commise, par son système de sanctions disci-
plinaires. En définitive, c'est donc essentiellement sur la capacité
d'autorégulation des avocats migrants que la protection du public
repose.

LE SYSTÈME FRANCO-QUÉBÉCOIS ET LE DROIT INTERNATIONAL ÉCONOMIQUE

Le système franco-québécois de reconnaissance mutuelle des qualifications professionnelles vise à faciliter la liberté d'établissement
des professionnels et des gens de métier entre le Québec et la
France, ce qui confère un avantage aux individus qui peuvent en
profiter. Bien que le système ne comporte aucune distinction fondée sur la nationalité,[117] il est prévisible que dans les faits, la majorité des individus qui en profitera sera de nationalité canadienne
ou française. Dans quelle mesure l'octroi d'un tel avantage aux
prestataires de service canadiens et français qui souhaitent s'établir
en France ou au Québec pour y exercer leur profession ou leur
métier, est-il compatible avec les obligations internationales du
Canada et de la France? Le principe de non-discrimination, qui
figure habituellement dans les accords commerciaux internationaux, sous la forme de la clause du traitement de la nation la plus
favorisée (clause NPF), interdit la discrimination entre les produits,
les services ou les fournisseurs de services similaires selon leur origine nationale, que ce soit *de jure* ou *de facto*. Il convient alors de
procéder à un examen très sommaire de la compatibilité entre
l'Entente France-Québec de 2008 et les principaux accords commerciaux internationaux qui lient le Canada et la France, et qui
touchent au commerce des services et au droit d'établissement des
prestataires de services.

115 *Code de déontologie des avocats*, R.Q., c. B-1, r. 1, art. 3.01.01.

116 *Ibid.*, art. 3.02.03.

117 Voir *supra* note 74 et le texte correspondant.

Compatibilité avec l'Accord général sur le commerce des services

Le système franco-québécois de reconnaissance mutuelle des qualifications professionnelles semble compatible avec les obligations juridiques qui lient le Canada et la France au plan multilatéral. Le Canada ou la France ne devrait pas faire l'objet d'une plainte à l'Organisation mondiale du commerce (OMC), pour violation de l'Accord général sur le commerce des services (AGCS) par une mesure d'exécution de l'Entente France-Québec de 2008.[118] Cela s'explique par le fait que l'AGCS ne couvre que les mesures affectant la prestation transfrontière *temporaire* de services, par une personne physique se rendant dans un État autre que celui ou elle est établie.[119] Une annexe à l'AGCS précise que "[1]'Accord ne s'appliquera pas aux mesures affectant les personnes physiques qui cherchent à accéder au marché du travail d'un Membre, ni aux mesures concernant la citoyenneté, la résidence ou l'emploi à titre permanent."[120] Il ne viserait donc pas les mesures qui touchent au droit d'établissement des personnes physiques dans un État d'accueil, afin d'y exercer une profession ou un métier de manière permanente, ce qui correspond précisément à l'objet du système franco-québécois de reconnaissance mutuelle des qualifications professionnelles.

Même à supposer que l'AGCS s'appliquerait aux mesures affectant le droit d'établissement des personnes physiques pour fournir des services dans un État d'accueil, il semble que le système franco-québécois de reconnaissance mutuelle des qualifications professionnelles serait néanmoins licite. Il est vrai que la clause NPF s'impose à tous les membres de l'OMC, en ce qui concerne les

---

[118] Accord général sur le commerce des services, Annexe 1B de l'Accord de Marrakesh instituant l'Organisation mondiale du commerce, 15 avril 1994, 1869 R.T.N.U. 221, 33 I.L.M. 1168 (entrée en vigueur: 1er janvier 1995) [ci-après AGCS].

[119] *Ibid.*, art. I:1 et I:2 d); Dominique Carreau et Patrick Juillard, *Droit international économique*, 3e éd., Paris, Dalloz, 2007, §§813, 952 et 953; Michael J. Trebilcock et Robert Howse, *The Regulation of International Trade*, 3e éd., Londres, Routeledge, 2005, à la p. 359; Éric H. Leroux, "L'*Accord général sur le commerce des services* (AGCS): règles propres à des secteurs particuliers," (2002) 43 *Cahiers de droit*, vol. 43 (2002), à la p. 427; OMC, "Mouvement des personnes physiques," disponible en ligne à: <http://www.wto.org/french/tratop_f/serv_f/mouvement_persons_f/mouvement_persons_f.htm>.

[120] AGCS, *supra* note 118, art. XXIX et *Annexe sur le mouvement des personnes physiques fournissant des services relevant de l'Accord*, para. 2.

fournisseurs de services similaires,[121] et que la clause interdit la discrimination entre ces fournisseurs, sur la base de leur origine nationale, que ce soit prévu de manière explicite dans une mesure ou que l'application de la mesure entraîne une telle discrimination dans les faits.[122] Le système franco-québécois pourrait donc constituer une discrimination *de facto* à l'endroit des fournisseurs de services similaires provenant de membres de l'OMC tiers, puisque ces derniers se trouveraient à recevoir un traitement moins favorable que les fournisseurs de services québécois ou français. Toutefois, le système serait compatible avec l'AGCS, en raison d'une disposition qui permet précisément aux membres de l'OMC de conclure des accords ou des arrangements de reconnaissance mutuelle des qualifications professionnelles obtenues dans un pays déterminé.[123]

Cette disposition — à supposer toujours que l'AGCS s'applique au droit d'établissement — imposerait cependant certaines obligations au Canada et à la France. Ceux-ci devraient informer le Conseil du commerce des services de l'existence de l'*Entente France-Québec de 2008*; ils devraient aussi ménager aux autres membres de l'OMC intéressés la possibilité de négocier un accord ou un arrangement comparable.[124] Enfin, le Canada — par le truchement du Québec — et la France ne devraient pas appliquer le système franco-québécois d'une manière qui constituerait soit un moyen de discrimination entre les pays, soit une restriction déguisée au commerce international des services.[125]

En terminant, il faut rappeler que des mesures compatibles avec l'AGCS peuvent quand même faire l'objet d'une contestation à l'OMC, au motif qu'elles annulent ou réduisent un avantage dont

---

121 *Ibid.*, art. II:1. Les mesures adoptées par des entités fédérées sont également soumises à l'AGCS, ce qui signifie que le Canada doit prendre toutes les mesures raisonnables en son pouvoir pour que le Québec respecte les obligations prévues par l'Accord (*Ibid.*, art. I:3 a)). Les membres de l'OMC peuvent par ailleurs exclure des mesures incompatibles avec la clause NPF, dans une liste nationale d'exemptions, mais aucune exemption ne concerne le système franco-québécois de reconnaissance mutuelle des qualifications professionnelles (*ibid.*, art. II:2). Par exemple, le Canada a inscrit sur sa liste d'exemption une procédure accélérée de validation des offres d'emploi pour l'admission *temporaire* de travailleurs agricoles originaires de pays avec lesquels le Canada a signé un protocole d'entente.

122 *Communautés européennes – Régime applicable à l'importation, à la vente et à la distribution des bananes (Plaintes de l'Équateur et al.)* (1997), OMC Doc. WT/DS27/AB/R §234 (Rapport de l'Organe d'appel).

123 AGCS, *supra* note 118, art. VII:1.

124 *Ibid.*, art. VII:2.

125 *Ibid.*, art. VII:3.

un membre aurait raisonnablement pu s'attendre à bénéficier, conformément à un engagement spécifique contracté par un autre membre.[126] Ces plaintes en situation de non-violation sont rarissimes à l'OMC;[127] une telle constatation n'a jamais été faite en ce qui concerne l'AGCS et les chances que le système franco-québécois de reconnaissance mutuelle des qualifications professionnelles fasse l'objet d'une telle contestation avec succès apparaissent extrêmement minces.

Compatibilité avec l'Accord de libre-échange nord-américain

La compatibilité des mesures d'exécution de l'Entente France-Québec de 2008 avec le chapitre 12 de l'Accord de libre-échange nord-américain[128] (ALENA), qui porte sur le commerce des services, semble également ne pas être problématique. Le raisonnement juridique à l'appui de cette conclusion ressemble beaucoup à celui qui concerne l'AGCS. En revanche, la possibilité que le système franco-québécois fasse l'objet d'une contestation au titre du chapitre 11 de l'ALENA, qui porte sur l'investissement, soulève des interrogations qui débordent le cadre de cet accord et qui interpellent de manière générale les traités bilatéraux sur l'investissement (TBI) auxquels sont parties le Canada ou la France.

À l'instar de l'AGCS, la libéralisation du commerce des services opérée par l'ALENA porte sur la prestation transfrontière *temporaire* de services par une personne physique, sur le territoire d'une autre Partie que celle où elle est établie. Le chapitre 12 s'applique aux mesures adoptées par une Partie, relativement au commerce transfrontière de services effectué par des fournisseurs d'une autre Partie, en ce qui concerne entre autres la production, la distribution, la commercialisation, la vente et la prestation d'un service ou encore la présence du fournisseur de service étranger sur le territoire de l'État d'accueil.[129] Toutefois, le chapitre 12 ne doit pas être

126 *Ibid.*, art. XXIII:3.

127 Le caractère exceptionnel du recours en situation de non-violation dans le secteur du commerce international des marchandises a été souligné par l'Organe d'appel de l'OMC. *Communautés européennes–Mesures affectant l'amiante et les produits en contenant (Plainte du Canada)* (2001), OMC Doc. WT/DS135/AB/R, para. 186 [ci-après Rapport de l'Organe d'appel].

128 Accord de libre-échange nord-américain entre le gouvernement du Canada, le gouvernement des États-Unis et le gouvernement du Mexique, 17 décembre 1992, R.T. Can. 1994 n° 2, 32 I.L.M. 289 (entrée en vigueur: 1er janvier 1994) [ci-après ALENA].

129 *Ibid.*, art. 1201:1 (a) et (d).

interprété comme "imposant à une Partie une obligation quelconque en ce qui concerne un ressortissant d'une autre Partie désireux
d'avoir accès à son marché du travail ou exerçant en permanence
un emploi sur son territoire ou comme conférant à ce ressortissant
un droit quelconque en ce qui concerne cet accès ou cet emploi."[130]

À nouveau, même à supposer que le chapitre 12 s'applique aux
mesures adoptées par une Partie relativement au droit d'établissement d'un fournisseur de services, et que le système franco-québécois
de reconnaissance mutuelle des qualifications professionnelles
viole la clause NPF,[131] celui-ci serait néanmoins compatible avec les
dispositions de l'ALENA sur le commerce des services. En effet,
une disposition semblable à celle prévue par l'AGCS permet aux
Parties contractantes de l'ALENA de mettre en place de tels systèmes
en vertu d'une entente avec un pays tiers.[132] Le Canada aurait cependant l'obligation de ménager aux États-Unis et au Mexique une
possibilité adéquate de démontrer qu'un tel système devrait aussi
être mis en place avec eux. À nouveau, l'hypothèse bien improbable
d'une contestation en situation de non-violation est aussi envisagée
par le mécanisme de règlement des différends interétatiques de
l'ALENA.[133]

La compatibilité du système franco-québécois avec le chapitre 11
de l'ALENA, qui porte sur les investissements étrangers directs,
pourrait être plus problématique. Le nœud du problème consiste
à déterminer si un ressortissant américain ou mexicain migrant au
Québec, dans le but d'y exercer une profession ou un métier réglementé, peut se qualifier d'investisseur au sens du chapitre 11. La
définition de ce concept opératoire est très large, puisqu'elle couvre l'individu qui *cherche,* effectue ou a effectué un investissement.[134]
Un "investissement" est entre autres une *entreprise,* un titre de participation dans une entreprise, un avoir dans une entreprise donnant droit à une part des revenus ou des bénéfices de l'entreprise,
ou encore des intérêts découlant de l'engagement de capitaux ou
d'autres ressources dans l'État d'accueil pour une activité économique exercée sur son territoire.[135] Un ressortissant américain ou
mexicain qui s'établirait au Québec pour y chercher à exploiter

---

[130] *Ibid.*, art. 1201:3 (a).

[131] *Ibid.*, art. 1203.

[132] *Ibid.*, art. 1210:2.

[133] *Ibid.*, art. 2004 et Annexe 2004.

[134] *Ibid.*, art. 1139.

[135] *Ibid.*

une entreprise fournissant des services professionnels pourrait-il remplir les critères de la définition d'investisseur?

Dans l'affirmative, cet individu jouirait de la protection juridique de l'ALENA à l'égard des investissements étrangers, comme la clause NPF[136]; cette dernière interdit la discrimination avec les investisseurs d'un pays tiers en ce qui concerne entre autres l'*établissement*, l'acquisition, la gestion ou la direction d'investissements. Le fait que les professionnels ou gens de métiers migrants de France au Québec bénéficient d'un système avantageux de reconnaissance de leurs qualifications professionnelles pourrait-il constituer un traitement moins favorable pour les professionnels ou gens de métier migrant en provenance des États-Unis ou du Mexique, en ce qui concerne l'établissement de leur investissement au Québec? Auraient-ils accès aux mêmes opportunités et aux mêmes conditions pour établir et exploiter une entreprise de services professionnels au Québec que les ressortissants français?

Il faut rappeler que les mesures adoptées par les entités fédérées ne sont pas exclues du chapitre 11 de l'ALENA. Le Canada pourrait donc voir sa responsabilité internationale être engagée par les mesures d'exécution de l'Entente France-Québec de 2008 prises par le Québec, si celles-ci devaient être jugées illicites par un tribunal arbitral. Les investisseurs étrangers qui s'estiment lésés par une mesure qui les concerne jouissent d'un recours international inconditionnel et immédiat auprès d'un tribunal arbitral, en vertu du mécanisme de règlement des différends du chapitre 11.[137] Ceux-ci pourraient réclamer des dommages-intérêts au Canada pour réparer le préjudice qu'ils auraient pu subir en raison de la violation de l'ALENA. Même si ces interrogations sur la compatibilité du système franco-québécois avec le chapitre 11 ne sont soulevées qu'à titre d'hypothèse, l'étude de l'utilisation par les personnes privées de leurs recours internationaux démontre qu'elles n'hésitent pas à les employer et à le faire de manière créative et originale, surtout lorsque ces recours sont inconditionnels.[138] Puisque le Canada et la France sont parties à de nombreux TBI qui peuvent prévoir des dispositions semblables au chapitre 11 de l'ALENA, ces questions méritent d'autant plus d'être posées.

---

[136] *Ibid.*, art. 1103.

[137] *Ibid.*, art. 1115–38.

[138] Charles-Emmanuel Côté, *La participation des personnes privées au règlement des différends internationaux économiques: l'élargissement du droit de porter plainte à l'OMC*, Bruxelles, Bruylant, 2007, aux pp. 304–6 et 510.

Compatibilité avec l'Accord de libre-échange Canada-AELE

Le système franco-québécois ne contrevient pas non plus au récent accord de libre-échange conclu entre le Canada et les États membres de l'Association européenne de libre-échange (AELE), c'est-à-dire l'Islande, le Liechtenstein, la Norvège et la Suisse.[139] Ce nouvel accord ne comporte aucune obligation significative en ce qui a trait au commerce international des services et au droit d'établissement. Il ne contient pas de clause NPF à cet égard, mais seulement une obligation à charge des Parties de s'efforcer d'informer la Partie qui en fait la demande sur toute mesure qui pourrait avoir des répercussions sur les échanges de services ou les investissements.[140] L'Accord contient en revanche une disposition très peu contraignante, suivant laquelle les Parties "encouragent" les organismes compétents sur leur territoire respectif à coopérer en vue de parvenir à la reconnaissance réciproque des licences et des certificats pour les fournisseurs de services professionnels.[141]

Compatibilité avec le droit communautaire

En ce qui concerne la France, la question qui se pose avec le plus d'acuité est celle de la compatibilité de l'Entente France-Québec de 2008 et de ses mesures d'exécution avec le droit communautaire. Cette question générale soulève une première sous-question, qui consiste à savoir si la France détient toujours le *jus tractatuum* en ce qui concerne la reconnaissance mutuelle des qualifications professionnelles ou si la capacité de conclure des traités à cet égard est désormais détenue en exclusivité par la CE. La deuxième sous-question soulevée est celle de savoir si la France peut prévoir dans un traité que certains professionnels ou gens de métiers établis sur son territoire recevront un traitement préférentiel à l'extérieur de la CE de la part d'un État tiers, pour s'y établir, au détriment d'autres professionnels ou gens de métiers établis sur le territoire français.

---

139 Voir Convention instituant l'Association européenne de libre-échange, 4 janvier 1960, 370 R.T.N.U. 203 (entrée en vigueur: 3 mai 1960).

140 Accord de libre-échange entre le Canada et les États de l'Association européenne de libre-échange (Islande, Liechtenstein, Norvège et Suisse), 26 janvier 2008, art. 12(2) (entrée en vigueur: 1er juillet 2009), disponible en ligne à: <http://www.international.gc.ca/trade-agreements-accords-commerciaux/agr-acc/efta-agr-acc.aspx?lang=fra&redirect=true>.

141 *Ibid.*, art. 12(3).

Un examen sommaire nous amène à constater que le système franco-québécois de reconnaissance mutuelle des qualifications professionnelles est probablement compatible avec le droit communautaire. Si l'on tente de circonscrire les accrocs possibles au Traité CE, il ne semble pas que les conditions respectives d'établissement en France des ressortissants européens et des ressortissants québécois soient problématiques, puisque le droit d'établissement en France des ressortissants européens est déjà largement garanti par le droit communautaire. Ce sont plutôt les conditions d'établissement au Québec des ressortissants européens autres que français qui pourraient être problématiques au regard du droit communautaire. Le système franco-québécois pourrait créer une discrimination *de facto* en faveur des ressortissants français, tel que discuté précédemment, puisque seules les qualifications professionnelles obtenues en France lui donnent accès. Une partie du problème pourrait être réglée par la suppression de la territorialité du diplôme, ce qui pourrait éliminer la discrimination *de facto* à cet égard, mais le problème de la territorialité du titre professionnel resterait entier, puisque le système vise la reconnaissance mutuelle des qualifications professionnelles obtenues en France ou au Québec. La question qui se pose est donc celle de savoir si la France peut, dans un traité, prévoir un système dans le cadre duquel les ressortissants européens seront moins bien traités que les ressortissants français? La jurisprudence récente de la Cour de justice des Communautés européennes sur ces questions, posée par les affaires dites "*open skies*," est particulièrement pertinente pour alimenter la réflexion sur ce questionnement.

Ces affaires découlent des recours en manquement introduits par la Commission européenne contre huit États membres qui avaient conclu des accords bilatéraux de transport aérien avec les États-Unis.[142] Le transport aérien avait déjà fait l'objet de plusieurs

---

142 *Commission c. Allemagne*, C-476/98 [2002], C.J.C.E. rec. I-9855; *Commission c. Autriche*, C-475/98 [2002], C.J.C.E. rec. I-9797; *Commission c. Luxembourg*, C-472/98 [2002], C.J.C.E. rec. I-9741; *Commission c. Belgique*, C-471/98 [2002], C.J.C.E. rec. I-9681; *Commission c. Finlande*, C-469/98 [2002], C.J.C.E. rec. I-9627; *Commission c. Suède*, C-468/98 [2002], C.J.C.E. rec. I-9575; *Commission c. Danemark*, C-467/98 [2002], C.J.C.E. rec. I-9519; *Commission c. Royaume-Uni*, C-466/98 [2002], C.J.C.E. rec. I-9427. Voir généralement Loïc Grard, "La Cour de justice des Communautés européennes et la dimension externe du marché unique des transports aériens: À propos des huit arrêts du 5 novembre 2002 dans l'affaire dite 'open skies'," *Cahiers de droit européen*, (2002), à la p. 695; A. Alemanno, "Note sous Cour de justice des Communautés européennes,"

instruments communautaires de droit dérivé qui visaient à mettre en place un marché unique dans ce secteur. Le principal problème posé par ces accords bilatéraux était qu'ils permettaient aux États-Unis d'offrir un traitement préférentiel uniquement aux sociétés aériennes de nationalité de l'État signataire, excluant du coup les sociétés de nationalité d'autres États membres de la CE qui sont établies sur le territoire de l'État signataire. Cela signifiait que les sociétés aériennes européennes avaient un accès fragmenté au marché américain, limitant leurs opportunités commerciales, tandis que les sociétés aériennes américaines avaient accès au marché unique européen. Ce déséquilibre dans les rapports commerciaux entre les États-Unis et l'Europe a poussé la Commission européenne à vouloir affirmer sa compétence externe exclusive dans le secteur du transport aérien.[143]

La Cour de justice a dénié la compétence externe de la CE de conclure des traités sur le transport aérien, tout en clarifiant sa jurisprudence antérieure sur certains aspects de la capacité internationale de Bruxelles. Il faut rappeler que le Traité CE prévoit explicitement que la CE jouit de la compétence exclusive pour conclure des accords commerciaux internationaux, depuis qu'elle a acquis les pleins pouvoirs sur la politique commerciale extérieure des États membres.[144] C'est sans doute pourquoi la France tient à ce que l'Entente France-Québec de 2008 ne soit pas considérée comme un accord commercial international.[145] Le secteur du transport aérien échappant à cette compétence externe générale,

---

(5 novembre 2002), *Revue du droit de l'Union européenne*, nᵒ 4 (2002), à la p. 838; Catherine Prieto, "Liberté d'établissement et de prestation de services," *Revue trimestrielle de droit européen*, nᵒ 3 (2003), à la p. 489; Henri Wassenbergh, "The Decision of the ECJ of 5 November 2002 in the 'Open Skies' Agreements Cases," (2003) 28 *Air & Space Law*, vol. 28 (2003), à la p. 19; Frank Hoffmeister, Commentaire de *Commission v. United Kingdom, Commission v. Denmark, Commission v. Sweden, Commission v. Finland; Commission v. Belgium, Commission v. Luxembourg, Commission v. Austria, Commission v. Germany. Cases C-466/98–469/98, C-471/98–472/98, C-475/98–476/98, 2002ECR I-9427, American Journal of International Law*, vol. 98 (2004), à la p. 567.

[143] Grard, *ibid.* aux pp. 696–701.

[144] Traité CE, *supra* note 10, art. 133. Voir Joël Rideau, *Droit institutionnel de l'Union et des Communautés européennes*, 3e éd., Paris, Librairie générale de droit et de jurisprudence, 1999, aux pp. 249–52.

[145] France, ministère des Affaires Étrangères et Européennes, "Informations pratiques sur l'Entente France-Québec en matière de reconnaissance mutuelle des qualifications professionnelles," disponible en ligne à: <http://www.ofiicanada.ca/entente.php>; Québec, ministère des Relations internationales, "Entente

la Commission européenne a cherché à fonder la capacité internationale de la CE sur deux autres chefs qui ont été dégagés par la jurisprudence communautaire.

Un premier chef de compétence externe exclusive de la CE sur une matière donnée découle du caractère nécessaire de la conclusion d'un traité sur cette matière, pour atteindre les objectifs du Traité CE, en combinaison avec l'impossibilité d'atteindre ces objectifs par l'introduction d'un instrument communautaire de droit dérivé.[146] Dans les affaires *"open skies,"* la Cour de justice a estimé que la CE aurait pu atteindre les objectifs du Traité CE visés par l'adoption d'instruments communautaires.[147] Cela fait dire à un observateur que la preuve de la satisfaction des critères de ce chef de compétence sera difficile à faire pour la CE.[148] Pour appliquer ce premier chef de compétence externe de la CE à la reconnaissance mutuelle des qualifications professionnelles, il suffit d'observer que plusieurs instruments de droit communautaire ont déjà été adoptés à ce sujet, et qu'il est probable que la preuve sera difficile à faire pour la CE qu'il est impossible de remédier aux problèmes qui pourraient être posés par l'Entente France-Québec de 2008 autrement qu'en négociant un traité communautaire sur la question. Au regard de ce premier chef de compétence, il semble probable que la France n'aurait pas perdu sa capacité internationale au profit de la CE.

Un deuxième chef de compétence externe exclusive de la CE sur une matière donnée découle du cas où les instruments communautaires de droit dérivé seraient "affectés ou altérés" par un traité bilatéral conclu par un État membre.[149] Les critères d'application de ce deuxième chef de compétence externe étaient imprécis et oscillaient entre une analyse quantitative, visant à déterminer si la matière est totalement ou largement couverte par la législation

---

France-Québec sur la reconnaissance mutuelle des qualifications professionnelles," disponible en ligne à: <http://www.mri.gouv.qc.ca/fr/grands_dossiers/qualifications_professionnelles/index.asp>.

[146] *Avis 1/76* [1977], C.J.C.E. rec. 741.

[147] *Commission c. Belgique, supra* note 142, para. 70 [seules des références à l'arrêt concernant la Belgique seront faites, mais le texte de tous les arrêts rendus dans les affaires *"open skies"* est pratiquement identique].

[148] Hoffmeister, *supra* note 142 à la p. 569.

[149] *Commission c. Conseil,* 22–70 [1971], C.J.C.E. rec. 263 [cette affaire est mieux connue comme l'affaire de l'Accord européen sur les transports routiers (AETR)].

communautaire, et une analyse qualitative, visant à déterminer si la législation communautaire touchait au traitement des ressortissants non européens ou à la négociation d'un traité avec un État tiers.[150] Les affaires *"open skies"* ont permis à la Cour de préciser les modalités d'application du critère qualitatif, qu'elle a préféré au critère quantitatif. La CE aura acquis la compétence externe exclusive sur une matière si les dispositions des instruments communautaires de droit dérivé régissent déjà le traitement à réserver aux ressortissants d'États non européens, si des dispositions de ces instruments confient à la CE la compétence de négocier un traité ou encore si ces instruments prévoient une harmonisation complète des dispositions nationales sur la question visée, par opposition à une harmonisation minimale.[151] Cela signifie que pour déterminer si la CE a acquis la compétence externe exclusive à l'égard de la reconnaissance mutuelle des qualifications professionnelles, il est nécessaire d'examiner la directive 2005/36/CE, qui est le principal instrument communautaire de droit dérivé en la matière. À première vue, il ne semble pas que cette directive couvre une de ces trois questions, ce qui signifierait que la France n'aurait pas non plus perdu sa capacité internationale en matière de reconnaissance mutuelle des qualifications professionnelles, sur la base de ce deuxième chef de compétence externe exclusive de la CE.

À supposer que la France ait effectivement perdu sa capacité internationale sur la reconnaissance mutuelle des qualifications professionnelles, le débat se déplacerait alors sur le terrain controversé du statut des ententes internationales du Québec. La question ne sera qu'effleurée, simplement pour rappeler que la position traditionnelle du gouvernement du Québec est que ses ententes sont de véritables traités au sens du droit international public, alors que la position traditionnelle du gouvernement fédéral du Canada est que les ententes du Québec sont dénuées de tout effet en droit international public.[152] Nous nous contenterons d'observer que la France a probablement intérêt à ne pas affirmer trop fort que

---

[150] Hoffmeister, *supra* note 142 aux pp. 569–70.

[151] *Commission c. Belgique*, *supra* note 142, paras. 95–98 et 107–8.

[152] Turp, "Doctrine Gérin-Lajoie," *supra* note 110 aux pp. 57–58; J. Maurice Arbour et Geneviève Parent, *Droit international public*, 5e éd., Cowansville, Yvon Blais, 2006, aux pp. 174–77; Jacques-Yvan Morin, "La personnalité internationale du Québec," *Revue québécoise de droit international*, vol. 1 (1984), aux pp. 256–75; André Trudeau, "La capacité international de l'État fédéré et sa participation au sein des organisations et conférences internationales," *Revue juridique Thémis*, vol. 3 (1968), aux pp. 244–46. Voir généralement Gibran van Ert, "The Legal

l'Entente France-Québec de 2008 est un traité au sens du droit international public, pour ne pas ouvrir le débat sur le statut de l'Entente et sur sa capacité internationale à conclure un tel traité au regard du droit communautaire. Nous avons pu recenser un document gouvernemental où la France affirme que "*L'Entente France-Québec* en matière de reconnaissance mutuelle des qualifications professionnelle est un *texte de nature politique* conclu par le Président de la République française Nicolas Sarkozy et le Premier Ministre du Québec Jean Charest. L'Entente *n'a donc pas à être validée par le Parlement français.*"[153] Paradoxalement, dans un dossier ou les relations France-Québec se sont approfondies, il apparaît que Paris pourrait être un allié objectif d'Ottawa dans le débat sur le statut juridique des ententes internationales du Québec. Mais nous pouvons aussi ajouter que ce cas en est peut-être un où le statut juridique ambigu de ces ententes offre une souplesse et une flexibilité qui sont positives pour les relations internationales du Québec.

Dans les affaires "*open skies,*" la compétence externe de la CE a été rejetée au titre des deux chefs de compétence précités. Cependant, la Cour de justice a donné raison à la Commission européenne sur la question de savoir si les accords bilatéraux de transport aérien étaient incompatibles avec le droit d'établissement garanti par le Traité CE. La disposition qui était problématique était celle qui prévoyait que les sociétés de transport aérien établies sur le territoire de l'État signataire, mais qui ne détenaient pas sa nationalité, pouvaient se voir refuser les droits reconnus par l'accord bilatéral. Il s'agissait de déterminer si un État membre peut prévoir dans un traité une disposition par laquelle un État tiers peut refuser aux ressortissants européens des droits qui sont reconnus par ce traité à ses propres ressortissants. La Cour de justice a décidé que

---

Character of Provincial Agreements with Foreign Governments," *Cahiers de droit*, vol. 42 (2001), à la p. 1093; Annemarie Jacomy-Millette, "Réflexions sur la valeur juridique des ententes du Québec," *Revue québécoise de droit international*, vol. 1 (1984), à la p. 93; Canada, Secrétariat d'État aux Affaires extérieures, *Fédéralisme et relations internationales* par Paul Martin, Ottawa, Imprimeur de la Reine et Contrôleur de la papeterie, 1968; Jacques-Yvan Morin, "La conclusion d'accords internationaux par les provinces canadiennes à la lumière du droit comparé," *Annuaire canadien de droit international*, vol. 3 (1965), à la p. 127.

153 France, ministère des Affaires Étrangères et Européennes, "Informations pratiques sur l'Entente France-Québec en matière de reconnaissance mutuelle des qualifications professionnelles," disponible en ligne à: <http://www.ofiicanada.ca/entente.php> [soulignés de l'auteur].

le droit d'établissement garanti par le Traité CE s'applique à toutes les sociétés établies sur le territoire d'un État membre, y compris lorsque les activités des dites sociétés consistent à fournir des servi- ces à destination d'États tiers.[154] Sur cette base, la Cour a jugé que les accords bilatéraux de transport aérien créaient une discrimina- tion illicite entre les sociétés aériennes nationales et les sociétés aériennes européennes établies dans l'État membre signataire, parce que les sociétés européennes n'avaient pas accès aux mêmes opportunités commerciales à l'étranger que les sociétés nationales.[155]

Le système franco-québécois de reconnaissance mutuelle des qualifications professionnelles viole-t-il le droit d'établissement garanti par le Traité CE? À nouveau la question du statut de l'En- tente France-Québec de 2008 en droit international public se pose pour donner application au raisonnement dégagé dans la jurispru- dence *"open skies."* Même à supposer qu'il s'agisse bien d'un traité au sens du droit international public, il semble à première vue qu'il n'y aurait pas de violation du droit d'établissement. En effet, contrai- rement aux faits dans les affaires *"open skies,"* l'Entente France- Québec de 2008 ne vise pas à ouvrir un marché d'exportation pour les fournisseurs de services établis en France. Il ne s'agit pas d'une entente visant à libéraliser le commerce international des services entre la France et le Québec, c'est-à-dire la prestation *temporaire* de services au Québec par des fournisseurs établis en France. Elle ne crée donc pas de distorsion économique sur le marché communau- taire entre les fournisseurs de services qui sont établis en France.[156] Elle cherche plutôt à faciliter *l'établissement permanent* au Québec de fournisseurs de services qui sont établis en France. L'Entente sem- ble échapper à la portée extérieure donnée au droit d'établissement par la Cour de justice des Communautés européennes. Par consé- quent, le système franco-québécois de reconnaissance mutuelle des qualifications professionnelles est sans doute compatible avec le traité de Rome.

À titre d'hypothèse, si le système franco-québécois devait néan- moins être soumis aux règles du droit d'établissement garanti par le Traité CE, il serait nécessaire de déterminer s'il prévoit un trai- tement préférentiel au profit des ressortissants français. Rappelons que le système interdit la discrimination fondée sur la nationalité,[157]

---

154 *Commission c. Belgique, supra* note 142, para. 133.

155 *Ibid.*, paras. 134–40.

156 Voir Grard, *supra* note 142 à la p. 704.

157 Voir *supra* note 74 et le texte correspondant.

ce qui signifie qu'il ne prévoit aucune discrimination *de jure* contre les ressortissants européens. En revanche, puisque les qualifications professionnelles doivent avoir été obtenues en France, il est raisonnable de penser que la grande majorité des individus qui utiliseront le système pour s'établir au Québec seront de nationalité française. Cette situation pourrait-elle constituer une discrimination *de facto* contre les ressortissants européens? La réponse à cette question deviendrait alors déterminante pour se prononcer sur la compatibilité du système franco-québécois avec le droit communautaire. L'interdiction de la discrimination fondée sur la nationalité nous apparaît en définitive être un élément très important de l'Entente France-Québec de 2008, qui contribuerait à maintenir sa licéité au regard du droit communautaire, dans l'hypothèse improbable où le système franco-québécois serait jugé soumis aux règles du droit d'établissement.

CONCLUSION

Le principal apport de l'Entente France-Québec de 2008 pourrait être d'opérer un changement de culture véritable chez les ordres professionnels, ce qui signifie que ses retombées pourraient dépasser les parties à l'Entente. Le gouvernement du Québec est engagé dans des discussions avec ses homologues provinciaux pour améliorer la libre circulation des professionnels et des gens de métiers au Canada, dans le cadre de l'Accord sur le commerce intérieur.[158] Des ententes intergouvernementales ont aussi été signées dans le secteur de la construction avec les provinces limitrophes du Québec.[159]

---

[158] Accord sur le commerce intérieur, 18 juillet 1994, art. 700–13 et annexe 708, disponible en ligne à: <http://www.ait-aci.ca/fr/ait/ait_fr.pdf> (entrée en vigueur: 1er juillet 1995; modifié pour la dernière fois par le Huitième Protocole de modification du 4 février 2009).

[159] Entente entre le gouvernement du Québec et le gouvernement du Nouveau-Brunswick sur la mobilité de la main d'œuvre et la reconnaissance de la qualification professionnelle, des compétences et des expériences de travail dans l'industrie de la construction, Entente intergouvernementale canadienne nᵒ 2008–112, disponible en ligne à: <http://www.saic.gouv.qc.ca/ententes_intergouvenementales/ententes2002au16avri12009.pdf>; Entente Québec-Ontario sur la mobilité de la main d'œuvre et la reconnaissance de la qualification professionnelle, des compétences et des expériences de travail dans l'industrie de la construction (2006), Entente intergouvernementale canadienne n° 2006–040, disponible en ligne à: <http://www.saic.gouv.qc.ca/ententes_intergouvenementales/ententes2002au16avri12009.pdf>; Entente entre

Le système franco-québécois de reconnaissance mutuelle des qualifications professionnelles offre certainement un modèle exportable aux relations avec d'autres partenaires étrangers du Québec. Le nouveau chantier transatlantique ouvert par l'Entente France-Québec de 2008 pourrait aussi jouer un rôle positif dans les négociations qui sont maintenant engagées entre le Canada et l'Union européenne en vue de conclure un accord de partenariat économique global.[160] Il pourrait s'agir d'un exemple où l'action internationale du Québec et l'action internationale du Canada peuvent se renforcer mutuellement, en plus de faciliter la vie quotidienne des nouveaux arrivants au Québec.

Toutefois, des ratés dans l'application de l'arrangement entre le Québec et l'Ontario sur la libre circulation des médecins, en raison du déséquilibre dans la migration des professionnels au profit de l'Ontario, ont récemment fait la manchette dans les journaux.[161] Ceci est un rappel que le suivi étroit des flux migratoires induits par l'Entente France-Québec de 2008, qui est confié au Comité bilatéral, sera un aspect important de sa mise en œuvre.

CHARLES-EMMANUEL CÔTÉ
Professeur à la Faculté de droit de l'Université Laval

ANNEXE

Le tableau qui suit présente de façon systématique l'état d'avancement au 1er juillet 2009 des ARM pour les professions prioritaires.

Québec et Terre-Neuve et Labrador sur la mobilité de la main d'œuvre et la reconnaissance de la qualification professionnelle, des compétences et des expériences de travail dans l'industrie de la construction, Entente intergouvernementale canadienne n° 1998–010, disponible en en ligne à: <http://www.saic.gouv.qc.ca/ententes_intergouvenementales/ententes-inter-1922–2001.pdf>.

160 Canada, ministère des Affaires étrangères et du Commerce international, "Canada-Union européenne: négociations en vue d'un accord de partenariat global," disponible en ligne à: <http://www.international.gc.ca/trade-agreements-accords-commerciaux/agr-acc/eu-ue/can-eu-report-intro-can-ue-rapport-intro.aspx?lang=fra>.

161 Lise-Marie Gervais, "Médecins: faut-il jeter l'entente avec l'Ontario?," *Le Devoir* (5 août 2009), à la p. A1.

ÉTAT D'AVANCEMENT DES ARM POUR LES PROFESSIONS PRIORITAIRES
au 1er juillet 2009

Profession	Échéance prévue	Conclusion ARM	Équivalence globale	Différences substantielles	Mesures de compensation
Architecte *Architecte*	30 avril 2009	9 avril 2009	Oui (pour le demandeur québécois)	Exigence d'expérience au Québec	Pour le demandeur français : • Expérience de 3 ans, ou à défaut, choix entre un stage d'adaptation d'un an ou une épreuve d'aptitude.
				Règles de la construction	Pour le demandeur québécois ou français dans l'année qui suit son inscription à l'ordre professionnel d'accueil: • *Formation complémentaire sur les règles de la construction.*
				Réglementation de la profession au Québec	Pour le demandeur français dans l'année qui suit son inscription à l'Ordre des architectes du Québec: • Formation complémentaire sur le contexte légal de la profession.
Arpenteur-géomètre *Géomètre-expert*	31 decembre 2009	9 juin 2009	Non	Exigence d'expérience professionnelle dans la partie d'accueil	Pour le demandeur québécois ou français: • Stage d'adaptation d'un an dans un cabinet de la partie d'accueil, avec possibilité de réduction de la durée selon l'expérience professionnelle;
				Domaines de connaissance en droit national	• Formation complémentaire sur les aspects juridiques de la profession.

▲

Profession	Échéance prévue	Conclusion ARM	Équivalence globale	Différences substantielles	Mesures de compensation
Avocat *Avocat*	31 decembre 2009	30 mai 2009	Non	Réglementation professionnelle et déontologie	Pour le demandeur québécois ou français: • Épreuve d'aptitude sur la réglementation professionnelle et la déontologie.
Comptable-agréé *Expert-comptable*	31 avril 2009	27 avril 2009	Non	Domaines de connaissance en droit national et en déontologie	Pour le demandeur québécois: • Épreuve d'aptitude en droit; • Formation complémentaire en déontologie.
				Champ de pratique et exigence d'expérience au Québec	Pour le demandeur français: • Expérience de 1 250 heures, ou à défaut, stage d'adaptation; • Formation complémentaire sur les normes professionnelles de mesure et de présentation de l'information financière; • Formation complémentaire sur les normes professionnelles en matière de certification; • Épreuve d'aptitude en droit et en déontologie.
Comptable général licencié *Expert-comptable*	31 avril 2009	27 avril 2009	Non	Domaines de connaissance en droit national et en déontologie	Pour le demandeur québécois: • Épreuve d'aptitude en droit; • Formation complémentaire en déontologie. Pour le demandeur français: • Formation complémentaire en droit.

Dentiste Chirurgien-dentiste	31 decembre 2009 signé le 17 octobre 2008	Engagement de conclure un ARM	s/o	s/o	s/o	s/o
Ingénieur Ingénieur	s/o	17 octobre 2008	Oui (pour les demandeurs (québécois)	Profession non en réglementée France à l'exception du titre Exigences de connaissances en matière de déontologie et de réglementation de la profession par le Québec	Pour le demandeur français: • Stage d'adaptation d'un an au Canada • Épreuve d'aptitude sur la déontologie et la réglementation de la profession.	s/o
Médecin Médecin	30 juin 2009	Engagement de conclure un ARM signé le 17 octobre 2008	s/o	s/o		s/o

Profession	Échéance prévue	Conclusion ARM	Équivalence globale	Différences substantielles	Mesures de compensation
Médecin vétérinaire *Vétérinaire*	31 decembre 2009	Engagement de conclure un ARM signé le 17 octobre 2008	s/o	s/o	s/o
Pharmacien *Pharmacien*	31 decembre 2009	Engagement de conclure un ARM signé le 17 octobre 2008	s/o	s/o	s/o
Sage-femme *Sage-femme*	31 decembre 2009	Engagement de conclure un ARM signé le 17 octobre 2008	s/o	s/o	s/o
Travailleur social *Assistant de service social*	31 mars 2009	27 avril 2009	Oui (pour les demandeurs français et dès la création dans les universités québécoises d'une formation sur le droit et les politiques sociales français)	Non	Pour le demandeur québécois, à titre transitoire: • Stage d'adaptation ou épreuve d'aptitude.

Summary

A New Transatlantic Workspace: The France-Québec Entente on Recognition of Professional Qualifications

The 2008 Entente entre le Québec et la France en matière de reconnaissance mutuelle des qualifications professionnelles *is undoubtedly the most important agreement that has been concluded by Québec lately. It aims at establishing a system of mutual recognition of professional qualifications between the two parties, to allow the permanent establishment of professionals in a jurisdiction other than that where they obtained their qualifications. Attuned to Québec's new international relations policy, the system has also been heavily influenced by the European Community's own system. Both systems are based on the principle that harmonization of professional education is not a precondition for recognition but, rather, that remedial measures may be required of migrants. An analysis of the implementation of the* entente *shows that professional bodies are actively involved in concluding mutual recognition arrangements but that the remedial measures imposed may vary greatly from one profession to another. Ambiguous provisions of the* entente *may in addition prove to be problematic in the future, most importantly in regard to its scope of application. Since the Québec-France system deals only with the permanent establishment of professionals, there seems to be no problem of conformity with international trade law or European Community law, with the possible exception of international investment law, with which some difficulty may arise. The new transatlantic workspace that has been opened up by the* entente *might serve as a model to be extended to other jurisdictions and may also illustrate the manner in which Québec's international initiatives may complement those undertaken by Canada, particularly as the latter is currently engaged in trade negotiations with the European Union.*

Sommaire

Un nouveau chantier transatlanique: l'entente France-Québec de 2008 sur la reconnaissance des qualifications professionnelles

*L'*Entente entre le Québec et la France en matière de reconnaissance mutuelle des qualifications professionnelles de 2008 *est sans doute la plus importante que le Québec a conclue au cours des dernières années. Celle-ci met en place un système franco-québécois de reconnaissance mutuelle des titres professionnels acquis en France ou au Québec, afin de* *permettre l'établissement permanent des professionnels sur le territoire d'accueil. Ce système, qui s'inscrit dans la nouvelle politique internationale du Québec, a subi l'influence significative du système général de reconnaissance mutuelle des qualifications professionnelles de la Communauté européenne. Les deux systèmes sont fondés sur le principe qu'il n'est pas nécessaire d'harmoniser le contenu des formations pour opérer leur reconnaissance, mais que des mesures de compensation peuvent cependant être prescrites aux professionnels migrants. L'étude de la mise en œuvre de l'Entente montre que les ordres professionnels sont activement engagés dans la conclusion d'arrangements de reconnaissance mutuelle, mais que les mesures de compensation prescrites varient grandement d'une profession à l'autre. Certaines dispositions ambigües de l'Entente pourraient également s'avérer problématiques, quant à son champ d'application en particulier. Le fait que le système franco-québécois porte exclusivement sur l'établissement permanent des professionnels migrants signifie que celui-ci apparaît compatible avec le droit international économique et le droit communautaire, mais certaines difficultés pourraient survenir avec le droit international de l'investissement. Le nouveau chantier transatlantique qui est ouvert par l'Entente pourrait être un modèle à suivre, en plus de constituer un exemple où l'action internationale du Québec renforce celle du Canada sur la scène internationale, alors que celui-ci s'engage actuellement dans des négociations commerciales avec l'Union européenne.*

Giving Effect to Out-of-Province
Judgments in Class Actions

INTRODUCTION

R ecently, on a number of occasions, Canadian courts have been
asked to recognize foreign judgments approving inter-
provincial[1] or international[2] class actions settlements involving some
non-resident plaintiff members of the class. Should such class action
settlements have a *res judicata* effect on its non-resident members
and prevent them from litigating again the same issues in the courts
of their residence?[3] Should the private international law rules applicable to the recognition and enforcement of foreign judgments
in force in common law Canada and in civil law Québec take into
account certain unique features of inter-provincial and international class actions proceedings since it is the settling defendant who is
seeking to enforce the foreign judgment rendered against him or
her approving the out-of-court settlement in order to preclude
further litigation?[4] Should the real and substantial connection test
and the principles of order and fairness apply to the non-resident,
absent plaintiffs who are members of the class action?[5] In *Canada*

---

[1] Class action brought in Canada involving residents of more than one Canadian
province or territory.

[2] Class action brought in Canada or abroad involving residents of Canada and of
one or more foreign countries.

[3] Civil Code of Quebec, art. 2848, para. 2, which deals with the authority of a
Québec final judgment deciding a class action. Such judgment has no *res judicata*
effect with respect to parties and members who have excluded themselves from
the group.

[4] See *Currie v. McDonald's Restaurants of Canada Ltd* (2005), 74 O.R. (3d) 321 at
329, para. 13 [*Currie*].

[5] *Morguard Investments Ltd v. De Savoye*, [1990] 3 S.C.R. 1077 [*Morguard*].

Post Corp. v. Lépine, the Supreme Court of Canada answered some of these questions in light of the relevant provisions of the Civil Code of Quebec (Civil Code).[6] However, parts of its decision may have important implications for the rest of Canada.

From a policy point of view, it is generally agreed that private international law rules should recognize that, in appropriate cases, it is important to have only one class action binding all of its members irrespective of their residences. Although, often, counsel in the various jurisdictions involved will co-ordinate the certification of the class actions and the settlement agreements to be approved by the courts in order to avoid the problems of the binding effect of the judgments rendered in these class actions, this is not always the case when non-resident absent members of the plaintiffs' class are involved.[7] In principle, there is no reason why Canadian courts should refuse to recognize foreign judgments approving out-of-court settlements of class actions. Yet, the special nature of this type of action may call for the adaptation of traditional rules of private international law.

Class actions provide greater access to justice for plaintiffs, and they improve judicial efficiency. By consolidating claims in a single proceeding, multiple suits can be avoided. This is particularly important when the individual claims are small and would be abandoned because of the cost of litigation. Taking such a result into account, Canadian legislatures have adopted statutes dealing with class actions, and Canadian courts have certified inter-provincial and international class actions. On the basis of comity, the same power should be recognized in foreign courts. However, Canadian courts must prevent abuses by counsel for the plaintiffs particularly with respect to the adequacy of compensation to be given to non-resident absent class members as the negotiated settlement may not always reflect the merits of the claims.

---

6   *Canada Post Corp. v. Lépine*, 2009 SCC 16 [*Lépine*]

7   The Uniform Law Conference of Canada has recommended means for co-ordinating class proceedings in Canada so as to minimize uncertainty arising from multi-jurisdictions class proceedings. Uniform Law Conference of Canada, *Report of the Uniform Law Conference of Canada 's Committee on the National Class and Related Inter-jurisdictional Issues: Background, Analysis and Recommendations*, Uniform Law Conference of Canada, Vancouver, 9 March 2005; and *Supplementary Report on Multi-jurisdictional Class Proceedings in Canada*, Uniform Law Conference of Canada, Edmonton, August 2006 <http://www.ulcc.ca>. In Québec, there is a central registry of applications for authorization to institute class actions kept at the office of the Superior Court. Code of Civil Procedure, art. 1051.

More important is the adequacy of the notice to be given to non-resident plaintiffs as to their rights in the action and settlement, including the right to opt in or out of the class, since the legislation applicable to foreign actions may be quite different from that which is in force where the absent defendant member of the class resides. In non-Canadian class actions, the adequacy of the notice may be more crucial than in Canadian class actions in order to protect the interests of the non-resident members of the plaintiffs' class since in Canada the provincial legislation is quite uniform and contains strict rules with respect to notice of class actions.[8]

The question of whether foreign judgments approving settlements of inter-provincial or international class actions should be recognized and given effect would seem to depend upon the contents of the relevant Canadian or foreign legislation applicable to class actions:

1. Where this legislation allows non-residents to opt in, the non-resident members of the class who did not opt in are obviously not bound by the foreign judgment.[9] Could they argue that, had they received an adequate notice, they would have opted in?

2. Where the legislation allows non-residents to opt out, which is the most common form, are the non-resident members of the class who did not opt out bound by the foreign judgment?[10] If they had received adequate notice, which is generally given after the certification of the class, but did nothing, can they be considered as having attorned or implicitly consented to the jurisdiction of the foreign court?[11]

---

[8] For the legislation in force in Canada, see <http://www.branmac.com>. In Québec, specific rules exist with respect to the approval of out-of-court settlements that are different from those of other provinces. Code of Civil Procedure, art. 1025.

[9] See, e.g., Alberta, Class Proceedings Act, S.A. 2003, c. C-16.5, s. 17(1) (b); B.C., Class Proceedings Act, R.S.B.C., 1996, c. 50, s.16(2); Newfoundland, Class Actions Act, S.N.L. 2001, c. C-18.1, s. 17(2).

[10] See, e.g., Manitoba, Class Proceedings Act, C.C.S.M., c. C-130, s. 16; Saskatchewan, Class Actions Act, S.S. 2001, c. C-12.01, s.18; Nova Scotia, Class Proceedings Act, S.N.S. 2007, c. 28, ,s.11(1) (f); Ontario, Class Proceedings Act, S.O. 1992, c. 6, s. 9; Québec, Code of Civil Procedure, arts. 1006 (e), 1007,1008.

[11] The legislation of several provinces specifically contemplate the inclusion of non-resident class members, e.g., Alberta, S.A. 2003, c. C-16.6, ss. 7(1) ,(3) and 17(1) (b); British Columbia, R.B.C. 1996, c. 50, ss. 6(2) and 16(2); Manitoba, C.C.S.M. c. C 130, ss. 6(3) and 16; Saskatchewan, S.S. 2001, c. C-12.01, s. 18(2); Newfoundland, S.N.L. 2001, c. C-18.1, ss. 7(2) and 17(2). In Ontario, the courts

Traditional private international law rules in force in common law Canada[12] and in Québec,[13] which deal with the recognition of a foreign judgment *in personam*, require, first of all, that the foreign court must have had jurisdiction to issue such a judgment. Jurisdiction must have been exercised appropriately in accordance with principles of order and fairness, which call for the existence of a real and substantial connection between the cause of action and the foreign court that rendered the judgment.[14] This is a constitutional obligation that applies inter-provincially and internationally.[15] Once this requirement has been met, the judgment can still be impeached for a variety of reasons, one of the most important of which is that the foreign proceedings were conducted in a manner contrary to natural justice — for instance, where the plaintiff failed to provide an adequate notice of the proceedings to the defendant or, more generally, where the defendant had not been given a sufficient opportunity to be heard.[16] In a traditional non-class action, there is no question as to the jurisdiction of the foreign court to bind the plaintiff since he or she is the one who initiated the proceedings. The main issue relating to recognition is whether the foreign judgment binds the defendant.

In a class action, the position of the plaintiff is not the same as that of a typical defendant. Since the non-resident class plaintiff is not brought before the foreign court and required to defend himself or herself upon pain of a default judgment as in the case of a defendant, it has been held that "[c]lass action regimes typically impose upon the court a duty to ensure that the interests of the plaintiff class members are adequately protected."[17] This is particularly important with respect to non-resident class plaintiffs who did not participate in the foreign proceedings due to a lack of notice

---

have allowed it as the *Class Proceedings Act*, S.O. 1992, c. 6, is silent on non-residents. The same is true in Québec. More generally, see Code of Civil Procedure, arts. 999 to 1051; and Civil Code of Quebec, art. 2848 (presumption of *res judicata*), and arts. 2897 and 20908 (prescription).

12 J.-G. Castel and J. Walker, *Canadian Conflict of Laws*, 6th edition (Markham: Butterworths, 2005), ch. 14.

13 Civil Code of Quebec, arts. 3134–3140 and 3155–3168, book 10, titles 3 and 4.

14 *Morguard, supra* note 5.

15 *Hunt v. T & N plc.,* [1993] 4 S.C.R. 289.

16 *Beals v. Saldanha,* [2003] S.C.R. 416 [*Beals*].

17 *Currie, supra* note 4 at 332, para. 20 (Sharpe J.A.).

of the class action and, therefore, did not avail themselves of the possibility of opting in or out.

With respect to the common law provinces, Justice of Appeal Robert Sharpe in *Currie v. MacDonald's Restaurants of Canada Ltd* attempted to develop new rules of private international law as he was concerned with the question whether Ontario should recognize an *international* class action judgment rendered in Illinois that approved a settlement against non-attorning Canadian resident members of the class who had not opted out and whether the notice given to them satisfied the requirements of natural justice.[18] Should such a foreign judgment preclude a non-resident, non-attorning member of the class from suing in Ontario? This raised first the issue of the jurisdiction of the foreign court. Applying the principles of order and fairness and real and substantial connection enunciated in *Morguard Investments Ltd. v. De Savoye,*[19] which are generally applicable to defendants, Sharpe J.A. extended them to the non-resident, non-attorning class member plaintiffs. Having done nothing to invite or invoke the foreign jurisdiction, the Illinois court lacked jurisdiction over them. His lordship pointed out that the recognizing court cannot approach the issue of jurisdiction simply by asking whether the foreign court would have had jurisdiction over the defendant at the suit of a Canadian plaintiff. The recognizing court must also have regard to the rights and interests of the non-resident members of the plaintiffs' class who did not participate in the foreign proceedings. Although there may have been a real and substantial connection between the defendant or the cause of action and the Illinois court, the principles of order and fairness require the recognizing court to consider the adequacy of the procedural rights of the non-resident, non-attorning class members. In assessing these rights, the recognizing court must examine the adequacy of the plaintiffs' representation, the adequacy of the notice given to them, the right to opt out, and any other factors that may strengthen or weaken the connection with the foreign court.

Sharpe J.A. was of the opinion that the right to opt out by a class member is a very important procedural protection afforded to non-resident class action plaintiffs that allows them to preserve their legal rights, which would otherwise be determined or compromised

---

[18] *Ibid.*

[19] *Morguard, supra* note 5. In Ontario, see *Mignacca v. Merck Frosst Canada Ltd.* (2009), 95 O.R. (3d) 269 (Div. Ct.) where it was held that a motion judge is not bound by principles of comity and full faith and credit to defer to a Saskatchewan order.

by the class proceedings. To be meaningful, the right to opt out must be properly notified to the plaintiffs. Similarly, in the provinces where non-resident plaintiffs must opt in class proceedings, proper notice must also be given to them. Therefore, the notice of the right to opt in or out must be adequate. In his conclusion, Sharpe J.A. stated the law to be as follows:

[P]rovided that

(a) there is a real and substantial connection linking the cause of action to the foreign jurisdiction,

(b) the rights of non resident class members are adequately represented, and

(c) the non resident class members are accorded procedural fairness including adequate notice, it may be appropriate to attach jurisdictional consequences to an unnamed non-resident plaintiff's failure to opt out. In those circumstances failure to opt out may be regarded as a form of passive attornment sufficient to support the jurisdiction of the foreign court."[20]

It must be noted that His Lordship uses procedural fairness to support the jurisdiction of the foreign court although the emphasis is on the lack of adequate notice. In the lexicon of foreign judgments, a lack of adequate notice amounts to a denial of natural justice.

Among recent Québec decisions dealing with class actions, the most important is *Canada Post Corp. v. Lépine*, which has addressed some important private international law rules for the recognition and enforcement of foreign/external class action judgments affecting the rights of Québec residents.[21] The facts are quite simple. In September 2000, the Canada Post Corporation had offered its customers a lifetime Internet access package using software designed and produced by Cybersurf. On 15 September 2001, the service was discontinued. As a result, in 2001, on behalf of all Canadian consumers who had purchased the package, the Alberta government filed a complaint against Canada Post and Cybersurf, which was settled in 2002. The same year on 6 February, the plaintiff, Michel Lépine, sought to represent in a Québec class action, any natural

---

[20] *Currie, supra* note 4 at 335, para. 30.

[21] *Lépine, supra* note 6. Note that the Supreme Court of Canada, at para. 14, called the Ontario judgment an external rather than a foreign one despite the language used in the Civil Code of Quebec: "foreign decisions, décisions étrangères" (at art. 3155 *et seq.*), which does not make a distinction since both types of judgments are treated the same way.

person residing in the province who had purchased the package. Similarly, on 28 March, Paul McArthur sought to represent in an inter-provincial class action in Ontario, any person in Canada who had purchased the package except persons in Québec. Finally, on 7 May, John Chain also sought to be authorized to represent in a class action in British Columbia any person residing in the province who had bought the package. Thus, in 2002, claims involving dissatisfied customers comprised one inter-provincial class action in Ontario and two local class actions — one in British Columbia and one in Québec — all arising from the same occurrence.

On 3 July 2003, the plaintiffs in the British Columbia and Ontario proceedings negotiated a national settlement the effect of which was to change the groups covered by the two proposed class actions. One group was to be made of British Columbia residents and the other group by the rest of Canadian consumers including those of Québec. Counsel for the Québec residents did not agree to participate in the proposed national settlement being negotiated by counsel for the parties in the other class actions. On 22 December 2003, the Ontario Superior Court of Justice certified the class proceeding and approved the settlement negotiated by the parties. The *Lépine* motion for authorization to institute the class action in Québec was approved on 23 December 2003 by the Québec Superior Court. On 7 April 2004, the British Columbia court also approved the settlement and, on 7 and 9 April 2004, notices were sent to members concerning the Ontario and British Columbia actions and published in Québec. These notices informed the parties that they had the right to be excluded from the settlement. Notices of the Québec class action were also sent to Québec residents by Lépine. On 11 June 2004, Canada Post attempted to have the Ontario judgment recognized and enforced in Québec and to seek the dismissal of the Québec class action on the basis of *res judicata*. The Québec Superior Court refused to do so — a decision that was confirmed by the Québec Court of Appeal and on further appeal by the Supreme Court of Canada.

The Superior Court judge[22] relied on a number of articles of the Civil Code, especially paragraph 3 of Article 3155,[23] which provides:

---

[22] *Canada Post Corp. v. Lépine*, 2005 Can LII 26419 [*Lépine* (Sup. C.)].

[23] Civil Code of Quebec, arts. 3134–37, 3148, 3149, and 3155, 3164, 3165, and 3168, which deal with private international law especially jurisdiction and foreign judgments.

3155. A Quebec authority recognizes and, where applicable, declares enforceable any decision rendered outside Quebec, except in the following cases:

(3) the decision was rendered in contravention of the fundamental principles of procedure.[24]

He also quoted extensively the remarks of Sharpe J.A. in the *Currie* decision to find that the notice given to the Québec members of the Ontario national class action was inadequate and violated the rules of natural justice. In his discussion of inadequate dissemination or circulation of the notice he stated:

However, far more important than the issue of dissemination and of the required notices and their publication as required by law, is that the notice itself be clear, adequate and sufficiently informative so as to permit the reader to take the appropriate steps to, in accordance with the notice itself, opt out which is the ultimate protection for an individual who does not wish to participate in the class.[25]

The Ontario notice was found to be inadequate and confusing for an untrained Québec person who had previously read the notice of the Québec class action. It did not adequately inform the members of the Québec class, nor did it distinguish their rights between the two parallel class actions. It was decided that this is why the Québec residents had not been treated fairly by the Ontario judgment.

In dismissing the appeal, the Québec Court of Appeal also relied primarily on Article 3155(3) of the Civil Code.[26] On behalf of the court, the Justice Pierette Rayle was of the opinion that the content and method of dissemination of the notice to members were two fundamental principles of procedure in class actions within the meaning of Article 3155(3) "as they alone make it possible for all members to personally define their positions and, as the case may be, to protect themselves from the release that the defendant could otherwise set up against persons who have not excluded themselves."[27] Like the trial judge, she found that "the notice to the

---

24 This article covers the defences to the recognition and enforcement of foreign decisions.

25 *Lépine* (Sup. C.), *supra* note 22 at para. 38.

26 *Canada Post Corp. v. Lépine*, [2007] R.J.Q. 1920 [*Lépine* (C.A.)].

27 *Ibid.* at para. 71.

Ontario member caused confusion for readers who had already read the Quebec notice. This constitutes a violation of the essential requirements of procedure, justifying the application of the exception in article 3155(3) C.C.Q. which was within the jurisdiction of the Superior Court to find."[28]

The Québec Court of Appeal, relying on Articles 3155, 3164, and 3168, held that the Ontario court had jurisdiction over the action brought by the Ontario consumer.[29] However, jurisdiction based on the real and substantial connection test between the forum and the cause of action must have been established for each of the members of the class, including the Québec non-residents, which had not been the case. The Ontario court should not have modified the composition of the class and should have declined jurisdiction over Québec residents on the basis of *forum non conveniens*.[30] Therefore, the Québec Court of Appeal refused to recognize the Ontario judgment, basing itself also on Article 3155, paragraph 1, which precludes recognition and enforcement of foreign decisions where "the authority of the country where the decision was rendered had no jurisdiction under the provisions of this Title." According to Article 3164, the foreign court must have had jurisdiction according to the Québec private international law rules of jurisdiction that include the doctrine of *forum non conveniens*,[31] adopted by Article 3135 of the Civil Code.[32] The court did not adopt the views of those

---

[28] *Ibid.* at para. 73.

[29] *Ibid.* at para. 62.

[30] *Ibid.* at paras. 69 and 90.

[31] *Ibid.* at para. 62; and Castel and Walker, *supra* note 12 at 14–23, para. 14–4e; G. Goldstein and E. Groffier, *Traité de droit civil, Droit international privé*, t. 1 (Cowansville, PQ: Yvon Blais, 1998) at 417, para. 175; H.P. Glenn, "Droit international privé," in *La Réforme du code civil*, t. 3 (Québec City: Presses de l'Université Laval, 1993) at 669, paras 116–19, and 769–73; and J.A. Talpis and J.-G. Castel, "Interpreting the Rules of Private International Law," in *La Réforme du code civil*, t. 5 (Québec City: Presses de l'Université Laval, 1993) at 801, paras 485–87 and 916–17. Civil Code of Quebec, art. 3164 reads as follows: "The jurisdiction of foreign authorities is established in accordance with the rules applicable to Quebec authorities under Title Three of this Book, to the extent that the dispute is substantially connected with the country whose authority is seised of the case." This is called the mirror principle since foreign rules of jurisdiction must reflect Quebec rules

[32] Civil Code of Quebec, art. 3135: "Even though a Quebec authority has jurisdiction to hear a dispute, it may exceptionally and on an application by a party, decline jurisdiction if it considers that the authorities of another country are in a better position to decide." This is called the little mirror since the foreign court

who believe that Article 3164 does not include the doctrine of *forum non conveniens*,[33] nor did it consider that the question of jurisdiction of the foreign court based on a real and substantial connection (*jurisdiction simpliciter*) is a question of law that should be separated from the discretion exercised by the court once jurisdiction exists.[34]

In reaching its decision, the Québec Court of Appeal could not understand

why the Ontario court was not guided by the same principle of comity with respect to the Quebec court before which it had been brought, before any other proceeding elsewhere in Canada had been commenced, a dispute that in no way infringed upon the exercise of jurisdiction by the two other Canadian provinces.[35]

If the Ontario court had applied principles of inter-provincial comity as mandated by the Supreme Court of Canada in *Morguard*, it would have excluded Quebec residents from the Ontario national class action.[36] The Québec Court of Appeal was also of the opinion that the Ontario judgment should not be recognized on the basis

---

in deciding whether to exercise jurisdiction must apply Québec notions of *forum non conveniens*, see the *Lépine* case, *supra* note 6 at para. 28. The rules found in arts. 3164 and 3135 were not part of Québec law prior to the coming into force of the Civil Code of Quebec on 1 January 1994 nor are they found in the 1975 *Report on Private International Law* prepared by the Civil Code Revision Office.

33 See G. Saumier, "The Recognition of Foreign Judgments in Quebec: The Mirror Cracked" (2002) 78 Can. Bar. Rev. 677 at 691–94. J.A. Talpis, *If I Am from Grand-Mère Why Am I Being Sued in Texas? Responding to Inappropriate Foreign Jurisdiction in Quebec- United States Crossborder Litigation* (Montréal: Thémis, 2001) at 109. Note that in *Hocking c. Haziza et HSBC Canada*, 2008 QCCA 800 (Bich J.A. for the majority of the Quebec Court of Appeal) at para. 181, Québec courts must first determine whether the requirements of Article 3168 of the Civil Code for personal actions of a patrimonial nature are fulfilled. Second, they must establish the existence of a substantial connection between the dispute and the foreign court that was seized of the class action by virtue of Article 3164 of the Civil Code. Third, they must assess the appropriateness of the foreign court's decision to exercise jurisdiction by examining how well that decision harmonizes with the general provisions of Québec's rules of private international law, including the doctrine of *forum non conveniens* in Article 3135. She added that the fundamental principles of order and fairness must also be considered when determining the jurisdiction of the foreign court (at para. 181).

34 Saumier, *supra* note 33 at 691.

35 *Lépine* (C.A.), *supra* note 26 at para. 89.

36 *Morguard*, *supra* note 5.

of *lis pendens* since at the time of this judgment the dispute, which had met the triple requirements in Article 3155(4) of the Civil Code,[37] had already been brought before the Québec court.[38] Finally, the Québec Court of Appeal was of the view that Article 3149 and 3168(5), which deal with jurisdiction with respect to consumer contracts and the effect of a waiver of the jurisdiction of the court of the consumer's domicile or residence, had no impact on the question of the jurisdiction of the Ontario court since this type of jurisdiction is not exclusive.[39]

In dismissing the appeal, the Supreme Court of Canada took a cautious approach to the recognition of foreign/external judgments approving the settlement of class actions involving some non-residents and, it is submitted, rightly so. The Supreme Court of Canada, like the courts below, was concerned with the interpretation and application of Article 3155 of the Civil Code since the dispute between the parties raised three issues, namely the application of the doctrine of *forum non conveniens* to ascertain the jurisdiction of the Ontario court, whether this court adhered to fundamental principles of procedure within the meaning of Article 3155(3), and whether the application for authorization in Québec and the application for certification in Ontario gave rise to a situation of *lis pendens*. The Court also offered some comments on the issue of inter-provincial judicial comity in the conduct of inter-provincial class actions.

From a Québec point of view, the most important point decided by the Supreme Court of Canada is its rejection of a literal interpretation of Article 3164 in light of Articles 3155(1), 3168, and 3135. Justice Louis Lebel, speaking on behalf of the Court, was of the opinion that "the Court of Appeal added an irrelevant factor to the analysis of the foreign court's jurisdiction: the doctrine of *forum non conveniens*."[40] To apply the doctrine of *forum non conveniens* found in Article 3135 (the little mirror) as part of the mirror principle adopted by Article 3164 to determine whether the court of

---

[37] "(4) A dispute between the same parties, based on the same facts and having the same object has given rise to a decision rendered in Quebec, whether it has acquired the authority of a final judgment (*res judicata*) or not, or is pending before a Quebec authority, in first instance , or has been decided in a third country and the decision meets the necessary conditions for recognition in Quebec."

[38] *Lépine* (C.A.), *supra* note 26 at paras. 75 and 78.

[39] *Ibid.* at paras. 59–61.

[40] *Lépine, supra* note 6 at para. 36.

another province or country should have exercised its discretion to decline jurisdiction over the case or suspend its intervention is not compatible with inter-provincial and international comity and defeats the liberal approach taken by the Civil Code towards the recognition and enforcement of foreign judgments.[41] The issue is simply whether the foreign court had jurisdiction based on Articles 3165 and 3168 and not how this jurisdiction was exercised.[42] The Supreme Court of Canada did not reject entirely the substantial connection requirement of Article 3164 as it recognized that "it may be necessary in considering a complex legal situation involving two or more parties in different parts of the world to apply the general principle in art. 3164 in order to establish jurisdiction and have recourse to, for example, the forum of necessity."[43] Applying this new interpretation, the Supreme Court of Canada found that the Ontario Court of Justice had jurisdiction pursuant to Article 3168 since the defendant, Canada Post Corporation, had its head office in Ontario. The Supreme Court of Canada did not address the question whether the Ontario court should have had jurisdiction over the non-resident plaintiff members of the class who failed to opt out, and, therefore, the Court impliedly rejected the approach taken by Sharpe J.A. in the *Currie* case who was of the opinion that "the notice issue bears upon jurisdiction."[44]

What prompted the Supreme Court of Canada to dismiss the appeal was the fact that the notice provided for in the Ontario judgment contravened the fundamental principles of procedural fairness within the meaning of Article 3155(3) of the Civil Code. Here, the Supreme Court of Canada developed further the general rule that the foreign proceedings must not have been contrary to natural

---

[41] *Ibid.* at paras. 35–36. "This approach introduces a degree of instability and unpredictability that is inconsistent with the standpoint generally favorable to the recognition of foreign or external judgments that is evident in the provisions of the Civil Code" (at para. 36).

[42] *Ibid.* at paras. 34–35. Art. 3165 deals with situations where the jurisdiction of the foreign authority is not recognized and art. 3168 lists the only cases where the jurisdiction of a foreign authority is recognized in personal actions of a patrimonial nature.

[43] *Ibid.* at para. 36. Civil Code of Quebec, art. 3136: "Even though a Quebec authority has no jurisdiction to hear a dispute, it may hear it, if the dispute has a sufficient connection with Quebec, where proceedings cannot possibly be instituted outside Quebec or where the institution of such proceedings outside Quebec cannot reasonably be required."

[44] *Currie, supra* note 4 at para. 31; see also paras. 21, 30, and 41–42.

justice since "a class action takes place outside the framework of the traditional duel between a single plaintiff and a single defendant ... For this reason, adequate information is necessary to satisfy the requirement that individual rights be safeguarded in class proceedings."[45] In other words, the requirement of procedural fairness is more demanding in class proceedings involving non-resident plaintiff members of the class. On the question of procedural fairness, the Supreme Court of Canada adopted the views expressed by the Québec Court of Appeal, which were based on those of the Ontario Court of Appeal in the *Currie* case:

Although it does not have to be shown that each member was actually informed, the way the notice procedure is designed must make it likely that the information will reach the intended recipients ... In light of the requirement of comity between courts of the various provinces of Canada, they are no less compelling in a case concerning recognition of a judgment from within Canada.[46]

This reasoning is quite important since in another of its decisions, which did not involve class actions, the Supreme Court of Canada had stated that with respect to Canadian actions "fair process is not an issue within the Canadian federation."[47] In the present case, the clarity of notice to the members of the class was particularly important in light of the parallel class proceedings in Ontario and Québec.

The Supreme Court of Canada also accepted the argument that the Ontario judgment could not be recognized on the basis of *lis pendens* pursuant to Article 3155(4) of the Civil Code. The application for authorization to institute a class action in Québec is a form of judicial proceedings between the parties for the purpose of determining whether a class action will in fact take place. Since the application for authorization was before the Québec Superior Court before 23 December 2003, when the authorization to institute the class action was approved, the three identities required by Article 3155(4) were met at the relevant time. No discretion was given to the Québec courts as in the case of Article 3137 of the Civil Code: "[T]he Quebec court has priority provided it was seised of the case first."[48]

---

45 *Lépine, supra* note 6 at para. 42.

46 *Ibid.* at para. 43.

47 *Morguard, supra* note 5 at para. 43.

48 *Lépine, supra* note 6 at para. 50.

Finally, it is interesting to note that the Supreme Court of Canada remarked that the creation of classes of claimants from two or more provinces "raises the issue of relations between equal but different superior courts in a federal system in which civil procedure and the administration of justice are under provincial jurisdiction."[49] To avoid friction, "[m]ore effective methods for managing jurisdictional disputes should be established in the spirit of mutual comity that is required between the courts of different provinces in the Canadian legal space."[50] This is an appeal for judicial co-operation based on comity, which the Québec Court of Appeal had found lacking.[51]

Although the Supreme Court of Canada was dealing with an interprovincial class action and Québec law, its pronouncements are equally applicable to international actions and, to some extent, to the rest of Canada. For Québec, the elimination of Article 3135 of the Civil Code from the scope of Article 3164 removes a serious obstacle to the recognition and enforcement of foreign judgments in general, as one discretionary power is better than two! With respect to both common law in Canada and civil law in Québec, the decision strengthens the procedural safeguards applicable to class actions especially with respect to non-resident, non-attorning members of the class. Finally, and also of great importance for the whole of Canada, the Supreme Court of Canada did not require jurisdiction to be established over each non-resident plaintiff member of a class. As in the past, all that is needed is the existence of a real and substantial connection between the foreign court and the cause of action or the defendant. It is not necessary to extend to non-resident class members who have not opted out and have not attorned to the jurisdiction the real and substantial connection test applicable to jurisdiction *simpliciter,* even if this test is adapted to class actions by adopting the expansive commonality of interest between the claims of resident and non-resident class members as a whole rather than the restrictive approach of actual connection between each non-resident member of the class and the foreign

---

[49] *Ibid.* at para. 57.

[50] *Ibid.*

[51] Note that the courts are not constrained by constitutional considerations from certifying an inter-provincial plaintiff class although it is not settled whether section 92 or 129 of the Canadian Constitution is the proper basis for provincial jurisdiction. See *Caron v. Bre-X Minerals Ltd.* (1999), 43 O.R. (3d) 441; and *Western Canada Shopping Centres Inc. v. Dutton,* [2001] 2 S.C.R. 534.

court as favoured by the Québec Court of Appeal. As T.J. Monestier explains, "the real and substantial connection required to ground jurisdiction over non-resident class members is found in the identity or confluence of interest that such non-resident class members share with resident class members in the resolution of common issues."[52] He continues: "[R]equiring a real and substantial connection between non resident plaintiffs and the forum in a class setting does not necessarily further the goals of order and fairness."[53]

By insisting on a more robust notion of procedural fairness to protect non-resident, absent members of the plaintiffs' class, the Supreme Court of Canada, without having to modify existing jurisdictional rules of private international law applicable to the recognition of foreign judgments, addressed their special situation, which, to some extent, is similar to that of the traditional defendants since the foreign court was not of their choosing. The Court should be commended for keeping jurisdiction distinct from the defence of lack of procedural fairness since this defence applies regardless of whether the foreign court had jurisdiction. Contrary to the opinion of Sharpe J.A., procedural fairness that relates to procedural safeguards such as the adequacy of the original court procedures, the adequacy of notice, the possibility of opting out, and the adequacy of representation should not be tied to jurisdiction. The lack of procedural fairness is part of the defence of natural justice and should only be raised if the original court had jurisdiction to hear the class action involving non-resident, non-attorning members of the plaintiffs' class. If lack of natural justice is associated only with jurisdiction, non-resident members of the plaintiffs' class who accidentally or unintentionally attorned to the original court would no longer be able to rely on such a defence.

Enhanced procedural fairness has now become the best defence available to named, unnamed, non-resident, non-attorning plaintiffs in inter-provincial and international class actions. In the *Lépine* case, at all levels, the courts insisted on the need for the adequacy of the notice given to the class members, which was an easier and less complex task from an analytical point of view than applying Article

---

[52] T.J. Monestier, *Personal Jurisdiction over Non-Resident Plaintiff in Multi-Jurisdictional Class Actions: Have We Gone the Wrong Road?* Working Paper no. 08–05 (23 October 2008) at 9, citing *McCutcheon v. The Cash Store* (2006), 80 O.R. (3d) 644 (S.C); and *Harrington v. Dow Corning Corp.* (1996), 22 B.C.L.R. (3d) 97 (S.C.), aff'd [2000] 193 D.L.R. (4th) 67 (C.A.).

[53] *Ibid.* at 22.

3155(4) of the Québec Civil Code. This defence covers the quality of the notice, which must be such that ordinary members of the class would have no difficulty understanding it. Its language must be clear and simple, and the implications of the proposed settlement on the legal rights of the class members must be set against any award they could receive as a term of any settlement. The right to opt in or out must also be clearly indicated including the consequences of the choice. In common law Canada, in the *Currie* case, the Ontario Court of Appeal was also particularly concerned with the breadth of dissemination of the notice to the class members. The mode used should be one to reach the maximum number of class members, which obviously raises the question of the standard of notice. Should it be the standard of the foreign court or that of the enforcing court?

Another issue is whether the quality of the representation of the members of the class and the adequacy of the settlement or award should be part of the notion of fairness? It would seem that order and fairness do not include an assessment of the suitability of the amount of the settlement or award. True, the plaintiffs want to maximize recovery although they may not necessarily want to participate actively in the proceedings. If recovery is inadequate, should the settlement, or award be enforced against non-resident, non-attorning class members, especially if the notice did not indicate what type of recovery could be anticipated? In *Beals v. Saldanha*, the Supreme Court of Canada did not consider that the enormity of the award was a factor that would prevent its enforcement against public policy.[54]

Therefore, it is arguable that, by an inverse analogy, an inadequate settlement or award would be enforced since Canadian courts do not examine the merits of a foreign decision.[55] In the case of an inadequate settlement or award, the only ground for attacking it would be to resort to the defence of a lack of procedural fairness if the foreign judgment was reached as a result of some unfair process such as the absence of adequate representation at the time of the out-of-court negotiation of the settlement. To conclude, it is comforting to know that in this age of globalization, the Supreme Court

---

54 *Beals, supra* note 16 at para. 76. The function of the award is the issue, not its size: *Kidron v. Green* (1999), 48 O.R. (3d) 775 (Gen. Div.), leave to appeal refused at 784.

55 Castel and Walker, *supra* note 12, ch. 14, para. 14.3. See also Civil Code of Quebec, art. 3158.

of Canada has recognized that the unique character and advantages of inter-provincial and international class actions require that they be finally decided in one jurisdiction and that judgments deciding or approving their settlement be widely recognized in Canada, provided that the interests of the non-resident, non-attorning plaintiff members of the class have been adequately protected. This is "order and fairness" at their best!

JEAN-GABRIEL CASTEL*
Distinguished Research Professor Emeritus,
Osgoode Hall Law School, Toronto

Sommaire

Exécution des jugements hors-province dans les recours collectifs

Dans l'affaire qui fait l'objet de ce commentaire, la Cour suprême du Canada avait à décider si les tribunaux québécois en instance et en appel avaient eu raison de refuser de reconnaître un jugement ontarien qui avait certifié un recours collectif et approuvé une transaction hors cour alors que certains membres du groupe résidaient au Québec. En affirmant les décisions des cours inférieures, la Cour suprême fut d'avis qu'en appliquant les règles québécoises de droit international privé, les tribunaux québécois ne devaient pas tenir compte de la doctrine du forum non conveniens *pour établir la compétence des tribunaux étrangers. Ce qui compte c'est l'existence de cette compétence et non les modalités de l'exercice de celle-ci. Par contre, ces règles de compétence ne s'appliquent pas aux demandeurs devant le tribunal étranger. Ce qui compte en ce qui concerne les résidents québécois, c'est de savoir si la procédure de notification du jugement étranger certifiant le recours collectif et approuvant la transaction hors cour avait violé les principes essentiels de la procédure. Enfin, la Cour suprême exprima le désir que des méthodes plus efficaces de gestion des conflits de compétence soient établies dans un esprit de courtoisie mutuelle entre les tribunaux des différentes provinces du Canada.*

* This text is based on a lecture given at the Faculty of Law, McGill University, on 2 April 2009.

Summary

Giving Effect to Out-of-Province Judgments in Class Actions

In Canada Post Corp. v. Lépine, *the Supreme Court of Canada upheld the lower Québec courts' refusal to recognize an Ontario judgment approving an out-of-court settlement of a class action that included Québec residents. In reaching its decision, the Supreme Court of Canada did not extend to the non-resident plaintiff members of the class the jurisdictional test applicable to defendants. The decision was based on the lack of procedural fairness accorded to the non-residents. The Court also rejected a literal interpretation of Article 3164 of the Québec Civil Code, which requires that the foreign court must have had jurisdiction in accordance with Québec rules, including the doctrine of* forum non-conveniens. *To apply this doctrine is not compatible with inter-provincial and international comity as it defeats the liberal approach taken by the Civil Code with respect to the recognition of foreign judgments. This settles a long-lasting controversy. As a result of this decision, enhanced procedural fairness has become the best defence available to non-resident, non-attorning plaintiffs in inter-provincial and international class actions. Finally, the Court hoped that, in the spirit of mutual comity, the provincial legislatures would develop more effective methods for managing jurisdictional disputes involving national class actions.*

Faut-il parler d'une "guerre" contre le terrorisme?

INTRODUCTION

En réponse aux attentats du 11 septembre 2001, les États-Unis ont déclaré la "guerre au terrorisme." Cette déclaration de guerre a pris forme dans un discours prononcé le 20 septembre 2001 par le président G.W. Bush lors d'une session mixte du Congrès américain.[1] Elle a été suivie par l'invasion américaine de l'Afghanistan, le transfert à la prison américaine située à Guantanamo, Cuba, de centaines d'individus soupçonnés d'appartenir à des groupes terroristes et l'instauration de mesures qui ont été condamnées par les organisations vouées à la défense des droits de la personne.[2] Près de huit ans plus tard, la lutte armée contre al Qaeda et d'autres groupes terroristes perdure dans différentes parties du monde. S'agit-il d'une guerre? L'expression est encore couramment employée mais elle perd du souffle. Ainsi, en janvier 2009, le ministre britannique des affaires étrangères a officiellement pris ses distances par rapport à cette expression.[3] De même, en mars 2009, le ministre américain de la défense a renommé ses opérations contre le terrorisme: il ne s'agit plus d'une "*Global War on Terror,*" mais

---

[1] Disponible en ligne à: <http://www.historyplace.com/speeches/gw-bush-9-11. htm>. L'existence d'une guerre contre le terrorisme international a été également soulignée dans le rapport de la Commission nationale d'enquête sur les attentats du 11 septembre: *The 9-11 Commission Report. Final Report of the National Commission on Terrorist Attacks upon the United States,* á la p. 363, disponible en ligne à: <http:// www.gpoaccess.gov/911/index.html>.

[2] *Amnesty International Annual Report* 2008, disponible en ligne à: <http://www. amnesty.ca/resource_centre/annual_report/>.

[3] Voir <BBC News.newsbbc.co.uk>; voir aussi "UK Ends Use of Phrase War on Terror," 16 avril 2007, disponible en ligne à: <http://www.msnbc.msn.com/id/ 18133506>.

plutôt de "*Overseas Contingency Operations.*"[4] L'évolution a sans nul doute un parfum politique, mais elle relance le débat sur la qualification juridique de la lutte contre le terrorisme. Les lignes qui suivent tentent de faire le point sur la question.

On notera d'abord que l'idée d'une guerre opposant des gouvernements à des groupes terroristes n'est pas nouvelle. Elle était déjà évoquée par la presse au 19ᵉ siècle pour décrire la lutte des gouvernements de l'époque contre les anarchistes.[5] À leur tour, en février 1944, des groupes terroristes juifs ont déclaré la guerre aux Britanniques en Palestine.[6] Pour sa part, l'administration Reagan est créditée d'être la première à avoir fait la guerre au terrorisme.[7]

Si l'idée d'une "guerre contre le terrorisme" n'est pas nouvelle, en revanche son application à la lutte contre certains groupes comme al Qaeda n'a jamais fait l'unanimité. Ainsi, suite aux attentats à la bombe commis à Londres le 7 juillet 2005, le Director of Public Prosecutions britannique a refusé de parler d'une guerre contre le terrorisme.[8] Il a préféré faire allusion à une lutte contre des activités criminelles régie par le droit pénal plutôt que par le droit des conflits armés.[9] En effet, la question de savoir s'il faut parler d'une "guerre" contre le terrorisme en dissimule d'autres.[10] L'une des plus marquantes concerne les règles applicables à la lutte

---

4   Scott Wilson et Al Kamen, "Global War on Terror is Given New Name," *Washington Post*, 25 mars 2009, à la p. A04.

5   Voir par exemple, "The War on Terrorism: European Measures for its Extermination," *New York Times*, 2 avril 1881, à la p. 1, disponible en ligne à: <http://query. nytimes.com/mem/archive-free/pdf? res = 9400EFDE133CEE3ABC4A53 DFB266838A699FDE>.

6   Robert A. Friedlander, *Terrorism, Documents of International and Local Control*, New York, Oceana, 1979, aux pp. 21–22.

7   David C. Wills, *The First War on Terrorism: Counter Terrorism during the Reagan Administration*, Lanham, Rowman and Littlefield, 2003.

8   "There is no War on Terror in the UK, says DPP," *The Times*, 24 janvier 2007, à la p. 12.

9   Cette position est conforme à la réserve britannique relative aux articles 1(4) et 96(3) du *Protocole additionnel I* (1977), disponible en ligne à : <http://www.icrc. org/ihl.nsf/NORM/OA9E03F0F2EE757CC125>. Pourtant, Tony Blair évoquait l'existence d'une guerre contre le terrorisme. Voir F. Mégret, *infra* note 10, aux pp. 363–64.

10 F. Mégret, "'War'? Legal Semantics and the Move to Violence," *European Journal of International Law* 13 (2002), à la p. 361. Voir aussi M.E. O'Connell, "When Is War Not a War: The Myth of the Global War on Terror," *ILSA Journal of International and Comparative Law*, vol. 12 (2005), aux pp. 535, 537.

contre le terrorisme international. Ainsi, si cette lutte correspond à une guerre, elle devrait logiquement être régie par le droit des conflits armés ou le droit international humanitaire. En revanche, s'il est question d'une lutte contre des activités criminelles, le droit pénal est pertinent. Les deux positions s'affrontent. Chacune repose sur un certain nombre d'arguments qu'il importe d'examiner.

LES ARGUMENTS POUR ET CONTRE LA "GUERRE" CONTRE LE TERRORISME

LES PARTISANS D'UNE "GUERRE" CONTRE LE TERRORISME

Les partisans d'une "guerre" contre le terrorisme mettent l'accent sur les points suivants:[11]

1. Les attentats terroristes commis à différents points du globe témoignent du fait que nous avons affaire à un phénomène nouveau qui menace l'ensemble de la communauté internationale. Ce phénomène se manifeste par des attaques armées menées par un réseau transnational de cellules terroristes qui peuvent frapper partout dans le monde.
2. Compte tenu de leur ampleur, les attaques terroristes dépassent la qualification de simples activités criminelles. Ce sont des actes de guerre[12] qui menacent la paix et la sécurité internationales.[13]
3. Le droit pénal n'est pas adapté à la lutte contre le terrorisme. Il est axé sur la répression plutôt que sur la prévention. Ainsi, il ne permet pas de prendre des mesures préventives afin d'éliminer les terroristes avant qu'ils ne frappent. Il intervient après coup, donc trop tard.

[11] "Le droit international humanitaire et les défis posés par les conflits armés contemporains, Extrait du Rapport préparé par le Comité International de la Croix-Rouge pour la 28e Conférence internationale de la Croix-Rouge et du Croissant Rouge," *Revue internationale de la Croix Rouge*, vol. 853 (décembre 2004), aux pp. 245, 265–66.

[12] Selon l'administration du président Bush, une seule attaque armée peut correspondre à un conflit armé. Voir l'article 5 de la *Military Commission Instruction No. 2, Crimes and Elements for Trials by Military Commission* (30 avril 2003), disponible en ligne à, <http://www.dtic.mil/whs/directives/corres/mco/mci2.pdf>.

[13] La Résolution 1368 adoptée par le Conseil de sécurité des Nations Unies le 12 septembre 2001 considère aussi que les attaques terroristes du 11 septembre constituaient, comme tout acte de terrorisme international, une menace pour la paix et la sécurité internationales. Dans le même sens, voir la résolution 1373 du 28 septembre 2001. La conséquence est énoncée en termes de *jus ad bellum*: ces attaques activent le droit de légitime défense.

4. Les tribunaux pénaux sont trop lents, les preuves requises contre les accusés sont trop exigeantes, la procédure pénale est trop lourde et elle profite aux terroristes.

Ces arguments conduisent les partisans d'une "guerre" contre le terrorisme à conclure que nous avons affaire à un nouveau type de conflit armé, une guerre pour leur permettre de revendiquer des pouvoirs exorbitants.[14] Or, cette "guerre" ne s'inscrit pas dans la classification des conflits armés telle que celle-ci résulte des Conventions de Genève du 12 août 1949. En effet, il ne s'agit pas d'un conflit armé international puisqu'il n'oppose pas des États. Il ne s'agit pas non plus d'un conflit armé non international parce que le conflit n'est pas confiné au territoire d'un seul État. En conséquence, il faut trouver une qualification qui corresponde à ce nouveau type de conflit armé[15] et surtout de nouvelles règles qui le

---

[14] En octobre 2001, le Congrès des États-Unis a adopté la *Authorization for Use of Military Force against Terrorists Act* (Pub. L. 107-40, 115 Stat. 224). Celle-ci autorise le président à utiliser toute la force nécessaire et appropriée contre les auteurs des attaques du 11 septembre 2001. Les autorités américaines ont fait appel à ce texte pour entreprendre des mesures de surveillance électronique sans mandat. Elles l'ont également invoqué sans succès pour fonder la légalité des commissions militaires établies par un acte exécutif pour juger les ennemis combattants transférés à Guantanamo. Dans *Hamdan c. Rumsfeld*, la Cour suprême des États-Unis a jugé que ces commissions militaires étaient ni conformes au *Uniform Code of Military Justice* ni conformes au droit de la guerre. De plus, selon la Cour, la *Authorization for Use of Military Force against Terrorists Act* n'autorisait pas la mise en place des commissions militaires telles que constituées (548 U.S. 557 (2006)). En réponse, l'administration du président Bush a fait adopter la *Military Commissions Act* (Pub.L. 109-366, 120 Stat. 2600 (2006)). Cette loi permet l'établissement de commissions militaires sur le modèle de celles mises en place en 2001. Elle interdit aux tribunaux américains de connaître d'une action portée devant eux par voie d'*habeas corpus* dont l'auteur est un ennemi combattant. Elle limite également la compétence des tribunaux américains de connaître d'autres recours concernant la détention, le traitement, le procès, etc., d'ennemis combattants aux mains des autorités américaines. Ces dispositions permettent de détenir ces ennemis indéfiniment sans les poursuivre devant les tribunaux sous un chef d'accusation précis. Elles ont été jugées inconstitutionnelles par la Cour suprême des États-Unis dans *Boumediene c. Bush/Al Odah c. United States*, 128 S. Ct. 2229 (2008). Depuis, la nouvelle administration américaine a abandonné la qualification "d'ennemi combattant": voir Louis Balmond et col., "Chronique des faits internationaux," *Revue générale de droit international public*, vol. 113, n° 2 (2009), à la page 399.

[15] Pour N. Berman, la lutte contre le terrorisme correspond à la définition du conflit armé donnée par le TPIY dans l'affaire *Tadic*. Voir "Privileging Combat? Contemporary Conflict and the Legal Construction of Law," *Columbia Journal of Transnational Law*, vol. 43, n° 1 (2004), aux pp. 32-33.

régissent.[16] Ces règles doivent être élaborées par la pratique des États et celle-ci doit être sans merci pour les terroristes. Ainsi, selon cette perspective, les terroristes sont des "combattants irréguliers." L'expression a plusieurs conséquences. D'une part, en tant que combattants, les terroristes sont des cibles légitimes. Ils peuvent faire l'objet d'attaques, y compris des attaques préventives où qu'ils soient et à tout moment.[17] Toutefois, comme combattants irréguliers, ils ont droit ni au statut ni au traitement de prisonnier de guerre en cas de capture, laquelle peut être obtenue au moyen d'un enlèvement. De plus, une fois aux mains de la puissance détentrice, les individus soupçonnés d'être des terroristes peuvent être soumis à des interrogatoires musclés et être détenus indéfiniment sans contrôle judiciaire. Finalement, en tant que combattants, ils ne sont pas protégés par la Quatrième Convention de Genève qui concerne les civils.

En d'autres termes, les personnes soupçonnées d'appartenir à des groupes terroristes n'ont pas droit à la protection du droit international humanitaire bien qu'elles participent à un conflit armé et puissent en subir les conséquences. Quant au droit de la personne, il cède le pas au droit international humanitaire qui, en l'espèce, est la *lex specialis*. Or, comme il vient d'être dit, celui-ci ne profite pas aux individus soupçonnés d'être des terroristes. La boucle est ainsi bouclée. Enfin, l'ensemble de ces mesures est justifié par la nécessité impérieuse d'assurer la sécurité de l'État.

LES OPPOSANTS À UNE "GUERRE" CONTRE LE TERRORISME

Pour leur part, les opposants à une "guerre" contre le terrorisme font état de plusieurs arguments:[18]

1. Le terrorisme n'est pas un phénomène nouveau. Ainsi, le mot "terrorisme" trouve sa source dans le régime de la Terreur mis en place par les Jacobins au cours de la Révolution française.[19] Il s'agissait alors d'un terrorisme d'État. Quant au terrorisme de groupe, il trouve des antécédents dans les activités meurtrières

---

16 Voir Michael Hoffman, "Rescuing the Law of War: A Way Forward in an Era of Global Terrorism," *Parameters*, vol. 34, n° 2 (2005), à la p. 18.

17 Avery Plaw, *Targeting Terrorists. A Licence to Kill?*, Aldershot, Ashgate, 2008, aux pp. 190 et suiv.

18 "Le droit international humanitaire," *supra* note 11 aux pp. 232 et suiv.

19 Friedlander, *supra* note 6 à la p. 6.

des Assassins qui, au Moyen Âge, s'attaquaient aux Chrétiens du Proche-Orient ainsi qu'à d'autres ennemis.[20] Dans le même ordre d'idées, on a vu que l'idée d'une "guerre" entre gouvernements et groupes terroristes n'est pas née en septembre 2001.

2. Traditionnellement, le terrorisme est considéré comme une activité criminelle qui relève de la compétence des tribunaux ordinaires. En attestent le droit pénal de la plupart des États[21] et les conventions internationales qui visent des aspects particuliers du terrorisme: actes d'interférence illicite avec les transports aériens[22] ou maritimes[23] ; attaques contre le personnel diplomatique;[24] attaques contre le personnel de l'ONU et le personnel associé,[25] etc. Selon ces conventions, les actes visés sont des délits internationaux et les États contractants s'engagent à coopérer pour les prévenir et les réprimer selon la formule *aut dedere aut punire.*

3. La nature transnationale du terrorisme actuel n'en fait pas un conflit armé. Cet aspect n'est d'ailleurs pas nouveau. Déjà, dans les années 1970, les groupes terroristes palestiniens coopéraient avec des bandes allemandes, italiennes et irlandaises. De plus, dans le cadre de la guerre froide, tous profitaient de l'appui de l'U.R.S.S. Ils disposaient aussi d'un vaste théâtre d'opérations. De leur côté, les Américains ont notamment soutenu les *contras* qui utilisaient des méthodes terroristes dans leur lutte contre le gouvernement sandiniste au Nicaragua.[26] Ces arguments tendent à établir que contrairement à l'opinion opposée, le terrorisme

---

[20] *Ibid.* aux pp. 7–8.

[21] Au Canada, voir Code criminel, L.R.C. 1985, c. C-46, Partie II. 1; en France, voir Code pénal, Livre IV, Titre II.

[22] Voir notamment Convention relative aux infractions et à certains autres actes survenant à bord des aéronefs (Tokyo, 1963), Rec. traités Canada (R.T.C.) 1970/5; Convention pour la répression d'actes illicites dirigés contre la sécurité de l'aviation civile (Montréal, 1971), R.T.C. 1973/6.

[23] Voir Convention pour la répression d'actes illicites contre la sécurité de la navigation maritime (Rome, 1988), R.T.C. 1993/10.

[24] Convention sur la prévention et la répression des infractions contre les personnes jouissant d'une protection internationale, y compris les agents diplomatiques (New York, 1973), R.T.C. 1977/43.

[25] Convention sur la sécurité du personnel des Nations Unies et du personnel associé (New York, 1994), R.T.C. 2002/7.

[26] Voir *Activités militaires et paramilitaires au Nicaragua et contre celui-ci (Nicaragua c. États-Unis d'Amérique)*, fond, arrêt (1986), C.I.J. Rec. 14.

actuel ne s'écarte pas du terrorisme traditionnel au point de justifier une nouvelle qualification de ce phénomène.

4. De plus, la thèse d'une "guerre" contre le terrorisme, régie par des règles particulièrement sévères est dangereuse. Elle tend à justifier des pratiques qui sont illégales au regard du droit international: torture, enlèvements, exécutions extrajudiciaires, détention arbitraire. Comme telle, elle remet en cause les acquis de notre civilisation et menace quiconque est soupçonné d'appartenir à un groupe terroriste, que ce soit vrai ou non.[27] Les résultats de la "guerre" contre le terrorisme ne sont pas d'ailleurs garantis.[28]

De même, la thèse d'une "guerre dure" contre le terrorisme remet en cause le principe de l'égalité des combattants au regard du droit international humanitaire. Selon ce principe, tous les combattants ont droit à la protection du droit humanitaire, que leur cause soit juste ou non.[29] La raison en est que le droit international humanitaire ne se préoccupe pas des causes d'un conflit armé. Il se préoccupe uniquement de la protection des victimes. À cet égard, le principe de l'égalité des combattants est un principe fondamental sans lequel le droit humanitaire ne saurait exister. En effet, sans lui, chaque partie à un conflit armé pourrait prétendre que sa cause est juste, mais que celle de l'adversaire ne l'est pas, de telle sorte qu'il n'a pas droit à la protection du droit humanitaire. C'est la position de certains États dans leur "guerre" contre le terrorisme.[30]

---

27 Voir le cas de Maher Arar. Jane Mayer, "Outsourcing Torture," *New Yorker*, 14 février 2005, disponible en ligne à: <http://www.newyorker.com/archive/2005/02/14/050214fa_fact6>.

28 Selon certains, la "guerre" contre le terrorisme aurait des effets contre-productifs. Antony Best, Jussi M. Hanhimaki, Kirsten E. Schutze et Joseph A. Maiolo, *International History of the Twentieth Century and Beyond*, 2e éd., New York, Routledge, 2008, aux pp. 527 et suiv.; Mark Tran, "US 'War on Terror' Backfiring says Thinktank," *guardian.co.uk*, 23 avril 2008, disponible en ligne à: <http://www.guardian.co.uk/world/2008/apr/23/usa.somalia>; Agence France Presse, "US-British War on Terror Backfires: Think Tank," 11 avril 2007, disponible en ligne à: <http://www.commondreams.org/archive/2007/04/11/466>.

29 Voir le préambule du Protocole I additionnel aux Conventions de Genève; *United States v. Wilhelm List et al.*, United States Military Tribunal, Nuremberg, *Annual Digest*, vol. 15 (1948), à la p. 632; H. Meyrowitz, *Le principe de l'égalité des belligérants devant le droit de la guerre*, Paris, Pédone, 1970; "Le droit international humanitaire," *supra* note 11, aux pp. 234–35.

30 M. Sassoli, "Terrorism and War," *Journal of International Criminal Justice*, vol. 4 (2006), aux pp. 959, 971.

Elle crée un défi pour le droit international humanitaire parce qu'elle suggère que ce dernier doit être revu à la baisse pour faire face à la menace terroriste. Adopter cette position serait s'engager sur une pente glissante. Elle constituerait un précédent qui pourrait être suivi dans d'autres cas n'ayant rien à voir avec le terrorisme. Finalement, les arguments retenus par les opposants à une "guerre" contre le terrorisme les conduisent à dire que la lutte contre le terrorisme actuel passe encore essentiellement par le droit pénal, tel qu'il est aménagé par le droit international des droits de la personne.

Cela dit, les opposants à une "guerre" contre le terrorisme reconnaissent que les actes terroristes commis au cours d'un conflit armé relèvent du droit international humanitaire.[31] Ainsi, le militaire qui, au cours d'un conflit armé international, commet des actes de violence dans le but de terroriser la population civile demeure un combattant. S'il tombe aux mains de l'ennemi, il aura droit au statut et au traitement de prisonnier de guerre, même si, par ailleurs, il peut être jugé pour crimes de guerre. De même, les opérations militaires menées dans le cadre d'un conflit armé non international contre des cellules terroristes alliées d'un groupe d'opposition armé relèvent du droit international humanitaire.

Les positions pour et contre une "guerre" contre le terrorisme ayant été exposées, il faut reconnaître que le choix pour l'une ou l'autre est souvent un choix politique nourri de considérations émotionnelles. La prise en compte de données juridiques devrait permettre un choix plus éclairé.

LA POSITION DU DROIT INTERNATIONAL

Le droit international révèle que la lutte armée contre le terrorisme s'inscrit mal dans la classification actuelle des conflits armés. Il recèle aussi les principes qui devraient inspirer de nouvelles solutions.

LA LUTTE ARMÉE CONTRE LE TERRORISME QUALIFIÉE SELON LE DROIT POSITIF

Traditionnellement, le droit international distingue les conflits armés internationaux des conflits armés non internationaux. Cette distinction est la pierre angulaire des Conventions de Genève de

---

[31] "Le droit international humanitaire," *supra* note 11, aux pp. 233–34. Voir aussi M. Sassoli, *supra* note 30, aux pp. 964, 967 et suiv.

1949[32] et de leurs protocoles additionnels de 1977.[33] Ainsi, les Conventions de Genève visent essentiellement les conflits armés internationaux qui sont définis comme des conflits armés entre États selon leur article 2 commun. Elles contiennent toutefois un article 3 commun qui concerne les conflits armés non internationaux. Le premier protocole additionnel s'applique aux conflits armés internationaux et le second s'ajoute à l'article 3 commun pour régir les conflits armés non internationaux de forte intensité.

Il est important de noter que le terme "guerre" n'est utilisé ni dans les Conventions de Genève de 1949 (quoiqu'il était utilisé dans les Conventions de Genève de 1929), ni dans leurs protocoles additionnels. Il a été remplacé par le concept de conflit armé qui est plus large (conflits armés internationaux/conflits armés non internationaux). En effet, selon le droit international classique, le mot "guerre" a un sens précis: il désigne un conflit armé entre États.[34] Ainsi, d'un point de vue strictement juridique, il est faux de parler d'une "guerre" contre le terrorisme. Cela dit, se pourrait-il que la lutte armée contre le terrorisme corresponde à un autre type de conflit armé et en particulier à un conflit armé non international? Les tribunaux américains se sont penchés sur cette question dans l'affaire *Hamdan c. Rumsfeld* dont le dénouement remonte à 2006.

Dans cette affaire, Hamdan, ressortissant yéménite, avait été capturé en Afghanistan puis transféré à Guantanamo pour y être jugé par une commission militaire mise en place après les évènements du 11 septembre. Hamdan contestait cette mesure. Il prétendait que son sort dépendait de l'article 3 commun aux quatre Conventions de Genève et que selon celui-ci, il avait droit d'être jugé par

[32] Convention de Genève pour l'amélioration du sort des blessés et des malades dans les forces armées en campagne (Convention I), 75 R.T.N.U. 31; Convention de Genève pour l'amélioration du sort des blessés, des malades et des naufragés des forces armées sur mer (Convention II), 75 R.T.N.U. 85; Convention de Genève relative au traitement des prisonniers de guerre (Convention III), 75 R.T.N.U. 135; Convention de Genève relative à la protection des personnes civiles en temps de guerre (Convention IV), 75 R.T.N.U. 287.

[33] Protocole additionnel relatif à la protection des victimes des conflits armés internationaux (Protocole I), 1125 R.T.N.U. 3; Protocole additionnel relatif à la protection des victimes des conflits armés non internationaux (Protocole II), 1125 R.T.N.U. 609.

[34] Dietrich Schindler, "The Different Types of Armed Conflicts According to the Geneva Conventions and Protocols," R.C.A.D.I., vol. 163 (1979), à la p. 125; Christopher Greenwood, "War, Terrorism, and International Law," *Current Legal Problems*, vol. 56 (2003), aux pp. 505, 512, 527.

un tribunal régulièrement constitué. Encore fallait-il que l'article 3 s'applique à lui. Or, l'article 3 ne définit pas son champ d'application, si ce n'est pour dire qu'il s'applique aux conflits armés "ne présentant pas un caractère international et surgissant sur le territoire" d'un État partie aux Conventions de Genève.

Dès lors, pour répondre aux arguments du plaignant, les tribunaux américains ont du déterminer si l'article 3 s'appliquait à la "guerre" contre le terrorisme en Afghanistan à l'époque où Hamdan avait été capturé, c'est-à-dire lors de l'invasion américaine. La question a divisé les tribunaux américains. En première instance, le tribunal du district de Columbia a jugé que l'article 3 était effectivement applicable. En effet, selon le tribunal, le conflit avec al Qaeda en Afghanistan était indissociable du conflit avec les Taliban. En conséquence le tribunal a statué que les Conventions de Genève étaient applicables dans leur ensemble, de sorte que Hamdan devait profiter du statut et du traitement de prisonnier de guerre jusqu'à ce qu'un tribunal en décide autrement.[35] En appel cependant, la Cour de circuit a renversé le jugement de première instance. Selon elle, l'article 3 n'était pas applicable à la "guerre" contre le terrorisme en Afghanistan pour deux raisons principales: (1) la "guerre" contre al Qaeda a une dimension internationale; (2) al Qaeda n'est pas un État; la nébuleuse n'est pas partie aux Conventions de Genève. La Cour a également expliqué que la "guerre" contre al Qaeda devait être dissociée du conflit avec les Taliban.[36]

À son tour, la Cour suprême des États-Unis a renversé la décision de la Cour de circuit, en faveur, cette fois, d'une interprétation littérale de l'article 3. Elle a ainsi statué que l'article 3 s'appliquait à la situation en cause dans la mesure où celle-ci correspondait à un conflit armé n'ayant pas un caractère international qui se déroulait sur le territoire d'un État partie aux Conventions de Genève.[37] Ce faisant, la Cour suprême a, pour les fins de l'affaire, limité son raisonnement à la lutte armée contre le terrorisme en Afghanistan, alors que la Cour de circuit avait, elle, considéré la lutte armée contre le terrorisme en général. Dans le premier cas, on peut effectivement justifier l'application de l'article 3 en adoptant une interprétation littérale de ses dispositions comme la Cour suprême l'a fait. Dans le second cas, la situation est différente: la lutte contre le terrorisme en général et contre al Qaeda en particulier, n'est pas

35 344 F. Supp. 2d 152 (DC 2004).

36 415 F. 3d 33 (2005).

37 126 S. Ct. 2749 (2006).

confinée au territoire d'un seul État; elle a bien une dimension internationale. En conséquence, la lutte armée contre le terrorisme n'est pas un conflit armé non international régi par l'article 3 commun aux Conventions de Genève.[38]

La dernière qualification qu'il convient de considérer rapidement est celle d'un conflit armé régi par l'article 1(4) du Protocole I des Conventions de Genève. Elle correspond à un conflit armé dans lequel un peuple lutte contre un régime colonial, une occupation étrangère ou un régime raciste dans l'exercice de son droit à l'autodétermination, tel que celui-ci est défini dans la Charte de l'ONU et dans la Déclaration sur les relations amicales et la coopération entre les États.[39] Cette qualification doit être rejetée d'emblée pour plusieurs raisons. Dans un premier temps, une organisation terroriste n'est pas un peuple. De plus, les conditions requises par l'article 96(3) du Protocole I pour que son article 1(4) s'applique exigeraient d'une organisation terroriste qu'elle respecte les Conventions de Genève et le Protocole I. En conséquence, elle devrait renoncer à exercer des activités terroristes[40] ainsi qu'à la perfidie.[41] Enfin, l'article 1(4) n'est applicable qu'aux États parties au Protocole I et nombre d'États qui font l'objet d'attaques terroristes ne sont par liés par ce texte.[42]

Finalement, il ressort de l'analyse précédente que la lutte armée contre le terrorisme ne correspond pas à la classification des conflits armés, telle que celle-ci découle du droit positif et en particulier des Conventions de Genève de 1949. Les partisans d'une "guerre" contre le terrorisme semblent bien avoir raison sur ce point. Cela ne signifie pas pour autant qu'ils aient raison sur toute la ligne.

LES PRINCIPES RÉGISSANT DE NOUVELLES SOLUTIONS

Si l'on persiste à assimiler la lutte armée contre le terrorisme international à un conflit armé, il faut lui donner une nouvelle qualification et élaborer des règles pour le régir. En ce qui concerne sa qualification, celle-ci doit tenir compte des éléments suivants:

• il s'agit ni d'un conflit armé international, ni d'un conflit armé

[38] En revanche, voir Sassoli, *supra* note 30 aux pp. 964–65 et 971.

[39] Schindler, *supra* note 34 aux pp. 133 et suiv.

[40] Voir notamment l'article 51(2) du Protocole I.

[41] Voir l'article 37 du Protocole I. Voir aussi Sassoli, *supra* note 30 à la p. 969.

[42] Entre autres, les États-Unis, Israël, l'Iran, l'Irak, le Pakistan, l'Inde, Sri Lanka, la Thailande.

non international au sens où ces types de conflits armés sont compris par les Conventions de Genève;

- il oppose des gouvernements à un réseau transnational de cellules armées;
- celles-ci utilisent le terrorisme comme méthode de guerre;
- les opérations contre les terroristes ont pour cadre le territoire de plusieurs États.

La lutte armée contre le terrorisme pourrait ainsi être qualifiée de conflit armé atypique opposant des États à un réseau transnational de cellules terroristes qui se déroule sur plusieurs fronts.

Quant aux règles applicables à ce nouveau type de conflit armé, il pourrait s'agir de règles coutumières, élaborées par la pratique des États en tenant compte des principes fondamentaux du droit international humanitaire. En effet, s'il s'agit d'adopter des règles juridiques destinées à régir un conflit armé, celles-ci doivent logiquement s'inspirer des principes qui sous-tendent le droit compétent, surtout si ces principes font partie du *jus cogens*.

Parmi eux, le principe d'humanité occupe la première place en tant que fondement même du droit international humanitaire.[43] Toutes les règles qui font partie de ce droit sont ancrées dans le principe d'humanité. Celui-ci était déjà mentionné dans la Déclaration de Saint-Pétersbourg de 1868.[44] Il a été repris dans le préambule de la Convention II de La Haye de 1899[45] et sans cesse répété depuis. Il trouve une expression concrète dans les règles visant à assurer la protection des victimes d'un conflit armé[46] comme dans celles régissant la conduite des hostilités.[47] Il s'exprime aussi à travers la fameuse Clause Martens adoptée dans le cadre de la première Conférence de la Paix réunie à La Haye en 1899.[48] Aujourd'hui, cette clause est toujours pertinente. Elle figure notamment, sous

---

[43] Jean Pictet, *Les principes du Droit international humanitaire*, Genève, C.I.C.R., 1966, à la p. 10.

[44] Dietrich Schindler et Jiri Toman, *Droit des conflits armés, Recueil des conventions, résolutions et autres documents*, Genève, C.I.C.R./Institut Henry Dunant, 1996, à la p. 101.

[45] Convention concernant les lois et coutumes de la guerre sur terre, dans Schindler et Toman, *ibid.*, à la p. 65 [ci-après Déclaration de Saint-Pétersbourg].

[46] Voir par exemple l'article 3 commun aux quatre Conventions de Genève.

[47] Voir notamment la Déclaration de Saint-Pétersbourg, *supra* note 45.

[48] Shigeki Miyazaki, "The Martens Clause and International Humanitarian Law," dans Christophe Swinarski, dir., *Études et essais sur le droit international et sur les*

une forme plus moderne, dans le préambule du Protocole II additionnel aux Conventions de Genève et a donné lieu à des applications jurisprudentielles.[49] Selon la Clause Martens, dans les situations qui ne font pas l'objet de règles spécifiques, les victimes d'un conflit armé demeurent sous la protection des lois de l'humanité et de la conscience publique. Dans la jurisprudence de la Cour internationale de Justice, le principe se retrouve à travers le concept de "considérations élémentaires d'humanité."[50]

En 1899, la Clause Martens a été adoptée pour compenser l'absence de protection juridique des partisans capturés dans un territoire occupé par l'ennemi.[51] Aujourd'hui, elle devrait être utilisée pour combler le vide laissé par le droit international humanitaire quant à la protection des personnes qui font l'objet de la lutte armée contre le terrorisme. En application de cette clause, la torture, les exécutions extrajudiciaires, les enlèvements et la détention arbitraire de personnes soupçonnées d'appartenir à des groupes terroristes sont illégales parce que contraires aux lois de l'humanité et à la conscience publique. Le droit international nous enseigne d'ailleurs que l'interdiction de la torture[52] et des exécutions extrajudiciaires[53] relève du *jus cogens*. Ainsi, pour reprendre une formule célèbre[54] le fait d'envisager la lutte armée contre le terrorisme

---

principes de la Croix-Rouge, Genève/La Haye, C.I.C.R./Martinus Nijhoff, 1984, à la p. 433.

[49] Voir notamment *Le Procureur c. Kupreskic et consorts*, IT-95–16-T, jugement du 14 janvier 2000, T.P.I.Y. (C.P.I. II), para. 527.

[50] Voir *l'Affaire du détroit de Corfou (R.-U. c. Albanie)*, arrêt, (1949) C.I.J. Rec. 4, 22.

[51] Frits Kalshoven, *Restrictions à la conduite de la guerre*, Genève, C.I.C.R., 1991, à la p. 15.

[52] Voir *Le Procureur c. Furundzija*, IT-95–17/1-T, jugement du 10 décembre 1998, T.P.I.Y. (Ch. P. II), para. 153. Voir aussi, *Le Procureur c. Kunarac et consorts*, IT-96–23-T & IT-96–23/I-T, jugement du 22 février 2001, T.P.I.Y. (Ch P. II), para. 466; *Al-Adsani c. Royaume Uni*, arrêt, 21 novembre 2001, Cour Eur. D.H. (Grde. Ch.), para. 61; *Regina v. Bartle and the Commissioner of Police for the Metropolis and others — ex parte Pinochet*, (1999) 38 I.L.M. 581 (H.L.); *Bouzari c. Iran* (2004), 71 O.R. (3d) 675, para. 65.

[53] Elles violent le droit d'un individu de ne pas être arbitrairement privé de sa vie. Ce droit fait partie intégrante du droit à la vie qui est reconnu par tous les grands textes internationaux destinés à protéger les droits de la personne. Voir l'article 6 du Pacte international sur les droits civils et politiques (999 R.T.N.U. 171); l'article 2 de la Convention européenne des droits de l'Homme (1950) (S.T.E. n? 005); l'article 4 de la Convention américaine des droits de l'Homme (1969) (O.E.A., Recueil des traités, no 36); l'article 4 de la Charte africaine des droits

comme un nouveau type de conflit armé ne donne pas aux États participants un choix illimité quant aux moyens de nuire à ceux qu'ils suspectent d'être des terroristes. Ces États restent soumis à l'obligation de respecter les principes fondamentaux du droit international humanitaire.

Les mêmes principes fondamentaux font aussi partie intégrante du droit international des droits de la personne. Ils sous-tendent les droits qui constituent le noyau dur des droits de la personne — ceux qui ne peuvent pas être suspendus en cas de guerre ou d'autre situation d'urgence menaçant la sécurité de l'État — tels qu'à titre d'exemple, le droit de ne pas être privé arbitrairement de sa vie, l'interdiction de la torture,[55] etc. De plus, les mesures susceptibles d'être prises pour faire face à une situation d'urgence nationale doivent être conformes à d'autres obligations découlant du droit international,[56] y compris du droit international humanitaire quand il est applicable, c'est-à-dire dans le cadre d'un conflit armé.[57] En d'autres termes, les mêmes droits fondamentaux doivent être respectés par les États dans leur lutte contre le terrorisme, que celle-ci tombe sous la coupe du droit international humanitaire ou du droit international des droits de la personne. Rappelons d'ailleurs que ce dernier s'applique en temps de paix comme dans le cadre d'un conflit armé. Dans ce dernier cas, il complète l'action du droit international humanitaire.[58]

Dès lors, peu importe que la lutte contre le terrorisme soit décrite comme une "guerre" ou comme une lutte contre des activités criminelles. Les mesures prises dans le cadre de cette lutte ne se limitent d'ailleurs pas à des opérations militaires; elles comprennent

---

de l'Homme et des peuples (1981), (1982), 21 I.L.M. 58. Le droit à la vie ne peut être suspendu en cas de crise menaçant la sécurité de l'État: *infra* note 56.

[54] "Les belligérants n'ont pas un droit illimité quant au choix des moyens de nuire à l'ennemi," article 22 du Règlement annexé à la Convention sur les lois et les coutumes de la guerre sur terre, *supra* note 46.

[55] Voir l'article 4 du Pacte international sur les droits civils et politiques, *supra* note 53; l'article 15 de la Convention européenne des droits de l'Homme, *ibid.*; l'article 27 de la Convention américaine, *ibid.* Aucune suspension des droits prévus n'est reconnue par la Charte africaine.

[56] *Ibid.*

[57] Voir *Licéité de la menace ou de l'emploi d'armes nucléaires pas un État*, avis consultatif (1996), C.I.J. Rec. 226, para. 25.

[58] *Ibid.* Voir aussi Dietrich Schindler, "Human Rights and Humanitarian Law," *American University Law Review* (1982), à la p. 935.

des interventions policières, l'action des autorités d'immigration, des tribunaux judiciaires, etc. Chacune de ces mesures doit, pour être légale, se conformer aux principes du droit international humanitaire, du droit international des droits de la personne ou à ceux qui sont communs à ces deux branches du droit international suivant les cas. Ainsi, dans le cadre d'une opération de police menée en temps de paix contre les membres d'une cellule terroriste, l'utilisation de la force, y compris de la force armée et plus particulièrement de la force létale est soumise au respect des règles internationales vouées à la défense des droits de la personne. Il en va de même en ce qui concerne l'arrestation des suspects, leur détention, les conditions dans lesquelles ils peuvent être interrogés, jugés, condamnés, punis s'ils le méritent.[59]

CONCLUSION

La thèse d'une "guerre" contre le terrorisme semble être inspirée par la volonté de contourner l'application du droit positif au profit de règles nouvelles, libérées des contraintes du droit international humanitaire et du droit international des droits de la personne.

Il s'agit ainsi de prétendre que l'on a affaire à un nouveau type de conflit armé, qui menace la communauté internationale et qui n'entre pas dans le cadre des Conventions de Genève, pour proposer une réglementation originale qui sacrifie la protection de l'individu à la sécurité de l'État. C'est oublier que les règles destinées à s'appliquer à tout conflit armé doivent respecter les principes fondamentaux communs au droit international humanitaire et au droit international des droits de la personne.

Ces principes tendent à protéger les individus contre les abus de l'État, conformément à l'évolution du droit international depuis la Seconde Guerre mondiale. Acquis au prix d'énormes sacrifices humains, trop souvent justifiés par la raison d'État, lesdits principes font partie des progrès de notre civilisation. Leur importance est soulignée dans les textes consacrés à la défense des droits de la personne: ils ne peuvent pas être suspendus, même en cas de crise menaçant la vie de la nation. En d'autres termes, ils doivent être respectés en toutes circonstances, y compris dans le cadre de la

---

59 Dans le cadre de la Convention européenne des droits de l'Homme, voir les articles 2,3,5 et 6. Dans la Convention américaine, voir les articles 4, 5, 7, 8 et 9. Dans la Charte africaine, voir les articles 4–7. Dans le Pacte international sur les droits civils et politique, voir les articles 6,7,9,10,14 et 15.

lutte contre le terrorisme. Il en va de même du droit international humanitaire selon l'article 1er commun aux quatre Conventions de Genève,[60] dont la Cour internationale de Justice nous dit qu'il découle des principes généraux de ce droit.[61]

Le respect de ces droits dans le cadre de la lutte contre le terrorisme est d'autant plus nécessaire que certains individus peuvent à tort être suspectés d'être des terroristes.[62] L'expérience montre aussi que la lutte contre le terrorisme n'est pas limitée à des opérations militaires. Elle passe également par l'application du droit criminel. Renforcée par la coopération entre États, cette application produit des résultats positifs.[63] Il importe enfin de rappeler que dans les pays civilisés, tout individu est présumé innocent jusqu'à ce qu'il soit déclaré coupable par un tribunal régulièrement constitué. Avant comme après, il doit profiter de la protection du droit.

C. EMANUELLI
Professeur, Université d'Ottawa

---

[60] Selon cet article 1er que l'on retrouve dans le Protocole I de 1977, les États parties aux conventions (et au protocole) s'engagent à les respecter et à les faire respecter en toutes circonstances. En conséquence, l'obligation de respecter ces textes ne dépend pas du principe de la réciprocité.

[61] Voir *Activités militaires et paramilitaires au Nicaragua et contre celui-ci, supra* note 26, para. 220. Ainsi, son application dépasse le cadre strict des conventions et de leur protocole I.

[62] *Supra* note 27.

[63] Des individus soupçonnés de terrorisme ont été jugés et parfois condamnés par les tribunaux pénaux de nombreux pays. Au Canada, voir *R. c. Khawaja,* [2008] O.J. No. 42444. Voir aussi "Khawaja Handed 10 1/2 Years," *Ottawa Citizen,* 13 mars 2009, à la p. A1. En rapport avec cette affaire, voir également *Omar Khyam, Salahuddin Amin, Jawed Akbar, Anthony Garcia and Waheed Mahmood* [2008], E.W.C.A. Crim 1612 (C.A.).

Summary

Should We Continue to Refer to the "War" on Terror?

Eight years after the events of 11 September 2001, the "war" on terror continues in many parts of the world. However, the expression "war on terror," as such, has lost much of its currency. This is so mainly for political reasons, but this evolution revives the debate on how to characterize, as a legal matter, the fight against terrorism. Following an examination of the pros and cons of the "war" on terror, this comment examines the position of international law on this issue. It concludes that the same fundamental principles apply regardless of the expression used and the legal system governing the fight against terrorism.

Sommaire

Faut-il parler d'une "guerre" contre le terrorisme?

Huit ans après les évènements du 11 septembre 2001, la "guerre" contre le terrorisme perdure dans différentes parties du monde. Toutefois, en soi l'expression "guerre contre le terrorisme" perd du souffle. Les raisons en sont essentiellement politiques, mais l'évolution relance le débat sur la qualification juridique de la lutte contre le terrorisme. Après un examen des arguments pour et contre la "guerre" contre le terrorisme, la présente étude envisage la position du droit international. Elle conclut que les mêmes principes fondamentaux s'appliquent quels que soient les termes employés et le système juridique applicable à la lutte contre le terrorisme.

Chronique de Droit international économique en 2007 / Digest of International Economic Law in 2007

I Commerce

RICHARD OUELLET

I INTRODUCTION

L'année 2007 en aura été une de fluctuations pour l'économie canadienne. D'abord, le dollar canadien est sur une lancée que les économistes n'hésitent pas à qualifier d'historique: en un an, il aura gagné près de 15 p. 100 par rapport au dollar américain. Le 21 septembre, pour la première fois depuis 1976, il atteignait la parité avec le billet vert.[1] Le 7 novembre, il atteignait les 1,10 $US, du jamais vu en 140 ans.[2] On s'entend désormais pour dire que la progression du dollar canadien est directement liée à l'augmentation du prix des ressources naturelles, puisque le Canada est un important exportateur de gaz naturel, de pétrole, d'or et de cuivre, entre autres. Le dollar canadien suit ainsi les fluctuations du pétrole assez fidèlement. D'ailleurs, en septembre, le prix du pétrole atteignait lui aussi un niveau historique, soit 84 $US le baril.[3] La performance économique des provinces dont l'économie repose en bonne partie sur les ressources naturelles a donc été excellente

Richard Ouellet est professeur agrégé à la Faculté de droit et à l'Institut québécois des hautes études internationales de l'Université Laval et membre du Centre d'études interaméricaines (CEI). L'auteur tient à remercier le CEI pour son appui financier et Mme Nadine Martin pour sa collaboration dans la préparation de la présente chronique.

[1] Radio-Canada, "Le dollar US a le teint vert," 21 septembre 2007, disponible en ligne à: <http://www.radio-canada.ca/nouvelles/Economie-Affaires/2007/09/20/001-euro-dollar-jeudi.shtml>.

[2] "Dollar: l'année du huard," *Le Soleil*, 31 décembre 2007, disponible en ligne à: <http://www.cyberpresse.ca/article/20071231/CPSOLEIL/71230089/5019/CPSOLEIL>.

[3] Radio-Canada, *supra* note 1.

en 2007, l'Alberta atteignant même un taux de croissance de 6,8 p. cent.[4]

On s'en doute, une telle progression de notre monnaie n'est pas sans impact sur l'ensemble du commerce international canadien. La hausse du dollar bénéficiait bien sûr tout d'abord aux consommateurs canadiens mais de nombreux secteurs dépendant des exportations étaient durement affectés par la hausse du dollar. Ce fût dramatique dans le secteur manufacturier où le Canada perdait 100 000 emplois seulement qu'au cours des derniers mois de l'année. Si du point de vue économique, l'année 2007 fut une année de tumultes pour le commerce canadien, du point de vue juridique, l'année fut relativement tranquille.

II   Le commerce canadien aux plans bilatéral et régional

A   les négociations commerciales aux plans bilatéral
      et régional

1   L'intégration hémisphérique

Les négociations pour un projet de zone de libre-échange au niveau du continent américain n'ont pas avancé en 2007 ni depuis le Sommet de Mar del Plata. Pourtant, l'idée d'une zone de libre-échange à grande échelle dans les Amériques persiste parmi les préoccupations du Canada. En octobre, la secrétaire d'État, Helena Guergis, soulignait que le Canada et les États-Unis avaient les relations commerciales bilatérales les plus importantes du monde et que l'Accord de libre-échange nord-américain (ALENA) est la plus importante zone de libre-échange au monde. Dans cette lignée, elle invitait le Mexique et les États-Unis à prendre appui sur l'ALENA pour renforcer les liens hémisphériques et créer une économie continentale plus concurrentielle.[5]

Si l'intégration hémisphérique stagne, l'intégration nord-américaine se poursuit. Les données économiques au sujet de l'ALENA rendues disponibles en 2007 ont éloquemment démontré que l'accord garde toute sa vigueur et continue de profiter au commerce canadien. Il a en effet permis d'atteindre des sommets

---

[4] Ministère des Affaires étrangères et du Commerce international Canada, *Septième rapport annuel sur le commerce international du Canada*, juin 2007, disponible en ligne à: <http://www.international.gc.ca/eet/pdf/07-1989-DFAIT-fr.pdf>.

[5] Gouvernement du Canada, *Communiqué de presse du 11 octobre 2007*, disponible en ligne à: <http://wo1.international.gc.ca/minpub/Publication.aspx?isRedirect=True&publication_id=385509&Language=F&docnumber=140>.

inégalés en matière d'échanges commerciaux: en 2006, les échanges entre le Canada et le Mexique ont atteint une valeur de plus de 20 milliards de dollars, soit une hausse de 349 p. 100 par rapport aux niveaux enregistrés avant l'entrée en vigueur de l'ALENA, en 1993.[6] De plus, près de 83 p. 100 des exportations canadiennes de marchandises sont destinées aux États-Unis et au Mexique[7] et environ 57 p. 100 des exportations canadiennes de services vont vers ces pays.[8]

2 *Les autres développements aux plans bilatéral et régional*

À défaut de la concrétisation d'une zone de libre-échange intercontinentale, le Canada s'est tourné vers d'autres partenaires commerciaux. En 2007, il concluait des négociations avec les pays de l'Association européenne de libre-échange (AELE), conduisant ainsi au premier accord de libre-échange en six ans pour le Canada. Le ministre du Commerce international, David Emerson, faisait remarquer à cette occasion que "le Canada ne devait pas se complaire dans sa situation et devait plutôt s'engager activement dans la nouvelle économie mondiale."[9] Cet accord de libre-échange est le premier conclu par le Canada avec des pays européens. Les pays membres de l'AELE (l'Islande, la Norvège, la Suisse et le Liechtenstein) se classent, collectivement, au huitième rang des destinations des exportations du Canada. L'accord éliminera notamment tous les droits de douane imposés par l'AELE sur les exportations canadiennes de produits industriels, notamment dans des secteurs clés comme les produits forestiers, les pâtes et papiers, les bâtiments préfabriqués, l'aluminium, les produits cosmétiques et l'automobile, ainsi que certaines subventions à l'exportation de l'AELE sur divers produits agricoles et agroalimentaires.[10] Des négociations ont aussi été lancées avec le Pérou, la Colombie et la République dominicaine.

---

[6] Ministère des Affaires étrangères et du Commerce international Canada, *Rapport du Canada en matière d'accès aux marchés internationaux 2007*, à la p. 15, disponible en ligne à: <http://www.international.gc.ca/assets/trade-agreements-accords-commerciaux/pdfs/ITC_MarketAccess_FRE_final.pdf>.

[7] *Ibid.*

[8] *Ibid.*, á la p. 16.

[9] Ministère des Affaires étrangères et du Commerce international Canada, *Communiqué de presse du 7 juin 2007*, disponible en ligne à: <http://wo1.international.gc.ca/minpub/Publication.aspx?isRedirect=True&publication_id=385204&Language=F&docnumber=76>.

[10] *Ibid.*

Le 4 octobre, le Canada fêtait les vingt ans de la signature de l'Accord de libre-échange (ALE) entre le Canada et les États-Unis, qui aura permis de tripler les échanges entre les deux pays depuis sa mise en œuvre.[11] On sait que c'est en s'appuyant sur cet accord que les États-Unis, le Mexique et le Canada ont construit l'ALENA qui aura permis, pour sa part, de doubler le commerce trilatéral de marchandises.[12] Depuis l'entrée en vigueur de l'ALENA, le Mexique est devenu la cinquième destination des exportations canadiennes et le troisième fournisseur du Canada.[13] Les deux pays collaborent aussi au niveau bilatéral, notamment grâce au Partenariat Canada-Mexique, et faisaient part de leur intention, en août, de créer un groupe de travail sur la mobilité de la main-d'œuvre.[14] Plusieurs travailleurs agricoles saisonniers mexicains viennent déjà au Canada chaque année.

En plus de chercher à améliorer la compétitivité de l'Amérique du Nord, la stratégie canadienne pour le commerce international vise aussi le développement des relations commerciales avec les pays d'Asie. En janvier, le ministre du Commerce international se rendait en Chine à la tête d'une mission commerciale ayant pour but de renforcer l'ensemble des relations commerciales en établissant des contacts avec les principaux décideurs chinois, autant dans le secteur public que privé, et de faire valoir l'expertise canadienne. Cette visite était couronnée de succès tout d'abord grâce à la signature d'un accord de coopération en science et technologie, qui favorisera une plus grande collaboration bilatérale dans le secteur de la recherche et du développement, notamment grâce à un mécanisme visant à faciliter les investissements des secteurs public et privé dans des programmes conjoints de science et de technologie.[15]

---

11 Ministère des Affaires étrangères et du Commerce international Canada, *Communiqué du 3 octobre 2007*, disponible en ligne à: <http://wo1.international. gc.ca/minpub/Publication.aspx?isRedirect=True&publication_id=385493& Language=F&docnumber=135>.

12 Ministère des Affaires étrangères et du Commerce international Canada, *Communiqué du 14 août 2007*, disponible en ligne à: <http://wo1.international.gc.ca/ minpub/Publication.aspx?isRedirect=True&publication_id=385374&Language =F&docnumber=111>.

13 *Supra* note 6 à la p. 17.

14 Ministère des Affaires étrangères et du Commerce international Canada, *Communiqué du 21 août 2007*, disponible en ligne à: <http://wo1.international.gc.ca/ minpub/Publication.aspx?isRedirect=True&publication_id=385384&Language =F&docnumber=115>.

15 Ministère des Affaires étrangères et du Commerce international Canada, *Communiqué du 15 janvier 2007*, disponible en ligne à: <http://wo1.international.

Le ministre faisait également la promotion du Canada comme porte d'entrée en Amérique et signait un protocole d'entente sur la coopération avec la Chine relativement aux portes d'entrée et corridors de commerce entre le Canada et la Chine.[16]

De plus, le Canada continuait de développer ses relations commerciales avec un autre marché clé en Asie: l'Inde. En 2006, les échanges bilatéraux entre le Canada et l'Inde atteignaient un chiffre record de 3,6 milliards de dollars, y compris une augmentation de 55 p. 100 des exportations de marchandises vers l'Inde. En mars, le secrétaire parlementaire du ministre du Commerce international y dirigeait une mission commerciale composée de chefs d'entreprises du secteur de l'infrastructure, visite qui concordait avec celle d'une autre délégation commerciale composée de membres du Conseil canadien des chefs d'entreprise.[17] Cette visite débouchait sur la signature, en juin, d'un accord de promotion et de protection de l'investissement étranger (APIE), lors du passage au Canada du ministre indien du Commerce et de l'Industrie. Les investissements directs étrangers bilatéraux entre les deux pays se chiffraient en 2006 à 528 millions de dollars, soit une hausse de 17 p. cent, ce qui laisse espérer que la signature de l'APIE permettra une croissance encore plus marquée pour les prochaines années.[18]

Finalement, en novembre, le Canada et la Russie signaient de nouveaux accords bilatéraux dans le but de renforcer la coopération économique entre les deux pays. Ils signaient notamment un protocole d'entente sur la coopération dans le domaine des pêches favorisant les possibilités de collaboration technique, scientifique et économique; un protocole d'entente sur l'Arctique afin de favoriser la coopération en matière de développement du Nord et de

---

gc.ca/minpub/Publication.aspx?isRedirect=True&publication_id=384752& Language=F&docnumber=7>.

[16] Gouvernement du Canada, *Communiqué du 16 janvier 2007*, disponible en ligne à: <http://wo1.international.gc.ca/minpub/Publication.aspx?isRedirect=True& publication_id=384755&Language=F&docnumber=8>.

[17] Ministère des Affaires étrangères et du Commerce international Canada, *Communiqué du 12 mars 2007*, disponible en ligne à: <http://wo1.international.gc.ca/ minpub/Publication.aspx?isRedirect=True&publication_id=384952&Language =F&docnumber=39>.

[18] Ministère des Affaires étrangères et du Commerce international Canada, *Communiqué du 16 juin 2007*, disponible en ligne à: <http://wo1.international.gc.ca/ minpub/Publication.aspx?isRedirect=True&publication_id=385227&Language =F&docnumber=82>.

questions autochtones et un protocole d'entente sur le commerce et l'investissement.[19]

B   LES DIFFÉRENDS LIÉS À L'ALENA ET À L'ACCORD SUR LE BOIS D'ŒUVRE RÉSINEUX IMPLIQUANT LE CANADA[20]

1   Bois d'œuvre résineux — Décision définitive positive sur la vente à un prix inférieur à la juste valeur — Requête en rejet

Le 5 janvier 2007, le Groupe spécial chargé en vertu de l'article 1904 de l'ALENA de réviser une décision de l'International Trade Administration (ITA) a accueilli une requête en rejet de l'instance qui avait été déposée par l'ITA et par le gouvernement canadien.[21] Cette requête a été accueillie au motif que l'Accord sur le bois d'œuvre résineux en vigueur entre le Canada et les États-Unis depuis le 12 octobre 2006 avait eu pour effet de révoquer l'ordonnance antidumping que devait réviser le Groupe spécial. L'ordonnance antidumping n'ayant plus de portée pratique, le Groupe spécial a considéré que l'instance engagée n'avait pas non plus de portée pratique.

2   Fils machine en acier au carbone — 2ᵉ examen administratif

En vertu du paragraphe 1904(2) de l'ALENA, le groupe spécial devait réviser un examen administratif effectué par le département du commerce des États-Unis. Cet examen administratif touchait des fils machine en acier au carbone et certains fils machine en acier allié vendus par Mittal Canada Inc. aux États-Unis. Parmi les nombreuses questions de fait et de droit soulevées, se trouvaient la question de l'application de la réduction à zéro. Dans un rapport

---

19 Gouvernement du Canada, *Communiqué du 29 novembre 2007*, disponible en ligne à: <http://wo1.international.gc.ca/minpub/Publication.aspx?isRedirect=True&publication_id=385648&Language=F&docnumber=169>.

20 Nous ne couvrirons pas ici les litiges en lien avec l'investissement, notamment avec le chapitre de l'ALENA. Ces litiges seront couverts par la chronique portant sur l'investissement.

21 Examen par un Groupe spécial binational constitué en vertu de l'article 1904 de l'*Accord de libre-échange nord-américain*, dans l'affaire *Certains produits de bois d'œuvre résineux en provenance du Canada: Décision définitive positive sur la vente à un prix inférieur à la juste valeur* — no USA-CDA-2002–1904–02, Décision du Groupe spécial concernant les requêtes en rejet, 5 janvier 2007, disponible en ligne à: <http://registry.nafta-sec-alena.org/cmdocuments/35cf2e05-b33f-48cf-b1d6-be41b7e8659d.pdf>.

de plus de cent pages et sur division — deux arbitres étant dissidents sur la question de la réduction à zéro — le Groupe spécial a confirmé en partie la décision du département du commerce américain mais a aussi renvoyé l'affaire en demandant au département du commerce de revoir certains de ses calculs.[22]

3 Bois d'œuvre résineux — Facteur d'ajustement

L'Accord sur le bois d'œuvre résineux comporte son propre mécanisme de règlement des différends. On est ici devant le premier différend porté devant un tribunal arbitral en vertu de ce mécanisme. Les États-Unis prétendent que le Canada a fait défaut d'appliquer correctement un facteur d'ajustement qui aurait dû permettre d'appliquer des droits à l'exportation sur le bois provenant de certaines régions du Canada et vendu aux États-Unis. Les États-Unis prétendent aussi que le Canada, lors d'une baisse du prix du bois aux États-Unis, aurait dû limiter le volume de ces exportations vers les États-Unis. Le Canada se défend évidemment d'avoir mal appliqué l'Accord sur le bois d'œuvre résineux. Les procédures ayant toutes été mises en place pendant l'année 2007, la décision du groupe arbitral devrait être connue au début de l'année 2008.[23]

III LE COMMERCE CANADIEN ET L'OMC

A LES DÉVELOPPEMENTS DANS LE SYSTÈME COMMERCIAL MULTILATÉRAL EN 2007

Selon les termes de l'Accord instituant l'OMC, l'année 2007 aurait dû en principe être l'année de la tenue de la septième Conférence ministérielle de l'OMC, deux ans après la Conférence de Hong Kong de décembre 2005.[24] Si cette septième conférence s'était

---

[22] Examen par un Groupe spécial binational constitué en vertu de l'article 1904 de l'*Accord de libre-échange nord-américain*, dans l'affaire *Fils machine en acier au carbone et certains fils machine en acier allié du Canada: Décision du Groupe spécial, 28 novembre 2007*, disponible en ligne à: <http://registry.nafta-sec-alena.org/cmdocuments/a3512a11–23cb-4818–810f-be6dbea934b5.pdf>.

[23] On peut retrouver tous les documents relatifs à cette affaire sur le site du ministère des Affaires étrangères et du Commerce international: <http://www.international.gc.ca/controls-controles/softwood-bois_oeuvre/other-autres/agreement-accord.aspx?lang=fra#settlement>.

[24] L'article IV:1 de l'*Accord de Marrakech instituant l'Organisation mondiale du commerce* prévoit que la Conférence ministérielle se réunira au moins une fois tous les deux ans.

tenue, on aurait pu espérer que 2007 soit une année faste pour le système commercial multilatéral. Ce ne fut pas le cas. Sans être une mauvaise année, l'année 2007 fut une année où l'activité à l'OMC fut au ralenti et livra peu de résultats.

On peut tout de même se réjouir, quant au membership de l'OMC, de la confirmation des accessions du VietNam et de Tonga qui ont complété en 2007 les dernières étapes du processus d'accession. Ces deux nouveaux Membres devraient rapidement être suivis par le Cap-Vert dont le Conseil général de l'OMC, à sa réunion du 18 décembre, a approuvé l'accession.[25]

Plus tôt dans l'année, le Conseil général, agissant cette fois à titre d'Organe de règlement des différends, a aussi procédé à des nominations de haute importance en désignant quatre nouveaux membres de l'Organe d'appel.[26] Mme Lilia R. Bautista des Philippines et Mme Jennifer Hillman des États-Unis ont été nommées pour un mandat de quatre ans commençant le 11 décembre 2007 en remplacement de Mme Merit Janow et de M. Yasuhei Taniguishi. M. Shotaro Oshima du Japon et Mme Yuejiao Zhang de la Chine ont été nommés pour un mandat de quatre ans commençant le 1er juin 2008 en remplacement de MM. Georges Abi-Saab et A.V. Ganesan.

La fin de l'année 2007 a aussi été l'occasion, dans le *Rapport sur le commerce mondial*, de souligner le 60e anniversaire du système commercial multilatéral. Le Rapport de 2007 a pris une facture particulière et a commémoré cet anniversaire historique en se livrant à une analyse approfondie du GATT, de l'OMC, de leurs origines et de leur évolution.[27]

1   Les négociations commerciales multilatérales

On se rappelle que les négociations du cycle de Doha avaient été suspendues en juillet 2006 à cause d'une trop grande divergence

---

[25] Organisation mondiale du commerce, Conseil général, *Compte-rendu de la réunion tenue au Centre William-Rappard le 18 décembre 2007*, 4 mars 2008, para. 5, disponible en ligne à: <http://docsonline.wto.org/DDFDocuments/u/WT/GC/M112.doc>.

[26] Organisation mondiale du commerce, Organe de règlement des différends, *Compte-rendu de la réunion tenue au Centre William-Rappard les 19 et 27 novembre 2007, 11 février 2008*, para. 6–7, disponible en ligne à: <http://docsonline.wto.org/DDFDocuments/u/WT/DSB/M242.doc>.

[27] L'observateur du système commercial multilatéral voudra consulter le *Rapport sur le commerce mondial 2007*, disponible en ligne à: <http://www.wto.org/french/res_f/booksp_f/anrep_f/world_trade_report07_f.pdf>.

de vue entre les Membres de l'OMC.[28] Ces négociations n'ont guère progressé en 2007. Pourtant, à la fin janvier, à l'occasion d'une réunion informelle à Davos regroupant des représentants d'une trentaine de Membres autour du Directeur général Pascal Lamy, on pouvait croire à un possible redémarrage des négociations. Les représentants canadiens exprimaient en tout cas un certain espoir.[29] Dans son rapport au Conseil général de l'OMC en février, M. Lamy faisait remarquer que les conditions politiques étaient plus propices à la conclusion du Cycle qu'elles ne l'avaient été depuis bien longtemps et annonçait que les Membres avaient repris les négociations dans tous les domaines.[30]

En juin, la réunion des membres du G4 (États-Unis, Union européenne, Brésil et Inde) n'a pas permis de rapprocher les positions de négociation.

La perspective d'un ralentissement économique mondial de même que l'insistance et la persévérance du Directeur général pour faire avancer les négociations, commençaient à donner des résultats en juillet. Le président des négociations sur l'agriculture et le président des négociations sur l'accès aux marchés pour les produits non agricoles (AMNA) — l'ambassadeur canadien à l'OMC, Don Stephenson — présentaient des textes de compromis sur le commerce des produits agricoles et des produits industriels.[31] Ces textes étaient le fruit d'importantes consultations avec les Membres de l'OMC et ouvraient la voie à un terrain d'entente sur des points où des divergences majeures s'étaient déjà fait entendre.

---

[28] Organisation mondiale du commerce, *Nouvelles de l'OMC — PDD modalités de juin/juillet 2006: résumé du 24 juillet,* disponible en ligne à: <http://www.wto.org/french/news_f/news06_f/mod06_summary_24july_f.htm>.

[29] Gouvernement du Canada, *Communiqué du 27 janvier 2007,* disponible en ligne à: <http://w01.international.gc.ca/minpub/Publication.aspx?isRedirect=True&publication_id=384792&Language=F&docnumber=16>.

[30] Organisation mondiale du commerce, Conseil général, *Compte-rendu de la réunion tenue au Centre William-Rappard le 7 février 2007, 19 mars 2007,* para. 2, disponible en ligne à: <http://docsonline.wto.org/DDFDocuments/u/WT/GC/M107.doc>.

[31] Organisation mondiale du commerce, Comité de l'agriculture, *Session extraordinaire, Projet de modalités concernant l'agriculture, 17 juillet 2007,* disponible en ligne à: <http://www.wto.org/french/tratop_f/agric_f/agchairtxt_17july07_f.doc>; Organisation mondiale du commerce, Groupe de négociation sur l'accès aux marchés, *Introduction du Président concernant le projet de modalites pour l'AMNA, 17 juillet 2007,* disponible en ligne à: <http://www.wto.org/french/tratop_f/markacc_f/namachairtxt_17july07_f.doc>.

En octobre, les négociations avaient recommencé à progresser, mais il restait encore du chemin à parcourir avant de présenter des projets de textes révisés, dont la remise était reportée au mois de janvier 2008. Optimiste comme il se doit, M. Lamy déclarait en décembre: "Si nous convenons de modalités au début de l'année prochaine, je pense que nous devrions pouvoir conclure le Cycle avant la fin de 2008."[32]

Dans son *Rapport en matière d'accès aux marchés internationaux* publié en 2007, le Canada rappelait qu'il est un partisan de l'élimination de toute forme de subvention à l'exportation dans le secteur agricole. Il souhaite de plus une forte réduction du soutien interne à l'agriculture ayant un effet de distorsion sur les échanges et une amélioration réelle et significative de l'accès aux marchés. Quant aux négociations sur l'accès aux marchés des produits non agricoles, le Canada recherche la réduction des droits de douane pour tous les produits et l'élimination de ces droits notamment pour les produits de la pêche, les produits forestiers, les produits liés à l'environnement et les matières premières.[33]

2   L'action canadienne à l'OMC en 2007

Le huitième examen des politiques commerciales canadiennes a eu lieu les 21 et 23 mars 2007. Le Canada fut généreusement félicité pour ses performances économiques et commerciales, pour l'ouverture de son économie, pour la transparence de ses politiques et pour sa participation active à l'OMC. Les membres de l'Organe d'examen des politiques commerciales ont tout de même adressé au Canada quelques remarques, souhaits et recommandations quant à certains aspects de ses politiques commerciales. Nous reproduisons ici des extraits des remarques finales du président de l'Organe d'examen qui nous apparaissent les plus importantes:

Les Membres ont émis des doutes concernant certains aspects du régime du Canada en matière d'investissement étranger, y compris les critères d'examen, les limitations de propriété et les prescriptions de résidence pour les administrateurs. Plusieurs mentions spécifiques ont été faites des

---

[32] Organisation mondiale du commerce, *Nouvelles 2007 — 18 décembre 2007*, disponible en ligne à: <http://www.wto.org/french/news_f/news07_f/tnc_chair_report_dec07_f.htm>.

[33] *Supra* note 6 à la p. 12.

restrictions à l'investissement étranger dans les secteurs des télécommunications et des transports aériens ... Les Membres ont demandé au Canada de faire en sorte que les taxes intérieures sur le vin et la bière n'exercent pas de discrimination à l'encontre des importations. En ce qui concerne les marchés publics, plusieurs Membres ont indiqué qu'ils souhaiteraient un meilleur accès aux opportunités découlant des marchés publics au niveau sous-fédéral ... Tout en rendant hommage aux efforts déployés par le Canada pour promouvoir la réforme de l'agriculture dans le cadre du PDD, certains Membres se sont déclarés préoccupés par la protection accordée à certains produits, surtout ceux dont les approvisionnements étaient gérés. Ils ont également émis des doutes sur les changements que le Canada se proposait d'apporter à son régime d'importation des produits laitiers qui éloigneraient encore plus certaines parties du secteur agroalimentaire des solutions fondées sur le marché qui avaient si bien fonctionné dans d'autres domaines.[34]

Dans un contexte bien différent de celui de l'examen des politiques commerciales, le Canada a su se faire valoir d'autres façons en 2007. En mai, le Canada faisait un don de 400 000 $ au Fonds pour l'application des normes et le développement du commerce (FANDC), en vue d'aider les pays en développement à améliorer leurs compétences et leur capacité à mettre en œuvre les normes internationales concernant la sécurité sanitaire des produits alimentaires, la santé des animaux et la préservation des végétaux.[35]

Le Canada faisait également un don de 400 000 $ au Fonds global d'affectation spéciale pour le Programme de Doha pour le développement, qui finance des programmes d'assistance technique et de formation pour les pays en développement, les pays les moins avancés et les économies en transition. Ces programmes visent notamment à aider les pays bénéficiaires à mieux adapter leurs pratiques et leurs législations aux règles de l'OMC et à mieux les intégrer au fonctionnement de celle-ci.[36]

---

[34] Organisation mondiale du commerce, Organe d'examen des politiques commerciales, *Examen des politiques commerciales du Canada, Compte-rendu de la réunion, Révision, 29 juin 2007, Remarques finales du Président*, para. 108, 110–111, disponible en ligne à: <http://docsonline.wto.org/DDFDocuments/u/WT/TPR/M179R1.doc>.

[35] Organisation mondiale du commerce, *Nouvelles 2007 — Communiqué de presse, 1er mai 2007*, disponible en ligne à: <http://www.wto.org/french/news_f/pres07_f/pr477_f.htm>.

[36] *Ibid.*

En octobre, le Canada était le premier pays à notifier l'OMC qu'il autorisait une société à fabriquer une version générique d'un médicament breveté à des fins d'exportation au titre des dispositions spéciales de l'OMC convenues en 2003.[37] En juillet, le Rwanda avait informé l'OMC de son intention d'importer un médicament de trithérapie du sida, le TriAvir, qu'il ne pouvait fabriquer lui-même. L'accord conclu en 2003 par les Membres de l'OMC permet l'importation de produits génériques à meilleur prix dans le cadre d'une licence obligatoire pour les pays confrontés à des problèmes de santé publique qui se trouvent dans l'incapacité de fabriquer eux-mêmes ces médicaments. La version générique du TriAvir pourra désormais être fabriquée au Canada et exportée au Rwanda.

B   LES DIFFÉRENDS DEVANT L'OMC IMPLIQUANT LE CANADA

Il est permis de qualifier l'année 2007 d'année paisible pour le Canada en matière de règlement des différends à l'OMC. On se rappellera qu'à la fin de l'année 2006, quelques affaires touchant le commerce canadien, dont la guerre canado-américaine sur le bois d'œuvre résineux, avaient trouvé leur issue. En 2007, quatre affaires impliquant le Canada ont connu des développements dignes de mention.

I   *Communautés européennes – Mesures affectant l'approbation et la commercialisation des produits biotechnologiques (DS 292)*

À la toute fin de l'année 2006, les Communautés européennes (CE) ont informé l'Organe de règlement des différends (ORD) de leur intention de mettre en œuvre les recommandations du Groupe spécial adoptées à la réunion de l'ORD du 21 novembre 2006. Dès le début de l'année 2007, le Canada, l'Argentine, les États-Unis et les CE ont avisé le président de l'ORD des modalités selon lesquelles ils allaient convenir ensemble du délai raisonnable de mise en œuvre des recommandations adoptées. En juin, ils ont avisé le président de l'ORD qu'ils avaient convenu que le délai raisonnable de mise

---

37 World Trade Organization, Council For Trade, *Related Aspects of Intellectual Property Rights, Notification under Paragraph 2(C) of the Decision of 30 August 2003 on the Implementation of Paragraph 6 of the Doha Declaration on the Trips Agreement and Public Health, Canada, 5 October 2007*, disponible en ligne à: <http://www.wto.org/english/news_e/news07_e/canada_notification_oct_e.doc>. Nous n'avons pu trouver en ligne la version française de cette déclaration.

en œuvre expirerait 21 novembre 2007.[38] Ce délai a ensuite été reconduit jusqu'au 11 janvier 2008.

2   Chine – Mesures affectant les importations de pièces automobiles (DS 342)

Le 29 janvier 2007, à la demande des parties, le Directeur général de l'OMC a déterminé la composition du Groupe spécial et chargé Julio Lacarte-Muró, Ujal Singh Bhatia et Wilhelm Meier d'entendre cette affaire.[39] Le rapport de ce groupe spécial n'était toujours pas rendu à la fin de 2007.

3   États-Unis – Subventions et autres mesures de soutien interne pour le maïs et d'autres produits agricoles (DS 357)

Par une longue demande de consultations datée du 8 janvier 2007, le Canada a demandé l'ouverture de consultations avec les États-Unis au sujet de trois catégories de mesures.[40] La première catégorie de mesures est composée de subventions et de soutien interne qui sont accordés aux producteurs et/ou aux exportateurs de maïs des États-Unis (le "secteur du maïs des États-Unis") ainsi que les programmes, la législation, la réglementation et les instruments réglementaires qui fournissent ces subventions et ce soutien. Les mesures comprennent des subventions et du soutien interne qui prennent la forme de programmes, de versements, de prêts, de certificats de produits, de bonifications d'intérêt pour avances, de garanties de crédit accordés au secteur du maïs des États-Unis depuis la campagne de commercialisation de 1996.

---

38 Organisation mondiale du commerce, *Communautés européennes – Mesures affectant l'approbation et la commercialisation des produits biotechnologiques,* Accord au titre de l'article 21:3 b) du Mémorandum d'Accord sur le règlement des différends, 26 juin 2007, disponible en ligne à: <http://docsonline.wto.org/DDFDocuments/u/WT/DS/292-29.doc>.

39 Organisation mondiale du commerce, *Chine – Mesures affectant les importations de pièces automobiles,* Constitution du Groupe spécial établi à la demande des Communautés européennes, des États-Unis et du Canada, Note du Secrétariat, 30 janvier 2007, disponible en ligne à: <http://docsonline.wto.org/DDFDocuments/u/WT/DS/342-9.doc>.

40 Organisation mondiale du commerce, *États-Unis – Subventions et autres mesures de soutien interne pour le maïs et d'autres produits agricoles,* Demande de consultations présentée par le Canada, 11 janvier 2007, disponible en ligne à: <http://docsonline. wto.org/DDFDocuments/u/G/AG/GEN74.doc>.

Le Canada est d'avis que ces mesures sont incompatibles avec les articles 5c) et 6.3c) de l'Accord sur les subventions et mesures compensatoires (Accord SMC). La deuxième catégorie de mesures est faite de mesures de soutien par lesquelles les États-Unis offrent à leurs exportateurs des taux de prime et d'autres conditions plus favorables que ce que le marché offrirait autrement. Les taux de prime au titre de ces programmes sont insuffisants pour couvrir, à longue échéance, les frais et les pertes au titre de la gestion des programmes. Ces programmes constituent, de l'avis du Canada, des subventions subordonnées aux résultats à l'exportation, en violation de l'article 3.1 a) et 3.2 de l'Accord SMC. Le Canada prétend aussi que ces mesures contreviennent aux articles 3:3, 8, 9:1 et 10:1 de l'Accord sur l'agriculture.

Des mesures de soutien interne composent la troisième catégorie. Le Canada considère que les États-Unis, par l'application de quatre lois relatives au financement agricole, accordent à leurs producteurs nationaux un soutien qui excède les niveaux d'engagement spécifiés dans la section I de la Partie IV de leur Liste, le tout à l'encontre de l'article 3:2 de l'Accord sur l'agriculture.

Plusieurs Membres de l'OMC, soit l'Argentine, l'Australie, le Brésil, les Communautés européennes, le Guatemala, le Nicaragua, la Thaïlande et l'Uruguay, ont rapidement demandé à être admis à participer aux consultations demandées par le Canada. Les États-Unis ont accepté ces demandes de participation aux consultations.

Le 7 juin 2007, le Canada a demandé que l'ORD, à sa réunion du 20 juin, établisse un groupe spécial pour entendre cette affaire.[41] L'ORD a reporté l'établissement de ce groupe spécial. Le 20 juillet, le Canada a demandé à participer aux consultations demandées par le Brésil aux États-Unis relativement à plusieurs questions similaires à celles soumises par le Canada. Le 8 novembre 2007, par une demande très détaillée dans laquelle étaient listées avec précision toutes les mesures états-uniennes en cause dans l'affaire, le Canada et le Brésil ont tous deux demandé l'établissement d'un groupe spécial.[42] Le 15 novembre 2007, le Canada a retiré sa première

---

[41] Organisation mondiale du commerce, *États-Unis – Subventions et autres mesures de soutien interne pour le maïs et d'autres produits agricoles,* Demande d'établissement d'un groupe spécial présentée par le Canada, 8 juin 2007, disponible en ligne à: <http://docsonline.wto.org/DDFDocuments/u/WT/DS/357–11.doc>.

[42] Organisation mondiale du commerce, *États-Unis – Subventions et autres mesures de soutien interne pour le maïs et d'autres produits agricoles,* Demande d'établissement d'un groupe spécial présentée par le Canada, 9 novembre 2007, disponible en

demande d'établissement d'un groupe spécial datant du 7 juin 2007. À sa réunion du 27 novembre 2007, l'ORD a reporté l'établissement d'un groupe spécial. À sa réunion du 17 décembre, à la suite d'une deuxième demande provenant à la fois du Canada et du Brésil, l'ORD a finalement établi un seul groupe spécial.

4 *Communautés européennes – Certaines mesures prohibant l'importation et la commercialisation de produits dérivés de phoques (DS 369)*

Le 25 septembre 2007, le Canada a demandé l'ouverture de consultations avec les Communautés européennes (CE) au sujet de certaines mesures prises par la Belgique et les Pays Bas concernant l'importation, le transport, la fabrication, la commercialisation et la vente de produits dérivés de phoques. Les mesures en cause sont décrites dans la demande de consultations.[43]

Une loi belge entrée en vigueur en 2007 (*Loi relative à l'interdiction de fabriquer et de commercialiser des produits dérivés de phoques*) prohibe la préparation pour la vente ou pour la livraison au consommateur, le transport pour la vente ou la livraison, la détention en vue de la vente, l'importation, la distribution et la cession de produits dérivés de phoques. Une autre mesure belge, l'*Arrêté ministériel modifiant l'arrêté ministériel du 15 septembre 1995 soumettant à licence l'importation de certaines marchandises* impose une prescription selon laquelle une licence d'importation doit être délivrée pour l'importation de produits dérivés de phoques. Enfin, une mesure néerlandaise, les articles 5 et 23 de la *Loi sur la flore et la faune* néerlandaise, lus conjointement avec le *Décret du 4 juillet 2007 modifiant le Décret sur la désignation des espèces animales et végétales* (*Loi sur la flore et la faune*) *et le Décret sur les espèces animales et végétales protégées (exemptions) en relation avec l'interdiction du commerce de produits dérivés de phoques du*

---

ligne à: <http://docsonline.wto.org/DDFDocuments/u/WT/DS/357-12.doc>. Voir aussi Organisation mondiale du commerce, *États-Unis – Subventions et autres mesures de soutien interne pour le maïs et d'autres produits agricoles,* Demande d'établissement d'un groupe spécial présentée par le Canada, *Communication présentée par le Secrétariat,* Corrigendum, 16 novembre 2007, disponible en ligne à: <http://docsonline.wto.org/DDFDocuments/u/WT/DS/357-12C1.doc>.

43 Organisation mondiale du commerce, *Communautés européennes – Certaines mesures prohibant l'importation et la commercialisation de produits dérivés de phoques,* Demande de consultations présentée par le Canada, 1er octobre 2007, disponible en ligne à: <http://docsonline.wto.org/DDFDocuments/u/G/TBT/D31.doc>.

Groenland et de phoques à capuchon ont pour effet de prohiber l'importation et le commerce de tous les produits dérivés de phoques du Groenland ou de phoques à capuchon quel que soit l'âge de l'animal. Cela inclut une prohibition interdisant la demande en vue de la vente, l'achat ou l'acquisition, la détention en vue de la vente ou du stockage, la vente ou la mise en vente, le transport ou l'offre en vue du transport, la livraison, l'utilisation à des fins de profit commercial, la location ou la mise en location, l'échange ou l'offre en vue de l'échange, le commerce ou l'exposition à des fins commerciales ou l'introduction ou la possession à l'intérieur ou à l'extérieur du territoire des Pays-Bas, de produits dérivés de phoques du Groenland et de phoques à capuchon.

De l'avis du Canada, ces mesures sont incompatibles avec les obligations des CE au titre des articles 2.1 et 2.2 de l'Accord OTC et des articles I:1, III:4, V:2, V:3, V:4 et XI:1 du GATT de 1994.

Au moment d'écrire ces lignes, la demande de consultations canadienne n'avait pas eu de suite. Du point de vue canadien, il est à craindre que les mesures belge et néerlandaise n'inspirent le Parlement européen pour un règlement qui couvrirait tout le territoire de l'Union européenne. Le Canada n'est vraisemblablement pas au bout de ses peines quant au commerce des produits dérivés du phoque en Europe.

IV Conclusion

Année tumultueuse au plan économique, année de stagnation au plan des négociations commerciales tant régionales que multilatérales mais année de relative paix commerciale quant aux différends impliquant le Canada, l'année 2007 est atypique à plus d'un égard. Il est à souhaiter que l'activité commerciale canadienne et le système commercial multilatéral reprennent leur souffle et fassent preuve de plus de dynamisme en 2008.

II Le Canada et le système financier international en 2007

compiled by / préparé par

BERNARD COLAS

L'apparition de perturbations sur le marché américain a été l'une des principales préoccupations de la communauté internationale en 2007. Dans ce contexte, la transparence, la surveillance, la gouvernance, la couverture des risques et la coopération des États ont été au centre de tous les débats. Parallèlement, la communauté internationale s'est intéressée à des sujets tels que la réforme des institutions de Bretton Woods, ou encore la lutte contre le terrorisme ou le blanchiment d'argent. Ces divers travaux ont été menés de concert par: (1) le Groupe des 20 (G-20); (2) les institutions financières internationales; (3) les organismes de contrôle des établissements financiers; (4) le Groupe d'action financière; (5) le Joint Forum. Au sein de ces institutions, le Canada joue un rôle de premier plan.

I Le Groupe des 20 (G-20)

La neuvième réunion du Groupe des 20 (G-20), s'est pour la première fois tenue sur le continent africain, dans le seul pays africain membre, à savoir l'Afrique du Sud. Pour leur rencontre des 17 et 18 novembre 2007, les ministres de finances et gouverneurs de banques centrales avaient choisi d'aborder le thème "Partage — Influence, responsabilité et savoir."[1]

Malgré une croissance mondiale stable durant cinq années consécutives et un premier trimestre vigoureux, les membres du G-20

Bernard Colas est avocat associé de l'étude Colas Moreira Kazandjian Zikovsky (CMKZ) à Montréal et Docteur en droit. L'auteur remercie Xavier Mageau, LL.M., de la même étude pour son importante contribution à cet article ainsi que Hélène Haulet.

[1] Communiqué, *Meeting of Finance Ministers and Central Bank Governors,* Kleinmond, Cape Town, Afrique du Sud, 17-18 novembre 2007, au para. 1.

ont mis en exergue des perturbations se matérialisant par une volatilité des cours des matières premières et des agitations sur le marché américain des prêts hypothécaires à risques. La durée et l'ampleur de cette baisse de croissance étant difficile à évaluer sur le long terme, ils ont préconisé d'accroître la surveillance financière, de s'armer de solides politiques macroéconomiques, d'exiger une plus grande transparence de la part de l'ensemble des acteurs ou encore de faire appel à des stratégies de couverture des risques.[2]

Les ministres de finances et gouverneurs de banques centrales ont également réaffirmé la nécessité d'asseoir la crédibilité et l'efficacité des institutions de Bretton Woods en réformant leur système de gouvernance. Ils ont en outre salué l'adoption de mesures relatives à la surveillance bilatérale des politiques des membres, les avancées dans l'élaboration d'un modèle de revenu du Fonds monétaire international (FMI) ainsi que les prémices d'un consensus concernant la réforme des quotes-parts et voix exprimées du FMI. Ils ont notamment profité de l'effort conséquent d'intégration des économies émergentes par la Banque mondiale pour rappeler au FMI de prendre des mesures dans le même sens.[3]

II LES INSTITUTIONS FINANCIÈRES INTERNATIONALES

En 2007, le Canada a principalement eu recours à ses 2,89 p. 100 des voix au FMI et 2,78 p. 100 des voix à la Banque mondiale afin d'obtenir la modification du système de gouvernance des institutions de Bretton Woods, l'accroissement de l'efficacité desdites institutions, le soutien aux pays fragiles et la réduction de la pauvreté.

A LE FONDS MONÉTAIRE INTERNATIONAL (FMI)

En 2007, les liquidités du FMI franchissaient le pallier record de 217,3 milliards de DTS.[4] Parallèlement, les nouveaux engagements de prêts généraux ont suivi une tendance inverse, enclenchée en 2003, en continuant à chuter. Leur montant ne représentait en effet que 237 millions de DTS en 2007[5] et n'atteignait donc même

---

[2] *Ibid.* au para. 3.

[3] *Ibid.*

[4] Direction des finances et des échanges internationaux, *Rapport sur les opérations effectuées en vertu de la Loi sur les accords de Bretton Woods et des accords connexes 2007, 2008*, à la p.17.

[5] *Ibid.* à la p. 29.

pas la quote-part de 6,3 milliards de DTS du Canada,[6] le neuvième actionnaire du FMI. Cette baisse est à relativiser étant donné qu'elle s'explique principalement par le remboursement prématuré de leur dette par la Bulgarie, la République centrafricaine, l'Équateur, Haïti, l'Indonésie, le Malawi, les Philippines, la Serbie et l'Uruguay mais également par l'efficacité des prêts à conditions de faveur[7] et des aides aux pays très pauvres endettés.[8]

En 2007, le Canada a largement pris part aux programmes de formation du FMI en apportant une aide conséquente aux centres régionaux d'assistance technique d'Afrique et des Caraïbes.[9] La même année, de nombreux pays ont bénéficié de "l'Instrument de soutien à la politique économique" (IPSE), créé en 2005 sous l'impulsion du Canada, permettant aux pays le désirant, d'obtenir un soutien et une évaluation régulière de leur politique économique interne.[10] Le Canada a quant à lui été le premier du Groupe des 7 (G-7) à expérimenter le Programme d'évaluation des secteurs financiers (PESF) à l'automne 2007. Cette évaluation s'est soldée par un franc succès puisque à son terme le FMI a conclu que "le Canada possède un régime d'encadrement et de réglementation des valeurs mobilières hautement sophistiqué répondant largement aux principes de l'Organisation internationale des commissions des valeurs (OICV)."[11]

Dans le rapport de fin d'année 2006, quatre grands objectifs avaient été mis de l'avant par le Canada: la refonte du système des quotes-parts et de la représentation des membres; le recours à des formules de prêts plus adaptées; la diversification et la consolidation des modes de financement du FMI; le perfectionnement des mesures de surveillance.

Ce dernier point relatif aux mesures de surveillance a connu un vif succès en 2007. En mars, le Bureau indépendant d'évaluation

---

6   *Ibid.* à la p. 17.

7   *Ibid.* à la p. 30. En 2007, dix pays ont bénéficié de ces prêts à conditions de faveur d'un montant total de 401 millions de DTS.

8   *Ibid.* à la p. 30. En 2007, vingt-quatre pays ont été admissibles pour recevoir cette aide aux pays très pauvres endettés d'un montant total de 1,7 milliards de DTS.

9   Le Cap-Vert, le Mozambique, le Nigéria, l'Ouganda et la Tanzanie.

10 Direction des finances et des échanges internationaux, *supra* note 4 à la p. 20.

11 Communiqué de l'Autorité des marchés financiers, "La qualité du système canadien d'encadrement des valeurs mobilières de nouveau reconnue," 15 février 2008, disponible en ligne à: <http://www.lautorite.qc.ca/pdf/com15fev2008-rapport-fmi.pdf>.

(BIE) a en effet publié un rapport relatif aux politiques de change; ledit rapport préconisant d'une part de renforcer la surveillance des activités du FMI et des crises à naître, d'autre part de mieux faire correspondre les déclarations du FMI avec ses véritables prestations et enfin d'améliorer ses outils d'analyses des taux de change. Encouragé par le Canada, le G-7 et le G-20, le Fonds a adopté, dès juin 2007, une nouvelle décision sur la surveillance bilatérale renforcée et uniforme des économies et des taux de change. En août, le Fonds a ensuite décidé de mettre en place un processus de déclaration des priorités de surveillance qui débutera dès 2008. Ce nouvel outil méthodologique permettra de se concentrer sur les éléments les plus pertinents et donc d'accroître l'efficacité du Fonds. Fin 2007, le BIE a également rendu son rapport sur l'évaluation de la conditionnalité structurelle des programmes appuyés par le FMI.[12]

En ce qui concerne la réforme des quotes-parts et la plus large représentation des pays émergents, le bilan est plus mitigé. En effet, même si cela assure une plus grande crédibilité au FMI sur la scène internationale, certains pays ne sont pas encore prêts à faire des concessions et à réduire le rayonnement de leur propre souveraineté. Ceci a conduit à une situation de blocage étant donné qu'une décision de cette nature suppose l'assentiment de 85 p. 100 des voix des membres. Le Canada ne fait pas partie des pays réticents et est très impliqué dans cette réforme. Il a notamment suggéré de réajuster le partage des quotes-parts en fonction de critères plus transparents, basés sur le produit intérieur brut et la parité de pouvoir d'achat. Ces propositions tendant à récompenser les économies dynamiques ou encore celles visant à augmenter les voix de base attribuées à chaque pays, ont été largement acceptées par les pays membres.[13]

Bien qu'une réforme du système des prêts soit considérée comme primordiale par le Canada, celle-ci a temporairement été mise en suspens. Dans ce contexte, le Canada a renouvelé sa volonté de doter le FMI d'instruments plus souples et plus en adéquation avec les différents besoins des membres. Enfin, le Canada ne semble pas opposé au remplacement de l'inopérante Ligne de crédit préventive (LCP), inaugurée en 1999, par une ligne de crédit pour l'augmentation des réserves.[14]

---

[12] Direction des finances et des échanges internationaux, *supra* note 4 à la p. 26.

[13] *Ibid.* à la p. 22.

[14] *Ibid.* à la p. 27.

Pour la première fois depuis des décennies, le budget d'administration du FMI a été déficitaire en 2007. Cette singularité a conduit les administrateurs à s'interroger sur l'efficacité des modes de financement du Fonds et sur une éventuelle réforme du système actuel. La grande majorité des membres du Fonds, le Canada en tête, ont reconnu la nécessité de restreindre les dépenses et de diversifier les sources de financement du Fonds. En ce sens, Dominique Strauss-Kahn, le nouveau directeur général du Fonds, a notamment annoncé de prochaines compressions de ressources humaines. En parallèle, le comité Crockett a remis son rapport sur les potentielles sources de financement du FMI. Les membres de ce comité ont dans un premier temps recommandé la vente d'une partie limitée des réserves d'or du Fonds. Ils ont ensuite invité le FMI à opter pour une politique d'investissement moins contraignante afin d'obtenir un meilleur rendement. De plus, ils ont émis l'hypothèse d'investir une partie des quotes-parts des pays membres puis d'en conserver les fruits. Le Canada a soutenu l'ensemble de ces propositions mais a conditionné son appui au respect d'un certain nombre de précautions telles que la prise en compte d'éventuelles retombées négatives sur les cours du marché de l'or.[15]

B   LA BANQUE MONDIALE

La fin de l'année 2006 a notamment été marquée par la quinzième reconstitution des ressources de l'Association internationale de développement (IDA) qui permet à cette institution de la Banque mondiale de disposer d'un budget triennal record de 41,6 G$US dont 4 p. 100 a été versé par le Canada (1,3 G$CAN). Afin d'accroître l'efficacité de ses contributions, le Canada a une nouvelle fois exhorté la Banque de cibler son aide et de se concentrer sur les États les plus fragiles en consacrant notamment 50 p. 100 de son budget aux pays africains.

Sous l'impulsion du Canada et de ses programmes d'aide en Afghanistan, au Soudan, à Haïti ou encore de sa campagne en faveur des pays touchés par un conflit, on note une véritable amélioration du comportement de la Banque vis-à-vis des États fragiles. Celle-ci a notamment mis en place un Fonds fiduciaire de l'Initiative d'aide aux pays à faible revenu en difficultés (LICUS) et a assoupli sa politique d'aide par le biais de l'IDA en instaurant un mécanisme de financements non remboursables. En parallèle, et ce, afin de combattre le cycle du "prêter et renoncer" qui a souvent pour effet

---

[15] *Ibid.* à la p. 28.

d'annihiler les efforts déployés par l'ensemble des acteurs, le Canada mène depuis 2000 une politique d'effacement des dettes. Son acharnement s'est soldé par un franc succès puisqu'en 2007, le Libéria a été le premier bénéficiaire d'un effacement de dettes à grande échelle.

La volonté de la Banque d'enrayer le problème de la corruption a également été d'actualité en 2007 puisque cette dernière a soumis, en partenariat avec le FMI, une stratégie de gouvernance et de lutte contre la corruption. Le Canada a évidemment soutenu ce projet et a une nouvelle fois insisté sur la nécessité de contrôler son efficacité en aval afin d'optimiser l'utilisation des fonds de la Banque.[16] Un des pans de ce projet consiste en un recouvrement des avoirs volés tandis que le second a trait à la ratification de la Convention des Nations Unies contre la corruption (CNUCC). Le Canada, fort de cette démarche, a procédé à des modifications législatives afin d'être en mesure, le 2 octobre 2007, de ratifier ladite Convention.[17]

Enfin, la Banque a inauguré en février 2007 la première garantie de marché, mécanisme permettant de financer et faciliter la recherche de vaccins nécessaires dans les pays en développement. Le Canada a contribué à hauteur de 200 M$ dans ce projet pilote relatif aux pneumocoques et censé sauver 5,8 millions de personnes d'ici 2030.[18] De plus, elle a inauguré une mutuelle d'assurance contre les risques liés aux catastrophes naturelles (CCRIF), dont le Canada est le principal bailleur de fonds. Ce mécanisme, dont le principal intérêt est la rapidité, offre aux États un délai pour prendre des mesures de soutien à plus long terme.[19]

III Les organismes de contrôle des établissements financiers

A Le comité de Bâle sur le contrôle bancaire

L'Accord Bâle I, également connu sous le nom Accord de Bâle de 1988, a été remplacé le 4 juillet 2006 par l'Accord Bâle II.[20] Un des

---

[16] *Ibid.* à la p. 53.

[17] *Ibid.* aux pp. 53–54. *Loi modifiant le Code criminel en vue de la mise en œuvre de la Convention des Nations Unies contre la corruption* (C-48). De plus, la *Loi sur la protection des fonctionnaires divulgateurs d'actes répréhensibles*, telle que modifiée par la *Loi fédérale sur la responsabilité*, est entrée en vigueur le 15 avril 2007.

[18] *Ibid.* aux pp. 56–57.

[19] *Ibid.* à la p. 58.

[20] Voir chronique de 2006.

principaux apports de ce nouvel Accord Bâle II est le remplacement du ratio Cooke par le ratio McDonough. La valeur de référence de 8 p. 100 de fonds propres a été conservée mais le ratio prend désormais en compte les risques de crédits et les risques opérationnels. Le système de pondération a également été remodelé. Le ratio McDonough permet une meilleure évaluation des risques. Toutefois, en raison de son caractère pro-cyclique, il semblerait que ce ratio puisse tendre à accentuer la récession en période de crise. De nombreuses institutions bancaires ont également regretté qu'en parallèle les valeurs de référence n'aient pas été réétudiées.[21] Bâle II repose donc désormais sur d'autres piliers que celui de la dotation en fonds propres, tels que la surveillance prudentielle à l'égard des exigences de fonds propres ou la surveillance de marché.[22]

Le Comité de Bâle sur le contrôle bancaire (CBCB) a vivement recommandé aux pays membres de transposer les dispositions de Bâle II dans leurs législations nationales avant le 1er janvier 2007. Toutefois, selon un sondage de l'Institut de stabilité financière, 95 organes nationaux de réglementation ont fait savoir qu'ils ne le feraient pas avant 2015.[23]

Les banques canadiennes se sont quant à elles engagées à intégrer la plupart des nouvelles pratiques du Comité de Bâle et à instaurer un cadre propice à l'application des dispositions de Bâle II avant le 1er novembre 2007 et le Bureau du surintendant des institutions financières (BSIF) a fait de cette transposition une des priorités de son mandat.[24] Les banques canadiennes ont notamment fourni l'ensemble des données nécessaires au BSIF pour que celui-ci puisse se prononcer sur l'utilisation de l'approche plus complexe des notions internes avancées de Bâle II.

---

[21] M. Navarro, *Troisième partie: Crise et régulation — La finance de bulle en bulle?*, 2008, disponible en ligne à: <http://www.cairn.info/revue-regards-croises-sur-1-economie-2008-1-page-243.htm>.

[22] J. Dupuis, *Les accords de Bâle sur les fonds propres*, Bibliothèque du Parlement, Division de l'économie, révisé le 30 octobre 2006, disponible en ligne à: <http://www.parl.gc.ca/information/library/PRBpubs/prb0596-f.htm>.

[23] Banque des règlements internationaux, *Implementation of the New Capital Adequacy Framework in non-Basel Committee Member Countries: Summary of Responses to the 2006 Follow-up Questionnaire on Basel II Implementation*, Bale, Banque des réglements internationaux, octobre 2006, à la p. 4.

[24] *Rapport 2007-2008 sur les plans et les priorités du Bureau du surintendant des institutions financières canadiennes*, disponible en ligne à: <http://www.tbs-sct.gc.ca/rpp/2007–2008/OSFI-BSIF/osfi-bsifo1-fra.asp>.

Enfin, le BSIF en partenariat avec les institutions responsables d'autres pays membres, et ce afin de faciliter les travaux du Comité de Bâle et la coopération entre les États, a procédé à l'élaboration d'un certain nombre de rapports tels que le *Sound Credit Risk Assessment and Valuation for Loans,* le *Supervisory Guidance on the Use of the Fair Value Option by Banks under International Financial Reporting Standards,* l' *Observed Range of Practice in Key Elements of Advance Measurement Approaches* ou enfin les *Principles for Home-Host Supervisory Cooperation and Allocation Mechanisms in the Context of Advanced Measurement Approaches.*[25]

B L'ORGANISATION INTERNATIONALE DES COMMISSIONS DE VALEURS (OICV)

La 32ème conférence annuelle de l'Organisation internationale des commissions de valeurs s'est tenue en avril 2007 à Mumbai, sur invitation du Securities and Exchange Board indien (SEBI). La Commission, créée en 1983, compte désormais plus de 181 adhérents.[26]

Comme relevé ci-avant aux vues du rapport rendu par le FMI dans le cadre de son Programme d'évaluation du système financier (PESF), le Canada agit en conformité avec les recommandations de l'OICV et son système financier est reconnu comme sain et stable. Ces conclusions ont corroboré le bilan rendu par l'Organisation de coopération et de développement économiques (OCDE) en 2006 selon lequel le Canada se place en seconde position mondiale concernant tout ce qui a trait à la qualité de la règlementation des valeurs mobilières.[27]

Les principaux enjeux abordés lors de cette conférence ont été l'Axe de coopération multilatéral (Multilateral Memorandum of Understanding — MMoU), les initiatives prises en matières de coopération internationale, la question du dialogue avec les représentants de l'industrie et enfin les agences de notation de crédit.[28]

---

[25] *Ibid.*

[26] En 2007, l'OICV a accueilli la Financial Services Commission des Îles vierges britanniques en qualité de nouveau membre ordinaire. Par ailleurs un nouveau membre associé, le Korea Deposit Insurance Corporation et sept membres affiliés, l'Autoregulator del Mercado de Valores of Colombia, l'Abu Dhabi Securities Market, le Dubai Financial Market of the United Arab Emirates, le Bombay Stock Exchange Limited, le Muscat Stock Exchange of Oman, le Tel Aviv Stock Exchange et le Jasdaq Securities Exchange of Japan ont été admis.

[27] Communiqué de l'Autorité des marchés financiers, *supra* note 11.

[28] Service de la communication de l'Autorité des marchés financiers française, *Communiqué final de la 32ème conférence annuelle de l'OICV,* 12 avril 2007, disponible en ligne : à <http://www.amf-france.org/documents/general/7714_1.pdf>.

Le MMoU est, à l'instar des années précédentes, un des axes majeurs de l'activité de l'OICV et de ses membres les plus actifs. Le calendrier prévoyant qu'avant 2010 tous les membres de l'OICV devraient être signataires (membres A) ou avoir mis en œuvre les moyens nécessaires pour être signataires (membres B) du MMoU a été réaffirmé lors de cette conférence. L'Autorité des marchés financiers du Québec, l'Alberta Securities Commission, le British Columbia Securities Commission et l'Ontario Securities Commission sont déjà signataires de cet accord qui a pour objet l'échange mondial d'informations et la coopération lors de procédures d'enquête.

En 2007, la transparence et l'indépendance ont été le fil conducteur de la politique menée par l'OICV. En effet, suite aux perturbations observées sur le marché américain des prêts hypothécaires à risques, les comités ont mieux réalisé l'enjeu central que constituaient ces éléments. Ils ont notamment décidé de créer un groupe de travail (*task force*) chargé de dresser un bilan des risques encourus et problèmes auxquels pourraient être confrontés les acteurs des marchés financiers et de proposer des solutions pour y faire face.[29] Ce groupe a basé son travail sur quatre principaux thèmes : la refonte des techniques d'analyse et de gestion des risques; la transparence; les modes de calcul des actifs; l'incontournable coopération avec le *task force* chargé de s'intéresser aux agences de notation, dont le mandat a été reconduit.[30] Ce groupe de travail, créé entre autre du fait de Bâle II, a beaucoup progressé dans l'adoption d'un code de conduite des agences de notation, et a notamment été encouragé par le comité à s'inspirer de systèmes ne recourant pas à l'autorégulation et dissociant davantage entre les activités de notation et les activités annexes afin d'éviter les situations de conflits d'intérêt.

Du point de vue de la gouvernance, l'OICV a reconfirmé l'importance d'une plus grande coopération entre les régulateurs des marchés financiers.[31] Il a aussi annoncé la création d'un groupe de réflexion portant sur les enjeux de l'intégration des actionnaires minoritaires.[32]

---

[29] Final Communiqué of the XXXIInd Annual Conference of the International Organization of Securities Commissions (IOSCO), 12 avril 2007, disponible en ligne à: <http://www.iosco.org/library/annual_conferences/pdf/ac21–27.pdf>.

[30] *Ibid.*

[31] *Ibid.*

[32] *Ibid.*

IV Le Groupe d'action financière (GAFI)

Au cours de la session 2007–2008, le GAFI a poursuivi ses efforts afin d'atteindre les objectifs lui ayant été confiés dans le cadre de sa lutte contre le terrorisme et le blanchiment d'argent. Ce mandat, initialement fixé en 2004, a été légèrement réactualisé. Les ministres du GAFI ont entériné les nouveaux axes de travail du groupe pour l'année 2007, à savoir l'élaboration de normes d'envergure internationale pour lutter contre le terrorisme et le blanchiment d'argent, la mise en œuvre efficiente desdites normes, le décryptage des méthodes utilisées par les délinquants afin d'être plus préparé à les contrer et enfin la coopération entre les parties prenantes. Les 40 + 9 recommandations du GAFI n'ont quant à elles pas été modifiées mais demeurent le fondement de la mission du GAFI.[33]

L'année 2007 a été marquée par la première réunion du GAFI avec le secteur privé. Depuis de nombreuses années, le GAFI ambitionne de mettre en place de tels partenariats, notamment par le biais de forum, afin de mieux interagir et de familiariser les acteurs du secteur privé avec les méthodes des délinquants. Le GAFI a en outre développé une nouvelle procédure de surveillance tendant à identifier les juridictions les plus faibles et peinant à mettre en place un système fiable. Le GAFI a publié à leur attention des lignes directrices adaptées à leur situation économique. Le cas de l'Iran a notamment été au cœur des discussions en 2007. Le GAFI l'a notamment exhorté de prendre des mesures dans les plus brefs délais afin de lutter contre le blanchiment des capitaux, le financement du terrorisme et plus particulièrement la menace de prolifération des armes de destruction massive.[34] Jusqu'à ce qu'il ait remédié à ce problème, le GAFI a exigé des pays signataires la mise en place de mécanismes de contrôle. Enfin, pour se conformer à la Résolution 1737 du Conseil de sécurité des Nations Unies, le GAFI a adopté de nouvelles lignes directrices sur la mise en œuvre des interdictions financières.[35]

---

[33] *Rapport annuel du GAFI 2007–2008*, 30 juin 2008, à la p. 11, disponible en ligne à: <http://www.fatf-gafi.org/dataoecd/28/47/42670151.pdf>.

[34] Déclaration du GAFI sur l'Iran et Résumé du Président de la réunion plénière, Paris 10-12 octobre 2007, disponible en ligne à: <http://www.fatf-gafi.org/dataoecd/45/23/39497320.pdf>.

[35] *Lignes directrices relatives à la mise en œuvre des interdictions financières liées aux activités couvertes par la Résolution 1737 du Conseil de sécurité des Nations Unies* (octobre 2007) et *Lignes directrices relatives à la mise en œuvre des dispositions financières des*

L'année 2007 a été sujette à de nombreux changements en ce qui concerne le Canada, l'un des leaders en matière de lutte contre les activités terroristes et le blanchiment d'argent. Ce dernier a notamment fait l'objet d'une évaluation mutuelle par le Groupe à l'issu de laquelle son système de surveillance a été jugé conforme et très efficace. De plus les rares bémols soulevés lors de cette procédure ont d'ores et déjà été comblés par les modifications de la *Loi sur le recyclage des produits de la criminalité et le financement des activités terroristes.*[36] Bien que le rôle du Centre d'analyse des opérations et déclarations financières (CANAFE) soit déjà actif, le Canada s'est également engagé à mettre en place une nouvelle génération de solutions de technologies et de gestion de l'information.[37]

V   LE JOINT FORUM

Créé en 1996, le Joint Forum est une assemblée composée de représentants des institutions de surveillance des banques, des négociants en valeurs mobilières et des assurances qui traitent de thèmes prudentiels transectoriels en vue de l'élaboration de normes de contrôle de conglomérats financiers.

En 2007, un groupe de travail a été chargé d'examiner l'obligation selon laquelle les prestataires financiers se doivent, du fait de leur devoir de loyauté et d'information, d'établir un lien entre les produits financiers et les clients (*customer suitability*) et de fournir un rapport à ce sujet. Un second groupe à quant à lui été chargé de procéder à un état des lieux de la manière dont sont appliquées par les signataires les recommandations du Joint Forum concernant les conglomérats financiers.

Ainsi en 2007, année notamment marquée par les importantes perturbations du marché américain, le Canada et les forums dans lesquels il intervient ont accru leurs mesures de transparence, de surveillance des politiques financières, de gouvernance des institutions, de stratégies de couverture des risques et de coopération

---

Résolutions du Conseil de sécurité des Nations Unies pour lutter contre la prolifération des armes de destruction massive (juillet 2007), disponible en ligne à: <http://www.fatf-gafi.org/dataoecd/28/47/42670151.pdf>.

[36] *Projet de loi C-25. Rapport relatif à l'évaluation mutuelle du Canada par le GAFI*, disponible en ligne à: <http://www.fatf-gafi.org/dataoecd/5/3/40323928.pdf>.

[37] *Rapport annuel du CANAFE 2007*, à la p. 2, disponible en ligne à: <http://canafe-fintrac.gc.ca/publications/ar/2007/ar-fra.pdf>.

entre les acteurs du système financier international. De plus, les institutions bancaires canadiennes ont pris des mesures afin de reconstituer leurs fonds propres et ont à ce titre affiché un seuil bien supérieur à celui fixé par la Banque des règlements internationaux et le BSIF.[38]

---

[38] Les institutions bancaires canadiennes ont affiché un ratio moyen de 11,9 p. 100. *Rapport annuel 2007-2008 du Bureau du surintendant des institutions financières,* disponible en ligne à: <http://www.osfi-bsif.gc.ca/app/DocRepository/1/RA/0708/fra/5.1_f.html>.

III Investissement

CÉLINE LÉVESQUE

I INTRODUCTION

Cette chronique est principalement consacrée à l'étude de deux décisions rendues sous le régime du chapitre 11 de l'Accord de libre-échange nord-américain (ALENA)[1] portant sur l'investissement au cours de l'année 2007. Toutes deux impliquent des enjeux de politique publique importants et comprennent une analyse de la relation entre le droit international des investissements et le droit international général.

La première affaire est *United Parcel Service of America Inc c. Canada.*[2] La sentence finale rendue le 24 mai 2007 a complètement débouté l'investisseur et mis fin à sept ans de procédures.[3] La plainte de UPS avait attiré l'attention, car elle semblait s'attaquer à la fourniture de services publics au Canada et en particulier aux activités de Postes Canada. Si l'issue de l'affaire a pu en rassurer certains, on peut déplorer le manque de rigueur dont fait preuve le raisonnement du Tribunal.

Céline Lévesque, professeure agrégée, Faculté de droit, Section de droit civil, Université d'Ottawa et Universitaire en résidence, Direction générale du droit commercial international, ministère des Affaires étrangères et du Commerce international (2008–2009). Les opinions exprimées dans cette chronique sont celles de l'auteure et ne reflètent pas nécessairement celles du Gouvernement du Canada.

1 Accord de libre-échange nord-américain entre le gouvernement du Canada, le gouvernement des États-Unis d'Amérique et le gouvernement du Mexique, 17 décembre 1992, R.T. Can. (1994) no. 2, 32:3 I.L.M. 605 (entrée en vigueur: 1er janvier 2004) [ci-après ALENA].

2 *United Postal Service of America Inc c. Canada*, UNCITRAL (24 mai 2007) [ci-après *UPS*] Arbitres: le doyen Ronald A. Cass, L. Yves Fortier, QC, et le juge Kenneth Keith.

3 Le coût total de l'arbitrage s'est élevé à 950,000 $US sans compter les frais des parties aux différends. Voir *UPS, supra* note 2 au para. 188.

La deuxième affaire est *Bayview Irrigation District et al. c. Mexico.*[4] Dans cette affaire, les demandeurs texans se plaignaient de mesures touchant l'eau et les droits relatifs à l'eau qui leurs appartenaient prétendument au Mexique. Le 19 juin 2007, le Tribunal a rendu une décision d'incompétence, car il a jugé que les demandeurs ne possédaient pas d'investissement sur le territoire du Mexique permettant de satisfaire aux conditions juridictionnelles de l'article 1101 de l'ALENA.[5] Bien que le Tribunal n'ait pas procédé à l'analyse du fond, certaines de ses constatations laissent présager du traitement qui pourrait être réservé à l'eau sous le régime du chapitre 11.

Une autre décision a été rendue dans l'affaire *Archer Daniels Midland Company and Tate & Lyle Ingredients America, Inc. c. Mexico* le 21 novembre 2007, mais la sentence a uniquement été rendue publique à l'été 2008 après la suppression des informations confidentielles.[6] On se rappèle que le Mexique, confronté à deux différences impliquant la même mesure, avait demandé la jonction de l'affaire *ADM* et de l'affaire *Corn Products International, Inc. c. Mexico.*[7] Dans une décision en date du 20 mai 2005, un Tribunal avait rejeté cette demande, au motif principal que la jonction serait extrêmement difficile, compte tenu du fait que les demandeurs étaient en concurrence directe dans le marché et que cela exigerait des arrangements complexes en matière de confidentialité.[8]

La sentence dans l'affaire *ADM*, rendue la première, a conclu que le Mexique avait manqué à ses obligations en vertu de l'article 1102 (traitement national) de l'ALENA en traitant les investisseurs américains de façon discriminatoire par le biais d'une taxe qui avantageait les producteurs de sucre mexicains et en vertu de l'article 1106 (prescriptions de résultats) en imposant aux investisseurs des obligations de résultat interdites. Par ailleurs, la sentence retiendra l'attention principalement quant au traitement de la défense de

---

[4] *Bayview Irrigation District et al. c. Mexico,* ICSID Case No. ARB(AF)/05/01 (19 juin 2007) [ci-après *Bayview*].

[5] ALENA, *supra* note 1, art. 1101.

[6] *Archer Daniels Midland Company and Tate & Lyle Ingredients America, Inc. c. Mexico,* ICSID Case No. ARB(AF)/04/5 (21 novembre 2007) [ci-après *ADM*].

[7] *Corn Products International, Inc. c. Mexico,* ICSID Case No. ARB(AF)/04/01 (15 janvier 2008) [ci-après *CPI*].

[8] *Corn Products International, Inc. c. Mexico* and *Archer Daniels Midland Company and Tate & Lyle Ingredients Americas, Inc. c. Mexico,* Order of the Consolidation Tribunal, ICSID Case No. ARB(AF)/04/01 (20 mai 2005) (ICSID Add. Fac.).

contre-mesures offerte par le Mexique et aux constatations sur la nature des droits que possèdent les investisseurs en vertu du chapitre 11 (c.-à-d. droits dérivés par opposition à droits directs). Étant donné l'intérêt à traiter ensemble des sentences dans les affaires *ADM* et *CPI*, elles feront l'objet d'une analyse comparée et approfondie dans une prochaine chronique.

Sur le plan des traités d'investissement, le Canada a conclu deux négociations en 2007 avec l'Inde et la Jordanie respectivement.[9] Aucune date n'est annoncée pour la signature et les textes ne sont pas publics. Un élément de la description rendue publique de l'Accord de promotion et de protection des investissements (APIE) qui sera signé avec l'Inde attire toutefois l'attention: "l'APIE canado-indien exigera que chacun des deux gouvernements: applique ses lois régissant l'entrée des investissements de façon objective et impartiale."[10] Ce libellé permet de penser que cet accord ne couvrira pas la phase pré-établissement de l'investissement. Si c'est le cas, il s'agit d'une rupture avec la pratique constante du Canada depuis l'ALENA et il en résulte une protection moindre offerte aux investisseurs canadiens en Inde en comparaison avec d'autres APIE. En effet, les seize APIE du Canada signés depuis 1994 s'appliquent tous à la phase pré-établissement.[11]

La ratification de la Convention pour le règlement des différends relatifs aux investissements entre États et ressortissants d'autres États,[12] signée par le Canada en 2006, se fait (sans grande surprise) toujours attendre à la fin de l'année 2007.[13] Par ailleurs, l'activité du CIRDI va toujours bon train. Trente-six nouvelles affaires ont été enregistrées par le Centre en 2007 ce qui porte le nombre des

[9] Voir Ministère des Affaires étrangeres et Commerce international Canada [MAECI], disponible en ligne à: <http://www.international.gc.ca/trade-agreements-accords-commerciaux/agr-acc/index.aspx?lang=fra>.

[10] Voir MAECI, Communiqué de presse (16 juin 2007), disponible en ligne à: <http://wo1.international.gc.ca/MinPub/publication.aspx?publication_id=385227&docnum=82&lang=fra>.

[11] Voir liste des APIE conclus par le Canada, MAECI, disponible en ligne à: <http://www.international.gc.ca/trade-agreements-accords-commerciaux/agr-acc/fipa-apie/fipa_list.aspx?lang=fra&menu_id=22&menu=R>.

[12] Convention pour le règlement des différends relatifs aux investissements entre États et ressortissants d'autres États, 18 mars 1965, 575 R.T.N.U. 160 (entrée en vigueur le 14 octobre 1966) [ci-après Convention CIRDI].

[13] Voir C. Lévesque, "Chronique de Droit international économique en 2006: Investissement," *Annuaire canadien de Droit international*, vol. XLV (2007), aux pp. 381–83.

affaires pendantes à la fin de l'année à 123.[14] On note aussi que dix-huit sentences ont été rendues en vertu des règles d'arbitrage ou du mécanisme supplémentaire du CIRDI.[15] Fait notable, cinq décisions ont été rendues suite à des demandes faites en vertu de l'article 52 de la Convention CIRDI qui permet l'annulation d'une sentence sur la base de motifs limités.[16] Étant donné leur importance institutionnelle, Emmanuel Gaillard consacre l'intégralité de sa chronique 2007 sur le CIRDI à l'analyse de ces décisions.[17]

II   *UPS c. Canada*

La sentence dans l'affaire *UPS* comporte plusieurs aspects inédits. Notamment, il s'agit de la première fois qu'un Tribunal interprète le chapitre 15 de l'ALENA portant sur la politique de la concurrence, les monopoles et les entreprises d'État. L'exception culturelle de l'ALENA a aussi été appliquée pour la première fois par un Tribunal saisi en vertu du chapitre 11. Malheureusement, en dépit de la nouveauté des thèmes, la décision est décevante sur le plan de ses apports au droit. De plus, la décision contient une dissidence.

A   FAITS ET QUESTIONS EN LITIGE

La compagnie UPS, notamment à travers son investissement UPS Canada, et la Société canadienne des postes (Postes Canada) se font concurrence dans le marché canadien. Bien que Postes Canada ait le monopole du transport des lettres de première classe, cette société de la couronne offre également des services de messagerie et de transports de colis en concurrence avec UPS Canada. Qui plus est, Purolator, la compagnie la plus importante de messagerie au Canada, appartient presque entièrement à Postes Canada.

UPS se plaint donc des comportements anticoncurrentiels de Postes Canada sur le marché non monopolisé et du fait que le gouvernement du Canada ne serait pas intervenu pour les empêcher. Elle se plaint aussi de mesures prises par l'Agence des douanes et du revenu du Canada (Agence des douanes) et du ministère du Patrimoine canadien (Patrimoine canadien) qui, selon UPS, placent

---

14 Voir E. Gaillard, "Centre international de règlement des différends relatifs aux investissements (CIRDI) – Chronique des sentences arbitrales," *Journal de droit international*, vol. 1 (2008), aux pp. 311–12.

15 *Ibid.*

16 Voir Convention CIRDI, *supra* note 12.

17 Voir Gaillard, *supra* note 14.

Postes Canada dans une position privilégiée et entraînent une injustice vis-à-vis de ses compétiteurs.

La sentence rendue en 2007 est en grande partie consacrée aux
allégations de manquement à l'article 1102 (Traitement national),
car dans une sentence préliminaire rendue en 2002 le Tribunal
s'était déclaré incompétent quant à la plupart des allégations de
manquement à l'article 1105 (Norme minimale de traitement) en
raison du fait qu'il n'existait pas de normes de droit international
coutumier en matière de concurrence.[18] Dans sa sentence finale,
le Tribunal a également tranché sommairement les allégations de
manquement aux articles 1103 (Traitement de la nation la plus
favorisée)[19] et certaines autres allégations mineures liées à l'article
1105.[20] Il a aussi décidé de certaines objections de compétence qui
avaient été jointes au fond.[21]

---

[18] Voir *United Postal Service of America Inc c. Canada,* Award on Jurisdiction, UNCI-
TRAL (22 novembre 2002).

[19] Voir *UPS, supra* note 2 aux para. 182–84.

[20] *Ibid.* aux para. 185–87.

[21] Un des arguments dont le Tribunal a traité dans sa sentence au fond mérite un
commentaire. Il concerne la computation du délai de prescription en cas de
"violation continue" d'un traité. L'article pertinent de l'ALENA prévoit qu'"[u]n
investisseur ne pourra déposer une plainte si plus de trois ans se sont écoulés
depuis la date à laquelle l'investisseur a eu ou aurait dû avoir connaissance du
manquement allégué et de la perte ou du dommage subi." La version anglaise
comporte l'expression suivante: "*from the date on which the investor first acquired ...
knowledge.*" ALENA, *supra* note 1, art. 1116(2) (c'est nous qui soulignons). Le
Canada a plaidé que l'investisseur connaissait depuis bien au-delà de trois ans
l'existence des manquements allégués et les dommages qui en découleraient.
La réponse de UPS, de façon générale, n'a pas été de contester la connaissance
mais bien d'avancer que chaque application d'une mesure qui continue dans le
temps et qui constitue un manquement à une obligation internationale renou-
velle le délai de prescription. Le Tribunal s'est dit d'accord avec le principe du
renouvellement en cas de violation continue. Selon lui: "*This is true generally in
law, and Canada has provided no special reason to adopt a different rule here.*" (*UPS,
supra* note 2 au para. 28). En conséquence, le délai de prescription n'est pertinent
que lorsque l'application cesse (*UPS, supra* note 2 au para. 26).
   Selon nous, pourtant, cette lecture semble priver l'article de son sens premier,
celui de forcer les investisseurs à se plaindre d'une mesure dans un délai de trois
ans lorsqu'ils ont connaissance (ou auraient dû avoir connaissance) du manquement et de la perte. Faute de quoi, le Tribunal ne pourra connaître de leur plainte.
Selon le texte même, le délai butoir commence à courir à partir de la connaissance avérée ou présumée et non pas à partir du moment où le manquement
prend fin. De façon notable, la sentence ne contient aucune référence à la décision dans l'affaire *Grand River Enterprises Six Nations, Ltd, et al. c. United States,*
UNCITRAL (20 juillet 2006) [ci-après *Grand River*] rendue en sens contraire et
appuyée d'un raisonnement étoffé. Voir *Grand River,* aux para. 53–83.

Afin de trancher cette affaire, le Tribunal a dû interpréter non seulement les dispositions du chapitre 11, mais celles du chapitre 15 portant sur la politique de la concurrence, les monopoles et les entreprises d'État. Étant donné que Postes Canada est une entreprise d'État et qu'elle détient un certain monopole, le Tribunal a dû se pencher sur la relation qui existe entre ces deux chapitres. La clef de voûte de cette relation est l'article 1116 qui prévoit que:

Tout investisseur d'une Partie qui estime avoir subi une perte ou un dommage en raison ou par suite d'un manquement d'une autre Partie à une obligation découlant

a) de la section A ou du paragraphe 1503(2) (Entreprises d'État) ou

b) de l'alinéa 1502(3)a) (Monopoles et entreprises d'État), lorsque le monopole a agi d'une manière incompatible avec les obligations de la Partie aux termes de la section A, pourra, en vertu de la présente section, soumettre à l'arbitrage une plainte à cet effet.[22]

La responsabilité de l'État, mise en œuvre par le biais de la procédure d'arbitrage investisseur-État du chapitre 11, est ainsi encadrée par les dispositions du chapitre 15 en ce qui concerne les comportements des monopoles et sociétés d'État.[23]

---

[22] ALENA, *supra* note 1, art. 1116(1).

[23] L'article 1502 (Monopoles et entreprises d'État) de l'ALENA, *supra* note 1, prévoit que:

(3) Chacune des Parties fera en sorte que, par l'application d'un contrôle réglementaire, d'une surveillance administrative ou d'autres mesures, que tout monopole privé désigné par elle, ou tout monopole public maintenu ou désigné par elle:

(a) agisse d'une manière qui ne soit pas incompatible avec les obligations de la Partie aux termes du présent accord *lorsqu'il exercera des pouvoirs réglementaires, administratifs ou autres pouvoirs gouvernementaux que la Partie lui aura délégués relativement* au produit ou au service faisant l'objet du monopole, par exemple le pouvoir de délivrer des licences d'importation ou d'exportation, d'approuver des opérations commerciales ou d'imposer des contingents, redevances ou autres frais; (notre souligné).

L'article 1503 (Entreprises d'État) de l'ALENA, *supra* note 1 prévoit que:

(2) Chacune des Parties fera en sorte que, par l'application d'un contrôle réglementaire, d'une surveillance administrative ou d'autres mesures, que toute entreprise d'État qu'elle maintient ou établit, agisse d'une manière qui en soit pas incompatible avec les obligations de la Partie aux termes des chapitres 11 (Investissement) et 14 (Services financiers) *dans l'exercice de pouvoirs réglementaires, administratifs ou autres pouvoirs gouvernementaux délégués par la Partie*, et notamment le pouvoir d'exproprier, d'accorder des licences, d'approuver des opérations commerciales ou d'imposer des contingents, redevances ou autres frais (c'est nous qui soulignons).

Les articles pertinents indiquent qu'un investisseur, pour porter plainte en vertu de l'article 1116, doit prouver:

(1) que le monopole ou l'entreprise d'État, selon le cas, a agi dans l'exercice *de pouvoirs réglementaires, administratifs ou autres pouvoirs gouvernementaux* délégués;

(2) que le monopole ou l'entreprise d'État, selon le cas, a manqué à une obligation prévue à la section A du chapitre 11, par exemple aux articles 1102 ou 1105.

Ces paramètres n'avaient pas de quoi plaire à l'investisseur qui s'est donc évertué à les contourner. D'abord, UPS a allégué que les agissements de Postes Canada étaient attribuables directement au Canada en tant que "Partie" en vertu des articles 1102 et 1105 (c.-à-d. qu'il n'y avait pas lieu de considérer le chapitre 15). Comme alternative, UPS a prétendu que la référence à l'article 1502(3)a), comprise à l'article 1116, permettait "d'ouvrir la porte" aux allégations de manquement à *toutes* les obligations de l'ALENA, et non pas seulement à celles de la section A du chapitre 11 (ce qui aurait eu pour effet de rendre admissible les allégations liées aux activités commerciales de Postes Canada). Se situant enfin à l'intérieur des paramètres fixés par les articles, l'investisseur a allégué que *tous* les agissements de Postes Canada tombaient dans la sphère des pouvoirs gouvernementaux et étaient ainsi couverts par les articles 1116, 1502(3)a) et 1503(2). À l'inverse, le Canada avait concédé un seul cas où Postes Canada exerçait des pouvoirs gouvernementaux, ce dernier lié aux douanes.

B   RAISONNEMENT DU TRIBUNAL

1   *L'attribution "directe" des comportements de Postes Canada au Canada en tant que "Partie" aux articles 1102 et 1105*

Le Tribunal a traité d'un point de divergence entre les parties quant à la pertinence du droit international coutumier en matière d'attribution pour l'interprétation des obligations du chapitre 11 et, en particulier, des articles 4 et 5 du *Projet d'articles sur la responsabilité de l'État pour fait internationalement illicite.*[24] Ces articles

---

[24] Voir *Projet d'articles sur la responsabilité de l'État pour fait internationalement illicite et commentaires y relatifs*, Rapport de la commission du droit international, cinquante-troisième session (23 avril au 1 juin et 2 juillet au 10 août 2001), Supp. No. 10 (A/56/10), Nations Unies, New York 2001 [ci-après *Articles sur la responsabilité de l'État*].

définissent les circonstances qui justifient l'attribution à l'État d'un comportement d'un organe de l'État (article 4) et d'une personne ou d'une entité exerçant des prérogatives de puissance publique (article 5).[25]

Selon UPS, l'un ou l'autre article permettait clairement l'attribution des comportements de Postes Canada au Canada pour les fins des articles 1102 et 1105 de l'ALENA. De son côté, le Canada a soutenu que le droit international coutumier en la matière était écarté par les règles spéciales prévues aux articles 1116(1), 1502(3) a) et 1503(2) de l'ALENA, ce résultat étant d'ailleurs conforme au caractère résiduaire des *Articles sur la responsabilité de l'État* reconnu à l'article 55 (*lex specialis*).[26]

Le Tribunal a donné raison au Canada et a conclu que les articles pertinents de l'ALENA, y compris ceux des chapitres 11 et 15, devaient être lus ensemble et non séparément.[27] Cette *lex specialis*, prévoyant l'existence, le contenu et la mise en œuvre de la responsabilité étatique en l'espèce, empêchait l'application du droit coutumier à titre résiduaire. Selon le Tribunal, les Parties ont clairement opéré une distinction entre elles-mêmes, d'une part, et les monopoles et entreprises d'État, d'autre part, et ont placé des limites à la responsabilité découlant des comportements des monopoles et des entreprises d'État. Par conséquent, l'interprétation de l'investisseur doit être rejetée, car elle prive les articles pertinents de tout effet utile.[28]

2   *Les plaintes en vertu du chapitre 15: les pouvoirs réglementaires, administratifs ou autres pouvoirs gouvernementaux*

Comme l'alternative, UPS a allégué que le Canada avait manqué à ses propres obligations en vertu du chapitre 15 en ne faisant pas en sorte que Postes Canada (à titre de monopole ou de société d'État) respecte les obligations du chapitre 11.[29] En réponse à cet argument, le Tribunal a fait trois remarques préliminaires:

(1)   Les obligations des Parties en vertu des articles 1502(3)a) et 1503(2) sont des obligations de résultat et non pas de moyens.

---

[25]   *Ibid.*, art. 4–5.

[26]   *Ibid.*, art. 55.

[27]   *UPS, supra* note 2 au para. 58.

[28]   Voir en particulier *UPS, supra* note 2 au para. 60.

[29]   *Ibid.* au para. 64.

(2) Les parties au différend, ainsi que le Tribunal, s'entendent pour dire que Postes Canada est une société d'État au sens du chapitre 15; le Tribunal ne décidera ainsi pas de la question de savoir si Postes Canada est aussi un monopole.

(3) La définition de "délégation" applicable à l'article 1502(3) sera aussi appliquée à l'article 1503.[30]

Ensuite, le Tribunal a rejeté l'argument que Postes Canada agissait toujours en vertu de pouvoirs gouvernementaux.[31] Il a conclu que l'expression *dans l'exercice de pouvoirs réglementaires, administratifs ou autres pouvoirs gouvernementaux délégués par la Partie* avait pour effet de limiter la gamme des comportements capables d'engager la responsabilité des Parties.[32] Cette limite était apparente à la lecture des autres alinéas des articles pertinents qui visent des activités de nature commerciale — des activités, d'ailleurs, dont un investisseur ne peut se plaindre en vertu du chapitre 11 de l'ALENA.[33]

Cette conclusion s'est avérée fatale, car elle a permis au Tribunal de rejeter plusieurs allégations clés de UPS quant à l'utilisation faite par Postes Canada de son infrastructure de monopole (à son profit dans le marché non monopolisé, mais aussi au profit de Purolator) au motif que ces activités étaient de nature commerciale et non pas gouvernementale.[34]

3 Les douanes et la violation de l'article 1102

Le Tribunal a énoncé le fardeau de preuve qui repose sur l'investisseur en vertu de l'article 1102 avant de rejeter les allégations de UPS en l'espèce. L'article 1102 de l'ALENA prévoit que:

1. Chacune des Parties accordera aux investisseurs d'une autre Partie un traitement non moins favorable que celui qu'elle accorde, dans des circonstances similaires, à ses propres investisseurs, en ce qui concerne l'établissement, l'acquisition, l'expansion, la gestion, la direction, l'exploitation et la vente ou autre aliénation d'investissements.

2. Chacune des Parties accordera aux investissements des investisseurs d'une autre Partie un traitement non moins favorable que celui qu'elle

---

[30] *Ibid.* au para. 69 où se trouvent ces trois remarques.

[31] *Ibid.* au para. 71.

[32] *Ibid.* au para. 72.

[33] *Ibid.* aux para. 73–74.

[34] *Ibid.* aux para. 74–78.

accorde, dans des circonstances similaires, aux investissements de ses propres investisseurs, en ce qui concerne l'établissement, l'acquisition, l'expansion, la gestion, la direction, l'exploitation et la vente ou autre aliénation d'investissements.[35]

Le Tribunal a noté que l'investisseur devait faire la preuve de trois éléments distincts, soit (1) la preuve d'un traitement en lien avec l'établissement, l'acquisition, . . . d'investissements, (2) la preuve que l'investisseur étranger (ou son investissement) était "dans des circonstances similaires" avec des investisseurs locaux (ou leurs investissements), (3) que l'investisseur étranger ou son investissement a été traité de manière moins favorable que les investisseurs locaux ou leurs investissements.[36] Selon le Tribunal, aucun renversement du fardeau de la preuve n'était justifié. Il a ajouté:

Failure by the investor to establish one of those three elements will be fatal to its case. This is a legal burden that rests squarely with the Claimant. That burden never shifts to the other Party, here Canada. For example, it is not for Canada to prove an absence of like circumstances between UPS Canada and Canada Post regarding article 1102.[37]

Le Tribunal a décidé que le "traitement" des articles livrés au Canada par UPS et par Postes Canada constituait bel et bien un "traitement"de l'investisseur. Il a ainsi rejeté la prétention du Canada que les articles plutôt que les investisseurs ou leurs investissements faisaient l'objet d'un traitement. Ainsi, le traitement accordé n'était pas uniquement celui des articles, mais bien celui des entreprises. Dans ce cadre, le Tribunal a noté que Postes Canada était un investissement et le Canada, à titre de propriétaire de Postes Canada, un "investisseur" pour les fins de l'ALENA.[38]

Le Tribunal a ensuite décidé que UPS et Postes Canada n'étaient pas "dans des circonstances similaires" quant au traitement douanier qu'ils recevaient. Il a ainsi rejeté (implicitement) la prétention de l'investisseur que la concurrence que se livrent UPS et Postes Canada dans le marché non monopolisé suffisait à conclure à l'existence de circonstances similaires.[39] Afin d'arriver à cette conclusion,

---

[35] ALENA, *supra* note 1, art. 1102(1) et (2).

[36] *UPS, supra* note 2 au para. 83.

[37] *Ibid.* au para. 84.

[38] *Ibid.* au para. 85.

[39] *Ibid.* au para. 87.

le Tribunal s'est concentré sur les différences qui existent entre le traitement en douanes du courrier international par opposition au traitement de la messagerie. Cette analyse lui a permis de conclure que le traitement différent se justifiait par les caractéristiques propres du courrier international et de la messagerie.[40] Le Tribunal a été rassuré par le fait que cette distinction est opérée dans de nombreux pays et est reconnue par les organisations internationales pertinentes.[41]

4   Exceptions pour les marchés passés par une Partie

Il restait un élément de la plainte de discrimination lié aux douanes à analyser, celui de savoir si le *Postal Import Agreement* (PIA) entre l'Agence des douanes et Postes Canada tombait dans le champ de l'exception de l'article 1108 (Réserves et exceptions) pour les marchés passés par une Partie. En vertu de cet accord, Postes Canada recevait un paiement de l'Agence des douanes pour l'exécution de certaines tâches accessoires, telles que la manutention, l'entrée de données et la collecte de droits de douane. UPS ne contestait pas le droit de l'Agence des douanes de contracter avec Postes Canada; elle alléguait plutôt que l'Accord offre un traitement plus favorable à Postes Canada qu'à UPS. De plus, elle alléguait que l'Accord n'était pas un marché passé par une Partie au sens de l'ALENA, mais bien un accord administratif entre deux entités gouvernementales qui ne tombait pas dans le champ de l'exception.

L'article 1108(7)a) prévoit que: "*Articles 1102, 1103 and 1107 do not apply to: (a) procurement by a Party or a state enterprise.*"[42] Après une analyse sommaire, le Tribunal a décidé que l'Accord était un marché passé par une Partie, car Postes Canada fournissait des services à l'Agence des douanes contre rémunération.[43]

---

[40] *Ibid.* aux para. 98–99.

[41] *Ibid.* aux para. 103–18.

[42] ALENA, *supra* note 1, art. 1108(7)a). Le texte français publié en 1993 ainsi que celui qu'on trouve à l'heure actuelle sur le site Internet du MAECI réfère aux "achats effectués par une Partie." Toutefois, l'expression "marchés passés par une Partie" nous semble plus appropriée, compte tenu du titre de la Partie IV de l'ALENA "Marchés publics" qui est en anglais "*Government Procurement.*" Il est a noter que la version française de l'ALENA n'est pas authentique.

[43] *UPS, supra* note 2 aux para. 130–36.

Le programme d'aide aux publications (PAP) et l'exception culturelle

Le PAP est un programme administré et financé conjointement par Patrimoine canadien et Postes Canada en vertu duquel des subventions sont versées aux publications admissibles à travers des comptes individuels de Postes Canada. L'argent versé dans ces comptes est utilisé pour défrayer la distribution des publications au Canada.[44] L'objectif de ce programme est, entre autres, de soutenir et de développer l'industrie de l'édition canadienne. Dans son analyse, le Tribunal a mis l'accent sur le rôle joué par Postes Canada en matière de politique publique et sur son obligation d'assurer un service universel.[45]

L'investisseur voyait plutôt dans ce programme un traitement plus favorable accordé à Postes Canada, car UPS n'était pas admissible en vertu de ce programme pour la distribution de publications. Selon UPS, si l'aide aux éditeurs tombait dans le champ de l'exception culturelle de l'ALENA, la livraison des publications par Postes Canada en était exclue.

Le Tribunal a jugé que l'effet de l'article 2106 et de l'Annexe 2106 portant sur les industries culturelles était d'exclure de l'application de l'ALENA (entre le Canada et les États-Unis) "toute mesure adoptée ou maintenu relativement aux industries culturelles."[46] Le Tribunal a jugé que cette exception était large et qu'elle avait fait l'objet de négociations. L'intervention du Tribunal aurait pour effet de rompre l'équilibre des engagements atteint par les parties.[47] Dans les faits, l'exigence de distribuer les publications à travers Postes Canada était liée rationnellement et intrinsèquement à l'aide à l'industrie canadienne de l'édition.[48]

Le PAP ne viole pas l'article 1102 . . . de toute façon

Le Tribunal a par la suite conclu que le PAP ne contrevenait pas à l'article 1102, car le Canada en élaborant et en administrant ce programme n'avait pas accordé un traitement "dans des circonstances similaires" à Postes Canada et à UPS.[49] Le Tribunal a constaté

---

44 Voir *ibid.* aux para. 150–54.

45 *Ibid.* aux para. 139–45.

46 Voir ALENA, *supra* note 1, art. 2106, Annexe 2106.

47 *UPS, supra* note 2 aux para. 162–63.

48 *Ibid.* au para. 168.

49 *Ibid.* au para. 173.

que le traitement en l'espèce était le choix de Postes Canada par Patrimoine canadien pour la distribution exclusive des publications ainsi subventionnées.[50] Le Tribunal ayant jugé que UPS n'avait pas la capacité de distribuer partout au Canada (une partie intégrante du programme), aucune comparaison ne pouvait être faite.[51]

Le Tribunal a ajouté:

> *As an aside, it is noted that this fact also illustrates that the rationale for providing distribution assistance through Canada Post does not comprise any nationality-based discrimination. Under the PAP, UPS Canada and Canadian courier companies – which, unlike UPS Canada and Canada Post, are indeed 'in like circumstances' – are treated in an identical manner.*[52]

En définitive, le Tribunal a conclu que les compagnies de messagerie canadiennes et UPS Canada étaient traitées de façon identique et donc qu'il n'y avait pas en l'espèce de discrimination sur la base de la nationalité.

5 *Dissidence de l'arbitre cass*

L'arbitre Cass a exprimé son désaccord avec la majorité à trois titres principaux: le traitement en douanes, le PIA et l'accès à l'infrastructure de monopole. Dans ces trois cas, il aurait jugé que le Canada avait manqué à ses obligations en vertu de l'ALENA. Quant au reste, il s'est dit en accord avec la majorité.

i Le traitement en douanes: l'article 1102 et les exclusions

L'arbitre s'est dit en désaccord avec l'interprétation de l'article 1102, en particulier quant au fardeau de la preuve qui repose sur les parties. Selon lui, le fardeau de l'investisseur était rempli dès que UPS avait fait la preuve *prima facie* de circonstances similaires – ici la preuve que les produits offerts par UPS et Postes Canada étaient en concurrence directe dans le marché. Le fardeau était alors renversé et il revenait au Canada de prouver pourquoi ces entreprises n'étaient pas dans des circonstances similaires.[53]

---

[50] *Ibid.* au para. 174.

[51] *Ibid.* en particulier au para. 176.

[52] *Ibid.* au para 177.

[53] *United Postal Service of America Inc c. Canada*, Separate Statement of Dean Ronald A. Cass, UNCITRAL (24 mai 2007) [ci-après: Dissidence, Cass] aux para. 17, 25–26.

En fait, il a jugé que les différences alléguées par le Canada entre le courrier international et la messagerie (et la conformité aux conventions internationales) n'étaient pas pertinentes. UPS se plaignait du traitement uniquement là où la concurrence existait. L'arbitre a critiqué l'approche prônée par le Canada qui, selon lui, viderait la protection de l'article 1102 de tout contenu.[54] Il a ensuite déterminé que le traitement accordé à UPS était effectivement moins favorable. Selon lui, l'article 1102 ne visait pas uniquement les cas de discrimination déclarée.[55] L'arbitre a accepté l'argument de UPS que le traitement objet de la comparaison devait être "le meilleur traitement" accordé à un national. Ainsi, il importait peu que le Canada ait accordé à d'autres entreprises canadiennes le même traitement qu'à UPS. Le Canada ne pouvait pas favoriser un "champion" national (Postes Canada) de cette manière.[56]

Sur la question du marché passé par une Partie, l'arbitre Cass est aussi en désaccord avec la majorité, car selon lui le PIA ne possédait aucun des attributs formels d'un marché passé par une Partie.[57]

ii   Le Programme d'aide aux publications: l'article 1102 et l'exception culturelle

Sur la question du PAP, l'arbitre Cass, contrairement à la majorité, a d'abord procédé à l'analyse de l'article 1102 et a conclu que le Canada avait manqué à ses obligations. Il a répété que UPS avait droit au "meilleur traitement" accordé à un national, ici Postes Canada. Il n'était pas pertinent que d'autres entreprises canadiennes aient été traitées également. Il a aussi conclu que Postes Canada et UPS étaient dans des circonstances similaires vis-à-vis du PAP, car elles étaient des concurrentes.[58] Il a jugé que le Canada n'avait pas réussi à prouver l'existence de circonstances dissimilaires en alléguant que seule Postes Canada avait la capacité de livraison partout au Canada. Il a noté que s'il n'était pas du ressort des arbitres de juger du caractère *raisonnable* d'un programme gouvernemental

---

[54] Notamment, il indique que: "*[i]f any plausible distinction suffices to eliminate a need for equal treatment even though the logic of the distinction would suggest a basis for better treatment of the complaining investor or investment, the NAFTA national treatment obligation would have precious little meaning.*" (*Ibid.* au para. 51).

[55] *Ibid.* aux para. 58–59.

[56] *Ibid.* au para. 60.

[57] *Ibid.* aux para. 71–75.

[58] *Ibid.* aux para. 94–96 et 101.

(ici, en particulier, le recours à une seule entreprise plutôt qu'à plusieurs), ils se devaient de juger de la *légitimité* de la justification présentée par le Canada.[59] À ce titre, il a conclu que la justification avait été montée de toute pièce par le Canada pour la défense de cette affaire. Pour l'arbitre, cette rationalisation *ex post facto* était inadmissible; la permettre revenait à laisser au Canada toute la latitude pour décider des cas où la protection de l'article 1102 s'appliquerait.[60]

Ensuite, l'arbitre Cass a rejeté la défense du Canada en vertu de l'exception culturelle. Il a jugé que le PAP visait davantage à subventionner Postes Canada qu'à promouvoir la culture canadienne.[61] (Par contre, il a jugé qu'il ne s'agissait pas d'une subvention au sens de l'ALENA, exclue de l'obligation de l'article 1102.)[62]

iii   L'accès à l'infrastructure de monopole: le chapitre 15 et
      l'article 1102

L'arbitre Cass a rejeté la définition étroite de "pouvoirs gouverne-mentaux" retenue par la majorité. Il aurait jugé que l'accès par Purolator à l'infrastructure de Postes Canada tombait dans le champ des articles pertinents du chapitre 15. Selon lui, le pouvoir "d'approuver des opérations commerciales" couvrait la décision de Postes Canada d'approuver la transaction assez complexe entre elle-même et Purolator.[63]

Passant à l'analyse de l'article 1102, il est arrivé à la conclusion que Purolator et UPS Canada étaient dans des circonstances simi-laires malgré le fait que Purolator appartenait en majorité à Postes Canada.[64] Il a finalement jugé que le gouvernement du Canada n'avait pas supervisé Postes Canada de façon adéquate afin d'éviter une violation de l'article 1102.[65] Bien que l'arbitre Cass ne l'ait pas souligné, cette dernière conclusion l'opposait à la majorité qui avait conclu que les obligations du chapitre 15 étaient des obligations de résultat et non de moyens.

---

[59] *Ibid.* aux para. 110–33.

[60] *Ibid.* aux para. 124, 127 et 132.

[61] *Ibid.* aux para. 147–48.

[62] *Ibid.* aux para. 158–63.

[63] *Ibid.* aux para. 177–88.

[64] *Ibid.* aux para. 197–98.

[65] *Ibid.* aux para. 199–204.

C   COMMENTAIRES

Le manque de rigueur dont fait preuve le Tribunal se remarque à plusieurs niveaux.

1. Le raisonnement du Tribunal ne respecte pas la structure de l'analyse dictée par les articles pertinents des chapitres 11 et 15.
2. La sentence contient un traitement confus des questions d'attribution.
3. L'approche quant à l'interprétation de l'article 1102 manque de rigueur et de cohésion.

1   Le raisonnement du Tribunal ne respecte pas la structure de l'analyse dictée par les articles pertinents des chapitres 11 et 15

Après le rejet par le Tribunal de plusieurs arguments fantaisistes de l'investisseur, il restait deux types d'allégations à trancher. D'abord, il devait décider du bien-fondé des allégations qui mettaient en cause les agissements de Postes Canada dans l'exercice de pouvoirs gouvernementaux, exercice que le Canada avait concédé dans un cas lié aux douanes. En second lieu, il devait se prononcer sur les agissements d'organes de l'État attribuables au Canada sans avoir à passer par le chapitre 15 (par exemple l'Agence des douanes et Patrimoine canadien).

Toutefois, le Tribunal a procédé à une analyse qui ne reflète pas clairement ces distinctions. Tantôt, le Tribunal traite du Canada en tant qu'investisseur et de Postes Canada en tant qu'investissement. Ailleurs, il traite des agissements de l'Agence des douanes et de Postes Canada sans faire les distinctions requises quant au rôle joué par Postes Canada (dans la perspective du chapitre 15). À l'occasion, le Tribunal confond le traitement *reçu* par Postes Canada (en tant qu'investissement) et celui *accordé* par Postes Canada. Ailleurs, encore, on ne sait plus très bien à qui est attribuable le comportement dont le Tribunal discute et à quel titre: Patrimoine canadien ou Postes Canada? Il en résulte, dans l'analyse, un manque de rigueur qu'on ne peut que déplorer.

2   La sentence contient un traitement confus des questions d'attribution

Bien que, selon nous, la conclusion du Tribunal sur la question de l'attribution directe des comportements de Postes Canada au Canada "en tant que Partie" soit correcte, le traitement général de l'attribution par le Tribunal laisse à désirer. Par exemple, lorsque le Tribunal traite du rôle des deux paragraphes à considerer, il note:

An essential purpose of the two particular paragraphs is to ensure that a State Party does not avoid its own obligations under the Agreement as a whole (in terms of article 1502(3)a)) or under chapters 11 and 14 (in terms of article 1503(2)) by delegating governmental authority to a monopoly (private or public) or to a State enterprise.[66]

Pourtant, si les Parties à l'ALENA n'avaient pas inclus de chapitre 15 à leur accord, les articles 4 et 5 des *Articles sur la Responsabilité de l'État* auraient été appelés à jouer leur rôle en matière d'attribution en ce qui concerne les sociétés d'État et les monopoles. Autrement dit, la responsabilité n'aurait tout de même pas pu être évitée, contrairement à ce que prétend le Tribunal. Par ailleurs, plusieurs autres énoncés relatifs à l'attribution prêtent à confusion.

3   L'approche quant à l'interprétation de l'article 1102 manque de rigueur et de cohésion

D'abord, le Tribunal dicte une méthode d'analyse de l'article 1102 qui contient trois éléments. Ensuite, il fait une affirmation sur le fardeau de la preuve qui est catégorique, affirmation qui pourrait laisser croire au lecteur non averti qu'elle va de soi. Pourtant, cette question a fait l'objet de nombreux débats et l'énoncé du Tribunal est en vérité unique.[67] À cette étape, aucune mention n'est faite de l'objet de l'article 1102, soit celui de prévenir la discrimination basée sur la nationalité. Le Tribunal en fait uniquement mention à la fin de la sentence, dans le paragraphe qui débute par: "*As an aside ...*" Cette façon décousue de procéder est à déplorer.

De plus, le traitement de l'exception culturelle par rapport à la règle de l'article 1102 est déficient. Notamment, dans son analyse du PAP, le Tribunal applique l'exception sur les industries culturelles *avant* de procéder à l'analyse de l'article 1102. Pourtant, l'exception n'est utile que s'il y a violation de l'article 1102 en l'espèce.

4   Un dernier mot sur la dissidence ...

Le raisonnement de l'arbitre Cass, bien que plus rigoureux que celui de la majorité, est tout de même contestable à plusieurs égards.

---

[66] *UPS, supra* note 2 au para. 70.

[67] Voir par exemple, *Feldman c. Mexico*, Award, ICSID Case No. ARB(AF)/99/1 (16 décembre 2002), aux para. 176–77 [ci-après *Feldman*]; *Pope & Talbot, Inc. c. Canada*, Award on the Merits of Phase 2, UNCITRAL (10 avril 2001), au para. 78 [ci- après *Pope & Talbot*].

Pour ne donner qu'un exemple, l'interprétation de l'article 1102 préconisée par l'arbitre semble faire fi du caractère *étranger* des investisseurs et des investissements, et a pour effet d'imposer à la partie défenderesse un fardeau plus lourd que celui qui repose sur l'investisseur. De façon plus générale, l'arbitre exprime souvent des préjugés quant à la signification d'une expression ou d'une exception. En conséquence, il ne se conforme pas de façon systématique aux règles d'interprétation de la *Convention de Vienne sur le droit des traités*.[68]

III *BAYVIEW C. MEXICO*

La sentence dans l'affaire *Bayview* est la première concernant l'eau rendue en vertu du chapitre 11 de l'ALENA. Des allégations de contamination de l'eau avaient été faites dans d'autres affaires,[69] mais l'eau et les droits relatifs à l'eau n'avaient pas fait l'objet d'une décision à titre d'investissement avant 2007. Il va sans dire que la préoccupation du public quant aux rapports entre l'eau, le commerce et l'investissement est bien antérieure à cette décision.

Les craintes liées à la gestion des ressources en eau avaient mené les Parties à s'entendre sur une déclaration en 1993 qui visait à préciser que l'ALENA ne crée aucun droit aux ressources naturelles en eau des Parties et que l'eau n'est visée par l'ALENA que lorsqu'elle devient un produit.[70] La plainte déposée par une compagnie américaine en vertu du chapitre 11 quelques années plus tard allait ranimer ce débat.

---

[68] Par exemple, c'est le cas en ce qui concerne les marchés publics, les subventions et l'exception culturelle. Voir Dissidence de l'arbitre Cass, *supra* note 53.

[69] Voir par exemple, *Methanex c. United States*, Final Award of the Tribunal on Jurisdiction and Merits, UNCITRAL (3 août 2005) [ci-après *Methanex*] et *Metalclad c. Mexico*, Award, ICSID Case No. ARB(AF)/97/1 (25 août 2000) [ci-après *Metalclad*].

[70] Déclaration faite en 1993 par les gouvernements du Canada, du Mexique et des États-Unis, disponible en ligne à: <http://www.scics.gc.ca/cinfo99/83067000_e.html#statement>:

> *The governments of Canada, the United States and Mexico, in order to correct false interpretations, have agreed to state the following jointly and publicly as Parties to the North American Free Trade Agreement (NAFTA):*
>
> *The NAFTA creates no rights to the natural water resources of any Party to the Agreement.*
>
> *Unless water, in any form, has entered into commerce and become a good or product, it is not covered by the provisions of any trade agreement including the NAFTA. And nothing*

En novembre 1998, Sun Belt Water Inc. a fait connaître son intention de poursuivre le Canada suite à l'adoption en Colombie-Britannique d'un moratoire sur les licences permettant l'exportation en vrac d'eau.[71] Bien que cette poorsuite n'ait jamais été interitée, les doutes semés par la plainte ont perduré. Il aura fallu près de dix ans avant qu'un Tribunal tranche une affaire concernant l'eau et les droits sur l'eau. Cette fois, la controverse concerne le Mexique et des allégations de détournement d'eau qui appartenait prétendument à des investisseurs américains.

Étant donné que le Tribunal s'est déclaré incompétent pour entendre cette affaire au fond, les enseignements de l'affaire *Bayview* sont limités. Par contre, les conclusions et le raisonnement du Tribunal sont révélateurs du traitement qui pourrait être réservé à l'eau sous le régime du chapitre 11 de l'ALENA à l'avenir.

A   FAITS ET QUESTIONS EN LITIGE

Les quarante-six plaintes dans cette affaire ont été jointes par consentement des parties au différend. Elles provenaient de districts d'irrigation (qui font partie de l'État du Texas), de détenteurs indépendants de droits relatifs à l'eau et d'une compagnie d'approvisionnement en eau. Tous prétendaient que le Mexique avait exproprié de l'eau leur appartenant, les avait traités, eux et leurs investissements, de façon moins favorable que les investisseurs et les investissements mexicains et ne les avait pas traités de façon juste et équitable, en violation respectivement des articles 1110, 1102 et 1105 de l'ALENA.[72]

La toile de fond de cette affaire est celle des relations centenaires entre les État-Unis et le Mexique en matière de gestion des eaux transfrontières. Cette relation est encadrée par différents accords,

---

in the NAFTA would oblige any NAFTA Party to either exploit its water for commercial use, or to begin exporting water in any form. Water in its natural state in lakes, rivers, reservoirs, aquifers, water basins and the like is not a good or product, is not traded, and therefore is not and never has been subject to the terms of any trade agreement.

International rights and obligations respecting water in its natural state are contained in separate treaties and agreements negotiated for that purpose. Examples are the United States-Canada Boundary Waters Treaty of 1909 and the 1944 Boundary Waters Treaty between Mexico and the United States.

[71] *Sun Belt Waters Inc. c. Canada,* Notice of Intent to Submit a Claim to Arbitration (27 novembre 1998), disponible en ligne à: <http://www.international.gc.ca/trade-agreements-accords-commerciaux/assets/pdfs/Sunbelt.pdf>.

[72] *Bayview, supra* note 4, Request for Arbitration aux para. 71–76.

dont un traité de 1944 intitulé Utilization of Waters of the Colorado and Tijuana Rivers and of the Rio Grande.[73] En particulier, ce traité alloue à chaque État une proportion de l'eau provenant de certaines rivières. Par exemple, une disposition du traité prévoit que les États-Unis ont droit à *"one-third of the flow of six Mexican rivers, but not less than an average of 350,000 acre-feet annually, averaged over a five-year cycle."*[74] Le traité contient également des exceptions qui s'appliquent en cas de sécheresse, période durant laquelle un État ne peut remplir ses obligations. Le Mexique s'est prévalu de cette exception durant les années 1992 à 2002, car le pays était en déficit d'eau vis-à-vis des États-Unis. Après des années de négociations, et de livraison d'eau, les deux pays se sont entendus en 2005 pour dire que le Mexique avait comblé son déficit.[75] Par ailleurs, en vertu du Traité de 1944, une commission internationale est chargée du règlement des différends sous réserve de à l'approbation des États.[76]

Le système qui existe au Texas pour répartir entre les usagers l'eau qui revient aux États-Unis en vertu du Traité de 1944 a été fixé par un jugement de 1969. Depuis, les droits relatifs à l'eau sont alloués par un *Water Master* sous la direction de la Cour de district. En l'espèce, les demandeurs étaient tous détenteurs de droits relatifs à l'eau au Texas. Ce dont ils accusaient le Mexique était de détourner "leur eau" au profit de l'industrie agricole mexicaine, tandis que les cultures américaines dans la Vallée du Rio Grande "se ratatinaient."[77] Ils alléguaient que le Mexique faisait fonctionner ses barrages et réservoirs d'eau de façon à manipuler le débit des affluents du fleuve Rio Grande. En conséquence, ils étaient privés de leurs droits relatifs à l'eau en violation de l'ALENA et réclamaient des dommages entre 320 et 667 millions de dollars américains.

Le Mexique a soulevé deux exceptions principales d'incompétence. D'abord, le Mexique a plaidé que la réclamation ne tombait pas dans le champ d'application de l'ALENA, car les demandeurs n'avaient pas d'investissement au Mexique. Ensuite, le Mexique a

---

73 Utilization of Waters of the Colorado and Tijuana Rivers and of the Rio Grande, United States and Mexico (3 février 1944) U.S.-Mex., 59 Stat. 1219 (entré en vigueur le 8 novembre 1945) [ci-après Traité de 1944].

74 *Bayview, supra* note 4, Counter-Memorial of Bayview Irrigation District et al. in support of jurisdiction (23 juin 2006), au para. 15.

75 *Bayview, supra* note 4, Memorial on Jurisdiction of the United Mexican States (19 avril 2006), aux para. 34–41 [ci-après Memorial on Jurisdiction].

76 *Ibid.* au para. 28.

77 *Bayview, supra* note 4, Notice of Intent, à la p. 3.

fait valoir que le Tribunal n'avait pas compétence pour décider des droits et obligations des Parties au Traité de 1944.[78]

B   RAISONNEMENT DU TRIBUNAL

Afin de trancher, le Tribunal a examiné les définitions d'investisseur et d'investissement comprises dans l'ALENA.[79] Les demandeurs avaient allégué qu'ils étaient des investisseurs et qu'ils avaient des investissements, notamment de l'eau et des droits relatifs à l'eau qui, selon eux, tombaient dans la catégorie des biens couverts.

La première question en litige était de savoir si un investissement *sur le territoire du Mexique* était requis. Les demandeurs avaient des investissements au Texas, mais est-ce que cela suffisait pour les fins d'une réclamation en vertu du chapitre 11 de l'ALENA? Le Tribunal a conclu que non — le chapitre 11 visait les investissements *étrangers* et non pas les investissements nationaux.[80] Quant à savoir ce qui constitue un investissement *étranger*, le Tribunal a conclu que la caractéristique fondamentale d'un tel investissement est qu'il doit être essentiellement réglementé par le droit d'un État étranger.[81] Les demandeurs n'étaient donc pas des investisseurs étrangers au Mexique, mais bien des investisseurs nationaux au Texas. De façon notable, le Tribunal a précisé que la dépendance économique n'était pas suffisante pour répondre au critère: "*[t]he economic dependence of an enterprise upon supplies of goods — in this case, water — from another State is not sufficient to make the dependent enterprise an 'investor' in that other State.*"[82]

La deuxième question était de savoir si les demandeurs avaient un investissement au Mexique. Le cas échéant, ils seraient considérés en tant qu'investisseur d'une Partie. Pour arriver à cette conclusion, le Tribunal devait accepter l'argument des demandeurs que de l'eau (ou des droits relatifs à l'eau) leur appartenait au Mexique. Le Tribunal a d'abord reconnu que les lois du Texas et du Mexique prévoyaient l'octroi de droits de prélèvement d'eau dans les rivières pour des périodes, quantités et des fins définies (sur leur territoire respectif). Il a ensuite conclu que ces droits relatifs à l'eau tombaient

---

[78] Memorial on Jurisdiction, *supra* note 75 au para. 25.

[79] ALENA, *supra* note 1, art. 1101 et 1139.

[80] *Bayview*, *supra* note 4 au para. 96.

[81] *Ibid.* au para. 98.

[82] *Ibid.* au para. 104.

dans la définition de "biens" comprise à l'article 1139 de l'ALENA.[83]
Toujours selon la définition, il a jugé que les droits relatifs à l'eau
acquis pour des fins agricoles étaient "acquis ou utilisés dans le
dessein de réaliser un bénéfice économique ou à d'autres fins
commerciales."[84]

En l'espèce, toutefois, le Tribunal n'a pas été convaincu que les
demandeurs avaient un investissement *au Mexique*. Il note:

116) *One owns the water in a bottle of mineral water, as one owns a can of paint.
      If another person takes it without permission, that is theft of one's property.
      But the holder of a right granted by the State of Texas to take a certain amount
      of water from the Rio Bravo / Rio Grande does not 'own,' does not 'possess
      property rights in,' a particular volume of water as it descends through Mexi-
      can streams and rivers towards the Rio Bravo / Rio Grande and finds its
      way into the right-holders irrigation pipes. While the water is in Mexico, it
      belongs to Mexico, even though Mexico may be obliged to deliver a certain
      amount of it into the Rio Bravo / Rio Grande for taking by US nationals.*

117) *Thus, the Claimants do not own any of the water within Mexico. Nor do the
      Claimants possess any water rights in Mexico and enforceable against the
      State of Mexico. Their water rights are granted by the State of Texas. Those
      rights are created in Texas and exercised in Texas.*[85]

Le Tribunal a justifié sa conclusion en signalant la difficulté con-
ceptuelle évidente et inéluctable que présente une réclamation de
droits de propriété sur l'eau coulant au Mexique et répartie en
vertu du Traité de 1944 une fois qu'elle atteint le canal principal
du fleuve Rio Bravo / Rio Grande.[86] Le Tribunal s'est également
référé au droit mexicain, en vertu duquel les demandeurs ne pouvaient pas avoir de "droits de propriété" sur l'eau. Des droits
d'utilisation et d'exploitation de l'eau pouvaient être concédés en
vertu du droit mexicain mais pas des droits de propriété.[87] Le Tribunal a également rejeté une prétention des demandeurs quant à
l'abandon de certains droits par le Mexique en vertu du Traité de
1944, car, selon lui, le Traité ne permettait pas de corroborer cette

---

[83] ALENA, *supra* note 1, art. 1139: "*investment (g) real estate or other property, tangible
or intangible, acquired in the expectation or used for the purpose of economic benefit or
other business purposes.*"

[84] *Ibid.*

[85] *Bayview, supra* note 4 aux para. 116–17.

[86] *Ibid.* au para. 115.

[87] *Ibid.* au para. 118.

interprétation.[88] Enfin, le Tribunal a souligné que si le problème (tel qu'allégué par les demandeurs) était un problème de détournement d'eau par le Mexique, avant qu'elle n'atteigne le territoire américain, il revenait aux États-Unis et au Mexique de le régler selon le mode de règlement des différends prévu au Traité de 1944.[89]

En définitive, le Tribunal a jugé qu'aucun des demandeurs n'avaient effectué un investissement au Mexique. En conséquence, le Tribunal ne pouvait connaître de cette affaire dans le cadre du chapitre 11 de l'ALENA.

C COMMENTAIRES

Que faut-il retenir de cette sentence? D'une part, elle confirme que le chapitre 11 peut s'appliquer à l'eau. D'autre part, elle révèle des limites quant à l'application des obligations de ce chapitre.

1   L'assujettissement de l'eau aux obligations de l'ALENA

Même si le Tribunal s'est dit intéressé à la question de l'eau en tant que produit, et que les deux parties se sont référées à la Déclaration de 1993, le Tribunal n'a pas vraiment eu à affronter cette question. Il est vrai qu'il a opposé, dans le passage cité plus haut, l'eau en bouteille à l'eau qui coule dans une rivière. Mais ces extrêmes ne soulèvent pas la controverse. L'aspect inédit de la sentence concerne l'eau en tant qu'investissement. En particulier, la reconnaissance par de Tribunal que des droits relatifs à l'eau (par exemple, un permis de captation d'eau pour des fins agricoles) peuvent être couverts par la définition d'investissement de l'ALENA. En conséquence, si un État choisit d'octroyer de tels droits et ensuite les répudie de façon discriminatoire, un Tribunal pourrait conclure à une violation de l'ALENA.

2   L'application territoriale de l'ALENA

Le Tribunal a confirmé, ce qui semblait pourtant évident, que l'ALENA vise la protection des investissements étrangers et non pas nationaux.[90] L'ajout de la précision concernant la dépendance

---

88 *Ibid.* au para. 120.

89 *Ibid.* au para. 121.

90 Voir dans le même sens, *Canadian Cattlemen for Fair Trade c. United States*, (UNCITRAL) (28 janvier 2008) [ci-après *CCFT*].

économique pourrait se révéler pertinente afin de limiter les ingérences étrangères dans la gestion des ressources naturelles des Parties à l'ALENA.

3   La cohabitation des traités

Le Tribunal n'a pas accordé une valeur juridique supérieure à l'ALENA par rapport au Traité de 1944. Il a interprété le Traité de 1944 afin de trancher l'argument de l'abandon des droits allégué par les demandeurs, sans considérer le rapport entre le Traité et l'ALENA comme incohérent ou conflictuel. De plus, il a affirmé que les demandeurs ne pouvaient pas faire appel au chapitre 11 pour mettre en œuvre les obligations des États Parties au Traité de 1944, en vertu duquel ils n'avaient aucun droit d'action. Cette interprétation semble conforme aux conclusions du rapport du groupe d'étude de la Commission du droit international de 2006 qui promeut "l'intégration systémique" et suggère que les traités environnementaux et de commerce et d'investissement pourraient cohabiter.[91]

4   Le rôle joué par le droit interne

Le Tribunal a tenu compte du droit interne mexicain, bien que l'article 1131 (droit applicable) se réfère uniquement à l'ALENA

---

[91] Voir Commission du droit international, *Fragmentation du droit international: difficultés découlant de la diversification et de l'expansion du droit international*, Rapport du Groupe d'étude de la Commission du droit international, A/CN.4/L.682, 13 avril 2006, aux para. 413–414: "On peut en particulier considérer que le paragraphe 3 c) de l'article 31 de la Convention exprime ce que l'on peut appeler le principe de 'l'intégration systémique,' processus étudié tout au long du présent rapport grâce auquel les obligations internationales sont interprétées par référence à leur milieu normatif ('système'). Le paragraphe 3 (c) de l'article 31 est ainsi conçu: 'Il sera tenu compte, en même temps que du contexte: (c) de toute règle pertinente de droit international applicable dans les relations entre les parties.'
On comprend aisément le bien-fondé d'un tel principe. Les dispositions conventionnelles reçoivent toutes leur force et leur validité du droit général et créent des droits et des obligations qui existent parallèlement aux droits et obligations créés par d'autres dispositions conventionnelles et règles de droit international coutumier. Aucun de ces droits et obligations n'a *intrinsèquement* priorité sur les autres. On ne peut aborder la question de leurs relations que par un raisonnement qui permet de les faire passer pour des éléments d'un ensemble cohérent et efficace." Disponible en ligne à: <http://daccessdds.un.org/doc/UNDOC/LTD/G06/610/78/PDF/G0661078.pdf?OpenElement>. Voir aussi ALENA, *supra* note 1, art. 104 (Rapports avec des accords en matière d'environnement et de conservation).

et aux règles applicables du droit international.[92] Ceci reflète une pratique de plusieurs tribunaux qui se sont référés au droit interne afin d'évaluer l'existence et l'étendue de certains droits.[93] Aussi, les tribunaux n'ont pas permis aux investisseurs d'utiliser l'ALENA pour faire reconnaître, en droit international, des droits qui n'existent pas en droit interne.[94] L'interprétation du Tribunal dans l'affaire *Bayview* s'inscrit dans cette logique qui reconnaît que la formulation de l'article 1131 n'empêche pas le droit interne de jouer un rôle important dans la détermination du manquement au traité.[95]

IV Conclusion

Dans la perspective de la protection du bien public et des services publics, les deux affaires étudiées dans cette chronique ont eu un dénouement qui peut-être rassurant.[96] Toutefois, vu à la nature ad hoc de l'arbitrage international en vertu du chapitre 11, on ne peut s'empêcher de penser que la menace demeure (presque) entière. En raison de à ses nombreuses faiblesses, les tribunaux futurs auraient intérêt à ne *pas* reproduire tel quel le raisonnement du Tribunal dans l'affaire *UPS*. L'existence de la dissidence est révélatrice: un autre tribunal aurait facilement pu arriver à un résultat contraire. En ce qui concerne l'affaire *Bayview*, on en a tiré des enseignements utiles, bien que l'analyse ait été limitée par le manque de compétence du Tribunal pour de décider de cette affaire au fond. Un scénario différent pourrait évidemment mener à un

---

[92] ALENA, *supra* note 1, art. 1131(1).

[93] Voir par exemple, *Robert Azinian, Kenneth Davitian et Ellen Baca c. The United Mexican States*, Award, ICSID Case No. ARB(AF)/97/2 Award (1 novembre 1999) [ci-après *Azinian*]; *Feldman, supra* note 67; *International Thunderbird Gaming Corporation c. United Mexican States*, Arbitral Award (UNCITRAL) (26 janvier 2006) [ci-après *Thunderbird*].

[94] La question est différente lorsque les droits sont reconnus par le traité même ou en droit international coutumier. Pour une analyse de la définition des droits de propriété en droit interne vs. international, voir Zachary Douglas, "The Hybrid Foundations of Investment Treaty Arbitration," *British Yearbook of International Law*, vol. 151 (2003), aux pp. 197–213.

[95] Voir aussi C. Schreuer, "The Relevance of Public International Law in International Commercial Arbitration: Investment Disputes" disponible en ligne à: <http://www.univie.ac.at/intlaw/pdf/csunpublpaper_1.pdf>.

[96] Voir S. Chase, "Canada Post NAFTA Win Sets Precedent," *Globe and Mail* (14 juin 2007), à la p. B3.

résultat différent. Et on sait maintenant que les droits relatifs à l'eau peuvent, dans certaines circonstances, être soumis aux obligations du chapitre 11. Un dossier à suivre.

Canadian Practice in International Law / Pratique canadienne en matière de droit international

At the Department of Foreign Affairs and International Trade in 2007–8 / Au ministère des Affaires étrangères et Commerce international en 2007–8

compiled by / préparé par

ALAN KESSEL

INTERNATIONAL ECONOMIC LAW

Application of Adjustment Factor in the Softwood Lumber Agreement (SLA) — London Court of International Arbitration — United States of America (Claimant) v. Canada (Respondent)

In its Statement of Defence dated 19 November 2007, Canada wrote:

The issue before the Tribunal is whether Canada properly and timely applied the adjustment factor set out in paragraph 14 of Annex 7D of the Softwood Lumber Agreement ("Agreement") ("paragraph 14"). The U.S. Statement of Case alleges that Canada has restricted its exports of softwood lumber to the United States to a lesser degree than the United States believes is required under the Agreement because Canada has not followed what the United States thinks is the proper interpretation of paragraph 14. More specifically, the United States asserts that paragraph 14 required, and requires, that Canada make an adjustment to "Expected United States

Alan Kessel, Legal Advisor, Department of Foreign Affairs and International Trade, Ottawa. The extracts from official correspondence contained in the survey have been made available by courtesy of the Department of Foreign Affairs and International Trade. Some of the correspondence from which the extracts are given was provided for the general guidance of the enquirer in relation to specific facts that are often not described in full in the extracts within this compilation. The statements of law and practice should not necessarily be regarded as being a definitive.

Consumption" ("EUSC") in two situations. There is no dispute on the facts. This dispute concerns exclusively whether the Agreement (a) requires Canada to apply the adjustment in paragraph 14 to Option A Regions of Canada, and (b) required Canada to make the adjustment in paragraph 14 in the period between January 1 and June 30, 2007, by applying the adjustment methodology to time periods before the Agreement or the relevant export measures were in effect.

Applying the principles in Article 31 of the Vienna Convention on the Law of Treaties (the "Vienna Convention") to the disputed provisions of the Agreement, the U.S. claims should be dismissed because Canada has complied with the Agreement according to its correct interpretation. Canada made, and is making, the adjustments that the Agreement requires.

Section A of Part II of this Statement of Defence addresses the U.S. claim that paragraph 14 requires an adjustment not only for Option B Regions of Canada, but also for Option A Regions. Applying the principles of Article 31(1) of the Vienna Convention, Canada will show that the U.S. Statement of Case (a) does not follow the ordinary meaning of the terms of the Agreement in their context, and particularly the exclusive reference to Quarters for which *quotas* are in effect; (b) improperly characterizes Annex 5B of the Agreement ("Annex 5B") as stating "a primary purpose" of the Agreement; (c) relies on an erroneous assumption that the paragraph 14 adjustment enhances the accuracy of export measures in relation to actual consumption; (d) claims support in alleged "subsequent practice" but fails to show any practice at all by Canada, much less a "subsequent practice in the application of the treaty"; and (e) ignores the negotiating history of the Agreement.

Section B of Part II of this Statement of Defence deals with the U.S. claim that the Agreement required Canada to make an adjustment to the monthly EUSC applied in the period January 1 — June 30, 2007, which Canada indisputably did not do. However, contrary to the U.S. claim, paragraph 14 did not require Canada to make adjustments based on how the adjustment formula would have affected EUSC in the first two Quarters of 2007 if the Agreement and quotas had been in effect in the last two Quarters of 2006. Canada did what paragraph 14 required as of January 1, 2007: Canada calculated the difference between EUSC and actual U.S. consumption in the first Quarter of 2007 — the first full Quarter under the Agreement and the first Quarter in which there were quotas. When Canada determined that the difference between EUSC and actual U.S. consumption was greater than 5%, Canada reduced EUSC for Option B Regions in the next Quarter for which quotas were determined. The U.S. claim amounts to an attempt to require Canada to make adjustments beginning January 1, 2007 to offset the fact that, if the Agreement had been in force earlier in 2006, there would have been a difference between EUSC and actual U.S. consumption that would have required an adjustment beginning January 1, 2007. The U.S. claim that Canada should have adjusted beginning on January 1, 2007 is not based on the language of the treaty, but rather on the flawed assumption that the adjustment is a mechanism that enhances the accuracy of EUSC.

Finally, before setting out Canada's argument as to the correct and timely application of the paragraph 14 adjustment factor, this Statement of Defence first presents relevant background information relating to trade in softwood lumber, the history of the dispute between Canada and the United States, and the Agreement itself.

Breach of Softwood Lumber Agreement (SLA) — Remedy — London Court of International Arbitration — United States of America (Claimant) v. Canada (Respondent)

In a Statement of Defence dated 30 June 2008, Canada wrote:

This second phase of the arbitration is to determine what measures, if any, are the appropriate consequences under the SLA, in light of the Tribunal's Award on Liability of March 3, 2008. In the liability phase, the United States challenged Canada's compliance with the SLA 2006 on the grounds that Canada (1) did not apply the adjustment factor in Annex 7D of the SLA with respect to Option A regions (a practice that was and is ongoing); and (2) did not apply the adjustment to Option B regions (a practice limited to the period January 1 — June 30, 2007, after which Canada did apply the adjustment to Option B regions). In its Award on Liability the Tribunal determined that Canada had not breached the SLA with respect to the first U.S. claim, in that Canada had no obligation under the SLA at any time to apply the adjustment factor to Option A regions. However, the Tribunal determined that Canada had breached the SLA 2006 by failing to adjust "Expected United States Consumption" ("EUSC") with respect to regions operating under Option B during the period January 1, 2007 to June 30, 2007.

It is common ground that the Tribunal's powers upon finding a breach of the SLA are set out in Article XIV, paragraph 22 which provides:

If the tribunal finds that a party has breached an obligation under the SLA 2006, the tribunal shall:

- identify a reasonable period of time for that Party to cure the breach, which shall be the shortest reasonable period of time feasible and, in any event, not longer than 30 days from the date the tribunal issues the award; and

- determine appropriate adjustments to the Export Measures to compensate for the breach if that Party fails to cure the breach within the reasonable period of time.

In its Statement of Case, the United States asserts that Canada has not cured the breach, but the United States is silent as to what the United States would consider "cure the breach" to be. Instead, the United States seizes a single line from the Tribunal's Award on Liability to assert that the Tribunal has already decided that Canada bears additional responsibility for the consequences of its breach beyond its action in applying the adjustment in Annex 7D since July 1, 2007. Seeking to avoid the central issue as to what "cure the breach" means, the United States argues that the only issue before the Tribunal is to determine "appropriate adjustments to the export measures to compensate for the breach" under paragraph 22(b). The United States then proposes four alternative adjustments, all premised on the assumptions that: (1) Canada has not cured the breach in this dispute, and (2) compensatory adjustments are authorized and appropriate to compensate for effects or consequences of breaches occurring prior to the end of the reasonable period of time for cure.

Both U.S. assumptions are false. The SLA is a "prospective" remedy dispute settlement system like that of the World Trade Organization ("WTO"), Chapter 20 of the North American Free Trade Agreement ("NAFTA") and other similar intergovernmental trade agreements. Prospective systems are those that impose no penalty and require no compensation for infringement of obligations that occur prior to a dispute settlement decision, plus some reasonable period of time to comply with a panel's ruling. Retaliatory or compensatory measures imposed under prospective systems are authorized to compensate for the continuation of a breach past the reasonable period of time and until such time as the breaching measures are terminated or brought into compliance with the obligations of the agreement. Unlike most commercial arbitrations and investor-state arbitrations under bilateral investment treaties or Chapter 11 of the NAFTA, there are no "retroactive" or "retrospective" remedies intended to compensate for past breaches.

Canada has cured the breach within the meaning of the SLA by applying the adjustment provided in Annex 7D since July 1, 2007 and therefore no compensatory adjustments are required or authorized by the SLA. Like its counterparts in other international trade agreements between sovereigns, Article XIV of the SLA provides for countermeasures only if the breach is not cured by the end of the reasonable period of time identified in paragraph 22(a), and compensatory adjustments are not authorized for prior breaches under the SLA unless specifically so stated. There is no need for the Tribunal to consider the alternative theories and rationales presented by the United States to justify the imposition of severely intensified export restrictions to compensate for a breach long cured.

In Part I of this submission, Canada will show, applying the interpretive provisions of the Vienna Convention on the Law of Treaties ("Vienna Convention"), that ceasing the breach of the Agreement constitutes a "cure," and that paragraph 22(b) does not contemplate or authorize compensatory measures for past breaches. It is not necessary to resort to negotiating history, but that history also confirms Canada's position.

In Part II of the submission, Canada explains why, even if the SLA were interpreted to require, as part of a cure, some compensatory action for past breaches, the U.S. proposals are unjustified. First, no further action is warranted in the circumstance of this proceeding because the "excess" of lumber exported by Option B regions to the United States as a consequence of the breach has already been more than offset by the degree to which those regions exported less than their full quota entitlements in the period since July 1, 2007.

Second, even if Article XIV(22)(b) authorized a compensatory adjustment in the circumstances of this dispute, and even if Canada's undership-ments since that period were disregarded, there still would be no justification for the alternative measures proposed by the United States. Canada will show that none of the four alternatives presented by the United States provide a justifiable form or quantum of adjustment under the SLA. Indeed, the muddle of different rationales and speculations contrived in the four alternatives, and the wide range of effects they could have, only provide further evidence to reject the U.S. assumption that a right to compensation for past breaches can or should be implied under the Agreement. Canada attaches the expert report of Joseph P. Kalt and David Reishus (the Kalt/Reishus Report) which provides an economic analysis of the four alternatives proposed by the United States and its expert Jonathan Neuberger.

General Agreement on Tariffs and Trade (GATT) — Border Tax Adjustment on Imports

In a memorandum dated 28 November 2008, the Trade Law Bureau wrote:

Article II:1 of the *General Agreement on Tariffs and Trade, 1994* (GATT 1994) prohibits a WTO Member from applying a customs duty higher than that set out in that Member's tariff schedule. Article II:1 also prohibits a WTO Member from imposing other types of duties or charges on imported products in excess of those imposed, or required to be imposed by legislation in force as of January 1, 1995. However, Article II:2 allows a Member to impose a charge that is equivalent to an internal tax on an imported product when that charge is imposed consistently with the requirements of Article III:2.

Article III:2, in turn, states that products from other WTO Members may not be subject, directly or indirectly, to internal taxes or other internal charges in excess of those applied to like domestic products. In other words, imported products may be subject to internal taxes or charges equivalent to those applied on like domestic products. This requirement has two elements. It must first be determined whether the domestic and foreign products being compared are "like." Second, the imported product must not be subject to an internal tax or charge in excess of that applied to the like domestic product.

With respect to the first element, the WTO Appellate Body has determined that "likeness," for purposes of this paragraph, should be assessed taking into account criteria such as the products' tariff classification, their end-uses in a particular market, consumers' tastes and habits, and the products' physical properties, such as their nature and quality [*Japan – Taxes on Alcoholic Beverages,* Report of the Appellate Body, adopted 1 November 1996, WT/DS10/AB/R, WT/DS11/AB/R, WT/DS8/AB/R, at p. 20.]. However, the jurisprudence indicates that these criteria are not necessarily exhaustive, and it does not tell us whether these have a hierarchy, or how much weight should be given to each criterion. The jurisprudence does emphasize that assessing "likeness" must be done on a case-by-case basis, and involves a certain amount of unavoidable discretion on the part of dispute settlement panels.

An important question that has sometimes arisen is whether a WTO Member can differentiate — and therefore tax differently — domestic and imported products that do not differ in their physical characteristics or end uses, but which have been produced or manufactured in different ways, particularly where the production or manufacturing process gives rise to public policy issues such as its impact on human health or the environment.

...

With respect to the second element, there are three further questions that must be addressed. First, *what is* an internal tax or charge? Second, is it applied *directly or indirectly* to a product? Third, is the tax or charge applied *in excess* of that applied to the like domestic product?

The third question on application "in excess" is answered fairly easily. The only question here is whether the like imported product is subject to higher charges or taxes; trade flows or trade effects are not considered. The first two questions, however, require some analysis and are considered in turn below.

1. Internal Tax or Charge

A customs duty, as distinguished from an internal tax or charge, is collected at the time of, and as a condition to, the entry of a product into the importing country and applies to an imported product only; that is, there is no similar charge collected on a domestic like product. In addition, a customs duty is normally levied pursuant to a customs tariff schedule and is subject to tariff binding commitments. Note Ad Article III clarifies that an internal tax or charge that applies to both a domestic and like imported product and is collected "at the time or point of importation, is nevertheless to be regarded as an internal tax or other internal charge ..." The determining factor, then, is not when the tax or charge is collected (i.e., whether the tax or charge is collected "at the border"), but rather that the tax or charge is applied equally on both domestic and imported products. A charge was defined in *Argentina – Hides and Leather,* where the panel found that "the term 'charge' denotes, *inter alia,* a 'pecuniary burden' and a 'liability to pay money laid on a person ... '" [Report of the Panel, WT/DS155/R, adopted February 16, 2001 at para. 11.143].

It is noteworthy that the reason for imposing a tax or charge is not a relevant factor in determining whether it is WTO consistent. In *US – Superfund* [*United States — Taxes on Petroleum and Certain Imported Substances,* Report of the Panel, adopted on 17 June 1987, BISD 34S/136, para 5.2.3–5.2.4], the GATT Panel found that,

> the tax adjustment rules of the General Agreement distinguish between taxes on products and taxes not directly levied on products; they do not distinguish between taxes with different policy purposes. Whether a sales tax is levied on a product for general revenue purposes or to encourage the rational use of environmental resources, is therefore not relevant for the determination of the eligibility of a tax for border tax adjustment.

This view was supported by the Appellate Body in *Japan – Alcoholic Beverages II,* which found that Members may pursue any policy objective through their tax measures so long as they do so in a manner that is consistent with Article III:2.

2. Directly or indirectly?

While it is clear that only indirect taxes are eligible for adjustment, it has not always been clear what constituted taxes or charges applied "directly or indirectly." The negotiating history of Article III:2 suggests that taxes on inputs, or at least certain types of inputs, to an imported product were to be eligible for BTAs. The US Draft Charter, which served as the basis for the GATT, originally read, "taxes and other internal charges imposed on or in connection with like products," a phrase that, apparently, was later redrafted due to the difficulty of translating it into French.

The view that inputs are eligible for a BTA is textually supported, at least with respect to inputs that are physically incorporated in the final product, by Article II:2(a), which provides that a charge equivalent to an internal tax, imposed consistently with Article III:2, may be imposed "in respect of an article from which the imported product has been manufactured or produced in whole or in part."

GATT jurisprudence has also supported this contention with respect to inputs physically incorporated into the final product. In *US – Superfund,* the GATT panel considered whether US import taxes applied on certain imported products to offset the effect of domestic taxes on inputs incorporated into the like domestic product were consistent with the GATT. The tax was imposed domestically on certain feedstock chemicals. At the same time, a parallel tax was established to be levied on imported chemical products made from the feedstock chemicals. The purpose of the tax was to be a border tax adjustment equivalent in effect to the internal tax imposed on the chemical inputs. The panel did not consider the reason for the border tax, designed to raise funds to clean up pollution caused by the chemicals, to be relevant to a determination whether the BTA was consistent with the national treatment obligation. It concluded that taxes on articles used for the manufacture of products and physically incorporated into the final product were eligible for border tax adjustments. Importantly, the panel noted that where foreign producers could establish that less of the taxable input in question was used in their final product they would be able to pay less tax.

In 1970, a report by the GATT Working Party on Border Tax Adjustments concluded that there was a consensus among the Contracting Parties (as WTO Members were known at the time) that taxes levied on products (i.e., indirect taxes) were eligible for tax adjustment and those not levied on products (i.e., direct taxes) were not. The Working Party also noted a "divergence of views" on whether "taxes occultes" were eligible for adjustment. Taxes occultes include taxes on capital equipment, auxiliary materials and services used in the transportation and production of taxable products, e.g., advertising, energy, machinery and transport. This suggests that taxes on inputs not physically incorporated in the final product are not eligible for BTA treatment.

We note, however, that this Working Party Report is almost 40 years old, and does not represent an official interpretation of GATT rules. Hence, it cannot be considered as conclusive evidence for this proposition.

...

The conclusions of the unadopted panel report in the first *Tuna-Dolphin* [*United States – Restrictions on Imports of Tuna*, Report of the Panel (unadopted), 3 September 1991 (DS21/R), and 16 June 1994 (DS/29/R)] dispute drew on these Working Party conclusions. The dispute stemmed from an import ban imposed by the United States on a product (tuna) based on the use of methods of production that killed large numbers of dolphins. At the same time, the US regulated its own tuna fishing fleets in terms of methods of harvesting, but did not impose any restrictions on the marketing of tuna, regardless of how it had been caught. The panel reasoned that, in line with the BTA Working Party Report, since only taxes levied on products were eligible for adjustment, only regulations that applied to a product, and not the process by which it was produced, fell within the scope of Article III. Since the US import ban applied to products, but the domestic measure advanced by the US as the corresponding internal regulation did not, the interpretive note to Article III did not apply, and therefore the import ban fell under Article XI rather than Article III.

While the *Tuna-Dolphin* report was not adopted, it has been understood to stand for the proposition that restricting imports of products based on their production process, where the process does not affect the product as such, is not a matter that falls under the non-discrimination requirements of Article III; rather, it falls under the more stringent terms of Article XI. However, we note that this inference has never been tested outright in a dispute, and there are reasons to doubt its applicability where the measure in question deals directly with the regulation of both domestically-produced and imported products, even where the basis for such regulation is the processing/manufacturing methods used.

In contrast to the Tuna-Dolphin panel report, the *Superfund* dispute stands for the principle that inputs physically incorporated into a final product may be taxed, as long as they are taxed in proportion to the inputs actually incorporated.

...

The problem with measurability was referred to in the BTA Working Party Report. For example, it noted cascade taxes (or cumulative taxes), taxes that are applied at each stage of production where those paid at prior stages are not taken into account at later stages, as presenting a problem because of the difficulties in calculating the amount of adjustment. This resulted in countries operating this sort of system of taxation in averaging rates of rebate rather than the actual tax levied on a particular product.

North American Free Trade Agreement (NAFTA) — Bar on Claims
— Merrill & Ring v. Canada

In a Counter-Memorial dated 13 May 2008, Canada submitted:

A. *The Investor's Claim Is Time Barred by Article 1116(2)*

1. Summary of Canada's Position

Article 1116(2) of NAFTA bars claims made more than three years after the investor *first* acquired knowledge of breach and loss. There is overwhelming evidence that Merrill & Ring had such knowledge for almost a decade, and certainly well more than three years, before it commenced this arbitration.

Merrill & Ring tries to evade the time bar by arguing that an investor cannot acquire the requisite knowledge for as long as the log export regime is operative ("continuing" breach). In addition, the Investor argues that each routine application of the regime in the most recent three years is a distinct measure in breach of NAFTA ("non-continuing" breach). These theories contradict the ordinary meaning of Article 1116(2), and cannot override the "*lex specialis*" time bar drafted by the NAFTA Parties.

This claim is clearly and entirely time barred. The Tribunal should dismiss it without further consideration of the substantive obligations pleaded.

2. Interpretation of Article 1116(2)

Article 1116(2) limits the time within which investors may commence a claim under Chapter Eleven. It states,

An investor may not make a claim if more than three years have elapsed from the date on which the investor first acquired, or should have first acquired, knowledge of the alleged breach and knowledge that the investor has incurred loss or damage.

Article 1117(2) is the same as Article 1116(2), but with respect to claims by investors of a Party on behalf of an enterprise.

(a) The Ordinary Meaning Is Clear

The wording of Article 1116(2) is abundantly clear. As Professor Reisman notes in his expert report filed in these proceedings,

It takes great effort to misunderstand Article 1116(2). It establishes that the challenge of the compatibility of the measure must be made within three years of *first* acquiring (i) knowledge of the measure and (ii) that the measure carries economic cost for those subject to it. If the challenge is not made within those three years, it is time-barred.

While perhaps obvious, "first" means "earliest in occurrence, existence." It identifies the start of a period or event, and not the middle or end of a continuing situation. Professor Reisman summarises this well when he notes, "an investor does not and logically cannot '*first* acquire' knowledge of the allegedly incompatible measure that constitutes the challenged 'breach' *repeatedly*."

The inclusion of "first" to modify the phrase "acquired knowledge" in Article 1116(2) was a deliberate drafting choice intended to mark the beginning of the time when knowledge of breach and loss existed. The provision must be applied as ordinarily understood and plainly drafted.

(b) The Context Confirms the Ordinary Meaning

The context for Article 1116(2) confirms that it is an absolute time bar, calculated from the moment the investor first acquires knowledge of breach and loss. Four aspects of context should be highlighted.

(1) Article 1116(2) Defines the Scope of the Right to Claim

Article 1116 creates an extraordinary right: the right of an investor to sue a State for breach of a treaty obligation causing loss to that investor. Absent this express language, investors would not have recourse to the treaty and would have to persuade their governments to espouse their claim in State-to-State proceedings.

Article 1116(1) carefully defines the circumstances under which the extraordinary right to arbitrate breach of a NAFTA obligation accrues to an individual investor.

It is no accident that Article 1116(2) directly follows conferral of the right to commence investor-State arbitration in Article 1116(1). Article 1116(2) is part of the definition of that right, prescribing its scope by virtue of when it may be exercised. The language of Article 1116(2), and in particular the inclusion of "first" in this context, clearly and intentionally limits the scope of the right to arbitrate and defines the time within which that right must be exercised.

(2) Compliance with the Time Bar in Article 1116(2) Is a Condition Precedent to Canada's Consent to Arbitrate

Article 1116(2) is also one of several jurisdictional pre-conditions to a Chapter Eleven claim. Article 1121 is titled "Conditions Precedent to Submission of a Claim to Arbitration," and allows a disputing investor to submit a claim under Article 1116 "only if" the investor consents to arbitration "in accordance with the procedures in this Agreement." Article 1122 of NAFTA conditions the advance consent to arbitrate given by the State-Parties on compliance with these conditions. Investors must fulfill Articles 1101 and 1116 to 1121 to take advantage of the State-Party's advance consent.

As explained by the *Methanex* Tribunal,

> In order to establish the necessary consent to arbitration, it is sufficient to show (i) that Chapter 11 applies in the first place, i.e. that the requirements of Article 1101 are met, and (ii) that a claim has been brought by a claimant investor in accordance with Articles 1116 or 1117 (and that all pre-conditions and formalities required under Articles 1118–1121 are satisfied). Where these requirements are met by a claimant, Article 1122 is satisfied; and the NAFTA Party's consent to arbitration is established.

Compliance with the time bar in Article 1116(2) is one of the pre-conditions to Canada's consent to arbitrate, and must be applied in accordance with its ordinary meaning to establish Chapter Eleven jurisdiction.

(3) The NAFTA Parties Used Deliberate Language for Time Frames in Dispute Settlement

A comparison of Article 1116(2) with other timing provisions in NAFTA further demonstrates its very specific meaning. Various provisions in Chapter Eleven establish times within which investor-State dispute settlement must be commenced or a step in dispute settlement must be taken. Generally, the NAFTA Parties inserted temporal conditions in an article by using phrases such as "within," "at least" or "no later than." No other article in NAFTA adopts the formula in Articles 1116(2) and 1117(2) of counting time from a date on which an investor "first" acquired knowledge. Nor does any provision on dispute settlement in other chapters of NAFTA impose a time limit in the same manner as Articles 1116(2) and 1117(2).

The formula in Article 1116(2) was a precise one intended to pinpoint the moment of first acquiring knowledge and to bar claims made more than three years after that time.

(4) The NAFTA Parties Anticipated Claims for Continuing Conduct and Designed the Time Bar Accordingly

The NAFTA Parties obviously contemplated that investors would challenge ongoing or continuing measures. Article 1101 authorises investors to make Chapter Eleven claims based on continuing measures when it defines the scope and coverage of the chapter by reference to "measures adopted or maintained."

Similarly, various substantive obligations envisage claims concerning on-going measures. For example, Article 1105(2) provides for non-discriminatory treatment by measures a Party "adopts or maintains" relating to losses owing to armed conflict or civil strife. Article 1108(1), (2) and (3) addresses non-conforming measures "maintained" by a Party. Article 1113 allows a Party to deny benefits as a result of measures it "adopts or maintains," while Article 1114 states that nothing in Chapter Eleven prevents a Party from "adopting, maintaining or enforcing" a measure to ensure investment activity is sensitive to environmental concerns.

Article 1116 itself demonstrates that the NAFTA Parties anticipated claims for conduct that was continuing at the commencement of an arbitration. Article 1116(1) uses the past tense, allowing claims that the Party "has breached" an obligation and the investor "has incurred" loss due to the breach. Article 1116(2) prohibits an investor from claiming if more than three years "have elapsed." No provision of the NAFTA even suggests that a measure must be finalised or spent to be the subject of an investor claim.

Knowing that continuing conduct would be challenged by investors, the NAFTA Parties must be assumed to have addressed the precise moment at which the time bar for such claims would apply. That time was counted from the "first" acquisition of relevant knowledge, not subsequent, repeated or ultimate acquisition of such knowledge.

Had the NAFTA Parties been willing to delay the time bar for continuing measures in the fashion suggested by the Investor, they would not have used the phrase "first acquire." It is only logical to conclude that the NAFTA Parties designed Chapter Eleven to permit claims for continuing measures while ensuring that such claims be asserted within a reasonable time. That reasonable time is clearly stated as three years after "first" acquisition of the relevant knowledge.

(c) The Ordinary Meaning Enhances Effective Dispute Settlement

The object and purpose of Article 1116(2) is consistent with one of the listed objectives of NAFTA: to create effective procedures for the resolution of disputes. This article enhances the effective resolution of disputes by ensuring that claims are raised as soon as the investor has the information needed to do so. It ensures that relevant evidence will be available and that allegations of non-compliance with NAFTA will be addressed rather than allowed to linger.

Article 1116(2) serves the usual purposes of a limitation period. First, it provides peace and repose by ensuring that an alleged breach of NAFTA Chapter Eleven is raised and arbitrated at the earliest reasonable opportunity. This allows the NAFTA Parties to address an allegedly non-compliant measure, or to adjudicate the matter and have its compliance with NAFTA determined by a Tribunal. If non-compliant, the NAFTA Party can take steps to cure, amend or repeal the measure. In turn, this creates certainty and stability for NAFTA Parties and investors.

Evidentiary concerns are also addressed by Article 1116(2). Requiring investors to raise claims when first known to them allows the disputing parties to collect relevant evidence. This may include testimony of witnesses or production of documents that might otherwise be lost with the passage of time. In turn, this contributes to a fair investor-State dispute settlement process.

Economic and public interest considerations are likewise fulfilled by Article 1116(2). Investment will be encouraged by providing investors with certainty about the legality of existing regulatory regimes. Allowing long-standing regimes to be challenged for decades after they have been in operation, in particular by entities that have operated for lengthy periods under these very regimes, can only contribute to uncertainty.

The Investor's interpretation of Article 1116(2) defeats the object and purpose of the time bar. It would allow potential claims to languish for decades; deprive State Parties of the opportunity to establish compliance with NAFTA or remedy a violation of NAFTA; deprive investors of confidence that a long-standing regime is not perpetually subject to challenge; and prejudice fair adjudication of a claim. The Investor's approach renders Article 1116(2) ineffective by allowing an investor to sit on its hands notwithstanding that it has all the knowledge needed to pursue a claim.

Professor Reisman also comments on the implications of the Investor's theory. In his view:

[it] would lead to a torrent of investor-state arbitral claims. It would also make a mockery of good faith interpretation of NAFTA Article 1116(2) ... [if] the 1998 policy regime established by *Notice 102* constitutes a "continuing violation" that may be challenged under Chapter 11, then it is difficult to see what laws and regulations that predated NAFTA would *not* be subject to challenge.

The Investor's approach to Article 1116(2) is antithetical to the object and purpose of that provision and must be rejected.

(d) Supplementary Sources Confirm Canada's Position

A Tribunal need not refer to supplementary sources if the meaning of a provision is clear from interpretation according to Article 31 of the *Vienna Convention*. However, Article 32 of the *Vienna Convention* permits resort to supplementary sources if necessary to confirm the interpretation under Article 31. Canada submits that in this case there is no need to refer to secondary sources. In any event, the supplementary sources on point confirm the interpretation of Article 1116(2) urged by Canada.

The first relevant supplementary source is the NAFTA negotiating texts. The first NAFTA draft containing a limitation period was proposed by Canada on June 4, 1992. It read,

[A]n investor is not entitled to initiate arbitration ... if ... (b) more than two years have elapsed since the date on which the investor first acquired, or should have first acquired, knowledge of the alleged breach that is at issue in the dispute.

The provision was revised on August 4, 1992 to read,

An investor shall not be entitled to submit an investment dispute to arbitration if more than three years have elapsed since the date on which the investor first acquired, or should have first acquired, knowledge of the alleged breach and knowledge that it incurred loss or damage.

At 1:30 a.m. on September 4, 1992, the text was altered minimally so that "shall" became "may" and "investment dispute" became "claim." At 1:30 (likely p.m.) on the same day, the provision was replaced by the language used in the earlier August 4, 1992 text. A final revision at 6 p.m. on September 4, 1992 changed the text to its current form.

These drafts establish that the Parties consistently retained the words "first acquired knowledge," showing that they intended a provision that did not allow an investor to delay commencing its claim once it had the requisite knowledge to do so. The Investor's approach here is inconsistent with this intention.

The other potentially relevant supplementary sources are the Canadian and American implementation statements. In commenting on Articles 1116 and 1117, the American Statement of Administrative Action simply states, "[A]11 claims must be brought within three years." This evidences the American view that the continuing nature of a measure does not affect the time for commencing an arbitration. The Canadian Statement of Implementation repeats Article 1116(2), with the exception of noting that knowledge of "a" loss is required.

North American Free Trade Agreement (NAFTA) — Transparency of Proceedings — Gallo v. Canada

In a Written Submission of Canada on Procedural Issues dated 26 February 2008, Canada wrote:

A. Open Hearings

Canada's proposed text at paragraph 14 of the draft Confidentiality Order states that hearings in this matter should be open to the public, except as required for the protection of confidential information. This position reflects Canada's commitment to transparency and public accountability under the NAFTA.

By contrast, the Claimant argues that hearings in this matter should be closed to the public. In this instance, the Claimant can avail itself of Article 25(4) of the UNCITRAL Rules.

Canada regrets that the Claimant has made this *in camera* election, and suggests that the better practice would be to open the hearing, except in circumstances in which the Arbitral Tribunal is satisfied there is a genuine issue of confidentiality.

Open hearings are consistent with the stated NAFTA objective of transparency. All three NAFTA Parties have reaffirmed this objective and have made clear commitments to holding open hearings in NAFTA Chapter 11 arbitrations.

On October 7, 2003, Canada issued a Statement on Open Hearings in NAFTA Chapter Eleven Arbitrations, affirming that:

Having reviewed the operation of arbitration proceedings conducted under Chapter Eleven of the North American Free Trade Agreement,

Canada affirms that it will consent, and will request the consent of disputing investors and, as applicable, tribunals, that hearings in Chapter Eleven disputes to which it is a party be open to the public, except to ensure the protection of confidential information, including business confidential information. Canada recommends that tribunals determine the appropriate logistical arrangements for open hearings in consultation with disputing parties. These arrangements may include, for example, use of closed-circuit television systems, Internet webcasting, or other forms of access.

The United States issued an identical affirmation on that same day. Mexico joined Canada and the United States in endorsing this policy following the meeting of the Free Trade Commission of 2004.

Canada therefore invites the Arbitral Tribunal to consider the clear intent of the NAFTA Parties and open the hearing, except in circumstances in which the Arbitral Tribunal is satisfied there is a genuine issue of confidentiality.

1. Recent NAFTA Chapter 11 Arbitral Practice Favours Open Hearings

Practice in the first NAFTA Chapter 11 proceedings under the UNCITRAL Rules was restricted to restating Article 25(4) and holding hearings *in camera.* However, since 2001, the parties in most NAFTA Chapter 11 proceedings have agreed to open hearings, including *UPS v. Canada, Glamis Gold v. United States, Grand River Enterprises v. United States, Methanex v. United States,* and *Canfor v. United States.*

In *Thunderbird International v. Mexico* the Arbitral Tribunal adopted a less transparent approach, where hearings were closed but transcripts were made public.

NAFTA Arbitral Tribunals have recognized through their practice over the past several years and by express rulings that there is a public interest in the outcome of NAFTA Chapter 11 arbitrations, and that this interest is best served through a transparent process, including open hearings. In the context of a ruling on *amicus* submissions, the *Methanex* Arbitral Tribunal found:

> The public interest in this arbitration arises from its subject matter [a challenge to an environmental regulation], as powerfully suggested by the Petitions. There is also a broader argument, as suggested by the Respondent and Canada: the Chapter 11 arbitral process could benefit from being perceived as more open or transparent; or conversely be harmed if seen as unduly secretive. In this regard, the Tribunal's willingness to receive *amicus* submissions might support the process

in general and this arbitration in particular; whereas a blanket refusal could do positive harm.

2. Claimant's Confidentiality Can Be Maintained

In practice, reasoned claims for confidentiality have been easily addressed in NAFTA arbitrations that have otherwise maintained open hearings. Necessary portions of the public hearings have been held *in camera* to ensure that there was no disclosure of confidential information. Claimant's particular concern about potential interference with the proceeding can be fully addressed, for example, by ensuring public access via live video-feed, which can be suspended briefly for the presentation of confidential information or at the request of either disputing party.

3. Conclusion on Open Hearings

For the foregoing reasons, Canada's position should be preferred, and the hearings in this matter declared open to the public, save for brief periods when confidential or privileged information is under discussion.
Alternatively, if the Arbitral Tribunal is inclined to close the hearings to the public by virtue of the Claimant's request under the UNCITRAL Rules for an *in camera* hearing, Canada notes that this simply means that the public is not allowed to be present at the hearings. It does not preclude the public from knowing about the arbitration or having access to pleadings, submissions, and award(s), nor does it prevent public access to transcripts of the proceedings, for example from an internet website.

World Trade Organization (WTO) — Compliance — Canada —
Continued Suspension (EC Hormones)

In a Written Submission to the WTO Appellate Body dated 13 June 2008, Canada wrote:

Contrary to the EC's contention, this case is not about procedural violations committed by Canada. At its heart, this case is about the EC's failure to demonstrate, after more than 10 years since the recommendations and rulings of the Dispute Settlement Body (DSB) in the *EC – Hormones* dispute, that it has finally brought itself into compliance.

Had the Panel's approach to the two series of EC main claims followed the logic and structure of the DSU, in a situation where, following the notification of Directive 2003/74/EC, Canada continued to suspend concessions *vis-à-vis* the EC pursuant to an authorization granted by the DSB, the Panel would not have found a violation of Article 23.1 and 23.2(a) of the DSU. In addressing the EC's main claims, the Panel was first required to determine whether the EC had established that the very specific conditions of Article 22.8 of the DSU for the termination of the suspension of concessions had been met.

The fact that the Panel in its report also found that Canada did not breach Article 22.8 of the DSU, because the EC had failed to demonstrate that the measure found to be inconsistent with the *SPS Agreement* in the *EC – Hormones* dispute had been removed, demonstrates the fundamental flaw in the Panel's approach.

The Panel's erroneous approach is rooted in its finding that DSU Article 23.2(a) and 23.1 can be examined in isolation from the three conditions set out in Article 22.8 for lifting the suspension of concessions. While examining the EC's claim of violation of Article 23.2(a), the Panel made the following statement:

> [...] the question before us in the context of Article 23.2(a) is not whether the European Communities has actually removed the measure found to be inconsistent [as required by Article 22.8], but whether it notified a measure which has not yet been subject to dispute settlement.

The Panel then went on to find that, because Directive 96/22/EC was removed and replaced by Directive 2003/74/EC (which amends the 1996 Directive in some respects, but continues the import ban of meat and meat-products from cattle produced with the same six growth promotants that were in issue in *EC – Hormones*), the latter measure was a different measure and as such "it is logical under Article 23 that Canada's prior authorization to suspend concessions or other obligation do not apply to this measure." Thus the Panel found that Canada, by maintaining the suspension of concessions, was "seeking the redress" of a violation of WTO obligations and had made a "determination" regarding the WTO consistency of the EC's implementing measure without recourse to the rules and procedures of the DSU, in violation of Article 23.2(a) and 23.1 of the DSU.

The Panel's approach and ultimate finding, which as stated by the Panel is premised on the mere existence of an EC implementing measure, is fundamentally flawed. It is inconsistent with well-established rules and principles of treaty interpretation in that:

> in accordance with Articles 31 and 32 of the *Vienna Convention,* a treaty must be interpreted in good faith in accordance with the ordinary meaning to be given to the terms of the treaty in their context and in the light of its object and purpose and should not be interpreted so as to lead to a result that is manifestly absurd or unreasonable;

the specific terms of a treaty must prevail over the general provisions of a treaty (the principle of *lex specialis derogat legi generali*); and

a treaty should not be interpreted so as to reduce whole clauses or paragraphs to redundancy or inutility (*i.e.*, the principle of effectiveness).

Each of these points will be addressed in turn below.

A. The Panel failed to apply relevant principles of treaty interpretation

The Appellate Body has repeatedly recognized that, in accordance with DSU Article 3.2, the provisions in the *WTO Agreement* are to be construed in accordance with customary international law rules of interpretation. Customary rules of treaty interpretation call, first and foremost, for an examination of the words of a treaty read in their context, interpreted in good faith in accordance with their ordinary meaning and in the light of the object and purpose of the treaty involved. These basic principles, codified in Article 31 of the *Vienna Convention,* have been summarized by the Appellate Body in the following terms [*US – Shrimp,* Appellate Body Report, at para. 114]:

A treaty interpreter must begin with, and focus upon, the text of the particular provision to be interpreted. It is in the words constituting that provision, read in their context, that the object and purpose of the states parties to the treaty must first be sought.

To interpret the terms of a treaty in their context, panels must look at the treaty as a whole and not interpret any particular provision in isolation. As was pointed out by the panel in *EC – Chicken Cuts* [at para. 7.153], this is clear from the *chapeau* of Article 31(2) of the *Vienna Convention,* which states that the terms of the treaty, including its preamble and annexes, qualify as "context" for the purposes of interpreting a particular provision.

1. The Panel failed to consider the context of the DSU in its interpretation of DSU Articles 23 and 22

The Panel should have interpreted the provisions of DSU Articles 22.8, 23.1 and 23.2(a) in the context of other relevant provisions of the DSU. Articles 21 and 22 of the DSU constitute a comprehensive "code" that provides detailed rules for the various situations that could arise after the adoption of recommendations and rulings by the DSB in a particular dispute. It is these detailed rules in their proper sequence that the Panel should have addressed in the post-retaliation stage of this case.

Article 21, entitled "Surveillance of Implementation of Recommendations and Rulings," sets out the fundamental principle that prompt compliance with the recommendations and rulings of the DSB is essential in order to ensure the effective resolution of disputes to the benefit of all WTO Members. In accordance with this fundamental principle, immediate compliance with the recommendations and rulings of the DSB is the preferred option. However, there is also a recognition that it may not always be practicable for Members to comply immediately with the recommendations and rulings of the DSB. Accordingly, Article 21 addresses, among other things, the establishment of a reasonable period of time to implement the recommendations and rulings of the DSB, and the determination of whether compliance with such recommendations and rulings has actually been achieved.

Under the heading "Compensation and the Suspension of Concessions," Article 22 addresses the potential consequences of a WTO Member failing to comply with the DSB's recommendations and rulings within a reasonable period of time. Article 22.1 specifies that compensation and suspension of concessions are "temporary measures" and reiterates the basic principle that neither of these temporary measures is preferred over the full implementation of the recommendations and rulings of the DSB.

Article 22.2 contains an obligation on WTO Members to negotiate in good faith on mutually acceptable compensation if timely implementation has not taken place. If compensation is not agreed on by the parties within 20 days from the end of the reasonable period of time, then the complaining party may request the DSB for authorization to suspend the application to the respondent of concessions or other obligations under the covered agreements. As a result, Article 22 provides a mechanism for WTO Members to obtain temporary relief from the nullification and impairment suffered when another Member fails to bring itself into compliance with its WTO obligations in a timely manner. The suspension of concessions also serves as an important inducement for the responding party to comply with the DSB's recommendations and rulings.

The suspension of concessions or other obligations must be equivalent to the level of nullification or impairment suffered. Thus, Article 22.6 and 22.7 of the DSU provide for an arbitration mechanism under which the level of suspension can be challenged as not being equivalent to the level of nullification or impairment suffered by the other party.

Key to this case is Article 22.8 of the DSU, which sets out the three conditions that must be met in order to have the suspension of concessions or other obligations terminated. Article 22.8 provides as follows:

The suspension of concessions or other obligations shall be temporary and shall only be applied until such time as the measure found to be inconsistent with a covered agreement *has been removed*, or the Member that must implement recommendations or rulings *provides a solution to the nullification or impairment of benefits*, or a *mutually satisfactory solution is reached*. In accordance with paragraph 6 of Article 21, the DSB shall continue to keep *under surveillance* the implementation of adopted recommendations or rulings, *including those cases where compensation has been provided or concessions or other obligations have been suspended* but the recommendations to bring a measure into conformity with the covered agreements have not been implemented [emphasis added].

Article 22.8 restates the temporary nature of the suspension of concessions and also articulates that the DSB must keep under surveillance the implementation of its adopted recommendations and rulings until actual compliance has been achieved, which in this case means until the EC's WTO-inconsistent measure "*has been* removed." The continuous involvement of the DSB suggests that it retains jurisdiction over the matter until its recommendations and rulings have been fully implemented. This is consistent with the ongoing obligation on the Member being retaliated against to comply with its WTO obligations, including the requirement to comply promptly with the recommendations and rulings of the DSB.

In order to ensure the effectiveness of the dispute settlement system, Article 23 of the DSU, entitled "Strengthening of the Multilateral System," sets out that the dispute settlement system is the exclusive means to redress any violation of WTO obligations. As such, Canada notes that there is a certain amount of parallelism between Article 23 and the structure of the dispute settlement process. That is, Article 23 as *lex generalis* begins by setting out general obligations that apply to what can be termed the pre-dispute settlement stage of a dispute and then proceeds by setting out specific obligations (*lex specialis*) applicable through the compliance and retaliation stages of dispute settlement.

Article 23.1 of the DSU contains the general obligation on Members to follow the rules and procedures of the DSU when seeking the redress of, *inter alia*, a violation of WTO obligations. In Canada's view, the context of Article 23 as a whole demonstrates that Article 23.1 is concerned with measures in respect of which no WTO dispute settlement proceedings have taken place. The EC's 2003 Directive does not fall into this category because it is not a new measure *ab initio*. Article 23.2 of the DSU goes on and lists what the Appellate Body in *US – Certain EC Products* has called a number of "specific and clearly-defined forms of prohibited unilateral action."

Each paragraph of Article 23.2 of the DSU follows a logical sequence with regard to prohibited unilateral action within the course of a dispute. Article 23.2(a) prohibits Members from making determinations that a violation has occurred, except through recourse to the rules and procedures of the DSU. In respect of the compliance stage of a dispute, Article 23.2(b) sets out the obligation to follow the procedures established in Article 21 for determining the reasonable period of time for compliance. Finally, in respect of the retaliation stage of a dispute, Article 23.2(c) sets out the obligation to follow the procedures in Article 22 to determine the level of suspension of concessions and obtain DSB authorization before suspending concessions.

While the panel in *United States – Section 301 Trade Act* recognized [at para. 7.45] that the examples of prohibited unilateral conduct contained in Article 23.2 are not exhaustive, the structure of Article 23 indicates that when a particular dispute has entered the compliance or retaliation stages, the relevant obligations are those in paragraphs (b) and (c) of Article 23.2. In those cases, the general obligations contained in Article 23.1 and Article 23.2(a) are no longer pertinent, as the only way for a complaining Member to have reached the compliance or retaliation stages is to have already satisfied those general obligations by having engaged the WTO dispute settlement process and obtained a DSB ruling that the responding Member has violated its obligations.

This interpretation of DSU Article 23 is consistent with its negotiating history. The primary concern of negotiators who favoured a provision obliging WTO Members to refrain from unilateral actions was Section 301 of the *Omnibus Trade and Competitiveness Act of 1988* of the United States, which was an example of a GATT party imposing trade restrictions on the basis of its own determinations. The Dunkel Draft Final Act, in Article 21, contained a compromise between the United States and other delegations. It stated that "Contracting Parties shall not make a determination to the effect that a violation has occurred [...] except through recourse to dispute settlement in accordance with this Understanding [...]." There does not appear to be any indication in the reports on the negotiations that the GATT parties contemplated the post-retaliation context when they negotiated what eventually became Article 23 of the DSU. Accordingly, the *travaux préparatoires* provide a further indication that DSU Article 23 was not intended to apply to a post-retaliation situation.

Thus it follows that, in this case, where Canada has had recourse to the rules and procedures of the DSU in the *EC – Hormones* dispute and is suspending concessions pursuant to a DSB authorization, Canada has already satisfied the obligations contained in Article 23.1 and 23.2(a). As suggested by the text of Article 23.2(c), the Panel, therefore, should have turned first to the provisions of Article 22, including the specific requirements of Article 22.8 that apply in the case of determining whether the suspension of concessions should be terminated.

In Canada's view, the Panel failed to follow, as outlined above, the basic architecture of the DSU in its approach to the first series of EC main claims. As a result, the Panel failed to first consider the specific provision of Article 22.8 of the DSU and thus erred in its finding that the first series of EC main claims was "completely unrelated to whether the European Communities implemented the DSB recommendations and rulings in the *EC – Hormones* dispute in substance." The Panel's approach resulted in its contradictory findings that, on the one hand, Canada, in continuing to suspend concessions, had made a unilateral determination that the EC was in violation of its obligations (contrary to Article 23.2(a) and, consequently, Article 23.1 of the DSU) and, on the other, that the EC had not removed the measure found to be inconsistent in the *EC – Hormones* dispute and, therefore, that Canada was not in violation of Article 22.8, which necessarily meant that Canada had every right to continue to suspend concessions.

2. The Panel failed to consider the object and purpose of the DSU in its interpretation of DSU Articles 23 and 22

The object and purpose of the DSU is set forth in Article 3.2, first sentence:

> The dispute settlement system of the WTO is a central element in providing security and predictability to the multilateral trading system. The Members recognize that it serves to preserve the rights and obligations of Members under the covered agreements, and to clarify the existing provisions of those agreements in accordance with customary rules of interpretation of public international law. [Emphasis added]

The objective of providing "security and predictability" is particularly germane in this case. The importance of this objective was discussed by the panel in *US – Section 301 Trade Act*. That panel found as follows [at para. 7.759]:

> Providing security and predictability to the multilateral trading system is another central object and purpose of the system which could be instrumental to achieving the broad objectives of the Preamble. Of all WTO disciplines, the DSU is one of the most important instruments to protect the security and predictability of the multilateral trading system and through it that of the market-place and its different operators. *DSU provisions must, thus, be interpreted in the light of this object and purpose and in a manner which would most effectively enhance it.* In this

respect we are referring not only to preambular language but also to positive law provisions in the DSU itself.

The ability of the WTO dispute settlement mechanism to provide security and predictability is linked intrinsically to the effectiveness of that mechanism and the remedies it provides. This is implicit in Article 21.1 of the DSU, which states:

> Prompt compliance with recommendations or rulings of the DSB is essential in order to ensure effective resolution of disputes to the benefit of all Members.

In this case, the Panel, by considering DSU Article 23 in isolation from other provisions of the DSU, arrived at findings that ultimately lessen the effectiveness of the WTO dispute settlement mechanism. The result of the Panel Report is that a Member authorized by the DSB to suspend concessions would have to terminate such suspension of concessions following the adoption of an alleged implementing measure by the non-compliant Member and the notification by the same Member of such measure to the DSB, unless it challenged the purported implementing measure pursuant to Article 21.5 of the DSU or in a *de novo* action. Put another way, a non-compliant WTO Member could avoid the duly authorized suspension of concessions by another Member merely by adopting an alleged implementing measure, notifying such measure to the DSB and waiting to be challenged. This is true even where the Member acts in good faith but mistakenly adopts a new implementing measure that is not consistent with the recommendations and rulings of the DSB.

The Panel specifically acknowledges in its report that its interpretation of Article 23.1 and 23.2(a) could lead to "recurrent litigations." In this regard the Panel states [at para. 7.230]:

> One could envisage that, in a complex case, a Member could notify in good faith an implementing measure which would be subsequently found not to fully comply with the original recommendations and rulings of the DSB. This Member would have to submit a revised measure which could, once again, be challenged and found to comply only partly with the covered agreements.

Although the non-compliant Member's alleged implementing measure may ultimately be found to be inconsistent with the recommendations and rulings of the DSB, the Panel's interpretation of Article 23 of the DSU has the effect of undermining the strength of DSB-authorized retaliation, thereby weakening an important incentive for Members to bring their measures promptly into compliance.

In Canada's view, such a result goes against the object and purpose of the DSU because it reduces the security and predictability of the multilateral trading system by effectively allowing a unilateral assertion of compliance by the previously non-compliant Member to override the multilateral authorization of the DSB to suspend concessions. In such a case, Canada is of the view that only a further multilateral determination by the DSB — this time of compliance — can set aside the DSB's prior authorization to suspend concessions. Thus, the Panel should have concluded that, if the EC, as the non-compliant Member, considered Canada's continued suspension of concessions to be in violation of DSU Article 22.8, it had the burden of initiating either a proceeding under DSU Article 21.5 or a *de novo* action against Canada's suspension of concessions (as the EC did in the present case). Such a result would allow the suspension of concessions to continue until the DSB determined otherwise. Also, the non-compliant Member is inherently in a better position to demonstrate that its alleged implementing measure has achieved compliance with its WTO obligations than the Member that has been authorized to suspend concessions. Such an approach would allow the real essence of such a dispute — whether the alleged implementing measure meets the recommendations and rulings of the DSB — to be litigated in a manner that leads to its ultimate resolution, in accordance with Article 3.10 of the DSU.

The Panel's approach is also inconsistent with the last sentence of Article 3.2 of the DSU, which provides that recommendations and rulings of the DSB cannot add to or diminish the rights and obligations provided in the covered agreements. The Panel's approach, if adopted, would diminish the right of Canada to rely on its validly obtained DSB authorization to suspend concessions against the EC. In Canada's view, the design of the WTO dispute settlement process, as evidenced by the structure of the DSU outlined above, is such that a unilateral action, such as the notification by the EC to the DSB of the adoption of the 2003 Directive, cannot alter the *status quo* and displace Canada's duly authorized right to suspend concessions without multilateral recognition that one of the three conditions for the removal of the suspension of concessions set out in Article 22.8 has been met.

3. The Panel's approach to the EC's claims disregards the principle of *lex specialis*

The interpretation and application by the Panel of the general language of DSU Article 23.1 and 23.2(a), in isolation from DSU Article 22.8, is also inconsistent with established principles of treaty interpretation, which have also been recognized by the Appellate Body. Article 32 of the *Vienna Convention* allows for recourse to "supplementary means of interpretation" to confirm the ordinary meaning of the terms of a treaty read in their context and in light of its object and purpose, or to determine the meaning in situations where the ordinary meaning is ambiguous or obscure, or leads to a result that is "manifestly absurd or unreasonable." One such supplementary means of interpretation that has been used by the Appellate Body is the application of the principle of *lex specialis, i.e.,* the principle that the specific terms of a treaty must prevail over the general provisions of a treaty.

In its approach to the EC's claims, the Panel determined that it was bound to address the main EC claims as elaborated in the EC's written submissions. The Panel stated [at para. 7.164] that it found "no reasons not to review the EC claims in the order followed by the European Communities in its submissions." However, the Panel appears to have failed to consider that the EC had misconstrued the obligations of the DSU in its main claims. By confining itself to the legal analysis elaborated in the EC's pleadings, the Panel committed an error of law in departing from well-established principles of treaty interpretation in the way it structured its analysis of the two series of EC main claims.

The Panel recalled that the Appellate Body in *Canada – Wheat Exports and Grain Imports* stated that [at para. 126], "[a]s a general principle, panels are free to structure the order of their analysis as they see fit." It went on to say, "[i]n so doing, panels may find it useful to take account of the manner in which a claim is presented to them by a complaining Member." However, panels must be careful not to simply follow the order of analysis as pleaded by a complainant, which may itself contain errors. In this case, the Panel appears to have accepted the EC distinction of its two main claims — the second relates to the presumed or actual compliance with the *SPS Agreement,* while the first does not. This distinction is not supported by the terms of the DSU and it obscures the central issue in this case: whether the 2003 Directive (amending the 1996 Directive) brought the EC into compliance with the DSB's recommendations and rulings in the *EC – Hormones* dispute as required by Article 22.8 of the DSU for the termination of Canada's suspension of concessions.

The Appellate Body has recognized that failure by a panel to consider provisions in their proper sequence may amount to an error of law. In *Canada – Wheat Exports and Grain Imports,* the Appellate Body stated [at para. 109]:

> Thus, in each case it is the nature of the relationship between two provisions that will determine whether there exists a mandatory sequence of analysis which, if not followed, would *amount to an error of law.* In some cases, this relationship is such that a failure to structure the analysis in the proper logical sequence will have repercussions for the substance of the analysis itself.

Therefore, panels must consider the repercussions of their chosen order of analysis so as not to give rise to an error in law. As such, panels are required to determine whether there exists a mandatory sequence of analysis dictated by the relationship between two provisions. In the determination of whether one particular provision must be analyzed before the other, panels should have recourse to principles of valid interpretative methodology. On this point, the panel in *India – Autos* stated [at para. 7.154]:

> Where the order of analysis of claims is concerned, it is important to consider if a particular order is compelled by *principles of valid interpretative methodology*, which, if not followed, might constitute an error of law.

In Canada's view, the Panel's approach gave rise to an error in law because by choosing to address DSU Article 23 in the abstract the Panel failed to consider the application of the rule of treaty interpretation that the specific rule overrides the general rule in a treaty (*i.e.*, *lex specialis*).

The principle of *lex specialis* as it relates to the order of analysis has been considered by the Appellate Body in *EC – Bananas III*. In its report the Appellate Body criticized the panel's approach and stated that it should have considered the more specific provision before the general. In other words, as stated by the panel in the *US – 1916 Act (EC)* case [at para. 6.76]:

> It is a general principle of international law that, when applying a body of norms to a given factual situation, *one should consider that factual situation under the norm which most specifically addresses it.*

In this case, the application of the *lex specialis* principle should have led the Panel to conclude that in the post-retaliation stage of a dispute it should begin its analysis by determining whether the conditions for the termination of the suspension of concessions set out in Article 22.8 of the DSU had been met.

In Canada's view, DSU Article 22 is the *lex specialis* for the post-retaliation phase of a dispute and, therefore, that provision, and Article 22.8 in particular, governs the issue at hand. In view of the very specific nature of DSU Article 22.8 and the general nature of DSU Article 23, it is DSU Article 22.8 that should have been applied first in this case, rather than DSU Article 23. As demonstrated above, Article 22 applies to situations where the DSB has adopted findings with respect to the WTO-consistency of a Member's impugned measure. Thus, this Article deals with the circumstances that can arise *after* that Member has failed to implement the recommendations and rulings of the DSB within a reasonable period of time.

In Canada's view, the Panel's approach to the first series of EC main claims is flawed because it fails to consider that the specifically applicable provision in this situation of post-retaliation is Article 22.8 of the DSU. By basing its approach on the mere existence and notification of Directive 2003/74/EC, the Panel failed to consider whether DSU Article 22.8 obliged Canada to end the suspension of concessions. This in turn would have required a determination by the Panel whether the EC's measure, as continued and marginally modified by the 2003 Directive, conformed in substance with the recommendations and rulings of the DSB in the *EC – Hormones* dispute.

4. The consequences of the Panel's disregard of the *lex specialis* principle

The Panel's failure to address DSU Article 22.8 and the underlying SPS issues when considering the first series of EC main claims resulted in contradictory findings: that Canada breached Article 23.1 and 23.2(a) of the DSU, even though the Panel also determined that the EC's measure found to be inconsistent with the *SPS Agreement* in the *EC – Hormones* dispute had not been "removed" within the meaning of DSU Article 22.8.

The Panel used two different and inconsistent manners of identifying the EC's implementing measure at issue. While examining the second series of EC main claims, the Panel gave a broad interpretation to the term "measure" in Article 22.8 of the DSU and recognized that the phrase "until such time as the measure found to be inconsistent with a covered agreement has been removed" means that the "illegality itself" and not only the originally impugned measure had been removed. However, in its approach to the first series of EC main claims the Panel based its finding of a violation of Article 23.1 and 23.2(a) of the DSU not on whether the EC had actually "removed" the inconsistent measure (in other words, actual compliance with the recommendations and rulings of the DSB) but rather on the fact that the EC had notified a measure that had not yet been subject to dispute settlement. This distinction is not supported by the terms of the DSU.

The Panel's approach to the first series of EC main claims ignores the procedural history of this case (as Canada argued before the Panel) and fails to take into account that the 2003 Directive is not a new measure *ab initio* but a measure taken in the context of the EC's ongoing obligation to comply with its WTO obligations, and more specifically with the recommendations and rulings of the DSB in the *EC – Hormones* dispute. Thus the EC's 2003 Directive should be situated in the post-retaliation context, to which specific provisions of the DSU apply, in particular Article 22.8. As such, the 2003 Directive cannot be considered to be a "new measure" for the purposes of Article 23.1 and 23.2(a).

Furthermore, the 2003 Directive amended the earlier 1996 Directive, which was at issue in *EC – Hormones;* however, it maintained the ban in respect of all six hormones that were at issue in *EC – Hormones* and made only marginal changes, the principal ones being the formal characterization of the ban in respect of oestradiol 17ß as a permanent ban and of the bans in respect of the other five hormones as provisional in nature.

As explained earlier, Canada has already sought and obtained redress in the *EC – Hormones* dispute for the EC's WTO-inconsistent measure. The central issue in this case is not whether the 2003 Directive has been the subject of recourse to the rules and procedures of the DSU but whether the measure genuinely removes the "illegality" of the measure at issue in *EC – Hormones,* such that one of the conditions for the termination of the suspension of concessions set out in Article 22.8 has been met.

Given that Canada obtained an authorization from the DSB in 1999 to suspend concessions *vis-à-vis* the EC because of its failure to implement the recommendations and rulings of the DSB within the reasonable period of time, the onus should have been placed by the Panel on the EC to provide a solution to the nullification or impairment of benefits, or reach a mutually satisfactory solution with Canada, or, in the event neither were possible, demonstrate to a WTO panel its compliance. In Canada's view, neither DSU Article 23.1 nor Article 23.2(a) should have been considered by the Panel in this context.

The implication of the Panel's approach to the EC's 2003 Directive under DSU Article 23 in the abstract and its conclusions on Canada's violations of DSU Article 23.1 and 23.2(a) is that the mere adoption and notification of an alleged implementing measure by a WTO Member that has failed to bring itself into compliance within the reasonable period of time could render the continuation of the suspension of concessions (a previously WTO-consistent and DSB-authorized measure) inconsistent with the DSU unless the Member suspending concessions has recourse, within a timeframe unspecified by the Panel, to the rules and procedures of the DSU to challenge the conformity of the alleged implementing measure. In Canada's view, such an interpretation is manifestly absurd or unreasonable within the meaning of Article 32(b) of the *Vienna Convention.*

Given the facts of this case, the Panel would not have arrived at the conclusion that Canada had violated DSU Article 23.1 and 23.2(a) if it had properly taken into account its conclusion that Canada had not violated DSU Article 22.8. Since DSU Article 22.8 is the more specific provision dealing with the termination of suspension of concessions, the Panel's conclusions in that regard should have taken precedence and should have precluded any adverse findings *vis-à-vis* Canada in relation to DSU Article 23.1 and 23.2(a).

5. The Panel's approach to the EC's claims disregards the principle of effectiveness

Another principle of treaty interpretation recognized by the Appellate Body is that of effectiveness, which holds that a treaty should not be interpreted so as to reduce whole clauses or paragraphs to redundancy or inutility. In this case, the Panel's interpretation and application of DSU Article 23.1 and 23.2(a) renders ineffective the substantive requirements set out in Article 22.8 of the DSU for the termination of the suspension of concessions and substantially narrows Canada's right to suspend concessions *vis-à-vis* the EC pursuant to the authorization granted by the DSB under DSU Article 22. This is contrary to the principle of effectiveness.

The principle of effectiveness has been affirmed by the Appellate Body in *US — Gasoline* [at p. 23]:

> One of the corollaries of the "general rule of interpretation" in the *Vienna Convention* is that interpretation must give meaning and effect to all the terms of a treaty. An interpreter is not free to adopt a reading that would result in reducing whole clauses or paragraphs of a treaty to redundancy or inutility.

In *Korea – Dairy*, the Appellate Body concluded [at para. 81] that:

> In light of the interpretive principle of effectiveness, it is the *duty* of any treaty interpreter to "read all applicable provisions of a treaty in a way that gives meaning to *all* of them, harmoniously." An important corollary of this principle is that a treaty should be interpreted as a whole, and, in particular, its sections and parts should be read as a whole.

In Canada's view, the Panel's approach to the first series of EC main claims misconstrues the field of application of Article 23 such that Article 22.8 of the DSU is given no effect. The Panel dealt with DSU Article 23.1 and 23.2(a) in the abstract and based its findings on the mere existence of the 2003 Directive as a "new measure" that had not been subject to recourse to the rules and procedures of the DSU. Such an approach fails to acknowledge that this case is at the post-retaliation stage of the dispute and that the EC's 2003 Directive should be interpreted in this light. Thus, the question is not whether a "new measure" has been notified to the DSB by the EC but rather whether this alleged implementing measure removes the "illegality" found in the *EC – Hormones* dispute such that Canada would have to cease its suspension of concessions.

Therefore, in Canada's view, the Panel's approach to the 2003 Directive in the second series of main EC claims is the correct one. In that approach, the Panel dealt with DSU Article 22.8 first and concluded that Canada was not in violation of DSU Article 23.1 because the EC had not established that it had removed the measure that was found to be WTO-inconsistent in the *EC – Hormones* dispute. This results in giving full effect to both DSU Articles 22.8 and 23. That approach does not deprive Article 22.8 of its application by ignoring the three substantive requirements set out in that provision for the termination of the suspension of concessions.

The consequence of the Panel's erroneous approach to the first series of EC main claims is that, in the post-retaliation stage of a dispute, a Member may no longer rely on a multilaterally rendered authorization by the DSB in the face of the mere assertion by a non-complying Member that a new implementing measure has brought it into compliance with the recommendations and rulings of the DSB. Therefore, the Panel's findings of a violation by Canada of Article 23.1 and 23.2(a) in the abstract must be reversed.

World Trade Organization (WTO) — Dispute Settlement Understanding (DSU) — Confidential Proceedings — United States Cotton

In a Written Submission to the WTO Appellate Body dated 3 June 2008, Canada, participating as a third party, wrote:

DSU Article 17.10

DSU Article 17.10, in its first sentence, states that "[t]he proceedings of the Appellate Body shall be confidential." Read out of context, this provision may appear to require closed oral hearings before the Appellate Body. However, when the key terms of the sentence — "proceedings" and "confidential" — are interpreted in accordance with the rules of treaty interpretation, in the context of the entire DSU and in particular Article 17 itself, it can be seen that the sentence does not and was not intended to operate as a bar to open hearings.

The word "proceedings" in DSU Article 17.10 refers to more than just the oral hearings before the Appellate Body. DSU Article 17.5 is instructive in this regard. The first sentence of Article 17.5 states: "[a]s a general rule, the *proceedings* shall not exceed 60 days from the date a party to the dispute formally notifies its decision to appeal to the date the Appellate Body circulates its report." [Emphasis added.] This indicates that the appellate *proceedings* encompass all the stages of the appeal, from the date a Notice of Appeal is filed to the date the Appellate Body issues its report to all Members. In every other instance in which the term "proceedings" is used in the DSU, *i.e.*, Articles 4.6, 4.9, 5.2, 10.4 and 26.2 (as well as paragraph 1 of Appendix 3) it is clear from the text that the term has a broad meaning. Also, in the Working Procedures, the term "proceedings" or "proceeding" is used to refer to the entire panel or appellate process. Rule 28 (1) of the Working Procedures, in particular, makes it very clear that an "oral hearing" is only a part of the entire "appellate proceeding." Consequently, the term "proceedings" in DSU Article 17.10 encompasses the entire appellate process.

Regarding the term "confidentiality," an examination of the context of DSU Article 17.10 and the practice of the WTO demonstrates that this provision does not require that the entire appellate process (or "proceedings") must remain strictly secret and out of the public's knowledge. If DSU Article 17.10 required absolute confidentiality, then all of the steps within an appeal would have to remain out of the public knowledge, including the initial Notice of Appeal and the final Appellate Body report. However, the Notice of Appeal, including the contents setting out the legal basis for the appeal, is not confidential because DSU Article 16.4 requires this notice to be formally notified to the Dispute Settlement Body ("DSB"). The WTO Secretariat then circulates this notice to all WTO Members and makes it available to the public on its website. Furthermore, at the final stage of the Appellate Body proceedings, the Appellate Body's report is circulated to all WTO Members prior to its adoption. At the same time as its circulation to the WTO Members, the Secretariat makes the Appellate Body report public on its website.

In addition, WTO practice demonstrates that the confidentiality of Appellate Body proceedings is not absolute. Appellate Body reports, which are made public, include whole sections of the parties' written submissions as well as the parties' arguments made during the oral hearing. In other words, many aspects of the Appellate Body's proceedings during the substantive portion of the appellate process are actually revealed to the public and are not subject to confidentiality under Article 17.10 of the DSU.

It is indeed appropriate that, as reflected in WTO practice, the scope of the term "confidential" in DSU Article 17.10 has been interpreted restrictively, to allow various stages of the appellate proceedings to be disclosed to the public. In addition, the fact that the initial and the final stages of the Appellate Body proceedings are disclosed to the public demonstrates that the confidentiality requirement of DSU Article 17.10 does not cover all stages of the appeal. DSU Article 17.10 cannot, therefore, be a bar to an open oral hearing before the Appellate Body.

DSU Article 18.2

A further consideration in relation to the meaning and context of DSU Article 17.10 is that DSU Article 18.2 permits parties to reveal their positions to the public. DSU Article 18.2 states:

Written submissions to the panel or the Appellate Body shall be treated as confidential, but shall be made available to the parties to the dispute. *Nothing in this Understanding shall preclude a party to a dispute from disclosing statements of its own positions to the public.* Members shall treat as confidential information submitted by another Member to the panel or the Appellate Body which that Member has designated as confidential. A party to a dispute shall also, upon request of a Member, *provide a non-confidential summary of the information contained in its written submissions that could be disclosed to the public.* [emphasis added]

Although DSU Article 18.2 states that written submissions to a panel or the Appellate Body are to be treated as confidential, this does not mean that all information contained therein must remain confidential at all times. First, a party is free, at all times, to disclose its own position in a dispute. Second, a party can be required to provide a non-confidential summary of its submission for public disclosure. Finally, as noted above, panels routinely disclose the parties' positions in their reports. The Panel in this dispute rightly noted:

The Panel notes also that Article 18.2 provides that "Members shall treat as confidential information submitted by another Member to the Panel or the Appellate Body which that Member has designated as confidential." We consider that this sentence clarifies the scope of the confidentiality requirement which applies to the Panel and to Members, and that panels have to keep confidential only the information that has been designated as confidential or which has otherwise not been disclosed to the public. Any other interpretation would imply a double standard, whereby panels would have to treat as confidential information which a WTO Member does not have to treat as confidential.

Members may, and in fact many do, openly publish or otherwise provide copies of their submissions *and oral statements* before panels and the Appellate Body to the general public. This is an important right that Members of the WTO have in order to be able to publicly communicate not only their positions in a dispute but also the specific way in which they have advanced those positions. Furthermore, it demonstrates that information regarding substantive aspects of the appellate proceedings, including written versions of oral statements, may be provided to the public contemporaneously with the hearings.

The Panel in this dispute addressed the issue of an open hearing resulting in a panel disclosing a party's position to the public. It concluded that disclosure of a party's position did not prevent a panel from holding open hearings:

The Panel is mindful that, by asking questions or seeking clarifications during the hearings with respect to written submissions of the parties, it may have itself "disclosed" the content of such submissions. However, the Panel notes that at all times the parties retained the right to request that specific statements of theirs not be broadcasted so as to remain confidential and that, in this case, the parties had made their written submissions public.

The Panel in this case went on to address the implications of the requests by the parties to a dispute for open hearings:

> The Panel also notes that, by requesting that the Panel hold hearings open to public observation, the parties to this dispute have implicitly accepted that their arguments be public, with the exception of those they would identify as confidential.

The same considerations and reasoning apply to the oral hearing at the appellate level.

As was recognized by the Panel, all three parties, by making a unanimous request for a public oral hearing in these two parallel appeals, are relying on their right, stated in DSU Article 18.2, to make their oral arguments public. DSU Article 18.2 does not prescribe a specific means of making a party's arguments public. Therefore, it does not matter whether such a right is exercised after the oral hearing or contemporaneously with the oral hearing.

Rules of Conduct

The Rules of Conduct do not present an obstacle to the Appellate Body holding open hearings. The relevant provision of the Rules of Conduct is Article VII.1, which provides that:

> Each covered person shall at all times maintain the confidentiality of dispute settlement deliberations and proceedings together with any information identified by a party as confidential. No covered person shall at any time use such information acquired during such deliberations and proceedings to gain personal advantage or advantage for others.

This provision requires confidentiality on the part of the members of the Appellate Body (as well as the Secretariat staff serving the Appellate Body) during its deliberations and proceedings. However, when Article VII is read with Article II.1 of the Rules of Conduct, it is evident that these Rules do not modify the rights and obligations of Members under the DSU nor the rules and procedures therein. Article II.1 provides that:

> Each person covered by these Rules ... shall be independent and impartial, shall avoid direct or indirect conflicts of interest and shall respect the confidentiality of proceedings of bodies pursuant to the dispute settlement mechanism, so that through the observance of such standards of conduct the integrity and impartiality of that mechanism are preserved. These Rules shall in no way modify the rights and obligations of Members under the DSU nor the rules and procedures therein.

The Panel in this dispute considered this issue in its determination of open hearings, and noted that "such confidentiality obligation on the covered persons during the panel proceedings is applicable to the extent not inconsistent with the DSU provisions" and that "[i]n [that] case, the parties [had] waived their right to confidentiality and requested open hearings." The Panel decided to adjust its working procedures and ruled that "[t]he Rules of Conduct should not be construed in a manner that would restrict the rights of Members under the DSU." Specifically, the Panel concluded "that Article VII [of the Rules of Conduct] [did] not prevent the Panel from holding hearings open to observation by the public."

The same considerations and reasoning of the Panel are applicable to the appellate proceedings.

Rule 16(1) of the Working Procedures

The Appellate Body has discretion under Rule 16(1) of the Working Procedures to respond favourably to the unanimous request by all three parties to the appeal in this case and to open the oral hearing to the public. Rule 16(1) states that "[i]n the interests of fairness and orderly procedure in the conduct of an appeal, where a procedural question arises that is not covered by these Rules, a division may adopt an appropriate procedure for the purposes of that appeal only, provided that it is not inconsistent with the DSU, the other covered agreements and these Rules." Since the DSU does not present an obstacle to an open oral hearing and there is no provision in the Working Procedures precluding or even addressing an open hearing, the Appellate Body may adopt such procedures for the purpose of this case that are consistent, *inter alia,* with the DSU, such as those which the Panel, or other panels that have agreed to hold open hearings, has adopted.

The request made by all three parties in these two parallel appeals is a stand-alone request. It does not affect the rights of the disputing parties in other appeals to request or not request open hearings as they see fit. Opening the oral hearing to the public in the present case would be consistent with the nature of the WTO as a Member-driven organization.

Moreover, practical arrangements can be made to accommodate any third participant who may not want to disclose its statements in the course of the hearing. Canada will elaborate below on such practical arrangements that could and should be made.

WTO Agreement on Subsidies and Countervailing Measures (SCM Agreement) — United States — Measures Affecting Trade in Large Civil Aircraft

Executive Summary of the Oral Statement of Canada, 25 January 2008:

1. Canada's oral statement will focus on three questions. First, whether "purchases of services" are covered by the list of financial contributions in Article 1 of the SCM Agreement. Second, whether the U.S. Department of Commerce's Advanced Technology Program, or ATP, is or is not specific under Article 2 of the SCM Agreement. Third, whether Article 6.3 provides an exhaustive or illustrative list of the forms of serious prejudice.

The Purchase of Services

2. This dispute is the first under the SCM Agreement to address the question of whether a government's purchase of a service can be the subject of a claim under Parts II, III or V of the SCM Agreement. In Canada's view, the answer is that it cannot be — provided, however, that the transaction in question is a legitimate purchase of a service and is not simply designed to camouflage a financial contribution that would otherwise fall within the list of financial contributions set out in Article 1.1(a)(1) of the SCM Agreement.

3. In responding to the Panel's questions, Canada agreed with the United States that the list of financial contributions in Article 1.1(a)(1) is an exhaustive list of the kinds of financial contributions that can give rise to a subsidy. Canada also agreed that the omission of any reference to the purchase of services from this list must be given some meaning — particularly since the purchase of services was included in the list in some of the negotiating texts before being dropped from the final text.

4. Brazil agrees that WTO Members should not be able to circumvent the disciplines of the SCM Agreement by mischaracterizing financial contributions as the purchase of services, Brazil disagrees that government purchases of services are excluded from the scope of Article 1.1(a)(1). Brazil speculates that the reference at the end of Article

1.1(a)(1)(iii) to the purchase of goods but not to the purchase of services may have been intended to maintain a separation between subsidization of goods and subsidization of services. Brazil argues that the omission of the purchase of services from the list of financial contributions in Article 1.1(a)(1) was not intended to create any carve-out from subsidy disciplines. Brazil has not provided any evidence that would support this view.

5. Furthermore, Canada notes that Article XV of the GATS indicates that the regulation of subsidies in respect of services is a task for a future work programme of the Members. Even if the Panel were to find some merit to the argument that this omission in the SCM Agreement was made in deference to the GATS, the incomplete work programme of the Members in respect of service subsidies provides a good reason for the Panel to exercise caution in this area.

6. Australia and Brazil have both advanced the argument that Article 8.2(a), now lapsed, is proof that no carve-out from subsidy disciplines was intended for the "purchase of services." Article 8.2(a), when in force, provided that "assistance for research activities conducted by firms or by higher education or research establishments on a contract basis with firms" was non-actionable if certain conditions were met.

7. In Canada's view, Article 8.2(a) does not establish that legitimate purchases of services were intended to come within the scope of the SCM Agreement. Article 8.2(a) only demonstrates that financial assistance for research activities provided on a contract basis was never categorically excluded from the SCM Agreement. However, "assistance" is not synonymous with "purchase," and it is the purchase of services that was omitted from Article 1.

8. Government assistance for a firm to conduct research, or for a firm to contract for research with another institution does not entail the purchase or acquisition of a service by the government. Rather, it is the firm that is conducting or contracting for the research. Therefore, the recognition in lapsed Article 8.2(a) that government assistance for a firm's research activities would be subject to the SCM Agreement, unless certain conditions were met, in no way conflicts with an exclusion in Article 1 for the purchase of services by a government.

9. Canada does agree with Australia and Brazil that the omission from Article 1 of any reference to the purchase of services should be interpreted narrowly to avoid circumvention of subsidy disciplines. A Member's characterization of one of its own transactions as a purchase of a

service should not preclude a panel from determining the true nature of the transaction at issue. This is a question of fact to be weighed by a panel and must be done on a case by case basis.

10. Notwithstanding the anti-circumvention concern, the silence in Article 1.1 respecting the purchase of services should be understood to exclude from the SCM Agreement those cases where a government can prove that it has genuinely purchased services, and that it is not attempting to disguise a direct transfer of funds or other form of financial contribution within the scope of Article 1.1 (a) (1) as the purchase of a service.

Specificity of the Advanced Technology Program (ATP)

1. The EC based its claim that the U.S. Department of Commerce's Advanced Technology Program, or ATP was specific to certain enterprises within the meaning of Article 2.1 (a) of the SCM Agreement on the assertion that ATP was explicitly limited by regulation to only those companies that perform research into "high risk, high pay-off emerging and enabling technologies." It also based its claim on the fact that eight particular ATP projects are limited to funding companies involved in manufacturing composite and metal structures, electrical components and improving logistics for manufacturing and supply chains.

2. Canada disputed these claims in its first written submission. Our concern with the EC approach is threefold: First, the universe of companies and industries involved in "emerging and enabling technologies" is extraordinarily diverse. Second, there is no commonality among the users of the ATP by reference to the products they produce. Third, it is inappropriate to assess the specificity of the ATP as a whole by reference to an unrepresentative sample of eight projects.

3. Australia has a somewhat different appreciation of the EC's specificity claim in respect of ATP. Australia's submission appears to assume that the EC is challenging each of the eight ATP projects at issue as "specific" under Article 2 regardless of whether the overall ATP is specific. Australia has suggested that the Panel look to the panel report in *Japan – DRAMS* for guidance in assessing the specificity of individual transactions under the ATP.

4. Australia may well be correct that the EC would like a specificity finding for each of the eight projects at issue regardless of whether ATP is specific. However, Canada is not aware of such a request from the EC. If the EC meant to make this request, Canada would have expected to see legal arguments in the EC's first submission as to why it was appropriate to do a transaction-level specificity analysis in the case of

these ATP projects. We would urge the Panel to avoid even considering such an analysis given the absence of an explicit request.

5. The specificity analysis is properly conducted at the program level when the subsidies at issue are provided under a generally available support program. If subsidies are provided under such programs in compliance with program guidelines, they are not specific within the meaning of Article 2.1. We note that the EC does not appear to have alleged that the eight ATP projects highlighted in its submission deviated in any way from standard ATP guidelines.

6. The *Japan – DRAMS* panel is the first and only panel to have assessed subsidies provided pursuant to a general framework program at the transaction level rather than at the program level. In that case, the *Japan – DRAMS* panel acknowledged that, as a general matter, individual transactions that flow from generally available support programs would not be "specific" within the meaning of Article 2.1 if they do not deviate from standard program guidelines. Even if the EC had requested a specificity analysis at the individual ATP project level, Canada does not believe such an analysis would be appropriate given our view that specificity should be assessed on a program basis. If, in any event, the Panel is considering such an analysis, Canada does not share Australia's view that the *Japan – DRAMS* panel report provides appropriate guidance.

7. The *Japan – DRAMS* panel found that an individual transaction would be "specific," "if it resulted from a framework programme whose normal operation (1) does not generally result in financial contributions, and (2) does not predetermine the terms on which any resultant financial contributions might be provided, but rather requires (a) conscious decisions as to whether or not to provide the financial contribution (to one applicant or another), and (b) conscious decisions as to how the terms of the financial contribution should be tailored to the needs of the recipient company." The *Japan – DRAMS* test does not provide appropriate guidance in this dispute for two reasons.

8. First, criterion 1 simply does not apply. Neither the EC nor the United States has claimed that ATP "does not generally result in financial contributions." Quite the contrary. Second, the *Japan – DRAMS* panel seems to have assumed, in criterion two, that a generally available support program can only be considered non-specific if the support it provides is granted automatically and without conscious decisions. This "no conscious decision" approach sets the bar too high to serve as a model for this or any other panel.

9. Article 2 of the SCM Agreement is intended to provide Members with real guidance as to what types of subsidy are or are not actionable under the SCM Agreement. It is rare for a government to establish a general support program that provides subsidies without any conscious decisions at all. A careful reading of Article 2 does not support the *Japan – DRAMS* panel's apparent view that the granting of a subsidy must be automatic, without conscious decisions, to qualify as non-specific. Article 2.1 (b) provides that specificity shall not exist for subsidies where eligibility is automatic based on objective criteria. Critically, however, Article 2.1 (b) refers only to automatic eligibility. The actual granting of support need not be automatic and unconscious.

10. To claim otherwise would be to ignore Article 2.1 (c), which presupposes some element of discretion in the granting of Article 2.1 (b) subsidies. Article 2.1 (c) sets out the *de facto* specificity test. It provides that programs that qualify as non-specific under Article 2.1 (b) may nonetheless be found *de facto* specific if discretion has been exercised inappropriately by the granting authority in the decision to grant a subsidy. Since the exercise of some discretion is assumed, it follows that not every exercise of discretion is disqualifying.

11. It is not necessary to find that the granting of a subsidy is automatic or unconscious to qualify a program as non-specific under Article 2. It is only necessary that the exercise of discretion not undermine a program's objective criteria governing eligibility for, and the amount of, a subsidy. Because the *Japan – DRAMS* panel overstated the relevant standard in its proposed test, it does not provide helpful guidance in this dispute.

12. As a final comment on ATP, Canada does not agree with Australia that the Panel should assess ATP using the *de facto* specificity criteria in Article 2.1 (c). The EC framed their specificity claim in respect to ATP under Article 2.1 (a) alone.

Serious Prejudice

1. In their responses to the Panel question on the issue of whether Article 6.3 of the SCM Agreement sets out an exhaustive list of the possible forms of serious prejudice that may be challenged under Article 5(c), the third parties took divergent positions. Australia and Korea took the position that Article 6.3 was an exhaustive list. Japan took the position that a successful serious prejudice claim requires the demonstration of an effect under Article 6.3, but stopped short of declaring that Article 6.3 was exhaustive. Brazil and China took no position on the

issue. Canada took the position, consistent with the views expressed by the panel in *Korea – Commercial Vessels*, that Article 6.3 does not set out an exhaustive list.

2. This divergence of views is not surprising since the relevant provisions appear to pull in different directions. Footnote 13 to Article 5(c) clarifies that the term serious prejudice is used in the SCM Agreement in the same sense as it is used in Article XVI of GATT and includes threat of serious prejudice. Article 5(c) brings into the SCM Agreement a broad understanding of serious prejudice forged over decades of GATT practice. Article 6.2, on the other hand, establishes that serious prejudice cannot be established if none of the effects listed in Article 6.3 exist. This suggests that Article 6.3 was an exhaustive list of the forms of serious prejudice. The language of Article 6.3 itself is open-ended, and refers the reader back to Article 5(c).

3. However, as discussed in Canada's written response to the Panel on this subject, there is a way to interpret these provisions harmoniously. Article 5(c) imports into the SCM an unbroken chain of meaning for the term serious prejudice, encompassing the concepts set out in Article 6.3, but also recognizing the possibility of additional forms of serious prejudice closely linked to those core concepts. Article 6.2 serves to indicate that Article 6.3 is a gatekeeper provision in that serious prejudice cannot be established if none of the core concepts in Article 6.3 are present. Article 6.3 itself is drafted broadly enough to permit the possibility of un-enumerated forms of serious prejudice, while providing particular guidance on the core concepts that must be established to found a serious prejudice claim. Treating Article 6.3 as the gatekeeper provision provides a mechanism for giving Article 6.3 its due weight without denying the legacy of 60 years of GATT/WTO practice that has adopted a broad understanding of the serious prejudice concept.

4. Canada is sympathetic to the concern raised by Australia that the possibility of undefined forms of serious prejudice could be seen as leaving a panel with no guidance for its examination of such a complaint. However, in Canada's view, such guidance is available in the jurisprudence of the GATT. This jurisprudence suggests that forms of serious prejudice that are not enumerated in Article 6.3 must have a real and substantial link to the core concepts that are set out in Article 6.3.

5. There is a practical reason why Article 6.3 may have been structured as a gatekeeper provision for the serious prejudice concept, while permitting a panel to consider the possibility of other forms of serious

prejudice once one of the effects in Article 6.3 is established. WTO dispute settlement is a limited resource. There is a logic to requiring a specific threshold before a Member can access the dispute settlement system to make a claim of serious prejudice. However, once a Member has reached that threshold, the benefits of an effective resolution of the dispute between the Parties may justify giving a panel some latitude to acknowledge other forms of serious prejudice that go beyond the confines of Article 6.3.

6. This type of gatekeeper structure is not unique in the WTO Agreements. An analogy can be made to Article 17.4 in the Antidumping Agreement that requires a complainant to delay its recourse to dispute settlement in respect to an anti-dumping investigation until an administering authority has taken one of three types of measures: a provisional measure of significant impact, a final action to levy definitive anti-dumping duties or acceptance of price undertakings.

7. The Appellate Body in *Guatemala – Cement* found that Article 17.4 of the AD Agreement meant that a panel request in respect of an anti-dumping investigation must specifically identify one of the required types of measures in order to give a panel jurisdiction over a dispute. However, as the Appellate Body clarified in *U.S. — 1916 Act,* once a Member has identified one of the three types of gatekeeper measures in its panel request, it may challenge the consistency of any preceding action taken by an investigating authority in the course of an anti-dumping investigation.

8. A gatekeeper interpretation of Article 6.3 in the SCM Agreement is justifiable for the same reasons that the Appellate Body gave for justifying the structure of Article 17.4 of the SCM Agreement in *U.S. – 1916 Act.* It avoids excessive use of dispute settlement, while seeking to provide a full and effective resolution to those disputes that do require formal dispute settlement.

Other Issues

1. Canada's first written submission also dealt with three other issues. First, the infrastructure challenged by the EC in this dispute that is generally available for use by the public. This infrastructure is not a financial contribution under Article 1 because availability for public use is a hallmark of general infrastructure. Second, the retention of intellectual property rights by a DOD or NASA contractor. This cannot constitute the provision of a good under Article 1 because property retained is not property provided. Third, the State of Washington tax

incentives are not export contingent within the meaning of Article 3 because eligibility for these incentives was tied to building an assembly facility. Eligibility was not tied to the export of the 787.

INTERNATIONAL ENVIRONMENTAL LAW

Licensing under the International Boundary Waters Treaty Act (IBWTA)

In a communication dated 23 October 2007, the Legal Bureau wrote:

We need to consider if a proposed irrigation project drawing water from and returning water to Lake Erie requires a license under the IBWTA. Must such a consideration include an analysis of the magnitude of the project and if it affects "levels and flows" [*sic*].

We were also referred to the following document which was an analysis prepared at the time of the introduction of our amendments to the IBWTA: http://dsp-psd.pwgsc.gc.ca/Collection-R/LoPBdP/LS/371/c6-e.htm.

I refer to it because its analysis segues nicely into my own interpretation of both the Boundary Waters Treaty (BWT) and the IBWTA. In particular, it has this particular discussion respecting the issuance of licenses:

Traditional uses, such as agricultural and industrial withdrawals that remained within the basin, would not be covered by the licensing system. The above provision would more effectively implement Article III of the *Boundary Waters Treaty.*

Now what the author David Johansen was getting at was the linked facts that Section 11(1) was intended to implement Article III of the BWT and that Article, while setting out the jurisdiction of the IJC to authorize various uses, obstructions or diversions, also provided that "such provisions [are not] intended to interfere with the ordinary use of such waters for domestic and sanitary purposes," that same exception being explicitly made clear by Section 11(2).

In my earlier opinion on irrigation and the Niagara River, I noted the IJC's own figures suggest that irrigation has been a considerable and uncontroversial use of the waters of the Great Lakes:

The 2002 IJC *Report on the Protection of the Waters of the Great Lakes* notes that consumptive use from the Great Lakes was approximately 4,270 cfs: Canada responsible for 33% and the US 67 %, although per capita use is roughly equal between the two countries. Of consumptive uses, the highest was irrigation (29% of the total). There are no figures of consumptive use as divided between the lakes above the falls and Lake Ontario below, but Tom McCauley from the IJC suggested a ballpark figure for consumptive use as a percentage of water flow at Niagara would be about 1.6%.

The logic of the report is that irrigation has already been well-established as a use for Great Lakes waters, and hence must be considered as a "domestic and sanitary purpose." Furthermore, as neither the IJC nor the two governments have sought to authorize or by special agreement permit withdrawals for irrigation, authorization for withdrawals is outside of the IJC's jurisdiction and remains within the undiluted exclusive jurisdiction of the United States and Canada (and their respective states and provinces), as the case may be. As Section 11 was intended to provide legal enforceability to the IJC Article III approvals, though a parallel system of the issuance of licenses and that its issuance of licences was not intended to cover "the ordinary use of waters for domestic or sanitary purposes" [*sic*], no license is necessary for withdrawals for typical municipal, industrial and agricultural uses regardless of whether they do or do not impact the natural level or flow of boundary waters, that latter being an entirely separate consideration. As the total consumptive use for all withdrawals from the Upper Great Lakes totals 1.6%, it is also implausible that any given new project factually would have anything more than a minimal impact.

Conclusion:

In my view, it is not necessary to inquire into whether the proposed project may affect levels and flows so long as we are convinced that it intends the ordinary use of waters for domestic and sanitary purposes, those purposes in my view necessarily including irrigation. In [*sic*] these facts, a license under the IBWTA is not required.

Shared Natural Resources

In response to the International Law Commission's questionnaire on state practice on shared natural resources, the Government of Canada provided the following observations, dated 20 March 2008:

Canada thanks the International Law Commission for its questionnaire on State practice on shared natural resources, distributed by the Secretariat of the United Nations by a note verbale LA/COD/45, dated 15 October 2007.

Canada would take this opportunity to provide the following few observations, followed by the response to the questionnaire:

A number of bilateral maritime delimitation agreements concluded internationally incorporate provisions regarding the possibility of finding a natural resource that straddles across [*sic*] a maritime boundary, as well as a procedure to be followed in the event of such a discovery. The obligations generally focus firstly on advising the other state that a transboundary field has been discovered, and secondly, on the necessity for states to seek to reach an agreement on some form of joint exploitation.

For the purposes of the present questionnaire however, Canada will focus on the *only* agreement that Canada has entered into relating to the exploration and exploitation of transboundary hydrocarbons, entitled the *Agreement between the Government of Canada and the Government of the French Republic relating to the Exploration and Exploitation of Transboundary Hydrocarbon Fields.* The *Agreement* governs the apportion [*sic*] of the reserves found in transboundary hydrocarbon fields straddling the maritime boundary between Canada and France.

Canada would like to note that providing answers to the Commission should not be interpreted as either agreement or acquiesce [*sic*] by Canada for the Commission to provide a set of draft articles on a subject matter, such as oil and gas, that is essentially bilateral in nature, highly technical, politically sensitive, encompasses diverse regional situations and requires a case-by-case solution.

Canada considers that any matters relating to offshore boundary delimitation should not be considered by the Commission.

QUESTION 1: Do you have any agreement(s), arrangement(s) or practice with your neighbouring State(s) regarding the exploration and exploitation of transboundary oil and gas resources or for any other cooperation for such oil or gas? Such agreements or arrangements should include, as appropriate, maritime boundary delimitation agreements, as well as unitization and joint development agreements or other arrangements.

Pursuant to the decision of the Arbitral Tribunal in the *Case Concerning the Delimitation of Maritime Areas between Canada and the French Republic of June 10, 1992,* Saint-Pierre-et-Miquelon only has jurisdiction over a narrow strip of maritime area that is 10 nautical miles in width and extends 200 nautical miles south of the islands, which is completely enclosed by Canada's exclusive economic zone.

As the 1992 Arbitral Tribunal definitively decided the permanent boundary between Canada and France (for Saint-Pierre-et-Miquelon) for all purposes, a need was felt for an agreement triggered by the possibility of petroleum fields straddling the Canadian-French boundary. Canada approached France in 1998 to suggest that both sides enter into a treaty to manage possible transboundary fields. Finally, in 2005, Canada and France signed an agreement to provide a management regime for hydrocarbon exploration and exploitation offshore Newfoundland, Nova Scotia and Collectivité de Saint-Pierre-et-Miquelon. The *Agreement between the Government of Canada and the Government of the French Republic relating to the*

Exploration and Exploitation of Transboundary Hydrocarbon Fields, containing 21 Articles and 6 Annexes, recognizes the need for a common approach to oil and gas management to ensure the conservation and management of hydrocarbon resources that straddle the maritime boundary, to apportion between the two countries the reserves found in transboundary fields and to promote safety and the protection of the environment.

The *Agreement* acknowledges that nothing is to prejudice or restrict the sovereignty or jurisdiction of either Party over their respective internal waters and territorial seas, or the exercise of sovereign rights, in accordance with international law, over their respective exclusive economic zones.

The *Agreement* was inspired by the 1976 Markham Agreement, which was used as a "framework" arrangement adapted to Canadian and French respective circumstances.

The *Agreement* has yet to enter into force, and Canada would therefore refrain from disclosing it at this time. That said, the following paragraphs will provide a general outline of the *Agreement.*

QUESTION 2: Are there any joint bodies, mechanisms or partnerships (public or private) involving exploration, exploitation or management of the transboundary oil or gas?

The *Agreement* envisages the creation of a joint Technical Working Group to examine technical issues that arise from the implementation of the *Agreement* or from any Exploitation Agreement (explained in Question 3), including information related to the regional geological setting and geological basins as well as any question related to the implementation of the Development Plan or Benefits Plan (explained in Question 3). The Working Group must allow the Parties to review information related to the regional geological setting and, at the request of one Party, meet to facilitate approval of a Development Plan or Benefits Plan by reviewing concerns or issues regarding such a plan or a preliminary version of it. The Unit Operator is normally to be invited to all or part of any such meetings.

The Working Group consists of individuals nominated by each Party (two Chairs and two Secretaries), as well as other persons which either Party considers should be present at any Working Group meeting.

QUESTION 3: If the answer to question 1 is yes, please answer the following questions on the content of the agreements or arrangements and regarding the practice:

(a) *Are there any specific principles, arrangements or understandings regarding allocation or appropriation of oil and gas, or other forms of cooperation?*

The *Agreement* is a framework arrangement which does not contemplate a single unified regime but instead is a means to facilitate the requirements of French and Canadian legislation to be fulfilled for any transboundary field [*sic*].

In addition to reiterating the definitive boundary between Canada and France for all purposes, the *Agreement*'s preamble recognizes proportionality based on respective share of reserves in a transboundary field as the basis of the *Agreement* and highlights the importance of good oil field practice, safety, protection of the environment and the conservation of resources in transboundary fields.

The following are the main features of the *Agreement* regarding allocation or appropriation of oil and gas, or other forms of cooperation:

- The *Agreement* envisages provision of information with a more comprehensive exchange once accumulation has been determined to be transboundary. The *Agreement* imposes a requirement for information exchange upon the drilling of any well within 10 nautical miles of the maritime boundary. Information exchanged cannot be further disclosed without the consent of the Party that provided it.

- The *Agreement* speaks about the notice to given [*sic*] to the other Party, with evidence, if data shows that accumulation is (or is not) transboundary. If the other Party is not convinced, that Party can: 1) request meeting of Technical Working Group; and/or 2) send the disagreement to a single expert for determination in accordance with procedure and timelines for using the expert outlined in the *Agreement*.

- The *Agreement* provides for determination and redetermination of hydrocarbon reserves in a transboundary field. Indeed, the Unit Operator is to submit specific proposals on which both Parties shall agree upon in a specific time frame. Should such an agreement not be reached, the disagreement is submitted to a single expert for determination, in accordance with procedure and timelines for using the expert outlined in the *Agreement*.

- Once agreement is reached or the expert determines that the accumulation is transboundary, the Parties must delineate an area for the exchange of comprehensive data. If a Holder of Mineral Titles, meaning a person or firm to whom one of the Parties has granted a subsisting mineral title or exclusive right to explore or exploit hydrocarbons in a particular area, is interested in production from the transboundary field, the Parties will start negotiation of an Exploitation Agreement. The Exploitation Agreement is defined as any agreement entered into between Canada and the French Republic in respect of a transboundary field.

- The *Agreement* envisages a separate Exploitation Agreement for each transboundary field. It imposes a time limit for the parties to enter into Exploitation Agreement since any commercial production in a transboundary field cannot commence until an Exploitation Agreement has been concluded. If the Parties are unable to conclude an Exploitation Agreement within a particular timeframe, either party may refer the finalization of the Exploitation Agreement to arbitration, in accordance with the arbitration procedure outlined in the *Agreement*. This provides certainty as to timeframes in which the Exploitation Agreement will be finalized.

- The *Agreement* requires that Mineral Title Holders conclude a Unitization Agreement that provides for: (a) combining respective rights in the transboundary field's hydrocarbon resources; (b) sharing costs and benefits; (c) operating the field as a single unit. The Unitization Agreement is subject to the prior written approval of both Parties. This is an operator-led confidential arrangement which incorporates provisions to ensure that, in the event of a conflict between the Unitization Agreement and the Exploitation Agreement, the terms of the Exploitation Agreement shall prevail.

- Exploitation of any transboundary field is to be undertaken in accordance with the Exploitation Agreement and the Unitization Agreement.

- A Development Plan and a Benefits Plan must be agreed upon for a particular transboundary field before production can commence. A Development Plan sets out in detail the approach to the development and operation of the transboundary field while a Benefits Plan ensures that, in developing the transboundary field, and subject to all applicable domestic and international legal obligations of the Parties, best efforts are made to ensure economic benefits are shared between Canada and France, taking into account the apportionment of hydrocarbon reserves as between the Parties. Upon submission from the Unit Operator, parties have a specific timeframe in which to approve a Development Plan and a Benefits Plan. Should the time period expire, either party can refer the matter to arbitration, in accordance with the arbitration procedure outlined in the *Agreement*.

- The Parties must ensure that exploitation of transboundary field [*sic*] is in accordance with approved Development and Benefits Plans.

- The *Agreement* provides that all disputes are to be resolved through negotiation except for disputes which are specifically to be submitted to an expert or to arbitration.

(b) Are there any arrangements or understandings or is there any practice regarding prevention and control of pollution or regarding other environmental concerns, including mitigation of accidents?

The *Agreement* contains provisions that address environmental considerations, including transboundary environmental impact assessments. The

Agreement provides for Parties to conclude arrangements or agreements dealing with search and rescue, marine pollution and transboundary impact environmental assessments. For instance, the Parties are required to enter into a side arrangement on implementation of the *Convention on Environmental Impact Assessment in a Transboundary Context,* Espoo, 1991 (available at: http://www.unece.org/env/eia/documents/legaltexts/conventiontextenglish.pdf).

The Parties have a duty to take all necessary measures to minimize adverse impact on the environment. The *Agreement* imposes a requirement for Mineral Title Holders to provide security, as determined by the Party having jurisdiction over them, to meet environmental damage caused by any hydrocarbon exploration or exploitation activity.

On a separate note, environmental considerations are part of the approval process for oil and gas activities under Canada's domestic legislation, and this would be true in the case of transboundary fields as well.

QUESTION 4: Please provide any further comments or information, including legislation, judicial decisions, which you consider to be relevant or useful to the Commission in the consideration of issues regarding oil and gas.

The Canadian area covered by the *Agreement* is governed domestically by the Canada-Newfoundland Offshore Petroleum Board, an independent body that regulates the offshore area on behalf of Canada and the Province of Newfoundland and Labrador. The pertinent legislation is the *Canada-Newfoundland Atlantic Accord Implementation Act* (available at: http://laws.justice.gc.ca/en/C-7.5/index.html).

In addition, there is a small transboundary area that could be subject to the *Canada-Nova Scotia Offshore Petroleum Resources Accord Implementation Act* (available at: http://www.cnsopb.ns.ca/generalinfo/pdf/ProvAct.pdf). Both pieces of legislation provide for the management of offshore oil and gas resources on behalf of the federal and provincial governments.

QUESTION 5: Are there any aspects in this area that may benefit from further elaboration in the context of the Commission's work?

While there is a growing demand for rules governing the use of shared or transboundary natural resources, Canada believes that the oil and gas issue is essentially bilateral in nature, highly technical and politically sensitive and encompasses diverse regional situations. As such, it should be left for resolution by negotiation between States involved. As a result, Canada is not persuaded by the need for the Commission to develop any framework or model agreement(s) or arrangement(s) or draft articles on oil and gas.

However, Canada does see the benefit of the Commission outlining elements that could guide states when negotiating agreements on partition of oil and gas. A "template of elements" on the practice applicable, including a review of the existing agreements and state practice, along with an identification of common principles and features, best practices and lessons learned, would be very useful, not only to Canada, but also internationally. Such a template could separate (a) circumstances where there is no delimitation agreement in place; and (b) circumstances where a delimitation agreement is already in place.

Should the Commission proceed with the consideration of the topic of shared oil and gas resources, Canada would not endorse the Commission examining matters relating to offshore boundary delimitation.

Transboundary Air Pollution

In a communication dated 7 May 2008, the Legal Bureau wrote:

You asked if the Canadian government had the authority or option of filing a notification under Article V the 1991 Air Quality Agreement in respect of the proposed expansion of the Shell Canada Refinery in Sarnia Ontario. The Article provides as follows:

> Canada-U.S. Air Quality Agreement
> Transboundary Notification Requirement Text
> Article V — Assessment, Notification, and Mitigation

1. Each Party shall, as appropriate and as required by its laws, regulations and policies, assess those proposed actions, activities and projects within the area under its jurisdiction that, if carried out, would be likely to cause significant transboundary air pollution, including consideration of appropriate mitigation measures.

2. Each Party shall notify the other Party concerning a proposed action, activity or project subject to assessment under paragraph 1 as early as practicable in advance of a decision concerning such action, activity or project and shall consult with the other Party at its request in accordance with Article XI.

3. In addition, each Party shall, at the request of the other Party, consult in accordance with Article XI concerning any continuing actions, activities or projects that may be causing significant transboundary air pollution, as well as concerning changes to its laws, regulation or policies that, if carried out, would be likely to affect significantly transboundary air pollution.

4. Consultations pursuant to paragraphs 2 and 3 concerning actions, activities or projects that would be likely to cause or may be causing

significant transboundary air pollution shall include consideration of
appropriate mitigation measures.

5. Each Party shall, as appropriate, take measures to avoid or mitigate the
potential risk posed by actions, activities or projects that would be
likely to cause or may be causing significant transboundary air pollution.

6. If either Party becomes aware of an air pollution problem that is of joint
concern and requires an immediate response, it shall notify and consult
the other Party forthwith.

The obligation to notify is triggered, in the context of the Shell refinery,
by a project "that, if carried out, would be likely to cause significant transboundary air pollution" and is "within the area under its jurisdiction" and
finally is also either "subject to assessment ... under its laws, regulations or
policies" or has become "an air pollution problem."

I am not aware of how significant the expansion of the refinery is, but
would assume for purposes of the Treaty that it would meet the test of
significant transboundary air pollution. But given the overall content of
the article, I do not see paragraph 6 as applicable when the "air pollution
problem" does not yet exist.

Therefore, we need to consider if our ability to notify in this case can be
derived from paragraph 2. That leads by a straight road to the question:
Is the project subject to assessment by Canadian laws, regulations or policies? I understand that the Refinery is undergoing a provincial environmental assessment and Shell Canada has actually engaged US state and
federal authorities, presumably respecting any potential impact to the air
quality of the state of Michigan. It is not obvious that assessment by a
provincial authority would be sufficient since the assessment must be triggered by the laws, regulations and policies "of the Party" (i.e. the Canadian
or US federal governments).

From my conversation with you, it is not clear if Shell also has to obtain
any federal permit for its expansion to go ahead (under the *Canadian
Environmental Assessment Act, 1999* or other federal statute) or if a federal
environmental assessment is required under the *Canadian Environmental
Assessment Act.* That you raise this issue is also suggestive that the federal
government may not also to [*sic*] have created a *policy* of making notifica-
tions where a project is capable of transboundary air pollution but is
outside of federal assessment or permitting authority.

Nevertheless, in my view the federal government may properly bring the
project to the formal attention of US authorities in accordance with the
procedures and forms established under the 1991 Air Quality Agreement.
Under the international law doctrine *sic utere tuo ut alienum non laedas* (use

your own property so as not to injure the property of another), states have a responsibility to prevent activities in their own territory that will cause pollution in another. This is partially enshrined in Article IV of the Boundary Waters Treaty ("boundary waters ... shall not be polluted on either side to the injury of health or property on the other"). The federal government has also given itself a nascent authority to combat transboundary air and water pollution under Divisions 6 and 7 of the *Canadian Environmental Protection Act,* including where the source involved is not a "federal source." As Canada has an international law responsibility to prevent transboundary pollution and has given itself a limited legislative authority and federal jurisdiction under the CEPA, all these together are sufficient to justify notification under the terms of the Air Quality Agreement even if no federal decision-making or permitting is present.

Ninth Conference of the Parties to the UN Convention on Biological Diversity, Bonn, 19–30 May 2008

In a report prepared in June 2008, the Legal Bureau wrote:

The Ninth Meeting of the Conference of the Parties (COP 9) to the UN Convention on Biological Diversity (CBD) was held in Bonn, Germany from 19–30 May 2008. The meeting had an extensive agenda concerning ongoing and new issues confronting the biological diversity of the planet. However, the central issue at the meeting was the continuing negotiation of the international regime on access and benefit sharing for genetic resources (ABS).

The COP began on May 19 with the installation of the new Conference President, Mr. Sigmar Gabriel, the Minister of the Environment for the Federal Republic of Germany. The Parties managed to adopt 37 new decisions, but not without extensive discussions and some acrimony. There were greatly divergent views on key issues such as biofuels, protected areas, genetically modified trees, and ABS. The following is a brief description of some of the main issues on the agenda.

Access and Benefit Sharing of Genetic Resources (ABS)

ABS was dealt with in a separate working group, presided over by the two co-chairs of the normal intersessional ABS Working Group. Many Parties, including the EU and Canada, wanted to deal with the draft COP decision exclusively, which will be the road map for the upcoming two years, in order to complete the work on ABS in time for COP 10 in 2010. However the Like-Minded Mega-Diverse Countries (LMMC) and the G77 wanted to enter into discussions on the substantive elements of the regime, so there was confusion at the start.

The co-chairs decided to work on the draft COP decision first. They also produced their own view of a road map, which called for a mix of technical expert groups on specific issues under the ABS regime, interspersed with ABS Working Group meetings to negotiate the elements based on the results from the expert groups. The discussions then went on to the terms of reference for the technical expert meetings. After 27 hours of negotiation, the Parties agreed to hold three technical expert meetings on the following: compliance; concepts, terms, definitions and sectoral approaches; and traditional knowledge associated with genetic resources. The Parties also agreed to hold three ABS Working Group meetings during the same period.

Discussions on the draft COP decision continued long into the second week. The Parties agreed that the draft elements of the international regime coming out of the last Working Group meeting in Geneva would be the basis for future work, putting aside for good the heavily bracketed draft text annexed to the ABS decision from COP 7. However, the Parties continued to have difficulties on directions to the Working Group regarding the type of regime to be negotiated. Canada, Australia, New Zealand and Japan maintained that a decision on whether the regime would be legally binding or not was premature, given that the elements of the regime are still to be determined. The LMMC and G77 wanted the COP to instruct the ABS Working Group to negotiate a legally binding instrument.

A final attempt to bridge the gap was made when Canada met separately with the G77 and a revised text as was agreed to follows:

> Further instructs the Working Group on Access and Benefit-sharing, after the negotiation of comprehensive operational text at its seventh meeting, to start its eighth Working Group meeting by negotiating on nature, followed by clearly identifying the components of the international regime that should be addressed through legally binding measures, non-legally binding measures, or a mix of the two and to draft these provisions accordingly.

By Thursday of the final week, the ABS working group had achieved its objective of a clear road map and a clean decision for the next two years. The road map however is a costly and ambitious one. The next two years on ABS will be very intense, with three technical expert groups and three ABS Working Groups. The difficult negotiations will only become more so, as Parties have to finally make decisions on the scope, nature and elements of the regime. Given the rudimentary nature of many Parties' positions on both domestic and international ABS regimes, the next two years will be difficult.

With one day remaining, the co-chairs bowed to pressure from some Parties to open discussions on the substantive elements of the regime. However, after 8 hours of discussion, very little was achieved. The draft elements remain the same.

Agricultural Biodiversity and Biofuels

The debate over biofuels was accentuated by the ongoing worldwide food security crisis, and the accusation that biofuel production is one of the main causes. The African group, backed by many NGOs, called for the suspension of new biofuel measures, while the EU called for the drafting of industry guidelines and certification schemes to ensure sustainability. Brazil and others did not agree that biofuel production should be curtailed, noting their own industry is sustainably managed and contributes to development, food and energy security. They, and others, blamed perverse agricultural incentives in developed countries for the food crisis. There was also concern that the CBD is not the forum to deal with the biofuel issue.

The debate over biofuels went on into the late evening and early morning of the last day of the Conference. It took the involvement of several Ministers in a smaller working group to get agreed language. The final decision called on Parties to promote sustainable production and use of biofuels, with supportive measures, in order to promote benefits and minimize risks to biological diversity. The decision was a recognition of both the potential benefits, and the potential negative impacts, of biofuels on biological diversity.

At the final working group meeting, a portion of the Arab group (Qatar, Saudi Arabia, Kuwait, Libya), which had not taken part in the final smaller group meetings, would not agree to the text. This group argues that biofuels impact on the food security of the poor. Although they continued their objection to the final plenary, this group did not break consensus on the issue after pleas from the COP President to respect the agreed text as negotiated.

Forest Biological Diversity

Divergent views on Forest Biological Diversity revolved around the control of trade in illegal timber, references to climate change, and genetically modified trees. Brazil and Colombia did not want any text on the tracking of illegally harvested forest products, seeing this as an issue for national governments, not the CBD. The African group called for suspending the release of all genetically modified trees, while the EU, Brazil and others favoured referring to the "precautionary approach" in terms of release.

Canada sought compromise text on the issue of forest governance and genetically modified trees, and a programme of work which addresses the objectives of the Convention in all forest types. Canada also sought to ensure that incentive measures, such as payments for ecosystems services, are implemented consistent with other relevant international obligations (i.e. WTO rules etc).

The final decision calls for a strengthening of forest law and governance at all levels. The decision references climate change by calling on Parties to ensure that possible actions for reducing emissions from deforestation and forest degradation do not run counter to the Convention's objectives. In effect, this reverses the focus from doing something about climate change, to making sure that what Parties do does not negatively affect the biological diversity of forests.

Regarding genetically modified trees, the decision reaffirms the precautionary approach, as contained in the Rio Declaration, and urges Parties not to authorize the release of genetically modified trees until the completion of studies on containment, addressing long-term effects, and a thorough, science-based and transparent risk assessment. It also acknowledges the entitlement of Parties to suspend the release of genetically modified trees, in accordance with their domestic legalization. This last provision was needed to assuage those Parties calling for the suspension of any release.

Marine and Coastal Areas Biodiversity

Discussions under this agenda item centred on the annexes to the draft decision, which outline scientific criteria and guidance in the establishment of marine protected areas, and the matter of the appropriate forum for addressing questions on biological diversity beyond national jurisdiction. Canada supported the scientific criteria in the annexes, and also the central role of [the] United Nations Convention on the Law of the Sea (UNCLOS) on questions regarding biological diversity beyond national jurisdiction.

The final decision reaffirms that UNCLOS sets out the legal framework within which all activities in the oceans must be carried out, and that its integrity needs to be maintained. The decision adopted two of the annexes, on scientific criteria and guidance in the development of marine protected areas, but only "took note of" the annex which outlines four initial steps to be taken in the development of representative networks of marine protected areas. The Parties called upon the Executive Secretary to transmit the annexes to the relevant United Nations General Assembly process. The decision also establishes an expert workshop to provide guidance on the identification of areas beyond national jurisdiction that meet the scientific criteria in the annexes.

The other key marine topic was ocean fertilization, the controversial theory that fertilization of selected areas in the ocean could sequester carbon dioxide from the atmosphere. The science on this matter is far from clear. The EU, Norway and the African group called for a moratorium on ocean fertilization. Canada, Australia, New Zealand and others did not want to call for a moratorium, but did want to ensure that the precautionary approach is utilised. Canada also called on Parties to agree that the forum for dealing with the issue is the London Convention on the Prevention of Marine Pollution by Dumping of Wastes and Other Matter. A compromise was reached at a High-Level Ministerial meeting, comprised of the precautionary approach, and ensuring that ocean fertilization activities do not take place until there is an adequate scientific basis to justify it. Many parties described this as a "moratorium without the name."

Protected Areas

This agenda item featured two main themes: The establishment of protected areas and the rights of indigenous peoples in these areas, and the need for increased capacity building and financial resources in managing these areas in developing countries. The final decision calls upon Parties to improve and strengthen protected areas policies by recognizing indigenous and local community-based organisations, and to establish effective ways for their participation in protected areas governance. The decision also recognizes the role that innovative financing mechanisms can play, but that they do not replace public funding and development assistance.

Traditional Knowledge

Article 8(j) of the CBD, calling on Parties to respect and preserve traditional knowledge relevant for the conservation and sustainable use of biological diversity, has been the subject of a Working Group and extensive work programme since COP 5 in 2000. The work programme encompassed two phases, the first with 12 tasks, and the second with 17 tasks. Over the years, the Working Group has dealt with several of these tasks, but not all. Many of the tasks went beyond the scope of the Convention and dealt with rights-based issues such as the repatriation of cultural property and the examination of intellectual property rights.

When the Working Group tasks were adopted in 2000, there was no other forum dealing with indigenous issues of this type, which explains in part why the tasks were adopted. However, there are now other venues for rights-based discussions of indigenous issues, notably the UN Permanent Forum on Indigenous Issues which was established in 2002.

Canada sought at COP 9 to refocus the work programme of the 8(j) working group back to the Convention text, i.e., traditional knowledge relevant for the conservation and sustainable use of biological diversity. This was supported by Australia and New Zealand. The EU agreed in part that a review of the work programme should take place. Latin American countries, supported by their indigenous NGOs, wanted to continue with the existing work programme, including several tasks that have yet to be started.

After several days of tense discussions, a compromise was reached. The existing tasks will be continued and the remaining will be initiated, but only in terms of information gathering. Parties will also provide submissions on a future strategy for the 8(j) Working Group, focussed on the conservation and sustainable use of biological diversity by indigenous and local communities, and aiming at strengthening their role in decision making. A review of the work programme, based on the submissions, will take place at COP 10.

"Consistent" vs. "Take Note"

Economic incentives, as part of Government policies or legislation, were a common component in many decisions. Brazil, New Zealand and Canada, amongst others, required these incentives to be "consistent with other relevant international obligations." This was needed to guard against the use of incentive programmes to skirt international trade rules. However, Norway, Switzerland and the EU objected to "consistent with," arguing that this subordinated the CBD to other agreements. They wanted these measures only to "Take note of" other obligations. This issue, which cut across several decisions, was not resolved until 5 p.m. on the final day, when the following phrase was agreed upon: "Consistent and in harmony with the Convention and other relevant international obligations."

Conclusion

COP 9 had an agenda filled with some of the most pressing and contentious environmental issues of the day, and the Conference did manage to agree on decisions that advanced in small ways many critical issues. But like all CBD matters of late, the ABS issue drew both resources and attention away from other work. The extensive ABS work programme over the next two years, although much of it funded by pledged donations, will still draw resources away from the Secretariat and other matters. But when the ABS working group was advised that the number of meetings envisioned would require the reduction of work programmes for other issues, one G77 delegate commented: "Let all the other issues be put in the fridge, all we want is ABS."

INTERNATIONAL HUMANITARIAN LAW

Cluster Munitions

In a report written in June 2008, the Legal Bureau wrote:

In light of failure to achieve agreement to negotiate a Protocol addressing cluster munitions within the traditional disarmament framework of the Convention on Certain Conventional Weapons (CCW), in February 2007, Norway initiated a separate process to negotiate a new Convention addressing cluster munitions. Subsequent pre-negotiation conferences within the 'Oslo Process' were held in Lima in May 2007, in Vienna in December 2007 and in Wellington in February 2008. Formal negotiation of the new Convention on Cluster Munitions took place in Dublin, 19–30 May 2008. At the conclusion of the Dublin Diplomatic Conference on Cluster Munitions, 107 participating States, including Canada, unanimously adopted a strong Convention text that *inter alia:*

(i)   bans all cluster munitions, as defined in the Convention text;
(ii) sets specific deadlines for the destruction of stockpiles of cluster munitions (8 years) and clearance of contaminated areas (10 years);
(iii) makes provision for risk education for vulnerable populations and assistance for victims, their families and communities;
(iv) obligates States in a position to do so, to assist affected States to fulfill their responsibilities under the Convention; and
(v)   allows States to (continue to) engage effectively in combined military operations with States not party to the Convention ('interoperability').

In addition to the 107 participating States present in Dublin, there were 21 observer States, 8 international organizations including UN agencies, the International Committee of the Red Cross and the European Commission, and 250 non-governmental representatives from around the world under the umbrella of the Cluster Munitions Coalition (CMC). Canada was widely regarded as a key participant throughout the Oslo Process and was commended by the Dublin Conference President in his final press conference for having made a "substantial contribution to the outcome of the Conference." The US, Russia, India, Pakistan, Israel and China are among those States that did not participate in the Oslo Process.

The two most contentious issues during negotiations were 'interoperability,' i.e. the capacity to engage in combined military operations with States not-party to any new legal instrument, and the 'definition' of a cluster munition.

Interoperability: Canada, UK, Australia, Germany, France and Japan were among the most active States in ensuring that the Convention does not limit States Parties' capacity to engage effectively in combined military operations with States not party.

Definitions: The negotiated definition of cluster munitions incorporated criteria used to distinguish between weapons that are inaccurate and unreliable and, therefore, prone to indiscriminate effect, and those that have more sophisticated technical features that make them more accurate and reliable. It was agreed that for a weapon with more than one explosive sub-munition *not* to be defined as a cluster munition, it must have: (i) sub-munitions over 20kg (which are usually dispensed in small numbers with few sub-munitions and pose less humanitarian risk), and *all* of the following features; (ii) fewer than 10 sub-munitions; (iii) sub-munitions capable of engaging a specific target within a prescribed area (sensor fuzing) (iv) sub-munitions with electronic self-destruct capability, and (iv) electronic self-deactivation capability. In addition, the Convention prohibits sub-munitions that weigh less than 4kg, in order to prevent increased risk that could result from developments in the field of miniaturisation.

The Convention on Cluster Munitions has been widely heralded as a major success by participating States, UN agencies, international organizations and civil society.

Canadian Position: The Convention on Cluster Munitions strikes an appropriate balance between humanitarian and military considerations. It establishes a high humanitarian standard with respect to cluster munitions, while preserving Canadian Forces' capacity to continue to engage effectively with allies such as the US, which likely will not become party to this Convention in the foreseeable future.

Next Steps: Authority to ratify the Convention will be sought once domestic legislation and other measures have been put in place to ensure Canada's compliance with the Convention's provisions. This is expected to be in place by mid-2009. In addition, as previously instructed by Cabinet, Canadian officials will continue to pursue a complementary, legally binding Protocol addressing cluster munitions, within the Convention on Certain Conventional Weapons.

LAW OF THE SEA

Ilulissat Declaration — Arctic Ocean Conference, Ilulissat, Greenland, 27–29 May 2008

At the invitation of the Danish Minister for Foreign Affairs and the Premier of Greenland, representatives of the five coastal States bordering the Arctic Ocean — Canada, Denmark, Norway, the Russian Federation and the United States of America — met at the political level on 28 May 2008 in Ilulissat, Greenland, to hold discussions. They adopted the following declaration:

The Arctic Ocean stands at the threshold of significant changes. Climate change and the melting of ice have a potential impact on vulnerable ecosystems, the livelihoods of local inhabitants and indigenous communities, and the potential exploitation of natural resources.

By virtue of their sovereignty, sovereign rights and jurisdiction in large areas of the Arctic Ocean the five coastal states are in a unique position to address these possibilities and challenges. In this regard, we recall that an extensive international legal framework applies to the Arctic Ocean as discussed between our representatives at the meeting in Oslo on 15 and 16 October 2007 at the level of senior officials. Notably, the law of the sea provides for important rights and obligations concerning the delineation of the outer limits of the continental shelf, the protection of the marine environment, including ice-covered areas, freedom of navigation, marine scientific research, and other uses of the sea. We remain committed to this legal framework and to the orderly settlement of any possible overlapping claims.

This framework provides a solid foundation for responsible management by the five coastal States and other users of this Ocean through national implementation and application of relevant provisions. We therefore see no need to develop a new comprehensive international legal regime to govern the Arctic Ocean. We will keep abreast of the developments in the Arctic Ocean and continue to implement appropriate measures.

The Arctic Ocean is a unique ecosystem, which the five coastal states have a stewardship role in protecting. Experience has shown how shipping disasters and subsequent pollution of the marine environment may cause irreversible disturbance of the ecological balance and major harm to the livelihoods of local inhabitants and indigenous communities. We will take steps in accordance with international law both nationally and in cooperation among the five states and other interested parties to ensure the protection and preservation of the fragile marine environment of the Arctic Ocean. In this regard we intend to work together including through the International Maritime Organization to strengthen existing measures and develop new measures to improve the safety of maritime navigation and prevent or reduce the risk of ship-based pollution in the Arctic Ocean.

The increased use of Arctic waters for tourism, shipping, research and resource development also increases the risk of accidents and therefore the need to further strengthen search and rescue capabilities and capacity around the Arctic Ocean to ensure an appropriate response from states to any accident. Cooperation, including on the sharing of information, is a prerequisite for addressing these challenges. We will work to promote safety of life at sea in the Arctic Ocean, including through bilateral and multilateral arrangements between or among relevant states.

The five coastal states currently cooperate closely in the Arctic Ocean with each other and with other interested parties. This cooperation includes the collection of scientific data concerning the continental shelf, the protection of the marine environment and other scientific research. We will work to strengthen this cooperation, which is based on mutual trust and transparency, inter alia, through timely exchange of data and analyses.

The Arctic Council and other international fora, including the Barents Euro-Arctic Council, have already taken important steps on specific issues, for example with regard to safety of navigation, search and rescue, environmental monitoring and disaster response and scientific cooperation, which are relevant also to the Arctic Ocean. The five coastal states of the Arctic Ocean will continue to contribute actively to the work of the Arctic Council and other relevant international fora.

TREATIES

Parliamentary Tabling Procedures — Albacore Tuna Treaty

In a communication dated 4 April 2008, the Legal Bureau wrote:

During the course of our Wednesday teleconference, a number of issues were raised about the processes surrounding our new treaty-tabling policy and about which my views were requested in the context of the Albacore Tuna Treaty.

The gist of the treaty-tabling policy is that treaties, after signature but before ratification, will be tabled in Parliament for possible consideration. If none takes place in 21 sitting days, the Government is free to proceed to ratification, typically by an exchange of notes in the case of bilateral treaties such as the Albacore Tuna Treaty. An MC [memorandum to cabinet] setting out negotiation goals must precede the commencement of negotiations. A further MC follows the successful conclusion of negotiations (often marked by the initialling of a finalized text) which will authorize proceeding to signature. Two Orders in Council will respectively authorize certain named individuals to sign the treaty on behalf of Canada (typically Ministers and/or the Ambassador) and a final one, obtained after the Parliamentary tabling process is completed, will authorize ratification and entry into force.

A number of possible issues may arise in the upcoming meetings in Vancouver. It is not clear at this point, with the US position both fluid and unclear, whether we are looking at simply administrative improvements, data exchanges already contemplated by the treaty, a renegotiation of various elements of the Treaty or termination. Certainly amendment and renegotiation will be considered treaty actions and will be undertaken in accordance with our treaty tabling and associated processes that are described above.

One specific issue was raised with regard to our flexibility to take the fishing regime out of its current default status. At this point, we must look at the provisions of the Treaty as well as a revised Annex C (negotiated in 2002).

Article VII of the Albacore Tuna Treaty provides that the Annexes may be amended through an exchange of notes. That provision is somewhat ambiguous since an exchange of notes does not in all cases, constitute an agreement between the parties (i.e. a treaty action). However, the August 21 and September 10, 2002 Exchange of Notes themselves by their own language "[constituted] an *agreement* amending the Treaty on Pacific Coast Albacore Tuna Vessels and Port Privileges." This exchange of Notes was itself authorized by Order in Council 2002–1236, dated July 17, 2002. It is therefore plain from language and our practice that amendments to the Annexes are to be accomplished by treaty actions as authorized by our processes for treaty tabling and conclusion of treaties.

Now the 2002 Amendments to Annex C provide for an elaborate multi-year process limiting fishing by each party's vessels in the waters under the fishing jurisdiction of the other party. The provisions are spelled out for the first three years of the agreement in Annex C, sections 3–5; the provisions for these three years described collectively as the "limitation regime" (or the "Regime").

Section 7 of Annex 3 provides for a period of time in which the possibility of the parties negotiating a new limitation regime or "extension of this regime for one or more years" [*sic*]. However, if no agreement is reached on either possibility, Section 8 establishes a "default" regime in which we are now situated that continues "until a new agreement is reached and implemented." It is possible that the Parties might have extended the limitation regime as provided for in the 2002 Annex C without a treaty action, but having not taken any action, that option is not now open by the clear application of Section 8. Once in default, the opportunity of extending the limitation regime through section 7 is lost.

Therefore, Section 8 freezes the default regime in place until a new "agreement" is reached between the parties. To do so will require an amendment at least to Annex 3 and, in any event, a treaty action undertaken as I have described in paragraph 2 above. This is so whether a new regime is concluded or even if the Parties decided to substantively return to the third year of the regime concluded in the current Annex 3 and which Section 7 provided for a possible extension. When section 7 was active, this extension may not have required a treaty action; however, it is effectively inoperative now that the Parties have entered the default regime set out in Section 8.

Lastly, I should note that there is a limited scope in the government's treaty policy for exemptions from tabling in the case of urgency, national security and/or national interest, and finally if the House is not sitting for a prolonged period. That possible tabling exemption, however, still does not exempt the treaty from the MC/OIC process.

Treaty Interpretation — Canada-US Boundary Demarcation Treaty — International Boundary Commission — Tenure of Commissioners

In a communication dated 7 July 2007, the Legal Bureau wrote:

As requested, this is background for your proposed conversation:

> The International Boundary Commission was established by the 1908 Boundary Demarcation Treaty and consists of a Commissioner for each Party. The two Commissioners were given responsibilities to survey and mark the border and the 1925 Treaty added the requirement that they also maintain a clear "vista" on both sides of the land border.

Both Article IX of the 1908 Treaty and Article IV of the 1925 treaty deal with vacancies in identical terms:

> ... the Commissioners appointed ... shall continue to carry out the provisions of this Article, and, upon the death, resignation or other disability of either of them, the Party on whose side the vacancy occurs shall appoint an Expert Geographer or Surveyor as Commissioner, who shall have the same powers and duties ...

Counsel appears to take from these words a restriction on the ability of either side to dismiss their Commissioner for any reason other than "death, resignation or other disability." However, I would argue that the obligation in that section is two-fold and owed by each Party to the other: firstly, Commissioners should be competent and secondly, vacancies should be filled promptly. There is no obligation created of tenure vis à vis the Commissioners because the two treaties cannot by definition create obligations at international law that are owed by each Party to their own commissioners. Nor is there a discernable interest for either Party (outside of ensuring brevity and competence) in the process by which the other Party nominates and dismisses its commissioners.

But can it be argued that these Commissioners together constitute an international organization and, as such, the two governments owe to the international organization an obligation not to interfere with the status of the Commissioners? This may be possible in legal theory but not in respect of this particular Commission. There is no intent in either treaty that suggests that the Commissioners are anything other than representatives of their respective governments. Nor has subsequent practice by either government changed that status. First, the Boundary Commission is not listed under Canadian or US legislation as an international organization, nor have the respective Commissioners been given privileges and immunities. As a practical matter, the Canadian Commissioner serves only so long as he is also designated as the Surveyor General (see P.C. 1996–876 of June 13, 1996). If he leaves that post, he also is no longer the Boundary Commissioner. The US Commissioners, up to the appointment of Mr. Schornack, have routinely offered their resignations when there is a change in administration, as do other presidential appointees. As such, they serve at the pleasure of the incumbent President.

It is somewhat less clear if the Commission has status under the domestic law of either Canada or the US, though it is not likely. Canada's implementing legislation enables the Commission (members, officers, employees and agents) to enter into any property to gain access to the border. The Commission can also grant permission for works that encroach on the 10 foot vista on the Canadian side and remove these works. However prosecutions for the construction of unauthorized works, or obstruction or defacing or altering border monuments are carried out by the Crown. Moreover, in the 1976 case, *Burnell v. The International Joint Commission*, the Federal Court held that the IJC did not have corporate personality at domestic law, and hence the ability to sue or be sued. There is nothing in the enabling legislation for the IBC to distinguish it from the *ratio* of the *Burnell* case.

There is considerable confusion to the extent which [*sic*] the Commission acts as a single entity or as separate Canadian and US Sections. For example, permission to construct a work that encroaches in the vista has been signed traditionally by both Commissioners but interestingly in the Leu case, only Mr. Schornack did so. The current Canadian Commissioner is not of the view that he should sign instruments respecting property in the US but consults extensively on the policies related to encroachments and individual cases as they arise. However, litigation against either of the Commission sections (putting aside whether the

Commission or either section has a legal personality) has been handled quite separately by each section. The *Qually* case in Canada was defended by a Justice lawyer in the Department's Vancouver office with no involvement by the US Section. Similarly, the *Leu* case was initially defended by a US Justice Department Attorney until Mr. Schornack took the fateful step of engaging his own counsel.

Parliamentary Declarations in 2007–8 / Déclarations parlementaires en 2007–8

compiled by / préparé par

ALEXANDRA LOGVIN

A STATEMENTS MADE ON THE INTRODUCTION OF LEGISLATION /
DÉCLARATIONS SUR L'INTRODUCTION DE LA LÉGISLATION

1 *Bill S-2: An Act to Amend the Canada-United States Tax
Convention Act, 1984 / Loi S-2: Loi modifiant la Loi de 1984
sur la Convention Canada — États-Unis en matière d'impôts*[1]

Mr. Ted Menzies (Parliamentary Secretary to the Minister of Finance):

Bill S-2 ... proposes to implement a fifth protocol to the tax treaty that we
signed [last September] with the United States ...

With the signing of this treaty ... we have strengthened the bonds of economic cooperation between our two countries. In doing so, we are modern-
izing a long-standing instrument for the betterment of individuals, families
and businesses on both sides of the border, including manufacturers.

This fifth update or protocol of the Canada-U.S. tax treaty will stimulate
further trade and investment between our two countries ... In today's
highly competitive global economy we need to continually explore ways
to grow, to expand and to compete. To that end, further improving and
refining our relationship with our neighbours to the south is essential.

Canada is a trading nation. The United States is by far our largest trading partner. Through NAFTA we have come together to create a competitive, open and connected marketplace, the largest marketplace in the world
... The bill ... represents the final step in this country in implementing that

---

Alexandra Logvin is a graduate of the University of Ottawa, LL.M. (2003) and LL.B.
(2009) programs. She is currently with Heenan Blaikie law offices in Ottawa.

[1] Editor's note: Bill S-2 was introduced in Senate by Hon. David Tkachuk (Acting
Deputy Leader of the Government) on October 18, 2007. The Bill received Royal
Assent on December 14, 2007; S.C. 2007, c. 32.

agreement. It also needs to be ratified by the United States before it comes into force.

This protocol will make our tax systems more efficient through initiatives such as eliminating withholding taxes on cross-border interest payments; extending treaty benefits to limited liability companies; allowing taxpayers to require that otherwise insoluble double tax issues be settled through arbitration; ensuring that there is no double taxation on immigrants' gains; giving mutual tax recognition of pension contributions; and clarifying how stock options are taxed ...

Within today's increasingly global economy and a more mobile population, tax treaties are increasingly important for Canada ... Canada's extensive tax treaty network consisting of over 85 countries includes our NAFTA partners, virtually all of the European Union and OECD countries, many members of the Commonwealth and the Francophonie, as well as other rapidly growing economies such as Brazil, Russia and China. However, Canada's tax treaty with the United States is unique, given our close relationship.

(House of Commons Debates, 26 November 2007, pp. 1350–52)
(Débats de la Chambre des Communes, le 26 novembre 2007, pp. 1350–52)

2   *Bill C-3: An Act to Amend the Immigration and Refugee Protection Act (Certificate and Special Advocate) and to Make a Consequential Amendment to Another Act / Loi C-3: Loi modifiant la Loi sur l'immigration et la protection des réfugiés (certificat et avocat spécial) et une autre loi en conséquence*[2]

Mr. Dave MacKenzie (Parliamentary Secretary to the Minister of Public Safety):

The *Immigration and Refugee Protection Act* ["the *IRPA*"] is important legislation as it sets out the rules by which people from across the globe may seek to come to Canada. As a country built by the imagination and dedication of many people, we truly understand the value of diversity within society. In fact, Canada is known internationally as a welcoming and compassionate country. Each year we admit more than 95 million people to our country, including 260,000 new immigrants.

While we encourage immigration, Canadians also insist on vigilance against people and organizations taking advantage of our generosity and openness. They pose a danger to our nation and, in some cases, to other

---

[2] Editor's note: Bill C-3 was introduced in the House of Commons by Hon. Stockwell Day (the minister of public safety) on 22 October 2007. The bill received Royal Assent on 14 February 2008: S.C. 2008, c. 3.

nations around the world. They have committed serious crimes, or violated human rights or even taken part in terrorism. These people are not welcome in Canada.

Canadians do not want our doors to be open to people who endanger our national security and the safety of our communities. The government wants what Canadians want. That is why we are unwavering in our determination to safeguard national security and to protect the safety and security of the Canadian public ...

The *IRPA* provides the government with a process to remove non-Canadian citizens who are inadmissible on grounds of security, violating human or international rights, serious criminality or organized criminality. When classified information is involved in support of the inadmissibility decision, the security certificate process may be used.

It has been in place for over 20 years, but it has only been used 28 times since 1991 in the most serious cases. Certificates have been issued against spies, terrorists and extremists. They can never be used against a Canadian citizen, and that is a very important part.

The reason Bill C-3 has been introduced is quite straightforward. Security certificates are used to protect Canadians. They are a vital national security tool. At the same time, when we take steps to protect Canadians and national security, we must also take steps to respect civil liberties and protect our core values. These values include freedom, democracy, human rights and the rule of law.

In February the Supreme Court of Canada confirmed the use of security certificates generally.[3] However, it found aspects of the security certificate process that required legislative improvement. In addition, various parliamentary committees have recommended changes to the *IRPA*.

The government has moved swiftly and is taking action. Bill C-3 is an essential public safety tool that enables us to continue to prevent inadmissible persons from remaining in Canada while ensuring that there is better protection of the rights of individuals subject to security certificates.

Bill C-3 would set into law the Supreme Court of Canada's ruling on security certificates, and takes into consideration the recommendations of both Houses of Parliament ... What changes did the Supreme Court of Canada say were needed?

It found that the in camera *ex parte* proceedings do not provide the person named in the certificate a sufficient opportunity to know the case against him or her and challenge that case. The Court ruled that a process

---

3 Editor's note: *Charkaoui v. Canada (Citizenship and Immigration)*, [2007] 1 S.C.R. 350 (finding that the procedure of the *Immigration and Refugee Protection Act*, S.C. 2001, c. 27, for the judicial approval of security certificates is inconsistent with the *Charter*, and hence of no force or effect).

had to be put in place to better protect the interests of individuals subject to security certificates. It also gave foreign nationals the same rights as permanent residents in the context of detention reviews. In that light, it stated that these reviews should occur 48 hours after arrest and at least once every six months thereafter for both foreign nationals and permanent residents. These changes took effect immediately upon the court ruling.

The special advocate function will help ensure fair court proceedings and provide a means to challenge classified evidence ...

[T]he Supreme Court indicated that a mechanism was needed to better protect the interests of individuals subject to a security certificate. Bill C-3 sets out that mechanism by introducing a special advocate in the Federal Court process to determine the reasonableness of the certificate ... It is important to appreciate that this model would strengthen an important public safety tool by making it fairer to the person subject to the certificate process, while recognizing the need to prevent the disclosure of confidential public security information ...

Other legislative changes proposed in the bill include: concurrent reasonableness hearings and risk assessments to streamline the proceedings and security certificate cases; permitting appeals of the decision on the reasonableness of the certificate upon certification, which is consistent with how all appeals under the *IRPA* are dealt with; confirming that foreign nationals have the same detention review rights as permanent residents, as the Supreme Court did express in its decision; and transitional provisions to provide for the treatment of existing certificate cases under the new law in the most transparent and fairest manner possible ...

(*House of Commons Debates, 26 October 2007, pp. 459–61*)
(*Débats de la Chambre des Communes, le 26 octobre 2007, pp. 459–61*)

3   *Bill C-5: An Act Respecting Civil Liability and Compensation for Damage in Case of a Nuclear Incident / Loi C-5: Loi concernant la responsabilité civile et l'indemnisation des dommages en cas d'accident nucléaire*[4]

Hon. Gary Lunn (Minister of Natural Resources):

This legislation will replace the 1976 *Nuclear Liability Act*.[5] The purpose of this bill is to update the insurance framework that governs the nuclear industry and protects the interests of Canadians.

---

4   Editor's note: Bill C-5 was introduced in the House of Commons by Hon. Loyola Hearn (for the minister of natural resources) on 26 October 2007.

5   Editor's note: Canada's *Nuclear Liability Act*, R.S.C. 1985, c. N-28, was passed in 1970 and came into force in 1976, after an agreement was struck with a group

The history of nuclear energy in Canada goes back some 75 years. For the past 30 years, nuclear power has been an important part of Canada's energy mix. Currently, there are 22 nuclear reactors in Canada providing over 15% of our electricity needs. These reactors are located in three provinces: Ontario, Québec and New Brunswick ...

The responsibility of providing an insurance framework for the nuclear industry falls under federal jurisdiction ... Canada addressed this responsibility with the enactment of the *Nuclear Liability Act* of 1976. This legislation established a comprehensive insurance framework for injury and damage that would arise in the very unlikely event of an incident ... Both this earlier legislation and Bill C-5 ... apply to nuclear power plants, nuclear research reactors, fuel fabrication facilities and facilities for managing used nuclear fuel.

The framework established under the legislation of 1976 is based on the principles of absolute and exclusive liability of the operator, mandatory insurance, and limitations in time and amount. These principles are common to the nuclear legislation in most other countries such as the United States, France, the United Kingdom, Germany and Japan. These principles are just as relevant today as they were when the original act was introduced ...

Although the basic principles underlying the existing legislation and insurance framework remain valid, the act is over 30 years old. It needs updating to keep pace with international norms and standards.

The bill is intended to strengthen and modernize Canada's nuclear insurance framework through an all-encompassing package of amendments. It would put Canada in line with the internationally accepted compensation levels and it would clarify definitions for compensation: what is covered and the process for claiming compensation ...

Canada's nuclear compensation and liability legislation should be consistent with international nuclear liability regimes. This requirement goes beyond financial issues related to liability and compensation. It extends to definitions of what constitutes a "nuclear incident" and what is a "compensable damage," and so on.

Consistency brings Canada a broader national benefit. It makes it possible for us to subscribe to international conventions we do not already belong to should we wish to subscribe in the future. There are two international

---

now known as the Nuclear Insurance Association of Canada to provide the liability coverage. (Canada, Senate Standing Committee on Energy, the Environment and Natural Resources, "Canada's Nuclear Reactors, How Much Safety is Enough" (Interim Report), June 2001, at 29).

conventions that establish compensation limits: the Paris-Brussels regime[6] and the Vienna Convention.[7]

In the case of the Paris-Brussels regime, the maximum compensation is approximately $500 million Canadian, available through a three tier combination of operator, public and member state funds.

The Vienna Convention sets the minimum liability limit at approximately $500 million Canadian. The operator's liability can be set at $250 million by national legislation, provided public funds make up the difference to $500 million.

Although Canada is not a party to either of these conventions, it has participated in them in order to monitor international third party liability trends and other issues of interest, such as definitions of nuclear incidents and the extension of time limits for death and injury claims. It encourages investment in Canada. It also levels the playing field for Canadian nuclear companies interested in contracts abroad. These companies may be inhibited from bidding because of uncertainty about liability and compensation issues.

Consistency is important for a more fundamental reason. It demonstrates Canadian solidarity with other nations on issues of safety and liability. And, as a major user and exporter of nuclear power technology, Canada must uphold its reputation for uncompromising excellence, responsibility and accountability.

The key change proposed in Bill C-5 is an increase in the amount of the operator's liability from $75 million to $650 million. The current limit of $75 million is outdated and unrealistically low. Changing this limit balances the duty for operators to provide compensation without burdening them with huge costs for unrealistic insurance amounts. This increase would put Canada on par with most western nuclear countries.

It is important also that what is proposed in this bill is consistent with international conventions, not only on financial issues but also in regard to definitions of what constitutes an incident, what qualifies for compensation

---

6 Editor's note: OECD Paris Convention on Third Party Liability in the Field of Nuclear Energy, 29 July 1960 (entered into force 1 April 1968) ["Paris Convention"]; Brussels Supplementary Convention on Nuclear Third Party Liability, 31 January 1963 (entered into force 4 December 1974) ["Brussels Supplementary Convention"]; at <http://www.nea.fr/html/law/legal-documents.html#agreements>. As of 20 April 2009, Canada was not a signatory to these conventions.

7 Editor's note: International Atomic Energy Agency, Vienna Convention on Civil Liability for Nuclear Damage, 21 May 1963 (entered into force 12 November 1977); at <http://www.iaea.org/Publications/Documents/Conventions/liability. html>. As of 20 April 2009, Canada was not a signatory to this convention.

and so on. These enhancements would establish a level playing field for Canadian nuclear companies that will welcome the certainty of operating in a country that acknowledges international conventions ...

Canada is a leader in the production of radioisotopes, an element produced by nuclear reactions. Isotopes have been put to dozens of uses that have improved agriculture and made industry more efficient. Their most significant applications, however, have been in medicine where they have performed wonders in the prevention, diagnosis and treatment of disease.

It is a little known fact that Canada supplies 50% of the world's reactor-produced radioisotopes for nuclear medicine and is used for the treatment of cancer and in over 12 million diagnostic tests each and every year. I believe the medical isotopes produced here in Canada are used in some 76,000 medical procedures each day.

The most widely used radioisotope is produced at AECL's Chalk River laboratory and prepared at MDS Nordion's facility in Ottawa. The short half life of this radioisotope requires efficient transportation around the world. Shipments are on airplanes within 24 hours of the material coming out of the reactor. Globally, an estimated 76,000 people benefit from these diagnostic procedures each day.

The improvements provided by Bill C-5 are now necessary for Canada to remain a leading player in the nuclear industry.

(*House of Commons Debates, 30 October 2007, pp. 536–38*)
(*Débats de la Chambre des Communes, le 30 octobre 2007, pp. 536–38*)

4   Bill C-8: An Act to Amend the Canada Transportation Act (Railway Transportation) / Loi C-8: Loi modifiant la Loi sur les transports au Canada (transport ferroviaire)[8]

Mr. Brian Jean (Parliamentary Secretary to the Minister of Transport, Infrastructure and Communities):

Bill C-8 is the third and final bill amending the Canada Transportation Act. Two previous bills, one on international bridges and tunnels and other provisions of the act, were passed in the previous session.

The *Canada Transportation Act* is the legislative framework that, among other things, regulates the economic activities of the railways, in particular services and rates. While the act generally relies on market forces, there are a number of shipper protection provisions to address the potential abuse of market power by the railways.

---

[8] Editor's note: Bill C-8 was introduced in the House of Commons by Hon. Lawrence Cannon (minister of transport, infrastructure and communities) on 29 October 2007. The bill received Royal Assent on 28 February 2008: S.C. 2008, c. 5.

... Bill C-8 is extremely important to shippers ... [It] strengthens the shippers' provisions in the act. By doing so, it improves shippers' leverage when they negotiate with railways, which contribute to better service and lower rates.

... The bill is also important to railways and their investors because it gives them ... regulatory stability ... Providing regulatory stability will improve the investment climate and facilitate investments by the railways and their networks, equipment and crews so they can maintain and even expand their operations.

Canada is a trading nation and railways are important to our future growth in our economy. This in turn will help shippers compete in domestic, continental and international markets. It will also facilitate the achievement of government objectives to improve the transportation gateways in corridors in western, central and eastern Canada.

... The main provisions in the bill [include the following additions.] "[S]ubstantial commercial harm" [need not be shown by a complaining] shipper pursuing a regulatory remedy. It is a serious matter for a shipper to seek a remedy under the Canada Transportation Act ...

The bill also contains a new provision that would allow shippers to complain to the agency if they were not satisfied with railway charges [ancillary charges such as fees levied for cleaning or storing cars] or the conditions associated with such charges, other than freight rates. The principal remedy for freight rates will continue to be final offer arbitration.

[Finally,] the introduction of group final offer arbitration, commonly referred to as group FOA, [is] a major element of Bill C-8 ... The concept of commonality in terms of both the matter and the offer is essential to group final offer arbitration.

The bill ... has been [awaited] ... since 2001 ... The economy of Canadians is tightly woven with the success of our shipping from coast to coast.

(*House of Commons Debates, 10 December 2007, pp. 1967–69*)
(*Débats de la Chambre des Communes, le 10 décembre 2007, pp. 1967–69*)

5   *Bill C-9: An Act to Implement the Convention on the Settlement of Investment Disputes between States and Nationals of Other States (ICSID Convention) / Loi C-9: Loi de mise en œuvre de la Convention pour le règlement des différends relatifs aux investissements entre États et ressortissants d'autres États (Convention du CIRDI)*[9]

---

[9] Editor's note: Bill C-9 was introduced in the House of Commons by Hon. Maxime Bernier (minister of foreign affairs) on 29 October 2007. The bill received Royal Assent on 13 March 2008: S.C. 2008, c. 8.

Mr. Deepak Obhrai (Parliamentary Secretary to the Minister of Foreign Affairs):

The [ICSID] Convention [10] was sponsored by the World Bank to facilitate and increase the flow of international investment. It establishes rules under which investment disputes between states and nationals of other states may be resolved by means of conciliation or arbitration [investor-state conciliation or arbitration]. It also creates the international centre for the settlement of investment disputes, known as ICSID.

Bill C-9 implements the ICSID Convention for Canada. It deals with enforcement of ICSID awards for or against the federal government and foreign governments, including the constituent subdivisions designated by foreign governments ...

The distinguishing feature of ICSID, what makes it uniquely valuable, is the enforcement mechanism which this legislation will implement for Canada ... An arbitral award from any other arbitral body is subject to review by a domestic court before it can be enforced, but an ICSID award merely has to be presented to a domestic court with a request that the court enforce it. Under Bill C-9 the award must be recognized and, with this recognition, enforcement mechanisms become available immediately.

In the great majority of cases the losing party in an arbitration will pay the award of an arbitral tribunal without the need for the successful party to take any enforcement proceedings. The same is true for investor-state arbitration.

In Canada, arbitral awards, including investor-state arbitral awards, are currently enforced pursuant to the New York *Convention on the Recognition and Enforcement of Foreign Arbitral Awards*.[11] The New York Convention permits a limited review of an arbitral award by domestic courts. It allows a court to refuse to enforce an award if to do so would be contrary to the

---

10 Editor's note: Convention on the Settlement of Investment Disputes Between States and Nationals of Other States, 18 March 1965, 575 U.N.T.S. 159 (entered into force 14 October 1966).

11 Editor's note: Convention on the Recognition and Enforcement of Foreign Arbitral Awards, 10 June 1958, 330 U.N.T.S. 38, (1968) 7 I.L.M. 1046 (entered into force 7 June 1959). Canada is a party to the convention by ratification since 12 May 1986. When ratifying the convention, Canada declared that it would apply the convention only to differences arising out of legal relationships, whether contractual or not, that were considered commercial under the laws of Canada, except in the case of the province of Québec, where the law did not provide for such limitation. Canada also declared that it would apply the convention only to recognition and enforcement of awards made in the territory of another contracting state.

public policy. In addition, it permits a state to exclude certain subjects from the application of the Convention and thus from enforcement.

The ICSID provides a better enforcement mechanism. It does not permit a state to exclude from dispute settlement any matter which the state has consented to submit to arbitration. The ICSID awards are enforceable as if they were final decisions of a local court. This simple, efficient mechanism guarantees better protection for Canadian investors abroad.

Clause 8 of the bill authorizes any superior court in Canada to recognize and enforce awards as described in the bill. The Federal Court is a superior court. The Federal Court would have jurisdiction over awards involving the Government of Canada and awards involving foreign governments or their constituent subdivisions designated under the Convention.

In addition, the ICSID Convention provides explicitly that the ICSID awards are binding between the parties and once parties have agreed to arbitration they cannot seek remedy before another body, such as courts of justice.

Therefore, it is not open to a foreign tribunal to refuse to enforce an award on the basis that the ICSID arbitration tribunal has exceeded its jurisdiction or was not validly constituted. These kinds of issues can affect enforcement of awards other than ICSID awards, thereby delaying resolution of the dispute. The ICSID does not permit such dilatory tactics.

There are numerous reasons to support Canada's adherence to the Convention. It would provide additional protection for Canadian investors abroad by allowing them to have recourse to the ICSID arbitration in their contracts with foreign states. It would also allow investors of Canada and foreign investors in Canada to bring investment claims under the ICSID arbitral rules where such clauses are contained in our foreign investment protection agreements and free trade agreements.

To date, 143 states have ratified the ICSID Convention. The majority of our trading partners are parties to it, except for Mexico, India and Brazil. Ratifying the ICSID would bring Canadian policy into line with our OECD partners. In a survey conducted by the ICSID center in 2004, 79% of the respondents said that the ICSID played a vital role in their country's legal framework and 61% said that the ICSID membership had contributed to a positive investment climate.

International investment arbitration is growing in importance. The stock of Canadian direct investment abroad in 2005 increased to a record $469 billion. As a result of the globalization of investment, the number of investment disputes has greatly increased in the last five years ...

Canada already has numerous links with the ICSID. Provisions consenting to ICSID arbitration are commonly found in contracts between governments of other countries and Canadian investors. The NAFTA in Chapter

11, the Canada-Chile FTA and most of our bilateral foreign investment protection agreements known as FIPAs all provide for the ICSID as a dispute settlement option that can be chosen by an investor if both the state of the investor and the host state for the investment are party to the ICSID. However, Canada and Canadian investors cannot benefit from this choice if Canada is not a member.

(*House of Commons Debates, 28 January 2008, pp. 2246–48*)
(*Débats de la Chambre des Communes, le 28 janvier 2008, pp. 2246–48*)

6 Bill C-14: An Act to Amend the Canada Post Corporation Act / Loi C-14: Loi modifiant la Loi sur la Société canadienne des postes[12]

Mr. Brian Jean (Parliamentary Secretary to the Minister of Transport, Infrastructure and Communities):

[T]his ... government [is] committed to helping Canadian businesses compete internationally. In Canada we have businesses involved in what is called remailing ... [R]emailers collect mail destined for international locations from large, commercial mailers. The remailer, or consolidator, then ships the mail outside of Canada to another country, a country with cheaper postal rates, ideally, a country that has been designated as a developing country by the Universal Postal Union.

The Universal Postal Union is an agency of the United Nations. It has been in existence since the late 1800s ... The Universal Postal Union ... established a single postal territory for the exchange of international mail ... This means that when we are mailing a letter out of the country, we can buy an international stamp to put on that letter.

Canada Post would keep the revenue from that stamp, but it would be a different postal administration delivering that letter. It is that other postal administration that is incurring the bulk of the cost for the delivery of the letter.

Therefore, under the Universal Postal Union system of international exchange of mail, Canada Post would need to compensate the country of delivery. This compensation is called "a terminal due."

The Universal Postal Union has classified its member countries as industrialized or developed versus those that are developing ... This classification affects the rate of terminal due a country is eligible to receive from another country for mail it has received and the rate it is obliged to pay another country for mail that it sent out.

---

[12] Editor's note: Bill C-14 was introduced in the House of Commons by Hon. John Baird (Minister of Transport, Infrastructure and Communities) on 29 October 2007.

It is a complicated issue, but remailers do not have to pay terminal dues and are therefore able to offer lower rates than Canada Post. The Universal Postal Union also allows remailing. There are other countries that allow remailing. However, Canada does not.

A few years ago Canada Post took a large number of remailers to court. The courts have rightly ruled, in reading the exclusive privilege of Canada Post,[13] that remailing is an infringement upon Canada Post's exclusive jurisdiction ... [T]he only way to adjust this exclusive privilege is to amend the Act ...

[T]he purpose of Bill [C-14] is to remove all outgoing international mail from Canada Post's exclusive privilege. This would actually enable remailers to operate in Canada without infringing on Canada Post's exclusive privilege. They would no longer be breaking Canadian law ...

[T]he business model of remailers is to collect large volumes of mail from commercial companies ... They offer Canadian businesses lower postal rates. This actually reduces the cost of those companies['] goods or services to Canadians, to consumers, which is ultimately a good thing for Canadians ...

The proposed legislation is not intended to allow the mail to come back into Canada ... The addressee of the letter is to be in a foreign country. We are not touching domestic mail. The addressee is to be outside of Canada. Remailers that attempt to send mail back into Canada will still be in contravention of the exclusive privilege of Canada Post after amended.

We are not proposing to let other postal sector players put stamps on their mail while it is in Canada. Some other countries also allow an Extraterritorial Office of Exchange, which is defined by the Universal Postal Union as:

> an office or facility, operated by or in connection with a postal operator, outside its national territory, on the territory of another country. These are offices established by postal operators for commercial purposes to draw business in markets outside their own national territory.

If a stamp is put on a letter while in Canada, it should have a Canada Post approved stamp. If Canada is to allow these ... Extraterritorial Offices of Exchange, there should be a licensing regime associated with it. We are not going there with this proposal. We are not allowing other countries to operate postal outposts in Canada. We want to help Canadian businesses compete internationally and we are attempting to do that with this legislation.

---

13 Editor's note: *Canada Post Corporation Act*, R.S.C 1985, c. C-10, ss. 14, 15.

The government has studied the issue. Canada Post has told us that it estimates it [ha]s currently foregoing revenues in the amount of $50 million to $80 million a year. This is an estimate based on what it has seen as a trend in its revenue stream since new rules were put in place by the Universal Postal Union in 2001. Canada Post does not know for sure how much business it has been losing to remailers operating illegally in Canada.

On the other hand, the industry itself has made claims of it being millions of dollars to hundreds of millions of dollars ...

Should this legislation get enacted, Canada Post estimates losing another $45 million to $50 million a year, so there are financial implications. Its employees will worry that this is a first step toward privatization. Let us be clear. This government will not privatize Canada Post and there are no plans to do so.

Canada Post is a very large institution. It is one of the largest employers in Canada. It has one of the largest retail networks in Canada. It provides services to Canadians from coast to coast to coast ...

We are enhancing competition in the outbound international mail business to benefit Canadians, to benefit small businesses across this country, and we are going to continue to support Canadian businesses.

(*House of Commons Debates, 20 November 2007, pp. 1126–28*)
(*Débats de la Chambre des Communes, le 20 novembre 2007, pp. 1126–28*)

7 *Bill C-23: An Act to Amend the Canada Marine Act, the Canada Transportation Act, the Pilotage Act and Other Acts in Consequence / Loi C-23: Loi modifiant la Loi maritime du Canada, la Loi sur les transports au Canada, la Loi sur le pilotage et d'autres lois en conséquence*[14]

Mr. Brian Jean (Parliamentary Secretary to the Minister of Transport, Infrastructure and Communities):

[Bill C-23] will support a more commercial operating environment for Canada Port Authorities. This proposal is a two-pronged strategy. It includes amendments to the Canada Marine Act, which is ... the legislative framework that governs ports, in combination with several policy measures. It is an approach that is responsive to industry concerns. It recognizes the importance of promoting strategic investment and productivity improvements, yet protects port lands for future transportation needs.

---

[14] Editor's note: Bill C-23 was introduced in the House of Commons by Hon. Lawrence Cannon (Minister of Transport, Infrastructure and Communities) on 16 November 2007. The bill received Royal Assent on 18 June 2008: S.C. 2008, c. 21.

In relation to the Canada Port Authorities, the national marine policy of 1995 emphasized the elimination of overcapacity, promoted cost recovery, mandated self-sufficiency, and instituted a consistent governance structure for all major ports ... Th[e]se objectives ... have largely been met through the Canada Marine Act, the legislation that introduced a commercial approach to managing the national ports system and marine infrastructure. CPAs have undertaken their management responsibilities in a sound and fiscally responsible manner and ports are well managed today as a result of that.

Budget 2007 positioned modern transportation infrastructure as a core element of our agenda. We have launched a national gateway and corridor approach which recognizes that transportation systems that enable us to move goods and people with world class efficiency are absolutely essential to our future prosperity. Specific initiatives, such as the Asia-Pacific gateway and corridor initiative, the Ontario-Québec continental gateway and trade corridor, and the Atlantic gateway initiatives are tailored to geographic and transportation opportunities in specific regions. These initiatives recognize that transportation infrastructure investment requires the cooperation of many parties ... These include Canada Port Authorities, representatives from all modes, all levels of government, and private investors. Each of these initiatives will provide concrete measures to contribute to a more productive economy and a stronger competitive position for Canada in international trade ... We are a trading nation, and trade is very important to our future.

... While the national policy and the legislative framework governing ports are sound and have met their intended objectives overall, these instruments need to be modernized to ensure that our ports can respond and take advantage of the significant opportunities in the current global markets. We have all heard the stories of Asia and the emerging markets in that area. Canadians need to take advantage of that in order to continue to have the best quality of life in the world.

We must make sure that the Canada Marine Act is not a barrier either for ports or for the federal government [, but] [i]nstead ... supports the government's ability to make funding decisions in the public interest and to position Canada advantageously within changing global supply chains ...

The proposed legislative amendments are wide-ranging. They focus on the following areas. First is financial flexibility, which is so important even in private business. Second is port access to infrastructure funding, which is important for the future. Third is environmental sustainability, which is the cornerstone of this government's policy and is on every Canadian's mind. Fourth is access to security funding. We want to keep Canadians safe, because without that we will not enjoy any future. Fifth is a commercially-based borrowing regime for larger ports. Sixth is supporting amalgamations and governance at ports if required and if in Canadians' best interests. [These are] targeted policy initiatives focused on a modernized national marine policy as it relates to ports, a streamlined mechanism for borrowing, and flexibility in the management of port lands for the future.

(*House of Commons Debates, 27 September 2007, pp. 8113–14*)
(*Débats de la Chambre des Communes, le 27 septembre 2007, pp. 8113–14*)

8   Bill C-38: An Act to Permit the Resumption and Continuation of the Operation of the National Research Universal Reactor at Chalk River / Loi C-38: Loi permettant de reprendre et de continuer l'exploitation du réacteur national de recherche universel situé à Chalk River[15]

Hon. Tony Clement (Minister of Health and Minister for the Federal Economic Development Initiative for Northern Ontario):

The extended shutdown of the [National Research Universal] reactor has resulted in a worldwide shortage of medical isotopes. These isotopes are used by physicians for cancer and heart disease treatment and diagnostic tests. This shortage has resulted in an intolerable situation in which cancer and heart disease treatments and diagnostic tests are being delayed or cancelled.

We have learned that many institutions have very limited supplies and some centres, particularly in the Atlantic provinces and in smaller communities across the country, are focusing on emergency patients only ... This is obviously a very critical situation, and resuming medical isotope production is an immediate priority for Canada's government ...

We have been working with our officials as well as national and international partners to identify alternative sources of supply in other countries, other isotopes that can be applied and other diagnostic options which may be available. We have worked diligently toward resolving the situation, but the best solution for Canadians would be to make these necessary medical isotopes available as quickly as possible. For this, we need to get the reactor at Chalk River up and running again.

(*House of Commons Debates, 11 December 2007, pp. 2049–50*)
(*Débats de la Chambre des Communes, le 11 décembre 2007, pp. 2049–50*)

---

[15] Editor's note: Bill C-38 was introduced in the House of Commons by Hon. Peter Van Loan (for the Minister of Natural Resources) on 11 December 2007. The Bill received Royal Assent on 12 December 2007: S.C. 2007, c. 31.

9   *Bill C-39: An Act to Amend the Canada Grain Act, Chapter 22 of*
     the Statutes of Canada, 1998 and Chapter 25 of the Statutes of
     Canada, 2004 / Loi C-39: Loi modifiant la Loi sur les grains du
     Canada, le chapitre 22 des Lois du Canada (1998) et le chapitre 25
     des Lois du Canada (2004)[16]

Mr. David Anderson (Parliamentary Secretary to the Minister of
Natural Resources and for the Canadian Wheat Board):

When we look at the tremendous accomplishments of our agriculture and
agri-food industry over the last 100 years, the Canadian grain sector stands
out as a great success story. Today, Canadian wheat, barley and other grains
are known by our customers all over the world for their outstanding quality, consistency, cleanliness and great innovation.

Each and every year, Canada's grain industry contributes over $10 billion
to the Canadian economy. These dollars of course drive the economies of
both the rural and the urban areas of Canada. They create and sustain jobs
right through the grain production chain, from farm input suppliers to
elevators, to transporters and processors ...

Canada's quality assurance system for grain is a key competitive advantage
for our farmers. The measures proposed in these amendments will build
on that competitive advantage ...

Canada's grain industry is changing. The legislative tools required to
keep the industry competitive need to change accordingly ... We face the
prospect of numerous new and growing competitors in South America,
the former Soviet Union and other regions around the globe. We need to
respond to those challenges ...

[T]he changes that we are bringing forward [include the following
measures]. First, inward inspection and weighing of grains will no longer
be mandatory. These amendments remove the requirements for costly
mandatory services that do not clearly contribute to the bottom line of
farmers and the grain industry ...

Second, the Grain Commission will get out of the business of collecting
and holding security deposits from licensed elevators and grain dealers
under the producer payment security program. This program has cost a
lot of money, since security is working capital tied up with no return ...

In addition, the legislation proposes several additional amendments ...
[that] will improve the clarity of the application and the enforcement of

---

[16] Editor's note: Bill C-39 was introduced in the House of Commons by Hon. Gerry
Ritz (Minister of Agriculture and Agri-Food and Minister for the Canadian Wheat
Board) on 13 December 2007.

existing provisions[,] ... reflect current practices[,] ... enhance producer protection [and] ... eliminate some of the provisions that are no longer applicable or no longer used.

(House of Commons Debates, 1 February 2008, pp. 2484–87)
(Débats de la Chambre des Communes, le 1 février 2008, pp. 2484–87)

10 Bill C-44: An Act to Amend the Agricultural Marketing Programs Act / Loi C-44: Loi modifiant la Loi sur les programmes de commercialisation agricole[17]

Mr. Guy Lauzon (Parliamentary Secretary to the Minister of Agriculture and Agri-Food and for the Federal Economic Development Initiative for Northern Ontario):

The Canadian livestock industry is a powerful driver of Canada's economy. Meat products are Canada's largest food manufacturing industry with over $20 billion in sales. The red meat sector is the largest employer in the food industry. Red meats are a major driver of Canadian exports.

[T]he future looks very bright for our livestock producers. The demand for animal protein is increasing globally, specifically in China, India and other emerging markets. Canada has a rich and robust resource base in place to meet that demand ...

We have taken every opportunity to further secure, protect and enhance access to the U.S. and to other key markets for the Canadian livestock sector. We have engaged through a friend of the court submission to fight the latest bid by R-CALF to once again close the border.

Canada has regained full beef access to the Philippines. Partial access has been granted for Canadian beef exports to Japan, Hong Kong, Taiwan, Indonesia and Russia. We are actively seeking to resume beef exports to Korea and China.

As well, the government has an ambitious agenda for the negotiation of bilateral free trade agreements. Canada is currently negotiating free trade agreements with several important markets for our beef and pork exports, including Korea which is of particular importance. Other markets include Colombia, Peru, the Dominican Republic and the Caribbean ... [A]ccess to Canadian breeding stock has recently been restored to Mexico as well as to Barbados ... The world wants our beef and pork products, and we are more than ready to deliver.

---

[17] Editor's note: Bill C-44 was introduced in the House of Commons by Hon. Gerry Ritz (Minister of Agriculture and Agri-Food) on February 25, 2008. The bill received Royal Assent on 28 February 2008: S.C. 2008, c. 7.

The legislation we are proposing is one more sign of this government's commitment to take action for Canada's hard-working beef and pork producers. [U]nder these proposed amendments ... a producer will have easier access to up to $400,000 in cash advances under the advance payments program. In other words, producers will no longer have to use these payments from business risk management programs as security for the loans. Instead, they can use their livestock inventories ...

Second, we are proposing to expand the triggers for emergency advances under the payments program. We will do this by adding severe economic hardship as a trigger, along with the existing triggers of weather and natural disaster. For those severe economic hardship situations, the amendments will raise the maximum payout from $25,000 to $400,000, of which $100,000 is interest free.

We are taking action to offer livestock producers repayable advances which could total up to $3.3 billion. We are also taking steps directly targeted to the hog sector to help those producers who wish to restructure and rationalize in the face of these realities.

(House of Commons Debates, 25 February 2008, pp. 3274–76)
(Débats de la Chambre des Communes, le 25 février 2008, pp. 3274–76)

11   *Bill C-55: An Act to Implement the Free Trade Agreement between Canada and the States of the European Free Trade Association (Iceland, Liechtenstein, Norway, Switzerland), the Agreement on Agriculture between Canada and the Republic of Iceland, the Agreement on Agriculture between Canada and the Kingdom of Norway and the Agreement on Agriculture between Canada and the Swiss Confederation / Loi C-55: Loi portant mise en œuvre de l'Accord de libre-échange entre le Canada et les États de l'Association européenne de libre-échange (Islande, Liechtenstein, Norvège et Suisse), de l'Accord sur l'agriculture entre le Canada et la République d'Islande, de l'Accord sur l'agriculture entre le Canada et le Royaume de Norvège et de l'Accord sur l'agriculture entre le Canada et la Confédération suisse[18]*

Hon. David Emerson (Minister of International Trade and Minister for the Pacific Gateway and the Vancouver-Whistler Olympics, CPC):

[18] Editor's note: Bill C-55 was introduced in the House of Commons by Hon. David Emerson (Minister of International Trade and Minister for the Pacific Gateway and the Vancouver-Whistler Olympics) on 5 May 2008. The bill is currently before the International Trade Committee of Parliament.

Canada has been, is now and always will be a highly trade dependent country ... Trade is Canada's lifeblood ... Therefore, it is critically important that Canada continue to develop trade relationships such as the one we are debating today ...

This agreement is with four countries: Norway, Iceland, Liechtenstein and Switzerland. It is really a milestone in terms of Canadian trade policy. It is a milestone for a couple of reasons. First, it is really our first substantial trade agreement in over a decade. Canada had a small agreement with Costa Rica in 2001, but ... the trade and investment numbers between Canada and the EFTA countries are nearly 30 times that of our relationship with Costa Rica. [O]ur previous most significant trade agreement was back in 1996–97, when we made the deal with Chile ...

[T]he combined exports and imports between Canada and the EFTA countries were over $13 billion in 2007. That is ... higher than our trade with Korea. It is a very substantial volume of trade and has grown rapidly in recent years ...

[T]wo way investment flows between Canada and the EFTA countries are in the $28 billion range as of 2007 ... [T]his is a very significant trade deal. These countries are relatively wealthy. Their GDP per capita is among the highest in the industrial world. They are technologically advanced countries ... [I]t is our first trade deal with a European bloc or country in terms of our bilateral free trade agreements ...

Canada ... is anxious to deepen our economic relationship with the larger European Union. To have shown that we can establish a free trade deal of the kind we have done with EFTA puts us in a very strong position to maintain and improve momentum in terms of doing a deeper trade deal with the European Union ...

Before this agreement, we have had free trade agreements with five countries through four agreements ... That is not good enough for a trade dependent economy like Canada's, which is why Canada is actively negotiating free trade agreements ... with some 27 countries. When we broaden it to cover air bilaterals, investment agreements and free trade agreements, we are negotiating presently with something in the order of 100 countries ...

This agreement has the best provisions on shipbuilding of any free trade agreement that Canada has ever signed. The tariff phase-out is 15 years on the most sensitive products and 10 years on the next most sensitive products, and the first 3 years is a period during which there would be no tariff reductions at all ...

I would also note on the agriculture front that this agreement does exclude the supply managed sectors ... [W]e have committed not to put those on the table in our free trade negotiations with other countries, and we have not done so in this case ...

This [agreement] is part of the government's approach to enhancing Canadian competitiveness and to recognizing that while we have had the strongest economy among the group of eight, certainly fiscally and economically, we do see risks on the horizon. Everyone knows there are some serious economic adjustments taking place in the United States and the rest of world. We are aggressively moving to ensure that Canada's economic performance in the long term is enhanced, because Canada's economic performance will be driven by our trade performance.

(House of Commons Debates, 9 May 2008, pp. 5661–63)
(Débats de la Chambre des Communes, le 9 mai 2008, pp. 5661–63)

B   STATEMENTS IN RESPONSE TO QUESTIONS / DÉCLARATIONS
     EN RÉPONSE AUX QUESTIONS

1   Environment / Environnement

(a) The Arctic / Arctique

Mr. Chris Warkentin (Peace River):

[W]hat action our government is taking to protect our country's sovereignty, specifically in the north?

Hon. Maxime Bernier (Minister of Foreign Affairs):

As part of asserting sovereignty in the Arctic our government will complete a comprehensive mapping of Canada's Arctic seabed. Never before has this part of Canada's ocean floor been fully mapped. New Arctic patrol ships and expanded surveillance will guard Canada's far north and our Arctic Rangers will also be expanded.

(House of Commons Debates, 18 October 2007, p. 106)
(Débats de la Chambre des Communes, le 18 octobre 2007, p. 106)

Mr. Chris Warkentin (Peace River):

Last week the Minister of the Environment held bilateral meetings with the United States Secretary of the Interior, Dirk Kempthorne, [and] ... discussed a number of important cross-border issues, including the protection of ... polar bear[s]. [Could the Minister provide] ... the details of that meeting[?]

Hon. John Baird (Minister of the Environment):

Protecting the iconic polar bear is a concern for our government because Canada is home to two-thirds of the world's polar bear population ... Last week Environment Canada agreed to work with the U.S. Department of the Interior to protect the future of the polar bear. [The] meeting ended with a signed commitment between our two countries to work toward the long term protection of Canada's polar bears ... We are committed to protecting the polar bear.

(House of Commons Debates, 12 May 2008, p. 5731)
(Débats de la Chambre des Communes, le 12 mai 2008, p. 5731)

Mr. Rob Clarke (Desnethé — Missinippi — Churchill River):

What further action [has] the government ... taken today to defend Canada's Arctic?

Hon. Gary Lunn (Minister of Natural Resources):

Today the Minister of Indian Affairs and Northern Development and myself have ... commit[ted] that will bring new research and information about our Arctic. We are investing $20 million in providing the scientific basis to demonstrate Canada's rights in the Arctic. As well, my colleague announced $5.2 million for projects to increase awareness of the Arctic research for Canadians.

(House of Commons Debates, 14 May 2008, p. 5851)
(Débats de la Chambre des Communes, le 14 mai 2008, p. 5851)

(b) Clean waters / Eaux dépolluées

Mr. Bruce Stanton (Simcoe North):

In budget 2007, our government took action to improve the water we drink, clean polluted waters, help maintain water levels in the Great Lakes, protect our ecosystems, and ensure the sustainability of our fish resources ... [L]ast week ... the government ... announced $12 million for the cleanup of Lake Simcoe in central Ontario ... [W]hat additional actions our government has taken to protect our precious rivers, lakes and oceans[?]

Hon. John Baird (Minister of the Environment):

The government is taking real action on environmental remediation to help clean our waters ... We are also putting major resources into cleaning up our oceans and our Great Lakes. For the first time ever, we are going to be banning raw sewage from being dumped into Canada's oceans, rivers and lakes.

(House of Commons Debates, 18 October 2007, pp. 106–07)
(Débats de la Chambre des Communes, le 18 octobre 2007, pp. 106–07)

(c) Climate Change / Changements climatiques

M. Bernard Bigras (Rosemont — La Petite-Patrie):

[L]e gouvernement dit qu'il veut inclure des cibles obligatoires pour lutter efficacement contre les gaz à effet de serre, mais ce qu'il ne dit pas, c'est que ce sont des cibles d'intensité et non des cibles absolues qu'il a en tête. Cela signifie que même si on pollue moins avec chaque baril de pétrole mais qu'on en produit plus, le résultat final est que la pollution, loin de diminuer, augmentera. Le [gouvernement] admettra-t-il que c'est cela la réalité? [...] Le gouvernement, [qui] prend aussi l'engagement de mettre en place une bourse du carbone, ... peut-il nous dire où, au Canada, il compte installer cette future bourse: à Montréal, à Toronto ou ailleurs?

L'hon. John Baird (ministre de l'Environnement):

Notre programme vise une réduction absolue des gaz à effet de serre alors que, pendant les 10 longues années où ce député a été porte-parole de son parti politique, on a connu une augmentation de 33 p. 100 des gaz à effet de serre. [Au sujet de deuxième question,] les directeurs des Bourses de Montréal et de Toronto ... disent que c'est le marché qui dicte cette décision ... Nous sommes très occupés à travailler sur ce dossier. Pour la première fois, on aura une bourse au Canada.

(House of Commons Debates, 17 October 2007, p. 22)
(Débats de la Chambre des Communes, le 17 octobre 2007, p. 22)

Hon. John Godfrey (Don Valley West):

The governments of 15 countries, 13 U.S. states, British Columbia and Manitoba met yesterday in Lisbon, Portugal, to expand their fight against climate change. Thirty governments have signed the International Carbon Action Partnership, which allows big industries to reduce greenhouse gases cheaply by allowing them to trade emission credits, but Canadians living outside of British Columbia and Manitoba are not being represented ... Why did the [federal] ... government not ... show up?

Hon. John Baird (Minister of the Environment):

The Government of Canada was represented at the meeting by our ambassador in Lisbon ... The Prime Minister provided real leadership at APEC. We have met with the Commission on Environmental Cooperation, with large emitters in Washington, and with the United Nations under the leadership of the Prime Minister in New York. We are committed to working on real global action on global warming, something that would see countries like the United States, China and India take action, but something that also would see Canada finally begin to take action.

(House of Commons Debates, 30 October 2007, pp. 573–74)
(Débats de la Chambre des Communes, le 30 octobre 2007, pp. 573–74)

Mr. Mike Wallace (Burlington):

The United Nations Conference on Climate Change is being held in Indonesia this week and next, where nations are meeting to chart a path for negotiating a post-2012 agreement on fighting climate change ... What [are] Canada's goals for this conference?

Mr. Mark Warawa (Parliamentary Secretary to the Minister of the Environment):

We believe that any post-2012 agreement on climate change needs to include all major emitters, countries like China, India and the United States, developed or in the developing world. The agreement must be fair and economically realistic without placing unfair burdens on any specific country. The agreement must be long term and flexible, and have a balanced approach that preserves economic growth and protects the environment. The agreement must call for real, absolute reductions in greenhouse gas emissions.

(House of Commons Debates, 7 December 2007, p. 1889)
(Débats de la Chambre des Communes, le 7 décembre 2007, p. 1889)

(d) Natural Resources / Ressources naturelles

Mr. Dennis Bevington (Western Arctic):

Gazprom in Russia just cancelled a major liquefied natural gas supply that was to service Québec's needs ... Why does the [Government] turn his back on a Canada first energy security strategy?

Hon. Gary Lunn (Minister of Natural Resources):

Our energy policy is based on free and competitive principles, respect for provincial jurisdiction, as well as targeted environmental initiatives. Under the International Energy Agency, Canada fulfills all of its obligations. With those obligations also come the benefits from the other member countries of their strategic reserves ... [T]here is no shortage and we do not anticipate anything. Canada's energy is very secure across the country.

(House of Commons Debates, 11 February 2008, p. 2889)
(Débats de la Chambre des Communes, le 11 février 2008, p. 2889)

(e) Ozone-Depleting Substances / Substances d'appauvrissement de la couche d'ozone

Mr. Rick Dykstra (St. Catharines):

Last month Canada was part of a major international deal that involved countries like China to phase out harmful ozone-depleting chemicals. Could the [Government] tell the House how Canada is ... showing ... international leadership on the world stage to fight pollution?

Hon. John Baird (Minister of the Environment):

Four weeks ago the world gathered in Montreal to tackle ozone-depleting substances. We built on the Montreal protocol,[19] which was first negotiated in 1987 by the then prime minister, Brian Mulroney. We were able to accelerate by 10 years the phase-out of these ozone-depleting substances, the worst being HCFC, which is a major and potent greenhouse gas.

(House of Commons Debates, 17 October 2007, pp. 26–27)
(Débats de la Chambre des Communes, le 17 octobre 2007, pp. 26–27)

(f) Shanker's Bend Hydroelectric Project / Projet hydroélectrique de Shanker's Bend

Mr. Alex Atamanenko (British Columbia Southern Interior):

A Washington State county is proposing to build a major dam on the Similkameen River near the Canada-U.S. border, which would inundate extensive areas of ecologically rich southern B.C. Half of the flood zone would be in B.C's dry Similkameen Valley, encroaching on close to 24 kilometres

---

19 Editor's note: Montreal Protocol on Substances That Deplete the Ozone Layer, 16 September 1987, 1522 U.N.T.S. 3 (entered into force 1 January 1989). Canada signed the Protocol on 16 September 1987 and ratified it on 30 June 1988.

of Canadian soil south of Keremeos and west of Osoyoos ... [W]hat concrete steps has [the Government] taken or will take to ensure this project never happens?

Mr. Mark Warawa (Parliamentary Secretary to the Minister of the Environment):

We are dealing with this with our counterparts in Washington State and also in the province of B.C. Canada takes the environment very seriously. That is why we announced the creation of a new national park on the east arm of Great Slave Lake. We announced $30 million to clean up Hamilton harbour. We announced $11 million to clean up Lake Winnipeg.

(House of Commons Debates, 7 December 2007, p. 1888)
(Débats de la Chambre des Communes, le 7 décembre 2007, p. 1888)

2   *Foreign Affairs / Affaires étrangères*

(a) Francophonie / Francophonie

M. Maka Kotto (Saint-Lambert):

Plusieurs, dont la ministre Gagnon-Tremblay, du Québec, présentent faussement l'entente Québec-Ottawa sur l'UNESCO comme une "entente historique." Or, en référence à des documents d'archives du ministère des Relations internationales du Québec, déjà, en 1968, Pierre Elliott Trudeau avait proposé la même chose à Daniel Johnson et celui-ci avait refusé, car cela ne correspondait pas à une réelle présence du Québec sur la scène internationale. [Le gouvernement présent] le savait-[il]?

L'hon. Maxime Bernier (ministre des Affaires étrangères):

La francophonie, c'est quelque chose d'important, et nous allons faire tout notre possible. D'ailleurs, j'aimerais l'informer que je m'en vais bientôt, dans quelques semaines, au premier Sommet de la Francophonie en Afrique. Cela me fera plaisir de parler des programmes que nous avons ici, au Canada, et d'expliquer l'importance de la francophonie pour les Canadiens et l'ensemble des Québécois.

(House of Commons Debates, 24 October 2007, p. 321)
(Débats de la Chambre des Communes, le 24 octobre 2007, p. 321)

M. Bernard Bigras (Rosemont — La Petite-Patrie):

En vue du prochain Sommet de la Francophonie, qui doit se tenir à Québec en 2008, la France dit être déterminée à faire des changements climatiques un thème central de la rencontre ... S'il croit au Protocole de Kyoto, le premier ministre doit mettre les changements climatiques à l'ordre du jour du sommet ... [L]e fera-t-il?

L'hon. John Baird (ministre de l'Environnement):

Tous les représentants des pays francophones travailleront fort pour lutter contre les changements climatiques. Dans un premier temps, nous pourrons le faire en Indonésie, lors de la réunion des Nations Unies, où le Canada travaillera très fort pour avoir un meilleur accord sur la lutte contre les changements climatiques. Il est absolument essentiel que tous les grands pays industriels travaillent ensemble, avec les autres pays dans la Francophonie. On peut être assuré de voir le véritable leadership des pays de la Francophonie.

M. Raynald Blais (Gaspésie — Îles-de-la-Madeleine):

Les changements climatiques ont des effets concrets aux Îles-de-la-Madeleine ... Une étude préliminaire du groupe Ouranos révèle que l'érosion des berges est telle que l'archipel pourrait se scinder en deux d'ici à 2012 ... [C]omment le gouvernement pourra-t-il justifier auprès des autres membres de la Francophonie son refus de porter le sujet à l'ordre du jour du sommet?

L'hon. John Baird (ministre de l'Environnement):

Ce n'est pas du tout le cas. On est toujours heureux de travailler avec les pays francophones. La meilleure façon de le faire, cette année, ce n'est pas d'attendre encore six mois pour tenir une réunion à propos de cette politique. On travaillera très fort avec tous les représentants des pays francophones, en Indonésie, pour s'assurer d'avoir un vrai plan d'action pour toute la planète après 2012.

(House of Commons Debates, 21 November 2007, p. 1155)
(Débats de la Chambre des Communes, le 21 novembre 2007, p. 1155)

(b) Iran / Iran

Mr. Gord Brown (Leeds — Grenville):

The government of Iran has told Canada's ambassador in Tehran to leave that country ... Can the [government] provide the House with some insight regarding these [events]?

Hon. Maxime Bernier (Minister of Foreign Affairs):

We regret Iran's decision to order our ambassador to leave Tehran, which is entirely unjustified. We stand behind our ambassador, who performs his duties with professionalism. Yes, we tried to come to an agreement with Tehran about the exchange of ambassadors for some time, but we did not succeed. I can assure the House that in the future we will promote human rights, the rule of law, and democracy in Iran and across the globe.

(House of Commons Debates, 5 December 2007, p. 1759)
(Débats de la Chambre des Communes, le 5 décembre 2007, p. 1759)

(c) Middle East / Moyen-Orient

Mr. Kevin Sorenson (Crowfoot):

Yesterday, Israeli prime minister, Ehud Olmert, and Palestinian Authority president, Mahmoud Abbas, agreed to resume long stalled peace talks. The first formal peace talks are to be held December 12, with Abbas and Olmert meeting every two weeks after that. This will be the first formal direct talks between the two sides in seven years. What is the government's assessment from the meetings that took place yesterday in Annapolis concerning the Middle East peace process?

Right Hon. Stephen Harper (Prime Minister):

Canada is optimistic about the meetings that took place yesterday in Annapolis. Prime Minister Olmert, in fact, called me just before question period regarding those meetings. I welcomed his recognition that peace in the Middle East will require painful compromises on all sides. I indicated ... that Canada stands ready to assist the process in any way that we can. This is an important issue. I do anticipate that I will be speaking to other leaders in the days and weeks ahead.

(House of Commons Debates, 28 November 2007, p. 1457)
(Débats de la Chambre des Communes, le 28 novembre 2007, p. 1457)

(d) Saudi Arabia / Arabie saoudite

Mme Caroline St-Hilaire (Longueuil — Pierre-Boucher):

Une saoudienne qui se trouvait dans un taxi en compagnie de quatre hommes a été victime d'un viol collectif. Le tribunal a condamné la victime plutôt que les agresseurs au motif que les hommes avec lesquels elle se trouvait n'étaient pas de sa famille. Elle a donc été condamnée à recevoir

200 coups de fouet ... [L]e ministre des Affaires étrangères entend-il intervenir auprès des autorités saoudiennes pour leur faire connaître la très forte objection du Canada devant un pareil traitement?

Mr. Deepak Obhrai (Parliamentary Secretary to the Minister of Foreign Affairs):

We have expressed concern on this issue. We will be talking with the government of Saudi Arabia expressing Canada's deep concern about the sentencing that was issued in this particular case.

(House of Commons Debates, 22 November 2007, p. 1244)
(Débats de la Chambre des Communes, le 22 novembre 2007, p. 1244)

(e) Tibet / Tibet

Mr. David Sweet (Ancaster — Dundas — Flamborough — Westdale):

Canada has a distinguished visitor this week. The 14th Dalai Lama, the 1989 Nobel Peace Prize laureate and our third honorary citizen, is in Ottawa. Could the [Government inform] ... the House about this meeting with the Dalai Lama?

Hon. Jason Kenney (Secretary of State (Multiculturalism and Canadian Identity)):

I had the pleasure of meeting [His Holiness the Dalai Lama] this morning and discussing issues related to pluralism, of which he is a world leader. He has just met with the Prime Minister and earlier met with parliamentarians from all parties of both houses. He is now on his way to meet with Her Excellency the Governor General. The government, the people, and I believe the Parliament of Canada, are proud to welcome this honorary citizen to Canada, this champion of peace and pluralism. We wish him and the Tibetan people all the best.

(House of Commons Debates, 29 October 2007, p. 502)
(Débats de la Chambre des Communes, le 29 octobre 2007, p. 502)

3   Health / Santé

Mr. Gary Goodyear (Cambridge):

Nearly 10 million children under the age of five die from preventable causes every year. Regrettably, half of all the child and maternal deaths in the world occur in Africa. Canada has been a world leader in terms of aid delivery in the fight against HIV-AIDS, tuberculosis and malaria ... [W]hat the government is doing to combat child mortality rates?

Mr. Brian Pallister (Parliamentary Secretary to the Minister of International Trade and to the Minister of International Cooperation):

This morning in Tanzania the Prime Minister launched the Canadian-led initiative to save a million lives. This program will deliver basic cost effective and lifesaving health services to mothers and children in countries where the needs are greatest. The Prime Minister said this morning that we will be delivering $105 million and training over 40,000 health care workers.

(House of Commons Debates, 26 November 2007, p. 1345)
(Débats de la Chambre des Communes, le 26 novembre 2007, p. 1345)

4   Human Rights / Droits de la personne

(a) Border Security / Sécurité à la frontière

Ms. Alexa McDonough (Halifax):

Retired U.S. colonel, Ann Wright, and CodePink co-founder, Medea Benjamin, were blocked at Canada's border because they appeared on an FBI watch list. Their crime was peaceful protest, time-honoured civil disobedience, in opposition to the Iraqi war. Why [has] the [Government] ... ban[ned] respected U.S. citizens from entering our country?

Hon. Stockwell Day (Minister of Public Safety):

In the exercise of our sovereign rights, we have very distinct guidelines in terms of who may come into the country and who may not. We exercise those vigorously for the protection and for the interests of Canada, and we will continue to do that.

(House of Commons Debates, 23 October 2007, p. 282)
(Débats de la Chambre des Communes, le 23 octobre 2007, p. 282)

Hon. Ujjal Dosanjh (Vancouver South):

In a ... report on the Canada Border Services Agency, the Auditor General concluded that shipments of goods and people who had been deemed "high risk" had been entering the country without being detained at their primary point of entry ... Why did the Minister of Public Safety allow it to come to this?

Hon. Stockwell Day (Minister of Public Safety):

We have adopted all the recommendations of the Auditor General. In fact, they coincided with a number of areas where we had increased investment just in the last year and a half ... We can see the results of that. There was a 50% increase in the amount of contraband seized at the border. There were 500 different cases where firearms were seized at the border. That is an increase of about 40%. About 12,600 people were deemed inadmissible and were removed from the country, many with criminal affiliations ... Of those who were pursued, there was over a 90% conviction rate.

(House of Commons Debates, 31 October 2007, p. 621)
(Débats de la Chambre des Communes, le 31 octobre 2007, p. 621)

Mr. Jeff Watson (Essex):

For decades communities on both sides of the Canada-U.S. border have depended on each other in times of emergency. Canada and U.S. border officials have traditionally respected this arrangement. Recently though, emergency responders have been delayed by U.S. border officials. In my region, a respected community activist twice revived after a heart attack, was held up in transit to emergency services in a Detroit hospital. The actions of U.S. officials have gone too far and it has to stop ... [W]hat the government is doing to ensure that emergency responders will not face this kind of unnecessary delay in the future?

Hon. Stockwell Day (Minister of Public Safety):

Canadians and Americans ... have been able to move quickly across borders and assist one another in ... times of crisis and times of need. We have raised a number of issues related to the western hemisphere travel initiative which is a U.S. law that has had some unintended consequences in terms of how it is interpreted at the border. I have communicated with the Secretary of State on this particular issue and the Department of Homeland Security. We have registered our concern. We do not want to see this continue. It has to come to an end.

(House of Commons Debates, 19 November 2007, p. 1039)
(Débats de la Chambre des Communes, le 19 novembre 2007, p. 1039)

(b) China and Tibet / Chine et Tibet

Mr. Chris Warkentin (Peace River):

Earlier this week we heard about hundreds of monks in Tibet who were staging peaceful protests demanding improved treatment and religious freedom. They are asking for human rights, yet we have heard that these protests have been met with force, monks have been detained, and monasteries have been surrounded by Chinese troops. [What is] the government's reaction to this news out of Tibet?

Hon. Maxime Bernier (Minister of Foreign Affairs):

Canada has one China policy. We have serious concerns about the human rights situation in Tibet. We have consistently urged China to respect ... freedom of expression, freedom of association, and freedom of religion for all Tibetans. These latest developments in Tibet are very troubling for us and for Canadians. We urge China to respect the right of Tibetans to peaceful protest and to take steps to improve the human rights situation in Tibet.

(House of Commons Debates, 13 March 2008, p. 4135)
(Débats de la Chambre des Communes, le 13 mars 2008, p. 4135)

(c) Durban Conference on Racism / Conférence de Durban sur le racisme

Mr. James Lunney (Nanaimo — Alberni):

Canada has already withdrawn from the conference on racism scheduled for Durban in 2009. Unfortunately, the last conference degenerated into controversy and disappointment, with open displays of anti-Semitism and anti-western rhetoric ... [Will] Canadian taxpayers ... be subsidizing NGO travel to the ... [2009] Durban initiative?

Hon. Jason Kenney (Secretary of State (Multiculturalism and Canadian Identity)):

Canada will not be participating in the racist Durban process. I am ... pleased to confirm today that we will not subsidize NGOs to attend the Durban conference.

(House of Commons Debates, 29 January 2008, p. 2310)
(Débats de la Chambre des Communes, le 29 janvier 2008, p. 2310)

(d) Housing / Logement

L'hon. Jack Layton (Toronto — Danforth):

[L]e délégué de l'ONU pour le logement adéquat a condamné le gouvernement: "Je suis très perturbé par la situation du logement au Canada."

... Le premier ministre va-t-il déposer un soi-disant mini-budget, oui ou non?

Le très hon. Stephen Harper (premier minister):

Le budget sera présenté au printemps, selon la pratique normale de cette Chambre et de ce gouvernement. De plus, ce n'est pas un secret que ce gouvernement diminuera les taxes et les impôts à l'intention de tous les citoyens du Canada.

L'hon. Jack Layton:

[B]ig corporate tax cuts are not going to fix the housing crisis ... Will the Prime Minister understand this basic proposition and start working for working families, yes or no?

Le très hon. Stephen Harper:

What this government understands ... is [that working families] do not want the government to spend Canada into oblivion. What they expect the government to do is use its surpluses to pay down debt, to invest in key programs and also to reduce taxes. We intend to pursue all those priorities.

(House of Commons Debates, 23 October 2007, pp. 275–76)
(Débats de la Chambre des Communes, le 23 octobre 2007, pp. 275–76)

Mr. Christian Ouellet (Brome — Missisquoi):

Au terme de sa mission d'observation, le rapporteur spécial des Nations Unies, Miloon Kothari ... a rappelé que si le Canada a ratifié de multiples traités internationaux reconnaissant le droit au logement, il reste énormément à faire pour que ce gouvernement puisse affirmer qu'il respecte sa parole. Le [gouvernement] peut-il confirmer ... qu'il suivra les recommandations de l'ONU et qu'il augmentera de façon significative le financement de logements sociaux et abordables?

Hon. Monte Solberg (Minister of Human Resources and Social Development):

We believe that people should have a roof over their head. We are concerned about this, which is why we put $1.4 billion into providing thousands of homes for people in this country. We provide $1.8 billion a year for social housing. The affordable housing initiative continues to create thousands of homes for Canadians. The homelessness partnering strategy is there to prevent homelessness.

(House of Commons Debates, 25 October 2007, p. 402)
(Débats de la Chambre des Communes, le 25 octobre 2007, p. 402)

(e) Immigration / Immigration

Mrs. Nina Grewal (Fleetwood — Port Kells):

How [is] our government ... assisting foreign trained individuals and new Canadians to access what they need to become accredited here in Canada?

Mr. Ed Komarnicki (Parliamentary Secretary to the Minister of Citizenship and Immigration):

Today we are pleased to announce that 75 Service Canada centres across Ontario are now providing in person foreign credential information and referral services. Ontario newcomers will now have more locations where they can go to receive information and in person help on how to get their credentials assessed and recognized more quickly. By the end of this year, these services will be available across the country at 320 Service Canada outlets. This is good news for new immigrants and it is good news for Canada.

(House of Commons Debates, 26 October 2007, pp. 448–49)
(Débats de la Chambre des Communes, le 26 octobre 2007, pp. 448–49)

Ms. Olivia Chow (Trinity — Spadina):

[W]e have thousands of families being cruelly split apart ... A Vancouver woman cannot bring her husband to Canada because she was born Christian and he is a Muslim ... She said, "I never thought my government would try to break my marriage up because of culture and religion." Do we have a Minister of Citizenship and Immigration that unites families?

Mr. Ed Komarnicki (Parliamentary Secretary to the Minister of Citizenship and Immigration):

In the last budget, we had $1.3 billion over five years to enhance settlement and immigration programs for newcomers, $13 million over two years creating the foreign credential referral office, $34 million over two years in selecting immigrants with skills and experience into Canada and $51 million over two years to improve the temporary foreign workers program. We are getting something done in the immigration portfolio ... [O]bviously we will not get into the specifics of any particular case but I will say that we treat all cases dispassionately, with merit and on a merit basis. All of the personnel working in immigration treat every case with utmost respect and with appropriate dedication.

(House of Commons Debates, 19 October 2007, p. 154)
(Débats de la Chambre des Communes, le 19 octobre 2007, p. 154)

Hon. Gurbax Malhi (Bramalea — Gore — Malton):

When will [the] government ... reform the visitor visa system?

Hon. Diane Finley (Minister of Citizenship and Immigration):

It is very important to this government that we maintain our reputation as a welcoming country. We have done that by raising our levels of acceptance for permanent residents to the highest in many years. We have worked to streamline our programs, so that visitors to Canada and temporary foreign workers can get here faster and easier. We have shown great progress on that as well. First and foremost, our job is to protect the safety and security of those who are already here, so we must make sure that those who are applying to come to this country are legitimate.

(House of Commons Debates, 6 December 2007, p. 1834)
(Débats de la Chambre des Communes, le 6 décembre 2007, p. 1834)

(f) Iran / Iran

Mr. Scott Reid (Lanark — Frontenac — Lennox and Addington):

The Iranian government is blatantly disregarding its commitments and its obligations under international law as well as its own domestic legal obligations. Canada, along with 41 co-sponsoring nations, brought forward a resolution at the UN this year to call attention to our serious concerns regarding Iran. [What is] the situation regarding th[is] ... resolution?

Mr. Deepak Obhrai (Parliamentary Secretary to the Minister of Foreign Affairs):

Yesterday the UN adopted a Canadian sponsored resolution calling attention to the continuing deterioration of the human rights situation in Iran. At the UN General Assembly meeting this September, the Minister of Foreign Affairs worked hard to build support for this resolution by his participation in almost 30 meetings with his foreign counterparts. United by our shared values of freedom, democracy, human rights and the rule of law, our government will continue to restore Canada's international leadership through concrete actions.

(House of Commons Debates, 21 November 2007, p. 1156)
(Débats de la Chambre des Communes, le 21 novembre 2007, p. 1156)

(g) Migrant workers and human resources / Travailleurs migrants et les ressources humaines

Ms. Libby Davies (Vancouver East):

Canada's temporary foreign worker program is fast-tracking thousands of people into Canada ... Workers are paying thousands of dollars to come to Canada ... [T]emporary workers must have the same opportunities for permanent residency as other immigrants and equal rights. Will the government ... halt the expedited labour market opinion program until there is a full review and compliance mechanisms are in place?

Hon. Diane Finley (Minister of Citizenship and Immigration):

There is no question that we have some challenges. In the west, in particular, there are significant labour shortages. We ... have been working with industry to expedite accessibility for foreign workers to keep our labour economy moving and to keep our businesses in business. We need to work with them and they need to work with the provinces to ensure that all labour laws are respected by all employers and all of the employees. We are working to make that happen.

(House of Commons Debates, 23 November 2007, p. 1293)
(Débats de la Chambre des Communes, le 23 novembre 2007, p. 1293)

Mr. James Rajotte (Edmonton — Leduc):

Last week the OECD released a report on jobs and youth ... [H]ow [does] Canada compare[] to other countries with respect to training and education for youth and what our government is doing to further advance these critical issues?

Hon. Monte Solberg (Minister of Human Resources and Social Development):

The OECD lauded Canada for its efforts to help young people enter the workforce. Today they are employed at record levels. The incidences of long term unemployment are at record lows ... [B]ecause of the new Canada student grant, no student in the future will ever be denied the chance to go to college, tech school or university.

(House of Commons Debates, 16 June 2008, p. 6995)
(Débats de la Chambre des Communes, le 16 juin 2008, p. 6995)

(h) Multiculturalism, cultural diversity, and heritage /
Multiculturalisme, la diversité culturelle et le patrimoine

Mᵐᵉ Johanne Deschamps (Laurentides — Labelle):

Reconnu dans toute la francophonie pour son expertise ... le bureau de Montréal du Centre Pearson pour le maintien de la paix ... a été mis sur pied en 1999 pour "renforcer la programmation francophone du Centre et pour qu'il joue un plus grand rôle dans le soutien des activités du Canada au sein de l'Organisation internationale de la Francophonie [...]" ... Le [gouvernement] peut-il nous assurer qu'il poursuivra le financement du centre?

Hon. Bev Oda (Minister of International Cooperation):

This government stands for good governance, democratic governments and human rights. The Pearson Centre plays an important role. There are no plans for the closure of that centre.

(House of Commons Debates, 13 December 2007, p. 2177)
(Débats de la Chambre des Communes, le 13 décembre 2007, p. 2177)

(i) Privacy / Vie privée

Mr. Mario Silva (Davenport):

Under the American secure flight program, Canadian airlines will be required to provide personal information on passengers who are not even flying to the U.S. This violation of privacy is without precedents. Who would want this kind of information in the hands of the [U.S.] administration?

Hon. Lawrence Cannon (Minister of Transport, Infrastructure and Communities:

This is a proposed new U.S. regulation. Our government has been working with the U.S. to minimize the impact on air travellers. So far, we have been able to ensure that almost 80% of flights will not be captured by the new U.S. law.

(House of Commons Debates, 23 October 2007, p. 280)
(Débats de la Chambre des Communes, le 23 octobre 2007, p. 280)

(j) Protecting Canadians abroad / Protection des Canadiens à l'étranger[20]

---

[20] See also *Extradition* in the International Criminal Law section later in this chapter.

L'hon. Irwin Cotler (Mont-Royal):

Saul Itzhayek, un citoyen canadien de mon comté ... croupit depuis cinq mois dans une prison en Inde. I spoke with Saul from his squalid prison cell, who advised me that he has been sentenced to three years for an alleged visa violation resulting from entrapment by Indian officials and has not received the needed consular assistance. Will the Canadian government take the requisite steps to assist and expedite the return of a Canadian citizen to Canada and his family?

Hon. Helena Guergis (Secretary of State (Foreign Affairs and International Trade) (Sport)):

I have been in regular contact through correspondence on Mr. Itzhayek's case ... [C]onsular affairs ha[ve] been in regular contact with him, with his family and with his lawyer. We have ensured that he is provided the consular services he is entitled to.

(House of Commons Debates, 18 October 2007, p. 106)
(Débats de la Chambre des Communes, le 18 octobre 2007, p. 106)

Mr. Wajid Khan (Mississauga — Streetsville):

Today in the United States House of Representatives foreign affairs committee, Secretary of State Condoleezza Rice admitted that the case of Canadian Maher Arar was not handled well by the United States. [What is our] government's reaction to this admission?

Right Hon. Stephen Harper (Prime Minister):

En janvier, notre gouvernement a présenté des excuses officielles à M. Arar et à sa famille de la part du gouvernement du Canada. Nous sommes encouragés par les commentaires émis par la secrétaire d'État Rice, aujourd'hui. We have raised this issue on many occasions with the Americans and we hope the U.S. government will act to fully address this matter.

(House of Commons Debates, 24 October 2007, pp. 322–23)
(Débats de la Chambre des Communes, le 24 octobre 2007, pp.322–23)

Ms. Yasmin Ratansi (Don Valley East):

Yesterday we heard Condoleezza Rice refuse to apologize or recognize the torture endured by Mr. Arar while in Syria. This contradicts Justice O'Connor's report that cleared Mr. Arar of any terrorist activity. Regardless, Mr. Arar is still unable to travel to the United States. When will the government ... have Mr. Arar's name removed from the no fly list?

Hon. Stockwell Day (Minister of Public Safety):

I wrote a letter today to my counterpart in the United States, the secretary of Homeland Security asking, in light of what the secretary of state said, for them to reconsider their designation of Mr. Arar and remove him from those look-out lists ... We have followed every one of the recommendations from Justice O'Connor, including compensation for Mr. Arar, including an apology from this government for what happened.

(House of Commons Debates, 25 October 2007, p. 399)
(Débats de la Chambre des Communes, le 25 octobre 2007, p. 399)

Mᵐᵉ Caroline St-Hilaire (Longueuil — Pierre-Boucher):

[U]n jeune garçon d'origine haïtienne adopté par des citoyens canadiens de ma circonscription aurait été abandonné en Haïti. Vendredi dernier, le garçon nous a suppliés de le ramener au plus vite au Québec pour avoir, selon ses dires, "une vie décente, soit manger, boire, dormir et aller à l'école." Le ministre des Affaires étrangères peut-il nous confirmer qu'il entend rapatrier l'enfant dans les plus brefs délais?

Mr. Deepak Obhrai (Parliamentary Secretary to the Minister of Foreign Affairs):

The Department of Foreign Affairs and International Trade officers in Ottawa and Port-au-Prince are working together with the authorities of the province of Québec to ensure the well-being of this child. [We are] working very closely with Québec social services, which is investigating allegations of neglect made by this child ... [T]he department is working hard toward facilitating the child's return to Canada as early as possible.

(House of Commons Debates, 21 November 2007, p. 1152)
(Débats de la Chambre des Communes, le 21 novembre 2007, p. 1152)

Mr. Scott Reid (Lanark — Frontenac — Lennox and Addington):

In 2003 Zahra Kazemi, who as we all remember was a Canadian citizen and a Montreal resident, was arrested while taking photos outside a Tehran prison. A few days later she died while in police custody ... Since this tragedy happened, the Canadian government has been demanding justice. Could the [Government] update the House on the Kazemi case?

Hon. Helena Guergis (Secretary of State (Foreign Affairs and International Trade) (Sport)):

Canada has long called for a new and credible investigation into the death of Ms. Kazemi. Iran has an obligation to the Kazemi family to ensure that the perpetrators of this terrible crime are brought to justice and the rights of the family are upheld. Today the media reports suggest that the Iranian supreme court has made a decision to reopen the case. Our government would welcome any decision to reopen this case and hope that it offers justice to Ms. Kazemi's family and to her memory.

(House of Commons Debates, 21 November 2007, p. 1152)
(Débats de la Chambre des Communes, le 21 novembre 2007, p. 1152)

Mr. Rick Norlock (Northumberland — Quinte West):

Brenda Martin remains in a Mexican jail awaiting trial ... [W]hat steps our ... government is taking with Mexico to advance Ms. Martin's case to ensure a speedy trial and her rights are being respected?

Hon. Helena Guergis (Secretary of State (Foreign Affairs and International Trade) (Sport)):

Our Canadian officials regularly supply Ms. Martin with consular services. We have raised her case at the highest levels in both letters and personal representation up to and including the president of Mexico. I returned last night from Mexico ... where I again raised Ms. Martin's case. I also met with state and federal officials, expressing our concerns for consular matters and Ms. Martin's need for a very speedy trial.

(House of Commons Debates, 31 January 2008, p. 2431)
(Débats de la Chambre des Communes, le 31 janvier 2008, p. 2431)

(k) Right to Food / Droit à l'alimentation

Mme Claude DeBellefeuille (Beauharnois — Salaberry):

Le rapporteur de l'ONU pour le droit à l'alimentation, Jean Ziegler, a dénoncé l'utilisation massive du maïs et des céréales pour la fabrication de biocarburants, ce qui fait grimper le prix de ces denrées de base et aggrave la crise alimentaire dans le monde. Est-ce que le gouvernement va corriger le tir ... en encourageant les biocarburants produits à partir d'autres choses que les cultures, tel l'éthanol cellulosique, par exemple?

Hon. Bev Oda (Minister of International Cooperation):

Canada will respond to the food crisis and we will do it in an effective and focused manner. There are many causes for the crisis and the impacts it is particularly having on developing countries. Not only is it the biofuel usage, but it is lower crops because of changes in the weather, drought, extreme winters, et cetera. The weather is having an effect. The efforts we have been making in agriculture have not realized their full potential yet.

(House of Commons Debates, 10 April 2008, pp. 4758–59)
(Débats de la Chambre des Communes, le 10 avril 2008, pp. 4758–59)

(l)   Rights of Women / Droits des femmes

Hon. Maria Minna (Beaches — East York):

The [Government ought] to take concrete and immediate measures, as recommended by the United Nations, to ensure that Canada fully upheld its commitments to women in Canada. Could [the Government] explain how [it] improves Canada's commitment to women's equality?

L'hon. Josée Verner (ministre du Patrimoine canadien, de la Condition féminine et des Langues officielles):

Notre gouvernement a augmenté au niveau le plus élevé le financement du Programme de promotion de la femme du Canada, une augmentation de 42 p. 100 [...] Encore récemment, j'ai accordé une subvention à l'organisation Actu-Elle, qui offre des opportunités et des outils qui aident les femmes à atteindre l'autonomie économique. De plus, une soixantaine d'autres projets seront annoncés au cours des prochaines semaines et 8 millions de dollars seront accordés au total.

(House of Commons Debates, 18 October 2007, p. 105)
(Débats de la Chambre des Communes, le 18 octobre 2007, p. 105)

5   *Self-Determination / Autodétermination*

(a) Indigenous People / Peuples autochtones

Hon. Anita Neville (Winnipeg South Centre):

The United Nations High Commissioner for Human Rights said the government's position against the UN declaration on the rights of indigenous people is incomprehensible and an astonishing reversal of [the] efforts [of [the previous government]] to support the declaration ... [I]s [the Prime Minister] ... unmovable [and] distant ... on this issue?

Hon. Chuck Strahl (Minister of Indian Affairs and Northern Development and Federal Interlocutor for Métis and Non-Status Indians):

After 30 years of waiting for first nations to have human rights like anyone else, like the hon. member has, do we know what she said in committee when the Liberals delayed this bill in the last Parliament? She said that they have "waited 30 years, what difference does a number of months more make ..." six months, ten months, a year, I do not see what the difference is. The difference is that it is time first nations had human rights on reserve and we are going to deliver that to them ... A shining example is to ... allow first nations to have the same rights as [anyone else]. In the last Parliament, we introduced legislation to do that [21] ... It is time for first nations to have human rights. It is time they were covered by the *Canadian Human Rights Act.*

(House of Commons Debates, 23 October 2007, p. 278)
(Débats de la Chambre des Communes, le 23 octobre 2007, p. 278)

(b) Kosovo / Kosovo

Mme Meili Faille (Vaudreuil-Soulanges):

Alors que la province du Kosovo s'apprête à proclamer son indépendance, plusieurs pays d'Europe ainsi que les États-Unis appuient la démarche d'une nation qui aspire à prendre en main sa propre destinée ... [Q]uelle position le gouvernement canadien entend prendre concernant la reconnaissance de l'indépendance du Kosovo?

L'hon. Peter MacKay (ministre de la Défense nationale et ministre de l'Agence de promotion économique du Canada atlantique):

Nous avons un intérêt sérieux à cet égard parce que le Canada a toujours participé à cet exercice. Il y a eu une discussion à l'OTAN la semaine dernière à ce sujet. Avec les autres membres de la communauté internationale, nous attendons les décisions sur le terrain au Kosovo.

(House of Commons Debates, 15 February 2008, p. 3173)
(Débats de la Chambre des Communes, le 15 octobre 2008, p. 3173)

---

[21] Editor's note: Bill C-44, *An Act to Amend the Canadian Human Rights Act,* was introduced in the House of Commons by Hon. Jim Prentice (Minister of Indian Affairs and Northern Development and Federal Interlocutor for Métis and Non-Status Indians) on 13 December 2006. As of 20 April 2009, the bill is before the Standing Committee on Aboriginal Affairs and Northern Development.

(c) Québec / Québec

M. Maka Kotto (Saint-Lambert):

Dans une lettre que la ministre des Relations internationales du Québec a adressée au chef du Bloc québécois, il est écrit qu'en cas de désaccord entre les deux gouvernements, le Québec ne peut faire connaître son opinion publiquement. Je la cite: "Le gouvernement du Canada remettra au gouvernement du Québec une note explicative sur sa décision." La ministre avouera-t-elle que le seul gain qu'a fait le Québec suite à l'octroi de sa présence à l'UNESCO est que, dorénavant, le Québec aura droit à une petite note explicative sur la décision unilatérale du fédéral?

Hon. Bev Oda (Minister of International Cooperation):

[The Government of Canada] recognize[s] the important role that Québec and Québeckers play in our international relationships and in our global scheme. We have enabled Québec to make representation at the United Nations and UNESCO because these things are important to all Canadians and we know these are things that Québeckers take a special interest in.

La ministre du Patrimoine canadien, de la Condition féminine et des Langues officielles signifiait le 30 août dernier au Centre international du film pour l'enfance et la jeunesse que le gouvernement fédéral ne le subventionnerait plus. Or, ce centre est une organisation associée à l'UNESCO. Comment [le gouvernement] peut-[il] expliquer qu'[il] fait sortir un organisme de l'UNESCO du Québec en lui coupant les vivres [et] ... prétend faire entrer le Québec à l'UNESCO?

L'hon. Josée Verner (ministre du Patrimoine canadien, de la Condition féminine et des Langues officielles):

Sous le gouvernement libéral précédent, le CIFEJ a été financé sous une autorité spéciale ministérielle. Or, ce processus n'a impliqué aucun processus formel d'application, aucune autorité spécifique du Conseil du Trésor, ni responsabilité minimale financière. En conséquence, notre gouvernement prend au sérieux son obligation d'utiliser de façon responsable l'argent des Canadiens. Cela étant dit, nous soutenons le récit de l'histoire canadienne par l'entremise de l'Office national du film, Téléfilm Canada et la Société Radio-Canada.

(House of Commons Debates, 22 October 2007, p. 204)
(Débats de la Chambre des Communes, le 22 octobre 2007, p. 204)

6   *Sustainable Development / Développement durable*

(a) Corporate social responsibility / Responsabilité sociale des entreprises

Mme Caroline St-Hilaire (Longueuil — Pierre-Boucher):

Hier, l'organisme Développement et paix a déposé des cartes signées par plus de 150 000 personnes pour demander l'application du rapport du groupe consultatif sur les tables rondes, qui dénonce l'attitude et le comportement des compagnies minières canadiennes en Amérique latine et en Afrique. Celles-ci ne respectent ni les droits de la personne ni l'environnement. Le gouvernement possède ce rapport depuis maintenant 210 jours ... [L]e gouvernement [a-t-il l'intention de] ... rappeler à l'ordre ces compagnies canadiennes?

L'hon. Maxime Bernier (ministre des Affaires étrangères):

Comme je l'ai dit à l'ONU lors d'un discours officiel du Canada, nous défendons, dans notre politique de relations étrangères, les droits de la personne, ... et la liberté d'expression, ... la démocratie, la *rule of law*, c'est-à-dire la règle de droit. Nous allons étudier ce rapport et nous allons y donner suite en temps et lieu.

(House of Commons Debates, 25 October 2007, p. 397)
(Débats de la Chambre des Communes, le 25 octobre 2007, p. 397)

Mr. Paul Dewar (Ottawa Centre):

First in Chile and now tomorrow in Tanzania the Prime Minister will lend credibility and promote the business interests of Barrick [Gold]. This Canadian company is operating in a most un-Canadian way: firing unionized workers, union busting, totally disregarding the environment, failing to protect workers' safety, and alleged tax evasion. Why is the Prime Minister promoting the un-Canadian practices of Barrick Gold?

Mr. Deepak Obhrai (Parliamentary Secretary to the Minister of Foreign Affairs):

The Prime Minister is in Tanzania because we have a great relationship with that country and we wish to promote Canadian businesses working in Tanzania ... [T]here is a round table conference on social corporate responsibility and the government will be giving its response pretty soon ... We expect all Canadian businesses to follow Canadian practices, Canadian

laws and Canadian regulations. We expect [the Barrick Gold] company to
do the same thing. That is why that company participated in the corporate
social responsibility round table. We are positive that all Canadian companies will follow the rules that have been laid down in Canada.

(House of Commons Debates, 22 November 2007, p. 1243)
(Débats de la Chambre des Communes, le 22 novembre 2007, p. 1243)

(b) Labour rights / Droits des travailleurs

Mme Johanne Deschamps (Laurentides — Labelle):

La situation des droits humains en Colombie est désastreuse. Selon Human
Rights Watch, l'administration Uribe est impliquée dans d'importants
scandales reliés au trafic de la drogue et on note une augmentation marquée des exécutions extrajudiciaires et des assassinats de syndicalistes.
Devant un bilan aussi sombre en matière de respect des droits humains,
comment le gouvernement peut-il vouloir signer un accord de libre-
échange avec la Colombie de Uribe, sachant que même le Congrès des
États-Unis a refusé d'entériner la signature d'un tel accord?

L'hon. Jean-Pierre Blackburn (ministre du Travail et ministre de
l'Agence de développement économique du Canada pour les
régions du Québec):

Effectivement, un accord de libre-échange est en négociation avec le Pérou
et la Colombie. À l'intérieur de cet accord, il y aura un accord parallèle
dans le domaine des droits des travailleurs. Au moment où je parle, les
discussions vont très bien avec les deux pays. Nous allons avoir l'accord le
plus robuste que nous n'ayons jamais eu avec des pays lorsqu'il y a des
accords de libre-échange.

Hon. David Emerson (Minister of International Trade and Minister
for the Pacific Gateway and the Vancouver-Whistler Olympics):

The government believes that if we are going to pursue human rights ...
and ... strengthen the governance and the democratic freedoms in a country like Colombia, we have to provide an economic basis that is legitimate,
that is legal, and that takes the country out of the cycle of violence and
poverty that it has been in. That is what we are doing. We are working on
trade. We are working across a series of initiatives that will help Colombia
build capacity to have a healthy and strong democracy.

(House of Commons Debates, 28 November 2007, pp. 1458–59)
(Débats de la Chambre des Communes, le 28 novembre 2007, pp. 1458–59)

Mr. Ron Cannan (Kelowna — Lake Country):

Canada has now concluded a free trade agreement with Peru. This agreement ... will provide greater market access for Canadian agricultural products, including wheat, barley and some boneless beef cuts, paper products, machinery and equipment in Peru. However, many Canadians have raised concerns about labour rights in South America ... [W]hat will this agreement mean for Peruvian workers?

Hon. Jean-Pierre Blackburn (Minister of Labour and Minister of the Economic Development Agency of Canada for the Regions of Québec):

[W]hen we have a free trade agreement with any country, we have a parallel agreement on labour rights. When I went to Peru I met with my counterpart, Ms. Pinilla, and we obtained an agreement on labour rights. The agreement means that Peru now agrees on a declaration of fundamental rights, as well as the abolition of child labour and the elimination of discrimination. Also, we ascertained that Peru is committed to providing protections for occupational health and safety at work and, if it does not respect what it signed, there will be penalties.

(House of Commons Debates, 28 January 2008, p. 2225)
(Débats de la Chambre des Communes, le 28 janvier 2008, p. 2225)

(c) Ukraine / Ukraine

Mr. James Bezan (Selkirk — Interlake):

This year marks the 75th anniversary of the Holodomor, the great famine in Ukraine. Millions of Ukrainians died during Holodomor in 1932 and 1933. Many Ukrainian Canadians survived the famine, while others had family and friends starve to death back in the Ukraine ... [What] initiative [has] Canada ... taken to commemorate the millions of lives lost in this tragedy?

Hon. Jason Kenney (Secretary of State (Multiculturalism and Canadian Identity)):

Canada is connected to this dark chapter in history by more than a million Canadians of Ukrainian descent, many of whom lost family during the Holodomor. On October 23, Canada co-sponsored a motion by Ukraine, which has been adopted by UNESCO, that honours the memory of millions who perished in the famine and acknowledges it was caused by the brutal communist dictatorship of Joseph Stalin ... [T]he government welcomes plans by the Ukrainian Canadian Congress to launch a year of commemorative events next month surrounding the great historic tragedy of the Holodomor.

(House of Commons Debates, 31 October 2007, pp. 621–22)
(Débats de la Chambre des Communes, le 31 octobre 2007, pp. 621–22)

(d) Zimbabwe / Zimbabwe

Mr. James Bezan (Selkirk — Interlake):

Zimbabwe held elections for all levels of government on Saturday, March 29. Based on preliminary results, the Zimbabwe opposition party, the Movement for Democratic Change, has claimed victory. [W]hat [is] Canada's reaction ... to the elections in Zimbabwe?

L'hon. Maxime Bernier (ministre des Affaires étrangères):

Nous demandons à la Commission électorale du Zimbabwe de faire connaître les résultats de l'élection sans tarder et le plus rapidement possible en respectant la volonté du peuple du Zimbabwe. Nous sommes aussi très préoccupés par les irrégularités survenues lors de la période pré-électorale et nous sommes profondément déçus du fait de ne pas avoir été invités alors que quelques pays ont été invités à superviser les élections au Zimbabwe. Toutefois, vous pouvez compter sur le Canada. Nous soutenons le peuple du Zimbabwe pour qu'il ait un pays plus libre et plus démocratique.

(House of Commons Debates, 31 March 2008, p. 4247)
(Débats de la Chambre des Communes, le 31 mars 2008, p. 4247)

7   *International Criminal Law / Droit pénal international*

(a) Extradition and death penalty / Extradition et la peine de mort

M. Michel Guimond (Montmorency — Charlevoix — Haute-Côte-Nord):

Le ministre de la Sécurité publique a justifié sa décision de ne pas réclamer la clémence pour Ronald Allen Smith, un Canadien condamné à mort pour meurtre aux États-Unis, au motif que la condamnation avait été rendue par un pays démocratique. Pourtant, le Canada refuse de déporter des réfugiés dans leurs pays d'origine, que ces pays soient démocratiques ou non, s'ils risquent la peine de mort. Comment le [gouvernement] peut-il rejeter ce même critère lorsque des citoyens canadiens, même s'ils ont été condamnés pour crime?

L'hon. Peter Van Loan (leader du gouvernement à la Chambre des communes et ministre de la réforme démocratique):

Nous ne ramènerons pas au Canada des meurtriers qui ont été inculpés dans un pays démocratique et condamnés selon la primauté du droit. Le faire serait envoyer un mauvais message ... Le Canada a pour politique de sévir contre la criminalité.

(House of Commons Debates, 2 November 2007, p. 744)
(Débats de la Chambre des Communes, le 2 novembre 2007, p. 744)

M. Michael Ignatieff (Etobicoke — Lakeshore):

Depuis plus de 30 ans, le Canada exerce son leadership dans la campagne internationale contre la peine de mort. Maintenant, le Canada ne demande plus la clémence pour un citoyen canadien condamné à mort au Montana. Le Canada ne parraine plus les motions de l'ONU contre la peine capitale. Pourquoi le gouvernement ... gaspille-t-il notre réputation internationale comme défenseur des droits de l'homme?

Hon. Rob Nicholson (Minister of Justice and Attorney General of Canada):

There are no plans to change the laws of this country and we will continue to seek assurances on extradition matters ... [M]ultiple murderers and mass murderers who are convicted in a democracy that adheres to the rule of law cannot necessarily count on a plea for clemency from the Canadian government and patriation back to this country. That message should be very clear.

(House of Commons Debates, 22 November 2007, pp. 1236–37)
(Débats de la Chambre des Communes, le 22 novembre 2007, pp. 1236–37)

(b) Illegal importation / Importation illégale[22]

M. Thierry St-Cyr (Jeanne-Le Ber):

La contrebande de cigarettes a repris de plus belle. Selon plusieurs études, les produits illégaux occupent le quart du marché au Québec et en Ontario, et les gouvernements fédéral et provinciaux perdent 1,6 milliard de dollars en taxes par année ... Le [gouvernement] est-il prêt à demander à la GRC de ... mettre fin à ce trafic illégal?

---

[22] See also, *Border Security / La sécurité à la frontière* in the Human Rights section earlier in this chapter.

Mr. Dave MacKenzie (Parliamentary Secretary to the Minister of Public Safety):

We have put additional funds into the border services. We are looking at ways and means to stop all contraband coming into the country. It is a serious issue and the [Government] certainly is well aware of it and is working toward an end to it.

(House of Commons Debates, 2 November 2007, pp.749–50)
(Débats de la Chambre des Communes, le 2 novembre 2007, pp.749–50)

Mr. Ed Fast (Abbotsford):

This morning the Minister of Justice tabled a bill that includes a mandatory prison sentence for criminals who profit from vulnerable drug addicts in our country.[23] The proposed legislation also provides an exemption whereby a drug treatment court can suspend the mandatory prison sentence if the offender completes a recommended treatment program ... [What is] the significance of this bill to our national anti-drug strategy?

Hon. Rob Nicholson (Minister of Justice and Attorney General of Canada):

[W]e advocate a balanced approach ... [W]hen we announced the national anti-drug strategy, we said that two-thirds of the new resources would go to prevention and treatment. At the same time, we have introduced a bill that provides mandatory jail terms for serious drug dealers, importers, those who get involved with grow operations. In summary, we want addicts in treatment and we want dealers in jail.

(House of Commons Debates, 20 November 2007, pp. 1114–15)
(Débats de la Chambre des Communes, le 20 novembre 2007, pp.1114–15)

(c) Money Laundering / Blanchiment d'argent

Hon. John McKay (Scarborough — Guildwood):

The proposed anti-money laundering regulations affecting the real estate industry are set for June 23 ... Will the government ... facilitate adjustment by the industry?

---

23 Editor's note: *An Act to amend the Controlled Drugs and Substances Act and to make consequential amendments to other Acts* (Bill C-26).

Hon. Jim Flaherty (Minister of Finance):

The regulations ... against money laundering are of great importance to the integrity of the financial system in Canada, the integrity of the financial system in the G-7 and in fact around the world; there are serious issues with respect to terrorist financing and with respect to money laundering around the world. That is why through FINTRAC we have taken certain steps ... They are resisted by the realtors, [as well as] ... various participants in our economy, but they are essential if Canada is going to play its role in combating terrorist financing.

(House of Commons Debates, 12 May 2008, p. 5731)
(Débats de la Chambre des Communes, le 12 mai 2008, p. 5731)

(d) Human Trafficking / Traite des personnes

Mrs. Nina Grewal (Fleetwood — Port Kells):

Yesterday the Future Group called on our government to take concrete steps to address the issue of human trafficking in light of the upcoming 2010 Winter Olympics ... [W]hat steps we have taken to address the issue of human trafficking while assisting the victims of these terrible crimes?

Mr. Ed Komarnicki (Parliamentary Secretary to the Minister of Citizenship and Immigration):

Our government is taking real action to address human trafficking and to prevent the exploitation of women and children. We have taken several initiatives, including a series of changes to the immigration guidelines that would address the unique needs of victims of human trafficking. Yesterday, we reintroduced Bill C-17, legislation to help prevent the exploitation and abuse of foreign nationals seeking to work in Canada.[24]

(House of Commons Debates, 2 November 2007, p. 750)
(Débats de la Chambre des Communes, le 2 novembre 2007, p. 750)

Ms. Olivia Chow (Trinity — Spadina):

During the second world war, 15-year old girls were subjected to torture and rape by countless men from the Japanese army ... Over 200,000 women suffered through that kind of torture. Four of the survivors of sexual

24 Editor's note: *An Act to Amend the Immigration and Refugee Protection Act*, introduced by Hon. Gary Lunn (for the Minister of Citizenship and Immigration) on 1 November 2007.

slavery are on Parliament Hill today asking us to join them in asking Japan to give a formal sincere apology. Will Canada be on the side of the comfort women?

Hon. Jason Kenney (Secretary of State (Multiculturalism and Canadian Identity)):

[The Government has] had an opportunity ... to meet with these living witnesses to an unthinkable evil that happened some 60 years ago. We commend them for their courage, bravery and dignity considering what terrible things took place. They inspire us all ... to join together in combating contemporary forms of slavery, sexual servitude and human trafficking ... The Prime Minister and the current and former foreign ministers have raised and discussed this matter with their counterparts in Japan. We in Canada truly believe that as Canadians we acknowledge moments of injustice in our own history but these women come to this country with a story that needs to be heard because we need to learn from the lessons of history to ensure they are not repeated. We need to do everything we can to be inspired by them to redouble our efforts in fighting similar kinds of violence against women and against children to ensure these things never again occur.

(House of Commons Debates, 28 November 2007, pp. 1457–58)
(Débats de la Chambre des Communes, le 28 novembre 2007, pp. 1457–58)

8   International Humanitarian Law / Droit international humanitaire

(a) Humanitarian intervention and aid / Aide et l'intervention humanitaire

(i) Afghanistan / Afghanistan

Mᵐᵉ Francine Lalonde (La Pointe-de-l'Île):

Alors qu[e le gouvernement canadien] vient de nommer un comité d'experts dirigé par John Manley pour faire le point sur la mission canadienne en Afghanistan, on nous apprend, dans le discours du Trône, que le mandat de la mission s'étendra jusqu'en 2011. Doit-on comprendre que le gouvernement a déjà décidé que le Canada restera dans la région de Kandahar jusqu'en 2011?

L'hon. Maxime Bernier (ministre des Affaires étrangères):

J'aimerais citer un extrait de la page 7 du discours du Trône qui est très précis à cet effet: "Notre gouvernement ne croit pas que le Canada doive simplement abandonner le peuple d'Afghanistan après février 2009." Cela est dit clairement. C'est une mission humanitaire, menée avec l'ensemble des pays des Nations Unies et aussi ceux de l'OTAN. Nous sommes fiers de cette participation pour défendre les droits humains en Afghanistan.

(House of Commons Debates, 17 October 2007, p.25)
(Débats de la Chambre des Communes, le 17 octobre 2007, p. 25)

Ms. Dawn Black (New Westminster — Coquitlam):

The [Canadian] government is spending $86 million a month on [the] war [in Afghanistan] ... How can the minister justify [this spending]?

L'hon. Maxime Bernier (ministre des Affaires étrangères):

Le 19 septembre, l'ONU a adopté la résolution 1776 engageant les États membres à fournir du personnel, du matériel et d'autres ressources à la Force internationale d'assistance à la sécurité en Afghanistan. Nous sommes dans ce pays en raison d'un mandat de l'ONU.

(House of Commons Debates, 18 October 2007, p. 104)
(Débats de la Chambre des Communes, le 18 octobre 2007, p. 104)

Mr. Wajid Khan (Mississauga — Streetsville):

Are [Canadians] and our allies winning the hearts and minds of the Afghan people? ... How [does] an average Afghan see the international mission?

L'hon. Maxime Bernier (ministre des Affaires étrangères):

[D'après] les résultats d'un sondage effectué par différents médias canadiens ... en Afghanistan ... 73 p. 100 des Afghans estiment que les femmes jouissent d'une meilleure situation à l'heure actuelle qu'il y a cinq ans. De plus, 84 p. 100 des Afghans font confiance à l'armée afghane et 76 p. 100 des Afghans font confiance à la police afghane. Enfin, 60 p. 100 des répondants croient que les troupes étrangères sont une bonne chose pour leur pays.

(House of Commons Debates, 19 October 2007, pp. 153–54)
(Débats de la Chambre des Communes, le 19 octobre 2007, pp. 153–54)

M. Gilles Duceppe (Laurier — Sainte-Marie):

Le gouvernement fédéral a accordé des contrats à la firme de sécurité privée Blackwater afin qu'elle forme des soldats qui se trouvent actuellement en Afghanistan. Cette firme, qui emploie d'ex-militaires ou d'ex-policiers que l'on compare à des mercenaires, se retrouve en pleine controverse depuis que ses agents ont abattu 17 Irakiens, dont plusieurs civils, dans des conditions qui demeurent nébuleuses. Comment le [gouvernement] explique-t-il qu'une firme privée aux méthodes plus que douteuses soit mandatée par son gouvernement pour entraîner des soldats qui sont actuellement en mission en Afghanistan?

Le très hon. Stephen Harper (premier ministre):

Ce sont des contrats pour obtenir les services de gardes de sécurité. On a souvent recours à ces services dans beaucoup d'édifices fédéraux ici et à l'étranger. Ces gens ne font pas d'activités militaires.

L'hon. Maxime Bernier (ministre des Affaires étrangères):

Nous avons engagé des gardes de sécurité pour l'ambassade du Canada à Kaboul ... Ces gens s'occupent de la sécurité des invités de l'ambassadeur et ils effectuent des opérations sécuritaires. Ce sont des gardes de sécurité traditionnels, et non pas militaires ... Ces contrats ont été alloués selon un processus très clair d'appel d'offres public, un processus complet qui respecte la réglementation et la législation.

(House of Commons Debates, 24 October 2007, pp. 319–20)
(Débats de la Chambre des Communes, le 24 octobre 2007, pp. 319–20)

(ii) Africa / Afrique

Mr. Gary Goodyear (Cambridge):

Canadians are becoming more and more concerned about the increase of violence and political unrest in Kenya. Recently, our government committed $1 million to the international Red Cross to support its efforts in Kenya and this is good news. [Does] the government plan[] on providing any additional help to the Kenyan people?

Hon. Bev Oda (Minister of International Cooperation):

Canadians are very concerned by the events occurring in Kenya and that is why Canada was one of the first countries to respond. I quickly announced $1 million in emergency funds to react to the violence arising out of the disputed election. Violence has increased, so today I am announcing an additional $3.3 million to alleviate the suffering of Kenyans. Canadians hope that a peaceful resolution can be found soon.

(House of Commons Debates, 30 January 2008, p. 2351)
(Débats de la Chambre des Communes, le 30 janvier 2008, p. 2351)

Mrs. Patricia Davidson (Sarnia — Lambton):

The Prime Minister committed to doubling aid to Africa by 2008–09 ... [Is] Canada ... on target to meet this commitment?

Hon. Bev Oda (Minister of International Cooperation):

The government is on target. Last week I announced $302 million to the African Development Bank, $72 million to the World Food Program and $17 million to strengthen governance in Africa. Last July the government announced $125 million to feed children in Africa. In November the Prime Minister announced $105 million toward improving the health of Africans. In this year alone our government has announced over $620 million. We will meet our commitment to double aid to Africa.

(House of Commons Debates, 12 February 2008, p. 2966)
(Débats de la Chambre des Communes, le 12 février 2008, p. 2966)

Mr. Ed Fast (Abbotsford):

Our Canadian government has expressed concern for the ongoing violence in Sudan and Chad. [Has] the government ... offered any humanitarian assistance to the region?

Hon. Bev Oda (Minister of International Cooperation):

Our government knows that the ongoing violence and instability in Chad and Darfur is devastating the lives of millions. Today, this government announced it is making a significant commitment to support the refugees in the region. Through organizations such as the Red Cross and Médecins Sans Frontières, we will be providing clean water and sanitation, emergency health care, food and shelter, and increasing coordination of emergency services.

(House of Commons Debates, 12 March 2008, p. 4047)
(Débats de la Chambre des Communes, le 12 mars 2008, p. 4047)

(iii) Bangladesh / Bangladesh

Mr. Patrick Brown (Barrie):

A category four storm with winds of 240 kilometres per hour brought torrential rainfall across much of southern and central Bangladesh. According to the Bangladesh Red Crescent Society, the death toll is over 3,100 and could climb to 10,000 once all the affected areas are reached ... [W]hat is Canada doing to help those affected[?]

Hon. Bev Oda (Minister of International Cooperation):

[L]et me first express condolences to the people and families who have been impacted by the disaster in Bangladesh. Canada has always responded to those less fortunate around the world ... Our government responded immediately with $250,000, and yesterday Canada committed $3 million to support recovery and humanitarian aid. We will continue to monitor the reports received over the next days and weeks.

(House of Commons Debates, 20 November 2007, p. 1117)
(Débats de la Chambre des Communes, le 20 novembre 2007, p. 1117)

(iv) Burma / Birmanie

Mr. Bruce Stanton (Simcoe North):

This morning we learned that Canada will impose the world's most strict sanctions on the reviled military regime in Burma ... [H]ow this morning's announcement furthers Canada's foreign policy of getting results through principled leadership?

Hon. Maxime Bernier (Minister of Foreign Affairs):

We have all seen stories about the repression taking place in Burma ... Yes, we will have the strongest economic sanctions against the military regime there ... I will be in Paris to speak with my counterparts [and] ... encourage our allies ... to do the same thing.

(House of Commons Debates, 14 November 2007, p. 861)
(Débats de la Chambre des Communes, le 14 novembre 2007, p. 861)

(v) Darfur / Darfour

Mr. Glen Pearson (London North Centre):

[W]hen will the [Government of Canada] ... create a course of action [in Darfur]?

L'hon. Maxime Bernier (ministre des Affaires étrangères):

L'engagement du Canada au Soudan, au Darfour, est un engagement très important pour notre pays. En effet, le Canada est le quatrième donateur au niveau de l'aide internationale pour l'Union africaine. Nous travaillons aussi avec l'ONU et l'Union africaine pour nous assurer de pouvoir arriver à un processus de paix dans ce pays. C'est pour cela que [le gouvernement a] ... bien dit que nous faisions la promotion des valeurs universelles que sont la liberté, la liberté d'expression, la démocratie. C'est cela que nous devons faire et nous allons continuer de le faire pour toujours, dans ce dossier-là tout comme dans d'autres dossiers aussi importants.

(House of Commons Debates, 17 October 2007, p. 25)
(Débats de la Chambre des Communes, le 17 octobre 2007, p. 25)

Mme Louise Thibault (Rimouski-Neigette — Témiscouata — Les Basques):

À l'aube de 2008, au Darfour, le gouvernement doit prendre les moyens nécessaires pour mettre fin à ce conflit meurtrier ... Il pourrait agir, mais ne le fait pas. Pourquoi?

L'hon. Maxime Bernier (ministre des Affaires étrangères):

Nous agissons en ce qui concerne le Darfour. Nous avons octroyé plus de 286 millions de dollars pour justement aider l'Union africaine à retrouver la paix dans cette situation difficile du monde. Nous avons aussi versé 441 millions de dollars pour aider les populations, soit pour aider plus de 4,2 millions de personnes en ce qui a trait à la nourriture, les médicaments et leur donner les besoins essentiels.

(House of Commons Debates, December 10, 2007, p. 1944)
(Débats de la Chambre des Communes, le 10 décembre 2007, p. 1944)

(vi) United Nations Central Emergency Response Fund / Fonds central d'intervention d'urgence des Nations Unies

Mr. Harold Albrecht (Kitchener — Conestoga):

Canadians are well aware of the major natural disasters that occur around the world ... But there are lesser known catastrophes that do not garner national media attention. The United Nations Central Emergency Response Fund was set up to deal with these emergencies ... [W]hat is Canada's government doing to aid this organization?

Hon. Bev Oda (Minister of International Cooperation):

Natural disasters around the world affect hundreds of thousands of the most vulnerable, particularly those in developing countries. Canada has responded to flooding and tropical storms in East and West Africa, Haiti and the Dominican Republic. Through the United Nations Central Emergency Response Fund rapid response is available. Today, Canada's government announced $192 million toward the United Nations Central Emergency Response Fund, so it can continue to do its work.

(House of Commons Debates, 13 December 2007, p. 2177)
(Débats de la Chambre des Communes, le 13 décembre 2007, p. 2177)

(b) Landmines and cluster bombs / Mines terrestres et les
    bombes à fragmentation

Mr. James Bezan (Selkirk — Interlake):

Mines and unexploded ordnances kill or injure on average 62 Afghans
each month and almost 50% of the victims are children ... [W]hat is our
government doing to help combat this situation?

Hon. Bev Oda (Minister of International Cooperation):

Canada supports demining efforts in 20 countries around the world and
we are making progress in Afghanistan. In fact, the lands contaminated
by land mines have been reduced by 20% and the number of communities
affected reduced by one-third. Today I was pleased to announce $80 mil-
lion over four years to the UN Mine Action Service. We will work with
Afghanistan to ensure that it becomes a mine free country by the year
2030.

(House of Commons Debates, 3 December 2007, pp. 1643–44)
(Débats de la Chambre des Communes, le 3 décembre 2007, pp. 1643–44)

Hon. Keith Martin (Esquimalt — Juan de Fuca):

Cluster bombs are much like landmines. They are vile killers of innocent
civilians. They violate basic norms of international human rights ... Will
[t]his government support an international ban on the production and
use of cluster munitions?

Hon. Helena Guergis (Secretary of State (Foreign Affairs and
International Trade) (Sport)):

Canada has given the direction to destroy any cluster munitions that we
do have in existence. Canada has never used cluster munitions. We supported the Oslo process.[25]

(House of Commons Debates, 6 December 2007, p. 1834)
(Débats de la Chambre des Communes, le 6 décembre 2007, p. 1834)

---

25 Editor's note: *Oslo Conference on Cluster Munitions*, Declaration, 22—23 February
   2007, at <www.clusterprocess.org/>. Canada is a signatory to the Convention on
   Cluster Munitions, 30 May 2008 (not yet in force; see at).

(c) Nuclear energy / Énergie nucléaire

Mr. Daryl Kramp (Prince Edward — Hastings):

Yesterday the Minister of Natural Resources announced that Canada has accepted an invitation to join the Global Nuclear Energy Partnership. This partnership focuses on enhanced safeguards, cooperative research and developing advanced technologies ... Could the minister ... explain what this announcement will mean for Canada?

Hon. Gary Lunn (Minister of Natural Resources):

First, the Global Nuclear Energy Partnership is an international partnership that promotes a safer, more secure, cleaner world. With respect to the spent nuclear fuel, there is absolutely nothing in the stated principles that requires Canada or any other country to take back spent nuclear fuel. We went even further. We have absolutely, explicitly stated that under no uncertain circumstances will Canada ever take back spent nuclear fuel at any time from any country.

(House of Commons Debates, 30 November 2007, p. 1587)
(Débats de la Chambre des Communes, le 30 novembre 2007, p. 1587)

Ms. Peggy Nash (Parkdale — High Park):

In 2005 the Liberal government was alerted ... to the very serious concerns about missing safety procedures and quality assurance in the Chalk River nuclear program. Now nearly 24 months later, the world is facing a critical isotope shortage due to the serious errors made at Chalk River. Was the minister aware that experts were telling the opposition the project was five years behind schedule and almost 300% over budget? If not, will he find out why these very serious concerns were totally ignored by the previous ... government?

Hon. Gary Lunn (Minister of Natural Resources):

With respect to the situation with medical isotopes ... our government is very concerned. Our first and foremost immediate priority is resuming production as soon as possible. Immediately upon learning of the situation, I was in immediate contact with both the CNSC and AECL with respect to this issue. [B]oth of these agencies are absolutely independent of this government. However, both the Minister of Health and I have written to both of these agencies today ... We are looking for an immediate response from both of these agencies to resolve this situation as quickly as possible ... We have also made available all government assets, if we can expedite this at all, to ensure that these radioisotopes come back online as soon as possible.

(House of Commons Debates, 10 December 2007, p. 1941)
(Débats de la Chambre des Communes, le 10 décembre 2007, p.1941)

(d) Prisoners of war / Prisonniers de guerre

M. Gilles Duceppe (Laurier — Sainte-Marie):

Hier, le ministre des Affaires étrangères a affirmé que les allégations de torture dans les prisons afghanes n'étaient que de la propagande talibane. Pourtant, selon la Commission afghane indépendante des droits de la personne, le tiers des prisonniers sont encore torturés ... Puisque des re-présentants canadiens ont visité les geôles afghanes à au moins 11 reprises, le [gouvernement] s'engage-t-il à rendre public le compte rendu de ses visites afin qu'on sache ce qui s'est passé?

Le très hon. Stephen Harper (premier ministre):

C'est dans la nature des talibans de faire de telles allégations. On ne doit pas présumer que toutes ces allégations sont vraies. Toutefois, en vertu d'un accord conclu avec le gouvernement de l'Afghanistan, lorsqu'il y a des allégations, ce gouvernement fait le suivi ... Le gouvernement de l'Afghanistan s'est engagé à faire certaines choses, et ce gouvernement peut faire le suivi pour assurer que cet accord est respecté. Jusqu'à présent, nos informations nous indiquent que ces accords sont respectés.

(House of Commons Debates, 30 October 2007, p. 571)
(Débats de la Chambre des Communes, le 30 octobre 2007, p.571)

Mr. Harold Albrecht (Kitchener — Conestoga):

In May of this year, our government signed an agreement with Afghanistan regarding the transfer of detained Taliban prisoners and insurgents ... [What are] the results of recent visits to detention facilities in Afghanistan?

Hon. Maxime Bernier (Minister of Foreign Affairs):

We are visiting and interviewing Taliban prisoners on a regular basis. Officials have conducted 32 interviews. As a NATO spokesman said yesterday, "We have no evidence of systematic torture of detainees." During a recent visit, Canada's officials did see a Taliban prisoner with conditions that concerned them. Our officials are following up on media reports that the Afghan government has announced an investigation. The allegation has come to light because we have a good agreement with the Afghan government.

(House of Commons Debates, 14 November 2007, p. 859)
(Débats de la Chambre des Communes, le 14 novembre 2007, p. 859)

(e) Refugees / Réfugiés

Mme Meili Faille (Vaudreuil-Soulanges):

Un jugement de la Cour fédérale faisant référence à l'affaire Maher Arar a virtuellement rendu caduque l'entente canado-américaine sur les tiers pays sûrs quant au traitement des réfugiés.[26] Selon ce jugement, les Américains contreviendraient aux conventions internationales en ne s'assurant pas que les réfugiés qu'ils déportent dans leur pays d'origine ne sont pas victimes de torture. Comme cette entente contreviendrait à la Charte canadienne et aux conventions internationales que le Canada a signées, le ministre entend-il renégocier les termes de cette entente?

Mr. Ed Komarnicki (Parliamentary Secretary to the Minister of Citizenship and Immigration):

A decision was rendered yesterday. That decision is being reviewed and after review, appropriate steps will be taken. In the meantime ... the safe third agreement continues to remain in effect.

(House of Commons Debates, 30 November 2007, p. 1584)
(Débats de la Chambre des Communes, le 30 novembre 2007, p. 1584)

9   *Trade and Economy / Commerce et économie*

(a) Automotive industry / Secteur de l'automobile

Hon. Karen Redman (Kitchener Centre):

Kitchener Frame announced that it is throwing 1,200 people out of work and this is a huge blow to the Waterloo region. [I]s [there] a strong role for the federal government?

Hon. Jim Prentice (Minister of Industry):

Kitchener Frame is a company that produced a frame for SUV vehicles. The market in the United States has fallen very significantly, causing a

---

26 Editor's note: *Canadian Council for Refugees v. Canada,* [2007] F.C.J. No. 1583 (F.C.).

significant problem for that company ... [O]ther corporations and companies in the auto sector continue to do well. There are plants that will be opening, a Toyota plant this fall, and there are also companies in the parts industry in places like Woodstock, Stratford, Simcoe and St. Thomas that are able to succeed in the current market ... [The Government] care[s] about our capacity to assemble automobiles in Canada. One out of every six automobiles that is produced in North America is produced in Canada. There are 158,000 workers in this industry, approximately a quarter of Ontario's manufacturing GDP. Two and a half million cars are assembled in Canada. It is something that we are extraordinarily good at. We are going to work together with labour and industry to make sure that we keep that competitive advantage.

(House of Commons Debates, 12 February 2008, p. 2963)
(Débats de la Chambre des Communes, le 12 février 2008, p. 2963)

(b) Canadian exports / Exports canadiens

Ms. Peggy Nash (Parkdale — High Park):

Last year, Korea sold $1.7 billion in auto products to Canada. Canada sold ... $11 million in trade to Korea ... When will the government put the brakes on a bad trade deal?

Hon. David Emerson (Minister of International Trade and Minister for the Pacific Gateway and the Vancouver-Whistler Olympics):

We do not have a free trade agreement with Korea. We are negotiating with a number of countries [, including] ... through the World Trade Organization. We are trying to level the playing field for Canadian exporters. We want Canada to be [a] strong [and] good exporter.

(House of Commons Debates, 23 October 2007, p. 281)
(Débats de la Chambre des Communes, le 23 octobre 2007, p. 281)

Mr. Francis Scarpaleggia (Lac-Saint-Louis):

The Chicago Mercantile Exchange has said that water is about to become commoditized and traded as a futures contract, along with pork bellies, oranges and lumber ... Last week at the Munk Centre a panel of water policy experts called on the government to create safety net legislation to effectively ban Canadian bulk water exports, now, today, before there is a crisis. When is the government going to act and close the door once and for all on bulk water exports [?]

Hon. David Emerson (Minister of International Trade and Minister for the Pacific Gateway and the Vancouver-Whistler Olympics):

Under NAFTA there is no obligation on the part of Canada or any of the NAFTA partners to export bulk water in any form. In fact, there is legislation in place that protects against the commoditization of water, as long as water remains in its natural state, and on boundary waters, it cannot be removed without the permission of the federal government under law, for export or for any other reason.[27]

(House of Commons Debates, 12 February 2008, pp. 2964–65)
(Débats de la Chambre des Communes, le 12 février 2008, pp. 2964–65)

(c) Economic competitiveness / Compétitivité économique

Mme Louise Thibault (Rimouski-Neigette — Témiscouata — Les Basques):

Les abattoirs canadiens commencent déjà à fermer. Nos producteurs de bovins doivent se conformer à grands frais à une réglementation des matières à risques spécifiées respectant de hauts standards de sécurité alimentaire, qui les obligent à éliminer des tissus de bovins abattus. Pendant ce temps, les producteurs américains nous vendent leur boeuf, qui ne répond qu'à 90 p. 100 de nos critères de sécurité, à des coûts quatre fois moindres. Qu'attend le gouvernement pour assurer la survie des producteurs canadiens et québécois de bovins sans diminuer les normes de sécurité qu'exige notre population?

L'hon. Christian Paradis (secrétaire d'État (Agriculture)):

Le gouvernement n'attend rien. Premièrement, il est attelé sur ce cas, qui est un cas très grave. Il a fallu rouvrir les marchés et nous les avons rouverts. On parle non seulement des États-Unis, mais on parle également de la Corée et de la Russie. Cela constitue de nouveaux marchés pour lesquels nos producteurs pourront tirer leurs profits à même le marché. Entre-temps, pour la première fois, il y a une direction claire de la part d'un ministre de l'Agriculture ... faisant en sorte que les normes de sécurité au MRS soient harmonisées aux États-Unis. Des gains sont déjà faits au plan de l'eau utilisée pour laver les bâtiments et autres.

(House of Commons Debates, 26 May 2008, p. 6001)
(Débats de la Chambre des Communes, le 26 mai 2008, p. 6001)

---

27 Editor's note: *International Boundary Waters Treaty Act*, R.S.C 1985, c. I-17.

Mme Denise Savoie (Victoria):

Huit mois après que le dollar canadien a atteint la parité avec le dollar américain, il y a toujours un grand écart entre les prix de chaque côté de la frontière. En moyenne, les consommateurs canadiens paient au moins 18 ¢ de plus que les Américains pour les mêmes produits. Certains produits coûtent de 30 à 35 p. 100 de moins aux États-Unis. Pourquoi le ministre des Finances ne prend-il pas les mesures nécessaires pour protéger les consommateurs canadiens?

Mr. Ted Menzies (Parliamentary Secretary to the Minister of Finance):

The strength of the Canadian dollar should actually be benefiting consumers. We think that it has in some cases. In fact, the price of cars, books and clothing has come down, but the strong dollar is also followed along with the lowest inflation rate in this part of the world, in fact lower than the United States. We would encourage our retailers to provide the lowest cost produce to Canadians that they can. We would also encourage consumers to force those prices to be as low as they can.

(House of Commons Debates, 12 June 2008, p. 6892)
(Débats de la Chambre des Communes, le 12 juin 2008, p. 6892)

(d) Financial crisis / Crise financière

Hon. John McCallum (Markham — Unionville):

The IMF has just reported that the global financial crisis could result in losses of $1 trillion ... [T]he British and the Americans have prepared detailed plans of action which they will be discussing at the G-7 finance meeting this Friday. What concrete plans or ideas will Canada's government be bringing to the table?

Hon. Jim Flaherty (Minister of Finance):

Canada and the performance of this government are complimented [in the MFN Report]. We have been specifically chosen by the IMF as an example of what governments should do because we did it on a timely basis last year on October 30 with the economic stimulus that this country needed to create jobs.[28]

(House of Commons Debates, 9 April 2008, p. 4676)
(Débats de la Chambre des Communes, le 9 avril 2008, p. 4676)

---

[28] Editor's note: Finance Canada, *2007 Economic Statement* (by Hon. James M. Flaherty, Minister of Finance), 30 October 2007, <http://www.fin.gc.ca/ec2007/speech/speech-discours-eng.asp>.

(e) Investments / Investissement

Mme Claude DeBellefeuille (Beauharnois — Salaberry):

Dans la vente d'Alcan, la compagnie Rio Tinto a réitéré les garanties qu'exigeait Québec, mais le ministre fédéral ... n'a pas utilisé les moyens que lui donnait la *Loi sur Investissement* Canada pour s'assurer que la transaction était à l'avantage du Canada. [Pourquoi] le ministre n'a pas ... exigé [que] Rio Tinto ... garanti[t] le plancher d'emploi et qu'elle assure un certain niveau de transformation de l'aluminium ici même?

L'hon. Jean-Pierre Blackburn (ministre du Travail et ministre de l'Agence de développement économique du Canada pour les régions du Québec):

[I]l y a d'abord la France, l'Australie et le Québec qui ont dit oui à cette transaction. Le ministre de l'Industrie a également approuvé l'acquisition de Rio Tinto Alcan parce qu'elle est à l'avantage du Canada. Rio Tinto s'est engagée à investir 3,9 milliards de dollars au Canada, dont 2 milliards de dollars au Québec. De plus, le siège social sera à Montréal et la majorité des cadres supérieurs sera au Canada ... De plus, Rio Tinto s'est engagée à verser un fonds de 200 millions de dollars à des oeuvres caritatives. En outre, le siège social demeurera à Montréal. Nous, du gouvernement, ... avons pris cette décision parce qu'elle était réellement à l'avantage du Canada.

(House of Commons Debates, 19 October 2007, p. 152)
(Débats de la Chambre des Communes, le 19 octobre 2007, p. 152)

(f) Labelling / Étiquetage

Mme Ève-Mary Thaï Thi Lac (Saint-Hyacinthe — Bagot):

Les règles régissant l'étiquetage des produits agricoles sont aberrantes. Elles tiennent compte, pour déterminer l'origine d'un produit, des coûts de transformation et d'emballage, ce qui, en matière agroalimentaire, n'a aucun sens. Ainsi, il est possible d'acheter à l'épicerie des olives étiquetées "produit du Canada." Le ministre admettra-t-il que les règles actuelles d'étiquetage des produits alimentaires ont pour effet d'induire les consommateurs en erreur et de priver les producteurs agricoles d'ici d'une part de marché?

Hon. Gerry Ritz (Minister of Agriculture and Agri-Food and Minister for the Canadian Wheat Board):

We are moving on that file ... We have begun the process for the consultations with industry. A product of Canada, of course, is a product of Canada. "Made in Canada" covers the lump of products that are brought in here, remanufactured, repackaged and sometimes exported back out.

(House of Commons Debates, 9 April 2008, pp. 4678–79)
(Débats de la Chambre des Communes, le 9 avril 2008, pp. 4678–79)

(g) Retail Industry / Marché de détail

Mr. Mike Wallace (Burlington):

While a number of retailers are reducing their prices, recent reports indicate Canadian prices for some goods are considerably higher compared to U.S. prices ... [W]hat is [the minister] hoping to achieve [when] ... he will be meeting with the retail industry representatives tomorrow?

Hon. Jim Flaherty (Minister of Finance):

There is clearly room to reduce prices in Canada, given the increased purchasing power of the Canadian dollar. This is important, not only for Canadian consumers, but it is also important for Canadian retailers so that they can maintain their sales volume. I have encouraged retailers to reduce their prices as soon as possible. Many already have. More are doing so. This is valuable for Canadian consumers. I encourage Canadian consumers to shop around so that the market will work well.

(House of Commons Debates, 22 October 2007, pp. 208–9)
(Débats de la Chambre des Communes, le 22 octobre 2007, pp. 208–9)

(h) Security and Prosperity Partnership of North America (SPP) / Partenariat nord-américain pour la sécurité et la prospérité (PSP)

Mr. Peter Julian (Burnaby — New Westminster):

The SPP involves the giveaway of Canada's energy and water resources and the dumbing down ... on lowering of regulatory standards in over 300 areas, including transportation safety, food safety, consumer and environmental standards. Will the Prime Minister respect Canadians and come clean on his ... SPP agenda?

Mr. Colin Carrie (Parliamentary Secretary to the Minister of Industry):

In a competitive global economy, Canada benefits from strong relationships with our North American neighbours. Under the SPP, we are working to ensure Canadian firms continue to have access to U.S. suppliers and American markets. We are working with our neighbours on smart border initiatives, infrastructure improvements and regulatory cooperation.

Mr. Brian Pallister (Parliamentary Secretary to the Minister of International Trade and to the Minister of International Cooperation):

We do not separate trade opportunities from human rights benefits. Human rights benefits can accrue to the people of other nations if we give them the opportunity to enter into trading relationships ... [W]e understand that opening doors to trading opportunities around the world is a way to advance human rights successfully, and we will continue to do that.

(House of Commons Debates, 23 November 2007, p. 1290)
(Débats de la Chambre des Communes, le 23 novembre 2007, p. 1290)

(i) Securities / Valeurs mobilières

Hon. Denis Coderre (Bourassa):

Private U.S. security firms operating in combat zones have raised some very serious questions about whether or not NATO countries can be held accountable by local authorities if laws are broken. The government has signed a contract to pay Saladin Security in Afghanistan, but Canadians have no way of knowing who will be held responsible if something goes wrong ... When will the government ... table the contract?

Hon. Peter MacKay (Minister of National Defence and Minister of the Atlantic Canada Opportunities Agency):

As we have seen on a number of other occasions, private security firms have been used from time to time depending on the issue and on the type of training required. That is standard practice ... We are very judicious when we enter into these contracts.

L'hon. Maxime Bernier (ministre des Affaires étrangères):

La réalité est la suivante: nous avons un système de contrats et nous l'utilisons. Toutes les procédures ont été suivies. Ce sont des procédures que nous suivons dans toutes les ambassades au pays et dans toutes les ambassades partout dans le monde.

(House of Commons Debates, 23 October 2007, pp. 277–78)
(Débats de la Chambre des Communes, le 23 octobre 2007, pp. 277–78)

Ms. Dawn Black (New Westminster — Coquitlam):

When I was in Kandahar last January, I met contractors who were employees of DynCorp. Recently a U.S. State Department audit found that little or no work was done for the $1.2 billion it paid to DynCorp ... Are the private security contractors hired by the government subject to the same rules of engagement as the Canadian Forces?

Hon. Maxime Bernier (Minister of Foreign Affairs):

The security firm employed by the Canadian embassy in Kabul operates in accordance with Afghan law.

(House of Commons Debates, 24 October 2007, p. 323)
(Débats de la Chambre des Communes, le 24 octobre 2007, p. 323)

(j) Softwood lumber/ Bois d'œuvre

Hon. Navdeep Bains (Mississauga — Brampton South):

We recently learned that Nova Scotia is poised to become the latest victim in the ... softwood lumber agreement[29] ... It has become apparent that the forestry program initiated by any provincial government will be sued by the United States. Will the minister tell us whose side he is on?

Hon. David Emerson (Minister of International Trade and Minister for the Pacific Gateway and the Vancouver-Whistler Olympics):

[T]he softwood lumber agreement protects our industry against trade actions of that kind in addition to putting over $5 billion back in the pockets of Canadian companies ... A number of major forest companies out there today would probably be in bankruptcy were it not for the timely refund under the softwood lumber agreement. The provisions in the softwood lumber agreement are ... flexible [to] protect Canadian forest policies.

(House of Commons Debates, 23 October 2007, pp. 279–80)
(Débats de la Chambre des Communes, le 23 octobre 2007, pp. 279–80)

---

29 Editor's note: Softwood Lumber Agreement between the Government of Canada and the Government of the United States of America, 12 September 2006 (entered into force 12 October 2006), <http://www.international.gc.ca>.

(k) Subsidized exports / Exportations subventionnées

M. Daniel Petit (Charlesbourg — Haute-Saint-Charles):

La communauté européenne a récemment décidé de subventionner ses exportations de porc. Cela crée des distorsions dans les marchés et fait très mal à nos producteurs. Avec raison, les producteurs de porc veulent que l'on agisse ... [Qu'est ce que] le gouvernement ... peut faire pour nos producteurs de porc?

L'hon. Christian Paradis (secrétaire d'État (Agriculture)):

Nous avons injecté 76 millions de dollars pour le circovirus porcin, en plus d'un montant supplémentaire d'un milliard de dollars en prêts additionnels pour l'élevage. De plus, il y a deux semaines, j'étais à Paris pour rencontrer le cabinet du ministre français de l'Agriculture et de la Pêche. On sait que la France assumera prochainement le leadership de l'Union européenne. J'ai dit de façon claire que nous étions très déçus de la décision européenne de subventionner les exportations de porc. Nous continuerons à dénoncer de telles pratiques.

(*House of Commons Debates, 30 January 2008, p. 2354*)
(*Débats de la Chambre des Communes, le 30 octobre 2008, p. 2354*)

(l) Tourism Industry / Industrie du tourisme

Hon. Bryon Wilfert (Richmond Hill):

Yesterday the Chinese government announced successful negotiations with the U.S., which means Chinese tourists can officially visit the United States. One hundred and thirty-four countries are now on China's approved destination list, but ... Canada is not. This failure will cost Canadian businesses millions of dollars. The previous ... government had reached an agreement in principle with the Chinese government to get this done. Did the government intentionally ruin our relationship with China, or did it just bungle it?

Hon. Diane Ablonczy (Secretary of State (Small Business and Tourism)):

These negotiations take time ... [W]e are continuing to have dialogue and bilateral talks on this ... issue[]. These will bear fruit.

(*House of Commons Debates, 12 December 2007, pp. 2088–89*)
(*Débats de la Chambre des Communes, le 12 décembre 2007, pp. 2088–89*)

Hon. Mark Eyking (Sydney — Victoria):

[W]ith ... the Canadian dollar strong, the government should be looking at ways to boost the ... tourism industry and bring tourists to Canada. [What] does the ... government spend[] on tourism?

Hon. Diane Ablonczy (Secretary of State (Small Business and Tourism)):

This government spends $800 million a year promoting tourism. That is nearly $1 billion and in fact our support for tourism has increased.

(House of Commons Debates, 6 February 2008, p. 2662)
(Débats de la Chambre des Communes, le 6 février 2008, p. 2662)

(m) Trade and trade-related agreements / Accords commerciaux et liés au commerce

M. Serge Cardin (Sherbrooke):

Le ministre du Commerce international négocie présentement des accords de libre-échange avec 28 pays. Le Canada est en déficit commercial avec ces pays, notamment avec la Corée du Sud. Comment le ministre peut-il se précipiter à conclure un accord de libre-échange tout en ignorant l'étude des Travailleurs canadiens de l'automobile, dévoilée ce matin même et qui fait état d'une perte potentielle de plus de 30 000 emplois au Canada, dont 8 000 emplois au Québec? La sauvegarde de ces emplois ne devrait-elle pas être une préoccupation primordiale pour le ministre?

Hon. David Emerson (Minister of International Trade and Minister for the Pacific Gateway and the Vancouver-Whistler Olympics):

The government is fully committed to free and open markets and to providing Canadian companies with access to foreign markets. Without free trade, the Canadian economy would be in much tougher shape than it is today. Yes, we are negotiating with Korea, [with which] we do not have a free trade agreement yet ... The government would not enter into a free trade agreement with Korea or any other country unless there were substantial benefits to Canada.

(House of Commons Debates, 23 October 2007, p. 277)
(Débats de la Chambre des Communes, le 23 octobre 2007, p. 277)

Mr. Dean Del Mastro (Peterborough):

Counterfeiting and piracy pose an ever-increasing threat to the growth of the knowledge economy and affect consumers and business in Canada and abroad ... [W]hat is the government ... doing in the fight against piracy and counterfeiting on the international stage?

Hon. David Emerson (Minister of International Trade and Minister for the Pacific Gateway and the Vancouver-Whistler Olympics):

Intellectual property theft is a particularly pernicious form of piracy. It hurts creators and innovators. It puts consumers in danger and it supports organized crime. I am, therefore, pleased to announce today that Canada, along with Japan, the United States, the European Union and Switzerland are entering into negotiations to develop an anti-counterfeiting trade agreement that will be a model of intellectual property protection for the world.[30]

(House of Commons Debates, 23 October 2007, p. 281)
(Débats de la Chambre des Communes, le 23 octobre 2007, p. 281)

Mr. Peter Julian (Burnaby — New Westminster):

[With the Government's endorsement of the EFTA, we will say] [g]oodbye [to the] shipbuilding industry. When will the government ... bring ... the EFTA agreement[31] to Parliament for a vote?

Mr. Colin Carrie (Parliamentary Secretary to the Minister of Industry):

Since late 2005, officials have held roughly 12 consultation meetings with various shipbuilding industry representatives. This FTA addresses domestic shipbuilding concerns in a number of very important ways. In response to concerns expressed by the shipbuilding industry, the draft agreement

---

30 Editor's note: Since October 2007, Canada has participated in preliminary discussions with the United States, Mexico, the European Union, Switzerland, Japan, South Korea, New Zealand, Australia, Morocco, and Singapore towards an Anti-Counterfeiting Trade Agreement. These discussions aim to develop international standards to better combat the trade in counterfeit trade-marked and pirated copyright goods (see the chronology of the discussions and public consultations in Canada, Foreign Affairs and International Trade, *Trade and Intellectual Property: Anti-Counterfeiting Trade Agreement,* at <http://www.international.gc.ca/trade-agreements-accords-commerciaux/fo/intellect_property.aspx>).

31 Editor's note: The Free Trade Agreement with the states of the European Free Trade Association, including Iceland, Liechtenstein, Norway, and Switzerland.

includes a 15-year tariff phase-out on the most sensitive shipbuilding products. The phase-out period includes a bridge period of three years, during which time tariffs will be maintained at their current levels under the FTA. These provisions provide Canadian shipbuilders with considerable time to adjust to duty-free environment. It is the longest phase-out period for Canadian tariffs in any of our free trade agreements.

(House of Commons Debates, 8 February 2008, p. 2834)
(Débats de la Chambre des Communes, le 8 février 2008, p. 2834)

Hon. Jack Layton (Toronto — Danforth):

[W]ould [the Government] agree ... that [re-negotiation of NAFTA] is an opportunity for Canada to put to the forefront reforms to the environmental and labour aspects of these trade agreements that could benefit working families[?]

Right Hon. Stephen Harper (Prime Minister):

We view NAFTA as a very positive agreement for all three of the countries, for Canada and the United States in particular, under which we have had tremendous growth in trade and tremendous growth in opportunity. Of course, if any American government ever chose to make the mistake of opening it, we would have some things we would want to talk about as well ... [U]nder this government and ... our trade arrangements, real disposable incomes of Canadians are up. Employment is up. That is a trend we want to keep going.

(House of Commons Debates, 28 February 2008, p. 3434)
(Débats de la Chambre des Communes, le 28 février 2008, p. 3434)

M. Daniel Petit (Charlesbourg — Haute-Saint-Charles):

Mercredi dernier, le Canada et la France ont signé un plan d'action conjoint pour accroître leurs relations commerciales ... Ce plan d'action sera[-t-il] avantageux pour le Canada?

L'hon. Lawrence Cannon (ministre des Transports, de l'Infrastructure et des Collectivités):

Entre autres, on peut souligner diverses actions conjointes, dont le renforcement de la coopération dans divers domaines, tels que les sciences et les technologies, et aussi le développement envers les petites et moyennes entreprises. Nous avons franchi une étape importante qui permettra de libérer et de libéraliser davantage notre commerce et nos investissements à l'étranger, surtout avec la France.

(House of Commons Debates, 12 June 2008, p. 6892)
(Débats de la Chambre des Communes, le 12 juin 2008, p. 6892)

(n) World Trade Organization (WTO) / Organisation mondiale du Commerce (OMC)

M. Denis Lebel (Roberval — Lac-Saint-Jean):

[Est-ce que] notre gouvernement ... se tient debout pour ce qui est de la gestion de l'offre à l'OMC?

L'hon. Christian Paradis (secrétaire d'État (Agriculture)):

Défendons-nous à la vie à la mort la gestion de l'offre à l'OMC? La réponse est oui. A-t-on invoqué l'article XXVIII du GATT pour défendre la gestion de l'offre? Oui. A-t-on mis en place des normes de composition pour le fromage? Oui. A-t-on mis en place des mesures de sauvegarde spéciales pour défendre la gestion de l'offre? Oui. Allons-nous continuer ... de défendre jusqu'au bout la gestion de l'offre? Oui.

(House of Commons Debates, 15 April 2008, p. 4951)
(Débats de la Chambre des Communes, le 15 avril 2008, p. 4951)

10 Law of the Sea / Droit de la mer

(a) 200 mile limit / Limite de 200 milles

Mr. Scott Simms (Bonavista — Gander — Grand Falls — Windsor):

In 2006 the [Government] promised custodial management outside the 200 mile limit ... Article VI, clause 10 allows NAFO to apply regulation inside Canadian waters.[32] ... Why has the minister ... sold out our sovereignty?

Hon. Loyola Hearn (Minister of Fisheries and Oceans):

No way has this government given away any jurisdiction inside the 200 mile limit. The only time any NAFO country or NAFO can come inside is if we invite them to do work for us and even then we have to agree to their coming. That is standard across the world [which] ... is acceptable [to Canada].

---

32 Editor's note: NAFO *Amendment to the Convention on Future Multilateral Cooperation in the Northwest Atlantic Fisheries* (GC Doc. 07/4; 28 September 2007), Art. VI (10) provides: "The Commission may adopt measures on matters set out in paragraphs 8 and 9 [conservation and management measures] concerning an area under national jurisdiction of a Contracting Party, provided that the coastal State in question so requests and the measure receives its affirmative vote."

(House of Commons Debates, 30 October 2007, p. 577)
(Débats de la Chambre des Communes, le 30 octobre 2007, p. 577)

Mr. Fabian Manning (Avalon):

For many years now overfishing has been a serious issue facing our country. Many communities, including several in my own province of Newfoundland and Labrador, have been devastated by the disregard by some foreign countries of international law that forbids these actions. Today ... the Minister of Fisheries and Oceans announce[d] that serious overfishing citations in the NAFO zone are at an all-time low ... [Has] the government ... fulfilled its commitment to bring about custodial management beyond our 200 mile limit?

Hon. Loyola Hearn (Minister of Fisheries and Oceans):

In a unanimous report to the House, the ... Standing Committee on Fisheries and Oceans said:

> By custodial management, the Committee did not intend that Canada should claim sovereignty over or exclusive rights to the resources of these regions of the ocean but that Canada should assume the role of managing and conserving the fisheries resources of the NAFO regulatory area in a way that would fully respect the rights of other nations that have historically fished these grounds.[33]

We have done that in spades.

(b) Fisheries / Pêches

Hon. Lawrence MacAulay (Cardigan):

The Minister of Fisheries authorize[d] a vessel 125 feet long, with 5,000 horsepower, towing a net five football fields wide and a quarter of a mile long ... [T]hese trawlers ... destroy everything in their path ... [W]ill [the minister] bring an end to this killing machine in the gulf region?

Hon. Loyola Hearn (Minister of Fisheries and Oceans):

[T]his boat and any other seiners who are fishing in the area are fishing their own quotas and not one herring above their quotas. They have a

---

33 Editor's note: Canada, House of Commons, Standing Committee on Fisheries and Oceans, *Custodial Management Outside Canada's 200-Mile Limit*, March 2003, at 1, <http://www2.parl.gc.ca/CommitteeBusiness/>.

certain amount to catch. It is prime product that will provide many hundreds of jobs in the New Brunswick area, an area that has been devastated because of the policies of the members opposite. If they only have a certain amount to catch, whether they catch it in a dory or in the *Queen Mary,* it does not make any difference.

(House of Commons Debates, 22 October 2007, *pp. 207–8)*
(Débats de la Chambre des Communes, le 22 octobre 2007, pp. 207–8)

Mr. Fabian Manning (Avalon):

The fishing industry remains a very important aspect of the economy of Newfoundland and Labrador ... Could the [Government] ... respond to the ... claim that NAFO reform would undermine Canada's sovereignty in our own waters?

Hon. Loyola Hearn (Minister of Fisheries and Oceans):

All of us remember a very short time ago when Canadian Coast Guard boats were tied up at the wharves because they could not afford fuel when the foreign fleets were ravaging our fish stocks. That is no longer the case. Our boats are out on surveillance missions. We have no more foreign overfishing because we changed NAFO as we said we would. This year we cemented these changes in the new convention ... that protects our stocks ... [and] our sovereignty now and forever.[34]

(House of Commons Debates, 23 October 2007, *pp. 280–81)*
(Débats de la Chambre des Communes, le 23 octobre 2007, pp. 280–81)

Mr. James Lunney (Nanaimo — Alberni):

[How is the Government addressing] concerns about illegal and unregulated fishing off the Pacific coast[?]

---

34 Editor's note: On September 28, 2007, at the 29th annual meeting of the Northwest Atlantic Fisheries Organization (NAFO) in Lisbon, NAFO members adopted changes to the NAFO Convention on Future Multilateral Cooperation in the Northwest Atlantic Fisheries, of 24 October 1978 (entered into force 1 January 1979), in the form of the Amendment to the Convention on Future Multilateral Cooperation (GC Doc. 07/4). The reformed convention implements ecosystem-based management measures that protect sensitive marine ecosystems and ensure the sustainability of straddling fish stocks in the Northwest Atlantic Ocean. The Amendment also protects Canada's sovereign rights over its 200-mile exclusive economic zone. (See, Canada, Department of Fisheries and Oceans, *Canada's Actions Against Overfishing,* September 28, 2007, at <http://www.dfo-mpo.gc.ca>).

Hon. Loyola Hearn (Minister of Fisheries and Oceans):

We are taking ... action over there. Just recently, during our Operation Driftnet patrol, six Chinese vessels were sighted using illegal driftnets. After reporting them to the U.S. coast guard, six were apprehended. The Chinese government has confiscated each vessel, sold five of them, and the owners have had their international fishing licences cancelled. Heavy fines were also imposed.

(House of Commons Debates, 5 March 2008, pp. 3665–66)
(Débats de la Chambre des Communes, le 5 mars 2008, pp. 3665–66)

11 *Sports / Sports*

L'hon. Bob Rae (Toronto-Centre):

Récemment, ... le ministre de la Défense nationale, a ouvert la porte à la possibilité d'un boycott des Jeux olympiques. En même temps ... le ministre [des Affaires étrangères] a parlé avec le ministre des Affaires étrangères de la Chine en disant tout à fait le contraire. [Pourrait-t-il le] ministre ... clarifier ... la position du gouvernement du Canada[?]

L'hon. Maxime Bernier (ministre des Affaires étrangères):

Notre position, celle du Canada, est très claire. Premièrement, nous ne prévoyons pas boycotter les Jeux olympiques. Cela étant dit, nous avons aussi une position claire envers les activités de la Chine en ce qui concerne les droits humains et les droits de la personne.Nous demandons au gouvernement chinois de respecter la liberté d'expression des Tibétains et de cesser la violence envers ces derniers. Nous avons une politique et nous voulons qu'il y ait un dialogue entre le gouvernement chinois et le dalaï-lama afin d'en finir avec la violence et d'avoir une situation qui respecte les normes internationales en ce qui concerne les droits humains.

(House of Commons Debates, 9 April 2008, pp. 4674–75)
(Débats de la Chambre des Communes, le 9 avril 2008, pp. 4674–75)

Treaty Action Taken by Canada in 2007 / Mesures prises par le Canada en matière de traités en 2007

compiled by / préparé par

JAQUELINE CARON

I BILATERAL

Belgium
Agreement between the Government of Canada and the Kingdom of Belgium Concerning the Working Holiday Program. *Signed:* Brussels, 29 April 2005. *Entered into force:* 1 January 2007

Bulgaria
Trade Agreement between Canada and the People's Republic of Bulgaria. *Signed:* Sofia, 12 February 1973. *Entered into force:* 7 January 1974. *Terminated:* 1 January 2007.

China
Agreement for Scientific and Technological Cooperation between the Government of Canada and the Government of the People's Republic of China. *Signed:* Beijing, 16 January 2007. *Entered into force:* 17 July 2008.

Czech Republic
Agreement between Canada and the Czech Republic concerning the Facilitation of Temporary Work Stays of Youth. *Signed:* Ottawa, 23 November 2006. *Entered into force:* 1 October 2007.

Dominican Republic
Treaty between the Government of Canada and the Government of the

Dominican Republic on the Transfer of Offenders. *Signed:* Santo Domingo, 22 June 2005. *Entered into force:* 25 January 2007. CTS 2007/4.

European Community
Agreement between the Government of Canada and the European Community Establishing a Framework for Cooperation in Higher Education, Training and Youth. *Signed:* Helsinki, 5 December 2006. *Entered into force:* 1 March 2007. CTS 2007/5.

Agreement between the Government of Canada and the European Community on the Conclusion of GATT Article XXIV:6 on Negotiations. *Signed:* Brussels, 25 June 2007. *Entered into force:* 25 June 2007.

Finland
Convention between Canada and Finland for the Avoidance of Double Taxation and the Prevention of Fiscal Evasion with Respect to Taxes on Income. *Signed:* Helsinki, 20 July 2006. *Entered into force:* 17 January 2007. CTS 2007/3.

Germany
Agreement between the Government of Canada and the Government of the

---

Jacqueline Caron is Treaty Registrar in the Legal Advisory Division of the Department of Foreign Affairs / Greffier des Traités, Direction des consultations juridiques, Ministère des Affaires étrangères.

Federal Republic of Germany on the Gainful Occupation of Members of the Families of Members of a Diplomatic Mission or Career Consular Post. *Signed:* Berlin, 11 December 2006. *Entered into force:* 1 May 2007.

Latvia
Agreement between the Government of Canada and the Government of the Republic of Latvia Concerning Exchanges of Young Citizens. *Signed:* Ottawa, 25 September 2006. *Entered into force:* 1 April 2007. CTS 2007/6.

Mexico
Convention between the Government of Canada and the Government of the United Mexican States for the Avoidance of Double Taxation and the Prevention of Fiscal Evasion with Respect to Taxes on Income. *Signed:* Mexico, 12 September 2006. *Entered into force:* 12 April 2007. CTS 2007/9.

Convention between the Government of Canada and the Government of the United Mexican States for the Exchange of Information with Respect to Taxes. *Signed:* Mexico, 16 March 1990. *Entered into force:* 27 April 1992. *Terminated:* 12 April 2007.

Convention between the Government of Canada and the Government of the United Mexican States for the Avoidance of Double Taxation and the Prevention of Fiscal Evasion with Respect to Taxes on Income. *Signed:* Ottawa, 8 April 1991. *Entered into force:* 11 May 1992. *Terminated:* 12 April 2007.

Netherlands
Agreement between the Government of Canada and the Government of the Kingdom of the Netherlands on Mutual Administrative Assistance in Customs Matters. *Signed:* Ottawa, 14 August 2007.

Peru
Agreement between Canada and the Republic of Peru for the Promotion and Protection of Investments. *Signed:* Hanoi,14 November 2006. *Entered into force:* 20 June 2007. CTS 2007/10. *Suspended:* 1 August 2009.

Romania
Trade Agreement between the Government of Canada and the Government of the Socialist Republic of Romania. *Signed:* Ottawa, 16 July 1971. *Entered into force:* 14 December 1971. *Terminated:* 1 January 2007.

Agreement between the Government of Canada and the Government of Romania on Cinematographic Relations. *Signed:* Bucharest, 23 January 1992. *Entered into force:* 11 September 2007.

United States of America
Air Transport Agreement between the Government of Canada and the Government of the United States of America. *Signed:* Washington, 12 March 2007. *Entered into force:* 12 March 2007. CTS 2007/2.

Air Transport Agreement between the Government of Canada and the Government of the United States of America. *Signed:* 24 February 1995. *Entered into force:* 24 February 1995. *Terminated:* 12 March 2007.

Exchange of Notes Constituting an Agreement Amending the Air Transport Agreement between the Government of Canada and the Government of the United States of America, signed at Ottawa on 24 February 1995. *Signed:* Ottawa, 20 January 2000 and at Toronto by Canada, 12 June 2000. *Entered into force:* 12 June 2000. *Terminated:* 12 March 2007.

Protocol Amending the Convention between Canada and the United States of America with Respect to Taxes on Income and on Capital done at Washington on 26 September 1980, as amended by the Protocols done on 14 June 1983, 28 March 1984, 17 March

1995, and 29 July 1997. *Signed:* Chelsea, 21 September 2007. *Entered into force:* 15 December 2008.

Exchange of Letters Constituting an Agreement Expanding upon Article XXVI of the Convention between Canada and the United States of America with Respect to Taxes on Income and on Capital, signed at Washington on 26 September 1980. *Signed:* Ottawa, 21 September 2007. *Entered into force:* 15 December 2008.

Exchange of Letters Constituting an Agreement Setting Out Various Understandings and Interpretations As They Apply to the Convention between Canada and the United States of America with Respect to Taxes on Income and on Capital, signed at Washington on 26 September 1980. *Signed:* Ottawa, 21 September 2007. *Entered into force:* 15 December 2008.

Joint Letter from the United States of America and Canada, pursuant to paragraph 5 of the Procedures for the Implementation of Article XXI of the General Agreement on Trade in Services (GATS) Relating to the Modifications Proposed to the GATS Schedule (GATS/SC/90) of the United States of America to Withdraw Its Commitment on Gambling and Betting Services. *Signed:* Geneva, 22 October 2007.

II MULTILATERAL

Bribery
United Nations Convention against Corruption, New York, 31 October 2003. *Signed by Canada:* 21 May 2004. *Instrument of Ratification deposited:* 2 October 2007. *Entered into force for Canada:* 1 November 2007. CTS 2007/7.

Culture
Convention on the Protection and Promotion of the Diversity of Cultural Expressions, Paris, 20 October 2005. *Instrument of Acceptance deposited:* 28 November 2005. *Entered into force for Canada:* 18 March 2007. CTS 2007/8.

Human Rights
Convention on the Rights of Persons with Disabilities, New York, 13 December 2006. *Signed by Canada:* 30 March 2007.

Narcotics
International Convention against Doping in Sport, Paris, 19 October 2005. *Instrument of Acceptance deposited:* 29 November 2005. *Entered into force for Canada:* 1 February 2007.

Private International Law
Amendments to the Statute of the Hague Conference on Private International Law, The Hague, 30 June 2005. *Instrument of Approval deposited:* 31 March 2006. *Entered into force for Canada:* 1 January 2007.

Science
Agreement among the Government of Canada the Government of the United Mexican States and the Government of the United States of America for Cooperation in Energy Science and Technology, Victoria, 23 July 2007. *Signed by Canada:* 23 July 2007. *Entered into force for Canada:* 24 July 2008.

Telecommunications
Final Acts of the World Radiocommunication Conference of the International Telecommunication Union — WRC-07, Geneva, 16 November 2007. *Signed by Canada:* 16 November 2007.

Trade
World Wine Trade Group Agreement on Requirements for Wine Labelling, Canberra, 23 January 2007. *Signed by Canada:* 23 January 2007.

Exchange of Letters Constituting an Agreement between the Government of Canada, the Government of the United States of America and the Government of the United Mexican States, amending

Annex 401 of the North American Free Trade Agreement between the Government of Canada, the Government of the United States of America and the Government of the United Mexican States. *Signed:* Washington, 10 October 2007, Mexico, 31 October 2007 and by Canada: Ottawa, 29 November 2007.

War
Protocol additional to the Geneva Conventions of 12 August 1949, and Relating to the Adoption of an Additional Distinctive Emblem (Protocol III), Geneva, 8 December 2005. *Signed:* 19 June 2006. *Instrument of Ratification deposited:* 26 November 2007. *Entered into force for Canada:* 26 May 2008.

I   BILATÉRAUX

Allemagne
Accord entre le gouvernement du Canada et le gouvernement de la République fédérale d'Allemagne sur l'exercice d'une activité rémunérée par des membres de la famille des membres d'une mission diplomatique ou d'un poste consulaire de carrière. *Signé à:* Berlin, le 11 décembre 2006. *Entré en vigueur:* le 1er mai 2007.

Belgique
Accord entre le gouvernement du Canada et le Royaume de Belgique relatif au Programme Vacances-travail. *Signé à:* Bruxelles, le 29 avril 2005. *Entré en vigueur:* le 1er janvier 2007.

Bulgarie
Accord de commerce entre le Canada et la République populaire de Bulgarie. *Signé à:* Sofia, le 12 février 1973. *Entré en vigueur:* le 7 janvier 1974. *Terminé:* le 1er janvier 2007.

Chine
Accord de coopération scientifique et technologique entre le gouvernement du Canada et le gouvernement de la République populaire de Chine. *Signé à:* Beijing, le 16 janvier 2007. *Entré en vigueur:* le 17 juillet 2008.

Communauté européenne
Accord entre le gouvernement du Canada et la Communauté européenne établissant un cadre de coopération en matière d'enseignement supérieur, de formation et de jeunesse. *Signé à:* Helsinki, le 5 décembre 2006. *Entré en vigueur:* le 1er mars 2007. RTC 2007/5.

Accord entre le gouvernement du Canada et la Communauté européenne sur la conclusion des négociations au titre du paragraphe 6 de l'article XXIV du GATT. *Signé à:* Bruxelles, le 25 juin 2007. *Entré en vigueur:* le 25 juin 2007.

États-Unis d'Amérique
Accord relatif au transport aérien entre le gouvernement du Canada et le gouvernement des États-Unis d'Amérique. *Signé à:* Washington, le 12 mars 2007. *Entré en vigueur:* le 12 mars 2007. RTC 2007/2.

Accord relatif au transport aérien entre le gouvernement du Canada et le gouvernement des États-Unis d'Amérique. *Signé à:* Ottawa, le 24 février 1995. *Entré en vigueur:* le 24 février 1995. *Terminé:* le 12 mars 2007.

Échange de notes constituant un Accord modifiant l'Accord relatif au transport aérien entre le gouvernement du Canada et le gouvernement des États-Unis d'Amérique, signé à Ottawa, le 24 février 1995. *Signé à:* Ottawa, le 20 janvier 2000 et *par le Canada* à Toronto, le 12 juin 2000. *Entré en vigueur:* le 12 juin 2000. *Terminé:* le 12 mars 2007.

Protocole modifiant la Convention entre le Canada et les États-Unis d'Amérique en matière d'impôts sur le revenu et sur la fortune, faite à Washington, le 26 septembre 1980 et modifiée par les protocoles faits le 14 juin 1983, le 28 mars 1984, le 17 mars 1995 et le 29 juillet 1997. *Signé à:* Chelsea, le 21 septembre 2007. *Entré en vigueur:* le 15 décembre 2008.

Échange de notes constituant un accord qui développe l'article XXVI de la Convention entre le Canada et les États-Unis d'Amérique en matière d'impôts sur le revenu et sur la fortune, faite à Washington, le 26 septembre 1980. *Signé à:* Ottawa, le 21 septembre 2007. *Entré en vigueur:* le 15 décembre 2008.

Échange de notes constituant un accord qui expose différentes perceptions et interprétations s'appliquant à la Convention entre le Canada et les États-Unis d'Amérique en matière d'impôts sur le revenu et sur la fortune, faite à Washington, le 26 septembre 1980. *Signé à:* Ottawa, le 21 septembre 2007. *Entré en vigueur:* le 15 décembre 2008.

Lettre conjointe des États-Unis d'Amérique et du Canada, conformément au paragraphe 5 des Procédures de mise en œuvre de l'article XXI de l'Accord général sur le commerce des services (AGCS) concernant les modifications que les États-Unis se proposent d'apporter à leur Liste d'engagements (GATS/SC/90) en retirant leur engagement concernant les services de jeux et paris. *Signée à:* Genève, le 22 octobre 2007.

Finlande
Convention entre le Canada et la Finlande en vue d'éviter les doubles impositions et de prévenir l'évasion fiscale en matière d'impôts sur le revenu. *Signée à:* Helsinki, le 20 juillet 2006. *Entrée en vigueur:* le 17 janvier 2007. RTC 2007/3.

Lettonie
Accord entre le gouvernement du Canada et le gouvernement de la République de Lettonie relatif aux échanges de jeunes citoyens. *Signé à:* Ottawa, le 25 septembre 2006. *Entré en vigueur:* le 1er avril 2007. RTC 2007/6.

Mexique
Convention entre le gouvernement du Canada et le gouvernement des États-Unis mexicanes en vue d'éviter les doubles impositions et de prévenir

l'évasion fiscale en matière d'impôts sur le revenu. *Signée à:* Mexico, le 12 septembre 2006. *Entrée en vigueur:* le 12 avril 2007. RTC 2007/9.

Convention entre le gouvernement du Canada et le gouvernement des États-Unis mexicains sur l'échange de renseignements en matière fiscale. *Signée à:* Mexico, le 16 mars 1990. *Entrée en vigueur:* le 27 avril 1992. *Terminée:* le 12 avril 2007.

Convention entre le gouvernement du Canada et le gouvernement des États-Unis mexicains en vue d'éviter les doubles impositions et de prévenir l'évasion fiscale en matière d'impôts sur le revenu. *Signée à:* Ottawa, le 8 avril 1991. *Entrée en vigueur:* le 11 mai 1992. *Terminée:* le 12 avril 2007.

Pays-Bas
Accord d'assistance mutuelle administrative en matière douanière entre le gouvernement du Canada et le gouvernement du Royaume des Pays-Bas. *Signé à:* Ottawa, le 14 août 2007.

Pérou
Accord entre le Canada et la République du Pérou pour la promotion et la protection des investissements. *Signé à:* Hanoï, le 14 novembre 2006. *Entré en vigueur:* le 20 juin 2007. RTC 2007/10. *Suspendu:* le 1er août 2009.

République dominicaine
Traité entre le gouvernement du Canada et le gouvernement de la République Dominicaine concernant le transfèrement des délinquants. *Signé à:* Saint-Domingue, le 22 juin 2005. *Entré en vigueur:* le 25 janvier 2007. RTC 2007/4.

République tchèque
Accord entre le Canada et la République tchèque relatif à la facilitation des séjours temporaires de travail pour les jeunes. *Signé à:* Ottawa, le 23 novembre 2006. *Entré en vigueur:* le 1er octobre 2007.

Roumanie
Accord commercial entre le gouvernement du Canada et le gouvernement de la République socialiste de Roumanie. *Signé à:* Ottawa, le 16 juillet 1971. *Entré en vigueur:* le 14 décembre 1971. *Terminé:* le 1ᵉʳ janvier 2007.

Accord entre le gouvernement du Canada et le gouvernement de la Roumanie sur les relations cinématographiques. *Signé à:* Bucarest, le 23 janvier 1992. *Entré en vigueur:* le 11 septembre 2007.

II   MULTILATÉRAUX

Commerce
Accord du Groupe mondial du commerce du vin sur les règles d'étiquetage du vin, Canberra, le 23 janvier 2007. *Signé par le Canada:* le 23 janvier 2007.

Échange de lettres constituant un Accord entre le gouvernement du Canada, le gouvernement des États-Unis d'Amérique et le gouvernement des États-Unis du Mexique, modifiant l'Annexe 401 de l'Accord de libre-échange nord-américain entre le gouvernement du Canada, le gouvernement des États-Unis d'Amérique et le gouvernement des États-Unis du Mexique. *Signé à:* Washington, le 10 octobre 2007, *à:* Mexico, le 31 octobre 2007 et *par le Canada à:* Ottawa, le 29 novembre 2007.

Corruption
Convention des Nations Unies contre la corruption, New York, le 31 octobre 2003. *Signée par le Canada:* le 21 mai 2004. *Instrument de ratification déposé:* le 2 octobre 2007. *Entrée en vigueur pour le Canada:* le 1ᵉʳ novembre 2007. RTC 2007/7.

Culture
Convention sur la protection et la promotion de la diversité des expressions culturelles, Paris, 20 octobre 2005. *Instrument d'acceptation déposé:* le 28 novembre 2005. *Entrée en vigueur pour*

le Canada: le 18 mars 2007. RTC 2007/8.

Droit international privé
Amendements au Statut de la Conférence de La Haye de Droit international privé, La Haye, le 30 juin 2005. *Instrument d'approbation déposé:* le 31 mars 2006. *Entrés en vigueur pour le Canada:* le 1ᵉʳ janvier 2007.

Droits de la personne
Convention relative aux droits des personnes handicapées, New York, le 13 décembre 2006. *Signée par le Canada:* le 30 mars 2007.

Guerre
Protocole additionnel aux Conventions de Genève du 12 août 1949 relatif à l'adoption d'un signe distinctif additionnel (Protocole III), Genève, le 8 décembre 2005. *Signé par le Canada:* le 19 juin 2006. *Instrument de ratification déposé:* le 26 novembre 2007. *Entré en vigueur pour le Canada:* le 26 mai 2008.

Science
Accord de coopération en science et technologie énergétiques entre le gouvernement du Canada, le gouvernement des États-Unis du Mexique et le gouvernement des États-Unis d'Amérique, Victoria, 23 juillet 2007. *Signé par le Canada:* le 23 juillet 2007. *Entré en vigueur pour le Canada:* le 24 juillet 2008.

Stupéfiants
Convention internationale contre le dopage dans le sport, Paris, 19 octobre 2005. *Instrument d'acceptation déposé par le Canada:* le 29 novembre 2005. *Entrée en vigueur:* le 1ᵉʳ février 2007.

Télécommunications
Actes finals de la Conférence mondiale des radiocommunications de l'Union internationale des télécommunications — CMR-07, Genève, 16 novembre 2007. *Signés par le Canada:* le 16 novembre 2007.

Cases / Jurisprudence

Canadian Cases in
Public International Law in 2007–8 /
Jurisprudence canadienne en matière de
droit international public en 2007–8

compiled by / préparé par
GIBRAN VAN ERT

Refugee protection — deserters — violations of international law in Chechnya

Lebedev v. Canada (Minister of Citizenship and Immigration), 2007 FC 728 (9 July 2007). Federal Court.

Lebedev was a failed refugee claimant from Russia whose Pre-Removal Risk Assessment (PRRA) was rejected. He applied to Federal Court to quash that decision. He argued that, if returned to Russia, he would be forced to perform military service in Chechnya, which would involve committing international crimes. The Refugee Protection Division concluded that Lebedev was afraid of prosecution not persecution, in that he had deserted the Russian army before fleeing for Argentina and, later, Canada. The PRRA officer found that Lebedev was not a conscientious objector and concluded that applicants cannot claim refugee status under the 1951 Convention Relating to the Status of Refugees[1] simply because they do not wish to perform military service.

Justice de Montigny allowed Lebedev's application and remitted the matter to another PRRA officer for redetermination. He deferred to the finding of fact that Lebedev was not a conscientious objector and noted recent authority that there is no internationally

---

Gibran van Ert is an associate with Hunter Litigation Chambers, Vancouver.

[1] Convention Relating to the Status of Refugees, [1969] Can. T.S. no. 6 [Refugee Convention].

recognized right to conscientious objection.[2] However, he considered that Lebedev might be able to establish convention refugee status on the basis that his performance of compulsory military service in Chechnya would involve acts contrary to international law. In this, de Montigny J. departed from the PRRA officer's decision, which acknowledged this exception to the rule that persons evading military service are not, without more, refugees but found that the international community had not condemned the conflict in Chechnya in such a way as to support Lebedev's claim.

Much of de Montigny J.'s decision on this point turned on the meaning and significance of paragraph 171 of the *United Nations Handbook on Procedures and Criteria for Determining Refugee Status*, which he described as "not binding on this Court" but nevertheless "a useful starting point in trying to interpret the Convention."[3] Paragraph 171 reads as follows:

Not every conviction, genuine though it may be, will constitute a sufficient reason for claiming refugee status after desertion or draft-evasion. It is not enough for a person to be in disagreement with his government regarding the political justification for a particular military action. Where, however, the type of military action, with which an individual does not wish to be associated, is condemned by the international community as contrary to basic rules of human conduct, punishment for desertion or draft-evasion could, in the light of all other requirements of the definition, in itself be regarded as persecution.

De Montigny J. observed that the concept of "international condemnation" has not been consistently defined, noting that paragraph 171 can be interpreted to refer both to a legal standard ("basic rules of human conduct") and a political assessment ("condemned by the international community").[4]

After reviewing Canadian case law on the point, de Montigny J. held that international condemnation will not always be required in order for a claimant to show that he falls within the purview of paragraph 171 of the handbook:

2   *Hinzman v. Canada (Minister of Citizenship and Immigration)*, 2006 FC 420, affirmed 2007 FCA 171; *Sepet v. Secretary of State for the Home Department*, [2003] U.K.H.L. 15.

3   *Lebedev v. Canada (Minister of Citizenship and Immigration)*, 2007 FC 728 at para. 28 (*Lebedev*).

4   *Ibid.* at para. 63.

An isolated breach of the basic rules of human conduct will clearly not be sufficient to fall within the purview of paragraph 171 of the UNHCR Handbook. Conversely, there will also be instances where political expediency will prevent the U.N. or its member states from condemning massive violations of international humanitarian law. This is why reports from credible non-governmental organizations, especially when they are converging and hinge on ground staff, should be accorded credit. Such reports may be sufficient evidence of unacceptable and illegal practices. But at the end of the day, condemnation by the international community can only be one indication of human rights violations. It should never be, in and of itself, an absolute requirement.[5]

The learned judge found support for this view in recent English authorities.[6] In particular, he approved the English approach to international condemnation, whereby the question of persecution does not turn on international condemnation in the political sense but on violations of international human rights and humanitarian law norms.

De Montigny J. concluded that the PRRA officer erred in focusing on evidence of the Russian military's intention to engage in planned and systemic human rights abuses. He observed that the PRRA officer "could not dismiss the issue, solely because there was no evidence that the Russian army intended to engage in human rights abuses." Instead, de Montigny J. held that "[t]ransgressions of international norms should always be taken into account in assessing a refugee claim, however they come about."[7] He went on to find that the war in Chechnya "has been broadly and unequivocally condemned across the board" and that the evidence in the tribunal's record of torture, disappearances, extra-judicial executions, and other gross violations of international law by Russian forces in Chechnya was uncontradicted.[8] The learned judge therefore held that the PRRA officer had erred both in fact and in law.

Security — espionage — jurisdiction to grant warrants to spy in foreign countries

Canadian Security Intelligence Service Act (Canada) (Re), 2008 FC 301 (22 October 2007). Federal Court.

[5] *Ibid.* at para. 70.

[6] *Krotov v. Secretary of State for the Home Department*, [2004] E.W.C.A. Civ 69; *B. v. Secretary of State for the Home Department*, [2003] U.K.I.A.T. 20.

[7] *Lebedev, supra* note 3 at para. 78.

[8] *Ibid.* at paras. 79–82.

This was an application by the Canadian Security Intelligence Service (the Service) pursuant to sections 12 and 21 of the *Canadian Security Intelligence Services Act*[9] for a warrant to investigate the activities of ten subjects outside of Canada. The subjects included Canadian citizens, permanent residents, and foreign nationals including refugees. Warrants had previously issued in respect of these same subjects for investigative activities within Canada. The question before the court was whether it could issue extraterritorial warrants. Justice Blanchard concluded that the act did not confer jurisdiction on the court to do so.

To assist in its deliberations, the court appointed an *amicus curiae*. The hearings were conducted in private. The court's judgment was given in October 2007 but was not immediately published and is only published now in expurgated form. This unusual procedure was seemingly adopted for security reasons, although the reasons do not expressly say so.

Section 12 of the act provides in part that the Service "shall collect, by investigation or otherwise, to the extent that it is strictly necessary, and analyse and retain information and intelligence respecting activities that may on reasonable grounds be suspected of constituting threats to the security of Canada." Section 2 defines "threats to the security of Canada" to include "activities within or relating to Canada directed toward or in support of the threat or use of acts of serious violence against persons or property for the purpose of achieving a political, religious or ideological objective within Canada or a foreign state." Section 21(3) of the act provides in part that, "[n]otwithstanding any other law but subject to the *Statistics Act*," the court "may issue a warrant authorizing the persons to whom it is directed to intercept any communication or obtain any information, record, document or thing and, for that purpose, (a) to enter any place."

The Service contended that the earlier-cited provisions of the act must be read as having an extraterritorial reach. It noted that section 16 of the act expressly limits the Service's collection of foreign intelligence to Canada, thus implying that the rest of the act's provisions are not subject to this territorial limitation. The Service apparently also argued that a warrant was required to ensure that agents engaged in executing the warrant abroad did so in conformity with Canadian law, and that a warrant was needed to authorize activities that might otherwise breach the *Canadian Charter of Rights*

---

9 *Canadian Security Intelligence Services Act*, R.S.C. 1985 c. C-23.

and Freedoms. These arguments are hard to follow. Surely, if no warrant was issued, the Service's agents would have no warrant to execute and would simply stay home. Implicit in these submissions seems to be that the Service intended to spy in foreign countries whether it had a warrant to do so or not.

The Service also submitted that section 21(3) of the act authorized the court to issue warrants notwithstanding international law. For this proposition, the Service cited the "secret reasons of Mr. Justice Heald" in an application ironically dating from the year 1984.[10] Continuing the Orwellian theme, the Service made the doublespeak submission that it was not asking the Court to authorize a violation of foreign law but nevertheless acknowledged that the activities to be authorized under the warrant were likely to constitute a violation of foreign law.

The *amicus* agreed with the Service that there was no territorial limitation on the activities of the Service as set forth in section 12 of the act. It followed, in the *amicus*'s submission, that any application for a warrant under section 21 to enable the Service to investigate threats to Canadian security may extend to investigations outside Canada. Yet the *amicus* contended that the Service could not execute a warrant so obtained without the permission of the country where the target resided and that without such permission the Service would be in violation of international law. These submissions appear to be founded on the decision of the Supreme Court of Canada in *R. v. Hape,*[11] a case concerning the extraterritorial application of the *Charter* (not the act).

Blanchard J. noted that the act does not expressly provide an extraterritorial mandate for the Service to engage in investigative activities of the sort contemplated by the warrant, nor does it expressly vest the court with jurisdiction to authorize such extraterritorial activities. The learned judge took the view that if the plain meaning of the act was unambiguous, he could not resort to "extratextual evidence of legislative intent, such as legislative history and international law," to contradict that plain meaning.[12] With respect, the rule that ambiguity must be found in the face of the legislation before having regard to international law is contrary to Supreme

---

10 The secret is partly out: Blanchard J. quotes from the decision, without citing it, at para. 28 of his reasons.

11 *R. v. Hape,* [2007] 2 S.C.R. 292. The *amicus* also cited *R. v. Harrer* [1995] 3 S.C.R. 562 and *R. v. Cook* [1998] 2 S.C.R. 597.

12 Reasons at para. 38.

Court of Canada authority.[13] In any event, Blanchard J. found the act sufficiently ambiguous to justify resort to legislative history and international law. He found legislative history to be insufficient to support a conclusion that Parliament intended extraterritorial activities of the sort contemplated by the warrant.

Turning to international law, Blanchard J. relied exclusively on Justice LeBel's reasons in *Hape* for the governing principles. The learned judge noted that legislation is presumed to conform to international law and that the principle of international comity will bear on the interpretation of our laws, "statutory and constitutional," where such laws could have an impact on the sovereignty of other states.[14] Blanchard J. also noted LeBel J.'s affirmation of the proposition that rules of customary international law are directly incorporated into Canadian domestic law unless expressly ousted by legislation, and LeBel J.'s restatement of the rule that Parliament may violate international law "but it must do so expressly."[15] Blanchard J. observed that the "intrusive activities contemplated in the warrant sought are activities that clearly impinge upon" the international legal principles of territorial sovereign equality and non-intervention. He added that the activities were likely to violate foreign laws and that absent a foreign state's consent these activities impinge upon that state's territorial sovereignty. The learned judge therefore concluded that the warrant sought would authorize activities "likely to breach customary principles of territorial sovereign equality and non-intervention, by the comity of nations."[16] In particular, he rejected the Service's contention that foreign "intelligence gathering operations" (better known as espionage) are recognized as a customary practice in international law.[17]

Blanchard J. therefore concluded as follows:

In construing the applicable provisions of the Act, I am guided by the principle of statutory interpretation that legislation is presumed to conform

---

13 *National Corn Growers Association v. Canada (Import Tribunal)*, [1990] 2 S.C.R. 1324 at 1372–3 (explaining that ambiguity may be patent or latent, and a latent ambiguity may only be discerned by having recourse to an underlying international agreement at the outset of the interpretive process). See also *Hape*, *supra* note 11 at para. 53 (explaining that international law values and principles "form part of the context in which statutes are enacted").

14 Reasons at paras. 46–7, citing *Hape* at paras. 47, 48, and 53.

15 Reasons at para. 48, citing *Hape* at para. 39.

16 Reasons at para. 52.

17 Reasons at para. 53.

to international law. Applying the above stated principles, I am unable to construe the applicable provisions of the Act, as drafted, as providing the Court with a jurisdiction basis to issue the warrant sought. To do so would require that I read into the applicable provisions of the Act, a jurisdiction for the Court to authorize activities that violate the above stated principles of customary international law. As stated earlier in these reasons, such a mandate must be expressly provided for in the Act. Given the principles of law in play, and guided by the teachings of the Supreme Court of Canada in *Hape*, I am left to conclude that, absent an express enactment authorizing the Court to issue an extraterritorial warrant, the Court is without jurisdiction to issue the warrant sought.[18]

While Blanchard J.'s judgment relies heavily on the principles enunciated by the Supreme Court of Canada in *Hape*, the same result could have been reached by applying an interpretive rule related to the presumption of conformity with international law, namely the presumption that domestic laws do not apply extraterritorially.[19] In a case such as this, the two presumptions emanate from the same normative imperative, namely respect for the rights of other nations. The presumption against extraterritoriality is perhaps the more directly applicable interpretive rule here, given that neither Blanchard J. nor the parties identified any specific international legal obligation that stood to be breached by issuing the warrant or conducting the foreign investigations. Rather, Blanchard J.'s analysis is founded on the general principles of sovereign equality and non-intervention described in *Hape*. In any event, the learned judge was surely right to find that the Federal Court's jurisdiction to authorize Canadian officials to spy on people in foreign lands must not be left to inference. If any state is to arrogate to itself such a legal entitlement, let it do so publicly and openly — and let it face the consequences.

Extradition — death penalty — absence of assurances

Karas v. Canada (Minister of Justice), 2007 BCCA 637 (24 December 2007). Court of Appeal for British Columbia.

Karas was charged in Thailand with the intentional murder of a Thai woman, a capital offence. Under the applicable extradition

---

[18] Reasons at para. 55.

[19] E.g., *Re Criminal Code ss. 275 & 276* (1897) 27 S.C.R. 461; *R. v. Libman*, [1985] 2 S.C.R. 178 at 208.

treaty,[20] Canada is required to deliver up fugitive criminals for the offences of murder and manslaughter (among others). Following a six-day extradition hearing under Justice Lysyk, a committal order was made for the non-capital offence of manslaughter. The minister subsequently ordered Karas's surrender to Thailand on terms that permitted Thailand to proceed with a charge of murder, without written assurances that Thailand would not impose the death penalty were Karas convicted. Karas therefore challenged the legality of the minister's surrender order on jurisdictional and *Charter* grounds. This challenge was heard by the Court of Appeal pursuant to section 57 of the *Extradition Act.*[21]

Justice Rowles, for the court, held that the minister was without jurisdiction to order Karas's surrender for an offence that substantively exceeds the offence supported in the committal order. The learned judge's reasons included important considerations of the application of the Supreme Court of Canada's decision in *United States v. Burns*[22] and the consequences in Canadian law of the legal inability of a foreign state to give assurances that the death penalty will not be imposed.

The minister's original surrender order was for the "conduct described by Lysyk J." in his committal reasons and was conditional upon Thailand providing assurances that it would not impose or carry out the death penalty against Karas. Thai authorities responded by a diplomatic note explaining that Thailand was unable to provide the assurances sought because of the absence of any provision in Thai law allowing its government to do so. Thailand explained: "Since the death penalty is prescribed in the Thai Penal Code as a discretionary decision of the court, such an assurance would prejudge the case."[23] The minister responded by amending the surrender order to manslaughter without death penalty assurances. The Thai authorities responded that it was not open to Thai authorities to amend the charges against Karas from murder to manslaughter in the absence of new evidence.

The minister responded by meeting with Thai government officials who advised, among other things, that when a foreign country has provided a diplomatic request seeking clemency from the King

---

[20] Treaty between the United Kingdom and Siam Respecting the Extradition of Fugitive Criminals, [1911] U.K.T.S. No. 23.

[21] *Extradition Act,* SC 1999, c. 18.

[22] *United States v. Burns,* [2001] 1 S.C.R. 283.

[23] Reasons at para. 40.

of Thailand with respect to one of its citizens sentenced to death there, the King has granted a pardon in every case. The minister also confirmed with the Department of Foreign Affairs that it would vigorously pursue clemency in the event of such a sentence against Karas. The minister was also advised by Correctional Services Canada that Karas was a psychopath who had been placed in solitary confinement for the protection of other inmates. On the basis of this information, the minister determined to surrender Karas without formal assurances from Thailand that the death penalty would not be imposed or carried out. The minister concluded that, in the words of the Supreme Court of Canada in *Burns,* it was not "reasonably anticipated" that the death penalty would result from Karas's extradition. The minister noted that Canada had no jurisdiction to prosecute Karas for a murder that took place on Thai soil and that a decision not to surrender him would ensure that he did not face justice at all and would promote lawlessness on the part of Canadians overseas. The minister therefore made a further amended surrender order that provided for Karas's surrender "for conduct described by Lysyk J." and without death penalty assurances.

In the interim, there was a military coup in Thailand (September 2006). The minister considered Karas's submissions on this point and concluded that surrender was still warranted and the extradition treaty between Thailand and Canada was still in force. Before the Court of Appeal, Karas challenged the further amended surrender order on jurisdictional and *Charter* grounds. The jurisdictional argument was that the minister had ordered surrender on the basis of the conduct described in Lysyk J.'s committal reasons rather than for the offence of manslaughter. The effect of these terms was to order the surrender of Karas for prosecution in Thailand on the Thai offence of murder. Rowles J.A. held that intention is an essential ingredient in the offence of murder both in Canada and in Thailand and that the minister exceeded his jurisdiction in effectively ordering Karas's surrender on the offence of murder despite Lysyk J.'s finding that only manslaughter was supportable on the evidence.[24]

Karas's *Charter* argument was that the minister violated his section 7 rights by ordering him to be surrendered to face a charge of murder without assurances from Thailand that the death penalty would not be imposed or carried out. This argument, of course, relied heavily on *Burns.* In particular, Karas contended that the

24 Reasons at para. 93. See also paras. 94–127.

minister had misapplied *Burns* and that the minister had erred in concluding (in the alternative) that his case fell within the "exceptional circumstances" contemplated, but not explained, in *Burns*.

The minister interpreted *Burns* as creating a threshold test to determine whether the death penalty was "reasonably anticipated" as a consequence of extradition. The minister concluded that the death penalty was not reasonably anticipated here given (among other things) the ability of the Thai court to convict on manslaughter instead of murder, the Thai practice of granting clemency to foreign death penalty convicts, and the intention of Canada to pursue such clemency if necessary.[25] Against this, Karas argued that *Burns* required the minister to ask not "What is the possibility of execution?" but "Is there a possibility of execution?" The court agreed.[26]

The minister's second position was that Karas's case constituted an exceptional circumstance of the sort contemplated in *Burns* wherein assurances need not be sought. The minister explained that Canada's inability to prosecute Karas here, combined with its failure to surrender him to Thailand, would make Canada a safe haven for fugitives. Before the court, the minister submitted that it was Thailand's legal incapacity either to grant assurances or to revise the charge against Karas that forced the minister to pursue alternative safeguards to formal assurances.

The court rejected this argument. It noted that *Burns* was founded in part on the international stance on capital punishment and concluded that the international trend towards abolition of the death penalty, described and relied upon in *Burns,* has continued since that decision was released (in 2001). In support, Rowles J.A. cited evidence of international practice from Amnesty International,[27] the entry into force of Protocol no. 13 to the European Convention on Human Rights[28] banning the death penalty in all circumstances, changes to the UK extradition practice prohibiting the secretary of state from extraditing to face the death penalty unless assurances are given,[29] and a recent article in *The Economist*

---

[25] Reasons at para. 135.

[26] Reasons at paras. 143–5.

[27] Reasons at para. 161.

[28] Protocol No. 13 to the Convention for the Protection of Human Rights and Fundamental Freedoms, Concerning the Abolition of the Death Penalty in All Circumstances, [2002] E.T.S. no. 187; Reasons at para. 162.

[29] Reasons at paras. 163–7.

describing the decline of enforcement of death penalty sentences from 1996 to 2006.[30] Rowles J.A. concluded:

All of the factors mentioned in the *Burns* analysis that weigh against surrendering Mr. Karas to Thailand for a capital crime without assurances are equally as compelling in the case at bar as they were in *Burns*. Further, since *Burns* was decided, the international move to abolish the death penalty has become stronger. I recognize Thailand does not at present have legislation enabling it to give the assurances required. However, Thailand can request the extradition of Mr. Karas to face the non-capital offence of manslaughter, rather than murder. Further, in the future, Thailand may pass the legislation allowing for extradition with assurances, as described in the Minister's letter. In my view, the argument that Mr. Karas will not face prosecution unless he is surrendered to Thailand to face murder charges without a death penalty assurance is unpersuasive ...

In my view, the fact that Thailand does not presently have domestic legislation to authorize the giving of assurances that the death penalty will not be imposed or, if imposed, will not be carried out does not bring the extradition case within the "exceptional circumstances" exception discussed in *Burns* ...

In my opinion, the constitutional requirement that Canada *obtain* assurances precludes the possibility of Canada asking for assurances, having those assurances refused, and then surrendering without assurances.[31]

Were it not for the comparative law analysis engaged in by the Supreme Court of Canada in *Burns*, one might doubt what the relevance of EU, UK, and other foreign legal practice was to the interpretation of the right to life, liberty, and security of the person guaranteed by section 7 of the Charter. Indeed, one might still doubt even after reading *Burns*, for the relevance of these comparative sources is not very clearly explained in that judgment. The striking fact about international practice regarding the death penalty, from a Canadian perspective, is surely that Canada has yet to ratify the second International Covenant on Civil and Political Rights Optional Protocol prohibiting the death penalty,[32] despite this country's effectively abolitionist stance. In any case, the Supreme Court of Canada opened the door to this sort of approach in *Burns*,

30 Reasons at para. 168.

31 Reasons at paras. 169, 171, and 174 [court's emphasis].

32 Second Optional Protocol to the 1989 International Covenant on Civil and Political Rights Aiming at the Abolition of the Death Penalty, 999 U.N.T.S. 302.

and the Court of Appeal can hardly be criticized for walking through it here. One is left to wonder, however, whether the exception contemplated by *Burns* has any content. If there is no exception on the facts of this case, is there really an exception at all?

Note: Leave to appeal to the Supreme Court of Canada was granted on 28 May 2009.

Judicial review of arbitral awards — Article 34 of UNCITRAL

Bayview Irrigation District #11 v. Mexico, 2008 CanLII 22120 (5 May 2008). Ontario Superior Court of Justice.

This was an application under Ontario's *International Commercial Arbitration Act* [33] which, by section 2, gives force to the UNCITRAL Model Law[34] in Ontario. Relying on Article 34 of the Model Law, the applicants sought judicial review of an award[35] made by an arbitral tribunal established under chapter 11 of the North American Free Trade Agreement[36] (erroneously described by the applications judge as the "North American Treaty Agreement"). Justice Allen dismissed the application.

The applicants, claimants before the North American Free Trade Agreement (NAFTA) tribunal, claimed ownership of a large quantity of water allocated to the United States under a 1944 treaty between the United States and Mexico.[37] The water rights allocated to the United States under the treaty were subsequently transferred to the state of Texas, which in turn granted them to the applicants, which consisted of seventeen irrigation districts, twenty-four individual water users, and a corporation. The applicants disputed Mexico's allocation of water between Texas and Mexico during the period 1992 to 2002, claiming that Mexico's actions breached NAFTA Articles 1102 (national treatment) and 1110 (expropriation). In response, Mexico challenged the tribunal's jurisdiction, arguing (among other things) that the applicants had no investment

---

[33] *International Commercial Arbitration Act,* R.S.O. 1998, c. I.9 as amended.

[34] Model Law on International Commercial Arbitration adopted by the United Nations Commission on International Trade Law, 21 June 1985.

[35] *Bayview Irrigation District No 11 and ors v. Mexico,* Award, ICSID Case no. ARB(AF)/05/1 (19 June 2007).

[36] North American Free Trade Agreement, [1994] Can. T.S. no. 2.

[37] Treaty between the United States of America and Mexico Respecting the Utilization of Waters of the Colorado and Tijuana Rivers and of the Rio Grande 1944, (1944) U.S.T.S. 994.

in Mexico and therefore could not avail themselves of the arbitral process provided for by NAFTA chapter 11. The tribunal agreed and dismissed the applicants' claims.

The applicants then resorted to the Ontario courts to set aside the award, Toronto being the agreed upon place of arbitration. Article 34 of the Model Law provides in relevant part:

(1) Recourse to a court against an arbitral award may be made only by an application for setting aside in accordance with paragraphs (2) and (3) of this article.

(2) An arbitral award may be set aside by the court specified in article 6 only if:

    (a) the party making the application furnishes proof that:

        (ii) the party making the application was not given proper notice of the appointment of an arbitrator or of the arbitral proceedings or was otherwise unable to present his case, or

        (iii) the award deals with a dispute not contemplated by or not falling within the terms of the submission to arbitration, or contains decisions on matters beyond the scope of the submission to arbitration, provided that, if the decisions on matters submitted to arbitration can be separated from those not so submitted, only that part of the award which contains decisions on matters not submitted to arbitration may be set aside

         ...

    (iv) or

    (b) the court finds that:

        (i) the subject-matter of the dispute is not capable of settlement by arbitration under the law of this State, or

        (ii) the award is in conflict with the public policy of this State.

As Allen J. rightly observed,

Article 34 sets out the grounds upon which a court can set aside an arbitration award. The court's role in reviewing an award is restricted to those grounds. Article 34(2)(a) establishes a claimant has the onus to prove one or more of the grounds under Article 34 is present. The Court is not permitted to engage in a hearing *de novo* on the merits of the Tribunal's decision or to undertake a review such as that conducted by a court in relation to a decision of a domestic tribunal. A high degree of deference is accorded on review by a court.[38]

---

[38] Reasons at para. 11.

Similarly,

> The standard of review of a domestic court of a decision of an internation-
> al commercial arbitral award is high. In the interest of comity among na-
> tions, predictability in decisions and respect for autonomy of the parties'
> chosen panel, it is only in exceptional circumstances that an arbitral deci-
> sion will be set aside. The grounds for refusing enforcement of an arbitral
> award under Article 5 are to be construed narrowly such that the award is
> not rendered invalid even where the tribunal wrongly decided a point of
> fact or law.[39]

Despite correctly identifying Article 34 as the sole basis for judicial
review of an international arbitral award, the learned judge nevertheless cited the most recent Supreme Court of Canada pronouncement on domestic standards of judicial review, *Dunsmuir v. New
Brunswick*.[40] This standard, and all domestic standards of review,
are quite irrelevant. Despite this citation, the overall tenor of Allen
J.'s observations on the all-important question of the applicable
standard of review is, with respect, very much in keeping with
Article 34. She observed that while international arbitral decisions
are not immune from challenge, there is a powerful presumption
that the tribunal acted within its authority. She added: "An arbitral
decision is not invalid because it wrongly decided a point of fact
or law."[41]

Allen J. quickly dispatched the applicant's "rather bare submission" that the tribunal had acted contrary to public policy (Article
34(2)(b)(ii)). The learned judge also rejected the applicants' complaint that the tribunal denied them a fair opportunity to present
their case. The allegation here was that the question of whether
water rights could constitute an investment for NAFTA purposes
was supposed to be left to the merits stage of the arbitration, yet
the tribunal proceeded to address the point, in Mexico's favour, in
their decision on jurisdiction. The applicants contended before
Allen J. that, in doing so, the tribunal dealt with a dispute not
within the terms of the submission to arbitration contrary to Articles
18 (equal treatment of the parties) and 34(2)(b)(iii) of the Model
Law. In rejecting these submissions, Allen J. noted that the applicants
made no objection during the hearings and did not seek an adjourn-

---

[39] Reasons at para. 13.

[40] *Dunsmuir v. New Brunswick*, 2008 SCC 9; Reasons at para. 60.

[41] Reasons at para. 63.

ment in order to present further evidence.[42] Oddly, Allen J. invoked the Canadian constitutional law concept of the "principles of fundamental justice" in scrutinizing the tribunal's decision on this point. This concept is unhelpful in this context, as it has no basis in Article 34 and is of uncertain ambit even in Canadian law.

Finally, Allen J. rejected the applicants' argument that Mexico was wrongly permitted to challenge the facts alleged by the claimants, contrary to settled arbitral practice that allegations are to be accepted as true for the purpose of determining jurisdictional points. She noted that the tribunal took the view that its jurisdiction depended on a determination of whether the applicants' claim met the threshold requirement under NAFTA Article 1101(1)(b) that the alleged water rights constitute an "investment." The tribunal concluded that such rights were not an investment. Allen J. expressly deferred to the tribunal's expertise, seeing no reason to intervene.[43]

This decision is encouraging in its affirmation of the very limited role domestic courts are given by the Model Law in judicial reviews of international arbitral awards. Were international arbitration to become only the necessary prelude to judicial review proceedings before domestic courts, international arbitration would become even more expensive and slow than it is now. Even in this decision, however, there are instances in which legal concepts particular to Canada seem to creep in at times, though thankfully not decisively.

Canadian Charter of Rights and Freedoms — extra-territorial application — Guantanamo Bay, Cuba

Canada (Justice) v. Khadr, 2008 SCC 28 (23 May 2008). Supreme Court of Canada.

In brief reasons ascribed only to "The Court," the Supreme Court of Canada held that a Canadian, detained by American authorities at the notorious US prison in Guantanamo Bay, Cuba, was entitled to disclosure from the government of Canada of documents in its possession relevant to the charges he faces. The detainee, Omar Khadr, sought this relief under section 7 of the Canadian Charter of Rights and Freedoms, relying on the well-established precedent of *R. v. Stinchcombe.*[44] The documents sought were the product of

---

[42] Reasons at para. 71; see also para. 73.

[43] Reasons at para. 76.

[44] *R. v. Stinchcombe,* [1991] 3 S.C.R. 326.

interviews of Khadr by Canadian officials in Guantanamo Bay in 2003. In granting the relief Khadr sought, the Court held that it did so as an exception to the "principles of international law and comity of nations, which normally require that Canadian officials operating abroad comply with local law."[45] The Court framed the issue as raising "the relationship between Canada's domestic and international human rights commitments."[46]

Khadr was taken prisoner by American forces in Afghanistan in July 2002. He was fifteen years old at the time. He is alleged to have killed an American soldier with a grenade and to have conspired with Al-Qaeda to commit acts of murder and terrorism against US and coalition forces. At the time of judgment, he had been held without trial in Guantanamo Bay for nearly six years. Canadian officials have attended at Guantanamo Bay to meet with Khadr on several occasions. Their visits do not appear to have been for the purpose of extending consular services. To the contrary, the officials, who included Canadian Service Intelligence Service (CSIS) agents, have interviewed Khadr for intelligence and law enforcement purposes, and shared the product of these interviews (or rather, interrogations) with US authorities.

After formal charges were laid against Khadr in November 2005, he sought disclosure from the Canadian government under *Stinchcombe* and was refused. He challenged the decision in Federal Court and was unsuccessful at first instance but successful on appeal. The Crown appealed, arguing that the Federal Court of Appeal erred in applying *Stinchcombe* given the decision of the Supreme Court of Canada in *R. v. Hape*[47] that Canadian agents participating in investigations abroad are not bound by the Charter. The Court explained *Hape* as "based on international law principles against extraterritorial enforcement of domestic laws and the principle of comity which implies acceptance of foreign laws and procedures when Canadian officials are operating abroad."[48] There was, however, an exception planted by the majority in *Hape*, namely that "comity cannot be used to justify Canadian participation in activities in a foreign state or its agents that are contrary to Canada's international obligations."

---

[45] Reasons at para. 2. No explanation is offered in the Reasons as to what the "local law" of the US military prison at Guantanamo Bay, Cuba, may be.

[46] Reasons at para. 1.

[47] *R. v. Hape*, [2007] 2 S.C.R. 292.

[48] Reasons at para. 17.

Rather, the courts should "seek to ensure compliance with Canada's binding obligations under international law."[49]

The Court therefore reasoned that if the "Guantanamo Bay process under which Mr. Khadr was being held was in conformity with Canada's international obligations, the Charter has no application ... However, if Canada was participating in a process that was violative of Canada's binding obligations under international law, the Charter applies to the extent of that participation."[50] The Court therefore purported to ask itself whether Guantanamo Bay is contrary to Canada's international legal obligations.[51] I say "purported" because the answer the Court gives does not quite match the question it claims to be asking. The Court observed that the Supreme Court of the United States has held that Guantanamo detainees were illegally denied *habeas corpus* and were subjected to violations of the Geneva Conventions.[52] Of course, the Supreme Court of the United States did not consider whether Guantanamo Bay was in violation of Canada's international obligations. That is obviously not a question for the US courts, and, in any case, it is hard to see how any state other that the United States could be regarded as internationally responsible for a prison operated by the United States on US-controlled lands. Nevertheless, the Supreme Court of Canada concluded that the US case law was "sufficient to permit us to conclude that the regime providing for the detention and trial of Mr. Khadr at the time of the CSIS interviews constituted a clear violation of fundamental human rights protected by international law."[53] To use a commercial term, the Court "outsourced" the international legal analysis to the Supreme Court of the United States, though it did note that Canada is a "signatory" (read: party) to the Geneva Conventions and observed, though without citation of Article 9(4) of the 1966 International Covenant on Civil and Political Rights or any other instrument, that *habeas corpus* is a fundamental right protected by international treaties.[54]

---

[49] Reasons at para. 18.

[50] Reasons at para. 19.

[51] Reasons at para. 20.

[52] Reasons at para. 21. The US decisions are *Rasul v. Bush*, 542 US 466 (2004) and *Hamdan v. Rumsfeld* 126 S. Ct. 2749 (2006).

[53] Reasons at para. 24.

[54] Reasons at para. 25.

The Court stated its conclusion as follows:

We conclude that the principles of international law and comity that might otherwise preclude application of the Charter to Canadian officials acting abroad do not apply to the assistance they gave to U.S. authorities at Guantanamo Bay. Given the holdings of the United States Supreme Court, the *Hape* comity concerns that would ordinarily justify deference to foreign law have no application here. The effect of the United States Supreme Court's holdings is that the conditions under which Mr. Khadr was held and was liable for prosecution were illegal under both U.S. and international law at the time Canadian officials interviewed Mr. Khadr and gave the information to U.S. authorities. Hence no question of deference to foreign law arises. The Charter bound Canada to the extent that the conduct of Canadian officials involved it in a process that violated Canada's international obligations.[55]

This is, with respect, a difficult argument to follow. First, it is hard to see how any foreign law might prevent or preclude Canada from disclosing documents to a Canadian citizen. Certainly, no such law was cited in the judgment. Furthermore, any such law would be objectionable on the very grounds of extraterritoriality and comity that the *Hape* court purported to rely upon in excluding the Charter's application in cases where Canadian officials operate abroad. No rule of international law or comity would require Canada to heed such a foreign edict. So the dilemma is doubly false: there is no international law requirement that Canada defer to a foreign law precluding it from disclosing documents to its own nationals, and there is no such foreign law at issue here in the first place. Second, the Court's determination that the Charter applies here turns on the holdings of the Supreme Court of the United States. The corollary seems to be that were Khadr imprisoned in a despotic country in which the legality of his detention could not be contested in the courts, or had the US court upheld the legality of Guantanamo, the Charter would not apply and Khadr would have no remedy — all in the name of international law and comity.[56]

---

55 Reasons at para. 26.

56 There is another possibility: perhaps if Khadr were detained in North Korea, for example, Canadian courts could find that the *Hape* exception applies, even without a ruling by that country's courts, by holding that North Korea's conduct was somehow contrary to international law. That may not be so, for the *Hape* exception purports to be directed at Canada's international obligations, not

The Court then proceeded to hold that Canada "participated in a process that was contrary to Canada's international human rights obligations" by "making the product of its interviews of Mr. Khadr available to U.S. authorities."[57] It is telling that the Court does not identify which of Canada's international human rights obligations it violated by sharing information with US authorities. It is far from clear that international human rights law really does include a right of criminally accused persons not to have information about them shared between states. The Court seems to anticipate this objection, for it observes that it "suffices to note that at the time Canada handed over the fruits of the interviews to U.S. officials, it was bound by the Charter, because at that point it became a participant in a process that violated Canada's international obligations." Again, the question is, which international obligations? I am sympathetic to the suggestion, implied if not made here, that the entire edifice of Guantanamo Bay is an international wrong and that any state participating in it might be internationally responsible for its participation. However, if that is the Court's meaning, it should have provided the analysis to support it.

The Court concluded that Khadr was entitled to disclosure of documents under Charter section 7, though not based directly on *Stinchcombe*.[58] Rather, the remedy granted here was said to be "for breach of a constitutional duty that arose when Canadian agents became participants in a process that violates Canada's international obligations."[59] I do not take issue with the result of *Khadr*, namely that documents be disclosed to the applicant along *Stinchcombe* lines. Yet this is a case note about public international law, not

---

those of foreign states (e.g., *Hape* at para. 101; *Khadr* at para. 18). Furthermore, it is not the usual role of domestic courts to sit in judgment of the international legality of acts by foreign states, and both North Korea and Canada might legitimately object to a court embarking on such an inquiry. However, the *Khadr* decision is hardly rigorous in applying the distinction between violations of Canada's obligations and violations by the US of its own obligations, as its exclusive reliance on US Supreme Court authority illustrates. Assuming that *Hape/Khadr* do permit (indeed, require) an applicant for Charter relief in such a case to establish a violation of international law by the detaining state, there is always the possibility that the conduct of that state might not actually be contrary to international law, in which case a person in Khadr's position would again be left without a remedy.

57 Reasons at para. 27.

58 Reasons at para. 37.

59 Reasons at para. 36.

results-driven reasoning. The ultimate question raised by *Khadr,* and perhaps even by *Hape,* must be: "Should international law come into the question at all?" Whether a Canadian is constitutionally entitled to document disclosure by the Canadian government is principally, and perhaps even exclusively, a question of Canadian law. The Court's mistake in *Hape* was to conclude that it is contrary to international law for a Canadian court to scrutinize the conduct of a Canadian official against Canadian laws where the conduct under scrutiny took place in a foreign country. In *Khadr,* that mistake is exacerbated by elaborating upon an exception to a rule that ought not to be.

Immigration — persecution or refoulement — Safe Third Country Agreement with the United States

Canadian Council for Refugees v. Canada, 2008 FCA 229 (27 June 2008). Federal Court of Appeal. Leave to appeal to the Supreme Court of Canada denied 5 February 2009.

The Canadian Council of Refugees, the Canadian Council of Churches, Amnesty International, and John Doe sought judicial review of sections 159.1 to 159.7 of the Immigration and Refugee Protection Regulations[60] and the Agreement between the Government of Canada and the Government of the United States of American for Cooperation in the Examination of Refugee Status Claims from Nationals of Third Countries.[61] They contended that the impugned provisions of the Regulation, and the Agreement itself, were *ultra vires* the Governor-in-Council's power under section 102 of the *Immigration and Refugee Protection Act.*[62] In particular, the applicants argued that a condition precedent to the exercise of power under section 102 was that the designated country (here the United States) comply with the non-refoulement obligations found in Article 33 of the Convention Relating to the Status of Refugees (Refugee Convention)[63] and Article 3 of the Convention against Torture and Other Cruel, Inhuman or Degrading Treatment or

---

[60] Immigration and Refugee Protection Regulations, SOR/2002–227.

[61] Agreement between the Government of Canada and the Government of the United States of American for Cooperation in the Examination of Refugee Status Claims from Nationals of Third Countries, [2004] Can. T.S. no. 2.

[62] *Immigration and Refugee Protection Act,* S.C. 2001, c. 27.

[63] Refugee Convention, *supra* note 1.

Punishment (Convention against Torture).[64] The applicants also relied on sections 7 and 15 of the Charter. The applications judge generally agreed with the applicants and granted the relief sought.[65]

On appeal, Justice of Appeal Noël for the majority of the Federal Court of Appeal reversed the applications judge on almost every point. Justice of Appeal Evans concurred in separate reasons. The impugned regulations serve to implement the agreement in Canadian law. The effect of the regulations is that if a refugee enters Canada from the United States at a land border point of entry, Canada will (subject to specified exceptions) send the refugee back to the United States. Under the agreement, the United States undertakes to do the same. This arrangement is known as a "safe third country agreement" because the participating states (Canada and the United States) are ones in which refugee claimants are said not be exposed to persecution, torture, ill-treatment, or refoulement. Section 102 of the act provides,

---

Regulations

102. (1) The regulations may govern matters relating to the application of sections 100 and 101, may, for the purposes of this Act, define the terms used in those sections and, for the purpose of sharing responsibility with governments of foreign states for the consideration of refugee claims, may include provisions

(a) designating countries that comply with Article 33 of the Refugee Convention and Article 3 of the Convention Against Torture;

(b) making a list of those countries and amending it as necessary; and

Règlements

102. (1) Les règlements régissent l'application des articles 100 et 101, définissent, pour l'application de la présente loi, les termes qui y sont employés et, en vue du partage avec d'autres pays de la responsabilité de l'examen des demandes d'asile, prévoient notamment:

a) la désignation des pays qui se conforment à l'article 33 de la Convention sur les réfugiés et à l'article 3 de la Convention contre la torture;

b) l'établissement de la liste de ces pays, laquelle est renouvelée en tant que de besoin;

---

64 Convention against Torture and other Cruel, Inhuman or Degrading Treatment or Punishment, [1987] Can. T.S. no. 36.

65 *Canadian Council for Refugees v. Canada*, 2007 FC 1262.

(c) respecting the circumstances and criteria for the application of paragraph 101(1)(e).

Factors

(2) The following factors are to be considered in designating a country under paragraph (1)(a):

(a) whether the country is a party to the Refugee Convention and to the Convention Against Torture;
(b) its policies and practices with respect to claims under the Refugee Convention and with respect to obligations under the Convention Against Torture;
(c) its human rights record; and
(d) whether it is party to an agreement with the Government of Canada for the purpose of sharing responsibility with respect to claims for refugee protection.

Review

(3) The Governor in Council must ensure the continuing review of factors set out in subsection (2) with respect to each designated country.

c) les cas et les critères d'application de l'alinéa 101(1)e).

Facteurs

(2) Il est tenu compte des facteurs suivants en vue de la désignation des pays sous le paragraph (1)(a):

a) le fait que ces pays sont parties à la Convention sur les réfugiés et à la Convention contre la torture;
b) leurs politique et usages en ce qui touche la revendication du statut de réfugié au sens de la Convention sur les réfugiés et les obligations découlant de la Convention contre la torture;
c) leurs antécédents en matière de respect des droits de la personne;
d) le fait qu'ils sont ou non parties à un accord avec le Canada concernant le partage de la responsabilité de l'examen des demandes d'asile.

Suivi

(3) Le gouverneur en conseil assure le suivi de l'examen des facteurs dans subsection (2) à l'égard de chacun des pays désignés.

The United States is designated a safe third country under section 102(1)(a) of the act by section 159.3 of the regulations.

In support of the application, the respondents relied on affidavit evidence from US academics and practitioners describing US asylum law and policy. The thrust of this evidence was that US practice was in violation of the Refugee Convention. The government's affidavit evidence sought to depict US practice as compliant with international law and to establish that a safe third country regime exists in the European Union.

The applications judge preferred the respondents' evidence. He interpreted section 102(1) of the act as requiring, as a precondition for concluding the agreement, that the United States comply with Article 33 of the Refugee Convention and Article 3 of the Convention against Torture. The learned judge wrote: "To interpret s. 102(1) of the Act as giving the Governor-in-Council the discretion to enter into safe third country agreements with countries that do not comply with the *Refugee Convention* and the *Convention Against Torture* would make a mockery of Canada's international commitments, of the very purpose of our domestic laws and even of the internal logic of s. 102(1)."[66] Having preferred the evidence indicating that the United States was in violation of its international obligations, the applications judge held that the Governor-in-Council's designation of the United States as a safe third country was *ultra vires* the act.

Noël J.A. began by considering whether the designation of the United States as a safe third country was a decision subject to judicial review. The generally accepted view is that the promulgation of regulations, like the enactment of legislation, is not subject to judicial review on administrative law principles, except where the allegation is that the regulation is *ultra vires* the enabling legislation. As Noël J.A. lucidly explains, "[a]n attack on the legality of subordinate legislation ... remains what it has always been; an attack on the impugned regulation *per se* and not on the 'decision' to promulgate it."[67] Noël J.A. therefore held that applications judge erred in conducting a pragmatic and functional analysis to determine the applicable standard of review. There was no need to do so because there was no decision to review here. Rather, the issue was *vires*, which is always a matter of correctness. Noël J.A. therefore concluded that the question properly before the Court was whether the impugned regulations and the agreement are *ultra vires* the act.[68]

Noël J.A. characterized the first instance decision as requiring "actual" compliance, or compliance "in absolute terms," with the

---

[66] Quoted in the Reasons at para. 67.

[67] Reasons at para. 56.

[68] Reasons at para. 64.

relevant international obligations.[69] Relying on the factors set out in section 102(2) of the act, Noël J.A. took the view that the Governor-in-Council could not lawfully designate a country under this section unless satisfied that the country's policies, practices, and record indicate compliance. Yet actual or absolute compliance was not required; the section requires only that the Governor-in-Council give due consideration to the factors set out in section 102(2). So long as the Governor-in-Council does not act in bad faith or for an improper purpose in making a designation, "there is nothing left to be reviewed judicially."[70] Similarly, Noël J.A. held that section 102(3) of the act does not require the Governor-in-Council to monitor the actual compliance of designated states with the Refugee Convention and the Convention against Torture but only continuing review of the section 102(2) factors.[71]

Noël J.A. also rejected the applications judge's findings of Charter breaches. He considered there to be an insufficient evidentiary basis for bringing a Charter challenge here, and that the Charter challenge should therefore not have been entertained.[72] Evans J.A. concurred in the result and agreed that the Charter challenge should not have been entertained. He observed, however, that "my colleague's reasons do not persuade me that the issues of statutory interpretation and the scope of judicial review raised by the respondents' application are so clear and incontrovertible that they warrant a departure from the guiding principle of judicial restraint that it is generally better to say less than more."[73] Instead, Evans J.A. preferred to allow the appeal on the ground that the relief sought was premature. His view was that a declaration invalidating the regulations was not required to ensure that they not be applied to refugee claimants in violation of either Canada's international obligations or the Charter.[74] He noted in particular that the Act "must be construed and applied so as to be consistent with Canada's international obligations." Thus, refugee claimants at the Canadian land border may not be turned back to the US if they can establish that, if returned, they would face a real risk of refoulement by the

---

[69] Reasons at paras. 77–8.

[70] Reasons at para. 78.

[71] Reasons at para. 92.

[72] Reasons at para. 103.

[73] Reasons at para. 108.

[74] Reasons at para. 130.

US to a country where they would have a well-founded fear of persecution or torture.[75]

As noted, Noël J.A. depicted the question before the Court in this appeal as whether the impugned regulations and the agreement are *ultra vires* the act. Yet the learned judge's subsequent analysis is devoted entirely to scrutiny of the regulations rather than the agreement. The issue of whether, and to what extent, a court may review the federal government's prerogative power to enter into treaties with foreign states is not addressed. Perhaps the course of judicial restraint recommended by Evans J.A. is appropriate here, and the issue better left to another day. But the question of whether Canadian courts have a power to invalidate treaties concluded by Canada is one that will need to be considered. It seems clear that a domestic court's pronouncement on the validity of an international agreement cannot affect that agreement's force or effect internationally. What consequence, if any, such a declaration might have in Canadian law, and whether such relief is available in the first place, is less clear than this case, and others, suggest.[76]

BRIEFLY NOTED / SOMMAIRE EN BREF

Charter of Rights and Freedoms — extra-territorial application — detention of persons by Canadian Forces in Afghanistan

Amnesty International Canada v. Canada (Canadian Forces), 2008 FC 336 (12 March 2008). Federal Court.

Application for judicial review seeking Charter relief in respect of persons detained by Canadian Forces operating in Afghanistan on the basis that arrangements between Canada and Afghanistan fail to provide adequate safeguards against exposure to the risk of torture. Justice Mactavish held that the Charter does not apply and dismissed the application. The Federal Court of Appeal has since upheld this decision, and leave to appeal to the Supreme Court of Canada has been denied. The appellate decision will be summarized in the next issue of the *Yearbook*.

---

[75] Reasons at paras. 122–3.

[76] E.g., *Chua v. Minister of National Revenue*, [2001] 1 FC 608 (TD).

Canadian Cases in Private International Law in 2007–8 / Jurisprudence canadienne en matière de droit international privé en 2007–8

compiled by / préparé par

JOOST BLOM

A JURISDICTION / COMPÉTENCE DES TRIBUNAUX

1 Common Law and Federal

(a) Jurisdiction *in personam*

Attornment to the jurisdiction

Note. See *Norex Petroleum Ltd. v. Chubb Insurance Co. of Canada*, [2008] 12 W.W.R. 322, 2008 ABQB 442, in which the Russian corporate defendant had filed a statement of defence and made a motion to strike out a pleading, but maintained that it never intended to attorn to the Alberta court's jurisdiction. Its intent was held irrelevant to the fact that it had attorned. Its attornment did not bar it from arguing *forum non conveniens,* but the court refused a stay, mainly on the grounds that there was a real risk that the plaintiff, the Canadian insured, would not get a fair trial in Russia and that the plaintiff's chairman could not travel to Russia out of a reasonable fear that he could be arrested and imprisoned on trumped-up criminal charges.

Non-resident defendant — claim arising out of business, investment, or professional transaction — jurisdiction simpliciter *found to exist — jurisdiction not declined*

Petroasia Energy Inc. v. Samek LLP (2008), 90 Alta. L.R. (4th) 373, 2008 ABQB 50 (Alberta Queen's Bench), affd. (2008), 94 Alta. L.R. (4th) 265, 2008 ABCA 323 (Alberta Court of Appeal)

The plaintiffs, an Alberta corporation (Petroasia) and its Netherlands subsidiary, claimed that Kaschapov, an individual resident

Joost Blom is in the Faculty of Law at the University of British Columbia.

in Kazakhstan, had been an officer and employee of the plaintiffs and had broken his fiduciary duty towards them by obtaining certain oil and gas concessions in Kazakhstan for the benefit of a corporation resident in that country (Samek), whereas he was supposed to be trying to obtain it for the plaintiffs. They also alleged breaches of four contracts that the Kaschapov, Samek, or both had made with the plaintiffs. The plaintiffs brought an action against Kaschapov, Samek, and a law firm in Kazakhstan, claiming, *inter alia,* an accounting of profits by Kaschapov and a declaration that Samek held the concessions in trust for the plaintiffs. Under rule 30 of the Alberta Rules of Court, the plaintiffs required leave to serve the defendants *ex juris.* The grounds for seeking service *ex juris* were that the claims were for breach of contracts made in Alberta (R. 30(f) (i)) and for breaches committed in Alberta of contracts made in or out of Alberta (R. 30(g)). Leave was granted *ex parte,* but the defendants sought to have the order set aside on the ground that the Alberta court lacked jurisdiction *simpliciter* because there was no real and substantial connection between the litigation and Alberta, or, alternatively, Alberta was *forum non conveniens.*

The chambers judge affirmed the order. The plaintiffs alleged that they had made an oral employment contract with Kaschapov — this would be a contract that by implication was governed by Alberta law, and a claim for the breach of it satisfied R. 30(f)(iii). A claim based on an alleged separate oral agreement with Kaschapov, to bid on oil and gas concessions, was insufficiently proved by the plaintiffs' affidavit evidence and could therefore not support service *ex juris.* A claim for breach of a third contract, one for services to be performed by Samek for Petroasia, satisfied the rule because the plaintiffs had made a good arguable case that the agreement was made in Alberta (R. 30(f)(i)). The alleged breach of the agreement, which was the failure by Samek to transfer the concession to Petroasia, took place in Kazakhstan because, on the evidence, the transfer would have had to be approved by the authorities there, and so the claim did not satisfy rule 30(g). The fourth alleged contract was a Loan and Conversion Transfer Agreement made between the two corporations. It was clear that it was negotiated, drafted and signed on behalf of Samek in Kazakhstan, and Petroasia's faxed acceptance was received there, which meant the contract was made there, not in Alberta. Nor was the alleged breach of this agreement committed in Alberta. Service *ex juris* was therefore available for claims based on breaches of the first and third alleged agreements. These claims had a real and substantial connection with Alberta.

The plaintiffs had also established that Alberta was the most appropriate forum to hear the action, despite the fact that the subject matter of the dispute was hydrocarbon rights in Kazakhstan and practical enforcement of any judgment would have to occur in Kazakhstan. The factors leading to this conclusion included evidence that suggested the Loan and Conversion Transfer Agreement might be void under Kazakhstan law whereas it appeared to be a valid contract as far as Alberta law was concerned, thus giving the plaintiffs a legitimate juridical advantage in Alberta. The Court of Appeal held the chambers judge was entitled to find the facts she did, for the purposes of the jurisdictional issues, on the basis of the affidavit evidence before her.

Wang v. Columbia Pictures Industries Inc. (2007), 49 C.P.C. (6th) 1, 2007 SKCA 133 (Saskatchewan Court of Appeal)

Columbia, a Delaware corporation whose motion picture business was based in California, brought an action in Saskatchewan against Wang, a resident of the province, for breach of an agreement granting the company an option on the film and stage rights to certain literary works in which Wang owned the copyright. Another defendant was Weinstein, a Delaware corporation, headquartered in New York, to which the rights had been granted. Ten days after Columbia brought the action in Saskatchewan, Weinstein began litigation in California against Columbia on essentially the same issues. The California court stayed Weinstein's action in deference to Columbia's Saskatchewan action. Both Wang and Weinstein applied to have the Saskatchewan court decline jurisdiction on the ground of *forum non conveniens,* and Weinstein, in addition, argued the Saskatchewan court lacked territorial competence (that is, jurisdiction *simpliciter*) in respect of the claims against it, applying the rules in the *Court Jurisdiction and Proceedings Transfer Act,* S.S. 1997, c. C-41.1. The motion judge dismissed both defendants' applications.

The Saskatchewan Court of Appeal affirmed that the Saskatchewan court had territorial competence in the action against Weinstein and was the *forum conveniens* for the actions against Wang and Weinstein. Columbia's claims fell within two of the categories in which section 9 of the act presumes the existence of a real and substantial connection with the province. The copyright in the works was movable property situated in the province because the holder of the rights resided in Saskatchewan. This brought the claim within section 9(a) (the proceeding "is brought to enforce, assert, declare or determine proprietary or possessory rights or a security interest in immovable or movable property in Saskatchewan"). Columbia's action was also for an injunction to restrain Wang and Weinstein from acting contrary to Columbia's option to acquire an interest in the works, which was within section 9(i) ("is a claim for an injunction ordering a party to do or refrain from doing anything (i) in Saskatchewan; or (ii) in relation to immovable or movable property in Saskatchewan"). The court also upheld the judge's decision that California had not been shown to be a clearly more appropriate forum for the claims against either defendant, applying the non-exhaustive list of factors in section 10(2) of the act that must be considered in exercising the *forum non conveniens* discretion. The central issue in the action was whether negotiations in Saskatchewan resulted in an agreement between Columbia and Wang. Even if California law was ultimately held to govern the issues, which was debatable, that law could be proved and applied in Saskatchewan.

Note. The fact that the action was for an order for the sale of immovable property in the province was held to provide a real and substantial connection in *Rakunas v. Scenic Associates Ltd.* (2008), 55 C.P.C. (6th) 293, 2008 BCSC 444, even though the property was owned by an offshore corporation and the dispute was between two foreign residents who held shares in the corporation.

Purple Echo Productions Inc. v. KCTS Television (2008), 76 B.C.L.R. (4th) 21, 2008 BCCA 85 (British Columbia Court of Appeal)

KCTS, a public television station in Seattle, Washington, made a co-production agreement with Purple Echo, a Vancouver, British Columbia-based provider of personal advice for a series of talk show television programs that included celebrity and person-on-the-street interviews. Purple Echo produced thirteen episodes. It claimed that KCTS did not perform its obligations under the agreement. KCTS applied to have the writ and statement of claim struck out, or the proceedings stayed or dismissed on the ground that the court had no jurisdiction or should decline jurisdiction. The chambers judge, applying the *Court Jurisdiction and Proceedings Transfer Act*, R.S.B.C. 2003, c. 28, held the court lacked territorial competence under section 3 and, in any event, should decline jurisdiction under section 11. He found that Purple Echo had not shown on a balance of probabilities that KCTS was ordinarily resident in British Columbia (giving territorial competence under section 3(d)) or that the action concerned breaches the contractual obligations that were substantially to be performed in the province (providing, by virtue of section 10(e)(i), a presumed real and substantial connection with the province for the purposes of territorial competence under section 3(e)). He also held there was no presumed real and substantial connection under section 10(h) ("concerns a business carried on in British Columbia") because the defendant did not carry on business in the province, notwithstanding its owning a corporation that raised funds in British Columbia for its operations in Seattle. The plaintiff's having a business that was carried on in the province was not enough. On *forum non conveniens* he held that the Washington courts were more appropriate as a forum for Purple Echo's action.

The British Columbia Court of Appeal reversed the chambers judge's decision, both on territorial competence and on *forum non conveniens*. On the former, it held that the judge had applied the wrong standard when he required the plaintiff to establish on a balance of probabilities the jurisdictional facts relating to the claims. When a defendant applies for a dismissal or stay of the proceeding on the ground that the court has no jurisdiction because the plaintiff has not pleaded necessary jurisdictional facts (rule 14(6)(a) of the British Columbia Supreme Court Rules) or because the court does not in fact have jurisdiction in respect of the claim (rule 14(6) (b)), the matter is to be decided on a "good arguable case" standard, since it is being decided at an interlocutory stage. The court contrasted those two rules with rule 14(6)(c), which permits a defendant to allege in a pleading that the court does not have jurisdiction. If a defendant does that, and jurisdiction remains an issue for trial, the factual questions must then be decided on the balance of probabilities.

This case concerned an interlocutory application and Purple Echo had met the good arguable case standard in respect of the pleaded facts and supporting affidavit evidence. It was arguable that KCTS was ordinarily resident in the province because it had a place of business there (section 7(c) of the act). As for the alternative ground of territorial competence, namely a real and substantial connection with the province, the court did not rely on the presumptions in section 10 but simply held that Purple Echo had made a good arguable case that the necessary connection with the province was present. Relevant in this context were the facts that obligations under the co-production agreement were to be performed to a significant extent in the province; that an objective of the agreement was the capitalize on KCTS's considerable audience and support base in the province; and that KCTS actively participated in the Canadian market and relied on it heavily for support.

As for *forum non conveniens,* the judge had failed to consider the interests of the parties as mandated by section 11(1) and, in particular, the *prima facie* entitlement of Purple Echo to its chosen forum, reflected in the principle that a more appropriate forum must be clearly established to displace the forum selected by the plaintiff.

Note 1. The distinction drawn between applying for dismissal or a stay because the court does not have jurisdiction (rules 14(6)(a) and (b)) and pleading and proving that a court does not have jurisdiction (rule 14(6)(c)) is an artifact of the rather awkwardly drafted British Columbia rules of court. If one wonders how a defendant can go to trial while still maintaining a jurisdictional challenge under rule 14(6)(c), the answer lies in rule 14(6.4), which exempts a defendant from being held to attorn to the jurisdiction, even if it defends the action on the merits, if a jurisdictional challenge is made under rule 14(6)(a), (b), or (c) within thirty days after entering an appearance. The exemption lasts until the court has decided the application (in the case of (a) and (b)) or decided the issue raised by the pleading (in the case of (c)). Another wrinkle is that the rule 14(6.4) exemption is worded so as not to apply if the defendant's jurisdictional challenge is limited to arguing that the court should decline jurisdiction. In other words, to protect its position the defendant must file a challenge, if only for the sake of form, to the existence of jurisdiction *simpliciter.* If this is not done, however, all may not be lost. In *Lin v. Huang* (2008), 59 C.P.C. (6th) 1, 2008 BCSC 288, the court held it could grant a stay on *forum non conveniens* grounds despite the fact that the defendant had attorned and a challenge to jurisdiction was filed too late to trigger the exemption. Taiwan was clearly a more appropriate jurisdiction, the dispute being between two Taiwanese businesswomen concerning a loan agreement written in Chinese, executed in Taiwan, and the subject of legal proceedings in Taiwan.

Note 2. At this point three provinces (British Columbia, Nova Scotia and Saskatchewan) and one territory (Yukon) have put their jurisdictional rules into statutory form in the *Court Jurisdiction and Proceedings Transfer Act* promulgated in 1994 by the Uniform Law Conference of Canada. As the above cases illustrate, one of the features of the Act is that it provides a list of cases in which a real and substantial connection with the province is (rebuttably) presumed.

Jurisdiction *simpliciter* was found under this provision in a number of other cases. In *Roeder v. Chamberlain*, 2008 BCSC 624, although the plaintiff lived in the United States and the defendant was a lawyer practising in Alberta, the negligence and breach of contract alleged involved consenting to the release of shares out of escrow in British Columbia. The claims therefore concerned a tort committed in the province and contractual obligations that to a substantial extent were to be performed in the province, two of the situations where jurisdiction *simpliciter* is presumed (S.B.C. 2003, s. 10(g) and (e), respectively). In *Stanway v. Wyeth Canada Inc.*, 2008 BCSC 847, claims against a drug manufacturer in respect of an insufficiently disclosed potential side-effect of a drug marketed, with the defendant's active involvement, in the province were within the categories of claims concerning a tort committed in the province (s. 10(e)) and a business carried on in the province (s. 10(h)). The fact that the plaintiff's business was injured in British Columbia was held also to bring the claim within s. 10(h), in *Timber West Forest Corp. v. United Steel, Paper & Forestry, Rubber Manufacturing, Energy, Allied & Service Workers Int'l Union*, 2008 BCSC 388. The defendant union was said to have made defamatory statements in Utah as well as British Columbia about the plaintiff's business, which constituted a tort committed in the province (s. 10(e)) because the statements were published and caused harm there. And the claim for an injunction against further statements was a claim for an injunction ordering a party to refrain from doing something in the province (s. 10(i)(i)). For another case under the Act, see the note of *Olney v. Rainville* below under (e) Infants and Children — Declaration of paternity.

In non-*Court Jurisdiction and Proceedings Transfer Act* provinces, jurisdiction *simpliciter* against a non-consenting defendant requires that the plaintiff show there is a real and substantial connection with the province. This test was met in *Wheeler v. 1000128 Alberta Ltd.* (2008), 87 Alta. L.R. (4th) 138, 2008 ABQB 70 (claims for conspiracy and for breaches of securities legislation against an Alberta company and its foreign parent companies); *Research in Motion Ltd. v. Visto Corp.* (2008), 93 O.R. (3d) 593 (S.C.J.) (claims for injurious falsehood, conspiracy, and wrongs under Canadian competition and trade-marks legislation brought by Ontario-based international company against Delaware company for statements made abroad but disseminated in Ontario); *Precious Metal Capital Corp. v. Smith* (2008), 297 D.L.R. (4th) 746, 2008 ONCA 577 (Ontario-based firm suing foreign defendants for breaches of fiduciary obligation that deprived it of business opportunities in South America); *Visram v. Chandarana* (2008), 291 D.L.R. (4th) 412 (Ont. Div. Ct.) (Ontario resident suing a number of defendants, some resident in Zambia, in respect of fraud in the sale of the assets of a Zambian company, with some of the relevant meetings and representations having taken place in Ontario); and *Big Sky Farms Inc. v. Agway Metals Inc.* (2008), 58 C.P.C. (6th) 357, 2008 SKQB 53 (action by Saskatchewan buyer against Ontario supplier for providing sub-grade roofing steel; defendant's third party claim against another Ontario company did not make Ontario court more appropriate).

Non-resident defendant — claim arising out of business, investment or professional transaction — jurisdiction simpliciter found not to exist

Note. An action by British Columbia-resident clients of an investment broker for mismanagement of their accounts was held to have no real and substantial connection with British Columbia in *England v. Research Capital Corp.*, 2008 BCSC 580. The plaintiffs' accounts were opened at the defendant broker's Calgary office and performed throughout in Calgary by the individual defendants, the broker's employees. The broker's being ordinarily resident in British Columbia for the purposes of the *Court Jurisdiction and Proceedings Transfer Act*, S.B.C. 2003, c. 28, did not mean the court had territorial competence under the act in respect of the claims against the individual defendants, and the broker's vicarious liability rested on the claims against the individuals. The court issued a request to the Alberta court to accept a transfer of the proceeding. In *Venterra Developments Inc. v. Weber*, 2008 CanLII 1953 (Ont. S.C.J.), the fact that a deposit on a sale of land in Florida was held in escrow by a real estate broker in Ontario was not enough to give the Ontario court jurisdiction *simpliciter* in an action for breach of contract by the vendor, a Florida corporation that was partly owned by Ontario residents, against the New Jersey-resident purchaser. Nor was the foreign defendant's doing business in Ontario via subsidiary companies a sufficient connection with the province to support jurisdiction in an action by a Canadian corporation against a foreign corporation for breach of a contract made in New York to settle — when approved by American federal and state regulatory agencies — patent litigation in the United States: *Apotex Inc. v. Sanofi-Aventis* (2008), 54 C.P.C. (6th) 182 (Ont. S.C.J.). Similarly, in *Schreiber v. Mulroney* (2007), 288 D.L.R. (4th) 661 (Ont. S.C.J.), there was no jurisdiction *simpliciter* in a claim by an Ontario resident against a resident of Québec for repayment of moneys paid under a contract the defendant had allegedly broken. Neither the contract, nor its performance, nor the effects of its breach were shown to be connected with Ontario.

Non-resident defendant — claim arising out of personal injury or damage to property — jurisdiction simpliciter found to exist — jurisdiction not declined

Penny (Litigation guardian of) v. Bouch (2008), 305 D.L.R. (4th) 412, 2008 NSSC 378 (Nova Scotia Supreme Court)

The plaintiff commenced an action in Nova Scotia, both as litigation guardian for her son and in her personal capacity, in respect of severe disabilities allegedly caused to her son by medical malpractice when he was born at a hospital in Red Deer, Alberta, in July 2004. The plaintiff had then been resident in Alberta for a year, but after three weeks in the hospital she moved back to Nova Scotia, where most of her family lived, taking the newborn and her older child. The three of them remained in Nova Scotia until July 2005, when they moved with the plaintiff's fiancé to Saskatchewan. Very shortly before the latter move, the son, who had been receiving further medical tests and treatment, was diagnosed with Spastic Dysplasia Cerebral Palsy. When the relationship with her fiancé ended in October 2007, the plaintiff and her children moved to Ontario so the plaintiff could provide support for her sick sister. It was during her residence in Ontario, in January 2008, that the plaintiff commenced the action in Nova Scotia. She returned to Nova Scotia in June 2008 so she could have the support of her family in raising her two small sons, one with a severe disability, and she intended to stay there for the indefinite future. The defendants applied for an order dismissing the plaintiff's action on the ground that the Nova Scotia court lacked territorial competence under the *Court Jurisdiction and Proceedings Transfer Act*, S.N.S. 2003, c. 2, section 3(e), because there was no real and substantial connection between Nova Scotia and the facts giving rise to the proceeding, and none of the defendants was resident in Nova Scotia or had attorned to the court's jurisdiction. Alternatively, the defendants sought a stay under section 12 of the act on the basis that Nova Scotia was *forum non conveniens*. Also in issue was whether the act applied to actions commenced before it came into force on 1 June 2008.

Wright J., following decisions in British Columbia on the same point, held that the act was substantially in the nature of a procedural statute having immediate application upon coming into force. It therefore applied to this action, although the outcome would be the same under the common law principles that it largely codified. The real and substantial connection test in the act, as well as in the preceding case law, was a flexible one, with the question of fairness in assuming jurisdiction to be considered from the point of view of all parties to the proceeding. The court considered the eight factors for jurisdiction *simpliciter* described in *Muscutt v. Courcelles* (2002), 60 O.R. (3d) 20 (C.A.), observing by way of preface that if the application had been heard when the plaintiff's action was first filed, the plaintiff would not have been able to meet the real and substantial connection test, but factual developments since that time must now be taken into account in considering the *Muscutt* factors.

(1) Connection of the forum with the plaintiff's claim. Although the events giving rise to the action were strongly connected with Alberta, the plaintiff's return to Nova Scotia with her son meant that the damage suffered by them had become sited in Nova Scotia and would continue to be indefinitely. The son had also received extensive medical treatment in the province in the first year of his life. Almost all of the plaintiff's witnesses, whether health providers or family members, also resided in Nova Scotia. The forum was therefore significantly connected to the claim. (2) Connection between the forum and the defendants. There was none, but a connection with the defendants, although important, was not a necessary factor. (3) Unfairness to the defendants in assuming jurisdiction. Although it was unlikely that anyone from Alberta would have to attend the trial for lengthy periods of time, considerable disruption to the professional practices of the defendants was inevitable, a factor weighing in favour of the defendants. (4) Unfairness to the plaintiff in not assuming jurisdiction. The plaintiff's predicament was that she was financially incapable of proceeding with the action anywhere other than Nova Scotia. She had no assets and only limited resources at her disposal. Her son's disability meant that he needed constant care and attention, and the plaintiff felt she could not leave him for extended periods to attend a trial in Alberta. The son's condition made it unlikely that he could accompany his mother if the litigation were in Alberta. Given the plaintiff's marginal resources and the difficulties in mobility for herself and her son, this factor was an access to justice issue for them. (5) The involvement of other parties to the suit. This was a neutral factor here.

(6) The court's willingness to recognize and enforce an extra-provincial judgment rendered on the same jurisdictional basis. This was also a neutral factor because each province would recognize a judgment from the other on the same jurisdictional basis. (7) Whether the case is interprovincial or international in nature. Although of minor weight, the fact that this was an interprovincial case meant that an assumption of jurisdiction more easily justified. (8) Comity and the standards of jurisdiction, recognition, and enforcement prevailing elsewhere. This factor was inapplicable, as the proceeding was interprovincial.

Wright J. concluded that this was one of those cases in which more than one forum was capable of assuming jurisdiction. Guided by the principles of order and fairness, he was satisfied that there was a real and substantial connection between the forum and the subject matter of the action and the parties. Turning to the *forum non conveniens* question, he noted that the burden was on the defendants to establish that Alberta was a clearly or distinctly more appropriate forum than Nova Scotia. The two main factors of those enumerated in section 12(2) of the act, as applied to this case, were the comparative convenience and expense for the parties and their witnesses, and the fair and efficient working of the Canadian legal system as a whole (paragraphs (a) and (f), respectively). These factors were fairly evenly balanced as between the parties. The defendants had not established that Alberta was clearly a more appropriate jurisdiction to try the action, which meant that the selected forum wins out by default. The plaintiff's action should therefore not be stayed.

Note. A characteristic of the *Muscutt* approach is that, in the name of order and fairness to the parties, it loads a good deal of what is essentially *forum conveniens* analysis into the "real and substantial connection" determination. Where, as here, the alternative forum is one to which the plaintiff in practical terms has no access, a court is almost driven to find, first, that there is a real and substantial connection with the local forum because it is the only one available to the plaintiff and, second, that the forum is at least as appropriate as the alternative one, thus precluding a stay on *forum non conveniens* grounds. The Nova Scotia Court of Appeal affirmed Wright J.'s decision, 2009 NSCA 80, with reasons that will be noted in next year's Yearbook.

In *Warner v. Edmonton Gen. Hospital,* 2008 CanLII 41829 (Ont. S.C.J.), a plaintiff also claimed for injuries to his shoulder suffered at his birth in an Alberta hospital, but the court found no real and substantial connection with Ontario. The plaintiff had moved to Ontario only when he was three, he was now twenty, and there was no evidence to suggest that it would be unfair to him to have to sue in Alberta.

Van Breda v. Village Resorts Ltd. (2008), 60 C.P.C. (6th) 186 (Ontario Superior Court of Justice)

The plaintiff couple booked a one-week stay at a Cuban resort with an agent in Ottawa, Ontario. The male plaintiff was a professional squash player and the two of them were to receive free accommodation in return for his giving lessons to other guests at the resort. The Ottawa agent specialized in arranging such opportunities for tennis, squash, and aerobic professionals at Caribbean resorts. The resort in question was managed by Club Resorts Limited, a Cayman Islands company. The female plaintiff was rendered paraplegic in an accident at the resort when exercise equipment she was using collapsed on top of her. After the accident, the plaintiffs moved to Alberta, where the female plaintiff's family lived, and then to British Columbia. The plaintiffs brought an action in Ontario against Club Resorts and two other companies, one incorporated in the Cayman Islands and the other in Jamaica, that along with Club Resorts were part of SuperClubs, a group of companies that operated or managed resorts in the Caribbean. None of the three was resident in Canada. Claims were made against each company in contract and in tort. The Canadian agent was also sued in contract and in tort. The defendants moved to dismiss the action on the ground that Ontario had no jurisdiction. Alternatively, they applied for a stay on the ground of *forum non conveniens*. Pattillo J., applying the *Muscutt* factors (see the note of *Penny (Litigation guardian of) v. Bouch* earlier in this section) held that there was a real and substantial connection between Ontario and the claims against Club Resorts, but not between Ontario and the two other companies. One was a holding company that controlled the companies that owned the SuperClub trademarks; there was no evidence that it had any involvement in or connection to Ontario. The other advertised in Ontario for resorts in the Bahamas and Jamaica, but there was no evidence that it had any direct interest in the Cuban resort or any involvement in its operations. Club Resorts had agreements with four operators in Ontario for inclusion of its resorts in tours promoted by them in Ontario. That by itself did not make it significantly connected to the province, but Club Resorts took a more active role in using the Ottawa agent to seek out racquet professionals to come to its resorts in Cuba for the purpose of providing, among other things, tennis lessons to its guests. That, coupled with the plaintiffs' arguable case that they had entered into a contract with Club Resorts in Ontario through the Ottawa agent, constituted a strong basis for assuming jurisdiction against Club Resorts. The assumption of jurisdiction would not be unfair against Club Resorts. It carried on business in a number of Caribbean countries and carried insurance against judgments given against it in courts in the United States or Canada. It was true that many of its witnesses would be residents of Cuba who could not travel to Canada because, in all likelihood, neither government would permit it, but means could be found for them to give evidence by teleconference if necessary. On the other hand, not assuming jurisdiction might be unfair against the plaintiffs, given uncertainty as to the fairness of the legal system in Cuba, owing to the control of the government over all matters including its judicial system.

On the *forum non conveniens* issue the judge held Cuba had not been shown to be clearly more appropriate as a forum. The defendants were planning to contest both liability and quantum. The key witnesses on liability on the plaintiffs' side were the plaintiffs themselves and another Ontario resident who helped them when the accident happened. The defendants' witnesses included many Cuban residents, but only a few of them were key. Evidence had been submitted to the effect that under Cuban law, the female plaintiff would have no claim for general damages for pain and suffering and her partner and other family members (who were also included as plaintiffs) would have no claim for damages for loss of care, guidance, and companionship. The inability of the plaintiffs to assert those claims in Cuba would constitute the loss of a legitimate juridical advantage available in Ontario.

Note. In the event, the advantages of Ontario law might not be available to the plaintiffs. Given that the accident occurred in Cuba, an Ontario court would almost certainly have to apply Cuban law, if proved, in order to determine the heads of damage for which the plaintiffs could recover. For a similar case to *Van Breda*, see *Robinson v. Fiesta Hotel Group Resorts*, [2008] 12 W.W.R. 152, 2008 ABQB 311, in which the court took jurisdiction in an action by an Alberta tourist who was injured at a resort in the Dominican Republic. The real and substantial connection with Alberta was supplied by the plaintiff's medical treatment there and the fact that the resort promoted itself to Alberta residents by distributing brochures in the province.

*Non-resident defendant — claim arising out of personal injury or damage
to property — jurisdiction* simpliciter *found not to exist*

Note. An action by the Ontario-resident victims of an automobile
accident in the American state of Georgia was brought in Ontario
against the estate of the Georgian resident who drove the other
vehicle. The court, applying the *Muscutt* factors (see the note of
Penny v. Bouch earlier), held there was no real and substantial connection with Ontario. The plaintiffs' residence in Ontario and their
having suffered harm there was insufficient, given the foreign location of the accident and the unfairness to Georgian residents if the
Ontario court took jurisdiction: *Pavacic v. Nicely Estate* (2008), 91
O.R. (3d) 49 (S.C.J.).

(b) Declining jurisdiction *in personam*

*Resident defendant — claim arising out of personal injury or damage to
property*

Note. A British Columbia resident sued a corporation with a registered office in British Columbia, as well as an individual defendant
resident in Alberta, for injuries suffered in a highway accident in
Alberta. Although the corporate defendant's ordinary residence in
the province meant that the court had territorial competence in
respect of the claims against it under the *Court Jurisdiction and Proceedings Transfer Act*, S.B.C. 2003, c. 28, s. 3(d), and there was a real
and substantial connection with British Columbia under s. 3(e),
the court declined jurisdiction, applying the factors in s. 11 of the
act. The activities of neither defendant could be said to involve a
sufficient risk of harm to non-residents of Alberta to warrant forcing
them to litigate in British Columbia: *Williams v. TST Porter* (2008),
[2009] 3 W.W.R. 126, 2008 BCSC 1315.

*Non-resident defendant — claim arising out of business, investment or
professional transaction*

Young v. Tyco International of Canada Ltd. (2008), 300 D.L.R. (4th)
385, 2008 ONCA 709 (Ontario Court of Appeal)

Young had worked for Tyco Canada (Tyco) in Ontario for eight
years when, in 2004, his position became redundant. Tyco agreed
that Young would continue to work for it and would perform temporary assignments in North America until a position opened up
at one of Tyco's other Canadian plants. After twenty-one months of

these temporary assignments, the last two-and-a-half months of which had been at a Tyco plant in Indiana, Tyco dismissed Young for alleged sexual harassment of certain female employees. Young, taking the position that he had really been let go for health reasons, brought a wrongful dismissal action in Ontario against Tyco and six other companies affiliated with Tyco. The motion judge granted Tyco's application for a stay, holding that Indiana was clearly a more appropriate jurisdiction for the lawsuit. This was based in large part on the judge's accepting Tyco's version of the facts, according to which the temporary assignment period had come to an end when Young accepted an offer of permanent employment in Indiana. Young denied that the 2004 agreement had been superseded.

The Court of Appeal held the action should not have been stayed. The majority judgment, given by Laskin J.A., enunciated three principles that should guide the exercise to stay a proceeding on the basis of *forum non conveniens*. First, the standard to displace the forum chosen by the plaintiff is high, in that the existence of a more appropriate forum must be clearly established. Second, the balancing of the relevant factors was not a mathematical exercise; the aim was to achieve the twin goals of efficiency and justice. Third, because a *forum non conveniens* application is heard early in the proceeding, the judge should adopt a prudential and not an aggressive approach to fact-finding. He or she should avoid drawing conclusions or making findings on important factual or legal disputes relating to the merits. If a *forum non conveniens* application cannot be decided without choosing between competing versions of the facts, the motion judge should accept the plaintiff's version as long as it has a reasonable basis in the record. This approach makes sense because the ultimate question is whether an Ontario court should take jurisdiction over the plaintiff's claim. In the present case, the motion judge erred in basing his decision on a finding that Young's version of the contractual situation between him and Tyco was less persuasive than Tyco's. Some facts on the record supported Tyco's version but Young's version also had a reasonable evidentiary basis when the circumstances of his employment at the time of his dismissal were examined. If his version was accepted the connections with Ontario were strong. In particular, the relevant agreement was made there, and Ontario law applied to it. Young was therefore entitled to claim the juridical advantages available to him in Ontario, namely, familiarity of courts with an employment regime apparently quite different from that in Indiana, an "at will" jurisdiction, and the practical advantage of being able to pursue his claim in his home jurisdiction against an employer more powerful than he. Tyco was a cross-border company and litigating in Ontario did not raise any serious access-to-justice concerns for it.

Simmons J.A. concurred but thought that the question should not be analyzed in terms of the motion judge's preferring one party's version of the facts to the other party's. Rather, the motion judge must recognize that if the competing versions of the facts both have a reasonable basis in the evidence, and if a *forum non conveniens* factor turns on which version of the facts is accepted, the factor should not be treated as if the plaintiff's version were established but should be treated as neutral because the two versions of the facts cancel each other out. If, taking that approach, the critical factors turn out to be neutralized by disputes as to the facts, the motion judge must exercise his or her discretion based on comparing the potential unfairness to the defendant if the stay is denied with the potential unfairness to the plaintiff if the stay is granted. Here, the two advantages that Laskin J.A. described the plaintiff as having in Ontario, if its version of the facts prevailed, were not clearly outweighed by the advantage to Tyco, if its version of the facts prevailed, of having an action governed by Indiana law tried in an Indiana court.

Note 1. The difference between the tests as defined by Laskin J.A. and by Simmons J.A. amounts to a difference in the onus on the defendant. On Laskin J.A.'s analysis, the defendant must persuade the motion judge that, even assuming the plaintiff's version of the facts (and the legal characterization of them) to be correct, the other forum is clearly more appropriate. Essentially, the plaintiff gets the benefit of the doubt as to what the disputed facts are. Simmons J.A., on the other hand, would allow the judge to say that if the relative appropriateness of the two forums cannot be determined on the basis of factual considerations, because the facts are disputed, the matter becomes one of comparing what is at stake for each party in the decision on the stay. On this approach, a defendant should obtain a stay if it can show that, assuming the defendant's version of the facts is correct, it clearly stands to lose more by the refusal of a stay than the plaintiff, on the plaintiff's version of the facts, stands to lose by the grant of a stay. Neither party gets the benefit of the doubt as to what the facts are, but the plaintiff gets the benefit of the doubt on which party, assuming its version of the facts is right, will lose more by an adverse decision on *forum non conveniens*.

Note 2. Jurisdiction was also not declined in *Pulse Ventures Inc. v. Ogee Tables & Chairs Inc.* (2008), 227 Man. R. (2d) 265, 2008 MBQB 51 (breach of contract action by Manitoba seller of custom furniture to buyer in Alberta; factors evenly balanced, therefore no stay); *Patel v. Kanbay Int'l Inc.* (2008), 67 C.C.E.L. (3d) 125 (Ont. S.C.J.) (wrongful dismissal and related claims by Ontario resident against the two Canadian companies for which he worked and their Illinois parent company). See also *Norex Petroleum Ltd. v. Chubb Insurance Co. of Canada*, [2008] 12 W.W.R. 322, 2008 ABQB 442, referred to above under (a) Jurisdiction *in personam* — Attornment to the jurisdiction; and *Warren v. ABC Wilderness Ventures Ltd.*, 2008 ABQB 258, referred to in the note after *Ledyit v. Bristol-Myers Squibb Canada Inc.*, under (c) Class actions — Non-resident plaintiffs — resident defendant — jurisdiction *simpliciter*.

Parallel proceedings elsewhere (lis alibi pendens)

Note. Jurisdiction was not declined in *VMAC Racing Ltd. v. B.R. Motorsports Inc.*, 2008 BCSC 685, a breach of contract action brought by the British Columbia seller of a custom automobile parts business against the California companies that had bought it. The contract was substantially to be performed in, and was probably governed by the law of, British Columbia. The fact that the defendants had begun a parallel action in California did not tip the scales in favour of a stay, especially because the California court had not yet decided the jurisdictional issue. Nor was jurisdiction declined in *Blue Note Mining Inc. v. CanZinco Ltd.* (2008), 305 D.L.R. (4th) 173 (Ont. S.C.J.), mainly because the defendants had agreed, in the contract that was the subject of the dispute, to the non-exclusive jurisdiction of the Ontario court and had also agreed that no party would plead *forum non conveniens* in any action brought in Ontario. There was no strong reason not to hold the defendants to that clause, although the dispute was about the plaintiff's obligation to indemnify the defendants for legal expenses arising out of litigation in New Brunswick and the defendants had made a claim against the plaintiff for the indemnity in the New Brunswick court. In *Invar Manufacturing, a Division of Linamar Holdings Inc. v. Giuliani, a Division of IGM U.S.A. Inc.* (2007), 52 C.P.C. (6th) 129 (Ont. S.C.J.), affd. (2008), 235 O.A.C. 202, 2008 ONCA 256, a stay was refused in an action by an Ontario buyer of custom industrial machinery against the Italian supplier that made and installed it, notwithstanding that the supplier had brought proceedings in Italy for breach of the same contracts. Those proceedings were begun a month before the Ontario ones but the Ontario buyer argued they were "torpedo" proceedings simply designed to pre-empt any Ontario proceedings. The judge regarded the potential conflict between proceedings as hypothetical at this stage and therefore only a weak factor in the *forum non conveniens* equation. And *Lilydale Cooperative Ltd. v. Meyn Canada Inc.* (2007), 84 O.R. (3d) 621 (S.C.J.), a decision referred to in (2007), 45 Can. Yearb. Int'l L. at 575, was affirmed (2008), 50 C.P.C. (6th) 1, 2008 ONCA 126 (refusal to stay Ontario proceeding in favour of earlier proceeding brought by same party in Alberta).

Jurisdiction was declined in *Buxar v. Lukich* (2008), 298 D.L.R. (4th) 489 (Ont. S.C.J. (Master)), in an action brought in Ontario against an Ontario resident by his former fiancée, resident in Michigan, for a declaration that her engagement ring remained her property despite the breaking-off of the engagement. Michigan was the more appropriate forum because the events relating to the engagement were mostly connected with that state. There was no reason why this matter could not be part of legal proceedings already brought by the fiancée in Michigan to determine her rights in immovable property the couple had bought there.

Forum selection clause

Commonwealth Insurance Co. v. American Home Assurance Co., [2008] 11 W.W.R. 690, 2008 MBQB 112 (Manitoba Queen's Bench)

An excess liability insurance policy was issued by Coromin, a Bermudan insurer that was part of the Anglo-American group, to the English holding company under which the group was organized. Coromin made the same coverage available to the other members of the group and solicited Hudbay, a Canadian member of the group, to subscribe to the coverage by written proposals sent to Hudbay at its office in Manitoba. Hudbay subscribed to the policy. Since Coromin was not licensed to carry on business as an insurer in Manitoba, the policy was actually issued to Hudbay by another company, American Home, on its usual coverage terms modified by a "difference in conditions" sheet to bring coverage into line with that in the Anglo American policy. The Anglo-American policy contained an express choice of English law to govern the policy and an exclusive choice of forum in favour of the English courts, but this clause did not appear in the written policy issued to Hudbay by American Home. Hudbay claimed against the Coromin policy in respect of a loss arising in North Carolina and Coromin paid the claim, but Coromin refused to reimburse the primary insurer, Commonwealth, for what Commonwealth said was Coromin's share of the defence costs. Commonwealth brought an action in Manitoba against Coromin. Coromin relied upon the exclusive choice of forum clause in its policy.

The clause was held ineffective for three reasons. First, it did not bind Commonwealth, which was a third party to the contract between Coromin and Hudbay. Second, the clause was nullified by the operation of sections 116 and 117 of the *Insurance Act*, C.C.S.M., c. 140. Since it solicited Hudbay's business in Manitoba, Coromin was deemed to be an insurer that carried on business in the province (section 22(2) of the act). The policy insured an insurable interest of a person resident in the province and was issued or delivered to Hudbay in the province and, consequently, was deemed to be made in the province and must be construed according to the laws of the province (section 116). This meant, in effect, that the policy was deemed to be governed by Manitoba law, not by English law. Nor could Coromin rely on the choice of forum part of the clause because Coromin never delivered the written Anglo-American policy to Hudbay, and section 117(1) of the act requires all of the terms of the policy to be set out in the policy. The third reason was that issuing the policy through American Home had the legal effect of making American Home the insurer and Coromin only American Home's reinsurer. The "difference in conditions" sheet did not include the English choice of forum, which meant that the exclusive choice of a Canadian forum in American Home's policy terms was the operative choice of forum in the contract.

Note. The *Marine Liability Act*, S.C. 2001, c. 6, includes in s. 46 an express override, in certain situations, of forum selection clauses in contracts of carriage by sea and affirming the jurisdiction of the Federal Court in actions brought on such contracts. *Mazda Canada Inc. v. Mitsui OSK Lines Ltd.,* 2008 FCA 219, following an earlier decision by the same court, held this provision only took away the effect of an exclusive choice of forum clause; it did not deprive the Federal Court of its discretion to stay a proceeding on the ground of *forum non conveniens.* A Canadian cargo owner's action against a Japanese carrier was stayed on the ground that Japan was clearly a more appropriate jurisdiction, particularly because all of the other actions arising out of the same occurrences at sea had been brought there and were proceeding expeditiously.

Arbitration clause

Note. A clause requiring arbitration in Russia was grounds for a stay of an Ontario breach of contract action by an Ontario seller of pigs against the Russian buyer, notwithstanding that the Ontario company had refused to participate in the arbitration because its chief operating officer had allegedly been the subject of death threats by the buyer's chief executive officer. The arbitration had taken place and an award been made. The Ontario company had not asked the motion judge to decide on the enforceability of the award in the light of the death threats, and the appeal court did not think it appropriate to decide that question itself. The effect of the alleged threats on the enforcement of the award could be raised if the Russian company took steps to enforce the award in Ontario: *Donaldson International Livestock ltd. v. Znamensky Selekcionno-Gibridny Center LLC* (2008), 305 D.L.R. (4th) 432, 2008 ONCA 872.

(c) Class actions

Non-resident plaintiffs — resident defendant — jurisdiction *simpliciter*

Ledyit v. Bristol-Myers Squibb Canada Inc. (2008), 58 C.P.C. (6th) 90 (Ontario Superior Court of Justice), affd. (2008), 53 C.P.C. (6th) 209, 2008 ONCA 372 (Ontario Court of Appeal)

In an Ontario class action suit against a number of defendants responsible for manufacturing and marketing a drug that was alleged to have harmful side effects, the brand name manufacturer, which had originated the drug, reached a settlement but the generic manufacturers and the other defendants did not. The plaintiffs were divided into subclasses depending on whether they had ingested the brand name or the generic version of the drug. Apotex, a generic manufacturer, applied to strike out the claims against it on the ground that the representative plaintiffs had used the brand-name version of the drug only. The application was dismissed because, with leave of the court, two residents of Québec who had used the Apotex version of the drug were added as representative plaintiffs. The judge's decision to add the Québec residents as plaintiffs was appealed on the ground that their claims had no real and substantial connection with Ontario, Ontario was *forum non conveniens,* and the amendment was an abuse of process. The Court of Appeal dismissed the appeal on the basis that Apotex was resident in and carried on business in Ontario, which itself gave the court jurisdiction *simpliciter.* Even if some other real and substantial connection of the proceeding with Ontario was necessary, it was present in this case, especially given that the representative plaintiffs were prepared to come to the jurisdiction. The *forum non conveniens* motion was premature because the only question was the addition of the representative plaintiffs. Apotex was not precluded from bringing a motion for a stay, in respect of the claims of non-residents, on appropriate material. On a further point, the motion judge was entitled to accept the plaintiff's counsel's assurance that parallel class proceedings in Québec would not advance pending the certification decision in the Ontario proceeding and, if certified, that the Québec action would not proceed. Finally, Apotex raised an argument that the new representative plaintiffs were unsuitable because their claims would involve the application of Québec law. The court thought this argument was also premature, particularly in the absence of any evidence that the applicable Québec law differed from Ontario law.

Note. Class actions that involve "national" classes, meaning classes of plaintiffs that include residents of provinces other than the forum, are providing many new conflicts issues. One obvious problem is coordinating class proceedings brought against the same defendant in different provinces on behalf of overlapping classes of plaintiffs. In the earlier case, this difficulty was met by an agreement between the plaintiffs in the Ontario action and those in the Québec action that the latter proceeding would be discontinued if the former was certified. In *Hocking c. Aziza* (noted under D. Jugements étrangers — 2. Québec — Compétence du tribunal étranger — Recours collectif en étranger — membres du groupe résidant au Québec), the Ontario action reached a settlement, but the plaintiffs in the Québec action were unwilling to accept it and the Québec Court of Appeal held that the Ontario settlement was not binding on the Québec-resident plaintiffs who were included in the "national class" in Ontario. (The *Class Proceedings Act,* 1992, S.O. 1992, c. 6, has no requirement that classes be defined by reference to the province or country in which the plaintiffs reside, which the courts have interpreted to mean that national (or even international) classes may be certified, which means that non-residents are included unless they opt out. The legislation of some other provinces stipulates that non-resident plaintiffs can be included in a class only if they opt into it.) In *Hocking,* the Québec residents were not bound because the Ontario court lacked jurisdiction over their claims under the Québec foreign judgment recognition rules in Article 3168 C.C.Q., and because the notice of the class action that was given to residents of Québec was inadequate. In *Canada Post Corp. v. Lépine* (2009), 304 D.L.R. (4th) 539, 2009 SCC 16, which will be fully noted in the next volume of this Yearbook, Québec residents were again held not to be bound by the settlement of an Ontario class action that included them in a national class. The Ontario court had jurisdiction with respect to their claims under Article 3168(1) C.C.Q. because the defendant was domiciled in Ontario through its head office being there, but notice to the Québec members of the class was again insufficient to bind them.

Jurisdiction *simpliciter* was held not to exist in a proposed class action on behalf of Canadians who had downloaded a screensaver, allegedly accompanied by undisclosed spyware, from the website of a company in the United States. This was said to be a violation of Canadian competition legislation relating to misleading practices. The court held there was no evidence that the defendant company had availed itself of Canadian laws or done any business in Canada through its website, and any alleged representations were made in the United States via a server in that country. There was therefore no real and substantial connection with Canada: *Desjean v. Intermix Media Inc.* (2007), 66 C.P.R. (6th) 458, 2007 FCA 365.

On the other hand, Newfoundland and Labrador residents have been held to be entitled to bring a class action against the federal Crown for harm caused to them by being exposed to Agent Orange at a Canadian Forces establishment in New Brunswick. Jurisdiction *simpliciter* was based on the presence in the province of the defendant and on the fact that the harm suffered by the plaintiffs continued when they came to live in the province: *Ring v. The Queen (No. 2)* (2007), 272 Nfld. & P.E.I.R. 348, 2007 NLTD 213. Newfoundland and Labrador was also the *forum conveniens*, especially given the expense and delay that the plaintiffs would suffer if they had to have their claims certified as a class proceeding in New Brunswick, which had enacted class proceeding legislation after certification proceedings had been begun in the present forum. It was also relevant that class actions arising out of the same events were not confined to New Brunswick. They were underway, as well, in six other provinces besides Newfoundland and Labrador, and in the Federal Court.

Jurisdiction was declined in a shareholders' class action on *forum non conveniens* grounds in *Warren v. ABC Wilderness Ventures Ltd.*, 2008 ABQB 258. British Columbia was a more appropriate forum. Most of the shareholders resided there, the corporations in question did business only in that province, and the individual defendants lived either in British Columbia or in Ontario. Jurisdiction was also declined in *Sollen v. Pfizer Canada Inc.* (2008), 290 D.L.R. (4th) 603 (Ont. S.C.J.), partly in deference to the fact that the Saskatchewan Court of Appeal had already held that there was no more appropriate forum for the claims than that province. The fact that the plaintiffs could apply for a national class on an "opt out" basis in Ontario, but only on an "opt in" basis in Saskatchewan, did not constitute a legitimate advantage in favour of Ontario because, if the class in Saskatchewan might be characterized as under-inclusive, the class in Ontario could equally be characterized as over-inclusive. As for the effect of a choice of forum clause in a class action, see the next case.

2038724 Ontario Ltd. v. Quizno's Canada Restaurant Corp. (2008), 89 O.R. (3d) 252 (Ontario Superior Court of Justice), reversed, 2009 CanLII 23374 (Ontario Divisional Court)

The plaintiff asserted that a restaurant franchisor, Quizno's, as well as its associated companies had systematically overcharged its franchisees for products and merchandise. The plaintiff sought to have the franchisees' claims certified as a class proceeding. One of the issues in the application was the effect to be given to an exclusive choice of forum clause in favour of the courts of British Columbia, a clause that featured in the agreements Quizno's had with about three-quarters of the franchisees. The defendants argued that the court should stay the proceeding in regard to the claims of these franchisees. Perell J. held that such an outcome was not desirable, necessary, or in the public interest. In relation to a class proceeding, the right approach was the one that courts in other provinces had taken when it came to arbitration clauses. The existence of a choice of judicial forum, like an arbitration clause, was to be considered as a factor in determining whether a class proceeding was the preferable procedure. There was no express statutory power to treat contractual choices of forum in this way. However, it was appropriate to see such a power as being implicit in the class proceeding legislation. To do so was compatible with the approach Canadian courts take to exclusive choices of forum, which is to consider whether there is strong cause to let litigation proceed notwithstanding the prior agreement to litigate in another jurisdiction. It was also analogous to reading down an illegal contract so as to bring it into compliance with the law.

Perell J. denied the certification application because of a lack of common issues among the plaintiffs, but, on appeal, the Divisional

Court held that there were common issues and certification should not have been denied. The defendants did not appeal against the judge's refusal to stay the proceedings on the ground of the choice of forum clauses, and the appellate court therefore did not comment on that part of his decision.

(d) Claims in respect of property

Matrimonial property

Note. In *Schulz v. Schulz* (2007), 45 R.F.L. (6th) 122, 2007 NSSC 319, a matrimonial property action was stayed because Germany was clearly a more appropriate forum. The husband had not attorned by seeking to have *ex parte* orders obtained by the wife vacated or by attending at a settlement conference.

Administration and succession

Re Foote Estate (2007), 84 Alta. L.R. (4th) 114, 2007 ABQB 654 (Alberta Queen's Bench)

Foote was originally from Alberta but had lived for the last thirty years of his life on Norfolk Island, an external territory of Australia. His widow still lived there, and their six children lived in various places, including one in Edmonton, Alberta. Foote devised his property by three wills, naming an individual resident in Alberta as executor in each. One will dealt with his (many) worldwide assets and was probated in the British Virgin Islands. The second dealt with his assets in Norfolk Island and was probated there. The third dealt with his Canadian assets and was probated in Alberta. Despite a "poison pill" provision in each will, according to which any beneficiary who contested the will would forfeit his or her inheritance, the widow and five children considered making family relief applications. They applied to the Alberta Court of Queen's Bench for directions as to the interpretation and validity of the "poison pill" clause, and a determination of Foote's domicile at the time of his death. The Lord Mayor's Fund of Melbourne, Australia, applied for a dismissal or stay of the proceeding on the ground that the Alberta court either lacked jurisdiction to determine Foote's last domicile or should decline it on the ground of *forum non conveniens*. The Fund was the residuary beneficiary under the Norfolk Island will and was also the designated recipient of half the annual distributions of the Foote Foundation Limited., a British Virgin Islands corporation, which received Foote's worldwide assets under the

British Virgin Islands will. The other half of the distributions went to the Edmonton Community Foundation.

On the question of jurisdiction *simpliciter,* Graesser J. held that the court had jurisdiction over the executor by virtue of his residence in Alberta, and this jurisdiction extended to his role as executor under the Norfolk Island and British Virgin Island wills, notwithstanding that the courts of those two countries also had jurisdiction with respect to his activities as executor of the wills probated there. On *forum non conveniens,* there was little to favour Norfolk Island over Alberta as the forum. Two of the parties, the executor and one of the applicant children, lived in Alberta, whereas the only party who resided in Norfolk Island, the widow, wanted the question of domicile to be heard in Alberta. The Fund claimed that it would be prejudiced if Alberta law was applied to the determination of domicile, because Alberta retained the common law rule that Foote's domicile of origin, Alberta, would have revived if he abandoned his domicile of choice in Norfolk Island, whereas under Australian federal legislation, which applied in Norfolk Island, Foote lost his Albertan domicile of origin once and for all when he first acquired a domicile of choice. The judge regarded this as a neutral factor. As a result of the different rules for determining domicile, the Fund would have an advantage in a Norfolk Island court whereas the applicants would have an advantage in an Alberta court; the difference did not point to either jurisdiction as more appropriate than the other. Also, the factual issues relating to domicile were likely to be more complicated and contentious than the legal issues.

Trusts

Gordon Estate v. Venables, 2008 BCSC 501 (British Columbia Supreme Court)

A British Columbia-resident trustee had taken over the trust from an Ontario resident who had exercised the office of trustee for thirty years and kept the assets in that province until the British Columbia resident took over and moved the assets to that province. The Ontario former trustee brought an action in Ontario to remove the British Columbia trustee and to pass the Ontario trustee's accounts. The British Columbia trustee subsequently sought an order for payment of trustee fees and for a declaration that the trust was now resident in British Columbia. The respondent Ontario trustee applied to have the court decline jurisdiction on *forum non conveniens* grounds. The British Columbia court granted a stay in order to avoid a multiplicity of suits where the Ontario proceedings, although not far advanced, were under way first and the other factors pointed moderately in favour of the other forum, including the fact that it was in Ontario that the trust had been administered for thirty years.

Bankruptcy and insolvency

Note. A British Columbia corporation that had acted as agent for a Liberian shipping company attempted to petition the Liberian company into bankruptcy in Canada, but the British Columbia court, sitting in bankruptcy, held it had no jurisdiction over the locality of the debtor, as the federal law of bankruptcy requires, because there was no evidence that the Liberian company was actively carrying on business in British Columbia: *North American Steamships Ltd. v. NASL Shipping Ltd.* (2008), 41 C.B.R. (5th) 230, 2008 BCSC 428.

(e) Infants and children

Declaration of paternity

Olney v. Rainville (2008), 83 B.C.L.R. (4th) 182, 2008 BCSC 753 (British Columbia Supreme Court)

The petitioner, a woman born and raised in British Columbia, married the respondent, a man from Québec, in Vancouver in 1990. After they both completed graduate study in England, the petitioner took a position with a United Nations agency in Geneva, Switzerland, in 1991, and both parties lived there and, later on, nearby in France. A son was born in 2000. The respondent had accepted a faculty position at a university in Québec City in 1993 and spent the teaching terms in Québec, where the petitioner joined him on her holidays. In 2002, the parties separated. A French court affirmed that the petitioner and the respondent both had parental authority. Since 2002, the son spent about ten weeks a year with the respondent, mostly in Québec. The son never lived in British Columbia but had visited it during most years with his mother or both parents. The petitioner and the respondent were divorced in 2004. The following year, the petitioner married M, an Australian citizen who also worked in Geneva. In 2005, the petitioner informed the respondent that M, not the respondent, was the biological father of the son and provided DNA test results to that effect. In 2007, the petitioner commenced the present proceeding in British Columbia seeking a declaration that M was the boy's father. The respondent was served with the process in Québec. The respondent sought a dismissal of the proceeding on the ground that the court lacked territorial competence under the *Court Jurisdiction and Proceedings Transfer Act*, S.B.C. 2003, c. 28, or, alternatively, should decline jurisdiction pursuant to section 11 of the act on the ground of *forum non conveniens*.

Kelleher J. held the court had no territorial competence (that is, jurisdiction *simpliciter*) and, in any event, should decline jurisdiction. Since the respondent was not ordinarily resident in the province and had not submitted to the court's jurisdiction, the only ground for territorial competence was in section 3(e), a real and substantial connection with the province. The case did not fall under any of the classes of cases listed in section 10, in which such a connection is presumed. It is open to a party to prove that a real and substantial connection nevertheless existed on the facts. The question here was whether, viewing the matter from the point of view of order and fairness, there was a real and substantial connection between British Columbia and the issues of the respondent's status as father of the boy and of the relationship between him and the boy. The petitioner argued that she and, through her, the son (under the *Infants Act*, R.S.B.C. 1996, c. 223, s. 28) were domiciled in British Columbia. Even if that were so, the judge was not satisfied that there was a real and substantial connection between British Columbia and the facts giving rise to the proceeding. There was no suggestion that the son or the petitioner was a resident of the province. It was noteworthy that section 10 of the act contained no reference to domicile as a basis for jurisdiction. The litigation was about the respondent and the son and neither had much, if any, connection with British Columbia. Nor did the petitioner's case meet either of the requirements in section 6 of the act for a court to take jurisdiction, even in a case in which it lacks territorial competence, where (a) "there is no court outside British Columbia in which the plaintiff can commence the proceeding," or (b) "the commencement of the proceeding in a court outside British Columbia cannot reasonably be required." On the evidence, the petitioner was entitled to commence her proceeding in Québec.

In any event, Québec was a more appropriate forum. The respondent was most closely connected with Québec, and Québec was the jurisdiction outside France with which the son had the strongest connections. A factor that favoured Québec was the choice of law rule for affiliation in Article 3091 C.C.Q., which allowed affiliation to be established using the law of either parent's domicile at the time the child was born, whichever is in the child's best interest. Thus, the petitioner would be free to argue in the Québec court that she was domiciled in British Columbia and that it was in the son's best interest to apply British Columbia law to determine paternity.

Contact order

Note. As in the previous case, the real and substantial connection test for jurisdiction *simpliciter* (common law rather than embodied in the uniform *Court Jurisdiction and Proceedings Transfer Act*, which Alberta has not adopted) was applied to a matter concerning a child in *S.(J.) v. W.(R.)* (2008), 95 Alta. L.R. (4th) 47, 2008 ABQB 358. A deceased mother's family sought a contact order in respect of a child that had lived with both parents in Alberta until the mother's death and then moved with the father to Newfoundland. The court held that, although the child was not ordinarily resident in Alberta, the court could exercise its *parens patriae* jurisdiction in respect of the child because the case had a real and substantial connection with Alberta. The father had not shown that Newfoundland and Labrador was a more suitable forum for hearing the application for contact between the child and his extended maternal family.

Custody — jurisdiction

M.(L.C.) v. S.(J.N.) (2008), [2009] 1 W.W.R. 299, 2008 ABQB 459 (Alberta Queen's Bench)

Although the mother had brought the child from the United Arab Emirates (UAE) to Alberta without notice to the father, the Alberta court took jurisdiction on her application for custody. Both parents lived in the UAE throughout their marriage but had arranged for the child to be born in Canada, of which the mother was a citizen, the father being a citizen of both Canada and Lebanon. The UAE was not a signatory to the Hague Convention on the Civil Aspects of International Child Abduction. In such a case, the Alberta court's *parens patriae* jurisdiction in custody was to be asserted, the test for jurisdiction being the best interests of the child. Part of the reason why it was in the child's best interests to have the matter heard in Alberta was that both parents agreed that issues of custody and access were to be determined in accordance with Canadian law, since the law of the UAE directs that Canadian law will apply to its non-Muslim non-national residents.

Note. In *Hynes v. Locke* (2008), 275 Nfld. & P.E.I.R. 230, 2008 NLUFC 10, the court declined jurisdiction in custody in favour of Alberta, where the child was habitually resident with his mother. The Newfoundland and Labrador court had jurisdiction under the *Children's Law Act*, R.S.N.L. 1990, c. C-13, s. 28(1)(b), which gives the court jurisdiction, even if the child is not habitually resident in the province, if certain conditions, including a real and substantial connection with the province, are met. But Alberta was a more appropriate jurisdiction on the facts. See also *Hoole v. Hoole* (2008), [2009] 4 W.W.R. 542, 2008 BCSC 1248, in which the court in British Columbia held it was appropriate to hold a joint hearing, by electronic means, with a court in Oregon to examine issues relating to custody jurisdiction, given that the father resided in British Columbia and the mother had recently moved with the child to Oregon.

Custody — jurisdiction corollary to divorce — foreign divorce

Quigley v. Willmore (2008), 272 N.S.R. (2d) 61, 2008 NSSC 353 (Nova Scotia Supreme Court)

This was one of a convoluted series of proceedings concerning the parents' divorce and custody over their child. The husband had obtained a divorce in Texas, which Williams J., in this case, held should be recognized under section 22(1) of the *Divorce Act*, R.S.C. 1985, c. 3 (2nd Supp.), because the father had been ordinarily resident in Texas for one year immediately preceding the commencement of the proceeding or, alternatively, had a real and substantial connection with Texas that supported recognizing the divorce as a matter of common law, which section 22(3) retained as a ground for recognition. The wife's Canadian divorce petition, which had been presented after the commencement of the Texas divorce proceeding, was stayed rather than dismissed because the wife was appealing in Texas against the divorce decree.

The parties being validly divorced by a foreign decree, the next question was whether the Nova Scotia court had jurisdiction in custody. The court held that it had such jurisdiction on either of two bases. One was that as long as the Canadian divorce proceeding was pending, even if stayed, the court had jurisdiction to make an interim order corollary to the proposed divorce under section 16(2) of the *Divorce Act*. The other was the court's *parens patriae* jurisdiction. Cases in Ontario and British Columbia had decided that once the parents have been divorced by a foreign decree, a Canadian court has no jurisdiction under the *Divorce Act* to decide on custody in connection with that divorce. As a result of the course legal proceedings had taken, the terms of section 18 of the provincial custody statute, the *Maintenance and Custody Act*, R.S.N.S. 1989, c. 160, did not support jurisdiction in custody, either. Therefore, if the parties were divorced by the Texas court, neither the federal nor the provincial statute applied to give jurisdiction. This gap must be filled by the court's *parens patriae* jurisdiction. It was appropriate to exercise this jurisdiction in light of the child's best interests, as well as the fact that both parties acknowledged that Canada had jurisdiction and the Texas court had encouraged the Canadian court to take jurisdiction to determine custody of the child. Custody was granted to the mother with access by the father to be determined.

Child abduction

Note. Decisions involving the Hague Convention on the Civil Aspects of International Child Abduction were *Kubera v. Kubera* (2008), 60 R.F.L. (6th) 360, 2008 BCSC 1340 (father's application for return of the child to Poland refused because the application was made more than a year after the wrongful retention and the child was now — meaning at the date of the hearing — settled into her new environment (art. 12)); *Cannock v. Fleguel* (2008), 303 D.L.R. (4th) 542, 2008 ONCA 758 (father application for child's return to Australia granted; judge entitled to rely on affidavit evidence in finding that the mother had not shown that return of the child would expose her to a grave risk of physical or psychological harm (art. 13(b))); and *Ibrahim v. Girgis* (2008), 291 D.L.R. (4th) 130, 2008 ONCA 23 (father's application for return of child to Florida granted; eight months' delay in applying was not acquiescence in the wrongful retention).

Child abduction — foreign court's decision not to order return

De Silva v. Pitts (2008), 289 D.L.R. (4th) 540, 2008 ONCA 9 (Ontario Court of Appeal)

The father, a United States citizen residing in Oklahoma, had a son with the mother, a citizen of Sri Lanka, who left the husband shortly after their son was born in 1993. An Oklahoma court granted the father custody in 1994, but in violation of the order the mother took the son to Sri Lanka and obtained a custody order from a court there. Neither order was subsequently varied. The mother later moved to Canada with the son, by then aged ten. When he was twelve, the son went to visit his father and did not return. The mother immediately obtained an *ex parte* order in Ontario for interim and permanent custody. She then petitioned a federal District Court in Oklahoma for the return of her son under the Hague Convention on the Civil Aspects of International Child Abduction. The court refused to order the return. A primary reason for the decision was the court's giving weight, as permitted by article 13(2) of the convention, to the fact "that the child objects to being returned and has attained an age and degree of maturity at which it is appropriate to take account of its views." The son, who by this time was almost thirteen, had expressed the wish to remain with his father, and the court held he was old enough that account should be taken of his wishes. Thereupon, the father, who had earlier succeeded on appeal in having the permanent custody part of the Ontario order set aside, applied to set aside the temporary custody order the Ontario court had made in favour of the mother, on basis that the Ontario court should decline jurisdiction in favour of the court in Oklahoma. The motion judge held that Ontario was the proper forum for custody and therefore refused to set the order for temporary custody aside and added an order for the return of the son to the mother. The mother sought unsuccessfully to have these orders confirmed by the Oklahoma court that had made the original custody order. In addition, the Tenth Circuit Court of Appeals affirmed the District Court's refusal to order the return of the son to the mother.

On the father's appeal from the refusal to decline jurisdiction in custody, the Court of Appeal held that the court should decline jurisdiction. The combination of comity, on the one hand, and of the need to preserve the convention's effectiveness, on the other, called for courts to avoid, as much as possible, interfering with foreign interpretations of the convention. The obligation to order the return of a child under the Hague Convention was not absolute. The District Court and the Circuit Court of Appeals had considered all of the relevant provisions of the convention in deciding that the boy should remain in Oklahoma with his father and, in particular, there was no basis to challenge the court's assessment that the son's wishes in that regard should receive persuasive weight.

2   *Québec*

(a) Action personnelle

Compétence territoriale — élection de for

STMicroelectronics inc. c. Matrox Graphics inc., [2008] R.J.Q. 73, 2007 QCCA 1784 (Cour d'appel du Québec)

Hewlett-Packard France (HP) a intenté une action en dommages contre Matrox en alléguant que cette dernière lui avait vendu des cartes graphiques défectueuses. Matrox a intenté par la suite une action en garantie à l'encontre de STMictroelectronics (STM), à titre de fabricant de l'une des composantes des pièces fournies à HP. Invoquant que STM lui avait fourni de l'équipement défectueux, Matrox a également intenté à son tour une action en dommages en son encontre. À l'encontre des actions intentées contre elle, STM a présenté deux requêtes en exception déclinatoire au motif que ces deux actions auraient dû être intentées au Texas. Elle a soutenu que les parties ont conclu un contrat sur la base des conditions standards de STM et ont choisi de soumettre leurs différends à une autorité étrangère. Matrox a rétorqué qu'elle n'a jamais accepté, ni explicitement ni implicitement, les terms et conditions (TC) de STM. Le premier juge a rejeté les deux requêtes en exception déclinatoire.

La Court d'appel a rejeté l'appel de STM. Dans la mesure où les discussions ayant mené au contrat-cadre entre les parties ont été fort générales et n'ont pas couvert tous les aspects de la relation contractuelle, on peut conclure que, vu l'usage en vigueur dans l'industrie, les parties s'engageaient implicitement à respecter les conditions et modalités additionnelles qu'elles pourraient ultérieurement se communiquer lors des ventes particulières, sans aller à l'encontre des termes du contrat-cadre. Cependant, quoique les parties soient mutuellement liées par les TC qu'elles ont échangés lors des diverses opérations de vente, et quoiqu'elles soient liées, en particulier, par la clause 19 de STM, il faut en conclure que cette clause n'a pas l'effet d'une clause d'élection de for. La clause 19 se lise,

This contract will be governed by and construed in accordance with the laws of the State of Texas ... Buyer agrees that it will submit to the personal jurisdiction of the competent courts of the State of Texas and of the United States sitting in Dallas County, Texas, in any controversy or claim arising out of the sale contract

Lorsqu'on tente d'établir le sens et la portée d'une clause dont on prétend qu'elle constitue une élection de for, on doit privilégier non pas une approche purement littérale mais plutôt une approche contextuelle, centrée sur la découverte de l'intention des parties. Il faut comprendre que lorsque la clause n'exprime pas la compétence exclusive du for étranger en termes absolument limpides, on doit alors se livrer à un exercice de lecture ou d'interprétation qui donne bien sûr une grande importance au texte, mais qui n'exclut pas l'examen du contexte. En plus, si les règles et méthodes d'interprétation usuelles ne permettent pas de fixer avec certitude le sens de la clause et que demeure une ambiguïté ou un doute insoluble, on devra alors recourir, à titre subsidiaire, à la règle *contra proferentem*, que consacre l'article 1432 C.C.Q. ("Dans le doute, le contrat s'interprète en faveur de celui qui a contracté l'obligation et contre celui qui l'a stipulée"). Le texte de la clause 19 n'a pas le caractère impératif ni le degré de clarté et de précision requis pour conférer une compétence exclusive à l'autorité étrangère. Devant l'impossibilité de résoudre le dilemme par les techniques d'interprétation usuelles, l'on doit recourir à l'article 1432 C.C.Q. et appliquer la règle *contra proferentem:* STM ayant stipulé la clause, on doit l'interpréter contre elle et, par conséquent, retenir ici l'interprétation suggérée par Matrox. Selon cette interprétation, la clause oblige Matrox à se soumettre aux tribunaux du Texas dans le seul cas où une action y est intentée contre elle, mais elle ne la force pas à intenter au Texas ses propres recours contre STM. Cette interprétation est raisonnable et s'accorde aux termes de la clause et à sa facture.

(b) Requête pour jugement déclaratoire

Motif légitime au sens de l'article 453 C.P.C. — but d'influencer un tribunal d'une autre province sur une question en litige

Royal Trust Company c. Webster-Tweel, [2008] R.J.Q. 2053, 2008 QCCA 1643 (Cour d'appel du Québec)

Brenda Webster-Tweel invoque ses droits de bénéficiaire dans trois fiducies mises sur pied au Québec par son grand-père au début des années 1940 au bénéfice du fils de ce dernier, le père de Brenda. En 1978, les actifs de ces fiducies sont transférés à Calgary en Alberta et sont administrés dès lors par Royal Trust Corporation et les impôts payés à titre de résidante de l'Alberta. En 1998, une nouvelle fiducie soit le "Protective Trust" est mise sur pied par le père au Québec. Tous les actifs des trois premières fiducies lui sont alors transférés incluant les actifs situés en Alberta. Cette dernière fiducie est administrée par Royal Trust Corporation à Calgary, les déclarations d'impôt sont déposées à cet endroit et les taxes et les impôts sont payés à titre de résidante de l'Alberta. Lors du mariage du père en 1998, son contrat de mariage instaure une autre fiducie appelée "Children and Grandchildren's Trust" pour laquelle Brenda est également bénéficiaire. Le père décède en 2004. Au début de 2005, Brenda demande une reddition de comptes aux fiduciaires situés à Calgary pour les trois fiducies du grand-père depuis leur création et pour celles du "Protective Trust" et du "Children and Grandchildren's Trust." En août 2006, en raison du refus des fiduciaires d'acquiescer à sa demande, Brenda entreprend un recours devant la Cour du Banc de la Reine de l'Alberta. Elle recherche du Tribunal albertain une ordonnance pour forcer les fiduciaires à rendre compte sur l'administration des fiducies dans lesquelles elle a un bénéfice. En février 2007, les fiduciaires déposent, au greffe de la Cour supérieure du Québec, une requête pour jugement déclaratoire dans laquelle ils requièrent du Tribunal une ordonnance de déclarer que c'est la loi du Québec qui s'applique à l'administration des fiducies dont ils ont la gestion.

En mars 2007, les fiduciaires présentent, devant le Tribunal de l'Alberta, une requête en irrecevabilité de la demande de Brenda selon la théorie du *forum non conveniens*. Ils allèguent que le Tribunal de l'Alberta n'est pas le forum approprié et que les tribunaux du Québec sont en meilleure position pour entendre tout le litige concernant la reddition de comptes. En juillet 2007, le juge albertain rejette la requête et conclut que le Tribunal de l'Alberta a juridiction pour entendre le litige et que la preuve n'établit pas que les tribunaux du Québec sont nettement en meilleure position pour l'entendre. Dans la requête pour jugement déclaratoire au Québec, les fiduciaires allèguent que l'application de la loi du Québec entraînera des obligations moins onéreuses pour les fiduciaires dans le cadre de la reddition de comptes alors que l'application de la loi de l'Alberta ou toute autre disposition de *common law* entraînera une reddition de comptes et des obligations beaucoup plus étendues. Craignant que le Tribunal de l'Alberta refuse d'appliquer la loi du Québec pour décider du mérite du dossier, les fiduciaires demandent à la Cour supérieure de déclarer que c'est bel et bien la loi du Québec qui s'appliquera quant à l'étendue des obligations et des modalités de la reddition de comptes dont la demande demeure toujours pendante devant le Tribunal de l'Alberta.

La Cour supérieure a accueilli la requête en irrecevabilité des défendeurs, Brenda et son époux, en qualifiant la situation à l'étude d'"espèce de litispendance." La Cour d'appel a rejeté le pourvoi. L'argument de litispendance ne pouvait justifier le rejet de la requête des fiduciaires. C'est le Code civil du Québec et non le Code de procédure civil qui régit tous les cas où la compétence d'un tribunal hors Québec entre en conflit avec celle d'un tribunal québécois. En application de l'article 3137 C.C.Q. et contrairement au cas de la litispendance interne prévu au paragraphe 1 de l'article 165 C.P.C., l'application de la litispendance internationale n'est susceptible d'entraîner que le sursis d'une procédure intentée au Québec et non sa rejet. Le jugement étranger non encore reconnu ne possède qu'en puissance tous les attributs de la chose jugée. Les distinctions entre la litispendance internationale et la litispendance interne s'appliquent aux conflits opposant deux tribunaux canadiens. Mais la requête en irrevabilité doit néanmoins être accueillie sur la base du moyen d'irrecevabilité pourvu dans le paragraphe 4 de l'article 165 C.P.C. ("Si la demande n'est pas fondée en droit, supposé même que les faits allégués soient vrais"). L'objectif poursuivi par les fiduciaires consiste clairement à influencer sinon à lier le Tribunal albertain sur la question de l'identification de la loi applicable. Il ne s'agit pas là d'une juste cause pour solliciter un jugement déclaratoire. La requête des fiduciaires ne fait pas voir qu'elle possède un motif légitime au sens de l'article 453 C.P.C. pour solliciter de la Cour supérieure le prononcé d'un jugement déclaratoire portant sur l'identification de la loi applicable aux fiducies en cause.

(c) Famille

Enfants — garde et droit d'accès — divorce à l'étranger

Droit de la famille — 082431, [2008] R.J.Q. 2391, 2008 QCCS 4493 (Cour supérieure du Québec)

Les parties se son mariées au Québec en 2001 et ont eu deux enfants au Québec. Les parties ont habité au Pays A à partir de 2004. Ils se sont divorcés en 2005 dans l'Abu Dhabi Sharia Court of First Instance, et ont signé une convention accordant la garde au père. La mère s'est remariée à l'étranger et a exprimé son désir de revenir au Canada avec les enfants. Elle a présenté, au Québec, une requête en modification des mesures accessoires au jugement de divorce rendu en Abu Dhabi. Le père oppose, par exception déclinatoire, l'absence de compétence des tribunaux québécois. En invoquant l'article 3142 C.C.Q. ("Les autorités québécoises sont compétentes pour statuer sur la garde d'un enfant pourvu que ce dernier soit domicilié au Québec"), il allègue que la mère réside de façon permanente à l'étranger. Il déclare avoir accepté de conduire les enfants au Canada afin de permettre à la mère de voyager avec les enfants et que la mère lui a caché son intention de ne pas lui remettre les enfants en juillet 2008. Il soumet donc que la Cour supérieure n'a pas juridiction, les enfants n'étant pas domiciliés au Québec. La mère soumet qu'elle et les enfants ont actuellement leur domicile au Québec. Subsidiairement, elle demande à la Cour d'entendre la cause car son recours est impossible à l'étranger. L'article 3136 C.C.Q. édicte que "Bien qu'une autorité québécoise ne soit pas compétente pour connaître d'un litige, elle peut, néanmoins, si une action à l'étranger se révèle impossible ou si on ne peut exiger qu'elle y soit introduite, entendre le litige si celui-ci présente un lien suffisant avec le Québec." L'expert en droit international du père soumet que la mère pourrait se voir redonner la garde des enfants malgré son remariage. L'expert de la mère soumet que lors du prononcé du jugement de divorce, il n'a pas été tenu en compte le principe de la primauté du meilleur intérêt de l'enfant.

La Cour a rejeté la requête en exception déclinatoire. La résidence habituelle des enfants est au Pays A. Mais, même si le meilleur intérêt des enfants favorisait un déplacement des enfants au Québec, le tribunal d'Abu Dhabi, étant lié par la jurisprudence islamique, devrait les maintenir au Pays A. La loi de 2005 du Pays A relative au statut personnel est plus progressiste que la Charia, qui s'appliquait antérieurement, mais contient des limites si importantes qu'il faut conclure que le principe de la primauté de l'intérêt de l'enfant ne s'appliquerait pas au recours de la mère au Pays A. Dans les circonstances, il serait déraisonnable d'exiger que la mère y dépose son recours. La naissance des enfants au Québec crée un lien de rattachement suffisant avec le Québec. Le tribunal québécois a donc compétence pour entendre le litige en vertu de l'article 3136 C.C.Q.

B PROCEDURE / PROCÉDURE

1 Common Law and Federal

(a) Trial procedure

Proof of foreign law — standard of review on appeal

General Motors Acceptance Corp. of Canada v. Town & Country Chrysler Ltd. (2007), 288 D.L.R. (4th) 74, 2007 ONCA 904 (Ontario Court of Appeal)

The plaintiff finance company was the assignee of the vendor's interest in a conditional sale contract for a 1999 Corvette that had been entered into in Québec on 24 November 1999. The plaintiff registered its security interest in Québec on 7 December, within the fifteen-day period during which such registration is deemed retroactive to the date of sale under Article 1745 C.C.Q. In the meantime, however, on 25 November 1999, the car was sold by a transferee from the original purchaser to Town and Country, a car dealer, who in turn resold it the same day to Devolin, an automobile wholesaler. The plaintiff registered its security interest under the Ontario personal property legislation on 24 January 2000, within the sixty-day period after the property came into the province during which the holder of a security interest can perfect it in Ontario. The plaintiff claimed damages against Town and Country and Devolin for interference with its rights in the chattel. The defendants argued that the plaintiff's security interest was not perfected as against them because, on the day that each purchased the vehicle, a search of the Québec registry would have produced nothing, and this, as a matter of Québec law, rebutted the presumption of knowledge that normally attached, under Article 2943 C.C.Q., to a registered security interest. The result, they argued, was that each, in turn, as a bona fide purchaser, acquired good title.

Both sides adduced expert evidence as to the law of Québec. The plaintiff's expert testified that a prudent purchaser, finding there was no registration in Québec, would either wait for the fifteen-day period to expire, or retain the purchase price until then, or inquire more closely into the chain of title back to the dealer. He did not address possible rebuttal of the presumption of knowledge. The defendants' expert said that the presumption of knowledge in Article 2943 was a simple presumption rebuttable by proof to the contrary under Article 2847 C.C.Q., referred to three cases that supported this view, and concluded that the defendants could succeed under Québec law if they acted in good faith. The trial judge, without referring to the evidence of either expert, held that under Québec law the defendants, even if they acted in good faith, were presumed to know of the plaintiff's security interest because of the retroactive effect of registration within the fifteen-day period, and that in any event they had not acted with due diligence.

On appeal, the first question was the standard of review of findings of foreign law. The court accepted the defendants' argument that the standard was not palpable and overriding error but correctness. The rationale that supported a high degree of deference for findings of fact made by a trial judge did not apply to findings and determinations made in respect of foreign law. The credibility of the expert witness testifying on legal issues was just as easily assessed on appellate review as at trial. The second point was whether the trial judge had erred in determining Québec law without reference to the expert evidence. The court accepted the defendants' argument that he had. His reasons included not one reference to the expert evidence. He appeared to have decided the case as if he were a judge sitting in a Québec court. That being so, the Court of Appeal was entitled to form its own view as to Québec law, based on the expert testimony. That view, however, was that the judge's conclusion, if not his reasoning, was correct. The standard of due diligence described by the plaintiff's expert was uncontradicted by the defendants' expert. The defendants knew of the sale in Québec and did not show due diligence, which rebutted any presumption that they had acted in good faith without knowledge of the plaintiff's security interest.

Note. On proof of foreign law and the role of an appeal court, see also *JP Morgan Chase Bank v. Kent Trade & Finance Inc.*, noted under D. Choice of law — 1. Common law and federal — (b) Property — Transfer of interest inter vivos — security interest in a ship.

(b) Local order to assist foreign proceeding

Evidence obtained locally for foreign proceeding — letters rogatory

Note. See *Lafarge Canada Inc. v. Khan* (2008), 298 D.L.R. (4th) 686, 89 O.R. (3d) 619 (S.C.J.), in which the court granted a request from a Nova Scotia court for the examination for discovery of a witness in Ontario for the purpose of an action in Nova Scotia. Although the *Evidence Act*, R.S.P. 1990, c. E.23, s. 60, provided only for letters of request from courts outside Canada, the provisions could be applied by analogy to a request from a Canadian court. Although the scope of the discovery would be according to the Nova Scotia rules, the procedure for dealing with objections should be that under the Ontario rules, which allow a witness to refuse to answer unless a judge orders otherwise, whereas in Nova Scotia the witness must answer subject to a subsequent determination by the court whether the question was proper. A witness being examined by order of an Ontario court was entitled to have that court supervise the process.

C   FOREIGN JUDGMENTS / JUGEMENTS ÉTRANGERS

1   *Common Law and Federal*

(a) Conditions for recognition or enforcement

Meaning of judgment — non-monetary order

Alsager v. Alsager (2007), 287 D.L.R. (4th) 237, 2007 SKCA 134 (Saskatchewan Court of Appeal)

A daughter who had obtained in British Columbia a committee-ship order in respect of her mother sought to register it in Saskatchewan, where most of the mother's property was, pursuant to the *Enforcement of Canadian Judgments Act*, 2002, S.S. 2002, c. E-9.1001. The chambers judge ordered a trial as to whether the daughter's appointment under the British Columbia order prevailed over a power of attorney in favour of her brother, which applied to the property in Saskatchewan. The Court of Appeal held that the British Columbia order was of no effect in Saskatchewan. It could not be registered in Saskatchewan under the act because the persons against whom it was sought to register it, the applicant's siblings, had not had adequate notice of the British Columbia proceeding and had not taken part in it. The siblings' participation in a reconsideration hearing six months later, after which the order remained intact, and their failure to appeal from the order, did not make the original order a judgment in a "proceeding commenced before this act comes into force and in which the party against whom enforcement is sought took part" (section 13(b) of the act). In any event, the order was clearly not intended to apply to the Saskatchewan property, as the master of the court in British Columbia had noted when he decided to leave the committeeship order in place.

Jurisdiction of the original court — real and substantial connection

Note. The real and substantial connection test for the recognition of an undefended foreign judgment was applied, and a Florida judgment enforced, in *Bush v. Mereshensky* (2008), 48 R.F.L. (6th) 450 (Ont. S.C.J.). The Florida action was brought by the plaintiff against her Ontario-resident former husband in respect of his wrongful withdrawal of funds from their joint bank account in Florida. A judgment from the Turks and Caicos Islands, in a lawsuit by a law firm in that country against its former client for unpaid fees, was enforced on the basis of a real and substantial connection in *Skippings Rutley v. Darragh*, 2008 BCSC 159.

In *Squire v. Yamatech Group Inc.* (2008), 297 D.L.R. (4th) 523, 2008 NBQB 278, an Ontario judgment was refused registration under the Canadian Judgments Act, S.N.B. 2000, c. C-0.1, because the plaintiff had brought his wrongful dismissal action in Ontario against a New Brunswick employer with no presence in Ontario, and the duties of his employment had been performed mostly if not wholly in New Brunswick. This did not fall under any of the categories of case — in effect, statutory real and substantial connection rules — in which a default judgment may be enforced under section 5(1) of the act.

(b) Defences to recognition or enforcement

Public policy

Bad Ass Coffee Co. of Hawaii Inc. v. Bad Ass Enterprises Inc. (2008), [2009] 1 W.W.R. 289, 2008 ABQB 404 (Alberta Queen's Bench)

The plaintiff franchisor obtained an arbitration award in Utah against two Alberta franchisees, Canadian federally incorporated companies, as well as their principal, who had guaranteed their debts as part of the franchise agreements. The claim was for damages from the franchisees for breach of their obligations under the franchise agreements and for indemnification by the guarantor in respect of those breaches. The plaintiff obtained a court order in Utah giving the award the status of a judgment and sued to enforce the judgment in Alberta. The master, whose decision is referred to in (2007) 45 Can. Y.B. Int'l L. 595, held the defendants were bound by the award and the judgment because they had attorned to the Utah court's jurisdiction by making numerous submissions on the merits in responding to the plaintiffs' application to compel arbitration. She also held the judgment enforceable in any event on account of a real and substantial connection between the litigation and Utah. Kent J. affirmed the Master's conclusions.

The main part of the reasons on appeal deal with the defence of public policy. The defendants argued that the *Franchises Act*, R.S.A. 2000, c. F-23, s. 16, expressly requires that it be applied to a franchise agreement notwithstanding any choice of law to the contrary. The choice of Utah law in the franchise agreements was therefore not bona fide and was ineffective. This meant that, under the act, Alberta law governed the agreements. That being so, the argument went, the principal's guarantees, which were most closely connected to

Alberta, were subject to the notarization requirements of the *Guarantees Acknowledgment Act*, R.S.A. 2000, c. G-11, and since they were not notarized they were not binding. Kent J. held, first, that on construction of the guarantees they incorporated the arbitration clause in the main agreements, which provided that the law of Utah was to apply. The *Guarantees Acknowledgment Act* of Alberta therefore did not apply unless by virtue of public policy. There was no breach alleged of the *Franchises Act*, only of the *Guarantees Acknowledgment Act*. It might be a fundamental value of Alberta to protect unsophisticated borrowers against taking on financial burdens, but here the guarantor was a businessman who knew the obligation he was undertaking. There was therefore no violation of Alberta public policy.

Natural justice

King v. Drabinsky (2008), 295 D.L.R. (4th) 727, 2008 ONCA 566 (Ontario Court of Appeal), leave to appeal to S.C.C. refused, 12 Feb. 2009

Investors in Livent Incorporated, an Ontario corporation that operated both in Canada and the United States, brought an action against the defendants, who were officers and directors of the company, in New York seeking damages for misrepresentations by the defendants as to the company's financial situation made in United States regulatory filings. The same matters were the subject of criminal fraud charges in both Canada and the United States. The defendants did not travel to the United States to give evidence in their defence at the civil trial but, instead, gave depositions in which they refused to answer certain questions on the basis of the immunity against self-incrimination granted by the Fifth Amendment of the United States Constitution. They also filed, in opposition to a motion for summary judgment, affidavit evidence of due diligence. The judge held the affidavit grossly deficient and granted summary judgment, which was affirmed on appeal. The plaintiffs now sought to enforce the judgment in Ontario. The defendants contended that the judgment should not be enforced for reasons of natural justice, namely, they had been unable properly to defend the civil action in New York because, had they given evidence that would incriminate them in the Canadian criminal proceedings, the evidence would not have been excluded from admission in the Canadian criminal proceedings by section 13 of the Canadian Charter of Rights and Freedoms. The argument was that this provision, which says that incriminating evidence given by a "witness who testifies in any proceedings" cannot be used in any other proceedings, applies only to evidence given in Canadian proceedings.

The Court of Appeal, affirming summary judgment in favour of the plaintiffs in the enforcement action, held that the defence of natural justice failed because the inability to defend the civil action had not been shown. It would have been open to the defendants to argue in the Canadian criminal proceedings that incriminating testimony given in the New York civil action was subject to the bar provided in section 13 of the Charter, since there was case law supporting the proposition that "any proceedings" should be interpreted as extending to foreign legal proceedings. The defendants could also have argued for exclusion of their testimony on the basis of a trial judge's residual common law discretion to exclude evidence in order to ensure a fair trial. A proposed "new defence" of lack of a meaningful opportunity to defend was rejected as indistinguishable from the natural justice defence.

Note. An undefended English judgment was refused enforcement under the Canada-United Kingdom Convention for the Reciprocal Recognition and Enforcement of Judgments in Civil and Commercial Matters, implemented by Part 4 of the Court Order Enforcement Act, R.S.B.C. 1996, c. 78, for reasons of natural justice and public policy. Notice of the proceeding to the defendant in British Columbia was not proved; service of process was improper because it was not made on the defendant personally and substitutional service was not shown to be authorized; the copy of the judgment exhibited was not certified; and it did not bear the seal of the English court as required by rule 54(3)(a) of the British Columbia Rules of Court: *Bank of Scotland PLC v. Wilson* (2008), 295 D.L.R. (4th) 128, 2008 BCSC 770. Another case in which the defence of natural justice succeeded was *Arcadia Int'l LLC v. Janmeja* (2008), 264 N.S.R. (2d) 82, 2008 NSSC 91. The default judgment was obtained in Minnesota for US $2 million. The action was initiated by publication of the action in a Minnesota newspaper, which the Minnesota rules permit in the case of absconding Minnesota debtors whose residence is unknown. The Nova Scotia judge held the publication was not reasonable notice; the plaintiff knew the defendant was in Canada but chose to make no effort to determine his whereabouts even when there were means available.

Limitations

Note. Yugraneft Corp. v. Rexx Management Corp., [2007] 10 W.W.R. 559, 2007 ABQB 450, noted in (2007) 45 Can. Y.B. Int'l L. 595 and 597, holding that an action to enforce an International Chamber of Commerce arbitration award from Russia was statute-barred under the Alberta limitations statute, was affirmed (2008), 297 D.L.R. (4th) 168, 2008 ABCA 274, leave to appeal to S.C.C. granted, 26 Feb. 2009.

(c) Effect of recognition or enforcement

Issue estoppel — who is bound

Monteiro v. Toronto Dominion Bank (2008), 89 O.R. (3d) 565, 2008 ONCA 137 (Ontario Court of Appeal), leave to appeal to S.C.C. refused, 24 July 2008

This litigation in Ontario was part of an international legal struggle between the plaintiff and her two brothers (one of whom had since died) concerning funds that were in a bank account that their mother, an Indian citizen resident in Kuwait, had at the defendant TD Bank in Toronto when she died in February 1993. The sons claimed their mother only had a life interest in the funds, which originally came from their father, that the funds belonged to them when she died, and that the mother's will, which left her entire estate to the plaintiff, was invalid. In 1994, the plaintiff commenced legal proceedings in Kuwait against her brothers to confirm the validity of their mother's will. The brothers defended the action. The Kuwait courts, including the highest court, upheld the validity of the will as a "grant contract" that, under Kuwait law, vested the mother's property in the plaintiff, including the funds in the TD bank account. In 1997, while the case was still being litigated in Kuwait, the plaintiff learned that in August 1993 the TD Bank, on the instructions of one of the brothers' lawyers, had transferred the funds in the account to the brother's bank account in Switzerland. It had done so without complying with its own procedures to verify the brother's entitlement to the funds. The plaintiff brought the present action against TD claiming payment of the funds on the basis that she was contractually entitled to them. TD's defence was that the funds were not the mother's property at the time of her death. The Superior Court of Justice granted summary judgment, holding that TD was bound by the outcome of the estate litigation in Kuwait, which confirmed the plaintiff's title to the funds.

The Court of Appeal dismissed the appeal. TD's argument, that it should not be bound by a judgment in a foreign legal proceeding in which it had no opportunity to participate, was misconceived. The parties to the estate litigation chose the Kuwait courts as the forum for the determination of the validity of the mother's will and to whom the assets referred to in it, including the TD account, were to be distributed. There was no sustainable argument that Kuwait was not a proper forum. The litigation was hotly contested, and all routes of appeal were exhausted. No one other than the plaintiff and her brothers could have an interest in the Kuwait litigation, except for some other person who claimed an ownership interest in some or all of the assets of the estate. TD was not such a person. Its status was not one of owner but one of contract debtor. The central issue decided in the estate litigation was the identity of the rightful owner of the contract of debt in relation to the TD bank account. TD had no interest in this dispute, being no more than a bystander that ought to be prepared to honour the obligation to the litigant who was found to be the rightful holder of its contract of debt.

Even if a simple interest in the outcome of the estate litigation was sufficient to entitle TD to participate in that litigation, on the facts of the case, the doctrine of issue estoppel applied to prevent it from re-litigating the issue of ownership. Issue estoppel applies where the same question has been decided in a final decision of a court of competent jurisdiction in a proceeding between the same parties or their privies. There was a real and substantial connection between the litigation and Kuwait and all the parties to the estate dispute had attorned to the jurisdiction of the Kuwait courts. TD was to be considered as privy in interest to the brother to whom it transferred the funds. A person may be the privy of another by blood, title, or interest. Privy by interest meant that there must be a sufficient degree of identification between the alleged privy and the actual litigant to make it just to hold that the decision in proceedings to which the latter is a party should be binding in proceedings to which the former is a party. Here, there was a total identification between the interests of the brothers and TD on the ownership issue.

This was not a case where TD was an innocent third party without notice or knowledge of the proceeding, the outcome of which is said to be binding on it. While it was true that TD was not a party to the Kuwait proceedings, the evidence was clear that it took no active steps to seek standing or to participate in those proceedings even though it had notice and knowledge of the Kuwait proceedings from an early stage. Nor was it a case in which the motion judge should have exercised his discretion not to apply issue estoppel. The discretion was based on fairness, but that required a balancing of the interests of both sides. It would be fundamentally unfair to the plaintiff to fail to recognize the judgment of the Kuwait court in her favour and to compel her to re-litigate her case in Ontario.

Note. In *Brown v. Miller* (2008), 62 R.F.L. (6th) 360, 2008 BCSC 1351, the court held that a husband was precluded from seeking the division of the wife's house in British Columbia as a matrimonial asset, which he claimed it was because it was bought by them jointly before they married and later, but still before their marriage, transferred into the wife's sole name to protect it from litigation. A court in Florida, in proceedings initiated by him as to the parties' property rights, held that it was pre-marital property to which the husband had no claim other than in equity, and the husband was therefore estopped from asserting a claim to the property in the British Columbia court.

(d) Enforcement by registration

Uniform Reciprocal Enforcement of Judgments statute — registrability of a judgment enforcing the original judgment

Owen v. Rocketinfo Inc. (2008), 305 D.L.R. (4th) 370, 2008 BCCA 502 (British Columbia Court of Appeal)

The plaintiff obtained a judgment against the defendant in Nevada and had it entered as a sister state judgment in California, which gave it the status of a California judgment. The plaintiff sought to register the California judgment under the uniform reciprocal enforcement of judgments legislation, which in British Columbia is contained as part 2 of the *Court Order Enforcement Act*, R.S.B.C. 1996, c. 78. California is a reciprocating state for the purposes of the British Columbia statute, but Nevada is not. The Court of Appeal, affirming the chambers judge, held the California judgment was not registrable because it was not a "judgment" that was "given in a court in a reciprocating state" within section 29 of the act. A "judgment," according to section 28(1), is "a judgment or order of a court in a civil proceeding if money is made payable." It was the Nevada judgment that made money payable by the defendant to the plaintiff. The California judgment did not make money payable but, rather, made the Nevada judgment enforceable in California. This interpretation was supported by other provisions in the act and by policy. To allow the plaintiff's judgment to be registered in British Columbia would have the effect of permitting the registration of a judgment granted by a court of a non-reciprocating jurisdiction, contrary to the intent of sections 29(1) and 37(1) of the act. The legislature did not intend to provide for registration by an indirect method when it was not permitted to be done directly.

2   *Québec*

(a) Compétence du tribunal étranger

Recours collectif en étranger — membres du groupe résidant au Québec

Hocking c. Haziza, [2008] R.J.Q. 1189, 2008 QCCA 800 (Cour d'appel du Québec)

Hocking a intenté un recours contre HSBC Bank Canada en vertu de la législation ontarienne sur les recours collectifs. Il voulait représenter tous les Canadiens qui ont remboursé par anticipation un prêt hypothécaire à HSBC et qui auraient fait les frais d'un calcul erroné de la pénalité associée à un tel remboursement. Les parties ont conclu à un règlement hors cour en Ontario. Haziza a intenté, à son tour, devant la Cour supérieure du Québec, un recours collectif de même nature, mais visant exclusivement les clients résidant au Québec. Le tribunal ontarien a certifié le recours collectif et approuvé l'entente de règlement. HSBC a alors déposé au Québec une requête visant à reconnaître et à déclarer exécutoire au Québec la décision ontarienne. La juge de première instance a conclu qu'il serait contraire aux principes d'ordre et d'équité d'ainsi contraindre des résidents québécois à s'intégrer à un recours collectif intenté dans une autre province, au choix du défendeur, alors que le tribunal de cette province n'a aucun lien direct avec leur réclamation.

La Cour d'appel (Chamberland J.C.A. dissident) a rejeté l'appel. Bich et Baudouin J.C.A. ont décidé que le jugement ontarien ne peut être reconnu au Québec, puisqu'il ne répond pas aux exigences formulées par les articles 3155 *et s.* C.C.Q. La compétence de l'autorité étrangère est en principe le "miroir" de celle que reconnaît aux autorités québécoises le titre troisième du livre dixième du Code civil du Québec, sous réserve de l'exigence d'un rattachement important. Par exception à la règle générale de l'application des dispositions du titre troisième à la détermination de la compétence de l'autorité étrangère, le législateur accorde dans l'article 3168 un traitement particulier aux actions personnelles à caractère patrimonial. L'exigence du rattachement important, composante invariable du principe structurant qu'exprime l'article 3164 C.C.Q., s'applique aussi bien lorsqu'on recourt aux dispositions du titre troisième que lorsqu'on recourt aux dispositions précisant ou restreignant les règles du titre troisième ou s'y substituant, comme par exemple les articles 3166 ou 3168 C.C.Q. En l'espèce, s'aggissant d'une action de nature personnelle à caractère patrimonial, il faut examiner d'abord l'article 3168 C.C.Q. puis, dans la mesure où l'un ou l'autre des paragraphes de cette disposition justifie à première vue la compétence étrangère, vérifier l'existence du rattachement important. L'article 3168 C.C.Q. doit être interprété et appliqué en fonction de la perspective des non-résidents auxquels on cherche à imposer le jugement étranger. Aucun des cas de figure énumérés par l'article 3168(1)-(5) C.C.Q. ne trouve application et ne peut justifier ici la compétence du tribunal étranger. La juge de première instance conclut que le paragraphe 3168(1) ("Le défendeur était domicilié dans l'État où la décision a été rendue") ne saurait fonder la compétence du tribunal ontarien puisque le siège social de HSBC Canada se trouve en Colombie-Britannique et personne ne revient sur cette question en appel. Le paragraphe 3168(6) C.C.Q. ("Le défendeur a reconnu leur compétence") repose sur la prémisse d'un choix de for effectué par celui qui a institué l'action: la reconnaissance par le défendeur de la compétence du tribunal étranger (*"attornment"*) prend alors tout son sens, se trouvant à avaliser le choix fait par le demandeur. Le seul consentement du défendeur ne peut pallier l'absence de compétence du tribunal sur des personnes qui n'ont pas elles-mêmes manifesté (et pas même implicitement) leur volonté de participer au recours collectif institué devant un for étranger, en rapport avec un litige qui, quant à elles, n'a aucun lien réel et substantiel avec le for en question.

En plus, le jugement ontarien a été rendu en violation des principes essentiels de la procédure, au sens de l'article 3155(3) C.C.Q., en ce que la juge saisie du recours collectif et, au même moment, de la ratification d'un règlement amiable, n'a pas examiné la question de savoir ce qu'il en était des intérêts des non-résidents (dont les québécois) visés par le recours, de la protection de leurs intérêts et de sa propre compétence sur ces justiciables. Le problème n'a pas été soulevé par Hocking et pas davantage par HSBC, mais cela ne dispensait pas la juge de se poser elle-même la question de sa propre compétence sur les justiciables non-résidants: on ne peut pas s'attendre à ce que celui qui a institué le recours collectif et proposé le groupe national fasse lui-même objection à la compétence du tribunal sur les ressortissants étrangers; on ne peut pas s'attendre à une telle contestation de la part d'un défendeur qui a tout intérêt à ce que le recours soit "certifié" et que le règlement proposé soit avalisé pour l'ensemble du groupe national visé. En omettant de se pencher sur cette question, la juge ontarienne a privé les justiciables québécois (sans parler des autres non-résidants) de la possibilité de se faire entendre sur une question cruciale.

En outre, l'avis destiné aux justiciables québécois était en l'espèce insuffisant et ne répondait pas aux exigences de la justice naturelle, dans le contexte. Il doit sans doute exister un certain degré de proportionnalité entre, d'une part, la nature et l'ampleur du recours collectif, compte tenu des remèdes recherchés, et, d'autre part, les efforts de diffusion. La modicité d'un recours collectif à portée limitée justifierait mal le déploiement de ressources de diffusion importantes. Mais les exigences de diffusion doivent être plus grandes lorsque le recours collectif vise un groupe national ou multiprovincial et inclut des non-résidants du for saisi. En l'espèce, l'avis a été publié, une seule fois, dans les quotidiens québécois *La Presse, Le Soleil* et *The Gazette,* qui n'est pas de nature à attirer l'attention; un tel avis aurit dû au moins être publié deux ou trois fois. On s'étonne aussi de ce que certains médias populaires aient apparemment été ignorés (comme le *Journal de Montréal* et le *Journal de Québec*). On ne peut pas économiser sur tous le fronts: si l'on admet le recours collectif national ou multijuridictionnel pour des raisons de commodité ou d'efficacité, on ne peut pas en même temps se montrer radin sur les avis destinés aux membres du groupe en question.

Bich J.C.A. a aussi discuté, sans exprimer une conclusion définitive, la question si le jugement ontarien peut être considéré inapplicable aux résidants du Québec par raison d'une atteinte directe au principe constitutionnel de territorialité. Le jugement fait apparemment en sorte de rendre applicable à tous les non-résidants de l'Ontario, et notamment aux Québécois, non seulement la procédure de reconnaissance applicable aux recours collectifs en Ontario, mais surtout le droit substantif de cette province. En effet, par ce jugement ontarien dont on demande la reconnaissance au Québec, les droits des justiciables québécois ayant contracté au Québec, avec un succursale québécoise de HSBC, un contrat hypothécaire relatif à une propriété située au Québec se trouveraient déterminés par le droit ontarien, alors qu'aucun lien de quelque sorte ne les rattache à celui-ci. Baudouin C.J.A. ne s'est pas prononcé sur la question de territorialité puisque cette question n'avait pas été spécifiquement soulevée devant la Cour.

D CHOICE OF LAW (INCLUDING STATUS OF PERSONS) / CONFLITS DE LOIS (Y COMPRIS STATUT PERSONNEL)

I *Common Law and Federal*

(a) Legal personality

Note. A Delaware limited partnership that was the defendant in an Alberta action was entitled to rely on its status under the law of Delaware with result that two limited partners, whom the plaintiff sought to examine for discovery, were not in law parties to the action and so could not be examined. The court rejected an argument that the limited partnership's failure to register as an extra-provincially created limited partnership under section 52(2) of the *Partnership Act*, R.S.A. 2000, c. P-3, deprived it of the advantages of that status in any Alberta proceeding: *Devon Canada Corp. v. PE-Pittsfield LLC* (2008), 303 D.L.R. (4th) 460, 2008 ABCA 393.

(b) Characterization

Substance and procedure — limitation period

Vogler v. Szendroi (2008), 290 D.L.R. (4th) 642, 2008 NSCA 18 (Nova Scotia Court of Appeal)

The plaintiff, a resident of Nova Scotia, commenced a personal injury action in that province for injuries he had suffered as a passenger in a motor vehicle accident in Wyoming in 2000. The defendants were the driver and the owner of the car, who were residents of Québec and California, respectively. The originating notice and statement of claim were issued on 20 January 2003, and a concurrent amending notice was issued on 23 January 2006. The owner was not served until 7 May 2006, and it was not clear whether the driver was ever served. The defendants applied to have the action dismissed on the basis that it was statute-barred under the four-year limitation period of the state of Wyoming. The rules of civil procedure in that state provided that an action is deemed commenced on the date of filing of the originating document if service is effected within sixty days, but on the date of service if it takes place more than sixty days after filing. The defendants argued that according to this rule the plaintiff had not commenced his action until the date of service, namely May 2006. The plaintiff argued that the applicable rule was that of Nova Scotia, which is that an action is commenced when the originating document is filed, not when it is served. The chambers judge considered that the Wyoming rule applied because it was part and parcel of the limitation law of Wyoming, which was substantive law and so must be applied as part of the *lex causae.*

The Nova Scotia Court of Appeal applied the Nova Scotia rule and held the action was therefore not statute-barred. The Wyoming rule must be characterized according to the conflict of laws principles of the *lex fori.* According to Nova Scotia conflicts law, substantive law defines the right and the remedy whereas procedural law defines the mode of proceeding by which the substantive right is enforced. Applying this distinction, the Wyoming rule about when an action is deemed to be commenced was procedural in nature. It dealt with how, not when, an action must be brought. This characterization was supported by considerations of policy. One is that the action being commenced is a Nova Scotia action, and it makes some sense to apply the Nova Scotia rule. Another is that commencing an action in a timely fashion is likely to face more obstacles in an interjurisdictional case than it is in a domestic one, and so applying the rule based on the issuing of process, rather than a later time, was likely to be more just as far as the plaintiff was concerned.

(c) Contracts

Statutory regulation of contract and related obligations — constitutional limits on territorial scope

Gore Mutual Insurance Co. v. John Deere Insurance Co. (2008), 65 C.C.L.I. (4th) 100 (Ont. S.C.J.).

An automobile insurer paid no-fault benefits to its insured under a policy issued in Ontario. The benefits were in respect of injuries suffered in an accident in New York state. The Ontario insurer sought reimbursement of the no-fault payments from the American insurer of the tractor-trailer that had struck the bus in which the plaintiff was riding. The right to reimbursement was created by section 275(1) of the *Insurance Act,* R.S.O. 1990, c. I.8. The act also required that claims to indemnity be determined by arbitration. Hoy J. dismissed the Ontario insurer's application for an order to appoint an arbitrator in respect of its claim. The Ontario legislation, as a matter of the province's constitutional capacity, could not impose obligations on an American insurer in respect of the consequences of an accident in New York. That would be legislating on subject matter not meaningfully connected with the province. No sufficient territorial basis could be found in the fact that the party seeking reimbursement was an Ontario insurer that paid benefits to an Ontario resident victim of the accident. The international context made this case an even stronger one than *Unifund Assurance Co. v. Insurance Corp. of British Columbia*, [2003] 2 S.C.R. 63, 2003 SCC 40, which circumscribed the territorial reach of the Ontario provisions in the interprovincial context.

(d) Property

Transfer of interest inter vivos — *security interest in a ship*

JP Morgan Chase Bank v. Kent Trade & Finance Inc. (2008), 305 D.L.R. (4th) 442, 2008 FCA 399 (Federal Court of Appeal), leave to appeal to S.C.C. refused, 4 June 2009

The *Lanner*, of Liberian registry, owned by a Liberian corporation and managed by a Greek corporation, was arrested in Halifax and sold by the Federal Court in an action *in rem* brought by the vessel's mortgagees. Three claimants asserted priority over the mortgagees on the basis that they were suppliers of necessaries to the ship who, under United States law, had maritime liens against her. None of the suppliers was based in the United States or Canada. Their supplies were provided under four contracts and delivered in, respectively, Spain, Canada, Trinidad, and Singapore. The first three contracts contained an express choice of United States law to govern the contract; the fourth contained a clause that disputes were to be submitted to arbitration in accordance with Washington State law. At first instance, a Prothonotary of the Federal Court held that the choice of law clauses did not operate to affect the rights of non-parties such as the mortgagees, and that none of the supply contracts was in fact most closely connected to the United States, which meant that the United States law on maritime liens did not apply. Since no other foreign law was proved, the claimants' rights were determined by Canadian law, which accords suppliers a statutory right *in rem* that ranks below the claims of a mortgagee. On appeal, a judge of the Federal Court reached the same result by a different route, holding the choice of law clauses were ineffective because the ship's owners had not been shown to be personally liable under the supply contract.

The Federal Court of Appeal reversed the decisions below and held by a two-to-one majority that all four supply contracts gave rise under United States law to a maritime lien that, applying the Canadian rule as to priorities as *lex fori,* ranked ahead of the claims of the mortgagees. The court recognized that maritime liens are *in rem* rights that arise by operation of law and not from contract, but took the view that choice of law clauses in supply contracts should generally govern maritime transactions, including the proprietary rights that may arise from them. The Supreme Court of Canada had emphasized the importance of comity, order, and fairness in determining conflict of laws issues. While the principles of comity and fairness will often be equivocal in maritime transactions, giving greater weight to the proper law of the supply contract would pay respect to the notion of "order" by promoting certainty and predictability in maritime transactions of a jurisdictionally diverse character. The court did not foreclose the possibility that a maritime transaction is so strongly connected to one jurisdiction that the law of that jurisdiction, rather than the law chosen by the contract, should govern the question of whether a maritime lien arises. That was not, however, the case in any of the four supply contracts here. The judge below was wrong in holding the personal liability of the shipowners on the contracts had not been shown. The authority of the manager, which had made the contracts, to bind the vessel was established by the documentary evidence.

The point on which the majority differed from the minority was on the state of United States law as proved. The expert evidence showed a division of opinion between the federal courts as to whether the federal statute conferring a maritime lien on suppliers of necessaries extended to supply contracts where neither the vessel, nor the supplier, nor the place of supply is connected with the United States. The Court of Appeals for the Eleventh Circuit had given a negative, that for the Ninth Circuit a positive, answer to the question. The majority concluded that because the Ninth Circuit decision was from 2008, it should be taken as representing a better view of the current federal law than the Eleventh Circuit decision from 1992. (The court said in passing that it was beyond the province of the expert witness to give "speculative and argumentative" testimony on the perceived strength or weakness of judicial decisions.) The minority thought that since a Court of Appeals decision from one circuit is not binding in the courts of the other circuits, and the claimants' rights therefore appeared to depend on the location of the court that decided the issue, United States law had not been proved one way or the other in relation to three of the contracts, and Canadian law should apply in default of such proof. The fourth contract provided for arbitration under Washington State law, which located it in the Ninth Circuit so that the law in that circuit, which granted foreign suppliers a maritime lien, applied.

Note. The creation of a maritime lien, unlike other forms of *inter vivos* transfer of an interest in a tangible movable, is usually not seen as a matter to be decided by the law of the jurisdiction where the movable is situated at the time of the transfer. This is presumably because the significance of the location of the ship is marginal in comparison with the other connecting factors in a typical maritime case, such as the flag of the ship, the states where the owners and the suppliers are based, the state where the necessaries are supplied, and the terms of the supply contract. If the location of the ship is not decisive, however, the determination of the applicable law becomes a matter of some intricacy. The Federal Court of Appeal's solution is to let the proper law of the contract play the dominant role unless almost all the geographical connections are with a single jurisdiction, in which case the law of that jurisdiction decides whether a lien arises. Essentially, the court draws the line between supply contracts that are truly international and those that are localized within a single jurisdiction, with the creation or non-creation of a maritime lien being a matter of party volition in the former but a matter of mandatory law in the latter. The line may not be easy to define. An example of the latter, which was cited by the court, was *Imperial Oil Ltd. v. Petromar Inc.*, [2002] F.C. 190 (C.A.), in which, notwithstanding an express choice of United States law to govern the supply contract, the supplier's rights *in rem* were determined by Canadian law because the ship's registration and the residences of the shipowner, the charterer, and the supplier were all Canadian. It is not clear whether all these elements, or only most of them, must be connected with a single jurisdiction if the parties' choice of governing law is to be overridden by that jurisdiction's law on maritime liens.

2   *Québec*

(a) Obligations

Contrats — désignation expresse de la loi applicable

Bal Global Finance Canada Corp. c. Aliments Breton (Canada) inc., 2008
QCCS 2749 (Cour supérieure du Québec), requête pour permission
d'appeler rejetée, 2008 QCCA 1420

Bal demande au Tribunal de déterminer la loi applicable au litige l'opposant à Breton, soit celle de l'Ontario ou du Québec.
Breton avait fait appel à Oracle pour l'implantation d'un système
informatisé de gestion intégrée d'inventaire et son financement.
Plusieurs contrats sont nés entre elles en plus d'un contrat de financement prévoyant notamment les modalités de financement.
Breton a consenté à toute cession éventuelle des droit et intérêts
d'Oracle dans le contrat de financement. Le contrat contenait
aussi une clause de déchéance du terme ainsi qu'une stipulation
que les obligations des parties à ce contrat sont régies par les lois
de l'Ontario. Oracle a donné à Breton quatre avis de cession de
créance sans implantation du système et Breton a dirigé ses paiements vers Bal. Celle-ci a poursuivi Breton à titre de cessionaire
pour défaut de paiement et a invoqué la clause de déchéance du
terme. Breton prétendait que les cessions lui étaient inopposables
et illégales parce qu'Oracle n'avait pas fourni un système perfor-
mant selon les règles de l'art et conforme à sa destination. Vu ces
manquements, Breton a invoqué la nullité des conventions entre
elle et Oracle, et donc celle des cessions, ainsi que le remboursement
des paiements effectués. Breton a ajouté qu'il s'agit de contrats
d'adhésion imposés comportant des clauses abusives et que la loi
québécoise doit s'appliquer. Bal prétendait que la loi de l'Ontario
doit s'appliquer.

La Cour a déclaré que la loi applicable au litige principal est
celle de l'Ontario. L'action principale est régie par le contrat de
financement contenant une clause d'élection de loi en faveur de
l'Ontario, qui implique le respect de l'expression de l'autonomie
de la volonté des parties selon l'article 3111 C.C.Q. Le fait que la
convention de services puisse être régie par les lois du Québéc ne
change en rien le fait que Breton ait choisi de procéder au financement du système sur la base du contrat de financement, un document distinct et indépendant de la convention de services qui
crée pour les parties des obligations distinctes et indépendantes
régies par les loi de l'Ontario. La désignation de la loi ontarienne
n'a rien d'abusif. L'élément d'extranéité est respecté puisque Oracle est domiciliée en Ontario. Breton ayant signé un contrat de financement valide et consenti aux cessions en redirigeant ses
paiements à Bal, a accepté l'application du droit ontarien.

Book Reviews / Recensions de livres

Forced Migration, Human Rights and Security. Edited by Jane McAdam. Oxford and Portland, OR: Hart Publishing, 2008. 316 pages.

This volume is composed of eleven papers initially presented at a conference held at the University of Sydney in November 2005. The selected papers were subsequently updated to reflect the law as of June 2007. The title of the book reflects the various issues covered. The first five chapters capture the whole of the title as they address the impact of some of the security measures adopted by states with respect to the international regime for refugees and other persons in need of protection. The next two chapters focus squarely on human rights issues. The last four chapters deal with a number of additional legal issues that will be of interest to scholars, practitioners, and non-governmental organizations working in the field of forced migration. While each author takes a comparative approach in discussing issues, the vast majority of the papers concentrate on Australian, New Zealand, and United Kingdom practice.

The opening chapter ("Forced Migration: Refugees, Rights and Security") is written by one of the foremost experts on refugee law, Guy S. Goodwin-Gill. Recalling a number of Security Council resolutions adopted since 11 September 2001, he questions why the Council has repeatedly insisted on linking border measures against terrorism with vulnerable persons seeking asylum. As he observes, "recognized refugees have rarely, if ever, been found among those guilty of terrorism or incitement."[1] This criticism, addressed both to the Council and some Western states leading the fight against

---

[1] Jane McAdam, ed., *Forced Migration, Human Rights and Security* (Oxford and Portland, OR: Hart Publishing, 2008) at 8.

terrorism, is also a frequent theme in other papers dealing with security in this volume. It is not the right of the state to protect itself that Goodwin-Gill and others question but, rather, an approach that, in the context of forced migration, fails to acknowledge the right to protection of both the state and asylum seekers and refugees. He reminds us that at the outset states were conscious of the need for balance, both in the general human rights regime as laid out in the Universal Declaration of Human Rights (UDHR) and in the 1951 Convention Relating to the Status of Refugees (Refugee Convention). These instruments include provisions meant to ensure that state security will not be endangered by the rights recognized within them. With regard to the Refugee Convention, limits are found in Article 1F (the exclusion clauses) and in Article 33 (the *non refoulement* clause). Of course, since then, and as many authors later discuss in some depth, these limits have been watered down by the international human rights regime.

In Goodwin-Gill's view, and in that of many of the other authors in this book, resolutions of the Security Council have tilted the balance towards state security at the expense of legitimate asylum seekers: "Indeed, it is arguable that the tenor of the Security Council's approach to refugees and asylum seekers has served to compound national measures which already seriously compromise their security, and impact negatively on the international regime of refugee protection."[2] Goodwin-Gill draws on US and UK practice to make this point, referring to various controversial legal provisions that have impacted asylum seekers and refugees and that have been challenged, in many cases successfully, as being contrary to fundamental human rights. The final part of the article highlights provisions, in resolutions adopted by both the Security Council and the General Assembly, which provide that anti-terrorism measures have to be "in conformity with the relevant provisions of national and international law, including international standards of human rights." Thus, while the author deplores the link that these resolutions have suggested between asylum seekers and terrorism, he emphasizes that this link did not do away with the obligation of states to ensure that the rule of law, notably as expressed in the international regimes on refugees and human rights, always prevails. Many of the subsequent chapters in this book suggest that some states have not yielded to this message.

[2] *Ibid.* at 6–7.

The next chapter ("Resolution 1373: A Call to Pre-empt Asylum Seekers? or 'Osama, the Asylum-Seeker'"), authored by Penelope Mathew, is a logical follow-up to the paper by Goodwin-Gill, as the first part of her paper focuses on the origin of Security Council Resolution 1373, one of the key resolutions linking refugees and terrorism adopted in 2001. She explains that some states hoped to rely on this resolution to more easily justify the exclusion of asylum seekers suspected of links with terrorist groups. In particular, paragraph 5 of the resolution provides that "acts, methods, and practices of terrorism" as well as "knowingly financing, planning and inciting terrorist acts" are "contrary to the purposes and principles of the United Nations." The latter wording is similar to the language found in one of the exclusion clauses — Article 1F(c) — of the Refugee Convention.

For Mathew, there are many reasons why a state would want to rely on this clause to exclude persons. First, there is not one generally agreed definition of terrorism at the international level, leaving it to each state to define it. Second, a terrorist threat does not have to be directed against the country of refuge to justify resort to the exclusion clause. Third, the exclusion can be resorted to without first determining if a person otherwise meets the criteria for a refugee. Fourth, no proportionality between the conduct of the excluded person and the risk of persecution upon return need be demonstrated. Finally, a low standard of proof is required to justify the application of an exclusion clause. In her view, the sum of these factors may lead states to exclude persons perceived as "undesirable" rather than legally undeserving of protection under the Refugee Convention. Whether this has indeed led to the exclusion of persons who are not linked to terrorism is difficult to determine. On the other hand, there appears to be ample evidence that, since September 2001, states have resorted more often to Article 1F(c) than in previous years. In the third and last part of her paper, Mathew provides some evidence of this trend though her study of states' reports to the UN Counter-Terrorism Committee established under Resolution 1373.

Mathew's analysis of states' reports also raises concerns that some states adopt an overly expansive and incorrect interpretation of exclusion clauses and/or justify restrictions to refugee rights based on a perceived threat of terrorism. The various examples she provides, all taken from states' reports, support her conclusion that "[o]n the whole, perusal of the state reports to the Counter-Terrorism Committee tends to show that states have been emboldened to frame violations of refugee law as counter-terrorist action."[3] Mathew also argues that "the Security Council's emphasis on denial of refugee status to terrorists may become a stalking horse for the erosion of the absolute protection against return to a place of torture currently guaranteed by general human rights law."[4] While she makes forceful and convincing arguments against states' attempts to dilute the absolute prohibition on returning someone to a risk of torture, it would, however, have been useful had she elaborated further on her fear that the absolute guarantee of *non-refoulement* to a place of torture will be eroded by Resolution 1373 and, as implicitly suggested, by a more frequent resort by states to Article 1F(c).

Contrary to Mathew and many other contributors to this volume, Rodger Haines, in the third chapter ("National Security and Non-Refoulement in New Zealand: Commentary on *Zaoui v. Attorney-General (No.2)*"), takes the view that there should be limits to the prohibition against *refoulement*. To make his case, he refers to a number of recent cases in New Zealand and, in particular, to *Zaoui v. Attorney-General (No 2)*.[5] In this case, the Supreme Court of New Zealand states in *obiter dicta* that, through the complementary protection of Article 3 of the 1984 Convention against Torture and Other Cruel, Inhuman or Degrading Treatment or Punishment (Convention against Torture) and Articles 6(1) and 7 of the International Covenant on Civil and Political Rights (ICCPR), there is an absolute prohibition against *refoulement*. Haines describes and comments on the relevant immigration and refugee law provisions in New Zealand and explains the status of treaties in domestic law. The core of Haines's argument is that the court has not provided any rationale for giving priority to the rights of refugees otherwise subject to *refoulement* over those of their past and potential future victims. Of course, the fact that the court was speaking in *obiter* may explain why it did not pursue a more in-depth analysis. Moreover, the court opted to rely on a number of international authorities that support its *dicta*. Haines would have rather preferred that the court take into account a number of policy reasons to right the balance in favour of past and potential victims of the refugee under threat of *refoulement*. The author appears to suggest that the court

---

[3] *Ibid.* at 58.

[4] *Ibid.* at 47.

[5] *Zaoui v. Attorney-General (No 2)*, [2006] 1 N.Z.L.R. 289 (N.Z.S.C.).

could and should have arrived at a different conclusion even if this meant inviting the state to act "in breach or potential breach of the *CAT* and the *ICCPR*."[6]

It is worth noting that while the title of the article refers to the case of *Zaoui*, much of the arguments made by Haines refer to *Baaiaty*, a case involving a refugee found guilty of a number of rapes. He was initially sentenced to nine years in prison. He reoffended soon after his release and was sentenced to a preventive detention sentence of at least seven more years. He appealed this sentence but was unsuccessful. Following this holding, the minister for immigration called for a report on the deportation issues raised by the case. Referring to this case, Haines asks: "[H]ow is it that his 'right' not to be exposed to the risk of being tortured trumps the right of New Zealand women not to be exposed to the serious risk that he will again commit rape in New Zealand?"[7] Given that the statement of the court in *Zaoui* is *obiter*, it is likely that this issue will resurface. At that time, the arguments raised by Haines will possibly be revisited. If so, one can well imagine that those in favour of the absolute prohibition against *refoulement* to a risk of torture will argue that the criminal system in New Zealand did punish Baaiaty and will ask whether one can distinguish, without offending universal human rights, on the basis of citizenship to justify sending some criminals to places where real risks of torture exist.

Increasingly since the 1980s, states have taken offshore measures aimed at more effectively controlling entry to their territory. In the fourth chapter of this volume ("Offshore Barriers to Asylum Seeker Movement: The Exercise of Power without Responsibility?"), Savitri Taylor provides a rich analysis of Australian actions in a great number of foreign airports aimed at intercepting individuals who try to reach Australia without valid authorization. First, she notes the deployment of Australian airline liaison officers (ALOs) in selected airports, most of them located in Asia. These officers are trained to detect fraudulent documents. They provide expert advice to immigration personnel, airport authorities, and airline employees in locations where they are posted. They also co-operate with other Western countries that have similar officers deployed in the same airports. Taylor describes the vast operational network of ALOs that Australia has been able to develop over the years through

---

6 McAdam, *supra* note 1 at 16.

7 *Ibid.* at 90.

memoranda of understanding and other arrangements with a number of countries. She observes that there are no clear processes for addressing asylum claims made by persons thus intercepted. Moreover, no records are kept on how many of those intercepted have made such a claim. Another Australian overseas control described by Taylor is the advanced passenger processing required from all airlines with regular passenger flights to Australia, which provides another means of checking whether those travelling to that country have adequate documents. Again, Taylor observes that this process does not seem to address the specific situation of asylum seekers. Australia, like a number of other countries, also sanctions air carriers that board persons with no valid visa. No provisions are made for reimbursement of penalties if one of those persons is subsequently granted refugee status.

Having described these measures and working on the assumption that they are effective in preventing asylum seekers from making a claim in Australia, Taylor examines, in the second part of her paper, whether Australia is, as a result, breaching its *non-refoulement* obligations. She further divides this question into two sub-questions: (1) do international rules on responsibility attribute all or part of the responsibility for these interceptions to Australia; and (2) do these interceptions amount to *refoulement?* With regard to the first question, she examines the now well-accepted rules by which acts of public and private actors are attributable to a state. Among key indicators is the identity of the decision maker—whether the decision is made by personnel of the private airlines or by Australian officials? Taylor's conclusions that "the conduct of Australia's ALO is definitely attributable to Australia, and the conduct of airline personnel in preventing a particular person from boarding an Australia-bound flight is conduct that is probably also attributable to Australia" appear legally sound. As to the second question, Taylor takes the view that Article 33 of the Refugee Convention, Article 3 of Convention against Torture, and relevant provisions of the ICCPR are engaged as long as actions of Australian officials overseas amount to effective control of the persons intercepted, a determination that will depend on the particular circumstances of each case. As she acknowledges, however, this view is not universally accepted. Finally, another key part of this sub-question is whether an interception can be characterized as *refoulement*. Some have suggested that this is not the case since the person intercepted can always opt to go to another country. Others have suggested that the choice of destination is illusory. As noted by Taylor, some countries in which Australia participates in interceptions are known to remove asylum seekers without a proper procedure in place to determine their claim. Moving on to the principle of joint responsibility, she concludes that an intercepting state cannot completely free itself from its responsibility by simply arguing that the state in which the interception took place is solely liable.

As will be apparent from the earlier discussion, the argument that Australia could be in breach of its international obligations due to its offshore immigration control measures is complex. For instance, it should be noted that Taylor starts from the premise that the article on *non-refoulement*, Article 33, does apply to offshore asylum seekers, noting, however, that the existing jurisprudence on this point is divided. This issue is a key one and, since we live in a world where many states give primacy to security and are increasing off-shore measures to control migration, it will no doubt be further addressed by various judicial authorities in the near future. Taylor's well-structured paper addresses this and other relevant issues and, as such, constitutes an important contribution.

The fifth chapter ("The Legal and Ethical Implications of Extra-territorial Processing of Asylum Seekers: The 'Safe Third Country' Concept"), written by Susan Kneebone, also deals with offshore measures aimed at controlling access to a state's territory, in this case the "Safe Third Country" concept (STC). While this concept originated in Europe, it has now spread to other parts of the world, notably to North America with the conclusion of a "Safe Third Country" agreement between Canada and the United States. Knee-bone questions the premises for this concept, notably that asylum seekers cannot choose their destination. In her view, too much importance has been given to the rights of states at the expense of individual rights. She revisits the interpretation of provisions that have been relied upon to justify STC, focusing on Article 14 of the UDHR and Articles 31 and 33 of the Refugee Convention. Her analysis leads her to conclude that while there is no positive duty on states to process asylum seekers, there are legal considerations that support giving some weight to the choice of asylum seekers. Moving from a legal approach to an ethical one, she invites the reader to further reflect on this issue by considering the view of political scientist Mathew Gibney who, like Kneebone, privileges a more nuanced view of the relationship between the respective rights and duties of states and asylum seekers than one in which, through the STC, states can unilaterally dictate where those fleeing persecution should claim protection.[8]

As mentioned earlier, the sixth and seventh chapters deal primarily with migration and human rights issues. Chapter 6 ("Re-thinking the Paradigms of Protection: Children as Convention Refugees in Australia") is an in-depth study by Mary Crock about unaccompanied child refugees, taking Australia as a case study. While in the first part of her paper she identifies some preconceptions that have contributed to a lack of sensitivity to child refugees in that country, in Crock's view, the more important factor to explain the inadequate response to these children has been "a general cultural failure to think about children as agents and as refugees in their own right."[9] In the remainder of the chapter, she demonstrates how one should read the Refugee Convention with "the image of the child front and centre."[10] She then revisits key elements of the definition of refugee (well-founded fear, persecution, convention grounds) with this image in mind. For instance, she identifies three different ways that a child can suffer persecution: (1) it can be similar to that suffered by adults; (2) it can be a persecution specific to children, such as the recruitment of child soldiers; and (3) it can be conduct that would not amount to persecution for an adult but could for a child because of his or her vulnerability, for instance, an action against a close relative that would traumatize a child and not an adult.[11] Her discussion also addresses many aspects of the process for evaluating children's claims to protection. For instance, with regard to the matter of evidence, she notes that the Australian Refugee Review Tribunal's Guidelines on Children Giving Evidence "recognize that children may be unable to present evidence in support of their claims because of their age, gender, cultural background or other circumstances. The Guidelines state that greater allowance should be made for inconsistencies in the evidence of children."[12] Throughout, Crock refers to, and comments on, relevant Australian case law and instruments. Her insights will be of interest to all those working with child refugees, whether in Australia or other countries.

---

[8] M.J. Gibney, *The Ethics and Politics of Asylum: Liberal Democracy and the Response to Refugees* (Cambridge: Cambridge University Press, 2004).

[9] McAdam, *supra* note 1 at 161.

[10] *Ibid.* at 158.

[11] *Ibid.* at 171.

[12] *Ibid.* at 162.

The seventh chapter ("Wearing Thin: Restrictions on Islamic Headscarves and Other Religious Symbols") provides an interesting comparative analysis of recent judicial pronouncements regarding the wearing of religious symbols in teaching institutions. Ben Saul examines and contrasts the recent decisions of the European Court of Human Rights in *Sahin v. Turkey*,[13] House of Lords in *R. (on the Application of Begum) v. Headteacher and Governors of Denbigh High School*,[14] and of the Supreme Court of Canada in *Multani v. Commission scolaire Marguerite-Bourgeoys*.[15] Each of the cases is analyzed with regard to its impact on the right to manifest one's religion and the right to education. The reader will appreciate the detailed treatment that Saul gives to each case. As he uses the same structure to examine each, the reader can more easily appreciate commonalities and differences between the three cases.

Saul's position is that liberal societies should be worried about too readily adopting measures restricting religious minorities' practices. As such, he is critical of the first two decisions, as he argues that the courts in these cases did not put to the test assertions by the governments involved that the religious practices in question represented a threat to the public interest. Not surprisingly, the concept of "margin of appreciation" played a great part in the decision of the European Court of Human Rights. The problem is not so much with the concept itself but, rather, with the fact that the court, in Saul's view, relied entirely on the assumptions made by the national government, in effect abandoning its supervisory role. Likewise, Saul emphasizes that the House of Lords relied very much on the opinion of the school authorities in its decision. In both cases, the result was to uphold a restriction on clothing, in universities in the first case, and in a school in the other. For Saul, these restrictions, often justified to promote unity within a diverse community, can have the reverse effect: "[O]ver the long term, cohesion and harmony are not possible if policies are accepted which eradicate difference, or render it invisible. Ultimately, harmony in a diverse society can only be built upon respect for difference, rather than its suppression in the name of public order or the pursuit of a vision of social cohesion that reflects a majoritarian

---

[13] *Sahin v. Turkey*, App. No. 44774/98 (E. Ct. H.R.: Grand Chamber, November 10, 2005).

[14] *R. (on the Application of Begum) v. Headteacher and Governors of Denbigh High School*, [2006] UKHL 15.

[15] *Multani v. Commission scolaire Marguerite-Bourgeoys*, [2006] 1 S.C.R. 256.

view."[16] This is not to say that he condemns all restrictions on religious clothing. He mentions, for instance, a number of cases in which the restrictions based on legitimate occupational reasons seem justified. Finally, Saul provides a number of reasons why the European Court of Human Rights and the House of Lords could learn valuable lessons from the decision of the Supreme Court of Canada, which allowed the wearing of a kirpan in school provided that this was done in a way that minimizes the risks to others.

The next chapter ("Objectivity and Refugee Fact-Finding"), by Arthur Glass, differs considerably from the others as it does not focus on human rights or security in a forced migration context. Instead, it identifies and discusses key elements that should be considered by decision makers to arrive at a decision on the facts of a case. While the chapter is rather short, it nevertheless clearly explains the role and importance of these various elements and will be greatly appreciated by anyone interested in better understanding how decisions on factual issues are made.

Since the provisions of the Refugee Convention are meant to be interpreted by the administrative tribunals and courts of the various states parties to the convention, it is to be expected that not all countries will have the same interpretation of those provisions. However, in the ninth chapter in this volume ("Towards Convergence in the Interpretation of the Refugee Convention: A Proposal for the Establishment of an International Judicial Commission for Refugees"), Anthony M. North and Joyce Chia argue that as much uniformity as possible should be sought in the interpretation of a convention meant to ensure the same, universal protections to all asylum seekers and refugees. In their view, there are currently too many important issues on which there is a diversity of interpretation, with grave consequences for some asylum seekers and refugees. They provide a list of these issues and could probably have added to it by drawing on examples mentioned in some of the other chapters in this volume. It should be noted that some of the references given here need to be updated. For instance, the authors note that the courts in Canada are divided on the issue of China's one-child policy, referring to decisions of the Federal Court of Canada in two cases instead of subsequent decisions of the Federal Court of Appeal in one of those cases and the Supreme Court of Canada in the other.[17]

---

[16] McAdam, *supra* note 1 at 203.

[17] *Ibid.* at 232, n. 22.

The authors then explain why existing mechanisms, at the regional or international levels, are not sufficient to promote the degree of consistency desired in the interpretation of the provisions of the Refugee Convention. Finally, they put forward a proposal to create, under the supervisory mandate of the United Nations High Commissioner for Refugees (UNHCR), an independent international judicial commission, composed of a small number of eminent judges and experts in refugee law, whose tasks would be to provide opinions on important issues in the convention that have given rise to divergent interpretations. The quality of the opinions formulated by this commission, its independence, its legitimacy (derived from its creation by the UNHCR) and a host of other factors discussed by the authors would, in their view, confer great value on the opinions of this commission. While the authors develop in some detail their proposal, they also stress that it could certainly be improved upon. This is apparent, for instance, in the section on the process for appointment of members to the commission, where the authors put forward only very general suggestions.

This proposal is certainly worth pondering as there is much to be said in favour of striving for greater consistency in interpretation of the Refugee Convention throughout the world. As pointed out by the authors, it is certainly unfair that similar claims for refugee status could be accepted in one country and rejected in another simply because of divergent interpretations of the same provisions of the Refugee Convention. There is, however, one important issue that the authors do not tackle in discussing their proposal, which is the risk that the creation of this commission would add to fragmentation of interpretation of the Refugee Convention instead of promoting a convergence of views. What if, for instance, an opinion of the commission were to differ from that of a conclusion of the Executive Committee of the UNHCR Programme or from a view expressed in the *Handbook on Refugees* published by the UNHCR? Why would national judicial authorities accord greater weight to the view of the newly established commission? It would be useful if in a subsequent paper on the topic the two authors would address this question.

The tenth chapter ("The Refugee Convention as a Rights Blueprint for Persons in Need of International Protection"), penned by the editor of the book, Jane McAdam, examines some aspects of the relationship between the Refugee Convention and the concept of complementary protection. As she explains, this concept "describes protection granted by states to individuals with international protection needs falling outside the Refugee Convention framework."[18] It could mean the legal protection offered under the Convention against Torture or the ICCPR or "more general humanitarian principles, such as providing assistance to persons fleeing generalized violence."[19] McAdam examines this concept in the context of its formulation as "subsidiary protection" in the EC Directive 2004/83 on Minimum Standards for the Qualification and Status of Third Country Nationals or Stateless Persons As Refugees or As Persons Who Otherwise Need International Protection and the Content of the Protection Granted adopted by the European Union in April 2004. While she recognizes the significance of this directive as the "first binding, supranational instrument on complementary protection," she deplores the fact that it does not provide for a regime of rights equivalent to those falling within the Refugee Convention.[20] (It would have been useful if McAdam had provided a few examples of these differences.) In McAdam's view, there is no legal rationale for providing different benefits to convention and extra-convention refugees, when both are protected by the obligation of *non-refoulement*. As alluded to by Goodwin-Gill in the opening chapter of this volume, McAdam reminds us that "[t]hough a specialist treaty, the *Refugee Convention* nevertheless forms parts of the corpus of human rights law, both informing and being informed by it."[21] She then explains why the Refugee Convention is a much more appropriate instrument than general human rights instruments to confer benefits on persons in need of complementary protection. She also demonstrates that the extension of the Refugee Convention's benefits to these persons is consistent with the origins of the convention, as a specialist human rights treaty, and with state practice. One particularly convincing argument made by McAdam to justify the extension of the benefits of the Refugee Convention to others is Recommendation E appended to the convention, in which the hope is expressed that states will extend the treatment provided by the convention to those in its territory who are in need of protection without being covered by the convention. This chapter adds an important new dimension to the concept of complementary protection, a concept already discussed in some of the previous chapters (in particular, those by Mathew, Haines, and Taylor).

18 *Ibid.* at 263–64.

19 *Ibid.* at 264.

20 McAdam, *supra* note 1 at 265.

21 *Ibid.* at 268.

Given that this book is composed of some of the texts initially presented at a conference, it is not surprising that its final chapter ("The Responsibility to Protect: Closing the Gaps in the International Protection Regime") is the text of an address presented at the time of the conference by an eminent speaker with the office of the UNHCR, Erika Feller. Widening the discussion beyond refugees, Feller urges the reader to ponder the capacity of the concept of "Responsibility to Protect" to close the gaps in the international protection regime in order to offer increased protection to other categories of persons in need, such as internally displaced persons, returnees, and stateless persons. The general tenor of her comments as well as a note at the end of her text indicates that the thinking of the UNHCR on this concept continues to evolve.

YVES LE BOUTHILLIER
Associate Professor, Faculty of Law (Common Law Section),
University of Ottawa

International Refugee Law and Socio-Economic Rights: Refuge from Deprivation. By Michelle Foster. Cambridge: Cambridge University Press, 2007 (paperback edition 2009). 442 pages.

In *International Refugee Law and Socio-Economic Rights,* Michelle Foster argues that the protection of the Convention Relating to the Status of Refugees (Refugee Convention) should extend to people fleeing abuses of internationally protected socio-economic rights. This argument sets her work squarely in the midst of the public and political contestation about the distinction between "real" refugees and "mere" economic migrants. It is this polemic that she deconstructs in this book, demonstrating its fallacies and its origins as well as the grain of truth that sustains it. In the pursuit of her central claims, Foster delivers a well-written and extensively documented text that provides a thorough canvass of the central tensions in contemporary refugee law.

The Refugee Convention's definition of a refugee is the most interpreted international law text in the world. In recent years, more than half a million decisions regarding asylum seekers have been made annually, each applying and interpreting the refugee definition, whether in a tent in the Sudan, a visa office in Islamabad, or the British House of Lords. Foster's work reads as a penetrating parsing of the definition, focusing in turn on each of its aspects, considering the ways in which deprivation of socio-economic rights may intersect with elements of its text. Too often in refugee decision making, the central jurisprudential elements of the definition — persecution, grounds, and nexus — have a three-dimensional seesaw interaction, with a positive finding in one area serving only to push vital issues into another heading. Foster tackles this tendency head on, carefully and deliberately anticipating the series of counters that might emerge to her propositions. She demonstrates how breaches of socio-ecomomic rights should be analyzed in relation to persecution but also addresses issues such as how "the poor" can be analyzed as a particular social group and how economic discrimination can be interrelated with other rights breaches.

Foster's central argument is familiar to refugee advocates, but her articulation of it is better than any I have encountered. Indeed, it is better than I had imagined it could be. She achieves this through extensive research, trenchant analysis, and crystal-clear articulation. This work will lend itself well to use in appellate argument, and, given the state of contemporary refugee law, opportunities for such argument are plentiful.

My favourite aspect of Foster's work is her engagement with James Hathaway's seminal text *The Law of Refugee Status* (Butterworths, 1991). She both supports and challenges his influential articulation of the relationship between "persecution" in refugee law terms and international human rights. Foster begins her engagement with Hathaway's analysis with a defence of his hierarchy of human rights obligations. She carefully distinguishes Hathaway's use of a hierarchical arrangement of state obligations to guide refugee decision makers in analyzing rights abuses from a normative hierarchy of human rights, such as that articulated by Jean Yves Carlier. Foster is right to draw this distinction and is correct in asserting that the distinction between these two genres of hierarchy has often been lost on decision makers and scholars. Hathaway's work may not need this defence, but Foster's adaptation of it does.

Having come this far, however, Foster is aware that without a principled method for distinguishing some rights abuses from others, decision makers will not be persuaded by her text. The elision between these two understandings of hierarchy has been persistently problematic for socio-economic rights in refugee law. In its place, Foster posits a "core" and "periphery" analysis of human rights breaches. Drawing on the work of the International Association of Refugee Law Judges, this approach focuses on whether a particular human rights breach is sufficiently serious to warrant a finding of persecution. This proposal circumvents the language of hierarchy but is not in tension with Hathaway's original conception. Foster stops short of an assertion that her approach should replace Hathaway's, arguing instead that it has more practical application in the area of socio-economic rights.

On its way to constructing her overall thesis, this book also serves as an excellent account of the current state of international human rights law. This is, of course, vital in pursuit of Foster's central claims, but she has carried off this canvass with extensive documentation and a thoroughgoing analysis. Much of this analysis is located in Chapter 4, where she argues against a normative hierarchy in international human rights and supports the argument regarding interdependence of these rights. Parts of this chapter could, and probably will, stand alone as a summary or teaching text regarding the contemporary status of international human rights.

Finally and most importantly, *International Refugee Law and Socio-Economic Rights* is a good read. It is well indexed and well supported. It can be read as a full argument or usefully excerpted as stand-alone chapters. It will have an enduring role as an important text in international refugee law.

CATHERINE DAUVERGNE
Canada Research Chair in Migration Law and Professor,
Faculty of Law, University of British Columbia

Making People Illegal: What Globalization Means for Migration and Law.
By Catherine Dauvergne. Cambridge: Cambridge University Press, 2008. 232 pages.

Catherine Dauvergne begins her original and fascinating monograph by noting the prevalence of contemporary discussion about the "problem" of "illegal" migration throughout the world and observing that the rise of the "moral panic" about this phenomenon is a marker of the twenty-first century. As she observes, "in contrast with the legalization of migration that took place at the outset of the previous century, we are currently witnessing the 'illegalization' of migration."[1] Against this background, her book

---

[1] Catherine Dauvergne, *Making People Illegal: What Globalization Means for Migration and Law* (Cambridge: Cambridge University Press, 2008) at 2.

examines the relationship between globalization and illegal migration, arguing that in "contemporary globalizing times," migration laws and their enforcement are increasingly understood as "the last bastion of sovereignty."[2] Her ultimate aim is to "make sense of the forces behind this illegality" and to "consider options for strategizing against it."[3]

In a powerfully written, lucid, and sophisticated analysis, Dauvergne takes the reader on a wide-ranging journey through the many categories and mechanisms "used to identify and construct extralegal migration" today.[4] As she explains in her introduction, by examining labour migration, trends in refugee law, trafficking and smuggling of human beings, and the migration/security nexus and shift in citizenship law, she aims to identify parallel arguments and common themes that emerge from an analysis of each of these developments. This approach enables her to move beyond the existing literature, which tends to focus on one or two discrete aspects of the modern story of illegal migration and, "using the dilemmas of globalization theory," "develop a story that emerges from combining these areas of study."[5] Of course, the immediate challenge that becomes apparent is the ambitious breadth of such a project. However, in order to respond to this challenge, Dauvergne has developed a highly original technique, namely to employ the "ice scientist's methodology of core sampling," which in this context means "drilling into each topic under consideration to extract a sample that in key ways reveals something about the whole."[6] The book clearly, then, does not aspire to be comprehensive, but this fact does not detract from the strength of the analysis and the original insights generated by this unique book. On the contrary, each chapter is worth reading in its own right. The fact that each of the excellent chapters is anchored in a strong theoretical foundation and drawn together in a thought-provoking conclusion makes this book an outstanding contribution to the literature.

Prior to moving to her "core samples," Dauvergne provides further background to the study in Chapters 2 and 3. In Chapter 2 ("On Being Illegal"), she examines the phenomenon of illegal migration, including explanations for its vast increase in recent times. As she

2 *Ibid.* at 2.

3 *Ibid.* at 8.

4 *Ibid.* at 3.

5 *Ibid.*

6 *Ibid.*

observes, an important account for its growth is the law itself, since the term "illegal" is empty in content and is circumscribed solely in terms of a relationship with law (compared with other identity markers such as visitor, guest worker, or refugee). This is an important insight because it assists to explain that while the law is a "necessary site for constructing illegality" it is "much less apt to remedying it."[7] She illustrates this point by undertaking an analysis of the ability of the law, especially the proliferation of human rights norms, to assist those deemed illegal. In this chapter, she lays the groundwork for a key point to which she returns, namely that human rights law has contributed little to the struggle for recognition and equality of "illegals." She argues that despite the promise of human rights law and, indeed, the claim by some that it is able or even has delivered significant benefits to illegal migrants, in fact "being merely human is not enough to ensure legal standing in many instances."[8] While she refers only briefly to general human rights conventions, she undertakes an excellent analysis of the background to, and content of, the International Convention on the Protection of the Rights of All Migrant Workers and Members of Their Families — a new treaty that entered into force on 3 May 2008. Her conclusion is that this convention "accords a greater place to sovereignty than to the rights of illegal migrants" and as such "is a paragon of the inabilities of law to address the new illegality of people."[9]

In Chapter 3, Dauvergne lays the foundation for the core sampling chapters to follow. Her contention is that "migration and the laws that regulate it are uniquely positioned to provoke insights about what is taking place under the banner of globalization."[10] One of the great strengths of this chapter (and the book in general) is her ability to traverse very large volumes of theoretical literature and distil the core salient points into her analysis. She is able to summarize complex theories and extensive literature in a way that is very accessible yet not simplistic. This is evidenced very clearly in her attempt to pin down the "shape shifter"[11] of globalization and identify its key features. She deftly traverses the extensive scholarship in the area and identifies four key questions at the heart of the globalization debate: whether globalization threatens the nation-state;

[7] *Ibid.* at 27.

[8] *Ibid.* at 21.

[9] *Ibid.* at 22.

[10] *Ibid.* at 31.

[11] *Ibid.* at 29.

whether it is essential to economic growth; whether globalization is simply a "transmission belt" for liberal values; and, finally, the question of global governance.[12] She explains that examining contemporary shifts in immigration law provides a way of assessing each of these debates. In particular, it allows an engagement with "legal accounts of the global," a prevalent theme of which is the notion that international law is becoming increasingly important and authoritative. This is, however, challenged by an almost "complete absence of international regulation of migration — a quintessentially international phenomenon that states are clearly desperate to control."[13] Drawing on the scholarship of Santos, whose work is characterized as being concerned with the social consequences of a "massive increase in law" and, in particular, with the question whether law can be emancipatory, Dauvergne explains that her challenge is to assess whether, in the illegal migration context, law has any "emancipatory potential."[14] This amounts to "addressing the question of whether law can draw its authority from any source other than the nation."[15] In particular, she explains that the book will focus on the "central pillar of jurisprudence" — the rule of law — and assess whether it is "an empty concept that will bear the weight of whatever political agenda it is conjured to support or whether it has its own emancipatory potential."[16] This is the challenge to which the remaining chapters respond.

Turning then to the "core samples," she begins in Chapter 4 ("Making Asylum Illegal") by assessing the emancipatory role of refugee law and how advocates may work to develop this. The "core sample" chosen is the background to, and consequences of, the story of the MV *Tampa* — a Norwegian container ship that rescued 433 asylum seekers close to Australia in August 2001. This event gave rise to one of the most destructive periods in Australia's history of refugee protection, culminating in the so-called "Pacific Solution" whereby asylum seekers were sent off-shore rather than be permitted to gain access to Australia's on-shore refugee protection system.[17]

[12] *Ibid.* at 33.

[13] *Ibid.* at 35.

[14] *Ibid.* at 37.

[15] *Ibid.*

[16] *Ibid.* at 38.

[17] It should be noted that this has been discontinued on the election of a new federal Labor government. See "Last Refugees Leave Nauru," Media release by the Minister for Immigration and Citizenship, 8 February 2008, <http://www.minister.immi.gov.au/media/media-releases/2008/ce08014.htm>.

This is a very apt choice as it indeed represents the increasingly effective attempts by many developed states parties to the Refugee Convention to engage in a wide range of non-entrée policies. The core theme of the chapter is the extent to which international refugee law has become "intertwined with the growing global concern about illegal migration," despite the fact that refugees are not illegal migrants.[18] While she correctly observes that states are pushing back against the threat to sovereignty embodied in the Refugee Convention in a myriad of ways, she also sees that there is some emancipatory potential in the willingness of states and courts to treat refugee law as a rule of law. She states that there is evidence that courts "are reaching for a rule of law beyond their own borders" and that this may signal the beginning of "unhinging law and nation."[19] The potential for such unhinging is then assessed in later chapters considering trafficking, the impact of national security concerns, and citizenship.

While the powerful, thought-provoking, and challenging analysis of current international responses to the problem of sex-trafficking (Chapter 5) does not yield a particularly hopeful conclusion ("in this area, the emancipatory potential of law is difficult to discern"[20]), Dauvergne finds a "glimmer of unhinging of law and nation" in her analysis of the response of the judiciary to the indefinite detention of non-citizens.[21] In Chapter 6, she undertakes an important and interesting analysis of case law on indefinite detention, which highlights that at least in some contexts courts have been willing to de-couple security and migration. As Dauvergne notes, in *A. v. Secretary of State for the Home Department,* the House of Lords found that the government's derogation from Article 5(1) of the European Convention of Human Rights was not valid because it discriminated impermissibly on the grounds of nationality or immigration status.[22] She explains that this decision recognizes that there is "a globalized understanding of the perceived threat" but that it "is not dependent on immigration status." There is "a line between us and

---

[18] Dauvergne, *supra* note 1 at 55.

[19] *Ibid.* at 68.

[20] *Ibid.* at 92.

[21] *Ibid.* at 117.

[22] For a recent important decision in this area, see the decision of the European Court of Human Rights in *A and Others v. United Kingdom,* Application No. 3455/05, 19 February 2009 (affirming the decision of the House of Lords).

them in this discourse, but it does not map onto the border of the nation."[23]

Part of the story told in these chapters links to an important theme identified by Dauvergne in Chapter 2 and picked up again in the conclusion (Chapter 9), namely the tendency of human rights proponents to overstate the importance and relevance of human rights in the context of "illegal" migration. Her key contention is that "human rights arguments have worked poorly for those without a legal right to be present."[24] One of the ways in which this theme is developed in Chapter 4 is by a consideration of the text of the Refugee Convention itself, which Dauvergne says gives rise to a "potentially disturbing human rights discourse" on the basis that many of the rights provisions in the Convention "address points that are well covered in other human rights instruments."[25] She states that either the presence of these provisions underscores that refugees have "human rights *too*," which might otherwise have been ignored, or it suggests that other human rights instruments are insufficient to guarantee the human rights of all refugees.[26] However, this seems to overlook the fact that at the time of drafting of the Refugee Convention binding general human rights instruments were yet to be drafted. The fact that the drafters referred in the preamble to the only relevant document in existence — the 1948 Universal Declaration of Human Rights — has led many commentators and the UNHCR to conclude that the Refugee Convention is in essence a human rights treaty.

Further, the dichotomy between refugee law and human rights law emphasized in this and later chapters may obscure the convergence of the two areas of law. There is no question that the subsequent general treaties can and do apply to refugees and asylum seekers.[27] In some cases, recourse to general human rights treaties is insufficient fully to provide the rights and entitlements that refugees require (for example, for refugee specific needs such as travel

---

23 Dauvergne, *supra* note 1 at 107.

24 *Ibid.* at 184.

25 *Ibid.* at 56.

26 *Ibid.*

27 See generally Human Rights Committee, *General Comment 15 on The Position of Aliens under the Covenant*, Doc. A/41/40 (11 April 1986), 117 at paras 1, 2, and 4–10; and Committee on Economic, Social and Cultural Rights, *Draft General Comment No. 20 on Non-Discrimination and Economic, Social and Cultural Rights*, Doc. E/C.12/GC/20/CRP.2 (9 September 2008) at para. 26: "[A]ll Covenant rights apply to everyone including non-citizens and stateless persons."

documents), but in many cases recourse to general treaties has been much more effective in protecting asylum seekers and others deemed to be "illegal entrants" given their superior enforceability mechanisms.[28] The general human rights treaties have considerably extended the category of persons to whom the core principle of *non-refoulement* is to be applied beyond the narrow definition in the Refugee Convention[29] and have also had a significant impact on the rights of asylum seekers and refugees. On the all important question of access to territory, human rights law has been important in reigning in some attempts by states to create spaces that are outside the law[30] or otherwise prevent persons from seeking asylum on racially discriminatory grounds.[31] It is undoubtedly true, as

[28] This is clearly evidenced in the context of the detention of "illegal" entrants, including asylum seekers. Since there is no international committee or treaty body to whom to complain of violations of the Refugee Convention, detained asylum seekers have resorted to lodging complaints before the Human Rights Committee under the ICCPR and have made out claims of arbitrary detention in this context in numerous cases. See, for example, *A v. Australia* (560/1993); *C. v. Australia* (900/1999); *Bakhtiyari v. Australia* (1069/2002), *Baban v. Australia* (1014/2001); and *Shafiq v. Australia* (1324/2004).

[29] See Convention against Torture and Other Cruel, Inhuman or Degrading Treatment or Punishment, Article 3 (1); Human Rights Committee, *General Comment 31 on Nature of the General Legal Obligation Imposed on States Parties to the Covenant*, Doc. CCPR/C/21/Rev.1/Add.13 (26 May 2004), at para 12: "Moreover, the article 2 obligation requiring that States Parties respect and ensure the Covenant rights for all persons in their territory and all persons under their control entails an obligation not to extradite, deport, expel or otherwise remove a person from their territory, *where there are substantial grounds for believing that there is a real risk of irreparable harm, such as that contemplated by articles 6 and 7 of the Covenant, either in the country to which removal is to be effected or in any country to which the person may subsequently be removed.*"

[30] For example, in *Ammur v. France*, [1996] 3 Eur. Ct. H.R. 827, the European Court of Human Rights found that France was in violation of the European Convention on Human Rights in depriving the applicants of their liberty when detaining them in the international zone of the Paris-Orly Airport (thus preventing them from making a refugee claim), even though France had deemed the airport to be part of an "international zone" and therefore outside French territory (and importantly, outside the reach of the European Convention).

[31] See *R. v. Immigration Officer at Prague Airport and another, ex parte European Roma Rights Centre and others,* [2004] U.K.H.L. 55, where the House of Lords found that the United Kingdom government was in violation of the *Race Relations Act* in stationing its immigration officers in Prague Airport to prevent Roma persons from travelling to the United Kingdom to claim asylum. As Lady Baroness of Hale explained: "In this respect it was not only unlawful in domestic law but also contrary to our obligations under customary international law and under international treaties to which the United Kingdom is a party" (at para. 98).

Dauvergne explains, that recourse to rights has "tended to trigger rights-based responses from states, drawing on states' sovereign right to exclude non-nationals and close borders."[32] However, recent trends in human rights adjudication suggest that human rights standards may equally provide a "space for marginal migrants within the law."[33]

For example, in *Adan*, a case concerning the legality of transferring asylum seekers from the United Kingdom back to Germany pursuant to the (regional) Dublin Convention, the applicant argued that the secretary of state's discretion to transfer asylum seekers under this scheme was circumscribed by both the Refugee Convention and the European Convention on Human Rights and that, accordingly, the secretary was under a duty to ensure that the asylum seeker would likely receive protection from *refoulement* in the receiving state (Germany) prior to transfer. In response, counsel for the secretary of state argued that the House of Lords should not require the government to ensure that each European Union (EU) state complies with the one "true autonomous meaning" of the Refugee Convention prior to transfer because this would "impose a complex and time consuming task that is inconsistent with, and would substantially frustrate, the objective of the 1996 act to implement the principles in the Dublin Convention and speedily return asylum seekers to other EU States for the merits of their claims to be considered."[34] The Lords dismissed such concerns, concluding that the obligation to monitor compliance of other states with the Refugee Convention was manageable and that "the sky will not fall in" as a result of this requirement.[35] Similarly, in *Limbuela*, a case in which the House of Lords found that the United Kingdom's policy of

---

[32] Dauvergne, *supra* note 1 at 184. The European Court of Human Rights has repeatedly emphasized that "[c]ontracting States have the right, as a matter of well-established international law and subject to their treaty obligations including the Convention, to control the entry, residence and expulsion of aliens." *Chahal v. United Kingdom*, Case 70/1995/576/662 (25 October 1996) at para 73. However, it has nonetheless held that the convention does impose restrictions on states' ability to expel or deport "illegal" migrants based on the consequences of return, especially where Article 3 (prohibition against torture and inhuman and degrading treatment) is at stake.

[33] Dauvergne, *supra* note 1 at 182.

[34] *R. (ex parte Adan) v. Secretary of State for the Home Department*, [2001] 2 A.C. 477; (2001) 2 W.L.R. 143 at 518 (H.L.).

[35] Further, in *Yogathas*, concerns about efficiency could not be said to obviate the need for rigorous scrutiny of the legality of a transfer: *R. (Yogathas) v. Secretary of State for the Home Department*, [2003] 1 A.C. 920 (H.L.) at para 9.

prohibiting asylum seekers from receiving welfare benefits when their applications were not filed "as soon as reasonably practicable" amounted to "inhuman or degrading treatment" in violation of Article 3 of the European Convention on Human Rights,[36] the House of Lords acknowledged the submission of the secretary of state that the legislation in that case was based on "a legitimate public concern that this country should not make its resources too readily available to [asylum seekers] while their right to remain in this country remains undetermined."[37] However, it remained firm that "engagement in this political debate forms no part of the judicial function."[38]

It may be, then, that human rights law and, in particular, the core norm of non-discrimination, either independently or in conjunction with the rule of law, may have greater emancipatory potential than is envisaged by Dauvergne. Regardless, Dauvergne's thorough and thoughtful analysis indeed achieves its objective of allowing us to see clearly the connection between the various facets of contemporary migration regulation and to understand that sovereignty "is part of the problem rather than part of the solution."[39] Further, as law is "deeply implicated in creating illegality," it is "at the very edge of law's potential to imagine using law to create 'not-law' — a space where people could not be made 'illegal.'"[40] In an engrossing and persuasive narrative, Dauvergne takes us to the very edge of this potential and challenges us to think beyond sovereignty and imagine a community "as something formed by values of equality, freedom and impartiality rather than people."[41] Dauvergne's highly original and incisive work deserves to be read widely and engaged with by all scholars of refugee law and migration studies, as well as advocates and policy makers willing to take a sophisticated approach to future policy development in the area of migration law.

MICHELLE FOSTER
Senior Lecturer and Director, Research Programme in International Refugee Law, Institute for International Law and the Humanities, Melbourne Law School

[36] *R. (Limbuela) v. Secretary of State for the Home Department*, [2006] 1 A.C. 396 (H.L.).

[37] *Ibid.* at para 13.

[38] *Ibid.* at para 14.

[39] Dauvergne, *supra* note 170.

[40] *Ibid.*

[41] *Ibid.* at 185.

Essays on War in International Law. By Christopher Greenwood. London: Cameron May, 2006. 700 pages.

In this important and immensely practical volume, Christopher Greenwood provides international lawyers, scholars, and students of international humanitarian law (IHL) with a useful and comprehensive collection of his fine works dealing with a complex and varied area of international law. Greenwood was elected to the bench of the International Court of Justice in November 2008. Immediately prior to this time, he was a professor of law at the London School of Economics in the United Kingdom, during which time he prepared this book. He has had a distinguished career in academia, is a prolific writer, and has represented the United Kingdom on numerous international legal challenges. Given his extensive qualifications, a collection of his works on IHL is long overdue.

Greenwood's purpose for this collection of essays is to examine the many facets of the law to discern "the ways in which international law seeks to contain and regulate the use of force by states."[1] In doing so, however, he "does not pretend [it] to be a comprehensive study of these subjects."[2] And so it is not. Nonetheless, it comprises a careful selection of topics, each independent of the other and yet necessarily interlinked. The volume can easily be used as a unique reference work. It is organized by theme into six parts, each containing varying numbers of chapters contributing to their respective part and, of course, the whole. Greenwood explains the theme of each part in his preface, which is fortunate because they are not otherwise immediately apparent: the parts are simply numbered and lack titles, which would have been helpful.

Part 1 deals with "the history and theory of international regulation of the use of force" and includes chapters dealing with the fundamental concepts of *jus ad bellum* and *jus in bello*; the current concept of "war" as a legal term of art; and a "stocktaking" of the subject at the millennium. This part includes, in Chapter 3, a particularly comprehensive and helpful report that he wrote on the centenary of the first Hague Peace Conference of 1899. Part 2 deals with the 1977 Protocols Additional to the Geneva Conventions of 1949 and seeks to winnow their impact on armed conflicts today, particularly the degree to which they are declaratory of customary

---

[1] Christopher Greenwood, *Essays on War in International Law* (London: Cameron May, 2006) at 7.

[2] *Ibid.*

international law. This is most important since, unlike the Geneva Conventions, which are universally ratified by the international community, the Additional Protocols are not. Part 3 deals with the conduct of hostilities and looks into the law of weaponry. It also returns to the relationship of the *jus ad bellum* and *jus in bello* and, in Chapter 8, considers the politically sensitive 1996 Advisory Opinion of the International Court of Justice on the *Legality of the Threat or Use of Nuclear Weapons*.[3] Part 4 focuses on the topical subject of terrorism, including the concept of "war on terrorism," while Part 5 looks at enforcement mechanisms both in the municipal courts of the United Kingdom and in the ad hoc International Criminal Tribunal for the Former Yugoslavia. Part 6 wraps up the collection with a review of, in Greenwood's words, "some of the most important cases in which force has been used in recent years."[4] In this most interesting part, he reviews the US bombing in Libya of 1986; Iraq's invasion of Kuwait; the Kosovo conflict; and the more recent Afghanistan and Iraq invasions by coalition states. In connection with these latter cases, he discusses the important legal challenges relating to pre-emptive self-defence.

The topics, as the reader will readily notice, are comprehensive and wide-ranging, representing the broad experience, great intellect, and incisive legal analysis for which Greenwood is widely known. Although it is always much too easy to critique a work for what it fails to address, the reviewer does so here briefly — not to indicate any fundamental flaw with the book but, rather, to express the hope that Greenwood will in future address other emerging topics of interest. Such topics could include private security companies, the meaning of "unlawful belligerents," a more detailed look at the expanding standards of IHL and their application to armed conflicts of a non-international nature (although the current work's contribution in this area is readily acknowledged), and, perhaps, a more in-depth treatment of insurgency as it relates to the principle of distinction. On the latter issue, Greenwood's reflections on the recent Gaza conflict would be most welcome in addressing allegations of insurgents' use of civilian areas from which to conduct operations and of Israel's use of white phosphorous smoke in urban combat zones.

---

[3] *Legality of the Threat or Use of Nuclear Weapons*, Advisory Opinion [1986] I.C.J. Rep. 225.

[4] Greenwood, *supra* note 1 at 9.

Before moving to a more detailed and substantive examination of some of the chapters comprising the book, some criticism should be levelled at several aspects of its organization and the quality of the editing. Some of these shortcomings are of a minor nature, whereas others ought truly to be addressed prior to another printing. First, the essays cover a significant time frame, with five of them being published in the 1980s, including one as early as 1983. The majority (nine) were written in the 1990s and another five were published in 2000 or later. Two chapters have no dates. Greenwood admits that he has "not attempted to alter any of these Chapters but ha[s] left them as they were when they first appeared."[5] This is regrettable since the reader must then remain on guard for the currency of the material. This could have been overcome, perhaps, by including a simple addendum to each chapter in which the author updates his views. Second, Greenwood's indication that he has not altered any of the chapters is preceded by the caveat "[b]eyond correcting a few egregious typographical errors."[6] If some such corrections were made, too many others were not. Needless to say, such errors detract considerably from a text of this type and require correction. Further, in some chapters, the Latin spelling "*jus*" (as in *jus ad bellum, jus in bello*) is used whereas in others it is rendered "*ius.*" Editorial consistency is important and consequently only one form should be used. Finally, an index, bibliography, and table of cases, all of which are lacking, would be most helpful and add greatly to this collection. These errors and omissions do not detract inordinately from the overall quality and usability of the text, but they should certainly be addressed in the next printing.

More substantively, some of the collection's chapters may be highlighted to provide the reader with a flavour of the whole. Chapter 1 is entitled "The Relationship between *Ius ad Bellum* and *Ius in Bello*" and was first published in 1983. It could properly be considered a primer on the examination of these fundamental concepts in IHL. Greenwood begins by noting that "[t]he rules of international law governing the legality of the use of force by states (*ius ad bellum*) and the rules by which international law regulates the actual conduct of hostilities once the use of force has begun (*ius in bello*) have seldom sat happily together."[7] He then provides an

---

[5] *Ibid.*

[6] *Ibid.*

[7] *Ibid.* at 13.

historical treatment and understanding of the terms, noting the significant separation they maintained as legal concepts prior to the implementation of the Charter of the United Nations. Greenwood carefully analyzes the two and defends their distinction.

Chapter 3, by far the longest at ninety pages, is also one of the most interesting. Entitled "International Humanitarian Law (Laws of War)," it was originally a report prepared for the centenary of the first Hague Peace Conference of 1899 and presented at a conference in honour of that occasion. It reviews the issues of concern at the 1899 conference and seeks to understand how the events of subsequent years were affected and influenced by them. Many of these issues are now clearly addressed by international law, but, at the time of the conference, they were novel and thoroughly debated. An example includes the establishment of the Permanent Court of Arbitration. While disarmament was discussed, it proved "to be the least productive" of the various committees.[8] However, the conference achieved the adoption of the Convention on the Laws and Customs of War on Land and its related regulations. The chapter also studies the scope and application of the laws of war and discusses the conduct of hostilities in international armed conflict, where it finds that the conference discussed all major areas of concern. However, in looking to the past century, Greenwood notes that five major areas dealt with at the conference are less than settled even today, including the entitlement to combatant status and the law of weaponry and targeting. The chapter notes that the law of naval warfare was outdated as it was written at the conference, although some improvements have since been made with the San Remo manual.[9] This chapter contains much more and alone adds immensely to an understanding of IHL. As such, it can be considered the centrepiece of the collection and is recommended for study by any serious student of IHL. It is so compendious, however, that it deserves its own table of contents for ready reference. Moreover, the format of the chapter is unlike that of any other, and such inconsistency is unfortunate. Nevertheless, its substance is excellent.

In Chapter 7, "The Law of Weaponry at the Start of the New Millennium," Greenwood provides a most interesting analysis of the law, its objectives, principles, and rules, and his prognosis for its future development. He notes that the law is often misunderstood

---

[8] *Ibid.* at 68.

[9] L. Doswald-Beck, ed., *San Remo Manual on International Law Applicable to Armed Conflicts at Sea* (Cambridge: Cambridge University Press, 1995).

by critics who do not comprehend its objectives and often have unrealistic expectations. The law is in essence developed to preserve core humanitarian values, but it "is not designed to prevent or deter states from resorting to force, and the constraints which it imposes must not, therefore, be incompatible with the effective conduct of hostilities."[10] To attain the law's objectives, therefore, weapons must not be indiscriminate, cause needless suffering, or have a substantially adverse effect on the environment. He notes that some criticisms of the law, by misunderstanding these objectives, appear to express concern about particular weapons because they are simply "unfair," and he illustrates this with historic complaints surrounding the advent of the crossbow and, much later, the submarine. He repeats the observation by one member of the 1899 conference who noted that "new weapons have always been denounced as barbaric."[11] He moves on to discuss the rules dealing with specific weapons and states that they can be grouped as limitations short of a ban — bans that allow possession and perhaps use in retaliation and bans on both use and possession. He then provides several examples including lasers, landmines, and chemical and nuclear weapons. In considering whether other rules of international law apply to the use of weapons, he examines the *Nuclear Advisory Opinion* in relation to international human rights and environmental law and concludes that their impact is likely to be minimal, particularly in relation to specific weapons. He finishes with a brief look to the future where he finds the law will, perhaps with difficulties, continue to be applicable even in such new contexts as cyberwarfare.

Chapter 12, dealing with "Terrorism and Humanitarian Law: The Debate over Additional Protocol I," provides yet another detailed and incisive analysis of the law as it pertains to terrorism. Greenwood argues that, from an analytical legal perspective, it is important to differentiate between two levels of debate. On the one hand is the "inner core" of terrorism, which at its heart pursues illegitimate targets (such as civilians, children, and hostages) and uses illegitimate means (such as indiscriminate weapons). In all cases, these are wrongful irrespective of cause or motive. On the other hand, there is a more political perspective of terrorism, with respect to which consensus is difficult to find as terrorists may attack legitimate targets (that is, military objectives) and use non-prohibited weapons.

---

[10] Greenwood, *supra* note 229.

[11] *Ibid.* at 232.

Greenwood refers to this as the "outer region" or "outer category."[12] He then engages in erudite analysis of the details of Additional Protocol I relating to terrorism and effectively undermines many, if not all, of the objections to the protocol originally raised by the United States. Interestingly, he notes that the particularly objectionable second sentence in Article 44(3) of Additional Protocol 1 was, in fact, a compromise proposal put forward by the United States and Vietnam. In short, this is a very thorough and helpful chapter for both the scholar and the serious student of IHL alike.

These chapters are but a sampling of the fine analysis that Greenwood brings to each subject in the book. This is not to suggest that some of his conclusions will be uncontroversial. For example, in his final chapter dealing with the pre-emptive use of force in Afghanistan and Iraq, he concludes that "those governments who resorted to force [in Iraq in March, 2003] were right to conclude that they could rely on the authorisation of military action in Resolution 678, read together with Resolutions 687 and 1441."[13] In Chapter 5, Greenwood relies upon military manuals to find state practice but does not explain why these manuals necessarily have such importance. For example, publications in the Canadian Forces are authorized by the chief of defence staff (CDS), but it is not at all clear that the CDS speaks for the government without specific authorization. Further, military manuals generally provide doctrine and policy guidance rather than having legal effect and may easily become outdated and therefore not reflective of current government practice. The situation may be different in other countries, but these considerations suggest that the author ought to have justified his reliance on such material.

Nonetheless, in this collection, Greenwood has provided the scholar, serious student, and interested layperson of IHL an excellent and generally well-presented collection of papers on a wide array of disparate yet related subjects. Many of the topics overlap, but far from being undesirable, this bolsters and complements the intellectual rigour that flows throughout the text. *Essays on War in International Law* is therefore highly recommended as an important addition to both public and private libraries alike.

H.A. HALPENNY
LL.M. Candidate, Faculty of Law, University of Ottawa

---

12 *Ibid.* at 387–88.
13 *Ibid.* at 699.

Human Security and International Law: Prospects and Problems. By Barbara von Tigerstrom. Oxford and Portland, OR: Hart Publishing, 2007. 254 pages.

International lawyers are likely aware of human security as an overarching political concept, but there has been relatively little analysis of human security from a legal perspective. *Human Security and International Law: Prospects and Problems,* by Barbara von Tigerstrom, begins to fill this gap. Von Tigerstrom is an assistant professor at the University of Saskatchewan College of Law. This book stems from von Tigerstrom's Ph.D. dissertation at the University of Cambridge and is current to early 2007. It begins by providing a history of the origins and development of the concept of human security. The term "human security" is traced back to the United Nations Development Programme's *Human Development Report* for 1994. This report defined human security as focused on people instead of states and on "safety [for individuals] from such chronic threats as hunger, disease and repression" as well as "protection from sudden and hurtful disruptions in the patterns of daily life."[1] The term was taken up in the late 1990s by national governments, regional and international organizations, and some non-governmental organizations and academics. One of the most prominent promoters of the concept was Canada, which adopted as a central foreign policy objective the promotion of a human security agenda through, *inter alia,* the eradication of anti-personnel mines, the creation of an International Criminal Court, and increased protection of civilians in armed conflict.[2] Japan also used and promoted the concept of human security, albeit differently from Canada. Former secretary-general of the United Nations Kofi Annan also embraced the concept, as have some — but not all — parts of the UN system. The 2005 World Summit on Sustainable Development outcome document committed to "discussing and defining the notion of human security in the General Assembly."[3]

---

[1] United Nations Development Programme, *Human Development Report 1994* (Oxford: Oxford University Press, 1994) at 23. Von Tigerstrom notes that the term was briefly introduced in the *Human Development Report 1993.*

[2] For a detailed explanation of the Canadian approach to human security, see R. McRae and D. Hubert, eds., *Human Security and the New Diplomacy: Protecting People, Promoting Peace* (Montreal and Kingston: McGill-Queen's University Press, 2001).

[3] *World Summit Outcome,* UNGAOR, 60th Sess., UN Doc. A/RES/60/1 (2005) at para. 143.

Von Tigerstrom starts Chapter 2 by observing that no universally accepted definition of the concept of human security exists. She outlines Canada's definition of human security as freedom from pervasive threats to people's rights, safety, or lives, especially protection from direct physical violence. She notes that some view this as a narrow version of human security and contrasts Japan's definition of human security as protection of the lives, livelihoods, and dignity of individuals and its use of the concept to focus on development assistance. Von Tigerstrom also highlights vigorous academic debate on how narrowly or broadly to define the term and on its utility. She identifies a threshold-based approach as a potential definitional middle ground, defining a threat to human security by its depth or severity as opposed to focusing on the source or nature of the threat. Von Tigerstrom argues that, despite the lack of agreement on a definition of human security, there are two key components of the concept: first, individual human beings — and not states — are the primary point of reference; and, second, the security of all individuals everywhere is a matter of common responsibility. The fact that there is no agreed definition for human security likely gives international lawyers pause: if the term cannot be precisely defined can it be applied or considered within international law? Von Tigerstrom answers this question by arguing that the concept can generally have agenda-setting, question-framing, and critical functions, including within the field of international law.

Chapter 3 provides the central analysis suggested by the book's title. In this chapter, von Tigerstrom admits that, on the one hand, proponents of human security value the rule of law, enforcement of international law, and legal accountability as essential components of human security and that, on the other hand, some view international law as a constraint on actions necessary to ensure human security. She argues that, while there is a complex relationship between international law and the concept of human security, they do share affinities. She points out that, while international law is focused on states and state responsibility, international law will only be incompatible with human security to the extent to which the law allows state security to be protected at the expense of individuals' security. She then argues for interpretations of international law that avoid such incompatibility, which are developed more fully in subsequent chapters. She also explores how international law already reflects the human-centred nature of human security in international human rights law, parts of international humanitarian law and some Security Council determinations of threats to international peace and security. She posits that certain areas of international law already reflect human security's idea that the security of the world's people is a matter of common concern or common responsibility, particularly international environmental and refugee law. She concludes that, although there are affinities between the concept of human security and international law, one cannot simply rely on these affinities to give effect to a human security approach, given that the basic structure of international law ties responsibility to sovereign jurisdiction in a state-based system. However, she also states that the human security concept can be used critically to scrutinize international legal developments to determine whether and to what extent the law actually provides protection to individuals.

The next four chapters analyze humanitarian intervention, internally displaced persons, small arms and light weapons, and health as joint human security-international law issues. Chapter 4 examines how the debate over humanitarian intervention is sometimes framed in terms of an opposition between the protection of individuals' rights and the protection of state sovereignty. Von Tigerstrom believes that this is a misleading dichotomy. She views a more helpful, human security-based, approach to be one that weighs these two considerations along with the effect of violating the prohibition on the use of force and the threat posed by military intervention to individuals' security. She also asks if the responsibility to protect doctrine might better refocus legal debate from the right of intervention to the obligations of states.

Chapter 5 explores the legal position of internally displaced persons (IDPs). Von Tigerstrom notes that legal discussion is usually focused on whether there is a right of humanitarian access to IDPs. She argues that a human security approach would reframe the analysis by, first, positing that sovereignty is responsibility and therefore a state has a responsibility to protect its own population. If it does not, other states must intervene provided such intervention is beneficial to individuals' security. Second, states must understand how their actions contribute to causes of displacement of other states' populations, and international law must consider what duties would be required to give effect to states' common responsibility for human security.

Chapter 6 discusses the regulation of small arms and light weapons (SALW). The joint discussion of human security and international law is not as clearly presented in this chapter as in the previous two, perhaps because the topic does not lend itself as easily to such an analysis. Regulation of SALW is complex and difficult because production, sale, and use of these weapons can be either legal or illegal, depending on the context. Von Tigerstrom argues that a human security perspective is useful because it pays greater attention to the potential for legally traded arms to be misused by a state. Such a perspective would militate in favour of mandatory consideration of the impact of arms transfers, even when such transfers would not necessarily be unlawful under current norms.

Chapter 7 focuses on the securitization of health risks, such as the spread of infectious disease, including a human security analysis of the 2005 International Health Regulations. The discussion in this chapter is especially interesting in light of the recent outbreak of the influenza A (H1N1) virus and the response of the World Health Organization and affected states. Von Tigerstrom proposes a human security analysis of health risks that focuses not on the impact of contagion on national stability or military security but, rather, on the vulnerability of individuals and communities to health risks and the degree to which threats to health in one state could be of concern to other states due to their severe impact. She argues that the International Health Regulations tend to reflect traditional conceptions of security and state sovereignty. In her view, a human security analysis reveals gaps that should be taken into account in their implementation, such as strengthened mechanisms to address economic impacts of, for example, the destruction of poultry stocks and the need to ensure that the response to one health threat does not take resources away from other pressing local health needs.

As can be seen from this brief review of Chapters 4 through 7, von Tigerstrom attempts to find a middle ground between human security and international law, usually by identifying questions that could be asked to better illustrate the impact of laws or legal decisions. Often, through these questions, von Tigerstrom is overtly or implicitly proposing shifts in, or additions to, existing international law in order to reach that middle ground. This is especially true with respect to questions about common responsibilities across borders and among states. As she concludes at page 212 in her final chapter, "[p]ut very simply, human security seems to offer a better way of asking questions, but does not provide us with many answers." She also acknowledges that those who want something more will be frustrated by this limitation.

Is a concept that essentially establishes a framework for posing questions a useful addition to international legal discourse? It is clear from von Tigerstrom's examples that human security provides a somewhat richer field for policy discussion than legal analysis. More than this, however, von Tigerstrom has made a compelling argument for the usefulness of human security as a framing mechanism, especially with respect to legal topics that have not traditionally been examined from the viewpoint of affected individuals. The questions raised by asking human security-related questions are helpful for understanding the full impact of the law in particular contexts. This becomes particularly important when legal decisions or documents are to be implemented through policy and programming, whether internationally, regionally, or domestically.

This book is well researched and generally written in an accessible, clear manner. It straddles legal and social science (international relations, international development, security studies, and political science) analysis, and its interdisciplinary nature is helpful for international lawyers who may not be aware of the richness of human security discourse in other fields. The book's main weakness is that it seems at times to struggle in placing international law squarely within a human security analysis. This is particularly so in the chapters on IDPs and SALW. However, this is likely because existing international law on these two issues is evolving and is, in many respects, more "soft" than "hard."

Human security may never become a central focus within international law. The concept is waning in influence in certain quarters, such as in Canadian foreign policy, but von Tigerstrom notes that it has taken on a life of its own and new interest and applications are appearing elsewhere.[4] Therefore, this book will be of interest to those who are interested in the legal aspects of this integrative policy approach, which is showing potential signs of growing.

VALERIE OOSTERVELD
Assistant Professor, Faculty of Law, University of Western Ontario

---

4 For example, the General Assembly held a thematic debate on 22 May 2008 on human security, <http://www.un.org/ga/president/62/ThematicDebate/humansecurity.shtml>. The UN's Office for the Coordination of Humanitarian Affairs has a Human Security Unit, <http://ochaonline.un.org/TheHumanSecurityUnit/tabid/2212/Default.aspx>. The Human Security report project publishes periodic reports on global human security, <http://www.hsrgroup.org/index.php?option=com_frontpage&Itemid=1>. There are social sciences journals devoted to the study of human security, such as the *Journal of Human Security*, <http://www.rmitpublishing.com.au/jhs.html>. There are also institutes focused upon human security, such as the Institute for Human Security at the Fletcher School of Law and Diplomacy (Tufts University).

The Historical Foundations of World Order: The Tower and the Arena. By
Douglas M. Johnston. Leiden: Martinus Nijhoff, 2008. 875 pages.

In May 2006, the international law community suffered a great loss
with the passing of Douglas Johnston, a profound thinker and pro-
digious writer. This book, his *magnum opus*, was the last in a publishing career that spanned forty-five years, during which he authored
or co-authored more than thirty books and some ninety articles. In
the words of his son Keith, who wrote the acknowledgments, the
book is "the culmination of five years of exhaustive research and
writing," and "the final chapter was literally completed from his
hospital bed just two weeks prior to his passing."[1] The work comprises 772 pages of text, a fifty-two-page bibliography, plus indexes
of subjects and names, and a list of Johnston's publications. The
reading is greatly facilitated by the use of short quotations only,
which are incorporated in the text without footnotes. The source
material is identified in parentheses by the name of the author or
organization followed by the year of publication — the full reference can be found in the bibliography.

In his introduction, Johnston explains that the focus on the concept of *world order* is to "capture the complexity of international law
in the modern world, now pervasive in almost every domain of human affairs."[2] The subtitle "The Tower and the Arena" is meant to
reflect the fact that "for more than two thousand years a balance
has been sought between the "idealists" of the *tower* and the "realists"
of the *arena*.[3] The work is divided into ten chapters grouped in three
parts: The System; Out of the Mists; and Into Clear View. These titles
indicate immediately the originality and inventiveness of the author.

Part 1: The System, covering 141 pages, consists of two chapters,
the first being "International Law in Action." Johnston's opening
observation is that "international law has become the central point
of reference in the quest for 'legitimacy' in world affairs." He argues
that most "ethicists and moralists seem to agree that the definite
expression of moral principle in world affairs today is international law."[4] He reviews the present system in the light of six topics:
diplomatic immunities, treaties, the law of transportation (aviation

---

[1] Douglas M. Johnston, *The Historical Foundations of World Order: The Tower and the
Arena* (Leiden: Martinus Nijhoff, 2008) at v.

[2] *Ibid.* at xvii.

[3] *Ibid.*

[4] *Ibid.* at 3.

and shipping), the law of the sea, the Arctic environment, and sovereignty and security. Johnston specifies that this "preliminary sweep over six areas of international law is intended merely to convey the range of norms, concepts, institutions and processes that contribute to its complexity and importance in the modern world."[5] These six topics are all viewed in their historical and political contexts, as is the case for all issues and principles examined by Johnston. For instance, he precedes his treatment of the law of the sea by recalling that the main event leading to the third Law of the Sea Conference was the 1967 speech of Arvid Pardo to the UN General Assembly, in which he proposed that the resources of the seabed be considered the common heritage of mankind, to be exploited mainly for the benefit of developing countries. Here, Johnston shows the importance he attaches not only to historical events but also to the personalities involved, devoting nearly two pages (57–58) to Pardo's personal background. It remains to be seen if Pardo's dream of a common heritage of mankind will eventually be realized, particularly with the enormous seaward limits of the continental shelf.

Another illustration of Johnston's attention to historical and political context is his observation, on the Arctic environment, that the two areas of international law that have expanded most rapidly in the last fifty years are human rights and environmental protection. Both, he notes, are "intensely ethical in orientation" and have attracted "the attention and allegiance of politically committed non-state groups and organizations."[6] About the Northwest Passage, he believes that, aside from being a shorter route than the Panama Canal, the passage "might also be more easily secured from terrorist attacks."[7] This might well be so, provided that Canada exercises full control over navigation and other activities in the passage.

In the second chapter, "Images of International Law," Johnston reminds us that the present system of international law took root in Western and Central Europe. This system, he judges, "is increasingly under challenge, especially from the international law community of the United States."[8] In his opinion, "[t]he influence of the civil law tradition associated with continental Europe can be seen by North Americans to introduce rigidities and formalities into

5 *Ibid.* at 103.

6 *Ibid.* at 63.

7 *Ibid.* at 64.

8 *Ibid.* at 108.

issue domains that may seem to call for a degree of flexibility and problem solving practicality."[9] The challenge arises from the difference between two main approaches to international law: the formalist approach of European scholars, represented mainly by Georges Scelle (France), Charles de Visscher (Belgium), and Rosalyn Higgins (England), as opposed to the counter-formalist or policy science approach of American scholars, represented by publicists such as Myres S. McDougal and Michael Reisman. Johnston gives, as an example of the divide between these two approaches, the controversy over the international legality of the US armed intervention in Iraq in 2003 "between the majority who focused on the rules against the unilateral use of force that limit such action to veto-free, majority decision-making by the UN Security Council, and the minority who invoked a wider range of community values believed to be at stake in an age of security concerns and outrageous human rights violations."[10]

In this chapter's last section, titled "Re-Examining World Order," Johnston surveys "eleven models of international law that serve as prisms or lenses, through which historians, social scientists and international lawyers themselves perceive world order, issues, goals and methods."[11] These models are: *order* ("a shield for the innocent or disadvantaged"); *autonomy* (one which would "prevent the recurrence of neo-imperial exploitation in the colonial era"); *regulation* (an "enhancement of an ever-expanding network of regulatory agencies and regimes"); *war prevention and management* (basically, the UN Security Council system); *world constitutionalism* (the UN Charter would become the nucleus of a world system); *conflict resolution* ("a world system that provides resolutive norms, institutions and procedures"); *system convergence* (among national legal systems); *civic benevolence* ("enlightenment through transnational, cross-cultural policies of benevolence," with emphasis on human rights and humanitarian concerns); *development* (through the "transnational promotion of economic and social development"); *environmental sustainability* (through the "obligation to preserve the vitality and variety of the planetary environment"); and *co-operation* (where "the central concern is the development of cooperative arrangements"). Johnston does not express a preference for a particular model but concludes instead that "[t]he functionalist, multi-model approach

[9] *Ibid.* at 109.

[10] *Ibid.* at 122–23.

[11] *Ibid.* at 125–35.

to the theory of international law, suggested above, commits the historian — and his reader — to a long story of slow and uneven human development: to a cross-cultural history of legal, moral, political, and psychological maturation."[12] That is the approach that he personally follows.

In his "final reflections" at the end of Part 1, Johnston deplores that "contemporary international law has undergone a process of fragmentation" and that "[i]t may be asking too much of 'theory' to create a unified field." He concludes that the questions to be addressed in a history of international law "should be framed around the eleven functions of the system."[13]

Part 2, Out of the Mists, comprising chapters 3, 4, and 5 and covering 176 pages, takes us from primitive antiquity to 1492. Johnston opens chapter 3 on "Primitive Order" by looking for ancient civilizations with a writing system. Writing seems to have been first developed in southern Mesopotamia and Egypt around 3100 B.C. and in China, Crete, and Greece around 1500 B.C.[14] Searching for the earliest forms of an inter-state system, he examines six domains of activity in primitive antiquity: religion, law, war, trade, bureaucracy, and diplomacy. Of these six, it is unquestionably ancient diplomacy that contributed the most to the development of world order. Long before the Greek city-states of the eighth-century B.C., "there were less well-documented accounts of diplomatic relations among the empires of the Near-East: those of Egypt, Babylonia, Assyria, the Hittites, and the Israelites."[15] Use was made of messengers and envoys, and immunity attached to the message, at least, if not always to the messenger. More importantly, it is in treaty making where we find the clearest evidence of developing international law: a famous treaty was the one "between Ramses II of Egypt and Hattusilis III of the Hittites, whereby each king acknowledges his obligation to the other on separate tablets."[16] Johnston concludes that, although "[p]rimitive antiquity is too early to find evidence of any of the twelve [*sic*] models of contemporary international law ... in certain early states we see rudiments of an ordered civic society."[17]

---

12 *Ibid.* at 139.

13 *Ibid.* at 140–41.

14 *Ibid.* at 147

15 *Ibid.* at 171.

16 *Ibid.* at 173.

17 *Ibid.* at 177.

In chapter 4, "Universal Order in Classical Antiquity," Johnston studies the principal contributions to international public order made by the Greeks, Romans, Chinese, Indians, and Africans. The Greeks, organized in city-states, concluded peace treaties and re- ferred some serious inter-state disputes to a single arbitrator. They also accorded special protection to their envoys, and these were often exempt from tax in the receiving city-states. The Romans were also organized in city-states by the eighth century B.C. and, being often in a state of war, not surprisingly developed the concept of "just war" to justify the resort to war (*jus ad bellum*) and certain rules for the conduct of war (*jus in bello*). As well, the Twelve Tables rep- resent "the first codification of Western European law, and the only official codification of Roman law before the age of Justinian in the 6th century A.D."[18] The Roman "*praetor peregrinus*," created in 242 A.D. with special jurisdiction over foreigners, developed a body of law called "*jus gentium.*" This was a private law system applicable to the settlement of trade disputes between Romans and non-Romans and had nothing to do with relations between nation-states. It was considerably later that the *jus gentium* (law of peoples) became the law of nations. Note, however, that the expression in French re- mained *le droit des gens.* On the substantive side, Rome's greatest contribution was its legal system, built over more than a millennium. Johnston concludes that "[d]espite the legal virtuosity of the common-law world, there is no doubt that the 'classical' system of international law, evolving through the 17th and 18th and 19th centuries, owed most of its inspiration to civil law inheritors of Roman law."[19]

In a way that is similar to the Greeks and Romans, the Chinese by the sixth century B.C. were grouped into nine states that were often at war with one another, and they developed rules observed in declaring and conducting war. They also concluded treaties of peace and used diplomacy to settle disputes. Johnston considers that "[t]he tradition of civic idealism in China is inseparable from the teachings of Confucius (551–429 B.C.)," which involved a com- mitment to personal virtue and ethical conduct. He maintains that ancient China's contribution to modern international law is "found chiefly in the Han experience seeking a balance between order and civic entitlement."[20] To discern the contribution of the Indians,

[18] *Ibid.* at 205.

[19] *Ibid.* at 225–26.

[20] *Ibid.* at 233.

Johnston reviews the early cultures, particularly after the emergence of the Mauryan Empire in the fourth century B.C. The Indians developed a theory of government reflected in the *Arthasastra*, which was "a compendium of traditional rules and precepts for the administration of the Indo-Aryan state of that period, written expressly for the guidance of the ruler and his ministers."[21] Although the king belonged to the upper class of *brahmans*, he considered himself a servant of the people and did not exempt members of his divine class from the heavy punishment for serious violations of secular law.[22] As for the contribution of Africans, it may be found only in the northern part of the continent. Since Egyptian peasants of the third millennium B.C. may have produced more than needed, "[s]urplus food production gave rise to a system of towns and the development of trade and culture associated with urban society."[23] Egypt also exported ivory, gold, ebony, and animal skins. However, in Africa generally there was no "law-based society with shareable values and principles."[24]

In Johnston's opinion, the appreciation of classical antiquity for its contribution to the development of world order depends considerably on whether one is a positivist or a natural lawyer. For the *positivists*, there is "little significance in classical antiquity except in the context of diplomatic privileges and, to a limited extent, in constraints on the conduct of warfare."[25] For the *natural lawyers*, they will find contributions in the concepts of natural justice, natural law, and civil rights, before and after Cicero. Johnston concludes that "the juridical legacy of Rome must be acknowledged as the most important influence on the modern 'legal mind.'"[26]

Part 2 ends with chapter 5, "Universal Authority in Pre-Modern History," which takes us to 1492. This period is viewed today as one dominated by religion: Hinduism, Buddhism, Confucianism, Christianity, and Islam. In particular, "[f]or 400 years, down to the late 15th century, the civil law tradition was heavily influenced by the natural law theory of Christian theology and ethics."[27] However,

---

21 *Ibid.* at 236.

22 *Ibid.*

23 *Ibid.* at 239.

24 *Ibid.* at 240.

25 *Ibid.*

26 *Ibid.* at 241.

27 *Ibid.* at 259.

this era of faith in the West was also marked by "the 100-year period of religious wars in and around the city of Jerusalem" during the crusades.[28] Still, in spite of the ferocity of the wars, a certain ethical standard of behaviour on and off the battlefield was introduced by the cult of chivalry and its noble knights.[29] Efforts were made to limit certain modes of killing, such as "the prohibition of the crossbow and arch [*sic*] by the Second Lateran Council in 1139."[30] This marks a distant beginning of humanitarian law.

A beginning was also made, in the area of international trade law between East and West, by the establishment of silk routes during the T'ang dynasty.[31] As well, "[t]he Mongols were the first to endow an extensive cross-cultural empire with a network of post stations for the support of mounted relay-teams of traders and other travelers."[32] Commercial law also evolved from the early fourteenth century, when "Venetians began an annual expedition of commercial vessels to the ports of the western Mediterranean, and beyond those of northern Europe."[33] Diplomacy and treaty making were developed during the pre-modern period in both the East, especially China, and the West through the Romans. Johnston affirms that "[i]t was the canonists, the specialists in canon law, who first developed the *theory* of diplomacy through a set of rules concerning the rights, privileges and duties of diplomatic agents."[34] The early fifteenth century saw the development of permanent bilateral diplomacy in the Italian inter-city relations and the birth of conference diplomacy with the Council of Constance from 1414 to 1418.[35]

As a final reflection on this pre-modern period, Johnston states that "the concept of *state autonomy* was just beginning to evolve as an alternative to central, imperial or religious, authority."[36] He concludes that "the idea of a *transnational convergence of laws* was a genuine creation of the pre-modern world in the context of commercial and maritime affairs."[37]

---

[28] *Ibid.* at 283.
[29] *Ibid.* at 291.
[30] *Ibid.* at 296.
[31] *Ibid.* at 298.
[32] *Ibid.* at 299.
[33] *Ibid.* at 302.
[34] *Ibid.* at 311.
[35] *Ibid.* at 314.
[36] *Ibid.* at 318.
[37] *Ibid.* at 319.

Part 3, Into Clear View, consists of the last five chapters, the first being chapter 6, "Shaping the Modern World 1492-1645." Johnston begins by a review of early maritime explorations, in particular, those of the Chinese, who are said to have circumnavigated the globe in 1421. Johnston was probably quite correct, at the time of writing, to state that most scholars outside China "are extremely dubious" about the Chinese feat.[38] However, Gavin Menzies, on whose 2003 book Johnston relied, has since published a second book producing additional and rather compelling evidence in support of China's discoveries (see Gavin Menzies, *1434: The Year a Magnificent Chinese Fleet Sailed to Italy and Ignited the Renaissance* (London: William Morrow, 2008). Johnston then surveys Western expeditions, especially those of Portugal, Spain, England, and France, leading to their rise as modern sovereign states.[39]

Although the concept of state sovereignty seemed to be sufficiently articulated towards the end of the sixteenth century to lay the foundation for a world order of secular authority, the religious conflicts were not conducive to civic order. In the Far East, "[o]nly in China did the force of cultural unity prevail over the duty of religious commitment."[40] In the Near East, "[t]he 1450–1650 period was also a period of crisis for Christians, Jews and Muslims."[41] In the West, Catholics and Protestants became fiercely divided and, although peace plans were put forward by scholars during the fifteenth, sixteenth, and seventeenth centuries, they did not produce any significant contribution to world order. The aggressive foreign policy of states was matched by a diplomacy of deceit. Hence, the injudicious definition of a diplomat as one who is sent abroad to lie and spy for his country. Nevertheless, overseas trade, capitalism, and greed developed and, along with these, the infamous slave trade, piracy, and privateering. Although these could not be brought within a system of justice during the sixteenth and seventeenth centuries, they did pave the way for the next period that witnessed the doctrinal emergence of modern international law.

In the early stages of consolidation of the international legal system, "there were still no clear boundaries separating the norms of the civil law, the canon law, and the common law as inputs into the doctrine of the law of nations."[42] This is evident from a review

38 *Ibid.* at 327.
39 *Ibid.* at 327–42.
40 *Ibid.* at 343.
41 *Ibid.* at 345.
42 *Ibid.* at 379.

of the contributions of international jurists such as the Dominican theologian Francisco de Vitoria (1480–1546); the Jesuit theologian Francisco Suarez (1548–1617); Alberto Gentili (1552–1608), civil law-trained but a practising barrister at Gray's Inn in London; and the famous civilian Hugo de Groot, or Grotius (1583–1645), who wrote extensively on the theological questions of his time in addition to making a singular contribution to international law. All of these scholars, except Gentili, believed that natural law was the basis of the law of nations. Suarez and Grotius maintained, however, that certain customs developed into positive law, whereas for Gentili "the law of nations needed to be developed doctrinally within the legal profession, like any other branch of law."[43] On the question of treaty obligation, Grotius insisted that "the principle of good faith must apply equally to Christian and Islamic treaty partners, just as it did to Catholic and Protestant states alike."[44] By the late sixteenth century, diplomatic privilege and the inviolability of ambassadors were established, but "the extension of inviolability to embassy premises did not become fixed into law until well into the 17th century."[45] With respect to the acquisition of territory, the accepted view was that "land not controlled by an entity internationally recognized to have the status of a sovereign state was deemed to be *terra nullius*."[46] Both Vitoria and Suarez rejected conquest "as a legal means of acquiring territory," as did Grotius, but the latter maintained that "it had to be recognized as a valid mode of acquiring territory, with certain limitations, based on the customary practices of States."[47] In his "final reflections" on this period, Johnston affirms that "[t]he development of law was just beginning to be perceived as a creative process with benefits for all."[48] Of the eleven models of international law that he identified in chapter 2, he found four that formed part of the debate among jurists: state autonomy, order, war prevention and management, and civic enlightenment.

Chapter 7, "Constructing the Imperial World System," covers the years 1618 to 1815. "These two centuries would provide the apparatus of permanent diplomacy and the conceptual framework for the law of nations, designed above all to empower the sovereign

---

[43] *Ibid.* at 387.

[44] *Ibid.* at 400.

[45] *Ibid.*

[46] *Ibid.* at 401–2.

[47] *Ibid.* at 402.

[48] *Ibid.* at 404.

state."[49] Indeed, this period begins with the Treaties of Westphalia (1648), ending the Thirty Years War, which incorporated the basic concept of state sovereignty. This incorporation triggered a revival of the old debate around natural law. In answer to Thomas Hobbes (1588–1679), who viewed the law of nations as being virtually limited to treaties, prominent natural law scholars such as Samuel Pufendorf (1632–94), Christian Wolff (1676–1756), and Emmerich de Vattel (1714–67) appeared on the scene. In his famous *Le Droit des Gens* published in 1758, Vattel argued that the law of nature applied to all men and nations and, "[s]ince men are naturally equal ... so too are nations."[50]

As part of his appraisal of the revival of natural law in political and legal debates, Johnston reviews the Enlightenment that was evident in France, Scotland, and the United States and concludes that "[i]n the history of international law, at least, the Enlightenment of the 18th century has a special resonance today because of the emergence of human rights law and cognate areas as the ethical core of the world law system." However, the Enlightenment did not prevent the imperial powers (France, Britain, Spain, Portugal, and Holland) from satisfying their lust for colonies and developing their military power, especially at sea.[51] Competition among colonial powers led to numerous political treaties devoted to alliances, war, peace, and neutrality. Consequently, the seventeenth and eighteenth centuries witnessed an important development of the law of treaties. In addition, positivists were brought to recognize that "the most fundamental principle of all in the law of nations was that agreements concluded in good faith must be observed (*pacta sunt servanda*)."[52]

During these developments in the Western world, China remained mostly outside the international scene, as "[t]he idea of a right to exchange diplomatic agents ... simply did not exist in China."[53] China's first international agreement on the basis of equality between the parties was the Treaty of Nerchinsk concluded with Russia in 1659, whereby the boundary in northern Manchuria was delineated.[54] Generally, it was very difficult to conclude treaties with

[49] *Ibid.* at 405.
[50] *Ibid.* at 417.
[51] *Ibid.* at 433 and 450-53.
[52] *Ibid.* at 465.
[53] *Ibid.* at 473.
[54] *Ibid.* at 475.

China or to establish diplomatic relations on an equal footing. Johnston affirms that "[t]he more the outsiders pressed for equality and reciprocity, the stiffer the Chinese resistance."[55]

During this period leading to 1815, principles of international law continued to evolve, in particular those relating to the modes of acquisition of territory (discovery and effective occupation), neutrality, privateering and prize, piracy, coastal state jurisdiction over a band of territorial waters (three to four miles), and slavery. The latter was the subject of condemnation by the Pope in 1639 and by France and Great Britain in the Paris Peace Treaty of 1814. In the light of the earlier developments, Johnston concludes that "[t]he political landscape of international law was transformed in the 17th and 18th centuries."[56] In his view, the principal contribution of those two centuries was "the reformulation of the *civic enlightenment* model of international law by Western intellectuals."[57]

Chapter 8, "The Ruling of the Modern World," covers the bulk of the nineteenth century (1815–1905) in 180 pages. This was a century marked by Great Power diplomacy and dominated by the growth of the British Empire, most of it under the reign of Queen Victoria. In his appraisal of the contribution of this period to the development of an international order, Johnston concludes that "[o]ne of the most durable contributions of the 19th century was surely the invention of constitutional government."[58] In particular, Britain contributed to the establishment of responsible and representative government in its colonies. During the same century, the concept of statehood and the main conditions for its recognition also emerged. However, the annexation of foreign territory by force or coercive diplomacy was still allowed, to wit in particular the British acquisition of Hong Kong in 1842.[59] The subjugation of indigenous peoples was also permitted, as exemplified in the colonial and post-colonial context in Latin America, the United States, Canada, New Zealand, and Australia.[60] Indigenous nations were generally considered part of the territorial acquisition and, since they were not recognized as state entities, treaties with them

55 *Ibid.* at 480.

56 *Ibid.* at 505.

57 *Ibid.* at 506.

58 *Ibid.* at 547.

59 *Ibid.* at 578–84.

60 *Ibid.* at 591–609.

fell outside the system of sovereign states and were not subject to the rules of the law of treaties. Within the system, however, the frequency and diversity of treaties increased tremendously. For instance, in one short eighty-nine-year period (1816–1905), some 477 multilateral treaties were concluded.[61] They related to international waterways such as the Suez Canal, the suppression of slavery, and, of course, war and peace.

This period also witnessed the adoption of two important conventions aimed at civilizing the conduct of war: the Treaty of Paris in 1856 and the Geneva Convention of 1864 on the conditions of maritime warfare. In addition, the First Peace Conference was held at The Hague and the Convention for the Peaceful Settlement of International Disputes was adopted in 1901. This convention provided for good offices, mediation, and inquiry commissions, plus an undertaking to organize a Permanent Court of Arbitration. Resort to arbitration became quite common. Johnston mentions a list by Evans Darby of "474 arbitral settlements after the three cases that arose out of the Jay Treaty" of 1794.[62] By 1905, international law was becoming institutionalized, with the involvement of prize courts, professional advisers, and negotiators. In spite of competing nineteenth-century ideologies (imperialism, nationalism, internationalism, colonialism, capitalism, socialism, and constitutional democracy), "state sovereignty retained an infrastructure status within the classical system of international law."[63] In his final reflections on the nineteenth century, Johnston highlights the progress on co-operation among states, while admitting that "classical international law rested on fragile foundations, as far as international justice was concerned," mainly because of the absence of international legal institutions.[64]

Chapter 9, "Contemporary World Order in Profile," is the last chapter and covers exactly one century, 1906 to 2006, the latter being the year Johnston passed away. In spite of the fact that the first half of the twentieth century was marked by the costliest wars in world history, it witnessed unprecedented steps in the creation of international legal institutions: the Permanent Court of Arbitration in 1907, the Permanent Court of International Justice in 1920,

---

[61] *Ibid.* at 612.

[62] *Ibid.* at 636.

[63] *Ibid.* at 686.

[64] *Ibid.*

and the International Court of Justice in 1945. Under the Covenant of the League of Nations, states bound themselves to submit "any dispute likely to lead to a rupture" (Article 12) to dispute settlement procedures, but the right to resort to war was not abolished. Abolition came in the Briand-Kellogg Pact of 1928, but it was limited to a renunciation of resort to war as an instrument of national policy (Article 1). In the UN Charter of 1945, not only is the right of states to resort to war prohibited but so is the use of force. The only exception is self-defence in response to an armed attack and, even then, only until the Security Council has taken the necessary measures (Article 51). However, the implementation of the UN collective security system, under the control of the Big Five (permanent members of the Security Council: China, France, Russia, the United Kingdom, and the United States), has proven to be most difficult. In the end, the preservation of international order in the second half of the century does not represent any real improvement over the first half.

Reviewing the efforts being made to find some answer to the perennial problem of world order, Johnston studies *world constitutionalism*, which "is often invoked as the best institutional defence against world disorder, violence and even terror."[65] He believes that "[o]ne of the most disturbing features of contemporary world order in the early 21st century is the prospect of a highly organized but dangerously asymmetrical universe in which the United States, as the only remaining superpower, has virtually total freedom to 'pick and choose' which parts of the newly-hammered-out global regimes and treaties to acknowledge as necessary components of world law and order."[66] After discussing some ten elements of the constitutional model (including protection of individuals and minorities, judicial review of ordinary legislation and allocation of powers to constituent entities), Johnston maintains that "[t]rends toward the constitutional model of international law are clearly visible in a number of contexts outside the framework of the original UN Charter: for example, in the rapidly expanding fields of human rights, international trade law and international criminal law."[67] However, he believes that constitutionalism is perceived by most Americans as being against their national interest, for various rea-

---

[65] *Ibid.* at 711.

[66] *Ibid.* at 712.

[67] *Ibid.* at 714.

sons, such as cultural diversity around the globe, the unrepresentative status of international judges, and the fear of changes in the
present power structure of the Security Council.[68] Of course, these
political objections are debatable and come not only from the
United States, as was seen during the World Summit on UN reform
in September 2005.

Another major question studied by Johnston is how to organize
the world community so as to facilitate obtaining its consent and
commitment. Although traditional treaties and international organizations have made an important contribution to world order,
the innovation of non-binding international regimes, such as the
one in the Helsinki Final Act of 1975 for European Cooperation
and the arrangements under the Antarctic Treaty of 1958, is proving to be an easier mode of obtaining consent than a formal treaty.
This innovation marks a departure from the firmness of international law and the "*strict legal culture,*" which had developed by
the end of the nineteenth century.[69] There is emerging in the *arena*
rather than the *tower,* writes Johnston, a preference for "soft law,"
which focuses "not on abstraction, such as norms, but on *instruments*
(or mechanisms) by which efforts to deal with compliance are actually executed in practice."[70] This phenomenon has been more
evident in the field of international environmental law, such as the
declaration of twenty-six principles adopted at the Stockholm Conference of 1972 and the Rio Declaration on the Environment and
Development of 1992.[71] The Kyoto Protocol of 1997, which imposes on parties strict, binding targets for the reduction of pollutant
emissions into the environment, is causing considerable controversy,
some leading polluters arguing that abiding by such heavy obligations would be most harmful to their economy. Johnston does not
expressly advocate following the soft law route in this case, but he
does suggest that "[t]he Kyoto provisions, in short, are likely to be
viewed as norms to 'guide,' rather than 'govern' matters of such
extreme national importance."[72]

Addressing the idea of "cultivating a benevolent society" towards
the end of his book, Johnston begins in a rather despondent tone

---

[68] *Ibid.* at 713–16.

[69] *Ibid.* at 735.

[70] *Ibid.* at 736.

[71] *Ibid.* at 748 and 750.

[72] *Ibid.* at 753.

by affirming that "[i]t requires an almost spiritual effort to extract from world history an optimistic view of our collective human capacity to deal intelligently and compassionately with the appalling list of challenges that we have inherited from the 20th century."[73] Still, he believes that it is with evidence of civic benevolence that "we must begin our search for the ethical foundations of the modern *human rights* movement."[74] It is in that movement, which began in earnest with the cause of minorities in the early twentieth century and was expanded under the UN to protect the fundamental rights of all individuals, that we must try to develop a benevolent society. We have already made a beginning towards such a society, where genocide and war crimes would not go unpunished, by the creation of special international criminal tribunals and even a permanent one in 2002. However, as is the case for the International Court of Justice, several states refuse to accept the jurisdiction of the International Criminal Court, and the prospects for a single world court with compulsory jurisdiction are not encouraging.[75]

Coming to the end of this phenomenal work, one is rather disappointed not to find any general conclusion, where Johnston could have made a general appraisal of the past and envisaged certain expectations. The only explanation this reviewer can imagine is that he was prevented from doing so by his terminal illness, having completed the final chapter from his hospital bed shortly before his passing. The same explanation also undoubtedly applies to the few typographical errors and the incorrect French accents in several of the references. As well, there is a partial repetition of text under the heading "Confronting the Agony of War" on page 616 — the half page text on that page is only the beginning of the full text found at pages 621–33. This oversight in proofreading necessarily occurred after Johnston's passing. Nonetheless, these peccadilloes of form and the absence of a general conclusion do not detract from the extraordinary contribution this book has made to the continuing quest for an international legal system that would make world order more possible.

This book will be of interest and benefit not only to students and scholars of international law but also to all those interested in world history. As a confirmation of Johnston's exceptional contribution,

[73] *Ibid.* at 754.
[74] *Ibid.* at 755.
[75] *Ibid.* at 761–65.

this book was selected by the American Society of International Law in March 2009, for its annual prize for "pre-eminent contribution to creative scholarship." This well-deserved recognition aptly complements the John E. Read medal for "outstanding contribution to the cause of international law" awarded to Johnston by the Canadian Council on International Law in 2006. Johnston deplored that public international law has always suffered from public anonymity, yet "this book will go a long way toward rescuing international law from that anonymity," writes Michael Reisman in his preface.[76] This reviewer would add that Johnston was perhaps the most encyclopaedic scholar of international law in Canada, and this work stands at the pinnacle of his numerous publications. It constitutes a seminal work challenging the traditional approach to the study of international law.

DONAT PHARAND
Professor Emeritus, Faculty of Law, University of Ottawa

International Humanitarian Law and Human Rights Law: Towards a New Merger in International Law. Par Roberta Arnold et Noëlle Quénivet, éditrices. Leiden: Martinus Nijhoff, 2008. 596 pages.

L'interaction entre le droit international humanitaire et le droit international des droits de la personne a attiré l'attention des juristes dès la solidification des normes de ce dernier en droit international positif, quelque part entre l'adoption et l'entrée en vigueur du Pacte international relatif aux droits civils et politiques. Jusqu'à ce point, le régime des droits de la personne faisait figure de parent pauvre du droit humanitaire, reposant sur l'assise fragile d'une Déclaration universelle au statut juridique contesté contrastant avec les centaines de dispositions détaillées des Conventions de Genève ratifiées par pratiquement tous les États. Bien que la Déclaration de 1948 et les Conventions de 1949 s'inscrivent toutes au nombre de l'héritage des expériences traumatisantes de la Seconde Guerre Mondiale, l'influence limitée de l'une sur les autres peut de prime abord surprendre. Malgré la convergence de l'objectif ultime poursuivi, la protection des intérêts fondamentaux des individus, chaque négociation a obéi à sa logique propre et impliqué des individus

---

[76] *Ibid.* at viii.

pour l'essentiel différents. L'interdiction de la discrimination sexuelle, raciale, nationale, religieuse et politique à l'encontre des personnes protégées par les Conventions de Genève semble le point de recoupement le plus net.[1]

Les choses ont changé au cours des années qui ont suivi, avec l'échec d'une tentative du CICR de développer des règles plus précises pour la protection des civils en période de conflits armés internes et le déblocage des négociations d'instruments avec force contraignante dans le domaine des droits de la personne. Soudainement, le droit humanitaire semblait frappé de stagnation alors que celui des droits de la personne prenait son envol avec de nouvelles normes assorties d'institutions universelles et régionales de mise en œuvre sans équivalent en droit de la guerre. L'empreinte des droits de la personne sur le droit international humanitaire apparaît beaucoup plus clairement dans les travaux de la conférence diplomatique de 1974 à 1977 qui déboucha sur l'adoption des deux protocoles additionnels aux Conventions de Genève de 1949. On peut mentionner entre autres l'impact du droit des peuples à disposer d'eux même, qui mène à requalifier les guerres de libération nationale comme conflits internationaux dans l'article 1 (4) du Protocole I, ainsi que l'article 75 de ce même protocole qui proclame une série de garanties procédurales dérivées directement du Pacte sur les droits civils et politiques. Cela dit, la conférence diplomatique souligne aussi la résistance des États à une réglementation serrée des conflits armés internes, qui ne jouissent dans le Protocole II que d'un squelette de régime humanitaire. C'est surtout le contexte de ces guerres civiles qui occasionnera une réflexion s'ouvrant de plus en plus à l'intégration potentielle des deux domaines du droit international, présentée par Noëlle Quénivet comme le cœur de l'investigation animant les textes du recueil collectif qu'elle dirige en compagnie de Roberta Arnold.

Le dernier, et sans nul doute le plus important tournant de cette relation trouble entre droit international humanitaire et droits de la personne résulte des attaques du 11 septembre 2001 et de la "guerre contre le terrorisme" qu'elles ont occasionnées. L'ampleur inégalée de ces attaques jumelée à leur caractère transnational a attiré une réaction s'appuyant sur la force militaire et, dans certains

---

[1] Voir l'une des seules études de cette époque sur le sujet: Claude Pilloud, "La Déclaration universelle des droits de l'homme et les Conventions internationales protégeant les victimes de la guerre" (1949) Revue internationale de la Croix-Rouge 252.

cas seulement, débouchant sur des conflits armés. La confusion des genres a ainsi été non seulement rhétorique mais aussi pratique: toutes les mesures, même celles n'impliquant aucunement le recours à la force armée, ont été rassemblées sous le vocable d'une "guerre" contre le terrorisme; des individus, interpellés par les autorités dans des circonstances ne suggérant pas la moindre trace de lien avec un conflit armé quelconque, furent classés "combattants illégitimes." Au même moment, la campagne anti-terroriste a mené à des conflits armés internationaux en Afghanistan et (plus nébuleusement) en Iraq, débouchant sur des occupations militaires ne cadrant pas avec les termes classiques de ce genre de situation, axés sur le statu quo, mais appelant plutôt une réforme sociale et démocratique. Cette confusion en a encouragé une autre, normative, quant à savoir lequel des droits de la personne ou du droit international humanitaire devait servir de cadre de référence fondamental pour jauger de la légalité des gestes posés dans ces contextes très éclatés de la "guerre" contre le terrorisme. C'est là l'environnement dans lequel les auteurs de cette collection se penchent sur une fusion éventuelle de ces deux domaines du droit.

Une manière d'envisager la possibilité d'une fusion entre droit international humanitaire et droits de la personne explore ce que l'on pourrait appeler la relation architecturale entre ces régimes. Ainsi, Conor McCarthy ("Legal Conclusion or Interpretative Process? *Lex Specialis* and the Applicability of International Human Rights Standards") se penche sur la portée qu'il faut accorder à l'énoncé de la Cour internationale de Justice dans ses avis consultatifs sur la licéité des armes nucléaires et, de façon plus détaillée, sur les conséquences juridiques de la construction d'un mur en Palestine à l'effet que les droits de la personne sont le *lex generalis* que vient compléter le droit international humanitaire à titre de *lex specialis*. Sur la base d'une lecture à la fois vaste et attentive de la manière dont le concept de *lex specialis* a généralement été appliqué en droit international public, McCarthy conteste une application trop binaire de ce dernier à la relation entre le droit humanitaire et les droits de la personne. Plutôt que d'une règle de préemption reflétant une vision formaliste et consensualiste du droit international, il faut comprendre le concept de *lex specialis* comme un principe d'interprétation téléologique liant la juste portée des normes à l'évolution organique du droit international humanitaire et des droits de la personne. On débouche ainsi sur une interaction qui laisse une place beaucoup plus grande à l'application simultanée et complémentaire des deux domaines.

Ces considérations architecturales sont directement liées à celle possiblement plus prosaïque de l'application extraterritoriale des droits de la personne, objet de l'étude de Ralph Wilde ("Triggering State Obligations Extraterritorially: The Spatial Test in Certain Human Rights Treaties"). En effet, sans application extraterritoriale il n'y a pas de concurrence possible entre droit international humanitaire et droits de la personne dans de très nombreuses situations de conflits armés, y compris toutes les situations d'occupation militaire. Les traités en matière de droits de la personne limitent en général leur portée aux droits des individus sous leur compétence, mis à part le Pacte international relatif aux droits civils et politiques qui visent "tous les individus se trouvant sur leur territoire et relevant de leur compétence." Ainsi que le rapporte Wilde, ces termes ont généralement reçu une interprétation assez flexible, même ceux apparemment plus restrictifs du Pacte pour lesquels la conjonction (territoire et compétence) a été interprété de manière disjonctive (territoire ou compétence). On note une tendance récente à accepter plus libéralement l'application extraterritoriale des traités sur les droits fondamentaux bien que, souligne Wilde, l'assise théorique de cette interprétation reste sujette à caution. Au-delà des concepts de la compétence, de l'exceptionnalisme, et de l'exercice de la puissance publique, il suggère que celui du degré de contrôle d'un territoire offre une flexibilité qui permettrait une application modulée des normes qui paraît souhaitable dans le contexte de l'occupation militaire.[2]

Au-delà des relations systémiques entre les droits de la personne et le droit international humanitaire, il est aussi utile et intéressant de s'arrêter à l'interrelation de normes qui offrent aux individus une protection parallèle dans l'un et l'autre régime. Le volume contient bon nombre de telles analyses, portant sur le droit à la vie, la protection des femmes, des enfants, des familles, des personnes déplacées et des réfugiés. Ainsi, par exemple, Agnieszka Jachec-Neale ("End Justifies the Means? Post 9/11 Contempt for Humane Treatment") offre une lecture de la prohibition de la torture et des traitements inhumains dans le contexte de la lutte contre le terrorisme. Grâce à une mise en contexte détaillée de la lutte contre le terrorisme dans le cadre du droit international public, tant en période de paix qu'en temps de conflit armé, elle souligne les dangers

---

[2] Cette question est étudiée en détail par la Cour d'appel de l'Angleterre dans une décision postérieure à la publication de ce texte: *R (Smith) c. Secretary of State for Defence*, [2009] E.W.C.A. Civ. 441.

d'une réinterprétation dans le célèbre "mémo Bybee" d'une prohibition que l'on voulait absolue. Une analyse de la jurisprudence nationale et internationale sur le sujet la mène à identifier l'essence de ce qui est universellement reconnu comme un traitement humain, une norme mise à mal à de nombreuses reprises par les gestes posés au nom de la lutte contre le terrorisme.

Dans un autre registre, Michael Schmitt ("Targeted Killings and International Law: Law Enforcement, Self-Defense, and Armed Conflict") se penche sur une pratique qui a fait couler beaucoup d'encre depuis l'exécution en 2002 d'un leader d'Al-Qaida au Yemen, tué par un missile lancé par un avion sans pilote de la CIA, pratique reprise à plus grande échelle par les États-Unis en 2003 dans leurs nombreuses tentatives d'assassiner Saddam Hussein au début de la seconde guerre du Golfe. Le dilemme de l'assassinat ciblé souligne bien la tension entre une approche centrée sur les droits de la personne et une autre sur le droit international humanitaire: au regard de la première, il s'agit d'une exécution extrajudiciaire difficilement justifiable, alors que selon la seconde une telle opération est entièrement licite en autant que l'individu visé puisse être qualifié de combattant. Au vu de la nature dorénavant acceptée d'une telle pratique, Schmitt dépasse un raisonnement binaire qui force un choix entre droits de la personne et droit international humanitaire pour suggérer une analyse contextuelle qui différencie trois types d'assassinats ciblés: d'abord celui qui vise à faire respecter la loi en arrêtant une attaque terroriste imminente détachée de tout conflit armé, auquel cas on doit essentiellement s'arrêter aux critères de nécessité et de proportionnalité; ensuite l'assassinat ciblé qui vise à assurer la légitime défense d'un pays attaqué par un groupe terroriste basé sur le territoire d'un autre État, auquel cas les critères de la légitime défense (nature immédiate du danger, nécessité, proportionnalité) vont s'appliquer; enfin, l'assassinat ciblé s'inscrivant pleinement dans le cadre d'un conflit armé, auquel cas la question centrale sera de savoir si l'individu visé participe directement aux hostilités. C'est là une manière d'envisager la question qui démêle un peu l'écheveau juridique entourant la pratique des assassinats ciblés.

S'ajoutent à ces textes une série de contributions qui analysent de façon institutionnelle la relation entre droit international humanitaire et droits de la personne. La dynamique va essentiellement du premier vers ces derniers, en raison de la faiblesse systémique et systématique des institutions propres au droit international humanitaire. On a bien créé une Commission internationale d'établissement des faits dans le Protocol I, mais trente ans plus tard on attend toujours la toute première enquête de cet organisme mort-né. À défaut, on a misé sur les structures beaucoup plus nombreuses et solides qui existent dans le domaine des droits de la personne pour pallier à cette faiblesse du droit humanitaire. Ainsi, Emiliano Buis ("The Implementation of International Humanitarian Law by Human Rights Courts: The Example of the Inter-American Human Rights System") se penche sur l'évolution du traitement du droit humanitaire dans le système interaméricain des droits de la personne. On rappelle les tensions entre la Commission et la Cour dans les affaires La Tablada et Las Palmeras, dans lesquelles la Cour a rappelé à l'ordre la Commission pour s'être reconnu une compétence pour appliquer directement les Conventions de Genève que ne semblaient pas vraiment lui accorder ses instruments constitutifs. Au-delà d'un débat partiellement sémantique, Buis conclut que le regard tourné vers les deux régimes vient enrichir l'interprétation et l'application des normes dans le système interaméricain, un modèle que d'autres organes de mise en œuvre des droits de la personne tardent à suivre. Giovanni Carlo Bruno ("'Collateral Damages' of Military Operations: Is implementation of International Humanitarian law Possible Using International Human Rights Tools?") vient compléter le tableau en examinant la contribution possible des tribunaux internes par le biais de la très intéressante question de savoir si un individu victime collatérale d'une opération militaire peut obtenir compensation. En analysant des décisions de tribunaux allemands et italiens, l'auteur en vient à conclure que de très nombreux obstacles comme l'immunité des États étrangers, la doctrine du forum *non conveniens*, et l'incertitude quant aux droits individuels conférés par le droit international humanitaire aux individus, se conjuguent pour limiter l'utilité de ce genre de recours.

Même s'il peut paraître un peu paradoxal de se pencher sur la fusion des droits de la personne et du droit international humanitaire en ces temps de débats sur la fragmentation du droit international, cette collection offre une réflexion utile qui certainement alimentera les discussions sur une question fondamentale autant au point de vue pratique que théorique.

René Provost
Professeur agrégé et Directeur, Centre sur les droits de la personne et du pluralisme juridique, Université McGill

International Law and Armed Conflict: Exploring the Faultlines: Essays in Honour of Yoram Dinstein. Edited by Michael N. Schmitt and Jelena Pejic. Leiden: Martinus Nijhoff, 2007. 590 pages.

INTRODUCTION

Recent events have led to a popular perception that international security and armed conflict have fundamentally changed. As a result, questions arise as to whether, in the context of modern hostilities, the international law governing resort to force (*jus ad bellum*) and armed conflict (*jus in bello*) are outdated and in need of reordering. In *International Law and Armed Conflict: Exploring the Faultlines*, editors Michael N. Schmitt and Jelena Pejic gather twenty-one international scholars and practitioners to address these questions, in honour of Yoram Dinstein's seventieth birthday.

While Dinstein has written on many areas of international law over the course of his distinguished academic career, he has focused on the *jus ad bellum* and *jus in bello*. As such, Schmitt and Pejic's collection addresses both areas of law. It aims to identify the fault lines that lie between and within the *jus ad bellum* and *jus in bello* and assess their consequences, in order to help scholars and practitioners anticipate pressure on both areas of law and react accordingly. This well-written and topically diverse collection largely succeeds in its objective, although — like many "in honour of" collections — it is theoretically limited and lacks thematic consistency and prescriptions for future research. Nonetheless, in light of Dinstein's extensive experience in international law, his service to the development and dissemination of this area of law, and the prevalence of his work in the literature on the use of force, the collection is ultimately warranted and appropriate.

ORGANIZATION

While not expressly indicated in the table of contents, the collection is divided into two parts. The first part examines topics related to the *jus ad bellum* and the second explores those related to the *jus in bello*. Within each part, no formal sub-headings are used. Thus, it is initially difficult for the reader to understand why the essays are organized as they are or how they relate to each other. Compounding this problem is the fact that the collection has no introduction or conclusion. While a preface and index are provided, the professional accomplishments of Dinstein are noted, and biographies of the essayists are included, there is little else to help the reader navigate this 590-page collection of twenty essays or learn what can be deduced from the collection as a whole.

That said, in reading the collection, informal organization is revealed. While not clearly grouped as such, the first part largely explores: (1) collective security; (2) self-defence; and (3) the relationship between the *jus ad bellum* and *jus in bello*. The second part primarily examines: (1) combatants; (2) occupation; and (3) other specific topics.

PART I: *JUS AD BELLUM*

As noted, a recurring topic in the first part of the collection is collective security. In "Rethinking Collective Security," Thomas Franck identifies gaps in the existing collective security regime. These include the failure of the UN Charter system to create a standing force and the threat and use of the veto by permanent members of the Security Council. These factors, Franck posits, weaken states' willingness to entrust their security to the UN regime. One response, he suggests, is to have the permanent members place voluntary restraints on the threat or use of the veto. While this remedy is noteworthy, Franck may overstate the problem to which it responds. For many non-powerful or non-Western states, it is the recent perceived erosion of the prohibition on the unilateral use of non-defensive force that most threatens their security, and less the historical shortcomings of the UN collective security regime.[1]

---

[1] For instance, in response to the North Atlantic Treaty Organization's military action in Kosovo in 1999, China, Russia, India, Namibia, Belarus, Ukraine, Iran, Thailand, Indonesia, South Africa, and the 133 developing states of the G-77 all reaffirmed that unilateral humanitarian intervention was illegal and unacceptable, and the UN General Assembly in September 1999 voted 107 to 7 (with forty-eight abstentions) in favour of a resolution rejecting "unilateral coercive measures." See M. Byers and S. Chesterman, "Changing the Rules about Rules? Unilateral Humanitarian Intervention and the Future of International Law," in J.L. Holzgrefe and R.O. Keohane, eds., *Humanitarian Intervention: Ethical, Legal, and Political Dilemmas* (Cambridge: Cambridge University Press, 2003) 184. Moreover, regarding the war on Iraq in 2003, 147 of the world's (then) 191 UN member states refused to participate in the US-led coalition. See S.D. Murphy, "Assessing the Legality of Invading Iraq" (2004) 92 Georgia L.J. 173 at 225. While the United States could argue that the inability or unwillingness of the Security Council to clearly authorize the foregoing uses of force suggests the shortcomings of that institution, opponents could argue that the Council *served* its founding purpose by refusing to sanction uses of force that could not be convincingly reconciled with the UN Charter and international law. See R. Falk, "What Future for the UN Charter System of War Prevention?" (2003) 97 A.J.I.L. 590.

Like Franck, Ruth Wedgwood identifies gaps in international law in her essay "The Military Action in Iraq and International Law." These include a lack of any automatic supply of police power in the collective security regime, the presence of the veto on the Security Council, and the lack of customary prohibitions on the acquisition of weapons by states. Unlike Franck, though, Wedgwood does not offer potential solutions. Instead, she justifies the 2003 Iraq war as legal and legitimate. While these arguments are sustainable, they are also contestable, and Wedgwood's minimal consideration of counter views is disappointing. For instance, she could have responded to John F. Murphy's view that the legal arguments in favour of the war are "unpersuasive," in his essay "US Adherence to the Rule of Law."

Concerned with a different problem than Wedgwood and Murphy, Ivan Shearer notes in "A Revival of the Just War Theory?" that, due to the inflexibility of orthodox international law, the United States did not feel required to legally justify the 2003 Iraq war. As this is a dangerous trend, he argues that just war theory, such as the 2001 *Responsibility to Protect Report*, be used to interpret the UN Charter. In doing so, he identifies a gap in the *jus ad bellum*, namely that unilaterally using force to stop a genocide is technically illegal. However, while Shearer offers a practical solution to this gap, he inadequately explores why "R2P" has attained less than broad support. One effect of the Iraq war was an increased hesitancy among states to endorse any unilateral uses of force. Thus, currently, just war theory arguably offers a limited basis upon which to reinterpret the Charter. While it may, as Shearer argues, allow a state to do what is "morally right," a private ethical justification avoids the challenge of modernity and the need to explain an action with reference to public and universal legal principles.

In addition to collective security, the first part of the collection explores self-defence. In "Claims to Pre-emptive Uses of Force," W. Michael Reisman and Andrea Armstrong explore how the US claim to a right of pre-emptive action has evolved and whether it is attaining customary status. Regarding US practice, the essay is very well researched and illuminating. Regarding non-US practice, however, while the views of eleven states are included, the evidence of these views is sometimes sparse and defence ministries are cited more often than foreign ministries. Further, in reviewing case law from the International Court of Justice (ICJ), the essay at times mixes the issues of whether self-defence extends to (1) pre-emptive action or (2) non-state actors. Nonetheless, the essay's final conclusions are analytically precise and practically useful.

The first part of the collection also explores the relationship between the *jus ad bellum* and *jus in bello*. In "Topographies of Force," Dino Kritsiotis seeks to delineate this relationship and explore how concepts within the two areas of law interact with each other. He largely succeeds in this task, outlining the normative landscape that comprises "force" in international law through detailed analysis of ICJ case law, state practice, and scholarly work. However, Kritsiotis's focus on the "minutiae" of law can lead one to lose sight of the broader issue. For instance, to benefit most from his analysis, one must be interested in the fact that the ICJ and UN General Assembly agree that ideological intervention is illegal, but they do so by different *methods*. That said, this is the most theoretically sophisticated work in the collection, and its complex findings are clearly summarized in diagrams.

PART II: *JUS IN BELLO*

As previously indicated, the second part of the collection examines the *jus in bello*. One of the topics explored is combatants. In "Combatants: Substance or Semantics?" Charles H.B. Garraway usefully notes that the meaning of "combatant" turns on whether one prioritizes a person's status or conduct. Thus, debate arises as to persons who do not formally qualify as combatants but nonetheless take part in hostilities. In response, Garraway argues that such persons are "unprivileged belligerents": civilians who lose their protections as such but remain protected by Common Article 3 of the Geneva Conventions and Article 75 of Additional Protocol I. This solution, he notes, aims to (1) refute the view that detainees at Guantánamo Bay are not legally entitled to humane treatment and (2) adapt old rules to modern conflicts.

In contrast to Garraway, Jelena Pejic argues in "Unlawful/Enemy Combatants" that "unlawful combatants" who fulfil the nationality criteria in Geneva Convention IV remain protected persons. While Pejic's view is supported by convincing treaty interpretation and a clever reference to a 1956 US Army manual, it may have unintended effects. These effects are noted in Garraway's essay, although the two authors do not expressly respond to each other. First, by Pejic's logic, a captured civilian who directly and continuously took part in hostilities but failed to comply with the requirements, for lawfully doing so would receive certain privileges that a combatant would not. Second, while Pejic notes that civilians who take part in hostilities may be prosecuted, the sheer number of "unprivileged belligerents" in modern conflicts arguably makes this impossible. Notwithstanding these differences, though, Garraway and Pejic agree on most other related issues. As was noted at the beginning of this review, explaining such scholarly differences and agreements in an introduction or conclusion to the collection would have helped the reader to better understand how the essays relate to each other and what can be deduced from the collection as a whole.

In addition to combatants, the second part of the collection explores the topic of occupation. In "The Adequacy of International Humanitarian Law Rules on Belligerent Occupation," Rüdiger Wolfrum notes that, while traditional rules limit an occupant's power to restructure an occupied state, the changes to Iraq's economy and political system introduced by the US-led coalition went "far beyond" these rules. Nonetheless, Wolfrum argues that Security Council Resolution 1483 legalized the political changes and "modified" traditional law. The theory behind his analysis is that, in light of the importance of preserving peace under international law, and the possibility that an occupied state's former political system was a cause of the war, limiting an occupant's power may no longer be appropriate. This theory, it should be noted, imports the objectives of the *jus ad bellum* into the *jus in bello*. This is, at best, erroneous and, at worst, dangerous. As Marco Sassòli notes in his essay "*Jus ad Bellum* and *Jus in Bello*," arguments under the former may not be used to interpret the latter. The separation between the two areas of law, Sassòli argues, is crucial for the survival of the *jus in bello* and for the effective protection of war victims.

In contrast to Wolfrum, Adam Roberts offers a more comprehensive analysis in "Transformative Military Occupation." By reviewing traditional law, emerging human rights norms, and state practice, he argues convincingly that "the law on occupations remains both viable and useful, and has proved reasonably flexible in practice."

Not all of the collection's occupation essays focus on Iraq. In "The Separation Fence in the International Court of Justice and the High Court of Justice," Fania Domb explores the similarities and differences between the decisions of the ICJ and the Israeli HCJ on the legality of Israel's "Wall" in the occupied territory. While the courts arrived at different conclusions, the ICJ noted that the normative basis upon which they relied was common for many issues. This view is largely confirmed by Domb's twelve findings. Nonetheless, she concludes that the ICJ decision is "controversial" and, thus, that it is doubtful that it will be widely accepted. Such a conclusion is arguably illogical, as "controversial" does not mean "incorrect"; and biased, as the unstated premise is that when the ICJ and HCJ disagree, the latter is correct. A more reasonable conclusion could be that, by inadequately explaining why the Wall's harm outweighs other interests, the ICJ risks eroding the principle of proportionality and widening the gap between "formal law" and state practice.

In addition to combatants and occupation, the second part of the collection also explores specific topics. In "The Law of Weaponry," Bill Boothby notes gaps in said law, such as the inadequate implementation by states of their obligation to review the legality of new weapons. As a solution, he argues persuasively that the way to get states to review weapons is to show how humanitarian law and operational effectiveness "converge." However, regarding the separate issue of how weapons law should be developed, Boothby's endorsement of the Convention on Conventional Weapons is less convincing, as it inadequately explores why many states and non-governmental organizations have turned to other approaches, such as the Convention on the Prohibition of the Use, Stockpiling, Production and Transfer of Anti-Personnel Mines and on their Destruction.

CONCLUSION

As noted earlier, Schmitt and Pejic's collection aims to explore the fault lines in the *jus ad bellum* and *jus in bello*, to help scholars and practitioners react accordingly and to honour Yoram Dinstein. This review suggests that the collection largely succeeds in this goal. Almost all of the essays identify gaps in the law, although some only do so implicitly. Furthermore, most of the essays offer potential solutions to these gaps. While some of these solutions are contestable, they offer fertile ground for future academic analysis and practical guidance for government lawyers. Finally, almost all of the authors refer to Dinstein's writing and pay tribute to him in their essays.

However, one of the reasons the collection succeeds is because its aim is limited. The collection does not seek to explain how the essays relate to each other, summarize its findings, or prescribe broad questions for future research. Moreover, even though the aim of the collection is limited to "exploring the faultlines," the sheer breadth of the topics included may have undermined this goal and obscured the collection's theme. For instance, while Theodor Meron's essay "Leaders, Courtiers and Command Responsibility in Shakespeare" reminds us of the timelessness of the problems to which the laws of war are directed, no other essay focuses on this subject or uses literature as a research method.

In addition to being limited, the collection's aim is theoretically questionable. The collection assumes that international security and armed conflict have fundamentally changed and that, as such, the *jus ad bellum* and *jus in bello* may be outdated and in need of renovation. Two critiques can be made regarding this theory. First, it may be empirically inaccurate. As Kenneth Watkin notes in his essay "21st Century Conflict and International Humanitarian Law," while 95 percent of armed conflicts are now internal, the 1999 Kosovo campaign, 2001 Afghanistan conflict, and 2003 Iraq war suggest that predictions about the demise of traditional inter-state conflict are "premature and unrealistic." Second, the collection's theory may be analytically inaccurate. By assuming that changes in armed conflict overwhelmingly affect international law, and not vice versa, the collection cannot fully explore the nature of the relationship between the two phenomena. Surprisingly, Boothby, a military officer, is one of the lone voices to note that by facilitating the development of battlefield norms, law, in time, directly influences military behaviour.

Nonetheless, all of the essays are well researched, written, and edited. Moreover, the academic authority of the essays — like that of Dinstein himself — is hard to contest, as many of the authors are leading or emerging experts in their fields. Finally, the essays represent a fairly broad range of views, as authors come from universities, institutes, courts, the military, and international organizations in North America, Europe, Israel, and Australia. The collection could have been improved, however, by including a broader range of perspectives from Africa, Latin America, Asia, or the Middle East. As one's opinion on the use of force turns so much on one's values and premises, including more views on the subject can only improve the comprehensiveness of "Western" scholarship. In sum, notwithstanding its identified shortcomings, the collection is a significant contribution to the literature on the *jus ad bellum* and *jus in bello*, a valuable resource for scholars and practitioners alike, and a worthy testament to Yoram Dinstein's life-long commitment to international law.

SEAN RICHMOND
D. Phil. Candidate, Oxford University, Oxford

Redefining Sovereignty in International Economic Law. Edited by Wenhua
Shan, Penelope Simons, and Dalvinder Singh. Oxford and Portland, OR: Hart Publishing, 2008. 470 pages.

The sovereignty of states is the foundation of the international legal
order. Yet both its contemporary meaning and legal significance
are uncertain and contested. Whatever sovereignty means, its effective scope is changing as a consequence of a variety of factors,
including the growing interdependence of states, the proliferation
of international treaties, and the globalization of business activity.
The nature and extent of these changes is also a matter of debate.
Redefining Sovereignty in International Economic Law responds to this
uncertainty through a collection of papers addressing how sovereignty has been affected by developments in international economic law. It brings together an outstanding group of scholars
representing both developed and developing countries who deal
with a broad range of issues from varied points of view. Following
four papers that meditate on the general question of the relationship between sovereignty and international economic law, *Redefining
Sovereignty* addresses the particular effects of international rules and
institutions related to trade, investment, and finance. The final
section is devoted to the interaction between international economic law and human rights. Even with such a broad reach, the
coverage of *Redefining Sovereignty* is inevitably partial. Nevertheless,
as the first work to address the relationship between sovereignty
and international economic law in a thoroughgoing way, it provides
the reader with a wealth of insights into the complex and multifaceted nature of sovereignty today.

The first section of *Redefining Sovereignty* provides ideas regarding
the essential nature of sovereignty from some well-known commentators on international economic law. The first paper ("Sovereignty: Outdated Concept or New Approaches"), by one of the world's
leading international trade experts, John Jackson, surveys the characteristics of the modern world that together have dictated a movement away from thinking of the state as sovereign in terms of
possessing an almost absolute power over its territory (referred to
by Jackson as "Westphalian sovereignty").[1] These include factors as
disparate as economic globalization, the expansion of international trade rules, and the development of international human rights

---

[1] Wenhua Shan, Penelope Simons, and Dalvinder Singh, eds., *Redefining Sovereignty
in International Economic Law* (Oxford and Portland: Hart Publishing, 2008) at 4.

norms. Concerned by unthinking continued use of out of date and illegitimate traditional sovereignty fictions, Jackson suggests that understanding sovereignty requires a new conception that he calls "sovereignty-modern."[2] This conception involves acknowledging that sovereignty is increasingly disaggregated, with different levels of state actors and international organizations exercising "slices" of sovereignty, and changes over time.[3] In this context, he hypothesizes that questions of sovereignty are really questions about what level of decision maker should be making a particular decision. For example, he suggests that when a state invokes sovereignty to justify not entering into a treaty, this means that it prefers that the subject matter of the treaty be dealt with at the state, not the international, level.[4] Jackson pursues this notion of power allocation by identifying a number of issues related to how such allocations should be made. He does so with a view to developing sovereignty-modern as an analytical tool to understand what is really at play when claims based on sovereignty are made.

The second paper ("State Sovereignty, Popular Sovereignty and Individual Sovereignty: From Constitutional Nationalism to Multi-level Constitutionalism in International Economic Law?"), by Ernst-Ulrich Petersmann, also argues in favour of a conception of sovereignty that recognizes an allocation of sovereignty among different levels of decision makers. Like Jackson, he acknowledges the increasing economic, political, and legal limitations on the political sovereignty of states, but his focus is on the effective transfer of state powers to individuals through the universal recognition of their human rights, including, in particular, their individual and democratic freedoms. For Petersmann, the effective protection of human rights requires redesigning the sovereignty of states in a manner that reconciles states' sovereignty with the human rights of their citizens. In his view, existing protection of human rights through national constitutions and international instruments is wholly inadequate. He argues for a multi-level constitutionalization of human rights. Petersmann goes on to identify some of the implications of constitutionalizing human rights at the international level for the rules of international economic law.

Robert Howse's contribution, "Sovereignty, Lost and Found," provides a kind of counterpoint to the first two papers by challenging

2 *Ibid.* at 7.

3 *Ibid.* at 15.

4 *Ibid.* at 11–12.

two commonly held views regarding globalization and sovereignty. Both Jackson and Petersmann conceive of state sovereignty as a limited and disaggregated concept in the contemporary world, due in part to economic globalization. Howse argues that economic globalization has not limited state sovereignty to the extent often thought. He provides evidence that states are not prevented from exercising their regulatory power by the threat that transnational corporations that are unhappy with government actions will withdraw from national markets. He cites Brazil, India, and China as countries that have achieved economic success by policies that aggressively regulate their markets. He also disputes the frequently heard claim that globalization has meant that international institutions have gained power at the expense of the nation state, suggesting that, in fact, globalization has weakened many international institutions such as the International Monetary Fund (IMF), whose role as the guardian of stable exchange rates has all but disappeared in a world where most rates float. Also, he suggests that states use international institutions strategically to enhance their sovereignty. For example, he suggests that national commitments under the World Trade Organization (WTO) agreements and bilateral investment treaties are sometimes used by states to lock in policies to which they are strongly committed, protecting them against changes by future governments. By enhancing the power of current governments in this way, Howse says state sovereignty is enhanced.

In his short piece "Sovereignty and International Economic Law," Vaughan Lowe, unlike the other contributors in this section, does not try to reconceive sovereignty in a way that makes it meaningful in the contemporary environment. Instead, he challenges the basic notion that sovereignty has sufficient explanatory power or specific content to be considered a helpful legal principle at all. Instead, he suggests that sovereignty is rather a "signifier" of a sort of claim that must be specifically unpacked to determine what it means in each case.[5] He prefers to call sovereignty a rhetorical flourish that may be used in political debate but that has little relevance as a legal rule.[6]

In the next section of the book, four papers take quite different approaches to the relationship between sovereignty, on the one hand, and trade liberalization and reform of the WTO on the other.

---

[5] *Ibid.* at 77.

[6] *Ibid.* at 79.

Like Lowe, An Chen ("Trade as the Guarantor of Peace, Liberty and Security?") is concerned about the political uses of sovereignty. He provides a critique of what he characterizes as selective strategic uses of different concepts of sovereignty, by the United States to further its own trade interests, and uses this to support an argument that developing countries should cling to traditional notions of sovereignty as a tool to protect them against US hegemony. Asif Qureshi also argues, in "Sovereignty Issues in the WTO Dispute Settlement: A 'Development Sovereignty' Perspective," that a strong form of state sovereignty is important to developing countries, but his focus is on the legal significance of sovereignty in the WTO. He argues that sovereignty of members is a key organizing principle of the WTO that is frequently invoked by them and often applied in dispute resolution cases involving the interpretation of WTO agreements. Qureshi is primarily concerned with identifying specific ways in which the sovereignty concerns of developing country members in the WTO — which he identifies as the preservation of domestic policy space and the recognition of differential levels of responsibility for countries at different levels of development — can be addressed within the WTO dispute settlement system, looking at both the existing system and proposals for reform.

The remaining papers in this section provide analyses of more technical issues related to sovereignty in the WTO context. Like Jackson and Petersmann, Phillip Nichols ("Sovereignty and Reform of the World Trade Organization") views sovereignty as a "tool for organizing relationships" with variable content depending on the circumstances.[7] He then discusses the particular legal conception of sovereignty used to determine eligibility for WTO membership — control over a customs territory — and considers whether this remains the right conception when WTO rules now cover much more than trade in goods, and political subdivisions within customs territories, such as California, are much more significant in terms of international economic activity and international economic regulation than most states. The final paper in this grouping, by Mads Andenas and Stefan Zleptnig ("The Rule of Law and Proportionality in WTO Law"), investigates the particular balance between WTO disciplines and members' freedom to regulate in pursuit of non-trade public policy objectives, such as health and environmental protection. Examining the general exceptions in Article XX of the General Agreement on Tariffs and Trade as well as the

---

[7] *Ibid.* at 151.

main obligations in the Agreement on Technical Barriers to Trade and the Agreement on Sanitary and Phytosanitary Measures, the authors argue for the adoption of a more structured approach to defining how these provisions preserve WTO members' policy-making sovereignty based on proportionality, a principle that has been adopted in other legal regimes, including, in particular, the European Union.

The third section of *Redefining Sovereignty* examines the relationship between international investment rules, largely created through the expanding network of bilateral and regional investment treaties and preferential trading agreements, and the sovereignty of the states that are hosts to foreign investors. In "The Neo-Liberal Agenda in Investment Arbitration: Its Rise, Retreat and Impact on Sovereignty," M. Sornarajah argues forcefully that international investment rules implement a neo-liberal agenda and have substantially undermined host state sovereignty, not just through the specific restrictions that they impose on state behaviour but also, more importantly, as a result of the expansive interpretation of these obligations by international arbitral tribunals. In Sornarajah's view, the erosion of sovereignty through arbitral decisions results from a variety of inherent characteristics of the international arbitration process, including the self-interest of arbitrators seeking to increase their opportunities for further work, and goes beyond the consent of party states. Sornarajah concludes by noting signs of a retreat from the neo-liberal investment agenda.

These developments, along with other current features of investment arbitration, are surveyed in Joachim Karl's paper, "International Investment Arbitration: A Threat to State Sovereignty." He reviews the threats to sovereignty identified by Sornarajah but concludes that, although cumulatively they may be significant, states retain considerable regulatory freedom, including, in most cases, the right to decide whether the entry of a particular investment will be permitted. He also emphasizes that any constraint on sovereignty in an investment agreement must be weighed against the benefits it provides by increasing the confidence of foreign investors regarding how they will be treated by host states and, as a result, encouraging them to invest. Although he concludes that the case for reform is not obvious, Karl goes on to suggest ways in which treaty provisions and arbitration practice could be improved to better preserve regulatory autonomy in host states while, at the same time, maintaining the role of investment treaties as inducements to foreign investment.

Wenhua Shan's paper, "Calvo Doctrine, State Sovereignty and The Changing Landscape of International Investment Law," deals with a fundamentally important sovereignty question in international investment law: to what extent should foreign investors be able to invoke international rules to complain about domestic measures of host states? He also considers the related question of whether foreign investors should be able to have their claims against host states resolved by forms of international dispute settlement that are not available to domestic investors. The "Calvo doctrine" (named after the nineteenth-century Argentine jurist, Carlos Calvo, on whose writings it is based), traditionally advocated by Latin American countries, precludes both. Shan describes the Calvo doctrine as embodying an "anti-super-national treatment" approach that guarantees a high level of host state sovereignty because it limits foreigners to exactly the same protections and remedies as local investors.[8] He provides a historical survey of the decline of the Calvo doctrine through commitments undertaken in international investment treaties, focusing on Latin America. He then describes several recent changes to the global context in which international investment law operates that have resulted in a global trend back towards a modified version of the Calvo doctrine, under which host state sovereignty receives greater protection while international obligations to foreign investors are more limited. The factors driving this trend, some of which are also discussed by Sornarajah and Karl, include the fact that some developed countries are now defendants in investor-state arbitration cases, investor protection under domestic regimes of host states has improved, and non-governmental organizations are increasingly engaged in the development of international investment law.

Part 4 of *Redefining Sovereignty* presents three papers on banking regulation and international financial institutions. The first, by Charles Chatterjee and Anna Lefcovitch ("Banking, Economic Development and the Law"), deals with the need for an effective domestic banking system as part of the foundation for national economic development. It also addresses the challenges faced by many developing countries in providing the right conditions for the establishment of such a system. Dalvinder Singh's paper, "The Role of the IMF and the World Bank in Financial Sector Reform and Compliance," nicely complements this analysis. Singh investigates the role of the Basel Committee on Banking Regulation and

---

[8] *Ibid.* at 249.

Supervisory Practices, the IMF, and the World Bank in domestic financial sector reform. He begins by exposing the global inter-connectedness of financial markets through a discussion of the financial crises in the 1990s. Interconnectedness gives virtually every state a stake in the effectiveness of every other state's regulation of its financial sector. He describes the international community's main response to these crises, which has been the core principles for the supervision of banks adopted by the Basel Committee. He notes that the legitimacy of this body as an international rule maker may be criticized because it is composed of an unrepresentative group of national central banks and bank regulators. The Basel Committee standards do not impinge on sovereignty directly, however, because they are non-binding and rely for their implementation on national bank regulators. In practice, implementation is far from universal. While this is due to political resistance in some states, a substantial challenge in many developing countries is limited domestic regulatory capacity. Singh describes how the World Bank and the IMF have expanded the scope of their activities to provide co-ordinated technical assistance for the purpose of enhancing domestic capacity to regulate and supervise domestic financial services providers and foreign businesses operating within their markets. Conditionality attached to IMF and World Bank technical and financial support, however, is used to push countries towards compliance with the Basel Committee's core principles and, more generally, financial sector reform.

The final paper in this section, by Jorge Guira ("International Financial Law and New Sovereignty: Legal Arbitrage as an Emerging Dimension of Global Governance"), describes the challenge to national regulation of financial markets posed by the ability of multinational businesses to engage in legal arbitrage, meaning quickly shift their activities to markets providing a regulatory scheme that imposes the lowest cost on them. Based on a comparison of US and UK securities regulation, he suggests that states can strategically respond to the possibility of arbitrage by being creative in how they regulate financial market participants, putting in place incentives to remain under national regulation that offset costly regulatory requirements. Such a strategy, he suggests, would permit states to, in effect, gain sovereignty at the expense of others.

The final section in *Redefining Sovereignty* contains three papers dealing with different aspects of the relationship between human rights and international economic law. Andrew Lang, in "Re-Righting International Trade: Some Critical Thoughts on the

Contemporary Trade and Human Rights Literature," argues that traditional human rights scholarship takes too narrow a view of this relationship, focusing largely on the constraints that trade rules impose on state measures intended to promote human rights. He suggests that trade rules also have a "teaching" effect regarding what kinds of trade policies are acceptable. Focusing only on tweaking the WTO rules to preserve policy space for human rights promotion will miss the impact of trade rules on the overall process of policy development.

Penelope Simons' paper, "Binding the Hand that Feeds Them: the Agreement on Agriculture, Transnational Corporations and the Right to Adequate Food in Developing Countries," is a comprehensive analysis of the role that trade law has played in contributing to food insecurity and undermining developing countries' ability to promote the human right to food. While this is the kind of analysis critiqued by Lang, it nevertheless effectively exposes the complex and sometimes indirect ways in which the provisions of the WTO Agreement on Agriculture operate to promote the interests of developed countries and global agribusinesses while further impoverishing developing countries, especially those that depend on agricultural exports. WTO rules have aggravated poverty by negatively affecting developing country agricultural producers, while at the same time constraining the policy options for developing countries to support their domestic agriculture sector as part of poverty alleviation strategies. Emphasizing the link between poverty and diminished food security, Simons concludes that WTO members have not taken seriously their human rights obligations in developing and implementing international trade rules in agriculture.

The last paper in *Redefining Sovereignty* is by David Schneiderman ("Realizing Rights in an Era of Economic Globalization: Discourse Theory, Investor Rights, and Broad-Based Black Economic Empowerment"). Like Howse, Chen, and Qureshi, he takes issue with the view that legal and economic factors associated with economic globalization have overtaken state sovereignty. He acknowledges that conflicts exist between human rights norms and foreign investors' interests. He describes the conflict between foreign investors in South Africa and the requirements of the Black Economic Empowerment (BEE) legislation that seek to correct historic discrimination by obliging businesses to transfer some ownership rights to local black investors. Notwithstanding such potential conflicts, he asserts that the state still has a role to play, noting that the South African government has been successful in negotiating carve-outs from bilateral investment treaties that shield the BEE legislation from challenge.

As noted at the outset, any collection of papers that seeks to deal with the fundamental but complex and multifaceted concept of sovereignty cannot address all of its aspects. *Redefining Sovereignty* does not discuss, for example, how issues dealt with for the first time in the Uruguay Round, such as services and intellectual property, affect sovereignty. Both the new substantive obligations in these areas as well as the innovative design of the agreements that impose them implicate new areas of state activity and, as a consequence, raise new kinds of sovereignty issues. As well, there is little in *Redefining Sovereignty* on the significant implications for state sovereignty of the evolving nature of governance of the WTO or other international institutions. A range of sovereignty issues like these remain to be addressed in some future work on sovereignty and international economic law.

Turning to the papers themselves, a couple of limitations may be noted. A few of the papers do not draw out the implications of their analyses for state sovereignty in much detail. For example, the paper by Chatterjee and Lefcovitch would have made a greater contribution to *Redefining Sovereignty* if the authors had devoted more attention to the linkages between state sovereignty and their otherwise compelling analysis of the challenges for developing countries seeking to create the conditions necessary for the development of an effective banking system. They do not refer to sovereignty at all until the last page of their paper, where they simply lament that states sometimes use their sovereignty as a reason not to accept expert advisers from the World Bank and IMF to assist them in developing their banking systems.[9] As well, while one of the strengths of the collection is its presentation of contrasting views and there were some examples of authors addressing one another's work (for example, Chen (104–5), Qureshi (160), and Simons (421)), the nature and extent of the divergence between the contributors could have been drawn out more effectively if they had more consistently responded to each other's arguments.

Nevertheless, these observations should not be seen as suggesting that *Redefining Sovereignty* is anything other than a very useful contribution to our current understanding of sovereignty in the context of international economic law. It provides an engaging and effective introduction to the issues as well as a strong foundation for future

9 *Ibid.* at 330.

research on the subject. In particular, readers will get a good sense of the divergence between Western and developing country scholars on conceptions of sovereignty and its continuing relevance.

As well, *Redefining Sovereignty* has a number of features that will ensure its utility as a reference work. These include an excellent index, a list of the sometimes bewildering abbreviations frequently used in international economic law, as well as tables of cases and international and national instruments showing where each is referred to throughout the volume. In short, the editors of and contributors to *Redefining Sovereignty* should be congratulated for producing a first-rate collection of papers that charts a path for future work on the relationship between sovereignty and international economic law.

J. ANTHONY VANDUZER

Associate Professor, Faculty of Law (Common Law Section),
University of Ottawa

Analytical Index / Indexe analytique

THE CANADIAN YEARBOOK OF INTERNATIONAL LAW

2008

ANNUAIRE CANADIEN DE DROIT INTERNATIONAL

(A) Article; (NC) Notes and Comments; (Ch) Chronique;
(P) Practice; (C) Cases; (BR) Book Review

(A) Article; (NC) Notes et commentaires; (Ch) Chronique;
(P) Pratique; (C) Jurisprudence; (BR) Recension de livre

Index of Cases /
Index de la jurisprudence

—

793